You Eat
What You Are

You Eat What You Are

PEOPLE, CULTURE AND FOOD TRADITIONS

BY THELMA BARER-STEIN PH.D.

FIREFLY BOOKS

A FIREFLY BOOK

Published by Firefly Books Ltd. 1999

Second Edition, First Printing

Canadian Cataloguing in Publication Data

Barer-Stein, Thelma,
  You eat what you are: people, culture and food traditions

2nd ed.
Includes index.
ISBN 1-55209-365-4

1.Food Habits. 2. Manners and customs. 3. Food – Terminology I. Title

GT2850.B37   1999   394.1'2   C98-932673-X

Published in Canada in 1999 by
Firefly Books Ltd.
3680 Victoria Park Avenue
Willowdale, Ontario
Canada M2H 3K1

Library of Congress Cataloging-in-Publication Data

Barer-Stein, Thelma,
  You eat what you are: people, culture and food traditions / Thelma Baer-Stein, Ph. D.
Exp. updated ed.
(544) p. : col. III., maps ; cm.
Includes bibliographical references (p.) and index.
Summary : Exporation of more than 100 culinary traditions worldwide and how food preferences and preparation reveal links with social structure, geography and history.
ISBN 1-55209-365-4
1. Food habits. I. Title.
394.1/2–dc21   1999   CIP

Published in the United States in 1999 by
Firefly Books (U.S.) Inc.
P.O. Box 1338, Ellicott Station
Buffalo, New York
USA 14205

Produced by: Denise Schon Books Inc.
Design: Gillian Tsintziras, The Brookview Group Inc.
Editor: Liba Berry
Front cover photograph: Greek market: Gillian Tsintziras

Printed and bound in Canada by Friesens, Altona, Manitoba

The Publisher acknowledges the financial support of the Government of Canada through the Book Publishing Industry Development Program for its publishing activities.

DEDICATION

To the memory of my father,
Michael Lion Barer,
who instilled in me a lifelong
love of learning
and
to my grandchildren,
Katelin, Daniel, Connor, and Austin,
who daily extend that learning.

1

CONTENTS

ACKNOWLEDGMENTS

If every author could foretell the difficulties, books would languish only in the mind. Like others, the fecundity of ideas, the eagerness of the people I interviewed, the excitement of the librarians who helped me, and the enthusiasm of my family drove my writing and possessed me in an unrelenting grip of single-minded excitement. Then, despite the chaos of divorce, the joys and demands of four children, the despair of 32 publishing rejections, and the happy delirium of graduate study, *You Eat What You Are* was recognized as a classic work by then editor-in-chief Anna Porter, and published in 1979 by McClelland & Stewart.

At that time – the late 1970s – a long list of individuals and organizations endorsed and supported this work. This list included the Ontario Folk Arts Council, the Commission on Canadian Studies, the National Museum of Man, the Canadian Dietetic Association, the Canadian Jewish Congress, the Canadian Home Economics Association, the Department of Public Health, Newfoundland, and many librarians across Canada. Tangible financial assistance was gratefully received from a Canada Council Explorations grant, the first Wintario grant to an author, and an Ontario Arts Council Award.

That seems long ago now, but the support of these organizations in this solitary task is still profoundly appreciated and will never be forgotten.

My sincerest thanks to Denise Schon and Michael Worek of Firefly Books Inc. and to my diligent copy editor Liba Berry.

Especially I am grateful for the blessings of my family. I cherish sharing their struggles and their achievements as they each grow in wisdom, enjoying every moment of life. Perhaps from those 32 rejections we all learned that rejection doesn't mean failure, it just means that we all try a bit harder.

More than ever, I wish to acknowledge the powerful love and never-ending support of my parents, who, even in memory, continue to guide me by their values and their belief in the worth of my efforts.

INTRODUCTION

HOW TIMES HAVE CHANGED!

Cultural understanding has progressed. We rarely hear the terms American "melting pot" or Canadian "multiculturalism." Instead the media, the academics, and the corporate world have converged on the term "diversity." For too long, the argument against recognizing and respecting differing cultural ways was to point out that, after all, we are all alike as human beings. The term "diversity" at least highlights dissimilarity and variance instead of demeaning it. And readers no longer question how I could have written a book about food with more than 450 pages and no recipes! Now that's progress!

Some things, however, stay the same. The English and the Scots still object to reference as an "ethnic" group even though, in Canada at least, they are no longer the dominant cultural groups. Changing the terminology from "ethnic" to "diversity" is a step in the right direction, but while it may connote positive action, it doesn't denote universal change or acceptance. Understanding and appreciation are only reached through a lengthy process of learning, but that process begins with awareness, so let's be optimistic and accept that as a good start.

For many years colleges and universities in North America have been providing courses in cross-cultural communication, global business management, and an increasing list of foreign language studies. Books on cultural issues line the library shelves (see Sources and References), and cookbooks from obscure regions are ablaze with color photos and exciting recipes. Supermarkets boast a large variety of fresh herbs and imported foods from world markets including fruits and vegetables, seasonings, varieties of vinegar, flavored oils, condiments and sauces that were not available even ten years ago. In larger cities in North America and many countries in Europe, special sections of food markets are devoted not only to international food but also to the food specialties for religious occasions such as Christmas, Ramadan, Passover, and Easter.

Cultural understanding has progressed to some extent from American "melting pot" and Canadian "multiculturalism" to the international expression of "global diversity." The diversity of people around the world is no longer the purview of social scientists, nor is its study focused on the remote tribal villages of interest to early anthropologists. Now diversity has become the byword of the global economy. Cross-cultural management, leadership and training have become imperatives seen as the basis for global market success and profit.

Toleration of cultural differences is very gradually giving way to curiosity, enjoyment and appreciation and, hopefully, understanding. Gradually the notion of understanding the differing behaviors, manners and customs of people is seen as a way of enhancing communication both for political and economic reasons. Diversity is a fact of daily life everywhere, and its understanding and appreciation has become an imperative rather than a choice.

Today the global economy must manage the workforces of international business, and "international" presupposes national and cultural diversity. While English is predominantly the language of international communication and business, it is now considered an advantage rather than a novelty to be proficient in other languages as well. Now, too, it is recognized that not only language but also the deeply embedded manners, customs, and ideologies of a people must be appreciated and religious beliefs and practices must be respected. Understanding and respectful practice must replace mere tolerance of difference.

The oft-quoted phrase "People are really all the same" is also gradually being replaced by the growing realization that we may all be human beings but the characteristics that we are born with – our race – and the habits and traditions that distinguish our daily life – our culture – do indeed differ. We are also learning that difference connotes neither inferiority nor superiority, it only points out how dissimilar we each are.

North American, Australian, and British food habits, to mention only a few regions, have changed more in the last twenty years than perhaps in hundreds of years previously. Increasing numbers of women in the workforce, struggling with home and family duties, has decreased time for meal preparation. In turn, this factor has led to the increase in production of processed, frozen and fast foods. Family restaurants, take-out meals, and even technological advances in kitchen appliances now available to those of average income all are changing.

In addition, the proliferation of international restaurants, "exotic" cookbooks and cooking classes tingle our taste buds, tantalize our imaginations, and challenge our food traditions. Travel has always extended our vision and our imagination whether we actually participated or only read about other places and other ways of living. Television and the Internet have compressed distance, speeded up communication. But the unchanging factors of natural disasters, political unrest, poverty and starvation still send refugees and immigrants in search of a better life, and wherever they go, their cultural traditions are part of their diversity.

WHAT IS CULTURE?

There are as many ways to describe culture as there are anthropologists and social scientists. Yet to define anything is to confine it. In attempting to understand what culture is, we can list its attributes, such as its offering each person a sense of identity, a feeling of belonging, an aura of security and comfort. Paradoxically, while we can describe the history, the language, the myths, the legends and superstitions and the religion and food traditions, we become aware of yet another quality. Culture is dynamic, it is always in a process of change because there are always those within each cultural group who strive for change and those who strive for the status quo. The challenges, misunderstandings, and dilemmas between generations are evidence of this dynamism.

Curiously, one's culture is the habitual aspect of daily life. Each of us, when pressed to describe or even explain the things we do but take for granted, find ourselves tongue-tied. More recently, because the cultural habits of others have been explored and discussed, we are beginning to realize that the way we greet people, eat our food, dress, or even how we walk and talk is just as odd to others as their daily ways may seem to us. Habituation is practical, it saves time, it wordlessly identifies us; cultural habits help us to retain that identity, solidity, and security that is so important to each human being.

Perhaps an adequate summary would be that unlike race, which is inherited, culture seems to represent the total of all aspects of the patterns of daily life that are learned by an individual and determinedly affects that person's behavior, providing a sense of order, security, and identity and yet paradoxically is in a state of continuous change.

WHY FOCUS ON FOOD TRADITIONS?

Food is only one aspect of cultural traditions, yet it is probably one of the most persistent. The term "soul food," although coined by the black peoples in North America, by no means applies specifically to them. There is no cultural group and no individual for whom at least one specific food – the memory, taste, or smell of which – does not evoke a pang of loving nostalgia.

There are many reasons for the indelible imprint of food customs and traditions on our cultural heritage. Food plays an inextricable role in our daily lives. Without food we cannot survive. But food is much more than a tool of survival. Food is a source of pleasure, comfort, and security. Food is also a symbol of hospitality, social status, and religious significance. What we select to eat, how we prepare it, serve it, and even how we eat it are all factors profoundly touched by our individual cultural inheritance.

Peoples of differing cultures inhabit most countries of the world. The human habit of migrating is as old as the history of humans. It is accepted that people move from place to place for reasons of religious or political freedom, for personal and family security, for a sense of adventure. What is often overlooked is something more basic: many peoples of the world have migrated to find food. Historically, this has frequently resulted in the necessity of relinquishing customary tastes according to what foods, seasonings, and even cooking methods are available to them in the new location. Finding new foods and new sources of foods and seasonings also motivated many adventurers and explorers and swelled the economy of countries.

Because of the centrality of food in our lives, many cults and religions impose feast days and fast days, and may list acceptable and prohibited foods. Special occasions, from funerals to weddings, from festivals and fairs to political holidays and religious celebrations – all of these would diminish in pleasure and importance if food were not a consideration. Various foods are given symbolic and even transformative connotations, and there is still no shortage of publications promising that a "magic food" will alleviate pain, increase sexual function, and promise almost everything but life after death. The ability to control one's appetite, in many aspects of life, but especially regarding food, may also be indicative of social status, and more recently is seen as critical for health and longevity.

WHY DO PEOPLE EAT WHAT THEY EAT?

Even a cursory glance at diets around the world reveals the strange fact that people do not only eat what is available; they eat only what they consider to be edible. What is considered a delicacy in one area and by one group may be considered an abomination by others. Sheep's brains and eyeballs, frog's legs, hot tea with fermented yak butter, or animal blood are not considered to be universal foods – nor are insects, but they are relished by some people. Further, eating food with one's fingers may be considered ill mannered by some, while others may consider eating with a knife and fork barbaric. An ancient Iranian saying suggests that eating with a knife and fork would be like making love through an interpreter.

THE PHASES OF IMMIGRANTS' ADJUSTMENT

Canada is not unlike many other countries that have opened their doors to refugees and immigrants. In most of these countries, history reveals successive and sometimes overlapping means of coping with these new citizens. In Canada, we have seen periods of assimilation, integration, hyphenated Canadians, biculturalism (French and English, the founding cultures), and in the late 1970s policies of multiculturalism. But while the Canadian government's policies regarding the immigrant population swayed over the years, the people themselves went right on with the imperatives of day-to-day living. Some of the newcomers had brought with them a host of material possessions, others brought education, still others brought only themselves and their family.

But all brought with them, consciously or subconsciously, overtly or tacitly, a cultural heritage.

Let's take a closer look at what happens to the generations when they arrive in a new country, settle in, and eventually become citizens. Immigrants and homeless refugees concern themselves initially with the basics of human survival: a job, a place to live, food. For the first generation, then, the urgency is simply survival. The second generation, having survived, concerns itself with the more sophisticated matters of "getting along" and "belonging." The first generation didn't have the time and the second generation didn't want to be "different" from what they viewed (for example) as being "Canadian."

And that is how cultural heritage for the most part remained in the suitcase in which it had arrived: never unpacked. Some cultural groups such as Ukrainians, Chinese, and Jews clung tenaciously to their language and other traditions, while others, like Icelanders, almost completely lost them.

For the third and fourth generations, a combination of complex factors evoked, among other things, the sense that something was missing from their lives. Increased prosperity and leisure time offered a chance for reflection, while the influx of later immigrants, mostly political refugees who were intellectuals and professionals (such as the Hungarians in the late 1950s), brought a tangible reminder and often a nostalgia for the richness of past traditions so long ignored. Reflection rekindled the need for a sense of individual and group identity.

Cultural heritage offers to everyday life not only a sense of collective identity, but pride and dignity, purpose, and stability. Cultural traditions like classic works of literature, art and philosophical thought survive because they offer solace to our thirsting soul. We can get along without these, but not for long. In the urgent press to survive, and the pressures to belong and to conform, these values and ideals are sometimes shoved aside. But eventually, in the pauses of daily life, we each, in our differing ways, come to the realization that life is not complete without the enrichment of our cultural heritage.

WHY A BOOK ABOUT PEOPLE, CULTURE AND FOOD TRADITIONS?

When the first edition of You Eat What You Are was published in 1979 – to the best of our research efforts – no other book on this topic was available. At that time this work was a novelty. I am heartened that now, close to a new millennium, the need to understand how people differ, and to appreciate that difference for the way such knowledge can enrich our own lives, is no longer a novel notion.

Tolerance is still rooted in the belief of superior and inferior peoples. The purpose of this book is to show, through studying the day-to-day lives of people and highlighting their food traditions, that we may discover there is something to be learned from everyone. And hopefully, that our attempt to understand and therefore truly appreciate others will be rewarded by their sincere efforts to understand and appreciate us.

For too long, at least in North America, we have persisted in the arrogant assumption that everyone eats or likes to eat what we ourselves do. And how is it that food professionals have persisted for so long in the equally arrogant assumption that only certain foods are the "right" foods? Perhaps in Canada, the United States, and Australia, where the existence of so many cultural groups has pressed forward our emerging awareness of just how different cultural traditions are, we have found that our own so-called national food customs have eluded definition.

Increasingly, awareness of the food traditions, and indeed the incredible variety of herbs and spices, fruits and vegetables, the countless enticing ways of food preparation and food service have enriched our individual food horizons and expanded our views of what constitutes a healthy diet. After all, healthy survival is not the possession of any one group.

Increasingly, too, it is becoming obvious that an understanding of many aspects of the cultures of others, including their food traditions, is indispensable in any human communication. This is true not only for professionals in the fields of education, medicine, social work, public health and nutrition, commercial food services, but is clearly recognized today in the global marketplace.

THE HOW AND WHY OF YOU EAT WHAT YOU ARE

While the conscious research for this book began in 1973, it has, in fact, been a lifelong fascination for me. The focusing of my interests in the diversity of peoples and their foods began with a realization of the narrow scientific content of both my undergraduate studies in foods and nutrition and my subsequent dietetic internship. Over the years I satisfied my own curiosity about "foreign foods" with informal study, travel, and recipe experimentation. Later I incorporated this learning into my professional work as a home service director, one of the first gourmet cooking shows on television, radio interviews, and later as an ethnic food consultant and lecturer with the Canadian Ethnic Studies Lecture Program.

In London, Ontario, teaching various courses in International Gourmet Cookery to more than 400 students further intensified my belief that foods of the world opened the door to deeper discussions of food. People wanted to learn more about these differing ways, and inevitably these discussions took as much time as the actual cooking lesson. My students were always questioning why people ate and served foods in differing ways, and I had to scramble to try to discover some of the answers. My desire to extend my knowledge of teaching adults as well as exploring the principles behind teaching and learning led me into graduate studies in education at the University of Western Ontario and the University of Toronto. There, as a Ph.D. candidate, I studied and researched the meaning of culture that led to my thesis on understanding cultural difference.

While this book is intended mainly as a useful resource for both the professional and the student, many gourmets and travelers may also consider this reference as a resource for their own cultural and culinary adventures. Hopefully, each reader will approach with curiosity the chapter of his or her own ethnic background and then, tantalized, browse through other chapters. To these ends, and mindful of the sometimes stuffy texts that I have researched, I can only hope that my own interests and enthusiasm have produced an accessible reference work.

So many variations occur in descriptions of food names from one region to another, and even from one author to another, that those definitions, like exact recipes, must remain open-ended. Similarly, a wide tolerance in the spelling of both terms and food names must be exercised.

A word about the use of B.C.E. (Before the Common Era) and C.E. (Common Era). This terminology is used in preference to the more common B.C. and A.D. with their more Christian reference, out of respect for the many religious and cultural viewpoints represented in this book.

AND FINALLY...

The subject of this work is unique and the scope vast. There will inevitably be omissions and perhaps areas of contention. I hope readers will continue to share these with me as willingly as they have in the past twenty years. Many suggestions and changes have been incorporated in this edition. As I have pointed out in the past, and will continue to point out – it is possible that in focusing on the "strange ways of others" we may fail to reflect on our own entrenched and indelible customs. But such reflection is not only invaluable to understanding, it is, in fact, the critical step in the process of learning. This book's title is frequently confused with Adele Davis' early book on popular nutrition entitled *You ARE What You Eat*. It is indeed possible that we really are what we eat – physiologically – but because our daily lives are embedded in our cultural heritage, it is even more probable that we eat what we are.

Thelma Barer-Stein, Ph.D.
Toronto

HOW TO USE THIS BOOK

YOU EAT WHAT YOU ARE – *People, Culture and Food Traditions* is a documented study of ethnocultural food traditions. ("Ethnic" refers to the minority group(s) in a larger culture within a specific region.) In this second edition, three new chapters have been added: Indonesian, Malay, and Singaporean; Thai; and Tibetan. In addition, each chapter has been updated, glossaries have been extended, and regional maps included. Cultural groups sharing a common region may be included in one chapter, others may be described in a separate chapter.

A historical, regional, and cultural overview begins each chapter, with particular emphasis given to factors or events that influenced food availability, selection, preparation and those food habits that have remained as traditions.

The section **Domestic Life** describes elements in family structure and the home, as well as specific cooking facilities and implements – especially where these factors touch on food traditions.

Foods Commonly Used is a quick-reference section that provides an overview of the basic diet preferences. These food preferences are then discussed in detail under the categories **Dairy Products, Fruits and Vegetables, Meats and Alternates, Breads and Grains, Fats, Sweets and Snacks, and Beverages.**

The section **Meals** and **Customs** describes general daily manners and customs – not just those pertaining to foods, wherever these may be helpful to understanding. Traditional meal and snack times including examples of foods and beverages, where and how they are eaten, noteworthy elements of manners and hospitality may also be included.

The section **Special Occasions** discusses the practices and symbolism of family and religious occasions, with special emphasis on those relating to foods. Where occasions are described but no particular foods are mentioned, this means that generous portions of daily fare are consumed instead of special dishes or treats. In this section too, reference to religious observances, superstitions, myths and legends are included especially as they pertain to foods.

Cooking Methods and **Regional Specialties** are described only for those groups where these factors are relevant and clearly differentiated.

Glossaries of Foods and Food Terms are included at the end of each chapter. For the most part, these are an extension of terms found within each chapter and highlight distinctive dishes, names for foods, food facilities or utensils. In some entries, foods similar to other cultural groups are listed, denoting differing names for similar dishes.

Sources and References for each chapter appear at the end of the book together with a detailed **Index**.

PUBLISHER'S NOTE
Languages, dialects and spellings vary widely throughout many countries of the world. Nowhere is this more true than in the world of food where names, spellings and even meanings are often determined by ancient custom rather than modern usage. In this book we have selected the most common and accepted words and spellings consistent with the usage of the region itself. The reader may be familiar with variant spellings and meanings depending on his or her personal background. Similarly, many languages have accents and other typographic symbols that are impossible to reproduce accurately in the English alphabet. Therefore all non-English words are used here without accents or other typographic marks that would be used in their native language. Finally, the maps are intended to help the reader locate the region or country discussed. However, cultural groups do not stay neatly within national boundaries so these maps are intended only as a guide.

CHAPTER 1

AFRICAN

Note: This chapter deals with the main regions of sub-Saharan Africa, including West, East, the Horn of Africa, Central and South Africa.

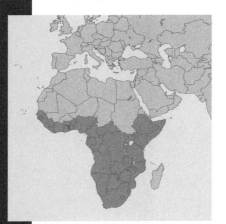

It has to be impertinence or at the least, a gross injustice, to attempt to squeeze into one chapter of a book a discussion of the world's second largest continent, with a population exceeding 580 million, speaking more than 800 languages, and living in more than 45 countries!

Africa's natural beauty and fascinating complexity has drawn and mystified travelers, while her violence, corruption, and poverty have horrified. There is no simple way to describe the contrasts that are Africa. Perhaps more than many other peoples, Africans, as de Villiers and Hirtie have noted, are a "work in progress, in always-unfinished evolution." As such, only moments in that continuing movement to progress can be captured.

To most people of Africa, the ancient past is as immediate as this moment. Stories, myths, traditions, and rituals from the spirit world guide and inform every daily activity, every celebration, and every decision. Throughout their thousands of years of history, tribal struggles, migrations, violence, and times of peace have threaded through their daily lives, melding into new tribes and new regions, and embracing new conquests. Nothing old is really ever discarded.

Over the centuries, other countries have conquered, explored, and exploited this continent's natural resources and its human beings, who were regarded as pagans to be converted or as merchandise to be shipped as slaves to other parts of the world. And though, for the most part, this predominantly tropical and sub-tropical continent clings to deeply embedded cultural traditions of its own, France, the United Kingdom, the Netherlands, Spain, and Portugal have left traces of their influence. After centuries of disease and neglect, attempts are being made – by a new and burgeoning middle class – to blend old traditions and modern developments for the benefit of the entire land. But change does not come easily to any country or people. The newborn states of Africa are struggling with problems of political and economic chaos, tribal rivalries, famine, poverty, and lack of education.

From the 1500s to the 1700s, African blacks, mainly from the area of West Africa (today's Senegal, Guinea, Sierra Leone, Gambia, Liberia, Ivory Coast, Ghana, Dahomey, Togo, Nigeria, Cameroon, and Gabon) were shipped as slaves to North America, Brazil, and the West Indies. For them, local and tribal differences, and even varying cultural backgrounds, soon melded into one common concern for the suffering they all endured. Music, songs, and dances as well as remembered traditional food, helped not only to uplift them but also quite unintentionally added immeasurably to the culture around them. In the approximately 300 years that blacks have made their homes in North America, the West Indies, and Brazil, their highly honed art of the cuisine so treasured and carefully transmitted to their daughters has become part of the great culinary classics of these lands. But seldom are the African blacks given that recognition.

Of African origin are such specialities as **gumbo** and **pralines**, West Indian **callaloo** and **duckandoo** (a dish of greens and a dessert based on sweet potatoes), the Brazilian condiments **dende oil** and spicy hot sauces. Jamaica's **bammy bread** and the **pan bread** so beloved in the southern United States are both said to have their origin in the flat round **cassava breads** typical of Africa. Seeds and the plants of sesame, okra, some melons, and certain varieties of greens as well as yams, together with many techniques of bread making, and the use and combination of spices, are also all credited to the ingenuity of the African cook.

It could be argued that every nation and every ethnic group has its own soul food. But the contemporary connotation of the term "soul food" refers to the gradual blending and developing of a peculiar style of cookery with its own dictionary of food terms: it is a blend of West African cookery begun in the southern United States and now very much a part of the cultural tradition of African-Americans, binding them proudly to their African heritage. "Soul food" incorporates an economical and satisfying cuisine based on cereals, vegetables (greens and yams), pork and pork offal as well as chicken.

When speaking of Africa, it is very important to differentiate between urban and rural populations. Not only are the urban people in many areas still more or less influenced by European customs and manners, they are also a part of the growing middle class that is creating a new, independent African image, culture, and cuisine. Although this middle class is growing, the dominant concern lies with the three-quarters of the African population who are rural and tradition-bound.

Because of the lack of large mountain ranges, the climate of Africa is consistently hot except for the southern more temperate areas. Most of its people belong to a pastoral society where life revolves around the seasons, the crops, the villages, and the tribes. In most areas a subsistence economy predominates: the concern is for survival not profit. This outlook has pragmatic roots. Food is more important than money; cattle are often more important as a status symbol than as food; food spoilage from rodents, humidity, or insects is prevalent; transportation to distant markets for trade or profit is difficult and often impossible because of lack of roads or vehicles or both. In fact, Jacques May reports that "given better seed, he [the African farmer] will rejoice not because it will give him a better yield, but because he will get the same result from a smaller plot ..."

The problems encountered by those attempting to introduce scientific agrarian methods are further complicated by general poor soil, lack of storage facilities, lack of trained technicians or available parts for mechanical equipment, and finally, the problems of a burgeoning population that absorbs more and more land.

While Canadians and Americans of African descent are proudly relearning their heritage and establishing themselves as valued members of their communities, the peoples of their homeland are still engaged in the long and difficult process of easing themselves – together with their cherished traditions, myths and stories – into the twenty-first century. Unlike the past history of conquest and exploitation from external powers, the future seems to promise a concerned and committed world increasingly aware of the needs of the global community.

DOMESTIC LIFE (RURAL)

Cookery methods rather than basic foods are what distinguish regional and ethnic dishes in Africa. Foods may be cooked over open fires or in pits heated with stones; either of these methods may be used indoors or outdoors. Commonly used cookery utensils include: perforated clay steamers, jugs and jars for storage, strainers, mortar and pestle, knives, enamel and clay and heavy iron cooking pots, wooden bowls and spoons (**fufu** or **ugali** is always stirred with a

FOODS COMMONLY USED

Although there are many ethnic groups in Africa, it is possible to make some generalizations about foods and food customs. In some areas, different names may be used but it is generally conceded that the principal African staple is a starchy mixture called **fufu** in western regions and **ugali** in eastern areas. It is eaten with spicy sauces and condiments. The starchy mixture may be prepared from any cereal or starchy vegetable or root by pounding into a paste and then cooking with water like a cereal. It is eaten with three fingers of the right hand by forming the food into a ball then dipping into flavorful and spicy sauces. Rice, yams, **cassava**, plantain, corn, millet, or **cocoyams** may be used. More sophisticated

versions may be formed into small cakes or fritters and fried, or formed into small balls and poached, then served much the same way as dumplings are in other countries.

The condiment sauces are skillfully prepared from locally available spices and herbs and often include onions, tomatoes, meats and bones, fish and seafood, and various root and green vegetables, even fruits, depending on availability. The use of fiery peppers and chilies of many types and distinct flavor and hotness is universal. Many a husband judges his wife's love and respect by the hotness of her sauces.

Considerable ingenuity is also displayed in the preparation and variety of breads, fried cakes, and

fritters prepared from flours made from cassava, millet, manioc, wheat, and corn.

Soups are the staple food of the nomadic tribespeople, moving from place to place in search of cattle food. They use milk and prepare butter but choose to collect wild vegetables and hunt occasional wild animals rather than use their herds for food.

Traditionally, fruit beers made from various cereals, and a slightly fermented beverage made from porridge water (**maheu**) are the beverages usually taken between meals rather than with food. More recently, sugar and honey-sweetened tea and coffee and commercial soft drinks are replacing the traditional and more nourishing beverages.

wooden spoon), graters, frying baskets. Grinding stones are used to mill grains; dried gourds and calabash shells are used as spoons and ladles – and many of these are beautifully decorated and carved.

Food storage is a great problem because of the climate and a prevalence of insects and rodents. However, elevated platforms, vessels and cages, strung and held up, and covered clay containers and woven covers of many types are used.

Eating and cooking, if not done outdoors, are often done in a special hut that may have floors finished with a paste of dried cow dung. A special ledge along one side may be used to store most of the cookery utensils, especially the treasured clay pots and jugs. In some areas, in addition to pits and the use of open fires, ovens built of dried mud may be used for baking.

Foods are generally used on a day-to-day basis, and the amount required is judged – seldom asked for by weight. Africa has an oral rather than a written tradition: events and traditions are passed by word of mouth and by careful demonstration, dance or song. The written word and such things as weights and measures were never important in traditional rural communities. Introduction of weights and measures is a slow process, whereas amounts are taught to, and somehow learned by, young children.

Cutlery is seldom used for eating except in cities and then often only in European company. Even in urban areas, the family evening meal will likely be a traditional **fufu** or **ugali** with condiment sauces all enjoyed in the traditional way from community platters and eaten with the fingers.

DAIRY PRODUCTS
Cow's milk, goat's milk, and sheep's milk, taken plain or soured or in the form of curds and whey, are used as available. Most often they are used for infants and young children as part of soups, gruels, and puddings. The Masai herdsmen are known to drink a beverage of milk and animal blood. Soured milk is preferred by adults in some areas. Farmers use dairy products less often than the nomadic tribes, who prefer to take dairy products in the form of soups and buttery sauces.

FRUITS AND VEGETABLES
Fresh fruits are eaten in season everywhere as they are available, whether wild or cultivated. Especially plentiful are varieties of mangoes and bananas, used green or ripe, to be eaten as they are or used in sauces. Other fruits include the whole range of tropical and sub-tropical fruits such as melons, **hacha**, **baobab**, **mushange**, **hwakwa** (African orange), **onde**, wild plums and berries, wild figs, dates, wild or **kafir oranges**, coconut, papaya, avocado, pineapple.

Most popular vegetables include plantains, green bananas, pumpkin, okra, yams, cocoyams, spinach, cress, mustard greens, and fresh corn. Cultivated vegetables include many varieties of beans, cucumbers, tomatoes, onions, garlic, cabbage, carrots, and potatoes. To these must be added the many local varieties of wild and indigenous roots, tubers, bush greens, and mushrooms.

MEATS AND ALTERNATES
In most of rural Africa meats from any source are an infrequent part of the usual diet. It will likely be the highlight of a special occasion or given to special guests. Most meats and fowl are tough and stringy and require long, slow cooking with moisture, so are most often used in soups or stewed or braised dishes. It should also be noted that most African women are experts at preserving whatever meat may be available by methods of salting, drying, pickling and/or smoking. In rural areas where cattle are still considered a sign of wealth and status, beef is seldom used for food, but it may be included in the urban diet. Some forest animals, pigs (not used by Muslims), goats and sheep, antelope, elephant, and oxen may be used for food. Many varieties of mice are eaten in season and there is also seasonal use of black and red ants and caterpillars as well as some types of grasshopper. Many taboos surround the eating of offal, chicken, and eggs, and care is taken to avoid a guest's particular taboo or superstition.

Fish and seafood are commonly only eaten close to their sources, such as in coastal areas, or near lakes, streams or rivers. Yet many experts have expressed strong feelings about the urgency and importance of improving fishing methods and storage and transportation facilities since this is an abundant resource that could greatly increase the general protein food supply.

There is a very wide variety of pulses used everywhere that form an important part of the diet. Peas, beans and lentils of many varieties are readily stored and easily cooked into soups, sauces, side dishes, in combination with vegetables, or mashed and fried as cakes.

Varieties of nuts and seeds are used depending on local preference and availability but most popular are **groundnuts**, the African name for peanuts. They are used in soups, stews, and sauces, and as garnishes. **Groundnut butter** is used as a seasoning.

BREADS AND GRAINS
The staple African food, **fufu** or **ugali**, prepared from almost any available starchy plant source, forms 80 percent of the daily calories consumed, while the average European diet contains only 30 percent calories

from breads or cereals. It must be stressed that the general African diet is high in fiber and carbohydrates, with proteins and fats forming only a small part. Principal sources for flours and **fufu/ugali** preparation are: maize, manioc, sorghum, millet, wheat, and rice. Plantain, green bananas, and yams are the favorites for **fufu**. Many varieties of bread are made from the flours and these are further varied by including recipes for breads that are both leavened and unleavened. Some flours are allowed to ferment first to improve taste.

Swahili yeast is the leavening agent prepared by mashing ripe plantain with a little water, sugar, and wheat flour, and allowing it to ferment in a warm place. It not only leavens the dough but adds a sourdough-type flavor to buns, breads, and fried cookies.

FATS
The most-used fats are oils prepared from vegetables, seeds, or coconut. In some areas olive oil or palm oil is used, as available. **Groundnuts** are sometimes used for their oil but the nuts themselves are more important; the pulp mash left after the oil extraction is also used as food.

SWEETS AND SNACKS
Desserts are mainly fresh fruits in season and as they are affordable or available. They are also nibbled as snacks. More recently there is a large increase in the use of sweetened tea and coffee as well as sweetened commercial soft drinks. An occasional snack or dessert may be of spiced and sugared fried pancakes or cookies; frying is more popular than baking because not everyone has an oven. Some honey and preserves are used as sweetening agents.

SEASONINGS
Blends of spicy, sweet, and various degrees of hotness in curries are widely used all over Africa. Many varieties of chilies and hot peppers are savored. Ground sesame seeds (plain or toasted), melon seeds, cotton seeds, as well as fresh and dried types of mushrooms, are also used. Special seasoning pastes are prepared from seeds that have been dried in the sun, then steamed and fermented. Small amounts of the resulting paste are used as a flavoring. One such is called **ogilie**.

It should be noted that all foods are not only hotly seasoned but well salted. Salt is obtained by burning certain grasses or tree barks and the resulting ash passed through calabash sieves, then boiled in clay pots until a residue of whitish salt is formed. Another salt source was from certain soils where animals are observed licking; the watery residue from repeated washings of such soil is boiled and leaves a salty residue.

BEVERAGES
Although the exact names may differ from one region to another, soured milk (from cow, sheep, goat, or camel), low-alcohol beer and wine made locally are all familiar beverages, as is the ever-present hospitable tea and coffee. Coconut milk and juices from fruits are also widely used both as drinks and as cookery ingredients. Commercial soft drinks are now increasingly used, but a wide variety of herb teas are also enjoyed everywhere in Africa.

MEALS AND CUSTOMS
The majority of rural Africans customarily eat one main meal a day and this is usually the evening meal. Upon arising, coffee, tea or milk or curds may form a small light meal while some people may be content to nibble on seeds. Throughout the day snacks of fruits, seeds, or nuts may be accompanied with beverages. In some areas a midday meal of **fufu/ugali** and relishes may be traditionally larger than the evening meal, which in this case would then be a cereal dish alone of gruel or **fufu.**

Infants are usually breast-fed on demand up to the age of two. Attempts to introduce bottle feedings have often met with sad results: sterilization of bottles and formula were poorly understood, formulas were diluted to last longer, and with the abandonment of breast-feeding, intercourse was resumed earlier than usual with a resultant increase in children who could be ill afforded. **Bota** is a thin gruel for babies, fed by pouring into the mother's hand and gently easing into the infant's mouth. Some foods and medicinal herbs if deemed necessary are pre-chewed by the mother then given to the infant.

Very young children are taught early that meat is a delicacy, but like other pleasures, they are also taught that they cannot always have everything they want: meat may be tasted and enjoyed, but it is generally not given until children are at least three or four years old.

In most parts of Africa, meals follow strictly specified rituals. At a very young age, children learn that handwashing and clapping of the hands must always precede a meal. Children must be silent while adults eat; further, they must never beg for food. Violations of these rules are punishable by beatings. Men precede women at meals but no one eats alone. Dining is always a group pleasure and a time of calm and serene enjoyment. In some areas it is considered that women are somehow self-sufficient, and no one seems concerned if they are left only the crumbs.

Often if new foods are introduced by aid groups from other countries, the food must be appealing to the men, for if refused by them no one else will touch it.

Hospitality is considered of great importance and also follows a predictable ritual of handwashing, clapping, and the offering of food. Even if one is not hungry, to refuse would be an insult.

Totemism is greatly respected and it is considered proper to inquire of a guest what their totem is so that it may be separated from the rest of the food. For example, if the totem of a certain guest is liver, then liver will be removed from the rest of the meats to be served and given to the others so that the guest will not be offended. Other strongly held traditions concern local clan, family, and tribal taboos: for example the eating of certain fish, eggs or parts of animals or fowl may be taboo, and for the Muslims pork is forbidden.

While food growing and harvesting is done by the men, women are responsible for collecting firewood and water and for food preparation. So seriously are these daily tasks taken that young children perform play ceremonies enacting their parts as men and women of the household. This parent-supervised ceremony is called *mahumbwe*. Very young girls make serious play of helping their mothers and grandmothers at their tasks.

Finally, it is important to remember that the customs and traditions recorded here are a part of traditional and rural African life, but by no means practiced consistently. A large and continually growing population of Africa is the new middle class: freshly educated, ambitious, sophisticated, and eagerly creating their own culinary and social arts liberally laced with ideas from their rich past, yet at the same time new. Three meals a day, school lunch programs, scientific fishing methods, and modern farming techniques have already made many of the traditions seem archaic.

REGIONAL SPECIALTIES

EAST AFRICAN

Uganda, Kenya, Tanzania and Mozambique are five countries within the region known as East Africa. It is a region where strong British influence is still felt although few British or East Indians remain.

Like West Africa, the vast expanses of land are inhabited by hundreds of differing peoples, each devoted to their rituals and traditions.

For the brief period that Europeans controlled East Africa, they introduced many dishes and eating customs from their own homelands. They also imported corn from America, which in a very brief time became another variety of **ugali** – now prepared from millet or corn flour.

The Portuguese explorer Vasco da Gama recognized the strategic importance of the area's trade route. In the early 1900s German missionaries established themselves in Tanzania, bringing with them their beer and schnapps, and their own recipes for roasting the plentiful wild game. The British, who viewed the region as a home-away-from-home, replaced German influence. Imported cereals, tea, and coffee and even fruits and vegetables as well as live cattle all helped to bring their dream to realty: England in Africa! To complete the illusion, the British hired East Indians who in turn added their influence to the food and manners of the region.

Today, East Africans enjoy their **ugali** prepared from maize flour as if it had forever been a part of their diet. Fine beef cattle roam the lands and Kenyans are proud of their pig production. Some of the best European cheeses are produced in excellent quality: **Swiss**, **Camembert**, **Cheddar**, **Gorgonzola**, and a variety of soft and fresh cheeses. Not only flowers that are typically found in an English garden, but also fruits and vegetables commonly found in European markets are now deliciously prevalent in East Africa, especially in Kenya.

Still, despite the availability of plentiful game, most East Africans are vegetarians, living on dairy products, grains, legumes, vegetables, and fruits. Meat may occasionally be a part of special celebrations or rituals. There is good reason for this. As in India, the animals (cows, sheep, goats) are more valued for their milk, dung, fleece, and hair. And in Africa perhaps more importantly, they are valued for the status they bring to their owners.

Rice is a favorite in many meals and dishes, but sorghum, millet, corn, and wheat are widely used as cereals, dumplings, and breads. **Pombe**, the national beer, is everyone's beverage, including children. **Manioc**, sweet potatoes, bananas, and plantain together with a variety of local fruits round out the average diet. In coastal areas fish and crustaceans are important. Snacks of fruits or sugarcane are enjoyed. Curry, chili peppers, coconut and coconut milk and groundnuts are the usual seasonings.

The foods of Tanzania are distinguished from the other regions mainly because of their increased use of tropical fruits and vegetables.

GLOSSARY OF FOODS AND FOOD TERMS

EAST AFRICAN

Huku Ne Dovi: Zimbabwe's version of the ubiquitous African chicken and groundnut stew, served with rice or **Sadza**.

Mealie-Meal: white corn flour.

Nhopi Dovi: cooked mashed pumpkin blended with a paste of **groundnuts**, salt and pepper. This is a good example of the many ways that **groundnuts** add protein to starch meals.

Nyama Ne Nyemba: along with **fufu** or **ugali**, beans of infinite varieties are important staples in African meals. This classic Zimbabwean dish is prepared with diced beef, garlic, chilies, curry, and a generous quantity of beans to bubble in the rich flavors.

Plantains: tropical fruits of the banana family, more often eaten in cooked form. The variations are amazing: thin crisply fried **plantain chips**, thick and smooth **mtori** (plantain soup), and crunchy **fritters**. Then add the countless ways that plantains are used as a vegetable in stews and casseroles with meats and fish. And there's even a wine.

Pombe Ya N'Dizi: another especially intoxicating use of plantains – richly flavored wine very popular in Tanzania.

Sadza: called a dumpling but in appearance and texture more like stiffly cooked cornmeal. **Sadza** can be prepared from maize or millet flour and forms the starchy base for a hearty stew of meat or fish with vegetables and spices. At least in Zimbabwe, **Sadza** would never be served without a delectably spicy hot sauce.

Supuya Papai: **Pawpaw** or papaya soup prepared simply with a basic light stock, the fried and mashed fruit, seasoned with lightly browned onions and smoothed with fresh cream. This Kenyan soup can be served hot or cool.

Ugali: a thick smooth porridge prepared from maize flour. **Ugali** can be mounded on individual plates or scooped into round balls for serving with hot peppery sauces and vegetables with meat and fish.

SOUTH AFRICAN

While the West African nations combine the most sophisticated of European, New World, and their

own indigenous food influences, and the area of East Africa is principally influenced by British, Indian and Islamic food traditions, South Africa is dominated by the influence of the Dutch. As early as 1651, Dutch settlers at the Cape created a colony with the sole purpose of supplying fresh food and other necessities to Dutch ships. "The richest, most complex and civilized contribution to the art of cooking in Africa evolved here."

The Dutch Free Burghers and their Muslim slaves from the East Indies, French refugees, Germans, other Europeans, and British all added their influence in customs, foods, and culture. The "Cape Colored" include those of mixed black and European background, strongly identifying with the Dutch, the French, and with Christianity. In some of the following typical foods and dishes can be seen the marriage of food customs that have created what is now typically South African fare.

The Cape Malay's (Indian) favorite dishes include:

Atjar: exotic pickles and preserves prepared from tropical fruits and vegetables which may be packed with brine, syrups or oils and seasoned with varying subtle or hot combinations of East Indian spices.

Bobotie: a soft moist mixture of ground lamb, softened bread, seasoned with a blend of curry spices, lemon juice, shredded apple and chopped almonds is baked slowly with an egg and milk custard topping. Of Malay descent this classic South African dish is everyone's delight.

Bredie: a specialty and often festive meat or fish stew redolent with onions and colorful with chunks of vegetables such as pumpkin, cauliflower, beans, etc. Takes its specific name from the predominating vegetable, e.g. **pumpkin bredie**.

Koesister: crunchy crullers fried to golden perfection and served with a tangy lemon and cinnamon syrup.

Sambal: refreshing salads prepared from grated fresh vegetables splashed with vinegar or lemon juice and zesty with chilies and cayenne pepper.

Slaais: related to **Sambals** and may combine unusual (for westerners) combinations such as layered dates and sliced onions sprinkled with vinegar; chicory and orange slices; fennel tomatoes and mushrooms, or the more familiar finely shredded carrots with raisins. All salads are usually well seasoned and could never be described as bland.

Sosaties (from the Malaysian **sate**): marinated meats, skewered and grilled; snack or main dish.

South African Cape Malay meals may include one of the traditional dishes above as well as salads, pickles, chutneys, and condiments (such as **blatjang**: nuts, garlic, sweet preserved fruits and spices), served with rice and rounded off with sweet bakery and candies. Dates are widely used and a combination of sugar-sweetened dates and sliced onions is a frequent side dish. The ubiquitous **tameletje**, basically a candy of caramelized sugar, is made in many versions too.

South African wines and brandies are known worldwide, as are their fish and shellfish (periwinkles, mussels, crayfish or rock lobster), fowl and pork dishes. Grape-stuffed chickens or roast suckling pigs take precedence and are eaten on Sundays or special occasions by South Afrikaners of European origin. The moderate climate produces vegetables so plentiful, varied, and popular that often half a dozen vegetable dishes or salads accompany the main meal. A plethora of both tropical and temperate fruits may be eaten fresh, preserved into jams and marmalades, dried, or used in desserts and bakery. Cookies of infinite variety (**soetkoekie**) and many types of buns (**mosbolletje**), as well as pies and tarts (**terts**), and doughnuts and crullers (**vetkoekies**) head the list of favorites that are nibbled for snacks or eaten at breakfast time with hot cocoa, tea, or coffee. And as with Dutch families the world over, bread on the table is an important element of every meal.

The native Bantu's staple diet includes milk from cattle, millet porridge, millet beer, and **mealie**. So popular is **mealie**, a porridge made from cornmeal but served in many forms, such as puddings, fried patties, etc., that many a South Afrikaner's meal is not considered complete without at least a side dish of **mealie**; with cream and honey it may be breakfast.

Braaivleis is the traditional South African outdoor meal of grilled skewered meats (usually lamb, huge rolled links of homemade beef and pork sausage) to be grilled, and many vegetable and salad side dishes with the traditional dish of **mealie**.

THE HORN OF AFRICA
The Red Sea, the Gulf of Aden, and the Indian Ocean wash the eastern tip of Africa known as the Horn of Africa. In this region lies the legendary ancient lands of Ethiopia and Somalia.

THE ETHIOPIANS

Ethiopia's very name conjures exotic visions of the Queen of Sheba, a legendary heritage of kings, and mythical tales of gold and hidden riches. Once called Abysinnia, this arid land of mountains and plateaus boasts the beautiful Lake Tana that flows into the mighty Nile River coursing through Egypt to the Mediterranean Sea. Ethiopia's name also conjures the aroma of some of the finest coffee in the world, one of her principal exports. Though impoverished and strife-torn today, Ethiopia's history speaks eloquently of bustling trade and prosperity beginning at least 4,000 years ago.

Arabs, Egyptians, British, Portuguese, and Italians each in turn entertained hopes of ruling the land. Today, these elements of Ethiopia's history are evident in her cultural and religious diversity. As well, Ethiopia's distinctive form of Christianity is impregnated with elements of Judaism, Islam, and paganism, setting it apart from eastern Orthodoxy or western Catholicism.

In the plateaus and mountains, primitive beehive-shaped *tukels* (huts) still exist in villages, while modern white skyscrapers pierce sunny skies in the large cities like Addis Ababa. Perhaps the huts are symbolic of the Ethiopian cultivation and love for honey. Guest are frequently welcomed with sweet dripping pieces of honeycomb and a bowl of curds and whey – literally the biblical milk and honey. While some Ethiopians have adopted western dress and some customs, their ties to ancient traditions remain, especially in their religion.

A meal begins with ritual handwashing. Water is poured from an ornate jug over the fingers of the right hand, which are wiped on a clean towel. Only those fingers are used for eating. Breads are held in the right hand too, to wrap, scoop, or dip into foods and sauces.

For the main meal of the day, a dome covers a small round table or a large metal tray. When lifted, a large "cloth" appears mounded with portions of stewed foods. The cloth is actually a very large thin pancake, an Ethiopian bread called **injera**. Often several other kinds of breads will appear as well as a variety of stews and combinations of meat and vegetables called **wots** and **alechas**. Diners enjoy the meal by tearing off bits of **injera** and scooping up foods. Frequently a partner or the host will combine a morsel of food and pop it into someone else's mouth. As can be imagined, mealtime is hospitable and lively when everyone is bent over the same "table."

Tej, the golden honey wine poured from traditional long-neck jugs, accompanies the meal while coffee with honey served in small cups concludes it. Dinner is over when the food and **injera** are all eaten. Later in the evening tiny spicy breads called **dabo kolo**, served with butter and honey, may be nibbled with fresh or dried fruits.

The large Ethiopian flat bread called **injera** obviates the need for tablecloths, cutlery, or serviettes. The two main types of meat and vegetable stews are **wots** – always spicy hot with chilies, and **alechas**, another type of stew sometimes quite mild. The most important sauce accompanying these dishes is **berbere**, and others include **mittmita** and **waaz**. The predominantly agrarian economy produces millet, barley, and sorghum. **Tef** is the millet-like grain used especially to prepare the sourdough for **injera**. Offal, especially tripe, is enjoyed in many dishes; beef, lamb, goat, and chicken are used by those who can afford them. For many, a diet of grains, potatoes, plantains, and legumes with some milk and cheese suffices.

GLOSSARY OF ETHIOPIAN FOODS AND FOOD TERMS

Abish: meat-stuffed fruits or vegetables usually cooked in butter, then served with breads or rice.

Berbere: a spicy aromatic mixture of seasonings such as ground cumin and coriander, nutmeg, cinnamon and ground cloves, an assortment of pepper and chilies all lightly and carefully toasted in a heavy ungreased skillet. **Berbere** has many versions – all hot and pungently delicious. The prepared mixture can be stored in an airtight jar for months.

Dabo Kolo: tiny spicy breads browned in an ungreased heavy skillet. These are enjoyed with butter and honey, often served with fruit for snacks and late evening nibbles.

Kitfo: raw minced beef seasoned with **berbere** or a similar spicy hot mix. This is served in patties or small balls as part of the meal.

Lab: a soft mixture of fresh cheese and herbs served with a variety of breads.

Miter Kebben: clarified butter simmered till golden then seasoned with onions, garlic, fresh ginger root,

and spices like nutmeg and cinnamon. The milk solids and the spices are then strained out and the clear oil stored.

Selatta: a bright spicy salad of cooked vegetables and/or legumes.

Shiro Wot: a stew made just with vegetables instead of meat.

Talla: a roasted and salted barley flour snack rolled between the fingers to form pellets, then eaten. The flavoring is an indigenous herb called **gesho**.

Wot: classic Ethiopian stew called **doro wot** if prepared with chicken and **beg wot** if prepared with beef. Sliced onions are simmered in butter or **ghee** (clarified butter) till golden, then tomato paste, water or broth, chilies or **berbere** and black pepper are added with chicken pieces and hard-cooked whole eggs. The mixture is slowly simmered until the meat is tender, then served with **Injera**.

SOMALI

The land of the Somalis consists of arid plains and plateaus, barren rugged mountains, and two main rivers under a harsh, hot and dry climate. The Indian Ocean, the Gulf of Aden, Ethiopia, and Kenya bound this area – the Horn of Africa. Archeological evidence indicates that the Somali people have occupied this region since before 100 C.E.

But the Somalis have not been alone. The present-day state is said to be "largely a creation of European colonialism," tempting others largely for its strategic and trade route importance. In the early centuries the region was ruled by Omanis, Zanzibaris, Yemenis, and Ottoman Turks before being regionally colonized by the British in the northwest, the Italians in the south, the Ethiopians in the west, and the Kenyans in the southwest. The segmented colonial control existed until Somali independence in 1960.

Civil war, the breakdown of health care services, drought, widespread malnutrition and famine, and the plight of refugees have plagued the Somalis since independence. After the fall of the regime of Mohammad Siad Barre in 1991, anarchy and civil war have added to the harsh realities of Somali daily life.

Officially Islamic and predominantly Sunni Muslim, the Somalis' ethnic groups consist of four pastoral nomadic clans: Dir, Daarood, Isaaq, and Hawiye and two agricultural or "cultivators" clans: Digil and Rahanwayn who dwell between the Shabeelle and Jubba Rivers. English and Italian are spoken by less than 10 percent of the population; the rest speak Somali in one of several dialects: Common Somali, Central Somali, and Coastal Somali.

While 95 percent of the population are Somalis, their hierarchical clans nonetheless segment them. Membership in these clans shape social status, individual obligations, and rights, while Islam permeates every aspect of daily life.

Traditionally Islamic, Somalis are polygamous and often marry four wives to produce as many children as possible. Population provides a workforce and fighting strength as well as political clout. The harsh lifestyle and the harsher climate take lives as well. Women are mostly involved with the care of the sheep and goats while the men concern themselves with the camels. The quality and quantity of camels confers prestige and wealth on the owners. Despite the importance of women's chastity, few are veiled and it is said that Somali women do not shrink from either assuming responsibility or expressing their opinions.

The Somalis' daily life and all festivities and saints' days emerge from and revolve around their religion of Islam. The *wadads*, the religious leaders, dispense – for a fee – blessings, advice, and magic potions and mediate in criminal proceedings and feuds. They also provide all religious services from birth to death. Pilgrimages, belief in the special powers of saints, charms, and amulets are all deeply interwoven in Somali daily life.

Frequently, the Somali pragmatism emerges from the religious mysticism and unabashedly accepts modern medicine, while at the same time promulgating traditions for ensuring the virginity of their women. Somalis recognized mosquitoes as the carriers of malaria before this was discovered by western science.

As with many nomadic peoples, the cultural literacy of Somalis is to be found in their oral tradition of reciting stories and poems, and in their encyclopedic knowledge of sayings and history. As might be suspected, Somalis enjoy talking!

Somali foods are based on dairy products, sheep, goats, and grains such as rice, sorghum, barley, and maize. Some vegetables such as varieties of squashes, sweet potatoes, and varieties of beans round out the meals. **Groundnuts** and sesame seeds, bananas and sugarcane find a place as well, when available.

A cautious suspicion greets strangers and new-comers, even amongst their own people. But Somali hospitality is legendary, with the finest they have to offer being proudly proffered to a guest. Differences in temperament are evident between the nomads and the cultivators with the latter being less aggressive and less suspicious than the former. However, the entire nation of Somalis unite in the celebration of Ramadan, as do Muslims the world over.

WEST AFRICAN

Long in touch with Europeans, and the most heavily populated area in Africa, West Africa includes Senegal, Gambia, Guinea, Sierra Leone, Liberia, Ivory Coast, Ghana, Togo, Dahomey, Nigeria, Burkinafaso, and Cameroon.

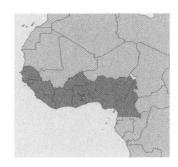

West African foods should not be a mystery to Americans, for it is from here that the slaves brought to North America the tastes and cooking methods that are now so deeply entrenched as to be considered part of American regional cookery.

Georgian and South Carolina rice was transformed into delectable casseroles after the blacks served it with black-eyed peas (called **Hoppin' John**), plantains, yams, or peanuts. Coarse leafy greens, long considered cattle food, came to the Southern table glistening with bacon fat, spicy with onions and garlic and tender from slow cooking. Southern **gumbo** dishes are derived from **okro** or **gombo** – West African names for okra. In fact, grilled meats and fish and varieties of vegetables and beans introduced by the black cooks extended the Southern American diet incredibly. And quite possibly, the black cook's penchant for washing hands may also have influenced cleanliness in American kitchens.

As in most of Africa, three-quarters of West Africa's population is rural. Staples of the farmer's diet include milk and curds and whey, varieties of wild cultivated green vegetables, dried peas, yams, corn, pumpkin, and several types of squash. **Yams, corn, cassava,** and **groundnuts** are indispensable in the West African diet. **Cassava** is used mainly for its flour – which when slightly fermented is called **gari** – and its leaves are used as a vegetable. **Groundnuts** are used in soups and stews and flavorful sauces. Eggplants, okra, garlic, onions, and tomatoes are important in many dishes too.

To the more sophisticated West African, **fufu** (made from yams or plantains) is still a staple but is prepared in more imaginative forms: fried cakes, dumpling-like balls, thin-fried chips, croquettes and fritters. To add variety, some of these are served sweetened and lightly spiced.

The rest of the diet is liberally laced with a wide variety of fish and seafood and there are many chicken dishes flavored with **groundnuts**. Beef and mutton are scarce; chickens require careful cooking to tenderize. Eggs are used liberally and are an important part of many dishes. Both urban and rural dwellers use fruits in season as their means permit: bananas, plantain, papayas, mangoes, pineapples, coconuts, limes and lemons, melons, oranges and the great variety of local tropical specialties.

This is an area where the new middle class is developing unusual and sophisticated dishes, combining indigenous fruits and vegetables in new ways.

GLOSSARY OF WEST AFRICAN FOODS AND FOOD TERMS

Callaloo: a dish for special occasions with the classic African combination of meats and fish extended with vegetables. Depending on the region may be served with fried rice cakes, cornmeal dumplings or breads.

Cassava: a West African staple also called **gari**. It has traveled to Brazil as **Farinhe de Mandioca**, and is known in North America as tapioca. Prepared from a tuberous root, it can be used as a pounded pulp or as a grainy powder. It is used like rice or couscous, by itself or as a base for other foods.

Chin chin: irresistible little fried balls (like doughnuts) made with wheat flour and yeast, and aromatic with nutmeg. These are a specialty of many festive occasions. **Maasa** are similar but prepared from millet flour.

Gari Foto: Nigerian dish based on **gari** (coarsely ground meal from **cassava** root). Gari is mixed with water, allowed to swell, then blended with egg and seasonings and eaten like a rice dish. In some areas it may be served as a casserole with tomato sauce, vegetables, and hard-cooked eggs.

Kyinkyinga: popularly sold by street vendors, hotly spiced kabobs of beef or offal. Served with bread or rice and a salad, they make a zesty meal.

Maafe: a hot spicy stew of chicken and groundnuts, claimed as original in many of the West African countries. Onions and chicken pieces are well browned then smothered in a spicy tomato sauce with vegetables and a sprinkle of cinnamon and paprika.

Usually served with rice, cooked vegetables, or potatoes.

Moi Moi: A chunky pate prepared from black-eyed peas that have been well cooked and seasoned with onions, tomato paste, and salt and pepper.

Okro Soup: Nigerian soup based on vegetables, seafood, and smoked fish thickened with okra and spiced with chilies. This soup is believed to be the origin of **gumbo**.

SPECIAL OCCASIONS

For the most part, Africans are part of a pastoral society and though many adhere to Christianity or Islam, they still, to a greater or lesser degree, retain elements of totemism and animism, and many of their special occasions revolve around the seasons, planting, and harvesting as well as family-life rituals. The land itself has a quasi-religious value to most Africans. This fact alone helps to explain (in spite of forced religious conversions) many cultural and religious ceremonies and the deep emotions relating to the dignity of work and respect for ancestors.

Land is not only the root of their culture and traditions, it also encompasses the whole realm of social relationships from duty to fellow tribesman to witchcraft. "Work is done as much in honor of ancestors and of the system as it is to provide food..." Knowledge of these deeply embedded traditions may help the westerner to also understand the African's seemingly stubborn resistance to mechanization and even to tools that are upsetting age-old traditions, that and result in the hateful pitting of one generation against another.

Aside from the cycle of seasons and crops, birth, weddings, puberty and death, visitors alone are reason enough for a "special occasion," and foods may seem festive merely because of the occasion. Or, depending on the area, the traditions, and the wealth and status, an animal or chickens may be specially slaughtered, special soups may be prepared with special ritual such as the **blessing soup** or **milioku ngozi** (a rich, hot chicken soup) of West Africa, or simply a more generous quantity of the usual fare may be offered.

In 1991, Eric Copage brought *Kwanzaa* to general public appreciation in the United States with his book by that name. This special week of African-American cultural celebration, celebrated the full week after Christmas, has been gaining wide practice since its creation in 1966 by Maulana (Ron) Karenga.

Central to the celebration are seven culturally and historically embedded symbols: fruit and vegetables, a straw place mat, ears of corn, small gifts, a communal drinking cup, a seven-branched candle-holder (*kinara*), and seven candles to be lit on successive days. Each of the candles in turn represent the seven principles of *Kwanzaa*:

1. Unity
2. Self-determination
3. Collective work and responsibility
4. Cooperative economics
5. Purpose
6. Creativity
7. Faith

December 31 is celebrated with feasting and entertainment. The foods, music, dance, and readings represent differing aspects and regions of African-American cultural heritage. *Kwanzaa* is a profoundly moving and meaningful example of cultural pride and thanksgiving that has survived centuries of hardship and repression.

GLOSSARY OF FOODS AND FOOD TERMS

Akara: popular breakfast dish made from mashed black-eyed peas seasoned with salt, pepper, and onion then deep-fried.

Akassa: Ghanian porridge made from corn flour and hot water.

Anu Ofia: term used for fresh meat from any forest animal. The meat is prepared by first singeing over an open fire then washing and cutting as preparation for smoking, drying, or cooking. Most African meats are tough and stringy and therefore best prepared by marinating (in beer, wine, various fruit juices, or soured milk) then cooking with moisture or used in soups and stews.

Asida: term used for a late morning meal usually consisting of **Fufu** and relishes.

Bamia: also called "ladyfingers." Both are names for **okra**, a green pod that can be cooked crisp or simmered to a gelatinous texture.

Bamie Bread: a moist bread made with okra.

Baobab Tree: as functional as the coconut palm. Fruit and leaves are edible; ashes of the wood are used as salt; seeds and pods are roasted to make a drink or snack; the tree trunk is a source of water.

Bajias: small seasoned balls of cooked mashed potatoes or yams, flour-coated then deep-fried. A favorite of African Indians.

Balila: term used for the evening meal, which usually consists of **Fufu** plus relishes. In many areas care is taken to eat this before dark so as to avoid evil spirits.

Bota: thin gruel often prepared from millet and given as a supplementary food for infants.

Buhme: locally made sweetened beer offered in small amounts to infants after six months of age.

Callaloo: a casserole of vegetables, various fish and seafood with meat and seasonings. A popular combination includes spinach, mixed seafood and cubed lamb seasoned with garlic, chilies, and tomato paste. The combination of fish, seafood, and meat is also popular in Portugal. Is it possible that the Portuguese traders and explorers brought this recipe home? (This is also the name of a Caribbean soup named for the coarse green callaloo leaves from dasheen or taro plant.)

Cassava: also called **manioc** is the tuber from which manioc flour and tapioca is made. Slightly fermented and ground into flour, manioc is used to prepare the classic **Gari** served with vegetable and/or meat sauces.

Chapatis: unleavened breads freshly made for a meal from almost any flour: rolled flat then deep-fried until they puff and brown. Well known in India and much favored by African Indians.

Chenga: a thick milk soup made with rice or corn and thickened with corn flour (cornstarch). Considered one of the chief foods of East Africa.

Chihengi: pineapple.

Chin Chin: deep-fried cookie leavened with **Swahili yeast.**

Cocoyams: variety of wild yams.

Dende Oil: the Brazilian name for the densely rich palm oil brought to Brazil by West Africans. Its reddish hue can be imitated by adding paprika to peanut or vegetable oil.

Dovi: paste of **groundnuts** (peanut butter).

Duri: mortar and pestle.

Fufu, **Ugali** or **Ampesi**: staple African food. Thick porridge-like mixture made by pounding then cooking any one of many starchy plant foods or mixtures of them. Corn, millet, rice, **cassava**, plantain, green bananas, or varieties of yams may be used. For eating, the mixture is formed into small balls with three fingers of the right hand then dipped into sauces or relishes made from fish, meat, or vegetables – almost always spicy hot.

Futari Yams: thick mixture of cooked potatoes flavored with **groundnuts**, tomatoes, onions.

Garri or **Gari**: a slightly fermented **cassava** flour used in cooking. A favorite of many, especially Ghanians.

Ghada: the midday meal, usually consisting of **Fufu** and relishes.

Groundnuts: peanuts, a staple food.

Gumbo: with a consistency between a soup and a stew, **gumbo** is derived from the African Bantu word for okra. Simmered gently with spicy seasoning, okra, and other vegetables, **gumbos** take their name from the main seafood or meat ingredient and are usually served over wild rice. In America, **gumbos** are a treasured part of Creole cuisine.

Hova or **Hobo**: bananas.

Imba: name given to main hut or house where cooking and eating take place.

Ininga: sesame seeds, when eaten cooked as a relish.

Injera: classic Ethiopian bread prepared like a huge pancake from **Teff** (fine millet flour). Then pancakes are placed, overlapping on a small table or large serving tray – at once becoming tablecloth, dish (for a stew of meat and/or vegetables) and then torn to scoop up the food.

Irio: Swahili word for a combination of cooked vegetables, cubed or chopped and seasoned with oil and salt and pepper. Favorite in East Africa.

Ji Akwukwo: very thick stew of many vegetables plus yams. Favorite in West Africa.

Keuke: corn bread prepared from wet fermented corn flour. Sour in East Africa, sweeter and whiter in West Africa.

Kikwanga: Congo name for disc-shaped bread made from cassava flour. The same bread in Jamaica is called **Bammy** and in the southern United States **pan bread**.

Kuli-Kuli: delicacy made from frying the residual groundnut paste after the oil has been extracted.

Madafu: immature coconut water, a beverage.

Maheu: traditional drink for women and children; slightly alcoholic sweet liquid left from soaking cooked **Fufu**.

Mahshi: almost any available variety of vegetable stuffed with a mix of ground meat or fish and rice and baked with tomato sauce.

Manhanga: term used to refer to many varieties of squash and pumpkin.

Manioc or **Cassava**: general name given to any starch roots from which tapioca and other flours may be made.

Manwiwa: watermelon.

Mealie: corn.

Milioku: soup.

Milioku Ngozi: also called **Blessing Soup**. A hot West African soup usually made with a whole chicken and yams. Soup is served first, then meat and vegetables sliced and served afterward. Usually served at planting and harvest celebrations.

Millet: the small grains of a cereal grass, used in preparation of some foods.

Mseto: Swahili word for rice or lentils; usually cooked into a thick sauce, highly seasoned and served with meat or fish.

Mudumbe: the succulent root fibers from the elephant ear plant.

Munyu: salt.

Mupunga: rice.

Muriwo: relish or sauces accompanying **Fufu**. These are an important part of the diet's nutrients, containing not only a wide variety of vegetables and seasonings (hot), but often meat and fish and bones, when available.

Naarjes: South African tangerines, deep in color and rich in flavor.

Nhopi: a **Fufu** or porridge made from pumpkin.

Nsiko: crabs.

Ofe Nsala: a fiery pepper sauce made with a base of meat or fish. This is one of the most popular things served to women with new babies and may comprise the main part of the diet, diluted as a soup or gruel, or eaten with **Fufu**.

Ogede: plantain.

Olilie: one version of the seasoning paste made from dried, fermented, and cooked seeds, used for flavoring.

Oka Esiri Esi: a corn and milk soup.

Olele: a baked or steamed Nigerian pudding made from ground peas, onion, and salt.

Oporo Ukwu: lobster.

Pan Bread: Southern United States name for a disc-shaped bread prepared from **cassava** flour.

Plantain: tropical plant bearing a fruit similar to the banana, usually eaten cooked.

Pombe: beer made from plantains or bananas.

Rupiza: thin porridge or gruel made from powdered dried beans.

Sabal Palmetto: the young sprouting leaves of coco-yams and sweet potatoes, cut and cooked as greens for relishes.

Sorghum: cereal grass grown for grain or fodder.

Surudzo: sieves.

Suya: cut up meats marinated in peanut oil then skewered and cooked.

Swahili Yeast: yeast made from the fermentation of ripe plantains, sugar, water, and wheat flour. Used as leavening agent for breads, buns, and fried cookies.

Teff: fine millet flour.

Tembo: palm wine.

Togwa: beverage made from fermented germinated sorghum.

Tseme or **Nhembatemba**: special pot used for storing **Dovi** (**groundnut** butter).

Tuwo: spicy okra sauce.

Tuwonsaffe: in northern Ghana, the daily **Fufu** is allowed to ferment in this "sourpot" and the **Fufu** needed for meals is scooped from the **Tuwonsaffe**.

Ugali: Tanzanian staple cornmeal porridge of **Fufu**.

Ulezi: a slow cooked porridge of milk and millet, flavored with butter and lemon juice. A food for convalescents.

Yam: the nutritious white yam is a powerfully symbolic staple food frequently staving off malnutrition and starvation, particularly in West Africa. Often of immense size, one African yam can easily feed a family. Feast days are common and yams figure largely in any festive occasion. Because the egg symbolizes fertility and therefore eternity, eggs often accompany yams in these special dishes.

CHAPTER 2

ALBANIAN

The people of Albania, mostly engaged in pastoral and agricultural pursuits, barely eke out an existence from their harsh, rocky land. They suffered through the 400-year domination of the Turkish Empire, when farmers were serfs to the sultan, and through the Communist period, when farmers were serfs to the state. It was said that with the establishment of a socialist republic under Hoxha in 1946, Albania became "one of the world's most thoroughly totalitarian states."

More recently, Albanians have struggled through the difficulties inherent in an emerging democracy. They gained some strength from the 1990 ruling that permitted private religious practice. Moreover, by 1993, 90 percent of farming had been privatized.

Yet troubles still dog the republic. Famine, illiteracy, malaria in the marshlands, and alcoholism plague the people. In 1997, complaints of widespread fraudulent financial schemes affecting thousands of families caused serious violence and looting. Past struggles, pain, and injustices press into the present, combining to make the Albanian's life difficult and insecure.

Accustomed to authority and foreign domination, the Albanian's insecurity is most evident in many of the mountain villages, where the dwellings are so cleverly camouflaged as to be indistinguishable from the native trees and rocks, providing them with a sense of security especially in turbulent times. Cultural influences include Italian, Greek, Turkish, and more currently, Russian. Progress is being made in medicine (control of diseases), agriculture (irrigation and diversity), and literacy. Cottage industries and increase in crop yields, such as rice, are slowly raising the general living standard.

While corn is the mainstay of the Albanian diet, rice is also much enjoyed when available, and a large variety of cheeses made from goat's and ewe's milk supplement the daily diet. In the country's eastern areas and the plains, Albanian cooking rivals some of the finest Turkish and Greek cuisine, but as one moves northward into the mountain areas where poverty and illiteracy increases, the diet is less sophisticated, based almost solely on corn, cheeses, and **kos** (yogurt).

DOMESTIC LIFE

Wealth and status vary from almost primitive conditions to a sophistication equal to that of any European city. Similarly, the range of family relationships, types, and styles of foods and food utensils are just as varied, although they may resemble those found in the neighboring countries of the Italians, Greeks, and the Southern Slavs (formerly Yugoslavians).

DAIRY PRODUCTS

As already mentioned, milk from goats and ewes is made into **kos** and many varieties of cheeses. Fluid fresh milk and butter are seldom used. **Kos** is used alone or eaten with other foods.

FRUITS AND VEGETABLES

Oranges, lemons, and figs are the main available fruits; some grapes and wild berries are made into fermented beverages. Mixed garden vegetables are used seasonally and as available. These include: cucumbers, onions, peppers, eggplants, zucchini, marrows, okra, squash (**kungull**), potatoes, and tomatoes. With the establishment of canneries, there has been a gradual increase in the consumption of canned fruits and vegetables.

MEATS AND ALTERNATES

The favored meats in the Balkan area (where meat is used) are lamb and mutton and sometimes chicken. Liver is considered a delicacy. Meats are usually prepared in types of stews or as pilafs with rice, or skewered and roasted over open fires. There is also a variety of nuts grown locally: walnuts, almonds, pine nuts, and hazelnuts. These may be used as nibbles, crushed (sometimes with garlic), and as sauces over meats and/or vegetables. (See also Greek.)

BREADS AND GRAINS
The most successful crops of the Albanian farmer have for centuries been grains. Predominantly corn, but also wheat, rye, oats, and barley are harvested. These grains have been used to produce a variety of flours for breads that are consumed mainly in coastal areas and cities. But the main type of bread – indeed the main food – is a flat pancake-shaped corn bread broken into pieces and enjoyed with **kos** or cheese.

FATS
Olive oil is the main type of fat used everywhere.

SWEETS AND SNACKS
Albanians enjoy very sweet and rich desserts made with nuts and syrupy sauces. The combination of thin, crisp pastries (identical to the Greek **phyllo**) with nuts, sugar or honey, cinnamon, and cloves, and finished with a heavy syrup, or very sweet puddings, are as beloved by the Albanians as they are by the Turks and Greeks.

SEASONINGS
A people who favor very sweet desserts will almost certainly also enjoy highly seasoned foods, and Albanians are no exception. Generous portions of garlic and onions, tart touches of lemon juice or lemon grating, and the more subtle enhancement of dill and parsley as well as cinnamon and cloves waft through Albanian foods. The combination of crushed or chopped nuts with garlic and oil, to be served with greens or chicken, as well as the combination of nuts and raisins either for nibbling or as part of exotic sauces, are all typically Albanian.

BEVERAGES
Cool soups made from pureed or chopped fruit or vegetables plus **kos** are often taken as cooling liquid refreshment. Small cups of mint and sugared tea, as well as tiny cups of Turkish coffee, often provide afternoon or hospitality refreshment. Sweet desserts and highly seasoned foods, as well as a difficult life, all seem to create a need for strong drink. Hardier local specialties include:

Dukagjin: a drink made from grape juice, sugar, and mustard.
Hardic: a drink made from wild berries.
Orme: an appetizer drink made from fermented cabbage, similar to the juice from sauerkraut.
Raki: a potent brandy, flavored from mulberries and served as an aperitif before meals or on special occasions.

MEALS AND CUSTOMS
Again a distinction must be drawn between the humble farmers and mountain-dwelling herders and the urban upper classes. For the mountaineer, flat corn bread is his staple, and since famine and starvation are not new, a deep appreciation of the importance of bread is expressed by the host, who always breaks the bread first and then shares it with all at his table; then, and only then, are any other available foods placed on the table.

In other areas, it is customary to bring all foods to the table, where they are shared by all the diners usually after appetizers (**meze**) with **Raki** or **Raki Manash** have been served. Three meals a day, similar to most western and European styles, are common except, again, to the humbler farmer or mountaineer to whom each meal will likely be the same – and gratefully received: **kos** and corn bread.

The late afternoon tea or coffee break is called *sille* and may include sweet pastries, nuts, and fresh local fruits.

FOODS COMMONLY USED

The staples of the Albanian diet include: corn; seasonal fruits, such as olives, lemons, figs, and oranges; and ewe's and goat's milk from which cheeses and **kos** are made. Albanians live simply. Only special occasions or social status differentiate the quantity or variety of food that is consumed daily. In some areas, water for drinking is so scarce that dishes are washed in goat's milk in order to conserve the precious water.

Because draft animals are valued for their power and by-products, they have, for many thousands of years, been considered too valuable to be used merely for food. As a result, the Albanian diet is mainly vegetarian except for the occasions or social status that permit the use of lamb, pigs (in Catholic areas), and sometimes chickens. Unfortunately, a lack of scientific chicken breeding has resulted in small and sporadic egg production, so that eggs have never formed an important part of the Albanian diet. The main source of protein in the mountain areas is cheese, while fish predominates along coastal areas and in cities. Everywhere, **kos** and cheese are much preferred over the use of fluid milk.

SPECIAL OCCASIONS

Culturally, the Albanians are said to be a "leftover of the Turkish Empire," with approximately 70 percent practicing Islam, eschewing pork and pork products, but relaxing the usual prohibitions against alcohol. In fact, alcoholic beverages are consumed freely.

Albanians are also strongly influenced by the heritage of two main ancestral tribes: the reserved but warlike Ghegs from the north, and the lighthearted, extroverted Tosks from the south.

Among both upper and lower classes throughout Albania, preparation of special occasion fare almost always results in an expansion in the quantity rather than the variety of foods. For the rural poor it may mean their first taste of meat in a very long time (they are vegetarian by necessity, not necessarily by desire), while for others the special occasion may simply be a feast of overabundance, as they eat their way through a formidable list of appetizers and repeated drinks of **Raki**, and have to make an effort to continue through the sumptuous and often exotic main dishes to follow.

Since Albania is a land not only of male dominance by custom, but male dominance by population, men are served first and treated with great deference and respect; this is not a custom reserved just for special occasions.

GLOSSARY OF FOODS AND FOOD TERMS

Corba: soup made with rice and flavored with lemon, sometimes containing chicken or chicken livers.

Dolma Me Vaj: rice and pine nuts (sometimes with ground lamb), seasoned with mint or cinnamon, and used as a stuffing for a variety of vegetables (e.g., peppers, tomatoes, zucchini), and oven-baked.

Dukagjin: beverage of grape juice flavored with sugar and mustard.

Ematur: cake made with almonds, cut into diamond-shaped wedges.

Hardic: a drink made from wild berries.

Kabuni: a sweet dish made with raisins, cinnamon, and rice. Used as a side dish.

Kafee: coffee; almost always refers to Turkish coffee.

Kos: Albanian yogurt made from goat's or ewe's milk.

Kungull: squash.

Kungull Me Kos: pieces of squash, batter-dipped and deep-fried then served with a garlic yogurt sauce.

Lakruar: a type of pizza made with vegetables, well seasoned and topped with cheese.

Meze: appetizers.

Moussaka: a baked casserole of layered vegetables, or vegetables and meats (classic version is eggplant and ground lamb). Of Greek origin.

Orme: an appetizer drink made from fermented cabbage, similar to the juice from sauerkraut.

Pelte: little cakes made with cornstarch and molasses, flavored with lemon.

Pilaf: a dish based on rice, which may include only nuts, raisins, and cinnamon, or almost any variety of vegetable, meats, and legumes. Of Turkish origin.

Quofte: meatballs.

Quofte Me Mente: meatballs made from ground lamb, fragrant with mint and cinnamon.

Raki: brandy distilled from grapes.

Raki Manash: brandy distilled and flavored with mulberries.

Revani Me Kos: simple sponge or nut cake finished by pouring hot, spiced syrup over, then cooling and cutting into diamond shapes.

Sille: afternoon refreshment, which may be either tea or Turkish coffee, sometimes served with fresh fruits or sweet pastries.

Supa Ves Limua: a rich soup based on chicken stock with rice, and tangy with freshly beaten eggs and lemon juice. Almost identical to the Greek **Avgolemono**.

Tarator: chilled refreshing soup of yogurt, with chopped cucumbers or other fresh vegetables as garnish.

Terituar: a finely chopped salad or pureed appetizer of cucumbers, walnuts, and garlic.

CHAPTER 3

AMERICAN

It is for good reason that Israel Zangwill's term "Melting Pot" for the name of a play in 1908 still serves as an apt description of the United States today. The United States is a nation of immigrants, each ethnic group retaining customs, festivals and food traditions with great pride and yet with a stamp that is unmistakably American.

Huge areas of fertile land, abundant natural resources, and some of the world's most advanced technology, marketing and transportation systems combine to give the U.S. one of the highest living standards in the world. Immigrants to America were dazzled by the space, opportunities, freedoms and diversity of things around them. Their glowing letters home spoke more of "you can get anything here!" than of the hard struggle to get ahead in a new land and often with a new language.

Though a visitor to the U.S. may conclude that the country's staple foods are hot dogs, hamburgers and french fries, washed down with soft drinks and topped off with ice cream, a more careful examination reveals regional as well as ethnic specialties.

The first generation of European immigrants had little time for Old World traditions. Making a living, creating a home and raising a family were the realities of everyday life. Food was whatever was available and affordable to fill an empty stomach. But as they became established, the newcomers found solace in grouping together in neighborhoods where the familiar languages, customs, and compatriots gave them strength for whatever the future might hold. It was good to share a glass of homemade wine, a pint of beer, or a schnapps. It was comforting to smell the familiar scents of cooking and baking and, even better, to drown a day's hard work in a homey soup or familiar stew. Adapting available foods to familiar recipes helped a little to make them feel at home.

But long before all the others, Aboriginal peoples, whose ancestors had probably crossed the Bering Strait thousands of years before the European had even heard of America, made their way southward in the great continent, founding villages and developing languages and social systems and adapting to the land in unique and often ingenious ways.

It was from the Indians that the earliest pioneers learned how to prepare such staples as corn, tomatoes, squash, peanuts, pumpkin, tobacco, turkeys, wild rice, pumpkins and squash, and even to tap wild maple trees for sweet maple syrup. In order to avoid cooking on the sabbath, the Puritans adopted the Indian clambake technique and used it to make slow-simmered beans cooked in the Indian way (today called **New England baked beans**) using a sealed bean pot buried overnight in a pit of embers. In its modified version – slow-baked overnight in the oven – it is enjoyed to this day.

As the pioneers settled into the land, they adapted the ethnic foods they brought with them to the new and different produce that was so plentiful. Ethnic foods melded into regional specialties, and although few writers dare to define the exact borders of these regions, distinctive ways of preparing, cooking, combining, seasoning, and even serving foods do exist.

Still another powerful influence came to America through the Atlantic slave trade from West African countries to the New World. The West African slaves adapted many New World foods to their own basic methods of frying, stewing, and preparing sauces for enhancing simple food. They introduced many flavorful, healthy varieties of greens to the European diet. They added grilled meats, wrapped foods in cabbage leaves (instead of banana leaves) for roasting in fires, and turned many of their own classic dishes like rice and black-eyed peas into Southern traditions like **Hoppin' John**. The use of a baffling array of peppers, spices, roots, tubers, and greens, and the skillful metamorphosis of every part of the pig or chicken into delectable morsels of food are all now imbedded not only in America's cuisine, but also in the cuisines of many Caribbean countries and Brazil.

DOMESTIC LIFE

Some of the earliest cooking by European immigrants used brick ovens and iron pots suspended over open hearths. Ironware, hearth-cooking, and brick ovens have not entirely disappeared from the American scene, but **Treen** (the variety of wooden cooking and eating ware) and many pewter pieces are now collector's items. Probably the most modern kitchens in the world, containing the most in cookery gadgets and small specialty appliances, are to be found in even average-income American homes today. Only imagination and the family budget limit the scope and variety of electrical appliances, plastic ware, cookware, dishes and serving utensils available, imported and domestically made.

Average American homes boast stoves and refrigerators, ample storage cupboards, cellars and home freezers (or rented freezer lockers), and a host of small appliances from juicers and food processors to bread machines and yogurt makers. Supermarkets and specialty food stores supply local specialties and fresh produce as well as an incredible array of imported delicacies.

DAIRY PRODUCTS

These products in every form – fluid, fresh, whole, skimmed or partially skimmed milk, buttermilk, butter, imported and local cheeses of many varieties, and all types and flavors of sherbets and ice creams – are all widely available and used. More recently, there has been an increase in the use of yogurt, both plain and sweetened or flavored. Moreover, as interest in travel and international cookery increases, so does the use of cottage cheese, sour cream, and some of the more unusual cheese varieties.

FRUITS AND VEGETABLES

Fresh and frozen, canned and dried fruits and vegetables, as well as local and imported produce, are available in most areas regardless of season, although out-of-season produce may be more expensive. All root vegetables such as carrots, potatoes, yams, and beets, are used and available in all parts of the country, with potatoes being a great favorite.

MEATS AND ALTERNATES

Beef is a great American tradition. Consumed in lesser quantities are pork and pork products, chickens,

ducks (domestic and wild), geese, game birds, veal, and lamb. Eggs are consumed almost daily, prepared in many specialty dishes such as omelets, souffles, and custards, and are used frequently as ingredients in many other dishes. Fish is used by certain ethnic groups and especially in coastal regions where it is freshly caught. It may be purchased as fresh, frozen, dried, and canned. Legumes are not widely consumed except as a budget dish, a regional or ethnic favorite. Nuts are used mostly as garnishes or tasty ingredients in desserts or baked goods. But peanuts and peanut butter are used so widely that in some households they could be considered a staple food.

BREADS AND GRAINS

White breads and rolls and dry prepared breakfast cereals are widely enjoyed. Wheat is most universally used in cereals and baked goods. Corn may be used as a vegetable (corn on the cob), for corn oil, or specially prepared as **grits** or as corn flour for regional specialty dishes. All grains are readily available but the kind used is largely based on personal, ethnic, or regional tastes. Use of whole grains in breads and cereals is increasing as people become more conscious of healthy lifestyles.

FATS

In the South, lard is the favored fat for all cookery, but butter is used at the table and for special bakery. Elsewhere, all varieties of oils, salted and sweet butter, many types of margarine, shortenings as well as lard and drippings are used according to individual preference. Olive oil and other vegetable oils are gaining increasing use for health reasons as well as for ethnic cookery.

SEASONINGS

Salt and pepper shakers and the bottle of ketchup, a spiced thick tomato condiment used to season virtually anything, are common sights in most highway restaurants, quick-serve food outlets, and on the average American table. The household spice shelf is

FOODS COMMONLY USED

With rapid transportation within the country and superior storage both in homes and in industry, Americans in almost any region can enjoy not only local seasonal foods and produce but an endless array of imported, frozen, dried, and canned foods available year-round. Almost every small town in the United States has its supermarkets, specialty bake shops, and quick-serve fast-food outlets. All types of foods are readily available, so that what is chosen for the day's foods will reflect personal preference, ethnic background, local custom, and state of health (special diet), rather than any market or seasonal limitation.

While Americans may conform to the traditional three-meals-a-day regimen, the prevalence of coffee breaks and snack foods make it seem closer to one continual daily meal.

stocked in amount and diversity by the household cook, and often reflects an ethnic background.

BEVERAGES

With the exception of very poor rural and inner-city areas, children consume large quantities of fresh milk, sweetened, flavored soft drinks and fruit juices, as well as many kinds of synthetic sweetened drinks. Adults enjoy coffee and tea, others beer and wine. With the increased cost of imported wines, more attention is being given to the fine wines produced in California and New York State.

MEALS AND CUSTOMS

In early times, daily physical exertion was the rule, and the hearty meals provided warmth and energy. But as technology made life easier, and as the workday became shorter, heavy meals were not only no longer necessary, they were impractical and expensive.

Today's trend is breakfast-on-the-run, which usually means simply orange juice and coffee. Typical lunches include sandwich, milk or coffee, and fruit or ice cream. Dinner in the evening is usually the only meal when most families are together, and the traditional pattern is soup or appetizer, meat or fish plus vegetables, a dessert, and tea, coffee, or milk to complete the meal.

Americans, like most of the western world, love to snack. Coffee breaks and coffee parties, the easy access of the corner variety store for candy, soft drinks, and chewing gum, or the fast-food outlet with ethnic specialties such as **tacos** or **pizza** as well as hamburgers, hot dogs, ice cream, and french fries, all seem necessary to keep the American fueled. More and more the pattern of three meals a day is blurring into a day-long fest of nibbling or "grazing" from breakfast to the late-evening show on television.

REGIONAL SPECIALTIES

Different regional food patterns and traditions are based on geography as well as ethnic lineage.

EASTERN SEABOARD REGION

New York, Delaware, New Jersey, and Pennsylvania were variously influenced by the early Dutch, Swedish, Quaker and German settlers. The latter, by the way, called themselves "Deutsch" (the German word for "German"), which became corrupted into "Pennsylvania Dutch."

Many all-American favorite flour mixtures such as pancakes, waffles, doughnuts, and even cookies are basically of Dutch origin. Even the dollop of coleslaw so prevalent in almost every American quick-serve restaurant is of Dutch origin.

The Pennsylvania Dutch produced hearty dumpling dishes, all kinds of sausages, cold sliced , molded aspic dishes, sauerkraut and pork combinations, pickled eggs and pickled vegetables salads that are now enjoyed all over the United States with little thought to origin.

Eastern Seaboard specialties include favorites like **Boiled Chicken Pot Pie**, and **Boova Schenkel** (also called Filled Noodles) which are made from noodle dough filled with seasoned mashed potatoes, sealed into half-moon shapes then boiled.

The broth from boiling smoked ham is used to make **Schnitz und Knepp**. Plump round yeast dumplings are poached in the ham broth together with dried apple slices (**Schnitz**).

Desserts and sweets include the wonderfully named **Shoofly Pie** made with eggs, molasses, flour and brown sugar scented temptingly with cloves, cinnamon and ginger, **Bloch Kucha**, a delicious buttermilk coffee cake, deep fried yeast doughnuts called **Fastnachts**, and **Funnel Cakes** made from batter dropped into hot fat are more treats.

HAWAII AND ALASKA

The two youngest states of the United States bring an offering of contrasts to the huge American table of foods. Hawaii offers touches from the South Pacific and Southeast-Asian cuisine like the sharp-salty fish sauces, exotic spices, an array of tropical fruits such as **taro**, coconut, passion fruit, guava, tangy-sour tamarind, as well as noodles, rice, pork, seafood and raw fish.

Hawaiian specialties include **Pupus**, fried or grilled snack foods or appetizers, which includes **Crab Rangoon** (hot spicy crab meat sealed in crispy fried won ton wrappers) and **Rumaki** which features grilled skewered chicken livers and water chestnuts wrapped in bacon. **Bagoong**, a salty fish sauce, is often used as a condiment and seasoning.

Perhaps the most famous festive occasion is the **Luau** during which a whole pig is cooked in a pit (**Imu**) heated with white-hot rocks.

Lomi Lomi Salmon, tender and juicy salt fish prepared with a mixture of tomatoes and onions, often served with **Poi**. A meal might end with **Haupia**, a sweet pudding made from coconut milk or feature **Mai Tai**, a heady Hawaiian drink prepared with rum, orange-flavored liqueur and lime juice.

Together with the bounty of nature – cloudberries, rose hips, blueberries, cranberries, salmonberries, huckleberries, rhubarb, fish and wild game (beaver, bear, venison, caribou, duck and ptarmigan) the early Alaskan pioneers brought two staples that still satisfy hearty appetites in the North. These are pork and beans and the famed sourdough from which breads, rolls, pancakes and biscuits are made.

The sourdough starter – a ferment of flour, yeast, and water – when once begun, lives in a crock in the kitchen, continually added to and a constant source of new doughs with a tantalizing aroma and taste. **Sourdough Cakes** are made by adding a little baking soda to a sourdough sweetened with sugar and baked on a griddle.

The native peoples taught the early trappers and miners how to prepare rolled sheets of dried berries. They also patiently shared their skills for salting, drying and smoking fish to last over the winter, and even how to keep sun-dried berries in airtight containers. The toasted seaweed that they crumbled over fish soap added a salty taste and valuable nutrients.

Alaskan specialties include **Matsuki**, only one of countless varieties of edible wild mushrooms, **Watapoo**, a mealy red tuber with a taste similar to chestnuts and **Camas**, a starchy bulb-shaped considered a staple wilderness food.

MIDWESTERN REGION

This region comprises America's dairylands and famed corn belt. Fine cheeses, butter, fresh milk and cream in abundance come from a country-quilt of well-kept farms. Eastern European delicacies vie with simple hearty meat-and-potatoes meals.

Scandinavian fruit soups and German beer soups vie for popularity with Ukrainian Borscht and Finnish cold buttermilk soup. Appetizers vary from Norwegian **gravlax** and pickled salt herring to French onion tarts and Danish liver pate. Homemade noodles, corn puddings and corn fritters, potato pancakes and hashed brown potatoes all find a place on Midwest tables with coleslaw, cucumbers in sour cream and 24-hour bean salad.

And who can overlook the wondrous variety of breads in this region? Sourdough rye and pumpernickle, Swedish rye, Finnish rye and Norwegian dark bread together with the array of fine sweet yeast buns, coffeecakes, tarts, pies and coffeecakes, **ableskivers** and **crullers**.

NEW ENGLAND REGION

Severe climate and non-arable lands probably molded the character as well as the diet of New Englanders. Hearty soups, steamed brown breads and the famed baked beans have all become synonymous with New England although these foods really know no regional boundaries. Blueberries and maple syrup, walnuts

and apples, and the well-known simple but hearty **New England boiled dinner** add to the fare.

Specialties include all kinds of **Chowder**. **Rhode Island** and **Connecticut Chowder** add tomatoes and are sometimes called **Manhattan Chowder**, while **New England Chowder** ignores tomatoes and stays with the classic chowder combination of a thick cream soup with added fish, seafood or chicken.

Scrod, fillets of young cod, and **Quahogs**, small edible Atlantic clams with thick shells, are popular. Perhaps almost as well known as chowder is the **New England Clambake** which features layers of fresh corn and seafood wrapped in seaweed steamed over white hot stones. Eager fingers and melted butter are the only accompaniments.

A **New England Boiled Dinner** isn't really boiled, but simmers for hours with pickled beef (corned beef), onions turnips and potatoes. **Red Flannel Hash**, is made using the leftovers of the New England Boiled Dinner chopped together, smoothed with cream and browned in a hot skillet.

Other New England favorites include **Rhode Island Jonny Cake**, prepared from white cornmeal served with butter and maple syrup. The rest of America calls them **Johnny Cakes** (spelled with an "h") and prepares them with yellow cornmeal. Favorites are: **Seventy-Fours**, deep-fried biscuits dipped into hot molasses, **Parkerhouse Rolls**, the roll with a deeply-indented fold, **Featherbeds**, yeast rolls made with mashed potatoes, **Anadama Bread** made with cornmeal, flour, yeast, molasses and melted shortening, and **Vermont Griddlecakes**.

For dessert New Englanders enjoy **Joe Froggers**, thick molasses cookies fragrant with ginger and cloves, **Indian Pudding** and **Boston Cream Pie**. Real **Boston Cream Pie** is not a pie at all but a soft sponge cake filled with vanilla custard and glazed with melted chocolate.

PACIFIC NORTHWEST REGION

This region is renowned for its salmon and trout, lingcod and other fine seafood and game. Areas in Washington State are still noted for their piglet barbecues while other

areas delight in wild game. Those who live near the coast enjoy fish and seafood grills.

If you can name a wild berry, it probably can be found in this breathtaking wilderness of immense evergreens, wild bushes and fields: blueberries, nectar berries, raspberries, strawberries, boysenberries and more. Apples thrive in this climate too: Gravenstein, Delicious, Gascoyne's Scarlet, Egremont Russet, Grieves, and American Mother are a few of the favorites.

NEW ORLEANS REGION

Here, a combination of French and Spanish settlers, native Choctaw Indians and the ingenuity of the African slaves have produced a cuisine that is considered to be one of the most unique in America.

The French (from France) and the "Cajuns" (Acadians from Canada) contributed sauces and roux. The Spanish their delight in fresh produce and light tastes in meat, fish and seafood. The Choctaw the use of powder made from dried sassafras leaves (later called **file**) to thicken soups and stews as well as to add delicate flavor. The Africans contributed **okra** and other greens, innovative uses of pork, cooking with lard and the use of heavy cast-iron cookware especially for **Jambalayas** and **Gumbos**.

New Orleans specialties include breakfast treats **Pain Perdu** (French toast with vanilla) and **Calas** (fried rice balls with nutmeg and vanilla) and peppery hot sausages called **Chaurice** enjoyed with red beans and rice.

Seafood favorites include **Shrimp de Jonghe**, **Pompano en Papillote** (fillets of pompano with a filling of chopped seafood blanketed with a thick white sauce), and **Oysters Rockefeller**. This delicacy is created by spooning a spiced white sauce mixed with cooked chopped spinach over fresh oysters nestled in their own half shell. A last sprinkle of grated Parmesan to brown on top and they are ready to be devoured. **Creole Bouillabaise** is a fish stew prepared from Redfish and Red Snapper fillets.

Creole pot roast (**Daube**) is beef browned in butter then slowly simmered to a juicy tenderness with vegetables and doused with sherry before serving.

Other delicacies include **Pecan Pralines** and **Pig's Ears**, a crispy Arcadian fried pastry served with a dribble of sugar syrup and a sprinkle of chopped nuts. And to end any meal in New Orleans there is **Cafe Brulot**. Black coffee is heated in a chafing dish, stirred with a curl of lemon and orange peel and a touch of spice. Sugar cubes soaked with brandy are ignited in a ladle then slowly lowered into the hot coffee. When the flames die down, the **Cafe Brulot** is ladled into cups.

SOUTHERN REGIONS

"Take two and butter 'em while they're hot!" refers to the southern predilection for a variety of delicious home-baked hot breads and beaten biscuits, which are eaten at almost every meal. As famed as southern hospitality are Virginia ham, southern fried chicken, **hog'n hominy** (pork and pork products served with **corn grits**), **cornbread**, **hoecake** and **cornpone** and a delectable array of desserts like tifle, **Sally Lunn**, **Tipsy Pie**, pecan pie and **George Washington cake**.

Many specialty dishes of African-Americans, enjoyed as "soul food" originated from the humble foods served with imagination by the early West African slaves. Well-cooked greens of all types, wild and cultivated, such as kale, collard and mustard greens, and chicory are enhanced with bits of salt pork, bacon fat or pig's innards, hocks or ears. Other dishes include those made with pork and chicken. Melons are the favored fruits, eaten sweet, juicy and fresh.

Specialties in the southern states include **Hush Puppies**, cornbread batter fried to golden crunchy perfection and **Southern Spoon Bread** prepared with white cornmeal and separated eggs baked high and fluffy, not unlike a souffle. In fact, it is so delicate, it requires a spoon to eat.

Beaten Biscuits with their silken texture are a Southern specialty properly served cold, split and filled like sandwiches. The ingredients are simple, just flour, lard, milk and salt. The trick is in the lengthy kneading or beating with a wooden rolling pin till the dough blisters. Then it is rolled out, cut in rounds and pricked with a fork before baking.

Southern Fried Chicken is famous across the United States but likely no two recipes are identical, and even the exact technique is dependent on location and tradition. Seasoned and floured chicken pieces may be browned in a skillet or deep fried.

Texas Barbecue Lima Beans are often served with barbecues. Cooked lima beans are layered in a casserole with a thick spicy tomato sauce laced with grated cheese. More cheese tops the casserole before it is baked till bubbly.

Candied Sweet Potatoes: In the South, 'potato' means yams, white ones are called Irish potatoes. Cooked potatoes are tossed in a skillet of bubbling butter and brown sugar. When glazed and heated, they are served, usually with ham. The same meal might feature **Vegetable Scrapple**, finely chopped cooked vegetables are stirred into cooked white corn-meal, then smoothed into a loaf pan, chilled, sliced thickly and browned in butter.

On a lighter note there is **Shortn'n Bread**, rich tender cookies made with flour, butter and light brown sugar. The traditional Christmas dessert **Ambrosia** is prepared with oranges, bananas or pineapple sprinkled with sugar and freshly grated coconut (if available) then chilled.

In the hot southern climate cool drinks are always welcome. **Raspberry Shrub**, a classic Southern summertime drink, is prepared from home-made raspberry syrup sharpened with cider vinegar. The syrup may be diluted before serving over crushed ice. An **Orange Julep** features orange juice, lime juice and sugar, carbonated water and ice, garnished with fresh mint and usually served with bourbon.

SOUTHWESTERN REGION

Strongly influenced by traditional Mexican and Spanish cookery, **tamales, tacos, enchiladas, fri-joles** all vie with local tropical and semi-tropical fruits and vegetables to create an usual and distinctive cuisine.

The influence of the Hopi, Pueblo and Papago Indians have also helped to make beans, squash, chili peppers, and corn staples of the southwestern diet.

The famed **Texas chili** contains no beans but is a slow-simmered stew of diced beef flavored with a mix of seasoning now known simply as "chili powder" (actually a combination of oregano, hot and sweet peppers, cumin, sugar and paprika) thickened traditionally with the same corn flour (**masa harina**) used to make **tortillas**. **Chili** is popularly served with a side dish of **Texas beans**, a hearty casserole of kidney or pinto beans simmered in water with onions and garlic.

Blessed with a mild climate and fertile soil and encouraged by efficient irrigation systems, California enjoys a diverse cuisine and is usually in the forefront of food trends.

An emphasis on fresh fruits and vegetables and simplicity in food preparation have always marked California cooking. Yet there is also a flare for the setting, for the presentation and for the combination of ingredients that somehow distinguishes California food traditions.

Barbecues are the specialty of southern Californians. Grilled meats, fish and seafood are often accompanied with a choice of several salads as well as tacos, enchiladas, caramel flan and other Mexican and Spanish specialties.

Sourdough breads, avocados and artichokes and the plentiful varieties of fish and seafood make eating a delight.

GLOSSARY OF FOODS AND FOOD TERMS

Note: The following is only a partial listing of food terms. To be complete, this glossary would have to include the glossary of almost every other chapter of this book. Please refer to the other chapters for specific ethnic food specialties.

Abelskivers: rich puffy Scandinavian pancakes baked in a pan with deep round wells.

Baked Beans: small white beans, slow-baked (often overnight), seasoned with salt pork, molasses, and mustard. (New England)

Boston Brown Bread: a steamed bread made of wholewheat flour, sour milk, and molasses. A favorite accompaniment to **Baked Beans** and both are traditionally served on Saturday night. (New England)

Cafe au Lait: in New Orleans that special taste and aroma comes from roasted chicory root.

Chili Con Carne: as the Spanish translated – "chili with meat" – suggests, this Southwestern favorite is made with chili seasonings and cubed beef thickened with **Masa Harina** (corn flour). Beans are served with it.

Clam Chowder: a creamy soup made with potatoes and fresh clams.

Coleslaw: a cabbage salad, finely shredded and dressed with vinegar. (Dutch origin)

Corn Oysters: a southern side dish of fritters made from corn dumpling batter blended with bits of bacon. Served with pot roast or chicken dishes.

Cornpone: a corn bread browned and cooked in a skillet.

Crullers: served with a drift of confectioners' sugar, these Scandinavian yeast twists are fried crisp.

Custard Corncake: a bland, baked custard of eggs, milk, and cornmeal.

File: the dried leaves of the sassafras plant, introduced by the Choctaw Indians to Creole cookery. It is used for flavor (something like thyme in taste), and to thicken foods just before serving.

Grits: Also called hominy grits, kernels of corn boiled in lye solution, hulled, washed and dried. The resulting hominy is then coarsely ground to form grits. Grits may be cooked like a porridge and served at any meal as a side dish, with everything from eggs to meat or fish. Slices of cold grits may be fried. Grits are the favorite Southern cereal food.

Gumbo: there are many varieties of gumbo – thick stews combining meats and seafoods or shellfish, almost always containing okra and served with rice. Okra, called **Gumbo** by the Choctaw Indians, helps to thicken the juices. (New Orleans)

Hash Browns: cubed potatoes and onions usually fried in patties to a crusty brown, most often served at breakfast with eggs. A favorite food at almost any meal, now almost across the United States.

Hoecake: crispy-browned pancakes made of white cornmeal, salt, and water, and cooked in bacon fat or butter.

Hooch: the Tilnglet people of Hooch-in-noo, Alaska are said to have originated a potent brew by adding molasses to ferment in the sourdough pot. It became known as "hooch".

Hoppin' John: traditional New Year's Day dish eaten in southern United States for good luck. Cowpeas or black-eyed peas are cooked and tossed with cooked rice. Usually served with ham hocks and collards, based on the cookery of the early West African slaves.

Jambalaya: a hearty Creole stew of fish, seafood, or chicken (many versions), thickened with **File** and served with rice.

Lagniappe: a menu conundrum for tourists until they discover it is an unexpected appetizer from the chef to you. (New Orleans)

Mile High Pie: New Orleans's dessert pie with a cookie crust layered with several flavors of ice cream crowned with meringue.

Pepper Pot: satisfying New England soup of vegetables, potatoes, and tripe, thickened with cream and flour.

Persimmon Pudding: a steamed pudding made with persimmon pulp and walnuts. Served with a custard sauce. (New England)

Poi: a syrupy mixture made from taro root. Poi is eaten with the fingers, dipping into it as "one-finger poi," "two-finger poi," etc. Efforts are being made to reintroduce it as an inexpensive, traditional and authentic Hawaiian staple food.

Pompion: early New England word for pumpkin.

Ponhaus: Pennsylvania Dutch dish of cubed pork feet, meat scraps, cornmeal, and oats all molded in aspic and sliced cold.

Pork Cake: New England spicy molasses cake made with minced fruit and finely diced salt pork.

Pot-likker: southern treat of melted salt pork, poured over breads or cooked greens.

Red (kidney) Beans and Rice: the ubiquitous classic of Louisiana, accompanying most meals and sometimes even breakfast. Can be a meal in itself. Usually served spicy-hot.

Red Fish Hash: an economical Pennsylvania Dutch dinner of leftover codfish molded into patties, fried, and served topped with poached egg.

Sally Lunn: a very light corn bread baked as a dropped batter on a baking sheet, then served hot and well buttered.

Shaker Salt Cod Dinner: Pennsylvania Dutch favorite of poached cod served with mashed potatoes and sliced cooked beets, a white cream sauce poured over all.

Tabasco: just the most famed of the many devilishly hot-pepper sauces in Louisiana.

Tipsy Pie: actually a bourbon-drenched pudding of cake slices, fruits, and custard decorated with whipped cream. Also called **trifle**.

Washington "Pie" or Cake: a light sponge cake filled with a soft creamy custard and glazed with melted chocolate. Also called **Boston Cream Pie**.

Wild Cranberry Ketchup: Alaska's specialty, said to put tomato ketchup in second place.

CHAPTER 4

Argentinian. See Latin American

ARMENIAN

An oval of mountainous land dominated by the lofty Caucasus Mountains, of which Mount Ararat in the Armenian Republic is the highest, stretches between the Caspian Sea and the Black Sea. This area, commonly referred to as the Caucasus, is made up of three republics: Armenia, Georgia, and Azerbaijan. Neither the people nor their languages are Slavic in origin, and even their foods bear more resemblance to Eastern Mediterranean cuisine than to Russian. But they do have several things in common: an incredible zest for life, unsurpassed hospitality, and the talent to use obscure excuses for feasting and merrymaking.

It is still a matter of considerable debate whether the Armenian Mount Ararat is actually where Noah docked his ark. What *is* known is that the Armenians are one of the oldest civilizations, dating back to the sixth century B.C.E., and one of the first peoples to accept Christianity.

Though Armenia is a landlocked country it has caught the eye of many conquerors because it forms a vital land bridge between the Black Sea and the Caspian Sea. A Mongol and Tatar invasion in the early 1200s wiped out Armenia as a state. Four hundred years later, Turkey and Iran partitioned the territory of Armenia, and shortly thereafter, czarist Russia took over eastern Armenia. During World War I, the Turks starved or killed more than a million Armenians for the "crime" of living too close to the border.

The arable land, though small in area, is highly productive and lovingly attended. The climate varies between subtropical and subtemperate and allows for production of a variety of crops: almonds and walnuts; rice, wheat and corn; stone fruits (peaches, apricots, plums), citrus fruits, grapes; tobacco; and olives. But perhaps more important is the valued production of wool, milk, and cheese from the goats, cattle, and sheep that nibble the tender greens of the high rocky slopes.

The general use of fresh food (frozen and packaged foods of any type are scorned) in season and the practice of drying, smoking, and pickling to preserve food for winter is common throughout the Caucasus. But where corn, walnuts, and many types of dried beans are the Georgian staples, Armenians prefer rice, wheat, and pine nuts. Many

writers feel that Armenian cuisine combines the finest of Persian (Iranian), Greek, and Turkish foods, while others consider that Armenians "cook mostly in the Turkish style." (See also Greek and Turkish.)

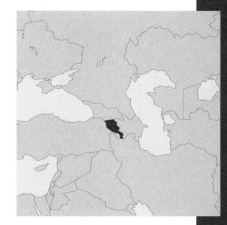

Researchers have long puzzled over the reasons for the almost legendary longevity of the people of this area. With an estimated "thirteen times as many centenarians as there are in every 100,000 people in North America," the question is intriguing. Senior citizens in North America are warned of the dangers of alcohol and tobacco consumption, yet strong brandy and wines are daily fare in the Caucasus and many people smoke heavily. And although the consequences of overindulgence in food are well-documented, it is also well-documented that Georgians and Armenians love nothing better than a party, one where the dishes on the table are so numerous that they must be piled one on top of the other. A party where each guest vies in toastmaking – everything from the favorable and unfavorable attributes of the host to a salute for world peace – as an acceptable excuse for draining the glass then promptly refilling it.

Perhaps these wondrously genial and generous people are so happy and hospitable because they have known lean times when bread and beans could constitute a blessed feast. Perhaps most of all, their personal warmth and longevity can be attributed to their inextinguishable philosophy of living life to the fullest.

DOMESTIC LIFE

The traditional lifestyle of Armenians can still be seen in the rural and mountain villages. The village is a family, with such an intertwining of caring and sharing that it is difficult to distinguish relatives from friends. Children are loved and respected as much as the oldest grandmother, and each person takes a share in work and activities. While modern electrical appliances and utensils are costly though available in urban centers, domestic life in rural areas still revolves around the traditionally simple but practical kitchen where woodenware and earthenware predominate. Heavy earthenware jugs and jars are used to store food in cold pantries and cellars over the winter months; garlic and onions, dried fruits and vegetables hang from walls and rafters; women share communal ovens.

DAIRY PRODUCTS

These products are plentiful and form an important part of the Armenian diet. Milk from sheep, goats, and cows is not used fresh but is cultured or soured as buttermilk or yogurt and used, sometimes diluted with water, as a drink or as a snack and often as part of other dishes. Fresh, hard, soft, and aged cheeses, some flavored with mountain herbs, are prepared all the time and used generously as appetizers, toppings, and as ingredients for many dishes.

FRUITS AND VEGETABLES

Citrus fruits, stone fruits such as plums, apricots, and peaches, grapes and melons, quince and apples are all abundantly enjoyed in season and mostly eaten fresh. Some of these fruits may be dried to preserve them for winter use.

Fresh and often wild herbs may be plucked from fields or paths and munched out of hand, minced and used generously in salads, or hung to dry for later use. Garlic and onions are used liberally in dishes and are often enjoyed raw. Leeks, green beans, squashes, okra, eggplant, salad greens, cucumbers, peppers and tomatoes, zucchini, pumpkin, and cabbages also may be plucked to eat out of hand, chopped into salads or soups, or eaten cooked in casseroles.

MEATS AND ALTERNATES

Lamb and chicken are the most favored meats, but beef and goat are also used. A variety of game birds also find their way to the table: pigeon, duck, quail, goose, plover, and partridge, teal, woodcock, and pheasant. Fish may be served boiled, steamed, baked, fried, or split and grilled on skewers. Some seafood is used where available fresh, such as oysters and mussels.

Eggs are widely used in cooking and baking, as a custard-like topping for vegetable casseroles and for the egg-lemon sauce (**avgolemono**) so popular in soups, meat, fish, and vegetable dishes. Many varieties of beans are used but **chickpeas** are the favorite.

The plentiful and nutritious nuts are used in sauces, where they are crushed or chopped sometimes with garlic and sometimes with spice and sugar. Nut filling for baked goods and nuts nibbled as a snack seem to be always at hand: pistachios, almonds, walnuts, chestnuts, pine nuts, and filberts. In fact, it is said that whenever two Armenians are talking there is probably a dish of pistachios between them.

BREADS AND GRAINS

The staple bread is the flat unleavened **pideh** or **lavash** made from wheat flour. **Bulgur**, coarse, dried whole wheat, is used in soups, as a side dish for meats, or mixed with chopped vegetables in a salad; it is also a frequent ingredient mixed with ground meats (See also Lebanese) and as fillings for vegetable dishes. Rice is also used in many dishes.

FATS

Every home has a supply of olive oil which is used in all cooking, as a basting for meats and fish, and as a base to dress salads. Clarified butter is used less frequently, sometimes for vegetables but mostly for special occasions that warrant pastries.

FOODS COMMONLY USED

The highly sophisticated and varied cuisine of Armenia encompasses a wide and well-balanced combination of foods. Lamb and chicken are the favored meats, fresh chopped vegetables are often eaten as salads, and vegetables are an important part of many one-dish meals. Soured or cultured milk and many types of fresh and aged cheeses are plentiful and eaten almost anytime with breads, fruits, nuts, or by themselves. Rice forms the basis of many **pilafs** and the filling of stuffed vegetables, while wheat is favored for breads of all kinds and cracked wheat (**bulgur**) is also used in many dishes. Refreshing yogurt and soured milk are consumed as beverages or snacks, wine often accompanies meals, especially parties, and brandy is taken for any reason.

SWEETS AND SNACKS

Besides ignoring the negative effects of overindulging in alcohol, tobacco, and food, Armenians also seem to destroy the commonly held notion that sweets may be detrimental to health. Armenians consume more sweets and pastries than other peoples of the Caucasus, and yet their indulgence in these foods doesn't seem to have a negative effect on their longevity. The usual dessert consumed is fruit and cheeses, but sugared and candied nuts appear to be widely available as snacks and desserts. The traditional syrupy-sweet desserts of thin, crisp pastries layered with nuts, spices, and sugar, so beloved around the Mediterranean, are just as welcomed by Armenians of any age. The availability of other sweet cakes as well as rolls filled with nuts and sweetened soft cheese fillings and brushed with egg and sugar toppings might even form the excuse for a party.

SEASONINGS

Garlic and onions head the list of seasonings, closely followed by a wide selection of cultivated and fresh and dried herbs. Nuts and seeds (sesame) add crunch and taste, vinegar and pepper add sharp hotness, while cloves, saffron, and cinnamon evoke the exotic. Greece's famed **avgolemono** (egg and lemon juice) sauce adds its tangy touch to many meals. A dribble of clarified butter and splash of homemade wine or fresh cream may also be a part of the cook's flourish.

BEVERAGES

Raki (brandy) is commonly taken as an aperitif, just in case any Armenian may be troubled with a lagging appetite, and if so, perhaps two **Rakis** would be better than just one. Homemade red and white wines usually accompany meals and are enjoyed by all ages. Yogurt and soured milk (**leban**) is usually more a part of lunch or a between-meal refreshment. **Soorj** (unsweetened coffee) is the common breakfast beverage.

MEALS AND CUSTOMS

Hospitality is a way of life and nothing is more enjoyed than inviting guests or wayfarers to partake of whatever food the family may have on hand. Whether the variety is wide or limited, somehow there is always enough to share. The women take great pride in preparing and serving the meals and usually hover in the background while the men feast and drink and merrily toast each other, the weather, the crops, the country, the world. Table service and manners are of secondary importance. Shared enjoyment is everything. Even when times are bad, and people have to survive only on bread and beans, these will be prepared in a variety of ways and served with the same joy as the most sumptuous meal.

The general pattern of three meals a day prevails. Breakfast is a simple spread of cheese, olives, and bread with coffee. The noon meal is usually a hot vegetable or vegetable and meat casserole, while the largest meal, dinner, usually takes place in the evening between seven and eight o'clock. This meal customarily begins with the potent **Raki** and more recently with vodka, to be followed by nibbles of cheeses, various types of olives (black, green spiced, salted, etc.), or sometimes a chopped green salad or gently simmered soup. The meal continues with roasted meat, fish, or fowl, together with more vegetables (often served cooked and cold), rice or **bulgur pilaf**, a choice of wines or **leban** or yogurt, to be finished with a dessert of fresh or dried fruits, nuts, and cheeses. Occasionally coffee may conclude a special dinner. Snacks throughout the day will be nuts or toasted seeds to crunch and munch almost continually, sometimes a break of pastries and coffee or wine, if there are guests, or just a humble refreshment of **leban** and fruit.

SPECIAL OCCASIONS

Armenian Christianity, recognized as one of the earliest branches of the Christian faith, dates from the work of Saint Gregory the Illuminator (third century). Armenians today are divided between the Uniate Church, which is similar to the Roman Catholic but uses an Armenian rite, and the Gregorian Church. A few Armenians are of the Protestant faith and some are Jewish. In America, the Armenian Apostolic Church is most closely identified with the Greek Orthodox Church.

It is the combination of the Armenians' warm family feelings and deep bonds to their faith as well as their inherent delight with parties that make family and religious events occasions for feasting, drinking, and merriment. Usually such a special occasion calls forth a vast array of all the traditional dishes, sweets and pastries, and all the brandy and wine the family can afford (and probably more than anyone can consume). Often a variety of spit-roasted game birds highlight many special occasions, but a specialty of weddings is a huge **saffron pilaf** made with rice, saffron, and flavored with rosewater.

GLOSSARY OF FOODS AND FOOD TERMS

Abour: soup.

Anoush: jams, or sweet preserves of fruits or vegetables.

Asma-Yaprak Dolma: a chilled dish of grape leaves stuffed with seasoned rice, cooked and flavored with olive oil, browned onions, and allspice.

Baklava or **Paklava**: many-layered with tissue-thin sheets of phyllo dough, this pastry is filled with nuts and sugar and finished with a dousing of hot spiced syrup.

Baluck Plaki: fish that is baked with a sauce of garlic, olive oil, tomatoes, and lemon.

Bami: okra.

Basterma: an Armenian favorite of salted dried beef, flavored with **fenugreek** then brined and dried again. Used all year but especially in winter dishes, or as an appetizer.

Bulgur or **Burgul**: wholegrain wheat cereal that has been boiled, dried, and cracked, and may be purchased as fine, medium, or wholegrain particle sizes.

Choerek: small, sweet rolls of yeast dough, sprinkled with sesame seeds.

Dolmas: generally refers to stuffed rolled grape leaves, but term may be used to refer to any stuffed baked vegetables.

Echmiadzinskaya Dolma: a dish of mixed stuffed vegetables, e.g., green and yellow pepper, tomatoes, zucchini, eggplant.

Feta: firm crumbly cheese made from sheep's or goat's milk, packed in brine, somewhat strong and tart in flavor. A favored cheese of Mediterranean as well as Armenian peoples.

Hariseh: traditional dish of broth-cooked **Bulgur** combined with shreds of chicken and beaten to an almost-smooth consistency.

Havabour: festive soup or chicken broth and rice flavored with beaten eggs and lemon juice, similar to Greek **Avgolemono**.

Iksir: homemade cherry brandy, often served with cheese.

Kchuch: Armenian vegetable stew like the Turkish/Bulgarian **Ghouvetch**.

Kebab: cooked meat. (**Shish Kebab**: on a skewer; **Tas Kebab**: in a pot).

Keshkegh: pilaf of bulgur and minced lamb or chicken flavored with butter, cinnamon, and pepper, all simmered in rich broth or chicken stock. National Armenian dish.

Keyma Koufta: meatballs made from well-seasoned, finely ground raw beef and fine bulgur.

Kharpout Koufta: cooked meatballs made with ground seasoned beef or lamb, bulgur, onions, and tomato sauce.

Kimionlou Shish Kebab: cubed meat (beef or lamb) marinated in olive oil and cumin seed, then grilled over an open fire on skewers and served on **Pideh**.

Koufta or **Kufta**: meatballs.

Lavash: thin, bubbled Armenian bread made from unleavened thin sheets of wheat flour dough, sprinkled with sesame seeds.

Leban: soured or cultured milk.

Matsun: yogurt.

Mezaa: appetizers, or those nibbles of food taken with drinks.

Nohond Basti: puree of well-cooked chickpeas flavored with small amounts of meat, stock, and onions.

Pacha Terbiehli: slow-simmered stew of beef or lamb cooked in their own juices, flavored with garlic, vinegar, and hot peppers.

Patlijan Moussaka: a casserole baked in the oven or on stove top, made of layers of fried eggplant, ground beef or lamb, and tomatoes.

Pideh or **Peda**: crispy-crusted white-wheat-flour bread leavened with yeast, shaped in rounds or long loaves, finished with a sprinkle of sesame seeds.

Prassa Basdi: a dish of sliced leeks cooked with beef or lamb, garnished with an egg-lemon sauce (**Avgolemono**).

Printz Abour: bland soup made with rice and flavored with salt, pepper, and lemon juice.

Raki: clear, anise-flavored brandy, taken as an aperitif.

Saffron Pilaf: pilaf of rice flavored with rosewater and saffron, a specialty at weddings.

Simit: a dessert cookie of twisted spirals of sweet dough sprinkled with sesame seeds.

Soorj: unsweetened coffee.

Sumpoog Letzvadz: eggplant stuffed with ground beef or lamb, bread crumbs, oil, garlic, and beaten eggs. This baked dish may be served hot or cold.

Tchorba: soup, usually refers to broths.

Tell Khadayif: a sweet dessert of finely shredded crisp wheat sprinkled with nuts and coated with syrup.

Tureli Ghuvedge: slow-simmered stew of mixed vegetables and meats flavored with tomatoes, salt, pepper, and mint.

Tushi: pickled vegetables.

Vousp Abour: thick soup of lentils, flavored with lemon.

Yaz Salata: a combination of chopped raw vegetables, sometimes including nuts and olives, all tossed with olive oil and lemon juice or vinegar.

CHAPTER 5

AUSTRALIAN

On the largest island and the smallest continent in the world more than 18 million people make their home among unusual flora and fauna and some of the most  unique animals in the world: the kangaroo, the dingo (a howling, doglike night hunter), the koala bear, and the platypus. One of the driest and most sparsely populated continents, Australia is mostly tropical in the north (Queensland) and temperate in the south (Victoria, New South Wales). More than half of the population live in cities and these are located in the irrigated and fertile coastal regions of the east, southeast, and southwest. For the most part, the vast interior of plateaus and eroded mountains – the outback – is all but uninhabited, with many areas remaining untouched and primitive.

Who are the Australians? It is believed that Australian Aborigines were the first settlers, arriving more than 40,000 years ago from Southeast Asia and evolving their culture in comparative isolation. By the early 1600s, seafaring Europeans arrived. Because of the gradual decline in Aboriginal population due to disease, loss of land, and faltering fertility, the colonials assumed they would soon disappear. On the contrary, the descendants of the early Aborigines are very much a vital, though small, part of the present Australian population.

Many of the great seafaring nations were probably aware of this great land mass in the South Seas, but it remained for Captain Arthur Philip, of the Royal British Navy, to unfurl the British flag at Sydney Cove on January 26, 1788. To this day, this is celebrated as Australia Day. By the 1800s, almost 5,000 white male prisoners and their guards formed a colony at Sydney, joining the first 700 convicts who had been unloaded from Captain Philip's ship on that fateful day. They may have been the first "citizens" of the "land down under," but it is estimated that more than 35,000 years ago, the ancestors of the present Melanesians and Australian Aborgines had already been living there in their own neo–Stone Age society. In the ensuing years, with allegiance to Britain, Australia's own parliament attempted to unite the population, but it took the First World War to weld the fiercely individual and independent population into a nation.

Unification finally occurred because of the strong link to Great Britain but also because the pressures of war caused shortages of essential goods. Self-sufficiency became an urgent necessity. Improvements in agriculture, mining production, and the development of new industries not only helped on the home front but set up Australia as an exporter to world markets. Iron ore, coal, and wool, as well as meats, wheat, and sugar became vital economic commodities.

Since the First World War increasingly diversified ethnic immigration add vitality to Australian lifestyles and generated heated debate in the country over the future of its preponderantly Caucasian population. Pride in "Aborginality" enhanced growth in the indigenous population, Asian-born Australians increased their presence, and refugees and displaced persons from many lands all added to the population by the late 1980s.

Up to the Second World War, Australia's population was more than 99 percent of British origin. Following the war, many of the displaced and war-weary of Europe migrated to Australia. These people included Italians, Dutch, Poles, Germans, Yugoslavians, Greeks, Ukrainians, and Latvians. These, then, are the Australians. Given this diversity, it is not surprising to find that one of the largest Australian cookbooks, *Australian and New Zealand Complete Book of Cookery*, should turn out to be a study of international cookery. Many writers then claimed that Australia lacked a distinctive cuisine, regional cooking styles, or even any great national dishes. Nonetheless, the combination of a wealth of seafood, good inexpensive lamb, delicious fruits, and the inspiration and ingenuity of immigrants long immersed in their own traditional cuisines, has now been recognized as a distinctive evolving Australian cuisine.

In fact, a current report on Australian food customs states: "Australians have thrown off the British yoke of pub grub and have embraced the great bounty from their own seas along with home-grown fruit and vegetables and the spices of Asia." The nostril-tweaking scents of Asian spices, the hot delight of chilies, the surprising pleasure of finger foods and dipping sauces are to be found not just in restaurants but on Australian tables everywhere. The palate-tantalizing flavors of Indonesia, Malaysia, India, and Vietnam, brought to Australia by travelers and immigrants, have found a new home and are creating a new tradition of fusion cuisine that is startlingly original, memorable and delicious.

Australian wines have long been making their presence appreciated in world markets, but more recently, visitors to the land down under are bringing back delicious accounts of **bush tucker**. The basic wilderness foods of the Aboriginals are gaining in popularity and sophisticated preparation. These include herbs like mountain pepper, watercress oil, and **wattleseed** (with a "coffee-hazelnut flavor") as well as rabbit, kangaroo, **wallaby**, crocodile, **emu**, and **bunya nuts**. Many fruits and vegetables unknown to most of the world await discovery. Examples of these include: greens called **warrigal**, **lemon aspin** that looks like a little pumpkin and tastes like citrus fruit, **munthari** berries with their apple-like taste, and tiny **kakadu plums**, their size belying their prodigious vitamin C content.

DOMESTIC LIFE
Australian kitchens are similar to those in North America, though smaller and probably boasting fewer appliances and gadgets. Electricity is favored over gas as a cooking fuel, but outdoor picnics and barbecues are frequent and preferred because of the pleasant climate. Home freezers are not yet common, so there are few frozen products available to the consumer. Ranges, refrigerators, and dishwashers are common, as are most of the small practical kitchen appliances familiar in North America. Most popular is the "hot water jug": available in different sizes, this small appliance heats water quickly to the boiling point – practical in a land where frequent cups of tea are the daily rule.

DAIRY PRODUCTS
Fresh whole milk is used in quantity by most Australian families: children drink milk at most meals and adults enjoy milk in puddings, soups, custards, and tea. Skim milk, 2 percent (partially skimmed) milk, and cottage cheese are not widely accepted, nor is skim milk powder. Cheeses are not a usual part of the dietary pattern and usually are only used in specialty dishes that call for cheese as an ingredient. There is a small but noticeable increase in the popularity of yogurt.

FRUITS AND VEGETABLES
Although there is a great variety of produce in Australia, the variety is mainly seasonal and local. There is even little importing of produce from one state to the other. Part of the reason may be storage and transportation facilities; frequently January floods affect supplies and cause price increases.

Fruits available include passion fruit, pineapples, pawpaws, many forms of coconut, fresh figs, **guavas**, melons, **chokos**, **tamarillos**, mangoes, mulberries, loganberries, **lichees, cumquats** (Australian spelling), kiwi fruit, **feijoas** (plums), and a range of citrus fruits. Exotic tropical fruits available are: persimmons, avocados, **custard apples, monsteria delicio**. Australia is also rightly famed for its fine-quality dried fruits; Australian raisins and currants are widely exported. Other popularly consumed dried fruits include peaches, apricots, pears, figs, prunes, and apples. Australians prefer to eat fruits that require minimum preparation, and more dried fruits are commonly eaten as snacks and desserts than in North America. A favorite accompaniment to a barbecued dinner of steak or chops is a large mixed salad that combines fruits and vegetables.

As with fruits, Australians prefer their vegetables with a minimum of "fixing"; not for them mysterious mixtures of creamed or sauced vegetables. Some Australian vegetables are called by names different than those used in North America: beets are commonly called **beetroots; capsicums** refer to green or red peppers. Australian "pumpkin" is unlike the pumpkin found in North America, as it is a dark

FOODS COMMONLY USED

The staples of the Australian diet can be described as "steak and eggs," and the preference for simple solid food shows up on the spice shelf too: salt and pepper and a few spices for baking. But inroads are being made in introducing "health foods" such as wholegrains and yogurt, and the preparation of more vegetables and the use of skim milk powder is becoming more widespread. Price rises in fresh beef will also encourage the use of other meats and meat alternates. Women favor tea, men enjoy beer, and children drink milk at most meals.

green vegetable with the shape and appearance of the familiar American pumpkin but a flavor and texture resembling that of carrots.

MEATS AND ALTERNATES
Beef in the form of steaks and roasts heads the popularity list on the Australian diet. Next come other cuts of beef, lamb, veal, and offal. Pork and poultry are not used with any regularity. Roasting, quick-frying, or barbecuing are the usual methods of meat cookery. Other meats used only occasionally include duck, goose, turkey, wild duck, crocodile, camel, marinated kangaroo meat, partridge, pheasant, venison, and wild pork. A famed dish is **carpetbaggers steak**: a thick steak that is split, stuffed with raw oysters, and broiled or barbecued.

There is no shortage of fish and seafood and there is wide variety: oysters, scallops, mussels, tohero (a shellfish with a distinctively green color), trout, salmon, red snapper, **mulloway, hapuka**, whitebait, **tarahiki, gurnard**, flounder, and bream. Following the Australian's preference for simplicity, fish is served fresh and prepared in a simple way by poaching, baking, frying, or grilling.

Legumes are used only in specialty dishes, but a growing vegetarian community is using legumes and soybean products extensively.

Finally, it must be noted that steak and eggs really are a classic favorite and considered the perfect breakfast, lunch, or supper and even – for heartier Aussies – a snack.

BREADS AND GRAINS
In home baking there is a definite preference for the use of self-raising flour, that is, flour containing a proportionate amount of salt and leavening agent. Fresh breads are usually purchased daily for meals and for teatime. Wheat flour is the staple but cornstarch is used in thickening desserts and sauces. Wholegrain wheat flour is called wholemeal. More recently, the Swiss breakfast favorite **muesli**, a blend of toasted oats, dried fruits, and nuts eaten with milk, has gained some popularity. Australians do not favor pancakes or waffles and seldom use sweetened breakfast cereals, although **pikelets** similar to pancakes are considered a dessert.

FATS
Margarine is the most widely used fat, and although generally priced the same as butter, many seem to prefer its flavor. **Cofa** is a solidified coconut oil used in making desserts.

SWEETS AND SNACKS
Dried fruits are popular snacks and Health Food Bars, made from nuts, sesame seeds, dried fruits, and honey are enjoyed by all ages. Fresh fruit is eaten as a snack in season.

SEASONINGS
Not for the Australian any complex form of seasoning. Cookery, service, and seasonings are all simple and basic. Salt and pepper and onions are the staples, for Australians have a strong preference for foods that "taste natural." Chutneys, pickles, and piquant sauces are often served with meals.

BEVERAGES
Australian wine is inexpensive, of excellent quality, and widely used. Local quality beer is the preferred beverage for most men and Foster's is the brand everyone knows; women enjoy frequent cups of tea daily; children prefer fresh whole milk but often have tea or coffee. Fruit cordials are popular, especially in hot weather. Strong spirits, cola drinks, and coffee are not as popular.

MEALS AND CUSTOMS
There are no particular rituals associated with meals in Australia. The three-meals-a-day pattern is prevalent, with morning and afternoon breaks usually consisting of tea or beer with a small snack. The Australian woman taking her lunch at home will eat sparsely; the working person will have an inexpensive hot plate of mince, potato, and peas, or a meat pie with beer. Most children eat their lunches at school, buying it at the tuck shop or cafeteria, and have a choice of cold but satisfying foods such as meat pies, sausage rolls, buns, salads, sweets, drinks, and potato chips. The evening meal at home will usually consist of meat and vegetables, potatoes, or bread. Potatoes are expensive and not as widely available as in North America. Pastries or fruit or simple puddings will be the dessert.

Avid outdoor people, Australians love any excuse for a picnic (the races, any races) or barbecue. Simple barbecued meats or fresh fish, vegetables, fruits, and perhaps biscuits and cakes, together with a good supply of beer spell good times and a festive occasion.

Many people still working in the isolated outback regions prefer to cook in bush ovens. A hole is dug in the ground and lined with hot coals. A special heavy, covered cooking pot is placed on the coals, covered with more coals, and finally heaped with earth. Although simple in principle, this method requires great skill, and for those who know how to do it, anything from meats and stews to cakes and breads can be cooked this way.

Aside from going to small casual restaurants and local bars to enjoy beer with friends, Australians are not generally keen about eating out. Tourists to Australia are often disappointed by what they consider to be mediocre hotel and restaurant standards. It is not that the Australians in any way lack hospitality, it is rather that they lack the ability to be servile. To the Australian, even his boss is his "mate," tipping is disliked because of its servile connotation, and Australians take great personal pride in the fact that theirs is a "classless society." It is most unfortunate that this pride of independence and love of equality is too often misconstrued as arrogance.

SPECIAL OCCASIONS

Freedom of worship prevails in Australia. There are many Protestant and Roman Catholic groups, and about one-third of the population belongs to the Church of England. Since Christmas occurs in the Australian summer, a typical dinner of salads and cold meats, with an ice cream cake or pudding for dessert, is common. Special occasions such as *Race Days*, or local sports events, are celebrated with picnics, barbecues, and plentiful beer.

Anzac Day, April 25, commemorates Australian soldiers who died in the First World War. The day is marked by a parade of "old diggers" (soldiers) and beer parties. *Australia Day*, on January 26, is marked by parties featuring barbecues of beef or lamb, salads, and the favorite dessert, **pavlova**: a whipped cream, meringue, and tropical-fruit confection.

GLOSSARY OF FOODS AND FOOD TERMS

Anzac Crispies: crisp oatmeal cookies.

Beetroot: common name for beets.

Biscuits: common name for cookies, many of which are also known as **Kiwi Crisps**, **Maori Kisses**, **Hokey Pokey Biscuits**, **Moomba Fingers**, and so on.

Brawn: a jelled mix of cooked cubed beef, veal, and pork.

Capsicums: common name for red and green sweet peppers.

Castor Sugar: finely granulated white sugar.

Chiko Rolls: snack food similar to small Chinese egg rolls.

Chooki: chicken.

Cofa: solidified block of coconut oil used mainly in desserts.

Cream Sponge: a light sponge cake, split and filled with whipped cream and fresh fruit.

Cumquats: a variety of tiny oranges, sour in taste and used especially in sugary preserves.

Damper: quick bread, mixed with a knife, and made with self-rising flour and milk or water. It may be baked in the oven or directly on coals (the outer crust would then be scraped off and discarded).

Egg and Bacon Pie: a quick luncheon or supper dish prepared by lining a piecrust with bacon strips, then breaking in the desired number of eggs, and finally topping with an egg/milk-glazed pastry, and baking till set.

Floater: a meat pie served floating in soup – usually pea soup.

Goanna: large fatty lizard, often eaten grilled.

Granny Smith: a variety of apple, bright green and crisp.

Hogget (or **Two-Tooth**): name given to sheep from nine to twenty months old, having passed the lamb stage but not yet matured.

Kabobs: meats that are sliced or cubed and threaded on skewers for barbecuing or broiling.

Kromeskies: mixture of diced cooked meats and seasonings, wrapped in bacon then dipped in fritter batter and deep-fried. These are served as appetizers and eaten dipped into tomato sauce (ketchup).

Kumera: sweet potatoes or yams.

Lamington Cake: butter cake, usually frosted with chocolate icing and coated with shredded coconut.

Mince: ground meat, usually beef. This term may also refer to any finely chopped mixture.

Molehill: a dessert of almond-filled prunes coated and mounded with a light mixture of gelatin, whipped eggs, and whipped cream, then topped with grated chocolate.

Muesli: dry breakfast cereal of Swiss origin made of toasted oats, nuts, and dried fruits and served dry or with milk. This mixture is also used in the preparation of many breads and biscuits.

Mutton: lamb that is more than two years old that has dark red flesh with hard white fat. Young mutton is twenty months to two years old.

Pavlova: a delicately baked meringue of egg whites and sugar topped with whipped cream and fresh seasonal fruits. Considered to be the Australian national dessert.

Pikelets: a quickly made mix of eggs, milk, self-rising flour, and sugar, similar to pancakes. The mixture is dropped by spoonfuls on a hot griddle and browned on both sides. They are eaten as a cool dessert.

Tomato Sauce: ketchup.

Sago: tapioca.

Spaetzli: small drops of soft dough either poached or fried before adding to soups.

Sucker: a very young spring lamb, less than nine months old.

Tohero: a shellfish with a distinctive green color.

Trifle: dessert of English origin prepared by layering fingers of plain cake with custard sauce and fruit then garnishing with whipped cream, glaceed cherries, and nuts.

Vegemite: a favorite Australian spread, brown in color and yeasty in taste. Said to be highly nutritious, it is as popular with Australians as peanut butter is with North Americans.

Wholemeal: Australian term for wholegrain (wholewheat) flour.

Yabbies: freshwater crayfish.

CHAPTER 6

AUSTRIAN

Small wonder that the Austrian is said to be preoccupied with the subject of food. For over 600 years the vast Austro-Hungarian Empire enveloped the languages, traditions, and food customs of more than a dozen nations. Even today, Vienna conjures up visions of opulent architecture, lilting waltzes, and mounds of whipped cream. And though 1918 saw the end of the empire and the opulence, the love of music and intense appreciation of an Austrian cuisine remains.

With seemingly endless appetite, the Austrian *feinschmecker* (gourmet) enjoys pastas, veal dishes, and tomato sauces from Italy, potato dishes and sauerkraut from Germany, dumplings in great array from the Czech Republic, vegetables and rice dishes from the Balkans, sour-cream cookery and soups from Poland and Russia, coffee from Turkey. But from Hungary, Austrians will only willingly admit to the acquisition of paprika. Their beloved **strudel** and **torten**, crescents and rolls, and fine breads are, however, of Austrian origin. When in Austria no one would dare argue otherwise.

If this claim of absorption with food seems unjustified, one should consider that although Austria is a predominantly scenic and mountainous country, its manicured farms, pastures, vineyards, and orchards produce all the necessities of the diet and do so relatively inexpensively. From Austria's granary in Lower Austria come wheat, barley, rye, and corn as well as grapes from the vineyards. From Styria, over 170 branches of the "Fresh Egg Service" supply eggs, while other areas produce fruits and berries, cattle and dairy products. And though Vienna is highly industrialized, the city is surrounded by areas engaged in mixed farming and animal husbandry. The smallest Alpine province, Vorarlberg, caters to the complete set of sweet teeth that every Austrian has, and produces famed chocolates and candies.

Despite an immersion in food, wine, and music, the country's history is not a happy one. As in most empires, those who were forcibly made a part of it resented their oppression. Torn between German and Hungarian affiliations, most immigrants solved the dilemma by referring to themselves not as Austrians but as Czechs, Slovaks, Slovenes, Croatians, Serbs, Magyars, Romanians, Ukrainians, Poles, Jews, Italians, or Macedonians. But in 1918, after Austria was established as a republic, almost 90 percent of her population was Roman Catholic and almost 99 percent were German-speaking.

Though most Austrian immigrants to America speak German and are German in spirit, they have – with the exception of the groups mentioned above – melded into North American society, caring little for Austrian newspapers or Austrian organizations, yet their ties and justifiable pride in Austrian cuisine remain.

DOMESTIC LIFE

The neat little Austrian kitchen has everything necessary to prepare fine foods lovingly, with everything in its special place. The kitchen may be the workshop, but the dining room is the stage; fine linens, fresh flowers, and sparkling dishes have retained their importance here.

Even with the presence of supermarkets and availability of prepared foods and mixes, canned and frozen delicacies, the Austrian homemaker prefers to shop daily in her favorite small specialty shops where she feels certain the proprietor will give her the best. Fresh fruits and tender fresh vegetables are still favored and their seasonal succulence is treasured. Because of the routine of daily shopping, large refrigerators are really not a necessity, but cold pantries are still filled with a proud array of home pickles and preserves, prepared when time permits.

Currently there is some deviation from this traditional pattern, as increasingly women are taking jobs and finding their cooking and shopping time limited. Supermarkets and the prepared-foods industry are expanding and even the long-established pattern of six meals a day is shrinking both in number and quantity of food consumed as people became more acutely aware of a healthier lifestyle.

DAIRY PRODUCTS

Fresh fluid milk is often served boiled rather than cold as a beverage. Sweetened condensed milk is widely used but skim milk and dried milk powder are not favored. Cheeses of all types, sour milk, and thick sour cream are used a great deal. Sweetened, whipped cream is so popular as almost to be classed as a daily staple.

FRUITS AND VEGETABLES

A wide range of seasonal fruits are used fresh or prepared as cold fruit soups, compotes, and other desserts, or are used as filling in baked goods. Some imported and canned fruits are consumed. Recently, citrus fruits and citrus juices are used regularly. This coincides with an increasing awareness of good nutrition.

Seasonal vegetables are purchased fresh and prepared with care as salads, pickles, well-cooked, or well-garnished, never plain. Winter staples include red and green cabbage, potatoes (prepared in an endless variety of ways), beets, **sauerkraut**, and pickles.

MEATS AND ALTERNATES

Pork, veal, and chicken are the favored meats; very little fish is consumed. Beef and lamb are usually served well-cooked and accompanied with rich gravies and sauces. Meats are used as main dishes but also form an important part of many snacks, which are often smoked, pickled, or cured meats or many types of sausages.

Eggs are most often eaten boiled, or hard-cooked as appetizers, as a garnish or as an ingredient in other dishes. Legumes are of little importance and used only occasionally in soups and sometimes as a side dish. Nuts are used only as garnish or part of rich desserts or candies.

BREADS AND GRAINS

Dried breakfast cereals served cold with milk or hot, cooked porridges have no place at the Austrian table. Many types of plain or sweet rolls with hot milk, tea, or coffee is a common breakfast. To the Austrian, grains do not comprise the morning meal, but are to be found as flour in the great array of breads of all kinds, dark and light, rolls, buns made with every combination of wheat and rye flours, sweet and soured doughs. Bread is present in some form at every meal and often is part of snacks as well.

FATS

Since sour cream, whipped cream, and eggs are very important in so many dishes, they also contribute a great amount of fats to the Austrian diet. Lard, oil, butter, and margarine are all used in cooking and baking.

SWEETS AND SNACKS

The Austrian sweet tooth is not easily satisfied. It begins with preserves and crisp rolls for breakfast, and requires refueling at almost any time of day in the form of chocolates and candies, sweetened coffee and occasionally tea (there is even a preference for sweet rather than dry wines), and of course, the almost legendary consumption of incredibly rich and tempting pastries and desserts, to which the true Austrian will often unabashedly add a generous dollop of **schlagobers** (sweetened whipped cream).

SEASONINGS

Most typical are paprika, caraway seeds, onions, and garlic, but there is also a judicious use of herbs and spices. Chocolate is the favorite dessert flavor, also vanilla and freshly zested rind of oranges and lemons. Wine and sour cream, sweet cream, and fresh butter are also typical flavors.

BEVERAGES

There is some consumption of fresh milk, by children, and some sipping of sweetened tea, but coffee in many varieties (flavored with chocolate, vanilla, or served with cream or whipped cream) is still most popular. When Austrians serve wine with a meal it will inevitably be a rich, fruity Rhine wine. This white wine is preferred no matter what the main course. Beer is considered a more casual beverage and more favored by men.

MEALS AND CUSTOMS

Gracious table manners are part of very early lessons for Austrian children. And these are readily learned, especially when the reward is a slice of **sachertorte** or **apfel strudel mit schlag**. Mealtimes are mannered and orderly with the father the first to be served, the leader in conversation, and the one whose opinion on everything from the **vorspeisen** (appetizers) to the **mehlspeisen** (desserts made with flour) is eagerly anticipated.

FOODS COMMONLY USED

A post–Second World War increase in the consumption of fresh milk and citrus fruits has added nutrients to a traditional diet based on veal, pork, and chicken, large consumption of breads and rich sweets, wine and beer, all somewhat balanced by an intake of seasonal fruits and vegetables.

Dinner guests are always on time and invariably bring a bouquet of flowers for their hostess. Entertaining and sociability are an indigenous part of the Austrian personality. If not taking a meal with a friend or entertaining guests at home, the gregarious Austrian will likely feel the need to communicate a few words to a pretty girl or even to a complete stranger at the next table in the *kaffeehaus*. Conversation, conviviality, and communication are as much a part of the Austrian soul as food and music.

The day usually begins with an "eye-opener" of small crisp rolls, preserves, and butter, with good coffee. Around 10:00 a.m. a small bowl of hot **gulyas**, or a sausage with bread and pickles, washed down with a beer, followed by a "real" lunch around 1:00 p.m. of soup (a "real" meal without soup is unthinkable), roast meat or chicken, bread, dumplings or noodles, a small salad of greens, followed by cheese, fresh fruit, or compote. To sustain one through the afternoon hours, one can always muse on which **torte** will accompany the afternoon *jause* of coffee and a pastry or two. By 7:00 p.m. businesses are closed and families are together for dinner, a meal suspiciously similar to lunch. After dinner, many Austrians will be off to the theater, opera, or out visiting friends and it would be most unusual if at about 11:00 p.m. one did not find them all chatting over a simple snack of sandwiches, cold salad plates, pastries, and coffee.

In Austria, movable *wurstel* (sausage) stands in strategic locations and cozy *kaffeehauser*, with their array of sweets, tease and tempt the passerby. Why try to avoid the inevitable? After all, who can deny that a little food helps to console and fortify one against the memories of the past and the uncertainties of the future. In almost any Austrian household that retains even a crumb of Austrian tradition, if there is not a serious discussion of the foods that are being eaten or were eaten, then visions are being conjured up of taste sensations yet to come. And what the father of the household desires will likely comprise the menu of the evening meal – or the next snack.

All of this represents the traditional Austrian viewpoint in matters of gastronomy. "Traditional" should be underlined. The contemporary desire by men and women alike for trim healthy bodies, and the fact that more women are working outside the home, have made inroads even to the Austrian table: meals and snacks are shrinking, waistlines are becoming increasingly visible. Despite this, however, nothing can diminish the opulence of Austrian cuisine.

SPECIAL OCCASIONS

The Austria of today is predominantly Roman Catholic, but many Austrians living elsewhere in the world may be Jewish or Protestant and celebrate their religious holidays accordingly. Elegant menus of game are often a part of special-occasion fare, together with a great selection of hot and cold garnished platters of other meats, salads, and molds, served with various breads and rolls, beer or Rhine wine, and completed with a tempting array of the country's famed pastries.

GLOSSARY OF FOODS AND FOOD TERMS

Dobosch Torte: many-layered sponge cake, with a chocolate filling, and characteristically topped with caramel-glazed wedges.

Fleischspeisen: meats.

Gabelfruhstuck: literally a "fork meal," referring to the traditional 10:00 a.m. snack usually of a small meat dish or sausage.

Gemuse: vegetables.

Gulyas: slow-simmered dish of cubed veal in a paprika-onion sauce, occasionally with potatoes and carrots added.

Gulyasuppe: the same as a **Gulyas**, with a thinner sauce.

Heuriger: name given to new young wine.

Jause: literally "gossip time"; refers to the pastry and coffee taken in the late afternoon. May occasionally be an elaborate spread of small sandwiches, pastries, and tea as well as coffee.

Kaisersemmel: crisp, artfully folded dinner roll, which, when baked, appears to have four sections in its top.

Kase: cheese.

Knodel (see also **Spaetzle**, **Spatzle**, **Nockerl**): dumpling made from flour and water and sometimes with added egg.

Krapfen: fried yeast cakes, similar to doughnuts.

Kuchen: a general name for what is considered "plain" cakes, i.e., pastry or yeast doughs with fruit or nut or cheese filling.

Linzer Torte: named after the great composer Franz Liszt, this is more a flan than a torte; a rich nut pastry filled with fine raspberry preserves, criss-crossed with more nut pastry, baked, then served with whipped cream.

Mehlspeisen: literally, a dessert made with flour, so many include pancakes, waffles, cakes, pastries, dumplings.

Nockerl: one name for dumplings.

Palatschinken: thin, small pancakes, similar to crepes, usually served rolled and filled with preserves, sprinkled with nuts or crumbs and topped with whipped cream.

Sachertorte: moist rich chocolate cake, glazed with chocolate and served with whipped cream. Named after the famed Frau Sacher, owner of the Sacher hotel, known for its chocolate cake.

Schlagobers or "**Schlag**": sweetened, flavored (usually with vanilla) whipped cream.

Spaetzli: tiny dumplings of flour and eggs, usually formed with a spoon dipped in broth or water.

Strucken: small, thin pancakes similar to crepes.

Strudel: very thin stretched dough made from flour, sugar, water, oil or butter, filled and rolled with sweet or savory filling. (Similar to **Retes** (Hungarian) or **Phyllo** (Greek).

Suss-speisen: literally, desserts with no flour, e.g., fruits, puddings, mousses, frozen desserts, gelatin desserts.

Teig: pastry or dough.

Torte: difficult to define, but commonly taken to mean a rich and often layered and filled cake usually made with little or no flour; instead, fine bread crumbs or grated nuts are used. Rich butter icing, chocolate or whipped cream complete it.

Vorspeisen: appetizers or hor d'oeuvres.

Wiener Backhendle: a Viennese specialty of egg-dipped, crumbed fried chicken pieces which are then finished by oven baking.

Wienerbrot: a Scandinavian term literally meaning Viennese bread, but which actually refers to pastries made from puff paste. (Known elsewhere as Danish pastry!)

Wiener Schnitzel: perhaps the most famous Viennese specialty; large thin (pounded) scallops of veal, egged and crumbed and crisply fried. The best are so thin and large, they literally bend over the edge of the plate.

Wurstel: refers to any one (or two) of a variety of spiced or bland sausages, large and small. Used sometimes as a term of endearment. In Austria, why not?

CHAPTER 7

BALTIC PEOPLES:

ESTONIAN, LATVIAN, AND LITHUANIAN

The almost 8 million Baltic peoples have many factors in common: a temperate climate and a rich harvest from the Baltic Sea, a land that is primarily agricultural and pastoral, but a bitter history of invasions, conquests, and humiliating oppressions. Estonia, Latvia, and Lithuania, the three countries that comprise the Baltic, have known foreign overlords controlling their lands, attempts at Germanization and Russification, and even extermination and deportation of their peoples.

For almost 500 years, and despite other conquerors who were tempted to rule over the Ests, the loosely knit tribes of Estonia, it was the Swedes who held sway from as early as the 1500s. To this day, Swedish architecture, names, signposts, and even many Swedish foods are strongly influential in Estonian life. Russification followed in 1721, when Sweden ceded Estonia to czarist Russia. A burst in Estonian culture resulted from the brief respite after the First World War when foreign influences in the land receded, but returned again in 1939, with the forced establishment of Russian military bases in key Estonian areas. By 1990, Estonia began the laborious trek to independence.

A glimpse into Latvia's history shows many similar and unhappy parallels. In 1201, the Germans swept over the rich fertile lowlands and sweeping forests of Latvia to conquer the tribes known as Letts, and established the capital city, Riga. By the mid-1500s, the German influence disintegrated, but in ensuing years the small land became the center of a struggle of three other powers: Poland, Russia, and Sweden. In 1795, Latvia officially became a part of the Russian Empire although much of her lands remained in the hands of German overlords. Like Estonia, Latvia was to taste brief independence following the First World War until 1939, when it too was forced to accept the establishment of Russian military bases on her land. By the mid-1990s, however, like Estonia, Latvia too was on the way to independence.

Lithuania's history shows her to be culturally and historically the strongest of the three Baltic countries. Lithuania not only successfully rebuffed early foreign invaders, but for a period of almost 200 years (1200-1400), actually expanded to exert control over much of the territory of Belorussia, the Ukraine, and parts of western Russia. The country's power might even have

extended farther with the marriage of Jagelo, Grand Duke of Lithuania and Jadwiga, Queen of Poland, but for a clash in religious convictions. The Polish-Lithuanian Roman Catholicism could not be reconciled with the principles of Orthodoxy of the Russian, Belorussian, and Ukrainian areas. By 1700, the tide of Russian power and influence was so strong that not only did these latter lands

wash back to Russia, but the tide of influence "backwashed" into Lithuania as well.

In the First World War, Lithuania was occupied by Germans, who seemingly supported the many Lithuanian nationalistic movements. But after Germany's defeat, a pro-Polish government was set up in Vilna (1920), and a part of Lithuania even united with Poland. This period was followed by an alliance with Estonia and Latvia but they too succumbed, as the others had, to Russian domination leading to the establishment of the Lithuanian Soviet Socialist Republic. By 1993, the last Soviet troops left, after much unrest, and like her sister Baltic countries, Lithuania too is struggling to control her own future.

In spite of such a history of foreign domination and influence, the Baltic peoples have staunchly retained a rich culture of their own and are famed for their literature, folk legends, athletic physiques, and joyous choral singing groups. Latvian and Lithuanian peoples share ethnic and language roots in the Slavic-Baltic division of Indo-European languages, but Estonian ethnic and language roots are to be found in the Finno-Ugric family, relating them more to the Finns and Hungarians.

DOMESTIC LIFE
Since the majority of people of these lands live a rural lifestyle it is this tradition that is considered here. While Latvia makes use of her peat bogs to supply fuel, Estonia and Lithuania depend more on the wood

resources of their forests. Electricity is costly and electrical appliances are not common except in the affluent homes of city dwellers. Wood or peat-burning stoves with built-in ovens are used to cook the family meals and in many cases also form the primary heat source for smaller homes. Heavy cast-iron cookware is favored for top-of-the-stove cooking; earthenware containers are used for oven baking and also for mixing bowls. The availability of wood makes it the ideal material for many kitchen utensils such as bowls, rolling pins, spoons, chopping boards, worktables.

Fresh seasonal foods are preferred and in many areas marketing is done daily. Any foods requiring storage are simply placed in a cool area of the house or in an icebox. Extra provisions for the long winters are frequently prepared in the home by drying, salting, pickling, smoking. Preserves and jams are also prepared for winter use.

DAIRY PRODUCTS

Soured milk, buttermilk. and sour cream are staples, while cottage cheese and pot cheese (Lithuanian: **suris**) are widely used for many dishes. A considerable amount of cheese is also consumed: fresh, aged, and with or without the beloved caraway seeds. Cheeses are prepared from the milk of cows or goats. Most families consider it very important that their children consume both milk and milk products. Milk is also used in many varieties of milk soups, and vegetables are often cooked in milk as well.

FRUITS AND VEGETABLES

Fruits are plentiful and enjoyed in season, fresh or stewed with sugar as fruit compotes, or served as fruit soups. Many jams, jellies, and preserves are prepared for winter use. **Korvits** is an Estonian sweet preserved relish made from chunks of pumpkin and traditionally served with meat. Estonian "fruit salad," traditionally served in winter, is a speciality of mixed preserved fruits. Berries are especially plentiful, both wild and cultivated, and Estonia's berries are noted for their quality and sweetness. The combination of fresh, dried, or preserved fruits, served or cooked with meats and fowl, is also much enjoyed.

Potatoes and cabbage are the staple vegetables and store well for winter use. A favored form of cabbage, especially in winter, is **sauerkraut**.

The common root vegetables – carrots, turnips, and beets, as well as the fresh seasonal favorites of cucumbers, radishes, tomatoes, and onions – are enjoyed fresh in salads and served with sour cream or a vinaigrette dressing. Wild mushrooms of many varieties are eagerly collected in season and many are hung and dried to add flavor to dishes year-round.

MEATS AND ALTERNATES

Pork, pork products, and poultry are the staples but are not used in great quantity. Domestic and wild fowl and game are enjoyed as available. Jellied pig's feet are a Lithuanian favorite and suckling pig is often prepared for festive occasions. Herring, sprats, and eels are the widely enjoyed harvest from the sea. Egg consumption is limited but steadily increasing due to increased supply and lower prices. Some dried legumes are used for soups, and Estonian children like to chew dried peas and beans as a snack. **Kama** is an Estonian soup served cold in summer and eaten as a refreshment any time of the day: it is prepared from a flour made from dried, ground, and roasted grains and legumes blended with sour milk and flavored lightly with salt or sugar.

BREADS AND GRAINS

Grains form one of the most important, satisfying, and economical staples of the Baltics. Bread is on the table at every meal and although this is usually a dark, sour rye bread, other breads made of wheat or

FOODS COMMONLY USED

The Baltics are noted for their grain crops of rye, wheat, oats, and barley, their high potato production, and their dairy farms. It is not surprising, therefore, that grains, potatoes, and dairy products form the staple foods of the Baltic diet, and are supplemented with smaller proportions of fish, pork products, and poultry. Because of the historical periods of influence, German, Scandinavian (See Danish, Swedish, and Norwegian) and Slavic (See Polish and Russian) cuisines have all made contributions to Baltic cuisines. German ethos prevails in the Lithuanian personality but it is the Slavic influence that prevails in the Lithuanian kitchen, although many so-called typical Lithuanian dishes are a part of German food traditions. Scandinavian influence, not surprisingly in view of history, predominates in Estonian cuisine, while Latvian cookery clearly shows threads of all three influences. The food of the Baltic peoples differs more in nomenclature than in substance; regional differences and specialties do exist, but many similarities are to be found as well.

combinations of flours may be served. Soups are often thickened with coarse flours or may even be made from grains; porridges and hot gruels are frequently served and may constitute a warming meal. Baked barley is a favorite side dish for meats and soups and barley flour is used for breads.

FATS

Oils are seldom used except occasionally for salads. Lard or bacon fat predominates in cookery while butter is used for baking, as a spread, and as a seasoning for foods. Fats are also consumed in the form of creams (sour cream, cream, and whipped cream), sour milk, and in many cheeses.

SWEETS AND SNACKS

The Baltic countries imported French pastry chefs, who opened their own little shops. The tradition of fine pastries, richly and elaborately prepared – by French chefs – is still maintained. Home baking includes satisfying buns, rolls and **kuchens** based on sweet yeast dough or firm cakes based on eggs. Sugared dried fruits are a favored snack to be nibbled anytime. Plain chocolate, either milk chocolate or bittersweet, is considered a special treat. A common snack in Latvia is paper cones filled with sauerkraut, eaten the way ice cream is elsewhere.

SEASONINGS

Caraway seeds head the list of favorites, and are also believed to be an aid for digestion. Poppy seeds, dill, parsley, and bay leaves add their touch to many dishes as well. Ginger, many varieties of honey, and allspice are used in baking. In general, Baltic foods are not highly seasoned; salty and sour flavors predominate. Most baked goods are rich simply with the aroma and taste of fresh eggs, butter, and cream.

BEVERAGES

Tea is taken frequently and sour milk is an anytime beverage. Coffee is also used but is considered a luxury in some areas, where a type of coffee may be prepared from ground, roasted cereals such as rye, and sometimes chicory. Beer, wine, and schnapps are enjoyed and vodka flavored with caraway is a favorite.

MEALS AND CUSTOMS

Although there is increasing mobility from rural to urban settings, more than half the Baltic population shares a common agricultural heritage that is reflected in a deep respect for land and nature and a humble religious devotion. Their thankfulness for the gifts of land and nature is shown in their preference for simple satisfying foods unadorned by sauces or excessive seasoning. Breads and soups form the mainstays of many meals. Lithuanians always begin a meal with a prayer of thankfulness, and Estonian children seldom leave the table without the words "Thank you, my Lord, my stomach has been filled." And though Latvian country homes are often isolated from each other, Slavic hospitality prevails in a flow of food and drink shared by all.

Together with individual pride in the family name, care is taken to hand down homemaking skills to the daughters and agricultural skills to the sons. Great respect is shown the father of the household: not only is his opinion consulted in all matters, he is also the first to be served at meals. Party foods are always presented buffet-style, while daily meals are commonly served family-style, with everyone helping themselves.

Based on the type of work done, heavier meals are usually served in the country, while lighter, more sophisticated meals are favored in the cities. A simple breakfast of porridge, bread, and beverage and a similar simple evening meal is balanced with the heavier meal taken at noon that consists of a hearty meat and vegetable or grain soup with bread and beverage and concluded with fresh or stewed fruits.

Many coffee and pastry shops provide snacks for city workers, while soup is often a refreshing snack for country people. Evening guests or quiet family gatherings enjoy tea with home-baked cakes, **kuchens**, or other sweets.

SPECIAL OCCASIONS

Religion has a profound influence on the lives of the Baltic peoples. Most Lithuanians are members of the Roman Catholic Church, while both Latvians and Estonians are members of the Lutheran Church. Nazi extermination of the Jews during the Second World War erased their population in the Baltic lands.

The Christian festivals of Christmas and Easter highlight the festive calendar, but occasions for festivities also include celebrations of seasonal flowers and foods, saint's days, harvesting and sowing, and family events such as births, weddings, and funerals. For example, the Estonian celebrations of *Leaf Month* (May), *Juice Month* (April), and *Candles* (February) indicate the deep ties of religion and nature. Thus the bounty of crops and orchards, religious and family events all intertwine in a heartfelt thanksgiving expressed in humble devotion and happy gatherings.

Traditional customs for Christmas in Lithuania include a meatless menu for Christmas Eve (called *kucios*), with twelve special dishes prepared from grains, fruits, vegetables, and fish to symbolize the twelve apostles. One of the oldest traditional dishes for **kucios** is a fermented poppy seed soup, **aguono pienas**, served with dumplings. Church services, visiting friends, and a buffet menu of ham baked in a sourdough crust, roast goose stuffed with apples and prunes, varieties of homemade sausages, and special winter salads completed with a display of special cookies and pastries (especially the poppy seed roll called **aguonines**) are part of the festive observances.

In the country areas of all the Baltic lands, the slaughtering of a pig for Christmas is followed by the many traditional activities involved in making sausages and blood puddings, curing and smoking hams and bacons, and rendering fat for lard. Again, roasted geese stuffed with apples and prunes share the table with salads of chopped herring and beets, potato dishes of many kinds, tart and salted pickles contrasted with sweet fruit preserves and all washed down with homemade beers and wines and even homemade vodka, faintly redolent of caraway. And while others favor richly sweet desserts to complete festive occasions, the Baltic pastries and yeast doughs owe their fragrance to roasted crushed nuts and poppy seeds and pot cheese: filling and delicious.

Concern and a special love for animals is exemplified by the Christmas Eve tradition of feeding small amounts of bread and barley to the farm animals before the family's evening meal. This is similar to traditions in Slavic countries.

Easter is celebrated with church services, and the menu reflects the joy of the spring season. Decorated eggs as well as fruits and berries are hidden for the children to find, and the game of *koksimine* (Estonian mischievous cracking of hard, and sometimes soft, eggs) is enjoyed by everyone. Communal buffet tables featuring family specialties are set up and prepared well ahead of time: a buffet of salads, meats, and fish and an array of good breads will be enhanced by the presence of the **pasha**: a Russian-inspired delicate cheese and whipped cream mold.

Weddings are often the excuse for the wearing of regional costumes and the presentation of distinct regional specialties in food, music, and dance. An Estonian country specialty is the serving of soup (**pulmasupp**) and farina and milk in wooden bowls traditionally eaten with wooden spoons. This wedding supper is accompanied by specially made beer drunk from wooden steins.

Similarly, traditional funeral practices often follow local or regional as well as religious customs. In some country areas of Estonia, the path for the funeral procession may be laid out with spruce boughs, a spruce wreath marking the house of mourning. Following the burial, a large meal prepared by friends and neighbors may include roasted pig, sausages, blood puddings, headcheese, winter salads, or fruit compotes and breads. Homemade vodka will be drunk in toasts to the departed one.

GLOSSARY OF FOODS AND FOOD TERMS

Berries: the finest and sweetest berries are said to be from Estonia. Here are some of the varieties:
   Karusmari: gooseberries.
   Klukva: large juicy cranberries. A favorite Estonian drink is vodka and cranberry juice called "The Rolling Estonian."
   Murakad: cloudberries.
   Pohlad: lingonberries.
   Punane Sostar: red currants.

Bliinid: Estonian version of Russian **Blini** (*See* Russian).

Estonian Fruit Salad: a combination of dried and fresh fruits (or just one type) cooked, then layered in jars and preserved with a syrup of water, sugar, and wine vinegar.

Halva: Estonian confection of a peanut-flavored flaky sweet. (Mediterranean **halva** is made from sesame seeds.)

Kama: a special flour that is made from a mixture of grains and legumes, dried, roasted then ground. This flour is then mixed with sour milk or cream and lightly flavored with salt or sugar to form a soup consistency. This cool soup is used throughout the summer in Estonia as a refreshing snack or beverage.

Kapsad: cabbage.

Kartuli-Tangpudru: a mixture of barley and potatoes, slowly baked in a casserole. Sometimes onions and ham are added. This often accompanies soup to make a filling meal. An Estonian favorite.

Koksimine: the Estonian "egg game" played at Easter time. The decorated hard-cooked eggs are knocked against an adversary's eggs, the object being to see how many eggs you can crack before yours is broken. Many jokes are played as part of this game, including decorating eggs that are not hard-cooked; even painted rocks have been known to become winning eggs.

Koogel-Moogel: an Estonian treat made of egg yolks, thickly beaten with sugar; eaten as a pudding.

Korbid: slightly sweetened cheesecake baked in a round shape.

Kugelis: baked Lithuanian potato pudding, often with eggs and onions.

Lekakh: Jewish Lithuanian honey cake. Also popular in Poland.

Lietiniai: Lithuanian soup accompaniment, made from tiny pancakes filled with the ground, seasoned soup meat. The tiny "parcels" are crisply fried then served with clear broth. Crumbled bacon garnishes the soup.

Ligzdinas: large juicy Latvian meatballs filled with mushrooms or a whole hard-cooked egg.

Mulgi Kapsad: Estonian casserole of **sauerkraut**, potatoes, and pork hocks or pork tails (or any pork cut), seasoned with salt, pepper, and bay leaf. So popular, it is almost a staple dish.

Pannkoogid: huge Estonian pancakes, which are almost a meal in themselves, eaten plain or with berries and sour cream.

Pirukas: Russian in origin, this Estonian soup accompaniment is made of plain yeast dough, filled with meat, vegetables, or grains, shaped into half-moons and deep-fried or baked.

Pudru: Estonian name for any porridge made from grains.

Pulmasupp: Estonian country-wedding soup, a rich soup of butter-browned meat, with dumplings and added vegetables. Traditionally eaten from wooden spoons and bowls for the wedding supper. Accompanied by beer in wooden steins.

Rassolnye or **Rossolye**: Estonian mixed salad of beets and potatoes, herring and meat, blended with sour cream dressing.

Solianka: Latvian fish soup.

Supp: soup.

Suris: white Lithuanian cheese resembling pot cheese, or the Italian ricotta.

Sult: Estonian specialty of sliced veal molded in its own aspic.

Tule-Homme Taas: literally, "Come back tomorrow," a satisfying Estonian pancake dish: huge pancakes wrapped around a filling. The filling may be cream cheese, spinach, carrots, or apples with sugar.

Vinegretas: Lithuanian version of **Rossolye**. An appetizer salad of beets, potatoes, herring and cubed meats, blended with a dressing of seasoned sour cream.

Virtiniai: Lithuanian soup dumplings made of filled noodle pastry. For Christmas Eve these are filled with mushrooms and served in a clear meatless beet stock.

Zalbarsciai: light Lithuanian soup made from grated beets and buttermilk. In the spring, the shredded beet greens are added.

Zrazy: rolled-up filled slices of beef or veal, made in individual servings or as a large roast to be sliced. A favorite throughout the Baltics.

CHAPTER 8

BELGIAN

In 1830, Belgium, a small heavily populated country bordering on France, Germany, and Luxembourg, detached itself from the Netherlands and became an

independent nation. Its history is a long story of other nations marching over Belgian soil, each leaving an imprint upon the people and their traditions: Romans, Franks, Spaniards, Austrians, Dutch, and especially the French.

Belgium is made up of two main groups: the Flemings in the north, a Teutonic people who speak Flemish (a dialect of Dutch related to German), and the Walloons in the south who are primarily a Celtic people who speak a dialect of French. It is said that Antwerp, the northern Flemish business city, represents its people's character: "salty, stubborn and proudly provincial," while Brussels, located in the heart of Belgium, and about four-fifths French-speaking, seems to represent the more emotional and flamboyant Walloons.

But wherever one goes in Belgium, North or South, despite the differences, some things are universal. Almost everywhere, except in remote rural areas, English is spoken and understood; Belgian husbands become emotional on the subject of food and argue about whose wife is the better cook; and Belgians like their food in ample quantity and of good quality. But although good food well prepared is a priority, Belgians are not adventurous cooks. They have little interest in experimenting with "foreign" dishes, remaining happily confident that the best is Belgian home cooking and the best of restaurant food is none other than the *haute cuisine* of France. And although the Flemish favor foods masked with velvety sauces of cream and eggs, and the Walloons make extensive use of pork in their dishes, the overall tone of Belgian cookery is definitively French.

The meticulous care with which Belgian cooks select their foods can best be illustrated by a walk through a Belgian supermarket, where even everyday items like butter and cream are carefully labeled with the proud producer's name, where an incredible array of exquisitely garnished cold meats, pates, sausages, salads, and prepared appetizers delight the eye, and where varieties of canned, packaged, and bottled goods line up in colorful profusion unparalleled elsewhere. Advertisements proudly proclaim:

"Butter from Namur" ... "Asparagus from Malines" ... "Pork and pork products from Pietron" ... "Walnuts from Bastogne" ... "Strawberries from Wepion."

The tremendous Belgian sweet tooth is not gratified in simply one bakeshop alone. A distinction is carefully made between the daily baked goods, which may be purchased from a *boulangerie*, and party specialties, which are selected from a *patisserie*. Candies and confections are so important they are sold in specialty stores called *confiseries*, where even a wanton glance seems to add pounds.

But gradually, as is happening in other parts of the world, some of the high standards of daily shopping and food preparation must be lowered to accommodate the modern lifestyle: the realities of traffic snarls, working mothers, and a shared international desire to narrow the waistline.

DOMESTIC LIFE
Most Belgian kitchens, though tiny by western standards, are well equipped, people commonly own freezers and dishwashers. Because there is still a strong preference for the use of fresh, seasonal foods, large storage areas and complicated equipment are really not a necessity. Family meals are often eaten in the home, but entertaining may often occur in restaurants, further obviating the need for complex preparation or large storage areas.

DAIRY PRODUCTS
Fresh milk as a beverage is not too popular; even children prefer to drink **cafe au lait**. Much fresh cream and whole milk are used in the preparation of soups, custards, and many sauces. Cheeses are often eaten with breads for breakfast. **Creme fraiche**, a thick and slightly tangy cream, is used both in France and Belgium for cooking, with fruits and in desserts.

FRUITS AND VEGETABLES

Fresh seasonal fruits are preferred and good variety and excellent quality are to be had in supermarkets, specialty stores, and open markets. A typical Belgian touch is to add dried fruits to many meat dishes, especially in the winter when vegetables are scarce and more costly.

Vegetables are of great importance in the Belgian diet and seldom served without distinction; they are usually served as a separate course, appropriately sauced and garnished, but often overcooked. Potatoes are a part of almost every lunch and dinner, especially when meat or fish is served. Cabbage, turnips, and potatoes are winter staples. Especially favored vegetables include cabbage, escarole, **Belgian endive**, cauliflower, brussels sprouts, **cressonette** (watercress), leeks, **hop sprouts**, and, of course, the ever-present potato, especially in the form of **frites**, served with some variety of mayonnaise.

MEATS AND ALTERNATES

Walloon cookery is noted for an extensive use of pork, but to all Belgians meat is an important part of dinner, followed by fish or seafood, which are also much enjoyed. But whether the main dish is meat or fish, the omnipresent side dish of some form of potatoes always makes the meal filling. Favored meats: pork, beef, veal, horsemeat; no lamb or mutton. Game meats are very popular and Belgians love to hunt: **marcassin** (wild boar), hare, rabbit, roebuck, wild deer, wild duck, grouse, snipe, quail, partridge, and thrush. Favored fish: salmon, mullet, trout, turbot, skate, **flounder**, pike, carp, whitefish, **dourade**, mackerel, **lotte**, cod, herring. All seafood and shellfish are savored, especially mussels, which are called "the poor man's oysters." Other seafoods enjoyed are: eels, scallops, clams, crayfish, small **crevettes**, and large shrimp, oysters, and lobsters.

Eggs are consumed mostly as part of other dishes: rich egg and cream sauces, mayonnaise, etc. Occasionally eggs may be part of light supper dishes. Nuts and legumes are not an important part of the Belgian diet.

BREADS AND GRAINS

Dry breakfast cereals or hot cooked porridges are seldom used. Crusty white bread is preferred either as the "Belgian family loaf" or as crusty small rolls called **pistolets**, which are a favorite late Sunday breakfast treat.

FATS

Unquestionably, the Belgians consume a considerable amount of fat in the form of dressings and sauces, mayonnaise accompaniments, fried foods, and butter, which is used lavishly. Butter preferences are as individual as wine preferences and the particular butter is selected by the name of the producer and the area it comes from, but whoever produced it or wherever it came from, the true Belgian will choose unsalted butter as having the superior taste. Both butter and lard are used in cooking and baking.

SWEETS AND SNACKS

The object of desire – sweets to satisfy the Belgian sweet tooth – are everywhere in evidence. And of course, Belgian chocolate and Belgian waffles (with strawberries and whipped cream) are legendary. *Boulangeries*, *patisseries*, and *confiseries* are never too far away. For any occasion, gifts of exquisitely packaged candies are appropriate and customary. A typical popular snack is the readily available Belgian waffles, served with butter and sugar or whipped cream and sometimes fresh fruit. Belgians also manage to consume, with ease, great quantities of crisp dry cookies (achieved by using ammonium carbonate

FOODS COMMONLY USED

"Coffee is a passion" and **frites** are so popular at home and as snacks everywhere that coffee and fried potatoes may be labeled Belgian staples. Belgium's national dish is **biftek, frites, salade** – also the usual lunch for almost everyone. **Biftek** is not a steak per se but is the general term used to describe any well-trimmed boneless piece of meat, whether it is beef, veal, pork, or horsemeat. The **frites** are usually eaten with varieties of mayonnaise, such as tartar sauce, Russian dressing or bearnaise sauce, accompanied with pickles or pickled onions. In fact, mayonnaise seems to appear almost everywhere in one form or another. Fish and seafoods are loved, deep-fried foods and potato-based soups enjoyed. The famed **waterzooi** is somewhere between a soup and a stew, made from fish or chicken in a well-simmered broth that is lightly thickened with eggs and cream and served in a soup plate accompanied with potatoes or buttered bread. As it sounds, it is a meal in itself. Sometimes the broth may be served first with the fish or chicken and the simmered vegetables served as a separate course.

instead of an equal amount of baking powder). The frequent cup of coffee is seldom served alone; usually it too is accompanied by a sweet baked product. Late afternoon ladies' gatherings also enjoy "cakes and gossip."

SEASONINGS

There is only a subtle use of onions and garlic in Belgian cookery and fresh herbs of all kinds are preferred. The favorite herb is chervil, while the favorite spice is nutmeg. The richness of butter, cream, and eggs stands alone as the flavoring in many dishes.

BEVERAGES

Estaminets are the popular beer taverns where businessmen are said to down unbelievable quantities of beer. Coffee is served to all ages at all meals and often between meals as well. Belgians are very knowledgeable about wine selection and usually purchase their wine with their groceries. Wine is frequently served with dinner.

MEALS AND CUSTOMS

Belgians are noted for their politeness, which is evident in business and at home. No dinner guest would ever be late, nor would a guest arrive without a bouquet of flowers or a beautifully wrapped box of candies. A short aperitif hour is customary, followed by a leisurely dinner with wine and likely one of Belgium's famed liqueurs with the after-dinner coffee: **elixir de spa** (pine-flavored), or **walzin** or **elixir d'Anvers**, both of which are similar to Benedictine, the liqueur prepared by the French Benedictine monks.

The usual Belgian day begins with a light breakfast of bread or rolls with jam, unsalted butter, and **cafe au lait**. A midmorning break of coffee and waffles or cookies is likely for the women and children, while men will enjoy a beer or two.

Traditionally, the noon meal is the main meal of the day: businessmen take a two-hour break and most children come home from school. This is the meal that begins with soup or **hors d'oeuvres**, then a hearty meat or fish dish with potatoes, followed by a separate course of salad or cooked vegetables. Frequently the meat is carved in the kitchen and the platter garnished with seasonal vegetables. It is interesting to note that vegetables and salads are almost a social status symbol – the higher the level, the more vegetables and salads are used. For most families, however, potatoes are the only vegetable requirement. A dessert for dinner would be fruit and cheese, a tart or pudding. Wine or beer is usually served as well.

Throughout the day, snacks of waffles, coffee, and cookies or **frites** to order, dunked in mayonnaise, are generously indulged in. The evening meal is usually a light supper of leftovers or simple egg, cheese, or fish dishes.

As in other countries in the western world, Belgian city dwellers are finding that the pressures of urban life make it increasingly difficult to enjoy that leisurely noon meal.

Sunday is a quiet day devoted to family and friends and often features a specially prepared dinner. For some families, Sunday is the day for dinner out, and in Belgium this is a delightful prospect, for all restaurants strive to achieve a high level of renown, especially since many gastronomic societies keep watchful eyes on the menus and specialties of these establishments.

SPECIAL OCCASIONS

Belgians, with few exceptions, are Roman Catholic, the Flemish being more religious than the Walloons. A specialty of Catholic Flanders' Friday menu is **botermelk met mavermout**, a meatless soup of buttermilk thickened with oatmeal.

Christmas is celebrated with no special menu, but with the best that each home has to offer. For many this may be a rich game dinner, for others pork or beef, but almost all will climax their Christmas dinner with a **buche de Noel**, a log of chocolate cake, trimmed to look like a fallen log, sometimes complete with mushrooms created of egg meringue.

Whitsun is a spring holiday welcomed after the long winter because it heralds spring's tender young vegetables and wild strawberries.

Family christenings are celebrated with afternoon tea or coffee; small packages of candied almonds are often sent to friends as a memento of the occasion. First communions, engagements, and weddings are often celebrated as formal occasions with elegant buffets and dances.

GLOSSARY OF FOODS AND FOOD TERMS

A la Flamande: "in the Flemish style," i.e., rich with smooth egg and cream sauces.

Amuse-geules: small cocktail tidbits.

Biftek: used to describe any trimmed, boneless piece of meat whether beef, veal, pork, or horsemeat.

Botermelk met Mavermout: buttermilk soup thickened with oatmeal, enjoyed on meatless Fridays in Catholic Flanders.

Boudin: sausage.

Boudin Blanc: mild-flavored sausage.

Boudin Noir: blood sausage.

Boulangeries: bakeshops specializing in "everyday" breads, rolls, cakes, and pies.

Carbonnades Flamandes: famous Belgian dish of stewed beef and onions simmered in beer.

Chicoon: French name for the variety of chicory from which the Belgian endive was first developed.

Confiseries: fancy bakeshops featuring party cakes and pastries.

La Cramique or **Rosynenbrood**: a loaf rich with raisins and eggs, served thickly sliced and buttered, with coffee. The favorite coffeebread of Belgium.

Creme Fraiche: slightly thick and flavorful cream available in both France and Belgium, widely used for fruits and desserts and in cooking.

Crevettes: tiny shrimp.

Elixir d'Anvers: one of the national liqueurs of Belgium, somewhat similar to Benedictine.

Elixir de Spa: Belgian liqueur with a taste of pine.

Estaminets: beer taverns.

Fondu Bruxelloise: a favorite appetizer of chilled thick cheese sauce, poured into a pan then cut in squares, breaded, and deep-fried.

Fraises des Bois: strawberries.

Frites: french-fried potatoes.

Fritures: any deep-fried food.

Hutespot: the Flemish **pot-au-feu**.

Keppebouillon: chicken soup.

Kervelsoip: light buttery soup, flavored with fresh chervil

Marcassin: wild boar.

Moules: mussels.

Padstools: a delightful appetizer of salmon-stuffed eggs arranged on end with tops of tomatoes to resemble mushrooms.

Patisseries: fancy bakeshops featuring party cakes and pastries.

Pistolets: traditional rolls for late Sunday breakfast.

Preisop: smooth pureed leek and potato soup.

Preskop: headcheese.

Rijspap: Flemish rice pudding made with milk, rice, and raisins, flavored with saffron and cooked in a large flat dish.

Speculaas: molded spiced breads and cookies.

Sprats: small herrings.

Tomates aux Crevettes: the favorite Belgian appetizer, tomato halves heaped with tiny shrimp in mayonnaise.

Walzin: Belgian liqueur with a flavor similar to Benedictine.

Waterzooi: between a soup and a stew, made with fish or chicken, its rich broth fortified with an egg and cream sauce. Served in a soup plate, it is accompanied by buttered bread or potatoes. The fish or chicken is usually served as a separate course.

Whitloof: Flemish name for the variety of chicory from which the famed Belgian endive was developed.

CHAPTER 9

BELORUSSIAN

Belarus is currently a nation of approximately ten and a half million people wedged into a tiny region between Russia and Poland. Formerly called Byelorussians or White Russians, the people of Belarus now call themselves Belorussian. They are members of the Eastern Slav nations which include Greater Russia and Ukraine.

In the early 800s they made up a part of several independent feudal princedoms, but in 1240, a Mongol invasion captured their territories and they became known as the Grand Duchy of Lithuania or Litva. The people we know today as Lithuanians were at that time called Samogitians. With the Treaty of Lublin, in 1569, the Grand Duchy of Lithuania merged with Poland until 300 years later when Poland herself was partitioned between Russia, Prussia, and Austria.

The hapless Litvanians were subjected to forcible Russification: the historic name of Litva was changed to White Russia and its language, traditions, and customs were suppressed. Despite the ensuing hardships that continually saw their lands as the battleground for nations around them, a slowly emerging Litvanian middle class found expression in the nationalistic movement around 1800. This emergence climaxed in the Russian Revolution, only to be dashed once again by the Bolsheviks, who claimed the land as a Soviet Republic in January 1919.

As if this were not enough, White Russia was again divided after the brief Polish-Russian War of 1919-1920. About 5 million Belorussians fell to Polish rule and 4 million to Russian rule. Following the Second World War, the entire country of about 10 million again ceded to total Russian domination.

Belorussians who emigrated to North America before the Second World War were largely illiterates from the poorer villages (the czar encouraged a deliberate state of illiteracy); those who came later were mostly political exiles, professionals, and intellectuals who stimulated the growth of cultural organizations in North America aimed at preserving their heritage.

For so long a part of Lithuania, Belorussia's cuisine most resembles that of Lithuania but also has strong elements of Polish and Russian traditions. Festive occasions are marked by devout religious observance: the Greek Orthodox Church in the East, the Roman Catholic Church in the West, with approximately 10 percent of the population estimated to be Jewish.

GLOSSARY OF FOODS AND FOOD TERMS

Buraki: a simple beet soup made with a rich meat stock, sliced cooked beets, a splash of lemon juice, and garnished with sour cream and sprigs of fresh dill.

Chiebny Kvas: A kind of cider drink prepared from dry rye bread. The dry bread is crumbled into a crock and boiling water is poured over. When it cools, dissolved yeast is added. The mixture is strained through a cloth, sugar and raisins are added and it is poured into bottles and tightly corked. After chilling for two days, the beverage is ready to drink. A little more sugar and some lemon juice is added to taste.

Chleb: bread.

Halubcy: cabbage rolls prepared with ground meat, beaten eggs, raw rice, and seasoning wrapped in steamed cabbage leaves. After frying the rolls in butter, diluted canned tomato sauce is poured over them and they are simmered for several hours over very low heat. These are usually served with cooked potatoes or fluffy boiled grains such as barley or **kasha** (buckwheat).

Hurkovy Rosol: a soup made with a meat stock and potatoes then flavored with chopped dill pickles and cooked chopped potatoes. A simple roux of flour and butter may be used to thicken the soup.

Kapusta: means cabbage but more often refers to **sauerkraut. Sauerkraut** is usually prepared in some way before serving as a side dish for a meal.

Sauerkraut is often drained, blended with butter-fried onions and a sprinkle of sugar then simmered slowly before serving hot. Other **sauerkraut** dishes combine cooked beets and/or potatoes as well as browned onions. **Sauerkraut** that has been fermented with apples and cranberries is also a favorite dish served with sour cream.

Kattlety: ground meat patties flavored with chopped onion and mushrooms, salt and pepper and bound with beaten raw egg. These are boiled or pan-fried or can be shaped then baked in the oven.

Kisiel: this fruit dessert can be prepared from any cooked summer fruits or berries. The hot cooked fruit is pressed through a sieve then returned to the heat and thickened with cornstarch and sweetened with sugar. While still hot, it is spooned into serving dishes to cool then served with light cream.

Kislaja Kapusta: soup made with pork stock and **sauerkraut** finished with sweet cream and slightly thickened with flour.

Krupnik z Hrybami a Miasam: barley and mushroom soup, thick and satisfying, usually prepared with a beef stock and garnished with sour cream.

Miadounik: a honey cake rich with sour cream, eggs, honey, and mixed spices such as cinnamon, cloves, and ginger. The top of the cooled cake may be frosted with chocolate icing.

Nadziavanaja Bulba: stuffed baked potatoes prepared by peeling large baking potatoes and baking till tender. The centers are gently scooped out and mashed with finely chopped boiled meat (usually from meat stock), onions, seasonings, and beaten eggs. The mixture is then heaped back into the potato shells, basted with butter and baked till lightly browned. These are served as a main dish.

Pirazki: little balls of unbaked yeast dough with fillings pressed into the center and the dough pulled over to seal. Left on a cloth to air-dry for about 20 minutes, they are deep-fried to a crispy brown, then served hot with sour cream as a main

FOODS COMMONLY USED

Belorussian foods are almost identical to Russian and Polish preferences and dishes, but the names of the dishes may vary. Dairy products used liberally include sour cream, milk and sweet cream as ingredients and as additions to prepared foods. As in Russian cuisine, there are few dishes that are not improved with generous additions of melted butter and blobs of thick sour cream.

Hardy vegetables such as onions, potatoes, beets, cabbage, pumpkin, and varieties of squash and mushrooms, especially wild mushrooms, are used almost daily, and fresh young vegetables such as tomatoes, green onions, cucumbers, sweet peas, radishes, spinach, and sorrel are enjoyed in season. Fermented **sauerkraut** and dill pickles are enjoyed year-round as side dishes to almost every meal. Herbs are used fresh in season and dried for winter use. Especially popular are dill and parsley. Wild and cultivated

berries and fruits such as plums, peaches, cherries, apples, and pears are a special treat when fresh but are carefully preserved for winter use.

Pork, beef, and chicken as well as some goose and duck are used for special occasions and use is made of every part including organs and offal. Very occasionally veal or lamb are used. If available, game is enjoyed. A wide variety of sausages and smoked meats add to the variety and even small amounts of meat, over-browned bones, and boiled soup meat is minced and used to flavor potato, cabbage, or grain dishes.

Pork fat and chicken, goose and duck fat are carefully rendered and used to flavor other dishes and may be used as a spread for bread. Cracklings are often served with dark heavy rye bread and a bowl of hearty soup as a meal.

A wide variety of breads including sourdough rye, pumpernickel, wholegrain rolls and breads

and many basic yeast doughs prepared as filled buns or dumplings round out meals. Boiled or baked grains such as barley, buckwheat, and coarse wheat and rye wholegrains are generously served with melted butter and sour cream. Baked, boiled, or fried dumplings filled with cheese, meat, or chopped vegetables are ingeniously served as appetizers, main dishes in soups, or with sweet fruit fillings as desserts. Baked desserts rich with butter, cream, and eggs also round out otherwise simple soup meals.

The Polish influence of adding sugar to heighten the taste of soups and salad dressings is also evident.

Like all Slavic food, Belorussian dishes excel in heartiness and ample portions, and are always served with the Slavic tradition of warm and generous hospitality that no amount of hardship can erase. (See also Baltic Peoples, Jewish, Polish, and Russian.)

dish. Prepared smaller, they may be served in clear soup.

Piroh iz Hreckich Krup iz Tvoraham: a main dish or a side dish prepared from cooked buckwheat mixed with cottage cheese, eggs, and sugar. This mixture is pressed into a buttered pan and topped with a custard mixture of beaten eggs, sugar, and cream. It is baked until the topping is set. Then melted butter is poured over as a finishing touch, and sour cream is added.

Scaujo Chaladnik: a springtime soup made with fresh sorrel, chopped and boiled. The soup is seasoned with salt and pepper then served with chopped green onions, cubed cucumbers, hard-cooked egg slices, and sprigs of fresh dill.

Zacirka: general name for egg barley, prepared by blending flour and a little salt into beaten eggs to form a thick mixture. This is then pressed through a coarse sieve or dropped in small bits from a spoon into boiling broth or water to form tiny dumplings. These can be served in soups, mixed with grains such as cooked barley or **kasha** (buckwheat), or served as a side dish to be topped with melted butter and sour cream.

Zapianka z Jablykami: a baked rice pudding dessert with apples. After slow baking, a buttery brown rice crust is formed and the apples cook fragrant and tender. The dessert is cut into large squares and served with sweet cream or sour cream stirred with sugar. Such a dessert often makes a light meal when served after a bowl of soup.

CHAPTER 10

Bosnian–Herzogovian. See The Southern Slavs
Brazilian. See Latin American
British. See English

BULGARIAN

Famous for its exports of fine fruits and attar of roses (used in perfume blending), Bulgaria is probably most renowned for the legendary vigorous health and longevity of its inhabitants. The Bulgarians themselves modestly attribute their health and long life to the properties of yogurt, which they claim was invented in Bulgaria. But a closer examination of their general dietary pattern shows it to be one of the healthiest in Europe, basically consisting of varied wholegrains, legumes, cheeses, yogurt, and fresh fruits and vegetables. Whether this diet is due to tastes, tradition, or to the almost "semi-permanent shortage of meats and meat fats" is difficult to assess.

Bulgaria is located in the heart of the Balkans bounded by Romania, Turkey, Greece, the former Yugoslavia, and the Black Sea. Bulgarian is the official language. Differing ethnocultural groups such as the Gypsies and Macedonians speak Turkish and several other languages. Bulgarian Christian Orthodox is the traditional church of Bulgaria, engaging more than 85 percent of the population, with smaller groups of Muslims (13 percent), Jewish (0.8 percent) and others (1.1 percent).

A continental climate of cold winters and hot summers prevails over the mostly hilly and mountainous terrain, but the fertile areas of the Dambian Tablelands and the Thracian Plains produce rich harvests of wheat, rye, corn, rice, and legumes, as well as orchards and vineyards famed for their quality fruits.

Bulgar means "man of the plow," and the predominantly agricultural people who call themselves Bulgarian are actually a blend of many ethnic groups: tribes from the Asiatic Steppes, and early Slavs who later melded with smaller groups of Turks, Greeks, Macedonians, Romanians, Serbs, Jews, Gypsies, Armenians, and Russians. In fact, most of the Bulgarians who came to North America before the Second World War were peasants and laborers of Macedonian origin from the Balkan Mountains. Later immigrants (after the Second World War) were mostly urban professionals and intellectuals who found themselves dispersed throughout Europe and were unwilling to return to their homeland because of Communist domination.

The long history of Bulgaria included acceptance of Christianity by King Boris I in the mid-800s, which led to the development of the first written Slavic in the form of church liturgy and the birth of the Cyrillic alphabet, also used by the Russians. Subsequent wars fought by the Russians and Serbs all left their mark, but it was mostly the 500-year domination by the Ottoman Empire that left Bulgaria with a Turkish imprint on its traditions and food customs.

DOMESTIC LIFE

The traditional Bulgarian kitchen is bright with homespun and hand-embroidered table linens and curtains, hand-painted pottery dishes, and carved wooden mugs. Strings of peppers and mushrooms of many varieties add color and aroma as they hang drying from the rafters. In country or city, the eating area is the heart of the home; hospitality centers around food and people and the sincere enjoyment of both.

In general, the present standard of living, though rising, is still low. The general housing shortage often means that two families live in a one-family residence. Average salaries provide for the necessities of life. Food shortages are common and kitchen facilities and dining areas meager. Food storage is not a problem since most foods are purchased on a day-to-day basis; and with most women working outside the home, there is little time for preserving and pickling, though Bulgarians are very fond of pickles and thick, sweet preserves.

DAIRY PRODUCTS

Sheep's and goat's milk are made into many types of cheeses or used as sour cream, milk, or yogurt. Yogurt itself may be used as a cooling refreshment or as a drink either plain or diluted with cold water. It is also used in soups, vegetable dishes, and served with cooked wholegrains, meats, and fish. Sometimes yogurt is used in desserts or served with fruits. Whatever the form of the dish, Bulgarians enjoy dairy products at every meal.

FRUITS AND VEGETABLES

Fruits and vegetables are also an important part of daily menus. Many main dishes are thick vegetable stews, sometimes including legumes, and sometimes served with cooked grains or hearty wholegrain breads. A meal is considered incomplete without at least one side dish of fresh greens, sliced onions, pickles, radishes, cucumbers, or tomatoes; in winter, olives and many types of pickles may be used instead. A usual dessert is fresh fruit or a compote of fruits cooked in a syrup.

There is wide variety and excellent quality in apples, plums, cherries, peaches, melons, watermelons, apricots, figs, and pears. The grapes are so famous that much of their crop is exported. Fruits may be eaten fresh, as jams or jellies, or as very thick **spoon sweets** to be served with glasses of cold water or Turkish coffee, made into fruit compotes, and occasionally into fruit drinks or fruit soups.

When it is necessary to export much of the fresh vegetable produce, the Bulgarian staples become beans, onions, potatoes, and rice. But fresh salad vegetables are eagerly enjoyed when available, and fresh seasonal vegetables become the center of the meal: eggplant, okra, squash, pumpkin, onions, potatoes, cabbage (**sauerkraut** is prepared and used widely). When possible, many vegetables are preserved with garlic and brine to create many interesting pickles for condiments, hot peppers being a great favorite.

MEATS AND ALTERNATES

Arguably, Bulgarians are mostly vegetarian by necessity rather than by choice, but if available, lamb and mutton are enjoyed. Pork and veal are seldom used, though pork may be part of a special occasion meal. Fish is mostly consumed near its source: the Black Sea and Bulgaria's rivers. Varieties include turbot, carp, shad, sturgeon, crayfish, mussels, and snails. Eggs are generally in poor supply but are used often as a custard to bake over the top of a vegetable casserole. Legumes are an important part of the diet in good times and bad: small white beans, yellow, red and brown lentils, other beans, and peas eaten fresh and dried. Very occasionally game may be enjoyed roasted or in casseroles with other vegetables: hare, duck, venison, partridge, pheasant, and quail. Nuts of all kinds are an important source of protein. They are chopped or crushed or ground to a fine powder and may be used in soups, salads, meat and fish dishes, with vegetables or with desserts. Locally grown nuts include: green and ripe walnuts, hazelnuts, and almonds.

BREADS AND GRAINS

Many breads are made with white wheat flour, wholewheat flour, rye flour, and cornmeal. Rice may be cooked into soups, mounded into **pilafs**, sweetened and made into desserts. Crushed wholewheat **bulgur** and **kasha** (buckwheat) may be cooked as a base for vegetables or as a side dish. The type of cereal or flour preferred depends on the area; nearer Romania, cornmeal prepared as a baked pudding or as a coarse bread can be as much a staple food as the Romanian **mamaliga**. Grains are also used to stretch the meaty flavor of rarely used meats (in the same way that meats and vegetables are often combined), especially in meatballs and many types of vegetables stuffed with ground meat and grain filling, then slowly simmered for deep flavor.

FATS

The most-used cooking oil is sunflower seed oil. Olive oil is also widely used both in cooking and as a dressing with garlic, onions, and lemon juice to add zest to crisp fresh salad vegetables. Cold cooked legumes may also be dressed this way and served as a side dish. Butter may be melted and used to prepare the sugary, nut-filled layers of **phyllo** pastry in many forms for rich desserts, and butter may also be eaten

FOODS COMMONLY USED

The Bulgarian cuisine is mainly adapted from Turkey and Greece but many native dishes can be traced readily to each of the neighboring countries. The staple and plentiful vegetables, dried white beans, peas and lentils plus yogurt, though seemingly simple foods, are used with such ingenuity that they become a variety of hearty and nutritious dishes: **guivech**, **dolmas**, **pilafs**, **tchorbas**, **musaka** (made with potatoes or the more traditional eggplant). And though onions and garlic are very much favored, Bulgarian dishes are not highly seasoned, but seasonings and natural herbs are used with a deft hand to bring out the inherent flavors of the food. As well as a love for pickles, olives, and peppers as condiments, Bulgarians enjoy tartly sour dishes, and in these the acid from lemon juice, natural yogurt, or **sauerkraut** add tang. Names of dishes vary slightly from one area to another, but the largest percentage of meals is based simply on wholegrain cereals, vegetables, cheeses, and yogurt.

with vegetables, but breads are often just broken and eaten plain or with cheeses.

SWEETS AND SNACKS

Bulgarians love to nibble on seeds of all kinds that have been toasted and/or lightly salted, as well as nuts of all kinds. Sweets are very much enjoyed, from a spoonful of fresh honey to thick sweetly preserved fruits with a glass of cold water or a tiny cup of strong Turkish coffee. Special occasions demand the presence of these rich sweets as well as the full range of delectable crisp and sweet nut-filled Middle Eastern pastries based on **phyllo** dough.

SEASONINGS

Onions, garlic, and oil are found in almost all dishes except desserts. Fresh herbs are used abundantly and often just munched out of hand as they are plucked from the fields. Mint, dill, savory, and a native tarragon called **ciubritsa** are all used generously. In fact, a combination of salt and pepper with freshly chopped **ciubritsa** is used as a dip for bread instead of butter.

BEVERAGES

Plain yogurt or yogurt diluted with cold water is the favored drink with meals, or is enjoyed as a between-meals refresher. Wine may be used with meals on special occasions. **Mastika**, a grape brandy, and **Slivovka** (plum brandy) are taken as a potent aperitif with a variety of **meze** (appetizers) before dinner or for special occasions. Turkish coffee, brewed in a special pot and served in tiny cups, is taken at the end of a meat or served frequently as a refreshment for guests.

MEALS AND CUSTOMS

Most Bulgarian meals are simple, hearty, and nourishing. Breakfast is usually bread with coffee; occasionally cheese and fruit may be added. Lunch would be a salad of chopped or sliced fresh vegetables mixed with nuts and cheese or lightly dressed with oil and lemon juice, followed, if available, by a meat or fish dish, and then by a dessert made with milk and cereal (e.g., rice pudding) or fruit and yogurt. A dinner may begin with an aperitif of **Slivovka**, black olives, and cheeses, a **tchorba** (stew of meat and vegetables), a side dish of cold dressed beans or lentils, all accompanied with wine and followed by fruits and Turkish coffee. The main difference between urban and rural meals would be the variety of foods presented and the presence of meat.

SPECIAL OCCASIONS

Although the more than 8 million Bulgarians include a variety of ethnic groups, almost 90 percent of them belong to the Bulgarian Orthodox Church, a branch of the Eastern Orthodox Church; about 9 percent are of the Muslim faith, and these include the Turks and the Pomaks (the name given to Bulgarian converts to Islam), and a part of the remaining 1 percent are of the Jewish faith.

When possible, Christmas is celebrated with a roasted suckling pig, while a young roasted lamb forms the highlight of the Easter dinner. Fish is especially important in festive menus for "meatless" days: the traditional baked carp, **sharan sawrehi**, stuffed with a rice and nut filling, or with raisins, walnuts, and onions.

Weddings often occur in civil ceremonies, but with the bride and groom in full traditional dress. A merry time with singing and dancing the circular *horo* or the famed couples' dance *ruchenitsa*, accompanied by heaped platters and full glasses – especially of **Slivovka** – complete the festivities. The wedding feast itself usually centers around a **guivech** (an oven-baked stew) of cubed lamb and succulent vegetables (an everyday **guivech** would be of seasoned vegetables only) to be followed by salads, condiments, and pickles, and a display of selected fruits in season, **baklava**, semolina puddings with rosewater, and finally Turkish coffee.

GLOSSARY OF FOODS AND FOOD TERMS

Banitsa or **Banitza**: Bulgarian national dish made with **phyllo** pastry filled with cheese, spinach, pumpkin, meat or fish mixtures. May be shaped as square or round pies, or small twisted shapes. For New Year's Day it contains small charms.

Bulgur Pilaf: dish made from rice browned in butter with onion and chopped calf's liver. Broth is poured over to complete the cooking.

Guivech: an oven-baked stew.

Selska Tchorba: slightly sour soup made with lamb broth, rice, and celeriac.

Sharan Sawrehi: festive Bulgarian New Year's dish and eaten on festive "meatless" days; a whole baked carp stuffed with rice and ground nuts, well seasoned, or with raisins, walnuts, and onions.

Shopska Salata: simple salad of layers of fresh greens and sliced tomatoes and cucumbers (or other fresh vegetables) sprinkled with walnuts and grated sirene cheese.

Sirene: fresh white goat's cheese, similar to the Greek **feta**.

Slivovka, **Slivova** or **Slivovitsa** or **Slivovitza**: potent plum brandy.

Soupa: soup.

Tarator: Middle Eastern chilled soup of cucumbers and yogurt.

Taskebap: stew similar to a goulash, made of veal, tomatoes, and seasonings.

Tchorba or **Chorba**: sour soup made of any greens cooked in water and finished with a delicate sauce of egg yolks and cream (or yogurt), flavored lightly with onion, garlic, salt, and pepper. The sourness is achieved with the addition of lemon juice, vinegar, or yogurt or sometimes sauerkraut juice added to taste.

Tokfozelek: delicious dish of strips of summer squash lightly cooked with butter, a little water, vinegar, sugar, and dill. Just before serving, the dish is blended with sour cream. Other vegetables and yogurt may be prepared in the same way.

Turlu Guivetch: basically a dish of stewed lamb to which a number of fresh cubed or sliced vegetables are added. The dish may be baked in the oven. Frequently served in soup plates with rice or pilaf.

Zelen Haiver: typical Middle Eastern appetizer of cooked, seasoned (much garlic and pepper) and puréed eggplant, which is spread flat on a large plate and eaten by dipping bread into it.

CHAPTER 11

CANADIAN:
ATLANTIC PROVINCES, FIRST NATIONS, QUEBEC

*Note: Canada, like the United States, comprises many different ethnocultural groups and regions.
All those studied in this book are Canadian – that is, have made their home in Canada –but considered
specifically in this chapter are those groups or regions that, by virtue of their lengthy histories,
have established their own distinctive food traditions.*

Canada, like the United States, is a land of immigrants. To really understand the cultural and food traditions of Canadians – as well as Americans – it would be necessary to read each chapter of this book, since each chapter represents one or more of the ethnocultural groups who consider themselves to be Canadian or American.

Canada was first settled by groups of Aboriginal peoples believed to have crossed the Bering Strait from Asia. It is they who first learned to adapt to their newfound environment of varying climate and geography. So symbiotic was the relationship of these ingenious peoples to their environment that without their help many of the Europeans who came a few thousand years later might never have survived. First Nations peoples taught them to use indigenous plants and crops and even brewed a tea from white cedar needles to cure scurvy.

In 1497, the explorer John Cabot wrote in his log: "The shoals of fish off the Grand Banks [Newfoundland] were so great as to impede the progress of the ship...." Shortly after this report was circulated, eager fishermen from Brittany, Normandy, the Basque provinces, and England came to reap the sea's harvest.

By the early 1500s, small villages were established on the Maritime coast. These soon became not only fishing centers but fur-trading centers as well. By the late 1500s, cod, "the beef of the sea," had become one of the economic staples of Northwest France, and each summer, as more and more Aboriginals came to the coast to exchange furs for European goods, a gradual transition took place. An increasing number of ships were sailing between France and Newfoundland but their trade soon had little to do with fish. And although the Basques from Spain had long established a whaling center at Tadoussac, it became widely known as a fur-trading center.

By the 1600s, wooden sailing ships were carrying other important cargo to Canada: English, Irish, Scottish, Welsh, French, Spanish, and Dutch immigrants, coming to make a new life in the new land. Life aboard these ships was grim at best and those who survived the sea journey had already passed the first test of pioneering. The ship's wood absorbed moisture and made it difficult to keep the stores dry.

Rats and insects multiplied rapidly in the dank holds. Aside from the highly salted pork packed in barrels and the small rations of water and **hardtack** (a saltless hard biscuit), the ship's stores often included butter, cheese, and beer. But too often before the ship was out to sea, the butter became rancid, the cheese moldy and tough, and the beer spoiled. **Skillygolee, lobscouse,** and **Scotch coffee** were a few of the names used to disguise the unpalatable slop created by soaking the hard "weevil-ridden" ship's biscuits with water. It was even considered a bit of luck if vinegar or a bit of salt pork was available for seasonings.

Fishing, fur trading, some farming, and cattle raising characterized the occupations of the first colonists to the Maritime region. During the first half of the 1600s, while the Europeans were grappling for footholds in the New World, the many Indian nations, once so free and independent, were in the throes of a cultural and technological revolution. As they became increasingly dependent on European goods, their old skills faded: metal replaced flint and bone, muskets replaced lances, bows and arrows, and European trinkets became status symbols. Worse, their old religious beliefs were undermined, wars were fought for extermination not domination, and the European's diseases and his alcohol degraded, debilitated, and finally eliminated them.

At this point in history, the mighty Huron Nation was almost destroyed. The Iroquois and Algonquins were next in the relentless path of fate.

The early 1600s were important years for Nova Scotia. De Monts had begun the work of colonizing Nova Scotia and it was largely as a result of his efforts that the Acadian colony grew. In 1605, the first wheat in Canada was both grown and milled in Acadia (Nova Scotia) in a mill that was claimed to be the first erected on the North American continent. Also about this time the first cuttings of apple trees were brought to Nova Scotia from Normandy. It did not take long before most farms boasted a small apple orchard, and soon specialty apple dishes and apple cider became a welcome part of the settler's fare.

In 1608, Samuel de Champlain founded the city of Quebec and within the next twenty-five years organized colonization of New France (Quebec) was encouraged by the Company of New France, or the One Hundred Associates. This very early attempt to settle New France was met with general apathy, but successful French settlement was occurring in small farms in Acadia where the rich soils produced vegetables and grains while wild berries and fruits helped to fill the larders, together with the rich bounty of game and fish.

The largest period of early growth for New France occurred in the late 1600s, when shiploads of *filles du rois*, hardy young women, arrived from France with dowries of "an ox, a cow, a pair of swine, a pair of fowl, two barrels of salted meat and eleven crowns ..." together with the addition of 2,000 new settlers and the protection of the Royal Troops. So important was population growth in New France at this time that early marriage and large families were encouraged by giving people annual grants and by making bachelorhood unpopular. Indeed, in some cases, fines were levied for this sorry state.

As early as the turn of the eighteenth century, the French in New France, deeply immersed in a new existence based on close family life and reverence for the soil, as well as vibrant adherence to ancestral traditions, began the break with the European French. In fact, tradition coupled with isolation were important factors in creating and maintaining a proud and independent self-sufficiency which was evident as early as 1675 and which steadily increased. Even in 1759, when New France capitulated to the English, she was firmly established as an agricultural society of French-speaking Catholics, albeit in an "English Canada."

From 1753 to 1755, the ominous rumblings of conflict between New France and the thirteen British colonies dealt their saddest blow to the almost 10,000 quiet farm people in the Annapolis Valley. Refusing to take an oath of allegiance to the British king, because they likely felt this would threaten their loyalties to France, the Acadians were deported and scattered throughout the British colonies. Some found their way south to New Orleans, where they were called Cajuns and soon adapted to the new life in the largely French city.

The English then sent out an urgent appeal for farmers to work the lands vacated by the Acadians. Many Germans came, a large group settling on the good land of Lunenburg. They were called Dutch (as they were called in Pennsylvania) as a mistranslation of the German "Deutsch." Their descendants became shipbuilders and fishers, and although they lost the German language early, to this day they still retain a recognizable Lunenburg accent.

The 1700s also saw the gradual immigration of settlers from other cultures. French and British Jews played important roles as early settlers and traders. French Jews came despite a French decree dating back to 1685 "which prohibited Jews and Huguenots (French Protestants) from settling in Canada or France's other North American colonies...." Nova Scotia counted almost 2,500 English settlers among its population while almost half of Newfoundland's population was Irish, brought in as passengers on English fishing ships calling at Irish ports on the outward journey.

New Englanders were also among those who came to take up the vacated Acadian farms, and they brought with them their famed trenchers and tureens and baked beans. Many Scots came in the late 1700s because of severe economic repression and the downfall of Scotland's chieftains. They settled in Cape Breton Island, in Pictou, Nova Scotia, and in the areas that later became Prince Edward Island and New Brunswick. Groups of United Empire Loyalists, some with their West African slaves, fleeing from the persecution and derision of the Americans for their loyalties to the British, were granted sanctuary and even given lands and some basic provisions to settle in the Maritime area and Upper Canada. A large percentage of these early Loyalists were Germans.

The flow of settlers continued into the nineteenth century. Polish soldiers and European political refugees, Scottish Highlanders from the Thirteen Colonies; German Mennonites from Pennsylvania; West African slaves escaping from the American Revolution; Irish fleeing the Irish Rebellion. Swedes joined the flow of British immigrants encouraged by the great areas in the new land, which afforded space that was at a premium in their homelands, where populations were burgeoning.

In their early struggles for survival, the immigrant settlers clung to familiar customs. They made do with available new foods and cherished some old food traditions too. Thus, the 2,000 West African slaves who came to Nova Scotia after the War of 1812 had a difficult time adjusting to freedom with its attendant responsibilities, and lived chiefly on rice, molasses, and Indian meal (corn), making a staple bread pudding called **padana**. The Scots took care to provide themselves with oats, molasses, and eggs; the Irish contented themselves "with a few herring" when they had to; German settlers produced **sauerkraut**, **kohl salad**, and **schmier-kase**.

In 1831, the earliest known cookbook published in Canada was *The Cook Not Mad*. But perhaps someone was "mad" when an identical book was published in the same year in Watertown, New York.

By the late 1800s, immigration became even more varied, not only in the immigrants' place of origin, but also in their place of Canadian settlement. By the 1840s, a small group of Maltese became Canadian settlers, preceded in 1836 by the first Maltese, Lewis Schikluna, who had established a shipyard at Welland Canal. Groups of Finns settled as far west as Vancouver Island; the Irish potato famine sent the evicted and forced-migrants from Ireland to Canadian soil; the first Hungarian Freedom Fighters emigrated to the United States and then to Canada after the 1848 revolt; Norwegians established settlements on the Gaspe Peninsula of Quebec; peasant immigrants from Prussian-occupied Poland fled the oppression in their homeland, some establishing the first Polish settlement in Wilno, Renfrew County, Ontario.

These later immigrants were probably oblivious to the changes that had occurred agriculturally and domestically in the lives of the pioneers. Food for cattle was widely grown and the ability to keep the animals in barns over the severe winter provided year-round supplies of milk, butter, cheese, and buttermilk.

Established settlers soon made cookstoves with ovens a special priority in their homes. And out of the ovens came baked goods leavened with baking soda that was made from burnt corncobs; or sourdough yeasts prepared from boiled hops or from **barm**, a soft dough of flour, salt, and warm water, allowed to ferment. The plentiful pumpkin was simmered into soups, baked into pies, and boiled down into molasses. Ingenious pioneers had perfected the making of gelatin from cow hides, and almost every household boasted its own homemade beer and apple cider.

In fact, many characterized the late 1850s as a time of "the food supply revolution." Coastal fisheries were expanding; railroad growth and development of new farm implements encouraged farming of virgin lands; improved passenger sailing ships helped to make the dreaded Atlantic crossing more pleasant. The increasing number of laborers in towns and cities, and the burgeoning landless middle class created a need for a wide range and steady supply of foods.

As well as increased technology and increasing need, the food revolution also extended to the home kitchen and inspired practical innovations. Catharine Parr Traill wrote *Backwoods of Canada*, a compendium of practical information and encouragement that included descriptions of the countryside and recipes for making candles, cheese, pickled beef, and maple sugar "sweeties." She culled ideas from friends and neighbors and wrote about preparing beer from beets, coffee from toasted dandelion roots, processing homemade starch from potatoes and bran, and even extracting the rennet from the first stomach of a suckling calf to use in cheesemaking.

Probably due to the patient persistence of one John McIntosh (1796), Upper Canada enjoyed an abundance of apples. McIntosh's patience was evident in his single-minded interest in learning the art of grafting and budding so that he could duplicate the apple trees on his father's farm. This man was responsible for producing acres and acres of crisp red apples known to this day by his name. Gradually apples began to replace pumpkins as a sweet and as a fruit. Dried apples were prepared in "paring bees" or were preserved like small fruits by boiling in sugar then sun-drying for winter storage.

The food revolution also resulted in the formation of new associations and new types of factories. Flour mills, tanneries, meat-packing plants, and breweries had accounted for most of the gross national product (GNP) but were being joined by expansion of heavy farm machinery by the Massey family, cornstarch manufacture by W. T. Benson, the first commercial cheese factories, and even the founding of the Canadian Fruit Grower's Association in the Niagara Peninsula to organize the marketing and storage of fresh fruits.

Changes and developments in Canadian foods and their production were also influenced by events in other countries. In 1860, forty years after the publication of Frederick Accum's book on food adulteration, the first British Food and Drug Act was passed. By 1876, the Food and Drug Directorate of Canada was established with a staff of four analysts – 100 years later it would employ more than 300. In Austria, a monk was pursuing a seemingly innocuous pastime that would revolutionize agriculture the world over. The monk's name was Gregor Mendel and he developed a genetic theory based on a fundamental law of heredity. In Canada Mendel's discovery led directly to the development of rust-resisting, high-yield wheat for which the prairies became famous. In 1861, a French engineer, Carre, experimented with ammonia gas as a refrigerant and provided a new means of preserving food without sterilization. By 1868, the first refrigerated boxcar was invented by coupling railroad transportation and the new process of refrigeration. With facilities for shipping, the meat and dairy industries expanded rapidly.

OPENING OF THE WEST

The biggest thrust of energy and publicity that would have an incalculable impact on Canadians occurred in the 1880s and centered around the building of the transcontinental railroad. It not only absorbed every available man for labor, it was even necessary to import labor from other countries. Italians, Chinese, and Finns all eagerly applied their efforts to forge the link between Eastern, Central, and Western Canada. Up to the 1890s, Canada's flour exports had steadily decreased, but with the new "opening of the West" the entire milling industry was stimulated. Shipping of food products by steamers increased with the development of the railroads and refrigerated boxcars were quickly linked with refrigerated chambers in steamers, making the export of perishables, such as butter and cheese, and later fruits and pork products, a practical enterprise.

STILL MORE IMMIGRANTS

The early 1900s also witnessed successive waves of immigrants from the British Isles, Europe, and the United States. Ukrainians, Doukhobors, Mennonites, Estonians from oppressed czarist Russia, economically deprived Romanian refugees, Greeks, Japanese, Lebanese, and Icelanders – all came, each group adding another dimension to the meaning of "Canadian."

Italians and Chinese were noted for their efforts in the building of the railroads; Icelanders helped make north-central Saskatchewan famous for its wheat; the Dutch proved their agricultural talents when they introduced strip farming into southern Alberta and put western irrigation districts into profitable production. Japanese settlers worked in British Columbia as farmers, fishermen, and skilled laborers in mining and construction. The simmering political problems of the Austrian Empire brought immigrants seeking calm and stability: Czechs, Serbs, Croats, Ukrainians, Jews, Magyars, and Romanians. In fact, 1913 was an almost record year of immigration to Canada: more than 400,000 immigrants came.

The experience of the First World War did little to unite Canadians. French-Canadian nationalism exploded against English management even though many conceded that the core problem was the French educational system, which was designed to produce priests, lawyers, and doctors but not the economists, engineers, and industrialists that were needed to promote and manage industry and agriculture in the province of Quebec. While Quebec simmered with deep-seated hostilities, "persons of the Asiatic race" – East Indians, Chinese, and Japanese – were denied the vote in British Columbia. Unaware of Quebec or Asiatic "problems" in Canada, immigrants contin-

ued their march to the land of hope. Armenians, Hutterites, Belorussians, Slovenes, and Hungarians fled political unrest in their countries and came to Canada.

Immigrants to Canada in the 1920s were met with the appearance of the first co-op food stores, electric ranges for domestic use, and home iceboxes in which to chill foods. They had a few years to enjoy these conveniences before the Great Depression turned the lives of North Americans into a nightmare.

Despite political and economic problems, industrial history was being forged. Strict grading standards and legislation were a great stimulus to both domestic trade and export. In 1928, Canada's per capita egg consumption was the highest in the world and a great expansion of the country's food industries took place because of increased public confidence in merchandise purchased. Ethnic tolerance increased as the newcomers proved their expertise in every area of the Canadian economy. And about this time, Quebec eased from a predominantly agricultural rural society to an industrialized urban one. New developments in agriculture further stimulated economic optimism, as did the development of dehydrated and concentrated food products, such as apples, and the worldwide interest in production and shipment of frozen foods.

Canada's story of growth is an intertwined tale of people and food. Representatives of more than 100 ethnocultural groups continue to make a place for themselves in Canada. And while making their place, each group adds, in its own way, to the tastes of Canada as a whole.

REGIONAL SPECIALTIES

There is little question that domestic life and food facilities as well as the range of foods commonly used by Canadians closely parallel those of Americans, as do the meal patterns and eating customs and the celebration of special occasions. As in the United States, area preferences blend with age-old cultural customs, personal preferences, economic and social status, and health, to determine what shows up on the table, how it is served, and even how it is eaten. Yet there are areas of Canada and ethnocultural groups with such lengthy histories that their food customs stand as distinctive: the Atlantic provinces, the First Nations, and the province of Quebec.

ATLANTIC PROVINCES

NEW BRUNSWICK

New Brunswick is considered to be the "home of the descendants of the Acadians and the Loyalists," since from earliest times Acadia included the areas of both

Nova Scotia and New Brunswick. The exception is Edmunston where Loyalists and New Englanders are a part of the population but the distinctly French character of the city is supported by its 85 percent French population.

From earliest times, forestry, fishing, and ship-building were the most important industries, and agriculture was, in comparison, neglected. Nonetheless, crops of wheat, rye, Indian corn, buckwheat, barley, and oats as well as peas and beans were produced; potatoes and root vegetables were popular but scarce; apples, plums, berries, and cherries were carefully cultivated together with small crops of pumpkins, cucumbers, melons, and varieties of squash. Some of the first Loyalists, arriving in New Brunswick in 1783, noting that the Malacite Indians were eating the young fronds of the ostrich ferns, plucked them too to use as a food. Today **fiddleheads** are eaten as a gourmet delight rather than merely as a hedge against hunger.

For the earliest settlers in the late 1700s, the basis of their daily diet consisted of the rations provided by the Royal Bounty of Provisions: "...one pound of flour per person, half a pound of meat, either beef or pork, an infinitesimal quantity of butter, about half a pound of oatmeal a week, an equal quantity of pease [sic], and occasionally a little rice..."

These daily rations could be supplemented with fish and game. The settlers even became adept at supplementing scarce wheat flour to make delicious corncakes, buckwheat pancakes, and steamed breads of dark flour. In fact, the ritual Saturday night baked beans and steamed bread were, and continue to be, a favorite meal of the entire East Coast, both in Canada and the United States. Wild berries and wild greens and the sweetness of maple sugar added variety too.

Wild fruits of the area include: strawberries, gooseberries, varieties of whortleberries, blackberries, raspberries, wild cherries, wild plums, and grapes. Some of these were used to prepare fruit cordials, teas, and wines. Others were made into jams and jellies or sun-dried for winter use. Teas were sometimes steeped from Labrador tea or chocolate root, or even from spruce or hemlock bark.

Early settlers enjoyed the abundant fish of the area: herring, both smoked and salted, mussels, lobsters, caplin, and of course, cod, which was the main staff of life. Cod heads were preserved by salting down; the cod itself was sun-dried. To use, cod could be soaked and then fried in deep fat or boiled and served with fried pork and mealy potatoes. Other fish like mackerel and caplin were spread on flakes (wooden racks) to dry and then cooked when needed.

For the settlers, molasses and maple sugar were the common sweeteners while varieties of vinegar (often made from apple cider) and salt served as the usual seasonings. For those with means, the *Halifax Gazette* advertised the availability of imported spices, white wine vinegar, brown sugar, and even rum, port, and sherry.

In later years, flour and potatoes became more plentiful and added to the extensive varieties of fish and seafood that were the continuing staples of the New Brunswick table. The ingenuity of the region's homemakers, then as now, produced cakes and breads and pies to round out the daily fare, and preserves and jams for winter months.

NEWFOUNDLAND

Britain's oldest colony, Newfoundland, became Canada's tenth province in 1949. Since before the mid-1500s, English fishing ships had come to the banks of Newfoundland. It is not known exactly when the crews began to leave men and women ashore to protect their shore buildings (where fish were stored and cured)

against the many rival and pilfering crews, but they became the first settlers. These English and the French intermarried with the Indians of Nova Scotia, the Micmacs, and so came to blend their lives and cultures. The Beothuck Nation gave no resistance to the settlers and are now extinct. The natural elements caused the toughest battles for survival in this land that the English called "a land of fog, bogs and dogs...." By the mid-1700s, about 50 percent of the population comprised Irish immigrants, who crossed the Atlantic agreeing to pay for their passage as soon as they had jobs.

Bankruptcy, fires, feuds, and "conquerors" – it all mattered little to the Newfoundland settlers who, from earliest times, lived their lives by the rhythm of the sea and used the same foods – potatoes, cabbage, and turnips from their little gardens – and somehow still managed to produce a hospitable table of tea, bread, and butter for guests. Living in weather-lashed, isolated fishing communities often dramatized positive human values and acts of daily heroism. Sometimes cod could be traded for flour, molasses, or even clothing; sometimes deer-trapping or seal-hunting supplemented the daily fish-and-potatoes diet.

The rocky island seemed to spurn life. Because they had to be built on rocks, the houses appeared to be asymmetrical. Fresh meats and vegetables were chronically hard to procure ("stringy cabbage and struggling turnips"). There was no place for cows or horses to graze. The extremes of weather were always a problem. In winter, bread was kept in people's beds to prevent its being frozen, while in summer the flies and mosquitoes and the stifling heat plagued people and spoiled foods.

Although in Newfoundland "fish" means cod, many other fish are part of the harvest: haddock, redfish, sole, halibut, salmon, mackerel, turbot, swordfish, and herring. The latter may be prepared by pickling, smoking, or serving with cream sauce. Occasionally lobsters and shrimp, squid and eels are enjoyed. Hunting may provide rabbit and hare, **ptarmigan**, caribou and, recently, small herds of deer provide meat as well. Otherwise, the main meat is salt beef or variety meats from pork.

Today, traditions of foods remain a treasured part of Newfoundland life. Many families have a few chickens, pigs, or sheep, and even a pony or two, but fish is still cod, and vegetables are still in large part potatoes, cabbages, and turnips. Considered to be the national dish is the one-pot meal of the "boiled dinner," consisting of turnips, potatoes, and cabbage boiled in a pot with salt beef or pork. Strong tea, soft drinks, or rum are the favored beverages, and only small amounts of either canned milk or skim-milk powder are used. The preference for salty foods in the Newfoundland diet may have come from the wide use of salt cod and salt beef and the flavor of the vegetables commonly cooked with them.

Another typical Newfoundland dish is **fish and brewis**, prepared from soaked hard bread (similar to ship's **hardtack**), served with cooked fresh or salt codfish, sometimes with a crispy topping of pork fat called **scrunchions**.

Few raw vegetables are eaten, but dandelion greens and turnip tops are cooked in the spring. Native berries – squashberries, blueberries, partridge berries, marshberries, and **bakeapples** – are used to make jellies and jams, baked and steamed puddings, and many cooked desserts. Homemade breads fill kitchens everywhere with delicious aromas, and a commonly prepared pastry, **smother**, covers fruit pies, leftover cooked-vegetable dishes, and one-dish meals of fish or meats. Commonly the source of many in-jokes, the seabird known as the **turr** or **murre** is

plentiful in coastal regions near the end of winter, and provides a welcome change of fare.

In cultural terms, Newfoundland was considered to be "an island-arrested society and a rich repository of European customs and folklore on the very threshold of the New World." Believed to have derived from British and Irish origins, "*mumming*," "*mummering*," or "*janneying*" are analogous terms for a living folk tradition and are an integral part of the high-spirited twelve-days-of-Christmas celebrations. Characterized by unique disguises, groups of mummers go from house to house presenting uninhibited performances and finally identifying themselves and joining in shared food and drink. Adult janneys are treated with beer, the young ones with candy, and all enjoy traditional **Christmas sweet bread**, eaten daily during the festive season. Since the kitchen is the center of the home, guests and mummers are treated to the best chairs around the table.

"Soup-suppers" and concerts highlight other festive evenings. The "soup-suppers" consist of communally prepared thick meat and vegetable stews of moose or caribou meat with vegetables, selling inexpensively for all to enjoy. **Scoff** is the name given to the big meal held at any time, but usually at night and consisting of leftovers from the "soup-supper" plus homemade **sweet bread**, **pork buns**, and good strong tea.

NOVA SCOTIA

The area of Nova Scotia and Cape Breton Island was early settled by French (Acadians), English, Scots, Irish, Germans, and Africans, all of whom shared their lives with the native Micmac Nation. The Scottish and French ancestors of the Cape Breton Islanders prepared simple meals consisting of fresh-caught fish or fried eggs accompanied by baked beans or panned potatoes. Occasionally, preserved berries were served as dessert or the meal ended with oatcakes or biscuits and pies with tea. For Cape Breton Islanders, breakfast is unchanging: porridge, strong tea, and fresh eggs with bacon.

Since the British government had offered free passage, land grants and even a year's basic provisions, English immigrants to Nova Scotia fared well. Although they often had to make do with *hardtack* and salt beef, the usual fare was hearty beef soup or mutton broths, and social status was identified by the type of sweet used: ladies used loaf sugar, apprenticed men enjoyed brown sugar, while servants had molasses.

Scots came without government support and subsisted at first on shellfish and wild fruits, adding their beloved oatmeal to their diet later, when gristmills could be built. Tea with oatcakes and scones marked the hospitality of the Scots, while **shortbread** was served for *Hogmanay* (New Year's Eve) and **forach** marked Halloween, when all guests dipped into a communal bowl of fine oats stirred stiff with sugar and whipped cream. The famed **haggis** marked St. Andrew's Day and Robbie Burns Night.

By 1760, the Irish made up half of Halifax's population. They submerged their traditions and adopted those of the English and Scots: oatmeal porridge became the morning and evening meals, while fried meat and potatoes formed the midday meal. A treat for the Irish was the serving of thin oatcakes with butter together with a glass of buttermilk.

With the dispersal of the Acadians by the British government, Germans came to tend the now-unoccupied farms and orchards. In 1753, they settled mainly around Lunenburg where their farms produced barley, rye, and oats and the rich fields yielded potatoes, cabbages, turnips, and cucumbers. Their diet of grains and vegetables was well supplemented with poultry and dairy products, veal and mutton, and many varieties of fish and seafood. German wedding fare consisted of ample servings of soups, mutton, goose, and hams and an array of home bakery. Typical of foods served at funerals was the **funeral cake**, a plain cake lightly flavored with cinnamon. Significantly, German cookery skills added many treasured foods to the tables of Nova Scotia: **barley bread, chicken noodle soup, Dutch mess** or **house bankin, soused eels, kohl slaw, sauerkraut**, many varieties of homemade sausages and puddings and **Solomon Gundy**, a type of pickled herring.

Like the Germans, many New Englanders came to Nova Scotia in the 1760s to take up the farms vacated by the Acadians. Those immigrants added **maize** to the crops, established the celebration of the New England Thanksgiving Day, and busied themselves brewing beer and making wines, apple cider, candles, soap, starch, and yeast. Some of the black people in Nova Scotia came with the New Englanders, while others came as slaves to the pre-Loyalists, and still others escaped during the American Revolution. Rice, molasses, and **Indian meal** (cornmeal) formed the staple foods for the blacks, with a favorite being **padana**, a bread pudding made from cornmeal.

PRINCE EDWARD ISLAND

As in the other Atlantic provinces, cod and potatoes were synonymous with survival, whether the settlers were English, Scottish, Irish, or French. From earliest times it was apparent that food stores from ships were not dependable and the settlers made ingenious use of shellfish, nuts, wild berries, and various roots. Lobsters, scallops, bar clams, salted herring, and smoked mackerel were, and continue to be, important foods and export commodities, but cod is still considered most important.

Although each of the island's cultural groups retains many traditionally favored foods, the ingredient that makes them especially "P.E.I." is potatoes. Famed for their fine quality, it is small wonder that potatoes are used in endless ways not only in meat and fish dishes and with other vegetables, but also as an ingredient in dumplings, cakes, breads, and candies. **Colcannon** is both Scottish and Irish and is made by mashing together cooked turnips, potatoes, and cabbage. **Pate a la rapure,** a dish of Acadian origin, consists of layered and seasoned mashed potatoes filled with cubed stewed chicken meat and topped with crumbled salt pork before baking in the oven. **Onesooe** is a one-dish meal of browned pork chops, onions, and potatoes. And who on P.E.I. is not familiar with the satisfying **potato bannock**?

In earliest times, bread, molasses, and tea, and later oatmeal porridge, were the staples that sated the Islander's hunger. Cordials and preserves prepared from wild berries, an occasional imported orange, and homemade wine and beer were considered special treats. Berries included raspberries, strawberries, bunchberries, blackberries, mulberries, black currants, rose hips, chokecherries, and **wild sarsaparilla**. These were also used as medicinal remedies, or for teas, preserves, or desserts.

Typical of P.E.I. hospitality to this day are the many homemade pickles and relishes that grace any meal and are part of any festive table. These include treasured recipes for **bread and butter pickles, chow chow** (a spicy relish of chopped tomatoes, onions, peppers, and celery) and **beet relish**. And what Islander's household does not boast a delightful array of homemade cookies, squares, baking powder biscuits, and quick breads? As in the British Isles, cherished family cookbooks often fill more than half their pages with pies, cakes, scones, squares, bars, and slices – all enjoyed as snacks with tea.

As in the daily menu, potatoes play an important part in many special occasion dishes on Prince Edward Island. Potato pancakes and potato soup are prepared especially for Lent. **Potted meat** or **head-**

cheese was served traditionally during Easter week. Traditional Christmas foods consisted of roast duck or goose with side dishes of potatoes and turnips, a special Christmas cake and **plum pudding**. The usual scones and sugar cookies would be replaced by **potato doughnuts** and **mincemeat pie** as special Christmas treats. Oysters are also a favorite of the festive season.

P.E.I.'s Acadians prepared a traditional specialty of their own, **pata**, to be eaten after the Christmas midnight mass. **Pata** is prepared with a mixture of meats, usually rabbit, chicken, and pork, and topped with a crust of pastry moistened with meat broth instead of water. Crusty rolls called **French cakes** are also traditionally served by the French at Christmastime.

THE FIRST NATIONS

The history of North American Aboriginals, as hunters, gatherers, or cultivators, is one of a tender balance between individual and environment. That is, until the European came. The term "Red Indians" is usually credited to Christopher Columbus, who thought he had found the Indies and therefore called the inhabitants "Indians." The probability that Columbus saw natives who decorated themselves with a paste of red ochre may explain the "red." So intimately were the lives of these Aboriginals interwoven with their environment that the distinctive lifestyles of each of the groups were largely determined by the nature of the land itself and the type and amount of food available.

Just as the various nations of Europe differ culturally and linguistically, and in terms of lifestyle and religions, so too do the languages, lifestyles, and dialects of the First Nations. Including the Inuit Nations, there are six main First Nations in Canada (see below), speaking eleven main languages and about fifty dialects. Elijah Harper, a prominent Aboriginal leader, describes the First Nations as "53 different nations ... with different tribes, cultures [and] languages." There are different ways of counting First Nations and it is possible to come up with

THE SIX FIRST NATIONS

Northwest Coast	Eastern Woodlands
Tlingit	Neutral
Haida	Five Nations Iroquois: Seneca, Cayuga, Onondaga, Oneida, Mohawk
Tsimshian	Huron
Kitamaat	Petun
Heiltsuk	Ojibwa
Kwakiutl	Ottawa
Nootka	Algonquin
Nuxalk (Bella Coola)	Abenaki
Northern Georgia Strait Coast Salish	Maliseet
Central Coast Salish	Micmac
Sub-Arctic	Plateau
Attikamek	Nicola-Similkameen (extinct)
Innu	Salish, Interior
Beothuk (extinct)	Kootenay
Arctic	Plains
Inuit:	Blackfoot
Labrador	Plains Cree
Ungava	Plains Ojibwa
Baffin Island	Assiniboine
Iglulik	Stoney
Caribou	Dakota
Netsilk	Sarcee
Copper	

The 1998 Canadian & World Encyclopedia. Toronto: McClelland & Stewart, 1997. (Used by permission, McClelland & Stewart, Inc. The Canadian Publishers.)

many divisions and subdivisions. What is most important is the respectful acknowledgment of the lengthy history of First Nations people, and their inalienable right to prosper.

Among the more obvious debts the European owes to the First Nations are the knowledge of plant cultivation, uses and techniques of preparation of certain foods as well as the use of implements and medicinal plants. These debts also include the cultivation, uses and preparation, and in some cases, preservation, of tobacco, corn (**maize**), potatoes, peanuts, some varieties of cotton, maple syrup and maple sugar, varieties of beans and squash, pumpkins, sunflowers, tomatoes, pineapples, and some melons; the domestication and cultivation of grapes, strawberries, gooseberries, raspberries, pecans, and other nuts. Forging forest trails and canoe routes, making and using sleds, canoes, toboggans, and snowshoes are all ancient skills of the Aboriginals of North America.

Considered to be "definitely the basis of Indian cooking in Canada" are the many versions of **nabos** or soups prepared from whatever is locally available. Although the name **bannock** is of Scottish origin, Aboriginals have long made a quick bread based on corn or wheat flour that can be baked over a fire or in a pan. Their name for it is **pakwejigan**. In fact, this type of bread accompanies most meals and can be eaten as a snack with preserves or enjoyed with wild herb tea as a breakfast. Traditional desserts are of wild fruits, berries, or nuts. Popular among many nations is **sagamite**, a thick mixture of meats with beans and corn simmered slowly in a cast-iron kettle, usually over an open fire. Traditionally, Aboriginals eat when they are hungry rather than following a rigid time schedule. Foods are often shared with other families. Menus are prepared according to area, season, and availability of ingredients.

While reading the following descriptions, remember that generalizations about any aspect of First Nations' daily life are as difficult to make as generalizations about Europeans.

BRITISH COLUMBIA COASTAL NATIONS

Because of the isolation caused by the Rocky Mountains on one side and the Pacific Ocean on the other, these nations evolved unique patterns of culture. Although there are at least four distinct groups of six languages, these nations share many common traditions. These include an elaborate mythology, the wearing of scanty clothing, high respect for their leaders, and the practice of lavishing them with gifts; the building of complex rectangular houses made from cedar planks (durable and aromatic); and their dependence on food from the sea.

Several species of salmon form the staple food and were traditionally caught by means of spears, dip nets, and damlike traps. Halibut was next in importance and was taken by barbed hooks or clubbed with hardwood clubs. Other foods from the sea included cod, whales, sea lions, **oolichan**, porpoises, sea otters, sea urchins, cuttlefish, and clams. Land animals formed only a small part of the diet: deer, caribou, and very occasionally bears, mountain sheep and goats (found inland). Plant foods included berries and roots, the inner bark of hemlock and other trees, edible seaweed, **eel grass**, and **cama**.

As with the B.C. Interior Nations, the Coastal Nations used two principal methods of cookery: boiling with hot rocks and pit steaming. Some fish was cooked by spearing on a stick and roasting over a fire. In earlier times, watertight wooden boxes and woven baskets sealed with spruce gum were made by the Haida and used both as storage utensils and cooking pots (hot-stone method).

Foods such as fish and berries could be readily preserved for winter use either by sealing in oil or by drying. Salmon and clams could be smoked then dried; seaweed and berries could be dried then pressed into cakes, berries sometimes being simply stored in oil. Although some tobacco was grown, it was not smoked but was dried, pounded to a powder, then chewed with lime made from burned clam shells.

Of great importance as a nutrient and as a condiment was the use of grease in the form of animal fats, and especially the use of oil from **oolichans**. These tiny fish were valued for their very high oil content, which could also be used as cooking fat. Sometimes they were called "candle fish" because a dried one, when lit at one end, would burn like a candle. Because of the prevalent custom of dipping foods, especially dried fish, into oil before eating, European explorers coined the name "grease feast."

Special diets were a traditional part of special ceremonies for both boys and girls upon reaching maturity. Boys were secluded with their uncles for a time and ate no "meat containing sinews or muscles." It was believed that to violate these taboos would affect the boys' prowess as hunters. During her initiation period a girl was secluded under her grandmother's care. She slept only in a sitting position, and stepped out of doors only if her head was covered so as not to offend the sea and land spirits. During this time, too, girls were not allowed to eat any fresh salmon and could only eat dried strips from the previous year's catch.

The most famed ceremonial of the B.C. Coastal Nations was the *potlatch*. This was an elaborate ceremony held for important events such as bestowing gifts, property or inheritance, but perhaps most important, to establish the status of a group or of certain individuals within it. For this occasion, huge quantities of foods were prepared. In fact, using the hot-stone method, foods could even be cooked in canoes, then spooned out with huge wooden ladles. Typical foods served were smoked salmon, caribou or venison, bear meat, berries prepared in various ways, tasty roots, small cakes made of dried berries and fruits and **squaw candy** (braided strips of smoked salmon).

In their arts and industries, customs and beliefs, these peoples differed greatly from all other Aboriginals of North America in having one of the most sophisticated cultures. The variety of mechanical and architectural skills they enjoyed were only matched by their skills in wood carving (totem poles), songwriting, and the staging of elaborate dance productions, often as special events for the *potlatch*. But this description scarcely does justice to the complex intricacies of games and pastimes and elaborate rituals or orders and status that were an integral part of each *potlatch*.

The West Coast Nations believed in a pantheon of deities of earth and heavens, some beneficent, some evil. The priest-doctor functions were traditionally performed by the local shaman, or medicine man, whose rituals included the use of beneficent magic, amulets, and medicinal herbs. Unlike others, the West Coast Nations also believed in monsters, dwarfs, ogres, and even in huge rocks of quartz that were believed capable of attacking man with electric-like charges. Considered to be the most powerful of all was the "thunderbird," believed to live on mountaintops and control man with lightning as the "ultimate master of the natural world."

The West Coast Nations, with their abundance of food and elaborate culture, recognized an aristocracy more sophisticated than the chief-systems of other groups. Their celebration of the potlatch and their "well-organized system of slavery" also serve to make them distinct. As Leechman states: "Prairie tribes put war deeds first – west coast people made wealth and gift distribution important in life."

BRITISH COLUMBIA INTERIOR NATIONS

Although the languages of the B.C. Interior Nations belong to three different language stocks, the customs of the people are similar. The most important food is salmon. Other foods include deer, moose, elk, caribou, bear, mountain sheep and goats, as well as roots and berries in season. Smaller animals such as rabbits, groundhogs, beaver, gopher, and porcupine as well as fish such as pike, trout, and whitefish may also be part of the diet. In some grassy areas, where grasshoppers are plentiful, the Aboriginals pluck them and eat them as a snack. Some berries may be pressed and dried for winter use. The inner bark of certain trees may be cut off in juicy slivers and also dried for winter use. Smoking, drying, and then pounding is a common method of food preservation, and because of the prevalence of fish in the area, a type of **fish pemmican** was commonly prepared for winter use.

Women of all ages traditionally had the difficult task of finding, digging, and preparing all types of roots and berries for winter storage. These included tiger lily roots, bitterroot, sunflower roots, yellow lily roots, and chocolate lily roots (**sa-qwa-aks**).

Traditionally, two principal cookery methods were preferred: boiling of foods with the use of hot stones, and pit steaming. The latter was done by digging a deep pit then layering it with hot rocks, grass, and the roots to be steamed, then packing over with earth, leaving a long stick buried down one side. This stick would later be pulled up to provide an airhole for all the layers. Rush mats or animal skins were used in sleeping, cooking, and eating, and even today many of these tribespeople prefer to sit on mats rather than chairs when eating.

INUIT NATIONS

The very name "Eskimo" conjures up visions of husky-dog teams and glistening igloos, furry parkas and mukluks, and vast drifts of blinding white snow whipped by howling winds. Actually, "Eskimo" was the name used by Europeans to represent the peoples they knew as "eaters of raw flesh." "Inuit" is the people's name for themselves and it means the "chosen and true people," while the singular form, "Inuk," means simply man.

The Inuit are scattered in the northern hemisphere from Greenland to Alaska and Siberia. They speak a single but complex language with six different dialects. Traditionally, they travel in search of food and live off the land with unparalleled skill.

Although the Inuit had had contact with Europeans as early as the 1500s, it was in the 1950s that the Europeans had the most shattering effect upon the tranquil Inuit lifestyle. With the sudden and rapid expansion of airlines, telecommunications, and settlements complete with homes, schools, stores, and even churches and hospitals, snowmobiles began replacing sled and dog teams, woolen clothing and rubber boots replaced traditional dress, permanent modest wooden homes replaced snowhouses and igloos and skin tents. Worse, sugar and tea, lard and flour quickly replaced much of the protein-filled meat/fish diet of the Inuit, and the serving of carbohydrate foods became almost a status symbol.

Today's Inuit live mainly in coastal areas, making forays inland primarily "to hunt caribou, or to fish in the lakes, to cut timber ... or to quarry soapstone for lamps and pots, returning always to the coast as their real home." The Inuit diet traditionally relied upon fish and sea mammals and land animals (depending upon the season), with small amounts of seaweed, sorrel leaves and other greens in the summer as well as berries and sometimes the partly digested greens from the stomach of land animals. Very occasionally some **ptarmigan** or ducks or small game animals supplemented the Inuit diet.

Raw meats and raw fish may occasionally have been nibbled as snack food or out of necessity, depending upon conditions, but traditionally, hot meat or fish, and the broths, was the usual fare. A soapstone pot simmering almost continuously over a seal-oil lamp with bubbling broth of meat or fish provided a warm and satisfying meal to anyone who was hungry. Specific hours or times of meals mean little to a people who never had timepieces and where, because of a Far North location, wintry nights sometimes last all day or summery evenings know no sunset. One ate or nibbled as hunger and food supply dictated.

Foods in excess of daily needs were always diligently preserved by freezing in caches, drying, smoking or preserving with oil bags made of seal skin called seal pokes. Fats were rendered for use in heating and lighting, some used for snacks and others used as a preservative for foods, such as seal meat or berries.

There seems to be little evidence of special festive or ceremonial foods as such. Special occasions were marked by an increase in the quantity of foods consumed and shared communally rather than by different types of foods. Some sources indicate that fermented berry juice was drunk to help mark special events.

Many Inuit have accepted Christianity yet still cling to beliefs in fortune-telling, the shaman, charms and amulets, inner spirits present in many objects. Traditional offerings of useful objects, such as tools or cooking utensils, indicate a belief in life after death.

The changes that have occurred in the traditional Inuit way of life have been so sudden and irreversible that today only the drifts of snow, howling winds, and all-too-brief northern summers remain aloof from the unrelenting clutch of 20th-century "civilization." As mentioned above, tea and flour, sugar and lard, together with canned and prepared food mixes have made tragic inroads into the traditional Inuit diet. Most foods are still boiled, most men still retain autonomy in their families, but increasingly the Inuit are suffering from obesity, acne

vulgaris, dental caries, diabetes, atherosclerosis, breast cancer, scurvy, and heart disease.

NORTHWEST TERRITORIES TRIBES

The nations of this area still live in dense forests and open tundra. They have a difficult life and experience many periods of food scarcity. All speak dialects of Athapaskan and are basically hunters and fishermen.

Caribou and salmon are the most important staples, but when available, other animals and fish are also used for foods: moose, buffalo, bear, musk ox, mountain goats, and sheep, and smaller animals. Very few vegetable foods are used. Occasionally berries, bulbs, and some tender spring shoots are enjoyed. Most foods were cooked by adding water and food to skin pouches then dropping in hot coals until the food was cooked to desired doneness. Fish and meats were also dried and stored in caches – high platforms built on poles. **Pemmican** preparation also served as a means of food preservation. In some areas sea mammals form an important part of the tribe's existence, both for food and skins: sea lions, sea otters, seals, and the beluga or white whale.

THE EASTERN WOODLANDS

Most of the nations inhabiting this region shared similar language and culture and lived in the area approximately from the Mississippi River and the western boundary of Ontario to the Atlantic coast. They were knowledgeable about the properties and uses of trees and plants: birch, beech, maple, basswood, elm, and ash. They made use of many wild foods, such as nuts and berries, fruits and wild rice, and prepared many medicines from flora. Except in the Far North, most practiced agriculture and raised corn, beans, tobacco, pumpkins, and squash, basing their survival on an intimate knowledge of natural resources.

The Algonquins were the first encountered by the European and also the first to disappear as a result of internecine war, disease, and intermarriage. It was from the Algonquins that the Europeans learned about crop cultivation and the taste and use of new foods. They also learned Indian words. Algonquins who were not involved in agriculture depended mainly on hunting and fishing and traveled as necessary for food supplies. These groups included the more northern nations.

Both the Ojibways and the Algonquins depended extensively on vegetable foods and on maple sugar and wild rice. Wild potatoes, wild onions, yellow water lily root, and milkweed, together with corn, beans, and squash formed the vegetable basics. The Winnebago steamed their corn in an underground pit filled with hot coals and alternate layers of corn and husks with just enough water added for steaming.

Women carried baskets to gather fruits and berries, wild herbs, and nuts: cranberries, gooseberries, Juneberries, cherries, chokecherries, black and red raspberries, grapes, butternuts, beechnuts, hazelnuts, white and pin oak acorns, hickory nuts. Wild rice was a staple food for the Woodland Nations and would be traditionally boiled and eaten with corn, beans, or squash and sometimes with meat, grease, or maple sugar added.

Fishing was a year-round occupation and often carried out by women, especially among the Chippewas. Fresh fish and various turtles would be eaten and the methods of preparation varied: spit-roasted, boiled, dried in the sun or over a slow fire, grilled, then smoked and dried and pounded into a powder that could be later added to cornmeal mush, or the fish could be added to cooking wild rice.

Deer, moose, fox, wolves, and some smaller animals would be the object of the hunt. The bear was never killed without a special apologetic ceremony, for the bear is much revered by the Woodland Nations. In fact hunting was treated with preliminary fasting and a sacrifice before the hunters entered the forest, and special charms would be carried for good luck and care taken to perfect the imitation of moose and deer calls. Reverence for animals was underlined in the need to treat even the remains of the game animals with deep respect by cleaning the bones and putting them in a special place.

Feast days were held to honor the first fruits, the first crops, or the first game killed by a young Aboriginal. Summer games and family gatherings were popular with the Micmacs, who also enjoyed lacrosse, a game similar to soccer, as well as dancing and storytelling and pipe smoking (in bowls made from lobster claws). The great spirit called *Po-Wah-Gen* or *Manido*, believed to inhabit everything, was offered first fruits or game as insurance for long life, good health, and safety.

For those who relied most on hunting, every part of the animal was used. The meats were prepared in pottery or metal pots, usually suspended on tripods over fires. In earliest times food was sometimes cooked by dropping hot coals directly into pots made from animal skins, stomachs, or bladders, which were then filled with water. If the food was not sufficiently cooked, more hot coals would be added. Meats would also be spit-roasted or dried over a fire or in the sun, then pounded and stored in birchbark containers. Grease would be rendered and used as a seasoning for rice and other foods; tallow would be rendered and made into soaps; bones pounded

into powder, then mixed with dried meat and grease, could be eaten at a later time uncooked. The leftovers would be carefully scattered as food for the dogs.

THE CREE NATION
The Cree follow similar food customs, and most Cree still maintain treasured traditions, more so than many other First Nations. They have a dislike for fishing, maintaining that it is "not worthy of a hunter or warrior." Some Cree, however, make practical use of fish: broth is prepared for infants, fish eggs are used in many ways and may even be blended with **bannock** dough, and a type of **pemmican** may be prepared from fish to be eaten with tea by trappers on the trail. Cree enjoy goose as a festive food and occasionally a bride and groom may eat bear meat.

THE WILD RICE PEOPLE
Wild rice has always been such an important staple to the Menomini that this nation became known as the Wild Rice People. According to their tradition, they believe the rice to be a gift of the "Underneath Beings."

To collect the wild rice, men pole canoes while the women and children share the task of knocking the ripened grain into the canoes, each family taking care to remain within their own rice area. As with fruits and game, the first collection of rice is cooked and enjoyed with great ceremony by all as an expression of thanks. Traditionally, after the gathering, rice is cleaned and dried in the sun. Then men wearing special "ricing mocassins" dance on the rice until finally it is separated from the chaff and ready to be stored.

THE BEAR
The bear has always been important to most of the Woodland Nations, but especially so to the Chippewas. For them the bear meat could only be eaten after specific rituals and ceremonies, the last of which would include the cooking of the bear's head, which had been sitting on a high scaffold for three days. Porcupine skins would be used to store the bear oil and grease, while strips of the bear meat were also preserved by storing them in some of the oil.

Maple sugar and maple syrup were also important to the Chippewas, as the principal part of their diet for almost a month in the springtime, and an important item for barter.

THE CARIBOU
For the Naskapi, the caribou was of prime importance and much formalized ritual was attached to

every aspect of the hunt, the kill, and the communal meals. Most interesting, one man's kill of caribou, valued so highly, was nonetheless ceremoniously and proudly divided into piles of meat and hide and shared with each of his hunting companions. Even today, the communal meal is an extension of this principle of sharing: all or none will be hungry. The communal meal of the caribou, called *mokoshan*, was designed to please the spirit of the animal and ensure future hunting success.

The ensuing ritual traditionally began with long bones placed on an outdoor scaffold, followed with elaborate routines of scraping meat from the skin, preparing a broth, crushing bones and marrow in preparation for a paste to be cooked, then freezing it in the snow for later eating. Men customarily ate first, followed by women and children. The traditional ritual of the *mokoshan* sometimes took twelve hours, ending with the throwing of bone splinters into the fire as a final gesture to the caribou spirit.

THE IROQUOIS

In the early 1600s, the settlements of the Hurons were graphically described as "stockaded villages in a fertile land." The people themselves were described as "content with what they have," living basically on corn and red beans. Soups, meal, and bread doughs could all be prepared from corn, with the addition of fruits, fish, or meats, with fat considered to be a delicacy. In fact, the Iroquoians, "alone among the Indians of Canada, seldom had fear of famine."

There was always an abundance of game and fish in the forests and lakes, and the fertile land that produced corn and many vegetables, as well as wild fruits and nuts, also yielded sugar and syrup from both maple and birch trees. Cultivated crops included corn, beans, squash, artichokes, tobacco, and pumpkin. Sunflower seeds were used to make oil as a condiment for certain foods and also as a cosmetic. Oils pressed from walnuts and hickory nuts formed a thick buttery cream also used with foods. Bear grease was used the way the European used butter.

Corn, the principal crop and staple food of the Iroquois, was roasted or steamed and eaten as corn on the cob. Cobs were also buried and allowed to ferment, then eaten as a treat. Hominy, succotash (a cooked mixture of corn and beans), and popcorn were all known and enjoyed. Corn ground into fine meal or coarse flour was used for breads and for thickening and flavoring soups and stews. It could also be dried together with meats, and these, with stored fats, provided good winter fare.

Some Iroquoians ate two meals a day, others one main meal. But for most it seems that food was at hand and eating when desired was the accepted custom. Skulls of old graves show that the Iroquoians had poor teeth (most other First Nations had excellent teeth) and this may be because of their use of soft-cooked foods, sugars, and syrups.

As with other Aboriginals, religion was traditionally part of daily life and the belief in spirits existing within nature (trees, rivers, rocks), as well as a Chief of all Good Spirits and a Chief of all Bad Spirits, was common. Interpretations of dreams and omens, and the importance of thankfulness, prayers, and fasting were and, in some cases, still are, all part of the lifestyle. Occasionally, wild turkeys would be part of festive meals; more often black bears would be penned and fattened for special feasts. **Sagamite**, the ubiquitous corn soup, formed a traditional part of every feast, together with dishes prepared from clams, fish, and turtles. Sagamite, to this day, forms the central dish of any Iroquoian occasion.

Traditional mid-winter ceremonials were preceded by several days of fasting (eating no foods); then Sacred Ceremonies followed, at which time animal meats – sometimes including fattened dogs as well as bears – would be ceremoniously prepared and shared, to be followed by sagamite, other meats, and breads. Other festivals were associated with crops and first fruits and even the successful collection of wild berries.

Among the most important of the festivals was the Feast of the Dead, which was held at 10- to12-year intervals. This solemn time would be celebrated by disinterment of corpses from temporary graves: flesh and skin would be stripped from the bones and burned, then the bones would be buried in a mass burial ground. Accompanied by great lamentations and tears, these tasks would be undertaken in the belief that the soul would take flight after the great ceremony ended. Long processions, bearing the bones to the burial area, would be followed by speeches and distribution of foods.

Keen agriculturalists with unique social and political patterns, the Iroquoians were "much superior in cultural development to all other Aboriginals with the possible exception of the Haida in B.C." They valued and practiced charity and hospitality and often welcomed large groups of impoverished peoples, even portioning land to them.

THE PLAINS (PRAIRIE) TRIBES

There were few animals that these tribes would not eat, but they were mainly dependent on the bison or buffalo. Some groups avoided fish. The Blackfoot considered bear too sacred to use as food. Others disdained dogs as food except for special occasions. The nourishing buffalo meat could be used fresh, or dried and powdered, and could even be preserved for years if necessary.

In fact, the uses of the buffalo were staggering in their variety and ingenuity. Not only was every part of the flesh and offal converted to food (fresh or dried), but the hides were used for blankets, bedding, clothing, wigwams, and furniture. Skins were stretched and treated for use as bridles, thongs, saddles, and lassos. Horns were shaped into spoons, ladles, and drinking cups. Bones were used for their marrow, which could also be dried and stored, or crushed and boiled to collect fat, which would be skimmed off and stored in animal bladders. Dried sinews could be used as threads for garments or for bow strings. Feet and hooves were boiled to extract glue. Even tail hairs were useful as a brush to kill flies and mosquitoes.

Buffalo meat was also used in making **pemmican**. It takes great skill to prepare pemmican. Large thin sheets of flesh are hung to dry over open fires, with the sun speeding the drying process. The dried and smoked sheets are then pounded into a powder and mixed with marrow fat, then packed into strong skin bags and sewn with sinews. The dried strips of meat are called **jerky**. Sometimes dried fruits, such as chokecherries or **saskatoomin** (blueberries) may be added to the **pemmican** mixture before storing.

Elk, deer, sheep, bear, wild fowl, and many varieties of fish supplemented the staple bison. Some tribes used wild rice and vegetables when available. Most groups enjoyed chokecherries, serviceberries, red willow berries, prairie turnips, **wild rose haws**, **bitterroot**, as well as the wild lily bulbs called **camas**.

Nearly all the Plains Nations shared similar beliefs concerning great spirits present in all things, especially the spirit Napi, the Old Man. Shamanism, charms, amulets, dreams, and magic were all an important part of daily life.

Traditionally hospitality has always been extended to anyone coming in peace. Common welcoming phrases include *ta-ta-wah*, meaning "There is always room for you," and *kes-poo*, meaning "May it satisfy you" or "refresh you." The importance of hospitality is underlined by the formalized three-step ritual customarily followed. Strangers are commonly called "cousin" or "brother-in-law," and are bidden first to share a smoke together, then speak to others present and, finally, share in food. In fact, the high point of most celebrations is the free distribution of foods that have been communally prepared. Refusal of hospitality or eating sparingly is considered rude.

QUEBEC

Quebec may be described as the area in Canada "where ancient France lingers," but it has attained a heritage and tradition distinctly its own. Modern growth and development, economics and politics may intrude but cannot erase the deeply rooted evidence: whitewashed stone houses, Roman Catholic churches with belfries and spires, outdoor bake ovens and wayside shrines, and most of all, the sense of home and family that is distinctly Quebecois.

The vitality of ancestral traditions coupled with isolation both from France and from the English in Canada served to direct Quebec on an independent course where often the spoken word, preserved in traditions of lore and songs and folk tales, as well as homey recipes passed from mother to daughter, made the oral tradition more important than the written word.

The food traditions of Quebec date back more than 350 years and are known for their richness: abundant eggs and meats, fresh rich cream and sugary maple syrup laced through a diet of plenty. The staple harvests of the early pioneers of corn, barley, oats, peas, lentils, beans, and asparagus combined with the plentiful game and fish. Potatoes (called "root") were not too popular in early times, but maize, adopted from the First Nations, became an important mainstay: coal-roasted and eaten off the cob; as a hearty stew with game or fish; ground into flour for pancakes and some breads; or as **sagamite**, a soup made from corn flour, dried fish, and dried peas. The mashed maize could be frozen and kept throughout the winter, often forming the base of the now-famed **habitant pea soup**. Abundant wild fruits were carefully picked and preserved as jams and jellies, relishes and compotes. Probably dating back to the basic stores of the *filles du rois* of the 1600s, salt pork is considered to be the mainstay of Quebec cuisine.

In fact, the traditional foods of Quebec and their method of preparation represent their history well. They blend English foods such as salt pork, beans and peas, molasses and spices, and many puddings and pies together with traditional favorites from France with dishes learned from the Aboriginals and culled from the new lands. From the traditional black cast-iron kettle came **pot-au-feu**: beef cooked in water with root vegetables and served with homemade bread; **soupe aux quatorze affaires**: pea soup with the main ingredients of corn, bread chips, salt, and butter; the **bouilli**: early vegetables simmered with chicken; **feves au lard**: simmered beans with pork.

Sugary fruit desserts and recipes with maple syrup abound in the repertoire of any Quebecois kitchen, for the "French love sweets." Cakes of maple sugar were stocked by the earliest colonists to last from one spring to the next. Syrup-drenched cakes and pies, butters and endless confections, as well as specialties such as **grand-peres au sirop**: dumplings served with maple syrup; **les toquettes**: hot maple syrup sprinkled on the snow to form a hard candy; eggs poached in maple syrup; chickens prepared with maple syrup; and servings of pancakes, bacon, and bread – all doused generously with maple syrup. Finally, the irresistible **beurree de sucre d'erable**: fresh heavy cream poured over inch-thick crusty fresh bread, then sprinkled with crushed maple sugar and topped with seasonal fresh berries.

For a people whose lives center around home and church, it is not surprising that the calendar is happily dotted with festive occasions. Although traditionally, "family life is lived in a world of rules, the definitions of which are taken from the Church's teachings," the rules for festivities take into account the joys of family and friends and good foods.

Christmas menus vary only slightly according to local traditions and family specialties, but most include a Christmas Eve – *Reveillon* – buffet of assorted pickled vegetables, breads and biscuits, soup or stew and, especially **tourtiere**: a savory thick pie of minced pork; **spate** (also called **six-pates**, **cipaille**, and **sea-pie**): a pie or casserole made with several pastry layers filled with game birds or other meats. Both of these dishes may be eaten hot or cold and served, sometimes alone, with homemade wines or coffee as the sole dish of the *Reveillon*. Another favorite traditional dish is **cretons**: a pork pate made from the crispy residues of rendered lard, sprinkled with spices (cloves, garlic, and cinnamon), and stored by covering with fat.

The festive Christmas meal ends with maple syrup desserts of dumplings or pies and cakes, a **buche de Noel** (chocolate-coated cake shaped like a Christmas log), tea, coffee, or milk. For many the traditional Christmas Eve sweet is the **Quebec apple dumplings**: whole apples stuffed with mincemeat, covered with pastry, and baked with butter, brown sugar, and cream, then served warm with rum-flavored cream.

Winter Carnival takes place before Lent begins and abounds in hearty dishes, such as roast pork loin with apples, thick pea soup with ham bone, roasted fowl with mashed potato stuffing, bread soup, spicy gingerbread, roasted and buttered squash or fried pumpkin, and of course, crusty breads baked in outdoor ovens.

Weddings and baptisms, Lent, Easter, autumn harvest, Christmas and winter carnival all embrace the best of cookery and the generous hospitality so typical of Quebec. Typical too is the Saturday night supper of home-baked beans with pork, served with brown bread, and the resulting Sunday breakfast of pork and beans.

GLOSSARY OF FOODS AND FOOD TERMS

Note: You will recognize many "Canadian" dishes in glossaries for English, Scottish, and Irish foods, as well as other ethnocultural groups.

Acointa: the hulls of dried peas or corn boiled with meat or fish to make a soup. An Iroquoian specialty.

Agutuk: Inuit "ice cream" made from various ingredients which may include whipped fats (caribou, moose, or edible beef tallow), fish, sugar, berries.

Andataroni: Iroquoian name for quickly prepared breads made from crushed, dried grain (corn) mixed with warm water, then baked by wrapping in corn husks. If no husks are available, the dough is washed after baking to remove charred particles. Sometimes cooked beans or small berries are added.

Bannock: a name of Scottish origin generally used for the many quick breads prepared by the Aboriginals from flour, salt, baking powder, and any fat. May be cooked in a pan over an open fire or oven-baked.

Blubber: the common Inuit name for the 4 to 5 inches of fat taken from a whale. Easily rendered, it is valued for fuel and light, used in cooking or as is. Sometimes fresh chunks are secured with a string to a baby's toe and offered as a pacifier.

Brewis: the Scottish name given to **hardtack**, a type of biscuit or bread with superior keeping qualities. May be used as is, or soaked then scrambled into soups, stews, or fish dishes. Popular in the Atlantic provinces as well as in Canada's North. (See also **Fish and Brewis**)

Bakeapples or **Bagh Apples**: native Newfoundland berry of a peach-apricot flavor; available fresh or canned.

Baked Cod's Tongues: Newfoundland dish of cod's tongues soaked in milk then rolled in crumbs and baked.

Berryhocky: a hot festive drink of berry juice spiked with rum. A favorite in Newfoundland.

"Canadian" Bacon: smoked back bacon, usually quite lean.

Chevreuil des Guides: a Quebec hunter's dish of well-seasoned deer meat cooked with beans and beer or ale.

Chow or **Chow Chow**: slow-simmered tomatoes and onions spiced with sugar, vinegar, cinnamon, and mixed pickling spice. A staple on every P.E.I. table. Islanders enjoy **chow** with almost any main dish, cold plate, or sandwich.

Cipate (**Cipaille, Six-Pates**, or **Sea-Pie**): pie or casserole of three pastry layers filled with cooked game or fowl and oven-baked.

Coinkia: Iroquoian specialty of twin dough balls wrapped in leaves then boiled rather than baked.

Cretons: Quebec dish of crisp pork cracklings spiced then stored in rendered lard and eaten as a pâté.

Croquignoles: twisted fried doughnuts dusted with icing sugar and served traditionally during Quebec's Christmas holidays.

Dutch Mess (**Hugger-in-Buff, Fish and Scrunchions**, or **House Bankin**): Nova Scotian dish of codfish and potatoes with browned onions, garnished with **scrunchions** (crunchy bits remaining after pork fat is rendered).

Eschionque: thick porridge made from fine meal of dried powdered corn and eaten with fat on top. An Iroquoian specialty.

Estoqua: the Iroquoian wooden paddle used to stir continuously (to prevent scorching) any pot or corn meal.

Fanikaneekins: in Nova Scotia, the German name used to describe "fried bread" or french toast: stale bread that is dipped in egg and milk then fried in butter or lard and served with syrup or preserves.

Fiddleheads: the young curled shoots of bracken or fern fronds just as they appear aboveground. Cooked lightly and served with butter, they taste much like asparagus.

Figgie Duff: Newfoundland dish of salt meat and vegetables cooked by suspending in a cloth bag in water.

Fish and Brewis: Newfoundland dish of soaked, drained hard bread (**Brewis**) served with boiled salt cod, or boiled fresh cod, then topped with scrunchions.

Fish Cakes: Prince Edward Island speciality of mashed potatoes blended with flaked cooked fish then made into patties and pan-fried.

Galette de Sarasin: Quebec buckwheat pancakes.

Gourgane: a Quebec dish of large flat beans used fresh as a vegetable in summer and served dried and cooked in the winter.

Grand-Peres: large dumplings cooked and served in Quebec maple syrup.

Grunt, Slump, or **Fungy**: Nova Scotian dish of stewed, sweetened fruit to which dumplings are added. Often served as a meal.

Herbs Salees: Quebec garden-fresh herbs layered in salt and packed in jars to preserve them.

Leindohy: Huron delicacy of small heads of corn fermented for several months in stagnant water or pits.

Les Toquettes: Quebec name for candied maple syrup cooled and hardened on ice or snow.

Muktuk: the outer covering of the white (beluga) whale including the white skin (1 to 2 inches thick) and the pink layer below. Usually eaten fresh after the kill, raw. Tender-crisp texture with flavor resembling fresh coconut. An Inuit specialty.

Oka Cheese: a strong pungent cheese prepared in Quebec by Trappist monks.

Ottet: Iroquoian cornmeal "mush" cooked with the wholegrain pounded and flavored with a little meat or fish.

Ouananiche: small freshwater salmon of delicate flavor from Quebec.

Pain Perdu Canadienne: dry bread or rolls are milk-dipped then egged and crumbled and butter-fried and served with a dusting of cinnamon and accompanied by maple syrup or fruit jellies. In honor of St. Anthony, served in Quebec.

Pate a la rapure or **Rappie Pie**: a type of pie with a top and bottom "crust" of whipped potatoes filled with cooked chicken meat. Common in Nova Scotia and New Brunswick.

Pate aux Bucardes (Acadian Clam Pie): New Brunswick dish of clams and onions baked on a biscuit dough and served hot with coleslaw.

Pate en Pate Acadienne: Acadian meat pie prepared from layers of uncooked mixed meats, potatoes, and biscuit dough, moistened with broth and topped with more dough then baked in a very slow oven for 4 to 5 hours. Served traditionally for Christmas.

Posies, Toddies, Toutons (or **Gandies** in Labrador): fresh bread dough formed in buns and fried till golden in pork fat and scrunchions.

Pot-au-Feu: a French method of making soup that provides a meal of soup, meat and vegetables. Each of these are served separately.

Poutines: potato dumplings served with the juice of the boiled dumplings or with molasses. Originally German, but a Nova Scotian speciality.

Poutines Rapees: New Brunswick "meat and potato pie" consisting of dumplings made of grated potatoes with a fried-crisp salt pork cube in the center. Eaten with wild-berry jam, sausages, or buttered cabbage, after slow two-hour simmering.

Pumpkin Soup: a puree of pumpkin stirred into a flavorful consomme base. Old Quebec specialty.

Sagamite: Iroquoian corn soup.

Salt Cod and Pork Scraps: Prince Edward Island traditional dish of salt cod and pork combined with potatoes, rutabagas, and onions.

Sarriete: one of the most frequently used herbs in Quebec cookery. Savory.

Scotch Cheese: cubed cheese and sliced onions baked in an egg/milk custard and eaten hot or cold. The Nova Scotian coal miners' dish.

Simnel Cake: a rich fruit-filled cake layered with almond paste. Traditional English cake made in Nova Scotia for "Mothering Sunday."

Solomon Gundy: Lunenburg (Nova Scotia) dish of herring pickled in vinegar and onions.

Sourdough: pastry fermented mixture of flour and water. A small amount is used as a leavening agent for any bread-type mixture and a small amount is always retained to begin the fermentation of the next batch.

Spruce Beer: old Loyalist brew from New Brunswick of boiled spruce wood sweetened with molasses and fermented with yeast then drunk as a beer after a few days of fermenting.

Switchel: Nova Scotian drink made from water, brown sugar, molasses, and spiced with vinegar and ginger then chilled.

Tourlouche d'Erable: rich Quebec cake served upside down and topped with maple syrup and walnuts then served with cold rich cream.

Tourtiere: traditional Reveillon (Christmas Eve) "pie" of seasoned minced pork baked in a double pastry crust and served warm or cold.

Turr or **Murre**: plentiful Newfoundland seabird, shot and eaten in season.

CHAPTER 12

Chilean. See Latin American

CHINESE

There is a pervasive sense of timelessness in everything Chinese. About one-quarter of the world's population – more than 1,221,591,778 – live in China. The Chinese emerged from a blend of many races and groups and theirs is considered to be one of the oldest civilizations extant, dating back more than 4,000 years. Their culture is firmly and deeply rooted in the history of their earth.

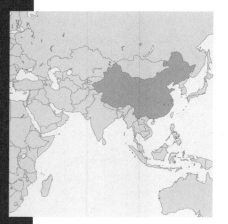

Dynasties and kingdoms, religions and philosophies, droughts and floods came and went, but one element in China remained steadfast: the humble peasantry. Long before invaders mounted their chariots or nomadic tribes saddled their horses, the peoples of Northern China tended their crops of millet, rice, and barley, and shepherded their flocks of sheep. Earliest evidence of rice cultivation dates back to 1800 B.C.E. By communal effort, fields were irrigated, tripod cooking pots of earthenware were constructed, and wine was made from fermented millet. Despite increasing numbers of invasions and political turmoil, the agrarian lifestyle of the Northerners – tending cattle as well as pigs, dogs, and hens, rearing silkworms, making plain white pottery, cultivating intense devotion to family – remained relatively undisturbed.

The earliest recorded period of Chinese history is sketchily referred to as the Shang Kingdom, some time before 2000 B.C.E. The people were late Stone Age Chinese whose communal efforts were in many ways superior to those of the primitive tribes and peoples around them. This kingdom was overrun by rough tribesmen from the West, and began China's longest dynasty: the Zhou Dynasty. It was in this period (1027-256 B.C.E.) that the plow and chopsticks were introduced, and the people called themselves "Central Nation," thus distinguishing themselves from the other peoples to whom they referred as "Barbarians." It must be noted, however,

that this distinction was cultural rather than political and it was actually by cultural influences (not domination or wars) that many of the bordering communities became gradually incorporated into the Zhou Dynasty. The Zhou evolved a feudal pattern of agriculture, traded with Turkestan for jade, and celebrated important agrarian seasonal rituals. Their ruler designated spring by ceremoniously turning the soil with a jade hoe and marked winter by making sacrifices to heaven.

The overthrow of the Zhou Dynasty signified a shift from central authority to the stronger peripheral regions and began a period of almost continuous warfare aptly called the Warring States Period (481-256 B.C.E.). To add to their miseries, nomadic invaders were such a relentless source of turmoil to the warring agrarian states that antagonism towards nomadic peoples has been a feature of Chinese thought ever since.

But as so often occurs in history, out of the darkest times come some of the greatest cultural achievements. So it was that while warriors battled amongst themselves and with nomadic invaders, peasants tilled fields and tended flocks and great minds began to philosophize on the meaning of man's existence. The period 550-280 B.C.E. was the era of prophets in Palestine, Zarathustra in Persia, Homer and Plato and Heraclitus in Greece, Buddha and Jina in India, and Confucius and Lao-tzu in the Central Nation.

"You know so little of the world, how can you concern yourself with spirits?" It was with such words that Confucius, the most influential of all Chinese philosophers, laid the groundwork of moral and ethical codes that exhorted humankind to concern itself with earthly matters and human relationships, yet at the same time not to deny the existence of spirits. It was Lao-tzu, reputedly the founder of Taoism, who taught followers the gentle philosophy of "Tao, the Way": a path of righteous living leading to happiness and peace of mind.

The period from 221-206 B.C.E. was the short but very influential rule of the Qin Dynasty, during which the Great Wall of China was built. This dynasty replaced feudalistic states with official-ruled commanderies and also began the first of several "literary inquisitions" in China's history by burning both books and scholars. Paradoxically, this was also the period that saw the establishment of standardized character writing or ideoforms. Thus was laid the cornerstone of Chinese culture: a method of written communication understandable to every citizen, regardless of dialect in spoken language. To this day it is the tie that culturally binds all peoples on whom the Chinese have had influence: Japanese, Korean, Vietnamese, and much of the rest of Southeast Asia. And though the Chinese themselves have never used the name "China" (as mentioned above, they called themselves "Central Nation"), it is from the Qin Dynasty that the name China originates.

Yet it was the Han Dynasty that was destined to be proudest of all. Even today among the many peoples who form the People's Republic of China, which includes the Mongols, Uighurs, and Tibetans as well as the Hui (Han peoples of the Muslim faith), the main body of the Chinese distinguish themselves as Han.

To the reforms begun by the brief Qin Dynasty were added the books of Confucius called "The Classics," as well as a stable political structure destined to last for 2,000 years. In fact, the features and conditions of the Han Dynasty made it possible to speak of Chinese people and Chinese culture. Furthermore, it was, a system in many ways superior to those of its neighbors, and hence became China's influence outward. The system was to remain largely unchanged until the arrival of the Europeans in the early 1500s C.E.

Perhaps most important, the firmly entrenched characteristics of the Han period were responsible for China's difficulty in adapting to modern times. China's ruling minority was chosen by competitive examinations based on The Classics of Confucius. While this principle made people regard education solely as a means to advancement, it also stifled creative, and particularly scientific, thought. Traditionally, any independence in the middle class or signs of liberalism in the commercial class that did not serve the ends of this ruling minority were persecuted and exterminated.

This is not to say that technological achievements were not important during this period. Indeed, it was at this time that the Chinese devised gunpowder, porcelain, paper money, and a simple seismograph, as well as complex irrigation schemes, techniques of slope-terracing, the use of animal droppings for fertilizer, and the wheelbarrow with its simple central wheel. In fact, as early as the first century, they had developed a harness that did not interfere with an animal's breathing, thus enabling animals to be used for draft.

Conquests of Vietnam and Korea, around 1000 B.C.E., introduced tea to China first as a medicine and later as a pleasing beverage. In turn, Chinese character writing was adopted by Korea and Vietnam and later introduced into Japan.

Between 1000 and 700 B.C.E., the age of poetry with Li Bai and Du Fu flourished, tolerance and interest in religions spread, and at the same time a new invention was changing peoples' eating habits: the stone roller. Rice had been the staple food of the people of the South and was planted wherever possible in the North, but the new stone roller made wheat more popular and more practical as a crop for the North China Plain. The wheat flour was prepared into doughs to form noodles, steamed buns and dumplings with many types of fillings, as well as lacy pancakes to enfold tidbits of meats, fish, and/or vegetables.

Tea drinking first appeared in China after the conquests of Vietnam and Korea but it is believed that the practice originated in ancient Tibet. It was during the 700s C.E. that Lu Yu wrote his classic *Ch'a Ching*, which describes every detail of tea from its cultivation to its ritual preparation. Lu Yu's writing probably led to the national acceptance of tea as a beverage. To this day Mongolians still use the method of pressing dried tea leaves into bricks and breaking off pieces as needed then boiling in water, which was the popular method in Lu Yu's time. It was about

FOODS COMMONLY USED

The traditional Chinese diet is confined almost entirely to plant foods. The staples of grains, legumes, and vegetables exist as such for the simple reason of economy. Imagination, necessity, and ingenuity have made satisfying and delectable dishes from a wide range of seeds, roots, tubers, and plants of many kinds. Rice is produced more readily in the South, hence it is the southern staple. Northern climates favor wheat production, so wheat flour made into noodles and steamed pastries are staples of the North. Traditionally, 98 percent of the diet is of plant origin, while only 2 percent is of animal or fish origin. Regional specialties and foods of minority groups represent interesting departures from usual daily menus. Seasonings are often limited but used deftly to enhance and add variety to natural food flavors. Cooking techniques also help to make similar foods taste and look different. Local rice wines and many varieties of teas are the common beverages.

300 years later (Sung Dynasty, 960-1280 C.E.) that the method of preparing tea by whisking powdered tea with hot water evolved. The Japanese continue to use this method in the honored classic tea ceremony and for preparation of rare teas. An abridgement of Lu Yu's classic text by Chen Chien in 1475 led to the ritual steeping of tea, popular in most of the world today.

There was never any defined period of stagnation in Chinese history but there was a period of general languidness (about 900 C.E.) when educated men grew long fingernails (indicating their disdain for manual labor) and contented themselves with watching a flower unfold while women hobbled about on tiny bound feet. But, as always, the stalwart masses tended fields and flocks and minded the voice of their fathers while their lives spun out in unremitting labor.

While it is said that "the enquiring mind died with the Sung Dynasty," it was then that the southward-pointing compass needle was invented, the abacus was used for counting, and acupuncture developed into a fine art of healing. Cities boasted clean streets, pure water, and even public bathhouses for the poor. Many varieties of tea and rice were readily available and delicate fruits were sent from distant provinces, packed in ice for city markets. Families enjoyed outdoor picnics and restaurant dining and wealthy homes boasted tiled walls and floors, and many servants.

The fall of the Mongol Empire (1200s to mid-1300s) brought population growth but also famine, peasant revolts, and the emergence of secret societies. The Ming Dynasty (1368-1644) came after the fall of the Mongol Empire. Having successfully overthrown the Mongol invaders, the Chinese, more convinced than ever of their cultural superiority, made isolationism a policy of the entire Ming period. They felt that their own culture was the ultimate, neither willing to give nor needing to take anything from the rest of the world. But this tradition would not last long either, for the clash with the great European naval powers was yet to come.

The Portuguese were the first to reach China by sea, settling in the port of Macao in the late 1400s and establishing an enviable system of trade that was to last 300 years, despite competition from other sea powers, particularly the Dutch and the British. Oranges, peaches, limes, and coriander, but mainly huge shipments of tea, filled the holds of Portuguese ships and gave Europe a taste of China. Jesuit priests entered Macao with the Portuguese and made their way to Peking (Beijing), the capital city, and later became allies of the Manchus who were to overthrow the Ming Dynasty in the mid-1600s.

Evidence of faltering strength of the great Han-inspired tradition began to show with the establishment of strict Manchu rule: contacts with the West were to be only religious or commercial; all Chinese males were forced to braid their long hair into a single pigtail or queue. By the early 1700s the Manchu influence had spread over China, Mongolia, Manchuria, Turkestan, Formosa (Taiwan), and Tibet. Paradoxically, in time, the Manchus themselves were to become "more Chinese than the Chinese," as a result of their eager adoption of Chinese culture.

A combination of factors inevitably and gradually led to a period of downfall. China's clash with European ideas and powers coincided with the end of the orderly Confucian system that had characterized the 2,000-year influence of the Han Dynasty. Savage wars, famines, floods, and widespread poverty were bad enough, but huge population increases dealt the final blow. Lack of arable land led to measures that attempted to increase the intensity of cultivation: new crops were introduced such as groundnuts, maize, and sweet potatoes, and the new technique of market-gardening was used wherever feasible. But the extraordinary increase of population density led to a sharp decline in living standards as well as an increasing problem of the middle society of minor officials and impoverished gentry who now saw diminishing opportunities. Moreover, strengthened in their ideals and resolve by previous minor revolts, their worsening living conditions led to renewed and more vigorous revolts of the once-placid peasants. The Manchus repressed the peasant revolts and blamed their troubles on the most convenient scapegoat: the foreigners.

The antiquated rigidity of the Confucian order proved not only inadequate but stultifying in the face of the machine age and industrial revolution occurring in the West. There was no middle class, no bureaucratic freedom, no liberation of new energy sources. The tragedy of the loss of millions of lives when the Yellow River changed its course was added to the humiliation of Hong Kong ceding to Britain in 1842 and British and French forces daring to enter Peking (Beijing). The rumblings of the T'ai P'ing Rebellion, then the Sino-Japanese War of 1894-1895, exploded in 1900 into the Boxer Rebellion, out of which the seeds for change began to sprout.

Into this confused, chaotic, and humiliating environment, rife with corruption and revolt, came Sun Yat-Sen, who cut off his queue as an act of defiance against the Manchus. He attempted to cure his country by making China into a republic. Meanwhile, western ideas of free enterprise and pursuit of personal profit gained ground as the Chinese became involved in world trade, which in turn led to the growth of a new middle class: the merchants. It was this group who strongly questioned the old Confucian order and patriarchal hierarchy. In fact, the claim that 'all men are equal' shook the very foundation on which the Confucian edifice rested.

Chiang Kai-shek (married to the sister of Sun Yat-sen's widow) helped foster the new national spirit and increasing westernization, but seemed blind to the desperate plight of the once stable peasantry. Increased Japanese aggression to China and the seeming inertia of Chiang Kai-shek's government stirred the growing spirit of Chinese Communists in Yenan, whose leader, Mao Zedong (Tse-tung), perceived that the peasantry holds the key position in all Asiatic countries. He determined to sinicize Marxism, took the slogan "Chinese do not fight Chinese," and proved the validity of his ideals when he proclaimed the People's Republic of China on October 1, 1949.

At the time, there were four distinct divisions of the Chinese populace. Mainland China, or the People's Republic of China, was politically separate from the China of Taiwan, which has been regarded both as a puppet of the United States and as a bastion of the Chinese nationalists. Both are also politically distinct from the Chinese populace of Hong Kong, then under British rule and now returned to Chinese sovereignty and most influenced by the West. Yet it remains the area in which most of the old flavor of Chinese traditions was retained. The fourth division consists of overseas Chinese. These include the many early emigrants who left China in the 1800s to seek their fortune in Canada, the United States, and Australia, as well as countries the world over. Their dream was to return home one day, but for various reasons they stayed on to become citizens of these countries.

Nonetheless, no matter where the Chinese may be located in the world and no matter what their position or profession, they still view Mainland China as the source and center of their great culture. There have been changes in the past and there will be changes in the future, but despite this, the timelessness and continuity that are China's heritage cannot be extinguished.

DOMESTIC LIFE

The success of Chinese culture throughout history lies partly in the country's adaptation of differing values to Chinese values and the view that allegiance to the state was simply an extension of the age-old allegiance to family. More than 2,000 years of Confucian values cannot be removed readily, but adaptation is possible and and this happens both in Mainland China and wherever the Chinese make their homes.

Traditionally, it was always Hsiao-filial piety or family duty that dominated life in China. Certain factors were common to all segments of society. Age demanded and received the respect and submission of youth. Women had no equality with men, and each extended family unit was autonomous in all life decisions such as education, religion, and festival observances, social organization, and economic activity. The Chinese view of society contrast with the Western world view. It is composed of families rather than individuals. One of the most treasured values is family harmony, and all family activities are responsibly disciplined to achieve this goal.

Overseas and Hong Kong families blend western ideals and values with their own traditions. The "new way" changes occurring in Mainland China during the Marxist period include: love matches replacing arranged marriages; family devotion replacing state authority and devotion to society's welfare; a leveling of opportunities for women; and increased status and opportunity as well as living standards for the ordinary person. To achieve this, the Marxists felt it was necessary to overcome "the respect for the intellectual elite who kept the masses on the edge of survival for literally thousands of years."

The traditional Chinese respect (bordering on reverence) for the scholar can be understood more clearly when the Chinese view of scholars is clarified. Because traditionally, prestigious posts were attained by competition in government exams of The Classics, education became synonymous with an elite upper class. Once the post was attained, election of family members to influential positions followed (familial piety). A family's sacrifice to educate one promising member could pay off and benefit all. Ideally, any son could aspire to such a role no matter what his origins. Even today this principle of family sacrifice to aid one talented member is a large part of Chinese practice.

THE TRADITIONAL LIFESTYLE

About one-fifth of the population of China today live in modest but modern accommodations in cities. But a look into the traditional homes and lifestyles, especially the "courtyard system," is significant to a basic understanding of life in China. Typical northern farmhouses were built of sun-dried bricks or pounded earth, because wood was too expensive and scarce. Houses were closely integrated around courtyards with the main living area facing south so that the warming rays of the sun could be caught. The few windows faced only to the inside of the courtyard and were covered by translucent oiled papers. To discourage thieves, no windows would be visible from the outside of the compounds. This system was widely copied in other lands because of its efficiency and practicality.

In part, aspects of a dwelling including placement of rooms, doors, windows, and even the most propitious direction for the front to face are based in great part on *Feng Shui* (Wind Water.) This theory preserved in Chinese *Feng Shui*, a spirit of sacred reverence for the divine powers of nature. Based on the 12th and 13th centuries C.E. teachings of Chu Hsi, *Feng Shui* men of today are consulted on every aspect from the site of a home to the rearrangement of existing rooms, windows, doors, and even mirrors to deflect evil spirits and conform to local currents of Wind Water.

Most courtyard homes consisted of a kitchen and separate living-bedroom called the *kang* room, so named because of the fire-heated brick platform in the center of the floor. Families always sat and slept with feet towards the warming *kang*. Generally, furnishings would be kept to the barest necessities. The privy building and the water well were located outside in the courtyard. Pigs, chickens, and draft animals were housed in a stable nearest the kitchen area.

The kitchen area of the courtyard home is of utmost importance Since fuel is scarce and expensive, classic Chinese cookery methods demand that all food be bite-size for quick cooking and all preparation be done before cooking begins. Simple, utilitarian utensils (still in use today) are stored on open shelves or hung on walls.

Many families in Mainland China still live in such traditional homes. But though others may enjoy more modern accommodations, kitchens are still the center of practicality since, even in cities, one kitchen may have to do for three families, even though they may have the convenience of gas or electricity to replace small fire-braziers.

Housing and facilities vary according to location. Yenan and Shensi people still make their homes in caves dug in the loess cliffs, yet some of these now have electricity. In Mongolia, people live in yurts: strong tents made of layers of felt supported on a lattice frame and anchored with ropes. In the center of smoothed earthen floors a stone area is set apart for fires made with dried dung, and a central chimney carries the smoke upwards. Many people in the South live in primitive huts thatched with palm, while others live in bamboo homes. And many other families make their homes aboard houseboats, eating and sleeping on the bobbing waters.

Most important of all, north or south, wealthy or poor, the main difference in domestic facilities was and even is today, more a matter of the number of working hands than the type of modern convenience available.

The Chinese kitchen is remarkably the same the world over. To the western eye it is incredible that such few implements can achieve such variety and artistry. Of course the answer lies in the heritage of thousands of years of techniques of preparation rather than actual recipes. Every Chinese kitchen contains the basic tools for Chinese cookery. These include chopsticks, bamboo or aluminum steamers, a wok (or large skillet or even electric frypan), a cleaver, a firm, heavy chopping block, and various sizes of strainers, skimmers, ladles, spatulas, many with bamboo handles that do not conduct the heat.

Most versatile of all is the Chinese cleaver, massive and awkward in appearance but incredibly practical. Depending on how foods are placed and held, the cleaver can be used for slicing, cubing, chopping, mincing, and scoring. The flat of the blade or handle can be used for crushing and grinding; the dull side of the blade can be used to pound and tenderize meats; the edge of the wooden handle can be used to crush and grind spices; the broad, flat blade can be used to scoop up all prepared foods and transport them neatly to the cooking pan.

The dome-shaped wok is also a marvel of ingenuity. It may be used for deep-fat frying, stir-frying, boiling, or simmering foods, or even as an improvised steamer. When special brown sugar is placed in the bottom with a rack of food above, and well sealed with a cover, it is possible to smoke-flavor any meat or fish. Using regular steamers, or an improvised steamer, it is possible to set layers of dishes one above the other in perforated bamboo racks and steam-cook an entire meal of many courses using only a single small heat source.

Food storage is seldom a problem in Chinese homes. Long ago the Chinese developed methods of food preservation that are unsurpassed even today: smoking, pickling, drying, and salting. Moreover, despite the availability of food storage facilities, it is a matter of great pride to use ingredients that are as fresh as possible. This might often mean bringing home a live squawking chicken or a still-wriggling fish. Food storage is only considered in more modern Chinese homes, which may use many western-style foods and beverages and a greater variety of fruits than commonly used in traditional Chinese homes.

DAIRY PRODUCTS

The Chinese have historically had a distaste for dairy products. Although many theories exist to explain this, none are conclusive. Logic points to the use of animals for work rather than for either milk or meat consumption. It is also possible that diseases and intestinal discomforts may early have been related to both milk and water sources. In early times too, cattle were considered sacred in certain areas. All that can be sensibly concluded is that the Chinese aversion to dairy products, especially milk, occurred very early in China's history. It is not known why they did not use milk as a food. There is no milk in the Chinese diet, but Chinese people living in other countries do consume some.

With the encouragement in modern Mainland China of minority folk customs, the pastoral peoples of Mongolia and Sinkiang have been encouraged to market many varieties of cheeses in city areas. Although dairy products have never been a part of the Chinese menu, recently some desserts are served with whipped cream, and ice cream is fast becoming a favorite treat in Mainland China.

Nutritionists concerned about calcium deficiency in this culture should note the delight Chinese people take in munching fish and poultry bones made tender by marinating and slow cooking. Soups and stocks are often prepared from simmered bones. Some regional customs include serving pig ribs cooked in a sweet-and-sour sauce of sugar and vinegar to new mothers. The acid of the vinegar and slow-cooking process may help to make the calcium in the bones more readily assimilated. Calcium requirements are also met in the fruits and vegetables, and meats and alternates discussed below.

FRUITS AND VEGETABLES
Good varieties of fruits and vegetables are probably more plentiful than ever before in Mainland China markets. Fresh fruits and vegetables are eaten in season, but fruits preserved and dried have always been considered a delicacy. Unless dried or salted, preference is given to vegetables purchased as late as possible before cooking. Nutrients are well retained by quick stir-frying, by steaming, or by adding vegetables to soups minutes before serving. Vegetables are seldom eaten raw but may be served cold after cooking and seasoning.

Problems of storage, climate, and transportation led to the development of preservation methods for vegetables: salting, pickling, and drying. Famines led to the ingenious use of any edible plant substance: buds, roots, fungi, sprouts, flower petals, seeds, and barks.

Peaches, apricots, apples, pears, and plums, as well as oranges and other citrus fruits, many varieties of melon and cherries are all grown in China and eaten mostly at the end of a meal or as a refreshing snack. Canned loquats, lichees, and pineapple are used in some areas together with meats and poultry. Fresh, cooked, or preserved (often spiced as well as dried and sugared) fruits are especially savored

on festive occasions.

The following list describes some unusual Chinese vegetables.

Note: phonetic spelling may vary.

Baak Choy: Chinese chard or Chinese cabbage, thick succulent white stems topped with deep green leaves and sometimes tiny yellow flowers.

Chung Choy: salt-preserved turnips. Only a small slice is used to add flavor, often to soups.

Doon Gwooh: blackish dried mushrooms requiring washing and soaking before use.

Gaw Pay: thin sun-dried strips of mandarin orange peel, especially used in duck dishes. Oldest and most flavorful is most expensive.

Gum Jum: also called "Golden Needles," these are dried brown lilies, soaked then snipped into thin strips to add a delicate flavor to fish, poultry, or vegetable dishes.

Haw Laahn Dow: tender green snow peas. Ends may be snipped and threads pulled in preparation for cooking, but they are cooked (usually stir-fried) and eaten, pods and all.

Hoong Jo: these look like wrinkled, red dates; also called **jujubes**. Used for color and sweetness in poultry and pork dishes or in soups. Must be pitted, washed, and soaked before use.

Jar Choy: preserved and spiced turnip greens used as a flavor accent in steamed or stir-fried dishes.

Jeet Quar: a hairy melon similar to fuzzy zucchini. Used for soups.

Jook Suen: fresh or canned bamboo shoots.

Kair: Chinese eggplant with a purple or white color and a cucumber shape; usually finer-grained than large eggplants.

Law Bok: Chinese turnips, large and creamy-colored. May be used grated raw as a vegetable, garnish, or condiment.

Lien Gow: lotus root. The underwater stem of the common water lily plant. Exterior is pinkish-brown and the interior is fibrous and mottled with holes.

Lom Gok: the very pungent cured strips of dried

black olives. Used mostly in steamed dishes.

Lut Gwoh: dried Chinese chestnuts prepared by soaking then cooking in water until tender.

Mah Tuy: crisp white water chestnuts, usually sliced very thin or cut in narrow strips before adding to dishes.

Mah Gwooh: whole button mushrooms.

San Geung: fresh gingerroot.

Seen Sun Yee: pickled bamboo shoots, usually canned in brine and used for marinated and steamed salad-type recipes.

Sun Ha: dried bamboo shoot membranes requiring soaking before use when they turn from dark reddish-brown to ivory.

Wun Yee: also called "Cloud Ears"; a type of fungi requiring washing and soaking before use.

Yien Waw: the nests of small birds or swallows. These are sold as dried cuplike nests which expand on soaking and are famed for the soup they are added to, **Bird's Nest Soup**. The natural glutinous quality of the nests gives the soup clarity and thickness. A costly but epicurean delight.

Yuen Sai: coriander leaves, also called "Chinese parsley." Used preferably fresh and sometimes dried.

It should be noted that all vegetables are carefully washed and trimmed before cooking is begun. Trimmings may be used as part of a stockpot to prepare a soup, broth, or sauce. If vegetables have been dried or salted, they usually require soaking before use. Vegetable pickles as well as their juice can be used as ingredients in dishes or served separately. The final step in vegetable preparation is the most time-consuming (for the cooking time itself is usually short): cutting, slicing, chopping, stripping, or dicing or roll-cutting exactly as may be required for each specific dish.

MEATS AND ALTERNATES

There is no question that animal foods are enjoyed and even preferred, but for the majority the cost of meats relegates them to use mainly on special occasions. Pork, poultry, and eggs are most favored. Mutton and fish are consumed regionally when available. Except for the Huis, there is a general disinclination toward beef-eating, probably related to ancient practices when cattle were much more important for work purposes than for food. Beef is seldom eaten, veal almost never.

Because of its general wide use and availability (most rural homes have a few pigs), pork can be considered the staple meat. Every part is carefully prepared for utmost flavor. For example, a full-flavored broth is commonly prepared by browning a few bits of pork in oil and garlic then adding cold water and simmering. Chinese sweet pork sausages are commonly steamed on top of a pot of rice. Ham is usually used as a flavoring for other dishes or as a garnish. Lamb and mutton are used primarily in the North where sheep-herding is common.

The customary bite-size or thin strips of meats are used because they cook quickly and spread flavor to other ingredients. Tougher meats are sliced as thinly as possible then marinated. Large pieces of meats or whole ducks or chickens are commonly cooked in commercial establishments where the consumer may then purchase any desired amount. (Home ovens are rare: top-of-stove cooking is common.) Whole roasted ducks or crispy-roasted pigs are specialties for festive occasions.

Poultry is enjoyed and is symbolic. Chickens, ducks, squabs (pigeons), geese, and pheasant are enjoyed from the skin to the bones and entrails. Male birds are considered to represent the positive and aggressive *yang* while ducks symbolize fidelity and happiness (*yin*). Pigeons are consumed not only for their intelligence but also for their filial devotion and longevity, traits that some believe are imparted to the diners.

The use of fish is increasing with development of the 3,000-mile coastline and numerous inland lakes and rivers as well as cultivation of artificial lakes for fish breeding. Dried fish and seafood (especially shrimp) are traditional favorites and available everywhere. The Chinese name for fish, *yu*, is pronounced the same as the idiogram for "bounteousness," and because fish are known for their rapid ability to propogate as well as for their speed and unconfined lifestyle, they further symbolize regeneration and freedom. Whenever a whole fish is served, it is customary to place the head of the fish (a succulent savored part) facing the guest of honor. Buddhists frequently serve fish at funeral banquets as a symbol of the departed person's new freedom from earthly restraints. Freshness in fish and seafood (unless preserved) is essential, so live purchase is preferred. Fishy taste and smell is abhorrent and is intriguingly disguised by marinating the fish in a splash of wine or sherry plus fresh sliced ginger, garlic, and scallions, before cooking.

Some unusual delicacies include: dried shark's fin,

which may be purchased in a whole piece or shredded and pressed into a block, from which small amounts may be used; dried jellyfish, thin and translucent and preserved in salt and alum; tiny dried shrimps; dried scallops. All dried foods are soaked before use.

Eggs may be used freshly beaten into small pancakes or omelets incorporating other foods; in steamed baked custards (not sweet); in prepared batters, coating foods to be fried. Egg noodles may be made by cooking beaten eggs in thin sheets then shredding, or by swirling beaten eggs in hot broth to create "egg drop." Eggs may be smoked; eggs may be hard-cooked then cracked and simmered in strong tea to give the whites a veined appearance – attractive as appetizers. **Thousand year eggs** are those that have been coated in lime clay and stored for 6 to 10 weeks. This is enough to give them a shiny-black look and soft smooth consistency. Used as appetizers, their flavor is more like fish than egg.

The soybean is called the "Chinese Cow" for good reason. The uses vary tremendously. Soybeans, like many other legumes, are used as dried beans or as bean sprouts. Fermented soybeans are used in the preparation of the favorite condiment: soy sauce. They may also be prepared into a firm white curd (called **Chinese cheese** or **tofu**) which can be braised, coated and fried, pickled, steamed with other ingredients, or eaten with sauces or as a garnish to soups. Soybean milk may be used often in the same way as westerners use cow's milk. Chinese vermicelli, called **bean thread**, is prepared from the soybean starch, is translucent and truly threadlike, but does not fall apart with long simmering. Nor is this all. **Bean curd sauce** is fermented bean curd that is packed in jars and sold as red bean curd sauce or white bean curd sauce. Both types have specific uses. Spiced, smooth bean pastes (almost like a date filling in texture and appearance) may be used to fill festive pastries.

The following list describes some other uses of soybeans in Chinese cuisine.

Note: Phonetic spellings may vary.

Dow Foo: bean curd or bean cake, usually kept covered in water. Fermented and sold in jars it is called **Foo Yu**.

Dow See: salted, fermented black bean paste often garlic-flavored and used in small amounts for poultry, pork, and seafood dishes and especially with steamed fish.

Mien Chiang (**Miso** in Japanese): thick syrup-like bean paste used for flavoring.

Tiem Jook: soybean milk sediment dried into thin sheets, broken, and soaked before cooking.

Wow Doo: dried black beans used in soups and slow-cooked dishes.

Finally, nuts are also an important protein source, usually purchased shelled and blanched, browned by stir-frying, and then added to dishes. Nuts may also be used as sweetmeats and treats but commonly are added to dishes in small amounts to give flavor and texture. **Ginkgo nuts** (**bok gor**) are used in soups and braised dishes, while walnuts, almonds, peanuts, and cashews are usually browned and crisped with stir-frying, then used.

BREADS AND GRAINS

Rice is the southern staple grain and wheat is the northern staple. But as grain production increases, both rice and wheat flours are used in steamed breads and dumplings to add menu variety. For all Chinese, rice is a symbol of all food, good omens, and fertility. "Have you had your rice today?" is almost the same as the western "How are you?" Most Chinese do not feel "satisfied" unless a meal includes rice. For the poor, rice may be the main part of the meal; for the wealthy, it may be served at the end of the meal as a symbol of plenty. To everyone, each grain of rice is sacred, for all are aware of the labor that went into producing it, and many people remember lean times when every grain was treasured. Upsetting a rice bowl is considered bad luck, while deliberately spilling a rice bowl is the worst insult. Long-grain rice is favored; glutinous rice is used mostly for desserts, while rice flour is a frequent thickener of sauces and soups.

Wheat flour is eaten in the North mostly in the form of noodles. Southerners consider noodle dishes snacks or quick lunches. Noodles and rice are never eaten at the same meal. Very long noodles are often served as a symbol of longevity. Barley, millet, maize, and buckwheat may be used in the form of flours to be made into noodles, steamed breads, buns, and filled dumplings of various symbolic shapes, or thin pancakes served rolled and filled, or to be filled by the diner at the table. **Jook** or **congee** is a thick rice gruel, almost a breakfast mainstay eaten with pickles or condiments.

FATS

Peanut oil, corn oil, and oils prepared from soybeans and rapeseed are all commonly used. Lard is sometimes used for frying but not as popularly as oils. Butter is not used. Sesame seed oil is used in small amounts and mainly as a seasoning, especially in vegetable dishes. **Joh yow**, strained pork suet, is used in pastry making.

SWEETS AND SNACKS

The Chinese have no conspicuous penchant for sweets; they prefer light savory foods. Tea is taken clear, and even sweet dishes are less sweet than usual western tastes dictate. Desserts, if any, will be fresh or preserved fruits, sometimes in a light syrup touched with anise or cloves. Savory nibbles such as steamed buns, egg rolls, or spring rolls, **won ton**, thinly sliced pickled or barbecued meats, vegetables, and eggs or noodles are favored as snacks. Sweet-and-sour sauces served with meat or fish dishes are enjoyed for their contrast in a menu. Occasionally, sweet preserved fruits may be served between courses at a banquet to arouse the appetite; but more likely, hot broths or slightly sweetened soups will be served for the same purpose.

SEASONINGS

The amount and use of seasonings varies regionally, as do their names, but the basic seasonings are the same throughout China. Onions of every type: scallions, leeks, chives, cooking onions as well as fresh garlic comprise a generous part of many dishes. Hot chilis are a part of many bean and garlic pastes used to season dishes in the North. Other seasonings include: fresh gingerroot, rice wine, bean pastes (**mien chiang**), chili pastes and fermented pastes, sesame seeds and sesame seed oil, sugar, many types of vinegars. Spices include: black pepper, star aniseed, cloves, **five spice powder** (fennel, clove, anise, cinnamon, and Szechwan pepper blended together). The flavor-enhancer monosodium glutamate is used sparingly by good cooks and is derived from wheat protein and more recently from corn or beets. It is called **meejing** or **wei ching**. **Cho** is rice vinegar and both pale and dark types may be interchanged with cider or malt vinegar. Not to be overlooked as flavorings are the many preserved, pickled, and salty-dried foods used in small amounts.

Chinese condiment sauces are as important in cookery as other seasonings and are used sparingly. Some are blended with other ingredients to make dipping sauces to be used at the table; others may be used for cookery; some are used both ways.

The following list describes some popular Chinese condiments.

Note: phonetic spelling may vary.

Duk Jeung (plum sauce): similar in taste and use to chutney sauce and used mainly as a dipping sauce.

Hom Hah: shrimp paste with strong flavor and aroma, used especially in Fukien cooking.

How Yow (oyster sauce): has velvety, chicken-like flavor and is used widely.

Hoy Sien Jeung (hoisin sauce): widely used as a flavoring ingredient. Excellent as a barbecue sauce for ribs.

Jeung Yow (soy sauce): not to be confused with **Shoyu** sauce, which is Japanese soy sauce and too sweet for most Chinese dishes. Used in all Chinese cookery and adapted in other lands. In use for more than 2,000 years. **Sang cho** is delicately light, while **Chan yow** is considered the best general type. **Chu yow** is dark and heavy and only for special tastes.

Mien See Jeung: pungent brown bean paste, salty and redolent of garlic. Used especially in steamed dishes for flavor.

BEVERAGES

Chinese seldom drink either water or milk. Most commonly enjoyed is clear hot tea as a beverage after meals and at any time. Wine is served at special or formal occasions and also used in cookery for the express purpose of neutralizing some flavors (as in fish) or to blend others.

Tea as a beverage was first known in China in the first and second centuries C.E., but was considered medicinal at first. Tea drinking as a general custom was promulgated with Lu Yu's classic *Ch'a ching*. **Ch'a** is the northern Mandarin word for tea, **chai** is the Russian word for tea (they got it from China), while the Amoy dialect on the southeastern coast called it **tay**. From this latter word the Dutch traders, who sold tea to the French, called it **the**, then the English called it tea. By any name, there are Chinese connoisseurs of tea that could vie with any world authorities of wines in their ability to distinguish quality, flavor, variety, and even the location of growth.

Some of the varieties include: **chang**, green tea; **hoong**, red tea (we call it black, but red has happier connotations to the Chinese), and a range of smoked, fermented, and partly fermented teas. The finest of green teas are considered to be **cloud mist** and **wun mo**. **Kemun** is one of the finest of the black teas, while **lapsang souchong** is a well-known strong smoky tea. **Oolong** is semifermented: the best grades make a clear straw-colored tea, lower grades yield a brownish-red brew. Scented teas such as **jasmine**, **lichee**, and **chrysanthemum** are shunned by purists but enjoyed nonetheless as an afternoon tea taken with pastries.

COOKING METHODS

Chinese cookery dates back thousands of years and China has one of the few cultures where "scholars wrote learned treatises on food and poets wrote cookbooks." In China, cookbooks are part of Chinese literature, rather than being a manual for practical cookery. Cookbooks per se are almost unknown in China. Instead, teaching was always by demonstration from mother to daughter or from chef to apprentice. With more than 80,000 distinct and separate dishes, Chinese cuisine stands unparalleled for its variety, ingenuity, originality, and practicality. Nothing edible is ever discarded and in times of famine even dogs and rats were prepared with some delicacy.

A classic Chinese recipe is basic and from it variations may be made according to necessity and preference. Minimal facilities and utensils are required for usual day-to-day meals. However, for occasions where many people are to be served, it is common to use the foods and services of commercial establishments. For example, the barbecuing of meats and preparation of holiday pastries are seldom tasks for the home kitchen.

The following methods of food preparation may be used singly or sequentially to prepare almost any Chinese dish. Soups and rice cookery are not included here.

Stir-Frying: all ingredients are prepared before cooking, by washing, and cutting into bite-size pieces. Usually all the foods for one dish are assembled in piles on a plate ready to cook. A small amount of oil is heated in a wok, seasonings and flavorings are added, then prepared ingredients are added and tossed and stirred, adding those requiring the longest cooking time first. (Sometimes tough meats or vegetables may be lightly parboiled to tenderize, or meats or fish may be marinated for the same reason before stir-frying.) The food is then heaped on a platter and served with suitable garnish. A quick rinse and the wok is ready to prepare the next dish.

Deep-Frying: out comes the same wok, only this time a cup or two of oil is added and allowed to heat until very hot. (When a wooden chopstick is placed in the oil and bubbles disperse rapidly from it, the oil is considered ready.) Again, prepared foods await on a plate; these may be filled doughs (such as spring rolls, egg rolls, or won ton) or they may be batter-dipped food morsels. To facilitate placing in the hot oil and removing when done, a bamboo-handled brass mesh strainer is used. Its wide shallow bowl is very efficient for scooping up the crisp-browned foods. Usually sauces or dips are served with fried foods.

Steaming: layers of lattice-bamboo or perforated aluminum trays that nest into each other and are covered with a tight lid are set over a pan or wok of boiling water. Into each layer of the steamer goes the serving plate or bowl with the food to be steamed cut into bite-size morsels (cut through bone and all) with a sprinkling of the desired seasonings, sauces, and garnishes on top. Those foods requiring the longest cooking are put on first. Leftover foods may be easily reheated this way without drying out or losing flavor. A whole meal of several different dishes can be steamed over one heat source. This method can be used for rice, meats, fish, poultry, dumplings, and pastries as well as individual steamed egg custards.

Slow Cooking: this term really refers to methods of braising (sautéeing in oil first then adding liquid) or stewing (cooking with water). "White stewing" refers to cooking with water or clear stock. "Red stewing" refers to cooking with the "master sauce," a mixture of soy sauce and spices, in which whole chickens and chunks of pork may be slowly cooked; the sauce is then cooled and stored for use again, increasing in strength and flavor and considered good for 100 years!

Roasting or **Barbecuing**: meats are oiled then brushed with marinade and always elevated or hung from hooks on racks so heat flows evenly around. A water pan may be set below to catch drippings. This is a commercial technique, as Chinese homes have seldom had ovens as part of the kitchen facilities. In any case, the convenience of being able to buy even very small portions of such meats is typical of any Chinese community.

Smoking: more a method of adding interesting flavor than a cookery technique. Burning brown sugar or moistened burning tea leaves are used to flavor and char previously cooked (usually by slow-cooking or steam-cooking) meats or fish. Smoked eggs are an appetizer treat.

REGIONAL SPECIALTIES

The Chinese royal courts had the finest chefs and could afford to produce magnificent, even legendary banquets. With the overthrow of the Ming Dynasty in the 1600s, court officials fled with their chefs. In this way the northern styles of cookery went with them and were adapted to regional foods. Regional styles developed for the same reasons as in other lands: climate, food production, local religion and custom. Taoists teach that foods should be served as close as possible to their natural state. Buddhists abhor the taking of life, so they may be vegetarians, often in the strictest sense. Muslims use no pork. Yet another reason for regional differentiation was difficulty of transport or storage between areas of production. Yet travelers have historically been the purveyors of traditions, foods, and customs as well as goods for trades, and so too in China, where many previously distinct regional dishes have been adapted to other areas, often making their origins difficult to distinguish.

Opinions even differ as to whether the regional specialties should be grouped by general area, by chief cities, or by province. Common Chinese restaurant terminology, such as Shanghai or Mandarin, used in western countries, is also misleading as the terms may be inclusive of many styles and only as good as the restaurant itself. The age of Chinese culinary traditions also makes origins difficult to pinpoint.

BEIJING (NORTH AND NORTHEAST)

Considered the classic Chinese cuisine, and most delicate, Beijing (Peking) is the most sophisticated and elegant. Onions, garlic, and leeks are used; steaming and poaching are the favored cooking methods.

Wheat flour dishes, such as noodles of all kinds, and steamed breads, buns, and pastries are served with most meals, while rice is reserved for banquets. Also included in the foods of this area is the Mongolian specialty, the **Mongolian hot-pot**: a steaming pot of broth is set in the center of the table and all diners dunk thinly sliced meat and vegetables to cook in the broth, then eat them with condiments. All northern nomadic peoples favor **hot-pot** cooking and eat lamb and mutton. Beijing's famed dishes include: **Peking duck**, **chicken velvet**, **spring rolls**, and **Yellow River carp with sweet-and-sour sauce**.

CANTONESE AND FUKIENESE (SOUTH)

Following Taoist principles, most foods are stir-fried or steamed. Because of nearby coastline and rivers, fish and seafood are a specialty and sugar is used in many dishes (to flavor not to sweeten), because it is grown in this region. Canton was the first port open to westerners and the embarkation point for many emigrating Chinese; therefore it has adopted western foods, such as tomatoes, peanuts, and corn as well as French pastries. The Canton region is also noted for its fruits — tangerines, loquats, plums, lichees, bananas, and the use of fruits and fruit juices in savory dishes. Cantonese specialties: **dim sum** (steamed filled dumplings), **shark's fin soup**, **bird's nest soup**. Chicken broth is often used as a cooking medium and flavoring and prized for its sweetness and delicacy.

SHANGHAI (EASTERN)

One of China's most important agricultural regions because of its location on the Yangtse River delta, both wheat and rice flourish here as well as vegetables, corn, barley, and soybeans. Peanut crops are used mainly to produce peanut oil used widely in cooking. The natural product of the many ponds, streams, and lakes – lotus leaves and roots – impart their delicate taste to many dishes.

Shanghai is not really a distinctly different cuisine but it is often singled out; there are many red-stewed dishes here, an abundance of sugar and fruits (like Cantonese), fine pickled and preserved foods. Pickled and salted greens are often cooked with meats. Most famous of these dishes is pickled cabbage, adapted in other lands as **kimch'i** in Korea and **sauerkraut** in Germany. Both Cantonese and Shanghai residents are fond of noodles, pastries, and dumplings, which are sold as snacks by street vendors.

SZECHWAN (CENTRAL AND WESTERN)

In China's largest province lying in a "great basin ringed by mountains," the climate gets colder, and the foods get spicier and oilier. This cuisine is famous for its liberal use of hot chili pepper and hot pepper sauces as well as for its rice-paper-wrapped chicken. Stir-fried nuts – cashews, walnuts, pine nuts, peanuts – as well as sesame seeds, add crunch and taste to many dishes. Many enjoy the flavor of chicken fat used to stir-fry vegetables.

MEALS AND CUSTOMS

In Chinese tradition, nothing is more cherished than an old friend. Love between a man and a woman is considered to be simply a corporeal need, while friendship involves the widest and highest range of human emotions. Thus, sharing the pleasures of food can never be greater than when in the company of old friends. The cook takes so much care and consideration to flavor, color, and artistry that diners at a Chinese table would be considered barbarian if they asked for added seasonings or even a knife. Seasoning and cutting are to be done in the kitchen. The diner may enjoy foods from any plate, eat them in any order, dip into any sauce or condiment or spiced salt according to taste.

An almost universal Chinese breakfast is a bowl of **congee** or **jook**: hot rice gruel cooked with small tasty tidbits or served with pickles, salty side dishes and always tea. Northern Chinese breakfasts are more likely to be steaming noodles or a wheatcake or hot steamed dumplings. In Mongolia, brick tea (loose tea pressed into bricks), cheese, and acrid butter may start the day, while Tibetans may wake to a meal of buttered hot tea and **tsampa** (roasted barley or **chingko** flour). For most of the Han Chinese, the local cereal grain comprises the main part of the meal, while anything else reflects either local custom or economic status. The noon meal in most areas is a smaller version of the evening meal: soup, a rice or wheat dish, vegetables, and fish or meat, if possible. For some, a favored noon meal may be varieties of **dim sum**, served with many cups of tea. For others, lunch is just right if it includes a bowl of noodles with condiments.

The Chinese are great snackers and enjoy nibbling on toasted seeds and nuts of all kinds, fresh fruits, dumpling dishes, assorted small plain cakes, and innumerable cups of tea. Snacks are important not only when a hunger pang strikes, but also whenever root eating becomes too monotonous. The preference is always for light savory foods, never for rich sweets.

The main meal is the evening or family meal, but with the addition of friends it can easily become a banquet. Tables seating eight to ten are favored since this makes eating and serving easier. Each diner's place is set with a rice bowl, teacup, chopsticks, and small dipping dishes as needed. Heaping bowls and platters are brought in several at a time and placed so that all may reach. Soup served from tureens may alternate with other dishes if the meal is lengthy. Normally the host will raise his chopsticks as a sign that the meal may begin with serving of soup.

In a typical family meal, care will be taken to consider variety in flavor, texture, cookery technique, and type of food. The meal will include at least one soup. Soup is a usual beginning but may be preceded by a cold selection of small appetizers. Small bites of foods are selected with one's own chopsticks and eaten over one's own rice bowl. The blend of flavors from casual drips of many sauces and juices makes the rice a flavorful dish to enjoy between other bites of foods.

The general etiquette of a meal is important too. Each person's rice bowl is held with the left hand, thumb resting on the top rim and always close to the chin. This way, rice may be scooped into the mouth without wasting any, and other morsels may add tasty juices to the rice itself. Eating rice from a plate is difficult, and wasting rice is considered an affront. Chopsticks are always used in pairs for eating but may be used singly to fold or stir in cookery. Each diner selects a morsel and either eats it at once or drops it in the rice bowl. Slippery noodles may be scooped into the mouth with chopsticks while holding the bowl close to the mouth. It is not polite to select the best tidbits for yourself, but someone else may pick up a special piece for you with the square end of the chopsticks and place it on your plate.

Over thousands of years, chopsticks of various sizes and materials have been the eminently practical cooking and eating utensil in every Chinese kitchen and at every Chinese meal or snack. Yet in 1995, at an archeological site in northwest China, a 4,600-year-old bone fork that predates the development of chopsticks was found. This discovery immediately dispersed the commonly held notion that forks were discovered, possibly, in early Roman civilization.

The use of chopsticks may seem awkward, but like everything else Chinese, they are both ingenious and practical. Like the porcelain wide-bowled soup spoons, they never burn the mouth or taste metallic. The general pace of eating is slow since only tiny morsels can be eaten at a time. Foods can never be drowned in sauces because, as the small piece is lifted, excess sauce immediately drains off. Children use slightly shorter chopsticks than average, and sometimes the host or hostess may use longer ones so as to reach and place special pieces on the plate of their guests.

Meals are concluded with the passing around of damply fragrant small hot towels to clean the fingers and refresh the diners. A lengthy banquet may include both the passing around of hot towels and the nibbling of dried preserved fruits partway through the meal, or the serving of hot soups between courses.

SPECIAL OCCASIONS

It is sometimes difficult to separate the Chinese calendar into specific occasions because there are many days that are deemed special only for certain family members, while others are designated for the entire family, and still others are shared by the community. These occasions revolve around life cycles, business ventures, or family or communal enterprises. Each may involve food offerings, incantations, spells, magic potions, or consultations of special calendars according to family or local custom.

Calculated on a lunar calendar, it is New Year's that evokes the greatest celebrations in Chinese life. Celebrated on the first day of the first month with dragon-led parades, incense and fireworks and banners of red everywhere (signifying good luck), New Year's is traditionally ushered in by family feasting, gifts of money in red envelopes for all unmarried children, and much visiting. Friends and relatives wish each other "hsin hsi" or "New Year happiness," or "kung hei fat chey" or "May you make money." New Year's is celebrated for the first fifteen days of the new year, especially for agrarian families who take this period as the opportunity for an annual rest as well as for visiting, feasting, and wearing new clothes. It is also a time when crowds throng to enjoy theater and film and watch chess tournaments, soccer, and other events.

In ancient times during the New Year's period, palace dignitaries were presented with purses embroidered with eight Buddhist symbols called "Eight Treasures," which they proudly hung on their chests. In more recent times this is recalled by the serving of a fruit-filled rice pudding called **Eight Treasures rice pudding**. Customary too at this time is setting around the room small bowls of lichees and longans, platters of steamed rice cakes and jujubes (red for luck), and salted seeds. During the festive dinner itself, red sweet-and-sour sauce is sure to be part of at least one dish, be it pork or fish. This is also the time to give the "Kitchen God" some sticky sweets so he won't give a bad report on the family.

Because of its strong connotations, the Chinese consider the New Year to be a male festival or one of yang spirit. But the Moon Festival, second in importance, is left to girls and women because of its cool yin connotations. In some areas, it was traditional to include many fertility rites and sacrifices to the Old Man in the Moon as the one who arranges all marriages on earth. In other areas, especially those under Taoist influence, it was believed that the moon was inhabited by a rabbit "forever busy pounding out the elixir of life." For this latter reason many moon effigies and rabbit images are burned with incense and money. Together with special parties for moon-viewing and the giving of boxes filled with **moon cakes** (round, filled pastries), symbolic paper lanterns are also used for gifts and decorations.

For every special occasion, small cups of rice wine are served to family and guests and feasting marks the special time. "Food makes the occasion ... food means contentment, even happiness, and happiness in turn calls for food to emphasize it." For those unable to add meat or fish to their usual daily foods, the major and minor special occasions of the Chinese calendar will surely bring the possibility of several special dishes rich with the welcome meat or fish.

Ch'ing Ming is the Chinese spring holiday. It is also called the Feast of the Tombs and is a time when families make a special effort (as at New Year's) to be together to make offerings to the dead in the hope that they may offer assistance to the living. There is also some evidence that originally this may have been a festival of spring rites which marked the renewal of life with many mating celebrations, although in time this was superseded by the cult of Ancestor Worship. More recently it has also been taken as the time of remembrance for all who gave their lives to worthy causes.

Some contemporary changes in the Chinese calendar have occurred in Mainland China: International Labor Day on May 1 and National Day on October 1. New Year's is still celebrated with a blend of both new and old traditions.

Other traditional days are marked with picnics of rice cakes and steamed dumplings. An old tradition of the fifteenth day of the seventh month, called the Festival of Lost Souls, is marked by setting lighted candles adrift in rivers and lakes, chanting Buddhist scriptures, and eating bitter foods. Other occasions mark a change of clothing for the season and agricultural events, such as harvesting or planting, and cold spells or hot spells of weather indicate special foods. For example, in shu fu (hot period), chunks of fresh fruits and ices are sold on the streets and many enjoy sour soups or drinks cooled with ice water. Many of these older traditions, however, are now relegated to history.

GLOSSARY OF FOODS AND FOOD TERMS

Note: While it would be impossible to detail the more than 80,000 classic Chinese dishes, those listed here represent some interesting types. Phonetic spellings differ, depending on sources.

Bark Fan: boiled rice.

Cha Chian Mien: noodles with meat sauce. Individual portions of hot cooked noodles are placed in bowls, topped with shredded vegetables, and spooned over with a thick meat sauce.

Ch'a Hsao Jou: barbecued pork. Thinly sliced as appetizers, and usually served cold, the pork may be coated with marinade and oven-roasted in a large piece or it may be simmered in a "master sauce" based on seasonings and soy sauce and meat stock.

Chi Pao Yu: paper-wrapped fish. Morsels of raw fish and dabs of seasoning are wrapped in wax paper, then the little parcels are deep-fried. The seasoning penetrates the fish and produces a succulent treat. The paper is not eaten.

Ch'ing Cheng Yu: whole steamed fish. Cleaned whole fish is laid on a serving plate inside a steamer then strewn with minced garlic and ginger, black bean paste, and other seasonings, as desired. After steaming is completed, the fish is sometimes finished with a poured-over topping of piping hot oil, which crisps the skin as it sizzles over.

Ch'ing Tow Hsia Jen: stir-fried shrimp with green peas. Because of its delicate taste and attractive color combination, this is a favored dish.

Chow Faahn: fried rice. Cooked rice is tossed and stirred with previously stir-fried bits of scallions, mushrooms, ham and raw egg beaten in, all lightly seasoned with soy sauce, which gives it the lightly browned or fried appearance. A good way to use left-over rice.

Chow Mein: this classic recipe of South Chinese origin is rice topped with "soft-fried" noodles. This means the parboiled noodles are tossed in hot oil with small bits of other foods and seasonings (stir-fried).

Ch'un Ping: Chinese pancake. Two small balls of noodle dough are pressed one on top of the other then rolled out thinly, brushed with sesame oil and cooked. After cooking, the two are pulled apart to form two thin almost lacy circles. Folded in quarters, and attractively served on a platter, the pancakes are accompanied at the table by many small bowls of assorted stir-fried dishes, and pickled vegetables, any of which may be selected as the filling. Each guest places a pancake on his or her plate and sets mounds of filling in the center with chopsticks. After rolling up with the fingers, the whole morsel is popped into the mouth.

Dim Sum: tiny dumplings prepared from thin wheat flour dough filled with various meat and vegetables then steamed. Served hot, they are enjoyed for brunch, lunch, or snacks.

Foo Yung: Chinese omelets, which may incorporate prepared vegetables and meats, fish, or seafood, as desired. Usually served with a light meat-flavored sauce.

Har Gow: steamed prawn dumplings.

Ho Pao Tan: fried eggs with sweet-and-sour sauce. A small amount of oil is brought to sizzling temperature then whole eggs cracked in. As each egg cooks on the bottom, it is folded gently in half to firm the yolk concealed inside. Then a delicate sauce of soy, sugar, and vinegar is spooned over before serving.

Hsiang Ch'ien Tou Fu: fried bean curd sticks. Fresh bean curd is sieved then mashed with flaked fish and egg white and smoothed into a small square pan. After steaming, the "custard" is cut in strips, coated with starch, and browned in hot oil.

Huen Tun (Won Ton): lightly seasoned filling of pork or finely minced chicken is placed in the center of a won ton skin. After folding in a triangle, the ends are pinched. These are cooked in boiling water then served in chicken broth garnished with shredded egg pancake and scallions.

Jee Bow Kai: well-seasoned cubes of raw chicken and celery wrapped in greaseproof paper and deep-fried. Unwrapped at the table and eaten from the paper with chopsticks.

Jook or **Congee**: soupy well-cooked rice gruel usually served with side dishes of condiments such as pickled vegetables.

K'ao-Pai-Ku: barbecued spareribs. Coated with a marinade of honey, hoisin sauce, soy sauce, and seasonings, the rack of ribs is hung in an oven and roasted.

Ku Lao Jou: sweet-and-sour pork. A colorful dish made by deep-frying starch-coated cubes of pork then adding them to stir-fried cubed pineapple, green pepper, and other vegetables, all lightly coated with a vinegar-sugar sauce colored with tomato paste or ketchup.

Lo Mein: a moist dish of tossed cooked noodles with bits of stir-fried foods.

Lou Han Chai: assorted fresh prepared vegetables cut in bite-size pieces and parboiled in broth. To finish, they are drained and quickly stir-fired with a little wine, sugar, and cornstarch to form a thin clear glaze.

Mien or **Mein**: noodles.

Pa-Ssu-Ping-Kuo: delicate dessert of apple wedges, batter-coated and deep-fried then served in syrup with a sprinkle of black sesame seeds.

Pei-Ching-K'ao-Ya (Peking [Beijing] Duck): a process of preparing duck in such a way as to produce the crispest, most succulent skin. Stages of drying are alternated with brushing of sauces and then finally oven baking. The completed golden-glazed duck is cut into serving pieces, skin and flesh on separate platters, with thin pancakes, scallions, and sauce nearby. Diners pick up the pancake, brush with sauce using the fanned tip of the scallion, add a morsel of meat or crispy skin (held with chopsticks) then roll and eat. A delicacy worthy of the effort.

Shao Mai: one of many examples of flower-like steamed dumplings.

Shih Chng Huo Kuo (Fire Pot Peking Style): one of many versions of the Mongolian **hot-pot** method of cooking. The shiny brass pot with white-hot charcoal in its chimney hold piping hot broth. Guests help themselves to the mounds of prepared delicacies in tiny pieces heaped in the broth. Broth is usually served at the end. Other versions provide uncooked tidbits to be cooked by the diners by holding the foods in the bubbling broth with their chopsticks, then dipping in individual condiment dishes both to cool and flavor the foods.

Siew Op: roasted duck marinated in a mixture of soy sauce, wine, sugar, ginger, tangerine peel, and five spice powder.

Subgum: means "many ingredients" or "mixed."

T'ang: soups. It would require another book to enumerate and describe all the soups of China, every one subtle in flavor, refreshing and satisfying, and often prepared in minimal time from few ingredients.

Tsung Tsu: sweet rice cake. Prepared by placing a mound of glutinous rice in the center of prepared bamboo leaves then a dab of bean paste filling. The wrapped and tied bamboo "packs" are boiled then untied to serve the enclosed sweet rice cakes.

Yen-Wo-T'ang (**Bird's Nest Soup**): richly flavored soup based on cornstarch-thickened chicken stock, prepared chicken velvet (a smooth light mixture of finely minced raw chicken breast and whipped egg whites) and dried crumbled bird's nest. The Asiatic swiftlet is a species of bird that uses saliva to build its nest. The Chinese collect this mucilaginous lining, dry it, and use it for this prized soup.

Yetcamein: a whole one-dish meal (usually a lunch) served in individual soup bowls: cooked noodles topped with sliced cooked meats, vegetables, then a rich broth poured over.

Ying Dan: steamed egg custard made with prawns or mushrooms.

CHAPTER 13

Colombian. See Latin American
Croatian. See Southern Slavs

CZECH AND SLOVAK

Czechoslovakia was born in October 1918, out of the disintegration of the Austro-Hungarian Empire after World War I. It would simplify our understanding of the people and the region if we could say that the mother was Czech and the father Slovakian. But as in real life, it has not been that elemental. Until 1992, the Czech and Slovak republics lived in relative harmony as Czechoslovakia, but with ensuing difficulties between the two republics' leaders, relations have plummeted. Increasing political differences between the two republics, with the Czechs' democratic reforms standing in stark contrast to the continuing "authoritarian leadership" and "oppressive rule" of the Slovak Republic, seem to be further intensifying differences.

Although it may seem that the two republics will continue on divergent political paths, there are also differences in their historical and cultural development that distinguish Czechs from Slovaks.

The name Czech derives from the spoken language, and this most westerly branch of Slavs make up 70 percent of the urban population of the region of Bohemia, Moravia, and Silesia. Bohemia's name is believed to have come from the early peoples who inhabited the area – the Boii. For 400 years, Bohemia was an Austrian province whose cuisine was strongly influenced by both Germany and Austria. Vienna was the spiritual capital of Bohemia and the people's ethos was predominantly Teutonic in nature: disciplined and orderly.

The Slovaks, on the other hand, speak a different though related language and their cuisine and their culture carry strong influences from their neighbor, Hungary. Most Slovaks are engaged in rural pursuits such as farming, lumbering, and cattle raising. And they take great pride in their indigenous dress and traditional festivals.

Up to the 1300s there was considerable German immigration into Bohemia and Magyar immigration into Slovakia. The hopes for a peaceful way of life seemed futile. Up to the mid-1800s continuous strife between ethnic groups, oppressive taxation, and forcible Germanization made daily life uniformly severe. The Austro-Hungarian monarchy was sympathetic only to its own cause, with the result that the period up to the end of the First World War was a tug-of-war between Hungarian and German dominance.

The joy at Czechoslovakia's birth in 1918 was short-lived. By 1939, Hitler had forced the surrender of Czechoslovakia to Germany and once more the people were torn and dispersed. Ruthenia went to Hungary, Bohemia and Moravia became German protectorates and Slovakia a puppet state. Forcible colonization, exploitation, and brutal oppression became routine again. In May 1945, with the end of the Second World War, a brief period of freedom was hungrily enjoy-

ed as Soviets entered Prague from the east and Americans from the west. But by 1948, the Communists' "bloodless takeover" occurred.

The food consumed in any land under stress bears little resemblance to the fare available under less burdensome conditions. Heavy exportation of food products and a frequent shortage of dairy products made the postwar diet predominantly carbohydrate, consisting mainly of bread, winter vegetables (cabbage and root vegetables), and potatoes. But strong in Czech memories are gravy-rich pork and veal dishes, famous hot sausages of endless variety, dumplings that were served throughout a meal, and a large choice of some of the finest beers in Europe. The land satisfied these tastes in abundance: Bohemia, traditionally an area of well-balanced industry and agriculture; Moravia, long the center of animal husbandry, with rich yields of wheat, corn, barley, and sugar beets; Slovakia, always well supplied from her own natural resources.

Sooner or later, no matter where Czechs and Slovaks may be, conversation is bound to turn to nostalgic arguments regarding the choice of the finest of beers, the lightest of dumplings and, among **parky** (sausage) connoisseurs, which *uzenazstvi* (beer and sausage tavern) was the best of all.

DOMESTIC LIFE

Postwar conditions of crowded housing and working parents, as well as the general scarcity of appliances, meant that the kitchens of Czechs and Slovaks contained the barest necessities. Food storage was not a consideration for most families because foods were usually purchased on a daily basis. More recently, with working parents, traditional home cooking is likely to be limited to weekends or holidays and further limited by what is available. Tiled ranges heated with locally mined coal have been the center of most Czech kitchens, complemented by handwoven table linens and brightly painted earthenware or fine china dishes. In better homes, the family's treasured collection of fine Czechoslovakian crystal would be used to grace the table for special occasions.

DAIRY PRODUCTS

Sour cream, pot cheese, sour milk, and buttermilk are used widely in many dishes, but milk is seldom used as a beverage. Frequently, hot milk is added to the breakfast coffee. Occasionally, **bryndza**, a sheep's milk cheese, finds its way to the table, and sometimes the Slovakian peasant specialty of **Liptovsky syr** (**Liptauer cheese**), made with a soft blend of sheep's milk cheese and seasonings, is heaped on rye bread, but for the most part, simple pot cheese is at the top of the list of favorites.

FRUITS AND VEGETABLES

Fruits and vegetables are used mostly in their cooked state. Fruits are served as compotes, fruit sauces, or fruit fillings for baked goods, and sometimes poached as a garnish for meat dishes. Vegetables are usually well cooked or served as pickles of many kinds. Berries and stone fruits are popular, but citrus fruits are seldom used. In public dining places, ascorbic acid has been added to salt to make up for this lack. Apples are widely enjoyed and used in compotes, fillings, and as sauces. The staple vegetables include potatoes, green and red and savoy cabbage, **sauerkraut**, wild mushrooms, rutabagas, cauliflower and kohlrabi, onions and garlic. Some fresh seasonal vegetables are also used sparingly, such as radishes and cucumbers.

MEATS AND ALTERNATES

Pork is the favored meat and every part of the animal is used. Other meats used include beef and veal, hare, all offal, goose, duck, and chicken, smoked and cured meats, and a great variety of sausages, served hot. Fish and seafood are not popular and are seldom served. Although carp and herring are usually available, they are mostly served only on traditional Christmas Eve.

The preference is for meats to be cooked until tender and juicy, and always served with a thick rich gravy, often including sour cream. Any meats that are not suited to this type of cookery are used in sausages, dumplings, or as a base for soups.

Eggs are used mostly as an ingredient for other dishes. Occasionally omelets are served, which incorporate bits of meats, vegetables, even potatoes, or pot cheese and sometimes fruits and fruit sauces. Legumes are of no importance in the diet and nuts are used only in bakery and desserts.

BREADS AND GRAINS

Wheat and rye predominate. Most breads are made with wholegrain flours, either wheat or rye, or a mixture of both, incorporated into a sourdough. Bread is never wasted. In fact, the Czech and Slovak use of slices or crumbs of stale bread vary greatly: in soups, in sauces, in cakes, and most often in dumplings. Wheat flour is consumed in bakery sweets. It must not be overlooked that the many types of dumplings are as much of a staple food as bread itself.

FATS

Preference is shown for butter and rendered pork or goose fats. More recently, use is made of margarines.

FOODS COMMONLY USED

Traditional Czech and Slovak cuisine borrows heavily from both Austrian and Hungarian tastes and are rich and satisfying. Plain meats, fresh crisp vegetables, fresh fruits, or small servings have no place here. The rich production of dairy products are ingredients in many baked goods, creamy gravies, and smooth sauces. Both vegetables and fruits are preferred well cooked and probably well garnished with appropriate sauces and syrups. Sour-cream-smothered vegetable dishes and fruits cooked in syrup predominate. A great variety of grains and flours are used in many types of breads and rolls, cereal side dishes, and especially in the many dumplings that can be found in soups, beside sliced gravy-rich meats, or on a dessert plate graced with a sweet fruit sauce or whipped cream. Whether one turns to Austria or Hungary, there is never a lack of richly elegant desserts. Beer is considered the national beverage for Czechs, while the Slovaks prefer wines.

SWEETS AND SNACKS

Desserts and candies have always been available and are a very popular snack. Women consume the most sweets both in the form of candies to nibble and rich desserts to take with a coffee break. For the most part, men prefer a snack of beer and hot sausages.

SEASONINGS

Spices and herbs are used with a light touch, since the natural taste of quality fresh foods requires little seasoning. The classic seasonings include poppy seeds, caraway seeds, garlic, onions, and mushrooms. Dried or toasted bread and/or cake crumbs may also be used as a seasoning. It cannot be overlooked that much of the rich flavor and aroma of traditional cookery is derived from the rich and abundant use of fresh dairy products.

BEVERAGES

Beer is considered to be the national beverage and the particular favorite of the Czechs, who will heatedly discuss the quality and merit of one beer over another. Red and white wines are made locally but do not travel well so are not usually exported. Many wines are homemade, especially by the Slovaks, who prefer wine over beer.

Slivovitz is a clear, very potent brandy made from plums. It is taken straight with any tiny excuse, from use as an appetite stimulant to medicinal use.

Coffee or a coffee-flavored brew made from malt or chicory is enjoyed for breakfast hot and strong, often liberally laced with hot milk or even rum.

MEALS AND CUSTOMS

Traditionally, Czechs and Slovaks prefer all meals to be served hot. When a variety of food is not abundant, they are satisfied with coffee and breads for breakfast; a quick hot lunch may be based on sausages or a potato or vegetable dish; dinner may be a soup with a second course of meat and gravy and a small dessert of dumplings, or a quick meat sandwich with pickles and potato salad.

These three simple meals will be complemented by hot snacks of sausages and beer or assorted pastries with coffee. *Gastronom* counters and taverns as well as pastry shops and coffeehouses and the famed *uzenazstvi* are present everywhere in cities and towns.

Friday was traditionally a meatless day, not as much for religious reasons as for a way to economize on meats. Friday dinner would be a traditional "false" soup with fruit dumplings for dessert. A "false" soup is made with a meatless vegetable stock, often starting with browned onions to add a pseudo meat taste.

Even in difficult times the Sunday dinner is almost always the biggest hot meal of the week. A rich hearty soup is followed by a special dish of pork or beef (or roast fowl) floating in smooth thick gravy, garnished with poached fruit or a huge sliced dumpling. The meal is completed with light sweet fruit dumplings served hot.

SPECIAL OCCASIONS

Most Czechs and Slovaks are Roman Catholic, celebrating traditional feast and fast days, while only about 10 percent are Protestants of the Reformed and Lutheran Churches. Of the more than 350,000 Jews living in Czechoslovakia before the Second World War, few remain. Those who were not killed during the Nazi regime emigrated.

Traditional festive fare consists of roasted goose or duck served with steamed dumplings, gravy, and red cabbage. Trout or carp, especially the spectacular **kapr na cerno** (a whole baked carp served with black sauce made of beer, prunes, raisins, sugar, and vinegar) may grace the festive table for Christmas Eve.

GLOSSARY OF FOODS AND FOOD TERMS

Bramborove Knedliky: potato dumplings.

Briosky: brioches. A rich light yeast bread or roll made with cream and egg yolks, shaped with the characteristic round knob on top.

Bryndza: cheese made from sheep's milk.

Buchty: sweet yeast buns baked with **Povidla** (thick plum jam) or apricot filling. Thin rolled squares of dough are dabbed with the preserves then pinched together so that the jam is sealed within, then baked.

Cevabcici: seasoned ground pork shaped into fingers, grilled, and eaten with onions and dark bread.

Chlebova Polevka: caraway-flavored soup thickened with stale rye bread crumbs and garnished with diced smoked meat or sliced sausages.

Dusene Zampiony: mushrooms sautéed with butter and caraway.

Falsche Polevka: an intriguing name, literally, "false soup," suggesting that any soup not made with meat is unreal! Actually a soup made with a vegetable stock, but a browned roux, or butter or goose-fat-browned onion helps to give the taste of meat.

Houskove Knedliky: one of the most popular dumplings made of flour, milk, and butter-browned bread cubes patted into a sausage shape and strung in a napkin for steaming. When cooked it is sliced with a strong thread and served with gravy by itself, or accompanying almost anything.

Husa: goose.

Jelita: blood sausage, served fried.

Jiternice: a sausage of lung and liver, served fried.

Kachna: duck.

Kapani: small drops of soft dough either poached or fried before adding to soups. Similar to the Austrian **Spaetzli**.

Kapr: carp.

Karbanatky: patties of ground meat, breaded and fried.

Kapr na Cerno: whole carp or steaks of carp served with the famed black sauce made from beer, sugar, vinegar, prunes, and raisins.

Klobasy: thick-skinned sausages that explode juicily when eaten.

Knedliky or Knedlicky: dumplings. The variety made is staggering. Anything that will form a stiff dough and can be steamed or poached seems to qualify – rice, potatoes, many vegetables alone or in combination, chopped or mashed, bread crumbs or cake crumbs, brains, liver, ham, smoked meat, marrow – all combined with enough egg, milk, and flour or crumbs to be shaped. May be served alone with sour cream, cream, chopped nuts, caraway seeds, poppy seeds, gravy, fruit sauces, or served with meats, fish, or in soups.

Kolace: round flat yeast buns with a dimpled hollow that is filled with jams, usually **Povidla**.

Kynute Houscove Knedliky: yeast dumplings with sautéed bread cubes blended into the batter before steaming.

Kynute Knedliky: simple yeast dumplings poached in salted water. Sliced with a thread to serve. Leftovers are breaded and fried.

Kure: chicken.

Liptovsky Syr: known as Liptauer cheese, a specialty of the Slovakian peasant. A delicious soft blend of sheep's milk cheese (sometimes cottage cheese) and seasonings. Served with dark bread and beer or wine.

Ovesna Kase Slana: a supper dish of oatmeal served with browned onions on top, eaten as a main dish.

Ovocne Knedliky: dessert dumplings filled with fresh or preserved fruit then boiled and served hot with sugar and butter or cottage cheese, sour cream, or buttered crumbs.

Parky: sausages. They are eaten at any meal and at any time as a snack, and people who live in Prague generally insist that all sausages, wieners, and frankfurters were invented there.

Pecena Husa: roasted goose, often accompanied with bread dumplings and red cabbage or sauerkraut. Traditional Christmas Day dinner.

Polevka: soup.

Polevka z Hovezi Ohanky: lightly spiced vegetable and oxtail soup. The meat is served separately.

Povidla: thick preserve of dark plums, usually simmered for two days. It is lightly spiced with cinnamon and anise.

Prazsky Salat (Prague Salad): julienne strips of meats, pickles, onions, and tart apples bound with mayonnaise. Other versions may include fresh or cooked vegetables lightly tossed with a vinegar and sugar dressing.

Pudink: pudding.

Raznici: thinly sliced ham or pork, grilled and served with chopped onion and dark bread, and eaten as a snack.

Slivovitz: clear potent plum brandy.

Smetane: sour cream.

Svacina: late afternoon snack of coffee and sweet breads.

Svickova: beef marinated in spices and vinegar then braised. The pan juices are blended with sour cream. Result: tender beef in sour, creamy sauce.

Uzenazstvi: beer taverns, where good beer and good talk is enjoyed.

Veprova Pecene se Zelim: roasted pork served with sauerkraut and flavored with caraway seeds.

Vursty: another name for sausages. Similar to the German **Wurst**.

Zajic na Cerno: cut-up braised hare simmered in a spiced sweet-and-sour sauce similar to the black sauce used on carp.

Zavin: stretched strudel dough.

CHAPTER 14

DANISH

The mainland of Denmark, together with its surrounding islands, juts into the cold and stormy waters of the Skagerrak and the Kattegat, the North and Baltic Seas, yet within the hearts and the homes of the Danes there is a special warmth. The Danes have their own word for it: *hygge*. It describes, in one word, that pleasant sensation when one is at ease with oneself and the world. *Hygge* is a feeling, an atmosphere, and a way of life. It is evident in the meticulously groomed dairy farms of the low rolling countryside. It is even reflected in the apparent contentment of the animals the Danes raise. The cows produce some of the world's finest milk, which is churned into butter and fermented into cheese. The pigs, which are cured into pork products, are of unparalleled quality. And chickens produce eggs so fresh, they are proudly date-stamped.

Today's Danish farmers are related to the early conquerors and rulers of England (1013-1035), and later expansions saw them ruling many shoreline areas of the Baltic Sea, Iceland and, even for a brief period, Norway and Sweden (the Kalmar Union, which lasted until 1523). Sweden won her independence then but it was not until 1815 that Norway, by the Congress of Vienna, was taken from Danish control only to find itself then ruled by Sweden. About this time, Danish trade expanded to the West Indies. (Perhaps the Danish fondness for rum desserts dates from this time.) But in 1917, Denmark sold the Virgin Islands to the United States and about the same time granted Iceland her independence.

The adventures of the Danes were not limited to northern Europe or even to the West Indies. As early as 1619, Captain Jens Munk landed at what is today Churchill, Manitoba, and claimed the land for Denmark, calling it Nova Dania. It is uncertain why his claim was not taken seriously, but what is known is that most of his crew succumbed to scurvy. Captain Munk and only two members survived that tragedy. Over 200 years later, more Danish ships brought settlers to establish what is today a community in Victoria County, New Brunswick.

DOMESTIC LIFE

The old Danish proverb "First flowers, then food on the table" explains the Danish delight in well-designed table appointments and cookware. These, together with a collection of candles and accessories that is present in most Danish homes, makes it difficult not to set an appealing table. And if flowers are not already a part of the setting, they will likely be brought by dinner guests.

Although Danes are practical enough to readily accept many convenience foods and labor-saving devices, they still enjoy certain tradition-tested customs. Probably from her mother and grandmother, the Danish homemaker has learned to adjust the embers in her iron stove to the perfect heat for **aebleskivers** (round puffed cakes) or for a cast-iron pot of yellow pea soup.

But if the coal stove is still a part of the country kitchen, the city kitchen is more in keeping with the times. Small appliances are widely used, colorful, lightweight cookware is preferred, and gas stoves and refrigerators are all very much a part of the modern kitchen. In fact, many new additions to the traditional Danish kitchen and way of cookery have combined to make Danish dishes just as good as mother's but prepared more quickly than grandmother's! Ekkodanmark, a branch of the Department of Agriculture set up to promote Danish foods, advises on canned and frozen goods, imported foods, and new recipe ideas.

The problem of food storage and preservation in Denmark, as in most of the northern countries, has always been carefully considered because extreme climate conditions can so easily spell hunger. Curing, salting, pickling, drying, and smoking were arts learned quickly because these techniques allowed meats and fish to last over long voyages or through periods of famine. Today, modern technology and storage methods lessen the need for these age-old approaches, but a distinct preference for salty foods persists, and even today salted meat and fish as well as dried or smoked foods are distinct Danish favorites.

DAIRY PRODUCTS

Milk, whey, or buttermilk are freely used often as refreshing beverages and also in soups and gravies. Cream is used generously in ice cream, whipped cream sauces (savory not sweet), as well as in desserts as sweetened whipped cream. In fact, plain cream, whipped cream, and sour cream are found in almost every dish: soups, salad dressings, meat and fish casseroles and sauces, and certainly in desserts. Coffee, however, is preferred black.

Danish cheeses, noted for their buttery richness and mild nutty taste, are exported all over the world. The Danes themselves enjoy cheeses for breakfast, as part of lunch, and often as a dessert with fruit or as a late evening snack.

FRUITS AND VEGETABLES

Fresh fruits in season are preferred, but fruits are also enjoyed when stewed then thickened with corn or potato starch and served with cream. The staple vegetables are potatoes and red or green cabbage, although the former are preferred. String beans and white asparagus are enjoyed when available, as are pickled cucumbers, pickled beets, a variety of summer vegetables, canned or fresh peas, and carrots. Danes use other vegetables, which are lovingly prepared: cauliflower, Belgian endive, onion of every type, kale, celeriac, and a great variety of local mushrooms. To the staples of potatoes and cabbage are added pickles or root vegetables in winter and greens in summer. Salad to the Danes means a mixture laden with meat or fish and bound with mayonnaise. Tossed salads with light dressings are largely ignored except by aristocrats.

MEATS AND ALTERNATES

Danish meat dishes are served moist and juicy. If the meats are naturally dry, they are accompanied by gravy or sauce. Broiling or dry-roasting methods are seldom used in meat or fish cookery. Though fish is plentiful, meats are the staple. Of these, pork is the favorite and all parts are used. Offal, sausages, and ground meats are often served for economy. Blood is used in soups and for sausages. Fish include: shrimp, eels, herring (used in countless ways), salmon, trout, mackerel, turbot, plaice, cod (fresh, dried, or salted).

Eggs are used occasionally for a light meal such as an omelet but mostly as an ingredient in or garnish for other dishes. The only legumes used widely are dried yellow peas, used at least weekly for a soup, **gule aerter**. Nuts are used in bakery and then almost always almonds.

BREADS AND GRAINS

Gruels or porridges of barley or oats are used only in rural areas or by children or invalids. Rice and pasta are also seldom used. Some oats are found in desserts or as oatcakes accompanying the traditional buttermilk soup. Most grains are eaten in the form of breads, rolls, and crispbreads. Heavy, dark, moist rye bread is sliced especially thin for **smorrebrod**.

Gruels and porridges of barley or oats still do form the staple peasant diet together with cabbage and potatoes and the very occasional addition of small amounts of fresh or cured home-raised pork.

FATS

Butter is used generously for everything. Unsalted butter is preferred. Danish margarine is also of fine quality and taste and is being used increasingly.

SWEETS AND SNACKS

Danes enjoy cakes, pastries, and crisp cookies often as snacks with coffee. The characteristic lightness and crispness of Danish bakery is attributed to **hartshorn salt** (ammonium carbonate) used instead of baking powder. In Canada and the United States it can be purchased in drugstores. Thick and sweet preserves as well as powdered sugar are often used to garnish desserts, especially pancakes.

SEASONINGS

Danish food is not highly seasoned. Cream, butter and eggs, mustard, horseradish, dill, onions, and leeks are favored. Poppy seeds and caraway seeds are used mainly in or on breads or rolls. For baked goods, the lightly spiced aroma familiar to Danes is the pungent one of cardamom, saffron, and toasted almonds.

FOODS COMMONLY USED

Good Danish food can be found both in homes and restaurants. Both types are prepared from fresh ingredients with simplicity and care taken to enhance natural flavors. Danish food is considered by some tastes to be bland; even the occasional curries are never spicy hot. Coffee and pastries are great favorites and all dairy foods have a daily place in Danish meals. Pork is the favorite meat; potatoes the favorite vegetable, but there may be a problem deciding between **akvavit** or beer. Solution: take both.

BEVERAGES

Black coffee in copious quantities vies with beer and **akvavit** as the favored drinks. **Akvavit** is a strong clear liquor distilled from grain or potatoes and always served ice-cold. In fact, it is traditional to serve **akvavit** from a frozen block of ice, syrupy, thick, and potent. Taken straight it is often followed by a chaser of beer and then nibbles of salted foods. Children consume large quantities of soft drinks; this is recent, not traditional. In cases of overindulgence, the Danes take a "cure" in the form of **gammel Dansk bitter**, a medicinally bitter brew (suspected of being alcoholic), said to clear the head and stomach.

MEALS AND CUSTOMS

Although Danes adapt readily to new ideas, they still relish foods in season, like tiny shrimps, which they heap on buttered white bread; the first delicate strawberries; new potatoes; fresh white asparagus. They still believe firmly that the best lunch is **smorrebrod** and that beer is the best chaser for the best drink – akvavit. Some things are too good to change.

Danes show their sophistication in elegant table settings and in their fondness for formal entertaining. It is almost second nature to set a table with candles and flowers. Dessert spoon and fork will be placed above each setting; no water glasses will be on the table; no host will wrestle with meat by carving at the table; the artfully arranged main dish platter is always prepared in the kitchen. The success of a dinner party will be judged by the abundance of food, the lateness of the guests' departure, and whether or not they asked for recipes.

Breakfast is usually very early since schools start classes and businesses open at 8:00 a.m. Lunch is invariably the **smorrebrod**, which is any artistic and flavorful combination of thinly sliced foods deftly balanced on thinly sliced pieces of dark rye bread. With beer or coffee, who needs more? Dinner may be a hearty soup and dessert or a multicourse meal introduced with akvavit and beer, nibbles of salted or smoked foods followed by one or two hot dishes, and later fruit and pastries with coffee. More usually dinner at home is a simple two-course meal of meat and potatoes or poached fish with sauce and potatoes or soup and dessert.

Danes seldom stay at home, and enjoy any excuse that takes them out to have a beer or a coffee, to take a walk, to see friends. Danes love a good joke and a hearty laugh. They love people and conversation and what better way than to enjoy both at the many small snacking restaurants, sidewalk cafes, stalls and booths and pastry shops? But who counts the number of drinks, snacks, or nibbles in any given day? When they talk about their meal patterns, average Danes don't consciously include them either.

SPECIAL OCCASIONS

Most Danes are Lutherans and the majority of those who aren't are Roman Catholics. But festivities celebrated are not always of a religious nature. Birthdays, Midsummer Eve, even the start of the crayfish season are all celebrated as avidly as Christmas, Easter, weddings, and christenings.

Drinking itself can be a special occasion and has a prescribed ritual. All Scandinavian countries share the custom of *Skoal* (or *Skal*). The host begins by meeting the eye of his guest. Together they wordlessly down their drinks without shifting their gaze. When the ritual is complete, the glass is raised with a slight bow of the head and lowering of the eyes. Women, particularly a hostess, are usually not part of this custom.

Although there are some distinctive characteristics in foods and customs from one Scandinavian country to another, festivities bring a delicious blend of wondrous cooking aromas and happy sharing of the very best food. Typically, repeated *Skoals* echo through any occasion, are washed down with beers and continual helpings of foods, and end with coffee and sips of **Cherry Heering** or maybe even a **Glogg** (hot spiced wine punch) or two.

Early in December, kitchens begin bustling with the furor of Christmas cookie baking, preparation of hams, **lutefisk** (traditional Christmas Eve dish made from lye-cured cod served with mustard sauce), liver pâté – the list is endless. Then there is the special Christmas **smorrebrod** with its array of fish, pickled and smoked dishes, salads, cold meats and hot dishes, breads of every kind, cheeses, cream-filled cakes, and crispy cookies.

Christmas foods are unquestionably the most outstanding but every festivity is celebrated with the best one has and always with one more helping. This can be fully understood when one remembers that even a gathering of friends is a special occasion to the gregarious Danes.

GLOSSARY OF FOODS AND FOOD TERMS

Aebleskiver: a round dimpled skillet used especially for cooking puffed apple-filled cakes of the same name. Often served with a dusting of cinnamon or icing sugar.

Aeggestand: baked custard of eggs and cream (usually in individual molds); the classic accompaniment to **Smorrebrod** fish or mushroom dishes.

Akvavit: clear potent liquor of Scandinavian countries, brewed from either grains or potatoes, always served icy cold – sometimes frozen dramatically in a block of ice, bottle and all – made in Aalborg, Denmark. Taken from a tall narrow glass in one smooth sip, often washed down with beer. **Akvavit** is called "aquavit" in English.

Brod: bread.

Buttermilk Soup: cold soup made by whipping raw eggs into chilled fresh buttermilk, lightly touched with lemon. Served with molded mounds of sugary, buttery toasted oatmeal.

Flaeskeaeggekage: traditional Danish thin omelet of bacon and eggs, garnished with a sprinkling of fresh chives.

Frikadeller: juicy Danish meatballs of minced veal and pork, browned in butter. Present at almost every **Smorrebrod**, and eaten at least once a day.

Frokost: lunch.

Gammel Dansk Bitter: the Danish solution to head and stomach troubles, a medicinal brew of probable alcoholic content.

Glogg: a festive hot spiced wine punch popular in winter, especially during Christmas entertaining.

Gule Aerter: a thick soup made from dried yellow peas.

Hakkebof: refers to minced or ground beef, but often means any ground meat. Danish ground meats are much finer-ground than those usually sold in North America.

Hartshorn Salt: used instead of baking powder to give cookies light crisp texture. Called ammonium carbonate in Canada and the United States, available in drugstores.

Kaernemaelkskoldskal: buttermilk soup.

Klukfaske: carafe for wine, used in all Scandinavian countries, so named because its dimpled sides cause the wine to come out with a *kluk-kluk* sound.

Koldt Bord: the array of cold dishes (meats, fish, cheeses, pates, salads) used to make up one's own **Smorrebrod**.

Konditorier: fancy cake and pastry shop where goodies are purchased especially for festive occasions.

Konditorkager: special name used to differentiate the fancy cakes purchased from the **Konditorier** from those that are home-baked. (An example of Danish honesty.)

Middag: evening meal, or dinner.

Morgenkaffe: breakfast.

Mycella: blue-veined Danish cheese, creamier and smoother than the famed **Danablu**. (Some other Danish cheeses: **Danbo**, **Elbo**, **Havarti**, **Samso**, **Tybo**.)

Natmad: lest Danish guests travel home the least bit hungry, this specially named late night sandwich snack is served just before guests depart.

Ollebrod: soup that is strong both in taste and smell, made from stale rye crusts and beer. A very old traditional country dish.

Pandekager: Danish pancakes eaten with powdered sugar, lingonberry preserves, or sometimes ice cream. Black coffee accompanies.

Risengrod: traditional rice pudding rich with eggs and cream and hiding a single lucky almond, served everywhere in Scandinavian countries on Christmas Eve. It is one of the few appearances of rice on the Danish table.

Rodgrod Med Flode: a favored dessert pudding of fresh fruits, usually berries, cooked with a little water and sugar and thickened with corn or potato starch, served with fresh cream.

Skal or **Skoal**: a formidable Scandinavian tradition begun when the host "eyes" a male guest, lifts his glass of **Akvavit**, and still eyeing his "partner," downs the icy brew, bows his head, and lowers his eyes. "Formidable tradition" because **Akvavit** is potent and because there is no end to **Skal**. Questionable whether this tradition is based on hospitality, fortitude, or the Dane's unquenchable thirst. (Women are usually exempt from the obligation to **Skal**.)

Smaretter: name given to several tasty hot dishes, such as creamed mushrooms, **Frikadeller**, that usually accompany the **Smorrebrod**.

Smorre or **Smorrebrod**: butter. **Smorrebrod** literally means "bread and butter," but Danish understatement makes whole lunches into just "bread and butter." It is an elaborate buffet of fishes, meats, cheeses, salads, breads, and usually a few hot dishes as well.

Snaps: common Danish name for **Akvavit**.

Snitter: miniature versions of **Smorrebrod** (open-faced sandwiches) served as appetizers.

Suppe: soup.

CHAPTER 15

DUTCH

For many people, "Dutch" is synonymous with a number of stereotypes: the clopping of wooden shoes, children skating to school in the winter, and a lone boy somewhere with his finger in a dyke. Some think of the Dutch as staid and stolid, settled placidly into a life of agriculture with days in the fields and evenings with the *goude frouw* knitting and the *burgher* puffing contentedly on his pipe.

In fact, wooden shoes are worn only in the muddy countryside; the Netherlands' year-round climate is so damp and misty that there are few days when ice actually forms on the canals; and in place of a little boy with a very sore finger, Dutch engineers have established a network of well-engineered dykes, dams, pumps, and sluices that not only keep back the North Sea, but are also draining and reclaiming the 25 percent of the Netherlands that is actually below sea level.

The 400th anniversary of the planting of the first tulip bulbs in the Netherlands was celebrated in 1994. One of the most awaited spring displays of glorious color, tulips excite delighted thanks to the Dutch. What many do not know, however, is that in many periods of hunger in Dutch history – as recent as the Second World War – tulip bulbs were ingeniously made into breads, stews, and soups.

Even the briefest glimpse into history reveals the Netherlands ("Holland" is the unofficial but popular name) as an important seafaring nation which once had global possessions: from the Arctic Ocean to Asia, Africa, Latin America, and even Staten Island in the United States. The Dutch East India Company is credited with introducing, in 1625, the Holland-Friesian breed of cattle to America, and in the 1800s it was Amsterdam bankers who were the first to invest in railroad building in Canada. It was the outspoken Dutch in the 1500s who fought the evils of the Inquisition and who to this day offer their land as a haven to religious and political refugees. Daring explorers, shrewd businessmen, and independent thinkers, the Dutch have also made great contributions to world art and literature.

Perhaps the image of the contented Dutch persists over the reality because so many Dutch contributions to our daily lives relate to the home. It was the early Dutch pioneers in New Amsterdam on Manhattan Island who introduced flower gardens

with imported bulbs from Holland, built their homes over food storage cellars, and even served pancakes, waffles, and cookies to neighbors who had never sampled such delights.

Even the ubiquitous mound of coleslaw on restaurant plates is of Dutch origin. Credited with introducing strip farming in southern Alberta, developing western irrigation districts, and starting market gardening in the Holland Marsh area of York County in Ontario, the sturdy Dutch emigrating to the New World from the most densely populated area of Europe found vast areas of good land awaiting their industrious ingenuity.

Because of the imports of the Dutch East India Company, the Dutch were among the first Europeans to make tea drinking a daily ritual. In fact, the Dutch are credited with initiating the 4:00 p.m. tea break, the rules of steeping for five minutes, and even the serving of tea from a tea cozy protected pot.

There are many who would argue that the most important Dutch contribution is the beloved tradition of Santa Claus. Although the Dutch Sinterklaas is the antithesis of the western world's commercially exploited Santa, he arrives annually in the Netherlands on December 6. (See Special Occasions.) Sinterklaas is a Dutch tradition specifically for the enjoyment of all children regardless of religion.

Dutch family life is of prime importance, and closeness of friends and relatives is retained with much visiting. In the Netherlands this poses no problem since more than 15.5 million people live in no more than 16,000 square miles. In Canada and the United States the Dutch maintain this visiting, regardless of the distance one has to travel. The sports-loving, health-conscious Dutch are also famous for their appetites. Though many are overweight, they still claim "Western Europe's longest life expectancy and one of the lowest death rates in the world." Perhaps then, the image of the *goude frouw* knitting and the *burgher* puffing on his pipe is more a symbol of inner peace and strength that contributes to Dutch health and longevity.

DOMESTIC LIFE

The spotless Dutch kitchen, boasting shiny rows of plates in the cupboards and a collection of spoons hung in a spoon rack, which was always so much a part of pioneer Dutch kitchens, is often still found today. Many Dutch have a fondness for delftware — earthenware dishes glazed in white and blue — as well as for copper utensils and accessories. North American home-styles are very much a part of Dutch life too, but the tradition of gathering around the kitchen table for good food and talk persists.

A part of the Dutch home that is shown with pride is the food cellar. Rows of home-canned fruits, vegetables, pickles, pickled meats, headcheeses, and bins of root vegetables are very much a part of home-making skills. Modern homes make full use of freezers and refrigerators, but the traditional pride in home preserving remains.

DAIRY PRODUCTS

Milk and buttermilk as beverages are consumed more by children than adults, although a substantial amount of milk is used in tea and coffee. The cheeses of the Netherlands are famous, such as **Edam**, **Gouda**, and the spiced **Leiden**, all named for the towns where they are produced. The Dutch traditionally prepare few dishes with cheese (although cheese dishes seem increasingly popular), nor is cheese used as a dessert. They enjoy their mild nutty cheeses thinly sliced and served with bread either for breakfast or as a snack with **Genever gin**.

FRUITS AND VEGETABLES

Frozen and canned vegetables are readily available, but fresh seasonal fruits and vegetables are preferred. Potatoes are used in an infinite variety of ways: boiled, mashed, puréed, fried, as a souffle, pudding, baked or sauteed. Vincent Van Gogh's famous painting, *The Potato Eaters*, is still representative of some rural areas in the Netherlands where the evening meal may consist of a huge bowl of potatoes centered on the table, each person spearing his or her own and dipping it into gravy or bacon fat before eating. White asparagus, red and green cabbages, cauliflower, Belgian endive, brussels sprouts, leeks, onions, kale, and carrots are favorites.

Apples are the most popular fruit. Other fruits are expensive and therefore used sparingly. Dried fruits often accompany cooked meat dishes.

MEATS AND ALTERNATES

Beef and pork are preferred and, frequently, offal and variety meats are imaginatively used for economy and flavor. All types of cured, smoked, and pickled meats and sausages are also enjoyed for flavor and economy. Fowl and hare are used only occasionally.

The favorite fish is herring, in many forms. Green or spring herring is lightly smoked and brined and called **Hollandse nieuwe**. These are usually purchased from street vendors, sprinkled with raw sliced onions, and eaten as a snack. Cod, haddock, plaice (flounder), and **snoek** (pike) have a place in the Dutch diet, too, as well as shrimp and eel. It is a New Year's custom to down as many oysters as possible. The Dutch generally prefer their meats well cooked, but enjoy their fish about raw.

Legumes are sometimes incorporated into several vegetables that are cooked, mashed, and served with butter or gravy. More common is the use of dried peas in the soup called **erwtensoep**. Nuts are only seen in bakery and then almonds are prevalent.

BREADS AND GRAINS

A great variety of breads made from wheat and rye flours are served at every meal and customarily eaten in quantity. Hot cooked cereals or cold prepared cereals are not used. The exception is **pap**, a hot cereal of oatmeal and milk, but more usually prepared from stale bread with hot milk poured over and served to children for breakfast.

FOODS COMMONLY USED

The Dutch eat traditional hearty fare at home, but prefer international dishes when they dine out. Cheese is one of their most important dairy products and is usually eaten for breakfast. Fruits and vegetables are well cooked and enjoyed in season, although preserves are also popular. Potatoes prepared in endless variations and breads of every type stand apart as the most important staples. Meats are used more sparingly and pork and beef are favorites. Of fish, herring is used most widely and in many ways. Seasonings are limited because the Dutch prefer the natural tastes of fresh ingredients. Tea, coffee, beer, and gin are the usual adult drinks, while children enjoy milk. It is customary that all cooked foods are well cooked.

FATS

Unsalted butter is the preferred fat. All the well-cooked meat and vegetable dishes are always served together with gravies or sauces, drippings or butter. "Dry" meats or vegetables are not served.

SWEETS AND SNACKS

Chocolate, cocoa, and candies are considered special treats. A great variety of baked goods, especially cookies and unfilled, un-iced cakes are eaten with tea or coffee as between-meal breaks. Red currant jellies and jams are used on bread or as dessert sauces. Snacks are often hearty meat sandwiches or fish specialties such as smoked kippers, sardines, and many varieties of herring.

SEASONINGS

Daily Dutch home cooking is well cooked but never highly seasoned. Onions, salt, and pepper with the added flavor from butter or drippings provide zest to soups, meats, and vegetables. Some fresh herbs are used when available. Ginger and cinnamon are used in baked goods with honey and molasses often providing sweetness as well as distinct taste and texture in honey cakes and honey and gingerbread cookies.

BEVERAGES

Milk is the children's beverage while adults prefer tea or coffee taken with milk and sugar. Afternoons often find women enjoying tea and cookies while men drink a few beers. The traditional dinner aperitif is **Genever gin**, sometimes called **Borrel** by the Dutch. The rest of the meal will be served with water or mineral water and, on special occasions, wine.

MEALS AND CUSTOMS

The average day in the Netherlands begins with an ample breakfast of many breads, unsalted butter and jams, sliced cheeses, and occasionally a fried or boiled egg. Young children often eat a breakfast cereal called **pap**. Adults drink tea with milk and sugar, while the youngsters have milk or buttermilk.

Lunch, called *koffietafel*, is principally a cold meal consisting of breads, cheeses plus sliced meats and sausages, and the addition of one small hot dish (a baked casserole, souffle, or omelet), perhaps a dessert of fruit or rice, or farina pudding. One thing is certain: lunch will be concluded with "endless cups of coffee," taken with milk and sugar. Note that both breakfast and lunch are "sandwich meals" and these are accompanied by either tea or coffee.

Six o'clock in the evening is time for a quick aperitif of Dutch **Genever gin** (strongly juniper-flavored) preceding the usual dinner time of 6:30 p.m. The often damp and chilly weather makes hot soup a popular first course, followed by fish or meat plus gravy and one of the many hot potato or vegetable dishes. A simple dessert pudding or **flensjes** (small crepes) finish the meal. Accompanying dinner is water or mineral water and sometimes wine but never tea or coffee. Juices or soft drinks also have no place at the dinner table. Occasionally men have beer at dinner.

The legendary Dutch appetite could hardly be appeased with a mere three meals a day. So at about 10:30 a.m. everyone stops for coffee and hot milk served with **koekjes** (cookies). At 4:00 p.m. there is a universal break for tea and cookies. But in between, if even the suggestion of a hunger pang strikes, all is in readiness: *pannekoekenhuisje* (pancake houses) dish up huge pancakes a-shimmer with butter and preserves; *broodjeswinkel* (delicatessens) stand by to serve sandwiches, especially the famed **uitsmijter**, a Dutch "snack" of bread and butter topped with sliced meat, fried eggs, and pickles. Then there are always vendors with herring and eel snacks.

Dutch cooks seldom experiment: simple and hearty traditional dishes are well loved. The most popular dining-out meal is the *rijstafel* or Indonesian "rice table." (See Indonesian.) This is a traditional feast centering on mounded rice flanked by platters of shrimp or pork or beef ready to be accented with an array of hot, sweet, spicy, crunchy, or cool condiments. What a contrast to the daily Dutch fare!

Such exotic tastes were brought to the Netherlands by colonists living for a time in previously Dutch-owned Indonesia. Three hundred years of Dutch occupation was long enough to bring home some Oriental food tastes. Many quick-lunch counters also feature a few of these specialties. The fact that most western Dutch import shops feature a section of specialty foods for the *rijstafel* is proof that adventurous Dutch will occasionally attempt this cookery at home.

SPECIAL OCCASIONS

More than two-thirds of the Dutch population belong to Protestant sects and the majority of these are members of the Dutch Reformed Church. Of the remainder, some 27 percent are Roman Catholics and about 5 percent are Jews.

Easter is celebrated with daffodils and tulips, **honingkoek** (honeycake) and **krentenbollen** (currant buns), while Christmas is quietly celebrated by going to church with family. New Year's Eve calls for happy family parties with **appel beignets** (fried apple fritters), **oliebollen** (deep-fried yeast doughnuts), and **appelbollen** (apples baked in puff pastry).

The happiest and most important celebration of the year is, surprisingly, neither religious nor patriotic, and is celebrated by everyone regardless of age or religion. This is the delightful festival of St. Nicholas, "a fixture of Dutch culture since the Middle Ages," and the patron saint of Amsterdam. Although no one seems to know why, as early as mid-November, Sinterklaas, dressed in bishop's robes and a long beard, arrives by boat from Spain, accompanied by his black helper Swarte Piet (Black Pete) and his white horse. Together they make the rounds of towns and villages, providing toys for good children and reprimands for naughty ones.

For many children, Sinterklaas, with his book of records about children, is scary. Yet, hopeful that they will receive toys, children eagerly prepare for the arrival of Sinterklaas and Swarte Piet by placing one of their shoes, filled with hay, carrots, or cookies for the horse, in front of the fireplace. For them, Sinterklaas and Piet may arrive by horse, barge, car, or even a bicycle. However, adults enjoy the festival with gifts accompanied by rhyming verses, treasure hunts, and practical jokes. Traditionally, a large solid chocolate letter (**boterleiter**) for each person's name marks their place at the festive table. Also enjoyed are marzipan and fondant candies, and other special cookies, rich with honey and fragrant with nuts and spices, are called **speculaas** and **taai-taai**.

Recently in the Netherlands, the rotund jolly Santa Claus, together with North American holiday jingles, have been encroaching on the Sinterklaas tradition. For those Dutch who retain Christmas as a calmly beautiful religious festival, such commercialization is profanity.

GLOSSARY OF FOOD AND FOOD TERMS

Amandelspijs: Christmas almond cake.

Appel Beignets: deep-fried apple fritters served with a sugar dusting. A New Year's Eve treat.

Appelbollen: apples baked in a puff pastry. A New Year's Eve treat.

Balletjes: small meatballs often used as soup garnish.

Bitterballen: small coated deep-fried meatballs used as appetizers.

Borstplaat: brightly colored flavored fondant candy, a specialty for St. Nicholas' Eve, December 5.

Boterkoek: rich shortcake enjoyed with "elevenses," the mid-morning coffee break.

Boterleiter: flaky puff pastry with almond or lemon filling, which may be formed into shapes. Typically enjoyed on St. Nicholas' Eve, December 5.

Chocolade Vla: chocolate pudding made with milk and thickened with cornstarch. (Cornstarch is called corn flour in Holland.)

Erwtensoep: most popular Dutch soup made with dried green peas, fresh greens, salt pork, and garnished with sausage slices.

Flensjes: tiny dessert crepes or pancakes.

Genever or **Jenever**: a strong gin, noticeably flavored with juniper and drunk straight while icy cold. It is the preferred Dutch aperitif.

Gestoofde Paling: stewed eel.

Groentesoep: a vegetable and rice soup with a broth base.

Haagse Bluf: favorite children's dessert made from whipped egg whites, syrup, and sugar to create a frothy light treat.

Headcheese: molded aspic made with chopped pieces of meat from pig's feet and head boiled in a bag then pressed into the cheese shape.

Hollandse Koffietafel: the traditional sandwich lunch of assorted sliced cheese and cold meats and sausages, occasionally accompanied by salads and perhaps one hot dish. Assorted rolls, breads and rusks, buttered, and endless cups of coffee complete the meal. Dessert seldom served, perhaps fruit.

Hollandse Nieuwe: the tiny or "green" spring herring eaten out of hand with a sprinkling of chopped raw onions. These are available only in the Netherlands as they are too delicate for export.

Honingkoeke: honeycake, lightly spiced.

Hutspot: a melange of well-cooked vegetables mashed together and served with butter or drippings. Sometimes meat or beans are included and sometimes the meats are sliced and served on the side. Typically a winter dish.

Izer or **Yser**: tea cakes baked on long-handled water irons often stamped with owner's initials. Eaten plain or rolled.

Jachtschotel: casserole made with layered cold (cooked) sliced meats and onions, apples, and potatoes, all baked slowly.

Kandeel: hot spiced wine thickened with egg yolks and traditionally offered to visitors after a baby's birth. Served in small cups and poured from a jug. Gender-appropriate decorations of pink or blue ribbons are tied to the cinnamon-stick stirrers.

Kool Sla: coleslaw. Literally, a cabbage salad dressed with vinegar.

Krentenbollen: shiny currant buns served with butter for Easter breakfast.

Oliebollen: traditional New Year's Eve treat of deep-fried yeast doughnuts sprinkled with sugar.

Olykoeks: "oilcakes." Yeast dough with raisins, lemon, and chopped apple shaped in rounds and deep-fried then rolled in sugar.

Ontbijtkoek: a moist lightly spiced cake often buttered and eaten on a slice of bread for breakfast.

Paling Soep: an eel soup popularly eaten with other fish and seafood dishes during meatless Lent.

Pap: children's hot breakfast cereal, which may be oatmeal but more usually is stale bread with hot milk poured over and flavored with cinnamon and brown sugar.

Pepernoten: spicy round crisp cookies eaten on St. Nicholas' Eve, December 5.

Puffertjes: puffards. Cookies baked in a "puffet pan" and eaten hot with cinnamon sugar.

Rijsttafel: the Dutch name given to the Netherlands version of an Indonesian feast, where a huge mound of rice flanked by many dishes combining meats, fish, and seafood with lightly cooked (stir-fried) fruits and vegetables are served, accompanied with deep-fried shrimp wafers and a selection of condiments from sweet, crisp, cool, to spicy hot. (See Indonesian.) This special dinner is usually eaten in restaurants, though it may be occasionally attempted at home. Some of the dishes may include the following:

Bahmi: Chinese noodles mixed with finely cut vegetables sauteed with meat or seafood and seasoned with the slightly sweet Indonesian soy sauce.
Gado-Gado: mixed sauteed vegetables with peanut sauce.
Ketimoer: a spicy cucumber relish.
Kroepoek: the small dried shrimp and tapioca flour wafers that billow out to fluffy crispness when deep-fried. Served as a bread accompanying the meal.
Loempiahs: similar to egg rolls or spring rolls.
Nassi: rice.
Nassi Goreng: fried rice.
Sambal: spiced combinations of crushed hot peppers made into very thick sauces. These are always added by the diner, not the cook.
Sateh or **Sate**: tiny cubes of meat, usually beef, threaded on thin, small wooden skewers and broiled.
Tauge: bean sprouts.

Rookworst: smoked spicy sausage eaten only after slow cooking, usually accompanies thick mashed vegetables.

Rolliches: lean beef and fat strips well seasoned and wrapped in tripe then boiled and pressed together with some of the broth into a loaf, chilled then sliced.

Speculaas: one of the many spiced cookies eaten on St. Nicholas' Eve, December 5.

Spekkie Sla: favored dish made of a cooked mashed mixture of potatoes and chopped endive, served in a soup plate with bacon drippings, vinegar, and freshly ground pepper.

Stamppot Witte Kool: white cabbage and potatoes cooked and mashed together and served with butter. A typical winter dish.

Taai-Taai: soft and chewy gingerbread cookies made in shapes of men and women, served at the place setting of each guest for St. Nicholas' Eve, December 5.

Uitsmijter: famed Dutch "snack" made of buttered bread topped with cold sliced meat and fried eggs, and garnished with pickles.

CHAPTER 16

EGYPTIAN

Sphinx, pyramids, pharaohs, and mummies all evoke vivid images of ancient Egypt. But so should a sip of cool frothy beer or a bite of warm crusty bread, because both are credited to the inventive genius of ancient Egyptians: an unnamed brewer and an equally obscure baker.

Perhaps it is from the land of Egypt that the expression "the sands of time" originates. It would be entirely appropriate. The study of Egyptology and the science of archeology have discovered keys to the ancient civilization under layers of dry sand. It is one thing to read about the histories of ancient peoples, it is another to view actual implements, original writings, artifacts, clothing, and even dried foods that were part of everyday life thousands of years ago. Credit must be given to the exceptionally dry climate of Upper Egypt (Southern) and the ease with which excavations may be made in sand.

Considered to be the direct living descendants of the ancient Egyptians are a group of present-day Egyptian Christians known as Copts. They clung to their faith even though in the 600s C.E. almost all Egyptians embraced Islam under the powerful influence of the Ayyubids, who established Egypt as the political and cultural center of the Islamic world. Although the overwhelming population of Egypt is Arabic, other groups, including Bedouins, Turks, Greeks, Syrians, French, Italians, and British, remain in Egypt as historical footprints of past conquests and foreign dominations.

Those influences have for the most part blended into general Egyptian culture but some threads are evident in the country's food styles. Excavations have yielded foods and writings about the foods that graced ancient Egyptian tables: leeks, onions, and okra; the large flat round yeast breads that are a staple of the Middle East even today; cakes rich with honey and dates; **fool** or **ful** – slow-simmered beans; and

tamiya, seasoned mashed bean patties, deep-fried. Even though thousands of years old, each is a part of Egyptian gastronomy today.

The processed **burgul**, used in many dishes, is likely of Syrian origin, but Greek and Turkish influence is evident in the following: **meushti**, stuffed vegetables; **shourba**, egg yolks laced with lemon juice and whisked into clear soup stock; and the many varieties of honey-drenched and nut-studded pastries made with phyllo dough. A popular classic Bedouin dish of lamb and rice, called **mansat**, is also much enjoyed on Egyptian tables. It is served over layers of carefully baked wholewheat sheets called **shrak**. **Couscous** is a Moroccan staple used in Egypt more as a dessert than an entree.

History credits both Arab civilization and the spread of Islam with bringing coffee to the tables of the world as a stimulant, refresher, and symbol of hospitality. Thought to have originated in Upper Ethiopia and Egypt, from an area called Kaffa, the Arabs first brewed coffee for use as an energizer and stimulant. Gradually the Greek and Roman Bacchic culture (so called because Bacchus was the god of wine and wine was their favorite beverage) was uprooted together with their vineyards as the Arab world spread its influence, and coffee came to be known as "the wine of Islam." It was not until the 1500s that coffee lost its exclusivity as its fame and aroma spread over Europe and, for many people, coffeehouses became their second homes. Coffee's importance never waned in Egypt. So important is the role of this beverage that people commonly have the name of their favorite coffeehouse inscribed on their business cards.

But of prime importance in Egypt and the Middle East is the oldest liquid of all – water. Egypt has been described as "a long fertile valley surrounded by desert." Only to the extent that water can be encouraged for irrigation can food be provided. Newer systems of canals and dams are helping to increase agricultural output and lessen the country's age-old dependency on the Nile River's annual flooding. More than 60 percent of the population is engaged in agriculture with the principal crop of cotton yielding not only high-quality fiber but also cottonseed oil used in cooking.

Berseem, the Egyptian clover, is used as a rotation crop for fodder to feed cattle, sheep, goats, and chickens as well as pigs, though pork is consumed only by the Copt community as the Muslims do not use it. The milk produced by these animals is used for yogurt and many types of cheeses. The gentle *gamoosa* (water buffalo) provides milk and is a dependable beast of burden and may even live with humble families as the winter heating unit. Donkeys are the preferred beasts of burden.

While upper-class Egyptians converse in Arabic, French, and English and enjoy a cosmopolitan lifestyle, the *fellaheen* (peasants) continue a way of life that has not changed in centuries. Working in fields with their *gamoosa*, they tend crops, vineyards, and orchards, and care for their animals and poultry but seldom eat what they produce. Meat, poultry, and eggs, as well as most vegetables and fruits, are sold. The *fellaheen's* staples are bread, onions, legumes, and copious drinks of very sweet tea. Their main protein source other than grains and legumes is **mish**, a white skim milk cheese stored in earthenware jars to ripen.

No one has torn down sphinx or pyramids in order to erect skyscrapers in Egypt. But today, modern skyscrapers, towering balconied condominiums, and bustling suburban streets hum with activity within sight of the ancient windswept pyramids of the pharaohs. Yet, Egypt remains, as always, a land and a people quietly aware of their ancient roots but absorbed in their daily tasks, all carried out with typical Mediterranean disdain for time, bustle, or punctuality. There must always be time for a sip and a chat.

DOMESTIC LIFE

The Egyptian's lifestyle and domestic facilities are sharply defined by class and gender. Modern ideas and technology have made great inroads in the educational, economic, and agricultural spheres, but the roles of male and female have changed little from ancient times. Upper-class women enjoy higher education and the help of servants but seldom accompany their husbands to restaurants or coffeehouses. Class is synonymous with wealth: servants, appliances, and the hand labor of many Muslim wives in a household (Muslim law allows a man four wives) indicate a family's status. *Fellaheen* conditions parallel those of many in subsistence economies, where most perishable foods are neither preserved nor stored but are consumed locally and seasonally as they are available. For this reason starvation may result when crops are poor.

DAIRY PRODUCTS

Fresh fluid milk is rarely used except occasionally in cooking. Some goat's milk is used but cow and buffalo milk are preferred. In the cities milk is sold from door to door and is always boiled before using. A variety of milk products are available in cities – pasteurized milk, condensed milk, butter, and cheeses. Yogurt, but primarily **mish**, is the rural staple. **Mish** (seasoned with red peppers and **fenugreek**) is considered peasant food, but is also much enjoyed by upper classes. A dried paste of soured milk blended with flour and seasonings, such as red peppers, is called **kishk** and is commonly cooked with water and eaten as the evening meal at rural tables with corn bread, onions, and sweet tea.

FRUITS AND VEGETABLES

Fruits are generally produced in small quantities and enjoyed mainly by the upper classes. In rural areas, seasonal fruits such as guavas, figs, and dates are used. Though quantity is limited, there is a wide range of tropical and subtropical fruits produced with peaches, pears, citrus fruits, and apricots being the most important. In addition, there are crops of apples, loquats, cherries, nectarines, plums, and quinces. Egypt ranks high in world production of dates, and there are also large crops of citrus fruits. (**Portoqal** are oranges, and limes are called **leimoon**.) Smaller crops of olives, bananas, pomegranates, grapes, and mangoes are also grown.

Onions and leeks are the most popular vegetable crops, dating from ancient times, and used year-

FOODS COMMONLY USED

Although there is a marked difference between the foods of the upper classes and the *fellaheen*, the general Egyptian fare is vegetarian. Even the wealthy serve meat only once or twice a week, while the poorest taste meat only on special occasions. Bread is the staple of all classes, from the leavened wheat breads of the upper class to the *fellaheen's* staple of unleavened corn breads flavored with **fenugreek** (similar in taste to anise). Meat, fish, legumes, and dairy products are a part of urban diets; skim milk cheese and legumes are the most important protein foods for the *fellaheen*, who supplement their diet with onions, tomatoes, and wild greens as well as very small amounts of local fruit. The wealthy consume fruits and vegetables according to taste. Tea is the rural drink, coffee is the urban drink, and all groups consume sweetened carbonated drinks.

round by all classes. Tomatoes are plentiful but eaten cooked rather than fresh. Other vegetables are consumed in very limited amounts in rural diets and only used seasonally on urban tables. Okra, potato, eggplant, cauliflower, cabbage, and spinach are other staple crops.

In cooler months, wild and cultivated leafy vegetables are eaten by all, but special favorites in the spring are the tender seeds and leaves of chickpeas and broad beans. **Millokhia** (spelled in various ways), is a green similar to spinach but with the gelatinous qualities of **okra**, and is especially popular in a classic soup of the same name which is based on chicken stock flavored with tomato paste, garlic, coriander, and pepper.

Occasionally radishes, carrots, lettuce, purslane, cucumbers, and even tomatoes are eaten raw as a side dish. Where storage is available some vegetables may be pickled in brine or vinegar during season: carrots, turnips, radishes, tomatoes, cucumbers, sweet peppers. Okra and **millokhia** are the only two that may be stored and preserved in a dried state for later use in soups, sauces, and slow-cooked casserole-type dishes.

MEATS AND ALTERNATES

Meats are not a frequent part of the Egyptian diet. When they are used, meats and fish are most often well seasoned and eaten mostly as part of a dish with legumes or cereal grains. Muslims not only do not eat pork but also prefer meats that have been ritually slaughtered (*halal*). Beef, lamb, kid, commercially raised rabbits, and even camel may be used by them as well. Traditionally, chickens are allowed to forage, which makes their meat stringy and tough and their egg production low. Most popular of all fowl are pigeons. Since young squabs are a special delicacy, pigeon nesting is encouraged everywhere.

Legumes are universally popular. Two classic Egyptian dishes: **ful** (slow-simmered beans) and **tamiya** (fried bean patties), are a popular dish at home and frequently purchased from vendors or eaten in restaurants. Lentils, chickpeas, broad beans, horse beans, vechling or the prass peas, and **moki** or lima beans are all used in soups and thick or thin stews. Sometimes they are mixed with meats or vegetables, and always they are well seasoned.

Because of its perishability, fish is used where caught. **Bouri** is a form of mullet fish most used: **fessikh** is salted **bouri**.

Small amounts of almonds, pistachios, and pecans are grown. They are used mainly as snacks or in rich desserts and pastries. Pine nuts may be used in some meat/vegetable dishes, or sometimes served with rice.

BREADS AND GRAINS

Corn, wheat, barley, rice, sorghum, and millet are the cereal crops produced in Egypt. **Baladi** is the wheat indigenous to the land, while **lindi** is a variety from India that has better baking qualities.

Bread is the most important staple for all classes and the poorer the family, the greater the ratio of bread consumed to other foods. Wheat breads are considered the finest, and **bettai** or **bettawa** is the classic Arabian bread leavened with yeast and baked in a fourteen-inch flat circle. The *fellaheen* make their breads from corn, millet, or sorghum (depending upon area) and spice it liberally with **fenugreek**. On special feast days they may add wheat to their usual breads to make them more festive.

Rural delta communities use corn as the staple, with only occasional use of wheat and rice. Rural southern Egyptians make breads from millet or sorghum with some wheat flour added. In common to all breads of rural areas is the sweet and fragrant taste of **fenugreek**.

Rice, **burgul**, and **couscous** form the main ingredients of many festive dishes and are often used as stuffings (well seasoned) for meats, poultry, including pigeons, and vegetables. **Burgul** is a nutritious wholegrain prepared from boiled, dried, and cracked wheat. It can be purchased from fine to coarse and has many uses. Cooked it can be used in many ways as rice; uncooked it is used by soaking first, then it may be combined with chopped vegetables and dressed with oil and seasonings. (See Lebanese; Syrian.) Another very similar grain dish is **farik** or **fireek**, which is made from green wheat.

Couscous is the favored dish all over North Africa, especially in Morocco. (See Moroccan.) Rural Egyptian families prepare it because it is economical and satisfying. Other Egyptians may make it as a sweet treat or dessert to be eaten with sugar and flecked with peanuts. Classic couscous is served with stewed meat and vegetables and a sidedish of very hot-seasoned sauce.

As if proof were needed that not a crumb of bread is wasted, witness **esh es saraya**, "Egyptian palace bread": made with bread crumbs stirred into a heavy syrup then poured out to cool. When cut into triangles and served with whipped cream, the rich honey and butter from the syrup and the smooth delight of the cream fit the name.

FATS

Fool sudani (peanuts) and **simsim** (sesame seeds) rank as the important crops used especially for oil production. Cottonseed is the source for most of the vegetable oil consumed in Egypt. Butter is usually used in the form of **samna** or **masli** – clarified butter.

SWEETS AND SNACKS

Large quantities of sugar are consumed in the very sweet desserts and confections, the well-sweetened tea and coffee, and the many carbonated beverages that are enjoyed. The pastry of the Mediterranean – phyllo – makes its sweet appearance in pastry shops in the familiar array of honey or syrup-drenched sweets. Exquisite sugared confections are sometimes specially created for desserts, but only in well-to-do homes. Sugar-coated nuts and sweets like **halwah**, which is a confection made from ground nuts, sesame seeds, and sugar, are snacked on whenever possible.

SEASONINGS

The aromas wafting from the bazaars of Cairo and Alexandria form a rich, heady blend of henna, sandalwood, myrrh, camphor, opium, and hashish. The rich scents wafting from Egyptian cookery may include coriander, mint, cumin, cinnamon, and the rich warmth of buttery honey syrups. Regardless of class, two favorite seasonings used are fenugreek and sesame, both as seeds and oil. While all of these lend their flavors to various dishes and breads, the most-used blend is garlic and onions with tomato paste or tomato juice. Egyptians love the sharp pungency of garlic and onions. Conversely, they also love very sweet drinks and desserts. Delicate pastries and fruit desserts are frequently enhanced with nuts, butter, honey, and often rosewater or orange flower water.

BEVERAGES

Sweetened coffee is the mainstay of the urban Egyptian, while sweetened tea is the frequent refresher of the rural family. Both beverages are enjoyed after meals and often as a "pick-up," or served just to express hospitality. Water is traditionally served with meals.

Soft drinks, carbonated beverages, and drinks made with prepared fruit syrups and plain water are used frequently. Meal beverages also include the following: **erkesous**, nonalcoholic beer flavored with anisette; **tambrahandi**, made from date palm juice; **shaier**, made from barley; **soubya** drink, made from fermented rice; **lubki**, a drink similar to ginger ale.

MEALS AND CUSTOMS

The abundance of gracious words, multiple cups of coffee, and a proliferation of heaped dishes that are all so typical of the unfailing Arabian hospitality can be explained in one word – *shaban*, meaning total satisfaction. The *shaban* of the guest is the joy of the host and nothing is spared to achieve this. Age, place, or wealth mean nothing. The best of what is available is proffered to the guest, and in great quantity.

Guests are seldom surprised by unusual foods.

Age-old traditions of food preparation, serving, and eating are well enshrined in Arab hospitality. City dwellers often prefer to take their meals in shaded courtyards during very hot weather. But whether indoors or out, the ritual is the same. Diners seat themselves informally on layered carpets while platters of food are placed on low wooden tables within easy reach. There are no individual plates, no cutlery. Foods are traditionally eaten with the fingers of the right hand only or are deftly scooped up with broken pieces of flat Arabic bread (from that big fourteen-inch flat circle mentioned above). Just in case there are some sticky fingers, bowls or brass jars filled with scented water are passed by servants between courses.

The quantity and variety of foods is further enhanced by the tradition of combining foods according to each diner's pleasure. Perhaps the eating is so enjoyable because there is always a different combination to taste.

Because the sheer quantity of foods offered is an important part of hospitality, some special dinners have as many as forty varied dishes, each one heaped and garnished in lavish display. Water or some form of light drink will be served with the meal. Sweet honey desserts might conclude a special meal, but fruits are the usual dessert. Small cups of Turkish-type black sweetened coffee and the smoking of the *narghile* or *hookah* (waterpipe) may be an after-dinner pleasure for some.

Hospitality is consistent, but foodstuffs may vary considerably. The humble home of the *fellaheen*, often shared by the family's animals, may be able to offer only bread, **mish**, and sweetened tea. A few dishes based largely on legumes, and occasional soups or vegetables, would be the only addition to the daily fare. Conversely, urban homes may rival the sophistication of gourmets anywhere with the exotica of typical Middle East specialties.

Morning begins very early for the *fellaheen* with a light breakfast of **ful**, bread, olives, **mish,** and sweet tea. In some areas local fruits may be eaten in season accompanying the bread and tea. Urban breakfasts are identical but coffee substitutes for tea.

The *fellaheen's* lunch will be a repeat of the earlier meal while dinner may include a legume-based soup (e.g. thick lentil soup) or **kishk** cooked with water. Olives with fresh onions and bread will complete the meal, while cups of sweet tea will be sipped to satiety.

There is usually not a great variety of foods in the peasant's meals but the staple legumes are prepared in many different ways and the adroit use of pungent and hot seasonings, along with the generous consumption of bread and tea, provides variety and satisfaction. Dried boiled legumes can be served as soup or stew, or drained and served as a "salad." Sometimes mashed cooked legumes are heaped in a mound and served with small amounts of meats or vegetables. Or they may be deep-fried in patties called **tamiya**. **Ful nabit** is yet another main dish prepared from sprouted beans.

Urban lunches also favor dishes prepared from legumes that are often eaten in restaurants. Dinners in upper-class homes feature all courses on the table at once and diners casually select each course to their own taste: a soup (eaten with a spoon), a legume dish, stuffed vegetables, couscous with meats and hot sauce, a plentiful supply of breads, and finally, fruits, followed by coffee.

Snack foods abound on city streets and even along roadsides, and again the favorites reflect the Egyptian love of legumes: **ful medamis**, simmered seasoned beans served with olive oil and lemon juice; **tamiya**, fried bean patties served with spicy-hot sauces; **kushari**, pasta, rice, and lentils topped with spicy tomato sauce and flecks of crisp browned onions. Vendors of sweet confections vie with those selling fresh fruits, toasted nuts, and crispy seeds. Coffeehouses locate themselves conveniently too. And at any time of the day, sweetened cola and other carbonated drinks, as well as fruit mixtures, are available to slake the thirst.

SPECIAL OCCASIONS

Since the majority of Egyptians are of Arabic origin (the Ayyubid, Muslim sect), Muslim feast days and fast days rule the Egyptian calendar. The small group of Egyptian Christians (about one and a half million) dating their lineage to the ancients celebrate Christian festivals. Proportionately smaller groups include Protestants, Orthodox Christians, and Jews.

Feast days for the *fellaheen* are marked whenever possible with the inclusion of meat, which is usually ritually slaughtered with ceremony fitting the occasion. The meat itself may be chicken, lamb, water buffalo (although rarely because the animal is more valued for work and for milk), and occasionally even a "very old camel – so tough it must be stewed for days before it can be eaten ..." Since wheat breads are considered of the finest quality, the inclusion of even some wheat flour into the daily bread is considered a treat for many *fellaheen*.

For many, however, special feast days are marked not only by visits from friends and relatives, but also by long days of preparation of the speciality dishes. These include **feta**, a classic holiday dish of layered bread, rice, and meats all moistened with rich garlic-flavored broth; **esh es saraya**, the rich sweet made from bread crumbs, honey, and butter, and served with **ishta** (whipped cream); heaping platters of **mehshi**, seasonal vegetables (e.g. eggplants, zucchini, peppers) stuffed with savory rice and meat mixtures; and variations of garnished sweetened **couscous**. The most dramatic dish of all, worthy of any festive occasion, is **ferakh bel borghul**. This is prepared by stuffing chickens with **farik**, or rice, then poaching them to tenderness and browning them to crispness and finally cooking them inside a boned turkey or lamb. With great ceremony the chickens are extracted as the awesome pièce de résistance, then carved in small pieces for the diners.

GLOSSARY OF FOODS AND FOOD TERMS

Asha: the evening meal.

Bamieh Bilahmeh: a stew of browned cubed lamb, garlic, and tomato sauce, completed with the addition of okra near the end of cooking time. Served with rice.

Bettai or **Bettawa**: classic Arab bread made of whole-wheat flour and leavening and baked in a large, flat fourteen-inch round. Eaten by breaking off pieces, and used to scoop up other foods. It is the mainstay of the Egyptian diet.

Bissara: lima bean and beef stew flavored with coriander and garlic. The cooked beans are puréed and mounded on a platter with the meat pieces arranged on top. Served with rice.

Boughasha: crisp pastry rolls filled with nuts and raisins.

Bourri: a most popular fish – mullet. When salted it is called **Fessikh**.

Couscous: Middle Eastern favorite prepared by dribbling water over flour and rubbing to form small granules. These are dried then steamed in a perforated pot over boiling water, or stew, or soup. Gentle stirring from time to time prevents lumps. In Egypt the *fellaheen* make this with small amounts of meat and vegetable sauce. Mostly it is prepared as a dessert sweet, sprinkled with **Samna**, peanuts, currants, and sugar.

Dfina: beef stew flavored with garlic and onions and simmered with sorrel and white pea leaves (spring greens).

Erfah: dessert coffee brewed in the usual way but lightly flavored with cinnamon as well as sugar.

Erkesous: a non-alcoholic meal beverage similar to beer but flavored with anise.

Esh es Saraya: classic festive dessert of bread crumbs cooked in heavy syrup and flavored with honey and butter. When thickened, it is cooled in a thin layer on a plate, cut into wedges, and served with whipped cream.

Farawla: a syrup of strawberries and sugar served in a glass with ice water or mixed with other juices to make a beverage.

Farik or **Fireek**: similar to bulgur (boiled, dried, and cracked wholewheat), but prepared from green wheat. Often used with seasonings as a stuffing.

Fenugreek: sweet aromatic powder or seeds used in large amounts to flavor bread and certain dishes.

Fessikh: salted mullet.

Ful, **Fool**, or **Ful Medamis**: dried beans boiled and served with oil. Classic dish especially for breakfast or lunch.

Ful Nabit: dried beans are covered with water and allowed to sprout, then cooked. A variation of **Ful**.

Ful Sudani: peanuts

Halawah: confection of finely ground sesame seeds and nuts molded to a rich delicious paste and sold by the piece.

Kishk: dried paste made of soured milk, flour, and various seasonings (usually hot and spicy). Commonly mixed with water and cooked as a part of the *fellaheen's* evening meal.

Kotelat: Egyptian-style meatballs made from ground beef and seasonings and cooked in water, oil, and saffron, served with egg-lemon sauce. Bread or rice usually accompany.

Maamoul: cone-shaped confection made from sweetened farina (cream of wheat), filled with nuts and perfumed with rose or orange water.

Meggadara: brown lentils and onions cooked with rice and served with yogurt and crunchy fried onions.

Millokhia or **Moulighia**: similar in appearance to spinach, a leafy green that yields a thick viscous liquid when cooked and used especially to prepare a classic soup of the same name, based on a stock of chicken or rabbit.

Mish: skim milk cheese, seasoned and allowed to ripen in earthenware jars for a year. The strong pungent taste is popular with all social classes and a small plate of sliced **mish** is a part of many meals.

Red Lentil Soup: a classic soup with the usual garlic and onion, and with coriander and cumin. Prepared without meat. Interestingly, red lentils cook up to a golden-yellow color.

Ruzz Dumyat: cooked minced giblets, butter, and pine nuts cooked with rice in a broth. The hot, fluffy, rich-flavored mixture is served with meat or other vegetables.

Samna: clarified butter.

Saniet Batatis: a baked casserole of meat and vegetables with the meat in the center and the vegetables arranged all around, seasoned with onions, garlic, and tomato juice.

Sayadia: a classic fish dish prepared by browning a blend of curry seasonings in oil then pouring over fillets or whole fish in a pan. Small amounts of water are added and the fish is cooked until tender and until the water boils away. The fish is served chilled with a garnish of fresh parsley and lemon wedges.

Shourba: rich stock meat soup finished with tangy egg-lemon sauce.

Simsim: sesame seeds.

Soubya: a mealtime beverage made from fermented rice.

Tahini: sesame seed oil used for cooking and flavoring and also for lighting and lubrication.

Tambrahandi: drink of date palm juice sometimes served with meals.

Tamiya: cooked mashed beans formed into small cakes and deep-fried then served as they are or, more usually, with spicy condiments.

Tanaka: Arabic name for the long-handled, narrow-necked, wide-bottom coffeepot used in Greece and Turkey where it is called an *ibrik*. Pulverized coffee, sugar, and water are added, allowed to bubble and boil up the desired number of times then poured ceremoniously into tiny demitasse cups. The exact amount of sugar, water, and coffee (as well as the type) and the number of times it is allowed to foam up produces an incredible number of variations. Sometimes spices are added.

Torley: casserole of ground meats and sliced vegetables arranged in layers. Flavorings and seasonings are tomato juice, onions, and salt and pepper.

CHAPTER 17

ENGLISH

It has been said that no one exhibits and exemplifies as much dignified self-control as the upper-class English. It is an image carefully cultivated. Appearance is everything. No matter what storms may rage in their minds or what chaos surrounds them, the English will quietly proceed with their reassuring cup of tea.

"British is best." "The Royal Navy always travels first class." "Britons never never shall be slaves." These are more than mere slogans or sayings or lyrics. This is the stuff of which tradition is made and nurtured. Although the English aristocracy of dignified mien, elegant dress, and cultured manners actually represents a minute proportion of the British population, it is this image that is considered typical of all English. It is a unique mixture of snobbishness and aloofness, a firm conviction of superiority that resides in even the humblest that leaves no doubt that the "stiff upper lip" will conquer all adversity.

How such a tiny island nation could have exerted and maintained so much influence on the rest of the world is a further tribute not only to the qualities the English have, but also to those qualities that they themselves believe they have. The quintessence of Englishness may be summed up in a description by Winston Churchill: "tenacity, national pride, and a sense of history."

But while a selective "sense of history" seems to buoy up the English image of the English, history in cold hard facts modifies the picture somewhat. The far-reaching effects of the Magna Carta in 1215; diplomacy and nationalism in Elizabethan times (1500s); and the great surges of industrialization and colonization in the early 1800s are indisputable historical highlights but they are intertwined with class and religious struggles, with poverty and disease.

EARLY TIMES

The early Celts and Germanic tribes that inhabited England – Angles, Saxons, and Jutes – were a brawny, boisterous mix of warring kingdoms, and it was only the threat of Danish invasions in the 800s C.E. that united them. After the Battle of Hastings in 1066, when William, Duke of Normandy, came from France to reign as king, some semblance of order and manners prevailed. French became the language of the aristocracy and this is when French words for meats

came into use: mutton from *mouton*, pork from *porc*, and poultry from *poularde*.

Medieval times were characterized by the building of castles and siege warfare, by the Peasants' Revolt and the Black Death. And while lords dined on gargantuan banquets of whole roasted animals, huge sausages, various puddings made with animal blood, and fruits and flowers preserved in honey, peasants huddled in their mud-daubed houses

and munched on coarse bread and a pottage of peas or beans washed down with homemade barley ale. Yet even in those early times it was the upper class that projected the image that made the continental Europeans refer to the English as "prodigious meat eaters."

The 1300s and 1400s saw the peasants gradually move from their humble status as tenants-on-the-land to the growing cities, where they became involved in craft guilds, industries, and merchandising. Slowly, prosperity and trade were making England into a viable nation and the English spoken in London became official "English" by the 1500s. With increased income, more people were able to make meat the center of their diet and increasingly the "cooked dish" became the focus of the meal.

ELIZABETHAN TIMES

It was both timely and lucky that the penchant for meat-on-the table coincided with Elizabethan England's emergence as a great maritime power. For while onions and garlic, wild and homegrown herbs flavored meats through spring and summer, imported spices from the Far East were almost a necessity to make meat palatable through the winter. In fact, it was so difficult to keep meat fresh after the customary September slaughterings (winter fodder was scarce) that Elizabethans actually became accustomed to eating spoiled and even putrid meats. Indeed, to this day, many maintain a preference for "high" game.

Salting down meats or spicing them heavily became standards of Elizabethan cookery. It was considered meritorious if diners could not recognize what they were eating. But probably most of all, the spiced "cooked dish" was so popular because it was so easily spooned up and could be eaten without chewing. These factors are of prime importance when dental fillings, artificial teeth, and dental care were scarcely known (the first metal fillings were used in 1542) and most of the population suffered from inflamed gums, dental decay, and a resultant general lack of teeth.

The Elizabethan had little dignity, elegance, or manners. In the late 1500s, foods were eaten with huge long-handled spoons (the forerunners of today's cooking spoons), knives were used to cut the tougher pieces, and unconcealed belching was commonly accepted. In fact, tablecloths were used mainly to wipe greasy fingers – if there were tablecloths at all. Even Queen Elizabeth the First herself was known to spit at courtiers and interrupt religious sermons. She even ended a feudal uprising by executing 1,000 people. Yet she did institute the Poor Law in 1601, which was the first governmental aid for the poor. She also tried to help the lagging fishing industry by instituting a three-day annual fast during which the consumption of meat was prohibited.

THE ENSUING YEARS

In the ensuing years manners did not improve. Gargantuan meals were accompanied by excessive drinking. The huge cupboards and sideboards common in the dining rooms of the time held chamber pots for use as soon as the ladies left the room. (Apparently, the after-dinner separation of men and women had more utilitarian purposes than talk and brandy sipping.)

If manners didn't improve, the variety of food on the English table did. Increasing travel and trade brought new imports to the English table. Cane sugar and fresh turtles came from the West Indies while the East Indian influence brought the taste of curries, spicy pickles, and tangy condiment sauces to add zest to the traditional bland English dishes. "Cheap and murderous gin" remained the most popular drink.

Meanwhile, evidence of yet another English characteristic was becoming obvious, at least to the non-English. This was the peculiar quality of insularism. No matter where in the far-flung British Empire the English chose to make their home, they carefully packed their language, manners, and traditions together with their other belongings. They never considered it important to learn either the language or the customs of the "foreigners," much less eat their food. Boiled mutton and steamed pudding was the menu in the cities of India, the jungles of Africa, or the mountains of New Zealand. Early housekeeping books published in England even as late as the 1800s show little evidence that the English kitchen had contact with anything but English foods.

In the 1600s, England's East India Company established a monopoly on tea. At the time, however, the English were enjoying coffee when they weren't imbibing gin. Some 2,000 coffeehouses dotted London by 1725. Some were the favorite haunts of the Whigs or Tories, others were frequented by academics or physicians. It was going to take another hundred years before tea, with its rituals of steeping, straining, and sipping, would overtake coffee and become entrenched as an English tradition. It is estimated that the average English adult brews and sips eight pounds of tea a year, while the Scots, Irish, Welsh, and English together brew and sip more than half the world's production of those tiny dried leaves.

FOODS COMMONLY USED

English cookery is not complex. The preference is for simple fresh foods well cooked and unadorned. However, even these deeply entrenched traditions seem to be wavering with the dual onslaught of immigration and the "new" healthy lifestyle. Meats, especially pork and pork products, beef and game, as well as locally caught fish and seafood together with well cooked vegetables form most of the main dishes in the English diet. But the fanciful endearing names of English dishes and baked food compensate for the simplicity of ingredients and preparation, making them irresistible. To the English, tea is indispensable. Tea with milk and sugar is served at all meals, at work breaks, and at the slightest provocation during the day. White breads and rolls and many quickbreads and biscuits and a great variety of cakes, pies, and steamed puddings still form a large part of the general diet. Bland meat and fish entrees are sparked with pickles, condiments, and spicy bottled sauces that are added to foods at the table. Fruits in the form of marmalade preserves and cooked desserts are more popular than fresh fruits. Many fine cheeses are produced in England and often form the "savoury" part of a meal (at the beginning or the end) or are eaten as a snack.

THE VICTORIAN PERIOD

From 1837, until her death in 1901, Queen Victoria reigned over the British Empire. Those 64 years, covering three generations, uncovered the excesses of the aristocracy and revealed a powerful and burgeoning middle class that was to be responsible in great part for England's world supremacy on the seas, in industry, and in banking and even as a model society. Members of the nobility continued to live in grand style and vied with each other for French cooks, Italian pastry chefs and gardeners. They were seemingly oblivious to child labor and the horrors of working conditions in the mines and factories that paid for their fripperies. A dandy called Beau Brummel became the gentry's idol. His elegant dress, exaggerated speech and mannerisms, and his proliferation of "delicacy of tastes" and "refinements of the palate" supplanted the previous coarseness and vulgarity. There is a tale describing his abrupt dismissal of a mistress because he "found out that she had eaten cabbage ..."

Generally, the Victorians were confident and self-satisfied. They had good reason. Education, arts, and literature flourished; workers became organized and vocal and even won a nine-hour day by striking. London's banks made her the financial capital of the world while her merchant marine and colonizers fortified the image of England as a supreme world power. The Victorian ideal centered around a happy domestic life and servants, ample families and ample tables. Mother, like Queen Victoria, ruled over all while father provided.

The example of the aristocracy, however, eventually filtered through the whole population and proved that one excess was as bad as another. A gradual change was occurring which often has been attributed to the Victorian era but in fact became noticeable in the late 1800s. Perhaps as a retaliation against the excesses of the past, the English developed a veneer of fastidious control and modesty that extended into every facet of life. A gray-brown pallor settled over conversation, homes, clothing, and even the food they ate.

Food, like sex, was considered an "unfortunate carnal necessity to be endured ..." Visible enjoyment of anything was synonymous with sin. Formality at meals, dressing for high tea and dinner, hushed dining rooms and silent eating became the national style. The subjects of food and cooking were considered bad taste and the pleasures of the culinary arts were considered unladylike. Children were banished to the nursery to eat their overcooked vegetables and bland milk puddings in the company of a gray-uniformed nanny. The ideal of genteel behavior metamorphosed into polite rigidity and an emotionless composure that left the English with an almost guilt-ridden viewpoint of anything that was at all pleasurable.

MODERN TIMES

The legendary British Empire has shrunk, but the traditionally English view of the English has not. They have successfully taken the excesses and eccentricities of the past and blended them with present practicalities. The post–Second World War period saw an influx of British subjects from far-flung countries, which gave England, and especially London, a colorful multicultural population, tastes, and customs previously unknown. Still more recently, tea drinking has declined to the point that the Venerable British Tea Council is encouraging the proliferation of the Guild of Tea Shops, selections of choice teas, and standards of tea preparation all in order to promote tea "as a gourmet accompaniment to food." Perhaps the traditional qualities of tenacity, national pride, and a profound sense of history still enable the English to believe that any discomforts are only temporary – even their reputation for a dawdling culinary affection. English restaurants provide delicious world fare, but English home kitchens seem oblivious to international culinary delights. The tradition of the Sunday roast lives on.

DOMESTIC LIFE

English food is honest and simple and so are English kitchens. There is a place for substantial wooden spoons, earthenware mixing bowls, pie pans and pudding bowls, but there is no place for exotic cookware or complex gadgetry. The biggest pot in the kitchen will likely be a soup kettle, but it will be used for cooking jams and jellies and shimmering marmalades. (The English are not given to soup-making.) Most important will be a kettle of boiling water, a teapot – beloved even if it is stained and a bit cracked – and a collection of teacups.

Thick frypans and electric or gas ovens have all but replaced hearth ovens and iron griddles or bakestones, but tea cakes, biscuits, and pastries are as expertly made and as much enjoyed as ever.

Although electrical appliances and gadgetry, and a wide range of exotic imported foods are available, especially in the larger cities, the English prefer their home preserves, homegrown fresh fruits and vegetables, and local meats, fish, and seafood. The English larder (a cool storage pantry) is still just as important as the refrigerator. Purchasing in small quantities is favored, so storage areas are not generally as important as in areas where food variety is not available year-round.

DAIRY PRODUCTS

Milk is mostly consumed in the form of fresh whole milk served with tea. Almost daily, children are served cream soups and milk puddings while adults prefer their milk with tea or enjoyed as cheese. **Cheddar, Cheshire, Stilton,** and **Caerphilly** are some of the best-known and locally produced cheeses. **Cornish cream** and **Devonshire cream** are thick-clotted creams usually eaten with breads and jams at teatime.

FRUITS AND VEGETABLES

The English countryside with its many small home gardens yield a variety of fruits, berries, and vegetables. Pears and apples (commonly **pippins**), peaches, apricots, cherries, quinces, rhubarb, and green walnut are occasionally enjoyed as fresh fruits but most often are eaten in some cooked and sweetened form. The most popular vegetables are potatoes, brussels sprouts, turnips, and cabbage. Salad and salad vegetables are not as popularly used, but their use is increasing. Many berries, fruits, and even some vegetables are made into jams, preserves, pickles, and chutneys. Vegetables are well cooked (usually in a lot of water) and sparingly seasoned. Sometimes they are cooked together with meats and fish or sausages to make a quick one-dish meal.

MEATS AND ALTERNATES

There is no shortage of meat in the English diet. Inexpensive cuts of meat form the basis for slow-cooked casserole-type meals. Steaks and chops and many types of sausages are fried or grilled for quick suppers. Pork, beef, lamb, and mutton, together with seasonal game, provide variety. Meats are usually grilled or pan-fried, stewed in a pot with vegetables, or oven-roasted. Game is usually well aged before cooking to tenderize. A "joint" of meat will likely be the center of the Sunday dinner table. Tastes run conservative when it comes to fish and seafood. Batter-fried **fish and chips** is a great favorite either as a snack or a supper. Jellied eels, cockles, and whelks are often bought from street vendors, but at home simple poached or fried fish, or even occasionally "soused" (pickled) fish may include a selection from kippers (smoked herring), flounder, salmon, sole, haddock (**finnan haddie**). Excellent dried, pickled, and smoked fish as well as crabs, prawns, crayfish, and oysters are all readily available.

Eggs appear frequently on the English menu, with bacon and/or pork sausages, or "mumbled" (scrambled) eggs for breakfast. Many a pub's "fork platter" (a lunch dish on one plate eaten with a fork) includes a poached or fried egg atop anything from spaghetti to beans or even a steak. Eggs are a part of the many custards and puddings, form the batter coating on fried fish, and are an integral part of the puffy **Yorkshire pudding**.

Legumes are not frequently used since, for the most part, beans are considered a food of necessity rather than a choice.

BREADS AND GRAINS

White breads and rolls made from wheat flour are preferred over wholegrain or rye breads. The English homemaker is adept at making many types of quickbreads, leavened, but not with yeast. Bakery with yeast is seldom attempted at home. Porridge is oatmeal and is almost always a part of breakfast, as is cold toast. The English prefer toast crisp (it is placed on toast racks after toasting), and when it is cold, it is spread with butter, thick preserves, or marmalade. Plain baked goods, lightly flavored and un-iced, accompany tea and form the major part of the four o'clock tea ritual.

FATS

During wartime, the English rendered and clarified fat from meats and poultry to be used in baking and cooking. But lard is preferred in cookery and butter finds a place on all tables as well as in much cooking. Oils are seldom used. Oil dressings for salads have a small niche in the English diet.

SWEETS AND SNACKS

In the English vernacular, "sweet" may refer to dessert or to taffies or hard candies. Such is the weakness of the English sweet tooth that almost half a pound of "sweets" (candies) are consumed per person per week. Sweets shops are everywhere and a little package of candies is to be found in almost every pocket or handbag for "quick energy." Much sugar is consumed in baked goods and many prefer their tea so sweetened as to be syrupy.

SEASONINGS

For several hundred years the spice shelf in the English kitchen was very important. Spices were not only enjoyed in heavily seasoned foods, they were frequently necessary to cover the rancid and fermented tastes of spoiled meats and fish. Since the Victorian era, however, salt and pepper, onions and a few homegrown herbs such as thyme, rosemary, sage, and garden savory have comprised the seasonings preferred by the English. There is some evidence of the English palate enjoying East Indian and African foods, but most commonly in restaurants, not at home.

BEVERAGES

The most important English beverage has been (but is declining) tea. Tea, well steeped and hearty of flavor and aroma, is served with fresh or canned milk and sugar many times during the day, at the slightest provocation – and after meals. Tea is considered a comfort and consolation, a break from work or other routines, a sociable time for friends, a cure, or at least a comfort, during illness, even a meal in itself. Pubs (short for "Public Houses," where simple sandwiches or one-platter lunch dishes are served with draft beer or ale as well as other alcoholic beverages) are so popular in England that most English people have "their" pub just as most Parisians have "their" café. Beer is the most popular alcoholic drink, but a wide variety of imported wines, gin, and whiskey (Scotch) are also consumed.

REGIONAL SPECIALTIES

Regional specialties are highly developed in England. A few are still available only in certain areas, but more are being enjoyed widely with the increase in transportation, communication, and the widespread interest and publication of regional pamphlets describing these dishes. Some are old favorites, beloved in almost every English kitchen: **brawn, bubble and squeak, tripe and onions, jugged hare, toad-in-the-hole, veal and ham pie, soused mackerel** or **herring, kippers, kedgeree, fish and chips, treacle tart, trifle** and **mince pie**. The most famous of the almost endless list of breads, biscuits, and cakes to accompany tea are: **crumpets** (**pikelets** in the North), **muffins, hot cross buns, Swiss roll** and **Victoria sponge**.

EAST ANGLIA

Norfolk turkeys and quail are highly prized in this region, but the area is most famous for the great variety of quality seafood: crabs, mussels, whelks, cockles, red and black herrings, and **Colchester oysters**. Local asparagus in season is so plentiful it is sold at roadside stands, and similar in taste, with a touch of chive, is **samphire**, a type of grass.

Ipswich almond pudding, a light custard flavored with almond, is a frequent dessert sweet.

The prepared mustard condiment is said to have originated here, and the world-famous Colman Mustard has its plant in Norwich.

EAST MIDLANDS: DERBYSHIRE, LEICESTERSHIRE, LINCOLNSHIRE, NORTHAMPTONSHIRE, NOTTINGHAMSHIRE

The most famous pork pies of all, **Melton Mowbray**, are made in this area from an age-old recipe that is widely copied elsewhere.

Many dessert pies and puddings are made from the local Bramley apples or green gooseberries, but probably the most unusual is a pie with a pastry crust that is filled with a sweetened mashed potato filling flavored with lemon and nutmeg. Dark tea cakes are the specialty here, often containing mixed dried fruits: **Melton hunt cake, Lincolnshire dripping cake** (dripping is the fat used), and **Lincolnshire yeast plum bread**, which is cakelike in texture and taste though rich with fruit and dried peel.

Derby, Colwick, Leicester, and **Stilton** are the cheeses produced here. A white wine, called **Lincoln Imperial**, is produced from the vineyards in Stragglethorpe.

NORTH ENGLAND

COUNTIES OF CLEVELAND, DURHAM, NORTHUMBERLAND, TYNE AND WEAR

From the Kielder forest comes venison, popular for steaks and roasts or stewed in casseroles with vegetables. **Northumberland pie** is made from several meats: beef, bacon, and **black pudding** flavored with onion and sealed in a pastry crust. **Stoveys** is a dish prepared from leftovers of meats flavored with bacon and onions and browned in a skillet with sliced potatoes. Leeks, potatoes, and dried gray peas called **carlins** are the most traditional vegetables served. Suet pastry, smothered with sliced leeks, is boiled in a cloth or "cloot" to make a **leek pudding**, while the carlins are soaked and boiled until soft, then fried and flavored with rum. The latter dish is a  specialty for Passion Sunday or Carlin Sunday, said to have originated when a siege, laid on Newcastle by the Scots, was broken by a French ship delivering a load of dried gray peas.

Tea favorites include **granny loaf**, a quick bread made with citron, raisins, and currants, and **Northumbrian aniseed cake**, a delicate brown sugar and honey cake spiced with anise. Probably most famed is the **singing hinny**: a large round scone-type cake baked on a griddle where it is said to "sing" as it cooks.

Flittin' dumpling got its name because this hearty steamed fruit pudding could be sliced and carried as a satisfying snack wherever the farmers worked. **Northumbrian sweet pie** is a Christmas tradition made as a deep dish pie of mutton chops, sweetened dried fruits, and peel enhanced with spices and rum all baked under a pastry.

Lindisfarne mead, a honey wine, and **Cotherstone cheese**, as well as **Lindisfarne mead**

sauce, made from mead and blackcurrants, are also regional favorites.

COUNTY OF CUMBRIA

Mutton, **Cumberland ham**, and the long strip sausage made of herb-flavored pork called **Cumberland sausage** are this area's famed meats. The Westmorland **tatie pot** is a lamb and vegetable stew cooked with **black pudding** (blood sausage) and served traditionally with pickled cabbage. **Yarb pudding**, a combination of leeks and spring greens boiled in a muslin bag with barley to form a pudding, can be served with meats or chilled and sliced then fried with bacon. **Atkinson's biscuits**, made with butter, honey, and almonds, **Grasmere gingerbread**, and **havver bread** (oat bread) vie with **Westmorland parkin** (an oatmeal sweet) and **Westmorland pepper cake** (a rich spiced fruitcake sharpened with black pepper) as teatime treats. Local **Mallerstang cheese** satisfies the savory taste, but the local sweet tooth may enjoy **Cumberland toffee**, **Kendal mint cake**, or a rich thick sauce called **rum butter** or **brandy butter**. The latter two are eaten on biscuits or scones or used as a sauce for mince pies or steamed puddings.

NORTHWEST COUNTIES OF CHESHIRE, DERBYSHIRE (HIGH PEAK ONLY), GREATER MANCHESTER, LANCASHIRE, MERSEYSIDE

Three meat dishes are unique to this area: **hindle wakes**, a poached chicken stuffed with prunes and bread crumbs and flavored with marjoram, served cold with a lemon sauce; the **Lancashire hot pot**, a slow-simmered stew of lamb, lamb's kidneys, onions, and potatoes and sometimes a few oysters; and the **Liverpool lobscouse**, a stew of mutton and/or vegetables topped with biscuits or cooked barley and served with pickled red cabbage.

Blackburn fig pie is a tart filled with stewed figs, treacle, and spices, while **Manchester pudding** consists of layers of apricot preserves and thick egg custard topped with meringue. From the Knotty Ash section of Liverpool comes **wet Nelly**, a syrup-soaked pudding made from cake and pastry scraps.

The tea cakes of this area are widely known and available in many bake shops. **Bury simnel cakes** are spiced fruit cakes, the **Derbyshire oatcakes** are more plebeian and can be served with butter and preserves or fried with bacon and eggs. **Eccles cakes** are round pastries rich with dried fruits and sprinkled with castor sugar (white granulated sugar).

Cheshire and **Lancashire cheese** are enjoyed locally and exported.

YORKSHIRE

Black pudding (also called **blood pudding**), a staple in most of North England, and **York ham**, cured by oak smoke, are widely enjoyed.

Curd tarts or **Yorkshire cheese cakes** are small tarts filled with curd (cottage) cheese, sweetened with sugar and currants. A traditional Christmas Eve dish, especially in Durham and Yorkshire Dales, is **frumenty**, a type of porridge made from soaked unhusked new wheat, oven-baked for three hours, and served with milk or cream. If served for Christmas Eve it would be followed by apple pie and cheese, and gingerbread. Yeast fritters redolent with spices, currants, and apples are the traditional dish for Shrovetide Tuesday and called **pately fritters**. **Fat rascals** is the endearing name given to raisin scones, and **Yorkshire parkin**, a spicy ginger cake made with oatmeal, is traditionally served around the bonfire on Guy Fawkes night, November 5.

But most famous of all is **Yorkshire pudding**, a light crisp batter baked in a smoking hot pan. When eaten in Yorkshire it is said to have a top and bottom but nothing in the middle. Traditionally it is served as a first course with gravy or raspberry vinegar, followed by roast beef and roasted brown potatoes, and likely the meal will be topped off with a stew of dates and rhubarb, or apple tart and the local creamy, tangy cheese, **Wensleydale**. **Wensleydale cheese** and **Bronte liqueur** made from herbs, honey, and brandy, are local treats.

SOUTHEAST ENGLAND

Steak and kidney pudding, beloved English dish, is said to have originated in Sussex.

Cherry brandy and **slow gin** are produced in this area as are wines from local grapes.

LONDON

All the regional specialties find their way to London, but the city itself is also famous for food specialties. **Jellied eels** are often bought from street vendors, while **beef and carrots** is boiled beef with carrots and onions served with **pease porridge** and **suet dumplings**. **Whitebait** is the local name given to young herring, sprats or pilchards, batter-dipped and fried and served with lemon wedges, brown bread and butter. Teatime or snack favorites are **Chelsea buns** and **London buns**: sweet dough crusted with sugar or icing.

SOUTHWEST ENGLAND: CORNWALL, DEVON, SOMERSET, WILTSHIRE

Wiltshire ham and **Wiltshire bacon** gained great fame even though the processed pork included not only local swine but also swine imported from Ireland. **Cornish pasties** originated in Cornwall, and the same pastry from Devon is called **taddy oggies**. Both are elongated cases of pastry filled with meat and potatoes and onion. **Devon pork pie** is also a meal in a pie dish: pork chops are topped with sliced apples and seasonings and covered with a crust. Warmed cream poured over the baked pie just before serving is the finishing touch. Devon is also famous for its fine salmon as well as snails, **Severn elvers** (tiny two-inch eels), and **stargazey pie**, a two-crusted pie with stuffed herrings in the center arranged so the heads are at the outer edges and all the tails meet in the center. The name describes the dish aptly.

Syllabub, a soft dessert of whipped cream and wine or brandy perfumed with lemon, sugar, and nutmeg, originated in this area. Large buns filled with candied dried peel and sugar-coated (**Bath buns**) and the sweet rolls split and filled with fresh clotted cream and jam (**Devonshire** or **Cornish splits**) are all part of the tea accompaniments.

A seaweed, called **laver**, is often eaten as a savory for breakfast either as **laver bread** or oatmeal coated and fried with bacon. **Sally Lunn**, a well-known dish throughout England, is a light golden corn cake split and buttered while hot.

THAMES AND CHILTERNS

Ducks from Aylesbury are famed, and the plentiful rabbits are often made into **Aylesbury harvest pie**: not a pie at all, but a rabbit stuffed with prunes and roasted with bacon and onions. A **bacon clanger** is a boiled suet pudding of bacon and onions, and **Bedfordshire** or **Hertfordshire clanger** is a filled pastry with a savory meat mixture at one end and a jam filling at the other end – a practical lunch in one piece! Baked marrow bones eaten with a long thin spoon and **Stockenchurch pie**, made with minced meat, macaroni, and hard eggs, are served as simple hearty suppers. **Poor knights** are fingers of egg-and-milk-dipped bread, fried, then sprinkled with sugar, while **hollygog pudding** consists of a flour and lard (or margarine) pastry spread with treacle, rolled up and baked in milk. **Banbury cakes** are similar to **eccles cakes**: oval pastries filled with dried fruit and spices.

THE ISLE OF MAN

Kippers (smoked herring) and **queenies** (scallops) are exceptionally good here, while a favorite tea treat is **dumb cake**: simply made from flour and water and baked in the ashes of a hearth fire. Legend suggests that young women eating a piece of **dumb cake** while walking backward will dream of their lover.

THE PLAIN OR HEART OF ENGLAND (CENTRAL REGION): COUNTIES OF GLOUCESTERSHIRE, HEREFORD, WORCESTER, SALOP, STAFFORDSHIRE, WARWICKSHIRE, WEST MIDLANDS

Meat pies are a great favorite here, but two other meat dishes are also specialties: **Shrewsbury lamb cutlets**, butter grilled lamb covered with aspic and served cold with green vegetables and mayonnaise; and **Stafford beefsteaks**, braised steak and onions served with a rich gravy and mushroom or walnut ketchup. **Fidget pie** is a harvest specialty of gammon (ham), onions, potatoes, and apples, while **Herefordshire pigeon pie** is a pastry-covered pie of pigeon and beef and carrots. **Shrewsbury pie** is 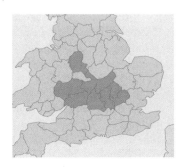 made with rabbit meat, dumplings of liver, baked under a pastry with a spiced wine sauce. **Herefordshire cod**, cooked with cider and mushrooms and sprinkled with cheese and lampreys (similar to eels), are the famed fish dishes.

Desserts include **Worcester beastings pudding**, a baked egg custard made from the first milk after calving (called beastings), and **Tewksbury saucer batter**, individual saucers of stewed sweetened fruit baked in the oven with a batter topping.

Warwick scones are rich with honey, **Shropshire mint cake** is pastry filled with currants and mint, while **Clifton puffs** are puff pastry triangles filled with chopped fruits and nuts warmed with nutmeg and brandy. **Coventry godcakes** were originally baked especially for presentation to godchildren on New Year's Day, and are pastry triangles filled with mincemeat. **Shrewsbury simnel cake** also has a festive connotation: this spiced round fruit cake, filled and topped with marzipan and decorated with twelve marzipan balls representing the twelve apostles (but sometimes only eleven to exclude Judas), is baked especially for Mothering Sunday, the fourth Sunday of Lent, and is also baked often for Easter.

Cider is not only a popular drink, it is also frequently used in many desserts and meat dishes, while **Double Gloucester** cheese, similar to **Cheddar**, is the local specialty together with the world-famous **Worcestershire sauce**.

MEALS AND CUSTOMS

The English reputation for composure under all circumstances is based on strict emotional control. It has been said that it is only in their relationships with their pets that the English "let themselves go." Seldom do they touch each other in public, even for a handshake, and the cool "How do you do?" though spoken as a question is never expected to be answered. This same control pervades conversations. Sometimes the English converse in a way that steers clear of the emotional or the heated argument. Yet, the delight of every English person is a sense of humor and the ability to take things and themselves not too seriously.

English composure at mealtimes is a point of etiquette. It is understood that one chews only small bites at a time, never speaks with food in the mouth, and uses knife and fork throughout the meal (setting the knife to rest while eating with the fork just isn't done). But it is also just as much understood that displaying any interest in the food on one's plate, whether of delight, distaste, or simple curiosity would be most ill mannered. There is some recent evidence of a change, especially when enjoying finger foods and ethnic specialties.

Tea is an English tradition. Tea is also a snack at 11:00 a.m., called *elevenses*. It is often a meal that brings out regional specialties when served at 4:00 p.m. and it is the English beverage. It also starts the English on their day, and there is even an automatic bedside tea machine on the market that can be set to have tea brewed and piping hot for the first morning stretch. This is sometimes called *bed tea*.

There is a traditional way to prepare tea, and the English consider themselves undisputed experts. Fresh cold water must be poured into the kettle, and only when it reaches a rolling boil is a little poured off into the teapot to "hot the pot." With the teapot thus warmed, the water is poured out, and measured black tea leaves are placed in the pot. The pot is taken to the bubbling kettle (never the other way around) to be filled. The lid is then placed on the teapot and a cozy (a cloth or knitted cover to keep the teapot hot) covers all but the spout while the five minutes' steeping time is carefully waited out.

The food accompanying the tea may be as simple as bread and butter or as elaborate as a buffet with hot savory dishes (often local specialties), to be followed by a variety of buns, biscuits, and cakes. The fare may be varied but the talk is not. Conversation around the tea table is as traditional and ritualized as the tea itself: the art of small talk is shown here at its artistic pinnacle.

Most English start their day with a simple breakfast of tea with milk and sugar, and some type of breads or buns. This is identical to the elevenses tea break. In the cities, especially London, lunch is frequently taken at a favorite pub. Here, sandwiches with thin fillings (a slice of cheese or beef), together with a pint of ale, are a usual lunch. Pubs also offer a variety of hot one-plate lunches, which may include almost anything served on toast, or anything hot (creamed meat or fish, spaghetti, beans), very often with an egg on top. A classic lunch is the **ploughman's lunch**: chunks of bread, wedges of cheese served with crunchy pickled onions, and a pint of ale. From 4:00 p.m. to 7:00 p.m. is considered "tea" time, or if the meal is to be ample, "high tea." A light evening supper may include roasted meat and well-cooked vegetables with a sweet, of a steamed or baked pudding, and tea.

It is considered good taste to serve foods in small, even portions. Second helpings may be offered but usually are declined more out of what is considered good taste than from lack of appetite. Among the upper classes it is still traditional for women to leave the men alone at the table after dinner for their brandy and cigars.

SPECIAL OCCASIONS

The Church of England, a Protestant denomination, is the state church and has a membership of more than 25 million. Other denominations include Roman Catholic, with approximately 9 million members; Methodist, with 760,000; Presbyterian, with 800,000; and Jewish, with 300,000. Freedom of worship prevails.

In England, as in much of the world, many festivals of the year, though ostensibly religious or secular, often trace their origins to ancient mystical pagan rites. Although the real Guy Fawkes was hung for attempting to blow up the Houses of Parliament in 1605, all of England commemorates the occasion on November 5, with huge bonfires and burning effigies — similar to the ancient Druid rite of building fires to replenish the waning strength of the autumnal sun. And instead of the human sacrifices of the Druids, gingerbread cookies shaped like men are gleefully consumed while the bonfires roar. Similarly, October 31, called *All Saints' Eve* or *All Souls' Eve*, is celebrated mostly in fun, although here and there one still finds a household that quietly sets out glasses of wine and little buns called **soulcakes** to satisfy wandering spirits.

Shrovetide is the name given to the days immediately preceding Ash Wednesday. This period before Easter is characterized by the "cleansing" of one's home and one's soul: houses are meticulously scrubbed and often painted; souls are cleansed by being "shriven," or subjected to confession of sins. Shrove Tuesday is the traditional pancake day, and in many areas races are held with women running while they flip pancakes in a skillet. The fourth Sunday of Lent is called *Mothering Sunday*, a traditional day for flowers and **simnel cakes**. The twelve marzipan balls that decorate the top of the cake are said to represent the twelve apostles. It is interesting to note that there are records of such a cake with similar distinct decorations dating to ancient Greek and Roman times. Similarly, the fragrant **hot cross buns**, so typical of the Easter season, can be shown to have pre-Christian origins – the cross representing the four seasons, and the roundness of the bun, the sun. Wider knowledge of this origin may make the buns more palatable to non-Christians.

Whether or not it can be proven that Christmas too has its origins in ancient mid-winter rites, there can be no doubt that it is the most beloved festival. Christmas in England is rich with traditions that are tenderly preserved and deeply cherished. It is a family time with wintry snows and cheering fires, warming punch bowls, caroling, gifts, and Santa Claus, but most of all the Christmas feast. Traditional hot wine punches are merely the prelude to a festive dinner of roast goose or turkey filled with fragrant sage dressing, accompanied by potatoes and turnips and brussels sprouts. Somehow room is left for sipping port wine and nibbling nuts and dried fruits followed by mince pie, or mince tarts.

In addition, the highlight in every English home has to be the **Christmas pudding**: a brandy-drenched sweet of fruits, nuts, and spices, served warm and flaming with cooling hard sauce or rum sauce. Almost as important as the pudding is the traditional **English Christmas cake**, prepared weeks in advance with fruits and nuts in a rich cake batter, all carefully set aside with a sprinkle of brandy and rum added now and then to aid in its mellowing. No one remembers exactly why anymore – perhaps for luck? – but everyone stirs the cake or the pudding at least once and only in a clockwise direction.

GLOSSARY OF FOODS AND FOOD TERMS

Note: because many Scottish, Irish, and Welsh dishes as well as food terms are also a part of the English glossary, please refer to those chapters. Additional foods are defined under the heading of Regional Specialties.

Blawn: process of wind-blowing in order to dry. Used mostly when referring to fish as "blawn."

Bloaters: red herrings.

Brawn: a dish usually served at the cold buffet table or for high tea. It is made from the chopped meat of pig's head and tongue, heart, and liver, which have been simmered in stock till tender. The meat is arranged in a mold and the stock poured over. When chilled and set it is served sliced.

Bubble and Squeak: a dish name for the way it sounds when it is cooking. It is a leftovers dish made from cold sliced meat, potatoes, cabbage, or sprouts (all previously cooked) and mashed together then crisply browned in a skillet.

Castor Sugar: finely granulated white sugar.

Chips: french-fried potatoes.

Clotted or **Clouted Cream**: cream, high in butterfat, that has been very slowly heated for many hours until it is yellow and when chilled turns firm. It can be eaten alone, with fresh fruits, or spread on a bun with jam.

Colcannon: a combination of potatoes, cabbage, carrots, and turnips well-cooked in water then drained and mashed, seasoned with salt and pepper and served with butter. Though the Irish lay claim to originating it, the dish is equally popular in Scotland and England, often the main dish of a late supper. This dish may also be called **Kailkenny**, **Kolcannon**, **Kohl Cannon**, or **Kale Cannon**.

Cornish Pasties: oblongs of pastry filled with meat, potatoes, and onions and oven-baked. Can be eaten hot or cold.

Crumpets: a flat round doughy type of bread about four inches in diameter. It is made from yeast batter shaped by a ring mold and cooked on a griddle. It is lightly browned and characteristically shows bubbles. Served with tea, hot and generously buttered.

Dried Currants: raisins.

Faggots: a ground meat mixture (can contain almost anything and often does) shaped into balls, wrapped in caul fat (sheer membrane veined with fat), and oven-baked.

Fish and Chips: English meal or snack made of batter-fried white-flesh fish, served with french-fried potatoes. Traditionally served wrapped in a newspaper cone (authentically *News of the World,* one of the English papers), and sprinkled with salt and malt vinegar.

High Tea: term used to distinguish from mere "tea." While "tea" usually takes place at 4:00 p.m., high tea may be served from 5:00 to 7:00 p.m., often as the last meal of the day in place of a later supper. It may consist of a buffet of cold meats and salads with a few hot casserole-type dishes finishing with cakes, tarts, and, of course, tea.

Horseradish Sauce: finely grated fresh horseradish root blended with a white sauce or thick cream and traditionally served with roast beef. In the early 1700s it was served with fish.

Jugged Hare: from September to March, hare is in season and classed as "game." It is hung for at least one week before being cooked slowly in wine or stock.

Kedgeree: the name and the dish are really a corruption of a Hindu dish. Made the English way, it is a curry-flavored mixture of flaked fish, hard eggs, and cooked rice. It is served as part of a breakfast buffet.

Kippers: smoked herring usually served heated for breakfast.

Laver: purplish seaweed found in the waters around England and Wales, usually served as a breakfast dish, coated with oatmeal and fried with bacon.

Mulligatawny Soup: also called "pepper water" or "curry soup," it is based on a hearty chicken broth well-seasoned with curry and afloat with rice and chicken meat. Originated in the early 1800s.

Mumbled: in the case of eggs it means scrambled; when referring to meat it means minced.

Neeps: turnips.

Pease Pudding: made from twice-cooked dried peas (boiled in a bag), pureed, and served either hot or cold. A popular dish in northeastern England.

Picalilli: spicy preserve of marrow, cucumber, and cauliflower chunks in a mustard sauce.

Ploughman's Lunch: a hearty platter of bread and cheeses served with large pickled onions and washed down with ale.

Raised Pies: refers to pies (usually meat pies) baked in pastry-lined molds with high sides (4 to 6 inches). Served in slices.

Rasher: a slice of meat, usually referring to bacon.

Rizzared: sun-dried. Usually refers to sun-dried fish but could mean someone's face.

Sally Lunn: a light golden cake split and buttered while hot.

Salsify: the cooked roots of this plant have a taste like salted fish, which accounts for its sometimes name of "vegetable oyster," but doesn't account for its other name – **Scorgonera**.

Samphire: a wild green with a taste similar to asparagus.

Scrowled: broiled.

Soused Fish: pickled fish with vinegar, onions, and spices.

Squash: if you ask for squash in England you won't get the vegetable, you'll be served a noncarbonated citrus-flavored drink.

Swede: rutabaga.

Swiss Roll: a thin light cake spread with filling or jam and rolled up. The slices show spirals of jam and cake.

Syllabub: a soft dessert of whipped cream and wine or brandy, perfumed with lemon, sugar, and nutmeg.

Toad-in-the-Hole: a light supper dish of pork sausages baked in **Yorkshire Pudding**.

Treacle: molasses.

Trifle: layered fingers of cake that have been soaked with sherry or Madeira then dribbled with a soft custard, sprinkled with sliced fruits, and topped with decorated whipped cream.

Tunny: tuna fish.

Victoria Sponge: round sponge cake filled with jam.

Vegetable Marrow: this term is used to describe most of the vegetables known in North America as the "squash family": hubbard, pepper, etc.

Water Souchy: a stewed mix of fresh fish and eels. Sounds similar to the Belgium fish soup called **Water zooi.**

CHAPTER 18

FILIPINO

A partially submerged mountain range in the southeastern Pacific Ocean forms a grouping of 7,100 islands and islets called the Philippines. Tropically hot and humid and frequently struck by torrential rains and earthquake tremors, more than 90 percent of these islands are an uninhabited tropical wilderness. In fact, more than 50 percent of them remain unnamed. Luzon and Mindanao are the two largest islands upon which more than 75 percent of the population of the Philippines lives and works.

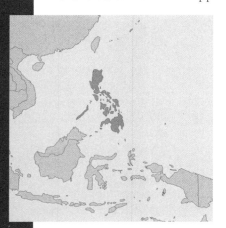

The natives of the Philippines call themselves Filipinos. Originally this term denoted a person of Spanish descent born in the Philippines, similar to the Creole of the Spanish-American colonies, but the name has been applied to the 80 percent of the population of Malays Christianized since the 1800s.

Arriving from the many Malay Islands and tracing their origins to approximately 3000 B.C.E., the aboriginal inhabitants arrived in successive waves and formed their own unique customs, lore, and dialects. Today these aboriginal dialects number more than 80 percent; as well, most people are fluent in English and Spanish. Since 1946, when the Philippines gained its independence from Spain, Tagalog, a Malayan dialect, has been declared the official language.

Although the Filipinos have long had trade contacts with the Chinese, Japanese, Portuguese and East Indians, the strongest influence came from the Spanish and the Americans. In the 1300s Arab missionaries brought the faith of Islam to some of the smaller southern islands and those who adopted the faith are called Moros. Perhaps the first Christian influence was the Portuguese navigator and explorer Ferdinand Magellan's landing in 1521, but the strongest was the Spanish rule and colonization which began in 1565 and lasted 333 years until the Treaty of Paris in 1898, when Spain sold the Philippines to the United States for $20 million.

So powerful was the influence of the Spanish rulers and the Roman Catholic missionaries that the small feudal units called *barangays* were not only quickly and easily conquered, they also rapidly embraced Spanish names, customs, and foods. Enraptured by the colorful Roman Catholic ceremonials, the Filipinos readily converted to the religion of Spain as well. Many vestiges of this protracted influence are still very much a part of daily life in the Philippines. Women stress modesty in dress and primness in behavior, and girls from fine families make public appearances usually only when discreetly chaperoned.

The Spanish custom of the late afternoon break called the *merienda* is much enjoyed by the Filipinos and frequently includes a variety of small or light savory snacks or dishes. The *merienda* is never considered to be a meal because it does not include rice. The Asian heritage insists that only when rice is present, at least in one of its many forms, is a meal a proper meal. Late evening meals followed by city-strolling is an older custom replaced recently by earlier dinner hours as the newer American influence presses in.

The 25 percent of the land under cultivation yields vital subsistence crops of corn, sweet potatoes or yams, and from ancient hillside terraces comes rice. Many tropical fruits including coconuts, bananas, mangoes, oranges, papayas, and **calamansi** (similar to lemons and limes) are grown. Each crop takes a place in an interesting cuisine that blends influences from China, Malaysia, Spain, and most recently, the United States.

China's staples of rice and noodles are also staples in the Philippines but in a form not used in China: served together in a dish called **pancit**. Many of Spain's dishes that mix ingredients in one casserole for a hearty main dish have found a place on Filipino tables: **puchidas** and **pucheros** are hearty variations on Spanish stews called **cocidas**, which are mixtures of slow-simmered legumes and vegetables with meats included whenever possible; the Spanish **caldereta** is a fish stew which becomes the Filipino **kaldereta**, a stew made with goat meat.

The Spanish *conquistadores* brought chocolate from their Mexican conquests to Spain, and the Spaniards brought it to the Philippines. Filipinos often enjoy a frothy hot chocolate for breakfast and a bitter-chocolate richness in the sauces of many chicken or duck dishes (similar to the Mexican **mole**). One of these is called **pato ng may tsokolate**.

The marriage of Chinese and Spanish cuisines together with the native tropical fruits and vegetables produces other interesting dishes. Chinese spring roll skins, those delicate, tissue-like pastry leaves, are used to produce **lumpia**. These are similar to spring rolls but are filled with a mix of ingredients that leave no doubt as to their Philippine origin: garlic, pork, chicken, bean sprouts, shredded cabbage, and finely shredded coconut palm hearts – a tropical touch with a nod to Chinese origins!

From 1898 to 1946, when the Philippines gained independence, American influences added yet another dimension to culture and customs. Freedom of speech, free elections, and free enterprise found a place in everyday Philippine life together with some incursions of American slang, hurry-up living, and convenience snack foods such as hamburgers and hot dogs and the slabs of meat Americans call "steak." In fact, in deference to American tastes, many native dishes tempered their garlic flavoring and removed the Filipino condiments made from fermented fish – **patis** and **bagoong** – pungently strong in taste and odor for American palates.

But the intricacies of a fine cuisine are not part of every Filipino's table. Though the tropical climate is a benign environment, many poor people subsist on little more than rice, sometimes stretched with the addition of corn. Others manage with rice lightly flavored with **patis** or **bagoong sauce**. Every grain of rice is treasured, as it is in all rice countries, and appetites are appeased by many types of dishes from gruels to puddings and treats made of glutinous rice as well as the more familiar fluffy rice.

DOMESTIC LIFE

The influence of American and Spanish occupations is apparent in both public and private life. The Spanish occupation brought with it increased religious participation especially by women. But the newer patterns did not replace ancient Asian kinship ties: the importance of family relationships and responsibilities are of prime concern. The new religion remained family-centered, not church-centered as in Spain. Family shrines became the worship centers, and on special occasions the entire family would join a procession carrying its own personal statues rather than those belonging to the community church. It was largely through the women's interest and devotion to Roman Catholicism that European ideas of dress, customs, and music made inroads in Philippine family life.

Though Philippine women enjoy equal status with men, and frequently are the "family treasurers," nonetheless like Spanish women, they manage in a very feminine way to make their husbands and sons feel dominant. The father makes all family decisions concerned with the outside world: schools, voting, business and community affairs.

The Filipino's family is of great importance for it represents the only source of love, sustenance, and security. There is almost nothing the Filipino will not do for the sake of family. *Lamangan* is a Filipino expression meaning more or less "by hook or by crook to get on top ..." It is also an expression that suggests some of the difficulty of accepting loss or defeat and the intense importance of self-esteem, pride, and dignity. In fact, the Filipino's supersensitivity is often considered to be a Malay trait called *hiya* and may be the underlying reason for the difficulty in giving or receiving criticisms.

As mentioned above, it was mainly through the women that European ideas were introduced, including ideas about food and its methods of preparation. Filipinos have always been alert not only to new food

FOODS COMMONLY USED

Filipinos enjoy salty, cool, and sour tastes. They love to combine many different ingredients in one dish, favor onions and garlic as a base to most preparations, and consider frying one of their favorite methods of cookery. Tropical fruits and vegetables blend happily with pork, chicken, and seafoods in an ingenious variety of dishes that borrow from China and Spain but end up definitely Philippine. Sourness is added with the frequent use of unripe fruits, the juice of the tart **calamansi**, or vinegars plain or spiced with chilis. Saltiness is most frequently added with the generous addition of either **patis**, the amber liquid prepared from fermented and salted fish, or **bagoong**, a popular shrimp paste also fermented and salted. These two condiments are on every meal table, much as salt and pepper shakers are always on the western table. Rice heads the staples list, closely followed by fish and pork, as can be afforded.

ideas but also to methods of sanitation and food preservation. In the larger cities, modern kitchens and appliances abound but contrast sharply with low-income homes where the barest minimum of food and equipment are available.

DAIRY PRODUCTS

The gentle *carabao*, similar to the water buffalo, is the farmer's workhorse and also provides milk from which a delicate white cheese is made. This cheese is widely used, especially at the end of meals. Fresh dairy products are increasingly available, using cow's milk, as well as canned evaporated milk and condensed milk.

FRUITS AND VEGETABLES

Fruits are abundant. Coconut is used in many ways: coconut oil, shredded fresh and dried coconut (**copra**) – even the gelatinous pulp of green coconuts called **buko** all find a place in the cuisine. Bananas too are used in many ways: wrapped in bacon, broiled, fried in slices, and even hawked by vendors as skewered barbecued treats. **Calamansi** and mangoes are also widely used.

Generally fruits find their way into a variety of dishes whether or not they are ripe. With their penchant for cool sour flavors, Filipinos make use of many green or unripe fruits, while overripe fruits are happily mashed together to make ice cream or cool fruit mixtures for refreshing desserts.

In fact, fruits are so widely used it is difficult to say which is most important: mango, banana, or coconut. Other native fruits include breadfruit, **dayap**, **atis**, **anonas**, jackfruit, guava, star apples, many varieties of bananas, and tamarind. Also to be added to the long list of popular fruits are: **chicos** (similar to dates), Mindanao grapefruits, pomelo, avocado pears, **magosteens**, and pineapples. These latter are believed to have been introduced by the Spanish and are mostly grown for export.

Most of the vegetables used today, such as leafy greens and some root vegetables, were introduced by the Chinese from the Asian mainland, brought by the Spanish either from Mexico or the Mediterranean, or grown for American tastes. Eggplant, **taro root**, **ampalaya**, and **patola** are examples of vegetables probably indigenous to the islands. Tomatoes and squash and some varieties of beans were almost certainly introduced by the Spanish, while mung beans (and sprouts) are of Chinese origin together with some types of cucumbers and melons, and perhaps some varieties of edible bamboo and bulbs. Like the fruits, many vegetables are used when still green, some when just sprouting, others when ripe. Fruits and vegetables are often used interchangeably. It is typical to find both fruits and vegetables combined in meat or fish dishes.

MEATS AND ALTERNATES

Pork is the most widely used meat: most farms have pigs, a few chickens, and several cows. It was the Spanish who added beef to the Philippines' traditional cuisine of rice-fish-pork-chicken, and the later influence of the Americans accentuated the taste for beef, as well as dairy products. Very insignificant amounts of duck, goose, pheasant, pigeon, and turkey are part of the Filipino diet.

Fish consumption usually exceeds available local supplies and a substantial amount of fish is imported to meet the demand. One of the favored special dishes is **inehow**: a whole baked fish (**bangus**) stuffed with **patis** and tomato-flavored rice and onion and garlic sautéed in oil. The whole stuffed fish is then wrapped in banana leaves and oven- or pit-baked.

Lumbag nuts, **pili nuts**, and **betel nuts**, as well as the more familiar cashew nuts, form very small crops on the islands and are not a large part of the cuisine. Also of minor importance to the cuisine are the bean crops: soybean, mung beans, garbanzos, and other varieties used mainly in some mixed dishes such as soups and stews, sometimes mashed with fruits as in **halo-halo**. This is a popular dessert of alternate layers of mashed fruit pulp (sometimes with mashed beans) and shaved ice, topped with cream.

BREADS AND GRAINS

Without rice, it is not a meal. So say the Filipinos. But rice is more than a mound of perfectly cooked fluffy granules. Rice may be found in fillings and stuffings, in soups and stews. Glutinous rice will often be the base of many confections and sweet desserts such as **suman**, a sweetened glutinous rice steamed in rolls or squares of banana leaves and eaten anytime as snack or dessert, or **malagkit**, a sweet pudding made with glutinous rice and coconut milk. Rice flour is used to make cakes, puddings, and delicious noodles. The delicate thin **lumpia** skins are made from a mixture of rice flour and water then filled and fried to golden crispness.

Rice is the chief food crop followed closely by corn and sweet potatoes. But while corn and sweet potatoes are found in many of the combination dishes that the Filipinos are noted for, there is no question that rice is the prime staple food.

FATS

Coconut oil and oil made from many local seed crops are widely used in cookery. Use of lard and olive oil became more prevalent under the Spaniards, while the use of butter together with other dairy products increased under American influence.

Filipino techniques for frying foods are artfully distinctive. Aside from the usual frying of stuffed foods, some preparations are coated with a meringue-like topping that forms a puffy brown crust (**rellenong alimango**). The delicious **ukoy** is a fritter carefully composed of a large shrimp and bean sprouts held in a light batter and deep-fried. Sometimes foods are quickly fried in slender strips (fish, meat, or vegetables) to create crispy garnishes.

SWEETS AND SNACKS

The Filipinos' eclectic mix of foods and cookery techniques also creates unusual combinations in the taste for sweets.

The late afternoon break called the *merienda* follows a Spanish tradition of consuming sweets in the form of a small afternoon meal. This was practical when the other Spanish tradition of a very late evening supper was also popular. Many Filipinos now follow American patterns of working hours and three meals a day. Yet for many others, the *merienda* is a custom too pleasant to break. Sweet cakes, tarts, and fritters are part of this tradition, but Filipinos also add small savory foods like **ukoy**.

Many sweet treats are made from a base of glutinous rice, richly sugared and often flavored with coconut. Ice creams and fruit mixtures also form snacks or desserts. Confections include those made of rice bases with added nuts and fruits and sometimes chocolate. The very sweet Spanish **flan** (baked custard) is almost a daily dessert, often with the tang of fresh limes or the sweetness of coconut.

SEASONINGS

Despite the triple influence of China, Spain, and the United States, Filipinos have developed a distinctive cuisine redolent of the tastes they enjoy. Salty, cool, and sour tastes, tropical fruits and vegetables, served with their many fried dishes, accompanied by rice and the surprise of very sweet snacks and dessert characterize Filipino cuisine.

Salty flavors are enhanced by using **bagoong** (salty fermented shrimp paste) and **patis** and **toyo** (salty light versions of soy sauce), and **hipon** (a salty sauce prepared from shrimp or anchovy). These may be used in food preparation as well as for dipping sauces. Other varieties of dipping sauces include vinegar, minced garlic, and seasoned salt with or without chilies.

Cool flavors are achieved using tart or unripe fruits, vinegar, or the juice of tangy citrus fruits such as limes or **calamansi**. The ultimate perfection of sour flavors is **sinigang**, a sour soup made with a meat broth and combined green tart fruits such as tamarind, guavas, green mangoes, **calamansi** or **kamias** (a sour fruit resembling a cucumber). Recipes for **sinigang** are family treasures.

Coconut milk, lime juice, ginger, turmeric, garlic, and brown sugar must also be included in the seasonings that distinguish Filipino food. For example, very sweet dipping sauce for **lumpia** (crispy appetizer rolls) is simply made from brown sugar and water gently thickened with cornstarch.

BEVERAGES

The most traditional beverages of the Philippines are those from the indigenous coconut tree. Both the milk from green to ripe coconuts and the sap that comes from the cut growing-tip of the tree can be consumed as sweet fresh drinks or fermented into an alcoholic drink called **tuba**. **Tuba** can also be made from the sap of the buri or nipa palm trees and likely is one of the oldest national drinks.

Cacao and coffee plants were introduced by the Spanish and have continued to be cultivated as the popularity of coffee as a beverage and the use of chocolate both as a drink and as a flavoring increase.

A great variety of cool fresh fruit drinks are popular any time of the day. Milk is increasingly used by children. Adults enjoy fruit drinks and also coffee with meals or as a refreshment break, while hot chocolate is often taken as a breakfast beverage. Tea or coffee may accompany the afternoon *merienda*.

MEALS AND CUSTOMS

As in all other areas of Philippine life, the origins of eating customs can be traced to the history of the islands themselves.

As in most Asian regions, rice is the most respected staple, for hunger is always a reality. Although many Filipinos enjoy a prosperous life and happily mingle foods, meal patterns, and eating customs that blend Malay, Chinese, Spanish, and American patterns, there are still many who cook and eat their meals traditionally, savoring every grain of rice and the slight taste of fishy condiment. Native fruits and vegetables in season fill many plates.

Traditional Filipinos begin their day with a meal of fish and rice, others enjoy fresh fruits and **ensaimada**, sugary yellow buns that are the Filipino coffeecake. For others, frothy cups of hot chocolate accompanied by crusty white sourdough bread (**pan de sal**) mean breakfast.

Diversity of tastes is less apparent in the other meals of the day, depending, of course, on economic circumstances. Lunch and dinner tend to consist of several dishes served buffet style, followed by fruits in season and then a variety of sweet desserts of which the **flan** is always one. The dishes presented often span several cultures, but somehow end up being unquestionably Filipino.

The *merienda*, the small, sweet meal served in the late afternoon with tea or coffee, is suffering competition from the many street vendors, cafés, and restaurants, as well as quick-snack bars in the American style. One can snack in almost any language, or at least with enough diversity to satisfy any taste, whether the hunger pangs arrive in the morning, afternoon, or late evening.

Despite its penchant for rice, the Philippines do not use chopsticks; western or European eating customs prevail. Hospitality is always gracious and the best dishes proudly presented to guests. Many Filipinos will even temper their own tastes for fermented fish condiments and heavy garlic to please what they believe to be an American palate, saving their traditional seasonings for when they are dining with family.

SPECIAL OCCASIONS

The population of the Philippines is 80 percent Roman Catholic. About 4 percent of the population follow the Muslim faith and are called (much to their resentment) Moros. The latter group live in independent groups faithfully following Islamic ceremonies and customs and are ruled by their own chieftain or sultan called the *datu*.

Mestizos is the name given to those of mixed native and Spanish heritage, but more recently this term is used to denote any mixed racial background. Mestizos are also sometimes called Cacique.

The predominantly Christian population of the Philippines is unusual in that it represents the largest body of Asiatic peoples converted to Christianity. Both the Spanish and American periods of influence have also left the islands with a more western culture than any other Asian country. Thus it is natural to expect that the Christian festivals of Easter and Christmas will have a special significance. Religion is more family-centered than church-centered and this makes for a special festive spirit on any occasion. Families gather and share special foods and their preparation brings a spirit of happy anticipation.

Sunday is a time of family relaxation, and is often celebrated with a special dinner of **puchero**. This special dish is a loving combination of several meats and many vegetables cut in large chunks glowing with a rich golden sauce of well-simmered tomatoes and yellow yams all bathed in a rich blend of sautéed onions and garlic. Served with mounds of rice, it is a Sunday meal for leisurely eating conducive to rest afterwards. With a **puchero**, other courses are hardly necessary!

Pork usually holds the center of attention for Christmas and Easter. Despite an ample array of many classical dishes arranged in bountiful buffet, the **jamon de Navidad**, a baked Christmas ham glazed with fruits and crusted with brown sugar, or the **lechon de leche**, charcoal-roasted suckling pig, will probably steal the scene. **Inehow**, the whole stuffed banana-wrapped baked fish, and **lumpia** will likely be other specialties on the menu. A full array of fresh fruits, cheese, and special sweet custards, puddings, and cakes as well as the **leche flan** will complete any festive meal.

GLOSSARY OF FOODS AND FOOD TERMS

Achara: generic name for a variety of sweet/sour pickles and relishes served with meat or fish.

Adobo: classic Philippine dish of slow-simmered chicken and pork (other meats may be used) cooked until the liquid evaporates. Oil is added to brown the meats, then the whole is served with rice. The rich sour taste and thick brown sauce is the result of first marinating the meats in mild palm vinegar liberally spiced with garlic and peppercorns, while the final browning in lard is accelerated with a dash of soy sauce. **Adobo** can also refer to foods cooked with vinegar, garlic, and soy sauce.

Apa: deep-fried filled **Lumpia** wrappers. **Apa** may be filled with many combinations of meat, fish, seafood, and vegetables, almost always distinguished from Chinese egg rolls by the addition of shredded tropical vegetables or fruits, sometimes even garbanzos. Another form of **Apa** is similar to Mexican tacos: crisp-fried open **Lumpia** are layered with fresh shredded vegetables, diced bean curd, and several varieties of beans then topped with spicy condiments.

A Pay Ng Naka: small chunks of liver simmered in a garlic-chili-lime-juice sauce with ginger and brown sugar and finished with a splash of coconut milk.

Bagoong: a thick paste made from fermented salted fish or shrimps, sometimes called the "Philippine caviar." It is used in cooking and as a condiment and often as an appetizer commonly served together with sliced green mangoes.

Buko: the gelatinous pulp of young green coconuts used in many fruit desserts. Sometimes this name is given to ice cream that is served right from the green coconut shell.

Calamansi: a local type of lemon with a taste between lemon and lime. It is used as a flavorful sprinkle on almost anything, frequently in cooking and in desserts.

Champorodi: small bowls of pudding made from glutinous rice (**Malagkit**), evaporated milk, coconut milk, and sometimes chocolate. Taken as a snack, and sometimes for breakfast.

Chinese Shrimp Toast: triangles of bread spread with a seasoned shrimp mixture and then deep-fried. Served hot as an appetizer.

Chorizos: garlic-flavored pork sausages used in many dishes. Brought to the islands by the Spanish.

Dilis: small cured and salted fish (similar to anchovies or sardines) dipped in batter, deep-fried then served as appetizers.

Empanadas: meat-filled pastry turnovers, served for snacks or as appetizers. The Spanish name reveals their origin.

Ensaimada: yellow saffron buns coated with a sugar glaze. A favorite with breakfast coffee.

Ensalada Itlog: Philippine version of potato salad with the addition of cooked rice, all tossed with French dressing.

Escabeche: sauteed fish, again with the cool sour taste imparted by the marinade, which is then poured over the cooked fish and allowed to chill to blend the flavors.

Estofado: any foods prepared with a brown sugar sauce, vinegar, and spices – usually meats.

Gazpacho: cool, tangy blend of fresh puréed summer vegetables forming a light soup. Served with small bowls of garnishes: croutons, chopped hard egg, minced scallions, etc. A Spanish import.

Ginesa: a dish of browned pork dice, shrimp, onions, and garlic seasoned with shrimp paste and **Patis**. Wedged tomatoes and any prepared vegetables at hand are steamed on top. The whole mixture is tossed before serving with rice.

Guisado: sauteed.

Halo-Halo: beloved Philippine dessert served in tall glasses and sometimes sold in cans. Layers of mashed mixed ripe fruits and sometimes beans, shaved ice and topped with cream.

Inehow: classic baked stuffed fish. A large whole fish is stuffed with a rice mixture including well-sautéed onions and garlic, tomatoes and flavored with **Patis**. The whole stuffed fish is then wrapped in banana leaves (or foil) and oven-baked or baked in a charcoal pit.

Kaldereta: similar to the Spanish fish dish **Caldereta**, a stew of goat meat, sometimes lamb, rather than fish.

Luglug: thick rice noodles also called **Bijon**, named for the noise they make both when being stirred and eaten.

Lumpia: the thin pastry wrappers or skins used for **Apa** or **Lumpiang**, prepared like crepes, but made with rice flour and water.

Lumpiang Ubod: **Ubod** is finely shredded coconut palm hearts, added to minced shrimp and chicken and wrapped in **Lumpia** before deep-frying.

Merienda: late afternoon break of sweets and tea. The Philippine version often includes savory dishes made from fish or seafood. Rice is not included in a *merienda*, as it is not considered a meal. Of Spanish origin.

Pancit Lulug Palabok: a dish of boiled rice noodles layered with a red sauce made from achiote seeds and shrimp juice, then a layer of browned diced pork and shrimp topped with a garnish of crushed garlic cracklings, flaked dried smoked fish, some shredded greens and wedges of eggs or salted eggs. The long noodles symbolize long life, making this a popular dish for special occasions.

Pancit Molo: a Philippine elaboration of Chinese won ton soup. **Molos** are similar to won ton: triangle shapes of noodle dough filled with finely minced chicken and pork, liberal with garlic. Some of the filling is browned, then chicken is stock added and finally the **Molos**. A sprinkling of chopped scallions is the garnish.

Pan de Sal: crusty white sourdough bread, taken with hot chocolate for a light breakfast.

Patis: the amber fluid prepared from salted fermented fish and used widely as a flavoring and condiment.

Pato Ng May Tsokolate: duck roasted with a dark tart sauce made with sherry, lime juice, and bitter chocolate.

Salabat: a refreshing tea steeped from fresh ginger and brown sugar.

Sinigang: classic sour soup made from mix of tart vegetables and a stock of chicken or pork hocks, finished with **Patis** and flavored with tamarind or calamansi.

Suman: sweetened glutinous rice steamed in rolls or squares of banana leaves. A popular snack at any time of day and often taken at *merienda*.

Ube: purple yams.

Ukoy: shrimp and bean sprouts held in a light batter and deep-fried into lacy rounds. Served as snacks, appetizers, or one of the courses of a *merienda*.

CHAPTER 19

FINNISH

Six hundred years of Swedish rule and a hundred years of Russian domination have left their stamp on the language and food customs of Finland but the character of the people remains unique.

The difficulty in understanding Finns becomes apparent when descriptions vary from "honest yet stubborn" to "slow and very quiet." Of course there are regional and individual differences, but certain general characteristics are evident. Finns are noted for their strength and athletic prowess, and Finn names will be found in the lists of pioneers clearing sites and building towns and highways in the United States. In Canada the Finns are famed for their work on the Canadian Pacific Railway and the Welland Canal. Their apparent slowness may be attributed to their meditative and philosophical natures, and their noted long periods of silence readily explained by saying, "There is nothing to talk about." Most of all, Finns possess a quality that can best be described by their own word: *sisu*, which is courage, stamina, and stubbornness rolled into one package. Others call it more simply "guts."

It must have been *sisu* that gave 420,000 Karelian Finns the endurance to move from their homes en masse during the Russian invasion of their beloved province of Karelia during World War II. It must have been *sisu* that caused the rest of the Finn population to open their homes to these refugees, to feed and clothe them and donate their own money and precious possessions to help the Karelians eventually build new homes. And surely it is *sisu* that provides the Finn with the kind of moral and spiritual sustenance to live in a rugged country visited by summer only two months of the year.

The Finns call their country Soumi, literally "marshland." Laced with more than 60,000 lakes, less than 8 percent of the land is fertile. This small arable portion consists mainly of the coastal regions. The rest of the land is largely stony or covered with forests. Crops are therefore limited. Principle ones are those that form staple foods: potatoes and a fine variety of grains including rye, oats, barley, and wheat. Flax is also an important crop and rural women are famed for their hand looms that produce rugs, cloths, mats, curtains, and clothing from the linen threads.

The exact ethnic origin of the Finns is obscure but they are believed to be of Mongolian descent.

Their height and fair skin, however, makes them appear to be closer to the Teutons.

Although 98 percent of Finns now speak Finnish, it was the publication of Finland's epic **Kalevala** in 1836 that led to the establishment of Finnish as the official language. Finns learn Swedish and Finnish at school and many also learn German, English, or Russian. Estonians and the Hungarian Magyars are the only other peoples who speak languages from the Finno-Ugric root, but only the Finns were part of the free world while the others were under Communist domination. Perhaps this too has something to do with *sisu*.

It is said that there are three things for which the Finn will be most homesick: the sour rye bread, the sauna, and the luminous summer nights when the sun forgets to set. **Ruisleip** – the sour rye bread baked flat and crisply hard with a hole in the center (western Finland) or thick, round, and crusty (eastern Finland) – is the staple of every meal.

The sauna is the eagerly anticipated Saturday night relaxation of Finn families and is much enjoyed by many others who have come to appreciate the pleasure of this warm steamy ritual.

Both **ruisleipa** and the sauna may be duplicated wherever Finns live, but the strangely mystical light of summer nights, when the sun does not set below the horizon, can only be appreciated in Finland and cherished in the memories of those who have witnessed it.

DOMESTIC LIFE

Because of the country's many rivers and streams, electrical power is used all over Finland, even in country barns. But wood and coal continue to be the common fuel for heating and cooking. **Ruisleipa** is still baked in brick oven – several times a week in eastern Finland, where the softer loaf is preferred, but sometimes only twice a year in western Finland, where the thin hard bread is preferred. The latter version is punched with a hole then hung on long poles to dry. It can be stored for months.

The most important room in the country house is the *tupa*. It is a combination living room and kitchen, typically with scrubbed wooden floors, wooden furniture and handwoven mats, table linen, and curtains. The important and often huge brick oven for baking bread is built into one wall of the house and the bread is placed inside and removed with a large wooden paddle.

Preferring fresh fruits and vegetables, urban homemakers shop frequently, but everyone makes preserves of berries and pickles of vegetables such as beets and cucumbers. All Finns have a strong preference for simplicity in their foods, enjoying the natural taste of wild berries and mushrooms, while fish and meats are frequently flavored only with salt or smoke. Although the *sauna* is primarily a bathhouse, legs of lamb and sides of bacon and ham are often smoke-cured there; quick post-*sauna* snacks of sausages are often grilled over a small fire and enjoyed there with **Kalja**, the light Finn beer.

DAIRY PRODUCTS

Much milk is consumed as a fresh whole beverage, as clabbered milk, called **viili piima**, or fresh buttermilk. Finland is famed for its great variety of quality cheeses: **Aura**, **Emmenthal**, **Kesti**, **Kreivi**, **Tilsitter**. There are also many local fresh-milk cheeses similar to pot cheese or cottage cheese and called simply "breakfast cheese." Both fresh rich cream and sour cream are used in many dishes.

FRUITS AND VEGETABLES

Because of the short growing season, fresh local fruits (mostly berries) and seasonal vegetables are greatly enjoyed. Preserves of berries and dried fruits (lightly sweetened or even quite tart) are often served with meats. Local fruits include blueberries, raspberries, cloudberries, lingonberries, cranberries, strawberries, and gooseberries, while citrus fruits are imported. Apples, rhubarb, and rosehips as well as dried fruits are also used. Fruits are eaten fresh, atop cereals, or as fillings in pastries and sometimes cakes. They are also served as dessert in the form of tart fruit soups, thickened puddings, whips, custards, and snows (with whipped egg whites). Fine liqueurs are made from some of the berries.

The staple vegetables are potatoes and cauliflower. Cucumbers, onions, beets, carrots, and radishes are used but not in any quantity and there is some resistance to increasing the consumption of vegetables. Salads of fresh vegetables are almost unknown. Many types of wild mushrooms are used both fresh and preserved in salt brine to be served during winter. Most vegetables are consumed as pickles, while potatoes and cauliflower are eaten in long-cooked (sometimes four to five hours) casseroles.

MEATS AND ALTERNATES

All parts of beef, pork, veal, and lamb are used: roasts, stews, jellied meat loaves, sausages, soups ("slaughter soup" is made from offal and blood). Bottled animal blood is sold as an ingredient for other dishes. Chickens are not plentiful. The Laplanders' domesticated reindeer is considered a great delicacy, especially reindeer tongue. Occasionally game birds, bear meat, and elk are consumed.

Although herring is the staple fish, other fish used include sprats, sardines, whitefish, bream, flounder, pike, and salmon. Freshwater fish from local rivers and lakes are most common. **Rapuja** are the tiny freshwater crayfish served in midsummer, while **muikko** are the tiny lakefish eaten whole.

Eggs are consumed mostly as an ingredient in other dishes, bakery, and desserts. But **munavoi** is a smooth spread of mashed hard-cooked eggs with butter. Legumes, other than the dried peas for soup, are not used.

BREADS AND GRAINS

Wholegrain bread is a part of every meal: slightly sour and filling. Porridges and gruels made from various grains are often the main dish at lunch and

FOODS COMMONLY USED

Breads and cooked grains form a part of almost every Finn meal and are often accompanied with herring, potatoes, or dairy products. Milk and cheeses are used generously. Because of the short growing season, fruits and vegetables are prized especially in season and accompany meats and fish in the form of preserves, pickles, and stewed dried fruits during winter. Meats and fish are used frugally, with nothing wasted. The staple fish is herring, prepared in many ways and used as appetizer or main dish. The Finns do not consume much concentrated sweets, preferring snacks of sandwiches or very plain cakes and cookies. Coffee is the national beverage, but beer, vodka, cognac, and strong tea have their place as well.

sometimes are eaten as desserts in smaller servings with berries added. Plain tasty yeast breads and crisp plain cookies are always served with coffee. Rye, barley, oats, and wheat are used singly or in combination for the many grain breads and dishes.

FATS

Much fat is consumed in the form of whole milk, butter, cheeses, cream, and sour cream. Butter is the main cooking fat although salt pork and bacon fat are also used.

SWEETS AND SNACKS

The Finns are not great sweet-eaters, preferring **viili piima** (clabbered milk), **kiisseli** (fruit soups), or fresh berries in season as a dessert. Between-meal snacks will usually be coffee and a sandwich or a variety of plain crisp cookies or yeast breads, pound cakes, or other un-iced baked goods. Really rich and elaborate desserts are seldom served except on special occasions or for guests. Even the many types of berry preserves enjoyed with meats are only slightly sweetened.

SEASONINGS

Finns prefer natural flavors but like them on the robust side. From the sour rye bread and soured-milk dishes to the tart pickles and fruit desserts, the Finn preference is not for sweet flavors. Seasonings include dill, onion, garlic, juniper berries, and pine needles, which may be rubbed on game or fowl. Because smoked meats and smoked fish are so popular, smoke must be considered a flavoring as well as the abundantly used fresh milk and cream.

BEVERAGES

Coffee is the national beverage, but milk, buttermilk, and clabbered milk are popular. There are a variety of homemade fermented beverages, especially **kalja**, which is similar to beer but is non-alcoholic and not sweet. Vodka is called **Ryyppy** and is served icy cold. Finland is reputed to be the largest importer of fine cognac from France. Tea and herbal teas are occasional beverages, but the Finns enjoy their tea brewed strong.

MEALS AND CUSTOMS

Finns wake up to a morning coffee, **pulla** (braided yeast bread), or open-face sandwiches of cheese and meats. Many Finns prefer coffee only and save their appetites for a lunch of **puuroa** (cooked cereal) or, in the country, a heartier meal of meat or fish with potatoes and gravy, bread and butter, and cheese. Not long after the noon meal comes a break when coffee, breads, and cookies or sometimes open-face

sandwiches are served. The evening meal is likely to be a baked casserole of meat and cereal, or potatoes, bread and butter, all served with fruit preserves, beets, and cucumbers. Later in the evening coffee will again be accompanied by yeast breads and cookies.

Voileipapoyta is the name given to the traditional Finn "sandwich table." In Sweden this is called *smorgasbord*; in Denmark it is called *smorbrod;* and in Norway it is known as *koltbord.* The basis of them all is bread and butter and upon this is built the rest of the meal – usually lunch, but occasionally a simplified version serves as breakfast. The Finn sandwich table is similar but differs with the inclusion of more freshwater fish dishes which abound in Finland, and small, hot, stuffed pastries. The ritual of the sandwich table requires that the smoked and salted fish (usually herring dishes) are eaten first, then a fresh plate taken for other fish dishes and cold roasted, smoked, or cured meats and jellied meat loaves. Still another fresh plate is taken for the variety of hot dishes. Fresh fruit or a compote of fruits with cheeses form the dessert. Coffee is served later, sometimes accompanied by simple yeast cakes and cookies.

The other Finn standby is the "coffee table," the favorite break of the day, anytime in the afternoon or evening, and the popular way to entertain guests. Although usually just a simple serving of yeast cake (**pulla**) and cookies with excellent coffee, it can be more elaborate for special occasions or special guests. In the latter case, the fare will likely include **pulla** glazed with egg and crusted with almonds and sugar, un-iced poundcake, several types of cookies, and a layered filled cake. Fine china coffee cups and a bread-and-butter plate will be placed before each guest and it will be expected that not only many cups of coffee, but also a generous helping of each of the cakes and breads, will also be consumed. Not to have tasted each of the baked goods (together with as many cups of coffee as needed) would be considered an insult. And while the plain cakes and cookies alternate with the cups of coffee, somehow room must be saved to enjoy a generous helping of the rich layered cake as the finale!

The roles of mother and father in Finn life are well defined. The rural woman considers not only the housecleaning and weekly baking as part of her work, but also the daily meal preparation and barn chores as part of her share, while the men do the heavy work in fields and forests. Urban women also accept a heavy workload of daily meals, weekly (usually Saturday) housecleaning, baking, as well as shopping. Most city people live in apartments.

THE SAUNA RITUAL

All Finn women follow housekeeping routines with almost religious fervor, but the bustle of Saturday's activities is rewarded and soothed with the relaxation of the Saturday night sauna. The ritual of the sauna occupies such a central place in the lives of Finns that often, as in pioneer times, it is either the first building built or the first item Finns seek out when they emigrate.

The sauna is a small house built of wood inside and out and often located near a lake or a backyard pool. One enters into a small dressing room and from there into the main room where the bathers rest or sit on sturdy wooden shelves. Heat is supplied by a small stove with hot rocks. From time to time water is splashed on the heated rocks to add steamy moisture to the air, and the bathers beat themselves (and others) lightly with a bunch of twigs called *vihta*. Bathers also douse themselves with cool water as a refresher. A soap-and-water scrub is followed by a shower or a leap into a lake or pool. Some hardy Finns have been known to run outdoors and roll in the snow.

But the sauna is more than a bathhouse. Because of its scrupulous cleanliness, the sauna has often been the scene of a birth. Because of its relaxed atmosphere, it has also been the scene of many business discussions and even sauna parties. Also sauna-cured and smoked meats are common. A snack always follows the sauna ritual: sausages are grilled over an open fire or snacks of salty fish with rye bread and butter may be washed down with homemade **Kalja**.

THE DAILY MEALS

The daily menus differ slightly between rural and urban dwellers. Commonly, rural Finns awaken early to coffee and **pulla**. This is followed between 10:00 and 11:00 a.m. with a substantial breakfast of potatoes, meat, and gravy (or fish) then rye bread and butter and a dessert of porridge. A rest period after this meal is followed by a "coffee table" and then all return to their work. In the country, the evening meal is served in the late afternoon (usually after the cows are milked) and is similar in content to breakfast. Later in the evening the rural Finn relaxes and completes the day with yet another "coffee table." Generally, the rural meal pattern consists of two hearty meals interspersed with coffee and plain yeast breads and cookies.

Just as rural meal pattern follows the routine of daily labor, so too the urban meal pattern adapts itself to working hours. It is not practical for city people to consume only two meals and to eat them at the odd hours popular in the country. Although breakfast for most is still little more than coffee and

pulla, men often have one or two open-face sandwiches of sliced cheeses and meats or fish. The city lunch depends on whether it is being eaten at home or in a restaurant. A home lunch will be little more than a bowl of **puuroa** (cooked cereal) and milk or buttermilk; while lunch eaten out will almost surely be the **voileipapoyta**: an array of fish and sliced meats, small hot dishes and then fruits and cheeses, all served with sliced dark breads. Often milk is the noon beverage, but men may take mild beers or **Kalja**.

The city dinner will be eaten when the men come home from work so that the family can dine together. If this is to be a late meal, the family may enjoy a late afternoon "coffee table" to appease hunger. Dinner will likely be a slow-baked casserole with potatoes and served with pickles, followed by a porridge or fruit dish for dessert. Coffee and breads will be enjoyed still later in the evening as a snack before bed.

SPECIAL OCCASIONS

Religious freedom prevails in Finland today. The Evangelical Lutheran Church claims a membership of 95 percent of the Finnish population while only 2 percent belong to the Greek Orthodox Church.

Christmas, Easter, and May Day are the main festivals but the Finns are also much affected in their mood and social life by the seasons. The long dark days of winter, relieved only by visitors or special family occasions, seem to cause a cloud of solemn quiet to fall over daily life. Even alcohol consumption increases dramatically in an effort to dispel the national winter depression.

The joyousness of the first of May (May Day) is celebrated with singing and dancing and a great sense of communal relief that the end of winter is in sight. **Sima**, the tangy fermented lemon drink, is served everywhere to happy visitors and even on the street together with the crispy-fried **tippaleipa**.

Midsummer Day, though less exuberant than May Day, is celebrated with special menus featuring fresh cheeses. Happy parties with crayfish feasts and sleepless nights during late spring and summer celebrate "the time of the long days" or *Pitkia Paivia* when the lingering mysterious Northern Lights add their special quality to the festivities.

Christmas is celebrated on December 24 with church services and a festive meal of well-cooked vegetable casseroles, **lutefisk** or **lipeakala** (the specially prepared salt cod dish), baked ham, garnished with dried fruits, and a creamy rice pudding. Later in the evening cookies and coffee are enjoyed while Santa Claus gives gifts to the children.

At Easter, a buffet is centered around a display of home-baked yeast breads. The most famed of these is the **paasiaisleipa**, of Karelian origin. Redolent with cardamom and chewy with nuts and candied fruits, it is baked in a high round tin that bears a striking resemblance to the Russian **kulitch**. From the rich spring butter and creams come the special cheeses that are served on the Easter buffet as well. One of the oldest traditional Easter dishes is served either as a pudding or a beverage depending on the area. **Easter mammi** is prepared from a mixture of molasses, water and rye flour flavored with raisins and orange peel, and the pudding version is traditionally baked in baskets.

GLOSSARY OF FOODS AND FOOD TERMS

Aamiainen: breakfast.

Besimarja: brambleberry liqueur.

Easter Mammi: a very old traditional Easter dish that is a baked pudding or a beverage depending on where it is served. Made from water and rye flour, molasses, orange peel, and raisins. The pudding version is traditionally baked and served in baskets.

Jaloviina: Finn brandy.

Kaalilaatikko: a supper casserole of shredded veal, cabbage, and whortleberries baked in layers.

Kalakukko: a dish of Karelian origin consisting of meat and fish (usually pork and herring or **Muikko**) baked inside a bread-dough crust for several hours. The resulting brown mixture is so well cooked that even the fish bones are indiscernible.

Kalja: mild non-alcoholic brew drunk like beer and prepared frequently in Finn homes.

Karjalan Piirakat: Karelian version of the filled noodle pastries or small filled yeast pastries known in Russia as **Piroshki**. The Finn version is filled with rice, potato, cheese, or meat, and the crust is made from rye flour.

Keitetty Muna: boiled egg.

Kesakeitto: a vegetable soup made with young sweet spring vegetables cooked together and finished with the addition of milk. A Finn spring favorite.

Lakka: Finn cloudberry liqueur.

Lanttulaatikko: a baked turnip casserole.

Lipeakala: Finn name for the Swedish **Lutefisk**, the dried salt cod given special preparation for Christmas Eve dinner. The cod is soaked in water for several days before being given a one-day soaking in a lye-and-ashes solution. This is followed by seven more days of soaking in fresh water before the fish is finally poached and served with a white sauce.

Lounas: lunch.

Maksalaatikko: a slow-baked casserole of liver and rice.

Muikko: tiny freshwater fish that are eaten whole.

Mustaa Kahvia: black coffee.

Pahkinakakku: nut cake.

Paistetut Sienet: a dish of fried wild mushrooms.

Paivallinen: supper.

Pannukakku: the baked Finn pancake made from eggs, milk, and flour similar to the batter and puffed crisp appearance of the English Yorkshire pudding.

Piimaa: buttermilk.

Poronkieli: reindeer tongue.

Poronliha: smoked reindeer meat.

Pulla: such a favorite, that there is seldom a Finn home without it. Scented with cardamom, this moist yeast dough is shaped into a braid and then thickly sliced after baking. Served with breakfast coffee or as part of a "coffee table." Leftover slices are oven-dried and eaten as rusks, dipped into coffee. These latter may be called **Korppua**. Sometimes sweetened with raisins.

Punajuuri Salaattia: cooked beet salad.

Puuroa: a bowl of cooked cereal such as rice, farina, or oats, served with milk. Finn favorite for lunch or dessert.

Rapuja or **Rapu**: the small freshwater crayfish served through the summer in Finland.

Sillisalaatti: herring salad, often including potatoes and hard-cooked eggs.

Sima: fermented lemon drink that is traditional for May Day.

Tallimestarin Kiisseli: a special dessert, literally "the stablemaster's fruit compote," it is a mixture of slightly sweetened stewed raspberries and red currants, served over toasted pound cake and garnished with whipped cream and jelly.

Tippaleipa: curlicues of thinly poured cruller batter, crisply fried and traditionally served with **Sima** for May Day.

Viili Piima: clabbered milk.

FRENCH

Impossible. Impossible to think of France without at once being pleasantly assaulted with a sensuous vision of velvety wines and tempting foods. Is this reputation a carefully nurtured legend or does it indeed have some basis in fact?

A great cuisine can only be developed where there are suitable and abundant natural resources, diligent and imaginative cooks, and enough sensitively appreciative palates to taste and enjoy the results. It would seem that France can give a nod to each point.

Watered by numerous rivers, blessed with a temperate climate and fertile soil, the rolling plains and valleys of France are dotted with orchards and vineyards, yield grains and varieties of delicate vegetables, and nurture cattle, sheep, and fowl in such abundance that, under normal conditions, France is actually self-sufficient in foodstuffs. Farmers, fishermen, and sheepherders have learned from centuries of diligent care and lessons handed down from one generation to the next how to coax the finest quality from their produce, be it grapes or chickens. And in a nation that can honor a chef with the Legion d'Honneur it is not surprising that the taste for fine wines begins with the very young at the family table, and the arts of the kitchen begin near *maman*.

Few nations boast culinary histories, gastronomic maps, and qualities of foods and wines that set world standards. Such is the case for France. Any library of cookbooks, while acknowledging most world cuisines, will have the weightiest shelves of books on French cookery. Not surprising when one glances at such tomes as Curnonsky's *Cuisine et Vins de France*, Brillat-Savarin's *La Physiologie du Gout*, the epic 2,984-recipe collection of Auguste Escoffier, or the meticulous cataloging of foods, techniques, and recipes by Antonin Careme. And it is indisputable that France's brandies and wines have set world standards and her cheeses defy imitation.

But it was not always so.

It was Auguste Escoffier who said: "When we examine the story of a nation's eating habits ... then we find an outline of the nation's history." France's history of food might begin with the meats boiled in huge pots together with fish and vegetables, or with whole wild boars spit-roasted and served with an assorted garnish of game and fowl. It was the comparatively civilized Romans who introduced their own spices, wine, and wheat to the Gauls. And in those early days before the Common Era, not only new foods but table manners also proved to be a novelty. The Romans taught the Gauls to drink from cups instead of from human skulls and to seat themselves at rough tables instead of squatting on the ground. But there was an exchange too. The Romans enjoyed milk-fed snails, oysters, and **foie gras** made from the artificially enlarged

livers of geese, and they in turn introduced these new luxuries "back home." But it was many years before both Romans and Gauls learned to eat with anything but their fingers, their teeth, and possibly a sword.

Charlemagne is credited with being the first gourmet in the history of French cuisine, ruling his feudal empire while dining on four-course meals and savoring the smoothness of **Brie cheese**, which he had "discovered" in a little abbey near Paris. He is also credited with helping establish France's wine industry, planting many orchards, and even developing fish ponds teeming with eels, carp, and pike. He left his intellectual mark as well, founding numerous schools and becoming a patron of scholars and artists as well as a devout Christian. In the late 700s C.E., Charlemagne struck a very early blow to male chauvinism when he allowed women to share his dinner table – a previously unheard-of circumstance.

The Dark Ages echo the plight of peoples all over Europe: gluttony and luxury for the upper-class few and almost unparalleled misery, poverty, and near starvation for the masses. Wars, diseases, and meager crops that failed resulted in the people scrounging for food from roots, barks, and even mixing earth with flour to make bread, and as a last resort the eating of human flesh.

France's "sense of mission" was perhaps born in the eleventh century with the Crusades. The First

Crusade was made up totally of French knights inspired to annihilate all of Christendom's enemies, and as they marched under the theme "God wills it," they massacred populations, destroyed towns, and even plundered Jerusalem. They did, however, also find time to enjoy dishes made with rice, and brought back to France not only rice but many oriental spices: cinnamon, cloves, thyme, aniseed, and bay leaves. At the same time, the feudal system was disintegrating, and while some peasants retained small plots of land, many others moved toward the towns. While small markets sprang up, storage, transportation, and food preservation were hardly adequate. The arrival and the use of spices greatly enhanced the palatability of available and inexpensive food such as whale meat.

The Middle Ages were characterized by gargantuan feasts and gross table manners: eating with hands, belching, and tossing scraps on the floor were all commonplace. However, many ate simply and bread and soup was a common meal. Joan of Arc is said to have enjoyed soups so much that she was known to eat five different soups at one meal and nothing else. Perhaps as a further influence from the Middle East, candied fruits, sugared nuts, and other sweetmeats became popular and Auvergne gained fame for its fine-quality **dragees** (sugared almonds). About the same time, a growing interest in food and its preparation was indicated by the publication of the first cookery books in French: *Menagier de Paris*, and Taillevent's *Viandier*.

THE BEGINNING OF FRENCH GASTRONOMY

The real turning point in the gastronomy of France was the arrival from Italy of a plump fourteen-year-old girl named Catherine de Medici. She came to Paris in 1533 to become the queen of Henry II. It was not she who revolutionized the tastes of France; it was her retinue of chefs, pastry makers, and gardeners, the finest from Florence. To realize what an impact this made, it is necessary to examine the culinary accomplishments of France's neighbor.

At the time of Catherine de Medici's arrival in Paris, the gastronomic arts had reached their epitome in Florence. The first modern cooking academy, the *Compagnia del Paiolo* ("Company of the Cauldron"), had been founded there in the early 1500s. Cookbooks had been commonplace in Rome since the first century C.E., with the writings of Apicius. Consumption of vegetables, especially cabbage, common boiled greens, and fava beans were all commonplace, as was the consumption of a variety of fruits such as apples, apricots, peaches, cherries, figs, and many types of melons. Herbs, spices, and many blended sauces were used both in cooking and as flavoring to be added at the table.

The Romans are said to have invented cheesecake, both a savory and a sweet dessert type using honey. More than a dozen varieties of cheese were known; they were used often after the meal as a dessert with fruits. Breads made with flour and yeast, pasta made from flour and water and shaped in a

FOODS COMMONLY USED

It does not matter which food you name: if it is prepared by a French cook it will look and taste "French." Therefore, we must conclude that the foods themselves are not French, but surely the preparation technique, the seasonings that enhance their flavors, and the way they are served make all the difference. *"Vive la difference!"* Mainly the French enjoy foods that take time and care and are as lovingly prepared today as they were a few hundred years ago: sauces, soups, and stews. It is understandable too that bread in many forms, but especially the ubiquitous **baguette**, must be a staple food, although regional "crusty breads" are gaining in popularity. How else to mop up those sauces, savor the soups, and accompany those stews!

Vegetables are treated with the respect they deserve and are always fresh, freshly cooked, and served as a separate course, while salads are stark in their simplicity, quivering with crispness, aglow with the shimmer of a simple **vinaigrette**.

Fruits may be served in many forms but none so eloquent as the choicest served on a plate with nothing but a drop of dew to assure its freshness and a wedge of cheese to accompany its juiciness. Water is for bathing, cleaning, and occasionally an ingredient of necessity, but to the French it is not something one drinks. The beverage of France is wine, which graces the table, whets the appetite, and enlivens food flavors. What could be more basic than wine? Ah, and the seasonings! Fragrant fresh herbs, a whiff of scallions or shallots, chives or leeks and, with a gentle hand, a little garlic.

variety of ways then dried, even the use of tomatoes and corn, newly arrived from the ships of the *conquistadores*, had some of their first experimental tastes in Italian kitchens. (See Italian.)

While Catherine de Medici dazzled the French court with her sumptuous banquets of unusual dishes, the greatest shock must have been her introduction of the fork! Spoons and knives had been used before, but to dine with a fork was revolutionary. The art of making breads, cakes, and pastries, the preparation of fresh vegetables, and the serving of fruits and cheeses were appreciated, but a great favorite was ices and ice cream. There is some disagreement as to whether the first ice creams were introduced by Catherine de Medici or by a Sicilian in Paris, Francisco Procopio, who reputedly opened the first cafe selling ice creams and ices of many flavors. It is certain that Catherine introduced the French court to the iced delicacies, but perhaps Procopio deserves credit for presenting it to Parisians.

From the kitchens of Marie de Medici, Catherine's niece who married Henry IV, came the present French classics: **sauce bearnaise** and **sauce mornay**. By now the culinary arts gained even wider appreciation, and while the next king, Louis IV, gorged on endless courses and enormous quantities of foods, Parisians were beginning to enjoy a new stimulation: the first public cafes (in 1669) serving coffee.

The 1700s saw many fads and fancies such as **bombe glacee**, **petits pois** (actually introduced by Catherine de Medici), **animelles** (ram's testicles), and truffled **foie gras** (imported truffles from Italy had started the French on a search for their own underground delicacies).

But it was through the efforts and writings of a French agronomist and economist, Antoine Parmentier, that the humble potato was finally accepted as a food. About the same time, restaurants began ·appearing, much to the consternation of the *traiteurs* or caterers who had more or less a monopoly on the selling of cooked meats. In 1765, an innkeeper named Boulanger is said to have used sheep's feet to flavor his soups which he sold as *restorantes*. This was construed by the *traiteurs* as an illegal way of selling cooked meats, but once the furor died down, more and more Parisians were enjoying eating out, and by the turn of the century more than 500 "restaurants" had opened their doors, each boasting long and different menus. This was the period of the development and codification of French gastronomy by four of the greatest French chefs and gastronomes: Jean Anhelm Brillat-Savarin (1755-1876) who labored for twenty-five years to produce *Physiology of Taste (La Physiologie du Gout)*; Antonin Careme (1784-1833) who wrote volumes on everything from the chronicling

of menus to the construction of confectionary architecture and was called "the king of chefs and the chef of kings"; George Auguste Escoffier (1847-1935) who was regarded as "the emperor of the world's kitchens," a title conferred on him by German Emperor William II; and the author of *Larousse Gastronomique*, Prosper Montagne (1865-1948). It was not uncommon, then as today, that cooks trained in the palaces and wealthy homes opened their own fine little restaurants when they retired.

FROM THE NEW WORLD

The New World was opening up (1700s) and its new foods trickled into Paris: roast turkey, squashes, tomatoes, and corn; even Indian corn pudding had its vogue on French tables. Both Benjamin Franklin (1706-1790) and Thomas Jefferson (1743-1826) brought enthusiastic impressions of the French cuisine back to America, not only in the form of recipes, cookbooks, and a newly honed sense of taste, but also in the form of cuttings from French vineyards with which it was hoped to begin an American wine industry.

However, credit for the first California vineyards goes to Spanish missionaries who, as early as the mid-1600s, had imported vines from France and Germany to assuage their well-developed wine-thirst. But more than the influence of either American leaders or European missionaries, the arrival in Louisiana of the worn and weary Acadians, routed from their homes in Nova Scotia by the English in 1755, gave Americans a true taste of the art and ingenuity of French cuisine. Having wandered for more than ten years and finally settling in the area of New Orleans, the French (called "Cajuns") had preserved little else but their bodies, language, and culinary skills. These they blended and adapted with the best that was at hand — and their "hand" proved a strong one in creating what is known today as the distinctive "Creole Cuisine."

TALLEYRAND AND CAREME

The French Revolution (1789-1799) did little to restrain the wonders of the French cuisine. In fact, there is some evidence that had Napoleon been more of a discriminating eater, he might not have suffered the debacle of 1813. He was suffering such a *crise de foie* (a digestive disorder so common among the French that it is listed in most gourmet glossaries) he felt he must have been poisoned, and he ordered his troops to retreat.

The post-revolutionary years (the French Revolution and the War of 1812) saw a surge of technical progress together with such an interest in the culinary arts that many famous names became associated with food. Napoleon's prime minister, Charles-Maurice de Talleyrand, and his chef, Antonin Careme, may not have been the first in history to combine diplomacy and gastronomy, but Careme quickly became famous for his splendid creations of architectural confections and his detailed books on cookery which included his own illustrations. While foreign courts enjoyed the secrets and the results of Careme's creations from the kitchen, Talleyrand was busy receiving diplomatic secrets from Careme!

AND OTHERS ...

Other names, trailing through French history, left immortal imprints on the gastronomic map. Marie Antoinette brought to Paris the recipe for a curved little bun, originating in the Turkish siege of Budapest in 1686. It was transformed into the buttery, flaky **croissant**. The deposed Polish king Stanislaus Leszczynski's favorite dessert of liqueur-soaked cake served with whipped cream became the **baba au rhum**. Francois Appert won a prize offered by Napoleon with his invention of preserving foods in jars; pirated by the English and the Americans, the canning industry was born.

Another Frenchman, Louis Pasteur (1822-1895), seeking to preserve wine and milk, stumbled on the process that bears his name. Yet another Frenchman, Charles Tellier (1828-1913), perfected the refrigeration system that has revolutionized the food industry. Still another Frenchman, Mege-Mouries, affected the world's eating habits with his invention of margarine in 1872. But powerful butter interests kept his product in disrepute for years. In fact, only during World War II did margarine gain respect.

Always inventive, adaptive, and willing to try something different, the French gradually standardized their cuisine so that eventually, with the mention of the name of a dish, everyone knew what it was and what it contained. Food discussion, then as now, centered mainly around the menu for the next meal or the exact degree of seasoning in a dish. The "settling" of the French cuisine, however, was preceded by some intriguing new tastes: in 1855 horsemeat was sold in Parisian markets for the first time and the *boucherie chevaline* is a common sight today. During the siege of Paris in 1870, the flesh of dogs, cats, and even rats and donkeys was sold as meat. About forty years earlier a more palatable dish in the form of **couscous** was introduced after the French took over Algeria, and in various forms it is still a part of Parisian menus.

CURNONSKY

During and after the two world wars, universal social and economic austerity made some of the extremes and excesses of the past seem more out of place than ever. While the war-weary soldiers yearned for the local wines and the good hearty cooking of *maman*, restaurants changed their fare too. Not only were the gargantuan displays and lengthy menus of the past distasteful because of the seriousness of the times, they were also no longer necessary because the new modes of transportation and food preservation brought fresh foods to every home. Expensive and time-consuming techniques were no longer practical or necessary.

The weighty gastronomic discourses by Careme and Brillat-Savarin were to move to the back of the bookshelf with the advent in Paris of a new philosophy propounded by a young chef from Angers, Maurice Sailland. He called himself Curnonsky, an appropriate variation on the Latin *cur non*, meaning "why not?" In 1927, 5,000 Parisian gourmets elected him prince (and he was to call himself Prince Curnonsky thereafter), whereupon all his pronouncements on food became legendary. Some, like the reduction of the menu to one main course from the previous three, were sensible. Others, like his statement that one should "never eat the left leg of a partridge, for that is the leg it sits on, which makes the circulation sluggish," detract from some of his more contemporary views.

Curnonsky classified the French cuisine into four categories: *haute cuisine, cuisine bourgeoise, cuisine regionale*, and *cuisine impromptu*. He said of *haute cuisine* that "like our haute couture it is the most beautiful manifestation of our national activity," and noted that it was not only the privilege of the elite clientele to enjoy, but it was propagated throughout the world by master chefs trained in the great French tradition. He defined *cuisine bourgeoise* as cooking in the family style, for "in France one always eats well." He defined *cuisine regionale* as being the best specialty dishes of the forty regions of France. His final category may be the most prevalent throughout the world: *cuisine impromptu*, or the hasty improvisations or what some cooks call "pot-luck" – a meal put together quickly from whatever is at hand.

Curnonsky not only ate well and cooked well, he also took his position as "the Prince" very seriously. His book *Cuisine et Vins de France* states in precise detail recipes representing the four types of cuisine, as well as strictly prescribed rituals for table service, carving, wine art, and wine service that in many places are still the guiding principles.

ESCOFFIER, THE GREATEST

Considered to be the greatest of all culinary authorities was Auguste Escoffier. He was decorated by the French government with both a Chevalier of the

Legion of Honor and the Rosette of the Officer of the Legion. Of all the sayings and writings of the gastronomic greats of France, the words of Escoffier were destined to point the way to the newest phases of French cuisine: the *nouvelle cuisine* as articulated by chef Paul Bocuse, and the *cuisine minceur* with which Michel Guerard experimented. The great master had entreated his students and readers to *fait simple*, and nearly thirty years after Escoffier's death in 1935, at the age of eighty-nine, French chefs and fine cooks the world over realized the timelessness and practicality of his words.

It is important to recognize that there are really three French cuisines. Exemplified in elegant restaurants throughout the world and preserved in the castles and homes of the servant-privileged is the classically elegant and extravagant *haute cuisine*. In the 1970s, chefs Michel Guerard and Paul Bocuse sought to simplify and lighten both ingredients and techniques to create *nouvelle cuisine*. Finally there is the soul-satisfying regional *cuisine bourgeoise*, time-tested and frugal but honoring the finest of regional produce.

DOMESTIC LIFE

Just as "much of French history is simply Paris history presented as a *fait accompli* to the provinces," so the French lessons of life are simply the family viewpoint presented as indisputable fact to the child. The principles of a sense of "belonging" and "favoritism" are inculcated early. In many ways, French mothers teach their children suspicion of lifestyles outside the family circle; schools teach a wariness of that which may be new; from families to schools to organizations the "French way" is carefully taught so that one will not "go astray." In some ways the French mother is as important a symbol to the family as Paris is to France herself: the occupation of Paris by a foreign power means defeat for the nation, while the liberation of Paris represents a victory for every French person in the entire world!

There is little question of *maman's* importance in the French family. She is often characterized as being hardworking and frugal. While all of this may or may not be true, what is irrefutable is her skill with food and every aspect of it. If she can afford to hire servants to do the work of marketing, preparing, cooking, and serving, there is no doubt that she will nonetheless be astutely knowledgeable about every detail and be able to offer criticism as well as advice. If she must do the chores alone, she will consider it her duty to rise early and shop almost daily for small quantities of the freshest and best herbs, bread, meats, fish, fruits and vegetables she can procure. Freezers and supermarkets and many brightly packaged quick-mixes are found in Paris, but there will always be a place for the farmer's and fisherman's market and for the small refrigerator. For the French there is no substitute for the freshest, the seasonable, the local, and the best.

In a French kitchen nothing is ever wasted. Bits of stale bread, the last of vegetables, the trimmings from the meat or the fish, all will find a place as stuffings, garnishes, sauces, or soups. French kitchens are frequently small and seemingly inefficient, but the miracles of cuisine they produce are never disappointing. The **batterie de cuisine** usually begins with a gas stove, although many have both gas and electricity just as in the "old days" the large country-estate kitchens used gas ranges for fast cookery but the old reliable woodstoves were preferred for slow simmering.

Quality pots, pans, skillets, double boilers, and casseroles are important to the French cook. Purchased once, they should last a lifetime (if not longer). A battery of sharp specialty knives, wooden spoons and wire whisks, the **tamis** (drum sieve), food mills and graters, and mortar and pestles to pound, grate, and purée foods are also found. More recently the electric blender has taken the place of some of the older utensils, and the food processor combines many kitchen functions in one unit.

DAIRY PRODUCTS

Milk by itself is not used as a common beverage except for very young children. Even so, it is more likely that they will join the rest of the family for the breakfast **cafe au lait** (sweetened coffee with hot milk) and **croissants** or **baguettes** with preserves. In the Basque area, foamy hot chocolate with whipped cream and golden warm **brioche** is the likely start of the day.

The French, however, make much use of milk and cream in soups and sauces. Some of the sweetest guises of milk and cream appear as **souffles, mousses, creme Anglais** (a light vanilla custard sauce), and the soft pyramids of sweetened whipped cream atop desserts for special occasions.

A variety of cheeses are a frequent ingredient in casseroles and **gratinee** dishes as well as sauces and garnishes. There is scarcely a region in France that does not produce a cheese specialty of the highest quality, either fresh or aged and made from the milk of cows, sheep, or goats or a mixture. But most important, cheese is carefully selected to complement the meal and to serve as the finishing touch, often sharing the plate with a small portion of juicy seasonal fruit. Cheese is the French dessert staple. This is true even when followed by a special sweet.

FRUITS AND VEGETABLES

Fruits are savored for their natural beauty and fresh taste and for this reason are purchased in small quantities and in season. To end a meal with one's last bite of bread spread with a creamy cheese and then to add the juicy coolness of any luscious fresh fruit.... But the French also prepare fruit tarts, fruit souffles, and fruit puddings (**clafouti**) as well as many types of homemade fruit wines, brandies, and clear potent liqueurs from many types of fruits.

The diligence of French cooks is similar to that of French farmers. Nothing is wasted: both manure and composts of trimmings, leaves, and kitchen wastes are returned to the earth with rhythmic precision. The reward is a seasonal delight of a great variety of fresh vegetables of every type.

Cooked vegetables are always served as a separate course, especially the first of the season. Others are cleaned and trimmed and appear at the table as the natural garnish of the meat or fish platter. All green or brightly colored vegetables are traditionally prepared by a short boiling, then after draining are plunged into icy cold water. The last step is a quick reheating just before serving by sauteeing in butter. Note that the vegetable water is not poured away, but will be used as the liquid addition to soups, stews, or sauces. Vegetables may also be served with sauces, tucked into crepes, simmered in soups, or pureed into souffles. They may also be chilled with oil, vinegar, and herbs (**vinaigrette**) to be served as a cold appetizer or salad. Artichokes, asparagus, green beans, green peas, cauliflower, brussels sprouts, endive (Belgian), broccoli, and spinach are special favorites. Potatoes, carrots, and tiny onions are most enjoyed lightly glazed with butter and sugar. A special vegetable melange called **ratatouille** smoothly blends the flavors of tomatoes, eggplant, and zucchini with garlic and onions.

Mushrooms (**champignons**) have a special place of honor at the French table. Finely chopped and blended with minced onions they form a flavorful thick sauce called **duxelles**, used alone or as the base for many other dishes. Mushrooms may be carefully sliced, chopped finely, or spirally fluted before using. They may be stewed, grilled, sauteed, or stuffed, but most elegant of all they may be served in simple splendor under a glass bell: **champignons sous cloche**.

Wonderful things happen to potatoes in the French kitchen, too. Although it took the writings of Parmentier to make the French take potatoes seriously as a food, they then made up for lost time. Mashed, scalloped, baked, and of course french fried, stuffed, made into crispy pancakes, hashed, rissoled – the list is almost endless. But the French top all their potato dishes with two triumphs of technique: **pommes Anna** and **pommes soufflees**. If these are not enough, the American potato and leek soup **vichyssoise** is based on an old recipe for French potato soup but served chilled. The French penchant for classification is clear even on the matter of potatoes; for each different shape, seasoning, and technique, there is a separate recipe.

Whether it is prudence, frugality, or simply an appreciation of food, the French give fruits and vegetables a place of great distinction on the daily menu. Freshness and care in cookery assure optimum nutritional content.

MEATS AND ALTERNATES

From the *boucherie* come the cuts of beef, pork, lamb, and veal as well as brains, liver, tripe, kidneys, tongue, and heart: meats as well as innards, each prepared with common-sense thriftiness. *Charcuteries* (shops that provide prepared meats) provide a huge variety of prepared, cured, smoked, and pickled meats and loaves and sausages of every type. Meats are often larded, that is, poked through with thin strips of fat to increase juiciness and flavor. Larding and the cooking technique of braising rather than dry-roasting are most commonly used for large meat cuts to increase flavor but mostly to increase tenderness.

Although there is a recent tendency to enjoy small cuts of meat that can be quickly prepared such as steaks and chops – served very rare – most French prefer to use age-old recipes for braising, stewing, and soup-making that take time while calling for the least expensive cuts of meats as well as offal.

Chicken, duck, goose, as well as rabbit, horsemeat, and any available game or fowl are all enjoyed in season and are economical. Special occasions may call for "a good piece of meat" but the type of meat depends more on the specialties of the region.

"Plainly almost anything that lives is edible, in France at least." The list includes snails (**escargots**), mussels (**moules**), frog's legs (**cuisses de grenouilles**), smelts or minnows (**goujons**), and sea urchins (**oursins**). More familiar to other tastes are crabs, shrimp, lobster, **langouste**, and a variety of fish found in French waters. Eels (**anguilles**) and scallops (**coquilles**) may also be added to the list of edibles prepared, like all fish and seafood, in a great variety of ways: grilled, deep-fried, ragouts, stuffings, etc. From Marseilles comes the famed **bouillabaisse**, a richly flavored soup-stew of fish and other seafood served with crusty bread and a spicy hot **rouille**. (But it is from the ancient writings of Atheneus that we learn it was the early seafaring Greeks who introduced their **kakavia** to the fishermen of Marseilles, where it quickly gained favor as **bouillabaisse**.)

That eggs are a useful addition to the French menu can be seen by the 282 separate recipes for egg dishes found in *Larousse Gastronomique*. This staggering list does not include the many variations of soufflés, omelets, and custards that are largely based on eggs. Incidentally, it should be noted that the omelet, thought of as French, was another of the many dishes introduced by Catherine de Medici's Florentine chefs: its origin seems to be an ancient Roman dessert of honeyed eggs called **ova mellita**. Eggs both as a dish and as an important cookery ingredient find themselves in many dishes but seldom at the French breakfast table, unless served as a simply boiled egg.

Legumes and nuts are not an important source of protein in the French diet but are used in some dishes. The most famous of bean dishes is the **cassoulet**, a specialty of the Languedoc region. Small white beans are well cooked and layered with several types of meats and sausages to form a richly flavored and filling dish. Nuts are used in desserts and confections.

BREADS AND GRAINS

For the French, the importance of daily bread cannot be overestimated. Crusty bread, usually still warm from the baker's oven, starts the day with steaming hot chocolate or coffee with milk. The main meal at noon would be incomplete without the bread basket that is only removed at the very end of the meal. The hearty soup that is the usual evening meal would be inconceivable without bread, and many a French snack relies simply on bread plus a few squares of chocolate.

French homemakers do not bake their own breads or rolls and seldom trouble to make pastries or cakes. Why should they when experts have opened shops in every neighborhood for the express purpose of providing the staple of the French diet? Meticulously demanding about the length, the width, the type of crust, and of course the freshness of their breads, bakeries cater to every whim. Most popular are breads made of white flour, and only when bakeries close do some families condescendingly nibble on "health bread" (that is, anything but white bread). **Croissants** and **brioches** are the best-known of small rolls, while the **baguette** in many sizes and shapes is the favorite of breads, although many varieties of each exist to tempt the mealtime tastes. More recently the Parisian French have taken to varieties of coarse, crusty, and chewy country breads.

The French bother little with wholewheat or rye or other flours, and never concern themselves with the category of food others call "cereals." Hot or cold cereals are almost unknown and even where known are not popular. Rice is used occasionally, mostly in combination with other ingredients to form sweet or savory dishes but seldom as a dish of any importance. France's ties with Algeria brought Algerian **couscous** to Paris in varying forms, some better than others.

FATS

Olive oil, butter, chicken fat, goose fat, and lard all have a place in French cuisine; mostly the preference is a regional one.

SWEETS AND SNACKS

The range of French desserts from light to rich is as impressive as the number of egg dishes in the national cuisine, yet the favorite dessert is fresh fruit and cheese followed by a demitasse of black coffee. Pastry shops and cafes abound so sweet snacks are available almost everywhere. Crusty white bread sandwiching a few squares of chocolate is a favorite of schoolchildren.

SEASONINGS

Used with the taste and skill of generations of patience, French cooks add to their basic foods only those seasonings necessary to enhance the original flavors. Scallions, shallots (with their delicate garlic-onion taste), leeks, onions, and garlic all have a special place. A tiny plot for a fresh herb garden is common and so too is a kitchen shelf near a bright window with freshly growing chives, tarragon, and chervil in small pots. If the herbs cannot be purchased fresh, they will be dried. Most used are tarragon, chives, rosemary, sage, thyme, savory, fennel, marjoram, bay leaf, parsley, chervil, and basil. Most commonly, several aromatic herbs will be tied together in a little bundle and placed in the cooking dish, to be removed just before serving. This is called a **bouquet garni**.

Two other commonly used techniques for seasoning are the **brunoise** and the **mirepoix**. Finely diced mixtures of vegetables are lightly browned in a small amount of butter or other fat and this mixture is added to other dishes to enhance flavor: soups, stews, casseroles, etc. The names can almost be used interchangeably except that the **brunoise** is always a vegetable mixture whereas sometimes the **mirepoix** may contain a fine dice of meat such as ham or salt pork.

Another category of seasoning techniques is the **roux**. Basically, the roux is the flour-and-fat mixture used for thickening, but depending on whether the roux is white, blond, or brown, different tastes are obtained.

Sauces could also be considered as seasonings and here again the list is almost endless. Some of the better-known are: **mayonnaise, hollandaise, bearnaise, vinaigrette** – in fact, "every kind of liquid seasoning for food" and Careme is said to have categorized more that 200.

Finally, the simplest and often considered "the most French" seasoning is the addition of wine to enhance flavor. A common misconception is that the poorest quality of wines may be used as "cooking wines." This is in fact a fallacy since in the process of cooking the alcohol evaporates and the flavor essence of the wine remains – either to enhance or ruin the original taste. Commonly for the French, the wine used in preparing a dish is also the wine served with the meal at table.

BEVERAGES
Cafe au lait or hot chocolate are the favorite morning beverages. Meals are almost always ended with a demitasse of fine black coffee, and the French take as many coffee breaks during the day as their taste dictates. Water is never seen on a French meal table unless it is in a vase containing flowers. Wine is not only the premier beverage of France, France's wines are of such quality as to set world standards in many categories. Regions have their distinct specialties, and certain wines are traditionally savored with special foods, but the final decision on what to drink with which dish is still a personal one.

REGIONAL SPECIALTIES
French food is often judged by *haute cuisine* and seldom by the more common *cuisine bourgeoise* or *regionale*. For this reason, the image of trays laden with heavily sauced and garnished foods and cold platters of stuffed extravaganzas masked with **chaud-froid** and glittering with **gelee** brings sighs of wonder and groans of, "Oh, I could never cook like that!" In fact, most French do not cook like that either.

Most vital to French cooking is the quality and freshness of the ingredients at hand. Invariably this means local produce that is seasonally fresh. Menus are never conceived ahead of time, but are mentally assembled at the market as the freshest foods and the best of buys are combined with prudence and skill. For this reason too the French have little use for large refrigerators or freezers.

Although processed and imported foods are available in most regions of France, the majority prefer to cook and eat in the traditional manner. This "preference" is of course strongly conditioned by climate and geography and in border areas by the influence of neighboring countries. And naturally when local markets offer the freshest and finest of local produce – young vegetables, ripe fruit, fragrant honey, and freshly cured *charcuterie* – who can resist? Each

community also boasts its own bakeries and bistros, daily serving an array of breads, rolls, and the special pastry delights of the locality. (Special bakeries in Paris also tempt with careful reproductions of provincial specialties.) Although no longer recognized as duchies or kingdoms, the provincial divisions of France mostly denote differences in culture, language, and cuisine.

ALSACE, LORRAINE
Many Alsatian food specialties are similar to those in bordering Germany. Alsatian pork and goose are famed for their quality and succulence. The pork is made into a variety of sausages and prepared meats, while goose livers are processed into **terrines** and **pates**. The hearty foods of the Alsatian table include **pate de fois gras, choucroute de Strasbourg**, and a string of dishes with German overtones: **kugelhopf, kaffeekranz, schenkele**, noodles, red cabbage with chestnuts, and **potatoes a l'Alsacienne**.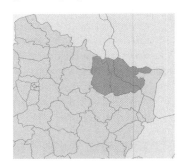

Plums, berries, and cherries are distilled into fine liqueurs: **Kirsch** (cherry), **Framboise** (raspberry), **Mirabelle** (yellow plum), **Quetsche** (red plum) – all clear, potant, and fragrant. The wines of the area, frequently disturbed in the past by political unrest (First and Second World Wars when many vineyards were overrun by the military), are returning to their deserved glory: spicy **Reisling**, sweet velvety **Traminer**, rich gentle **Gentil**, the musky **Muscat**, and the light **Sylvaner**.

The rich, satisfying foods of the Lorraine kitchens echo many of the same tastes found in Alsace: fine pork products, rich goose and goose livers, red cabbage and sauerkraut, potato and noodle dishes, filling soups. But most famous of all is **quiche Lorraine**, a rich custard of eggs and cream baked with strips of bacon in a tart shell. Coffee cakes, macaroons, but especially the **madeleines** from Commercy, deserve special note. Light and dark ales are the favored beverages together with a selection of fine **Moselle** and **Meuse** wines, fruit liqueurs, and specialty cheeses.

ARTOIS, FLANDRE, PICARDIE
Meats, orchards, and produce of these ancient provinces in the north of France are not of exceptional quality and the main food resources come from the sea. Beer and hard cider are the principal beverages of the region. Beer and leek soup, **hotch-potch**, and jellied eel have a strong taste and resemble

similar dishes of Flemish origin. There are a great variety of herring dishes: baked, fried, pickled, smoked with hazelnut leaves salted and oil cured. Apple and red plum tarts and preserves are found among the sweet specialties. Pork and rabbit and especially the **andouillets** (pork sausages) are among the best meats of the area.

BORDEAUX

Masterful cooks and winemakers, the people of the Bordeaux region use fine produce from both land and water as basic ingredients. Originating from this region are many dishes made with **bordelaise sauce**: the sauce itself is made from a base of white or red wine enriched with marrow, but the term can also refer to a dish with the addition of mushrooms called

cepes, or the sauce may be based on a **mirepoix**, or finally the dish may be garnished with tiny potatoes and artichokes. Many dishes also contain more than a taste of garlic, and as one moves southward towards the Spanish border, many fine Basque dishes have found favor in Bordeaux such as the **piperade**, an omelet of eggs and vegetables, and the thick cabbage soup flavored with salt pork: **carbure**. Specialties include **entrecote**, lampreys, and lamb as well as chicken served *a la Bordelaise*. Game and the flavorful **cepes** abound in the forests. And here too is the home of armagnac and cognac, the finest brandies in the world.

BOURGOGNE

There are always those who will dispute it, but it is the considered opinion of the experts that the province of Burgundy is "undoubtedly the region of France where the best food and the best wine are to be had." Certainly with so many dishes known as *a la Bourguignonne*, with such famed wines and even the fine mustard known as **Dijon**, named for Burgundy's capital, there is substance to the claim.

The sauce which has added fame to the region is prepared from the local dry wine to which is added a garnish of fluted mushrooms and tiny whole glazed onions. Meats prepared with this sauce are usually enriched with lardoons and a whiff of garlic but the sauce is also used for fish and poultry (**coq au vin**) and **escargots**. Rich is the word not only for the arrays of wines, but also for the fine poultry from the district of Ain, and the fine cattle, winged game and the famed **escargots** from Bresse. Only the fish found in Burgundian waters can be described as delicate. Fruits are of exceptional quality and the black currants are made into a liqueur called **Cassis**. Pigeon, duck, hare, woodcock, all are pre-

pared with special skill. Fine preserves, jams, biscuits and cakes, and sweets such as meringues, macaroons, fondants, and nougats stand high on the gastronomic list. The Cote de Beaune region produces white as well as red wines, while the Cote de Nuits area produces the great reds.

CHAMPAGNE

This is the area of chalky soils, vineyards, and cool caverns yielding the sparkling wines that have made the province's name synonymous with elegant special occasions.

There is a distinct and interesting difference between both the people and the cuisine of southern and northern Champagne. The tall, blue-eyed blondes in the north of the province prefer substantial dishes of cabbage and potatoes, enjoy strong cheeses, and relish the strongly flavored wild boar and prefer to wash it all down with beer. The shorter, dark-haired populace of the southern area of the province have lighter tastes, and prefer fish and

chicken dishes, and wine as their beverage. Pork products of fine quality, mutton, and poultry as well as local cheeses, fine fragrant honey, and of course the famed hillside vineyards are the produce of the land.

ILE-DE-FRANCE

This area literally pulses with Paris at its heart. Here, all the culinary specialties as well as the finest produce of land, sea, and rivers come together with the historically great chefs to produce the *haute cuisine* for which France is world renowned. Further, the very area surrounding Paris is reputed to be one of the most fertile in all of France, and from here come the freshest delicacies of the earth to Parisian markets. Pork, beef, and poultry specialties are too numerous to mention, fish and seafood dishes, such as **sole marguey** and **coquilles Saint Jacques a la Parisienne** are imitated

throughout the world; sweets such as **Paris brioche**, aniseed breads, barley sugar, and candied almonds and the countless **vol-au-vents**, **flans**, and **tarts**.... The name Paris is at once the impetus for and the summary of fine cuisine.

LOIRE VALLEY

The Loire Valley is an elegant region where ancient castles and estates dot the landscape of sweeping

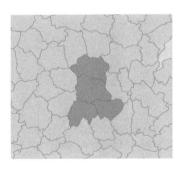

fields and gardens. Fine salmon and trout, truffles from nearby Perigord, an abundance of cream and butter and tiny shallots to flavor almost any savory dish as well as the lesser-known dry or sweet vouvray wines are the regional specialties.

LYONNAIS, FRANCHE-COMTE, SAVOY

The Lyonnais district is a small plains area with fertile fields and much industry. Fine vegetables, orchards with stone fruits, and chestnut trees flourish. Especially fine potatoes produce notable dishes such as when meats, tripe, potatoes, or onions are combined in **Lyonnaise sauce** or "a la Lyonnaise." Typically this is a fine cream sauce with onion, white wine, and white vinegar. Lyons sausage, chicken sausage, black sausage, dishes with chestnuts or walnuts (both plentiful), and delicate chicken and veal dishes are all well known. **Quenelles**, poached balls of ground fish (especially pike), are also a specialty. Desserts include pumpkin cake and **matefaim**, a coarse, heavy pancake, and fritters of acacia blossoms.

The area of Franche-Comte shares many gastronomic specialties with neighboring Switzerland. In fact, **Comte cheese** is considered a type of French gruyere. Almonds, chestnuts, and walnuts find their way into many desserts and sweets. Hearty culinary specialties include a type of cornmeal porridge, a

puree of cooked bread and butter served as a soup, and a range of soups made with garden-fresh vegetables and fruit soups, especially cherry soup. Many pork products such as variety meats, hams, sausage, and bacon are of excel-

lent quality. Cheese dishes, hearty breads, simmered meat and fish dishes with wine, and preserves of local fruits – quinces, bilberries, and whortleberries – as well as some rare and unusual wines, are produced in this region.

Mostly mountainous, the area of Savoy produces cereal grains and potatoes and some cattle for beef, milk, and cream. Orchards on the hillsides supply temperate climate fruits such as apples, pears, and plums as well as chestnut and almond trees. In the shadows of the woods are found mushrooms and tiny wild strawberries. **Civet** is a specialty dish of hare and pork with a sauce combining spices, wine, and animal blood with cream. The abundant crops of nuts make nut oil a favorite for cooking, adding a unique flavor to many dishes. Satisfying cheese dishes, noodle dishes, and potato specialties also resemble many dishes of Switzerland.

NORMANDY AND BRITTANY

Reaching out to the English Channel in the northwest corner of France, these two provinces are famed for their rich production of milk, cream, and butter. From the sea comes a wide variety of fish, shellfish, and seafood. Conger eels are made into the dish of the Breton fisherman, a soup-stew called **cotriade**. Shad, salmon, and trout are especially delicate.

Mutton and lamb feed in the salt marsh areas, giving them a distinctive taste. The residents prefer to serve their lamb and mutton rare and bloody: **mouton pre sale**.

The common beverage is hard cider made from the bounteous apple crops. The potent apple brandy, **Calvados**, as well as the liqueur, **Benedictine**, are made in Normandy.

Brittany's pancakes and griddle cakes are famed, but especially the wide thin lacy ones called simply **crepes Bretonnes** and served in casual folds enclosing sweet or savory filling. Buckwheat is used in soups and as a flour in

some of the Breton pancakes and griddle cakes.

Almost all the culinary specialties of the area are noted for their use of cream. In Normandy, **graisse Normande** (seasoned pork fat and suet) adds distinctive flavor as well. Normandy's cheeses have international fame, among them **Camembert**, **Pont-L'Eveque**, and the rich double-cream **Gervais Petit Suisse**.

PROVENCE

Formerly a part of Italy, Provence still retains the flavors of olive oil, garlic, tomatoes, and black olives. Garlic is used generously but is not considered to be either as strong or as bitter as its counterparts elsewhere. **Aioli** is a type of mayonnaise sauce made with mashed garlic, egg yolks, oil and lemon juice, and is served with many dishes but especially as a sauce for the fish in a **bouillabaisse** or the simpler **bourride**. Provencal foods include **mariage**, a thick meaty soup with rice, and **pistou**, a thick vegetable soup with green beans, potatoes, pasta, garlic, and tomatoes served with fresh basil and grated cheese. **Loup** is a wolf fish prepared in many ways, while **brande de morue** is an appetizer of finely puréed codfish with oil and garlic. The **pan bagna** is similar to a favorite lunch of Malta: crusty bread moistened with olive oil and layered with anchovies, tomatoes, and capers. **Pissaladiere** is an open tart

(similar to a pizza) laid out with sliced onions, anchovies, and black olives. **Panisso** is a cooled mash of cornmeal or chickpeas fried in oil then eaten with sugar. Not only the olives, olive oil, garlic, and tomatoes but also the chickpeas, rice, and many forms of pasta add up to satisfying pungent food with the taste of the sea and Italy.

ROUSSILLON, LANGUEDOC

Pungent flavors and hearty foods with a definite Spanish and Mediterranean taste are found in this region. *"A la Languedocienne"* applies to the many dishes that are served with a sauce or garnish of tomatoes, mushrooms, and eggplant. Garlic is one of the most-used seasonings.

Soups that are substantial meals in one pot are those that include in the broth a whole stuffed chicken; beef ribs and other meats with white beans and cabbage; stuffed goose neck, and so on. Potatoes, cabbage, and beans occur again and again in combination with omelets or poached eggs, veal, beef, and

mutton. Most famous of all is the **Roquefort** cheese and the ancient dish of Roman times, **cassoulet**, a layered white bean casserole with many meats. A little farther north, Auvergne gives its name to cabbage specialties coming so abundantly from the good soil: **pote Auvergnate**, a hearty cabbage soup, and **oeufs a l'Auvergnate**, poached eggs served on a bed of sausages and cabbage. Other pleasures include mushrooms and truffles, chestnuts and snails. Good local wines from heavy and rich to sparkling and rose as well as white accompany the meals.

THE BASQUE COUNTRY

The Basque are different. They speak their own language called *Euskera*, populate three provinces in France and four in Spain, and consider themselves at once citizens of both countries and individualists above all. They dance the *fandango* in their rope-soled shoes called *espadrilles*, place a rakish beret on their heads, and defiantly claim that their gourmet clubs (for men only) are the finest in the world. **Tripochka** and **loukinka** are two of their mountain sausages; **chipirones** is a type of cuttlefish served in its own ink, and **ttoro** is a savory fish stew related to **bouillabaisse**. It is here too that the Basques sip their foamy hot chocolate and munch tender egg-rich **brioche** for breakfast; play *pelota* (a ball game similar to *jai celai*) at the *fronton* (a building with indoor court for playing *pelota* and betting on the outcome of the games), find time also for church, which is very important in their lives, but forsake everything each autumn to hunt the *palombe*, a wild pigeon with a deliciously haunting taste.

It is believed that the taste for hot chocolate as well as chocolate in other forms was brought to

Bayonne, the capital city of the Basque region, by the Jews escaping from the Inquisition in Spain and Portugal in the early 1500s. They brought with them their secret recipes, and from Basque the ways of cookery were introduced to the rest of France.

MEALS AND CUSTOMS

Food is a subject of prime importance to every French person. It is not uncommon for suggestions for the day's menus to be discussed by family members at the breakfast table over a hot drink, breads, and preserves. Traditional recipes are treasured and the happy purchase of a young vegetable or a fine piece of meat will send the whole family into rapturous anticipation of the "special dish."

The morning meal is light but each of the simple items must be "just so" – the exact proportion of hot milk to well-prepared coffee, the freshest bread of exactly the length, width, and crust favored by the members of the family, and choice preserves to each one's taste. The noon meal is usually dinner, the special meal of the day, although in cities this pattern is changing somewhat as more women move into the workforce.

A traditional dinner would begin with **hors d'oeuvres**, literally "aside from the main work," and meant to be small appetite teasers. These may be taken with a light aperitif, a favorite being **Kir**; directions for its preparation include opening a lightly chilled bottle of Chablis and pouring off one drink (for the server) then replacing that amount of wine in the bottle with **Creme de Cassis** which gives the pale wine a rosy glow.

The fish course would be followed by a course of meat, poultry, or game, never carved at the table. In homes the carving is usually done in the kitchen and the foods are presented attractively arranged by a servant holding spoon and fork in what is commonly called "French service." Carefully prepared vegetables may be cooked and served as a garnish to the main course or immediately after as a small separate course.

A serving of salad greens, cool, crisp, and shiny with a simple **vinaigrette**, will always follow the main course. Family dinners will end with cheese and fruits either fresh or poached and a demitasse of coffee. One wine may be chosen that will complement all the courses or a separate wine will be served for each course, always proceeding in the order from light dry wines to heavier and sweeter. Wine may be on the table but is never taken with a green salad (the vinegar in the salad would disturb the palate's appreciation of the wine).

The staple food to the French is bread. At every meal, the bread basket is placed on the table and remains as a part of each course, the last crust to be enjoyed with cheese. Only the fruit, the sweet dessert (if there is one for a special occasion), and the demitasse coffee will be taken without bread. Bread is not only considered a symbol of hospitality and satiety, it is also viewed as important to cleanse the palate for the appreciation of the flavors of the various courses.

Water is never on a French table; wine is served throughout the meal to everyone at the table, regardless of age, and black coffee signifies the end of the meal. The French also do not add water to sauces or casseroles – how can one add water when stocks, vegetable juices, and wines are always at hand?

French banquet menus follow traditional patterns too. The courses are usually multiplied, depending on the grandeur of the occasion. Commonly, soup either hot or cold followed by hot **hors d'oeuvres** then a course of cold **hors d'oeuvres** would precede the fish course. A course of poultry or fowl may precede a more substantial entrée of roasted meat or game. Carefully chosen vegetables garnishing the entree will accompany the meat. Or a course consisting of cooked vegetables by themselves or in the form of small casseroles may be served preceding a small course of green salad to clear the palate. Cheese and fruit would then be followed by an array of sweet desserts, the choice depending again on the type of occasion. After-dinner liqueurs may accompany the demitasse coffee. In a gathering of true gourmets, it would be considered bad taste to smoke during a meal as this would disturb the taste sensations and thus the appreciation of the diners.

French table service differs only slightly from that in other western countries. It is customary to place cutlery with the fork prongs and soup spoons facing downwards to the cloth. Dessert spoon and fork are placed above the dinner plate setting with the fork at the top and the spoon below.

French family supper menus most frequently consist of a good satisfying soup or casserole, bread, and wine. It is a lighter, simpler meal than that the noon meal. But as in other countries, this pattern is changing as people dine out in restaurants, *bistros*, and even fast-food outlets.

SPECIAL OCCASIONS

The majority of the population of France is Roman Catholic with a minority being Protestant and some of the Jewish faith. The two most important religious festivities of the year for Christians are Christmas and Lent. Christmas is ushered in with the celebration of midnight mass followed by *Reveillon*, a festive meal at home for all the family. This meal is usually a carefully prepared series of dishes that reveal not only traditional family favorites, but regional specialties as well. White or black puddings (made with light meats and fats or animal blood) will almost always be a part of the dinner. A fat goose or a stuffed turkey will be the center of the menu while family specialties may shine after the nuts and cheese course. Special desserts such as **buche de Noel** may represent generations-old recipes or the best from the *patisserie*.

In contrast to the feasting of Christmas, Easter is preceded by forty days of fasting from Ash Wednesday to Easter itself. In early times the fasting prohibitions of this time forbade the inclusion of any foods of a "live nature." Thus breads, fruits, and vegetables as well as legumes made up the limited menus. Meats, fish, and seafood as well as butter were excluded. In more recent years fish and seafood have been permitted together with the use of eggs and butter, yet there is a sense of restraint in the forty days of fasting menus. In many French homes, the foods of Lent are considered a matter of individual choice.

GLOSSARY OF FOODS AND FOOD TERMS

Au Gratin: any dish that is sprinkled with buttered crumbs and/or grated cheese then placed under a broiler so that a lightly browned topping is formed. Sometimes a light cream sauce may mask the ingredients before sprinkling toasted bread crumbs and cheese on top to form a crunchy crust.

Babas au Rhum: light sweet yeast dough, traditionally baked in small flowerpot-shaped tins. After baking, the dough is pricked and a light sugar syrup poured over while both are warm. A sprinkle of rum, a garnish of candied fruit, and a dab of whipped cream complete the dessert.

Baguette: the famed Parisian long bread, well browned and crusty with a spongy white center. Used to mop up the last morsel of almost any French dish.

Bearnaise: slightly different from **Hollandaise Sauce** in that it is more piquant. A strongly steeped mixture of boiled wine vinegar, white wine, shallots, tarragon, salt and pepper is prepared then strained into a thick blend of cooked egg yolks and butter. This sauce is served with meat, fish, eggs, or vegetables.

Bouillabaisse: the classic soup-stew of Marseilles. Actually this dish is prepared all along the southern coast of Provence. A good bouillon of cleaned vegetables is set to cook then a layer of crustaceans placed in, followed by a layer of several varieties of fish both firm and tender of flesh. Included in the seasonings are olive oil, saffron, salt and freshly ground pepper, onions, tomatoes, garlic (generous), cloves, fennel, parsley, and even a piece of orange peel. A brisk boiling for only fifteen minutes and it is done. Bouillabaisse is served in a deep soup plate with **Marette** (the specialty bread of Marseilles) and **Aioli Sauce** (a type of garlic mayonnaise).

Bouquet garni: any arrangement of aromatic fresh herbs tied together or wrapped in cheesecloth: parsley, thyme, bay leaf, etc. After cooking, it is removed before serving the dish. Small wire baskets with a hook to secure them against a pot can also be used.

Bourride: a simple fish soup in which the stock is strained after cooking, then the crouton placed in the soup plate, the soup poured over, pieces of cooked fish garnished with **Aioli** and served with bread.

Brioche: a very rich, yellow (from the addition of eggs and/or yolks) yeast dough baked into many different shapes. The most usual and classic is the fluted muffin size with a shiny brown knob on top. A wash of egg yolk just before baking assures the shine and rich brown color.

Brunoise: a flavorful medley of cubed raw vegetables cooked in butter till lightly done then added to any other dish to intensify flavor.

Cassoulet: the ancient Roman meat and bean casserole, specialty of the Languedoc region. Small white beans are simmered till tender then layered with several different types of meats, each cooked separately. A crust is allowed to form on the baking cassoulet by sprinkling with crumbs.

Champignons: mushrooms. It should be noted that many different types are to be found, **Cepes** and **Morels** being two. **Truffles** are found only in certain areas, and are routed out by trained pigs or dogs.

Chantilly: sweetened, flavored whipped cream.

Chaud-froid: an aspic glaze to cover cold cooked foods, especially meats or fish. Cream is usually added to the aspic gel so it is not transparent.

Clafouti: a traditional country fruit dessert served warm from the oven. A light batter of eggs, flour, milk, and sugar is poured over any prepared, sugared fruits then the whole dish is oven-baked.

Coeur a la Creme: a classic French dessert prepared from a blend of cream cheese and cottage cheese pressed into a heart-shaped basket to drain off the whey. Unmolded, this dessert is served with sugared fresh berries and crusty French bread.

Couscous: a North African dish dating from earliest times and served in Parisian Algerian restaurants. The tiny pellets of couscous can be made from millet, semolina, or even ground rice. Steamed then served with meat and vegetables in a rich spicy sauce. Tossed with nuts, raisins, and sweet spices such as cinnamon, and drizzled with honey, couscous can be served as a dessert.

Creme Anglais: a delicate custard sauce of cream, egg yolks, and sugar usually flavored with vanilla, served warm or cold with desserts.

Crepes: a thin batter of eggs and flour is poured into a small skillet and cooked on both sides. May be filled with sweet or savory fillings, may be sauced, flambeed, gratineed, and served as appetizer, main dish (a light one), or dessert.

Daube: any braised meat cooked with vegetables in a covered pan in the oven or on top of the stove.

En Gelee: any dish that is served coated with a jelly. Usually this is taken to mean a fine clear bouillon preferably gelled with its own good stock or with the addition of gelatin to form a clear but firm mixture after chilling. Sometimes several coats of the warm or cooled aspic are poured over meat, eggs, fish, or fowl with a layer of carefully arranged decoration between. Superb for cold buffets or as appetizer dishes.

Farci: stuffed or filled.

Hollandaise: a sauce of lemon juice and butter thickened with egg yolks.

Marrons: chestnuts.

Mayonnaise: an emulsion of egg yolks, lemon juice, and oil, lightly flavored with a touch of mustard and salt.

Mirepoix: the same as **Brunoise**, except may sometimes have the addition of cubed meat such as ham or salt pork.

Omelets: originated by the Romans, a simple dish prepared by beating eggs then easing them into a hot buttered pan and cooking with care to assure a setting and a light but tender browning. The omelet may be flipped to brown the other side; it may be filled with any desired mixture, or it may be served rolled on itself – a beautiful golden oval.

Pate: a very finely ground blend of meats, usually including liver for smoothness, light seasonings, Madeira wine, or cognac then smoothed into a pan

and baked. Served cold. May also be used as a filling for other foods.

Pate a Choux: otherwise known as "creampuff pastry," this is created by bringing to a boil a measured amount of water and butter then plopping in an amount of flour and stirring vigorously. One by one a few whole eggs are beaten in till the dough is glossy and ribbon-like. Dropped into little dabs or spread into a ring mold, the pastry rises to a high, crisp roundness with a hollow center. Upon cooling, this ingenious "opening" can be filled as desired. **Gougere** is this same mixture baked to any shape but flavored with grated cheese.

Petits Pois Frais a la Francaise: a dish delightful in appearance and flavor and typifying the French love for delicate fresh vegetables. Young fresh peas are boiled quickly with lettuce wedges on top and a buttery glaze at the end. Peas and lettuce in their shimmer of butter may be eaten, deservingly, as a separate course.

Pommes Anna: deceptively simple dish of layers of raw, sliced potatoes and fresh butter baked in a round pan in the oven or in a hot straight-sided skillet. The trick: to unmold as a crusty whole.

Pommes Soufflees: another deceptively simple dish of oval thin potato slices which are twice fried in deep fat. The second time the fat is hotter in temperature and the slices puff and crisp like crunchy pillows of air.

Quenelles: actually a mixture of **Pate a Choux** plus a very fine puree of ground raw fish, chicken, or veal. Formed into oval balls and gently poached in bouillon, then served cold or hot.

Ratatouille: a delicious mixture of baked layers of browned onions, tomatoes, eggplant, and zucchini slices.

Riz a l'Imperatrice: a velvety, molded rice dessert made with milk-cooked rice blended with fruits and **Creme Anglais**. More fruit to garnish.

Roux: mistaken as the name of a sauce, quite simply the mixture of fat and flour that begins a sauce. It becomes a sauce after liquid has been added, which is thickened by the roux.

Sauce Aioli: a garlic-mayonnaise prepared by pounding (or using an electric blender) moistened bread with garlic till a fine puree is obtained. The addition of egg yolks, then drop by drop of olive oil yields **Aioli**.

Savarin: a light, sweet yeast dough usually baked in a tube pan and poured over a Kirsch-flavored warm syrup then cooled and served with Chantilly.

Soubise Sauce: a delicate onion sauce prepared by cooking onion in butter till golden, then stirring in a little flour and the desired liquid (white wine, stock, milk, or cream). After straining, the sauce may be served.

Souffle: a thick sauce of any sweet or savory mixture incorporating the carefully beaten egg whites. Baked in the oven then eaten with great pleasure.

Supremes de Volaille: any dish made with chicken breast, and served with a garnished sauce. The term **supremes** may be used to refer to the breast meat of fowl or animals.

Tarte or **Flan**: a baked or unbaked shell into which any sweet or savory filling may be poured, set, or arranged then garnished, topped, or glazed as desired. Commonly called a pie (open-face) in North America.

Terrine: the loaf-shaped pan traditionally used for baking **Pates**. Thus the baked **Pate** sometimes takes the name of the pan and is called a **Terrine**.

Vinaigrette Sauce: the simplest of salad dressings for the finest and freshest greens. A blend of fine oil, wine vinegar, salt, freshly ground pepper, and any desired seasonal herbs. Garlic is added in southern France.

CHAPTER 21

GERMAN

He who doesn't love wine, women and song
remains a fool his whole life long.
—German proverb

As early as 100 C.E., the Roman historian Tacitus described the Germans as a "warrior nation, hard-drinking, honest and hospitable." He spoke of German food as "simple" but hearty, that included breads and gruels made from oats, millet and barley, wild fruits and berries and wild game and fowl roasted whole on huge spits. Milk and cheese added variety, especially on the occasions when game was lacking. By 800 C.E. Charlemagne had joined the many Germanic tribes into a huge empire that included not only present-day Germany but also France and parts of Italy. It was Charlemagne too who encouraged monasteries in their cultivation of vineyards, orchards, and gardens, especially herb gardens.

Charlemagne's Holy Roman Empire existed for a time, but parts of it broke away and became distinctive united nations. This was also to be the fate of Germany. In fact, at the time of Tacitus's writing, the term "Germans" referred rather loosely to all the "barbarian" tribes north of the Alps and the Rhine River including what are today known as English, Dutch, and Scandinavians. The Latin word *Germania* used in so many early Roman and Hellenistic writings is believed to be of Celtic origin while the later term *Deutsch* has a more complex origin linking both early Teutons and Saxons and referring to language as well as people. It is thought that by a mistranslation of the word *Deutsch*, the Germans emigrating to Pennsylvania came to be known as "Pennsylvania Dutch."

Although Charlemagne had tried, and the people themselves dreamed of it, the hope of a united Germany was not to be. The problems which prevented unification were first, the lack of natural boundaries, and second, the fact that the German language was also spoken in other lands, so it could not be used as a unifying factor.

However, the influence of the Romans and other Europeans brought improvements at least in foods. By the Middle Ages, Germans were quaffing their hot-spiced wine from gold and silver-plated vessels and downing not only spit-roasted oxen but also spiced sausages and blood puddings, smoked meats and pickled fish, a great variety of fresh and dried fruits, and even spiced honeycakes. Strict adherence to church fasting days, which prohibited the consumption of meat, meant that fish was in greater use and prepared in even more ways than in present times. Spices were especially important, not only to help preserve foods but to help improve the taste of spoiled meat.

Accepted Germanic manners and customs date from Charlemagne's time, and although there were some gradual adaptations, the prevailing pattern of manners was rigidly adhered to by all. It is believed that Charlemagne introduced the custom of dining alone with his faithful leaders while the servants were the last to eat. Later, couples often dined together, sometimes sharing a plate and eating with the fingers (before cutlery became popular), but the women would retire promptly after eating, leaving the men to their drinking and singing.

In the Renaissance period, the establishment of the Hanseatic League helped to organize and increase trade, bringing a greater variety of fish, spices, fruits, oil, and even precious sugar to German tables. Cattle and poultry production was increased both in amount and quality by special breeding. Following the ideas used in the kitchens of noblemen, foods were cooked in cauldrons suspended on hooks over open fires. There were even some primitive kitchen ranges with metal rings over wood fires to hold huge pots in which bubbled mixtures of meats, vegetables, and fragrant herbs. Local inns served sausages with white and black radishes and mugs of wine, cider, or beer, and favorite dishes included lentils or beans cooked with chunks of cured and smoked pork.

In cold weather, dried fruits were served with cured meats, and pears, apples, and plums were commonly set into banked ovens to dry after the bread had been baked. Two other dishes were already old favorites: steak Tartar, adapted from the scraped raw meat of the marauding Tartar horsemen from Mongolia, and **sauerkraut**, a tart fermented dish the Tartars had learned from the laborers on the Great Wall of China.

Germany as a political entity came into being on January 18, 1871, when peace was finally signed with France and Chancellor Otto von Bismarck welded the nation together. But the area itself was still far from unified. There were still pronounced regional differences in religion, customs, dialects, and even temperaments. Wars and dissension had torn the land: the Thirty Years' War (1618-1648) had produced incredible devastation and starvation – people ate dogs, cats, rats, acorns, and grass. Generally, it was felt that the unification of 1871 was only a superficial one. Despite every effort, the fiercely individualistic regions could seldom reach agreement, with the result of a lack of national identity.

The discovery of America had brought many new exciting foods to European tables, but it took almost 200 years and the strong insistence of Frederick the Great of Prussia in 1744 that German peasants plant potatoes against hunger, before the potato found a firm place in German cuisine. It now appears in dozens of delicious forms from soups, thick sauces, pancakes, dumplings, and puddings, even to the making of schnapps. Cocoa and turkey came to be known, but coffee was to suffer a lack of popularity because of the national preference for beer. Brewed everywhere and enjoyed everywhere, beer was

considered a food in liquid form, evidenced by a corpulence seldom seen before. Beer began and ended the day, was a part of many dishes – **bierhals**, **bierfreund**, **biersack**, etc. – and was the beverage for all gatherings from weddings to funerals. It's thought that the beer preference has to do with Germany's long history of strife and wars, for the processing of beer is quicker and easier than the culture of wines.

The 1700s not only saw new foods enter the German cuisine, there were also some new customs. French influence was becoming paramount in everything to do with food and drink. Small glasses replaced huge drinking mugs; coffee, tea, and chocolate came to be sociable drinks and were served from specially made porcelain sets. Fine light bakery and flaky pastries replaced the heavy honey and spice cakes of old. The carving of huge roasts was refined to an art and matching silver sets of cutlery and carving utensils came into vogue. Even Frederick the Great of Prussia preferred speaking French to German. French cooks and cookbooks, French manners, all became an intrinsic part of the cultured upper classes and, as always, this newer protocol was rigidly adhered to.

But the German peasants, workers, and the many poor made do with their homemade beer and filled their stomachs with **kraut** and bacon, lentils and peas, firm satisfying breads and light dumplings. By the 1800s more than four-fifths of the German population were peasants, and their own pigs were the mainstay of their diet. Thanks to Frederick the Great,

FOODS COMMONLY USED

Pork, beer, potatoes, **sauerkraut**, and black bread are not only German staples, they are simple hearty foods that German ingenuity has raised to gastronomic heights of perfection and diversity. With newer trends to lightness and simplicity, people increasingly forgo soups as being fattening, and eat less bread and potatoes but more eggs. It is a pity that soups are losing popularity (except in rural regions where they are still a staple), for German soups are always richly satisfying, based on vegetables, flour-thickened, and flavored with smoked pork. No part of the pig is wasted and much of the pork produced finds its way into the dozens of varieties of

sausages as well as hams, bacon, chops, and roasts.

Beer is the national drink and is of exceptional quality everywhere, with many areas specializing in several distinctive types. Potatoes are served in every conceivable form and guise but none so wondrous as the fluffy dumplings of Thuringia. **Sauerkraut**, too, shows up in soups, stews, blended with fruits, or dotted with caraway seeds – the perfect bed for roast goose or plump sausage.

German bakery is renowned not only for its flavor – the honest taste of good fresh ingredients – but also for its lack of coloring, additives, or chemicals, which the

Germans dislike. Throughout, honest natural flavors of good fresh foods in hearty servings all washed down with fine beer represent German cuisine at its best.

German cuisine can also be divided into cookery based on wine and cookery based on beer. At one time only the aristocracy was permitted to hunt and dine on game and wine; today it is only a question of taste and preference. Wines are served mostly in a *Weinkeller* and foods are more apt to be light and delicate from main dish to airy desserts. Beer is served in a *bierlokal*, *brauhaus*, or *keller* and is the hearty partner to filling savory dishes usually served in generous portions.

it could be said that by the end of the 1800s, "potatoes were such a regular item that smoke coming from a cottage chimney at night was almost a certain sign that inside, potatoes, bacon and onions were frying."

Kaiser Wilhelm II ruled from 1888 to 1918. He introduced many English customs to the court since his mother was a daughter of Queen Victoria. Most popular was the introduction of large satisfying English-style breakfasts, and inns called *weinstube* featuring lodging and good food and wine. Kaiser Wilhelm also insisted upon menus being written in German instead of French, and he was not above enjoying robust peasant dishes. It was not long before the tastes and manners of the court were reflected in fine hotels and the burgeoning middle classes.

The industrial revolution that swept Great Britain took another hundred years before it took hold in Germany. For too long, the Germans lacked well-established political and economic systems: Germany's many fragmented provinces and states often had separate currencies and different trade tariffs. But within three years after the 1871 unification, more mines, ironworks, and blast furnaces were producing than had existed in the past seventy years.

The expansion and power of the great Krupp works paralleled the growth of Prussian power. Educational systems were keyed to industrial education and research, and this trend, together with the vast riches of natural resources and the growth of fast communication systems, spurred German genius. Welding industrial development to scientific research and careful use of resources were vital factors in Germany's success. But so was another point: business and industries were enriched by aggressive personalities who regarded politics as too conservative.

Yet the dream of a unified Germany was still shared by political conservatives, intellectuals, and powerful businessmen. The gradual rise of the Social Democrat Party and a large working class that chafed under the collar of hard work and submissiveness expected of them caused rumblings of concern. In their gigantic industrial leap forward, they had pushed aside the periods of Classicism and Romanticism that other nations had gone through, and this lack added yet another rift to the many inner conflicts of the German people.

After the First World War, the great progress of the Second Reich was abruptly ended. New interpretations and fabrications of German history attempted to overcome the people's sense of national failure. These theories drew largely on popular legends, on the German composer Richard Wagner's revival of Germanic mythology, and on Gobineau's race theory, and not least on the philosopher Friedrich Nietzsche's "superman" and "blond beast." Every misfortune came to be attributed to the deceit of others: "the crafty Jews, the perfidious British, the treacherous Italians" and so forth. Lacking established values and traditions and leaning heavily on a lack of reality and with a sense of despair and inferiority, the ground was laid for the horrors that came with the Second World War.

For a time Germany was split yet again into East and West. But the autumn of 1989 to the end of 1990 saw dramatic changes. The dismantling of the notorious Berlin Wall was triggered by the influx of East Germans fleeing to West Germany through Czechoslovakia and Hungary. Coinciding with the collapse of the Honecker government, the dismantling of the Berlin Wall gained a wave of unrelenting support. By the end of 1990, a unified Germany held elections for the first time in fifty-eight years. Subsequently, the reality of everyday life, economic restructuring, attacks by neo-Nazi gangs, and the pressing influx of immigrants dimmed the euphoria of unification.

Despite the current struggles, Germans are regaining their deep traditions of respect for authority and orderly living. Their great zest for life, boisterously dramatized in their festivals, is also bringing them renewed industrial and agricultural advances as well as a high general standard of living. There is a new and growing pleasure in regional German cuisine, and the celebration of regional dialects, customs, and festivals. Yet some admirable old ways remain ingrained: politeness and formality especially in names and titles, the importance of cleanliness and neatness in dress, and a strong sense of responsibility even in very young children.

DOMESTIC LIFE

The German home is an orderly one and German cleanliness is legendary. Children are taught very early to be polite, courteous, and responsible. There are some regional differences that are noted by Germans themselves. Northerners feel that Bavarians (in the south) take life too easily, are too fond of good living, and speak with an unintelligible dialect. But the southern Germans counter this with the opinion that northerners are too dour and serious even if they grudgingly admit that northerners are honest and very hardworking.

Whether from the north or south, in most German households there is little argument that father is the head. More recently the traditional view that the "woman's place is in the home" is fast disappearing as increasingly women join the workforce.

Kitchens are small but efficient and make use of modern gadgets and electrical appliances. Small appliances are of high quality and often perform several functions. Earthenware mixing bowls, strong wooden spoons, pudding and cake molds, rubber, wooden, and metal spatulas, as well as wire whisks all find a place in the German kitchen. Even if the weekdays are busy ones, the *hausfrau* will find time to prepare a special dinner at least once a week, while home baking for the holidays is traditional. Many kitchens boast specialty baking utensils: the **kugelhopf** tube pan with its diagonal spiral fluting; springform cake pans; flan and torte pans; a **springerle** roller or wooden **springerle** molds for cookies. Utensils are chosen for use and for quality and all are bought to last.

In rural areas cold cellars are used for winter storage of root vegetables, fruit, the family crocks of pickles and **sauerkraut**, and shelves of home preserves and jams. But food storage is not such a necessity in the city. Germans prefer their foods fresh. Baked goods, and often vegetables, fruits, and meats are bought daily. Many specialty stores, small open-air markets, and huge supermarkets and hypermarkets with incredible selections of local and imported goods make shopping a delight. Still other specialty shops feature a wide range of fine foods such as imported cheeses, different breads and rolls, and sausages and meats of every description. Milk too is not delivered to homes and is often bought daily at nearby dairies.

DAIRY PRODUCTS

Milk is not a favorite beverage except for children, pregnant women, and nursing mothers. Milk is used in custards, puddings, and cream fillings. In East Germany where the cuisine tends to retain its traditional tastes, there is a more prominent use of sour cream than in the rest of Germany. In Northern and Eastern Germany buttermilk is often used to marinate and tenderize game. Breakfast and afternoon **kaffee** (coffee) is taken preferably with canned milk. Sour cream called **schmand** is added to soups and gravies.

Many fine imported cheeses are available and these are enjoyed mostly as a dessert, especially after a cold meal. Sometimes sliced cheeses join platters of assorted cold meats and sausages for a light supper with rye bread to form open-face sandwiches, which are eaten with a knife and fork. **Topfen**, the farmer's firm fresh cheese, is widely used in baking and cooking. **Quark** is a creamy form of fresh cottage cheese.

FRUITS AND VEGETABLES

Apples, pears, cherries, and plums are produced in quantity in many areas of Germany. Increasingly, more varieties of fresh vegetables and exotic fruits are filling market displays. The Rhineland is famed for grapes and these are pressed into many varieties of fine wines. Fruits are enjoyed fresh as a snack but most often are cooked into compotes, that is, wedges of fresh fruits poached in sugar syrup sometimes scented with fresh lemon zest or lightly spiced.

Dating from olden times, dried fruits still play an important and interesting part in the German cuisine. They can be made into jams and spreads, fillings for tarts and yeast doughs, and they can also add their natural sweetness and color to many meat and game dishes. Fruits such as crushed pineapple, orange wedges, or chopped apple are often also added to **sauerkraut** dishes. Cold fruit soups and soups made from fresh crushed berries, sweetened and slightly thickened with cornstarch, are popular especially in Northern and Eastern Germany. Dried fruits may also be cooked as a colorful compote and then served as a side dish with game or meat roasts. Raisins and apples are frequent tasty partners to quick suppers of liver or sausages. And of course fresh fruits and nuts are a special treat at holiday time.

In Germany, vegetables are treated with the respect due their special "status." Cabbage, turnips, and potatoes can be mashed, sliced, grated, shredded and cooked, boiled, fried and braised into dozens of delicious dishes. But the highest praise is reserved for Germany's flavorful wild mushrooms and exquisite white cultivated asparagus. Mushrooms and asparagus are considered company treats. Many varieties of cabbage, cauliflower, hop sprouts and cabbage sprouts, carrots, turnips, and peas find their way into the German vegetable pot.

If the vegetables are not intended to add their flavor to a soup or a stew then they are cooked in the special German way. First a thorough cleaning then shaping and cutting as desired, a quick tossing in hot bubbling butter, a little addition of moisture and the vegetables steam to a perfect tenderness, forming their own sauce. Old or fibrous vegetables may be cut up and boiled first then given the glorious butter and steam treatment. Sometimes a little flour, toasted bread crumbs or a dollop of sour cream adds the final flourish. Vegetables cooked this way are served separately as they deserve to be.

MEATS AND ALTERNATES

All over Germany pork reigns supreme. The Germans have found so many delicious ways to serve every morsel of pork that the variations are endless. Beef and veal find a smaller place on the menu, but Germany's plump chicken, duck, and especially goose are famed. There is also some competition from wild game and fowl, which is plentiful in Germany's mountains and forests, and which is marinated to tenderness and slowly cooked in covered dishes that bring out the best flavors. Every part of the animal is used: tongue, brains, ears, kidneys, heart, lungs, tripe, milt, sweetbreads, palates, heads, shanks, tails, hocks, trotters, and udders. The quality of Germany's smoked bacon and cured hams is legendary.

It would take another book to describe Germany's sausages. The seemingly endless varieties of **wurste** (sausages) can, however, be placed in general categories: **rohwurst** is cured and smoked sausage ready to slice and eat; **bruhwurst** is sausage that is smoked then scalded and usually eaten heated; **kochwurst** is smoked sausage already well cooked and may be eaten as is or heated; **bratwurst** is the large category of sausages that are sold raw (but may be spiced, smoked, and cured for flavor) and usually pan-fried before eating. Animal intestines are often well cleaned and used as casings for sausages; animal blood too finds a place as fried blood (**gerostetes blut**) or more commonly in black or blood pudding (sausage).

Almost as important on the menu (but not quite) is herring. In Emden it is even possible to be served an entire meal with appetizer, main dish, and salad made with herring. Fresh-caught herring is called "green" and is often served fried. Herring salad may be prepared by mixing diced herring with chopped cooked potatoes; herring may also be served jellied, grilled, cooked *au bleu*, grilled or fried in wax paper packets, chopped and spread on toast. Nor does the list end there. There are also **rollmops** or **Bismarck herring**, fillets of herring rolled around onions and pickles; **brathering**, fried sour-pickled herring, and **matjeshering**, a quality fat herring served simply with boiled potatoes.

Herring is not the only fish consumed here. German waters provide crayfish, lobster, eels, mussels, flounder, plaice, turbot, sole, and the noted salmon and trout especially from the Rhine River. **Forelle blau** or **trout au bleu** is a method of fish cookery reputedly devised in Germany: live fish (scales and all) are plunged into acidulated water to cook briefly and then are served immediately. Traditional German accompaniments to all fish dishes are potatoes in some form, usually simply boiled and garnished with minced parsley or chives and fresh butter. Other partners with most fish meals are cucumbers, asparagus, and green salad.

Eggs are widely used not only soft-cooked for breakfast but also at other times in many forms, most under the heading of **eierspeisen**. These include scrambled, fried (**spiegeleier**), poached, as plain or fluffy omelets, eggs with sauces, and **kaiserschmarren** – "torn" (pulled into irregular pieces with two forks) egg pancakes served with cinnamon sugar and buttered raisins. Eggs are also used generously in savory and dessert soufflés, blended into soups and

sauces, and add their golden richness to the many fragrant baked goods.

Legumes are also important in the German cuisine. Yellow and green dried peas are used in thick soups or as side dishes of puréed peas. Lentils and white beans are also used both in soups and in many one-dish (**eintopf**) meals.

BREADS AND GRAINS

Bread is on the table at all meals whether in the home or at a public dining room and it is the undisputed "staff of life," only slightly more important than the ubiquitous potato. While chewy dark breads made of rye flour come immediately to mind, German bakeries also turn out an incredible array of soft and hard, crisp and chewy, seeded or plain breads and rolls of every shape and size. Rye and wholewheat flour, barley and oats all have a place in German breads and rolls. Many are sprinkled with cracked wheat grains, coarse salt, and crunchy sesame or poppy seeds.

With such an array to choose from it is not surprising that dry breakfast cereals are not too popular, although children are sometimes served hot cooked oats or rice at breakfast, usually sweetened with sugar and raisins and sometimes flavored with cinnamon.

Pastas are increasingly popular, especially as quick light meals – more so in cities than in rural regions.

FATS

Lard, bacon fat, and butter head the list of most-used fats in Germany. Olive oil is used only infrequently for special salads or dishes. Vegetable shortenings and margarine are gaining popularity among health-conscious Germans. Many homes (especially in the country) still enjoy the taste of fats rendered from geese, ducks, and chickens and these are used as spreads on breads and in general cooking. Fats for deep-frying include lard, rendered fat from fowl, and even horse fat.

SWEETS AND SNACKS

Sweet preserves with the breakfast bread, plenty of sugar in the **kaffee**, something sweet to finish the midday meal – and how depressing it would be to contemplate a day without afternoon **kaffee** that included at least a little **kuchen**, **strudel**, or **torte**! And what kind of a holiday would Christmas be without the warm aromas of **weihnachtsgeback** and **konfekt**?

It is all right to list beer, sausages, kraut, and potatoes as hardy old traditional German staples, but let no one forget the rich baked goods available if not from mother's oven, then from any number of exquisite *konditoreien*, where one can relax, chat a while, and sip delicious **kaffee** while choosing from a bewildering display of sweet nibbles.

One is further reminded – in the nicest way – of the German sweet tooth with the serving of many meat and fish dishes gently afloat in sweet and sour sauces and sometimes including a melange of dried fruits to heighten the tart-sweet tastes. Don't forget, too, that not only are many popular German summer soups made with fresh fruits, but if none of these is available the canny *hausfrau* will use sugar and vinegar.

SEASONINGS

After Charlemagne encouraged the monasteries (in olden times very advanced in both the growing and preparation of food) to plant herb gardens, it did not take long for the people to use the fragrant herbs – lovage, woodruff, parsley, chives, garlic, and dill – in many dishes. Seeds quickly found a place in German cuisine too: caraway, dill, sesame and poppy seeds.

German cookery could generally be described as hearty but bland. Strong flavors and strong seasonings are not the rule; even garlic is used with a heavy hand only in certain sausages, while onions, chives, and leeks are preferred. Adding a distinctive touch to German cuisine is the prevalent use of sweet-sour, usually created by blending vinegar or lemon juice with brown sugar. The best of German cookery relies on the delicate natural taste of fresh ingredients: fresh eggs and butter, choice meats and fish, tender young vegetables, fragrant ripe fruits. Sweet and sour dishes are often further enhanced with the addition of raisins or currants and spices like cinnamon and nutmeg, and thickened with the dried crumbs from honeycake or gingerbread. Other frequent tastes include: anchovies, apples, capers, fresh dill weed, horseradish, juniper berries, and many varieties of mustards.

The tang of sour cream and dark rye bread and the smoky taste of bacon permeates many meals especially in Northern and Eastern Germany.

BEVERAGES

Beer is the favorite German beverage and if natural thirst and good fellowship are not enough, there are any number of salty, sour, tangy, or tart **vorspeisen** (appetizers) to lure the thirst. German thirst is not only first and foremost quenched by frothy mugs of beer, the containers come in different materials and sizes (from a small glass to a huge stein) and the beer itself comes in many tastes and brews from mild to strong. If that is not enough, there may be a **schnapps** to drink before the beer and even fruit syrups to add to them for variety. Germany is considered to be "the greatest brewing country in the world and Munich the greatest brewing city" but every area and every town and, in many cases, most homes brew specialties of their own. Types of beer include among many others: **Helles**, light Munich beer; **Dunkles**, dark; **Heller Bock**, strong and light; **Dunkler Bock**, strong and dark.

Many fine German wines are also produced, both reds and whites, but the whites are more widely known than the reds. Rhine and Moselle wines offer many delicate flavors. The sweetest ones are for sipping while the drier fruity types are for special occasion meals. Generally, Germans have a preference for sweet rather than dry wines.

Kaffee begins the day as a warming, stimulating breakfast drink. The coffee served in the late afternoon usually has the connotation of a friendly hospitable gathering to which is added the sweet touch of fine pastries. Coffee and a sweet is a German tradition. Tea has a medicinal connotation and is usually taken to "cure" something. Of the many types of herbal teas, camomile and mint are among the favorites.

REGIONAL SPECIALTIES

While the various regions of Germany were independent and autonomous communities until relatively recently, it is not surprising that they also developed special regional foods. There is a common factor: almost everywhere, these regional foods are based on the country's favorite staples of beer, pork, potatoes, and cabbage, yet they are different in the technique of cooking, seasoning, or the way they are served. In general, there are three main divisions of German cuisine: Central, Northern, and Southern.

CENTRAL REGION

The Central region also includes hearty meals and foods, especially the famed Westphalian ham and dark heavy pumpernickel bread. Pork is important here and many dishes favor a heavy touch with freshly ground black pepper. Gravies are thickened with dried bread crumbs more often than with flour. **Pannhas** is a thick, simmered porridge made from buckwheat and may be eaten hot or cold and sometimes sliced and fried. **Pannhas** may have been the origin of New England "scrapple," with cornmeal rather than buckwheat used in the United States. Frankfurt is known for a special herb-flavored green sauce, **grune sosse**, which is similar to the **pesto alla genovese** based on basil.

One cannot think of Thuringia without images of fluffy round dumplings, for here is the home of the feathery **klosse**, made only from potatoes and flour – the best made even without the leavening help of eggs. The foods in Saxony are similar but they take even more pleasure in sweets: **schnitten**, **stollen**, and fruit **kuchen** in delicious variety.

Apple cider in different alcoholic potencies is a familiar drink throughout this region.

NORTHERN REGION

The Northern region, influenced by its proximity to the Scandinavian countries and the Netherlands as well as by the damp, cold climate, is characterized by thick soups, pickled and smoked meats and fish, dried fruits, smoked bacon, sour cream, and many

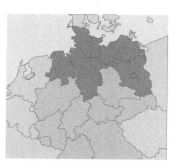

dishes with goose and eels. Most interesting is the traditional North German meal of **lab-skaus**: a one-dish meal of meat and fish plus vegetables which became a sailor's specialty and earned the name **lob-scouse**. **Schlachtplatte** or slaughter plate is also a Northern specialty of a variety of meats and sausages – the byproducts of a slaughtering day – served with bread and pickles.

Berlin, considered part of the Northern cuisine district, is famed for its ground meat dishes: **strammer max**, a snack of buttered rye bread with a thick slice of ham and two fried eggs resting on top; **Berliner pfannkuchen**, luscious plump jam-filled doughnuts (the inspiration of those in other countries); and **baumkuchen**, rich eggy Christmas layered logs glazed and browned with chocolate. Here too, **kummel** (caraway) as a flavoring and as a liqueur is important and beer is taken with schnapps to accompany most foods. Occasionally beer **mit schuss** indicates a shot of raspberry syrup in the beer for a change. Every Berlin bar carries a good supply of **Kurfurstlicher Magenbitter**, a bitter potent cordial said to do wonders for the stomach.

SOUTHERN REGION

Southern German cuisine has a characteristically lighter touch. Wine is more prevalent than beer, due to the grape cuttings planted by the Romans almost 2,000 years ago. Here, dumplings are called **knodel**, and some very special potato dishes are prepared: puddings, pancakes, diced potatoes and bacon and the famed **himmel und erde**: equal amounts of pan-fried sliced apples and potatoes with crisply fried slices of blood sausage, aptly translated as "heaven and earth."

MEALS AND CUSTOMS

Early risers, the Germans like a light breakfast of bread or rolls with butter and preserves and coffee with canned milk and sugar. Children may be served a porridge of oats or rice flavored with raisins and cinnamon. But since that first meal of the day is served before the real German appetite has fully awakened, most people take a few sandwiches of meat or cheese to work or school, to be eaten around ten o'clock as the second breakfast or snack. In some areas a few sausages with beer fill the hunger "pocket."

Traditionally the noon meal is the largest of the day and many try to eat at home with the family, although this is becoming increasingly less feasible with more and more women working outside the home. A hearty soup, a meat and vegetable **eintopf**, and a dessert (**susspeisen**) make up the midday meal.

Since supper is customarily served around 7:30 p.m., an afternoon snack of "coffee and a sweet" helps tide one over. A light evening meal frequently comprises soup and a dessert, a selection of cold meats, sausages, and cheese with bread or rolls accompanied with salad is served. Occasionally a late evening hunger pang may be assuaged with sausages and beer or a thick goulash-type soup. Restaurants serve every variety of food in generous portions and eating out is almost a form of sport to many Germans.

One can understand the delight in eating out with only a glance at what is offered: good eating places have special names such as *gasthofe, ratskeller, weinstuben, bierhallen, restaurants, schnellimbiss-stube* (quick lunch counter), *milchbars* for cool milk or milkshakes, *eissalons* for refreshing ices and ice creams of all types, *konditoreien* for pastries and coffee, summer beer gardens, and even special cafeterias at places of business to provide that hot midday meal. And there is a *wurstlerei* just for beer and sausages. Increasingly, Turkish, Italian, Thai, and other ethnic restaurants in the cities provide delicious alternatives to traditional German fare.

Entertaining at home is enjoyed with close friends, family, and the children's friends. In fact, for most Germans, the friends of their children are not only welcomed as family, they are often considered as extended family. Many Germans retain the old traditions and formal etiquette associated with entertaining in the home. These include punctual arrival, some hand kissing is still customary, and almost always, a bouquet of flowers will be proffered to the hostess. Handshaking is a definite point of etiquette, and reputedly, more handshaking goes on in Germany than in many other countries.

Entertaining for business purposes or with casual friends takes place not in the home but in the many types of restaurants and cafés. Should it be necessary to bring people into the home to discuss business, the hostess rarely serves anything.

Family and close friends coming for dinner or lunch will always be served with the best linen, and if possible any fine treasured pieces of china, especially coffee sets. Rhine and Moselle wines or a punch bowl accompanied with appetizers of small salted pastries and nuts will be offered first. The more sophisticated may sip Scotch, bourbon, or brandy, but generally cocktails are not in the German entertaining tradition. Home dinner parties are usually prompted by some special family occasion such as a confirmation or engagement. Often a lengthy evening may conclude with the hostess serving casually prepared sandwiches or plates of sausages with beer.

A particularly delightful custom is that of presenting children with a huge gaily decorated cone filled with sweets for their first day at school. Perhaps this sweet beginning adds pleasure to learning.

SPECIAL OCCASIONS

Present-day Germany is almost equally divided between Roman Catholics and Protestants and each group celebrates not only religious and saint's days but also join in beer and wine festivities, regional holidays and, in some areas, harvesting and planting festivities.

Hundreds of local and regional festivals and holidays are celebrated throughout Germany and vary according to locale, as do customs and foods. The South is predominantly Catholic while the North is mostly Protestant. Plain cakes, bread, and cheese are served at funerals, while the happier family occasions such as weddings, engagements, and confirmations call forth wines and opulent meals from the best of the regional and family specialties.

The wedding-eve party is called *polterabend* and, aside from the special treats and wine that are served, guests traditionally bring baskets or armloads of old crockery and these are cheerfully smashed because "broken dishes bring good luck." Humorous and teasing speeches and songs for the new couple help make a boisterous and fun-filled evening. Another traditionally German evening is the *herrenabend*, an evening for men only. Not quite the same as the familiar "stag party," the *herrenabend* usually takes place for the purpose of discussing business or politics while eating and drinking. Of course no one minds if, towards the smaller hours of the evening, drinking predominates over conversation.

Spring and fall see the proliferation of many local beer and wine festivals but none as overwhelming as the Munich *Oktoberfest* held annually for a sixteen-day spree of beer-drinking, singing to the oompah-pah bands, dancing, and snacking on roasted chickens, sausages, and whole spit-roasted oxen all in gargantuan quantities. The fest, which originated in 1810 to celebrate Crown Prince Ludwig's marriage, proved to be such a good idea that it has been an annual event ever since. The boisterous good fellowship has spread to other countries where citizens of German origin make their homes, and, as with the Irish Saint Patrick's Day parade, everyone, regardless of ethnic background, happily joins in. Together with the fun and frolic, eating and drinking, nearby amusement parks offer all manner of games and rides as well.

The German's annual calendar is rung in with a quiet family evening on New Year's Eve centered around the traditional specialty of Polish carp: a whole carp gently poached in a rich sauce of beer, gingerbread crumbs, lemon peel, almonds, and raisins all traditionally served with **kartoffelklosse** and **kraut**. The festive meal is served with a flaming punch bowl and completed with an array of baked treats. Catholics eat no meat on New Year's Eve, Protestant families may enjoy other local food favorites.

Three King's Eve, Epiphany or *Dreikonigsabend* signifies the end of the Christmas season (Twelfth Night) and is greeted with the serving of wine or punch and **konigskuchen**, a loaf cake with raisins, almonds, and rum.

Arriving in bleak mid-winter is the brightest carnival of them all: *Fasching* (elsewhere called Mardi Gras and Shrove Tuesday), usually a three-day bash of costumes, masks, parades, processions, parties, and revelry unmatched at any other time of year. Crullers called **fastnachtkrapfen** are the special treat everywhere but feasting and drinking before the Lenten restrictions is the general rule. The new spring beer, called **Bock**, is celebrated during this time as well and is enjoyed with **bockwurst** sausages that are the specialty of the season. Holy Thursday (just before Good Friday) is also called *Grundonnerstag* and the spring festival is heralded with the serving of a green vegetable soup made of fresh spring vegetables, while other dishes made with eggs and spinach are also traditional. Good Friday or *Karfreitag* is a solemn day when all businesses and shops are closed. For the pious, no meat is eaten; only fish dishes are allowed. Churches open their doors revealing huge displays of fresh flowers and flickering candles.

Easter or *Oster* arrives with the special aroma of home-baked fruited breads and cakes, candies in the form of eggs and rabbits, and a traditional Easter dinner featuring ham served with pureed peas. For the children, the Easter Bunny does his job of hiding colored eggs throughout the house and in gardens.

A pleasant spring ritual is the Whitsun Festival or *Pfingstausflug*, a traditional spring outing when good luck is considered to be the prize of the first person to hear a cuckoo, and everyone enjoys communing with nature.

Germany is the land where many of Christendom's cherished Christmas traditions originated. These include the Christmas tree, many Christmas legends and hauntingly beautiful Christmas carols, as well as some of the earliest stagings of Christmas nativity scenes (by Saint Francis of Greccio, 1225) and primitive Christmas plays.

The holiday begins early with the many fairs held at this time of year, especially the one held annually at Nurnberg. Here one finds every conceivable decoration and toy for Christmas: a fairyland of color, design, and fun. And for those who get hungry while shopping, there is the famed Nurnberg **lebkuchen** and **pfefferkuchen** (spiced squares and cakes).

While the first taste of Christmas may be at the fairs, the real beginning of the festive season is on Saint Nikolaus' Day, December 6. The evening before, all children hang up socks or boots and find them filled in the morning with sweets and small gifts. But the real excitement is the house-to-house visit of Saint Nikolaus himself with his helper, Krampus, a horrid furry little monster who carries a switch for bad children. But most children have been good and therefore happily receive the saint's good cookies and good wishes. Delicious smells drift from every home as mothers almost daily prepare batches of honeyed and spiced cakes, cookies and fragrant breads all called **weihnachtsgeback**. And everywhere little *naschkatzen* (pilferers of sweets) are nibbling tastes of **stollen**, **lebkuchen**, **spritz cookies**, **springerle**, and **spekulatius**.

Christmas Eve brings tree-lighting and carol-singing and most families go to church. Surprise gifts from Kris Kringle appear mysteriously under the tree after everyone returns from church services. Since pious Christians refrain from eating meat on Christmas Eve, the traditional dinner of Polish carp baked in all its glory with beer, nuts and raisins is usually the highlight of the meal surrounded with potato dumplings and dishes of **kraut**. Punch or wine and fine bakery end the meal while others still nibble on fruit and nuts. Christmas Day is a quiet family day in Germany and the special dinner will likely be the regional specialty of roast hare, roast pork, or a fine fat roasted goose. Marzipan fruits and little figures are part of the decorations and the nibbles too.

GLOSSARY OF FOODS AND FOOD TERMS

Apfelkuchen: a short rich pastry is pressed into the bottom and sides of a springform pan. Sliced apples, bread crumbs, currants flavored with rum and grated lemon rind are arranged over the pastry, then baked. Twenty minutes before removing from the oven a creamy egg custard is poured over the cake to form a topping.

Auflaufe: souffle.

Braten: the favorite German technique for cooking most meats. If necessary, meat is larded first then browned in a heavy pan with fat, onions, and seasonings. Liquid is added and the dish is covered to cook slowly. To finish, the gravy is thickened with potato paste, bread crumbs, or flour. Sometimes wine, beer, or sour cream is added. Meat is sliced and served with accompanying vegetables and sauce.

Baumkuchen: a many-layered egg-crusted log glazed with chocolate. A Christmas specialty.

Der Westfalische: a Westphalian pudding made of grated chocolate, pumpernickel crumbs, lemon zest, cinnamon, and slivered almonds blended with eggs and baked. It is served with vanilla sauce.

Einbrenne: used as the basis for most German sauces and to thicken soups, vegetable liquids, and gravies. Flour and fat are heated and blended together, then the liquid slowly added. This differs from the French roux, because the German **Einbrenne** always has the flavor of onion. Chopped onion is added to the fat while heating or a half onion is allowed to brown in the fat for flavor and may then be removed before blending with the liquid.

Eintopf: a one-dish meal related to the casserole, usually of meat, vegetables, and gravy.

Feinkostgeschaft: literally a "fine food shop," and actually the next step up from the usual delicatessen in that such a shop carries not only an exceptionally wide range of fine local and imported foods, but also foods which feature exceptional quality and unusual packaging.

Gans: goose. But in Northern Germany a goose is not just a goose. It may be **Spickgans**, pickled and smoked goose breast; or **Ganseklein**, bits of goose meat stewed with vegetables and finished with dried cooked fruits and finally served with dumplings; or **Schwarzsauer von Gans**, goose blood and vinegar thickened with flour and spiced. Or it could be a dish of pickled goose stomach minced and blended with onion and seasonings and used as a spread on bread.

Hausgebackenes: home-baked goodies, cakes, and small cookies.

Himmel und Erde: South German specialty of pan-fried apple and potato slices served with fried slices of **Blutwurst** (blood sausage).

Huhn im Topf: chicken simmered with wine and vegetables.

Kalbfleisch: veal.

Kartoffel: potato.

Kartoffelpuffer: potato pancake.

Kase: cheese, of which the two most used types in Germany are **Topfen**, a dry farmer's cheese, and **Quark**, a moist creamy cottage cheese.

Kasseller Rippenspeer: roast pork served on sauerkraut with mashed potatoes and a rich wine and sour cream gravy.

Klopse, **Knodel**, **Klosse**, **Klosschen**: only a few of the many names for dumplings. **Klopse** are those made with finely ground meat; **Knodel** is the South German name for the North German **Klosse**, which are fluffy potato dumplings, while **Klosschen** is an endearing name for little dumplings.

Konfekt: a confectionary, a place where sweets of all kinds can be purchased.

Konigberger Klopse: an example of dumplings fit for a king. Mixed finely ground meat and soaked bread (in milk) is shaped into small balls and poached, usually in a light broth, then served with a cream sauce. What sets the dumplings apart are the anchovies and capers in the sauce.

Kuchen: generic name for yeast dough, pastry or cakes baked with fillings and shaped in a log, square, or round.

Napfkuchen: fruit cakes.

Pfefferpotthast: a beef short-rib stew with onions, knob celery, and carrots all browned in bacon fat. Served with potatoes and beet salad in the winter but with a fresh salad of lettuce, tomatoes, and cucumbers when they are available.

Pickert: a yeast-risen wheat or potato-flour bread. A specialty in the central region.

Potthucke: a baked pudding of raw and cooked potatoes, eggs, and milk, sliced and fried to serve.

Rindfleisch: beef.

Rostbratl: roasted pork basted with dark beer.

Rotwein: red wine.

Sauerbraten: a marinated pot roast of beef with a rich dark gravy sweet with sugar and gingerbread crumbs and sour with a touch of vinegar. Traditionally served with cooked red cabbage and fluffy potato dumplings.

Schinken or **Speck**: cured bacon or ham.

Schnippelkuchen: a large egg-rich potato pancake served in wedges.

Schwarzwalder Kirschentorte: Black Forest cherry cake. Layers of chocolate cake filled with whipped cream and cherry preserves, the layers having first been given a dousing of rum and/or kirsch. The cake is coated with whipped cream, the sides pressed with chocolate flakes, and the top decorated with chocolate-dipped cherries.

Schwein: fresh pork.

Soleier: pickled eggs, a common snack in most drinking places in Germany.

Strudel: a log of thin stretched dough enfolding juicy fruit or cheese filling. Favorites are sliced apples and currants, cherries and almonds, or cottage cheese and raisins. Reputedly of Austro-Hungarian origin, and never forgotten by those who have tasted it!

Suppen: soups.

Sussspeisen: the general name for all the sweet dishes that may happily end a meal – puddings or farina, rice or tapioca, apple or fruit pancakes, apple or fruit dumplings served with sauces, egg custards, sweet egg omelets or souffles, and finally wine or fruit jellies.

Topfbraten: a thick stew made from pigs' ears, snouts, kidneys and heart with the sauce thickened with both gingerbread crumbs and plum jam. A specialty of "Slaughtering Day."

Vorspeisen: appetizers, either hot or cold. Germans prefer a one-plate appetizer rather than a choice of many small bites.

Weihnachtsgeback: this includes all the special bakery for Christmas – especially the crisply delicious array of small cookies.

CHAPTER 22

GREEK

Pleasures drive out pain and excessive pain leads men to seek excessive pleasures ...
—Aristotle

The above was spoken by a Greek, and more than twenty centuries later it is still the core truism of Greeks everywhere. No characteristic is more typically Greek than the inherent ability to balance pain and pleasure delicately and live life to the fullest.

Ten million Greeks living on the mainland and on 1,400 Greek islands suffer the daily realities of existence in a harsh meager land where political problems simmer and where poverty and hardship are old neighbors. But while the body may subsist on bread, cheese, and olives as rural daily fare, the Greek soul is spiritually nourished by the mystically dazzling landscape of endless blue skies, the clarity of a strong white sun, and the warmth of rustic red earth.

These are the same elements that bore witness to the "Glory of Greece." This included a brilliant span of 200 years from 500-300 B.C.E. when Athens became the light-source of the western world and spawned a plethora of literature, philosophy, mathematics, democracy as well as a sophistication in style of living seldom equaled. While the rest of the world was gnawing on roasted meat, the Greeks were savoring many varieties of fruits and seafoods, experimenting with cooked mixtures of meats and vegetables, developing sauces and dressings (white sauce, mayonnaise, marinades of oils and seasonings), blending seasonings, and even writing cookbooks.

Because reminders of Greece's past greatness are everywhere visible in the civilized world of today, the past and the present are one reality to the Greek. It doesn't matter what subject is under discussion, Greeks will have an opinion – and a word for it. It is the incredible blending of past greatness, living the present to the fullest, and unflagging faith in the future that makes simple survival the ultimate Greek pleasure. With bold words and classic gestures, with intense curiosity and endless enthusiasm together with an age-old ability to dramatize, the Greek brushes aside pain and troubles, gently disdains time, and plunges fully into the enjoyment of life.

Others may point to the closeness of Greek family life or to the stability of the Greek Orthodox Church as central to Greek optimism and self-confidence. But it is all of these factors and something more. It is an ancient tradition that Greece is somehow more than a land or a people but rather a special image that was nurtured by the ancient gods of Greece and preserved for all eternity by an omnipotent "god of Greece." That innate Greek faith is rooted firmly in the belief that while other gods may be alive or dead, the "god of Greece" will somehow forever intervene just when things seem hopeless. And a glance at Greek history bears out this philosophy.

When the great Hellenistic age came to a crushing end with the Roman Conquest of 197 C.E., Greek schools declined and Greek democracy disappeared, yet Greek language and culture survived. The novelty of Greek cuisine – varieties of wild animals, fruits, and seafoods, the ingenious uses of sauces and seasonings, recipes and utensils – was a revelation to the Romans. They unabashedly adopted Greek foods, together with Greek art and architecture, Greek philosophy and refinements. And they valued their Greek chefs above all. While the Greeks helplessly watched as Athens gave way to Rome as the center of the western world, they must have also experienced some satisfaction in seeing that Hellenistic influence proved stronger than armies.

The embers of Greek language and culture that flickered during the Roman domination were fanned to a bright flame during the thousand years after the fall of Rome. The period of the Byzantine Empire with its center in Constantinople actually took its name from the ancient Greek community on which it stood: Byzantium. Christianity was introduced by the Emperor Constantine as the state religion of the Roman Empire around 325 C.E., much to the credit of the early Christian theologians who incorporated many Greek ideas into Christianity that the latter flourished even though Rome was later sacked by hostile pagan tribes.

Again, however, this Greek flowering of influence was abruptly cut off in 1204 C.E. as the

Crusaders captured Constantinople and parceled it out to Frankish knights. The new rulers crushed everything Greek. Latinization was the goal, Greek ships and trade were turned over to the Venetians, and strong attempts were made to impose Catholicism. It did indeed seem that the Franks dominated every aspect of life, with one exception. Greek women quietly saw to it that the children they bore never forgot that they were Greek.

The continuing benevolence of the god of Greece was about to meet the strongest test. On Tuesday, May 29, 1453, the Byzantine Empire was crushed completely with the capture of Constantinople by the Turks. So deep is the memory of that terrible day that even to the present, Greeks consider Tuesday a bad-luck day and the entire month of May fraught with grim symbolism. Yet historians see a positive aspect in that the mass dispersal of thousands of Greeks throughout Europe (as a direct result of the Turkish conquest) may have been responsible for the revival of learning that led to the Renaissance.

The suppression and cruelty of the Ottoman domination lasted 400 years. And while the Greeks learned, among other things, to enjoy sipping Turkish coffee, smoking the *narghile* (water-filtered smoking pipe), and preparing meat on skewers, which they called **souvlakia** (from the Turkish **sis kebab**), the Turks, who were previously a nomadic people, very quickly developed a taste for Greek cookery. Not surprising then, in the manner of all conquerors, they also gave Turkish names to classic Greek dishes.

It seems the Greek's hopeful confidence, that age-old faith in the god of Greece, was to be renewed again. In their 400-year occupation, the Turks made two fateful errors: first, they gave the Greeks concessions in trade, shipping and administration, at once unwittingly creating Greek leadership and a Greek navy; and second, they decided to place the Orthodox Church leaders in charge of their communities. The Greek leadership and navy were the seeds of the subsequent Turkish downfall, while the authority and strength of the Church in small communities unified Greeks everywhere and served to preserve their language and culture. While the rest of the western world at that time became a blend of Roman and Turkish culture with only echoes of Greek taste apparent, to the Greeks themselves their vital roots remained strong.

When people are suppressed, their only daily concern is survival. They have neither the time nor freedom to devote to the arts, literature, philosophy, or the delicacies of the palate. Choice lands were cultivated by the Turks and the Greeks were forced to retreat to barren rocky lands and mountain areas, often surviving on cheese made from the milk of mountain goats, wild herbs, olives, and whatever crops they could nudge from the unwilling land. The Turks called the Greeks *Rumis* and it is from this bitter time that Greeks still refer to the noble and creative part of themselves as *Hellene* and any bursts of stubbornness or selfishness as *Romios*.

Of necessity, then, Greek cuisine became an art of the past. It was so successfully adapted, transformed, and renamed mostly by the Turks and Italians that its Greek origins were all but forgotten. Yet one piece of ancient writing remains: *The Banquet of the Learned* (*Deipnosophists*), written in 200 C.E. by Athenaeus, a Greek philosopher living in Rome. His detailed descriptions of foods eaten, their methods of preparation, and even cooking utensils and cutlery as well as menus for dinners and banquets are remarkable in their sophistication. It is from Athenaeus that we learn of **kakavia**. A seafood stew introduced to Marseilles by seafaring Greeks, **kakavia** later became world-renowned as **bouillabaisse**. The book discusses sauces in loving detail: that emulsion of eggs, lemon juice, and olive oil called **mayonnaise**; a thick white sauce called **bechamel**; and even cruets of oil and vinegar to be set on the table and used to dress fresh or cooked vegetables. The use of blends of curry probably was introduced in Alexander's time after his conquest of northern India, but Greek cooks were already long familiar with fragrant thyme and oregano, mint and marjoram, and the Isle of Rhodes was noted for a ginger-flavored bread.

There is more. The general acceptance of small nibbles of food with drinks as "provocatives to eating" not only added graciousness to dining but may even be the ancient root of the Greeks' predilection never to drink without the accompaniment of food.

FOODS COMMONLY USED

To the casual observer, it seems that Greeks are either enjoying a feast day, or submitting to yet another fast day. The Greek calendar is studded with both. Foods for fast days coincide with foods that are the staples for most rural Greeks: bread, olives and olive oil, fruit and nuts and legumes. Food for feast days includes roasted meats such as lamb or chicken, varieties of fruits and vegetables, cheeses and yogurt and specialties of delicate pastries and cookies. The abundant fresh lemons and wild herbs season most dishes while homemade wine is the beverage of choice.

Athenaeus further describes many stuffed, baked vegetables and leaves, tiny meatballs called **kefthedes**, light crusty breads and thin crispy pastries, polenta and dumplings, capers and pine nuts, force-fed geese, herb-grilled fish and seafood, and unusual combinations of meats cooked with vegetables. The flavored beverage was a light drink of wine diluted with fresh water and sometimes flavored with honey or spices. It is incredible to think that these commonly known culinary cornerstones of today were part of daily fare even before 200 C.E.

The Greeks have been suppressed and forced to survive on meager rations for so long that it was often Greek emigrants rather than native Greeks who revived interest and pride in culinary pursuits. The first large wave of Greek emigrants followed that fateful Tuesday in May 1453. But other events in Greek history have spurred waves of emigrants, especially to North America. In 1891 a combination of serious crop failures, especially in Laconia and Arcadia, as well as fear of conscription in Turkish lands, sent emigrants out of the country in waves that continued even after the First World War. The combined shortages and suffering that the Greeks endured during the Second World War and during the subsequent civil strife once again sent them to seek a better, more peaceful life elsewhere. Arguably, it is this recent memory of pain that motivates Greeks in North America to take every advantage of the results of hard work, enterprise, and education.

Greeks know and treasure their deep roots in the past. Against a backdrop of painful history, their own pride and determination, together with the help of the god of Greece, have kept alive and vital a culture, language, and cuisine that have few equals. Despite an occasional fretful fingering of the worry beads, the Greek has learned to find pleasures in day-to-day living and to brush aside the painful events of the past with a hopeful sigh to the future. It is a feat of survival and pride that Aristotle himself would enjoy reading the many Athens newspapers of today, Greeks from the Byzantine Empire would be at home in the worship and rituals of the Greek Orthodox Church, and even Athenaeus would be happily familiar with today's Greek table.

DOMESTIC LIFE

Greek survival is attributable, in large measure, to the closeness of family ties and responsibilities. There is no doubt that the Greek male child is favored and loved by mother and sisters, but in later years he returns this affection with a strong devotion which often includes the postponement of his own marriage in favor of seeing his sisters provided for. And the Greek male's lifelong devotion to his mother is legendary: it is said that with the slightest look or gentlest sigh from his mother, the Greek male capitulates to her wishes.

Every Greek feels himself or herself a strong part of an extended family that includes concern for someone from the same village or area. Greek emigrants do not need to be told where to seek advice or help; they will automatically seek out relatives no matter how distant, and former villagers or neighbors. This kind of help and shared responsibility comes naturally to a people whose history is flecked liberally with examples of the need for mutual aid, without which survival would have been impossible.

Except for the upper classes, where women exhibit considerable independence, male and female roles in the traditional Greek family are clearly defined. The men not only enjoy their favored position, they carry this loving confidence with them into their work and into their male-oriented leisure hours. Every village, no matter how small, boasts a *plateia* or village square where the men congregate to enjoy Turkish coffee, a sip of **Retsina** or **Ouzo**, or where they lounge on chairs reading the paper or listening to the talk. It is a male preserve and the women neither complain nor intrude. In fact, most Greek women contentedly follow the saying of Euripides: "A woman should be everything in the house and nothing outside it...."

The women concern themselves with homemaking and crafts, with child-rearing, with the kitchen garden and – in rural areas – the goats, sheep, and chickens. Not for them the problems of fields or businesses, money or education. Nor do they envy the male social life. They find fulfilment in their weekly visit to the church, and their daily trip to the village well or market. Even in North America, with increased accessability and opportunities for women, many Greek women choose to retain this traditional role.

The rural Greek family home commonly comprises two large rooms: one for sleeping (Greek children usually go to bed when their parents do), and one for everything else. Firewood and stores are kept under the house. Large earthenware jars are used to store and cool fresh water taken daily from the local wells. In the main room of the house the walls are lined with open shelves displaying cooking and table utensils, strings of garlic and onions and colorful jars of sweet preserves (spoon sweets). Day-to-day baking is done outside in beehive-shaped ovens, while the local *fourno* (bakeshop) shares its facilities for special occasion baking. This is also one of the few times that young boys share in household tasks: it is their job to bring home the fragrant baked foods from the *fourno*. Villagers also share wine and olive presses, for each home makes its own olive oil and ferments its own wines.

Recent government programs encourage the arts of butter-, cheese-, and yogurt-making, dispense information on nutrition, and educate people about various methods of food preservation that include drying, canning, salting, and pickling. Traditionally, Greeks favor fresh seasonal foods, an understandable preference considering that storage and transportation, together with low annual incomes, frequently meant that the available food was the day's menu. But it should also be noted that preference for fresh seasonal foods is also distinctly shown by those with a discerning palate.

Modern methods of food storage and preservation are available to those in the larger cities, as of course are an increased variety of foods both local and imported.

DAIRY PRODUCTS

Milk is not a favorite beverage for the Greeks, whose dairy products of choice are yogurt and cheese. Yogurt, usually made at home, is used as a snack or ingredient in many dishes. Cheeses vary from mild to strong and may be grated for use in cookery or cut into cubes for salads or appetizers. Most popular is **Feta**, a pungent goat's-milk cheese preserved in brine. Other cheeses used are: mild **Kasseri**; **Mizzithra** made from ewe's milk and resembling cottage cheese; and **Kefalotiri**, which is a salty and hard grating cheese. **Manouri** and **Graviera** are used much like **Feta**; all three lend a pronounced flavor to **tyropitas** and **spanakopitas**, a marriage of **phyllo** pastry with the cheese as filling. **Saganaki** is an appetizer of deep-fried flour-dusted cheese squares served hot and sprinkled with fresh lemon juice.

FRUITS AND VEGETABLES

As in most Mediterranean countries, Greek fruits are noted for their luscious ripe tastes and are enjoyed fresh or lovingly preserved in thick heavy syrups to be served to guests accompanied with a glass of fresh cold water. Served in this way, fruits are called spoon sweets. Sometimes these are also made from selected tiny vegetables such as tomatoes. Lemons and other citrus fruits are used most widely. In season there is also a choice of grapes, figs, quinces, strawberries, cherries, apricots, plums, peaches, and many varieties of apples. Special autumn favorites are **peponi**, a Greek melon resembling both a honeydew and a cantaloupe, and **karpouzi**, a richly flavored type of watermelon.

Vegetables have a special place in the Greek menu and they are used frequently. Carrots, potatoes, and small beets are year-round staples, while **aubergine** (eggplant) and **courgette** (zucchini) head the list of seasonal favorites. These may be made into pickles, stuffed and baked, or sliced and layered into casseroles with sauce and cheese. Even the zucchini flowers are considered a special treat and served batter-dipped and fried. **Kolokithokorfades** is a zucchini-flower specialty where the flowers are gently filled with a cheese mixture before being dipped in batter and fried. Artichokes, okra, broad beans and lima beans, cauliflower, fresh peas, tomatoes and cucumbers as well as many wild greens such as mustard, dandelion, and spinach are collectively known as **horta**.

Horta is cleaned, chopped and boiled, then served with lemon juice and oil. But other vegetable preparations may be more elaborate, including **bechamel sauce** and cheeses; layered between **phyllo** pastry and cheeses; or scooped out and baked with fillings. **Dolmadakia** are meat- and rice-stuffed vine (grape) leaves. Vegetables can also be a part of pilafs (with rice), yeast doughs, and sometimes breads (**zucchini bread**) and vegetables can be a light meal when combined with eggs to make omelets or souffles.

A meal (other than breakfast) without fresh or cooked vegetables of some kind is rare. A main course of meat or cheese is accompanied by **salata**. This term is loosely used to include cooked, chilled vegetables served with oil and lemon and a sprinkling of herbs or the **Greek salata**, a carefully constructed mountain of fresh greens (sometimes over a mound of potato salad), garnished with black olives, cubed **Feta**, tomato and cucumber chunks all shimmering with oil and lemon juice and fragrant with fresh oregano.

Olives are of special importance in Greece. Greeks prefer their olives black, but these may be brined, pickled, or even spiced and are a part of almost every meal. Sometimes bread and olives form a simple meal.

MEATS AND ALTERNATES

Goats are plentiful in Greece, but because they are generous with their milk they are seldom used as food. Goat's milk, and the **Feta** cheese made from it, are important staples in the Greek diet. Some pigs and chickens are available, but the staple Greek meat is lamb. Meat is generally scarce and expensive, so every part of the animal is used and the main cookery methods promote tenderness and "stretch" the flavor. The sweet nutty flavor of lamb blends well with all vegetables, and often a dish is considered different because of the different herbs used: spearmint, rosemary, oregano, and even cinnamon. Lemon juice and/or yogurt flavor as well as tenderize.

Eggs are not plentiful in Greece but are used in

pastries, omelets, and the famed **avgolemono sauce** used to finish soups, glaze fish and meat dishes, top casseroles, and add a golden lemon touch to vegetables.

People living on the islands and near coastal regions enjoy fish and seafood dishes prepared from recipes that date to Greece's Golden Age: grilling with herbs, oil and lemon juice; baking in parchment, and baking fish on a bed of chopped vegetables. Dishes may include eels (a traditional Christmas dish), squid, octopus, prawns, cod, red mullet and sun-dried **petalia**. Those who do not live near the sea make every effort to obtain fresh fish and seafood for they are great favorites.

Fish roe is considered a special delicacy and may be made into small cakes and fried in oil (**tarama kefthetes**) or made into **taramosalata**, the popular dip used as an appetizer. This creamy mixture is made by pureeing soft white bread, fish roe, onions, olive oil, and lemon juice. It is served either from a bowl garnished with bread chunks and black olives, or as a filling for scooped-out cucumbers and small tomatoes.

Another valuable source of protein is available in the many varieties of nuts: almonds, pine nuts, walnuts, pistachios, and chestnuts. These are used in pastries and confections and often mixed with rice as a stuffing for vegetables or as a pilaf. Sometimes choice nuts will be arranged on a serving platter and honey poured over to be served as spoon sweets for guests.

Thick and hearty lentil soup (**faki soupa**) and bean soup (**fasolada**) are favorites in Greek cuisine. They have often satisfied appetites in hard times, and also are the Lenten staples when the consumption of meat is forbidden.

BREADS AND GRAINS
Bread is on the table for all meals. **Kouloura**, a crusty white bread baked in a ring shape and sprinkled with sesame seeds, is typical. Some wholegrain breads are used with appetizers (**mezedakia**) and some specialty dishes, but white breads are preferred. Wheat flour is used for breads and pastries.

Rice and pastas are eaten in small quantities, mostly in soups, in occasional casserole dishes or in pilafs to add variety to the menu. **Pilaf** is the name given to a rice-based dish of Turkish origin where sauced meat and/or vegetables are served either with molded rice or over a mound of rice.

Phyllo pastry is one of the most versatile. Modern Greek women buy the commercially made paper-thin sheets ("phyllo" means "leaves"). Liberally spread with oil or melted butter, they can be folded, rolled, layered, or twisted into endless sweet or savory delights.

FATS
Olive oil is of prime importance in the Greek kitchen. Some fats and margarines are made with olive oil and flavored like butter. Butter is used especially for its taste in baked goods.

SWEETS AND SNACKS
The traditional ending to a Greek meal, and a favorite snack in itself, is fresh fruit. But this is not to say that Greeks don't have a sweet tooth. The offering of sweets is an important symbol of hospitality in the home, and a sweet pastry with Turkish coffee makes a pleasant break any time of day. Special breads and baked goods are made for festive occasions and these are crunchy with nuts and spiced with cinnamon, ginger, and cloves. **Baklava** (layered nut-filled phyllo), **kataifia** (sweetened shredded wheat), and even a simple semolina cake called **ravani** are all enhanced with a drenching of hot thick syrup right after baking. Other confections include fritters (**loukomathes**), rich buttery cookies (**kourabiedes**), beignets (**svingi**), and sugared nuts and dried fruits.

Sweets are always served with a drink – Turkish coffee, **Ouzo**, or a simple but welcome glass of cold water.

Homemakers take great pride in preparing treasured recipes for spoon sweets. Choice fruits in season are carefully preserved in thick sugar syrups and enjoyed with guests anytime but especially in winter when fruits are not available. They may be made from citrus peels (lemon, limes, oranges), grapes, fresh figs, cherries, and even eggplant or tiny tomatoes.

SEASONINGS
Garlic, leeks, and many types of onions are widely available and used in most fish, vegetable, or meat dishes. In fact, the classic **stefado** (beef stew) owes its rich flavor to slowly simmered onions. Except for **skordalia** – a potent garlic mayonnaise, forerunner of the French **aioli** – garlic is used in moderation. A surprise to some tastes is the use of cinnamon, either stick or powdered, in many meat dishes.

Greek cooking has a pleasant freshness that comes from the generous use of fresh lemon and wild herbs. Together with lemon, garlic and onions, parsley and celery leaves, mint, oregano and green dill (not the dill seeds) are most frequently used. Camomile and sage are used as herbal teas, while both marjoram and basil are used as potted plants rather than seasonings. In fact, most Greek homes have a little pot of basil for good luck and to give as a sign of affection – and to keep away flies and mosquitoes.

Greeks were among the first to use capers pickled in wine vinegar and used in sauces or as a garnish.

SOME SEASONINGS AND THEIR USES

English	Greek	Uses
oregano	**rigani**	seasoning
mint dill	**thiosmos**	seasoning
bay leaves	**anitho**	seasoning (not the seeds)
rosemary	**daphni**	seasoning and also boiled with linens to impart fresh smell
thyme	**thymari**	seasoning, especially with lamb, also to freshen black dresses (that have been stored) leaves fed to snails to impart flavor, also added to oil-preserved olives

Baked with bread, sesame seeds are a favorite, and sesame seed oil is used in the confection called **halva** (there is also a cake called **halvas** made from semolina). Pureed seeds are used in the appetizer called **tahini**, a popular dip in many Mediterranean countries.

Three other flavors tease the palate: **orange flower water**, **retsina**, and **mastic**. Orange flower water is extracted from the oil of orange blossoms and is used in delicate sweets. **Retsina** is pine-flavored resin extracted from pine trees and gives its name to the well-known white Greek wine. **Mastic** is made from a resinous shrub and gives its clean pungent flavor to sweets, breads, and even chewing gum, and is popular in many Balkan countries too. The most widely known use of mastic is in the potent drink **Mastika** distilled on the Greek island of Chios.

BEVERAGES

Water, thirst-quencher, refresher, and symbol of hospitality, is the most frequently used beverage in Greece. Natural wellsprings are respected and cherished and many mark the location of monasteries and villages. Water and a sweet will be offered to a stranger even before the individual's name is known; water brings men to the *tavernas* and the *zacharoplasteion* (pastry shops) where sometimes the classic water may be replaced with **Ouzo** or Turkish coffee prepared exactly to taste. Water brings women to the wells to fill their jugs and also to socialize.

Ouzo, reputedly the favorite drink of Alexander the Great and believed to be the inspiration for **Pastis** and **Pernod**, is prepared by infusing distilled grape spirit with a blend of fennel, aniseed, saponaria, and mastic. The predominant flavor is licorice-like; it can be taken straight or with water when it turns milky.

Turkish coffee is a pleasant relic from the Turkish occupation and is always prepared to individual preference: **glikos**, very sweet; **metrios**, half sugar and half coffee; **schetos**, black. Actually, "to taste" means

that there are more than thirty precise levels of flavor and preferred sweetness.

The usual beverage with meals is either cold water or homemade wine; more recently, children have been encouraged to drink milk. **Retsina**, the white resin-flavored wine considered so typical of Greece, is actually only one of many varieties, both red and white, and not all are treated with resin. Many legends describe the origins of the resin-flavored wine but the most persistent tells of Greeks pouring the resin over their wines during the early part of Turkish domination to prevent their conquerors from taking their wines. Later, when the Greeks tasted the resinous wine, they enjoyed it. Most visitors react like the Turks and drink something else. **Fix** and **Alpha** are Greek beers; imported ones are preferred.

MEALS AND CUSTOMS

Greeks don't like being alone and don't think that anyone or even any thing should ever be alone. For example, a drink must always be accompanied with food and food must always be enjoyed with friends. Greek men can always find an excuse to be with other men and consider it an unparalleled honor to have guests – even strangers – to share their home and food. Greek women seriously value their reputation as hostesses and the very finest will be provided to the guest even if it sometimes means that the family must do without.

So deeply valued is the concept of hospitality that it is closely interwoven with a sense of self-esteem in the Greek word *philotimo*. Since a part of hospitality is a display of generosity, members of the Greek family happily extend every courtesy and the best of their food to their guests. This, however, can have adverse effects. Greek women may be insulted if only one helping of food is taken; they firmly believe in the Arabic saying, "The food equals the affection." Greek men may feel shamed if their offers of hospitality are refused. Moreover, it is often true that any failed gesture in the ritual of hospitality on the part of guest or host can be construed as either a personal insult, a family or communal insult, or even disdain of the ancient gods themselves.

Perhaps it is not even correct to suggest that the treatment of guests is any kind of "ritual" to the Greeks, for their enjoyment of people and their warmth of affection are sincere. Thus, if one's appetite is limited, it may be best to visit during the late afternoon rather than at mealtime. In Greece, from five to nine o'clock is considered late afternoon when visitors would be treated to spoon sweets, fresh cool water, and perhaps **Ouzo** and pastries. The Greeks delight in their children and it is expected that visitors will admire the little ones and bring small gifts for them. But should the guests' admiration extend to a particular object in their home – in the generosity of most Mediterranean peoples – the Greek family would probably make you a gift of the admired item.

Age-old tradition even accompanies the offering of refreshments to visitors. It is the Greek hostess who serves all food and drink while the host remains at all times to converse with the guests. The oldest guest is served first. Traditionally, a spoonful of the homemade sweet is taken together with a glass of water and, before partaking, the honored guest extends good wishes to the entire family and ends with the expression: *"Yiasus!"* This means, "To your good health!" Everyone then sips the water and tastes the sweet preserves. This will be followed by general conversation. **Ouzo** or whiskey may then be served accompanied by the tasty small pastries that Greek homes never seem to be without, especially when guests arrive.

The pattern of the day's meals varies from rural to urban dwellers. The Greek farmer rises early, often with little more than grape juice or fruit brandy to start his day. His noon meal will be brought to the fields for him by his wife or daughter and the basket will contain a hot soup, bread and cheese, perhaps olives and raw onions, tomatoes and cucumbers and occasionally a sweet pastry or fresh fruit. The farmer eats his evening meal after sundown when the chores are completed. The meal is similar to the noon one except that a meat dish may be added if meat is available or if it is not a fast day. The table is set with colorful woodenware and the women place the meal on colorful cloths woven from goats' wool.

Turkish coffee begins the city dweller's day, while the noon meal may extend for much of the afternoon and even include a siesta. Many cosmopolitan menus are available to those in cities, and it is only in private homes that often the really authentic Greek dishes are preserved and treasured. Typically a visit to the coffeehouse or *taverna* ends the workday from the smallest villages to the cities, and is a habit continued even in emigrant countries – but only for men. Traditionally dinner is served very late in the evening – ten o'clock is considered the usual time. And even after dinner at home it is not considered too late for an evening visit to the taverns or *kafeneion*.

Although mealtimes form a pattern there is always time for snacking, always a place to provide what the mood dictates. The *kafeneion* is the Greek café where Turkish coffee in its many varieties will be individually, ceremoniously prepared in a long-handled pot called a *briki*. It is also a place where a man may enjoy animated conversation or a quiet snooze while sprawled out on several chairs. *Zacharoplasteions* are strategically located shops which offer tempting varieties of honeyed pastries, nutted sweets, and fabled candy confections to be enjoyed with Turkish coffee whenever the urge for sweets insinuates itself. Hunger, whether for a meal or a hearty snack, may be assuaged at the *psistarya*, eateries whose specialties include charcoal-roasted lamb rotated on spits and served with simple green salad, Greek bread, and the husky red house wine.

And then there are the *tavernas*, second home to most Greek men. Why not? For it is here that anything from a small drink to a complete meal can be enjoyed with conversation and often with debate and frequently with the insistent and soulful rhythms of the *bouzouki*. It is in the Greek *tavernas* that the guests are expected to walk directly to the kitchen to make their selections of food (a word or two of advice to the chef is in order too). Platters are placed on a table and diners help themselves or they may choose their foods directly from the cooking pots. The meal is always enjoyed with crusty white bread and wine. It is also in the *tavernas* that the lusty combination of good food and drink, good friends and music together well up in the Greek soul and burst forth in the controlled exuberance of impromptu dancing. The Greeks have a word for that impulsive ecstasy of the spirit – they call it *kefi*.

The Greeks are a people to whom the word *zenos* means both stranger and guest; to whom *philotimo* expresses the sincerely natural rituals of hospitality; and to whom the height of spiritual pleasure blends people, food, drink, and music into a spontaneously joyous burst of *kefi*. Why shouldn't the Greeks have the right words for the things they do so well?

SPECIAL OCCASIONS

To outsiders it seems that "Greeks are always either feasting or fasting." There is good reason: 98 percent of the Greek population is Greek Orthodox and the calendar revolves around the fasts and festivals of the Church and all public and private activities are geared to it. Feasting preceded by fasting actually only occurs during five important holidays of the year: Christmas, Carnival Time (Lent), Saint George's Day, Assumption, and Easter. Other festive days are usually marked with special foods, most significantly with the inclusion of lamb or kid. Other occasions include name days, saint's days, weddings, funerals, baptisms, planting or reaping crops, or the opening of a new business.

Fasting, in Greek Orthodox tradition, is a strictly observed discipline which includes vegetables, fruits, grains (bread), and olives but no animal products such as meat or fish and not even wine or oil. Greek homemakers are scrupulous in their observance of fast days even though their ingenuity in preparing meals is heavily taxed.

Such piety can be understood when it is realized that for the Greek, the Church is not just a Sunday matter but an integral part of traditional everyday life. *Papas* (the priest) with his long hair, beard, and flowing robes is deeply involved with every family, and presides over every occasion with ceremonies, blessings, and often advice. During the 400-year Turkish occupation, the Church was credited with saving Greek culture and language and became the source of hope and security to each Greek family. Having proven itself in the most difficult times, this faith is still a source of comfort. When talk and worry beads can't solve a problem, many Greeks prayerfully light a candle to a special saint, consult the *papas*, or (when in Greece) make a special pilgrimage to a holy site.

Although traditional daily life is strongly interwoven with the Church, there is also a deep belief in the immortal god of Greece. Within this fabric of mysticism are also some threads of ancient superstitions that are so much a part of Greek life that it is difficult to draw a line between custom and belief.

The ten or twenty beads on a string commonly called Greek worry beads do not have the religious significance of the Catholic rosary; they are used by all classes as an aid to meditation, a substitute for nervousness, or simply to "chase the bitterness away." Furthermore, the casting of spells, the fear of the "evil eye," the concern for "bad-luck Tuesdays," or the grim connotation given events in May – like the worry beads – are often practiced more as a custom than out of any tangible conviction. Nonetheless superstitions persist. Rural children and animals often wear necklaces of blue beads, and May Day wreaths often include whole buds of garlic, the blue beads and fresh garlic considered effective means of warding off the evil eye. The cutting of cloth for clothes, the scheduling of weddings, and even the planting of flowers during the month of May are all considered activities fraught with bad luck.

One of the most prevalent superstitions occurs each year in the days between Christmas and Epiphany (January 6). At this time, it is believed that strange crippled ghosts known as *kallikandzaris* rise from the earth's depths to poison foods and frighten people. For this period of time all edibles are carefully hidden or disguised; torchlight searches from house to house and strong crosses nailed on doors and over windows are believed to help ward off evil attacks. In the evening, sieves are placed on windows and in doorways because it is believed that the ghosts become fascinated by the holes in the sieves and spend the night counting them rather than inflicting harm. The frightening season of the *kallikandzaris* comes to a close when the *papas* blesses the waters on January 6, and all the ghosts are believed to return from whence they came.

For the Greeks and for many other people with ancient roots and traditions and profound religious feelings, myths and even pagan traditions have become such an integral part of daily life that distinctions or rationalizations are often difficult to make and the prevailing principle seems to be quite simply, "Why take a chance?"

The most important festival for the Greeks is Easter, with its emphasis not on Crucifixion, but on Resurrection. *Apokria* (carnival time or a "farewell to meat") is gaily ushered in with parades, costumes, and many parties filling two weeks of merrymaking before Lent. The forty days of Lent are solemnly observed with a diet of bread, olives, vegetables, grains, legumes, and fruits. Invertebrate seafoods are used in coastal areas. Most Greeks observe these fasting traditions strictly during the first and last week of Lent, while the devout follow the ascetic diet for the full forty days. But even for them, the usual daily fare of bread and olives and boiled beans and sliced raw onions may be relieved by a traditional sweet called **halvas**, made from farina or semolina, and flavored with almonds and sugar.

The week preceding Easter Sunday is called Holy Week and is busy with the preparations of the holiday which even include "spring cleaning" indoors and the exterior whitewashing of all homes. On Maundy Thursday or Holy Thursday, the lambs are killed and hung, and eggs are hard-cooked then dyed red and rubbed with oil to make them shine. On Good Friday, the **tsoureki** (Easter bread), fragrant with caraway seeds and nestled with the red eggs, is baked. The evening meal is traditionally bean or lentil soup flavored with vinegar to represent the vinegar believed given to Christ when he thirsted. Saturday includes the joyful marketing and preparations of the festive foods for Easter Sunday. But through all these preparations, the fast continues with the austere bread, olives, legumes, and fruits.

The spiritual climax of the Easter festival is the midnight service on Saturday when all lights in the church are extinguished while the *papas* chants. Finally the announcement of *Christos anesti* is greeted by the lighting of everyone's candles from the priest's three-branched candelabra. Then, carefully shielding the flame, people carry each candle home to be reverently placed before the family's icon. Now the happily traditional midnight meal of **myeritsa soup**, olives, **tsoureki**, and citrus fruits is enjoyed by all. After the meal, the game of egg-cracking keeps everyone laughing.

Easter Sunday finds most of the men busily preparing a shallow trench filled with glowing charcoal over which the **souvla** (spit) of lamb will be cooked with an occasional basting of olive oil and lemon juice. Soup, stuffed vegetables, and many sweet pastries will be a part of the festive meal. Understandably, after the austerity of Lent, it will be the **mayeritsa** and roasted lamb that will be relished most.

By comparison, Christmas is a much quieter and less significant festival on the Greek calendar. Fish is traditionally eaten on Christmas Eve and eel dishes are especially popular. Special sweets such as **kourabiedes** (buttery cookies), **christopsomo** (walnut and sesame seed breads topped with a cross of dough), and fried treats such as **diples** and **loukomades**, crispy fritters dusted with cinnamon sugar or served with sugar syrup, are the highlights of the season.

January 1st is called Saint Basil's (Vassilio's) Day and this is the day not only for exchanging gifts (Saint Basil was known to be a philanthropist), but also for enjoying old rituals designed to foretell fortunes in the coming year. Splitting open a pomegranate and counting the seeds is used to suggest the abundance of the coming year. The evening is spent singing *kalandra* (carols) and then at midnight, **vasilopeta** (Saint Basil's Cake) is served. Everyone watches the serving with suspense, for somewhere in the cake a good-luck coin is embedded. Tradition states that the first slice is for Christ, the next for Saint Basil, and if one of these should have the coveted coin, a donation must be made to the church. But if one of the family or guests receives the slice with the coin, good luck is said to be theirs for the coming year.

Like other Greek occasions, funerals too have a share of both religious and superstitious ritual. Surviving family members usually eat a quiet meal of fish, bread, and wine followed by Turkish coffee. Special memorial services are held on the fortieth day after the death and also on the first- and third-year anniversaries of the death. A special plate of **kolyva** is prepared for blessing at the church, then it is eaten by all the family. **Kolyva** represents one of the most symbolic dishes: the wheat for everlasting life, the raisins for sweetness, and the pomegranate seeds to symbolize plenty. A very old tradition holds that when Greeks leave a house of mourning, they must sprinkle themselves with water to drive away the spirit of death. Modern Greeks leaving a funeral will seldom return directly home, but will stop at a pastry shop to eat and drink. This seems to be a form of ritual purification similar to the older one of water sprinkling.

GLOSSARY OF FOODS AND FOOD TERMS

Note: Variations in spelling may be noted, especially the interchange of "d" and "th."

Anginares: artichokes. Jerusalem or root artichokes are not known in the Greek kitchen; this term refers to the small globe variety.

Arni: lamb, the favorite Greek meat and highlight of feasts.

Avgolemono: egg-lemon sauce prepared by adding fresh lemon juice to whisked eggs. This frothing tangy sauce may then be used to flavor any white stock (made from either fish, veal, or chicken) by carefully adding a little hot stock to the egg-lemon mixture, then returning all to the hot but boiling stock. Or the egg-lemon mixture may be used for fish, vegetables, or casseroles.

Baklava: famed Mediterranean pastry whose origin may be debatable but whose crispy sweetness is not. Made from many layers of butter-brushed, nut- and sugar-sprinkled layers of phyllo pastry, gently cut in diamonds and secured with whole cloves. Immediately after baking, a spiced hot syrup is poured over. The crisp diamond wedges are served together with the oozing syrup, the only accompaniment an icy glass of water or a demitasse of coffee. Who needs more?

Barbouni: red mullet, a favorite fish usually served grilled or fried. The cheeks and liver are considered special delicacies.

Bechamel Sauce: by this name, the sauce's origin is attributed to Louis de Bechamel, of the court of King Louis XIV. However, it should be noted that this same sauce – a roux of fat and flour whisked with a liquid, usually milk or cream – was described by Athenaeus in 200 C.E. and widely used in Greek cuisine.

Bourekakia: a Turkish name covering all the tiny appetizer pastries made from **Phyllo** pastry and filled with many different savory fillings – vegetable, meat, cheese, etc. In Greece they commonly take their name from the filling, for instance **Kotopitakia**, chicken; **Tiropitakia**, Feta cheese, etc.

Dolmadakia: with *akia* being the diminutive, and *dolma* meaning any stuffed food, this term refers to tiny stuffed foods such as small rolls of cabbage, spinach, or vine leaves or tiny scooped-out vegetables. These are filled with savory mixtures such as bechamel sauce and cheese or rice with seasonings.

Domates: tomatoes.

Fakki: meatless brown lentil soup, a standby for fast days and a staple soup when meat is scarce.

Fasolada: a meatless bean soup.

Fava: a yellow lentil soup served hot and thick and garnished with a little olive oil and lemon juice and a sprinkling of chopped raw onions.

Feta: most widely known of all Greek cheeses, firm and white and made from goat's or sheep's milk, usually stored in a salt brine.

Galactoboureko: Phyllo pastry with a rich custard filling.

Halvas: the homemade version is a simple egg and semolina cake over which is poured a sizzle of hot syrup. The commercial version is a firm paste of pureed nuts and seeds, predominantly almond and sesame, and may be colored and/or flavored with chocolate or pistachio.

Horta: general name given to assorted cultivated and wild greens enjoyed by simply boiling, draining, and serving at room temperature with olive oil and a squeeze of fresh lemon juice.

Imam Bayaldi: slowly baked eggplants stuffed with tomatoes and sliced onions and flavored with garlic. Literally "the caliph fainted." So named because the dish was exquisitely delicious, and the priest was said to have fainted – here the stories differ – either when he tasted it òr when he was denied a taste.

Kafes: coffee. Turkish coffee introduced into Greece and brewed in a long-handled pot called a *briki*. In Greece it is called Greek coffee, but it is still made in thirty-three variations, as is the Turkish.

Kalamarakia: baby squid.

Kataifia: very fine shreds of a wheat flour pastry rolled up with chopped nuts and served with a spicy sweet syrup.

Kefalotiri and **Kasseri**: names of two Greek cheeses that are aged and hard and suited to grating. Very similar to the Italian Romano or Parmesan.

Kefthedes or **Keftethes**: tiny meatballs prepared with finely minced meat (any kind) blended with bread crumbs and eggs then seasoned with garlic, mint, oregano, and salt and pepper. The mixture is formed into tiny balls and fried in oil till brown. Usually a part of appetizers.

Kolokythia: called baby marrows in England, courgettes in France, and zucchini in Italy. Greeks enjoy the flowers freshly picked, stuffed, and fried.

Kouloura: one of many Greek breads. This one is made from white wheat flour and baked in a ring shape, light and crusty.

Kourabiedes: rich buttery shortbread-type of cookie baked in round balls then liberally sprinkled with rosewater or orange flower water and dusted with icing sugar. Piled in a mound, these are a Christmas specialty.

Latholemono: oil and lemon sauce.

Lathoxitho: a vinaigrette sauce of oil, lemon juice, or wine vinegar plus seasonings.

Mastica: the powdered resin from a small evergreen grown mostly on the Greek isle of Chios. Used for flavouring yeast doughs. There is also a liqueur by the same name.

Mayeritsa: the eagerly anticipated soup of lamb entrails finished with avgolemono sauce and enjoyed after the midnight services of Easter Sunday.

Melitzanosalata: a popular Mediterranean appetizer of pureed eggplant seasoned liberally with onion and vinegar and garnished with black olives and tomato wedges.

Melomakarona or **Finikia**: traditional Christmas cookies similar to **Kourabiedes** but flattened and finished with a drenching of honey syrup and a dusting of nuts.

Moussakas: browned eggplant slices layered with tomatoes, cheese, onions, and ground meat finished with a bechamel sauce. Typically Greek, there is a faint taste of cinnamon.

Meze: a simple term to cover the complex array of delicious small nibbles that may accompany drinks.

Octapothi: octopus. Ancient technique of rubbing the fresh-caught greenish octopus with a rock until it is a pearly gray color and well tenderized was long ago perfected by Greek fishermen.

Pastizzio: a baked layered casserole of cooked pasta sprinkled with cheese and a layer of seasoned minced meat. The casserole is finished with cheese and bechamel sauce then cut in squares to serve.

Phyllo or **Filo**: another food whose origin is difficult to pinpoint but this paper-thin pastry is usually made commercially of egg, flour, and water. Sold in packages of many sheets, it is the basis of many Greek appetizers (**bourekakia**), pies (pita), and sweet nut-rich pastries. The Greek word **phyllo** means leaf. The thin sheets are brushed with butter or oil then layered, filled and stacked, flipped into triangles, or rolled and twisted.

Pilaf: cooked rice with melted butter poured over then pressed into a mold. Unmolded, it is then served with any variety of sauces, seasonings, and garnishes as may occur to the imaginative cook, and named according to the ingredients.

Psaria: fish.

Saganaki or **Tiraki**: any firm cheese cut in squares, dusted with flour, and quickly fried in hot oil and served as an appetizer.

Salata: salad.

Saltsa: sauce.

Skordalia or **Skorthalia**: a smooth thick sauce made with oil and lemon juice and soft white bread and as much garlic as desired.

Souvla: the name of the spit used to roast lamb.

Souvlakia: skewered cubes of lamb with onions, green peppers, and tomato wedges, all marinated then broiled.

Spanakopita: baked in a rectangular pan, this "pie" is made of buttery layers of phyllo with a center portion of chopped cooked spinach and Feta mixed with bechamel. The pie is cut into squares to serve, and may be a light main dish or one of many dishes accompanying a feast.

Spanakorizo: spinach and rice. A favorite Lenten dish of browned onions, tomatoes, and chopped spinach with water and rice added, then the whole cooked till dry and fluffy.

Stefado: a method of cooking used for any meats or game. Literally a stew. Cut-up pieces of meats are marinated overnight in a bowl with cut-up vegetables and seasonings, white wine, vinegar and oil. The next day the pieces of meat are browned then simmered slowly with the strained marinade. Most traditional accompaniment is onions. The dish is eaten with bread and wine.

Tahini: smooth puree of sesame seeds.

Tarama: fish roe, usually referring to carp roe.

Taramosalata: smooth creamy dip made of roe, white bread or potato, garlic, oil, and lemon juice.

Tyropita: layered phyllo pastry (or otherwise shaped), filled with cheese.

Tzatziki: a tangy dip of plain yogurt, minced cucumber, and garlic, salt and pepper.

Vasilopita: made especially for Saint Basil's Day, this sweet yeast bread is perfumed with grated orange rind, cinnamon and **mastica**.

Yaourti: plain natural yogurt.

CHAPTER 23

HUNGARIAN

Hungarians do not take anything lightly, least of all food. The romantic, volatile, and soulful Hungarian uses food the way most other people use psychology, politics, literature, material acquisitions, and even medicine. Food is the prelude to a mood, the buffer for difficult situations, and the solace – even the cure – for adversity. Food elevates the spirit, food promotes confidence, food is a comforting symbol of success and status. But most important of all, in the Hungarian mind, food, love, and music are inextricably interwoven with one's very existence.

The Hungarian coffeehouse symbolizes the uniquely Hungarian viewpoint. Softly lit and comfortable, well supplied with sumptuously sinful pastries and good coffee, it is here that the Hungarian finds inspiration and sustenance, even on occasion, solace. No Hungarian could survive a day of business without repeated fortifications of smoothly rich pastries and sensuous whipped cream floated gently down on a wave of strong coffee. And how could one sustain oneself in the suspenseful prelude to a love affair, the inner strength required and then the agony at the breakup, without a coffeehouse?

Hungarian restaurants are so much a part of daily life that not even the vicissitudes of wars, the reversals of economics, or the upheavals of politics could empty their tables or close their doors. When all else in life falters, food, love, and music remain steadfast in the life of the Hungarian. It would be unthinkable to make love on an empty stomach, conclude a business deal, or even survive a normal day without fine food and wine to the accompaniment of Gypsy violins. Who but the Gypsy violinists could understand one's every mood and knowingly accompany it with melodies that can be at once tender and passionate or haunting and sad?

And when on those rare occasions all seems to be moving well in life, the Hungarian can still find a reason for sadness that requires consolation. It seems that no Hungarian ever had a happy childhood. Mournful recollections of that "unhappy childhood" are always considered suitable excuses for further gastronomic indulgence. Just why there seem to be so many unhappy Hungarian childhoods is uncertain. Perhaps mother and father were too preoccupied with love and food? Perhaps a rich little pastry became the substitute for parental love? Perhaps too the unhappy childhood is fabricated. No self-respecting Hungarian could indulge in food and love (with musical accompaniment) without reasons.

Given such vital significance, can the finesse of the Hungarian cuisine ever be underestimated? Hungary's history is witness to the many influences that resulted in the complex subtleties so much a part of the Hungarian table.

A part of Hungary's earliest history concerns the Khazar Kingdom which occupied a strategic position between Asia and Byzantium and spread to much of the area that is Hungary today. In 740 C.E., these tribes converted to Judaism. Although many reasons for this dramatic change are given, the most logical seems to be that both Islam and Christianity had political and military underpinnings while Judaism allowed the Khazars to retain neutrality. For a long time they maintained the Jewish laws of Kashruth and no pork was eaten.

Although the Khazars were believed to be of Magyar origin, they were defeated in 896 C.E. by seven other Magyar tribes. Finally driven to a small area near the Bosporus Sea, the Khazar Kingdom came to an end, defeated by the Russians. Many Hungarian towns still bear names believed to be of Khazar origin (Kozar and Kozardie), the language of the Khazar Jews is still spoken in parts of Poland, Lithuania, and Hungary, and the agriculture, handicrafts, commerce, and wine making that they introduced are still very much a part of Hungary.

Hungary's appeal to conquerors was not only its strategic location in central Europe but also the fertility of the vast Hungarian Plain. Here a mellow climate and a rich land yield orchards and vineyards, grain fields and pastureland – a plentiful reservoir of abundance that probably more than anything else has made the Hungarian a lavish and appreciative cook. It would be difficult to find a farm without pigs, an abundant supply of fruits, vegetables, and grains, and cool pantries without fresh cream, sour cream, and butter.

To this natural abundance, the 150-year Turkish occupation introduced to Hungary not only many tropical fruits and nuts but also coffee and many seasonings, the most important of which was **paprika**. Today Hungary's production of quality paprika is highly regarded. The Hungarian uses paprika with the deft understanding of a connoisseur. Although paprika, a favored seasoning, is not used exclusively, it is used widely in Hungarian cookery.

While Hungarians are willing to admit that many things were the result of Turkish influence, it would be more difficult to get them to admit that the beloved Hungarian **retes** (identical to the Austrian strudel) probably had its origin in the paper-thin crisp Turkish pastries made from **phyllo** – the most famous of which is **baklava**. And these Turkish pastries, in turn, originated from Greek influence.

Further influences on Hungarian cuisine, now so deeply embedded that they are difficult to separate, are Slovakian, Serbian, Croatian, Romanian, Russian, Polish, and German. This vast span of influence was mostly due to the fact that Hungary was for almost 200 years more or less under Hapsburg (German) rule and a part of the Austro-Hungarian Empire until its breakdown after the First World War. Extended uses of sour cream, dumplings, noodles, sauerkraut, and the art of making soup, pastries, and sweet delicacies may well be the only pleasant aspects of this period for it was also one marked with almost continuous inner strife and feudalism.

If nothing else, both the very rich and the very poor in Hungary always shared a love of food. Just as a laden table was essential to the Hungarian aristocracy, so the filled larder was essential to the Hungarian peasant. In fact, it was the Hungarian Baroness Orczy (1865-1947), who lived both in Hungary and in England, who coined the much-quoted phrase: "I would say the Englishman lives like a king and eats like a pig, and the Hungarian lives like a pig, but God knows he eats like a king." To this day, good eating is synonymous with good living to every Hungarian regardless of background.

Finally to the many influences of colorful and hearty foods that found their way into the Hungarian cuisine came the refining influences of the sophisticated Italian cuisine from Queen Beatrice, and the subtle French culinary arts from Queen Anne. King Matthias of Hungary wed the Italian Queen Beatrice in 1475 and enriched Hungarian aristocratic cuisine with all the delights of the Italian courts – including ice cream and forks. The gentling effects of French and Italian cuisine still evident in Hungarian cookery include wider use of sweet cream instead of sour cream, a preference for butter, especially in bakery, and a general lightening of seasonings, especially the use of garlic.

Where else but in Budapest could so many *cukraszdas* (coffee and pastry shops) flourish? And where else but the Hungarian capital could the world's first museum dedicated to catering and gastronomy be opened, or a holiday be declared to celebrate a cake – the **dobos torta**?

But the history of the Magyars, speaking their Hungarian language of Finno-Ugric origin, is not just one of gastronomy. It is also one of defeats and partitions, of conversions and peasant uprisings. Hungary was defeated by the Turks in 1526 and partitioned into three main areas: the part that is half of today's Hungary and partly Czechoslovakian and partly Russian, the area west of the Danube; the Great Hungarian Plain, which is today also part of Romania and Yugoslavia; and Transylvania in the Eastern Carpathian Mountains, which is today mostly Romania.

In the early 1700s, fighting between the Turks and the Hapsburgs (Germans) resulted in a tug-of-war with Hungary, forced conversions to Roman Catholicism and even compulsory Germanization. It had been King Stephen who, in 1001 C.E. converted his people to Christianity, so the main objection 700 years later was not to religion, but rather to the

FOODS COMMONLY USED

The staple foods of the nomad Magyars in earliest times included meat from their herds of sheep (lamb, sheep, mutton), game, millet and groats, some fish and **Zsendice**, a fresh cheese made from sheep's milk. Foods were cooked mainly over open fires on sticks or in huge kettles. Later, pork, lard, paprika, and sour cream were added to these staples. As the Magyars settled down, adaptations from other cultures were added to the staple diet: more fruits and vegetables, onions and other seasonings, noodles and dumplings. But the cornerstones of the Hungarian cuisine continue to be pork and lard, onions and paprika and sour cream. Tea and **kumis** (fermented mare's milk) were the earliest beverages, and are still used; but coffee and the fine locally produced wines are today's staples.

enforcement of the German language and customs.

The first Hungarian to emigrate to Canada was Stephen Parmenius De Buda who accompanied Sir Humphrey Gilbert to Newfoundland in 1583. But the first real wave of immigration came after the 1849 Hungarian defeat against the combined strength of the Austrian and Russian armies. October 6, 1849, is still remembered as a day of mourning in Hungary. These first "freedom fighters" were to be followed by many subsequent emigrations of fiercely independent peasant rebels seeking a free life. Most came to Canada via the United States, working as miners, farmers, and industrial workers.

It is interesting that up to 1930, 90 percent of Hungarian emigrants were from the poorer classes of Hungary, especially the rural areas. From 1930 to 1945, the class of Hungarian emigrants changed to include professionals, intellectuals, and members of the aristocracy – mostly Jews or those whom Hitler classified as being Jewish – fleeing from Nazism. Even after 1945, the flow of upper-class emigration continued, culminating in 1956 when the October Revolution was crushed by the Russians, and 175,000 people left the country.

For about forty years, between 1949 and 1989, Hungarian politics, economics, and cultural life were dominated by Communist tenets. The industrialization that began then altered the nature of the Hungarian economy, shifting it from agriculture to industry. Collectivization of agriculture was enforced but most collective farms disbanded with the 1956 Hungarian Revolution. Museums and free public libraries, sports clubs, radio and television, and a widespread system of education prevail, but somehow, for many, the zest for good living and attention to food and cooking have been reduced to necessities and fast food. This change may also be the result of more women joining the workforce, although men still remain dominant in family life.

Although Hungarian organizations in North America have attempted to unite all Hungarians, they have met with limited success. The reasons burrow deeply into Hungarian culture, where until recently feudalism and class distinctions were a way of life. These differences in manners, customs, and even appearance survived the pressures of the North American way of life. Moreover, the importance of kinship patterns, similar to those in Poland, Germany, and Italy, have had a profound influence on family life. These kinship patterns include primarily one's obligation towards helping and maintaining the status of the family, which may include relatives, in-laws, godparents plus all their families, rituals of marriage, birth and death and assistance in education or business. To add to this complexity, the once-privileged

classes have reconciled themselves only slowly, if at all, to the democratic way of life in North America. Many still cherish dreams of returning to the life they once knew.

The final difficulty in attempting to unite Hungarians is the result of the frequency of changes in the Hungarian borders which at various times included Poles, Serbs, Germans, Romanians, Jews, and Austrians. Although each of these peoples was officially classed as Hungarian when they emigrated because of their having shared for so long in the social and political culture of Hungary, once they reached a new land many reverted to their former identity and united with cultural groups other than Hungarian.

But the Hungarian pattern of life in North America has closely followed that shown by many other ethnic groups. The first generation of immigrants clung together not only in their kinship patterns but also in their manners, appearance, and language. The original intention of many was to work hard and save money in order to return to their former homeland. In many cases, as in the case of the Hungarians, the conditions that they left behind changed, but not for the better. They were fortunate to escape from the system of land estates and rigid class distinction where there was no hope of owning more land, advancing their position in life, or gaining an opportunity for education. Later emigrants sought to escape religious persecution and the Communist regime which seemingly favored the labor classes, but which in fact further suppressed social, religious, and political freedoms.

The changes that occurred in North America were gradual but profound. In Hungary the kinship pattern promoted the success of the whole family as a unit rather than individual success. In the new country, schools lauded individual achievement, newspapers and store catalogues advertised materialism, and the opinions of neighbors and peers gradually took on more importance than those of distant members of the Hungarian's family. Gradually, too, Hungarian calendars marked with special name days and saint's days were lost, and with them went many holiday rituals.

As ties with the Old World and the old traditions weakened, Hungarian immigrants regarded themselves more and more as Americans and Canadians. But Hungarians, together with many other ethnic groups, have witnessed and are happily participating in a partial reversal of this apparent assimilation for there is currently a newfound pride in old crafts, songs, customs, and traditions and increasingly these are being revived.

There may be evidence of Hungarians adapting and even integrating into the community that is their home. There may even be intermarriage. But one thing is certain: so long as there is even a trace of Hungarian soul there will be an appreciation of fine food and wine, and somewhere a Gypsy violin will play the haunting melodies that will bring tearful reminiscing about unrequited love and unhappy childhoods – and the consolation of sumptuous pastries.

DOMESTIC LIFE

Class distinctions were very much a part of Hungarian daily life until shortly after the Second World War. In the homes of aristocrats, lavish meals of many courses, each with intricately prepared dishes, were possible because of the availability of cooks, gardeners, and servants. Finely crafted tableware and luxurious eating began as early as the late 1400s. It was the influence of King Matthias and his Italian wife, Queen Beatrice, that soon made the work of artisans and the arts of gastronomy very much a part of the life of the upper classes. Abundance of good produce, servants, and the appreciation of good foods well prepared were the true beginnings of the excellence of the Hungarian cuisine.

While the nobility wined and dined on what the world came to know as "Hungarian cuisine," the peasants lived on their monotonous diet (except for festivals) of bacon, bread, and soup. The bacon was often cooked on an open fire, the bread baked in outdoor communal ovens, and the soup slowly simmered in a big kettle called a *bogracs*. The delightful food specialties of the upper classes – known as "national dishes" – likely were unknown to the rural family because they had neither the time to prepare the more traditional complex foods nor the money for the ingredients. To this day many white outdoor ovens, still used for cooking and baking, may be seen in the countryside.

Class distinctions with their inevitable polarities of luxury and poverty were said to diminish under communism. Huge kitchens with fine facilities and many chefs prepared meals for workers. Individual homes had minimal kitchens as most meals were taken outside the home. Except for special occasions and restaurant fare (especially for tourists) food in Hungary was simplified to pork and poultry dishes, potatoes, cabbage, and quantities of bread. Cattle, pigs, poultry, eggs, and wine were mainly for export.

The Hungarian cuisine is seen at its finest in restaurants, and only occasionally in Hungarian homes when time permits the loving attention that great cookery requires. Hungarian women tend to prepare traditional foods mostly on weekends and of course for festive celebrations.

DAIRY PRODUCTS

Fresh milk is seldom used as a beverage, but it is used in many dishes, especially puddings, custards, and milk soups. Variations of **Zsendice** – a staple so long ago – are still popular in certain areas and fresh curd is the type of cheese most used both as a spread with added seasonings or as an ingredient for fillings in baked goods and dumplings. Fresh sweet cream and sour cream are used liberally whenever possible.

FRUITS AND VEGETABLES

Traditionally fruits and vegetables have been produced in fine quality and great quantity. More recently most have been used for export, leaving those available for local sale often too expensive for large or even adequate consumption. Apples, plums, apricots, peaches, and many types of melons are not only available in season but are also used as preserves and in the production of fine fruit brandies.

Cabbage, potatoes, onions, green pepper, tomatoes, and cucumbers are not only the staple vegetables, they are the most popular, most used, and the basis for many stews, soups, and pickled vegetables. Raw salads with fresh greens are seldom if ever used. When income permits, a much greater variety of vegetables is used, preferably those that are fresh and seasonal. Vegetables are never served simply boiled; they are braised, baked, or boiled then drained and blended with a sauce of onions, paprika and sour cream, buttered crumbs, or prepared as stuffed vegetables, vegetable puddings, vegetable souffles, or fresh vegetable soups.

Lecso is a well-cooked blend of lard, onions, tomatoes, and green peppers. This basic sauce is of South Slav origin and is used throughout Hungary not only as a basic sauce but also as an appetizer. With added sausages or meats it becomes a main dish. By itself a little may be added to stews and soups or vegetable dishes to enhance flavors.

MEATS AND ALTERNATES

The time of the Khazar Kingdom was the only time in Hungarian history that pork was not the number-one meat. In many areas, especially Transylvania, *Disznotor* (pig-killing day) is set aside as a feasting holiday and every part of the animal is either used fresh or preserved by smoking, brining, drying, or sausage-making. Cattle-, sheep-, and pig-raising are basic industries and game is widely available, so meat is usually a big part of the diet if income permits.

Hungarians are very fussy about the freshness of their fish and would rather eat locally caught fresh fish than imported varieties. Fish may be prepared as a soup, smoked, or baked whole as a main dish; but fish is not consumed in great quantities. Most fish used in Hungarian dishes originate in the Danube and Tisza Rivers: carp, perch, pike, sturgeon, trout, **fogas**, **silure** or catfish, and small amounts of tiny crabs and crayfish, the latter usually used for soups.

All types of offal and variety meats are used efficiently in sausages, stews, soups, and casseroles with vegetables. Goose liver is considered a luxurious treat, comparable to caviar in Russia.

Legumes are not an important part of the Hungarian diet, occasionally only used in soups or a bean casserole called **somogyi**. Nuts and poppy seeds are an important ingredient in the many fine cakes, tortes, **retes**, yeast pastries, and breads. Nuts and poppy seeds tossed with buttered noodles are often a side dish to meats, or a snack or dessert.

BREADS AND GRAINS
Bread is much revered in Hungary and seldom is a table set without a display of a variety of breads and rolls made from wheat or rye flours. In fact, **bankoti** (Hungarian wheat) is considered one of the finest in the world and high in gluten content. In the 1840s the introduction of iron rollers for milling white wheat flour caused the wheat germ to pop out without crushing, thus resulting in the whitest milled flour available anywhere. Breads, cakes, and pastries baked with this new white flour quickly became a status symbol.

Tarhonya, one of the staple foods of the nomadic Magyars and still a favorite accompaniment to meat dishes and a soup garnish, is made from eggs and flour blended to a stiff dough then grated to form tiny pellets. After drying, these tiny pellets or grains may be stored for long periods and cooked as needed. Noodles and dumplings are widely used as well. Cereals in the form of dried breakfast flakes or cooked porridge are not traditionally used.

FATS
Lard is the most widely used fat in Hungary. Butter is also used, especially for baked goods and sometimes to add flavor. Hungary's margarines and oils are considered of inferior quality and are seldom used.

SWEETS AND SNACKS
The Hungarian sweet tooth prefers cakes and rich pastries over candy. The national preference for temptingly sweet baked goods both as a snack with coffee and as dessert (as well as reward, consolation, and medicine) makes the intake unquestionably high. Sugar is also a major ingredient in the fruit brandies, wines, preserved fruits, and the many cups of coffee enjoyed daily.

SEASONINGS
Paprika, onions, tomatoes, green peppers, and sour cream are the staple seasonings of the Hungarian kitchen. Of course, it is impossible to describe traditional Hungarian cuisine without emphasizing the importance of paprika. Hungary's paprika is not only considered among the finest in the world, it also ranges in flavor from sweet to very hot. Most Hungarians prefer the mildest. Because of its sugar content, it is always allowed to cook with great care together with the melted lard and gently simmered onions to create the base and rusty-red hue of countless meat, fish, and vegetable dishes. Hungarian cooks would never turn their backs for even a moment on the careful simmering of this lard-onion-paprika combination. A touch too much heat or a little too long cooking and the mixture may well be discolored or taste bitter.

The range of seasoning extends to many herbs such as dill and tarragon, and in some areas black pepper takes precedence over paprika. Poppy seeds, apricot preserves, and nuts often form a part of the flavors or fillings of desserts and pastries, and chocolate and whipped cream are great favorites.

BEVERAGES
Coffee, wine, and brandy are the main beverages consumed in Hungary and by Hungarians everywhere. They are not tea drinkers and seldom is beer consumed.

Breakfast coffee is often served with hot milk. Afternoon coffee with a dollop of whipped cream seems the only fitting accompaniment to the staggering array of pastries offered. But by evening perhaps a little guilt has set in, for the coffee after dinner is usually served black.

Hungary produces many fine wines and is famed for her tokay variety. Wines and fruit brandies are produced everywhere, but Transdanubia and Northern Hungary are famed for their vineyards and it is the area in Northern Hungary called Paloc that produces the red wine called bull's blood or **Egri Bikaver**.

REGIONAL SPECIALTIES

BUDAPEST
The capital of Hungary, Budapest is actually a union of three cities, Buda, Pest, and Obuda, which joined in 1873 to form, among other things, what is, arguably,

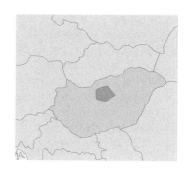

the pastry and coffeehouse capital of the world. Reputedly the city of "romance, wine and Gypsy music," Budapest is also the city where the pastry and confection makers happily cater to at least two million connoisseurs. All of Hungary's great dishes and regional specialties may be tasted here in fine restaurants, coffeehouses (*cukraszdas*) and stand-up strudel shops where strudels may be sampled crisp and warm in a great variety of sweet fillings: fruit, nuts, noodles with cheese, poppy seeds, and even with savory fillings of cabbage, potato with onion and cheese, and many others.

As mentioned above, it is Budapest that staged a festival to honor a cake – the incomparable **dobos torta** – and even opened a museum dedicated to the history of catering and the gastronomic arts.

NORTHERN HUNGARY

This area is called Paloc, and extends from the Danube River to the Soviet border. It is as famed for

its many local crafts and embroideries as for the wine called bull's blood or **Egri Bikaver**. Here in small villages, life has continued with little change almost since medieval times. Baking foods in ashes, collecting the eggs of wild birds, and even grinding flour continue unchanged. Fish caught locally is still dried, salted, or smoked for use during the winter, and cheeses are dried and smoked in sausage shapes and hung from cottage rafters. The planting and harvesting of both wheat and grapes to make wine are intertwined into many local and colorful festivals which go back to ancient times.

THE HUNGARIAN PLAIN

The rich, fertile Hungarian Plain is populated mostly by peasants and shepherds who have little formal education and who live in isolated villages. Paprika, grains, orchards, and rolling pastures with sheep and cattle all add to the produce of the area. It is one of the

few areas in Hungary that does not produce noteworthy wines, but the fruit brandies are so good they are a part of the daily peasant breakfast together with bacon roasted over an open fire and eaten with bread. Often the lunch and

dinner of the people who inhabit this region will be identical to the breakfast. Cabbage and sauerkraut, pickled cucumbers, and many potato dishes add some variety to the usual meals. A fresh sheep's cheese called **Gomolya** is also enjoyed.

TRANSDANUBIA

The area west of the Danube is famed for its vineyards and matchless wines. But the residents like to drink, in addition to their own wines, bottled mineral waters. This is one of the few places in Hungary where milk is drunk as a beverage and milk and home-baked breads are a usual lunch.

Many mushrooms grow wild in this area but most famous of all are the truffles carefully sniffed out by trained dogs. The area is also noted for its many goose farms, especially for the huge goose livers from specially fattened geese.

Local specialties include **white hurka**, a sausage made more from grains than meat. It is first boiled and then fried. Curd cheese and browned onions fill noodle squares that are pinched together then poached and eaten with a thin sauce of paprika cooked in lard. Many simple milk soups (meatless), pastries, strudels, and dumplings using fresh curd cheese are much enjoyed in this region.

TRANSYLVANIA

This area, populated by the Szekely people, has variously been considered Hungarian, German, and Romanian. Presently it is a part of Romania. The forests and mountains, as well as the people themselves, have contributed to the lore that is part poetry, part legend, and part mythology. Stories of ghosts, trolls, and spells abound and seem somehow to fit into the atmosphere of misty forests and dark mountains.

But a fine cookery tradition is also prevalent and it includes many dishes or versions of dishes that taste differently than the general cuisine of Hungary. From Romania, the Transylvanians have adapted cornmeal and use it for breads and dumplings; and from their own fields they have plucked tarragon and summer savory which they use as abundantly in their cookery as the rest of Hungary uses paprika.

Sauerkraut is a part of the Transylvanian **szekely gulyas** and forms the base of many casseroles with pork or noodles. **Tokany** is a delicious pork and beef stew simmered with wine and finished with sour cream. Flax is eaten as a vegetable and many main dishes are created around grape leaves or cabbage leaves stuffed with imaginative mixtures of finely chopped and seasoned meats and vegetables. Cross-cut wooden slabs provide the wooden platters for the famed grilled dinner of pork and sausages, pickled cabbage (especially **cika**, the cabbage core) and cucumbers with potato salad. This grilled dinner on a wooden platter is called **fatanyeros** and is often served as a specialty in many Budapest restaurants.

Pork is an important staple and pig-killing day (*Disznotor*) means much work in slaughtering the pigs, smoking, curing the meats, and preparing many types of sausages. But it also means special feasting foods, almost all based on pork: **paprikas**, soups, roasted meats, sausages, all accompanied with pickled vegetables and much wine.

The area also makes good use of locally prepared fresh curd cheese, cream and sour cream. Often these too differ in flavor because they may be prepared from sheep's or even buffalo's milk.

MEALS AND CUSTOMS

The dishes comprising the Hungarian cuisine form the distilled essence of centuries of adaptations based on their native ingredients and the fine recipes from other peoples that have been a part of Hungarian history. What sets these dishes apart and makes them so distinctly Hungarian is more than a matter of lard, paprika, and onions, it is passionate attention and appreciation.

Sauces and salads are of little importance in the Hungarian menu. Soups, main dishes, cooked and pickled vegetables, fine breads and pastries – these are the cornerstones. Probably most important of all is the art of soup-making. Hungarians can make a flavorful and satisfying soup from almost anything: an onion browned in fat, flour browned in fat, milk and noodles, cabbage and sour cream, endless combinations of simple and complex vegetable soups and of course soups made with meats or game. Given so many types of soups, so many satisfying main dishes – **tokany**, **gulyas** (goulash), **paprikas**, and many others – and desserts of incredible delicacy and richness, is it any wonder that appetizers join sauces and salads as being of little importance? In fact, appetizers are only served in aristocratic homes or in restaurants.

Whether Hungarian breakfasts are the peasant meal of brandy, roasted bacon and bread, or the urban meal of coffee with hot milk, rolls and preserves, they are small. Mid-morning snacks are common everywhere: factory workers may have a small bowl of **gulyas**, shepherds may pause for bread and onions, others may take coffee with bread or rolls, similar to a breakfast.

The largest meal of the day is usually served at noon. Invariably it begins with soup, and if it is in a poor home, it may be only soup and bread. The main dish following the soup will likely be of meat with cabbage, potatoes or noodles forming a part of the dishes or a side dish. Dessert is almost as necessary as

soup and may be stewed fruits, thin dessert pancakes called **palacsintak**, dumplings served with sweet sauces, fritters or noodle desserts, souffles, custards or puddings. Traditionally the noon meal is eaten at home with all the family together. Increasingly, however, children are taking this hot meal in school cafeterias, industrial workers in factory restaurants, while those working in the cities often enjoy restaurant or fast-food dining.

The afternoon coffee will be taken with honeycake or coffee cake if it is just for the family. But there will be a choice of fine pastries, cakes, **strudel**, and **tortas** if there are guests or if this snack is taken in a coffeehouse.

The evening meal is usually a light supper of leftovers from the noon meal. Sometimes soup and dessert are enough, other times soup with bread or light dishes made from eggs will be served. The evening meal is traditionally eaten between seven and nine o'clock.

SPECIAL OCCASIONS

It is estimated that two-thirds of the Hungarian population is Roman Catholic, the remainder Protestant. The large Jewish population that was for so long a part of Hungary was either exterminated under the Nazis or escaped to other lands; few remain. Religious practice was not encouraged under the Communist regime and most religious orders and monasteries are now state properties. However, the Hungarians are not a deeply religious people. Religious occasions are enjoyed more for their festive foods and gathering of friends and family than for prayer or ritual.

The Magyars have always been noted for their colorful costumes, spirited music, and lavish feasting. No matter what the rest of the year may be like, a festival is for merrymaking, eating and drinking, friends and music. This includes religious occasions, weddings, christenings, funerals, name days and saint's days and many special celebrations associated with the crops and the seasons. Although the agricultural celebrations are usually local events, they represent old traditions and are much cherished.

Probably the most important religious holiday in Hungary is Easter. *Husvet* literally means "the taking of meat," and begins on Shrove Tuesday. This date also coincides with the time of much spring planting: vegetables, poppy seeds and the preparation of maize for sowing. Dwellings are cleaned and often painted. In preparation for Lent when no meats or greasy foods may be eaten by the devout, even the dishes and pots used to cook meats and greasy foods are carefully set aside and replaced with others.

The traditional pancakes enjoyed on Shrove Tuesday actually begin the forty days of meatless and greaseless meals. But ingenious Hungarian cooks provide an imaginative supply of breads of all kinds and baked goods, filling noodle and dumpling dishes, meals based on fish or cottage cheese, and many soups and main dishes based on cabbage and/or potatoes. The fare is simple but satisfying. Ash Wednesday marks the start of Lent and the abrupt ending of all festivities. Even the customary bright tablecloths are exchanged for somber dark ones. Sour eggs and herring salad are the symbolic foods for Ash Wednesday.

The Easter week after Lent is the time to enjoy new spring vegetables, layered Easter cakes, and painted eggs all culminating in a Good Friday dinner of wine-flavored soup, stuffed eggs, and baked fish. The chiming of bells on Holy Saturday signals the end to Lenten restrictions and the eagerly anticipated Easter Eve feast. This is considered to be the biggest and most important meal of the year. A rich chicken soup is served with dumplings or noodles followed by roasted meat (ham, pork, or lamb) then several pickled vegetables, stuffed cabbage rolls and finally a selection of sweet cakes and black coffee. Easter Sunday is a continuation of the feast with roast lamb and "blessed" ham as the traditional main dish and more cakes and pastries served to all.

April 23 is an annual country festival celebrating the rounding up of the flocks and the hiring of shepherds, all accompanied with feasting and drinking.

A week of celebrations everywhere in Hungary centers around August 20, the birthday of the beloved King Stephen. November 1 is All Saints' Day and it is also the final day for sowing winter wheat – and more feasting. Mid-October brings the vintage festivals, for wine is the national drink as the Hungarians remind themselves in an old folk song:

> The Slovaks all drink brandy
> The Germans all drink beer
> The Hungarians drink wine only,
> The very best, my dear.

Christmas is celebrated quietly with the day preceding it observed as a fast day, that is, no meat is eaten and the Christmas Eve meal is traditionally a simple one based on fish and potatoes and the serving of cakes and tortes made with nuts and poppy seeds.

It was King Matthias and his Italian wife, Queen Beatrice, who introduced turkeys, which have been popular ever since (when available) for the Christmas Day dinner. The turkey is accompanied with roasted potatoes, stuffed cabbage, and desserts of brandied fruits or fruit compotes with wine and more cakes of nuts and poppy seeds. In more modest homes,

chicken or goose will be the main course, but everyone enjoys cakes.

Weddings are gala occasions involving not only many days of preparation but often three days of celebration.

Perhaps one of the best examples of local festivities is the *Disznotor* or pig-killing day celebrated in most rural areas but especially in Transylvania. The day begins with spiced wine or brandy and coffee cakes and then the work begins. By 11:30 a.m. a **paprikas** has been prepared from pigs' brains, and pork is roasted with potatoes or layered cabbage. The meal itself will begin with a cabbage or potato soup. Throughout the day pigs are slaughtered and prepared into cuts to be separated as fresh meats and as those to be used for brining, smoking, curing, and sausage-making. Most trimmings go into the latter, but some, such as the snout and ears, are saved for a special soup for the evening meal. The pig soup, freshly prepared sausages, and roasted pork are eaten with bread and wine as well as pickled peppers, cabbage, and cucumbers.

In order that urban dwellers may not miss this type of pork feasting, many restaurants make a feature of *Disznotor* presenting a special menu of soup made from pigs' trimmings and a main dish of varied fresh pork sausages and **flekken** (loin pork slices flour-dipped and crisply fried) served with rice, noodles, and assorted pickled vegetables.

GLOSSARY OF FOODS AND FOOD TERMS

Bankoti: name given to the high-gluten content Hungarian wheat.

Barack: apricot brandy.

Csipetke: literally "pinched noodles" made by preparing a stiff dough from eggs, flour, and water then pinching off tiny pieces and dropping them in boiling salted water to cook.

Cukraszda: one name that spells the finest array of delectable cakes, tortes, and pastries, all prepared with fine ingredients readily identified by the sweetly fragrant aroma of creamy cheeses, fresh lemon zest, toasted nuts and poppy seeds, rich chocolate and of course whipped cream. All of this and coffee too.

Disznotor: the country celebration and feasting centering around pig-killing day. Except for breakfast, which is usually spiced wine or brandy and coffee cakes, the menus of the day feature soups, roasts, stews, and sausages all made from fresh pork and pork trimmings. City restaurants attempt a duplication of this by presenting a special *Disznotor* menu featuring soup made from pork trimmings and a main course of varieties of pork cuts and pork sausages accompanied with pickled vegetables and bread.

Dobos Torta: great arguments ensue when attempts are made to decide who invented this masterpiece. Hungarians will insist emphatically that it was of course a Hungarian. (Don't argue – just eat it.) It is made by preparing a light round sponge cake, which is split and filled with a rich smooth chocolate filling (five to seven layers are usual). The top layer of the torta is scored into narrow wedges and coated with a hot caramel that hardens almost immediately. These caramel-coated wedges are then arranged in spiral fashion with alternate rosettes of chocolate cream as the finishing touch. **Dobos Torta** lovers save the caramel wedge for last and daintily eat it from their fingers.

Fatanyeros: Translyvanian specialty of assorted grilled meats served on a wooden platter garnished with pickled vegetables, and potato salad.

Galuska: soft "noodles" prepared by dipping pieces of a soft dough batter into simmering water or broth; they congeal as they hit the heated liquid and swell as they cook.

Gomboc: dumplings.

Gomolya: a fresh cheese made from sheep's milk.

Gulyas: a stew made with cubed beef or pork and a base of gently simmered onions, lard, and paprika. Only cubed potatoes are added and the final result is a hearty dish with plenty of gravy to enjoy with **Galuska** or **Csipetke**. This dish is not finished with sour cream.

Habart Bableves: a sweet and sour soup with fresh green beans, the thin vegetable broth flavored with cream, vinegar, and sugar. Probably of Romanian origin.

Kaposztak: cabbage in any form, even sauerkraut.

Lecso: an all-purpose thick sauce made of simmered onions, tomatoes, and green peppers, usually well flavored with garlic. It may be used to flavor other dishes or soups, eaten cold as an appetizer, or cooked with sausages or meats as a main dish.

Meleg Tesztak: refers to the variety of sweet noodle dishes that are so typically Hungarian. They are always served hot, usually as a dessert but often they follow soup and complete a light but satisfying meal. The dish may be as simple as hot buttered noodles tossed with cinnamon sugar and chopped nuts or poppy seeds, or a more complex mixture involving sieved cottage cheese, nuts, raisins, freshly made noodles in strips or squares all lightly folded with beaten separated eggs then baked. Other versions are filled noodle squares simmered and served with nuts, sour cream, or preserves.

Metelt: noodles. (If this is confusing remember the importance of noodles and dumplings in the Hungarian cuisine – hence the many names.)

Palacsintak: very thin delicate pancakes similar to French crepes, Czechoslovakian **Palacinky**, and Austrian **Palatschinken**. The Hungarian version is used in as many ways, for sweet dishes mostly but occasionally filled with vegetables or meat preparations. They may be layered, folded, or rolled and are almost as frequently seen on the menu as the many noodle and dumpling dishes.

Paprikas: may be made from any meat, fish, or vegetable prepared with an onion and paprika base and finished with a generous stirring-in of sour cream.

Porkolt: a stew similar to **Gulyas** only thicker and with more onions.

Pulsizka: similar to the Romanian **Mamaliga**. A thick cornmeal porridge used only in certain areas (Transylvania).

Retes: the Hungarian name for all strudels, those crisply delicious rolls of thin pastry enveloping almost any mixture of fruits, nuts, cheese, potato, cabbage, meats. The sweet ones are only at their best with whipped cream close by.

Szilva: plum brandy.

Szekely Gulyas: a **Gulyas** of mixed meats or pork only, prepared with the usual lard-onion-paprika base, but then layered with sauerkraut. Breaking the **Gulyas** rule, this dish is finished with sour cream. A Transylvanian specialty.

Tarhonya: a type of egg barley prepared from a stiff flour and egg dough grated into tiny bits resembling rice or barley. These are well dried then prepared by boiling or baking with liquid. One of the oldest Magyar dishes still widely enjoyed.

Tokany: another type of Hungarian stew where the meat is cut into very small cubes or small strips, less strongly flavored with the lard-onion-paprika base and often made with variations such as peppers, mushrooms, and sour cream.

Toltott Kaposzta: meat-and-rice-stuffed cabbage rolls.

Tor: a feast.

Tortak: tortes. Since *tor* means "feast" ... what better way to feast than on **Tortak**!

Zona: the name given to that mid-morning snack usually composed of a small portion of **Gulyas**, sometimes scrambled eggs or an omelet, sometimes assorted cold meats with scallions, radishes, and cucumbers.

CHAPTER 24

ICELANDIC

Ingolfur Arnarson guided his Viking ship towards a northerly land and threw some logs overboard. Wherever they would drift would be the location

of his settlement. Whether it was the will of the gods or simply the drift of the tides, Arnarson found that his logs had drifted ashore at a place he called Reykjavik. That was in the year 874 C.E. Today the city is the capital of Iceland and with a population of about 103,000 it claims one-third of the country's population in its treeless, dogless but sun-filled streets.

Although the name "Iceland" is a misnomer, it ensures a pleasant way of life for Icelanders and means they avoid the influx of tourists and new settlers that many other countries experience. Moderate winters, cool summers, and only one-eighth of the country covered with glacial ice indicate that the name is inappropriate. Since only 1 percent of the land is arable, the main harvest is from the sea, while meat is obtained from the sheep and cattle that nibble seaweed and mosses from between lava rocks.

Iceland is located just south of the Arctic Circle and there is evidence that before people arrived with their sheep and goats, their fire and their axes, there were woods of birch trees. Mostly because of people, but also because of wind erosion and volcanic eruptions that scorched the earth with fiery lava, vegetation is minimal despite efforts at reforestation.

The Vikings, however, were not the first to step on this land. There is evidence that adventurous Irish were there first. These early Irish were said to be Celtic monks in search of solitude. As the Viking settlements grew, they brought with them not only logs and provisions, but also animals for food (there were no herbivorous animals on Iceland) and Celtic women and bondsmen. It is said that the Norse and Celtic strains remained without change for a thousand years. Later, very small groups of other immigrants

came to the land and intermarried. But all continue to live in a tolerant and classless society.

Early Icelandic history matched the pattern of the country and its climate. Tribal blood feuds, fiery volcanic eruptions, silent snowy winters followed by glacial floods, the plague of the Black Death, the ravaging raids of English and Algerian pirates, and finally cattle disease and famine gradually took their toll of hope and life. The Black Death in the early 1400s killed two-thirds of the population, but it was not until the "greatest recorded eruption and lava flow in history" in 1783-1784 – horror that decimated livestock as well as people – that the first groups of emigrants left Iceland for North America. Many of those first settlers made their homes in Saskatchewan and it is said that today more Icelanders reside in Manitoba than in Iceland's capital.

It is understandable that their history would give Icelanders an empathy for the suffering of others, as well as a fierce desire to maintain their independence. Offers of aid from other countries are met with the reply, "We'll do it ourselves when we are able." And so they have. They have built roads, highways, and huge greenhouses heated with piping hot springwater. In fact, the heating of all homes in Reykjavik is by the same system of harnessing the heat and water of the many underground springs. Where else in the world can one turn a tap for instant hot water and enjoy hot-water heating all supplied from deep underground springs?

Another characteristic of Icelanders, whether in their native land or abroad, is their insatiable love of books and reading. The humblest home proudly displays a well-stocked bookshelf, and Iceland reputedly has more publishers, more published books, and more daily newspapers than any other country in the world.

The Icelanders' capacity for alcohol does not quite match that for books, but it is considerable. Icelandic wives dutifully bring the black coffee – it is still a man's world in Iceland. This is clearly visible in the after-dinner separation: men in one corner to talk, while women gather in another to "chat." Many parties finish only in the small hours of the morning, for the men take great pride in "finishing the bottle."

Icelanders adapt well into almost any society and live in almost every Canadian province. Their rapid integration has made them a valued part of the Canadian lifestyle. The deep importance in their daily lives of books and their profound desire for self-education has always placed them on an elevated intellectual level even though they may make their living at humble tasks. Most Icelandic families enjoy the custom of evening and Sunday reading. Icelanders are also said to have the healthiest and wealthiest society in the world, but visitors are apt to be shocked at the high prices of lodging and meals they encounter.

DOMESTIC LIFE

Since wood is scarce and bricks expensive to import, most homes in Iceland are built of concrete blocks. Most Icelanders use the living room for company and the kitchen as the center of family living and eating. Actual food preparation areas are described kindly as "step saving": tiny by any standards. Yet Icelandic women retain a proud tradition of home cooking, baking, and preserving.

Electrical appliances tend to be expensive (prices for almost everything are said to be the highest in Europe) but the Icelandic homemaker will save her money for a first purchase of an electric iron, teakettle, and electric mixer; later acquisitions may include a toaster and a vacuum cleaner. Some homes have refrigerators with freezers, but most manage with "cold closets." These are small alcoves built into the kitchen wall, enclosed with doors and ventilated to the outdoors. They are fine in winter, but of little use in summer.

Because of inadequate storage, the homemaker shops almost daily for the needs of the family. The number of department stores and supermarkets are increasing, but most still shop in specialty stores.

DAIRY PRODUCTS

A glass of fresh cold milk is a common accompaniment to almost every meal, and soups made with milk and dried pureed fruits are often enjoyed. But the favorite dish of all and an Icelandic staple is **skyr**. It is made from pasteurized skim milk fermented with rennin. The resulting curd is eaten with a sprinkling of sugar both as a snack and a dessert. The slightly soured whey is used to preserve many types of meats and fish. A brownish, smooth-spreading cheese called **Mysostur** is eaten as a spread on bread much as peanut butter is used in North America. Other cheeses are sliced and enjoyed in open-face sandwiches or as part of the cold buffet. Cream is used in cookery and whipped cream is a part of many cakes and desserts.

FRUITS AND VEGETABLES

Wild berries and rhubarb grown locally and imported dried fruits such as raisins, prunes, and apricots are used. These may be made into preserves with sugar, sugared fruit soups (with added cream or milk), or dessert puddings that are sweetened with sugar and thickened with potato flour. Fresh fruits are scarce.

Use of imported and canned vegetables is increasing, but potatoes are the staple vegetable and are served daily, often at more than one meal. Salads are all but unknown.

MEATS AND ALTERNATES

Icelandic lamb, the staple meat, is sold ground, in fresh cuts, spiced, smoked, salted, and served in the form of many varieties of sausages and frankfurters. It also comes in a meat paste made with ground mutton or lamb blended with potato flour. This paste is used to make fried meat patties.

Smoked, salted mutton is a Christmas tradition, while **blodmor**, a sausage made from salted sheep's blood thickened with barley or rye flour and boiled in the cleaned sheep's intestines, has been made from earliest times. Another sausage called **lifrapilsa** is made from sheep's liver. Still another traditional dish that is often the Sunday dinner is **svid** – smoked or fresh whole lamb's heads served boiled. **Svid** is sometimes prepared into headcheese – meat from the lamb's heads jelled in its own aspic.

Cattle are mainly used for dairy products, rarely for beef. Pigs are all but nonexistent; pork is rare and expensive and said to have a fishy taste because of the pig's diet. However, horsemeat is a frequent part of the menu and is more available and more tender than beef.

FOODS COMMONLY USED

Icelandic cuisine revolves around the plentiful sea harvest supplemented by dairy products, wholegrain and white breads, and potatoes. Vegetables and fruits are often scarce and expensive, but canned products and the produce from local greenhouses, which include bananas, grapes, and tomatoes, are helping to increase the variety.

Vitamin supplements are widely used to help make up for the lack of greens and fruits. Lamb, the favored meat, is prepared in unusual ways. The traditional Scandinavian cold buffet and love of coffee together form the traditional ways of entertaining: buffet and coffee parties are common.

Icelandic fish is of excellent quality, relatively inexpensive, and abundant. Herring in many forms – salted, fried, pickled, smoked, raw, baked – form an important part of many meals and especially the cold buffet table. Whole baked stuffed fish and Icelandic fish cakes called **fiskibollur**, made with minced fish, eggs, and seasonings fried to golden brown patties, are special treats. **Hardfiskur** is a traditional Icelandic dish of wine-dried fish, usually haddock. This fish is not cooked, but is pounded until it reaches a soft crumbly texture, then it is dipped into butter and eaten with the fingers.

Still another uniquely Icelandic fish dish is **hakarl** – cured shark meat. Shark meat is not considered edible until it has been cured. The meat is cut in strips and laid in clean gravel beds for several weeks. Finally it is washed and air-dried in special sheds. As is the case with most pungent but delicious foods, the taste is an acquired one; however, it is widely agreed that washing it down with icy Icelandic **Brennivin** (brandy) adds to the pleasure.

Icelanders have a deeply rooted objection to eating birds of any type, so the poultry that is raised supplies eggs but not meat to the Icelandic table. Eggs are often served with smoked mutton in the same way that bacon and eggs are used. Eggs are also used widely in the many fine baked products and also blended with sugar and milk or cream to make a type of eggnog soup.

Dried legumes and nuts are used minimally.

BREADS AND GRAINS

Grains in the form of porridges, flour for thickening, and baked goods comprise a large and important part of the Icelandic diet. Oatmeal together with bread and butter is an almost daily breakfast, while breads made from wholegrain wheat flour, barley flour, rye flour, or white wheat flour are present at every meal and often accompany coffee.

Homemakers pride themselves on the many breads, cakes, and cookies they bake and there always seems to be "a little something baked" to go with coffee, no matter the hour. Potato flour is used for thickening soups, gravies, sauces, and puddings. Rice is used seldom and then only in the form of a milky dessert pudding.

FATS

Much fat is consumed in the form of cheeses, coffee and dessert cream, ice cream, and also in many fried foods where any fat – from margarine and butter (all unsalted) to sheep's fat and horse fat – may be used. Icelanders like the rich taste of fat fish and meats and seldom skim soups or gravies.

SWEETS AND SNACKS

Icelanders do not hedge about their love of sweets. They add granulated sugar to almost everything from appetizers to soups and even in mashed potatoes. They sweeten their many daily cups of coffee and enjoy them with a great variety of sweet baked and fried cakes, often adding an extra sprinkle of white or brown sugar on top.

SEASONINGS

The Icelandic spice shelf is a minimal one. Salt, pepper, and onions are the few added seasonings; most food is enjoyed for its natural fresh or smoked flavor. Salt is seldom added, and to most other tastes, Icelandic food often seems like part of a salt-free diet. But it should be remembered that Icelanders enjoy many salted meats and fish so that the contrast of bland dishes is a welcome one. Fresh cream and fresh unsalted butter are frequent additions, but most often sugar is used to heighten natural flavors, and with a liberal hand.

BEVERAGES

Young and old enjoy a glass of cold milk with almost every meal, but there is little doubt that good strong coffee with cream and sugar is the number-one beverage. While milk accompanies meals, coffee does too, but goes on to be the snack beverage as well as the drink to discuss business, chat over old times, and entertain friends.

Icelanders, together with most Scandinavians, also share a predilection and capacity for alcohol seldom equaled elsewhere. The idea of a "good time" is never complete without the other idea of "finishing the bottle," and the men are quietly indulged by patient wives waiting with the sobering strong coffee. Imported wines sometimes accompany meals, though beer and ale are more common. The national drink is **Brennivin**, similar to brandy and taken straight and icy cold.

MEALS AND CUSTOMS

The normally reserved, independent, and industrious Icelanders become talkative, gregarious, and even humorous after a few drinks. But it should be noted that the usual alcoholic beverages are confined to meals and most especially to evening gatherings in homes or nightclubs. Morning breaks are not the rule, but an afternoon coffee break with bread and butter and several cakes and cookies is enjoyed. Snacking and street vendors are not as much a part of Icelandic life, but coffee shops are as popular here as anywhere else.

Mornings begin with a breakfast of oatmeal porridge, bread and butter, milk and coffee. Lunch is usually a hot meal of meat or fish with potatoes, followed by a sweet fruit soup and a glass of cold milk. From about 2:30 to 4:00 p.m. most Icelanders will be enjoying their coffee with open-face sandwiches or bread and butter, and/or a variety of layer cakes, tortes, quick breads, and cookies. At 7:00 p.m. the family enjoys either another hot meal based on meat or fish and similar to the noon meal, or sliced meats and cheeses may be enjoyed as open-face sandwiches with rye and wheat breads. **Skyr** will be the usual dessert eaten with a sugar topping or sugar and cream. The day would not be complete without an evening coffee and pastries around 9:30 p.m. If there are guests, the evening will not be concluded until all have enjoyed coffee, though probably much later than 9:30.

Icelanders are casual about meal service, preferring to place food on the table and allow diners to help themselves. Bread and butter is part of every meal. Given the country's lack of vegetation, it is understandable that Icelanders have a great love for flowers and these are a part of the table setting whenever possible. Preferring to talk in separate groups, men and women disperse after the meal, it still being considered "odd" or "forward" if women join in men's conversations.

SPECIAL OCCASIONS

Most Icelanders are of the Lutheran faith. Although they are not devoutly religious, many go to church services while others prefer to listen to the services at home on the radio. Others spend the day quietly resting and reading. But almost all Icelanders know it is Sunday when **svid** (lamb's heads) and potatoes appear as the main dish and the favorite **skyr** as dessert.

Perhaps it is because of their Viking heritage that many Icelanders believe in psychic phenomena such as communication with the dead and a belief in haunted houses. Telling ghost stories is a favorite pastime and these tales are listened to with more than casual interest. Though not strict in their own religious beliefs, Icelanders are most tolerant of other beliefs.

Christmas is the main annual celebration with **hangikjot** (smoked mutton) being the specialty of the feast, together with a variety of special sausages, many cured and smoked meats and fish, and an array of special baked treats. **Astarbollur** are baking powder doughnuts made as a Christmas specialty and richly studded with currants. All in all, it is a veritable "groaning table" of hot and cold buffet dishes to please all family tastes and those of callers.

GLOSSARY OF FOODS AND FOOD TERMS

Astarbollur: Christmas specialty of deep-fried doughnuts leavened with baking powder and rich with currants.

Brennivin: Icelandic brandy drunk icy cold and straight.

Blodmor: formerly a staple in the Icelandic diet, today a traditional favorite. It is made from salted, diluted sheep's blood thickened with barley or rye flour and boiled in intestine casings. To preserve the boiled sausage, they are stored in sour whey.

Fiskibollur: Icelandic fried fish cakes made by combining finely minced fish with chopped onions and separated eggs. The flattened cakes are fried till golden then gently steamed by adding a little broth.

Flatbrau: Icelandic griddle cakes made from whole rye or wholewheat flour blended with boiling water to make a dough. Served with sugar or preserves of rhubarb or berries.

Hakarl: cured shark's meat prepared by cutting the fish meat into strips and storing in clean gravel beds for several weeks. Following this, the strips of fish are washed then air-dried in special sheds. Although strongly pungent, the flavor is much prized and is enjoyed with **Brennivin**.

Hangikjot: the Christmas specialty of smoked cured lamb or mutton. Often enjoyed throughout the year, thinly sliced and sometimes served with fried eggs.

Harkfiskur: fish that is wind-dried till brittle. It is eaten uncooked but pounded till soft and crumbly. The torn strips of fish are butter-dipped to eat.

Kaupfelagi: the name for Icelandic cooperative supermarkets, offering reasonable food prices – a balm to the tourist after the exorbitant cost of restaurant meals.

Koefa: simmered meat (usually lamb, occasionally veal) ground then packed into a loaf mold with some of the broth. The jelled chilled loaf is sliced to serve.

Kringlur: pretzel-shaped yeast dough flavored with cinnamon and caraway seeds.

Lifrapilsa: a baked liver pate or boiled liver sausage made from sheep's liver, oats, flour, and milk.

Mola Kaffi: strong coffee served with loaf (cube) sugar.

Mysostur: a brown smooth-spreading cheese.

Ponnukokur: simple light pancakes served cold as a dessert or with coffee. They are usually served in rolls, sprinkled with brown sugar.

Rullu Pylsa: pickled rolled lamb, served cold as a sliced meat with buttered wheat or rye bread.

Rusks: sweet plain yeast dough in buns or slices that have been oven toasted till crisp and dried.

Skyr: a curd dish somewhere between yogurt and cottage cheese in flavor, prepared by fermenting pasteurized skim milk with renin. It is served with sugar or with sugar cream. Icelandic staple and favorite dessert and snack available everywhere.

Steiktir Partar: thin wafer-like pastries filled with sweetened whipped cream.

Svid: general name for singed sheep's or lamb's heads. These may be smoked or boiled or simply boiled and served, often as a Sunday specialty. The heads may also be simmered in a stock, the meat removed and jelled in the stock aspic to be chilled and served sliced as headcheeses.

Svidasutla: head cheese.

Vinarterta: called "Viennese torte," an Icelandic specialty made with many layers of cookie-like pastry filled with cardamom or cinnamon-flavored pureed prunes.

INDIAN, PAKISTANI, AND SRI LANKAN

In Northern India, against a background of sweeping sandy plains and crumbling rocky hills, men in intricately wound turbans of coral, magenta, acid green, and ethereal blue, vie with the brilliantly patterned swirling skirts, snug bodices, and floating shawls–rather than saris–of graceful women. On city streets, teetering trucks and bicycles bulging with produce sway along dusty roads past snooty camels, lumbering elephants, and careening goatherds. Towering lacy turrets of pink palaces and the palatial splendor of ancient gardens impress the mind with the glories of Rajasthan, India's elegant northwest state, home of the maharajas and heart of one of the most exotically complex cuisines in the world.

Historically, it was the northern provinces of India, centering around the capital of Delhi, with its fabled riches and benign climate that proved to be the most tempting area for conquests both military and ideological. Greek thinking in 300 B.C.E. and Buddhism in the 200s B.C.E. were followed by Hindu beliefs in 100 B.C.E., and gradually filtered throughout India and Pakistan. Later battles by Huns and Turks only added to the anarchistic state of affairs that had prevailed for several hundred years.

By 1000 C.E., yet another power arose: united by the beliefs of Islam, a succession of Muslim rulers prevailed as Delhi sultans for several hundred years. They were followed by the Mogul Dynasty, led by Saber in 1526. This period of religious tolerance and cultural splendor peaked in the mid-1600s when the famed Taj Mahal was constructed, then declined abruptly by early 1700, coinciding with the firm entrenchment of the Sikhist faith. Later, Persian plunderers added to a chaotic and violent era fraught with war.

The indigenous crops of fine teas and spices also made northern India into an arena for European conquest, ostensibly for reasons of trade. The Portuguese in the 1400s were followed by the Dutch East India Company in the 1600s, with the British taking a share of the trade monopolies in the late 1600s.

On August 15, 1947, the republics of India and Pakistan were born amid cheers and parades. With a history of warring kingdoms drawn into temporary peace only to burst again and again into cultural or political explosions, the end of British occupation and independence for India and Pakistan has provided a period of relative peace, economic growth, and cultural harmony, which was, however, accompanied by a mutual wariness.

India is 80 percent Hindu, 14 percent Muslim, with small minorities of Christian, Sikh, Buddhist, and Jains. Religious diversity, however, is only one factor in the great complexity that is India. In the huge tropical subcontinent of India and Pakistan reside almost one-fifth – 18.87 percent – of the world's population, representing eight distinctive ethnic groups, many religious and religion subgroups, endless local and regional cultural traditions, 19 regional languages, more than 179 different languages, and more than 500 dialects. Add to these figures the staggering population growth rate, food production problems, and the difficulties of education and communication, and one can see that the problems India confronts are indeed complex.

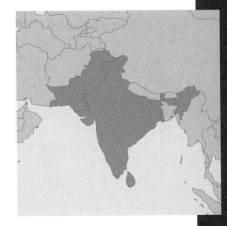

Since the 1970s, the Green Revolution in India, improving irrigation, and types and qualities of crops, has resulted in food self-sufficiency for the first time since the 1800s. Still, much of the area's agricultural lands are deficient and frequently lack water. Other countries use compost from crop residues and other organic wastes. In India crop residues are used together with animal dung for cooking fuel and building materials. Although improved irrigation systems have been introduced, primitive farming methods frequently prevail, often with family hand labor. Since animals and fowl compete with people for the land and the food, the animals are lean, milk production is low, chickens are scrawny and their egg production is also low.

Common to other areas where subsistence agriculture is practiced, the low crop production as well as dairy and eggs are usually consumed in the local villages. There is seldom any kind of surplus. Despite superior systems of air and train travel, transportation is often by bullock cart over primitive roads to distant markets. Storage facilities are limited or nonexistent.

If it seems that discussions of the food problems of India and Pakistan focus on the poorer classes, it is because they represent more than one-half of the rural population living below the poverty line, and their dietary intake is also controlled by local availability, economic status, traditional religion and culture, along with the vagaries of nature, which can bring drought or flood.

Despite the prevalence of poverty in the country, India has a thriving and large, well-educated middle class. There is also a rapidly developing industrial and technical economy and increasing foreign investment. Only periodic political chaos and community violence mars an otherwise thriving economy.

As the noted anthropologist and author, Marvin Harris, notes, "The picture of a ragged farmer starving to death alongside a big fat cow conveys a reassuring sense of mystery to Western observers." For the Hindus, the cow is the symbol of all life and as such is venerated and protected. But the almost 200 million cows that freely roam the countryside and some cities of India (helping India to have the largest cattle population in the world) are rarely either big or fat. Cows and bullocks provide critically important power for plowing, hauling, threshing, and pumping water from wells where old water wheels are still used. They produce milk that is used for cultured dairy foods and cheeses. Perhaps most important, their dung is avidly collected and dried for use as fertilizer, cooking fuel and, mixed with mud, it provides concrete-hard floors for farm tasks and kitchens. As valuable and venerated as cows are, there is little food for them and most survive on litter and garbage (incidentally helping to keep the roads clean) and are therefore usually lean.

Unlike many other lands and cultures, the most decisive factors in India's cuisine are not the influence of invaders and conquerors, but the natural resources available, local tradition, custom and status, as well as the complex stipulations of religion. These reasons support the idea that India's cuisine is set apart mainly by use and varieties of spices, and that although the foods of different regions appear to be different, they are in fact only different in methods of preparation rather than composition.

DOMESTIC LIFE

Domestic life depends upon region, cultural traditions, and economic status.

There are more than a half-million villages in India and Pakistan with populations just under 2,000, which are run by *panchayats* or local councils. People in the villages subsist on local produce mostly secured by hand labor, dependent on the weather. Sometimes women stay behind as men leave the village to seek work. For most, life is hard, and primitive methods prevail in home and field.

The kitchen and dining areas of most homes are held in some degree of reverence and shoes are never worn there. Kitchen facilities may vary but most have open shelves to store copper and brass utensils as well as spices, seasonings, and staples such as cereals, legumes, flours, and pickles. Cooking is done over small charcoal or dung-burning "stoves"–usually a container to hold the burning fuel fitted with a grate on top. Cooking utensils include some type of griddle for breads and a deep pot to be used for rice cooking, heating water, deep-frying, and pickle making.

The rounded griddle is called a **tava**, while the

FOODS COMMONLY USED

The most important factors that differentiate Indian foods from other cuisines are the use of seasonings and the methods of preparation, while the variable factors include economic status, local traditions, religion, and availability. All regions of the country depend mainly on cereals, followed by legumes and only small amounts of vegetables and fruits. Dairy products are enjoyed as often as possible by all. Meats and fish pose problems: the poor can seldom afford them and religious taboos affect the use of these foods. Some taboos may be locally overcome. For example, Hindus (especially in coastal areas) may eat fish by considering them "fruit of the sea" rather than flesh; others may eat beef in restaurants but never allow it to be cooked in their own homes. More frequently people are vegetarians for economic reasons rather than by choice.

The basic cereals are rice, wheat, corn, millet, and barley. Pulses are commonly used in at least one daily dish, often in a thick sauce called **dal**, which can be served over grains, used as a side dish or as a thickener for other dishes. Vegetable oils are the staples but **ghee** (clarified butter) is preferred by the upper classes. Potatoes and onions are the staple vegetables. Other vegetables and seasonal fruits are consumed mostly in the form of condiments, sauces, and pickles. Tea is the favored beverage in the North, while coffee is preferred in the South.

dome-shaped utensil used specifically for frying is called **karhai**. Some method of grinding and crushing the many blends of spices used for different dishes is a vital part of kitchen equipment. These may be as simple as a long flat stone with a smooth round one to roll over the spices, or a stone vessel with a deep pit and a stone pounder to form a type of mortar and pestle.

City homes of some social and economic stature would use electric blenders. **Chimta** is the name given to long tongs with smooth flat edges. These and several sizes of ladles and mixing spoons constitute basic equipment. Especially popular in the Punjab region is the **tandoor**, a clay oven used to barbecue meats and bake breads that are slapped onto the sloping sides of the pit-like oven.

A collection of small bowls and individual **thalis** (trays) are used for meal service and these reflect the economic status of the home. Most households also have at least one **paraat**, a wide-brimmed brass tray used for kneading bread doughs, but it can also be used for serving foods on special occasions.

Just as kitchen facilities vary according to the family's economic status, so do storage facilities. These are nonexistent for most of the population. Dry flours, cereals, and legumes are stored high on shelves in closed jugs and jars to keep their contents free of vermin and insects – always a problem in tropical climates. Thus, fruits and vegetables in the form of pickles, seasoning sauces and chutneys, oils and other condiments keep well. Oil, brine, or sugar may be used to preserve the fruits and vegetables as pickles, which vary from salty to very sweet, spicy, and hot or sour. Only in the wealthiest urban homes do electrical appliances, and especially refrigerators, make an appearance.

DAIRY PRODUCTS

Milk is a staple of some vegetarian meals, when available. Fresh milk, whether from cows, buffalo, or goats, is always boiled before using. Yogurt relishes, milk desserts, and drinks prepared with buttermilk or yogurt sometimes diluted with water are used as often as possible. Powdered and canned milk products are widely used. The British introduction of tea drinking replaced many traditional frothy hot milk drinks and cool fruit beverages.

Milk also forms the base of most of the very sweet desserts. For example, boiled milk, sugar and spices with grated carrots, flours, or raisins transforms into the exotic pudding **gajar halva**. **Kulfi** is similar to ice cream, made with frozen boiled milk, chopped nuts, and cardamom. **Khoya** is evaporated milk boiled to an almost solid cream. **Gulab jaman** (fried milk balls) are prepared from boiled milk blended with cream of wheat then formed into balls and deep-fried and finished with a plunge into hot syrup. Many desserts are also made from fresh curds, similar to cottage cheese. One of these, a cloudlike ethereal delight of light cheese dumplings in a rose-water-scented milk sauce is **ras malai**.

FRUITS AND VEGETABLES

Fruits and vegetables are eaten in season only sparingly; more are consumed in the form of pickles, condiments, and chutneys. The latter may be made from any fruits including mangoes, dates, lemons, melons, citrus fruits, coconuts and flavored with tamarinds, ginger, mint. These are preserved with both sugar and spices. **Achar**, or pickles, are made by all women in a household when seasonal vegetables are in their prime. Cleaned and cut vegetables are prepared in combinations that may be cherished family recipes and, together with distinct seasonings, are preserved in brine or one of several types of oils. Condiments may include finely chopped fresh or dried fruits or vegetables prepared sometimes just before the meal as taste-tingling and complementary side dishes.

While general vegetable consumption is low, greens of all kinds are used when they are available: mustard greens, fenugreek greens, spinach, radish greens, gram and chickpea greens. A Punjabi favorite is creamed mustard greens served with corn bread and with buttermilk to drink. When fresh greens are not available, pulses may be soaked and sprouted; they are often eaten in their fresh form. In many areas it is also common to preserve vegetables by cleaning and slicing then drying them in the sun. Aside from greens, onions and potatoes are frequently used. Other vegetables consumed (but not widely used) include: cauliflower, okra, eggplant, many types of mushrooms, lotus stems, water chestnuts, tomatoes, radishes, and cucumbers.

Fruits also include many of those available in temperate climates: varieties of apples, pears, cherries, berries, melons, plus the great variety of tropical fruits including **cheekoos** (like brown persimmons) and **kulu pears**.

MEATS AND ALTERNATES

To most Indians, it is the "alternates" that are vital. The Brahmins (upper-caste Hindus) are reputed never to touch meat, eggs, or fish, but traditions are sometimes stretched. Buddhists and Jains are strongly against killing. Some Jains go so far as to wear masks lest they inhale any minute insects. Vegetarianism reflects the doctrine of *ahimsa*, the reverence and concern for all living things, and this is a fundamental precept of daily life for many Buddhists, Jains, and upper-class or orthodox Hindus. Muslims do not use pork. Most Indians, however, are so poor that they cannot afford meat of any kind. They are vegetarians by necessity not choice. In fact, the term "vegetarian" is misleading since the bulk of their diet does not comprise vegetables but cereal grains, pulses, and dairy products.

It is said that "when an Indian sits down to eat meat, it is nearly always goat meat." But whether it is goat, lamb, buffalo meat, or chicken, the likelihood is that the meat will be finely chopped or ground or well marinated before cooking because most available meats are lean and tough. A great favorite is any kind of meat cooked on the bone so that diners may eat with fingers and enjoy sucking out marrow and nibbling tidbits. Many ground meat dishes are popular: **koftas** (of Persian influence), which are many sizes and types of meatballs served with special sauces; **kheema**, a spiced ground meat sauce served with rice or **chapatis**, **dal**, or sometimes vegetables. Other meats may be prepared as barbecues (**tandoori**), or curried.

Chickens are usually bought in the cities, ready for use, fresh, or frozen. In rural areas they will be purchased still live from markets or poultry men hawking their wares from door to door. Most chickens are skinned before use in cookery, then cut up, leaving the bones for nibbling. Generally, chickens are considered a luxury food and reserved for special occasions.

Fish and seafood are used mostly in coastal areas, where caught, and in cities, where refrigeration is available. Fish production and intake are low. Eggs are in short supply and even when available, often fall under so many religious taboos that they are not used. Nuts of all kinds are widely used and served toasted and salted as ever-present nibbles or appetizers and are often crushed or ground to form part of sauces, confections, and desserts.

Of great importance are pulses (legumes), called by the general name **dal** in most of India. (Dal also refers to a sauce of cooked pulses.) Varieties and uses are many. There are several varieties of lentils, peas (called **gram**) including: **Bengal gram**, **black gram**, **green gram**, **red gram**. There are also many varieties of beans, including soybeans. Dal is eaten minimally at one meal each day and everyone eats some form of dal; cooking methods and seasonings vary by locale.

Dal is usually thick except in the South where it is traditionally served soupy-thin. Cooked dal is served in tiny bowls or poured over rice, then seasonings that have been precooked in oil are poured over. In Punjab, whole unhulled dals are cooked slowly in the **tandoor**, and often a spicy dish of chickpeas served with puffy deep-fried bread accompanies

a meal and is called **chana batura**. In Delhi the dal may be cooked as hulled and split **moong dal**, spiced with cumin and browned onions and given a tangy splash of lime juice. In Bombay, a hot, sweet and sour **toovar dal** is prepared by adding **jaggery** (raw sugar) and tamarind paste to the cooked dal. The oil and spice mixture used to finish the dal may be called **tarka**, **baghar**, or **chhownk**.

Beans and chickpeas and other pulses may also be marinated in peppery mixtures of tamarind and hot spices and nibbled as snacks. Cooked mashed dal figures prominently in many fried snacks. There are also many flours made from legumes and these are used in making desserts, breads, noodles, and snacks. Legumes may be also served as **curries** in small side dishes and are often sold by street vendors in many forms as quick snacks, such as **beelpuri**: a mixture of lentils and puffed rice well seasoned and served with wheat-flour chips. Similar spicy snacks are available even in movie theaters.

BREADS AND GRAINS

In the South and the East rice is the staple grain. In the North and the West, many varieties of breads are made from their staple of wheat. In wealthier homes, both rice and wheat may be used, while the poorest may eat only barley or millet. Valuable nutrients are lost when rice is well washed before using, cooked in large amounts of water and the water is drained off. In some areas, though, the drained rice water is saved and used for breakfast.

Basmati or **basumati** rice is considered the best of long-grain rice and cooks with a sweet fragrance. It is usually well aged and comparatively expensive. But like pulses, rice too comes in many varieties in India and each is meant to be used in special ways. It may be polished or unpolished, brown or parboiled, long, short or round grain, freshly harvested green rice or rice that has been aged for several years in clay-walled storerooms. There is also pressed rice, puffed rice, rice flakes, beaten rice, and rice flour. Rice flour blended with varying amounts of ground lentils, then cooked flat like little pancakes, or baked, could be used to form almost endless varieties of hot little crepes and breads popular in the South for breakfast, following coffee and fruit.

Rice is commonly cooked into fluffy mounds and served garnished with dal and seasonings or with curried accompaniments, or may be made into rice balls, rice gruel, or sweet rice desserts. The latter are prepared from sticky or glutinous rice. Two popular rice preparations are **pillau** or **pilaf**, in which meats, fish and/or vegetables with seasonings are cooked together with the rice. **Biryanis** are similar, but more ornate and garnished with nuts, flowers, raisins, varka (silver leaf). Many sweet dishes may be made with rice or rice flour in the form of puddings or sweet confections. Saffron, coconut milk, and milk are most commonly added to rice for flavor.

At Hindu weddings rice is thrown into a fire to symbolize fertility. One explanation has it that rice is not fertile until transplanted to another field. A girl therefore becomes fertile when transplanted to her husband's home.

Breads are mostly made from wheat flour and cooked unleavened. But they can also be made from chickpea flour, maize, millet or barley flour, bean, rice or lentil flour, and from white or various types of wholewheat flour. Most breads are deep-fried or griddle-cooked as ovens are usually improvised by heaping a covered pan with hot coals.

Chapatis are made with only wholewheat flour and water, rolled into flat rounds – which puff when cooked on a griddle – and then held over a flame with tongs. **Puris** or **pooris** are the same as **chapatis** only they are puffed by deep-frying. **Parathas** are similar to pancakes. Two richer breads are **bhatura** (favorite of the Punjabis), a deep-fried bread made with white flour, yogurt, baking powder, and egg, and **naan**, a yeast and baking powder–leavened rich white bread baked in huge flat ovals by slapping quickly on the sides of the **tandoor** or under a broiler. **Roti** is the general name given to all Indian breads.

FATS
The use of butter and **ghee** (clarified butter) is mostly confined to the middle and upper classes. Mustard oil is popular in the northeast, peanut or groundnut oil is used where cultivated, while coconut oil is restricted mainly to the west coast. Northern India uses ghee where it can be afforded, but peanut oil and **gingilli oil** (sesame seed oil) are widely used. Seasonings are always first well cooked in fat or oil before other ingredients are added. Oils are used for deep-frying, a popular method of cookery where fuel and space is limited. Oils are also used in the preparation of **achar**, various types of pickles and condiments. General fat intake may be quite high because fats are used liberally in cooking.

SWEETS AND SNACKS
Indian sweets may vary greatly in composition but they all have one thing in common: they are very sweet. Sweet desserts may be made in a number of ways, from cooked thickened milk, from a rice base with added raisins and nuts, from very thin Indian vermicelli cooked with milk and flavored with rosewater, almonds, and **jaggery** (unrefined palm sugar). Sweets may also be made from doughs prepared with legume or rice or wheat flours–even cooked mashed vegetables, such as eggplant, potato, sago palm–all deep-fried in different shapes then plopped into hot spicy syrups to give them a fragrant and sticky glaze. Many of these sweet treats are purchased from street vendors as well as prepared at home.

There is also a definite taste for spiced, salted, and even sour snacks. These include green or unripened fruits dipped into spicy sauces or simply salted and then nibbled. Crisp, thin flakes or chips are made from various fruits and vegetables then salted and spiced and eaten as snacks. Of course salted roasted nuts are high on the list of nibbles too.

Most meals end with a light dessert of fruits, usually peeled or cut into pieces by the women of the family, and passed first to the children. Really sweet confections and desserts are saved either for teatime, between-meal snacks, or special or festive occasions.

SEASONINGS
It is the unique use and preparation of freshly ground seasonings that set Indian cuisine apart from others. The selection, preparation, and use of spices and herbs in India differs from most other cultures, because of the medicinal properties attributed to them by the 4,000-year tradition of *Ayervedic* medicine. Chilies, paprika, and black pepper are noted for their vitamin C content; garlic is thought to provide energy and stimulation; ginger is used as a remedy for flatulence and other digestive disturbances; whole cloves for fever, and so on. And while many people believe that all India's dishes are as fiery as those in Madras, in truth, the dishes are spicy but few are fiery hot. In fact, many Indians state calmly and firmly that they "do not take hot."

In fact, it is the *vasana*, or aroma, of food that is of prime importance to the Indian. This is not to say, however, that appearance and taste do not also play an important part. Each household has its special treasured recipes that indicate exactly what type and amount of spices or herbs may be used in preparing each dish. The mixture of freshly ground seasonings is called **masala**. The Indian palate carefully distinguishes between a full range of tangy, sour, piquant, peppery, hot, briny flavors, as well as sweet.

The much-misused all-encompassing term "curry" actually refers to a "highly seasoned stew with plenty of sauce." The word "*curry*" is said to have originated from the Tamil word *kari* meaning simply meat or food, but that which is prepared in a manner to appeal to all of man's senses. Bottles of seasoning sold in the western world as "curry powder" consist of a blend of spices and herbs and vary greatly in flavor and quality. In India the term "curry" refers to a meal based on rice with a spiced and sauced meat or fish dish surrounded by several smaller bowls of accompaniments such as chopped vegetables, nuts, chutneys and pickles, toasted chips or flakes of fruits or vegetables – all to be eaten in the order desired and usually with a spoon and a fork but just as often with the fingers.

Sometimes fresh or green spices may be ground with liquid such as water, coconut milk, etc., in which case they are called "wet masalas." Wet masalas blend smoothly into sauces, but one rule should be noted: all seasonings are always well cooked, whether in fat or oil or liquid, before being added to a dish, or before other ingredients are combined.

The list of spices used in Indian cookery is almost endless: cardamom, cloves, cinnamon, mace, nutmeg, saffron, turmeric, many types of peppers and chilies, fennel, dill, cumin seed, mustard, bay leaf, aniseed, coriander seeds, asafeetida (of fetid smell but delicious taste), dried garlic, ginger. The masala may be hot, spicy, burning, tangy, mellow, rich, light, but never on any account should it "catch the throat!" Many arguments ensue on the subject of which spice or herb, how much, and whether fresh or dried should be used for what dish and in combination with what other seasonings!

BEVERAGES

Tea is the favored hot drink in the North, coffee in the South; both are served well sweetened, and usually with boiled milk. Yogurt and buttermilk are much enjoyed as cooling beverages as well and are often served diluted and sometimes lightly salted or sweetened. **Lassi** is the name given to salted or sweetened diluted yogurt. Hot tea and coffee are commonly served as a breakfast beverage but may also be taken at other times of the day between meals. They are rarely served at the end of meals.

In many countries, but especially in India, the gentle art of serving the right beverage at the right time to a desired effect is elevated to an art form. While tea and coffee are commonly taken as part of hospitality, to refresh and to stimulate, special varieties of teas and other beverages are taken to calm, to aid digestion, to heat or to cool the body. Some of these include homemade preparations of tangy diluted iced drinks and shakes prepared from sweetened or lightly salted mixtures with water, yogurt, and sometimes fruit juices or flavorings such as orange or rosewater added. Spiced tea prepared according to treasured family recipes is a specialty of Bombay; tropical fruit juices lace cooling yogurt drinks in the South.

Some wines are made in India but are not highly regarded or served often. There is also Indian beer, which is of lesser importance as a beverage. Frequently after a large feast a glass of water is served and this is taken with the left hand. Some fruit drinks, called **shurbut**, make a cool refreshment. These are made from fruit juices or crushed fruit pulps and iced.

REGIONAL SPECIALTIES

Indians and Pakistanis share characteristics both in their food customs and in their basic diets. For example, both groups show a strong preference (whether for religious, regional, or economic reasons) for cereal foods, legumes, and dairy products, with little meat, fish, fruits, or vegetables consumed by the majority of people. Yet there are some interesting regional preferences and differences that are worth noting. Included below are the general customs and food specialties of East, West, South, and Northern India, and Pakistan as well as Sri Lanka (formerly Ceylon). The cuisines of all these areas, however, may be called Indian.

EAST INDIA

This area includes the northern part of the eastern coastal provinces of India, centering around Calcutta and the Bengal province. Here parboiled rice is the staple food. Fish is important because the area is really a maritime state and many types of fish are used, as well as fish meal. Plantains, potatoes, tubers, beans, and water lily roots are eaten here more than anywhere else. Thinner and sweeter curries, usually including fish and vegetables, are served for  one meal of the day. In general, foods and food preparation are simpler than, say, in the central northern regions. The favorite bread is called **loochi** (elsewhere known as **puri**), and is prepared from white or wholewheat flour, fried until puffed. Mustard seed oil and **gingilli** (sesame seed oil) are used predominantly. Milk sweets include **sandesh, rasgulla, gulab jamun**: well-boiled milk sweetened and served as thickened puddings. **Dum aloo** is a dessert made from potatoes with almonds, raisins, and yogurt. One typical meal may be **loochi, dum aloo**, and fried eggplant; another may be a fish and vegetable curry with rice and dal and fruit in season.

NORTH INDIA

This is the area of India most influenced by the cuisines of the conquerors, for Delhi seemed like a magnet for foreign invaders: here came the Greeks, under Alexander the Great, the Kushan kings, the

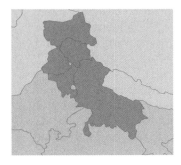

Muslims, the great Mogul Empire adding Bengal and Kashmir to the domain, then the Persian kings. From the courts and palaces came the cuisines that were to influence the cookery of all of India. Delhi cuisine is considered the epitome of India's cuisine. The people of the area admired and happily adopted dishes from Persian cuisine: **pilafs**, imported fruits such as melons, pomegranates, figs, plums, dates and nuts. They also traditionally used ice from the Himalayas to cool their drinks and to prepare chilled dishes. This area was ideal for the creation of a great cuisine because of its fertility and temperate climate, conditions which are most conducive to the growth of crops and orchards.

For modern-day residents of Delhi, electric appliances and efficient kitchen facilities as well as a wide variety of prepared-food mixes make the preparation of traditional meals a simple matter.

Of Punjabi origin is the **tandoor**: the clay oven partially submerged in the ground and used for barbecuing skewered meats and baking flat oval breads (**naan**) by slapping them against the hot sides. The brick and plaster charcoal stove called **chula** is mostly used. In some areas the **chula** is made from smoothed mud.

The North is the great wheat and tea area of India. However, rice dishes, meats, fish, fruits and vegetables are used as lavishly as income permits. Cereals and pulses are nonetheless an important part of all meals. Here the fabulous **biryani** and rich **pellao** or **pilafs** are served, and there are a great many wheat breads, each with similar ingredients yet prepared differently so they add great variety to the menu: **chapatis**, **pulkas**, **parathas**, and **naan**. **Korma** is a thick, rich curry, well browned with added poppy seeds and coconut flavoring, of meat that has first been tenderized by yogurt marination.

SOUTH INDIA

The people of the South are great rice eaters who prefer their foods cooked simply. However, their **masalas** (curries) are much hotter than in other areas of the country. Some say that where the standard of living is the lowest there is an increase in the intake of pungent spices and condiments as though the increased depth of flavors somehow helps one to overcome the oppressive heat of the tropical weather and the monotony of simple meals. **Gingilli** oil, or sesame seed oil, is predominantly used, and most foods are thinned with coconut milk. **Sambar** is the general name given to all vegetable and legume or pulse dishes. **Pachadi** is a cooling "salad" made of chopped fresh vegetables or fruits blended with yogurt similar to a **raita**. **Rasam** is a clear spicy broth much enjoyed here but unusual since soups and broths are not generally a part of Indian cuisine. Desserts are commonly made from a base of rice, vermicelli, or pulses that have usually been boiled in milk then sweetened well with sugar or molasses and served at the end of most meals. The southerners are great coffee drinkers and hot well-sweetened coffee served with fruit begins most days. They are also fond of snacking and enjoy **idli**, fermented and steamed mounds of pulses and rice; or **masala dosa**, large crisp-fried potato-filled crepes served with sweet or sour chutneys.

The poorest of this region eat millet, called **raji**, or **sholam**, which is small millet ground into flour then boiled or steamed in little balls. Wheat for breads is available only in wealthier homes. In the area of Cochin, in Kerala province, foods are very plain, and rice and coffee prevail. Rice and fish, vegetables and seafoods make up the diet, and the considerable use of coconut and coconut milk makes their foods milder than in most other areas of the South. Tropical fruits are freely available here and form an important part of the diet: bananas, pineapple, papaya, custard apples, mangoes.

WEST INDIA

This area is on the northerly part of the west coast of India and includes the provinces of Gujarat and Maharashtra, with Bombay the principal city. The vegetarian peoples here are the Gujaratis and the Maharashtrians, while the Parsee and the Goans (from Goa, under Portuguese influence) are non-vegetarians. Rice is favored especially in the coastal areas. Both the Gujaratis and the Maharashtrians serve a sweet dish as a first course with a vegetable dish and **puri**. However, the Gujaratis like to eat wheat dishes first and rice dishes last, while the Maharashtrians reverse this order. The Parsee specialty is **paneer**, like firm cottage cheese, served first and last at every

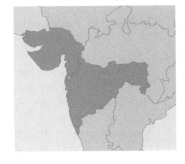

wedding feast, and prepared frequently in every home. The Parsees also like **dhan sak** (plain fried rice) that is served with any combination of meats or fish, vegetable or dal dishes. **Bombay duck**, taken as a salty, fishy-tasting condiment, is enjoyed frequently by the Parsees: it is a small fish that may be served fresh either curried or fried.

The Goans have their food preferences too. Accompanying their rice they enjoy finely chopped fresh vegetables dressed with salt and lime juice. **Foogaths** is the general name given to many mild mixtures of coconut and vegetables, while **vindaloo** is a vinegar-marinated meat and spice dish.

Throughout West India, **neeri**, a drink made from coconut palm, is sold everywhere. Breads called **bel puri** and **khasta kachuri** are sold by vendors everywhere for snacking. Milk sweets are also a favorite here, and are called: **jalebis**; **barfi**, a type of fudge; **doodh pak**, a type of milk rice pudding; and **shrikhand**, a semi-solid sweetened yogurt.

PAKISTANI

The areas of Pakistan are more than 80 percent Muslim. Here, the rules of Islam prevail, and when available, meat comprises the main part of the meal. Pakistanis have many beef, lamb, and chicken dishes, but do not eat pork. The **kababs** and **koftas**, and even the **biryanis**, have more of a hint of the Arab

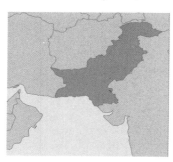

lands than of India, although the region's taste for rice and seasonings is definitely Indian. Rice and wheat are the main crops, and of the pulses, chickpeas are the most popular. Small quantities of fruits and vegetables are available, mostly in West Pakistan: both fruits and vegetables represent temperate and tropical produce.

There are some differences between East and West. Bangladesh (formerly East Pakistan) is densely crowded, has abundant water, and is in constant threat of floods. The principal crops are rice and tea. The people of Bangladesh speak Bengali, while the Pakistanis speak Urdu. The West is a much larger area that is sparsely populated and that frequently suffers from droughts. Wheat is the main crop in the West, but corn, rape, mustard, sugarcane, barley, and chickpeas are also produced. Hydrogenated vegetable oils are used in both East and West, principally mustard and rape seed oil.

In both areas, although meats are much favored, production of meat and poultry is sparse: the ani-

mals again compete with people for the land, meat is lean and chickens yield few eggs. Sadly, the Pakistani and Bangladeshi diets are considered among the poorest in the world, being low both in calories and nutrients.

Breads, cooking of rice, and dairy products are similar in name and preparation to those in most of India. **Halwah** may be sweet wheat or carrot puddings, called **halwahgajar**. Pakistanis enjoy their foods highly spiced and often their pilaus or **biryanis** are flecked with beans or split peas (**kishris**) or with vegetables and lentils, called **bhajias**. Sometimes wheat flour is used in West Pakistan to prepare lamb and potato-filled pastries, resulting in a **samosa**.

SRI LANKAN (CEYLON)

In the hot, humid equatorial island country of Sri Lanka, two main groups struggle: the Tamils, of southern Indian descent, and the Buddhist Sinhalese. Both in language and religion (the Tamils are Hindus) the groups differ. Curries, onions, red chilies, and fish dominate the diet, together with rice and wheat flour. Torrid curries with rice or "stringhoppers," fried noodle patties, are favorites. The third main

group of the island are of the Muslim faith. Dietary habits among the three groups differ largely according to religious custom: the Buddhist Sinhalese do not eat meat, although there are some exceptions; the Muslims have the widest range of foods, eschewing pork but permitting beef, and they have no strong objection to milk; the Hindu Tamils refrain from eating any flesh, but drink milk whenever possible.

A dish unique to Sri Lanka is **hoppers**. Taking its name from a round-bottom fry pan, hoppers are made, rather like omelets (and with as much variety) by tossing and browning bits of vegetables, and/or meats or fish in hot oil then pouring in a beaten egg mixture. When the mixture has almost firmed, it is tossed to cook the flip side. Hopper pans are made of tin and sold at roadsides.

A meal pattern of four meals a day is commonly followed by all: a morning meal, a noon meal, a late afternoon meal, and an evening meal. The morning meal is prepared from rice or rice flour or occasionally wheat breads. The noon meal consists mainly of rice with grated coconut as the curry base, and **mellum**, a well-spiced preparation of shredded vegetable leaves cooked with grated coconut as the usual accompaniment. The number of dishes varies according to the economic standard. Sometimes accompanying the breakfast cereal food is a **sambal** made of various spices with onions and chilies and usually grated coconut; if income permits, a curry may also be part of breakfast. A small late afternoon meal will consist of sweetmeats and sweetened tea, while the evening meal will be similar to either breakfast or the noon meal. Served at the end of each meal is sweetened tea.

Cereals and spices form the main part of the Sri Lankan diet, and there is a general lack of fruits and vegetables.

MEALS AND CUSTOMS

The majority of South Asians have two main meals a day. The morning meal is usually based on the regional preference of rice or wheat and this is accompanied by the regional preference of either tea or coffee. Region, however, plays no part in what is added to the beverage: all enjoy their tea or coffee well sweetened and preferably served with boiled milk. Sometimes **sambals** (sauces) of spices accompany the rice breakfast and either fruit or **achar** (pickles) may also be a part of the meal. In most areas the evening meal is based on rice plus dal plus vegetables, then, according to religion, means, and area, a meat or fish curry and a sweet milk dessert may complete the meal. The time between morning and evening meal is often sated with the many foods hawked by vendors in almost every part of the country: beverages, milk sweets, fresh fruits, or snack foods made from a cereal or pulse base served with spiced sauces.

In most regions, it is customary to sit on the floor or the ground for meals. The area used as the table is covered with carpets which in turn are spread with cloths. In the South, meals may simply be taken in a cool area and smoothed ground may be the table. In hotels and in upper-class homes, meals may be taken at large tables or at short-legged individual tables. Most commonly each diner is served a *thali* (tray) of metal, upon which rests many small ornate metal bowls, each containing a different sauce, dish, or condiment. It is up to the diner to mix the foods and eat them in whatever order they find pleasing. In the South, banana leaves may substitute for the *thali* and portions of foods may be placed directly on the diner's leaf or placed in small earthenware bowls that are discarded after the meal.

But North or South, hands are always washed before and after eating, and foods are always prepared and eaten only with the use of the right hand. If any cutlery is used, it will be a spoon or fork. Knives never make an appearance except in the kitchen to prepare foods. Northerners pride themselves on their ability to eat deftly with only the fingertips of the right hand, while southerners eat their foods with great relish and use their right hand right up to the wrist if need be.

Inviting people for dinner is as pleasant a way to entertain guests in India as it is anywhere else. A leisurely meal is often served buffet style and typically, the mother of the household takes the role of the hostess, the father circulates and sees that everyone is conversationally engaged. If the extended household also boasts sons and daughters-in-law, the sons will be part of the evening socializing, but the daughters-in-law will often be in the kitchen preparing food and keeping the buffet table replenished. This division of roles is common even in homes with servants.

Another tradition in Indian entertaining is to serve dessert a long time after everyone has finished dinner. There is good reason for this. Visitors may be surprised to see that after dessert there is a prompt and courteous exit of the guests – a custom that could be emulated elsewhere to solve the problem of extended visiting!

There is one further custom that is greatly enjoyed by everyone. This is the nibbling of fragrant, piquant **paan** after a meal. The paan is a heart-shaped leaf which is wrapped around special spices (including betel nuts and leaves, aniseed, cardamom, and cloves) and usually served to guests as they are departing, or else purchased from street vendors. It is believed to freshen the breath and aid digestion. Many homes have an ornate box called a *paandaan*, especially made for storing paan, or for keeping a loose mix of after-dinner spices to be nibbled. Sometimes lightly toasted aniseed are chewed.

SPECIAL OCCASIONS

Probably in no other country in the world do so many diverse religions play such a prominent part in the daily lives of as many people as they do in India.

While there is a small minority group of Christians in India, the majority populations are represented by Hinduism, Buddhism, Muslim, Parsis, and Sikh. Note that there are many variations within each religious discipline as to beliefs and practices, particularly where food is concerned. Sometimes it is the family tradition that is followed, sometimes the local traditions, and frequently availability and necessity dictate dietary patterns. It is also important to bear in mind that religious restrictions alone seldom are responsible for malnutrition. According to Dr. Rajammal Devadas, principal of Sri Avinashilingam Home Science College for Women in Coimbatore, India, "People used to think cultural factors affected better nutrition, but the absence of nutritional education and poverty are the deciding factors. If these are remedied, people will eat better."

The following describes the general principles of India's major religions.

HINDUISM

Hinduism is the religious denomination of 80 percent of the Indian population and has roots reaching back to the Indus Valley civilization which flourished some 3,000 years before Christ. There is a mixture and a borrowing of many customs and beliefs in Hinduism and Hindus themselves represent diverse elements from many ethnic sources. Although in modern times efforts have been made to abolish several tenets of the ancient religion, such as *purdah* (the separation and seclusion of women), *suttee* (the mournful self-cremation of a widow on the funeral pyre of her husband), and the caste system, remnants of each remain in some areas.

The chief features of the newer Hinduism are the movement towards social purpose and a type of puritanism. Many other ancient traditions are slowly being dissolved either by newer tradition, or in some cases, by India's newer legislation; some of these traditions are child marriage, animal sacrifices, and the concept of untouchability. The caste system developed from the belief that an individual was born into a certain class and was destined to remain in it for life. There are four main classifications: the Brahmins, representing the upper or priestly class; the Kshatriyas, representing the warrior class; the Vaisyas, representing the traders and agriculturalists; and finally the Sudras, or menial classes, destined to serve the other three castes, considered the Aryans.

Hinduism embraces an enormous pantheon of gods and lesser gods in three main groups, called *vaishnava, saiva,* and *sakta.* Many seemingly contrasting principles and beliefs are often held by one individual. This becomes even more complex when it is understood that the many gods can also be worshiped in any of their incarnations (of which there are eight). In addition, there are many local divinities and demigods, and some of the incarnations may also have sons. Animals as well as plants may be considered sacred. For example, the cow, one of Hinduism's best-known deities, is considered holy as a representative of "Mother Earth herself." Even parents and teachers are thought of as gods – as is the husband by his wife.

There are two main writings – the *Vedas* and the *Puranas* – as well as six different schools of philosophy emphasizing different means for the individual to achieve the main spiritual goal to rise above the "cycle of transmigration and achieve union or close

contact with the ultimate Being." Tradition (*aryan dharma*) punctuates the life of the Hindu with frequent ritual acts and disciplines. Subordinate to *moksha* (the winning of salvation) are the three aims of religious merit, prosperity, and pleasure – the Hindu's general ethics. Strict vegetarianism is practiced by the upper classes, and this includes abstention from beef – in fact, all flesh or that which may have the seed of life, such as eggs. However, these rules vary, with some considering water-buffalo steaks appropriate fare, and fish as the "fruit of the sea."

The vast complexities of the ancient Hindu faith can be further appreciated by any attempt to catalog the number of festivals and special occasions celebrated. Unlike the Muslims, Christians, or Jews, there are no singular festivals celebrated universally. Instead, there are regional festivals, local temple feasts, and traditional family occasions. However, these are not always celebrated annually. Often there is a space of several years between the celebrations, and many may be based on differing lunar calendars with differing intercalations. Eight popularly celebrated occasions are discussed here.

DIVALI (OR DIWALI)

Arguably the almost universal Hindu festival of light, it is a time of renewal, bright lights, new clothes and painting of homes, games of chance, fireworks and the distribution of sweetmeats to all. A modern addition is the sending of cards wishing: "A Happy Divali and a Prosperous New Year."

Divali is celebrated in Hindu homes everywhere. One room in the house displays an altar to the family's special gods and is decorated with glowing dishes of ghee lit as lamps. Outside the home, tiny colored bulbs are strung around the windows and often through the trees. Special welcome is offered to the god Lakshmi, the goddess and giver of wealth. Drinks, sumptuous trays of food, and sweets are offered to friends and family and often fireworks are part of the three-day festivities.

DUSSARA

A festival celebrated differently in different regions of India. This can be more readily understood when it is realized that this is the ten-day festival worshiping Devi, Shiva's wife, who is widely considered to be all things to all men. Generally the festival is celebrated with pomp and pageantry.

HOLI

A springtime festival with elements of primitive fertility orgies and pranks similar to those played on April Fool's Day. The festival is presided over by Kama and Krishna, the deities of pleasure. There are many lively dances and singing and the scattering of color dyes in powder form so everyone and everything is bright and colorful. Some choose to stay indoors when the festivities become rambunctious.

SHIVARATRI
A solemn all-night vigil with hymns and the reading of sacred texts. It is believed to bring material prosperity and life after death for those who keep this festival sacred.

JANMASHTAMI OR GOKUL ASHTAMI
The birthday of Krishna, believed to be the eighth incarnation of Vishnu, is celebrated with pyramids of young men reaching high to break hanging curd (yogurt) pots. This unusual practice is based on the legend that the child Krishna was particularly fond of milk products and used to steal, with the help of friends, butter and curds, hung high in earthen pots in the kitchen to be out of reach of children.

GANESHA CHATURTHI
Celebrated as the birthday of the jovial elephant-headed Ganesha, whose well-rounded potbelly symbolizes a god of plenty and appetite. Offerings of milk, fruits, and puddings are presented. The center of these festivities is Bombay where three-day processions crowd the roads.

RAKHI PURNIMA
Mainly a festive occasion for upper castes, i.e. the Brahmins, who ceremoniously discard old sacred clothes and put on new ones. The coconut plays a symbolic role for it is believed to represent the three-eyed Shiva. It is therefore considered auspicious to break a coconut at a shrine or whenever one is embarking on a new enterprise. An amulet called *rhaki* is tied on men's wrists by women to signify that from that point on their relationship will be only brotherly.

RAMA NAVAMI
A celebration of the birth of the seventh incarnation of Vishnu, Rama, one of the most beloved of deities. This is one of the most important festivals and is celebrated by all castes and sects. Because it is believed that Rama was born at noon, traditionally this festival begins at noon with a coconut placed in a cradle while a priest announces the birth of Rama to the rhythmic incantations of the diety's name. Afterward, dancing and stage shows and effigy burning of evil spirits take place.

BUDDHISM
Many legends surround the birth and life of Siddhartha Guatama, the Buddha and founder of Buddhism 500 years before Christ. He denounced animal sacrifices and the caste system and pronounced his philosophy in the form of four "Sublime Verities":

1. sorrow is inherent in life
2. sorrow has a cause
3. removal of sorrow leads to cessation of sorrow
4. removal of sorrow can be affected by Right Living

"Right Living was all that the Buddha wanted of his followers." His teachings were especially appealing at a time when it was thought that only royalty or the upper castes could attain nirvana. His teachings were easily adopted but were confined to India during the Buddha's lifetime and for about 300 years afterward. Gradually Buddhism became a world religion largely due to the missionary zeal of Emperor Asoka who spread its teachings to China and Japan and most of Southeast Asia. However, in India itself, Jainism and a newer version of Hinduism struggled for supremacy over Buddhism. This was followed by the Muslim invasion.

Generally, Buddhists abstain from eating meat because of their belief in the sanctity of all living things.

The most radical sect of Buddhism is Zen Buddhism; described as "... what I do and my mind and my soul are one ... anything that absorbs one fully is in effect – Zen." Severe dietary restrictions believed to help one on the way to achieving *satori* (enlightenment) are roundly criticized by food professionals because the special dietary system claims that there is "no disease that cannot be cured by 'proper' therapy which consists of natural food, no medicine, no surgery, no inactivity." The special dietary regime recommended begins at the lowest level with an intake of 10 percent cereals and gradually reaches the "highest level" of 100 percent cereals, with the documented result of emaciation, starvation, and death.

MUSLIM
The Islamic faith has much in common with both Judaism and Christianity and indeed recognizes all the sages of both the Old and New Testaments. Muslims comprise approximately 80 percent of the population of Pakistan. While Sunday is the holy day for Christians and Saturday for the Jews, Muslims hold Friday as sacred. It is obligatory that they abstain from work on this day and say the main prayer in the mosque.

All Muslim celebrations are based on a purely lunar calendar with no intercalations, so that the named months do not necessarily fall in the same seasons. For example, Ramadan or Ramzan Id may occur in winter or summer. Indian Muslims celebrate similarly to others but add some local festivals such as death anniversaries of saints.

Generally, Muslims abstain from eating pork and any flesh that has not been ritually slaughtered. Although alcohol (from the fruit of the vine) is also a part of the abstentions, many make concessions and enjoy alcohol from other sources.

Two popularly celebrated occasions are described below.

UD-UL-AZHA OR BAR ID

Enjoined in the holy writings of the Koran, this festival commemorates Abraham's willingness to sacrifice his son as a sign of obedience to God's command. (In the Muslim version of the account Ishmael – believed to be the progenitor of all Muslims – not Isaac is the object of sacrifice.) On this day the wealthy sacrifice animals to give meat to the poor. Special benedictions are repeated while killing the animal, as the meat of an animal not killed according to sacred ritual is not considered fit for human consumption. Generally, it is a day when new clothes are donned and there is widespread feasting.

RAMZAN ID OR RAMADAN

This celebration is one of the pillars of the Muslim faith. It is celebrated by abstention from food, drink, and smoking, from the hours of sun-up to sundown for the whole of this month. Those who are ill may make up the fast days at another time. Light meals are taken before dawn and after sunset, while communal prayers are often accompanied by the gift of a set amount of alms in the form of grains or fruits. It is believed that after death those who do not keep these traditions will remain suspended between heaven and hell.

PARSEE

The Parsee are a group of people who came to the Bombay region of India when the Arabs conquered Persia and imposed upon everyone the faith of Islam. In order to preserve their beliefs and customs, these people of ancient Persia, members of the faith of Zoroaster, or Zarathustra, fled. From the early 600s C.E. they made their home in the province of Gujarat, spoke Gujarati, and absorbed many of the manners and customs of the Hindus around them. However, they retained certain characteristics of their own despite adopting many western ideas from the British. They still believe in a supreme deity called Ahura

Mazda and a lesser evil power called Ahriman, and they consider that the universe is a battleground of continuous warfare between Ahura and Ahriman (good and evil). They believe also that the path of heaven is over an "accountant's bridge," where each person's good and evil deeds are said to be balanced and the decision made on his entry to heaven or hell. Most Parsee disputes center around the dates of festivals, and these disputes have led to three sect divisions, each with its own calendar. Most festivals are marked by parades and pilgrimages and charity to others.

SIKH

This is the newest and most liberal of Indian religious groups and was founded by Guru Nanak in 1469 after the Muslims had established their power in North India. This was a period of some moderating influences: many Hindus were personally troubled by their polytheism and idolatry and yet many Muslims found their ideas being "tamed" by Hindu influences. These changing ideals found expression in two cults that came into being about this same time: the Hindu Bhakti cult and the Muslim Sufi cult. Both developed many mystical ties in common by referring to a loving God-man relationship and it is felt that the Bhakti cult influenced Nanak in founding his religion. Further, these new cults found their leadership from the common people not the intellectuals, and the principles they propounded were general enough that they found sympathy with both Hindus and Muslims.

Nanak's followers were known as Sikhs, from the sanskrit *Sishya* (disciple) while Nanak himself was known as the teacher or *Guru*. The concept of the Guru developed until he was not only the acknowledged teacher but also the head and leader of the community. Gobind Singh, the tenth Guru, is credited with building the Sikhs into a powerful community and instituting the Granth (literally, the book) in place of the series of Gurus.

Because Gobind Singh's father, the ninth Guru, had been slain by Moghuls, Gobind swore vengeance and developed the militant aspect of the religious order. It was he who developed the institution of the five Ks that are still a part of the Sikh community:

kes–unshorn hair
kirpan–sword
kacha–short pants
kankan–steel bangle
kangha–the comb

Together with the rejection of the caste system, the advocacy of monotheism, and the rejection of idols for worship, most Sikhs have also added the suffix Singh ("lion") to their personal names to further designate their pride and beliefs. In general, their faith is a flexible one with none of the Hindu's elaborate taboos. Sikhs observe many Hindu festivals as well as their own. Two of these are discussed below.

BAISAKH OR VAISAKH

The first day of the month of Baisakh (April-May) is most important for Sikhs and is celebrated as the day that Guru Gobind founded the Khalsa. The Khalsa is an "elect" group of five men. The formation of this group is based on the story that the Guru wanted to create a special council and asked for the lives of five men only. It is said that 80,000 men came to offer their lives. Of these, five were selected and after each selection, the Guru entered into a tent with the man and came out with a sword dripping with blood. At the end, the whole ceremony was revealed to be merely a test, for the five brave men were alive and five goats had been sacrificed. The five great men came to be known as the *Panch Pyare* ("beloved five") and these five are represented for their devotion and bravery in all important Sikh festivals.

This festive occasion is marked with processionals and religious music, usually led by five leaders with drawn swords in memory of the *Panch Pyare* of the Guru Gobind Singh. Following this, everyone joins in feasting and dancing.

GURPURAB

These celebrations represent the many festive days marking the births of all the Gurus and are observed by all Sikhs as holy days.

GLOSSARY OF FOODS AND FOOD TERMS

Amchoor: raw mangoes are dried and ground into a powder. The tangy sour flavor is used as a seasoning.

Asafetida: literally fetid, stinking. A strong-smelling gum resin obtained from plants of the carrot family. It is bought in lump form and used in tiny amounts in vegetarian dishes.

Bahatura: favorite bread of the Punjabs: deep-fried puffed bread made with yogurt, egg, and white flour and leavened with baking powder.

Barfi: general category of many types of sweets prepared from evaporated milk with the addition of sugar, colorings, and flavorings such as rose or orange flower water, coconut, or nuts.

Biryani: the most elaborate of rice dishes, usually presented on the largest platter available. A layered mixture of cooked rice, nuts, and raisins, and well-seasoned prepared meats in bite-size pieces. The whole presentation is decorated with **Vark**, fresh flower blossoms, and artistic arrangements of the ingredients.

Bombay Duck: fermented dried fish used as a side dish or condiment.

Chapatis: wholewheat flour and water are the ingredients. May be cooked in rounds on a griddle then held over fire to puff. When deep-fried they puff almost immediately and are then called **Pooris** or **Puris**.

Chholas: fresh green chickpeas (garbanzos), eaten raw or cooked.

Curry: not a single seasoning but a blend of spices. In India, these spice mixtures are called masalas and are treasured family recipes. Curiously, there is also a green herb called the curry plant whose leaves exude an aroma similar to the spicy masala.

Dal: classic dish of legumes or pulses cooked to a thick sauce. This is eaten daily in all parts of India and Pakistan, but each state has favorite methods of preparation and seasoning. These cooked legumes are often the best source of protein for the poor.

Dum Aloo: potato dish made with almonds, raisins, and yogurt.

Ghee: clarified butter similar in appearance to vegetable shortening. Purchased in tins, and used in cookery.

Halwah: common name given to sweet baked pudding made from semolina or finely grated carrots.

Idli: fermented and steamed mounds of pulses and rice served with condiments and eaten as snack food. Sold by many street vendors.

Kababs: general name for marinated skewered meats.

Kalonji: black onion seeds, used as seasoning.

Karhi: northern Indian dish made from buttermilk and chickpea flour.

Kari: thick sauce, possible origin of *curry*.

Kheema: dish of freshly ground spices cooked in fat then blended with ground meat and canned tomatoes. May be used as a sauce for rice or **Chapatis** or **Dal** plus vegetables, or the mixture may be used to stuff other vegetables.

Kheer or **Khir**: well-cooked milk flavored with cardamom and sugar and thickened with rice or vermicelli, then garnished with toasted nuts and **Vark** and served as dessert.

Khoya: boiled milk cooked until it is in almost semi-solid form.

Kitcherie: a porridge or mixture of cooked rice and lentils or any leftover pulses. Possible origin of British "kedgeree."

Koftas: meatballs of smoothly ground beef or lamb with a tiny stuffing of blended seasonings popped into the center, served with a well-seasoned tomato sauce. **Nargisi Koftas** are much larger versions of the meatballs, only stuffed with hard-boiled eggs, then served cut in half with the sauce.

Korma: thick, rich brown curry dish often with poppy seeds and coconut and prepared with meat that has first been marinated in yogurt.

Kulfi: dessert or treat of frozen boiled-down milk seasoned with cardamom and chopped nuts.

Lassi: popular beverage made with diluted yogurt served with the addition of either salt or sugar.

Masala or **Garam Masala**: general term for a blend of freshly ground spices and herbs to form the basic seasoning of a dish. A masala is always added to fat and well cooked before adding the other ingredients of the dish. It is never sprinkled in before serving.

Masala Dosa: crisp-fried potato-filled pastries redolent with cumin, coriander, red chilies, onion, and black mustard seeds, eaten with chutneys and **Sambar** and sold by vendors as snacks.

Moghul Foods: the variety of rich Persian meat and rice dishes that together with the Hindu vegetarian dishes became the base of what is today called the Delhi cuisine.

Naan: leavened bread baked in bubbly flat ovals or rounds.

Paan: the large heart-shaped Paan leaf is wrapped around special spices to form a small packet that is served at the conclusion of a meal or to departing guests. The box that stores the Paan is usually highly ornamented and is called a **Paandaan**.

Pakoris: batter-fried bite-size chunks of vegetables served as appetizers.

Papad: condiment to garnish rice made from fired or roasted thin sheets of wheat or lentil flour, which puffs when fried.

Papadums or **Papars**: called **Papadums** in the South and **Papars** in the North, these appetizers are made by drying and forming prepared **Dal** into small balls then deep-frying and serving with condiments.

Pilau or **Pilaf** or **Pellaos**: a dish prepared with a base of fluffy cooked rice topped with a sauce of vegetables or meats or fish.

Raitas or **Raytas**: cooling salads of buttermilk or yogurt dressed with chopped fresh fruits or vegetables. Served as a side dish.

Roti: the general East Indian name for bread made from any one or a mixture of many flours and may be prepared by baking, deep-frying, or cooking on a griddle. Some of the more popular varieties of Roti cooking include: **Bahatura**, **Chapatis**, and **Naan**.

Parathas: griddle-cooked breads similar to pancakes.

Sambar: a mixture of vegetables and pulses, especially lentils, and all richly spiced. A popular dish in southern India.

Samosa: snack or appetizer prepared from dough-wrapped filling of diced cooked potatoes, onions, and carrots spiced with garam masala, turmeric, ginger, and fried black mustard seeds.

Tandoori: yogurt-marinated barbecued chicken cooked in the **Tandoor** or clay ovens.

Thandai: cooling summer drink made from pulverized almonds, milk, and cardamom.

Varka: very thick edible silver leaf used to decorate special dishes and desserts.

Zaafraan: saffron. Poorer families substitute turmeric for yellow coloring in dishes, but care must be taken as turmeric in quantity tastes bitter.

CHAPTER 26

INDONESIAN, MALAY, AND SINGAPOREAN

On any map of the world, the sprinkling of islands lying on the equator in the South China Sea, flanked by Australia and Southeast Asia, are easy to over-look. They seem like dots on the vast blue of the South Pacific Ocean, and on many maps their names are so small it is almost impossible to read them. But that is only if you are looking at a map. In reality, the 180 million inhabitants of Indonesia, the 20 million people of Malaysia, and the 3 million citizens of the city-state of Singapore are impossible to over-look.

Migrants, traders, colonizers, and astute leaders created this transformation. And today the three regions boast a fascinating cultural mix of Chinese, Indian, and Malay populations, with others, that are working hard to blend their people, cultures, and traditions into a multicultural and multiracial success story.

INDONESIA
As early as the first century C.E., Indonesian ships were trading off the coast of Africa while merchants from India may have been trading with the Spice

Islands several hundred years earlier. Any country with seaworthy ships struggled to monopolize the trade routes that would control the burgeoning worldwide trade in spices. The fabled Spice Islands fueled world trade with the quality and variety of their local spices used to enhance cuisine, pre-serve foods, and even provide medicines and aphrodisiacs. These pungent and aromatic spices became indispensable to world cooks and diners, and who can even conceive of cakes, cookies, or apple pies without ginger, cinnamon, and cloves? Where would pilafs, curries, and stews be without peppercorns, turmeric, chilies, and cardamom?

By 1000 C.E., the Arab domination of the east-ern world and the spread of Islam replaced the early Indian traders. The Arabs not only purchased spices from the islands, it is believed that they were responsible for introducing coriander, caraway, dill, fennel, and maybe even cumin to the Spice Islands.

In turn, the Spice Islands were to trade with the Portuguese, the Spanish, the Dutch, and the Eng-lish. And as the rest of the world was finding these entic-ingly aromatic addi-tions to their cuisine indispensable, the Dutch East India Company and the enterprising Dutch traders gained dom-

inance in Indonesia and remained until the Japanese invasion of 1942. Incidentally, while the Dutch plied the trade of spices, they brought home something else to jar the bland Dutch cuisine – **rijstafel**. This was the Indonesian rice table of exotic dishes and pungent fiery sauces all served with rice. This novelty for the Dutch palate is still enjoyed today.

By 1949, the Indonesians won independence and gradually since then, trade in spices gave way to international trade in oil, copper, and manufactured goods. Coffee, rubber, and coconuts are still pro-duced for export, while sweet potatoes, rice, and cassava are produced for local consumption.

It is no surprise that Unity in Diversity is the national motto of Indonesia today, for Indonesia boasts more than 250 dialects among more than 300 ethnic groups. Indonesians live scattered over many islands including Sumatra, Kalimantan (Borneo), Java, and Sulawesi. This tropical paradise of lush vegetation and fascinating wildlife co-exist with rum-bling volcanoes and earthquakes while periodic slashing monsoon rains threaten to wash away vil-lages. Yet daily life continues in predominantly Muslim ways while hovering in the air everywhere is the penetrating sweet smell of cloves from Indonesian cigarettes.

MALAYSIA

Malaysia is one country with two parts: Western Malaysia on the southern tip of the Indo-Chinese Peninsula south of Thailand, and Eastern Malaysia –

mostly rain forest, sharing an island with Kalimantan. The South China Sea separates the two regions, and the Indonesian islands lie just southward.

Recently discovered archeological relics in the limestone caves near Sarawak point to Malay civilization at least 50,000 years old. Much later in their history, people from Cambodia and South Vietnam began to migrate southward looking for a better life. A lack of land resources and increasing population pressures in their own lands prompted this migration. It is believed these people arrived in the Malay Peninsula in two large migrations: the first was more than 7,000 years ago and a later large migration arrived in Malaysia between 500 B.C.E. and 100 B.C.E.

By the early 1500s, Malacca (south of Kuala Lumpur) was a thriving trading port until the Portuguese conquered it in 1511. These first colonizers, eager to take advantage of the region's spice production, were followed by a Dutch takeover in 1641, and finally by British domination in 1811. Although colonial times are only a memory now, ruins of the early foreign settlements in and near Malacca can still be seen, and English is widely spoken and understood.

The Malay states of the Malay Peninsula finally gained their independence in 1957, to be followed by Kalimantan and Singapore together with Malay, forming the Federation of Malaysia in 1963 with its capital at Kuala Lumpur.

SINGAPORE

Most accounts describing Singapore today marvel at how a swampy island once dotted with primitive disease-ridden villages, opium dens, rickshaws, and

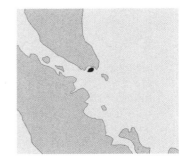

piracy has transformed itself into a prosperous city-state of world-class distinction. Her population of more than three million has also been transformed with intensive education, continuous training, and strict laws of behavior, from labor-intensive service industries to a highly specialized world-class technology and finance center.

FOODS COMMONLY USED

Indonesian, Malay, and Singaporean food is a tantalizing blend of basic Chinese, Indian and Thai foods all caressed with chilies and coconut milk, but with the elegant presentation left to hotels and fancy restaurants. Whatever the food mood, there is probably a restaurant to cater to it. Specialty restaurants abound serving Thai, Chinese, Indian, and even regional Malay, and Indonesian dishes, with larger hotels offering typical western meals including breakfast.

Since Indonesians and Malays are predominantly Muslim, they do not eat pork and prefer to dine in restaurants or purchase snacks from vendors who are *Halal*, that is, who prepare their foods according to Muslim religious ritual and custom.

Aside from the northern Mogul curries, adaptations of Indian foods tend to be those from southern India where seasoning with hot chilies, steaming rice in banana or coconut leaves, and eating nimbly with the fingers of the right hand is common. In southern India as in these countries of Southeast Asia, banana leaves may be used as a *thali* (plate or tray), with foods arranged in mounds.

It is interesting that this region's foods are characterized more by cooking style than by ingredients. There are variations of food preferences in the different regions, but all cooking categories include curries, **sambals**, **sayurs** (soupy stews of meat and vegetables), and grilled, fried, or steamed foods. Coconut, chilies, and a rich

mix of enticing spices flavor most dishes. Only rice is traditionally served in its steaming white perfection, untouched by salt, spice, or garnish. But no meal is complete without it.

Chilies and spices are necessary to stimulate flagging appetites in the intense heat and to help preserve foods that spoil readily. The cuisine is essentially peasant food, eating is just a necessity; originality and creativity appear to be reserved for crafts, arts, and literature.

Singaporean food is so cosmopolitan that there is probably a restaurant, vendor, coffee shop, or snack bar to satisfy the most exotic food whim whether Asian or western.

Remnants of Singapore's colonial past remain in the names of streets and the old colonial buildings. Sir Stamford Raffles (1781-1826) is remembered as the British representative who set up Singapore as the trading post for the British East India Company. In fact, while Raffles successfully negotiated an agreement with the existing rulers to establish the post, it was Colonel William Farquhar who, as Resident (like a governor), attempted to abolish slavery and piracy, and set up tariff-free trading. These measures started Singapore on its thriving course. In 1822, however, Raffles returned to Singapore, and within one year reorganized the city's layout and its government and, with the powerful backing of the British navy, established it firmly as a free port. This was quite an accomplishment, since piracy was still rampant until about 1870.

Modern Singapore is relatively free of corruption and crime in great part because of the People's Action Party of social programming. While some decry the rigid laws regarding the importation of chewing gum, eating or drinking on the public transit systems, littering or even failure to flush a urinal, others support the necessity of enforcing strict rules for the people of this area.

But it can't be too hard to swallow tough cleanliness rules and strictness in education when order and cleanliness, and a tangible and continuing increase in living standards and prosperity for the city-state as a whole are so evident. Modern efficient high-technology industries are replacing support services that used to characterize Singapore's economy. Workers are encouraged to continually upgrade their skills and phase out labor-intensive trades in favor of knowledge and skill-based finance, commerce, and technology. And no one can deny the value of the free and compulsory education system where each child learns English as well as one of the three other official languages: Tamil, Malay, or Mandarin.

Singapore is also known for its diverse population. The efforts made by the government to create unity within this multiracial land – 76 percent Chinese, 15 percent Malay, 6 percent Indian, some Arabic, and the remainder Eurasian – are staggering. Essentially a Chinese city with strong western influences, Singapore still retains distinct ethnic regions such as Little India, Chinatown, the predominantly British Orchard Road, and the mosque-centered Arab Street. Bastions of the British colonial period stand today as distinctive landmarks.

Along with Chinese, Malay, and Indian cultures, there are still descendants of the earliest Chinese immigrants in Singapore who married Malay women. Today they are known as the *peranakans*, which is the Malay name for half-caste. They quickly became wealthy traders who exhibited their wealth in ornately terraced and tile-decorated homes, specially carved and inlaid furniture, and embroidered silk clothing decorated with filigree jewelry. Today, while some of these remain, the remnants of their culture are most evident in their *nonya* cooking: an exotic blending of classic Chinese dishes with Malay's tropical ingredients and spices.

While young Singaporeans enjoy western popular culture in food, clothing, and music, scarcely below the surface there remains a stolid attachment to traditional customs and values – an intricate braiding of Chinese, Indian, and Malay time-honored ways.

DOMESTIC LIFE
In this region of Southeast Asia, rural village people live and cook in ways unchanged from earliest times. This is a contrast to city dwellers who rapidly become accustomed to the modern conveniences and technology available in large cities anywhere.

In rural areas, Southeast Asian foods are prepared in simple outdoor areas. A small stovetop using wood, charcoal, or dried dung provides the fuel. A wok is used for most of the stir-frying, frying, and steaming, and a mortar and pestle for grinding and combining spices and seasonings. Other special utensils are used for grating coconut; boards and cleavers are used for chopping vegetables and herbs. Rice is cooked in a large pot first and set aside to fluff in its own steam while other dishes are prepared.

INDONESIA
As everywhere in the islands, feasts and banquets, whether for religious or special family occasions are frequent. But food is never just a matter of satisfying hunger or expressing hospitality. The Indonesians call their banquets *selamatan*. This is a name suggesting the spirituality they associate with food and its appeal to all the senses. With small portions of food offerings set aside to honor the spirits – for ancient animism is still ever-present – the *selematan* celebrates a time of rejoicing as well as of thanksgiving.

Dutch traders, impressed with Indonesian feasts and the ceremony of the parade of dishes from the kitchen brought to the main table by servants, took this custom back to the Netherlands. The Dutch called it **rijstafel**, meaning "rice table." But for the Indonesians, this term connotes the Indonesian period of colonization, so **rijstafel** is really only seen on menus for tourists.

The food specialties of the various islands reflect their people, their culture and the food traditions gradually evolving over the years.

MALAY

Before 1970, most Malays of the thirteen states of Malaysia lived in traditional villages, but the increasing movement into the cities has now almost evenly divided the Malay population between cities and villages. The recent surge in economic prosperity has increased the general standard of living with the services, infrastructure, and consumer goods rivaling those of any upper-middle-class society. Villages, however, have no electricity, sanitation, or water supply other than wells and rivers. Nonetheless, many traditional family and food customs are integral to everyday life whether the Malays live in a village or a city.

Since more than 99 percent of Malay people are Muslim, Muslim traditions in behavior, foods, and special occasions prevail.

Within the home there is no question of male dominance, but general responsibilities are shared between male and female members.

Outside the home, there is strict separation of the sexes, and a strict code of behavior. Men and women do not shake hands with each other, although men may shake hands with each other. When men and women greet, the woman will likely cover her hands with a cloth first. A particularly touching welcome is shown by one man touching the other man's hands then pressing his own hands to his heart as if to say, "I greet you with my heart." Effusiveness and superlatives decorate everyday speech and are not unusual.

Muslim life centers on the home and family, and while women do not pray or eat together with men, men do share in child-rearing. Families not only care deeply for their members but also extend their support and care to those less fortunate in the community. Most special occasions include extra foods that are given to the poor and needy. Muslims do not consider dogs clean and so prefer birds, cats, and fish as pets.

Other traditions include the removal of shoes before entering a home since shoes may soil the floor used for prayers. In many other Southeast Asian communities as well as in the Malay community, it is considered offensive for anyone to point with the forefinger or the thumb. Men may walk hand in hand in public and openly hug each other, but it is considered impolite to openly display affection between men and women, even when married. However, some of these traditions are not so zealously practiced in the Malay cities.

CHINESE

No matter where they live, Chinese families retain distinctive traits and customs. Similar to Chinese people worldwide, the Chinese living in Southeast Asia may consult an astrologer for auspicious dates and times to do business, to get married, to build a home, or to engage in a business venture. They will likely consult a Feng Shui practitioner for advice on the layout of their home regarding windows, doorways, and even the placement of furniture. A house with a front door facing south is preferred. These precautions are taken not only to ensure luck and success but also to avoid enraging evil spirits or the spirits of the ancestors.

The Chinese have few food taboos. Some, however, remain – for example, the care taken to remove the flesh of a steamed or grilled whole fish so as not to turn it over. This tradition follows the belief that turning over the fish also capsizes a fishing boat in the China Sea. Many other traditions are adhered to with respectful piety, especially during Chinese festivals and the important life passages of birth, weddings, and funerals. Despite the different Chinese ethnic groups and religious persuasions, all share ancestor veneration, obedience to authority, and pursuit of prosperity. Children are especially important for the veneration they will give their own dead parents in the never-ending cycle of respectful ancestor worship.

The Chinese have no specific customs or rules regarding the wearing of shoes in the home. Visitors to the brilliantly colored Chinese temples are expected to be respectful, but are not forbidden from wearing shoes there too. Temple doors are always open so that spirits may freely come and go.

Chinese religion today is a deft blending of Confucianism, Taoism, and Buddhism, as well as strands of animism and ancestor worship. Nor is the astrologer overlooked, for, as mentioned above, it is important to determine auspicious dates for special occasions. Like other aspects of Chinese life, things and ideas are layered on rather than discarded or replaced.

The auspicious time for weddings is considered to be during the fifth and eighth lunar months of the year. The young couples invite their parents to the Chinese tea ceremony and receive gifts of money wrapped in red paper for good luck. The wedding celebration takes place during the serving of many elaborate banquet courses, and tradition ordains that the celebration ends when the food is finished. In a similar way, at home or in restaurants, when the meal is concluded, the evening is ended.

Similarly, tradition reigns during a funeral, when the family may use funeral parlors or may erect a large canopy outside their housing area complete with burning joss sticks and many floral arrangements. For as long as three days, family and friends will visit and partake of food and drink.

INDIAN AND TAMIL

Indians from India and Tamils from Sri Lanka came to Singapore first as merchants and traders and then as laborers, with the Tamils comprising the largest portion. The traditions they practice today, whether Muslim, Hindu, Buddhist, or Christian, are similar wherever they live.

Shoes are always removed on entering homes or temples. Many Hindu homes have their own altars and images or statues where prayers and food offerings are presented in the light of flickering oil or *ghee* lamps. Friday is the day for temple prayers and offerings of fruits blessed by the priest.

Births, weddings, and funerals follow Muslim traditions provided that the people share similar caste and class. Today, marriages may be arranged or people are permitted to choose their partners. Engagement parties take place several months before the wedding when rings are exchanged and an auspicious date is set for the wedding. Traditional wedding day rituals include the planting of a tree to symbolize new life and a gift of new clothes from the groom to the bride symbolizes his new responsibility to care for her.

When there has been a death, *ghee* or oil lamps will be left burning continuously in the house of mourning for sixteen days, since it is believed that the departed one's spirit only leaves after that period.

EURASIAN

Just as the Chinese who married Malay women are called *peranakans*, similarly, the offspring of marriages between European men and Chinese or Malay women are called Eurasians or *serani*. Many have Portuguese or Dutch names and many earlier marriages followed Roman Catholic traditions. The Eurasians are closely related and therefore share a strong communal spirit. Whenever there is a celebration or special occasion, the gatherings are large because of all the relatives who attend. Moreover, they have their own organizations and sports clubs, which further unites this group.

Since there are no food taboos and a general fusion of Southeast Asian and European cuisine combined with tropical fruits and vegetables and Malay spices, the **Nonya** cuisine has great variety in everything from stews and casseroles to curries, sambals, and satays as well as sandwiches and cakes. Alcohol, especially beer, is a European tradition and it requires no special occasion to be enjoyed liberally.

DAIRY PRODUCTS

Milk, cheese, and yogurt are consumed with regularity mostly by the Hindu community. Others may on occasion use canned condensed milk for desserts and enjoy ice cream from vendors. Sweetened condensed milk is also enjoyed in tea and coffee.

FRUITS AND VEGETABLES

Southeast Asians enjoy an immense variety of tropical fruits and vegetables since these are permitted by all religions. From the New World, the Portuguese introduced tomatoes, squashes, corn, chilies, and sweet potatoes, and may have brought peanuts and okra from Africa and eggplant and oranges from the Middle East. The Dutch reputedly introduced cauliflower and broccoli, and likely the Chinese taught them to stir-fry it with their many greens.

A wide range of tropical fruits including mangoes, bananas of many varieties, jackfruit, durian, papayas, and varieties of oranges are all used in season.

Many salads are served that combine a variety of cooked, chopped, or sliced vegetables, and some of these may also include noodles, tofu, or tempeh as well as seafood. **Gado-gado** is a classic salad of mixed cooked vegetables (European and Chinese) garnished with egg slices and either drizzled with spicy hot peanut sauce or the sauce may be served as a side dish.

Sliced vegetables such as cucumbers, tomatoes, onions, and various greens and herbs are often a side dish and served together with the main dishes of the meal. Garlic, okra, turnips, varieties of cabbage, potatoes, baby corn, yams, and other vegetables are eaten in quantity and always purchased fresh from the markets.

MEATS AND ALTERNATES

Many varieties of seafood and fish are the primary sources of protein, with chicken, duck as well as pork, and beef used less often. Many Buddhists are vegetarians and use tofu (soy bean curd) or tempeh (fermented soy bean curd). Muslims eschew pork but enjoy chicken, duck, and beef as well as fish and seafood. The Chinese enjoy pork and chicken, all fish and seafood, and use offal and organ meats as special delicacies.

Fresh fish is usually steamed in banana leaves, deep-fried whole, or marinated in chili paste then grilled. Most meats and poultry are cut into small pieces or thin slices then stewed or curried, usually in coconut milk. The sauces resulting from the cooking are not thickened as in Chinese cookery. Thin slices of chicken and less usually pork or beef are threaded on wooden skewers, marinated then grilled. These **satays** accompany meals or may be enjoyed with spicy peanut dipping sauce whenever a hunger pang or a whiff of the grilling meat makes snacking imperative.

Eggs find many uses in Southeast Asian cuisine. Hard-cooked eggs in wedges or slices are frequent garnishes and chopped fresh vegetables with small amounts of shredded seafood or chicken may be stirred into beaten eggs then fried or steamed as omelets. These would be served as one of several dishes for a meal with rice.

Another Chinese cooking style is to pour some beaten egg into a lightly greased soup ladle, heat it over a flame, sprinkle with filling then fold over the omelet to seal. These small egg pockets are served in soups or together with stir-fried vegetables.

In smaller quantities, tropical nuts are used. The candlenut called **kemiri** tastes sweet and mealy similar to macadamias.

BREADS AND GRAINS
Long-grain white rice and short-grain glutinous rice are used. Rice is enjoyed in the form of fried rice, rice noodles, rice wrappers, and rice cakes. The preference for rice together with steamed, filled dumplings is of Chinese origin.

For Indonesians, rice is more than just the staple food. Meal planning begins with rice, and other foods are added only as the family budget permits. Rice is cooked so that each grain is dry and separate. Mixed with other moist foods, the rice holds together and can be scooped up with the fingers. Although Muslim, Indonesians, honoring their ancient gods, offer a **tumpeng**, a golden cone of rice, symbolizing their sacred mountain, at almost every special feast.

Southeast Asians also enjoy many different breads. Since ovens are scarce, Asian breads are usually of the flat type that can be prepared quickly on heated griddles or fried in oil, or they may be steamed. **Roti** is the generic Indian name for breads; in Malaysia thin lacy pancakes are called **roti jalah** and are quickly cooked from a thin batter then used instead of utensils or fingers to dip into curries.

Chinese-style steamed breads are also popular. These are made from tiny rounds of simple yeast or baking powder dough pressed with a chopstick to form a fan shape and then steamed. They are delicious served quickly after steaming. Some may be filled with minced vegetable, meat, and seasonings.

Mung bean starch or flour is used to make transparent vermicelli and bean starch sheets that are used as wrappers for other foods. Mung starch may also be used to thicken pudding-like desserts to be served with fruit. Another useful starch is made from the cassava root and processed into tapioca flakes, balls, or starch. These are used in desserts and served with fruit.

FATS
Fats are consumed in peanut garnishes, peanut oil, palm oil, and peanut sauces. Coconut milk and coconut cream, both high in fat, grace many dishes, and often curries and other dishes are afloat in shiny pools of oil. Plain rice makes a perfect base for such dishes and fat is not disdained.

SWEETS AND SNACKS
A wonderful variety of very sweet and often sticky desserts are enjoyed after meals or for snacks. These may include fruits, smoothly thick coconut puddings, glistening gelatin desserts molded with fruits, sweetened sticky rice cakes or rice balls, often dusted or rolled in shredded coconut and tinted in bright pastels. Bean flour steamed buns are also a popular sweet.

SEASONINGS
It is impossible to ignore the variety and degrees of "fire" of chilies when discussing Southeast Asian cuisine. Black and green peppercorns were used generously before the Portuguese traders introduced chilies from Mexico. All so-called peppers are really varieties of capsicums and range from Hungarian sweet paprika and sweet banana capsicums to the blast-furnace hot of the green chilies.

Spices are important in this cuisine. Turmeric is a necessary curry ingredient to add the deep yellow color and pungent scent together with garlic, cumin, pepper, and onions. For tang and to bring out flavors, the citrus freshness of tamarind, lemon grass, limes, as well as rice wine and palm vinegar are part of all kitchen staples. Other seasonings include: cinnamon, nutmeg, cloves, mace, dried fish or shrimp paste, chilies, either fresh, dried, or in flakes. Also used is a sweet soy sauce called **ketjap**, which is of Chinese origin.

BEVERAGES
Malaysian water is safe to drink but as in other Southeast Asian countries, cooling fruit juices, local and imported beer, as well as soft drinks, are enjoyed with meals and as refreshment.

Arak is a potent liquor (much like whiskey) distilled from palm tree sap. It is not only enjoyed as a drink but is used as an ingredient in some curries. **Anchor Beer** is the favored drink of Eurasians (i.e. people of mixed European and either Chinese or Malay origin).

Tea and coffee are popular everywhere. Coconut milk is not only prevalent in many cooked dishes, it is also often served salted and with a splash of lime juice, and even a sprinkle of nutmeg or cinnamon as a refreshing drink.

MEALS AND CUSTOMS

Meal patterns are similar all over Southeast Asia. Without an ample serving of rice, no meal is considered to be a meal. A huge mounded platter of turmeric rice with garnishes will often be the centerpiece for festive tables, especially in Indonesia. The day begins and ends with rice as the base and other foods as accompaniments. In Indonesia, the day may begin with rice and fried eggs or fried plantains or other vegetables. Elsewhere, some may enjoy the rice gruel called **congee**, while still others may prefer a bowl of garnished noodles.

During the day, hunger is abated with frequent and readily available snacks of rice cakes, leaf-wrapped mixtures of fish or meat, or just vegetables, all well seasoned and served with chilies and other garnishes and dips. Tea and other beverages are always available from vendors, and sweet snacks such as sugary rice cakes go well with sweetened tea. If families are together for lunch, rice with two or three cooked dishes will be served and beer may be the beverage. The evening meal usually takes place at dusk and is a larger version of lunch with several cooked dishes such as fish, meat, a curry, and vegetable dishes accompanying the rice. Dessert may consist of fruit.

Food vendors line roads, streets, parking lots, and markets. Some vendors specialize in one dish; others provide full meals of curries, sambals, and rice. There is always a nearby cafe, restaurant, or food vendor to refresh one's thirst or satisfy a hunger pang.

Chinese, Indian, and Portuguese foods and customs can be readily identified in Indonesian and Malay meals. This variety of foods not only is part of daily fare for most, but is also available in restaurants and supplied by food vendors everywhere. People usually entertain their visitors at restaurants rather than at home. It is customary for the host to inquire many times through the meal if the guest would like more to drink or eat. Asians will often decline the first time and accept subsequently.

Indonesians and Malays prefer to dine with their fingers. And as in other areas where eating with the fingers is common, only the thumb and fingertips of the right hand may be used. The left hand is used for holding serving spoons or a drinking glass and for passing plates of foods to others. The *kendi* is a water jug passed around the table to wash hands before eating and the use of finger bowls after dining is common. Chopsticks are used whenever Chinese foods are served, and spoons are provided for soups or wet dishes (**sayurs**). Forks are readily available and increasingly used.

Like most Southeast Asians, Malaysians are conservative in both manners and dress. Formality, whether on business or social occasions, is important to them. Malaysians are polite, and restrained in emotions, physical contact, and gestures. Malaysians avoid displays of anger or annoyance, and especially avoid confrontation. In such a situation they may smile to cover embarrassment. Certain hand gestures such as pointing with the index finger or curled thumb or beckoning with the palm of the hand are considered rude. Slapping the fist in the palm of the hand or pounding a table, pointing with the foot or showing the sole of the foot when sitting cross-legged are considered impolite for both men and women.

Polite general conversation with gracious serving of heavily sweetened tea or coffee usually precedes a business meeting, and often precedes the serving of a meal. It is polite to take at least a sip, but refusal is almost insulting.

The meal patterns and manners of most Southeast Asians are also found in Singapore. But here, contact with businesspeople and tourists from all over the world, in addition to the presence of many cultural groups, have added a big-city sophistication to daily life. Table manners and behavior, however, remain distinctly Southeast Asian.

SPECIAL OCCASIONS

INDONESIAN

The majority of Indonesians are Muslim, their beliefs tempered with Hindu and animism. Many Indonesians of Chinese descent embrace Buddhism. While people are free to worship and celebrate freely, Muslim manners, customs, and celebrations predominate.

MALAY

Any multi-ethnic society celebrates many special occasions and Malaysia is no exception. There are even three separate New Year's celebrations: Muslim New Year, Chinese New Year, and the Christian or Roman New Year. In addition, other religious holidays, as well as Independence Day, August 9, are celebrated by most.

The musical ensemble called *gamelan* often accompanies special occasions such as weddings, Thanksgiving meals, and New Year's Day. Their music is rendered with gongs, bamboo flutes, drums, xylophones, and metallophones, and offers various moods from hauntingly sad contemplative music to upbeat dance music. The traditional Malay dances representing ancient tales of princesses and sultans as well as those inducing trances and for celebrating courtship are being revived by Malay choreographers eager to preserve their culture.

Special occasions also include the special rites of passage of the traditional Muslims. *Naik Buaian* is a ceremony for the baby's first cradle or bed, and *Potong Jambul* is the shaving of the young child's head as a cleansing ritual.

Many traditions and superstitions surround pregnancy and birth. Some superstitions include a fear of sewing or of harming any living thing for fear these activities will harm the unborn child. Girls are circumcised in infancy with ceremony and special rituals. Boys are usually circumcised before puberty, between the ages of seven and twelve and their ceremony is followed with a banquet. The circumcision of a boy is an occasion for rituals and feasting, and while this ceremony was traditionally carried out in the home, families increasingly have the circumcision performed in hospital.

Today, Muslim weddings are rarely arranged, and have been considerably simplified in their rituals. Engagement often lasts at least two years and the engagement is celebrated with a large feast and celebration almost like the wedding itself. *Akad nikah*, the wedding ceremony, is always held on a Saturday for the signing of marriage certificates. On the Sunday, the *bersanding*, the wedding reception, is held with a fine array of foods and sweets, music and dancing.

In the villages the biggest event is a wedding, usually attended by all in the village with everyone helping in the preparation and the ceremonies. The scattering of scented leaves and flower petals at both the bride's and the groom's homes is part of the ceremony and precede the feast.

There are a number of rituals connected to funerals. Since Islam requires burial as soon as possible after death, prayers are offered by family and friends to the deceased in their own home. The deceased is wrapped simply in a white cloth preceding the burial. The mourning period lasts for a hundred days.

Rice is not only the basic food of the people, it is also considered important for the spirits, and small piles of freshly cooked rice are left in rounded mounds on paths and on windowsills throughout the year to appease wandering spirits and bring good luck.

SINGAPOREAN
(See also Chinese and Indian)
The list of special occasions in Singapore is long. Almost everyone takes part in these many celebrations and festivals. Public holidays include: January 1, New Year's Day; May 1, Labor Day; and August 9, Independence Day. These are celebrated by everyone with parades, feasting, fireworks, and street parties. Even tourists and visitors join in the festivities if only as onlookers.

CHINESE
The Chinese community celebrates festivals that are similar to those in China. However, Chinese hospitality doesn't await major festivals – the Chinese can always find a reason to gather family and friends and enjoy a banquet. Banquets always include many courses, of which **Peking duck** and accompaniments will be only one. Diners are usually refreshed with at least one or two soup courses in between, while wine flows throughout the meal. Usually the last course is the serving of a whole colorfully decorated, steamed or grilled fish, with the head pointed toward the host.

When major festivals arrive, families go all out to celebrate and of course banquets are as elaborate as budget allows. Such gatherings are always noisy not only because of the guessing games and drinking games that celebrants playfully engage in, but also because it is always a good idea to make lots of noise to scare away any hovering bad spirits.

The two-day Chinese New Year is celebrated with parades of red dragons, dancing in the streets, feasts, parties and gifts for everyone, which includes *hong boa*, small red packets of money for good luck and good fortune in the new year. Lots of noise and the color red everywhere are believed to frighten away bad spirits that may dare to spoil happiness in the new year. So any Chinese word that even sounds like luck, prosperity, or good fortune is eagerly embraced in some way: mandarin oranges – *kam* – sounds similar to *kat*, the word for gold; peaches similar to Chinese word for longevity; carp and other fish similar to the Chinese word for good luck.

Especially for the new year, houses are cleaned and decorated with lanterns and banners, incense is burned, and children receive gifts. Throughout the house, special snacks and sweets await guests and nibblers: litchies, longans, red jujubes, and steamed sweetened rice cakes filled with dates or red bean paste. Of course tea is always served. For the festive meals, many dishes are cooked in or served with red sauces since red is a color of happiness and good fortune. Not to be forgotten at this special time are the family ancestors: special offerings of rice, fruits, and cups of wine as well as burning joss sticks decorate the ancestral altars and family pictures in the home.

A more solemn Chinese occasion is *Qing Ming Jee*, or the Feast of the Tombs. This is the day for family visiting of graves and remembrance of ancestors. The family usually dines privately and quietly. A simple cold meal is served the evening before, and the day itself is spent in quiet remembrance.

For a weekend in June, the Chinese community – and everyone else, Chinese or not – enjoys watching the Dragon Boat Races and munching on rice and minced pork dumplings garnished with mushrooms, and shrimps wrapped in leaves. *Song Yuan Jee* is the Hungry Ghost Festival or Festival of the Lost Souls, which usually falls near the end of summer. It is considered an unlucky period and is reserved for honoring ancestors by leaving out offerings of wine, food, and rice and by burning joss sticks.

Song Chin Jee, the Moon Festival, falls in late autumn, and is a time for delicious moon cakes and rice wine, and the recitation and writing of poetry. Red lanterns are hung everywhere and when families stroll in the evening, the children carry small red lanterns too. Everywhere people are snacking, buying, and giving **moon cakes**. These are sugary sweet, thick buns filled with lotus seeds, fruits, nuts, and spices, especially delicious with rice wine.

INDIAN

The many festivals for gods and special occasions celebrated all over India also find their place on the Indian Singaporean calendar. And again, almost everyone takes part as guests, family, or onlookers. The participants are many, since Indian special occasions include Muslim, Buddhist, Parsee, Sikh, and Hindu festivals as well as many smaller special regional ones. Festivals in Singapore are predominantly Buddhist, Hindu, or Muslim.

Early in the year Indians celebrate the harvest festival of *Thai Poggal*. Homes are cleaned, old clothes and old cooking utensils are burned or discarded. On the morning of the festival, bathing and the pleasure of wearing new clothes starts the day. A special pot of new rice is cooked together with milk, nuts, and raisins and new young shoots of plants are arranged around the edge of the pot. Together with other offerings of vegetables and sugarcane, the food is blessed in the temple. At the family altars too, food offerings are blessed and the doorways of the homes are decorated with a paste of rice flour and water called **kholan**. The day after the festival, cattle are washed and fed boiled rice as the final celebration of the harvest festival.

Hari Raya Puasa, the three-day spring celebration to mark the end of Ramadan, the Muslim month of fasting and prayer, is anticipated as a special time of celebration. *Hari Raya Haji*, the Muslim festival to honor those who made the Mecca pilgrimage, is celebrated about one month later. This holiday also focuses on Ibrahim's willingness to sacrifice his son Isaac, when God substituted a lamb instead. With this in mind, lambs are ritually slaughtered (this is called *Korban*) and prepared for the feasting with portions going to the poor.

November brings the most important Hindu festival – *Divali*, the festival of lights. Some fast for several weeks before the festival, chanting special prayers, carrying food offerings and flowers to their temples. In the home, shimmering ghee lamps burn around images of the gods, and floral decorations are everywhere in the home as guests enjoy a sumptuous buffet of many dishes.

All Buddhists celebrate *Vesak Day*, which honors Buddha's birth and his enlightenment. Meditations, processions, and offerings representing all of man's worldly needs are placed on altars both in homes and temples. The family celebrations are a time for togetherness and reflection.

The rest of the year is dotted liberally with other traditional Chinese, Malay, and Indian festivals drenched in pageantry, tradition, and feasting. Some offer specialty foods such as those proffered for the summer Singapore Food Festival, celebrating Singapore's glorious array of truly international cuisine.

GLOSSARY OF FOODS AND FOOD TERMS

Adjam Panggang: Indonesian barbecued or grilled chicken seasoned with garlic, lime juice, and sweet soy sauce called **Ketjap**. Freshly grated ginger root and **Sambal Oelek** (hot chili sauce) add zip and pungency.

Agar-Agar: a type of gelatin processed from seaweed that is commonly used to gel desserts. Because it is of vegetable origin, it is acceptable to all religions. It has the advantage of being readily available in powdered form, in strands or sticks ready to dissolve in boiling water. It will set firmly without refrigeration, and can be colored and flavored as desired.

Air Batu Campur: also called ABC. The Malay version of the American ice cone. Only this one is a mound of chipped ice drizzled with sweet red syrup or topped with crumbled palm sugar then served with sweet garnishes of red beans, brightly colored cubes of jelly, and sweet corn.

Bayam: also called **Amaranth** or pigweed. It is an edible weed of several varieties. Usually the tender top leaves are plucked and cooked much like spinach. Popular and plentiful all over Southeast Asia.

Bean Curd: also called **Tofu** or **Tempeh**. Popular not only in Asian countries, but also increasingly in western countries as a low-cost and excellent source of protein. Its most important characteristic is its ability to soak up other flavors. Aside from the well-known varieties of soft tofu and pressed tofu (firm) as well as fermented bean curd called **Tempeh**, prepared bean curd is also widely available as dried-frozen. This form can be quickly hydrated and cooked with any foods or sauces for a healthy meal.

Bumbu: a basic spice-paste mixture thinned with coconut milk then used with food as a sauce.

Chee Chong Fun: a dish of steamed stuffed noodles or dumplings with a filling of pork and seafood with seasonings. Of Chinese origin.

Chye Tow Kway: sometimes called carrot cake in English. This is not a dessert, but an omelet of vegetables and eggs, served as part of a meal or as a snack.

Kalio: sauce densely flavored with fresh coriander and coconut.

Katjang: Indonesian spicy peanut sauce that usually is made with freshly ground roasted peanuts, oil, and seasoned with browned onions, garlic, and a liberal firing up of **Sambal Oelek** (hot chili sauce).

Ketjap: a sweet soy sauce.

Krokets: flat cakes, peaked cones or balls of mixtures of vegetables with seafood or meat finished by deep-frying. This dish and the Dutch name for croquettes was introduced by the early Dutch traders.

Laksa: a vegetarian broth based on fish stock with added chilies and gentled with coconut milk. Enjoyed in Malaysia.

Lombok: generic Indonesian and Malaysian name for chilies. Malays also call some varieties **Cili** and **Cili Padi**. Chilies are used fresh as well as dried, powdered or flaked or as a paste. Chilies sliced in thin rounds or long strips are also available pickled. Chili oil is also widely used as a flavoring and can be prepared by simmering oil with chili paste or flakes and some added sugar, salt, and tamarind. When deep brown in color it is cooled and stored for later use.

Nasi Goreng: Indonesian-style fried rice that is liberally doused with **Sambal Oelek** (hot chili sauce), and chopped garlic together with thinly shredded vegetables and cubed shrimp or meats. **Ketjap** (sweet soy sauce) adds color and brings the flavors together. This dish is served as part of the meal with other dishes and with plain rice.

Nasi Lemak: the Malay version of Chinese **Congee**, a rice gruel enjoyed for breakfast. In the Malay version, rice is cooked in coconut milk and garnished with eggs, anchovies, cucumbers, and chopped peanuts.

Nasi Pedang: rice served in the Pedang way in which a central bowl of steaming rice is flanked by dishes of **Rendang**, seafood, vegetables, and grilled fish. In a Pedang-style restaurant, all the dishes are displayed, diners take what they wish and pay only for what they have eaten.

Nonya Cookery: Peranaken or Nonya cookery combines both Chinese and Malay ingredients and seasonings. People learn recipes by watching their mothers and grandmothers choose and prepare foods and judge measurements, each in her own way. Pungency comes from ginger root, lemon grass, shallots, shrimp paste, and generous amounts of garlic and chilies. Essential to Nonya cookery is **Rempeh**, a heady mixture of spices pounded together in a mortar then fried in oil to enhance the flavor.

Palm Sugar or **Jaggery**: called **Gula Jawa** or **Gula Aron** in Indonesia, and **Gula Melaka** in Malaysia. This sugar is made from palm juice and sold in solid cylinders or blocks. For use, the hard sugar is sliced or scraped off. Brown sugar can be used as a substitute.

Pisang Goreng: a dessert of fried bananas.

Poh Pia or **Popiah**: filled pancakes, Singapore style, in which the diners choose their fillings and sauces. Fillings may include seasoned minced pork, chicken, or seafood and an array of fresh greens and herbs, bean sprouts, and crisply fried garlic. Small bowls of dipping sauces are also provided. Diners arrange greens on a wrapper then garnish, and add sprinkles of sauces as they please. The wrappers are rolled up with the ends tucked in so all is sealed, then immediately eaten.

Rempeh: a mixture of seasoning and spices that is basic to Nonya cookery. The chopped garlic is always fried to a golden crispness before Rempah is added, much as various prepared spice mixtures are used in other ethnic cookery. Precise ingredients for Rempeh are always treasured family recipes.

Rendang: a favorite Malay dish with meat or poultry, spices, and coconut milk, enjoyed as part of a meal with other dishes of seafood, fish, and vegetables.

Sambals: small side dishes or condiments fiery with chilies and redolent with fragrant spices and citrus tang.

Satay Babi: Indonesian skewered slices or small cubes of pork marinated with coriander, garlic, lime juice, and ginger. Note that satays never combine meat with vegetables on the skewer.

Sayurs: meat, fish, seafood, or vegetable dishes that are cooked with lots of sauce that can be dipped into with rice balls held in the fingertips.

Sirap Bandang: a refreshing Malay drink prepared from palm sugar and red coloring. Ice cubes chill the beverage and canned condensed milk turns the red to pink. This drink is popular in vendor's stalls.

Soto: a Javanese chicken soup differentiated from chicken soup anywhere else by its addition of rice and bean sprouts.

Tahu or **Takwa**: bean curd. **Tahu** is the Indonesian name for it and **Takwa** is the Malay name for it.

Tepung Hon Kwe: the name used in both Indonesia and Malaysia for mung bean starch or flour.

The Taruk: a popular beverage especially in Indian or Malay restaurants, prepared with hot steeped tea and condensed milk. Just before serving, the mixture is poured rapidly between two mugs then the frothing tea is set before the thirsty diner.

Tumpeng: the sacred mound of rice shaped like a cone and decorated with coconut, slivered and curled chilies, salty fish, vegetables and aromatic herbs. This is prepared with symbolic rite and is in honor of ancient gods, but is intended to be eaten at the end of the ceremony by men only. Women may dine with the same ingredients but from side dishes instead of from the main rice cone. Even the colors of the garnishes have symbolic meaning with the white rice standing for purity, the red chilies for anger, yellow vegetables for greed and so on.

CHAPTER 27

IRANIAN

In 1935, the Shah Mohammed Riza Pahlevi changed the name of his country from Persia to Iran. Changing a name is simple, but shifting an ancient nation into the high gear of modern western civilization is a monumental and complex task.

Beginning with the shedding of women's veils and the doffing of men's traditional fezzes, the Shah's reforms spread widely and thrust deeply into many aspects of Iranian life.

In 1979, with the forced exile of the Shah, and the return from exile in France of Iran's dominant religious leader, Ayatollah Ruhollah Khomeini and his reversal of the Shah's reforms, clashes between religious factions and between the urban middle class and the disenfranchised poor left a bloody trail of thousands killed or arrested. Despite the death of the Ayatollah in 1989, and a more moderate regime, Iran was politically and economically stagnant. Whether the Shah's reforms and modernization will gradually seep back to renew and restore ancient pride and vitality in this lustrous land remains to be seen.

Yet in this harsh dry land, despite illiteracy and poverty, foreign dominations and religious disputes, some things remain constant: the innate artistry of Iran's people and the Iranian philosophy of duality, evident not only in issues of morality but also in balancing sweet and sour, hot and cold, and even light and dark.

Ancient Persian culture abounds with eloquent tales of wit and exquisite paintings. Her cities reflect the genius of sculptor and architect and her peoples participate in crafts of carpet weaving, delicate metalwork, and pottery that have been handed down from generation to generation since prehistoric times. Persian artisans throughout history absorbed the new and subtly blended it with the familiar old ideas, perhaps with some inner vision that their skills would long outlive conqueror and conquered.

Persia, like many other countries, experienced periods of power and times of suffering. It was the Persian, Cyrus the Great, who united the tribes of Medes and Persians and established the Persian Empire about 540 B.C.E. By the time of Darius in the fifth century B.C.E., the mighty Persian Empire dominated the countries from India to Greece and its power was only subdued with the might of Alexander the Great in the early 300s B.C.E. This was the period of great commercial expansion: increased trade, use of coins, building of roads and irrigation tunnels, all of which also included the exchange of ideas. Long ago, Oriental tea and rice had revolutionized Persian cuisine and Persian expansion in turn had spread crafts and arts. With Greek conquests, Hellenistic influences touched everything from the foods on the table (sauces, stuffed vegetables, and methods of food preparation) to architectural design.

A change in religion came with the Arab domination in 640 C.E. Zoroastrianism had been the Persian faith since its founding by the Persian prophet Zoroaster (about 600 B.C.E.). The dualistic faith of Zoroastrianism, teaching that the principles of good and evil struggle for mastery in the universe, was suppressed and replaced by the faith of Islam which appealed to Persians because of its simplicity and emotionalism. Small pockets of Zoroastrian believers are still found in areas of Iran and the Near and Middle East as well as among the Parsees in Bombay, India.

But foreign influences and dominations were not to end with the Arabs. In the next 800 years, Turks and Mongols vied for control of Persia. It was a period that all but wiped out the country's ancient culture and artistry. In the crumbled small kingdoms of the ancient Persian land, only small pockets of learning kept alive arts, science, and literature, while in the homes parents quietly passed on their skills to their children.

The brief Persian resurrections, under Ishmail I in 1499, who established the Persian Islamic sect of Shiism, and later the rule of Shah Abbas I, who restored order and even promoted trade with the British East India Company, were squelched in 1722 by an Afghan army. Later, a tug-of-war between Russia and Great Britain further weakened Persian rulers and increased foreign influence to the point where the despair of the people resulted in the growth of a nationalist movement. This climaxed in 1923 with the election of Riza Kahn Pahlevi as prime minister. The shift to independence, renewal of ancient pride, and vitality had begun.

DOMESTIC LIFE

The traditional walled-in houses and picturesque gardens of Iranian homes reveal a deep respect of old ways. Traditionally, while the men pursued their trades, crafts, or other work, the women spent long hours lovingly preparing fresh seasonings and the intricate ingredients for favorite dishes. Besides meal preparation, their work included the care of children, animals, and often crops.

More recently, despite their traditional *chador* (a long drab cloth draped to cover the body and most of the head and face), women are increasingly educated and working in professions. The week's routine of work is broken by the Muslim day of rest: Friday. On this day, picnics are customary and the men of the family take turns accompanying a chattering group of girls, aunts, mothers, and grandmothers for a country outing. As in most other Middle Eastern countries, men prefer to enjoy the company of other male friends in local *ghavakhane* (a name meaning "coffeehouse" although tea is the favored beverage).

In a land where ancient arts are prized, it is no surprise that the ancient arts of the kitchen are also prized and taught with great pride by mothers to their daughters. In the larger cities, modern conveniences and appliances are increasingly available; but to many Iranians the arts and skills of the kitchen are still best performed in the old way – squatting on rug-covered floors and working on trays, blending seasonings using mortar and pestle, cooking foods with patient care over a small stove.

DAIRY PRODUCTS

Ten percent of Iran's population consists of nomadic tribes who herd goats and sheep. Fresh milk is not practical in a hot climate; goats and sheep can forage for food in dry scraggy areas where cattle could not survive; hence the title of "poor man's cow" bestowed on the goat, the producer of milk that makes excellent cheeses and that is also fermented to produce rich buttery yogurt. Most homemakers prepare their own yogurt simply by adding a little yogurt to fresh milk and allowing it to ferment. Spread on a cloth and allowed to dry in the sun, the yogurt culture can be transported as a dried powder then reconstituted. Yogurt is used as it is or diluted with water and lightly salted to form a refreshing beverage. Because yogurt is mildly acidic, it is also used as a marinade to tenderize meats, and as an ingredient in many dishes.

FOODS COMMONLY USED

The classic Middle Eastern staples of lamb, wheat bread, eggplant, and yogurt are also the staples of Iran. But Iranian cuisine sets itself apart by the cultivation and use of rice for almost every meal. "A loaf of bread, a jug of wine" may have satisfied Omar Khayyam, but the fact that the Iranians themselves pay highest tribute to their poet Firdausi, who wrote the *Shah-nama* – an epic poem to the ruler said to have invented cooking – clearly marks their valued appreciation of gastronomy.

Thus the Iranian diet, along with a base of expertly cooked long-grain white rice, includes seasonal fruits and vegetables, meats and fish, all subtly touched with fragrant spices and herbs and accompanied with liberal servings of some form of yogurt as well as flat wheaten bread. Very little seafood is used and pork is forbidden since Iran is a Muslim land. It should be emphasized that Iranian foods are mildly seasoned, often using saffron or turmeric and the aromatic cinnamon, clove, and cardamom, while orange flower water and rosewater perfume many confections. Sweet hot tea in tiny cups is the anytime beverage, while succulent sweetness keynotes not only the tea but also snacks and treats and even some of the fruit sauces that are part of meat dishes.

As in most Middle Eastern countries, there is great disparity between the diet of the wealthy classes and that of low-income groups both in rural and urban areas. The fine intricacies of the Iranian cuisine and the selection of many dishes for a meal are the privilege of the upper classes alone. Zoroastrian duality is still very much a part of food selection into "hot" and "cold" and eaten in accordance often with body temperaments, such as illness, fatigue, stress, and so on.

For others, cereals supplemented with dairy products, and small amounts of fruits and vegetables in season washed down with huge quantities of sweet tea, form the basic diet. Meats are used rarely. In the wheat-producing areas, rice, the staple of most Iranians, is considered a luxury for the poor, while in the rice-producing areas, the poor enjoy wheat bread as if it were cake.

FRUITS AND VEGETABLES

While the climate of the Middle East is conducive to the growing of fruits, the orchards and vineyards of Iran produce fruits of legendary flavor and size. These are not only enjoyed fresh and ripe as desserts but are also imaginatively combined with meats and form unusual accompaniments to the main dishes. When fresh fruits are not available, a large variety of excellent dried fruits such as dates and figs, dried apricots and peaches are used instead. The list of fruits includes: fresh dates and fresh figs, many citrus fruits, apricots, peaches, sweet and sour cherries, apples, plums, pears, pomegranates, and many varieties of grapes and melons.

While the eggplant is "the potato of Iran," Iranians are fond of fresh green salads dressed with olive oil, lemon juice, salt and pepper, and a little garlic. Vegetables such as pumpkin, spinach, string beans, varieties of squashes, and carrots are commonly used in rice and meat dishes.

Tomatoes, cucumbers, and green onions often accompany a meal. A small sweet variety of cucumber is popularly served as a fruit. The term **dolmeh** is used to describe any vegetable or fruit stuffed with a rice or rice-and-meat mixture: grape leaves, cabbage leaves, spinach, eggplant, peppers, tomatoes, even apples, and quince (**beh**).

To underline both the skill and imagination of Iranian cookery, a few examples of the main ingredients in national specialties would include: duck, pomegranates, and walnuts; lamb, prunes, and cinnamon; spinach, orange, and garlic; and chicken and sliced peaches sauteed in onions and butter, seasoned with cinnamon and lemon juice.

The above are only a few examples of the combinations of meats and vegetables, or meats and fruits plus unusual seasonings that may go into **chelo koresh**, the favorite Iranian dish that is served at least once daily. This dish of crusty baked rice is topped by one of the sauces listed, or one of dozens more, limited only by price and availability of ingredients.

MEATS AND ALTERNATES

Lamb is the favored meat. Young, sweet, and tender, lamb is treasured for its taste and texture and is usually combined with rice to form **chelo koresh**, **tah chin** (layered rice, yogurt, and lamb) or the many **dolmeh** dishes. Next to lamb in importance is kid (young goat), and very occasionally beef and chicken. Many varieties of local fish are eaten, but almost no seafood.

An important source of protein is found in the large quantities of beans, legumes, and nuts Iranians consume almost daily. Chickpeas, dried fava beans, white and red beans, dried yellow and green split peas and lentils are used not only in stews with vegetables and bits of meat but also mixed with rice and even toasted and salted to be enjoyed as appetizers. Nuts in rich profusion, especially pistachios, walnuts, and almonds, are used widely as ingredients or garnishes as well as appetizers or to nibble lightly toasted and salted like the beans.

Iran's beluga caviar, lightly salted sturgeon roe, deserves special mention for it is world famous. Sturgeon and swordfish are served skewered as a specialty dish of the Caspian Sea region, but these fish are also good smoked.

BREADS AND GRAINS

Unpolished long-grain rice or **patna** is an Iranian staple. Many say that the preparation of rice in Iran is unequaled elsewhere in the world. The exact method of cookery – whether or not to pre-soak, and how long to cook – depends on the age of the rice. Who else but Iranians concern themselves with the age of rice? The scores of unusual food combinations are actually based on two simple rice dishes: **chelo**, in which the brown crustiness of the rice is encouraged with the addition of melted butter and egg yolks, then the rice is topped with sauces; or **polo**, similar to pilaf in which the many ingredients are mixed and cooked together with the rice. **Khoresh** is the name given to the many sauces that can top a **chelo** and these are usually only limited by season, not by imagination.

Aside from main dishes, rice may also be heavily sweetened with sugar, syrup, or honey and flecked with almonds and pistachios to prepare a type of **shekar polo**, a very sweet **polo** used for special occasions. Finally, rice will likely be the principal ingredient in many stuffed fruit or vegetable dishes called **dolmeh**.

Second only to rice is the production and use of wheat. There are more than forty types of wheat breads, from very dark to very light, from crisp to limp, and at least one type of flat bread will be a part of every meal. **Nane lavash** is an example of the thin crisp bread with good keeping qualities, while **nane sangak** is a fresh yeast bread, baked on hot stones and eaten while still warm. **Nane barbari** is a flat thick bread sprinkled with cornmeal and sesame seeds and enjoyed warm from the oven.

Some barley is produced but it is used mainly as food for animals and only occasionally for human food when wheat crops are poor.

FATS

Olive oils, clarified butter, and fat from the "fat-tailed sheep" are used in cooking and salads. Butter is clarified mainly to remove the milk solids and enhance its keeping qualities.

SWEETS AND SNACKS

Fresh fruits are the usual dessert, but the insatiable Iranian sweet tooth finds some satisfaction in the many fruit **khoreshes** used in **chelo**, the many cups of hot sweet tea (herbal and regular), candied and dried fruits, and the special occasions when **shekar polo** and pastries like **baklava** are prepared in profusion.

SEASONINGS

One of the distinctions of the Iranian cuisine is the subtlety of the seasonings. The traditional Iranian politeness even extends to limiting garlic in cookery so as not to offend others. Onions and garlic are used only with discretion, but cinnamon, cloves, cardamom, saffron, paprika, fenugreek, marjoram, savory, nutmeg, turmeric, and dill are used with artistry: never overpowering, always gently enhancing the main ingredients.

To balance the natural sweetness of fresh and dried fruits used so often in cookery, the Iranian cook adds judicious amounts of tartness by using one of the following: **verjuice**, the sour juice of unripened grapes; lemon or lime juice; strips of dried limes; dried tangerine peel or tamarind. Powdered **sumac**, with its chili-powder appearance and sour taste, is a seasoning often used for broiled meats. Pomegranate juice and seeds are often used both for color and tartness. Sweetness and tartness: a skillful balance in Iranian cuisine.

BEVERAGES

The national beverage of Iran is sweet clear tea, often sipped through a sugar cube. Sweet tea starts the day, breaks the work hours, may accompany social or business engagements and sometimes meals. Tea called **chai** is always appropriate. But so are the special herbal teas called **tisanes**, used for a variety of medical "cures," steeped from flowers such as roses, violets, jasmine, camomile, and spices such as ginger, saffron, and anise: all fragrant, flavorful, and aromatic.

Next in importance is coffee – more important in some areas than in others. Special rituals surround the preparation and serving of tiny cups of coffee (discussed below) but it is taken with little or no sugar.

Yogurt, diluted with water or sparkling mineral water and lightly salted, is served as a refreshing drink – often with meals – and is called **dugh** or **abdug**.

Although Muslims do not drink wine, they sometimes allow themselves beer (often taken with the addition of salt), cognac, or **Aarak**, a clear potent liquor redolent of anise. Large quantities of carbonated beverages and soft drinks are also enjoyed.

Not to be overlooked are the many refreshing non-alcoholic drinks prepared from fresh fruits called **afshoreh** and from fruit syrups called **sharbat**. Unique syrups include those made from quince, rose petals, rhubarb, lemon, and even from vinegar scented with fresh mint. Fresh fruit drinks can be made from varieties and combinations of orange, berries, cherries, and melons.

MEALS AND CUSTOMS

Consideration of others and refinement of manners are as much a part of the Iranian character as appreciation of and dedication to artistry. Shoes are traditionally removed before entering a room and the main meal of the day is always preceded by ceremonious hand-washing and the serving of tea.

The traditional Iranian dinner is set out in serving dishes set on a large white cloth spread over many beautiful carpets. The diners sit around the cloth on soft cushions. It is customary for the diners to eat all foods with the fingers of their right hand. Special short-handled spoons are used for soups and soft desserts, and sometimes visitors are given forks. However, all food is prepared and served in such a way that knives are never needed or used at the table. A simple meal would traditionally observe all of these customs, a more elaborate meal or banquet would differ only in the number and variety of dishes presented.

Where coffee still takes precedence over tea, there is a special ritual to its preparation and serving, and special implements are used. For the purist, the coffee beans are roasted and crushed immediately before brewing. **Mihma** is the special spoon for roasting the beans, **qashuga** is the name of the long rod to stir the roasting beans, while **hawan** is the special brass mortar used to crush the hot, freshly roasted coffee beans. In fact, in some homes, the early morning pounding of the coffee beans and the baking of crisp breads for breakfast is a pleasant awakening for the family.

The rounded Iranian coffeepots, with their long spouts and narrow necks, seem always ready with a fresh brew, whether the woman of the house is being hospitable or the merchant is doing business. In fact, to refuse the offer of coffee is considered an insult. Traditionally, coffee is offered three times after the guests' arrival and always it must be drunk. This is not a difficult matter as the handleless cups are very tiny and when one excludes the sediment, there is really not too much to drink. As with food, the cup of coffee is always received and drunk with the right hand. The use of the left hand is considered impolite, but the noisy sipping of the beverage, or rather the thick brew, is indicative of pleasure.

Three meals a day are usual and they begin with a light and early breakfast of sweetened tea or coffee and breads. Sometimes the breads are served with local cheeses. Lunch and dinner are usually similar meals based on hearty portions of rice either made as **chelo** or as a **polo** and frequently accompanied with fresh seasonal vegetables, bread and cheese. Iran has a small but fine repertoire of soups but these are not as popular as dishes prepared with rice as a base. In fact, *ash*, the word for soup, is really part of the Persian word *ash-paz* or "cook." This means "the maker of the soup." For most meals, fresh ripe fruits are the usual dessert.

Throughout the day nibbles of crunchy toasted nuts of all kinds, crisp dried seeds, and roasted beans, all lightly salted, are enjoyed everywhere.

Juicy snacks of fresh fruits and the frequent social sipping of tea or coffee allow little opportunity for real hunger. **Ajeel** is a traditional mix of nuts and seeds that have been simmered in lime juice then salted and toasted. The familiar arrangement of selected fresh fruits that graces tables and is sold by vendors is called **miveh**.

SPECIAL OCCASIONS

The largest religious group in the ancient land of Iran is Muslim, with much smaller groups of Christians, Jews, and Zoroastrians.

Friday is the Muslim day of rest and Iranian women relax by enjoying a form of a country picnic, chaperoned by the men of the family. The traditional dish is **kuku** or **kukune**, which is like a large omelet or pancake cooked on top of the stove and prepared from cooked and lightly browned vegetables bound with beaten eggs. It can be enjoyed hot or cold accompanied by breads, cheese, and fruits.

The Iranian New Year (**Norouz**) is joyously celebrated on March 21, the spring solstice. Like so much in Iranian life, the end of the year is seen as symbolic of death and darkness, while the beginning of the new year is seen as rebirth and light.

Several weeks before, houses are cleaned, new clothes are sewn, and sweet baked goods are prepared. A special ceremonial *sofreh* (embroidered white cloth for the new year) is set up ready for the feasting. The eve of the last Wednesday before the new year is called Red Wednesday, a night for bonfires, costumes, even the wearing of painted faces and shrouds, to symbolically chase away bad spirits.

In addition, to help chase away the spirits of darkness, a special *sofreh* is placed on the carpets or table to be laid out with seven symbols of good angels, to symbolize "life, rebirth, health, happiness, prosperity, joy and beauty." Close to the *sofreh*, a mirror is placed to reflect the beautiful symbols, and candles to represent the number of children in the home are lit. With the singing of songs and readings from the Koran, the family ushers in the new year.

Iranian families prepare many special sweet dishes for the new year and always among them are the **shekar polo**, a sweet and syrupy rice dish flecked with almonds and pistachios, and the traditional **baklava**. Shoots of wheat to symbolize the very roots of life adorn the festive table together with a mirror on which eggs are arranged. The first jiggle of the eggs symbolizes the very moment when the legendary bull tosses the whole earth from one horn to the other. There follows a happy time of family visits and gift-giving and many sweets and treats to nibble and munch for thirteen days of festivities when all schools and businesses enjoy a holiday too. Traditional outdoor picnics end the days of New Year's celebrations.

GLOSSARY OF FOODS AND FOOD TERMS

Aarak: a strong colorless liquor (possibly Chinese in origin) made from fermented rice and molasses, taken as an aperitif and sometimes diluted with water. Because it is not made from grape fermentation, for some Muslims it somehow circumvents the prohibition against alcohol, more specifically wine. In Iraq, **Aarak** may be made from dates and flavored with *mastik*; Iran's **Aarak** may be flavored with the addition of anise or fennel.

Abdug or **Dugh**: a refreshing tangy drink of yogurt diluted with plain or mineral water and lightly salted. Often served with meals or as a refreshment by itself.

Abgusht: a thick soup of chickpeas and onions, flavored with lamb or mutton. Accompanied with bread and pounded to a smooth puree, this dish is the staple of workmen.

Abgusht Miveh: a thick soup made with lamb, beets, red beans, and lentils. In the last hour of cooking, a cup of assorted dried fruits is added.

Adviel: spice mixture of fragrant cinnamon, angelica, nutmeg, crushed dried rose petals, and cumin.

Ajeel: a mixture of nuts and seeds simmered in water and lime juice then salted and toasted and eaten as an appetizer or snack.

Ash or **Aash**: general name given to thick soups prepared from several beans and lentils plus vegetables and sometimes meat. Lemon or lime juice is added at the end and the thick soup is served topped with yogurt as a meal. Frequently, many thick Iranian soup-stews are served as a strained clear broth to be followed by the soup ingredients neatly chopped or pounded into a smooth mound, this second course to be eaten with bread and crisp fresh vegetables.

Bademjan: eggplant.

Basmati or **Patna**: unpolished long-grain white rice, the basis of traditional Iranian dishes.

Borani: salad of freshly steamed and drained spinach dressed with a sauce of yogurt, lemon juice, garlic, and crushed walnuts. Toasted sesame seeds and sprigs of fresh mint are the final garnish.

Chai: tea. In Iran, tea is taken clear, strong, and sweet, usually in small cups.

Chelo or **Chilau** or **Chello**: classic Iranian dish of rice (long-grain and unpolished) cooked lightly for eight to ten minutes, then allowed to fluff over low heat. The addition of melted butter and sometimes egg yolks to the last step results in a crispy-brown crust on the bottom of the pot. **Chelo** is served in a mound, topped with the broken crisp crusts and poured over a **Khoresh** (sauce) is poured over to make a main dish. Sometimes a raw egg yolk in its shell and a sprinkling of **Sumac** is added by the diner.

D'Abdugh: popular summer dish of diluted **Mast** (yogurt) mixed with chopped cucumbers and seasoned with powdered rose petals and dried raisins. Served as a chilled soup.

Fesenjan: a whole duck or cut-up duck pieces are lightly browned in butter then set aside while the sauce is made of crushed walnuts, pomegranate juice, or syrup all lightly flavored with onions and cardamom. Served over **Chelo**, this may be considered a **Khoresh**. Chopped walnuts and sections of fresh tangerines are the garnish.

Firni: powdered rice starch used for thickening soups and desserts.

Fustuck: pine nuts.

Geisi Polo: a pilaf of cooked lamb, rice, raisins, and dried apricots.

Gushe Barreh: similar to Italian ravioli. Small noodle dough envelopes filled with finely chopped meat and vegetable mixtures, usually served in soups.

Halva: popular sweet made throughout the Middle East, but varying from place to place. Iranian **Halva** is a pasty mixture of browned butter and flour blended with syrup and takes its color and taste from saffron. It is served as a dessert or eaten on bread.

Harisa: a thick puree resembling a porridge and made of burgul (coarse wheat), mutton, and chickpeas with butter and cinnamon, served hot.

Joojeh: a dish of stuffed roasted chicken. The mildly flavored stuffing is made of cooked rice or burgul (coarse wheat), cooked chickpeas, slivered almonds, and salt and pepper.

Kabab: marinated meat, broiled. Marinade is most often lemon juice with finely grated onion.

Kabuli Polo: a mixture of cooked rice and lamb scented with saffron, allspice, and cardamom, strewn with cooked slivers of almonds, carrots, and white raisins.

Keysava: a rich conserve of dried apricots and nuts. Served as a dessert garnished with yogurt or whipped cream.

Khoresh or **Koresh**: general name given to any one of dozens of exotic combinations of seasoned fruits, meats, nuts, vegetables. Prepared as a thick sauce served over **Chelo**. Ingredients depend on season.

Kufta: of the whole "meatball family" this one is probably the largest. Finely ground meat (lamb or mutton) is blended with ground chickpeas, rice, and seasonings and shaped to form a large ball. Chopped prunes and hard-cooked eggs are tucked into the center and the Kufta is gently simmered in broth. Broth may be served as a soup, while the Kufta is sliced and served separately.

Kuku, **Kukune**, or **Coucou**: classic Iranian picnic dish, delicious whether hot or cold. It is actually a large omelet full of chopped vegetables; potatoes, leeks, onions are the usual ingredients (plus eggs of course).

Mahi Dudi: smoked fish.

Mast: yogurt.

Mastva Khair: a salad of chopped cucumbers with white raisins, mint, onion, salt and pepper and dressed with yogurt.

Miveh: a mix of fruits, usually fresh, sometimes dried.

Nane Lavash: thin crisp wheat bread with good keeping qualities.

Nane Sangak or **Sangak**: fresh yeast bread, baked on hot stones and eaten while still warm.

Paludeh: any crushed or coarsely grated fresh fruit, sprinkled with lemon juice and heaped in a serving dish. Garnished with mint or cinnamon, it makes a quick and refreshing dessert.

Panir: a firm white goat's cheese similar to the Greek **Feta**.

Polo: general name for a layered mixture of fruits, vegetables, meats, and rice. Similar to **Pilaf**.

Rogan: clarified butter.

Sabzi Panir: appetizer platter of dark bread, slices of goat's cheese, walnut halves, and sprigs of coriander served separately and to be assembled according to taste by the diner. May be accompanied with **Aarak**.

Seranjabin: a sweet and sour syrup prepared from sugar, water, vinegar, and mint. Used as a basis for cool summer drinks (as are other fruit syrups) combined with water and sparkling mineral water. Also may be used for dipping Romaine lettuce as a light dessert.

Shekar Polo or **Polou**: classic Iranian sweet rice dish prepared as the highlight of all special occasions. Cooked rice is sweetened with heavy syrup and flavored with saffron. Finely chopped almonds and pistachios complete the dish.

Shirini: cubed pumpkin is cooked in a heavy syrup and served with walnuts, cinnamon, and topped with clotted cream. Traditional Kurdish dessert. (Kurds are Muslims scattered over Iran, Iraq, and southeast Turkey, mainly farmers or herders.)

Shish Kabab: Iranian dish well known in the western world. Cubes of meat marinated in lemon juice, onion, and salt. The meat, usually lamb, is arranged on skewers and broiled.

Sofren: elegantly embroidered cloth spread over rich floor carpets upon which is placed the platters of foods for meals and special occasions. Often a mirror is placed to reflect the beauty of the foods.

Tah Chin: classic Iranian dish of lamb marinated in yogurt both for flavor and tenderizing, then layered and cooked with rice (**Chelo**).

CHAPTER 28

Iraqi. See People of the Fertile Crescent

IRISH

The Irish are one with their land. Warm, sprightly, and whimsical on the outside, the Irish character occasionally surfaces to reveal mercurial ups and downs of temperament firmly rooted in steadfast stubbornness. The land is the same. A moderately moist climate gently washes over the idyllically green land, which is dotted with lakes and encircled with mountains, and which only occasionally breaks to reveal the limestone of the plains or the granite and basalt of the Highlands. Even the softness of the peat bogs belies their vital importance for fuel and power. The Irish people and their island homeland exhibit both tenderness and strength and bear witness also to the contrasts inherent in their history.

After the arrival of St. Patrick in 432 C.E., Christianity spread over the many separate kingdoms of the Emerald Isle and for the next 400 years Catholicism, monasteries, oatmeal, milk, and leeks occupied the souls and filled the stomachs and the working days of the Irish. Aside from those in the religious life most of the population were farmers and shepherds. Then this somewhat peaceful existence was shattered with Viking raids and even the brief establishment of Viking rule. Although seldom openly attributed to the Viking conquest of 832 C.E., could it be possible that the Vikings left an inheritance of mischievous trolls and bottomless imbibing that remains to this day so much a part of the legends and customs of the Irish?

For the next 700 years after the Viking occupation, the Irish had to stave off raids, invasions, and pressures from first, the Normans (who had already established themselves in England) and then the English. Both Queen Mary and Queen Elizabeth in the 1500s and early 1600s gradually supplanted Irish landowners with Scottish and English owners. The Irish (Catholics and Protestants alike) now became tenant farmers on what was their own land. This non-resident ownership of land together with strong grievances in many other areas of Irish life came to a head and erupted in the conflicts of the 1700s.

But a specter more ominous than religion or politics was looming. The wheat, oats, and barley that the Irish grew for their landlords, and the pigs, mutton, and beef pastured on their lands never saw an Irish hearth. Adopted by the Irish peasants as their staple food, potatoes in every possible form became the

basis of every meal. The usually gentle climate became endless days and nights of alternately drizzling and torrential rains and in 1821, the uneducated, mis-governed pauper peasants suffered famine, fever and death from the first failure of the pota-to crops. Increas-ingly, the majority of the Irish population lived on misery and little else. Some, at this point, assured that there would be priests and a goodly supply of potatoes in the New World, set out for life in North America.

Those Irish who decided not to emigrate managed to survive and the next year enjoyed, if nothing else, a profusion of potatoes so plentiful that it is said they were even used as fertilizer. The respite in the form of food for all, however, hardly made up for the almost slave-labor conditions in the cities and the general oppression in the countryside. England and Scotland were glutted with unskilled labor; poverty, disease, and death were commonplace. And the blighted potato crops of 1845 were only the fore-shadowing of the disastrous total crop destruction in 1846. The beleaguered government chose a poli-cy of eviction and forced emigration, a far less costly strategy, they decided, than attempting to support the starving disease-ridden thousands in workhouses.

So it was that almost two million Irish – almost 40 percent of the population – prematurely aged, hag-gard, sick with cholera, typhus, and dysentery, allowed themselves to be herded onto filthy ships to the New World. Many died on board, others soon after landing. Those who managed, by miracle or inner fortitude, to survive were given three-quarters of a pound of bread and the same amount of meat for six days and then they were on their own.

While the Irish back home fought for survival as well as independence from the English, those in the New World applied their inner stubbornness to build-ing roads, homes, and sawmills and clearing land for their own farms. Others became soldiers or political and religious leaders. But always the lilt of Gaelic (Irish language) and laughter could be heard over the clink of glasses wherever the Irish gathered. And as memories of the misery of their lives in Ireland softened with time (although it is said that the Irish have a long memory) they kept alive too the memories of leprechauns, hearth-baked soda bread, St. Patrick's Day and the Blarney stone (whoever kisses it will have a "golden tongue").

What other holiday is celebrated with such a mixture of wistful sadness and uninhibited joy? Who but the Irish could turn their St. Patrick's Day Parade (wherever in the world it is held) into an event felt and celebrated by all ethnic groups? Perhaps it is that March 17, St. Patrick's Day, is more than "the wearin' o' the green," more than parades and drinking and sad lamenting songs; perhaps St. Patrick's Day is celebrated by so many because most of all it portrays a yearning memory of a dear homeland, beloved in spite of suffering. Most peoples of the world can share that.

The struggle for independence from the English culminated in the Foundation of the State in January 21, 1919. Disagreements, treaties, and violence were not to end. The Irish flag, a tricolor of green, white, and orange, was adopted in 1848. It was not until 1948 that the Republic of Ireland finally gained British recognition, but Northern Ireland has remained under British control. The green represented the Gaelic and Norman-Irish while the orange symbolized the William of Orange supporters, mostly English and Scottish. The field of white on the flag, then as now, was meant to symbolize peace between the Irish factions. Sadly, violence still disrupts the Emerald Isle, but hopes for lasting peace have never burned as brightly as in the closing years of the twentieth century.

More than political miracles have been happening. It has been said that the Irish care more about what comes out of their mouths than what goes in. This too is changing. A food revolution of a happy sort is erupting everywhere, and not just in restaurants. The Irish are awakening to the luscious possibilities of their homegrown succulent lamb, creamy Irish cheeses, the freshness of rain-washed vegetables, and the rich bounty of the waters around them. Homegrown Irish ingredients touched more boldly with fresh herbs and seasonings and prepared with loving perfection can now take their place in any cuisine of the world.

DOMESTIC LIFE

The emigrant Irish may dream of potato fields, turf-roofed cottages, and a hearth with bubbling stew, and they could return to Ireland today and see much unchanged. Modern Irish cities, however, are as noisy and crowded as most around the world, but one need not travel far into the countryside to find examples of life as it has traditionally been lived and as it will likely continue for a long time.

Accustomed to a frugal existence and hard work, many rural Irish still find deep contentment in simple daily life. The huge hearth for cooking and heating a cottage, and open shelves to store dishes and groceries are used today much as they were several hundred years ago.

The term "to take pot luck" reputedly originated with the three-legged iron pot that the Irish homemaker hung over her fire to cook potatoes, make a soup or a stew, and even bake breads and cakes. Skill was necessary to bank the coals of the fire just so, and to raise or lower the "bastable oven" as the three-legged pot is sometimes called. A kettle for boiling water, a churn for butter, and a sturdy wooden board for making dough (mostly quick breads) as well as mixing bowls and stirring spoons comprised the important utensils of the Irish country kitchen.

FOODS COMMONLY USED

Conservative Irish cookery in the home has not moved far from the traditional staples known and enjoyed for centuries. The earliest staples were oatmeal, dairy products, and leeks. Oatmeal is still used; dairy products are still favored, although tea and stout are more popular as beverages; leeks still appear in traditional dishes, although they have been widely replaced by onions. The biggest change over the centuries was the replacement of oatmeal with potatoes. Fish was and continues to be the principal source of protein (next to milk) because it is readily available and generally less expensive than meat. To most Irish, "meat" most often means variety meats, sausages or pork products, not by preference, but for economic reasons. So adept are the Irish at putting together a satisfying meal economically, that at least this Irish saying is based more on fact than legend: "When it comes to knocking up a light savory meal you can't beat the Irish." But increasingly the spice shelf and supply of herbs and vegetables are expanding.

City kitchens, like those in most of the rest of Europe, are efficient and compact, and contain as many electrical or gas conveniences as needed. However, the Irish cook, like the Scottish, prefers simple substantial meals with no frills so there is little need for many of the gadgets and "conveniences" found in so many western kitchens. Although this too is changing.

DAIRY PRODUCTS

Milk is used in cooking oatmeal and making soups. Buttermilk is a beverage often taken with a light vegetable meal. Cottage cheese, called "curds," is eaten occasionally and used in **Irish curdcake**, a type of cheesecake made with curds, eggs and flavored with butter and lemon, all baked in a pastry shell. Local Irish cheeses are gaining heightened appreciation.

FRUITS AND VEGETABLES

Apples are the most popular fruit and are used in applecakes, **fruit fools**, **flummery**, and the toffee apples prepared especially for Halloween. Oranges are a special treat, not daily fare. Blends of fruits, such as plums and apples, and berries are made into preserves.

Potatoes are the number-one vegetable; although many others are available, they are not used in quantity. Cabbage, carrots, and onions are used year-round because of their keeping qualities, but purple broccoli, asparagus, chicory (Belgian endive), endive (curly green leaves), leeks, kohlrabi, marrows, mushrooms, peas, and parsnips also are used. **Sloke** is a sea "spinach" which must be cooked four to five hours, and **dulse** (also called **dillisk** or **dillesk**) is a type of reddish brown seaweed often added to soups, fish or vegetable dishes or mashed potatoes (**dulse champ**).

The variety of delicious and satisfying dishes produced from and with potatoes makes their popularity understandable. People near the sea enjoy potatoes freshly boiled in seawater, and boiled potatoes often form at least a part, if not the main part, of a meal. Whether boiled in seawater or saltwater, their appeal is national. **Champ** is a mound of hot mashed potatoes served in a soup plate with a pool of melting fresh butter; each spoonful of potato is dipped in the butter. **Colcannon** is a dish of Scottish origin, using mashed potatoes and other vegetables (usually cabbage or turnip) well cooked and blended with the potato. Leftover cooked potatoes may thicken a soup or stew, or be blended with flour to form a potato dough or bread, or formed into patties to be fried as pancakes called **boxty bread** or **boxty pancakes**. **Cumberland pie** is a hearty dish of two layers of the potato pastry filled with rolled slices of bacon and beaten eggs, all well baked. **Haggerty** is another main dish made with thinly sliced potatoes and onions fried in bacon fat to form a large crisply browned cake. **Dublin coddle**, a traditional Saturday night dish guaranteed to prevent hangovers, is a piping hot casserole (like a thick soup) of bacon and sausages topped with sliced potatoes and onions.

Casseroles, vegetable dishes, pancakes, and soups do not complete the lengthy list of uses for potatoes. Ingenious Irish cooks have developed delicious recipes using potatoes – usually leftover cooked ones – in pastries, cakes, biscuits and breads. A mouth-watering baked pudding is called **potato-apple cake**, layers of sliced apples between a potato "pastry" sweetened with sugar and spiced with ginger, are baked till golden brown and the apples meltingly tender. This is almost a meal, served hot with sweet cream. It wouldn't be unusual to have a three-course meal with potato in some form in each dish!

MEATS AND ALTERNATES

Pork is the country mainstay and a favorite throughout Ireland. But budgets seldom permit roasts, chops, and other expensive cuts. The ingenuity of the Irish cook, however, produces a proliferation of delicious dishes based on **trotters** (pig's feet), **Bath chaps** (cured cheeks and tongues eaten breaded and fried), **brawn** (pig's head cooked in spicy broth then chopped and gelled), **griskins** (odds and ends of pork trimmings pounded flat then breaded and fried), and the wide use of bacon fat to flavor dishes based on cereal or vegetables.

Beef is enjoyed but expensive for frequent use. Mince is the name given to ground beef, brisket is used for simmered **corned beef and cabbage**, while **spiced beef** is a traditional Christmas treat. Chickens are used occasionally, mostly in soups or stewed dishes, and goose is a holiday specialty. Game finds its way to the table less often: quail, grouse, hare, pheasant, snipe, partridge, woodcock, duck, and venison. Local lamb is increasingly enjoyed.

Herring is a regular part of the diet and Irish fish soups are a specialty. **lough negh pollan** (a freshwater herring) and **potted** or **soused herring** make good companions to potatoes. Fish that is baked slowly in a pickling mixture keeps well and may be eaten hot or cold: this is called **potted** or **soused**. Many other fish are readily available: mackerel, trout, cod, haddock, whiting, flatfish, and smoked or fresh eels. **Willicks** or **willocks** are winkles or periwinkles that have been boiled in seawater then eaten out of their shells with a pin, sometimes accompanied with vinegar and salt or lightly dipped in fine oatmeal. **Blocking** and **lythe** are two fish commonly sold dried and filleted. Crab and lobster are available but the large **Dublin prawns**, whose fat tails are sometimes exported as **scampi**, are special favorites, as are freshly shucked oysters.

Eggs are enjoyed with ham, bacon, or sausages, often as a breakfast dish, but more often as a dinner. Eggs are also a frequent ingredient in other dishes. Peas and dried beans are used less frequently. Nuts cannot be considered a protein source as they are infrequently used in baking, and only on special occasions (Halloween) as a treat.

BREADS AND GRAINS

A hot cereal for breakfast in Ireland means oatmeal. Oats and wheat flour (often wholegrain wheat) are used widely in preparing the many breads and biscuits that are a part of most meals and always accompany tea. Frequently, fine oatmeal or coarse wheat flour kneaded into leftover mashed potatoes will form the dough for a stomach-filling bread or even a main-dish piecrust.

FATS

Bacon fat is the most widely used fat for cooking and baking and even as a spread. Butter is used when it can be afforded, most often to lend taste. Increasingly, oil is finding its way to Irish kitchens.

SWEETS AND SNACKS

Traditionally, simple cooked fruit desserts, custards and milk puddings made with **carageen** (a fresh moss used as a thickening agent), and bread puddings are the usual desserts. Cakes are for special occasions only (Christmas and weddings) and most baked goods are not heavily sweetened if they are indeed sweet at all. Honey, treacle (molasses), and white sugar are the usual sweeteners. **Yellowman** is the traditional Irish sweet: a hard candy similar to the brittle in peanut brittle. Sugar is also consumed in tea. The Irish also enjoy homemade jams and jellies eaten with breads and biscuits. Newer Irish cuisine is borrowing gourmet recipes and using fresh Irish fruits and cream to create spectacular delights.

SEASONINGS

The Irish spice shelf is a small one but growing! Salt and pepper together with onions and leeks are the daily seasonings. Caraway seeds are used in breads, cakes, and pancakes, cinnamon and nutmeg and mace enhance rich festive fruitcakes together with nuts, dried fruits, and currants. Butter and bacon fat also add flavor to vegetables and fish. More recently, fresh herbs, more spices and even garlic- and butter-simmered vegetables are being enjoyed and not just by tourists.

BEVERAGES

Tea is the beverage accompanying every meal and most snacks. The Irish have a reputation for their love of alcoholic beverages, stout being the usual, but occasionally whiskey or mixed drinks too. The Irish don't linger over their drinks, the reason perhaps found in one of their many sayings: "Don't sip a cocktail, drink it quickly while it's still smilin' at you!"

Of the milk drinks, buttermilk is enjoyed over whole or skim milk as a drink for refreshment or with meals.

MEALS AND CUSTOMS

From a many centuries' tradition of "having to endure," the Irish have found some consolation in their "pint o' stout," their pot of potatoes, and probably even in the whimsical names lovingly given to the humblest of their dishes. Three meals a day is a fine pattern to follow if you can. But many Irish can make little distinction from one meal to the other so long as it is warm and filling. Tea, potatoes, and **soda bread** (made from flour, buttermilk, leavened with soda, and marked off into floury **farls**) may well serve as breakfast, lunch, and supper with only an occasional fish or two as a supplement. With peace and increasing prosperity, the table is expanding too.

Traditionally, the Irish like to awaken to a steamy cup of tea taken with milk and sugar. For some, breakfast may also include oatmeal, bacon and eggs, soda bread and preserves. Around eleven, most people pause for a "wee bite of pastry" taken again with tea and sometimes with coffee. The main meal often takes place at about one o'clock and may include a hot and hearty soup of fish and vegetables or a casserole. Either dish is accompanied by soda bread, potato bread, or potato pancakes. Irish stout or fresh buttermilk is the likely beverage, and a pudding the likely dessert. Late afternoon tea may include a few small sandwiches and little cakes or even a hot fish dish. The evening supper around eight o'clock is light and often cold, prepared from the leftovers of the noon dinner.

SPECIAL OCCASIONS

Most Irish are of Celtic origin and about 95 percent are of the Roman Catholic faith. The majority of Protestants live in the north. Freedom of worship is guaranteed by the constitution.

A Christian country, Ireland celebrates Christmas

and Easter, but since there is still more than a small belief in the "wee people" and in spirits and fairies, Halloween is also still very much a part of the festival calendar.

Christmas is the most lavish family celebration of the year with many specialty dishes that are also very much a part of holiday tradition in Canada and the United States. The traditional dressed boar's head is sometimes replaced with a potato-stuffed roast goose or turkey, and homemade spiced beef is a frequent holiday delight. Spicy-sweet plum puddings, hot mince pies, and traditional iced rich Christmas cake round out the meal. New Year's is a more important celebration in Scotland than in Ireland, but the Irish do celebrate it with the Scots currant bun and Scottish shortbread.

The austerities of the Lenten season are ushered in with Shrove Tuesday, when pancakes highlight every meal and homemakers happily attempt to win the many pancake-flipping races held locally. Lenten dishes are based on fish, cereal, and vegetables and are really not too different from the rest of the year. Soups like **brotchan** and **brotchan roy** made from an oatmeal-thickened vegetable broth and sometimes garnished with grated cheese as in the meatless **cottage soup**, **champ**, and **colcannon**, and dishes like **mealie greachie** (pan-fried flaked oatmeal served with fried eggs) are all examples of filling and meatless dishes.

Easter is welcomed with the spicy warm fragrance of **hot cross buns**, **simnel cake** (marzipan-topped fruit cake), and **Easter biscuits** made with currants, grated lemon rind, and egg yolks.

Halloween is celebrated with parties and fireworks. Roast goose is part of the traditional menu, topped off with apple cake, toffee apples, and nuts in the shell. Often tiny charms are wrapped in paper and baked in the cake or in dumplings to add to the fun of the evening. A must with the goose dinner is the making of dozens of **boxty pancakes**, gobbled up as fast as they are fried. The large potatoes grated for the pancakes are usually too big to store and no one objects to this method of storage. **Barmbrack** is the fruited yeast bread for Halloween.

There could not be an Irish wedding or christening without a many-tiered darkly rich fruitcake, beautifully iced and decorated. Because it is considered good luck to share this cake with the guests, all are given a small finger of it, often specially wrapped. The top tier of the wedding cake is the smallest one and is often stored away to be used for the christening of the first child. Sometimes the middle tier is saved for a 25th wedding anniversary. If these wedding customs have a familiar ring, now you know their source!

GLOSSARY OF FOODS AND FOOD TERMS

Balnamoon Skink: a traditional special rich chicken broth and vegetables finished by beating in egg yolks.

Barmbrack: one of the few yeast-leavened breads made in Ireland. Increasingly more varieties are being added. This delicious fruited bread is a special treat for Halloween when tiny charms are often tucked inside, bringing luck to the finder.

Bastable: the three-legged iron cookpot still very much in use in Irish country kitchens. It is hung on a hook above the peat fire in the open hearth and is used for soups, stews, potatoes, and even baking. The famed Irish soda bread is made in a covered bastable.

Bath Chaps: the lower half of the pig's cheeks together with the tongue, cured like bacon and sold breaded and fried. They may be eaten hot or cold.

Black Pudding: a thick sausage made from well-seasoned lard and oatmeal with the addition of pig's blood. It is served sliced and fried, often with eggs, as a supper.

Boxty Bread: a flat round bread, marked in floury farls and made from mashed potatoes, flour, and buttermilk, and leavened with soda.

Boxty Pancakes: dough similar to the **Boxty Bread**, only fried in bacon fat instead of baked.

Brawn: a jellied dish of simmered pig's head and sometimes vegetables. The meat is chopped and set to gell in the cooking broth.

Brotchan: an oatmeal-thickened soup.

Brotchan Roy: Brotchan, with the addition of leeks.

Carvies: caraway seeds.

Caveach: boned and fried fillets of fish (usually mackerel) stored in a crock covered with vinegar. This dish is served cold, often with potato salad.

Champ: hot mashed potatoes served with a pool of melted butter. Each spoonful is dipped in the butter. An Irish favorite.

Chicken Broody: oven-roasted chicken, cut up and served with a cheese sauce, potatoes, and mushrooms.

Chocolate Sandwich: a layered cake prepared from mashed potatoes, eggs, flour, and melted chocolate. After baking, the layers are filled with mashed potatoes blended with melted chocolate, butter, and sugar. More filling is spread over the cake before serving.

Coddles or **Dublin Coddle**: traditional Saturday night supper in Dublin said to prevent hangovers. Chunks of bacon and pork sausages are stewed with sliced onions and potatoes, seasoned with salt and pepper and served like a thick soup.

Colcannon: Scottish dish of hot potatoes mashed with another well-cooked vegetable (often cabbage or turnips) and served with melted butter.

Corned Beef and Cabbage: pickled brisket is slowly simmered in water. Near the end of the cooking time, wedges of cabbage are added and cooked till tender. The meat is sliced and served with the cabbage wedges; the broth is reserved to use as a soup base for another meal.

Cottage Soup: a meatless vegetable soup seasoned with salt and pepper and a dab of butter, finished with a roux and sprinkled with grated cheese.

Crubeens: pig's feet.

Cumberland Pie: a two-crusted pie made with a potato and flour pastry filled with rolls of bacon and beaten eggs. Cut in wedges after baking.

Curd Cheese: cottage cheese.

Dublin Coddle: slowly baked stew of ham, sausages, onions and potatoes served with hot soda bread.

Oaten Biscuits: a mixture of lard, oats, flour, and milk (no leavening) that is rolled thinly, cut in rounds then baked. Thin, crisp, and nourishing, these may be eaten with morning tea or for a snack.

Scrooch: chunks of beef brisket, mutton, and vegetables boiled together with a little salt and pepper, served as a soup or a meal.

Singin' Hinnies: hot griddle cakes scented with cinnamon and studded with currants. These are usually prepared after pig-killing – so extra lard is added. Sizzling of the lard accounts for their name.

Skirlie-Mirlie: a mixture of cooked potatoes and turnips whisked with boiling milk and butter until light and fluffy. Served with toast triangles or fried bread.

Skirts and Bodices: pork trimmings and pickled spare ribs cooked with water, salt, pepper, and onions. A traditional Cork dish.

Slainte: the one word meaning "good health" that is heard before the stout or whiskey disappear.

Sloke: also called **Sea Spinach**. Requires four to five hours' cooking, then drained and served with butter and lemon.

Stirabout: what else would you be callin' oatmeal porridge that is made by stirring the water about then adding the oatmeal (fine not flake) in a stream?

Tripe and Onions: English fare adopted by the Irish and served as a Sunday breakfast specialty. Boiled onions and tripe are drained, mixed in a white sauce, and served over toast.

White Puddings: a type of thick sausage made from well-seasoned oatmeal and lard boiled in sausage skins. Usually sliced, then breaded and fried before serving.

Willicks or **Willocks**: another name for winkles or periwinkles. They are boiled in seawater then eaten out of their shells with a pin. Sometimes vinegar and salt are sprinkled over them or they are dunked in fine oatmeal before popping in the mouth.

Yellowman: crisp brittle like the brittle in peanut brittle; sold in broken pieces. An Irish treat made from melting sugar till it browns then pouring quickly into a buttered pan or baking sheet to cool.

CHAPTER 29

ISRAELI AND JEWISH

... and to bring them up out of that land unto a good land and large, unto a land flowing with milk and honey ...
—Exodus III(1)

It is touched with biblical mystique and drenched in history, but on any map of the world you can hardly see it. This small strip of land called Israel is strategically located between three continents: Asia, Africa, and Europe. It has known the conquests of almost every great civilization in ancient history and is revered as the Holy Land by three great religious groups: Judaism, Christianity, and Islam.

In earliest times the land was called Canaan and was divided into many fragmented kingdoms inhabited by various Semitic groups known as Canaanites, Ammonites, Moabites, Amorites, and others, as well as the historically more important Phoenicians, Philistines, and Israelites. The gradual conquest of Canaan by the Israelites took place over a period of several hundred years (around 1200 B.C.E.) when most of the world was between the Bronze and Iron Ages.

It is to the credit of the Israelite monarchy (1000 B.C.E.) that the dissident tribes and kingdoms finally achieved political unity and historic significance. Under King Solomon, the Hebrews made pilgrimages to the Temple in Jerusalem bringing offerings of fine flour, first fruits, and the fattest of their calves to celebrate the three main festivals of the year: Passover or *Pesach*, Pentecost or *Shavuoth*, and Tabernacles or *Succoth*. Jewish dietary laws regarding the eating of clean and unclean flesh were strictly observed and the Sabbath (Saturday, the seventh day of the week) was honored with rest, prayer, and simple food cooked ahead of time. An orderly lifestyle prevailed. Trade and commerce flourished on land and sea with Solomon's merchant fleet of ships and his camel caravans.

But idol worship and the increasingly luxurious lifestyle of the wealthy caused rumblings among the workers and farmers of the Hebrew nation. They were not content with their "fragrant brown loaves and roasted goat meat, their barley, oats, vegetables and olives." Finally, full-scale anarchy broke out and idolatry was widely practiced; the nation was disrupted and fragmented, leaving it vulnerable to the devastating conquest of King Nebuchadnezzar of Babylon.

In 586 B.C.E., he swept through the Kingdom of Judah, destroyed the great Temple of Solomon, and exiled most of the Israelites to Babylon as captives. The few poor farmers remaining had to eke out a living from the destruction left; their exiled compatriots, mindful that Jerusalem and the Temple had been the symbol of their faith, intoned: "If I forget thee O Jerusalem, may my right hand forget its cunning...."

While the Jews agonized over their fate, other parts of the world were awakening to the inspirational words of philosophers. Already Confucius was propounding his ideas and ideals in China; Zoroaster was prophesizing in Persia; soon in India, the great Gautama Buddha would reveal his profound wisdom. But the Jews already had known more than 1,200 years of history recording ideas and ideals, prophecies and revelations.

In fact, the Jews did not fare so badly in Babylon. Most important, they were to set a pattern of Jewish survival for the next 2,500 years and more. Without a Temple, Jews grouped together wherever they could to pursue daily study and worship. Study, worship, and prayer – the direct communion of each person with God – replaced Temple offerings and sacrifices; in many cases, teachers replaced the priestly ruling class. These were the steps that provided the means of survival and created a spiritual and democratic bond within a people that is unparalleled in history.

Many Jews were later allowed to return to Jerusalem and Temple worship was restored. But the Greek Empire was now rising, and the Syrian Seleucids under their king, Antiochus Epiphanes, attempted to Hellenize their conquered territories. The Kingdom of Judah was no exception. Greek ideals and aesthetics, dietary customs, even dress and gymnastics all held much allure to the culture-conscious Jews. The Hellenic conquest threatened to be a spiritual and cultural one as well as a conquest of land.

This threat became the impetus for a small band of Hebrews – zealots who called themselves Maccabeans – to rally the Israelites to the cause of religious freedom. In what was at that time an almost unprecedented form of guerilla warfare, they succeeded in routing the Syrians and restoring a semblance of order to the Temple and a rededication to the symbols, worship, and principles of the God of Israel. It must be noted that this revolt was probably the first example in recorded history of a battle fought solely for religious and spiritual freedom: it was as much an attempt to rally the Israelites together as to stem the tide of Hellenization. From this episode in 165 B.C.E., Jews the world over celebrate the festival of *Chanukah* with lighting of candles and eating of potato pancakes and sweet fritters.

The Romans were the next to bring desolation, suffering, and slavery to the inhabitants of this tiny strip of land. In memory of the second destruction of the Temple in 70 C.E., the ninth day of the Hebrew month of Av is a day of fasting (total abstinence from food and drink for twenty-four hours) and mourning for all Jews. At that time, stripped of their homes and lands, the Jews were shipped to Rome where, as slaves, they built the great structures for the Emperor Titus.

In the fourth century C.E., Jerusalem was rebuilt again, this time with churches and monasteries to celebrate the official religion of the Roman Empire: Christianity. While Hebrew and Aramaic continued to be the languages of the Jews and the lands they inhabited, yet a third language and influence was rising: Arabic, the Arab Empire, and the faith of Islam.

Muhammed founded the religion of Islam in the 600s C.E. and, like the Christian church, modeled the mosque after the synagogue. For a time, there was great affinity between the Arabs and Jews since many customs including prayer, circumcision, dietary laws, and family life all followed Jewish models and precedent. With the Arabic conquest of Palestine in 638 B.C.E., Islamic holy sites were added to the others and the Arab caliphs ruled for almost 500 years.

In the ensuing years, fraught with the desire to set down roots but continually singled out for their "isolationism," Jews were to be found in Italy, France, Germany, Spain, and Portugal. No longer permitted to own land and pursue a life as farmers or shepherds, Jews turned to whatever trades were open to them.

Jewish communities were also found in the British Isles (until the Expulsion Edict of 1290 C.E.). The Jewish entry and subsequent expulsion from the

FOODS COMMONLY USED

There is an incredibly complex blending of food and culinary habits together with variations in *Kashruth* observance, and as yet no clear-cut Israeli cuisine has emerged, but certainly it is "in process." However, there seems to be a preference for the age-old food favorites of the Middle East: legumes, lamb, fresh and saltwater fish, **leben** (a drink made from cultured skim milk), the unsaturated oils of seeds and nuts, olives and grapes as well as the produce of local fields and orchards.

This low-cost, nutritive, and well-balanced diet is not enjoyed by all. For example, many Europeans consider vegetables (with few exceptions) as "mere grass." However, the newly emerging general cuisine shows a strong preference for meat soups with rice or noodles, salads of all kinds, eggplant in many forms, **hamoutzim** (pickled vegetables), lamb on a spit or in kebab form, **houmous**, **tehina**, **felafel**, cottage cheese and **lebenia** in many forms and combinations. Those of Oriental and Sephardi background prefer rice and oil while the Europeans enjoy potatoes and butter, using oil for meat or *pareve* dishes. Canned, quick mixes and frozen foods sell primarily to westerners or are for export; Israelis have no doubt about their strong preference for fresh foods. But as in other parts of the world, the busy pace of daily life makes prepared foods increasingly attractive and even necessary.

In reference to Israeli foods and food customs definite distinctions exist between the three main divisions of Jewish people. These are divisions which distinguish cultural differences only, and not religion, for the people that make up these groups are all Jews. The Jews from Central and Eastern Europe are called Ashkenazi Jews; those from the countries of the northern Mediterranean and those who speak Spanish or Ladino (a mix of Spanish and Hebrew) are called Sephardi Jews; those from the North African and Middle Eastern countries are called Oriental Jews. In common, all use Hebrew as the language of prayer and study, have special local foods for all the Jewish holidays, and use the Torah (the Five Books of Moses or the Pentateuch) as their holy book.

British historical stage represented, in microcosm, the tale of Jewish life in almost every other European land. First came the encouragement to enter and settle because of their known ability as statesmen, lawyers and judges, physicians and merchants. Second came the rumors, allegations, and edicts leading to their victimization, degradation, and persecution. The final step was the command to leave, usually with the penalty of loss of home and possessions.

This repeated saga may have been the reason for the preponderance not only of the educated professionals among the Jews, but also of the continuing emphasis of the individual home as a sanctuary and haven of Judaism.

It was the Inquisition that caused a turn in the movement of Jewish emigration. From steadily westward, now it was back to the only direction left, to the area known as the Levant: Egypt, North Africa, Arabia, Syria, and Palestine. In 1178 C.E., the area was taken over by the Muslim leader Saladin, and Muslims subsequently reigned for 300 years; by 1517, it became part of the Ottoman Empire. The tormented Jews of Europe were offered help by the Ottomans and were welcomed for their linguistic abilities and their business and professional acumen. The Turks were mostly militarily or agriculturally inclined and content to leave matters of trade and business in the hands of the Armenians, Greeks, or Jews.

It was to take yet another 300 years of persecution, pogroms, and the seeds of human rights sewn by both the Russian and the French Revolutions that instigated the first utopian plans in the hearts of Jews to return to Palestine and create a Jewish homeland.

The new city of Jerusalem, begun with the suburb of Yemin Moshe in 1860 as a religious settlement, grew slowly. There and in other areas settlers experimented with vegetables, orchards, and chickens on lands that had been dustblown and neglected for centuries. Ancient lands yielded to the persistent but increasingly familiar coaxing of Jewish farmers. In the 1880s, vineyards financed by Baron Edmund de Rothschild and cultivated from French vineyard cuttings were to start a new industry. The long-forgotten "Turkish province" began to bloom with the toil of these new-style farmers: mostly idealists with intellectual and professional training who had to learn the hard way how to work with their hands.

Set aside too were the languages and even the familiar foods of the lands the settlers had come from. Hebrew was revived as the daily language, agricultural schools were established, and the typical meals were garnered from whatever the land and cattle offered: mostly dairy foods, fruits and vegetables, as well as grains.

The Turkish Empire broke down completely during the First World War, and in 1917 Turkish rule in Palestine was turned over to the British army. While political Zionists pressed leaders to implement the Balfour Declaration of 1917, which viewed "with favor the establishment of a Jewish homeland," the League of Nations also gave recognition to the Jews' right to settle in Palestine.

Now a new European immigration wave joined the early pioneers (chalutzim). Many of them were merchants, artisans, and laborers eager to ply their trades. It was they who gave impetus to the growth of factories, industries, schools, and research institutes. This new wave joined not only the chalutzim but also the Oriental Jews who had long lived in the land and devoted their lives to study and the strict religious and ritualistic observance of Judaism. The population of Palestine was now made up of Arabs as well as Ashkenazi Jews from Russia, Poland, Lithuania, the United States and Canada, and the Oriental communities from Yemen, Arabia, Persia, Syria, Morocco, Turkey, and the Balkans as well as the Sephardi Jews from Spain, Italy, and Portugal.

After the Holocaust and the creation of the Israeli State in 1948, the small state absorbed as many of the homeless, orphaned, and war-weary souls as it could. The new citizens of Israel had come from more than a hundred countries of the world, speaking almost as many languages, and bringing with them (if nothing else, and often it was nothing else) their culture: language, customs, and foods. Thus this tiny "new" nation once again made a historical impact on the same land shown to them by Moses: the little strip of land he called the Promised Land some 3,270 years ago.

DOMESTIC LIFE

The earliest Israelites were mostly farmers and herdsmen living in simple homes with simple furnishings. In hilly, rocky areas they were able to build homes of stone; in the plains they built their homes out of sun-dried mud bricks. The poorest homes in rural areas were put together with thatch and straw, using smoothed clay for the floors. In towns, the more permanent dwellings were often joined at the rooftops and this became the place for strolling and meeting one another after the working time. Rural homes would be furnished with tables, stools, straw mats for sleeping and with vessels of earthenware, clay, and wood in the kitchen. Town homes would use some metal utensils as well as the earthenware ones both for cooking and for storage. (To this day, huge porous earthenware jugs are used to keep water cool.) Small clay dishes filled with olive oil and lit with a flaxen wick would provide light in the evenings.

It is believed that the secret of yeasts for baking was discovered by the Egyptians, but the ancient world had long known the secret of fermentation to produce wines. In the early days of Israel's history, wheat and barley grains were ground in stone millstones then pounded with a mortar and pestle to make fine flours. Kneaded bread doughs were then baked by laying them in hot ashes (a technique still used by modern-day nomadic peoples), or by placing them into rudimentary earthenware ovens heated with charcoal embers.

Oil was pressed from both olives and sesame seeds; cheeses and butter were prepared from the milk of cows and goats; wine was made from fermented grapes. (Later this art fell into disuse in the Middle East because of the Muslim prohibition against wine; Israel today has the only flourishing wine industry in the region.) Onions, leeks, garlic, and cucumber were commonly used, and fruits such as dates, figs, and grapes added variety to the diet. Natural honey was the source of sweetening.

Modern-day Israel, like the many peoples that make up the nation, has many kitchens. It is not enough to consider merely foods that are "Israeli" or that are "Jewish." One must ask the further questions: "What is your country of origin?" and "Do you keep the laws of *Kashruth*?"

A Yemenite Jew following orthodox observance will eat and serve differently than a reform Jew of German origin. Yet, all are Jews – or Israelis. Tastes and origins may vary, but the observance of the Jewish dietary laws (called *Kashruth*) also varies from strict to negligent. And the observance of these laws further affects not only the foods on the table, but the facilities within the kitchen itself.

THE KOSHER KITCHEN

There is no more complex set of food rules in the world than those that govern the "kosher kitchen," and they are observed voluntarily.

It is believed that discipline as well as thankfulness in regard to food has played an important role in Jewish awareness and survival. The laws of *Kashruth* were first described in the Book of Leviticus in the Five Books of Moses, and were later codified and amplified by schools of the learned into what is known as the *Shulchan Aruch* and the *Talmud*. Observance of *Kashruth* varies not only between Jewish households (as it did throughout the Diaspora), it also varies in observance between the cooperative settlements.

In following the interpretation of the rule that states, "Thou shalt not seethe a kid in its mother's milk," strict separation of meat foods and dairy foods is observed, to the point of maintaining separate dishes, cookware, towels, and cutlery. Thus in the observant kosher kitchen, each item required in the preparation and serving of foods (as well as the cleanup) will be stored in duplicate – often in different colors – one set for dairy foods and one for meat foods. This rule carries on to the meal itself, for no dairy foods may be served at the same meal with meat foods.

There is a classification of both foods and dishes that may be considered to be *pareve*: that is, they are inherently kosher and are considered "neutral," neither meat nor dairy. This group covers grains, fruits, vegetables, beverages (except dairy products), and seasonings. As far as dishes and utensils, all glassware is considered to be *pareve* or suited to both meat or dairy use (but at separate meals). Packaged or processed products may be marked *pareve* on the package; often soaps and detergents may be so marked as well.

Yet another duplicate set of dairy and meat dishes and utensils may be found in the *strictly* observant kitchen – stored in a separate cupboard – and these are for use only during the eight days of *Pesach* (Passover), when the prohibition of all leavened foods adds still more restrictions.

Kosher or *Kashruth*, meaning "fit for use," covers all foods used in accordance with the biblical laws. The term *glatt kosher* signifies the observance of the strictest rules.

In effect, the Jewish dietary laws place foods into three categories: those that are inherently kosher or *pareve*; those that require some processing to make them kosher, as in preparation of meats; and those that are not kosher. Foods that are not kosher include pork products, shellfish, any fish without scales or fins, and any meat from animals that do not have split hooves or chew their cud. This prohibition also relates to the ingredients in prepared products; for example, gelatin in dessert products or candies must come from a kosher source. To distinguish prepared products that may or may not be kosher, several international label markings are used – K, U, or COR, for example – which indicate the designation of rabbinical approval.

Depending on degree of Judaic observance then, the kosher kitchen may have to be a large one, and in some cases may mean two separate kitchens (as in many institutions) in order to observe the letter of the laws of *Kashruth*.

DAIRY PRODUCTS
Dairy products are plentiful and of excellent quality in Israel. **Leben** is cultured from skim milk, **lebenia** is prepared from whole milk. Other refreshing cultured milk drinks include **zeevda**, yogurt, and **kefir**.

All these clabbered milk drinks are nutritiously similar but are made from different cultures yielding slightly different flavors and textures. All have proven historically to be good ways of using milk in hot climates.

Cottage cheese is one of Israel's favorite foods, appearing in countless dishes and frequently eaten for breakfast. Filled pastries of many types (and with origins from many countries) use cottage cheese as their basic ingredient: **blintzes**, **knishes**, strudel, tarts and turnovers as well as cheese pies and cheesecakes. Cottage cheese smoothed with sour cream may also be blended with other ingredients to form tasty snack spreads that may be colorful with vegetables, spicy hot, salty with olives or anchovies or sweet with carrots and honey. Other cheeses include mild firm cheeses of the Gouda, Edam or Swiss cheese types as well as cheeses made from sheep's and goat's milk.

FRUITS AND VEGETABLES

Among Israel's principal crops are citrus fruits, olives, figs, corn, and tomatoes. Although citrus fruits and drinks made from fruits head the list of Israeli favorites, varieties of melons, dates, bananas, and grapes are also produced as well as smaller amounts of other fruits. Apples, pears, plums, peaches, apricots, pomegranates, avocadoes, pomelos, mangoes, rhubarb, quinces, pawpaw, strawberries, and persimmons are quickly becoming not only a part of the Israeli diet but an addition to the country's lists of exports. Compotes of stewed mixed dried fruits are Sabbath favorites because they can be slowly simmered, keep well, and smell delicious. Dried fruits used include: prunes, raisins, dates, figs, apricots, apples, and pears.

The most widely used fresh fruits are of the citrus family, especially oranges. Wedges of juicy orange are used in many salads and fresh fruit dessert mixtures. The *tapuach zahav* (golden apple, the name given to the orange) is also made into preserves and marmalade, refreshing drinks and iced sherbets. The peel is shredded for flavoring other dishes, for use in baked goods, and candied as a special treat called **pomerantzen**.

The most symbolic fruit is the **sabra**. Although with sharp prickles on the outside, once peeled this juicy fruit from the cactus-type plant is a joy to eat. Native-born Israelis are called Sabras after this plant because they too, though prickly on the outside, are believed to be soft within.

To many tourists and visitors it must seem that Israelis are vegetarians. Many interesting and nourishing dishes are made from vegetables, which are even a part of the breakfast menu, while sliced tomato served with milk as a beverage is a common morning snack in homes for older citizens. The popularity of vegetables stems from the bountiful growing season and new agricultural techniques which combine to produce as many as three crops in a year. The *kibbutz* (a community agricultural settlement based on collectivist principles) way of serving vegetables (sometimes called a Ben-Gurion salad) is to place whole washed vegetables on the table. Each diner selects and peels his own – peels are placed in a special bowl called a **kolbonick** that is standard on most tables – then dresses the vegetable selection with fresh lemon juice and oil. Since nothing is wasted, the vegetable peels probably enrich the soup pot or compost.

Tomatoes and potatoes are the largest and most enjoyed crop of vegetables. But many others come year-round or in seasonal plenty, including greens of all types, cabbages, cauliflower, cucumbers, peppers, onions, eggplants, and carrots. Potatoes, tomatoes, and onions are popular with all the population. These and other vegetables are often cooked in combination dishes that form hearty soups or stews, sometimes in combination with meats, fish, or legumes. Vegetable consumption, both raw in salads and cooked, is greatly increasing despite the original distaste of the central Europeans.

Other vegetables consumed include asparagus, artichokes, fresh peas, and green beans of many varieties, especially the favorite **pul** or broad bean of antiquity, brussels sprouts, beets, cabbage made into sauerkraut, and carrots sweetened with honey and made into **tzimmes**, leeks, **khubeisa** or **haalamit** (greens), okra or **bamia**, squash or **kusa** or **kishuyim** (plural in Hebrew), marrows, calabash or Israel's pumpkin-like squash, yams and sweet potatoes, turnips and celery.

One has only to think of the blend of cuisines and cultures that comprise Israel's population to understand that it would not be difficult to think Israelis were indeed vegetarians. The range of non-meat dishes includes savory stuffed vegetables of the Mediterranean countries, the dozens of legume soups and stews of the Orientals, the endless potato and cabbage dishes from European Ashkenazim and the new flavors and recipes that are being developed and that combine such tastes as carrot and orange.

MEATS AND ALTERNATES

In Israel it is mostly the "alternates" that are important on the menu. Land is too scarce and too valuable to support large herds of beef cattle. While lamb, mutton, poultry, and fish are more frequent on the menu, beef is much enjoyed when available and within the family budget.

The rules of *Kashruth* demand that only meats from those animals that chew their cud and have a cloven hoof may be eaten. The animal must be slaughtered in the ritual manner by a *shochet* (ritual slaughterer) and *kashered* (made fit, in this case especially in regard to blood removal) by soaking the meat in cold water for a half-hour. Then the flesh must be salted with coarse salt for one hour on a slanted board so that the released blood may drain away. After a final washing, the meat is considered *kashered* and fit for use. Small variations in the *kashering* of meats are based on regional, familial, and cultural customs.

In most lands where Jews make their homes, the hindquarters of animals are part of the dietary prohibition. But in Israel, the hindquarters are used because skilled butchers are able to cut the meat free of the main blood vessels. Thus the meat is called *treibert* and is fit for use. Most modern-day kosher butchers, both in Israel and in other countries, perform the added service of *kashering* meats for their customers.

Those of European background prefer to roast or stew their meats and like to eat meat whenever possible. Oriental families have lived for generations with little meat in their diet and have become accustomed to stretching the meat taste by using small amounts in combination with vegetables or legumes or both in many hearty soup or stew dishes, stuffed vegetables, or rice dishes. Grilled meats or kebabs are also popular.

Again, as with vegetables, the popular listing of meat dishes reads like an international cookbook: **sauerbraten** and **rouladen**; **cholent** (hamim or defina), **stefado**, **puchero**, **beef stroganoff** (the cream sauce is a "mock," creamed with a non-dairy creamer or blended with mayonnaise for a creamy taste and appearance), **Romanian karnatzlach, klops**, (Dutch meat loaf), **kirseh** (Yemenite tripe dishes), **wiener schnitzel, vitello arrot olati** (Italian rolled stuffed veal), **Persian ju-ju** (stuffed lamb), **kibbe, moussaka, dolmas** (**sarmali** or **malfouf**) (stuffed grape leaves), and **kefta** or **keftedes** (round meatballs or hamburger).

Poultry can be prepared in as many languages as well – flavored with orange and honey, prepared as a curry or even prepared with olives and pickled lemons in the Moroccan way, Tunisian chicken with **seleriac** (the Israeli type of root celery), chicken a la king ("cream" sauce made with egg yolks, chicken stock, and flour), chicken pilau, chicken paprikash, and **galantina di pollo** (Italian boned and stuffed chicken). Turkey, goose and duck, even quail and pigeons find a place on the menu. The giblets from all fowl are enjoyed in specialty dishes which make use of the gizzards, necks, hearts, and livers. The large piece of skin from the neck of the fowl is often cut off separately and stuffed then roasted beside the bird; it is called by the Yiddish name **helzel**.

Fish too are used in accordance with the traditional laws of Kashruth. Carp and tuna are the most-used fish and are taken from the Sea of Galilee, the Red Sea, the Mediterranean, and also from what are popularly known as the "gefilte fish ponds" – the artificial ponds created on many of the farms for fish production. Only fish with scales and fins are used in traditional Jewish homes; eliminated are all seafood and shellfish. Fish is a must as part of the Sabbath Eve dinner on Friday night, often eaten in the form of pickled fish, or poached fish balls called **gefilte fish**. But many methods and many different preparations are used to make fish dishes interesting. Besides carp and tuna, herrings in many preparations are great favorites, as well as bream, sole, sardines (fresh), grouper, red snapper, mackerel or drum fish, and **palamida** (little tuna).

While meat, poultry, and fish are enjoyed when available, the real protein staples aside from dairy foods are legumes. Not only are they the ancient standbys of Arab and Bedouin meals, they are used widely in contemporary Middle Eastern cuisine. Their popularity comes from the many ways they can be prepared as well as the fact that they are filling, satisfying, and inexpensive.

Chickpeas, also called **nahit, houmous, bob**, and **hamtza**, are used in many ways. They are even sold by street vendors and nibbled as salted peanuts. **Felafel** is made from ground, seasoned, and cooked chickpeas which are formed into balls and deep-fried. They are served with spicy hot sauces and vegetable shreds often all tucked into the pocket of a **pita**. **Pul** or **Phul**, dried broad beans, are more popular than small white navy beans which are also used. Legumes (also lima beans, lentils of several varieties) may be served as an appetizer by mashing and serving them as a well-seasoned dip. They also may be mashed and added to thicken soups and stews, served as a spiced side dish for meats, or cooked and tossed in with salads. Israelis never eat greens alone as a salad, always as a mixture.

Legumes are also used to make hearty soups, and often a meaty flavor and color is obtained by browning shredded carrots in oil or using onions with their skins on. Finally, legumes are often used together with cereals in combinations like beans and rice, lentils and **burgul**. Soybeans are of great importance too. They are used to feed cattle and poultry, in the production of oils and margarine, and by law all breads must incorporate at least 2 percent soya flour.

Eggs are plentiful and widely used, with most

Israelis consuming at least one egg a day and often two: one at breakfast and another as part of the lunch or supper meal. In homes for the aged and in institutions, many dishes are prepared with eggs so that consumption could be listed as one egg per day. **Chatchouka**, a whole egg poached and served in a hot sauce, and **tetchouka**, the same ingredients but served as an omelet, are North African favorites. **Hamidas**, long-cooked browned eggs, are holiday favorites for Sephardi Jews because eggs symbolize the mystery of life; they also turn brown and flavorful when cooked in the Sabbath bean specialty **cholent**. Hard-cooked, soft or scrambled, made into omelets or souffles, or combined with many other foods, eggs form a staple part of the Israeli diet.

BREADS AND GRAINS
It is easy to tell the origin of a family by watching to see which breads or grains the members favor. Whether prepared in the homes or bought from street vendors or at bakeries, all form an important part of the daily diet. Varieties used include wheat, rye, rice, barley, oats, **burgul** (coarse wheat), **orezon** (fine and coarse wholewheat grits), cornmeal, noodles and pasta, **kasha** (**cousemet** or buckwheat), and **hirshe** (**dochan**, **durra** or millet). Between 50 and 60 percent of the day's calories come from grains.

European light and dark breads and rolls, egg breads, bagels, rolls, **matzohs** (unleavened Passover bread), and **pita** (Arab flat bread, hollow in the middle) are available everywhere. Oriental Jews prefer **burgul** and rice, while many Sephardim use cornmeal (**polenta**). Cereals are used with milk for breakfast, cooked with meat, fish or vegetables, in soups, and often in desserts. For example, rice is often used as a kibbutz breakfast cereal by cooking it with milk and cinnamon, and is eaten with sugar and margarine; hospitals and Sephardim often cook a rice pudding (flavored with egg and fried onions) instead of the bean **cholent** for the Sabbath. **Mouchalabeh** is a popular Middle Eastern dessert of diluted milk thickened with rice flour and aromatic with rosewater and spices then garnished with chopped nuts. **Farina** is used as a thickener in cooking. It is also cooked then spread in a pan to cool and cut in cubes which may then be served as a soup garnish or breaded and fried then served with grated mild cheese or sprinkled with cinnamon sugar. Oatmeal finds its way to the table as a cooked cereal, as **muesli**, in pancakes, cakes, cookies, breads, and in meat mixtures and soups.

International breads include: **anbeissen stuten** (Germany); **keylitch** or **challah** (twisted egg bread); **khubs** and **lakhoach** (Yemen); **pita** (Middle East); **kayek** (Syria); **croissants** (France); **zemel** or **pam-palik** (Russia); **bobke** (Polish); **krentenkranenbrood** (Dutch); and **Chelsea buns** (England).

FATS
Olive oil and sesame seed oil are most used for cooking, baking, and as dressings for salads and pickles. Margarine (that contains no dairy product) is preferred over butter because it is made *pareve* (that is, it can be used both for meat and dairy dishes) and because it is less expensive. Butter is used when possible but not at the same meal with meat dishes.

Techina is the name for sesame seed oil, adding its delicate roasted seed taste to many dishes. It is becoming very popular for any dish with legumes.

SWEETS AND SNACKS
There are many ways to satisfy a sweet tooth in Israel. Chocolate and candy factories produce tempting products, but the Israeli sweet tooth is not a strong one. In fact, many prefer sour or salted nibbles. Salted legumes, salted roasted seeds of all kinds such as melon and squash, pumpkin, sunflower, and treats made of ground and roasted nuts and seeds such as **halvah** are common wares of the street vendors. Fresh fruits and fresh fruit drinks and juices are popular. Candied nuts and many types of dried candied fruits, candied peels, and sweets made with seeds or nuts plus honey are popular too. **Marzipan**, a sweet made from ground almonds, can also be made from cereals such as oatmeal, farina, and semolina. **Turkish delight** or **rahat el halkum**, flavored with rosewater, is a special sweet treat.

SEASONINGS
It would be impossible to describe a group of seasonings as typically Israeli. As yet, there is no one group of tastes that is predominant to the young country. To get a better understanding of the complexity, see "Ethnic Specialties" below.

BEVERAGES
Heading the list of beverages, perhaps even before tea or coffee, is the special orange-flavored citrus syrup made by many Israeli homemakers and kept on hand to be mixed with icy cold soda water for a refreshing beverage. This may be lightly spiced or refreshed with rosewater, even a little wine.

Coffee is the most popular hot beverage, but the number of ways of serving it is staggering. Here again, the cosmopolitan population of Israel demands that each specialty be available. Here one can find **cappuccino**, instant coffee, **cafe au lait**, Turkish coffee, **espresso**. You can also have coffee with sugar (varying amounts in each type), coffee with hot milk, coffee with cold milk, coffee with cream, and coffee with whipped cream. If that does not satisfy, you can also have your coffee warmed with ginger (Yemenite style), with hale or cardamom (Middle Eastern), with chocolate (Italian), or in the basic American style.

Tea is also not a simple matter. Do you want it Russian style with a slice of lemon and a sugar cube? Moroccan style with mint? English style with milk and sugar? Do you want your tea served in a glass or in a cup and saucer?

Israeli wines probably began with Noah, or even before. But in Israel the modern wine-making industry became established in the 1880s thanks to the generosity of Baron Edmund de Rothschild in both finances and cuttings from French vines. Beer is made and used as a beverage as well as in cooking, as are the many types of wines.

ETHNIC SPECIALTIES

Israel is too small a country and as yet too young to have distinct regional specialties but these are emerging. However, because of the interesting mix of Jews from many countries of the world, food specialties not only exist, but many are preserved with great pride and taught to the younger generation. Some are beginning to take a special place in the emergence of an Israeli cuisine. While information and cookbooks abound on the foods of most Mediterranean and European countries – and the Jews from these countries have adapted all of these specialties with suitable changes for the "kosher kitchen" (see above) – the food specialties of the Oriental Jews are most intriguing because little general information is known. Many of these minor groups are listed here; their food specialties can be traced back hundreds of years. Unusual specialties from other groups are also included.

Special ethnic favorites for festivals are listed under "Special Occasions." For further information, consult chapters on other ethnic groups, for Jews have made their homes and adapted the foods of most countries in the world.

AFGHANISTANI JEWS

These Jews do not like soups or the taste of sharp hot peppers. They often prepare meat dishes that include dried fruits cooked together. They enjoy a pilau of rice as a main dish, and favor onions, cinnamon and mild pepper as seasonings. Lamb and chicken are the favorite meats, **leben** the beverage. Some specialty dishes include **tashkebab**, tender lamb slices marinated in **arak** (a potent anise-flavored liquor) with salt and pepper, cinnamon, and turmeric plus sliced onions. This prepared lamb is then placed on skewers alternately with tomatoes and onions and browned quickly on a grill. The cooking is finished in the same marinade.

Most interesting is the Sabbath **cholent**. In order not to break the prohibition against working on the Sabbath (and cooking is work), a double boiler is used to prepare two hot meals. In the bottom pot is placed cut-up chicken and vegetables while in the upper pot fish, oil, and a little water are set together. The double pot is simmered very slowly overnight to form the main meal of meat and vegetables and the evening meal of fish for the Sabbath.

Another special dish is **kondy**. This is a layered casserole with rice, meats, and vegetables prepared with great attention to detail. Slightly cooked rice is mixed with egg and placed in the bottom of a pot to be topped with a layer of braised lamb and vegetables, then a further layer of plain precooked rice. The whole mixture is slowly simmered or baked for one hour.

Other favorites include preserved sweet lemons (layers of sliced lemons and sugar served as a pickle); sugared rhubarb eaten boiled or raw; and tiny squash or pumpkins hollowed out and filled with a stuffing of meat, rice, mixed chopped vegetables, raisins, plums, cinnamon, and turmeric then stewed or baked till tender.

ARABS

Most Arabic families cling closely to traditional food customs. The nomadic Bedouins in the Negev Desert depend largely on their own flocks for dairy products and meats, and their crops for barley and other grains. Dried fruits make up the balance of the diet. Most Arab farming in Israel is still based on the subsistence principle so that food produced is mostly for domestic consumption and perhaps enough extra for trade to buy a few other necessities. Crops are neither scientifically grown nor irrigated although many modern changes are occurring. Arabs have flocks of sheep and goats and cultivate crops of olives, wheat, barley, maize, millet, cucumbers, potatoes, and other vegetables. (See also People of the Fertile Crescent.)

ASHKENAZI JEWS

If not the earliest, the largest migrations of Jews to North America were from Central and Eastern Europe. It is their food preferences that North Americans think of as "Jewish food."

Most sources refer to the Jews from central and Eastern Europe as Ashkenazim, their food preferences as Ashkenazi specialties, and their common language, Yiddish. The Ashkenazi cuisine was based on foods available in the *schtetls* (small Jewish villages) and later became sophisticated to include many of the refined dishes of the Austro-Hungarian Empire. From as early as 900 C.E., Jews have made their home in Poland, Bohemia, Russia, Ukraine, the Southern Slav states of the former Yugoslavia and the Baltic States of Latvia, Riga, and Lithuania.

Ashkenazi food preferences, even among second- and third-generation Ashkenazim in North America, indicate a reluctance to eat a variety of fresh or even cooked vegetables; meats are confined to cuts of beef, veal, and poultry. Favored breads are **challah** (egg bread, especially for the Sabbath and holidays) and many varieties of sour rye, pumpernickel, bagels, and crusty rolls. Their favorite beverages are usually small sips of hard liquor like **Slivovitz, vodka,** or **brandy,** but most often tea. Nor is it surprising that preserves, jams, and cooked fruits (compotes) are served more often than fresh fruits; fresh fruits and vegetables were only available regionally and were often costly. Exceptions were those fruits and vegetables that could be stored, such as apples, pears, cabbages, potatoes, and onions. The wondrously satisfying dishes and meals prepared from simple basic ingredients have become the Ashkenazi classics of **kugels, perogy, blini** – the list is a long one!

BALKAN JEWS

Balkan Jews include Jews from Romania, Bulgaria, Greece, and the former Yugoslavia, most of whom speak Ladino (a mix of Hebrew and Spanish). Definite elements of the great Greek cuisine are apparent in their preferences and specialties. They use yogurt and **avgolemono** sauce, stuffed vegetables, goat cheese, thin sheets of **phyllo** pastry in many dishes, olives and spinach and legumes in many forms.

Eggplant dishes abound, shredded pumpkin is enjoyed cooked, and there are many desserts rich with honey, sugar, syrups, and nuts, finished with whipped cream. Bulgarians make delicious vegetable croquettes, breaded and browned then simmered with lemon juice and sugar. Romanians enjoy a corn-meal pudding (**mamaliga**) baked and served with **lebenia** (similar to yogurt) or fresh cottage cheese and butter (also called **malai**). Sweet red peppers or pimentos are a special pleasure and are called **gamba,** while a marinade of pickled pimentos with vinegar, honey, onions, and spices is called **gamba marinade.**

BUKHARAN JEWS

Bukharan Jews prepare Oriental foods with a special touch, using olives, rice and oil as staples, **pita** as their bread, and **leben** or **lebenia** as their beverage. **Yacini** is a dish of combined pickled meats and boiled chicken served with **pilau** and salads of fresh and cooked vegetables. Bukharan **pilau** consists of rice cooked over a savory bed of meats, carrots, and raisins. **Basch** is another rice dish of cubed meats, parsley, and liver cooked and served with rice.

Hasamoosa is a complex flaky layered pastry leavened with yeast, rolled very thinly, and filled either with a meat filling or a sweet almond mixture. Traditional holiday fare is fried fish dipped into a mixture of garlic, water, parsley, and salt – served in a small dipping bowl at the table with thin crisp pitas and **lebenia.**

CENTRAL ASIAN JEWS

Central Asian Jews represent some of the underdeveloped Israeli communities because they had previously lived in remote areas and in some of the "darkest ghettoes of the Near East." They prepare a dish of stuffed cabbage rolls similar to Russian style but often using lamb as the meat and tomato sauce as the seasoning. **Pastlikas** are small rounds of yeast dough topped with a filling that may be prepared from meats, cheese, spinach or other chopped vegetables, or eggplant well seasoned. A brushing with egg and a sprinkle of sesame seeds precedes oven baking. **Oroto** is the name given to a sliced cucumber salad tossed with olive oil and lemon juice and flavored with both garlic and mint leaves.

COCHIN JEWS OF INDIA

From the west coast of India and now largely "transplanted" to Israel, this small group eats typical Indian fare, but conform to traditional kosher food laws. They use **carcum** (turmeric) instead of the costlier saffron, and many vegetable and fried dishes characterize their menu. (See Indian.)

EGYPTIAN JEWS

Egyptian Jews have brought many typical Egyptian dishes with them to Israel. They often fry fish, then cook it with rice, and meats are seldom eaten alone but always in combination with vegetables or legumes. **Moussaka** (from Greece) is a layered dish of eggplant, rice, and sometimes includes chopped meat. **Bamia** or **okra** is popularly cooked with a tomato sauce. (See Egyptian.)

IRAQI JEWS

The largest emigration of Iraqi Jews to Israel occurred in 1948, adding another element to the Israeli cuisine. This group likes to combine vegetables with meat, fish or rice and enjoys eating a large variety of foods including cheeses and **leben** (which in Iraq was made from buffalo milk). Although they are not fond of soups and usually serve them only when someone is ill, they do make a bean soup that is more a stew than a soup. Oil and **samneh,** the fat from the tail of sheep, is their favorite. **Rubbeh** is the national dish made from **burgul** paste filled with chopped meats and nuts, then fried or cooked. They enjoy a thick paste (similar to Indian dal) made of pureed lentils, cumin, and garlic with a touch of salt and pepper. Curry blends are the favorite seasoning. Others include cinnamon, cardamom, garlic, cloves, cumin, rosemary, orange blossom and rosewater, **carcum** (turmeric), cayenne, and salt and pepper. However, their food cannot be considered highly spiced.

Traditionally, Thursday night supper is cheese, lentils, and rice, for this is a traditional meatless day. Another favorite is a filled fried yeast pastry stuffed with lentil or meat paste. Among the staples are rice, burgul, semolina, chickpeas, beans, and lentils, while **techina** (sesame seed oil) is used on vegetables, meats, and fish.

Vegetables used include eggplant, **bamia**, sweet pumpkin preserves, vegetable marrow stewed and served with **leben** or tomato sauce. Fresh dates are the most popular fruit; **dibs** is a syrup made from fresh dates; unripe dates are preserved with sugar, lemon, cinnamon, and cloves.

Burgul is used as in Lebanon and Syria. Made into **kibbeh, baked kibbeh,** filled and fried, the Iraqi touch is the addition of eggs and the steaming of the **kibbeh** before frying to make the mixture lighter.

Other Iraqi (as well as Lebanese and Syrian) specialties include **mishmish**, dried apricots sold in a firm block or as halved fruit and often cooked with meats; **cousa**, zucchini; **kibbeh chalab**, fried patties of mashed potatoes and rice, onions and ground chicken meat; and **rechem**, a mixture of chopped embryos (unlaid chicken egg yolks), lungs, giblets with seasoned rice used to stuff cleaned intestines, tripe or ovary sacs or vegetable leaves. **Agasi adama** are **camheen truffles**, an underground fungi that look like wrinkled potatoes but are used and eaten like mushrooms. (See Iraqi.)

KURDISTAN JEWS

Kurdistan Jews enjoy drinking **arak** (potent anise-flavored liquor) with **meza** (appetizers) of cooked sliced potatoes, hard eggs, and chopped meat steamed in oil. They eat all the **kibbee (burgul)** dishes, stuffed vegetables, and leaf dishes, and prefer a soup made from leeks and added rice. They enjoy, as a treat, **mamoul**, a slow-baked semolina cake with chopped nuts, cinnamon, and rosewater.

ORIENTAL JEWS: MOROCCAN, TUNISIAN, AND TRIPOLITANIAN

With an especially rich and intriguing cuisine, Oriental Jews bring these specialties to add to Israel's pot. **Tagines, couscous** and special spices and aromas mark this group's exotic cookery. In some areas, a marked Italian influence in the preparation of pasta and pizza dishes is also noted. A **tagine** is a mixed stew of pulses, rice or potatoes and other vegetables and may or may not contain meat or fish. Pickled lemons, a staple of the cuisine, are prepared by layering lemons that have been cut in halves or quarters with red hot peppers and coarse salt, and allowing them to stand for about three weeks. They are evident in jars on the counters of restaurants everywhere in the Middle East.

Couscous is a basic staple prepared in many ways and the time and fuel-saving couscous pot is indispensable. Esthetically pleasing and eminently practical, the two-tiered pot can be used to cook a meal with only one heat source. The bottom of the pot stews meat and vegetable mixtures richly fragrant with spices and herbs while the upper pot, perforated on the bottom and closed with a tight-fitting lid, gently steams the couscous while capturing some of the spicy flavors. To serve, the fluffy pellets of couscous are mounded high in a serving platter then the well-cooked melange of vegetables and meats is spooned over. Traditionally the couscous meal is completed with spicy hot sauces, flat breads for dipping, and an array of herb-scented room-temperature salads of lightly cooked or pickled vegetables. (See also Moroccan.)

The Italian influence in Tripoli shows itself in the prolific use of garlic, tomatoes, and tomato sauce. Desserts are not customary: fresh fruits, toasted seeds, and nuts are the usual finale to a meal.

Schiksuka is a vegetable melange casserole finished by pouring over beaten eggs then serving when the eggs are set. **Crousha** is another vegetable dish made by frying leeks and onions in oil then adding a little water and fresh green peas and simmering till tender. **Moussaka** is also popular in Tunisia and Tripoli, as is **arrosto**, a stew of browned beef or lamb with vegetables added and then served with rice or couscous.

Moroccan Jews never combine onions and garlic in the same dish; they prefer saffron to season and color their rice, while the poor settle for turmeric. Favorite seasonings include cinnamon, cloves, marjoram, allspice, thyme, and sharp red hot peppers. To wash it all down they enjoy green tea steeped with mint – a beverage as popular as coffee. **Hout crafs** is a Moroccan dish of poached fish balls served with the broth in which a whole head of celery plus leaves have been simmered, giving it a fresh taste. **Phul** or **fool** is a dish of fried or deep-fried broad beans that are then simmered to tenderness. Popular too are many meat and fruit combinations – exotic by western standards. Eggplant, leeks, onions, and squash are widely used, while dates, pomegranates, and sesame seeds are probably the most popular fruits and seeds.

A favorite Moroccan dish after the Yom Kippur fast is a **tagine** of chickens, pickled lemons, and olives, served with couscous.

PERSIAN (IRANIAN) JEWS

For Persian Jews, rice with meat forms the main dish for special occasions, while rice with legumes provides the everyday fare. Many pickles are used and they are made with undiluted vinegar, turmeric, cumin, and cinnamon bark. Between meal courses, this group enjoys drinking strong alcoholic beverages or strong and very sweet tea flavored with **hail** (cardamom). **Joindee** is a typical dish of pounded meats, legumes, and vegetables formed into tiny balls and cooked in soup, stews, or in vegetable or legume casseroles. A **moussaka** dish is layered sliced potatoes with a filling of ground meat, eggs, and spinach all topped with beaten eggs. (See also Iranian.)

SEPHARDI JEWS

Sephardi Jews have made their home in Palestine for centuries. They are for the most part the descendants of the large Jewish communities living in various areas around the Mediterranean after their forcible expulsion from Spain in 1492 (and some from Portugal at a later date). They settled not only in Palestine, but also in Italy, the Balkans, Egypt, and Greece. They speak Ladino (a mix of Hebrew and Spanish), while others speak Arabic or the language of their native land. The Jewish cuisine of these areas is of course largely a reflection of the general cuisine, but also features many Jewish specialties.

Among the many typical foods of this group are the following specialties: **berekes** or **pastilikes** are meat-, cheese- or spinach-filled baked goods made with thin flaky phyllo pastry; **kadros** are meat-stuffed artichoke hearts fried lightly to brown, then simmered in lemon water and served with meat sauce; fried fish is also touched with lemon and frequently topped with crunchy pine nuts; **haminadas** are eggs that have been hard-boiled in water containing onion skins to help turn the shells and egg whites brown; sharp pickles are an important part of the cuisine and are made from almost any vegetables including turnips, peppers, cabbage, cucumbers, and of course the ubiquitous pickled lemons, all with the indispensable ingredients of sharp vinegar and tiny hot peppers; **machshee**, a high point of Sephardi cookery (and an Israeli favorite), are carefully stuffed vegetables flour-dipped then fried in oil and arranged in a baking pan with lemon water and sometimes tomato sauce (*machshee* is an Arabic word representing a dish that has been loved in the Mediterranean area for centuries). Garlic and lemon suffuses almost any dish except a sweet dessert; and when it comes to desserts, many pastries and cookies are honey-drenched, sprinkled with sesame seeds, and nibbled to the accompaniment of Turkish coffee.

Sephardi fish dishes also bring the lemon-garlic aroma and taste to many versions of baked, stewed, and fried fish dishes. Rice is frequently a part of many dishes, or may be cooked and served separately. **Katcheval** is a mild cheese (similar to Italian Cacciocavelli) used grated or sliced and breaded, then fried or grilled as a light main dish. Still another dish is **chenagee**, consisting of boiled chicken boned and cut up, then baked in an egg custard with walnuts and served either hot or cold.

Served with mint tea or Turkish coffee, small cookies made with a rich dough and sesame seeds, then drenched in a sweet syrup are frequent favorites. So too are date-filled cookies or rolls (**ajvah**) and rich cookies called **oogiot sumsum** made from toasted ground sesame seeds.

SOUTH AFRICAN JEWS

Many Jews from South Africa are of Lithuanian origin. They like fried fish covered with a marinade (like **escabeche**), and a flaked fish pie that consists of layers of flaked fish with crumbs and an egg-milk custard poured over and then baked. This baked fish pie is served with a sauce of sour cream mixed with anchovy paste and chives. Other South African Jews bring dishes from their country of origin blended with dishes they have enjoyed in South Africa. (See South African section of African.)

YEMENITE JEWS

Coming from the southern tip of Saudi Arabia, an area called Yemen, these were the Jews who were airlifted to Israel. Their transport to Israel on planes seemed to fulfill the ancient prophecy that they would return to their land "on the wings of an eagle." They make up a very religious group of Jews who have always spoken Hebrew but have lived in a community unaccustomed to modern civilization. They have distinct tastes and definite preferences. For example, except for the Yemenites from Aden who eat a cooked clabbered milk called **zhum**, they do not eat cheese or drink milk in any form. They use most foods in their natural, unprocessed state, prefer meats, and use all parts of the animals. Their staple foods are meats, legumes, raw whole vegetables, and dried roasted nuts and seeds. Lemon and salt are used for pickling but not vinegar.

Hilbe is a watery paste made from soaked **fenugreek** seeds, ground and seasoned with **zhug**, which is a fiery combination of garlic, cumin, coriander, and dried hot spicy red or green peppers. **Hilbe** with **zhug** is an ever-present staple used in soups, on breads, meats and vegetables – as indispensable on the Yemenite table as salt and pepper is on the Canadian. All leafy greens are used, but garlic, sharp hot peppers, cumin, coriander, and cardamom are the staple seasonings. **Semneh** is clarified butter containing garlic and sharp spices; other fats used are oils made from olives and seeds. **Zhum** is the flour-thickened **leben** made with garlic, salt, pepper, and **semneh**. This is served with **zhug** and mint.

Many hearty soups are prepared: **ftut**, a fat meat and vegetable soup, to which torn pita is added in the last five minutes, is served with **hilbe** and **zhug**. Stews and soups are made almost daily for at least one meal and always contain meats and vegetables and often legumes. Tripe, lungs, and brains are used in many dishes, and **kebabs** of grilled meats are also popular. Marinated **kebans** of meat are called **shishlick** and are alternated on skewers with tomatoes and onions. All meat dishes, whether soups, meat stews, or grilled meats, are well seasoned.

Yemenite beverages display the same love of spicy tastes. Tea is prepared by boiling tea leaves with cinnamon or mint; coffee is made with ginger or cardamom; hot lemonade is served as a beverage "good for the ears" and prepared with onions, ginger and honey. But **arak** is the national drink and **kat** refers to the leaves of a narcotic shrub that the Yemenites like either to chew or brew into a tea.

Sabbath is special to the Yemenites as it is to all pious Jews. The morning meal is hot spicy tea served with **kubaneh**, fragrant warm brown bread made with flour, yeast, water, and **semneh**. It is allowed to rise and then is placed in a tightly sealed, greased pan and baked very slowly overnight. For Sabbath afternoon a soft yeast dough will be baked into pancakes and eaten with **hilbe**; these are called **lechuch**. Other types of breads include **hubs** or **salouf**, flat rounds of yeast dough baked on the sides of a preheated earth oven called a **taboon**.

MEALS AND CUSTOMS

The emerging Israeli food pattern is one that makes imaginative use of plentiful local food products and adapts to the lifestyle of the different peoples and areas of the country. Already well known and often emulated in western brunches is what is referred to as the "Israeli breakfast." This was started in the communal dining rooms of the farming settlements (*kibbutzim*). It includes a wide variety of fresh local vegetables, some served as "Ben-Gurion salad" (an array of whole fresh vegetables) and others made into various combinations of chopped and shredded vegetables mixed with different light dressings and including herring, fish, cheese, olives, and various cooked legumes. Eggs cooked in several ways, hot cooked cereals (oatmeal, cooked rice with cinnamon), and a variety of cheeses – cream cheese, cottage cheese, **Al Kerish**, **Katoush**, **Brindza**, **Safad** – breads, butter, fruit preserves, and honey provide a hearty and satisfying meal to start the day. Coffee, tea, or **leben** is the morning beverage.

The midday dinner usually begins with an appetizer made of beans or vegetables – **houmous techina** or **chopped eggplant** – followed by a hot meaty soup or a vegetarian soup. Israelis are great soup lovers and soup is frequently the most important part of the menu, notwithstanding the strong individual ethnic preferences. For example, many peoples of the Middle East do not care for soups since most of their main dishes are juicy stews; those of Polish or Russian origin prefer meat-based soups but enjoy a meatless borscht; Yemenites may forgo any course except the soup to which they always add bread and **hilbe**; Oriental Jews do not care for vegetable soups but prefer soups of legumes – and so it goes. One can only imagine the headaches of menu planning in any large institution!

In general, jellied soups and those based on fish are not popular, but the central European cold soups of fruit are well liked. These include tangy soups made with dried fruits as well. After the all-important soup comes the main dish of stewed meat or fish accompanied with either rice or potatoes and pickles. The dinner will be completed with fresh or stewed fruit or a simple pudding.

The evening supper is usually served between seven and eight o'clock and is a light meal of an egg or cheese dish accompanied with a mixed vegetable salad, bread, margarine, honey, and hot tea or coffee.

Tea breaks are usually taken in mid-morning about ten and again in the late afternoon at about five. "Tea" may actually include tea, coffee, milk, or a fruit drink served with simple sandwiches or cakes, or may even be a snack of fresh fruit. In the cities, people take frequent snacks of hot or cold beverages and the many nibbles offered by vendors: pita, **felafel**, pizza, salted and toasted nuts, seeds of every kind, and fruits.

Hospitality and sharing is a way of life for the Israeli. Most especially is it considered a *mitzvah* (divine commandment, and thus a righteous deed) to extend hospitality to the stranger. Every effort is made to see that no stranger is left without a home or family to share a festive meal of the Sabbath or any other holiday. This hospitality is also extended to the stranger visiting a synagogue, who is often given special honors during the services simply because he or she is a visitor.

Israeli eating customs are influenced by daily lifestyle, by the tradition of hospitality, and also by the distinct customs that each ethnic group has brought from other lands.

SPECIAL OCCASIONS

The recurring festivals celebrated by Jews the world over are based on a lunar calendar. But other special occasions dot the months of the year and these include the *bris* or *bris milah* (circumcision ceremony of the male baby at eight days), the *bar* or *bat mitzvah* (the coming-of-age ceremony usually at thirteen years), and of course weddings and mourning. All special occasions, whether happy or sad, traditional or personal, are based on biblical traditions thousands of years old, and are undeniably touched by the customs and rituals emerging from the communities where Jews have made their homes.

Israel's population is not only Jewish. Of the non-Jews, many are Muslims and a small minority are Christians. The smallest group of all are the Druses. Religion and government are separate, but the Jewish holidays are celebrated nationwide.

The seventh day of each week is a special occasion – *Shabbat*, the day of rest. Like all Jewish holidays, the *Shabbat* begins at sundown the evening before. Late Friday afternoon a hush falls over business and work areas, and throughout the cities of Israel men and women can be seen hurrying home with a bouquet of fresh flowers for the *Shabbat* table. A white tablecloth and blessings over the Sabbath candles that are lit to usher in the day of rest precede the blessings spoken over the traditional *Kiddush* cup (of wine), and the two loaves of Sabbath bread, and then the eating of a peaceful family dinner, where the presence of guests is considered a blessing.

A typical Ashkenazi menu comprises a small serving of some fish dish – **gefilte fish**, poached jellied fish or pickled fish – which serves as the appetizer before hot soup. A chicken main dish is then served accompanied by cooked vegetables and a **kugel** (a baked pudding based on noodles or potatoes). Dessert is usually fresh or stewed fruits followed by tea and small cakes.

Sephardi homes will reflect the foods more typical of many Mediterranean countries: fish with **avgolemono** sauce, chopped eggplant, roasted lamb, stuffed vegetables, rice and, to finish the meal, a honey-soaked cake or pastry nibbled with strong, sweet Turkish coffee.

Since work of all types is prohibited on the *Shabbat*, and the day is devoted to prayer, spiritual study, and family togetherness, cooking is done the day before. Hence the enormous popularity of slow-cooking casserole dishes usually based on legumes and called by various names: **cholent, cholendt, hamin, defina**. These can be combined (often with a huge single dumpling in the center or with eggs in the shell to bake to a soft brown) and then set either in the home oven or into a commercial baker's oven where the banked coals provide a slow even heat throughout the night. The next morning, after Sabbath morning services, the family can enjoy a filling hot meal. The Sabbath evening meal usually consists of cold fish dishes, bread, and wine.

The youngest holiday celebrated in Israel is Independence Day, which falls on a different date each year as it is based on the Hebrew lunar calendar. Thus while officially, Israel achieved independence on May 14, 1948, the actual date of celebration may differ from year to year. Some Israelis spend the holiday promenading the city streets and stopping at cafes for coffee and rich sweet pastries like **dobos torte** or a rum savarin with whipped cream; others celebrate with meals at home composed of **felafel** and pita, eggplant dishes and breads with varieties of cottage cheese spreads. Dinners may include chicken, Israel's favorite meat, cooked with some citrus addition, as, for example, orange wedges and honey. Sephardi Jews will make **haminadas** (24-hour cooked eggs, brownish in color and creamy soft in texture), while others may enjoy meals of herring and salads or poached jellied carp. Sesame seed and honey sweets as well as candied nuts and citron peels are nibbled by all.

Other special occasions are those shared by Jews the world over. These include: *Rosh Hashana* (New Year's), *Yom Kippur* (Day of Atonement), Succoth (Feast of the Tabernacles, or Thanksgiving), Chanukah (Festival of Lights), *Tu-Beshvat* (Tree Planting), *Purim*, Passover, *Lag B'omer*, and *Shavuoth* Pentecost. These are celebrated in only slightly differing ways, depending on the country of origin and the types of foods traditionally available, and are discussed below.

ROSH HASHANA

Celebrated in the early autumn, this is the traditional New Year's festival observed for one day in Israel and for two days in the diaspora. Its observation is marked not by hilarious celebration but with prayer and quiet contemplation of the past year's deeds, relationships and accomplishments. Families attend synagogue services and share festive family meals. *Rosh Hashana* features foods to celebrate the hope of a sweet year. A hearty main meal of fish, appetizers, meats and honeyed vegetables (**tzimmes**) is customary. Many sweet dishes of nuts, fresh fruits and dried candied nuts and fruits are served, as are special cakes and cookies that are rich with fruits, nuts and often honey. **Mandelbroit** and **leckach** (honey cake) are traditional.

YOM KIPPUR

The solemn ten-day period of prayer and introspection ushered in by *Rosh Hashana* culminates in the solemn day of *Yom Kippur*. The day starts the evening before when each family partakes of a simple, bland meal to be eaten before sundown. Foods are chosen that are not thirst-producing, for this is the occasion when every Jewish person over the age of thirteen submits voluntarily to a 24-hour fasting period that is not even broken by so much as a sip of water.

The light chicken soup served in the traditional meal the evening before *Yom Kippur* is often afloat with meat-filled **kreplach** or **kisonim** and the rest of the menu may include boiled chicken, mashed potatoes, a mixed green salad with lemon juice and a dessert of quince or apple compote, a light sponge cake and tea.

The entire day of Yom Kippur is filled with traditional synagogue services. Families are weary, thirsty and hungry from the ordeal but spiritually uplifted and usually come home to a light and refreshing meal. The meal after the fast may be a buffet of fish and pickled herring dishes, salads, breads, cakes, and tea. Moroccan Jews traditionally break their fast with a **tagine** of chicken and olives; German Jews enjoy a chicken-rice dish; Italian Jews may serve a cold, stuffed turkey breast.

SUCCOTH

Many families build their own "booth" (*succah*) complete with a branch-covered ceiling open to the stars, for it is a *mitzvah* (divine commandment) to partake of at least one meal during this eight-day festival of thanksgiving in a *succah*. All the fresh harvested fruits of the season are enjoyed and are used to decorate both the *succah* and the festive table. Filled foods of all kinds like strudels, **kreplach**, and stuffed vegetables are traditional, as are sweets made with nuts, fruits, and poppy seeds.

CHANUKAH

Occurring in the last month of the year, this eight-day festival commemorates a battle not for land or power, but for religious freedom, instigated by a small group called the Maccabeans (in 165 B.C.E.) when they united the Jewish people and restored the Temple. This is celebrated by the lighting of candles in a progression from first to last night so that all eight candles brighten the holiday table on the final evening. Families play games with nuts and *dreidels* (small spinning tops) and everyone enjoys the special holiday foods.

For central European Jews the treat is the making and eating of stacks of crisp potato pancakes (**latkes**) served with sour cream or applesauce. But for Jews from most other areas, the festive foods include sweet treats that are deep-fried in oil: Greek Jews serve **loukomades**, honey-drenched fried dumplings, and Persian Jews serve **zelebies**, made from a simple flour batter dribbled into hot oil then plunged into a pot of boiling honey. In Israel, too, all of these are served as well as many types of jam-filled doughnuts lightly dusted with sugar called **pounchikot** or **soufganiot Chanukah**. Fruits, nuts, and sweet treats are served in every home and children are given small gifts.

TU-BESHVAT

Occurring sometime in February, this is the day for tree planting. But throughout the world, even in areas where the wintry weather may not be conducive to tree planting, the fruits of trees and vines are enjoyed: fresh and dried fruits of all kinds as well as toasted and candied nuts. Sephardi Jews chant a special prayer in which many popular fruits are mentioned by name and it is customary to sample each one: pomegranate, apple, nuts, carobs, and mulberry.

PURIM

Amid parties, costumes, masks and carnivals, the festival of *Purim*, celebrating Jewish deliverance from the wicked Haman (the king of Persia's minister who plotted to kill all the Jews), is joyously celebrated. Poppy seed cakes and cookies, prune and poppy seed-filled **hamantashen** (three-cornered filled cookies) and three-cornered shaped **berekes** and **kreplach** are traditionally eaten to remember Haman's three-cornered hat. Greek and Italian Jews prepare a rich confection called **mustatchinoni** or **escravaniya**, with almonds and decorated with confetti sprinkles. Toasted and salted seeds are eagerly cracked and nibbled while handfuls of peppered chickpeas are munched and everyone has a good time.

PASSOVER

This festival of freedom commemorating the Jewish exodus from Egypt more than 3,000 years ago after suffering 400 years of slavery is vividly celebrated in every Jewish home as though the event had just taken place. After a thorough housecleaning and the replacement of the daily dishes and utensils with special Passover dishes and utensils, the family sits down to a symbolically set table and members taste a little of each of the special foods. The service, in which each person at the table partakes, is called the *seder* (*seder* means order) Throughout this eight-day festival no foods that are made with leaven may be eaten; in fact many families observe stringent food rules that may be traditional in their families because of local or regional rituals.

The service and precise sequence of the *seder* meal are performed similarly the world over, but one

ASHKENAZI & SEPHARDI FOOD PREFERENCES
A BRIEF COMPARISON OF BASICS

FOODS/ SEASONINGS	ASHKENZI PREFERENCES (Basic)	SEPHARDI PREFERENCES (Basic)
VEGETABLES	potatoes, onions, cabbage, beets, mushrooms	eggplant, peppers, artichokes, cardoons, leeks, okra, fennel, zucchini, tomatoes, fresh fava beans, olives
SEASONINGS	onions, garlic, parsley, sugar, dill, vinegar, fermented brines (from sauerkraut, pickles)	onions, garlic, dill, mint, parsley, coriander, lemon (fresh & salted), bay leaf, tahini paste
SPICES (also see spice mixtures below)	paprika, salt, pepper, dried herbs, dill, parsley	cinnamon, clove, sumac, cardamom, hot chili, cumin, fenugreek, tumeric, saffron
FLAVORINGS	vanilla, chocolate, lemon	almond essence, rose flower water, orange flower water, carob, tamarind, mastika (a resin)
GRAINS	wheat, barley, buckwheat (kasha)	rice, couscous, semolina, bulgar (Turkish) or burgul (Arabic)
FRUITS	apples, pears, cherries, currants	melons, apricots, persimmons, peaches, oranges, lemons, limes, figs and dates (dried and fresh)
FATS & OILS	chicken or goose fat, butter, vegetable oils, corn oil	olive oil, ghee, sunflower seed oil, corn oil, walnut oil, sesame seed oil
DAIRY PRODUCTS	sour cream, pressed farmer's cheese, cream cheeses	yogurt, goat & sheep cheeses
MEATS	beef, veal, chicken, duck, goose (served in large portions)	lamb, innards & bones, chicken (served in small portions)
LEGUMES	dried peas & dried white beans	lentils, fava beans, garbanzos, red or white kidney beans
OTHER	walnuts, almonds	almonds, sesame seeds, pine nuts

To Life! Setting a New Standard for Delectable Healthy Eating within Cherished Kosher Traditions. Barer-Stein, Schwartz & Vandersluis. Toronto: Culture Concepts Publishers. 1996. Reprinted by Permission.

SOME TYPICAL CLASSIC DISHES

ASHKENAZI	SEPHARDI
Strudel or **Retes**	Paper-thin pastry: **Phyllo** or **Fillo** (Greek) **Warka** (Moroccan) **Yufka** (Turkish) **Brik** (Tunisian)
Kasha, Barley, Wheat or Rye flour	Couscous, Bulgar or Burgul, Rice, Semolina, Wheat or Barley Flour
Cholent (European) **Schalet** (German)	**Dafina** (Spanish) **T'Fina** (Libyan & Tunisian) **Chameem** (Israeli & Indian)
Knish (Central European) **Kroppkakor** (Swedish)	**Bestil** (Libyan) **Bantage** (Indian) **Croquette** or **Pastel** (Moroccan) **Huevos Haminadas** (long-cooked brown eggs)
Lesco (Hungarian mixture of well-cooked onions, peppers, tomatoes, sugar, paprika)	Spice Mixtures: **Garam Masala** (Indian) **Queman** (Ethiopian) **Advia** (Persian) (cinnamon, cloves, ginger, cardamom, pepper)
Omelet	**Frittata** (Italian) **Tortilla** (Spanish) **Moussaka** (Greek) **Givetch** (Romanian)
Meat Stuffed Dishes: **Kreplach** **Perogi** **Vereniki** **Kulebiaki** **Holupchi** or **Holishkes** (stuffed vegetable leaves)	Meat Stuffed Dishes: **Borek** (phyllo pastry) **Dolma** (stuffed vegetables) **Saprakos** (stuffed vegetable or grape leaves)

To Life! Setting a New Standard for Delectable Healthy Eating within Cherished Kosher Traditions. Barer-Stein, Schwartz & Vandersluis. Toronto: Culture Concepts Publishers. 1996. Reprinted by Permission

dish on the table may show the family's origin more than any other. This is the **charoset**, a reddish mixture of fruit, nuts, and wine eaten as a symbol of the bricks made by the Jewish slaves in Egypt. Israelis prepare their **charoset** with chopped nuts, grated carrots instead of apples, orange juice and grated rind, honey and matzoh meal with wine to bring it to the right consistency. Oriental Jews use a cooked mixture of dried fruits and nuts finely minced and seasoned with lemon, sugar, and cinnamon. Yemenite Jews, always with a preference for the hot and spicy,

make theirs with chopped nuts and dried fruits, cayenne, sugar, and ginger. Jews of the western world prepare their **charoset** with chopped apples, nuts, honey or sugar, cinnamon and wine.

The most important symbolic food of the Passover festival is of course the unleavened bread or **matzoh**. This is eaten not only in place of leavened bread, but is also used in many dishes that are prepared specially for this festival. **Matzoh meal** and **matzoh cake meal** (finer in texture) also form the basis for most cakes and cookies during this holiday.

MAIMUNA

Many Sephardim from Mediterranean countries and particularly from North Africa add a ninth day of festivities called *Maimuna*. There are several explanations for this special day, ranging from a derivation of an Arabic word meaning wealth and good fortune, to a day in memory of the death of the beloved Rabbi Moses ben Maimon (Maimonides, the famed physician and philosopher), affectionately known as Rambam.

For Sephardim this day has long been a happy day of marriage proposals, gifts for brides and grooms, masquerades for boys and girls, and a time for picnics and visiting. Today in Israel, Maimuna has become a major festival of picnics, concerts, and artistic events enjoyed by Jews of all origins.

Because yeast bakery of any kind is not used throughout Passover, *Maimuna's* food specialties include sweet yeast bakery of all kinds, symbolic pitchers of milk and honey, and especially **muffletta**, delicious yeast pancakes eaten in quantity and dripping with melted butter and sweet honey.

LAG B'OMER

The days between Passover and *Shavuoth* (festival of the Giving of the Law) are sadly counted as days of mourning in remembrance of the suffering that Jews in Palestine endured under the Romans. The 33rd day, however, was set aside as *Lag B'Omer* to celebrate the harvest of barley. In Israel this is a day of weddings, picnics, dances, and pilgrimages to the tomb of the great scholar Rabbi Simeon Bar Yohai, near the town of Safed. Candles and lamps are lit to the accompaniment of dancing and singing. It is customary to eat colored eggs as a symbol of life and joy, also chickpeas, **felafel**, and seasonal fruits and nuts. In some areas of Israel, bonfires are lit in celebration.

SHAVUOTH

Falling exactly seven weeks after Passover, the festival of *Shavuoth* is really a threefold holiday celebrating the ripening of the first fruits, the harvesting of wheat, and the giving of the Torah to Moses on Mount Sinai. The festival is also celebrated by the serving and eating of the seven first fruits mentioned in the Torah: wheat, barley, grapes, figs, pomegranates, olives, and dates. Traditional the world over among celebrating Jewry is the eating of dairy foods: cheesecakes, cheese-filled pastries of all types including strudels, knishes, blintzes, and **kreplach**.

But in Israel, once again, the country of origin is a factor in some traditionally different and interesting ways of celebrating this festive occasion. Aden Jews (Aden is located in southern Yemen) make special cakes of almonds, honey, and coconut; Persian Jews serve a pudding of rice and dates; Yemenite Jews serve fried potato cakes; Kurdistan Jews prepare a meal of wheat ground in sour milk and rissoles of cheese and butter; Afghanistan Jews prepare butter-cooked rice and serve it with diluted yogurt poured over top; Ladino-speaking Jews from Middle Eastern communities prepare a huge seven-tiered egg bread (**challah**) filled with sweetmeats (fruits, nuts) to represent the seven weeks of counting *Omer* (a measure of grain brought to the Temple during the barley harvest between Passover and *Shavuoth*; the "measure" was usually the first sheaf cut during the barley harvest) and the seven heavens to which it is believed Moses ascended on his death; Sephardi Jews bake **Sinai cakes**.

GLOSSARY OF FOODS AND FOOD TERMS

Assie: tomato ketchup.

Assis: pomegranate juice, or a fruit drink made from it.

Bamia or **Bamja**: a dish of okra stewed in tomato sauce or tomato ketchup and served over rice.

Bashal Yirakim: a method of cooking fresh vegetables by suspending them in a cloth bag over boiling water.

Ben Gurion Salad: an array of fresh whole vegetables.

Berekes or **Bourrekas**: paper-thin pastries (made from strudel or phyllo pastry) filled with spinach and/or cheese and folded into triangular shapes. Usually made very small and served as appetizers.

Chazilm Frikadellen: minced eggplant, grated cheese, or sieved cottage cheese plus flour and egg blended into a "dough" then shaped into small balls or patties and fried. Served with rice or potatoes.

Cheeses: many varieties are made in Israel, the most popular being the fresh cheese or mild ones. Of the fresh cheeses **Al Kerish** contains 9 percent butterfat, while **Katoush** is a pressed white cheese with low fat and salt content. **Brindza** is a brined goat's milk cheese; **Safad** is a brined cow's milk cheese. Many varieties of processed, semi-hard, and aged cheeses are also made.

Chickpeas: these are staples in Israel, but are known by many names: **Hamtza, Houmous, Nahit, Bob**.

Cholent: a hearty meal-in-a-pot prepared especially for the Sabbath as it can be left on a low heat overnight ready to eat hot after the Sabbath morning services. The classic **Cholent** is made with a mixture of beans and barley flavored with onion and garlic and the addition of a piece of meat such as brisket, but many variations exist.

Dag Katsoots: chopped pickled herring garnished with tomato wedges, hard-cooked egg slices, and scallions.

Felafel: a spicy mix of mashed chickpeas formed into balls and deep-fried. Most commonly served by street vendors in Israel inside pita. The diner adds spicy hot sauce and cooling shredded fresh vegetables to taste.

Gefilte Fish: the origin of these fish dumplings may be obscure but this dish is one of the Ashkenazi Jewish festival favorites. Usually two types of fish (a lean and a fat one) are ground together then blended with eggs, crumbs, or matzoh meal and seasoned with finely minced onion, salt, and pepper. Sometimes finely ground almonds or finely grated carrots are added. Then, with moist hands, the mixture is shaped into small ovals and poached in a court bouillon (a French term for a fish broth prepared from fish heads and bones, carrot, celery, onion, and fresh herbs simmered in water. This is usually strained before adding the uncooked **Gefilte Fish**. Served chilled with a garnish of a thin slice of cooked carrot. Usually accompanied with red (colored with grated, cooked beets) or white freshly grated horse radish.

Genetsh or **Givech**: a layered casserole of stewing meat, rice, and vegetables well seasoned with onions, tomatoes, and green peppers.

Glidah: everyone's favorite – ice cream. There are many versions of ice cream made with margarine and egg yolks but containing no dairy products. Other types of "ice cream" may be made with non-dairy creamers and thus can be used after meat meals without violating the prohibition of mixing meat and dairy foods in the same meal (*Kashruth*).

Haminadas: whether simmered over low heat for 4-5 hours in water, or baked slowly overnight in Sabbath dishes, these eggs become lightly browned inside and develop a rich smooth flavor.

Hatzil Katsoots: cooked eggplant chopped with garlic, salt, and pepper and chilled. Served as a dip or appetizer with breads.

Hilbe: the Yemenite staple of soaked fenugreek seeds crushed and prepared in a watery paste. This is used in preparing **Zhug**.

Kisonim or **Kreplach**: meat- or cheese-filled triangles of noodle dough that are poached in boiling water or cooked in soup before serving.

Kugel: a baked pudding based on noodles, or more usually, potatoes.

Leben or **Lebenia**: cultured milk slightly thickened and tangy in taste, similar to yogurt. **Leben** is made from skim milk, while **Lebenia** is made from whole milk.

Pita: bread made from a simple dough of yeast, flour, and water with a little sugar and salt. The dough is rolled into thin rounds then baked briefly in a hot oven where it puffs up, hollow in the middle. It is a simple matter to poke a hole to the hollow then fill it as desired to form a **Felafel**. Or the bread may be folded and used to scoop up foods in the Arab style or rolled up and dipped into foods in the Yemenite way.

Pul or **Phul**: broad beans.

Rossel: the tangy sweet and sour juice made from fermented beets. The juice alone may be served in small glasses as an appetizer.

Semneh: fat used by the Yemenite Jews, made from clarified butter flavored with garlic and sharp spices.

Tarnegal Paprika Oreez: paprika chicken served over rice.

Techina (variously spelled): an Arab specialty made by blending sesame seeds with water in an electric blender, or purchased already prepared. It is thick and creamy in appearance and may be peppered and flavored with garlic to be dipped into with pita as an appetizer. Usually served spread on a flat plate with a swirl or olive oil and a light sprinkle of minced parsley.

Tivaleen: appetizers.

Yerak Marak: a strained vegetable broth liberally seasoned with minced fresh herbs.

Zhug: a hot spicy blend of garlic, cumin, dried red or green peppers, and coriander. Used to season **Hilbe**. Both are Yemenite staples.

CHAPTER 30

ITALIAN

The profoundly civilizing influences of Italian kitchens and table manners touch almost everyone. Even a brief examination of Italian cuisine offers convincing evidence that Italy's mission of civilizing the world may have had its deepest impact on gastronomy.

All of this seemed to have been predicted in 100 C.E., when Pliny the Elder claimed Italy "mother of all nations with a mission to civilize mankind" and 1,200 years later, Dante, too, spoke of a politically united Italy that would have a "special place as the sacred garden of Christendom." The universalism of Imperial Rome was one thing, but the sense of unity and mission collapsed with the Western Empire in the late 400s C.E.

When the Romans conquered the Greeks in 197 C.E., they enlarged their empire and profoundly enriched their culture in the form of arts and architecture, literature and philosophy. Greek became more than ever before the language of the literate and the language of international trade. Therefore, educated Romans, unlike the Greeks and unlike most early peoples, had to learn to use a second language.

Early Romans had learned to evaporate seawater to provide salt for their sheep and this skill became a profitable export to the Greeks in the South and the Etruscans in the North. In fact, the valuable salt exports increased with the expansion of the Roman Empire, but the language of trade was Greek.

Despite the many tales of exotic, gargantuan Roman feasts, all classes of early Romans valued frugality and simplicity and nowhere were these values more evident than in their food customs. Wheat, the staple food, was served at *jentaculum* (the early light meal) in the form of wheat pancakes, biscuits or breads, then served again at *cena* (the main meal) in the form of a boiled gruel or porridge. Milk, honey, olives, and dates would accompany the main dish at either meal. Sometimes the wealthy would add **gustato** or **promulsio** – hors d'oeuvres of salads, radishes, mushrooms, eggs, oysters, or sardines – to the basic typical meal, and desserts of honeyed cakes and fruits would complete the special meal.

While **puls** or **pulmentum** was the staple porridge-like dish for all, early Romans also enjoyed cottage cheese, the use of iron kettles to boil their mutton, types of dumplings called **gnocchi**, even omelets and cheesecakes. Some of the earliest Roman kitchens made knowing use of bakery molds, cutting knives and round chopping knives, cooking spoons and measuring spoons, mortar and pestle. Small portable brick ovens were used for keeping foods hot in the dining area. An arrangement of one pot inside another and set in hot water was used to keep other foods warm but not cooking. There can be little doubt that this latter technique was the forerunner of the French **bain-marie** and the western double boiler.

Dishes chilled with snow, vessels treated with pitch to keep foods cool, inspectors to check the freshness of meats in butcher shops, commercial bakers, and even commercially prepared seasonings were all familiar. **Garum** or **liquamen** was one such seasoning prepared from fish and salt; **defrutum** was a syrup made from wine and honey or grapes and honey; **agrodolce** (said to have been developed by Apicius) was a sweet-sour sauce prepared in many ways. Honey and vinegar were widely used but so was **silphium** or **laserpitium**, a prized flavoring prepared from **assafoetida** (a sour-tasting spice with a strong aroma used in Indian cookery).

By 200 C.E. all these foods, seasonings, and techniques were commonplace for the Romans. Gradually the commercial bakeries became so widespread and dependable that all but the very poor relied on them for fresh daily baked goods. Those who could not afford to buy breads relied on the old gruels and porridges. Small stones pressed into larger concave stones probably represent the earliest forms of grinding, to be followed by mortar and pestle, but it was about 200 C.E. that a small hand mill called a **mola versatilis or quern** became a prized item in Roman kitchens.

Apples were plentiful and popular but it took later conquests to bring the taste (and the plants) for cherry trees home from Asia. Apricots and peaches were brought from Armenia and Persia, melons from both Persia and areas of North Africa, and dates from Africa. Rome's returning Asiatic armies also brought back sophisticated ideas of seasoning and tales of Oriental dishes.

By the 800s C.E., Islamic conquests began to influence European foods. The Saracens are reputed to have introduced spinach (the special ingredient in so many Florentine dishes) to Italy from its native Persia. Many unusual desserts were also introduced at this time, most notably **gelati**, the whole range of ice creams and sherbets that the Muslims had learned

FOODS COMMONLY USED

The consideration of foods, facilities, and food customs of ancient times is not for historic interest alone: many parts of Italy and many Italian families still live in much the same way. In ancient times, the majority ate mostly wholewheat in many forms and vegetables, while the wealthy ate the kinds of meals that have promulgated the legends of Roman banquets where "the wealthy ate till they vomited and often vomited in order to eat more." The wealthy have long moved to an elegantly conservative pattern of eating and drinking, but many of Italy's poor still live in earthen huts with dirt floors and open fireplaces for warmth and for cooking. Their staple foods may well be plain bread and chicory, not pasta or a sandwich of bread and olive oil with tomatoes and garlic. Pasta may even be considered a luxury food reserved for special occasions, while a thick vegetable soup-stew prepared when fresh greens are available may constitute a special meal. The poor seldom eat eggs because their sparsely fed chickens do not produce very many. Some areas have no milk or cheese as cows are too expensive to keep. Yet even in areas where a sparse diet is familiar, the Italian spirit finds sustenance in an enjoyment of life, music, and wine. Those who cannot find such sustenance emigrate.

Despite innumerable provincial variations and specialties, Italian cookery can be roughly divided into a dominance of milk, butter, rice, and **polenta** (cornmeal) in the North; olive oil, wine, **pasta** in the South; and a meeting place for both areas in central Italy, particularly in Tuscany. Aside from these generalities, it is difficult to discuss details of foods and food customs without specifying an area. This is more true of Italy than almost any other country. Interaction and exchanges between regions are recent; previously, lack of transportation and self-imposed pride and isolationism prevented communication. The familiar Italian "pasta image" is well founded, for most emigrants hail from Southern Italy, and most Italian restaurants in Canada and the United States are Neapolitan (from Naples, in Southern Italy), although this has changed. In most large European and North American cities, fine Italian restaurants provide a variety of Italian regional food specialties. In North America, pizza has become as familiar as hamburgers.

The staple foods of Italy revolve around cereals, vegetables, and cheeses. Breads and pasta made from wheat, innumerable rice dishes and, in some areas, **polenta** made from corn is served at least once a day. Great varieties of vegetables are plentiful: staple root vegetables, fresh beans and peas, greens of many kinds, all types of squash, eggplant and zucchini, artichokes and asparagus. Each area produces cheese specialties and traditional ways of nibbling cheese, as appetizers or snacks, topping dishes, fillings, savory fried foods, sauces and even sprinkled into soups. Fresh-

dried bunches of herbs – parsley, borage, myrtle, rosemary, sage, oregano, and basil – are familiar in every kitchen, as are onions and garlic in varying proportions. Olive oil and butter are the favored fats and the best olive oil is said to come from Lucca in Tuscany. Rice (Italy is Europe's largest producer), vegetables, and all types of pasta are enjoyed al dente, that is, chewy and not overcooked. Meats and products of the sea are enjoyed and cooked with imagination but are served in smaller amounts than is customary in other countries because they are both more expensive and less available. Fruits and cheese are a usual dessert when dessert is served. Elaborate desserts are reserved for special occasions or restaurant dining.

Many regional wines of Italy are world-famous. Others that are equally as good are not known simply because they do not travel well. Italy's high rate of alcohol consumption and low rate of alcoholism can be explained by many factors. Wine is considered a food and all children grow up accustomed to wine as part of a meal. The strong moral influence of the close-knit family structure and the national distaste for drunkenness are powerful factors as well. While daily wine is commonplace, it should be stressed that wine always accompanies food, and the cosmopolitan sipping of the pre-dinner cocktail is practiced only by very sophisticated Italians.

from the Persians and East Indians. There is evidence that the earliest record of frozen desserts and ice- or snow-chilled foods accrue to the Chinese. Although the Arabs knew about sugar cultivation, they found it difficult to introduce it successfully.

The Romans also introduced culinary ideas to other lands. From earliest times, the Greeks thought of the Romans as a wine-producing nation and learned from them wine fermentation and processing techniques as well as the drinking of wine diluted with water and often sweetened with honey. Most of the world had been content to dine on spit-roasted meats, but the Romans seem to have introduced the notion of boiling and stewing in kettles. Various boiled greens (many considered weeds today) were commonly used in many lands, but the Romans brought with them the conviction that cabbage was worth cultivating since it contained medicinal properties. (Yet cabbage prepared in many ways – even fermented like Germany's **sauerkraut** and Korea's **kimchi** – predates Roman times as it was known and used in early China.) In fact, Europe took the Romans' word that oysters were delicious and even set about cultivating them in many lands. Similarly, edible snails were introduced to European palates by the Romans and remain a French favorite today.

The Roman belief in the efficacy of almonds as an aid to sobriety may have been the forerunner of salted almonds as a cocktail snack in many parts of the world, especially Spain. Central Europe's penchant for sausages in endless variety may have derived from the many types of spiced sausages, stuffed meats and fish that were common at the time of Apicius, a gastronome of the 1st century C.E., who wrote the first non-Asian cookbook.

At the time of the Crusades (around 1000 C.E.) some new culinary touches were introduced to Italy and some old ones revived. Indian salt was the name given to sugar, used at first as a condiment and later as a base for desserts and confections. Believed to have originated near Jerusalem and named for the Saracens, buckwheat (called **sarracin** in French, **sarraceno** in Spanish, and **saraceno** in Italian) was brought back by the Crusaders. Use of many spices was revived and the use of the tangy lemon was reintroduced to replace the green grapes and other fruits that had been used both to flavor and to tenderize meats. The present-day **carciofi alla Giudia** (literally "artichokes in the Jewish way") may have dated from the Crusades or from even earlier times when the Jews were brought back to Rome as slaves. In any case, the Italian enjoyment of **carciofo** remains.

Encouraged by the meal styles they had enjoyed abroad, the Crusaders are also responsible for the return of the meal pattern including appetizer, main course, and dessert. The prevailing custom in the Middle East of serving foods on large heaped platters also found a place on many Italian tables.

The question of the origin of **pasta** seems to have no ready answer. Once again some of the earliest references to types of noodles come from Chinese sources (wheat is the North China staple and noodles are the most popular form of preparation). Some believe that it was the Venetian explorer Marco Polo who brought dried noodles to Italy. Others believe that Italians were eating forms of pasta before Marco Polo but its importance and use were limited. What cannot be argued is that the varieties of pasta today are nowhere greater than in Italy.

The next most significant period in Italy's culinary history occurred in the late 1400s and 1500s when the country's great cities were the merchant centers of the world and her gastronomic achievements had no competitors. The gluttony accredited to ancient Roman leaders had long given way to a general inclination for simplicity and frugality, so much so that in many areas, traditional favorites would have been lost to succeeding generations were it not for the monasteries that preserved the great recipes and encouraged their monks to interpret them with taste. Sugar, coffee, and ice cream were introduced to the rest of Europe via Venice, together with many of the culinary details that had long been commonplace in Italian kitchens (stewing, frying, elaborate breads and baked goods and efficient utensils).

At the same time, growing world explorations were bringing back to Europe New World products such as corn, red and green peppers, varieties of beans, turkeys, and potatoes (of limited popularity in Italy). Most significantly, the **pomo d'oro** (golden apple) – the name given to the early tomato which was of a yellow variety – was lifted to gastronomic heights in Southern Italy's ubiquitous tomato sauces. But there is also some evidence that original Italian tomatoes were started from seeds brought back from a missionary trip to China by Monk Serenio in the Middle Ages.

While it may seem from the foregoing that food and food customs in Italy are the same throughout the country, this is not true. Nor are the Italians themselves homogeneous. Unfortunately, however, the predominating western view of Italy, Italian food, and Italians has been a blur of dark hair, emotional personalities, and pasta, tomato sauce, garlic, and wine. In fact, the peoples of Italy developed from early migrations of tribes throughout Europe and even Asia and North Africa. Italians, like other people, have red hair (from the northern region), may have gentle personalities, and enjoy a far greater variety of food than just pasta! And while geography played some part in isolating areas from each other, much more important was the part played by the battles between the popes and the emperors, each courting towns and eventually favoring development of northern and central Italy as almost independent states.

The fragmentation of the states left Italy vulnerable to powerful outside influences: French, Spanish and, later, Austrian. Most especially, Southern Italy, Sicily, and Sardinia fell under Spanish control and exploitation for 250 years (from 1559 to the early 1800s), which resulted in great part in the poverty, pestilence, disease, and famine relieved only by the great charities and hospitals run by religious orders.

The Spanish oppression of Southern Italy had many other effects as well. The debt-crushed peasants rebelled by forming secret societies and strongly emphasizing the power of the family unit, both of which exist to this day. As recently as 1958, Edwin Banfield's study of Southern Italy confirmed the prevalent attitudes of "family first and family against everything else," and Luigi Barzini takes care to explain this same phenomenon by stating that *mafioso* (with a small "m") means "... a subtle art of promoting one's own interests without killing anyone," while *Mafioso* (with a capital "M") includes everything else.

Probably from the influence of the Saracens and their Muslim ideals of womanhood, as well as the later influence of the Spanish, Southern Italians are possessively proud of their women, and consider honor a matter of life and death. Also in keeping with Mediterranean influence, the people of the South take a leisurely view of time in general and punctuality in particular, enjoy afternoon siestas, and spell happiness with the conviviality of boisterous friends and an open bottle of wine.

In 1713, Italy came under Austrian influence but was not isolated from the effects of the French Revolution. These events bound the Northern Italians in a *risorgimento* of culture, stressing the commonality of all of Italy's great cultural heritage and hoping for political unity. Even the proclamation of King Victor Emanuel of Piedmont as King of Italy in 1861 could neither allay the South's economic distress nor cement the cleavage between North and South.

Northern Italy remained strongly influenced culturally, economically, and politically by Europe, and later construction of railway tunnels in the mountains increased this influence. The peoples themselves became diffused with Germans, French, Austrians, and Slavs, gave their women considerable freedom, were too busy to consider siestas (nor did the climate warrant the rest periods), and cultivated conservative but elegant taste in everything from manners and clothing to food and wine.

DOMESTIC LIFE

Most of Italian daily life from ancient times to today is spent in the streets and squares of cities, towns, and villages. Home is the place to eat dinner but the streets and squares truly represent Italian life. The squares provide fountains and wells, markets and a place to gossip, a playground for the children and a place to see and be seen.

Early Roman kitchens, with their cooking hearths, metal and earthenware pots, and efficient utensils, were highly practical. In many areas all are in use today, even earthenware jars to store oil and wine. The older ways are more prevalent in rural and southern areas, while the cities of the North produce ultramodern appliances and kitchen designs that are not only used in wealthy Italian homes, but also exported worldwide.

REGIONAL SPECIALTIES

Discussion of Italy's particularly important regional specialties are divided into the North, Central, and Southern regions. The provinces of Piedmont, Lombardy, Veneto, and Emilio-Romagna will be considered as North; Tuscany, Umbria – The Marshes, and Rome-Lazio as Central; the Southern area will include the provinces and islands – Abruzzo-Molise, Naples-Campagna, Calabria-Lucania, Apulia, Sicily, Sardinia, and Corsica.

Perhaps nowhere else in the world are regional food specialties so passionately and proudly defended and enjoyed. And of all foods, none receives more passionate dedication in Italy than bread. Carol Field notes that "bread is so fundamental to everyday eating" that meals are described as what will accompany the bread. Breads for every occasion are found in plentiful supply in thousands of specialty bakeries throughout Italy, and many treasured family recipes begin by advising the cook to "take the baker's bread dough and add ..." What is deftly added creates the family's snacks, meals, and holiday specialties. Varieties and uses include **pizza, grissini, panini, crostini, bruschetta, foccace, bread salads, bread soups,** and country cakes made from bread crumbs. Holiday breads include **panettone, pandoro, bolzanese, veneziana, pizza de pasqua,** and **gubana** – all sweet and light and many studded with raisins, nuts, and chopped fruits, and scented with spices, vanilla, and fresh lemon zest.

NORTHERN ITALY

It is believed that the early merchants from Venice, Genoa, and Florence were responsible for introducing exotic spices from the Orient. Yet the pervasive general preference in northern foods is for subtle tastes with the aromas of herbs rather than spices.

Rice was introduced into Italy by the Spaniards in the 1400s and is used mainly as a first course where it "competes with the pasta." Originally a distinction was made between rice dishes, where the rice was cooked first in water then seasoned, and **risotto**, where the rice is cooked and gently stirred in hot oil or butter with seasonings then finished with a broth, creating a soft, moist dish. Cold and colorful rice salads are also popular in this region.

EMILIO-ROMAGNA AND LIGURIA

The main city of Liguria on Italy's northwestern coast is Genoa. Often called the richest city in Italy, Genoa is also known for its conservative elegance and fine taste in everything from small cars to discerning food. Basil grown in tiny pots on windowsills represents not only the wild weed that grows in every meadow, but also a beloved flavor. Genoa's traditional sauce **pesto** is prepared from generous amounts of fresh green basil, pine nuts or walnuts, Parmesan cheese, and olive oil. Garlic may or may not be an ingredient in the pureed sauce that is served over pasta. Traditionally, mortar and pestle are used to pound the herb and nuts into a smooth fine paste, but electric blenders are also used.

The **focacce** of this region are likely to be dimpled and studded with anything from sea salt to fresh herbs, olives, or **Gorgonzola** thinned with a little fresh cream and sprinkled with thyme.

Fish and vegetables are so popular that they blend together to form many of the most famous classic dishes of the area. One is **burrida**, in which a variety of fish (*rospo* or frogfish, dogfish, mackerel, octopus, eels, etc.) is sauteed in a flavorful sauce of oil, garlic, parsley, and tomatoes, then thickened with pounded walnuts, blended with white wine and finally served in its cooking pot with toasted bread. **Ciuppin** is another fish soup but prepared with pureed mixed fish.

Liguria is also famed as the area where **ravioli** was invented, where many tempting candies and sweets are prepared daily, and where fine wines complement each meal.

Salami, **mortadella**, **bologna**, and **zamponi** represent only a few of the famed sausages varying from bland to hot and spicy that prove the popularity and ingenuity of pork in the region of Emilio-Romagna. Parma is believed to be the area that originated Parmesan cheese. Not only Parmesan goes with pasta, but also the famed Bolognese sauce called **ragu** prepared from a blend of well-cooked vegetables, mushrooms, and meats. The most famed pasta of the region are the many versions of **tortellini** (ladies' navels). In general the cookery of the area is considered to be the "fattest" of Italy: rich and well seasoned with spices and garlic.

LOMBARDY

The city of Milan, bustling and industrialized, dominates the plains of Lombardy. In the 1300s foods were sometimes gilded in the belief that gold was curative; the poor could not imitate this except by the use of saffron and the generous addition of golden butter to as many dishes as possible. This tradition is common in many Milanese dishes such as **risotto** and **costolette alla milanese** (butter-fried veal cutlets). Another famed dish is a version of **minestrone** which includes toasted bread, poached eggs, and a sprinkling of cheese with the soup poured over top. **Buseca** (tripe with white beans), **vitello tonnato** (cold roasted veal served with tuna sauce), and **osso bucco** with **risotto** (veal shanks braised then served with a **gremolata** of minced garlic, parsley, and grated lemon rind) are such beloved dishes that they are part of fine international cuisine and are found in countless cookbooks.

Panettone, the richly sweet yeast cake eaten throughout Italy both for Christmas and Easter festivities, is humorously believed to have been originated in Milan by a baker called Tony whose delighted customers then continued to ask for "**panne** Tony" (Tony's bread) but other provinces claim it too. **Gorgonzola**, the creamy-rich, blue-veined cheese also known worldwide, is the product of Lombardy. Many other cheeses are produced but are mostly used locally.

Lombardy wines include: **Cortese**, **Barbera**, **Montelio**, **Sasella**, and many others.

PIEDMONT

White truffles, **fonduta**, game dishes, **risotto**, and enticingly sweet desserts are the famous specialties of the region. So insistent are the Piedmontese on the freshness of produce that most families use the fresh-picked seasonal vegetables and herbs from their own backyard gardens. Many varieties of mushrooms are used and the special vegetables include **cardi**, similar to an artichoke in flavor but resembling celery and delicate asparagus. Grapes, strawberries, and small russet pears are grown throughout the area, while cherries come from Pecetto or Ceresolo, and peaches from Casale. In the rice-growing areas, carp is raised in the water of the paddies, and tench (a fish of the carp family) and frogs abound. **Rane dorate** is a specialty of skinned frogs, flour-dipped then fried in olive oil. In mountain regions, wild goat, the white hare, wild boar, and chamois await the hunter.

Pasta is used but rice is preferred, and rich and satisfying dishes are made from **polenta**. Wild and cultivated herbs are used with a generous hand and, in this area, so is garlic. One of the famed dishes redolent of garlic is **bagna cauda**. A selection of fresh crisp vegetables like celery, cardoons, green peppers, and **grissini** are dipped into a hot pot of blended olive oil, butter, anchovies, and garlic. **Bagna cauda** may be a first course – as rice, pasta, or polenta usually are – or it may be the entire meal.

The area is also known for its production of fine cheeses: the spicy **Robiole d'Alba**, crusty **Toma Veja**, and aged yellow **Fontina**, whose quick-melting properties are enjoyed in **fondata** or **fonduta**, which is served over bread, rice, or polenta. Cream, milk, and butter are found everywhere and used to add rich flavor and light texture whenever possible.

Sweets and desserts are almost an art form: pastry shops resemble exclusive jewelry shops and the Piedmontese often enjoy leisurely snacks of pastries and tea. In mountain areas sugar is considered important to provide energy and calories, in case anyone needs an excuse to nibble candied chestnuts, macaroons, **caramelles**, **gianduiotti** (hazelnut chocolate), and **turcet**, the plain cookies baked in horseshoe shapes. Ladyfingers, anise cookies, and the famed fried cookies known as **cenci** or **bugie** delight every taste. Many sweet puddings and egg custards, especially **zabaglione**, a wine custard of Marsala and whipped eggs, are believed to have originated in this area. The long thin crisp bread sticks called **grissini** are thought to have been created by a Turinese baker to tempt the flagging appetite of a young prince.

This region claims also to have invented vermouth. Some of the finest red wines come from this region as well: **Barolo del Piemonte**, **Barbera**, **Grignolino**, **Friesa** (semi-sparkling with low alcohol content), **Gattinara** and **Dolce della Langhe**. Sparkling wines include **Asti Spumante** (white) and **Muscato d'Asti** (sweetly sparkling). **Cortese** is the best of the local white wines served dry and chilled. Commonly a *digestivo* is offered after a meal: **Grappa del Piemonte**, **Genepy** (mountain herb liqueur), or **Acqua del Po**.

VENETO

The great staples of this province include **polenta**, **radicchio rosso** (a reddish form of chicory or curly endive), rice, and fish of all kinds including the imported salt cod.

It was in Venice that the first sack of dried corn reputedly was unloaded in Italy, and Venetians have retained their affection for it ever since. It was also in Venice where the first fork and cloth serviette accompanied elegant dinners while the rest of the world ate with their fingers and wiped them on their clothes and anything else available. The height of Venice's glory was in the 1400s – like an elegant lady with the confidence and breeding that comes from 300 years of supremacy as a cultured city, intellectual center, and merchant harbor to much of Europe. Not surprisingly, her sophistication encouraged a cosmopolitan cuisine and to this day, dishes such as sausages and sauerkraut, casseroles of salt cods, stews of offal, turkey, and goose are reminiscent of other European and Mediterranean lands.

While almost every region of Italy and each small village delights in their own version of **biscotti**, it is believed that this twice-baked crisp little bread originated from the standard (plain) Venetian **pani biscotti**. From earliest times the large round dried flatbreads and smaller crisp breads were considered essential food for journeys even by Marco Polo and Christopher Columbus.

Typically, too, the classic dishes of the region are prepared with loving precision. **Polenta** may be served hot or cold, boiled, roasted, sliced and fried, layered with fish, cheeses, meats or vegetables into baked dishes, or served from a wooden slab or copper pan. Fish is cooked principally in one of three ways: poached in a broth, deep-fried in oil, or grilled quickly over red-hot charcoal. Although rice is widely used it is not prepared as in Lombardy. No saffron is used here nor is rice eaten by itself. Rather, it is cooked and served with a variety of other ingredients which may include meats, fish or seafoods, or even beans or raisins. Most famous is **risi e bisi**, a famed first course of cooked rice with tiny green peas, grated cheese, and bits of bacon or ham. Flat noodles accompany many meat dishes and may also be served with grated cheese as a first course. Game and all types of meats and sausages abound, and frequently it is the added grated cheese that distinguishes Venetian dishes from those of Austria, Germany, or Hungary.

Cabbage, zucchini, fennel, squash of all types, potatoes (especially in the form of **gnocchi**) are all used in abundance, together with tomatoes, peppers, onions, and other common vegetables.

Some of the more exotic dishes of this region include: **sopa coada**, a soup made of young pigeon squabs; **arrosto di maiale al latte**, browned pork flavored with rosemary and garlic then stewed in milk; and **capon a la canevera**, capon stuffed with beef and guinea-fowl meat then placed in a pig's bladder and sewn up with a bamboo pole as the vent – the bladder is discarded after boiling and the meat is cut for serving.

CENTRAL ITALIAN PROVINCES

ROME-LAZIO

While most of Italy balances its cooking between butter and olive oil, Rome prefers matured pork fat called **strutto**. In other ways Rome is different too: vegetables grown in the surrounding volcanic soil are said to have a distinct taste, and sheep, suckling lamb, and suckling kid (slaughtered often when only weeks old) become specialty dishes. Romans take

their traditions very seriously. With a common saying, "Bread and water are fit for a dog," every home and every small restaurant proudly serves the very best, fully confident that their tradition truly is the best. With knowing skills the Romans do indeed select the best from north and south and create from it a distinctively Roman cuisine.

Pizzas are everywhere, but Rome has an elegantly simple one that defies imitation. Gently warmed from the oven, the **pizza alla Roma** is stretched to six feet long before being baked and finished with brushings of olive oil, chopped garlic, and rosemary or maybe just a blush of fresh chopped tomatoes graced with olive oil and pepper.

Crostini (toasted bread and cheese) takes on distinctive Roman flavor because it is made with Roman **Provatura**; **spaghetti all amatriciana** is a spaghetti tossed with a delicate sauce of peeled and seeded tomatoes caressed with onion and bacon; **suppli** are cheese croquettes filled with a mixture of northern rice, meats, and dried mushrooms; and **stufatino** is a Roman version of Milan's **stufato** (beef and tomatoes), but cooked in lard and garnished with cardoons. Tripe is beloved in many dishes throughout Italy, but Rome's version is cooked with either meat gravy or tomato sauce, then served with grated cheese touched with minced fresh mint. **Carciofi alla Giudia** dates from ancient times and bases its tenderness on the quality of artichokes grown near Rome.

Roman cuisine also includes batter-fried squash flowers, stuffed zucchini, tomatoes, peppers and squashes; casseroles of simmered vegetables; fava beans and white beans served as thick soups or hearty casseroles with cheese or sausages – and if the fresh tenderness of young vegetables are not enough, there is the haunting flavor of **strutto**, the matured pork fat used in so many dishes and heightened with sage, rosemary, garlic, and anchovy paste.

Specialties of Rome include cheesecakes and filled pastries made from **Ricotta**; fruit tarts prepared with **visciole** (sour cherry jam); tiny cookies shaped like beans (**favi dolce**), and crisp fritters.

Each of the many villages around Rome produces its own famed wines and most of the **Vine Dei Castelli** are white.

TUSCANY

In the 1400s, which city dined first with a knife and a fork and dabbed elegantly with a napkin? Venice, the Venetians, of course, claim, but the Florentines claim it was Florence, in Tuscany. Also in the 1400s, not only was pasta and ravioli of many varieties commonly cooked, wines of many types were also enjoyed, and a favorite dish was **fegatelli**, a type of liver sausage. Rules of behavior and good manners were carefully listed in *Galateo* by Giovanni Della Casa. Among them were admonitions against eating noisily, burping, or sniffing at food before eating. Furthermore, drunkenness was considered repugnant (but the book noted that in Germany and France drunkenness was considered amusing if not manly). In the late 1400s, Florentine doctors were prescribing cabbage as a general cure, a panacea that was to be taken into many other lands.

One of the best known Tuscan breads is the salt-free **panne toscano**. Made from white or wholewheat flour, it is the perfect foil for the region's spicy sauces and gravies, salamis and sausages. More commonly it is enjoyed with a generous rubbing of fresh garlic and a drizzle of first-pressed olive oil. Leftover breads are cubed or crumbled and anointed with a simple dressing as part of a bread salad, or to add substance to a simple country soup.

The cuisine of Tuscany is noted for its classic simplicity and strict insistence on the finest and freshest ingredients prepared with passion and artistry. While olive oil is important throughout Italy, in Tuscany only the finest from their own presses at Lucca can be considered. The Florentine steak **bistecca alla fiorentina** is judged by the animal the meat came from, the perfect degree of heat for cooking, and the final flourish of a seasoning with salt and pepper and a brush of fine oil. Most meats are spit-roasted or grilled; vegetables are cooked with loving care, and in coastal areas fish gets the same kindly attention to detail.

Fritto del mare (a mixed plate of fried fish and seafood) and **cacciucco** are two classics, the latter a spicy fish stew inspired anew by each cook from the fish and seafood at hand. Pork, wild boar, guinea fowl, kid, and hare take their turn on grills and spits. Rice is widely used here too but in some specialties not known in other areas: **riso nero**, black rice prepared with cuttlefish ink, and **risotto alla toscana** that includes livers and kidneys. Dried white (haricot) beans are a staple and are prepared in soups with ribbon noodles, as a main dish with sage, tomatoes, and garlic, and sauteed with tomatoes and chunks of tuna fish. **Fagioli nel fiasco** is a dish of beans cooked in a flask. Tuscany pastries and sweets are often distinguished by being prepared with chestnut flour. **Chianti Brolio** is one of the great chianti wines.

Throughout Italy, but especially in Tuscany, recipes using beans often date from the Middle Ages or earlier, and much Tuscan cooking still centers around the skills of the grill and the roasting spit.

UMBRIA-THE MARSHES

This area is famed for its use of **porchetta** (pork) cooked with fresh herbs, fine threadlike noodles called **maccherocini**, spit- and oven-roasted meats, black truffles, and such a rich variety of fish that the local fishermen are reputed to be the best in Italy. **Orvieto** and **Verdicchio**, the latter having a faint greenish cast, are considered to be among Italy's finest white wines. Versions of pizza are prepared here, but the garnishes are kneaded into the bread dough rather than sprinkled over the top as in southern areas. Chicken, turkey, goose, game birds, and pigeon may be served when pork is not. But many versions of homey fish soups and fish stews served with garlic-rubbed bread also provide hearty meals.

SOUTHERN ITALIAN REGION

Southern Italy is characterized by an inexpensive but hearty cuisine based on bread, together with milk and cheese, incredible variations of vegetable dishes, and an unquenchable taste for very sweet confections and desserts. In some areas such as Calabria,  meat is used only on special occasions and the mealtime beverage is mineral water. Soups are often a mainstay of meals: fish and seafood soups in coastal regions and vegetable and pasta soups inland. Some pork and chicken may be used for meat but cattle are more important for their milk and cheese; offal forms inexpensive and nourishing meaty dishes.

CALABRIA, LUCANIA, APULIA

Calabrian cookery is based mostly on pasta, many varieties of vegetables, and cheese. Most coastal towns have their own specialties in fish dishes and these are usually types of fish soups which may be based on fish and/or seafood: **brodetto**, **zuppa di pesce alla marinara**, and **zuppa di vongole**, using mussels, clams, or **vongola**, a shellfish similar to a snail.

Tomatoes, artichokes, and peppers find numerous expressions in filling dishes but none so often as eggplant. Spinach is another favorite but wild greens may also be used when available. Bread is so important and so revered that it is identified with Christ the Life Giver and often pieces of bread are offered to beggars rather than money. Bread doughs are leavened by saving a small piece from the previous batch. So entrenched is the tradition and reverence for bread baked at home that it is easy to understand the Italian resistance to commercially baked bread.

While Naples-Campagna indulges itself with ancient symbols, rituals, and superstitions sometimes with a "why not?" or a "just in case" attitude, here in the deep south, ancient customs, so closely intertwined with poverty and the ancestral history of conquests by the Turks, Greeks, and others, have left a distinct mark on the inhabitants. Time has stood still. Yet orchard groves, olive trees, and lean cattle producing milk contribute at least to physical nourishment.

Pork is the most important meat, and pig-killing is a festive occasion fraught with tradition and great rejoicing. Local hams and fine pork sausages in many varieties, including **capocollo** and **pezzente** (made from sinews, livers, and lungs), are well spiced with pepper and garlic. Lard is an important fat and the children love the crisp cracklings called **frittoli** or **ciccioli**. Chicken, kid, or rabbits add variety to the menu as well.

Apulia's cuisine is similar to Calabrian but the inhabitants consider themselves the champion pasta eaters of Italy. They add cabbage, turnips, broccoli, and cauliflower to their casseroles, soups, and even sauces more often than others in Italy. Vegetables, bread and pasta, with cheese in and on almost everything, is the staple diet, but around the coastal areas there is also abundant fish and seafood and the oysters are considered special. Fish soups, stuffed shellfish, and squid stew are among the specialty dishes. Almonds are so abundant that some say there is an aroma of bitter almonds even in the local olive oil. The specialty cheeses include **Caciocavallo**, **Scamorza**, **Mozarella**, **Ricotta**, and **Parmesan**. Apulian wines are known for their heavy-rich flavors and some are even used for blending with other Italian wines of lesser stature.

CORSICA

Politically, Corsica is a part of France, but her geography, history, and language are linked inexorably with Italy. Most distinctively, Corsican cuisine is noted for its imaginative use of chestnuts, which are used whole or ground into a fine flour that forms a part of many types of dishes and adds distinct flavor. Many people maintain that even sausages and hams produced from crossbred pigs and boars have a special taste because chestnuts form an important part of the animals' diet. The importance of chestnuts in Corsican cuisine stems from the ingenuity of the peasants of the Middle Ages who decided to grow chestnuts instead of the grains that were so heavily taxed by foreign conquerors.

NAPLES-CAMPAGNA

The Neapolitans who emigrated to other lands also made famous their city's two great dishes: pizza and spaghetti. They also popularized **pommarola**, the tomato sauce that graces pizza and most pasta dishes. Many North Americans, therefore, are surprised by the great variety of foods in Italy. But it is not surprising that these simple foods have gained such popularity: they are easy to eat, tasty, satisfying, and inexpensive.

From Naples to the world! Since before the 1700s, the bakers of Naples transformed simple bread dough and the produce of their gardens into a food enjoyed almost everywhere. The classic Neapolitan **pizza** may have only sliced garlic, a brush of olive oil, and a final sprinkle of fresh basil, oregano, or rosemary. A more elaborate version will be graced with the addition of freshly chopped tomatoes, slivers of anchovies, and shredded **Mozarella** all baked to perfection in a brick-lined oven.

But Neapolitan food is not all pizza and spaghetti. This area also boasts an array of fish and seafood dishes that include octopus, clams, mussels, sea truffles and sea dates, eels, sea scorpion, shrimps and prawns, swordfish, dogfish and skate. These may be grilled, boiled, or fried; served dressed with olive oil, garlic and tomatoes or capers and black olives; they may be simmered in savory soup-stews or cooked and chilled then served in salads with lemon juice and olive oil.

Neapolitans love the idea that their foods and their lively temperament symbolize Italy for much of the world. They treasure their traditional recipes as much as they enjoy indulging themselves in old songs and folk music, in ancient superstitions and modern pleasures. They enjoy eating on the run: tiny folded pizzas called **libretti**, snacks of fresh seafood, and small containers with oysters and even small servings of vegetables that can be hurriedly enjoyed.

Many cheeses are used but **Mozarella** made from buffalo milk is the favorite for pizza. It is also used to top many vegetable dishes and in hot-fried cheese sandwiches such as **mozarella in carroza**. Other versions of mozarella-inspired foods include **panzarotti**, turnovers of tender yeast dough filled with several cheeses such as Parmesan, Mozarella and Provolone then deep-fried to seal the melted cheese mixture within, and **fritto di mozarella**, squares of cheese, egg and crumb, dipped then deep-fried and eaten while hot.

While pasta of every description creates so many meals, this is not to say that rice and **polenta** have not reached the South. The famed **sartu di riso alla napoletana** is a magnificent rice mold layered with cheese and meat sauce, seasoned rice and tiny meatballs alternated with a filling of chicken livers, crumbled sausage meat and peas, plus more slices of Mozarella. The dish is baked then unmolded. With similar Neapolitan flair, **polenta** finds itself sliced and layered with pork sausages, Parmesan, and Pecorino cheeses and baked into a golden casserole called **migliaccio napoletana**. Whenever possible, Neapolitan dishes exhibit the same bursting exuberance as the people who cooked them – and those who happily eat them.

The first ice cream shops or **gelateria** opened in Tuscany in the 1500s, but the Southern Italians are believed to be responsible for the popularity of ice cream in North America. **Spumone** is the specialty of Naples: a layered oval mold of several flavors of ice cream and sherbets with mixed fruits. But there are at least five distinct types of **gelati**: **granita**, a crystal-like sherbet usually flavored either with lemon or coffee; **gelati**, the familiar firm ice cream made with fruits, nuts, etc., in a rich creamy base; **coppe**, several flavors of **gelati** served in a dish and garnished with fruit, etc.; **cassata**, a decorative ice cream cake or mold layering several **gelati** with whipped cream and fruits; and finally the **semifreddi**, a type of soft foamy ice cream that also comes in many flavors. Most of these are usually served in dessert dishes with a topping of whipped cream and sometimes a liqueur as well.

But the **gelati** do not satisfy every Neapolitan sweet tooth. Some like to indulge in the many crisply baked or deep-fried little pastries, honey-dipped and candy-sprinkled as well: **zeppole** or **struffoli**.

SICILY AND SARDINIA

These two islands represent an unspoiled tradition of what is believed to be the earliest Italian cuisine. The cuisine stems from many influences, especially the early Greeks who conquered Sicily and the early Phoenicians (Lebanese) who conquered Sardinia. It is a tradition dating back more than 2,000 years; this is the tradition of fine cuisine that touched the Romans and all of the Roman world. But there is also a lengthy tradition of poverty, of feuding peasants and landlords, of insularism and a proclivity for traditional lifestyles.

Most notably, there is a difference in the personalities of the Sicilians and the Sardinians, the former known for their explosive exuberance, the latter similar to the Spaniards – quieter and more reserved.

SICILY
It is believed that the Saracens in the 800s C.E. introduced to Sicily a taste for sophisticated sweets such as the **cassata**, **cannoli**, and the crisp candied almonds thrown at the wedding couple for a "fruitful and sweet life." So famed are Sicily's sweets that monasteries still compete with treasured recipes of candies, confections, and ice creams.

Their varieties of white and crusty bread and rolls include an unleavened bread that is enjoyed by dipping in olive oil and eating with saltfish. **San vito pizza**, pizza dough topped with sardines and **Caciocavallo** cheese, or **scacciata**, a type of Sicilian bread pie where two rounds of dough are sandwiched with a filling of ham, anchovies, tomatoes, and seasonings, then baked and served in wedges.

Fish of all kinds are important in the Sicilian diet: salt fish, freshwater fish, seafood of all kinds, and especially tuna and sardines, each of which may appear in pasta dishes such as **pasta con sarde**, a layered pie of macaroni with a sardine sauce that includes fennel, anchovies, pine nuts, and white raisins.

The list of Sicilian staples includes pasta and rice, fish of all types, meats in the form of meatballs and sausages, and a good variety of cheeses. Vegetables are important too: tomatoes, capers, olives, eggplant (**melanzane**), zucchini, cauliflower, artichokes, and onions. Fennel, oregano, mint, and sesame seeds highlight fresh natural flavors. Citrus fruits, cactus fruits, and prickly pears, melons and fresh or dried figs are special snacks or desserts in season. Grapes are enjoyed as a fresh fruit and also in the production of fine wines including **Marsala**, the richly sweet dessert wine used in making **zabaglione**; many fine white wines including **Corvo** and **Etna**, as well as muscatel wines. Walnuts, almonds, and hazelnuts are used in the many rich confections, cakes, and ice cream desserts. The abundance of pasta and breads, fruits and vegetables as well as cheese and wine make it no surprise that the typical country lunch is usually one of sausages, bread, and cheese refreshed with local wine – a fine Sicilian meal.

SARDINIA
Sardinian meals are heartier and more frequently use meats than do Sicilian meals. Pit or spit-roasted pig,

lamb or kid braised over the smoking embers of natural woods add a special smokiness to the Sardinian **furria furria**. Wild sheep, bears, many birds, wild boar, and hare are usually prepared by boiling them first (to tenderize) with their innards, then flavored by placing them in bags lined with myrtle leaves. Bread is more of a staple here than pasta and two types include **pan frattau** and **carasau**, thinly crisp and usually baked unleavened. **Pecorino** is Sardinia's best-known cheese. Sardinia's wines are unusual: **Vernaccia**, a rich amber wine redolent of orange blossoms and traditionally served with fish, and especially **Malvasia**, more popularly known as **Malmsey** and said to have come to Sardinia from Greece.

MEALS AND CUSTOMS
The influence of Roman gastronomy on the foods and customs of countless peoples is unquestionable. It was a sophisticated influence that included meat inspectors, bakeries, private caterers, and even slave cooks. Early meal patterns comprised two or sometimes three meals a day. *Jentaculum* or *ietaculum* was a light breakfast of bread or a type of pancake with cheese or honey and sometimes olives or dates, with milk as a beverage. *Prandium*, a type of lunch, was served infrequently but included eggs, fish, or pork served with prepared vegetables or mushrooms and often fruit as dessert. Diluted wine was the meal's beverage and *mulsum* (honey-sweetened wine) was possibly an appetizer.

The main and most important meal of the day was the evening meal, called *cena*. For many this meal was actually served in the late afternoon and for the average family it included a bowl of wheat porridge stirred with milk and served with honey. For the wealthier, it began with appetizers called **gustato** or **promulsio** (salads, fresh vegetable relishes, oysters, sardines, olives, etc.) and proceeded through six or seven main dishes prepared from fish or meats with vegetables and served with white bread and *mulsum*, and ending with sweets and fresh fruits in season. Occasionally the *cena* for the poor included vegetable soup and coarse bread.

By 200 B.C.E., the hour for the *cena* had gradually moved to the later part of the day, obviating the need for what had come to be known as the *vesperna*, a light snack before bedtime. The later *cena* became the practice as more and more people preferred to take a large meal after their daily public bath. Coinciding with the later *cena*, the *prandium* gained in importance. For many it was simply bread and cheese (similar to today's sandwich), but occasionally it may have been a more formal miniature meal similar to the *cena*. As a rule, only slaves and young children did not recline while eating their meals.

Common practice in old Roman tradition was the silent offering of wheat, salt, and wine to household gods at the conclusion of the *cena*.

Modern Italians in most urban areas have a wide choice of both location and menu for their meals. Cities boast simple or sophisticated *ristorante*, casual family-run *trattoria* featuring low-cost meals, or a choice of many *rosticceria* where a limited menu offers simple, inexpensive dishes and quick or stand-up service, and the *osteria* for quick light snacks. Innumerable street vendors, corner **cappuccino** and **espresso** cafes and pastry shops also eagerly offer sustenance to the passerby.

Throughout Italy, a hot morning drink of tea, coffee, or hot chocolate together with bread and jam or marmalade form the most typical breakfast. Lunch and dinner (the former usually about 1:00 p.m. and the latter usually about 7:30 p.m. and later in Rome) are similar meals but may vary in the number of courses depending on status and occasion, and perhaps appetite. Seven courses may be distinctly delineated in the most formal meal: **antipasto**, a variety of small servings of appetizers; **minestra** (soup) or **asciutta**, which may include either **risotto** or a pasta dish but in a small serving; **pesce**, one of a number of fish or seafood dishes; **carne**, meat dishes usually served with separately selected **contorni** or vegetables; **fromaggio**, some form of cheese so important in any Italian meal; **frutta**, selections from a platter of fresh fruits in season; and finally **dolce**, very sweet confections, pastries, and desserts.

Traditionally, the Italian stomach has required some small mid-morning and mid-afternoon sustenance called *merende*. This is usually a snack based on bread like **crostini**, **bruschetta**, **focaccia**, **farinata** (a bean pancake), **fritelli** (fritters), **calzone**, **paniccia** (fritters made from garbanzo dough) **pizza**, bite-size squares or cubes of **polenta** fried or grilled. *Merende* may also be a snack at home from leftovers like **frittata**, or a few fresh vegetables plucked from the garden and dipped in salt and olive oil. Or *merende* may be simply bread, cheese, and/or fruit nibbled out of hand and washed down with – likely – wine.

Italians have some distinct preferences: they like their pasta *al dente* (chewy, not mushy), their rice tender and moistened with a sauce, and their tomatoes green unless specially ripened for sauces or specially requested as red. Italians also think it important to select carefully the piece of fresh fruit they would like to eat, so touching, pinching, and even sniffing for ripeness are all considered proper. Once Italians have finished eating, plates are immediately removed. It is almost a breach of etiquette both at home and in a restaurant to leave an obviously finished plate in front of the diner.

SPECIAL OCCASIONS

Almost all of the people of Italy profess the Roman Catholic faith, and according to many observers, the Church comes second only to the family in daily importance. From early infancy, through education and social services, festivities and special occasions, the Church plays a meaningful and important role. Yet, like Italian foods, personalities, and lifestyles, there is great variation throughout the country and generalities are difficult. Each village – indeed, each family – have special festive traditions. Together with the specialty foods, most festive occasions begin with devotional prayers and end with singing, dancing, wine-drinking, and feasting.

Natale – Christmas – is one of Italy's most important holidays. In many regions the festivities begin with the setting up of miniature nativity scenes in the homes. Carolers visit from house to house, and the *zampognari* are the shepherds who descend into cities and villages playing ancient instruments such as flutes and *ciarmeddi* (bagpipes).

Traditionally a 24-hour fast precedes Christmas Day, which generally means that no meats or meat products are eaten. Eels for Christmas Eve are a great favorite, but in many areas tuna, clams, or squid with pasta form the main dish or may be served as an accompaniment to **capitone** (charcoal-grilled eels and bay leaves). Some may prefer **frito misto di verdure**, an array of precooked batter-fried vegetables. The pre-Christmas tradition of meatless meals is climaxed with a display of treasured regional desserts, cookies, and sweets, many made only at Christmastime, such as **cullurelli**, the sweet pastries from Calabria-Lucania made by deep-frying small balls of dough then serving hot with sugar; the traditional Neapolitan sweet called **struffoli alla napolitana**, made with tiny drops of fried dough bound in a rich honey syrup and garnished with tiny colored candies; the special Christmas treat prepared in Abruzzo-Molise called **calciuni di molise**, actually a type of sweet ravioli filled with a puree of chestnut and chocolate then fried and served with cinnamon sugar; and Bologna's traditional Christmas cake, **certosina**, a rich dark honey cake with bitter chocolate, fruits and nuts and the aroma of anise seeds and cinnamon. The Ferrara region of Emilio-Romagna boasts a rich chocolaty yeast cake delicately scented with lemon and almonds. It is eaten from before Christmas to Twelfth Night and is called **pampepato di cioccolato**.

Christmas trees are not a usual part of Italian festivities, but the treasured displays of the nativity scene are. Also typical almost throughout Italy is the rich egg-yolk yeast bread dotted with chopped candied fruits and slivered nuts called **panettone** which everyone enjoys with **cappuccino** or **espresso** coffee throughout the holiday. Christmas is a time for family and friends and the day begins with coffee and **panettone** and often cups of **zabaglione**, the warm fluffy dessert made from whipped eggs and Marsala. Dinner on Christmas Day is often a feast of the best the family can afford, sometimes following the traditional seven-course menu of homemade family specialties of antipastos, pastas, vegetable dishes, fish or seafood, with a traditional main course of stuffed roasted capons to be followed by brandied fruits, nuts, cookies, cakes, and fine liqueurs.

New Year's follows many local and familial traditions too. For Sicilians, on Notte di Capo d'Anno, the doors are opened to sweep out the old year and the windows are opened to let in the new year. In Southern Italy, the new year is welcomed by the clatter of clay pots tossed from windows. Hopefully, there are no serious injuries, just good fun. Plates of cut-up herring are enjoyed as a symbol of luck, while lentils, a symbol of health and wealth and also the traditional staple of the poor, are consumed. Mistletoe is yet another symbol of luck. Money gifts (*strenna*) for the children and flowers sent for friends and relatives add excitement to the day. The traditional dinner is stuffed pig's legs and lentils, **zampone di modena**.

In some areas, children receive gifts at Christmas from the legendary *Befana*, the witch who travels on her broom in search of the Holy Child after hearing about the birth of Christ from the *zampognari* (shepherds). In other homes, children and family exchange gifts, and still others give only money gifts at New Year's.

There are many other special days on the calendar but these vary from region to region, as do the customs and foods. December 13 is traditionally the Feast of Santa Lucia when **cuccia**, a mixture of wheat and chickpeas (garbanzos), is eaten for each meal of the day. The Feast of St. Agatha is bright with parades and everyone enjoys nibbling on snacks of roasted seeds, nuts, beans, and cookies made with almonds and pistachios. February 15 is the special day for celebrating almond blossoms; sugar-coated almonds play an important role in many occasions such as weddings, anniversaries, graduations, and baptisms, while chopped or ground almonds and nougat and marzipan confections sweeten and flavor many festive dessert plates.

Throughout Italy, March 19 is celebrated as the Feast of St. Joseph (*San Guiseppe*), the patron saint of hearth and home. In consideration for the poor, meatless feast tables are set up with fish and seafood, vegetable and cheese dishes and breads and fresh fruits. Most homes share this meatless day by serving appetizers of fruits, vegetables, and olives; for example, orange slices, fennel, and black olives. The main meal of the day may follow the appetizer with a soup then fish and vegetable dishes. Again each area and family often prepares its own St. Joseph Day specialty dish. **Bigne de San Giuseppe**, deep-fried beignets dusted with sugar join the list of traditional sweets with fresh oranges and sweet yeast breads. Sicilians prepare **sfinge**, crisp crullers with cheese filling.

Pasqua (Easter) once again ushers in the familiar pattern of devotional prayers and gatherings of family and friends to feast together. Roasted whole suckling lambs, spring salads, eggs, roasted artichokes, and **fugazza di pasqua**, an egg-rich yeast bread lightly touched with orange, vanilla, almond, or lemon replace **maritozzi quaresmali**, the light fruity buns eaten throughout Lent.

Other festivals often retain more regional than national importance. For example, Rome celebrates Midsummer Night or St. John's Eve with family gatherings where the traditional feast includes garlic-simmered snails garnished with fresh mint and tomato. May 9 and 10 are the special Sicilian dates for eating marzipan fruits (made from ground almond paste) and **cuscusu**, a dish patterned after the North African couscous but made with coarsely ground semolina and fish. Many areas of Italy celebrate July's summer weather with day- or week-long festivities that include stewed snails and suckling roast pigs (**porchetta**). In Sicily the first two weeks of August are known as Ferragosto, the Feast of the Madonna; streets are brightened with religious floats and parades, and everywhere vendors sell grilled sausages and peppers, pizzas and **polpi** (octopus). And in case anyone still feels hungry, there are always seeds, candies, or nuts, or delicious ice cream for cooling refreshment.

On November 2, most Italians celebrate All Souls' Day, a time of feasting and a warm remembrance of dead loved ones. No one seems to know why anymore, but beans have long been symbolic of death and the souls of the departed, so it is not surprising that **fave dolci** (sweet almond cookies shaped like fava beans) are eaten especially on All Souls' Day.

GLOSSARY OF FOODS AND FOOD TERMS

Abbacchio: suckling lamb.

Alla Cacciatora: prepared according to the "hunter's style," which means slowly simmered in a sauce of vinegar and water liberal with garlic, minced anchovies, rosemary, and sage.

Alla Fiorentina: prepared according to the Florentine style, which often (but not always) means that spinach is included.

Bagna Cauda: literally, a "warm bath." Simmered mixture of olive oil, butter, garlic, anchovies, and sometimes other ingredients such as cream. A specialty of Piedmont and Turin.

Bottiglierie: a wine shop that not only sells wines of all types but also often serves soups, all to the accompaniment of wandering musicians and troubadours.

Brodetto: fish soup or chowder with as many variations as there are soup pots. Yet each **Brodetto** is made with fish and usually served with bread, the local variations depending on the available fish and seafood.

Bruschetta: that's what they call it in Rome; in Tuscany they call it **Fettunta**. By any name, it began as stale bread, rubbed with garlic and drizzled with newly pressed olive oil. More recently it has undergone a metamorphosis to become a popular appetizer topped with finely cubed fresh vegetables, freshly chopped herbs, and maybe a drift of cheese, served warm and crispy from the oven.

Budini: puddings.

Caffe: a coffee shop that also serves as a meeting place, club, or office. Also a place to read a paper, write a letter, or just watch people. Specialty coffees (caffe latte, cappucino, espresso, iced coffee) are served with sweets or snacks.

Caffe Latte: equal amounts of hot coffee and hot milk. Usually served as a morning beverage.

Cannelloni: tube pasta or crepes that are stuffed with meat then rolled and sauced and baked with cheese. Specialty of Rome.

Cannoli: Sicilian dessert of thin fried pastry tubes stuffed with a creamy filling based on Ricotta cheese and rich with fruits, nuts, chocolate, etc., then finished with a dusting of sugar.

Caponata: a Sicilian dish of chilled and well-seasoned eggplant, anchovies, and capers served as a side dish or appetizer.

Cappuccino: frothy hot coffee prepared from steamed milk and espresso, served with whipped cream and a sprinkle of cinnamon or cocoa. It's named for the light brown color of the robes of the Capuchin monks.

Carciofi alla Guidia: the Jewish style of cooking artichokes – flattened and fried. A specialty of Rome.

Cassata: the traditional Sicilian cheesecake made from Ricotta cheese and blended with grated chocolate and chopped candied fruits then chilled in a mold. **Cassata Gelata** is the ice cream version prepared in a special metal mold and consists of an outer layer of rich ice cream and an inner layer of softer cream and chopped fruits.

Con le Vongole: served with clam sauce.

Costolette alla Milanese: a crisp breaded veal cutlet fried in butter. Sounds Austrian, but it is believed that this dish was introduced into Vienna by the Austrian General Joseph Radetz who discovered it in Milan in the 1800s.

Crostini: literally, "toasted bread," but there are many versions that vary from alternating slices of bread and cheese grilled on skewers to toasted bread slices over which a sauce is poured, cheese is melted, etc. Used as a snack or appetizer.

Espresso: prepared by forcing steam through finely ground black coffee producing a strong richly flavored drink. Usually served black in small cups.

Fagioli: beans. One of Italy's staples.

Fegatelli: a Renaissance dish prepared by rolling a fine membrane around a chopped-liver stuffing then slicing and serving as an appetizer.

Focaccia: another bread of Southern Italy, reputedly introduced by the Greeks. Flatly shaped yeast dough in a large oval or square liberally sprinkled with available herbs and olive oil.

Frito Misto: literally means "mixed fried foods," and includes small morsels of cooked vegetables, fish, seafood or meats or even left-over rice or noodles that are bound with eggs – all deep-fried then served piping hot.

Gelateria: ice cream shops, the first believed to have been in Tuscany in the 1500s.

Gnocchi: a specialty of Rome but prepared all over Italy. A dough is made from flour and eggs with either semolina, polenta, or potatoes, then formed into small shapes and poached. To finish, they are drizzled with melted butter and sprinkled with cheese and oven-baked until bubbling hot. Street vendors serve a snack called **Bom-Bolini**, which are crumb-crusted and deep-fried **Gnocchi**.

Gremolata: finely minced fresh garlic, fresh parsley, and grated lemon rind.

Grissini: thin crisp bread sticks believed to have originated in Piedmont.

Minestre or **Minestrone**: a hearty vegetable soup with pasta and/or beans that can be a whole meal and which the Genoese claim to have invented. Often served with a spoonful of **Pesto Sauce**.

Osso Bucco: a typically Milanese dish of veal shanks simmered in a sauce of wine, tomatoes, and onions then served with **Risotto Milanese** and garnished with a sprinkling of **Gremolata**.

Osteria: a quick-snack shop.

Panettone: a light egg-rich yeast dough studded with chopped fruits and nuts and baked in a tall cylindrical mold. Commonly eaten throughout Christmas festivities for breakfast with coffee but also enjoyed anytime. Believed to have originated in Northern Italy.

Polenta: thick cornmeal prepared in a copper pot then served as the base for any meal. Traditionally cooked fresh daily in Milanese kitchens.

Porchetta: spit-roasted suckling pig.

Ravioli: typical Genoese dish of small squares of pasta dough filled like little pillows with a meat or vegetable mixture then coated with sauce or melted butter to serve. Prepared in many versions (both sweet and savory) throughout Italy and sometimes with different names.

Risi e Bisi: the Venetian **Risotto** of rice and peas cooked in a rich stock as a side dish of soup yet always eaten with a fork.

Risotto: the Northern Italian way of preparing rice – well cooked and well flavored, usually in a broth with added cream and butter.

Saltimbocca: literally, "jump in the mouth." Slices of ham and veal seasoned with fresh sage and browned in butter and wine.

Sambuca: Rome's favorite clear anise liqueur served after dinner with a coffee bean floating on top to be crunched while sipping.

Spaghetti alla Carbonara: hot pasta is tossed with beaten raw eggs, crumbled salt pork or crisp bacon and grated cheese.

Stufato: stewed beef and tomatoes.

Torta Pasqualina: a layered "pie" of buttery pastry and cheese-spinach filling, similar to the Balkan cheese pies made with phyllo pastry and the Greek **Spanakopita**.

Zabaglione: a soft warm custard of eggs and Marsala wine served in tall glasses and eaten with a spoon.

Zuppa alla Pavese: Milan's soup of bouillon afloat with toast carrying a poached egg and dusted with Parmesan cheese.

Zuppa Inglese: literally, "English soup" but it is neither English nor a soup and its name may be a gentle aspersion. One thing is certain: it is a delicious dessert of layered rum-soaked cake and custard.

CHAPTER 31

JAPANESE

The Japanese call their homeland *Dai Nihon* or Nippon, meaning "origin of the sun." It is from this name that Japan has also been called "Land of the Rising Sun." It is an apt name. For in the short span of about a hundred years, Japan has shaken off the shackles of an ancient feudal system and hundreds of years of isolation from the rest of the world, united her people, elevated her standard of living, and today proudly stands prominently as a world class industrial nation.

The four main islands that make up Japan – Hokkaido, Honshu, Shikoku, and Kyushu – are 80 percent mountainous. Picturesque lakes dot the mountain areas and small rivers water the rolling plains. Only 15 percent of the land is arable but it is from this that diligent Japanese farmers coax rice and other grains, vegetables, and a wide variety of fruits. From the surrounding seas come cold and warm currents and air masses that give Japan a climate that varies from short summers and severe winters in the North to torrential rains and whipping winds, hot days and humid nights in the South. But from the seas also come Japan's great harvest of fish, seafood, and edible seaweed.

Japan's first outside contact was with Korea in the early 300s C.E. Chinese industrial arts, crafts, and learning found their way through Korea to Japan. Shintoism, Japan's indigenous cult of imperial and ancestor worship, existed side by side with Buddhism since the latter was introduced from India (through Korea and China) in 538 C.E. Gradually the cult of ancestor worship blended with Buddhism and deeply affected many aspects of Japanese life. Appreciation of nature and a cultivation of simplicity and grace in everyday life influenced not only food and dress, but also literature and the arts.

One of the most exquisite examples of the infusion of the blend of Buddhism and Shintoism into art and thence into everyday life is found in the Japanese art of *tsutsumu*. This is the art of packaging, and includes everything from a farmer's quantity of eggs delicately laced in rice straw, to a gratuity that is not placed directly in the hand, but is wrapped in folds of delicate paper to resemble a flower. *Tsutsumu* represents utility as well as beauty and simplicity. Materials and colors for wrapping, as well as the completed shapes, delight the eye and symbolize the spiritual essence of nature.

In this same way, although Japan adopted crafts, arts, language, industries, and even religion from other lands, she has given each an indelible Japanese stamp. From the Chinese and Koreans the Japanese learned how to write by using Chinese ideograms, but soon simplified and refined the complex characters (in the 700s during the Heian Period) into two native *kana* syllabaries: *katagana* and *hiragana*. The Japanese word *kana*  means a symbol representing a syllable. This resulted in a flourishing of Japanese literature and learning previously unsurpassed.

It was in the Meiji Period (1867-1912) that the next great advances occurred. With the government centered in the emperor, Japan became unified for the first time and boldly stepped into expanding school systems and new industrial techniques based on western patterns. The western influence in music and art, in transportation (steam engines and electric trolleys), lighting, household appliances, telephones, and even western-style skyscrapers was mostly apparent in the cities. Rural areas continued their traditional ways, but not for long.

After a taste of territorial expansion – Japan for a time during the Second World War gained control of Okinawa, Formosa, Korea, Inner Mongolia, Southern Manchuria, and several Pacific Islands – the country laid down her arms in unconditional surrender on August 11, 1945. So began the American occupation. Once again Japan was to accept outside ideas, this time those of democratic government, land reforms, franchise for women, and the demotion of Shintoism from state cult to minor sect. This latter meant that with the government no longer sponsoring Shintoism, the emperor of Japan was no longer considered to be divine and no longer could the government impose religious education or activity on the Japanese people.

By 1952, Japan had taken her place as one of the great industrialized societies of the world – and also shared in many of the ensuing problems. Yet it is surprising that although living and working conditions in Japan seem to parallel those of the western world, differences remain. For although outward circumstances undergo rapid change, "the traditional aspects of the society are retained."

This is worthy of closer examination because it reveals differences of thought and custom that are often incomprehensible to the western mind. In Japanese tradition, it is the group as a whole that matters: individuals are as important as the group they belong to. Further, traditional views maintain that only diligent hard work leads to success: if one does not succeed in life it is simply because one has not worked hard enough. These factors lead to intense familial and company loyalties as well as fierce competition. It often also leads to a lack of communication between occupations because workers may belong to rival companies.

Japanese social life, too, differs from that of the West. There is a sharp distinction and division between social pleasures – enjoyment of friends, meals, and entertainment – and the world of business, education, and politics. Logical, philosophical, religious, business, or even political discussions have no place when friends gather for a meal or a few drinks. "The ability to seek pleasure in a world that has no logic may appear as a kind of art in the eyes of foreigners." But the ability to relax completely both mentally and physically in congenial sociability may explain, more than anything else, the traditional Japanese resistance to stress-related illnesses.

For Japanese who emigrated, the story is only slightly different. Wherever they went – to Hawaii, the United States, or Canada – the first emigrants left Japan for financial reasons. Their dream was to work hard, live frugally, and then one day return to retire in their native Japan. But conditions frustrated their dreams. It was these enclaves of frugal, hardworking Japanese quietly retaining their language, dress, foods, and traditions that aroused the unwarranted indignation of their western neighbors. Differences are seldom tolerated. But when it became evident that the dream of returning to their homeland was not going to be realized, their resistance to social change broke down.

Issei (first generation Japanese in North America) sadly watched as western education changed traditional family patterns. Schools emphasized individuality and the *nisei* and the *sansei* (second and third generations) wanted nothing more than to belong. Western dress and manners were readily adopted, and the Japanese language was lost by many.

For most, assimilation was the rule and Japanness was evident only at mealtime. The simplicity and symbolic qualities of Japanese foods and cookery could not be supplanted by western ones. The separately savored flavors of Japanese foods are as artistically presented as the colorful and different dishes upon which they are served. Japanese still eat sparsely and with appreciation.

The traditional aspects so deeply a part of the people of Japan have not deterred her from becoming a bustling industrialized nation. They only somewhat deterred western and Japanese mutual understanding and communication. But the rituals and beauty inherent in simplicity and restraint – so much a part of Japanese life and food customs – may prove a valuable lesson to be viewed in a new light by westerners, just as the notion of separating daily work from daily leisure.

FOODS COMMONLY USED

The staples of the traditional Japanese diet are rice, fish and seafood, vegetables and tea. Although some meats were taken occasionally as medicine, and records show that the people often hunted and ate wild animals, it was not until the American diplomat Townsend Harris's visit to Japan in 1856 that beef was considered a food. After Emperor Meiji's enjoyment of beef became widely known, its popularity, together with that of pork and chicken, rose steadily. Today most main dishes are combinations of vegetables with meat or seafood. Fruits in season are the usual desserts.

While the Japanese have borrowed from the foods and cookery techniques of Korea and China, there is no other cuisine in the world that can match the delicate artistry of the Japanese table. The Japanese cook is the artist, food the medium, and the table its frame. The subtle influence of both Buddhism and Shintoism are felt and expressed in the simplicity and oneness with nature so evident not only in the food and its arrangement, but also in the garnishes, eye-appealing combinations, and unmasked natural flavors all served in small appealing portions.

DOMESTIC LIFE

Present-day mass production of everything from electrical appliances to instant and frozen foods has made the urban Japanese kitchen similar to any in the West. The main difference is size. In Japan, refrigeration and storage space are minimal for several reasons: the prevalence of small-size homes, the preference for foods purchased fresh daily, and the custom of entertaining guests outside the home.

But Japanese women are well trained in the arts of the kitchen, in decoration, flower arranging, poise and good manners. Many are graduates in home economics, belong to cooking clubs, and love to watch food shows on television. But since most entertaining is done outside the home, and since very often the Japanese wife is not even sure if her husband will be home for the evening meal, most home cooking is of a much simpler nature than that found in restaurants. Yet the great care taken in the appearance and arrangement of both the table decor and the food itself is never neglected.

Harmony and identity with nature is a constant theme. Metal is used in cooking and cutting utensils out of necessity. But when it comes to wrapping foods – meats are often wrapped in large bamboo leaves – serving or eating foods, the elements of nature are preferred. Dishes and chopsticks are made of bamboo, ivory, or lacquered woods. Soup spoons are not used: larger pieces are picked out with chopsticks and then the broth is sipped from the bowl.

Japanese homes have a serene simplicity and so does the cooking. Hidden behind sliding shutters are folding furnishings and decorations that can transform the atmosphere and even the use of one room. In the same way, one basic cooking method can make flavor differences in many different foods. Or reversed: one type of food cooked by many different methods will seem like a totally different dish. Again, a Japanese dining room with low table and soft cushions can be pushed to one side as mats, blankets, and pillows transform the room into a bedroom.

In the same way the **tokonomo**, which is a small alcove in the main room, is completely transformed by changing the wall hanging and the flower arrangement to give one a sense of another time or season. All of this is part of the complex artistry and creativity entwined with a oneness with nature that in Japanese hands comes out looking so naturally simple.

Every Japanese kitchen has a colorful collection of teacups, soup and rice bowls, handled teacups and saucers (for western coffee and tea), china plates, platters and tiny dishes of different shapes to be used for special dipping sauces. Chopstick rests made in a variety of materials and shapes complete the table collection. For decoration, many styles and colors of mats, cloths, and vases for arrangements of blossoms, twigs, and leaves add that special Japanese touch.

Kitchen utensils include a variety of sharp, strong knives and cleavers. Many have specific uses such as vegetable-cutting knives, fish knives, etc. The mortar and pestle is probably one of the oldest utensils and is used for grinding herbal medicines, tea leaves, and pounding rice for New Year's cakes. Other basics include a wooden spatula (rice paddle) to ladle rice, bamboo lattice mats for molding **sushi**, sieves made of wood and horsehair, bamboo baskets for steaming, draining, and straining, a tub for cooking rice, graters, ladles, pots and pans.

DAIRY PRODUCTS

Although dairy products have been known in Japan since ancient times, they have never been an important part of the diet. More recently (since the American occupation after World War II) more milk is consumed but still not significantly. Perhaps in its place, the many products derived from soybeans are used. Broths made from simmering bones, and the eating of tender fish bones all add calcium and phosphorus to the diet.

FRUITS AND VEGETABLES

Japan's variable climate and the careful cultivation of the soil is responsible for a wide variety of fruits and vegetables enjoyed both in season and later when dried, salted, pickled, and more recently, frozen.

Fruits familiar to other temperate and subtropical areas are common. Many varieties of oranges form the staple fruit. Loquats, berries, persimmons, summer mandarins (**natsumikan**), and pear apples (**nijusiki**) are among the favorites for simple refreshing desserts.

Japanese enjoy all available vegetables, seed, and bean sprouts, and they enjoy them not only cooked by many methods (stir-fried, steamed, boiled in soup) but also as salads. Japanese salads are actually lightly cooked vegetables chilled, thinly sliced, slivered or grated and dressed with seasonings. Vegetables may also be salted or pickled and used as appetizers or separate courses like the salads to be served after the main course.

Yams and taro were introduced to Japan in ancient times and often form the staple food in mountainous areas, as well as in times of famine when rice and grain crops have failed. Burdock, lotus roots, leeks, onions, and white radish (**daikon**) are great favorites, but it would be difficult to find a vegetable not enjoyed. Several types of seaweed and many varieties of local mushrooms such as **shitake** (tree mushrooms), **shoro**, **kotake**, **shimeji**, and **hatsu-dake** are also used. **Tsukemono** is the name given to pickled vegetables, while **sunemono** refers to vine-gared vegetable dishes.

MEATS AND ALTERNATES

Meats are available and used according to means. These include all varieties of cuts – including offal – of beef, pork, veal, and lamb. Some poultry is used, as well as game meats, as available. Japanese **kobe** beef has gained a great reputation; it is beef fattened on beer shipped from the port of Kobe. Also famed and even more expensive is **wadakin** or **matsuza-ka** beef raised in special dark sheds, fed on hot mash and even massaged regularly.

Although the precepts of Buddhism have been gently bent to permit meat-eating, the Japanese still eat only small quantities; their fish intake is reputedly five times that of North Americans. Unquestionably the abundant supply and the great variety of seafood from nearby waters makes the harvest from the sea the Japanese staple. Edible seaweeds, abalone, clams, squid, shrimp, prawns, oysters, cuttlefish, blowfish, as well as salmon, cod, sardines, trout, herring and shark, tuna, flounder, sea bream (**tai**), and bonito all find their way into delectable dishes.

In areas distant from the sea, fish is most often prepared from dried or salted varieties. In fact, it forms such an important part of all festive occasions that where marine food could not be obtained or afforded, seaweed or even salt was then substituted.

Sashimi is a dish of sliced varieties of raw fish, arranged in a pattern on a plate and eaten by dipping into a sauce. Sometimes slices of raw chicken are also called **sashimi** and eaten in the same manner. But most dramatic of all is the daring Japanese custom of eating raw blowfish called **fugu**. Fugu-eating is dramatic because each year many people die from consuming raw portions of this fish (the liver and ovaries are poisonous, so the fugu chef must be especially skilled).

Eggs are consumed in quantity often as appetizers in the form of fried egg yolk squares, boiled or pickled quail, duck or pigeon eggs, garnishes and rectangular-shaped omelets.

Bean pastes are used as seasoning and as ingredients in desserts. For instance, **red bean cake** is a type of candy made from agar-agar and red bean paste. But most widely used are the products made from soybeans, which include **shoyu**, a sweetish soy sauce made from wheat and barley, soybeans, salt and water; and **miso**, mostly used for flavoring thick soups and made from fermented bean paste.

Tofu or soybean curd is so widely used in Japanese cuisine that it can safely be considered a staple. Its smooth, white custard-like texture and bland taste make it an ideal ingredient. So versatile is it – it happily absorbs any other flavors – that restaurants in Japan take great pride in their tofu dishes.

Chestnuts and **ginkgo nuts** are enjoyed by themselves but more frequently in desserts and main dishes.

BREADS AND GRAINS

Rice is the staple grain in Japan. But rice is more than food, it is also an indispensable symbol in Shinto religious ceremonies. It has always had a place of reverence and has sometimes been considered medicinal. However, contrary to wide belief, rice is not the only important grain in the Japanese diet. Noodles made from wheat or buckwheat flour are so popular that they often form not only a main dish, but also a snack food. Rice may be eaten as a base for other foods or it may be eaten from its own separate bowl. **Red rice** is rice that has been cooked with the juice of red beans, then served cold garnished with salt and black sesame seeds.

Perhaps most popular is **sushi**, the rice sandwich. Basically, sushi is vinegared or sweet and sour cooked rice wrapped around colorful and flavorful food tidbits. **Sushi** is eaten with the fingers, often as a snack, picnic food, or appetizer with swallows of tea in between. It is sold in shops and by street vendors. Many types exist, each with a specific name indicating the ingredients. There are three main types of sushi:

Nigiri-Zushi: vinegared rice with raw or cooked fish, seafood, or eggs garnished with **Wasabi** (grated horseradish).

Norimaki-Zushi: vinegared cooked rice and tiny tidbits of fish, seafood, or meat and edible seaweed or laver rolled up like a jellyroll then sliced into bite-sized pieces.

Chirashi-Zushi: the most artful and complex sushi of all, made from nine ingredients prepared in nine special steps.

Japanese noodle dishes are very popular and may be served hot or cold. Noodles are served in one of two ways: **kake**, which means the cooked noodles are placed in a bowl and hot soup poured over; and **mori**, which means the cold or hot cooked noodles are served on a bamboo plate and mouthfuls picked up with chopsticks and dipped into sauce before eating. **Soba** means fat noodles, while **udon** refers to thin noodles. Usually the name preceding either **soba** or **udon** indicates the garnish. Buckwheat noodles (**toshikoshisoba**) are believed to be good luck, are eaten on New Year's Eve, and are considered an appropriate house gift, especially when wrapped in red paper and ribbon. In eastern Japan buckwheat noodles are favored, while wheat noodles are most popular in the western part of the country.

Besides rice and noodles made from wheat or buckwheat flour, barley and millet are also grown and used in Japan. Barley is also used to make a mild refreshing tea. Roasted barley grains are brewed in a pot and served either hot or cold.

FATS
Little fat is used in food preparation as many dishes are eaten raw, pickled, steamed or boiled, barbecued, or as soup. Few dishes are fried and this is mostly done in seed oil.

SWEETS AND SNACKS
Japanese do not eat many sweets in the sense of consuming candies, cakes, pastries. However, much sugar is used in the seasoning of dishes rather than in actual sweet desserts. Sugar came into use in Japan in the late 1500s and has been an indispensable ingredient ever since. Even the Japanese soy sauce called **shoyu** is considerably sweeter than the Chinese version. Japanese snacks are not sweets. Most often they are snacks of skewered broiled meats, **sushi**, or noodle dishes.

SEASONINGS
Since the goal of Japanese cuisine is to present foods with artful simplicity and natural beauty, seasonings are always subtle. Any flavor that is pronounced, such as horse radish or scallions, is most often added by the diner at the table so the powerful tastes do not override the delicate ones. It is also interesting to note that in Japanese cookery seasonings are added only one at a time and in a strictly specified order, never all at once.

Shoyu, **miso**, **dashi**, and **aji-no-moto** are the most popular seasonings. **Shoyu** is slightly sweetened soy sauce. Made from fermented bean paste, **miso** is mostly used to flavor thick soups called **mis-oshiru**. **Dashi** is clear base made from a broth of dried fish and dried seaweed. It can be purchased commercially prepared but is usually made at home. A small square of **kombu** (dried kelp) is placed in water and brought to a boil then removed. Shavings of **katsuobushi** (dried piece of bonito with green mildew on it) are then added and removed as soon as the broth returns to a full boil. The resulting liquid, seasoned with a dash of **aji-no-moto** (Japanese monosodium glutamate) is **dashi**.

Vinegar and sugar are widely used. **Sansho**, a native pepper, and **yuzu**, citrus flavoring from peel, as well as sesame seeds (black and white), red peppers, hot mustard, horse radish, **shiso** leaves and berries, fresh ginger root, and occasionally peanuts, ground walnuts, and **ginkgo** nuts round out the seasoning "shelf" of the Japanese kitchen.

Rice wine called **sake** and fortified rice wine called **mirin** or **toso** are often used to enhance flavors as well.

BEVERAGES
Tea is the number one drink in Japan. Tea accompanies meals, is taken as a refreshment, and is the indispensable ingredient and symbol in the exquisite **Chanoyu** (tea ceremony). Green teas are favored and there are many different types. **Matcha** is the fine powdered green tea reserved especially for the **Chanoyu**, while **gyokuru** (literally, "gem-dew") is considered next to **matcha**. Other green teas include **aoyagi** or **aoyanagi**, **sen-cha** and **ban-cha**, which are coarser, and **habu-cha**. **Kombu-cha** is a tea made from seaweed, while **mugi-cha** is a tea brewed from toasted wheat or barley grains and taken cold, especially in hot humid weather.

Sake is made from fermented rice in a process similar to beer making. This mild yeasty-flavored wine is served warm in tiny cups called **sakazuki** and poured from an individual porcelain or pottery flask called **tokkuri** to accompany meals. **Mirin** is the type used in cooking. **Toso** is used for special occasions. **Sake** contains about 20 percent alcohol – most wines are about 10 percent – so despite its gentleness on the tongue, it is potent. Beer is also enjoyed, usually brewed from inferior rice or sweet potatoes, called **sochu**. There is also a growing demand for Scotch whiskey.

Coffee enjoys some popularity in Japan. Water is never drunk as such, milk very seldom.

JAPANESE COOKING METHODS
There are abundant opportunities for creativity in Japanese cooking. There is great joy in tasting something for the first time and a concentration of skills in producing an original dish or garnish. It is considered commonplace to repeat what was a successful dish – one must always strive to improve. It is for this reason that Japanese cookbooks stress cooking methods rather than recipes, techniques rather than ingredients.

The following are some of the basic methods:

Tempura or **Tendon**: In 1550, batter-dipped and fried shrimp was introduced to the Japanese by Portuguese traders. The Portuguese did not eat meat on Catholic Ember Days (four times annually); these days came to be known as Quatuor Tempora and the fried shrimp that became the specialty was called **Tempura**. **Tempura** now refers to the Japanese cooking method of coating cleaned cut or sliced foods in a light batter and frying quickly in a light vegetable oil. **Tendon** refers specifically to fried crustaceans. These foods so prepared are served with a base of rice or noodles, accompanied by sauces for dipping.

SAUCES: Aside from those sauces providing obviously contrasting flavors – for instance, **shoyu**, hot mustard or grated horse radish – most sauces are made from the boiled stock of trimmings and entrails. Sauce is well reduced then finished with a small amount of **dashi**, **shoyu**, grated fresh ginger-root, or horse radish.

Sushi: See Breads and Grains for discussion.

Sashimi: a method of preparing thinly sliced raw fish or chicken and sometimes raw lobster, shrimp, or clams garnished with paper-thin slices of raw vegetables. They are eaten by dipping into a light sauce seasoned with **shoyu** or horse radish. Sometimes **sashimi** is prepared by dipping the raw slices of fish or vegetables very briefly in boiling water before eating. Fresh ocean fish is best for this method.

Fugu Sashimi: the highly skilled preparation of raw blowfish. Since the liver and ovaries contain a lethal poison, incorrect handling or preparation could contaminate the meal. More than 100 dead each year are mute testimony that eating this delicacy is fraught with danger.

SOUPS: There are basically three types of soups:

Suimono: clear broths made from bits of meat, fish, bones, trimmings, entrails, skins, etc. These are strained and flavored lightly with salt, **shoyu**, and **dashi**.

Misoshiru: thicker and heavier soups made with the addition of **miso**, fermented bean paste. Substantial soups that are more like chowders or thin stews and make a meal in themselves, these may be made from fish or chicken.

Zoni: this is a special soup made for New Year's, comprising a rich chicken broth with slivers of chicken meat but flavored with Japanese herbs (**nanakusa**) and fish paste (**kamaboko**). Threads of lemon and spinach and sprinkles of **shoyu** and **dashi** complete the soup. To serve, **Zoni** is poured over specially made cakes called **o-mochi**.

SUKIYAKI: *suki* means a plow and *yaki* means roasted. This dish is cooked at the table in front of the diners, with the ingredients artfully sliced and arranged on a platter. **Sukiyaki** is usually made with prime quality tender beef and an array of vegetables which may include onions, leeks, types of seaweed, carrots, radishes, squares of **tofu**, **shirataki** (Japanese noodles), spinach, bean or bamboo shoots or sprouts, **konnyaku** (devil's foot squares), and **mitsuba** (marsh parsley). The liquids to be added are water, **sake**, and **shoyu**. **Nabe** is the frying pan which is placed over a *hibach* or *hibachi*, an earthenware cooking pot heated with charcoal embers.

The cooking ritual of **Sukiyaki** begins with the sauces heating in the pan, then the meat slices are browned, and finally the vegetables, pushed each to one side as they are cooked.

The meal is begun with a clear soup, **sake** or beer served throughout, rice served before or after the **Sukiyaki**. Foreigners like to eat the rice with the sauces; to the Japanese this is unthinkable. Rice is revered and is savored usually by itself. The meal concludes with fresh fruit and then tea.

Beef is the classic meat, but any other fish, meat, or seafood and any vegetable variety may be used.

YAKITORI: Spit-roasted meats or foods grilled on tiny wooden skewers are prepared by this process. Often the meats are marinated first, basted with the marinade while roasting (**miso** or **dashi-shoyu** marinade), and dipped in sauces while eating. Finely minced ginger or horseradish may enhance the flavors. **Teriyaki** is one version using **shoyu** and **mirin** as marinade.

NIMONO: This refers to boiled foods. This is also called one-pot cooking and may be done at the table or in the kitchen. Meats or seafood (in appropriate pieces) are boiled in the broth then removed and kept hot. Vegetables are then added and boiled until done, then removed. The cooked, slivered vegetables and sliced meats are well drained, placed on a plate, and served with a little broth as sauce.

MUSHIMONO: This is the classification that includes all steamed foods. There are three main methods:

1. Various ingredients are steamed in individual bowls and served in the same dishes.

2. Foods are steamed in one large platter or in layers of platters in a large steamer and then portioned out individually.

3. Prepared foods are arranged over hot coarse salt in a special earthenware (unglazed) dish called a *horoku*. The fresh foods placed on the scalding-hot salt release their own moisture to steam-cook the foods. The dish is covered during cooking time.

Dobin: a small teapot used for steaming single dishes.

Chawan-Mushi: Classic dish of sliced chicken, shrimp, mushrooms with chestnuts or ginkgo nuts layered in individual dishes with an egg custard poured over. After steaming till set, the dishes are garnished with a sprinkle of lemon juice and lemon slivers.

Odamaki-Mushi: Similar to **Chawan-Mushi** except that on the bottom is a layer of noodles that are topped with ham, sliced fish paste, vegetable slices, and finally the egg custard. A sprinkle of lemon juice sharpens the taste before eating.

AGEMONO OR **KARAAGE** style: *Kara* means empty and *age* to fry. **Tendon** and **tempura** are part of this style, although generally the term refers to foods pre-dipped in cornstarch and lightly fried in a little oil.

SALADS: Japanese "salads" are made from pre-cooked vegetables, meats, fish or seafoods, cooled and dressed and served as **zensai** (appetizers), side dishes, or small separate courses. Each of the ingredients may be arranged in little mounds and sliced, chopped, grated, or shredded. The dressing is called **aemono** (or mixture). **Tsukemono** refers to pickled vegetables while **sunemono** means vinegared dishes. These are usually eaten accompanied with many rounds of **sake**. Pickling is done with salt or salt and rice bran to aid fermentation.

MEALS AND CUSTOMS

Many factors intrude on the strict maintenance of the traditional meals and customs of the Japanese; nonetheless, there is an increasing Japanese pride together with the delight and curiosity of foreigners that is causing even *nisei* (second-generation Japanese) to turn to the traditions of their ancestors. Many Japanese have discarded all facets of their culture with the single exception of their food customs.

Umeboshi, a powerfully tart little red plum that so many Japanese pop into their mouths first thing in the morning, is one food that defies artful and delicate descriptions. It is not artful or delicate. It is potently sour, and the punch it packs is intended to waken all but the dead. It clears heads and freshens mouths. Breakfast is either a hot rice bowl garnished with a raw beaten egg which cooks as it touches the hot rice, or **nori** (dried laver), but most often a steaming bowl of **misoshiru**, a thick nourishing soup made with fermented bean paste. Tea may be included.

Lunch is usually taken in restaurants, snack bars, or eaten from little lacquer boxes in the form of a picnic if the weather permits. The mother who is at home is most often alone for lunch and will frugally make her meal from leftover rice topped with tidbits from last evening's meal.

Dinner may frequently be enjoyed in a general or specialty restaurant in the company of relatives or special guests. If it is an evening when the husband is out with his friends, or if it is to be a family dinner at home, most likely the meal will be a boiled or steamed dish, accompanied with sake or beer, preceded by hot clear soup. After the main course, rice and pickles will be eaten. A dessert of fresh fruits will complete the meal.

Street vendors, snack bars, and the temptation of delicious aromas from many types of restaurants make snacking a way of life. Almost anything cooked in any form can be purchased in small amounts for hasty nibbling.

Good manners have a special place in Japanese life and there are probably more words in Japanese to indicate etiquette, humility, and honor than in any other language. While men could enjoy themselves in a more uninhibited way, women were traditionally taught to be gracious, obedient, and humble. They were also taught to make the household skills the center of their life. Japanese women were never expected to be all things: the Japanese wife should be an able homemaker and mother – scintillating conversation, musical ability, and graceful dancing belonged to the realm of the geisha. But these traditions too are changing with women increasingly taking on professions and moving into the workforce.

Whether in Japan or abroad, many Japanese cherish the time-honored etiquette that surrounds hospitality and meals. Guests remove shoes and slip into tiny slippers before entering the home. Hot towels to refresh the hands and a cup of hot green tea are presented almost immediately. A traditional meal begins with the guest saying, *"Itadakamasu"* ("Now I will eat") and the host replies, with a small bow, *"Dozo,"* ("Please go ahead"). Meals conclude with the gracious, *"Gochiso-sama-deshita"* ("This has been a delicious dinner"). To which the host again ceremoniously replies, *"Arigato-Gozaimashita"* ("Many thanks").

Rice accompanies every traditional meal and it has specific rituals based on the deep reverence for it as a food together with the awareness of the hard work that went into producing it. The rice bowl is always received or removed with both hands, and children are taught this very early. Since the rice bowl is placed at the left of the table setting, its cover should be removed also with the left hand and placed to the left of the bowl. Rice is never eaten all at once, but in separate mouthfuls between other foods and usually after the main course or dishes. Since after-dinner tea is often served in the same bowl as the rice, one must never leave even one grain. However, if you wish more rice, a spoonful left in the bottom indicates this desire.

There are traditions surrounding the use of chopsticks too. They must be picked up with the right hand, using the left to arrange them comfortably. To take foods from a platter, the chopsticks are reversed, and when not in use they are to be laid one inch apart in parallel position on your own tray or place mat.

Since great skill is needed in making soups and broths, it is considered polite to praise the soup. To eat the tidbits from the soup bowl, the dish is lifted near the mouth and the pieces eaten with chopsticks. Finally the broth is sipped. Hot foods are eaten first, then room-temperature foods, and finally chilled foods. As in most societies, it is considered thoughtful to wait for older persons to begin their meal before partaking.

Since sake usually flows generously in almost any social situation, but especially during meals and in gourmet sake bars, it is wise to understand the rituals honed over thousands of years. The wine is traditionally poured for you ("you must never fill your own cup") from an individual flask called a **tokkuri** into a tiny cup called a **sakazuki**. The cup is held in the right hand between the thumb and two fingers and steadied on the bottom with the first two fingers of the left hand. With an average alcohol content of 20 percent, and usually served warm, sake packs a punch and what some describe as an "awesome" hangover. Hold your hand over your cup to decline refills.

But of all the Japanese traditions associated with food, **Chanoyu**, the Japanese tea ceremony, is the most profoundly significant. Although it was developed in the late 1400s by Murata Juko, it has been handed down through generations almost unchanged. Most of the masters of this ceremony are men, but women are often taught the ritual as much for its beauty as for its profound effect on grace and poise, dignity and discipline.

Every step of the ceremony itself, each movement and each utensil as well as one's clothes (which should be of quiet colors) and the little teahouse, the garden and the details of the room are all part of the experience. **Chanoyu** is strongly influenced by Zen Buddhism, "the aim of which is, in simplified terms, to purify one's soul by becoming one with nature."

The special powdered green tea called **matcha** is prepared and served in an atmosphere of serene simplicity with specially made foods called **kaiseki**. This food too came under the Zen influence of simplicity, lightness, and harmony with nature. **Kaiseki** is thought to represent Japan's highest aesthetic form of food.

Chanoyu is far from being a disappearing art: factories, many schools, and clubs all have special classes in **Chanoyu**, for its significance as one of Japan's most beautiful traditions is well appreciated.

Although *nisei* (second-generation Japanese) in Canada, Hawaii, and the United States retain many traditions, for the most part they comprise three groups: traditionalists who have retained the Japanese eating customs but have added a few western foods, for example, breads, hamburgers, and hot dogs (prepared with **shoyu**); the relatively acculturated group who prepare and eat traditional foods in decreasing frequency – this is the largest group; and those who have completely westernized themselves, even changing their names, rejecting their heritage, and intermarrying.

Gradual increase in the consumption of protein, fats, sugars, and the switch to a western-style breakfast are the most notable changes. While the gradual dietary changes have led to increased stature and life expectancy, they have also unfortunately increased the Japanese incidence of cardiovascular disease and dental caries.

SPECIAL OCCASIONS

The Japanese constitution of 1946 guarantees religious freedom to all as well as separation of religion and state. Virtually all Japanese, except those converted to Christianity (numbering more than one million), are Shintoists. But Shintoism, indigenous to Japan, is regarded as a cult rather than a religion, and includes aspects of ancestor worship, faith healing, belief in spirits, and purification rites. Confucianism is regarded as a moral code rather than a religion. Thus, it is possible for a Japanese to intertwine not only Shintoism and Confucianism, but also Buddhism. The latter is the predominant religion of Japan's more than 125 million people and has more than 200 sects and denominations. It is not unusual for a Japanese person to follow Shinto rites for marriage and Buddhist rites for a funeral.

Although modern in many ways, the Japanese mother takes great care to have the special symbolic foods that are traditional for each of the many festivities of the year: weddings, funerals, birthdays, visits to the shrines, Children's Day (May 5), and Girls' Day (March 3). November 23 is the memorial day for Kobo Daishi, the great Japanese teacher who united Shintoism and Buddhism in the late 700s under one doctrine called *Ryobu Shinto*. The biggest festival, often lasting three or four days, is New Year's when families gather and meals comprising many courses of symbolic foods are enjoyed together with visits to the shrines.

Red is considered a joyous and lucky color so it is found in abundance on festivals, whether in clothing, ribbons, decorations, or foods. But most symbolic of all is rice. Most typical Japanese feast foods are **mochi** (rice cakes) and **dango** (dumplings made from rice flour, steamed or boiled then finished by broiling and eating with bean-jam, a sprinkling of soybean flour or sauce.) **Shitogi** is another ceremonial food made from powdered rice that is steamed or boiled. It is usually prepared as an offering rather than a food.

Foods for holidays are always deliberately different in color and flavor from those eaten the rest of the year. Red beans are popular and a sweet rice wine called **amazake** is served often. For the Girls' Day, also called Doll Festival, **mochi** is made in diamond shapes colored pink, pale green, and white. The Boys'

Festival Day (May 5) is celebrated with **mochi** wrapped in oak or bamboo leaves.

But perhaps most interesting is the individual symbolism given to certain other foods. For example, lobsters are considered an indispensable part of the birthday celebration, the hump of the lobster suggesting the bent back of old age. By partaking of this food, it is hoped the person celebrating the birthday may also live to old age.

The New Year's customs and foods are so varied that often they differ from one family to another and certainly from region to region. A whole fish broiled in salt (**tai**), sweet sake, red beans, **mochi**, and many other dishes add to the merriment.

GLOSSARY OF FOODS AND FOOD TERMS

Aji-No-Moto: the Japanese name for monosodium glutamate, white crystalline powder prepared from wheat gluten and sugar beet residue, that heightens flavors without adding one of its own.

Cha: tea. In Japan, green tea is commonly used.

Chanoyu: ancient Japanese tea ceremony strongly influenced by the principles of Zen Buddhism.

Chawan-Mushi: most famous of the individual steamed custard dishes. It is made of layered chicken, shrimp, ginkgo nuts, greens all covered with beaten egg then steamed. Eaten with lemon garnish.

Daikon: long white radish. Turnips make a good substitute for daikon.

Dashi: a basic broth and seasoning used to enhance flavor in many dishes, sauces, and soups. It is made from dried fish (**Katsuobushi**) and seaweed (**Kombu**) briefly boiled in water and the flavor is heightened with **Aji-No-Moto**. Aji-No-Moto may be used as a substitute for **Dashi**.

Dipping Sauces: served in tiny individual dishes, these accompany most main dishes and may include a simple vinegar, soy sauce and salt mixture, (e.g., **Nihai-Zu**) to a more complex cooked sauce thickened with egg yolks and cornstarch (e.g., **Kimi-Zu**).

Fu: wheat gluten.

Ginnan: ginkgo nuts.

Gohan: rice meal or may refer to rice dishes.

Hakusai: Chinese cabbage. The appearance is similar to celery, except stalks are succulent, smooth, and white and the leaves are pale to deep green. Taste somewhere between cabbage and radish.

Hashi: name given to the chopsticks used at home. They are cleaned after eating and are often valuable.

Hibach or **Hibachi**: small portable earthenware or cast-iron grill heated by charcoal embers or sometimes gas. Used for table cooking.

Japanese Ways of Cutting and Slicing: is an art and each technique has a name. Artistic cutting and slicing to form designs and special shapes has its own vocabulary, distinct from routine ways of cutting.

Hangetsu-Giri: cutting round slices in half to form crescents.

Icho-Giri: cutting round slices in quarters to form wedges.

Kakumuki: cutting to remove both ends and then peeling in thick slices.

Katsura-Muki: using a broad cutting blade to slice off thin wide sheets.

Koguchi-Giri: slicing.

Kushigata-Giri: slicing to form quarters, as in slicing an apple into quarters.

Men-Tori: peeling the surface thinly.

Mijin-Giri: slicing food into long thin strips, bunching them together then slicing finely crosswise to form a fine mince.

Naname-Giri: cutting long narrow food strips diagonally, the piece of food is rolled with one hand while it is cut with the other.

Sainome-Giri: chopping food in chunks or coarsely by slicing into strips then slicing the gathered strips into rounds or squares coarsely.

Sen-Giri: slicing thin sheets of food into narrow strips.

Tanzaku-Giri: cutting flat sheets of food into narrow rectangles.

Wa-Giri: slicing long round food like carrots, parsnips, etc., in round slices.

Kabayaki: eels split and broiled on skewers.

Kaiseki: the natural and appealing foods artfully prepared for **Chanoyu** (tea ceremony), said to be the epitome of excellence.

Kama: name for the pot used for rice cooking. In many Japanese homes today this has been replaced by the electric rice cooker which is accurate for rice cooking and excellent for rewarming rice.

Kamado: a cooking range built from baked mud, used in rural areas especially to hold the deep iron rice pot called **Kama**.

Katsuobushi: dried bonito fish with a residual greenish mildew. It is shaved and used especially for making **Dashi**.

Kombu: tangle or dried kelp, a species of seaweed used in many dishes as a seasoning but an especially basic ingredient for making **Dashi**.

Matcha: the finest-quality highly prized powdered green tea used in **Chanoyu** (tea ceremony).

Mirin: sweet rice wine.

Miso: a fermented soybean paste with added salt and malt used as a basic seasoning. Comes in two types: **Shirumiso**, which is white, and **Akamisu**, which is reddish.

Misoshiru: a strong broth of **Dashi** and **Miso** served with various garnishes, enjoyed most often for breakfast. **Aji** oil may sometimes be added; this oil is spicy hot because of the addition of **Aji** peppers.

Mushi Imo: steamed sweet potatoes lightly seasoned with salt and pepper. Sometimes a quick, inexpensive meal, most often an after-school snack for children. The children's food is often prepared separately from the adults' and made milder, less seasoned, and often sweeter.

Mushimono: general category of foods prepared by steaming.

Nasubi: Japanese eggplant.

Negi: leeks.

Nimono: general category of foods prepared by boiling. Most often this refers to the boiling broth pot set on the table. Slivers of meat, fish, and vegetables are cooked separately and served over rice. The clear broth completes the home meal.

Okazu: relishes or salads of fresh vegetables lightly dressed with **Shoyu** and sesame seeds or a mixture of egg yolk and vinegar.

O-Shinko: Japanese version of sauerkraut. Pickled shredded **Hakusai** (Chinese cabbage).

Owanrui: soup stock.

Oyatsu: general name for snacks. Most recently these may be tea and pastries or carbonated drinks.

Sashimi: sliced raw fish usually, although sometimes may be raw breast of chicken, or seafood, and occasionally the raw slices may be dipped in boiling water before eating. Most commonly the term refers to thinly sliced fresh raw fish dipped in relish or sauce before eating.

Shabu-Shabu: like **Sukiyaki** and **Mizutaki** (made with chicken), this is a winter dish. Named for the sound of the chopstick-held beef slivers as they are swished in a broth of **Dashi** and chicken stock. Morsels are dipped into various condiments; finally **Tofu** and **Hakusai** (Chinese cabbage) are cooked in the broth and eaten. The last step of the ritual occurs as noodles are added and the soup is enjoyed as a finale to the meal. Many restaurants specialize in this.

Shoyu: Japanese soy sauce, sweeter than the Chinese version.

Shumai: steamed filled dumplings. Can be made with filled dough or with a thin flour batter poured over the mounded fillings before steaming to cook. A Chinese dish much enjoyed in Japan.

Soba: buckwheat noodles, considered symbolic of luck and happiness, therefore eaten on festival days and given as gift to people in new homes.

Suimono: clear broth soups.

Sukiyaki (pronounced **Skee-yah-kee**): *Suki* means plow, *yaki* means roasted. But, in Japan, "roasted" really means grilled or broiled, and in the case of this famous dish, stir-fried. Thinly sliced meat, fish, or seafood plus vegetables are cooked in specified order in a *nabe* (frypan) at the table. The meal begins with clear broth, sake served throughout, and white rice eaten with or after the main dish.

Sunemono: relishes or salads of cooked or raw vegetables, finely sliced, grated or shredded and prepared with vinegar.

Suribachi: a wooden bowl with finely grooved lines on the inside. When ingredients (especially herbs or seeds) are rubbed against the grooves with a wooden pestle, they are quickly reduced to a pulpy mass.

Sushi: the name for the general category of vinegared rice snacks or appetizers – classical Japanese foods – made in many forms – wrapped, sliced, cakes, balls. Their different names indicate their style and ingredients. Because they are picked up and can be eaten with the fingers, they are a favorite snack or picnic food.

Tai: sea bream, a common fish, widely used.

Tamago: a rectangular pan with a handle, used to prepare rectangular omelets.

Tempura: batter-fried shrimp. Both the batter and the frying oil in the Japanese cuisine are light and delicate in appearance and flavor. Sliced meats, fish, and vegetables are in turn batter-dipped and fried right at the table. Diners may dip the foods in sauces before eating. Originated from Portuguese traders.

Teppanyaki: Japanese cooking technique common in restaurants. Sliced foods are cooked by the stir-fry method in front of diners. The table center is actually a huge gas or charcoal-heated plate on which the food is cooked.

Teriyaki: generally refers to morsels of foods marinated in **Shoyu** and **Mirin** then broiled on skewers. But it may also refer to the process of spit-roasting or barbecuing. In any case, it is the sauce used as marinade, cooking, and dipping sauce that gives the foods an appealing brown glaze.

Tofu: soybean curd, used in soups and dishes, much loved. A staple in the Japanese diet.

Tsukemono: vegetables that have been pickled with salt or a salt and bran mixture to hasten fermentation. Used as relishes or salads.

Udon: Japanese macaroni.

Unagi Domburi: popular dish of split grilled eels served over rice and with dipping sauces.

Warihashi: chopsticks used in restaurants. Sometimes paper-packed, they are made from one piece of wood and must be pulled apart – this ensures that no one else has used them. They are inexpensive and discarded after use.

Yakitori: spit- or skewer-roasted pieces of marinated chicken.

Yuba: dried soybean curd.

Yuzu: a limelike citrus fruit, the peel of which is often dried and powdered and used for flavoring and garnish.

Zensai: appetizers.

CHAPTER 32

Jewish. See Israeli and Jewish
Jordanian. See People of the Fertile Crescent

KOREAN

Choson or *Tai Han* is the name the Koreans give to their beautiful mountainous country. The name means "Land of the Morning Calm," a name perhaps representing more hope than fact.

As a strategic land bridge between north Asia and the outside world, especially the islands of Japan, the mountainous peninsula of Korea traces its origin to a legend. According to this, it was Tangun the great Divine being who descended from heaven and claimed leadership of the many Mongol tribes said to have inhabited the area more than 4,000 years ago. Archeological findings confirm the presence of migratory Ural-Altaic tribes around the tenth century B.C.E. throughout the peninsula and in southern Manchuria as well.

The Land of the Morning Calm first faced invasions by the Han Dynasty of China which brought the introduction of bronze metal-working skills as well as the gradual division of the land into three kingdoms: Koguryo in southern Manchuria and northern Korea; Paekche around the basins of the Han River in central Korea; and Silla in the south of Korea. Chinese living styles, Buddhism, and later, Confucianism formed the foundations of Korean civilization.

From 1392 to 1910, the Yi Dynasty in Korea took many steps to unify the people and the country. All government officials had to pass a national examination based on the Chinese classics, especially Confucianism; a phonetic alphabet of the Korean language was developed. This latter achievement and a much earlier one – the invention and use, before 1392, of what is believed to be the world's first metal type system, inaugurated with the printing of the Buddhist scripture the *Tripitaka Koreana*, are credited by many as being two of the most important unifying features of the time. The phonetic alphabet was called *Hangeul* and its 24 precise letters were used in the publication of many precious books. This

rich period of relative calm and great cultural achievement was broken in 1591 by Japanese invasions.

In the past, although Korea had taken much from China, her "elder brother," the hundreds of years during which Korea experienced relative isolation helped to develop customs and distinctive ways of life that are uniquely Korean. So it was that although much suffering came with the Japanese occupation from sporadic conflicts after 1591, and for a long period between 1910 and 1945, another cultural layer was superimposed on the Korean foundation. While the walled towns and cities and the many Buddhist and Confucian temples suggested Chinese influence, it is equally obvious that modern-day Korea's many rapid transit and highway systems and even the electrical and telephone systems as well as new consumer habits resulting from mass production of cheap goods, the development of mines and factories and expanded seaports, all trace their origin from the western world via Japan.

Although the Japanese can be credited with preserving the unity of Korea during their occupation, other results were not so favorable. It was both the increase in population and the pressures of politics that resulted in a large emigration of Koreans abroad. And with the Japanese withdrawal following World War II in 1945, the vacant administrative posts in government and executive positions in industry were left to be filled by untrained Koreans with the sad result of a period of economic corruption.

Communist North Korea and the Republic of South Korea differ markedly, and not just in political outlook. With a total Korean population of more than 70 million, North Korea has close to 25 million predominantly engaged in agriculture, while South Korea has a population of almost 46 million with more than two-thirds located in cities and engaged in business and manufacturing. From the plains and lowlands of both regions come the major agricultural crops of maize, rice, wheat, vegetables and fruits as well as pigs, poultry, and cattle.

Presently, although North and South Korea have been on divergent ideological paths, the severe famine in North Korea in the spring of 1997 seemed to bring negotiations closer to a lasting peace between the two regions. Many Koreans living at home and living overseas feel they will win the struggle for the restoration of their unique national culture and gain liberty once again so that their land of Choson will truly be the Land of the Morning Calm.

DOMESTIC LIFE

There are sharp contrasts between the domestic life of Koreans in farming villages and those who live and work in cities. The majority of Koreans live in farming villages, for even fishermen in seashore communities pursue some form of agriculture. The villages are mostly democratic, each tending to be an almost independent social unit.

Many urban homes as well as almost all of those in the countryside follow traditional styles and decor. As the extended family grows, rooms and wings are added to the basic L-shape, U-shape, or hollow square homes built of earth, clay wattle, brick, or concrete blocks. Old straw-thatched roofs are giving way to tiles, metal or plastic styles, but the heating system remains "age-old." Under baked clay floors which are neatly covered with glazed paper, stone flues carry heat from either the kitchen or outside fire pits. Thus there is heat for cooking, hot water, and warmth for the occupants of the house as they sit on mats or sleep on quilted mattresses at night.

In rural homes as well as in many urban homes, the kitchen is the special domain of the woman. Pine branches may be used for fuel in the iron, stone, or clay fire pits. Traditionally, three large globular iron pots of varying size are sunk into pits in the stove. The largest of these pots may be used for heating laundry water or cooking grass as food for oxen; the smaller pots are used for rice and other foods. An inverted dome of the iron pot is used as a griddle. Open shelves as well as at least one food cabinet are used for general storage, while foods needing storage in a cool place may be kept in the ground or in huge stone jars. Trays for dining, baskets and brooms add to the decor of the kitchen together with the family's brass ladles hanging on the wall.

A special area of the traditional rural home is the outer porch or patio area, made with a floor of smoothed clay and often sheltered with a roof. This area is called the *matang*. Shoes are placed here before entering the home, but more important, it is here that old and young congregate to do odd jobs, talk, and watch the children. It is said that "he who does not know the *matang* will never understand Korea." In fact, for the men, the *matang* is the summer social area, while women prefer the kitchen or the tiny walled garden accessible from the kitchen entrance.

While sliding rice-paper panels within the homes are reminiscent of Japanese design, Chinese influences are stronger. Borrowed from the Chinese is the village arrangement of homes clustered together around the courtyard. So too are the small market gardens near each home, the pine tree and bamboo groves surrounding the villages, and even the typical walls surrounding the towns.

Upper-class Koreans living in the larger cities live in towering modern apartment buildings or western-style homes, many with modern appliances such as refrigerators, gas stoves, and piped-in hot water.

Gradual changes are occurring in family life. Father and son still form the primary family relationship, but the large extended family living in one home unit is gradually giving way to the nuclear family consisting only of father, mother, and children.

Respect for elders and ancestor worship are almost as deeply inculcated in the Korean as fundamental

FOODS COMMONLY USED

The foods that are the daily staples reflect the produce of agriculture: rice, barley, and many varieties of beans, cabbages, potatoes, and squash. Pear and persimmon trees are most common, but peaches, chestnuts, and walnuts are also enjoyed. While the Chinese introduced market gardening and irrigation methods, the Japanese influence was greater in increasing the yields of the fishing industry and it is believed that the Japanese introduced the culture of maize and tobacco.

Rice and rice dishes – that is, rice mixed with barley, beans and potatoes – head the list of staple Korean foods. Two Korean specialties include the brined, pickled and hotly, even fiery spiced **kim-ch'i** and the bland tea called **sungyung**, which is made by throwing cold water on the burned rice or barley at the bottom of the pot. This latter is served as a beverage at the conclusion of the meal.

Koreans enjoy soups immensely and show their appreciation by slurping, which is accepted etiquette. Many Chinese and Japanese dishes find a place together with these distinctly Korean specialties, while barbecued and roasted meats and many intricate dishes add to the great variety. Chinese cuisine is still the richest and most varied, Japanese the sweetest, and Korean tastes include both, yet again with special touches that make it different, like **sinsun-lo**, the Korean "hot pot."

Garlic, chili peppers, and sesame seeds are the outstanding seasonings.

Confucian values. Among these is the belief that "a good life depends on knowledge and observance of proper behavior between one individual and another." This is outlined in the five Confucian categories: parent and child (especially father and son), king and minister, husband and wife, elder and younger brother, and between friends.

These fundamental traditions persist even among Koreans who profess the Christian faith. First Chinese, then Japanese, and more recently Russian and American cultures, religions, and lifestyles have all been superimposed on traditional Korean ways, but they do not replace them.

Following this age-old pattern it is not difficult to understand that even if the modern-day Korean woman works outside her home, the likelihood is strong that within the family she is the "inside master" while her husband is the "outside master." That is, while the Korean family may live in a modern multi-story apartment building and enjoy modern conveniences, a scratch on the surface will reveal ancient codes and beliefs.

DAIRY PRODUCTS
As in China and Japan, the use of dairy products such as cheeses and butter and cultured milk products is not a part of the Korean menu.

FRUITS AND VEGETABLES
The persimmon and the Chinese pear are the most common fruits. However, fruits are not a staple part of the menu, nor are they served with any frequency. In city homes or in upper-class families, fruits may be part of a snack or a treat offered to guests. When strips of raw meat are served (after marinating in garlic and sesame seed oil) it is customary to accompany the dish with thin slices of Chinese pear.

Vegetables offer important nutrients and variety to the diet. Many types and varieties of vegetables are grown and prepared in a number of ways: white potatoes, sweet potatoes, pumpkin, many squashes, onions, leeks, Chinese cabbage, turnips, red and green peppers, **daikon** (Oriental radish), many types of mushrooms, cucumbers, garlic, and many types of beans (red beans, green beans, soybeans, and pea beans).

Unquestionably the most important Korean vegetable dish present at every meal is **kimch'i**. There are almost endless combinations but the general categories of **kimch'i** include **daikon kimch'i** made in large cut, small cut, salty, very salty, pickled, and summer; **cabbage kimch'i** made with shredded Chinese or round cabbage; and **cucumber kimch'i**. This national dish is made by layering cut vegetables with varying amounts of salt and onions and allowing it to ferment for a short time. After rinsing, the prepared vegetables are seasoned with peppery spices, garlic, leeks, and ginseng. A great variety of other special ingredients may be added to create the **kimch'i** specialty of the household, such as dried or fresh shrimp, fish or other seafood, pine nuts, meats, chestnuts, pears, or apples.

In some households, **kimch'i** and rice may be the entire meal. Huge earthen jars are used to store the **kimch'i** and these are placed either underground or in cool places during the summer.

Cucumber and eggplant are greatly favored and are prepared in a variety of ways: stuffed, fresh, cooked, pickled, steamed, roasted, or as a salad with vinegar.

More than 1,000 varieties of seaweed or laver are found around the shores of both Korea and Japan. Edible seaweed is called **nori** in Japan and **kim** in Korea. It is popularly served by dipping in sesame seed oil and soy sauce then toasting. It can also be toasted then crushed and mixed with soy, sugar, sesame seed oil, and red pepper. Another way is to cut the greens into small pieces, paint with rice powder and seasonings cooked together, then dust with sesame seeds, sun-dry, and finally fry.

Other vegetables in the category of greens are parsley leaves, spinach, bean sprouts, lettuce, celery, bamboo shoots, and carrots. A delightful "lettuce lunch" called **sang-chi-sam** is prepared by washing fresh green lettuce leaves (a few drops of sesame oil in the last rinse water makes the leaves shine). The leaves are arranged on one platter, and various tidbits such as varieties of seafood, bean paste, slivered meats, **kimch'i** (many types), and other greens are arranged on other platters. Diners choose their fillings, roll up their lettuce leaves, and eat. This dish is often served with soup.

An important ingredient and condiment is hot pepper mash made from sun-dried red peppers. Seeds are knocked off (they add bitterness) and the peppers are pounded into powder. The resulting powder is then mixed with soy sauce, sticky rice, and seasonings of onions, leeks, and spices. This may be eaten as a side dish, condiment with other foods, or in soups.

Finally, proper distinction must be given to the soybean, one of the most ingeniously used crops in China, Japan, Korea, and Southeast Asia. Aside from using the dried soybeans as any other dried legume (mixed with rice or vegetables), six other distinctive uses are made. Soybeans may be used in soy sauce, as soybean mash; as raw beans that are toasted in an iron pot then ground up and used as a garnish over rice cakes or plain rice (children enjoy eating the toasted coarser bits not used in the toasted meal); sprouted into soybean sprouts to be eaten lightly cooked as a vegetable; prepared into **tu bu** or soybean curd.

Tu bu is sometimes called "Oriental cheese" because of its creamy white appearance and smooth spongy texture. It is prepared by grinding soaked soybeans with water. The liquid is strained, boiled, and eaten as is, or it may be strained through a hemp bag into a shallow bowl; the curds left in the bag form a firm cake which may be cut, dipped in soy sauce, or fried in sesame seed oil and eaten. Oil can also be made from the soybeans, but it is not commonly used or prepared.

MEATS AND ALTERNATES

In many households, meat and fish are considered dishes for special occasions. Pork, chicken, fish, and many types of seafood are enjoyed when available. Fish is probably more plentiful than meats, though all rural households maintain a few pigs and chickens. Bits of fish or meat may be used in the preparation of **kimch'i**, soups, in casseroles and other dishes where the combination of grains and vegetables stretches the flavor of the more expensive meats and fish. Marinated dried beef is a favorite for appetizers; some may be toasted before serving. Raw beef strips are enjoyed after marinating in garlic and sesame oil, and served with slices of raw pear.

Charcoal fires are frequently used for barbecues. Strips of chicken or beef are marinated in mixtures of ground sesame seeds, sugar, soy sauce, minced garlic and green onion with a little sesame oil added near the end of marinating.

Eggs are used as available. They are scrambled, formed into small pancakes with vegetables or **kimch'i**, or made into steamed custards generally eaten for breakfast and, finally, sometimes used as soup garnishes.

The tiny Korean kitchens make ingenious use of their facilities: fish or meats are usually grilled over hot coals in a little pot stove; a cook may scramble eggs and add a few other ingredients and set the little filled bowls to steam over the rice in the rice pot; frying can be accomplished by using the top of the iron pot upside down; finally, great varieties of soups are begun in the Chinese way with the simple browning of tiny bits of meat or seafood in the bottom of a pot, followed by a sprinkling of soy sauce or other seasonings and the adding of water to make a basic broth.

Foods from the sea include sea cucumbers, oysters, crab, cuttlefish, cod, herring, whitebait (**baingo**), sea bream (plentiful and eaten with vinegar soy sauce), clams, crab, shrimp, and jellyfish.

Pine nuts, chestnuts, and walnuts are also used and must be considered for their texture and flavor as well as for the protein they provide. **Kochujan**, which is a seasoned red pepper bean paste, may be mixed with minced pine nuts, green onions, and sesame seeds to form a popular condiment used with pickled cucumbers and vinegar soy sauce. Many other dishes use pine nuts collected from the five-needled pine tree whose nuts are thought to have the essence of longevity.

Finally, two exotic foods enjoyed by Koreans are crickets and silkworms. Crickets are boiled whole then mixed with soy sauce usually as a special dish for babies and children in the autumn (said to prevent drooling), also as an upper-class delicacy for urban dwellers. Children also enjoy boiled silkworms when available.

BREADS AND GRAINS

Koreans do not generally eat breads as known in the western world. Rice is the staple and most important food. As a rule the rice is washed four times before cooking. The first rinse water is given to the pigs, the second may be used in the soup pot. Distinct personal preferences exist about exactly how much water to use for cooking the rice and the exact degree of hardness or softness desired. Rice accompanies every meal and often only rice with **kimch'i** comprises the entire meal. Rice may be served plain or mixed together with barley, cubed potatoes, sorghum, millet, or as a dish of rice, barley, and potatoes.

Rice flour is used in making special occasion cookies, steamed dumplings, and for the very special **tuk-kuk** or New Year's rice cake soup. For the rice cakes, the rice flour is steamed then kneaded.

Barley is the next most important grain. It is grown in between the season for the rice crops and is considered important especially when rice is scarce. Since it takes a long time to cook, barley is often boiled separately first and is always served combined with other foods. It is considered a "low-level food" but nonetheless important.

Although corn is grown in some areas, it is not used as a grain. It is considered more of a children's food and is cooked by steaming the ears of corn on top of the rice pot. The youngest children and babies are given cooked corn or white potato to gnaw on when they are hungry.

The buckwheat grown in Korean fields is widely enjoyed in the form of buckwheat noodles. In fact, noodles are frequently homemade from a dough of buckwheat flour, salt, rice flour, or cornstarch and water. The stiff dough is then pressed through a Korean noodle cutter placed over a pan of boiling water. Noodles are called **myun**. Noodles are considered a lunch dish, whether served hot or cold. **Naing-myun** is a cold plate of cooked buckwheat noodles served with a garnish of chopped **kimch'i**, strips of beef or chicken and sliced pear and sliced hard egg; chilled broth is poured over. A similar dish served hot and said to be a favorite of the masses – especially enjoyed by men as they eat sitting cross-legged – is **jaing-ban**. The heated meat and condiments are enjoyed with wine, the noodles are eaten last, and the entire platter is kept hot over small fire pots placed on the low tables.

FATS

Sesame seed oil is used both for cooking and frying. Frequently the flavorful oil, reminiscent of toasted sesame seeds, is also used to give a sheen to washed greens or roasted (grilled) meats.

Other fats consumed include those contained in pork crackling and chicken skin and in the actual meats themselves.

SWEETS AND SNACKS

Considering that a small Korean child is commonly given a cooked potato or a steamed cob of corn to gnaw on as a snack between meals, as opposed to the early western introduction of sweet cookies and sweetened desserts, it can be seen that the Korean sweet tooth is an insignificant one.

Desserts are not part of traditional Korean meals but they are served when special guests come and also for holiday and feast occasions. **Chun Kwa** is the name given to a variety of candy-coated thinly sliced vegetables; the prepared vegetables are dipped into a syrup then allowed to cool and harden. Many types of dried fruits – sometimes candied – are also enjoyed. Steamed and kneaded glutinous rice can be made into many types of small cookies and pastries often flavored with honey and nuts. Some are even sun-dried then deep-fried. **Kai-yut** are sesame seed candies, and a candy treat made from glutinous rice powder, chestnuts, honey, dates, and cinnamon is called "flower paste" or **ju-ak**. **Ju-ak** is shaped and fried in sesame oil then sprinkled lightly with sugar.

Pine cakes or **song-pyun** are specially festive and often used as offerings to the spirits of ancestors. They are made with rice powder dough pressed into small cup shapes then filled with red beans, chestnuts, and raisin mixture. The unusual taste comes from steaming them together with fresh pine needles. Another festive favorite is **kyung-dan**, sweet dumplings which are also prepared from glutinous rice powder dough. Red bean paste and chestnut paste are popped into the center then rolled in a ball which is finally coated with yellow bean powder or very finely chopped walnuts or dates.

Interestingly, although these festive and dessert specialties are considered to be sweets, many are also considered medicinal because of their content of nutritious ingredients such as honey, raisins, etc.

Sometimes fruits are poached in a light syrup and flavored with ginger root. Such a dessert is **su-jun-wa**, made from persimmons.

The traditional children's treat, particularly in rural areas at New Year's, is **yot**. This is ritually prepared from ground barley powder mixed in a ratio of one-to-three parts of boiled rice, then heated carefully with water (overheating makes it bitter). The thick part is gradually spooned off and the remaining liquid is allowed to boil until it thickens into a rich syrup. This is much enjoyed by dipping rice cakes into it.

SEASONINGS

The taste and distinctive aroma of sesame seeds is characteristic of Korean cooking because sesame seed oil is the preferred fat, and sesame seeds are used in many dishes. Garlic, green onions, ginger root, pine nuts, and monosodium glutamate are all used generously. Pears and pear juice are often used both as seasoning and as condiment. Soy sauce, vinegar soy sauce (a combination of two parts soy sauce, one part vinegar and monosodium glutamate), and **kochujan** are the condiments. The latter is a red pepper and bean paste made from a blend of soy sauce, bean paste, and powdered red peppers in equal parts. Another condiment is prepared from a base of **kochu-jan** with minced green onions, crushed pine nuts, and sesame seeds. This pine nut condiment is served with pickled cucumbers.

Commercially prepared soy sauce, of course, is widely available, but many households in Korea still prepare their own. Prepared in the autumn, the boiled and pounded soybeans are molded into a cone shape and set to dry hard. Then they are wrapped with rice straw, hung from ceilings, and allowed to ferment for several weeks. (Such fermented cones may be winter-stored in huge rice straw bags kept in a cool place.)

In the spring, bits of the cone are broken into a water-filled jar to which is added salt, spices, red peppers, and a few charcoal lumps. This is left in the sun a few days until the molded soybean clumps float on top and the resulting liquid turns black. The final step is the ladling out of the black liquid which is then boiled to become soy sauce. The remaining contents of the jar are used as soybean mash.

BEVERAGES

Water is an anytime drink. Well water is considered superior but spring waters are considered to have medicinal value. In wintertime (November to February) hot water is sometimes taken with lunch.

It was the Japanese who introduced tea as a beverage in the cities and towns, but it is almost nonexistent in the villages. **Sungyung** completes every meal: the color and flavor are derived by pouring hot water over the charred rice or barley in the bottom of the pot. Sesame seed tea is also enjoyed.

There is a great fondness for wine and spirits although at all times drunkenness is considered very offensive, while an inebriated woman is simply intolerable. However, there is leeway in what is considered drunkenness. One village saying insists that a man may not be considered drunk so long as he can still move an arm.

T'akju is a light wine that has an alcohol content of about 10 percent, a bit stronger than beer. **Yakju** is a stronger version of **T'akju** with about 15 percent alcohol content and is considered medicinal, as are many other good things. **Soju** ("burning wine") is a spirit so named because of its effect and probably because of its 25 percent alcohol content.

Omija-wha-chai is a refreshing beverage made either in the home or commercially. It is a seasonable drink prepared from fresh or dried fruit, parts of tart or sour flowers and is sweetened with honey or sugar. **Shikhe** is another sweetened drink, prepared from fermented rice and sugar and lightly scented with citron.

MEALS AND CUSTOMS

Koreans disagree whether breakfast or supper is the main meal of the day. Generally breakfast is more important in the country, while supper is the main meal in the city. Considering the work patterns, this emphasis can be understood. Since rice and **kimch'i** are present at every meal, the additions of soup, meat or fish, and vegetable dishes and more probably, the amount and number of courses, would signify which is the most important meal of the day. Many Koreans prefer rice for breakfast and supper, while a noodle dish with meat or fish and vegetables and sometimes soup provides a satisfying lunch.

Meals are usually taken while the family and guests sit cross-legged around a floor mat upon which are placed separate low-legged trays with the foods for each diner. Sometimes foods are arranged banquet or buffet style and each diner takes his or her portion to eat with rice.

Ladles made from gourds as well as crafted ladles from brass are used for spooning out foods, but brass chopsticks and spoons are used for dining. Rice, soup, and **kimch'i** may be eaten with the aid of spoons; liquid, soup, **kimch'i** juice and wine can also be loudly and appreciatively sucked from bowls.

The etiquette of chopsticks demands that they be held close to bowl and mouth. Further, they should always be held close to the top ends for it is said that those who hold their chopsticks near the working end will have a bad wife. It is considered bad taste to make a scratching sound with chopsticks or spoons against the food bowls.

It is expected that liquor will be served at funerals, weddings, sixty-first birthdays (sixty-one is considered a significant age), at any old man's birthday, at all ceremonial festivals. Wine is poured graciously into a bowl and passed around, while the men sit on their heels and sip. The largest wine bowl (about 4 inches) is for **T'akju**; **Yakju** is served in a smaller one; and the potent **Soju** is presented in a tiny winecup. The many forms of **kimch'i** are nibbled in between sips of the wine as an hors d'oeuvre.

Both men and women enjoy pipe tobacco at any time. In the cities and towns people enjoy smoking cigarettes, but these are too expensive for most villagers who simply grow and dry their own tobacco suited more to pipe smoking.

Children are nursed till about two years of age but in the villages it is not uncommon to see even six-year-olds occasionally nursing. This is no embarrassment to anyone. Weaning is accomplished by the simple expedient of dabbing the nipples with pepper. Children are fed whenever they cry. As the child becomes older he or she may be given a corn cob to nibble or a cooked potato or even a **daikon** soaked briefly in saltwater.

Social life in the villages centers on the *matang*, and guests are always welcomed. The only exception to this is the few days after childbirth when it is understood that the family would prefer to be alone. In the cities, many fine restaurants abound and men enjoy bars, cafés, and nightclubs. Upper-class men enjoy the company of *kisaeng* (female entertainers like the *geishas* of Japan), while upper-class women for the most part live a secluded and isolated life, spending their free time sewing and embroidering when the details of managing the home are completed. However, Korean cities, like large cities everywhere, are changing with the pressures of modern society and more and more women are venturing into the business and professional world.

SPECIAL OCCASIONS

Similar in pattern to their culture, the religion of Koreans is gently layered. That is, although many are Christians today, their Christianity does not dispose of, but somehow rests amiably with, the traditional "layers" of Buddhism, Confucianism, spirit worship, and animism.

Special occasions may be divided into those concerning family rites and those which are widely celebrated holidays. The first and the sixty-first birthdays are considered the most important and the most festive.

A child's first birthday is celebrated by dressing the youngster in bright colors and serving treats of rice cakes, cookies, and fruits. The whole family delights in the ceremony where the child is placed in the midst of symbols representing possible future careers and everyone enjoys predicting which symbol the child will grasp. For example, should he grasp a coin, it is believed he will be a businessman. The sixty-first birthday, especially of a man, is greeted with festive foods and much wine and rejoicing; this is called *hwangab*.

Traditional weddings and funerals have recently been much simplified. Elaborate processions, numerous guests (or professional wailers and mourners), and huge presentations of food and wine have been reduced to simple meaningful rituals more consistent with the times. Weddings are most often performed amidst flowers and music in special wedding halls. There is still a treasured tradition that requires parental approval of the match before the wedding, and sometimes even the astute services of a matchmaker.

On New Year's Day (usually in February on the lunar calendar) families surround the ancestral shrine in the home of the eldest son with plates of fruits and cookies, rice cakes and "sweet wine" (a non-alcoholic mix of liquid **yot** with the residue previously spooned off). Everyone dresses in his or her best clothes and pays respect by bowing to the elders in the family. Small treats of foods and gifts of money are given to the children. Families and close friends visit one another; those in mourning may receive visitors but do not pay calls.

Bibim-bab is a specialty dish often prepared for festive nights and New Year's. A variety of mixed fresh and dried vegetables are individually cooked and carefully shredded together with a beef and egg pancake; each of the ingredients is artistically arranged on a rice bowl and is mixed just before eating. This colorful and substantial dish becomes a meal with soup and **kimch'i**.

On special occasions as always, Korean children are taught to drop their eyes to show respect, and always cup both hands when receiving any gift, sweet, or special treat. (Koreans stare into each other's eyes only in anger). While festive occasions are times of happy chatter, there is always a hush when the trays of foods are served, for Koreans prefer to give their attention to the food at hand rather than to converse while eating.

In Korea most traditional holidays are based on the seasonal farming cycle and the dates are from the lunar calendar. In the villages these festive days are

observed as in olden times but in the towns and cities and amongst emigrant Koreans, the observance of the holidays varies greatly. Some will prepare the festive foods out of nostalgia and enjoy them with family and close friends, others will retain the ancient traditions of ancestor tributes, while many take the occasion as a day of rest or partying. There are few Korean homes, however, that do not keep a traditional lunar calendar with the special occasions clearly marked.

The fifteenth day of the first month on the lunar calendar is celebrated with singing and dancing and wrestling contests (*ssirum*). This is called *Taeborum* or *Dongsin-je*. The first full moon of the new year is called *Dal-magi* or *Talmaji* and is celebrated by torch-light parades to the highest hill in the area to view the moon clearly while huge bonfires are lit expressing hopes for fruitful crops, longevity, and the good things of life.

Cold Food Day or *Hansik* is celebrated approximately 105 days after the winter solstice. People offer tributes of wine and cold foods near the graves of their ancestors; later, the foods and wine are eaten by the family picnic style. In some areas the festival is marked by tree planting. Later in the same month some homes mark Buddha's birthday by processions, banners, and lanterns; some shrines and homes are specially decorated as well.

Tano is a day of sports events, including wrestling for the men, contests of seesawing for the women, and swinging for the children. It is celebrated on the fifth day of the fifth lunar month. Those who are too old to participate content themselves with watching and musing on the strength they enjoyed when they were younger.

The day of the full moon in the eighth month brings the beautiful harvest festival of thanksgiving called *Chusok*. Foods and wine are offered at the ancestral shrines. Celebrations include feasting, dancing, village bands, and much rice wine. One need not be in the countryside to enjoy and treasure the abundance of this festival, for it is celebrated everywhere.

During the traditional period of the winter solstice, women cook and sew while men enjoy a respite from the hard work of the fields. On *Dongji*, the day of the winter solstice, foods are prepared with red beans both in **juk** (porridges of rice) and in **kuk** (soups). Special sweet cakes made with glutinous rice also mark the day.

Korean Christians mark Christmas in quiet family gatherings. Many attend church services. For those living in Korea, this season is their winter, so Koreans enjoy a "white Christmas" too.

Special and ceremonial dishes include the following: roasted chicken; oysters, sea cucumbers;

soups of beef, pork, and seaweed; grilled pork, fish or beef dishes; fried eggs with pumpkin or dryfish; fried bean curd; tiny boiled bean sprouts or Chinese "flower bell"; steamed rice cakes; glutinous rice cakes; **kimch'i**; pumpkin, flour-dipped and fried; **yot**; white rice; sweet wine and varieties of wine spirits.

GLOSSARY OF FOODS AND FOOD TERMS

Bam-Kyung-Dan: dessert of spiced puréed chestnut formed into balls, rolled in honey then chopped almonds.

Bibim-Bab: literally, mixed rice; a variety of fresh and dried vegetables all individually cooked plus beef and egg shredded pancake. All of these are precisely shredded and sliced then arranged over a bowl of rice to be mixed just before eating.

Bin-Ja Tuk: a pancake made from soaked mung beans. After the batter is poured on a hot griddle (inverted pan), small strips of pork and **Kimch'i** are placed on top then flipped. Good inexpensive meal eaten with rice and other **Kimch'i** with vinegar soy sauce as a dip.

Bulkoki or **Bulgogi**: small tender patties of good beef fillet marinated in spicy hot sauce, briefly cooked in sesame oil then eaten by dipping in more fiery spiced sauce.

Chun-Kwa: treats made from thinly sliced vegetables coated with sugar glaze.

Hobahk-Juhn: ground beef and slivered zucchini stirred with beaten eggs. Spoonfuls of the mixture are dropped into hot sesame seed oil to form small, 3-inch omelets. This is served with rice and a dipping sauce called **Cho Jung** (mixture of soy sauce, vinegar, sugar, minced onion, and toasted sesame seeds).

Hong-Haisam: a festive dish using sea cucumbers, for special occasions like weddings and sixtieth birthdays.

Juk: rice "porridges" made with addition of white sesame seeds, or red beans or pine nuts or soy beans – all served in little bowls with sugar. Sometimes made with meat and vegetables.

Kalbi-Kui: barbecued short ribs of beef. The meat is deeply scored in criss-cross fashion then marinated three hours or overnight in a sauce of soy, garlic, ginger, green onions, sesame oil and seeds, with the addition of sugar, vinegar, and pepper. The chunks of meat are then drained and barbecued over hot coals. A barbecue meal is usually served with a salad of blanched greens (watercress), soybean sprouts dressed with soy, sugar, onions and toasted sesame seeds, and rice and **Kimch'i**.

Keran-Chikai: steamed egg custard prepared in small dishes. Ground beef and mushrooms are mixed with the stirred egg then garnished with threads of red pepper and green onion on top. Served as a breakfast dish.

Kimch'i: the national dish of Korea. Can be made many ways but the classic is **Baichu-Kimch'i**, made from salted, fermented, spiced and chopped Chinese cabbage. The *baichu* may be layered with other items such as sliced onions, shredded radishes, dried shrimp, cuttlefish, squid, garlic, ginger root, sugar, anchovy sauce, etc. Other types include: **Kaktuki**, pickled radish or *daikon*; **Nabak-Kimch'i**, slightly different variation on the *kaktuki* often served on New Year's; **Oi-Sobaki**, small cucumber pickles; **Put-Kimch'i** (green pickles), salted, seasoned and fermented spring greens such as turnip greens, watercress, mustard greens, etc. (made in small quantities and used quickly); and **Tong-Chimi**, another type of pickled radish (bigger pieces). The juice of the latter is sipped while eating **Tuk** (rice cakes) on New Year's. *Note: While the many varieties of* **Kimch'i** *may be considered in the category of pickles it should be noted that they are not only served with every meal as a side dish or condiment, they are also used as ingredients in other dishes. Even the tangy fermented juice is enjoyed as a beverage and as a flavoring in stews and soups.*

Kochujan: a hot red pepper and mashed bean paste blended in equal parts with soy sauce. Used as a condiment alone or in combination with other flavorings.

Ku-Jul-Pan: a special dish with separate compartments used especially for the attractive arrangement of mixed appetizers.

Kuk: the general name for soup. Most soups are prepared with minimal ingredients and maximum flavor. Tiny strips of meat and vegetables are tossed and browned in a little oil, then the second rinse water from the rice is poured in to make the stock base (of Chinese origin). Soups are great favorites, especially in cool weather, and many types are made. Examples include: **Kori-kuk**, oxtail soup; **Aitang-kuk**, a spring soup prepared after a family outing to collect the first greens, usually mugwort; **Yukkai-Jang-Kuk**, a rich beef broth garnished with green onions eaten especially in the hottest summer weather in order to "maintain strength and give heat relief"; **Muik-Kuk**, a broth made from seaweed. The latter is believed to have many healthful properties. It is given to mothers four or five times a day after childbirth. It is also the soup served on birthdays, perhaps to remind one of his or her birth. It is as common a birthday dish as cake is in the western world. *Note: An important ingredient in many soups, used to add flavor, is Joki, a white-meat fish that is purchased brine-pickled, dried, or salted. When not available, salt cod can be used.*

Kyung-Dan: "sweet dumplings" made from glutinous rice powder dough with chestnut paste or red bean paste placed in the center. Tiny balls are then rolled in yellow-bean powder and, finally, chopped dates or nuts.

Myun: noodles. The Korean favorite is noodles made from buckwheat flour.

Naing-Myun: a dish of cooked cold buckwheat noodles swirled on a plate and topped with attractively arranged chopped **Kimch'i**, stripped beef, chicken, sliced pear, and hard egg. To serve, a chilled broth is poured over. Side condiments include mustard, red pepper, or vinegar.

Na-Nul-Jan-A-Chi: whole heads of fresh garlic pickled in vinegar, soy, and sugar. Served sliced very thinly crosswise and with wine and rice.

Sang-Chi-Sam: the "lettuce lunch" which is considered a meal, and usually served with soup. Fresh lettuce leaves are well washed. The addition of a few drops of sesame seed oil in the last rinse assures shiny leaves. The leaves are arranged on a platter with a second platter of variously prepared tidbits of fish, seafood, meats, vegetables, condiments, bean paste. Morsels are chosen as desired, placed in a lettuce leaf, then rolled up and eaten.

Sinsun-Lo: the "hot pot" of Korea. Traditionally made up of nineteen different ingredients, today much simplified but still popular. Consists of several meats and fish slivered, dipped, and fried in sesame oil. It also contains tiny meat omelets arranged in sliced rolls, sliced onions and watercress, and flour and egg dipped then fried. All of these prepared foods are artfully arranged in a special utensil called **Sin-Sul-Lo** (like a Mongolian hot pot). Red charcoal is placed in the center chimney and as soon as the meats sizzle, hot broth is poured over and eaten by all.

Tahk-Kui: chicken, marinated then barbecued. See **Kalbi-Kui**.

Tongtak Juk: roasted chicken. A special occasion dish flavored with garlic, ginger, and sesame seed oil.

Tu Bu: soybean curd.

Tuk: rice cakes.

Tuk-Kuk: New Year's rice cake soup. One of the important festive dishes traditional for New Year's, it is prepared by steaming then kneading regular rice flour. The soup is garnished with crushed dried *kim* (seaweed) and black pepper. A popular festive soup garnish is shredded egg pancakes.

Yot: a thick, sweet syrup boiled from barley and rice then dipped into with rice cakes. A great treat, especially for children, who regard it as a candy.

Yuk-Po: dried beef

CHAPTER 33

LATIN AMERICAN:

ARGENTINIAN AND URUGUAYAN, BRAZILIAN, CHILEAN, COLOMBIAN AND VENEZUELAN, PERUVIAN

For the adventurous Spanish explorers and navigators who first touched western lands, new lands to conquer were the lesser goals; hope of riches was the driving force that pushed them through uncharted waters, steamy jungles, and over defiant mountains.

But the Spaniards were in fact not the first. Many centuries before them, tribes of Aboriginal peoples had migrated from north to south, settling in areas along the way, adapting themselves to their surroundings and even building temples and cities of incredible grandeur. They staked out their territories, in many cases set up complex systems of government and systematically cultivated a number of crops. These included many varieties of beans, the whole family of squashes and pumpkin, sweet and white potatoes, tomatoes, hot chili peppers and tobacco. Pineapples, papayas, bananas, coconuts, and many varieties of corn found many uses. In ancient Tenochtitlan (Mexico), corn was revered as a deity. Chocolate from cacao and vanilla from leathery brown pods were also cultivated and used by many Aboriginal tribes. While the Spaniards may not have been the first, their arrival was to instigate a period of savage wars.

How could the Spaniards have known that the gold they sought would be so tainted with blood? Or that the countries they fought to establish would in later years suffer still more bloodshed in fighting for their independence? And how could they have known that the cargoes of foodstuffs and plants that they would bring back to the European continent would spread to many countries and effect far more profound and lasting consequences than gold?

In a similar way, the many peoples, herds of cattle, swine and sheep, and the many plants that would migrate to South America would change the topography, the lifestyle and even the food habits of the inhabitants, for the Europeans brought with them the culture of wheat and rice and the taste for domesticated meats such as beef, lamb and chicken and the use of fats in cookery. Onions and garlic added piquancy to the bland and the hot flavors of indigenous herbs and peppers. A quickly spreading taste for sugary sweets was another influence from the Old World.

One of the most important products introduced to the New World was coffee. Coffee was reputedly discovered in the ancient Arab world, and took hold in Europe in the 1700s. But it owes its introduction to the western hemisphere to a Frenchman, Gabriel Mathieu Desclieux, who brought a cutting of the coffee plant to the French-owned island of Martinique in the West Indies in the 1700s. It was from there that other cuttings were taken to French Guiana and from there to Brazil. Today it is Brazil and Colombia who lead world coffee production.

Early food patterns in Central and South America before the arrival of the Europeans still form an important part of the basic food patterns of today. The early subsistence foods of corn and beans in fact are the same subsistence foods in Mesoamerica today. The preparation of the corn itself involved a lime water soaking (incidentally adding valuable minerals to the diet), then a crushing and grinding to prepare the **masa harina** (corn flour) used to form the flat corn cakes called **tortillas**. (See Mexican.) This is the core staple of Mexican food, while simply crushed corn forms the modern-day Panama staple.

In the mountainous Andes area, corn is more commonly eaten green (both in early times and now), supplementing the indigenous potato and other tubers such as **oca**, **ulluco**, and **mashwa**. Grain, such as the Andean grain called **quinoa**, is also a staple, supplying protein to the diet – and incidentally becoming a popular grain in North America.

The agricultural Indians along the Atlantic coast, in the Caribbean and in the northern part of South America survived by hunting and fishing and by cultivating a poisonous bitter plant called **manioc**. There are many varieties of this tuberous plant, called sweet **cassava** in North America and **yuca** in South America. But it was the bitter and poisonous **manioc** that the Indians somehow not only discovered how to eat and prepare, but most important, how to process to remove the toxic quality of the juice. They did this by patiently grating the pulp and allowing it to hang in a mesh basket till all the juice dripped through. By boiling the juice they were able to make it into a palatable sauce. By toasting the dried pulp they formed **manioc meal** or **farinha de mandioca**. Modern Brazilians still enjoy the absorbing quality of the meal and sprinkle it liberally on almost any juicy food. Today in Brazil the processing of **manioc** is of course commercialized; the rest of the world enjoys it too in the form of tiny pellets called **tapioca**.

The Spanish conquests of the 1500s brought the complete destruction of many tribes and ancient civilizations; they also added wheat and rice to the diets, and introduced the use of fats in cookery, particularly sauteeing and frying. The cattle, swine, and fowl that the Spaniards managed to bring on their sailing vessels became the initiators of domestic herds of cattle, swine, and flocks of chickens and ducks. It was not long before large quantities of meats became readily available and an important part of the Latin American diet.

Before this, only those meats from successful hunting were a part of meals and in many areas, such as Mesoamerica, wild game was often reserved for royalty and seldom became a part of the daily meals of ordinary people. In fact, a sad commentary on the "modern diet" may be that it has moved too far from the basic nutritious diet of the native Indians, and the wealthier classes may in many cases have a poorer diet, too heavy in sweets, fats, and breads.

The effect on the diet of the native peoples in the Andean Highlands was negligible as they had little contact with the Europeans. However, one of the most notable shifts in consumption for the lowland peoples was the introduction and acceptance of rice as a staple in areas as distant as the Panama to many

of the lower jungle areas of the entire Andean range. But the general trend throughout Central and South America, aside from the foods mentioned, was the impressive use and adaptation of the range of indigenous staples by the new European population.

Although the Amazon floodplain has a strong potential for growing rice, it is still mainly a **manioc**-corn-beans area, following the Aboriginal patterns. In fact the areas where heavy meat-eating becomes the pattern together with areas where wheat, milk, and rice consumption is dominant, are clearly those areas where the native Indian population is diminished or no longer exists and urbanization has taken over.

The vast size of South America with its varying climates and topography and differing ethnic populations makes generalizations difficult, but some food items are common to most countries, and the diligent cultivation by native Indians is responsible for the enjoyment of so many of these foods and products in almost every country of the world: chocolate and vanilla, pineapples, bananas, squashes, potatoes and pumpkins, tobacco, tomatoes and hot chili peppers. These indigenous foods gradually blended with those introduced by the Europeans: rice, wheat, milk and cheeses, garlic and onions, coffee, sugar and rum. The introduction of domesticated animals and fowl has resulted in a much greater increase in meat consumption.

The very old staples of corn, beans, and **manioc** are still the subsistent foods for millions of Latin Americans, while high in the Andes, native Indians still survive on the staples of potatoes, **quinoa** flour, and dried llama meat as did their ancestors. In coastal and river areas fish and seafood form an important part of the diet while the grassy Pampas provides a diet high in beef for those of the area. Urban popu-

FOODS COMMONLY USED

Quantities of milk and varieties of cheeses are produced in both Argentina and Uruguay but both these products are used mostly in cooking. Cheeses and fruits are a part of dessert selections among the upper classes. The favorite meat of Argentinians is beef, and for the *gauchos* it is also their sole staple, washed down with a tea-like drink called **yerba mate**. Uruguayans also add mutton and lamb, while in both countries outdoor grilling of meats provides the

favorite cooking method. **Asado** (outdoor roasted meats including many types of sausages and organ meats), **matambre** (rolled stuffed meat served in colorful slices) and **empanadas** (meat-stuffed pastries of Spanish origin) are great favorites too. Fish, eggs, and legumes are available but are less commonly used except in coastal areas, where a wide variety of fish and seafood is enjoyed. Vegetable staples include the many varieties of both squash and potatoes as

well as corn and pumpkin. They form the basis of many soups and stews and are used by all classes. Fruits are mostly enjoyed by upper-class urbanites as are certain vegetables and salad greens. But all have a penchant for richly sweet desserts and pastries as well as highly sweetened beverages such as **yerba mate**, coffee, or fresh fruit punches. Rum and many fine local wines as well as strongly brewed coffee add to refreshment.

lations in any country enjoy the indigenous staples together with European staples and blend them into different cuisines. (See Regional Specialties.)

Rum (prepared from sugarcane) and coffee are the most widespread beverages, although some areas produce grapes for wine production. **Mate** and various fruit juice punches and soft drinks are important too.

In South America as elsewhere, domestic life and the facilities for preparing, serving, and storing foods vary according to class prestige, economic ability, local customs, and taboos. Obvious differences in family relationships and household facilities must exist between the *gauchos* (cowboys) of the Pampas and the Andean herders, between the native Indians in remote jungle areas and the sophisticated urban population of the large cities.

ARGENTINIAN AND URUGUAYAN

Argentina and Uruguay share many similarities in history, climate, people, food production, and food customs. The gentle temperate climate, the rolling

grassy Pampas and the many river systems attracted increasing numbers of hardy and adventurous Spanish settlers who brought with them their cattle and sheep, horses and hogs. Settlers enjoyed the natural beauties of the area, but natural growth and productivity was marred in subsequent years by battles for independence from Spain.

Still weakened from battles with Spain, the Portuguese in Brazil took advantage of Uruguay's weakness and annexed the **Banda Oriental**, as the area was called. Argentina's unrest centered on freedom from Spanish rule and this was attained in 1835, while Uruguay was granted independence only a few years earlier in 1828.

Civil wars as well as political unrest and economic downturns have plagued both countries. From 1930 to 1955, Juan Peron's successful populist strategies and economic development policies brought Argentina to a new level of achievement. But authoritarian military rule stepped in when three events coincided to crush his popularity and power: the death of his charismatic wife, Eva; the diminishing markets for Argentine exports; and clashes with the Catholic Church. In the years from 1966 to 1973, under brutal authoritarian rule, more than 20,000 Argentine citizens simply disappeared without a trace,

in what came to be known as the "Dirty War." However, following the Falklands/Malvinas war with Britain, the military government was ousted with the civilian election of Carlos Menem. Suffering economic instead of political hardship now, nonetheless the people of Argentina continue to strive for a better life for all citizens.

Uruguay too suffered under repressive military rule from 1973 to the early 1980s during which human rights and dignity were severely abused. But by 1984, Sanguinetti won a civilian election, approved amnesty for the military and, by increasing foreign investment and liberalizing trade, set Uruguay's economy on a firm but steady course forward. Ousted briefly, he was returned to office again in 1994.

Both Argentina and Uruguay have very high literacy levels among their predominantly European populations. Most claim Spanish or Italian heritage, but others include French, German, Russian, and Turkish in Argentina, while aside from Spanish and Italian, Uruguay's citizens claim Brazilian and Argentinian as well as French heritages. Uruguay is particularly proud to be the only nation in the western hemisphere where all levels of education from public school to postgraduate studies are free. In both countries the official language is Spanish and the predominant religion is Roman Catholic.

Men in both Argentina and Uruguay typically work on a ranch or in some area of the food processing industries. Most women tend to occupy themselves with caring for the home and family. Domestic life is of great importance and the saying *"Mi casa es su casa"* is meant in the warmest sense of rich and generous hospitality. Entertaining in one's home is preferred although casual meetings in cafés and inns are as much enjoyed as in Spain or Italy. Gatherings of friends and guests are always loud and lusty with comparative quiet only coming while everyone eats.

DAIRY PRODUCTS

The Argentine dairy cattle, **Holando Argentino**, and Jersey breeds produce quantities of fresh milk used in similar ways as in North America. Urban populations consume some fresh milk but most is used in custards, **flans**, and puddings, such as rice puddings, where the cereal is cooked in milk. Many varieties of cheeses are produced similar in appearance and taste to the prized European ones. In Argentine mountain areas cheeses are made from goat's milk; other areas produce fine cheeses from sheep's milk. Grated and sliced cheeses are used in many dishes such as soups, casseroles, pasta dishes, and for dessert with fresh local fruits.

FRUITS AND VEGETABLES

Fruits, fruit desserts, and fruit jams are widely used, but mostly in urban areas and among the upper classes. Many varieties of apples and pears, quinces, peaches, and apricots, cherries and grapes as well as bananas, coconuts, pineapples, and other tropical and semi-tropical fruits are available. The varying soils and climates are suited to different types of fruit cultivation. Many types of preserves and jams form a part of breakfast with breads and a beverage, while fresh fruits are more likely to be a part of desserts at lunch or dinner. Typical of Argentina is a dessert of cheese served with a jam made from quince or sweet potatoes.

Pumpkins and many types of squashes, sweet potatoes, and mealy white potatoes and corn are the principal vegetables used. Salad greens and other vegetables are mostly used in urban areas. *Gauchos* seldom eat either fruit or vegetables, surviving mainly on large quantities of roasted or boiled beef and **yerba mate**, sipped from a silver or metal straw called a **bombilla**, which is placed in a gourd that contains the tea-like beverage.

Both squashes and corn are used in many interesting ways. Squash soup, squash fritters, baked squash puddings, and chunks of squash in stews such as **carbonada criolla** add color and rich smooth flavor. In the **carbonada**, the rich beef stew is served in a hollowed-out squash shell. In other dishes the chunks of squash are allowed to cook till they disintegrate into a thick golden mass, enriching the sauce by coloring and thickening it and, incidentally, adding valuable nutrients.

Corn is used imaginatively as well. Small chunks of corn are cooked together with beef and other vegetables in the **carbonada**, but grated green corn also forms the most important ingredient in **humitas**, a spiced mixture of grated corn served as a side dish, or the mixture may be spooned into corn husks called **chalas** then wrapped, tied, and steamed. The **humitas en chala** are prepared exactly as they were hundreds of years before by the ancient Aztecs; the Mexicans call them **tamales**. Corn flour cakes, buns, and puddings abound in many variations. **Chuchoca** is the name given to maize toasted on hot coals, **timbales de polenta** betray the Italian name for corn (**polenta**) and refer to a type of cornmeal porridge, while **mazamorra** is the name given to sugar-sweetened maize cooked in milk.

MEATS AND ALTERNATES

The favorite meat of the Argentine is beef. Huge quantities are consumed and it is not uncommon for beef to appear in each meal of the day. Uruguayans also enjoy sheep and lamb. In both countries, open-air grills called *parrilla* are so commonly used to prepare **asado** (roasted meat) that it is said the tantalizing smell of meats roasting over wood fires may be called "the national aroma."

The Argentine appetite for meat can be noted in two popular appetizer dishes that often precede a hearty meal: **matambre** (roasted rolled steak with vegetable stuffing) and **empanadas** (meat-filled pastries). Probably it is the *gauchos* of the Pampas who introduced the **asado con cuero**, meats in their natural state, that is with hide and hair intact, roasted over open wood fires. Huge sides of beef, lamb, kid, and sometimes pork may be cooked by this method. On smaller grills, together with meat chunks, many parts of the animal are grilled also in their natural state: chunks of intestine, liver, etc., all become part of the **asada**. Restaurants specializing in such mixed grills are called *churrascarias*. **Matambre** is a prepared piece of flank that is rolled up and stuffed with attractively arranged vegetables. After moist roasting or steaming, the roll is sliced and served hot or cold. **Empanadas**, from Spain, are half-moons of pastry well filled with meats, olives, and raisins. Pitchers of wines and assorted fruit punches wash down the appetizers and stave off hunger while the diners await the **asada**.

Fresh fish and many varieties of seafood are available but do not form nearly as important a part of the diet as the meats. Eggs are poached or fried and often top steaks or chops as a garnish. Eggs are also part of the caramelized **flan** that is a frequent dessert. Beans and nuts are not a widely used form of protein, although nuts may be used as snacks or as ingredients in desserts and confections.

BREADS AND GRAINS

A wide variety of breads, buns, and rolls prepared from wheat, rye, and cornflour is served at most meals. Abundant use of corn is seen in flours and finely ground meal like **masa harina** as well as **hominy** and **cornstarch**. Bread is especially important for breakfast when it is usually served with butter and jams. Corn and rice become part of many dishes as well.

FATS

Beef fat, butter, and olive oil are used in cooking, baking, and salads. Lard is popular in baking and frying while other fats such as duck and goose fat, palm and coconut oil may also be used.

SWEETS AND SNACKS

Much sugar is taken in coffee, sugar-sweetened fruit punches, and soft drinks. Jams are a part of every breakfast. Many types of **flans**, custards, and sweet puddings as well as confections made of fruit pastes, ground seeds (squash seeds, for instance), and nuts heavily sweetened and colored may be seen often for desserts or on special festive occasions. As in Spain and Portugal, many convents are famed for the sweet confections and special occasion cakes they prepare. **Dulce de leche** is a thick, jam-like sweet that is prepared from the slow cooking of milk and sugar.

SEASONINGS

In most of South America, onions, garlic, and tiny hot peppers are the predominant seasonings. Mostly the fresh natural flavors of fresh produce and ingredients prevail. Chocolate, sugar, and vanilla are used in desserts as are the tangy flavors of fresh citrus juices or the grating of their rinds. Also used are **achiote** or **annatto** seeds (which add red color) from the annatto tree, coconut in many forms, rum, and a variety of fresh herbs.

BEVERAGES

Argentina and Uruguay produce sufficient quantities of grapes to produce some fine local wines, both white and red. Coffee is a favorite beverage but is taken so sweet that often even the beans are roasted with sugar. **Mate** is drunk mostly by country people who still brew this tea from the dried leaves of a holly tree. The liquid is steeped and drunk from a small gourd, by sipping through a **bombilla**, a straw which has a perforated, rounded base that acts to strain the leaves. **Yerba mate** is popular in Argentina, Paraguay, and parts of Chile and Brazil, its high caffeine content providing a powerful wake-up.

BRAZILIAN

Brazil, occupying nearly half the South American continent, is the fifth-largest country in the world. The climate varies from tropical to sub-temperate

and ranges over a topography that includes the highlands of the Brazilian Plateau to the Amazon River Basin, which is largely an area of floodplains and tropical rain forests. Rapid depletion of these valuable and pristine rain forests is causing international environmental concern.

Brazil boasts the highest and most rapidly growing gross national product (GNP) in all of South America. In addition, Brazil is now the world's leading producer of not only coffee but also sugarcane, soybeans, papayas, oranges, and **cassava**, with cattle and pig stocks ranking among the highest as well. Brazil's avocado, tangerine and mandarin, cocoa bean and banana exports also rank high among world production and export. Crops of rice and edible dried beans as well as a thriving fishing industry add to the nation's table and the general economy.

Brazil differs from every other country in South America. More than 60 percent of the population is of European origin and Portuguese is the official language rather than Spanish, which is common elsewhere. To the staple indigenous foods of beans and manioc, the Portuguese added the use of wine in cooking and as a beverage. They also added the many fish dishes for which the Portuguese are famed, especially those including **bacalhao** or salt cod. The Portuguese added their **cocidas** (stews) and, most important, elevated the humble **feijoada** of Portugal into an elaborate national buffet meal of Brazil still called by the same name, **feijoada completa**.

Another important and different influence on the cultural development of Brazil was the importation of slaves from West Africa. Far from being absorbed, the slaves not only retained their own cultural traditions, taboos, and food customs, they successfully made them a part of Brazil. To the basic African food crops of bananas, coconuts, yams, okra (**okro**), and many beans, spices and the small hot pepper called **malagueta**, the Africans added the native corn, beans, and manioc. **Dende oil**, so characteristic of West African cooking and noted especially for the dense yellowish color it adds to so many dishes, is extracted from an African palm. The African slaves quickly became respected cooks, and wherever they cooked they also brought with them their basic utensils: mortar and pestle, gourds that were fashioned into bowls, measures, scoops and cooking utensils; grinding stones used to crush corn, beans, or rice and earthenware or clay cooking utensils and wooden spoons. Many of these utensils were felt to have special magic properties and others related to certain taboos.

The rice originally brought by the Spaniards and much favored by the Portuguese quickly became a staple food. In Brazil, the combination of black beans and white rice sprinkled with **manioc meal** is eaten at least once a day and often twice by every class of people, and is considered so basic that few salads or vegetables are served. Black beans and rice are looked upon in the same way as bread on the table in many other countries. In fact it is known that servants and workers will not remain in a place where beans, rice, and **manioc** are not part of the meals.

Cozinha Baiana or Bahian Cuisine is the name given to the distinctive contributions of Brazil's African population. Bahia represents the area near the port of

Salvador where the slaves were first brought to Brazil. The Bahian kitchen staples include dende oil, coconut milk, fresh coriander, dried shrimps, sweet red or green peppers, ground almonds or peanuts. The hot pepper sauce made from crushed *malagueta* peppers in **dende oil** is always on the table, in the same way as salt and pepper graces North American tables. Because sugar was often a luxury in Europe, the African slaves in charge of Brazilian kitchens used it lavishly for many dishes and to produce many intriguing sweet desserts, to the delight of the Portuguese.

Native Indians, Portuguese, and West Africans have influenced the culture and food customs of Brazil, but so have other immigrants. Germans, Italians, and Japanese have all brought with them food traditions that have gradually become a part of the general cuisine. Evidence of the French cuisine is also a part of the Brazilian blend.

DAIRY PRODUCTS

Milk as a beverage is seldom used but much milk is consumed in custard-type desserts such as the Portuguese **pudim flan**, the caramelized baked custard so loved in Spanish-speaking countries as well. Many varieties of cheeses are used with pastas, in creamy cheese sauces for vegetables, and sometimes with fruits for desserts.

FRUITS AND VEGETABLES

Coconut and coconut milk are basic staples used in many dishes. Bananas and oranges are favorite fruits. Fruits familiar to North Americans are widely available together with persimmons introduced by the Japanese, fresh figs, pomegranates, melons of many types, breadfruit, citrus fruits, quinces, and more than twenty-six tropical fruits unknown to North Americans. Fruits are combined in salads with fresh vegetables, and sometimes fruits are a part of casseroles with meats and vegetables.

Palm hearts, avocados, and artichokes are great favorites; stuffed avocados are often part of a buffet meal. **Manioc**, the Brazilian tradition prepared as a flour from the tuberous root, was one of the ancient Indian crops together with corn and sweet potatoes. **Tamales** or **humitas**, that is a seasoned corn mixture wrapped and steamed in corn husks or banana leaves, is made in both Mexico and Brazil. (See Mexican.) Salads and vegetables simply cooked by themselves are not popular in Brazil, but their use is increasing.

The Afro-Brazilians enjoy greens that take to long cooking, especially **taioba** (also called "elephant's ears"), collards, okra, and cabbage. The Japanese, especially around Sao Paulo, have been responsible for an increase in vegetable consumption through the produce of their truck gardens: asparagus, broccoli, beets, carrots, lettuce, leeks, scallions, parsnips, radishes, cucumbers, cauliflower, etc.

The *salus* is a special container lined in a black substance containing powerful germicides. All vegetables to be eaten raw are placed in the *salus* for one hour before serving.

There is also a special place on the menu for the many squashes, gourds, pumpkin, chayotes, and the many types of yams such as **cara** and **inhame**.

MEATS AND ALTERNATES

As in Argentina, beef is the most important meat eaten in Brazil. Some veal, pork, and chicken are also used as available and where budget permits. **Charque** (also called **carne seca**) is a popular form of beef, especially with the working classes. Strips of beef are sun-dried while being brushed with a solution of salt and water. Brazilian laborers in the north and northeast areas live on black beans, rice, manioc, and **charque**. Southern laborers depend more on freshly barbecued meats (meat is more plentiful in the south), **manioc**, and **mate**, the popular beverage. **Churrasco** is the name for barbecue; most barbecued meats are prepared simply by grilling over a fire with the occasional salt-water brushing for flavor. *Gauchos* make their staple meal of the grilled meat dipped in **manioc** then washed down with **mate**.

FOODS COMMONLY USED

The staples of Brazilian cuisine are rice, black beans, and **manioc meal**. To these may be added, according to income, location, and class, the Portuguese contributions of codfish dishes and other fish preparations, stews called **cocidas**, and the use of wine as a beverage and in cooking; West African slaves brought the tastes for **dende oil** and hot **malagueta** peppers, condiments and sauces, coconut and coconut milk, dried shrimps and groundnuts (peanuts). These form an interesting cuisine when native fruits, grains, and vegetables are added, and even more interesting when considering the countless variations of **farofas** and **piraos**.

Farofas are based on **manioc meal** and, like the **piraos** based on cornmeal or rice, may have any combination of vegetables, seasonings or even raisins, cheese, coconut, or olives added. These are considered side dishes and are part of most meals. Wine, **yerba maté** and coffee are the favorite beverages.

Beans are the third great staple food of Brazil, together with rice and **manioc**. Brazilians produce many types of beans but prefer the tiny black beans. Their great national and festive dish, **feijoada completa**, is based on black beans; the name is taken from the Portuguese word for beans, **feijao**. Basic preparation involves cooking the beans till they are soft. A portion is removed and mashed with lard, chopped onion, and minced garlic; returned to the bean pot this forms a flavorful smooth sauce to bathe the rest of the beans. **Tutu de feijao** is the basic bean dish with **manioc** added to thicken it. Sometimes the beans are cooked with meat and sometimes with coconut milk.

To the Brazilian family to whom the three staples are daily fare, the table setting is routine: a plate of prepared beans is garnished with a mound of cooked rice; there will be a shaker of hot pepper sauce and another of the fine grainy **manioc**. The **manioc** is similar to the North American farina and, sprinkled on the juicy beans, absorbs the moisture and flavors and adds the final filling touch.

Many types of fish and seafood are used but two are outstanding in Brazilian cuisine: **bacalhao** or dried salt cod and the dried shrimps so much a part of Afro-Brazilian cuisine. **Bacalhao** dishes are of Portuguese influence, while the dried shrimp strong in sea taste show up in sauces like **nago**, a blend of dried shrimp, lemon juice, cooked and sliced okra, and **malagueta** peppers, served as a condiment with stews. **Moqueca**, originally a meat or shrimp mixture seasoned with **dende oil** and coconut milk then packed in banana leaves to steam, has more recently been prepared in a pot then served with rice that has been cooked in coconut milk. **Acaraje** is a puffy deep-fried dumpling made from the dried shrimp and mashed bean paste. **Caruru**, the traditional stew of Bahia, incorporates fresh shrimp, sliced okra, shredded coconut all thickened with **manioc** then flavored with **dende oil** and crushed peanuts at the end – a blend of Brazil and Africa.

The Portuguese have never given up their taste for very sweet and often intricate desserts, many of which are made with incredible numbers of egg yolks or egg whites. It takes a skillful cook to prepare the **fios de ovos**, threads of egg yolks cooked in sugar syrup. These may be eaten as part of a dessert or used as a garnish for many other dishes.

Brazilians enjoy soups especially for lunch. Most of these are rich hearty preparations thick with beans or rice and often containing many vegetables such as corn, yams, squash, or pumpkin. One regional soup features peanuts and rice cooked in small cakes then served in bowls with a rich broth poured over.

Peanuts have a small but special place in Brazilian cuisine. They are grown in Brazil and the Afro-Brazilians are familiar with their use in sauces (either crushed or chopped), for in Africa, where they are called groundnuts, they are widely used.

BREADS AND GRAINS

Since wheat production is low in Brazil, wheat breads, made mostly in the cities, are prepared from imported wheat. The most common type of bread is similar to the long crusty white French loaf and is called **pao frances**, with the smallest variety called **bisnaga**. Many other types of breads are available as well as rolls, twisted breads, breads rich with milk and eggs like **cuca**, which, with its topping of heavy cinnamon sugar and butter, is more of a coffee cake than a bread. The name **broa** is applied to any breads made with cornmeal, and originates from the Portuguese bread of the same name.

Most Brazilians, however, do not eat breads in the European or North American sense. Their daily "bread" is the **manioc** so generously sprinkled on all dishes from a shaker called a *farinheira*.

Rice is another basic staple cereal. Brazilian rice is well seasoned and cooked light and fluffy. The rice is first tossed in a pan with fat or oil along with any desired seasonings. When all the grains are coated, the liquid for cooking is added. This may be water, broth, or often coconut milk. Desserts are prepared by cooking rice in milk and adding sugar, eggs, and sometimes raisins and nuts.

Probably the great variety of breads in the cities of Brazil, and the great variety of desserts and types of puddings and cakes, are due to the many types of flours available. Rice flour, cornmeal and corn flour, manioc meal as well as many types of wheat flours all add variety. Tapioca, hominy, and crushed rice also thicken many desserts. The poor make porridges and a type of bread from the **farinha de mandioca**.

Cereal grains and flours form the basis of many special Brazilian dishes. **Farofa** is the soft porridge-like dish made by cooking toasted manioc meal in water and butter. Many added ingredients can change it into different dishes that can be used as stuffings, side dishes to meats or fish, or into a small meal in itself. **Pirao** is a bland molded pudding made very simply from cornstarch, crushed rice, or rice starch flour. Unmolded and served on a platter, it is used as a bland foil to spicy dishes of meats or fish.

FATS

Dende oil is the most typical Brazilian fat. But beef fat, olive oil, and butter are widely used as well. Lard is used in the flavoring of bean dishes and often for deep-fat frying.

SWEETS AND SNACKS

Brazilian "snacks" include hot dogs, hamburgers, and wedges of hot pizza as well as tamales, humitas, empanadas, and tasty morsels familiar in the Spanish **tapas** (appetizers). Brazilian desserts are very sweet puddings, cakes, custards, and the classic **pudim flan**. They also enjoy **dulce de leite**, the thick caramel-like sweet made from slow-simmered milk and sugar. Gelatin desserts and many kinds of pudding mixes are also popular. Fantastic confection and candy creations and many special occasion cakes are prepared by cooks in wealthy homes, and many convents finance schools by selling the exquisite sugar creations of their artistic nuns. These are especially famous in the area of Pernambuco which happens to be the area of highest sugar production in Brazil.

The only similarity between the specialty dish called **cuzcuz** and the North African **couscous** is that they are both steamed in colander-type pots set over boiling water. The **cuzcuz** of northern Brazil differs from the **cuzcuzeiro** made in the southern part. The northern version is a sweet dessert like a steamed cake made from starchy flour such as rice flour, cornstarch, corn or **manioc** flours flavored with coconut milk, grated coconut, and sugar. The southern version is not a sweet at all but a showy main dish where the starchy flour is mixed with meats, fowl, or fish and well seasoned and garnished like a steamed savory pudding.

SEASONINGS

Brazilian seasonings are usually thought of in terms of mixtures or sauces that are distinctively either African or Portuguese in origin. The native Indians ate their foods simply natural.

Refogar is the Portuguese art of marinating, or the technique used to cook almost any meat, seafood, fowl, or vegetable by first sauteeing in a mixture of fat, onions, garlic, peppers, tomatoes, herbs and seasonings. Then the appropriate liquid is added and the cooking completed as desired. The very simplest Portuguese **refogar** consists of marinating the food in wine then cooking.

Tempero means seasoning. Typical Brazilian **tempero** is a blend of onions, garlic, parsley, and tomatoes. The typical Afro-Brazilian **tempero** is a blend of **dende oil**, coconut milk, and malagueta peppers.

Four typical sauces accompany all Afro-inspired dishes:

Acarje Sauce: a blend of dende oil, onions, ginger, dried shrimp, and **malagueta** peppers.

Dende Oil and Vinegar: a simple vinaigrette used for fish and seafood.

Nago Sauce: served with stews, a blend of **dende oil**, lemon juice, dried ground shrimp, and cooked sliced okra.

Pepper and Lemon Sauce: hot peppers, lemon juice, salt, dende oil, garlic, and onions. (Considered most popular.)

BEVERAGES

Sweetened coffee served with milk begins the day for most Brazilians. Other meals are always concluded with a demitasse of coffee, and the same little demitasses of strong sweet coffee are part of meetings, chats, breaks, and probably twenty other excuses to account for the average Brazilian intake (at least in urban areas) of 12 to 24 demitasses in a day. The most popular method of preparing coffee is the filter method. Without **cafezinho** what would a Brazilian do?

Probably the next favorite beverage would be **guarana**, a soft drink based on the flavoring extracted from a shrub of the same name. Innumerable fruit punches could also quench thirst and accompany snacks and meals as could wines for the sophisticated and **mate** for the *gauchos* who claim that **mate** reduces hunger pangs and fatigue. The fiery white **cachaca** mixed with sugar and lemon juice may be downed between courses of the festive **feijoada completa**. Its alcoholic potency, however, is only for the experienced few.

MEALS AND CUSTOMS

Afro-folklore and superstitions have become a part of Brazilian cookery. Perhaps with the attitude of "Why take a chance?" or simply because in many European homes the cook was of West African descent, many rituals and customs are a part of the daily meal preparation. Corn is believed to possess special virtues, beans are only considered good if cooked in a clay or earthenware pot, and special dishes based on vegetables and with minimal seasoning are often prepared as offerings to the gods.

The early *dona de casa* (Brazilian housewife) was of pampered Portuguese background and only too pleased to hand over the tedious and skilled details of cookery to the African slaves. The West African women were not only skilled, they were pleased to find many familiar ingredients, and enjoyed the challenge of combining familiar old sauces and ingredients with the new meats, fruits, vegetables, and sugar. It was they to whom most of the credit for the ingenious Brazilian cuisine must go.

The wealthy Brazilian middle-class families follow French meal planning and service, and their menus are often a cosmopolitan blend of cuisines. Coffee is a symbol of hospitality at all times and always concludes lunch or dinner.

Breakfast in most of South America is a simple affair usually consisting of strong, sweet coffee with hot milk and a variety of breads and rolls served with butter and jams. Lunch is most often the heaviest meal of the day, featuring five or six courses usually including soup. The hot lunch is the rule whether taken at home or in a restaurant. Sandwiches are only served in small forms for appetizers or for teas; American-style hamburgers, hot dogs, and pizza wedges are more likely to be nibbled as between-meal snacks. Wednesday and Saturday lunches as well as any festive occasions are the traditional times to serve **feijoada completa**.

Almoco is the name for lunch, while *lanche* means an afternoon snack usually consisting of a beverage plus cookies or cakes. Formal teas are still a popular social event and the array of fancy pastries and cakes adequately illustrate the Brazilian love of sweets.

SPECIAL OCCASIONS

Most special occasions are marked by an elaborate presentation of the **feijoada completa**, preceded by appetizers of **empanadas** in small shapes either baked or fried and filled with mixtures of meats, raisins, and seasonings. Family occasions may be marked by a huge cook-out and much drinking.

Christmas dinner is centered around a huge roast turkey with many side dishes or a roast suckling pig. Easter features some dish based on the dried salt cod **bacalhao**. But both occasions would be incomplete without a course of **rabanados**. This is a rich dish of crusty white French bread dipped in a mixture of eggs and port wine then fried in butter and served with generous dustings of cinnamon sugar and much coffee.

St. John's Day, June 24, is celebrated everywhere by preparing and eating dishes made with pumpkin or corn. In Bahia, the traditional sweet pudding of hominy and cinnamon is called **mungunza**. It can be prepared as a creamy pudding of hominy cooked in milk and well spiced with cinnamon and cloves, crushed roasted peanuts and rose water, or it may be made very thick and served in pieces.

CHILEAN

South America has many unique characteristics. The Andes mountain range is the longest in the world, running 20,000 miles. The driest region in the world is the Atacama Desert of northern Chile. And Chile itself has a Pacific coastline of 2,600 miles, making it the longest country in the world in a north-south direction. The Andes Mountains that rise like a wall between Chile and her neighbors are the reason for her relatively calm history and the fact that monkeys, jaguars, and poisonous snakes do not mar her

tranquillity. It is in the Central Valley, with its temperate climate, that Chile grows her crops of grapes for wine and all the familiar temperate-climate fruits as well as wheat, potatoes, corn, oats, rice, and legumes such as chickpeas, beans, and lentils. Sheep, cattle, and pigs graze on some of the lands but only about 25 percent of the Chilean population is involved in any aspect of agriculture. More than 60 percent is urban and many are involved either in the huge fishing industry or the copper of which Chile is said to have the largest deposits in the world.

The Chilean settlers in the northern part of the country are mainly native Chileans, while settlers in the south are immigrants, predominantly Germans. The original Indian descendants live in southern reservations and are called simply the *Auracanians*, but are actually the remnants of many tribes. The majority of Chileans are a homogeneous group of *Mestizos*, that is, a mixture of Spanish and Aboriginal peoples. Only the land shows great diversity, from snow-tipped mountains to arid deserts and areas of rich agricultural yield.

From a slow and bloody beginning – the early Spanish settlers fought almost continually with the powerful *Auracanian* Indians – Chile has emerged from the colonial stage with many firsts. It was the first country in South America with the material signs of progress: railways, steamships, and telegraphs, as well as one of the largest navies. Some say the Chilean's calm and energetic personality is due to the temperate climate, while others trace it to the "Nordic stock" – from the many Germans, British, Irish, and Scandinavians who were among the early settlers.

Chileans enjoy large generous meals with many courses and enjoy beef as much as their Argentine neighbors, except that there is more seafood available than meats and fowl. In kitchens that are often painted a deep blue to keep away flies, Chilean cooks prepare their **cazuelas** or **curantos**. Preceded by appetizers, the **cazuela** is a rich rice-vegetable soup well filled with chunks of meats or fish. Its origin is said to be from the pork stews of Milan called **cassolas**; these were brought to Chile by the *conquistadores* who had fought in Italy. **Curanto** is also called Chilean stew and is a slow oven-baked casserole of alternating layers of many different types of meats and sausages with shredded cabbage and seasonings that harken to Central European tastes.

Albondigas, poached meatballs, **empanadas**, the half-moon filled pastries, and **sopaipillas**, the fritters made with yams or pumpkins and served with brown sugar syrup, all hint of their Spanish background.

Chileans begin their day with a light breakfast of buttered rolls and coffee with sugar and boiled milk. Lunch will feature appetizers, a **cazuela**, a vegetable or fish course, a course based on legumes or pastas, a steak with french-fried potatoes, all served with any of the number of fine Chilean wines, and followed by desserts in the Spanish manner (more than one and very sweet) or fresh fruits and finally coffee. Afternoon tea is common and consists of a brew of tea blended with **mate** and served with boiled milk and sugar. A variety of tiny sandwiches and pastries and an array of rich layered cakes will also be served. By eight in the evening, the average Chilean is ready for dinner. A clear or cream soup will be followed by a fish course, then a meat course with a salad and finally a light dessert and coffee.

Chilean bread is usually a long white crusty loaf resembling the long French bread stick, but many other varieties are made as well. Corn is used abundantly, and is given an imaginative range of tastes by being used in many forms from green to very ripe, each stage giving unique taste and texture to dishes. **Pastel de choclo** is a classic Chilean dish rather like a meat pie with a topping of fresh ground corn baked to a custard rather than a piecrust. This is served in a large casserole or individual earthenware ones. Beans in many varieties are used as abundantly as corn, because both grow in the country and are readily available.

Chilean cuisine features two unique sauces. Heating garlic and paprika in fat produces a warm, rich color and fine zesty taste that is sometimes pepped up with **aji**, those small fiery hot peppers. This sauce, either bland or peppery, is called **color**. **Pebre** is a more complex sauce of onions, garlic vinegar and olive oil plus chili and coriander. Like **color**, **pebre** may also be zipped up with the addition of the hot **aji** peppers. Both sauces and their variations are household standards much as salt, pepper, and ketchup are in North America.

COLOMBIAN AND VENEZUELAN

Both Colombia and Venezuela were explored and settled by Spaniards. Since the few local Indian tribes in the area proved primitive and unresisting to the Spanish conquest, the Spaniards found that their search for gold was far more hampered by the tangle of jungle and pestilence-ridden rivers. But beyond the jungle-rimmed ocean fronts, they were surprised

to discover temperate and pleasant valley areas, plateaus with jungle tropics on the one side and high mountains on the other. For many hundreds of years these early settlers created their own lifestyles, almost completely isolated from the rest of the world, while honing the arts of agriculture and cuisine and making the most of land, climate, and skills.

Corn, many kinds of potatoes, **yuca** (sweet cassava), avocados, green bananas, plantains, and beans became the staples of their kitchen together with whatever fresh tropical fruits the jungles below them yielded. Lean, grass-fed cattle, hogs and chickens multiplied and provided variety for the table as did the many types of seafood that could be caught or brought in.

From the early Spanish and Indian beginnings, the lands now possess rich oil reserves in Venezuela, while Colombia is famous as the world's second-largest producer of fine coffee. Many cereal grains and vegetables, sugarcane, rice, and bananas, as well as coconuts, pineapples, peanuts, and cacao today more than round out the foodstuffs for a varied table.

Because of the low rate of immigration, the population is fairly homogeneous in both countries, being predominantly a mix of Spanish, Indian, and some West African ancestry, almost all Roman Catholic and Spanish-speaking.

The jungle peoples of Colombia and Venezuela are either strongly Indian or African and live on a subsistence level with **yuca**, plantains, corn, and beans as their diet mainstays. The diet is occasionally supplemented with any animals or birds they can hunt and, at certain times of the year, with varieties of ants that are considered a delicacy. The rest of the population occasionally dine on some exotic tropical animals and birds too, but their mainstays are not much different from those used by the rest of South America.

Beef, veal, pork, and chicken are usually prepared by cooking slowly in a sauce that is well seasoned and often sparked with chunks of vegetables such as white and sweet potatoes, **yuca** (cassava), plantain, and squash. One such typical Colombian dish is **sancocho especial**. When the richly flavored stew is cooked, the savory broth is served from a tureen and the meat and colorful vegetables (plus chunks of corn on the cob) are served from an attractively arranged platter. Okra is another vegetable that is used in many stew and soup dishes. Avocado lends its smoothness to sauces, dips and soups. Coconut, grated coconut, and coconut milk sweeten many dishes and desserts: **pato con coco** is duck in a coconut sauce, while **arroz con coco y pasas** is a side dish of rice and raisins cooked in coconut milk. Potatoes, **yuca**, and plantain are often served as crispy nibbles or snacks by slicing them thinly then deep-frying to form chips.

It is no surprise that in Colombia, a country that grows both coffee and sugarcane, there would be many delightful recipes for drinks featuring coffee well flavored with rum. The people of both Colombia and Venezuela enjoy many demitasses of coffee throughout the day and always to end a meal.

PERUVIAN

In Peru, a land where mountains, jungles, and gorges make transportation and communication difficult, the llama is an eminently sensible and reliable beast of burden. The Indians who live here pursue a simple life. Many are shepherds, while others reap crops of corn, potatoes, barley, **manioc**, beans, and **quinoa** (Peruvian wheat). The sheep help to alleviate the

perennial shortage of meat, while their wool is important for the Peruvian textile industry. Sugar, rice and coffee are important crops as well.

Like most other South American countries, Peru has witnessed a turbulent history. It began with the Spaniards who were attracted by the legends of gold and silver said to be in the area, then remained to rule over the Quechua peoples (sometimes referred to as Incas who at a time in their history ruled over them). Their huge empire even before 2000 B.C.E. stretched over today's Colombia to Argentina. Extensive highways, advanced water and irrigation systems and methods of agriculture set them far ahead of other parts of the world.

For 200 years, discontent rumbled and finally exploded into an Indian revolt in 1780. This was crushed but was then led in subsequent years by revolts of Creoles (those of Spanish descent born in America) who resented the Spanish aristocracy's exploitation. In almost every country of South America it was these revolts that led finally to the independence of each country, with Peru's being in 1821.

The early Quechuas lived quite well on crops of corn, barley, potatoes, **quinoa**, beans, various roots, jungle fruits, and fish. The Creole cuisine that later evolved from a mixture of ancient Indian customs and traditions brought by the Spaniards is said to be one of the best in South America. The Creole cuisine of the coastal areas reflects the greater abundance and variety of foods that are available, while that of the mountain areas unfortunately reflects poverty and hungry times.

In the worst of times, potatoes serve as the mountain staple. They are eaten simply boiled, sometimes with a hot **aji** pepper sauce, and in better times they are served with a cheese and milk sauce (a side dish on the tables of wealthier coastal Peruvians). **Papas a la huancaina** is a dish that combines the good yellow potatoes of the Indians with the cheese of the Spaniards. **Cuy** or **South American cavy** is said to be the ancestor of the guinea pig and is widely used both in the coastal and mountain cuisines. The flavor and texture is said to resemble rabbit and many interesting grilled and stewed dishes are made from it.

The festive occasion in almost any Andean area demands the careful preparation of a **pachamanca**. A deep pit is dug to form the basis for the earth oven which is then filled with wood and straw and topped with rocks. After the wood has burned and the rocks are red-hot, moist green leaves form a base for all the good foods — whole young pigs or goats, casseroles or rice, many types of potatoes and vegetables — all to be eaten many hours later when well cooked, together with drinking and dancing.

Coastal Peruvian cuisine reflects the wealthy homes, well-staffed kitchens, and the heritage of their owners. Spanish dishes prevail, but certain Peruvian specialties are valued too. Grilled cubed heart on small skewers are called **anticuchos**, much enjoyed as street snacks or appetizers in large homes. Fried fish slices and the pickled raw fish called **ceviche** (also popular in Mexico) may also be served to start an ample meal. Shrimps and scallops in many forms may also be offered as appetizers, the scallops often served raw with sauces. A hearty soup with several kinds of meat, wheat, rice, and many vegetables usually follows. Only the broth is served to the guests; servants eat the boiled parts of the soup. Another soup similar to a fish chowder is called **chupe** and still other soups become the whole meal with the broth served first, then other ingredients attractively arranged and served with a variety of peppery and spiced sauces afterward.

The main course of meat may come to the table as stews, roasts, or in a heap of fine shreds. This latter technique of serving boiled, tough meat makes it easier to chew and more attractive in appearance. It is also a common technique in Mexico.

Peanuts, believed to be originally from South America (peanuts have been found in ancient pre-Inca tombs) are widely used, mostly crushed and as a flavoring and thickener in sauces. Some recipes use boiled peanuts, in which case they have little taste but add a mealy texture.

Bananas are widely used also. When green they are thinly sliced and fried to form appetizer chips. The people of Ecuador (which produces huge banana crops), frequently use mashed bananas simply mixed with flour and other ingredients to create a great variety of breads and pastries. Sauteed bananas is one of the simplest desserts in Central and South America and almost as popular as the **pudim flan**. Slit, peeled bananas are warmed and coated in a sauce of butter and brown sugar then flambeed with rum or brandy, or both. Served as they are, or with ice cream or whipped cream, they make a delightful ending for any South American meal.

GLOSSARY OF FOODS AND FOOD TERMS

Acaraje: a dried shrimp and mashed beans mixture formed into patties and deep-fried in lard or **Dende Oil**. Brazilian.

Aji. See **Malagueta**.

Anticuchos: cubed heart grilled on skewers. A favorite snack or appetizer of Peru.

Asado: grilled meat.

Asado con Cuero: Argentine specialty of huge sides of meat with hair and hide intact. Grilled over slow wood embers.

Batida: a mixed drink with a base of strong white Brazilian rum called **Cachaca**. Made with lemon or lime juice it is called **de Limao**; **de Coco** is made with coconut milk; **Abacaxi** is made with pineapple juice, and **Maracuja** is made with passion fruit.

Batido de Frejoles: mashed and seasoned red beans that are cooked, spread in a casserole then topped with mild grated cheese and oven-baked. This dish, together with fried rice, a side dish of fried bananas, and **biste arrebozado** (beef or lamb steaks breaded and fried) would make a classic Peruvian dinner.

Bombilla: the silver or metal straw that is used for sipping **Mate** from a gourd. The straw has a perforated bulbous end so that the tea leaves may be strained while drinking.

Cachaca: strong white Brazilian rum.

Carbonada Criolla: a rich beef stew chunky with cobs of corn, yams, and peach halves. Traditionally served from a hollowed-out squash or pumpkin shell. This is a classic dish of Argentina.

Caruru: cross between a soup and a stew and related to the West Indian **Callaloo**. It is made from dried ground shrimp, **Dende Oil**, ground almonds, coconut milk and served with rice. Brazilian.

Causa: a Peruvian dish of artful simplicity. Cooked mashed potatoes are smoothed over the bottom of a large deep dish and ingredients as desired are decoratively arranged on top – chopped hard eggs, olives, corn kernels, cheese cubes, chopped onions, etc. Diners scoop out the combination they like.

Cazuela: the soup of Chile derived by a circuitous route from a dish in Milan, Italy, called **Cassola**. Chileans turn it into a soup or rich meat, vegetables and rice.

Ceviche: firm-fleshed white fish marinated in lemon or lime juice plus seasonings and onion. It turns opaque and white but is in fact raw. It is served as an appetizer.

Chicha: national drink of Chile, alcoholic and pleasantly effervescent. Comes in strong, strong-sweet, and sweet.

Chimichurri: a spicy green sauce from Argentina made from minced fresh garlic, parsley, chilies, and olive oil seasoned to taste with salt, pepper, and a splash of vinegar. It is served as a condiment especially for meats.

Chorizo: spicy, juicy sausages prepared from beef parts and grilled. Served on bread or a bun, it's called **Choripan**.

Chupe: Peruvian fish chowder with corn, potatoes, and usually shrimp.

Color: an orangey flavoring mixture kept close at hand in Peruvian kitchens, made with oil, garlic, and paprika. Sometimes is spicy hot with **Aji** peppers.

Dende Oil: a bland orange oil made from an African palm tree. It adds a golden color to many dishes.

Empanadas: half-moons of meat and raisin-filled pastries that may be baked or deep-fried, eaten as a whole meal (in which case they will be made large) or as an appetizer (in which case they will be small).

Spanish original but with some kind of version in almost every country of the world.

Escabeche: South American specialty originating in Spain. Fish slices are breaded then fried and finally immersed in a vinaigrette with onions and chilled.

Farofa: kind of seasoned porridge made with **Manioc** meal and served in a mound sometimes garnished with eggs and olives. Brazilian.

Feijoada Completa: a large platter of individually prepared meats of all kinds. Boiled, roasted, pickled, all are sliced and arranged attractively. Side dishes include sliced oranges, cooked greens, **Farofa**, black beans, rice, and several spicy, tangy, and peppery sauces. The festive and national dish of Brazil, a much-glorified version of the original Portuguese dish.

Humitas or **Hallacas**: a mixture of corn flour or cornmeal, with such added ingredients as dried shrimps and peppers, spooned into green corn husks or banana leaves, then set carefully in a large kettle to steam.

Malagueta or **Aji**: tiny, fiery peppers that give zip to many dishes and special hot sauces.

Manioc: a grainy flour sprinkled on almost everything. The peeled pulp of the **manioc** tuber or bitter **cassava** is shredded then hung in bags or otherwise pressed to remove all the liquid which is poisonous unless separately boiled. The dried pulp is then pounded into a grainy flour. No table is complete in Brazil without its shaker of manioc flour.

Manjar Blanco: a caramelized milk pudding made from milk and sugar. This is the name for it in Peru. In Brazil it is called **Doce Leite**; in Argentina, **Dolce De Leche**.

Matambre: literally, "kill hunger." This is an Argentine appetizer that amply illustrates the Argentinian appetite for beef. A flank steak rolled up with colorful vegetables then steamed and browned and served sliced and cold, usually with assorted sausages, **Empanadas**, and wines to precede an **Asado**.

Mate: the South American tea-like drink of the *gauchos* (cowboys) said to relieve both hunger and fatigue. It is brewed in a gourd from the dried leaves of the **Yerba Mate**, sipped through a **Bombilla** (straw made of wood or metal), and packs a powerful caffeine punch.

Okopa Arequipena: an original Indian dish from Peru. In order to provide food while traveling, provisions of dried shrimp, corn flour, dried vegetables, roasted peanuts, and hot peppers would be carried. Simply adding water and heating to form a thick hot sauce made a substantial and tasty meal when served over fire-roasted or boiled potatoes. Coastal Peruvians serve the sauce over a large platter containing an arrangement of cooked seafood, hard eggs, olives, and cooked potato chunks.

Parrillada: Argentinian meat platter of assorted grilled beef parts and **Chorizo**, including entrails.

Pastel de Choclo: a stew of meat and mixed vegetables arranged either in one large casserole or in individual ones. The difference is the topping of a corn custard that is baked in the oven. Chilean.

Pebre: a Chilean seasoning and flavoring sauce, always at hand. Made from onions, garlic, and olive oil sharpened with vinegar, chili, and coriander. Similar to the Argentinian **Chimichurri**.

Picadillo or **Picadinho**: a soft ground beef mixture flavored with tomatoes, onions, peppers, and garlic and served over rice.

Picante de Cuy: Peruvian dish of roasted or boiled guinea pigs.

Pisco: a fragrant clear brandy of exceptional quality produced in Peru.

Quinoa (pronounced **Keen-Wah**): a staple grain crop cultivated in the high Andean valleys of Chile and Peru. The small cream-colored seed is high in protein content.

Sancocho: a Venezuelan fish stew with chunks of pumpkin added to the usual ingredients of fish, garlic, onions, and tomato.

Vatapa: an intricate dish made with a sauce of dried shrimp, ground almonds, **Dende Oil**, and coconut milk. Any meat or seafood may be added. It is served with a molded starchy pudding made from rice flour.

Xin-Xin: pieces of chicken cooked in a "sauce" of dried shrimp, **Dende Oil**, onion, tomatoes, hot peppers, and coriander. As the sauce evaporates, the chicken cooks then browns in the remaining oil. Served with rice and peanuts to garnish.

CHAPTER 34

Lebanese. See People of the Fertile Crescent
Macedonian. See The Southern Slavs
Malay. See Indonesian, Malay, and Singaporean

MALTESE

Homer called it "the navel of the sea" and most maps show Malta as a dot in the Mediterranean between Sicily and the North African coast of Tunisia. Actually, Malta is an archipelago of several islands, the three largest and inhabited ones being Malta, Comino (named for the abundance of wild, fragrant cumin-seed plants), and Gozo. History has considered Malta more than a mere dot on the map. Its strategic location and the sheltered harbors lured so many great maritime powers that it is impossible to dismiss either Malta or the Maltese as insignificant.

The Maltese are believed to be descended from adventurous settlers from Sicily who made their home on the islands more than 6,000 years ago. Excavations of animal remains reveal that Malta may once have been connected to Sicily: the animal remains are of European origin, not African. There is no doubt, however, about the later succession of occupations by the Phoenicians, Greeks, Carthaginians, and Romans. It was during the Roman occupation in 60 C.E. that the ship carrying St. Paul to his trial in Rome was reputedly wrecked on Malta's shores. Deeply impressed by the warmth and hospitality of the Maltese people, St. Paul was apparently equally impressive to them, for it is from that date that the islands were converted to Christianity. Now, with almost 100 percent of the population being Roman Catholic, Malta is often described as being "more Catholic than the Pope."

Byzantine conquest followed the Romans, but it was the subsequent domination of the Arabs, who held Malta from 800-1000 C.E., that left deep imprints on Malta's architecture and language. Present-day Maltese is an Arabic dialect strongly etched with the later addition of Italian, Spanish, French, and even English words. It is the only Semitic language written in the Latin alphabet.

The long line of conquerors did not end with the Arabs. Normans and Spaniards took their turn at the strategic islands, but it was the Knights of Saint John who were to leave the next lasting marks upon the Maltese.

It was King Charles V, Emperor of the Holy Roman Empire and King of Spain, who "rented" Malta to the Knights of the Order of Saint John of Jerusalem after the Turks had driven them from Rhodes. The "rent" took the form of an annual tribute of one falcon – thus the legendary but mystical importance of the "Maltese Falcon" dating from 1530 and immortalized much later in Dashiel Hammett's novel of the same name. Both the falcon and the Knights' eight-pointed cross (the Maltese Cross) remain today as Maltese symbols. Lesser known but of more importance are the many hospitals and charitable organizations that the Knights left behind in Malta and which operate to this day.

Although the Knights of the Order of Saint John were able to help the Maltese withstand a powerful Turkish siege, their rule collapsed in 1798 without a shot being fired. It is believed that Napoleon seized Malta for France with the secret aid of some of the Knights. Nonetheless, French rule was only a brief two years, and was brought to an abrupt end by a Maltese revolt aided by the British. In 1814, the Treaty of Paris officially gave Malta to the British and the 150-year British rule was to leave its indelible mark. Although the British preferred to retain their own traditions, the Maltese cheerfully adapted the habit of "elevenses" and four o'clock tea, bright red postboxes, helpful police officers and driving their cars on the left. They even developed a taste for beer.

Despite the long tiresome hold of so many conquerors, the Maltese have stubbornly retained their distinctive language, their Roman Catholicism, their many traditions and festivals and their national flag. In 1964 they achieved their independence, and in 1974 the international status of a republic.

They have also retained something else. In spite of the successive dominations by so many foreign powers and in spite of the density of population on the tiny islands, the Maltese are known for their courtesy and good humor and they are never too busy to take a stroll or chat with friends. Perhaps these are the very qualities that enabled them to endure such relentless hardships as the incessant bombing raids in World War II. So incredible was the courage of this tiny nation of over 350,000 people living on 122 square miles, that in 1942 King George VI awarded the nation the George Cross for "heroism and devotion" and in 1943 President Franklin D. Roosevelt also presented the nation a special citation.

Perhaps the sunny disposition of the Maltese comes from the moderate Mediterranean climate that basks the islands for most of the year in a pleasant warmth. Two winds occasionally disturb the tranquility of climate: the hot *sirocco* blowing during August and September, and the *gregale*, a sharp northeasterly that can whip the sea to a froth and cause problems for fishermen.

The climate also helps the scanty topsoil to coax forth enough potatoes and onions for export, but of the other vegetables, fruits, wheat and barley, only enough for local use are grown. Goats are still used for meat and milk but are mostly supplanted by the sheep (lamb and mutton) and the dairy farms of cows introduced by the British to supply cream, milk, and butter. The island's main sustenance comes from the sea. Even with skill and ingenuity, almost 80 percent of Malta's food needs must be imported.

Retaining their identity and cheerful disposition despite a lengthy list of conquerors is a tribute to such a tiny, vulnerable nation, and so is their legendary hospitality. Out of a desire to please others, it is actually easier to find cosmopolitan restaurants in Malta than it is to find local cuisine, but the increase in tourism (more than 800,000 visitors annually) and increasing pride in "things Maltese" is changing this.

Malta may be small in population and size but her people are content to stay put; traveling three to ten miles is considered quite a distance and a family living only a few miles from the sea may actually visit the seashore only once or twice in a lifetime. Further, size has nothing to do with the ability to distinguish "local" customs and even varying dialects of Maltese.

The most interesting and notable example of the Maltese view of native differences are the Gozitans. These inhabitants of the island of Gozo are viewed by other Maltese as "the Scotsmen of our islands"; thrifty, industrious, and plain-speaking, the Gozitans can be singled out as leaders in business and church. The island of Gozo is said to be the most fertile because of the persistent and patient toil of her people. And there is a saying that if a fisherman brought in a record catch, he was probably a Gozitan.

DOMESTIC LIFE

Density of population brings with it both noise and a lack of privacy. Neither of these appear to bother the Maltese. Only in their own home do they treasure quiet and privacy. Once outside, they bask in the crush of cars and people and the cadenza of horns, noisy talk, and church bells. The Maltese have an extended home; the city streets are part of their living room and they are friendly and gracious to everyone (the Maltese have a phenomenal memory for names and faces). The church is their second home, a place for help and prayer, thanksgiving and consolation.

Maltese cooking and hospitality is probably best symbolized by sourdough Maltese bread and white fresh **Rikotta** cheese. Simple and honest, these foods are a part of almost every meal and form the edible centerpiece of the table. They are not only sustaining in themselves but also represent a blend of tastes and textures that would cause a Maltese mouth to water anywhere in the world. The crusty white sourdough bread shaped in a gentle golden oval, eaten with creamy mild **Rikotta** cheese, may form the appetizer, the main dish or merely a side dish of any meal. Add a glass of Maltese wine and you have the quintessence of hospitality.

The delicious aromas that pour forth from Maltese kitchens belie their tiny size. Sideboards and open shelves store groceries and utensils, while a small refrigerator holds perishables. Maltese enjoy fresh seasonal fruits and vegetables and prefer to shop daily in nearby stores for their needs. Although supermarkets and a wide range of prepared mixes are slowly changing old ways, the pot of soup simmering on the small petrol stove is so much a part of the meal pattern (and the aroma of Malta) it is difficult to visualize it being preempted by a cold sandwich for

FOODS COMMONLY USED

The foods of the Maltese table are simple and satisfying. Unquestionably, many dishes can trace their origins to foods introduced by historic invaders: Greeks, Romans, Arabs, French, and British. The latter left a taste for beer, mutton, lamb, turkey, Christmas pudding, and probably also the custom of a "roasted joint with potatoes" for Sunday dinner. Crunchy Maltese sourdough bread and **Rikotta** cheese are certainly staples but these are well rounded with hearty soups, stews, and pasta dishes that deftly spin out the flavors of meats and fish. Vegetables are preferred cooked; salads are few and usually seasonal. Local fruits are relished as snacks or desserts but are expensive. Wine is the commonest beverage and knows no age limit.

lunch. Freezers for the home and small kitchen appliances such as blenders, pressure cookers, and so on, are not common in Malta. Baking is usually done in commercial communal ovens, carefully watched over by the local baker.

DAIRY PRODUCTS

With fresh milk for drinking, canned milk for tea and coffee and the daily use of cheese with bread or as part of a sauce or casserole (pasta dish), milk is obviously high on the list of priorities. The famed **pastizzi** or Maltese cheesecakes may be large or tiny and although usually made with puff pastry and a filling of **Rikotta**, they still retain the same name when they are made with anchovies or even peas and onions. So popular are the **pastizzi** that they are available everywhere in bars and coffee shops and commonly form a mid-morning snack with tall glasses of tea or coffee. Many varieties of hard or aged cheese are used, shredded or grated for rice or pasta dishes. **Gbejniet** are the small fresh cheeses made by farmers' wives and sold fresh, dried, or peppered, and preserved in olive oil and vinegar.

FRUITS AND VEGETABLES

If you want someone from Malta to become nostalgic, just mention prickly pears. These are by no means the only native fruit – just the favorite. Also included and eaten mostly fresh and juicy are pampamousse, small round watermelons, dates and figs, oranges and apples and many small berries. Most home gardens grow their own pampamousse and grapes. Fresh fruits are the usual dessert.

Vegetables are more than a garnish or accompaniment; they are cooked in a variety of ways and often form the main dish of a supper. From the Greeks the Maltese adapted a number of stuffed vegetable dishes; from the French they adapted the method of "refreshing" – a brief boiling of the fresh vegetables then a dunking in cold water, thus retaining both color and texture. Favorite vegetables include pumpkin (ripened on Malta's flat rooftops), **aubergines** and **courgettes** (eggplants and zucchini), broad beans and artichokes. Many varieties of squashes and gourds, leafy greens, cabbage and cauliflower and of course potatoes and onions are cooked in satisfying and imaginative ways. These include not only the stuffed vegetable recipes already mentioned but also breading and frying, layering in casseroles, baking as a filling in crispy pastry pies, as patties and fritters and even as steamed, molded puddings to be served with cheese and bechamel sauce.

MEATS AND ALTERNATES

In a Maltese cookbook, the recipes for fish will likely precede the recipes for meats. Not only are there many varieties of fresh fish and seafood and dozens of ways to prepare and serve them, but even with the lifting of the ban of meat on Fridays, most Maltese prefer to make Friday a fish day. Many others also abstain from meats on Wednesdays.

Most famed is the **lampuka**, also called **dorado** or **dolphinfish**, closely followed by varieties of mackerel, tunny fish, mullet, bass, grouper, and many more. **Lampuka** is poached, baked, fried, stewed, or made into fish soup. **Torta tal-lampuka** is a meal-in-a-dish: between two layers of pastry is placed a combination of **lampuka** and a sauce of vegetable chunks surprisingly tasty with olives, sultanas, and walnuts. Salt cod, cuttlefish, turtle, snails, and sea urchins (**rizzi**) are also enjoyed.

Meat in any quantity is usually reserved for a Sunday or festive dinner with the best and largest cut going to the father, head of the household. The rest of the family round out their meal with potatoes and other vegetable dishes, bread and cheese. Maltese homemakers value meats and nothing is ever wasted. Not only are bits of meats and bones used to flavor casseroles, stuffed vegetables, and soups, there is also a long list of appetizing dishes prepared from offal, including tripe, brains, liver, and tongue. **Zalzett ta' Malta** (Malta sausages) are composed of a mixture of fat and lean pork seasoned with garlic and coriander and stuffed into pork intestines and hung for two to three days. Beef and pork, lamb and rabbit, chicken and game birds add variety to the menu.

Eggs and legumes are not a special part of the Maltese menu. Eggs are used occasionally as a light meal or snack but most often as an ingredient in other dishes. Dried legumes are seldom used except for the large brown lentils which are popular in **soppa tal-ghazz**, a thick lentil soup simmered with vegetables and pig's feet.

BREADS AND GRAINS

Bread and pasta, the staples of the Maltese diet, are both prepared from wheat. But the Malta bread is memorable because it is baked from a sourdough starter which gives it a particular taste and coarse texture. The crispy crust is enhanced by the traditional baking of the bread on the floor of the oven rather than on a pan. This bread is not only part of every Maltese meal, it is also the main dish for lunch or even a light supper when hollowed out and stuffed with tomatoes, anchovies, and cheese, and drizzled with olive oil. Rubbed with a pungent clove of fresh garlic and sprinkled with salt and olive oil, Malta bread makes a quick savory snack.

And every Maltese is familiar with **hobz biz-zejt**, thick slices of bread rubbed with fresh tomatoes, sprinkled with olive oil, salt and pepper, then topped with any combination of sliced onions, garlic, herbs, capers, olives, or anchovies. This quick snack satisfies laborers' appetites for lunch, children for "elevenses" (mid-morning snack) and whole families as an easy light supper served with local wine. **Galletti**, **krustini**, and **biskutelli** are small breads sometimes made at home.

Pasta dishes abound, but most are complex. **Timpana** is really a version of a similar Sicilian dish where puff pastry forms the outside layer of a center filled with layered cooked macaroni, bits of brain, liver, and pork seasoned with tomato paste, Parmesan, and onion. Carefully baked, the dish is unmolded and served in slices. (Today **timpana** is a main dish; in previous times it was merely an appetizer.) **Ravjul** (ravioli) and many types of pasta cooked to perfection and topped with delicate sauces of cheese, vegetables, or fish are a part of every Maltese menu.

Close in importance to both bread and pasta is rice. Rice is used in stuffings for meats and vegetables and in many dishes in the same way as pasta. One of the classic Maltese dishes is **ross fil-forn**, literally "baked rice." It is made from a mixture of ground meat, seasonings, raw beaten eggs, and tomato paste blended with stock or water and raw rice. The whole mixture is slowly baked in the oven to a golden crustiness.

It should be noted that while few Maltese cooks bother to bake their own bread, it would be difficult to find one who was not an expert maker of light flaky puff pastry (the downfall of cooks elsewhere) and who did not possess an old treasured family recipe for filling **pastizzi**.

FATS
Maltese use many fats for cooking, baking, and as a spread. Lard, margarine, and salt butter are used widely for cooking and baking. Margarine is used at the table but fresh **Rikotta** cheese is the favorite spread. Olive oil and a variety of vegetable and seed oils are also used.

SWEETS AND SNACKS
The popular Maltese dessert is usually fresh fruit and sometimes cheese. Sweets in the form of pastries, candies, and rich desserts are usually reserved for special occasions and most often purchased from the confectioner's rather than prepared at home. A listing of specialty sweet dishes sounds like an international roll call of sweetmeats because it includes the many specialties known in other countries: chestnut fillings, almond, chocolate and nougat, sesame seeds, dates and treacle, trifles and steamed puddings, pine nuts and crunchy meringues.

SEASONINGS
Maltese food may be simple and hearty but it is seldom subtle. Strong flavors are enjoyed and these often include the pungency of garlic and onions cut with the bright acidity of tomatoes. In fact one of the most basic seasonings is actually an all-purpose sauce of fried onions, garlic, and tomato paste known as **toqlija**. Freshly ground pepper, spicy hot curry blends, and fresh aromatic herbs are all used with a generous hand. These include mint, parsley, marjoram, basil, and rosemary.

BEVERAGES
Beer was introduced by the British, but local wines are still the favorite accompaniment for the evening meal. Coffee and tea with canned milk is taken by adults for breakfast and lunch, for "tea" at four and for "elevenses" in mid-morning. Children drink milk except at the evening meal when they will often have a glass of wine.

MEALS AND CUSTOMS
Maltese restaurants, snack bars, coffee shops, and street vendors satisfy the taste whims of most tourists, but the Maltese prefer to eat hearty, simple, well-seasoned food at home.

Breakfast for most is a small light meal of bread and cheese, honey and ham accompanied by coffee and milk. If that seems a light beginning for the day, a snack of tea or coffee and **pastizzi** around eleven will hold any Maltese till lunchtime.

Maltese homemakers begin early in the morning to prepare the ingredients and simmer their soups over small petrol stoves. Soup for lunch is a tradition broken only by the laborer who cannot get home for the meal. Then a bundle of **hobz biz-zejt** (bread rubbed with tomatoes, drizzled with oil and seasonings, and topped with garlic, sliced onions, and herbs) and a glass of wine will ease their hunger till evening, when a hot meal – probably a pasta dish or a meat and vegetable stew – will be savored.

Homemakers, businesspeople, laborers and children all stop their day's routine for a short break at four for tea and small cookies. The tea break is especially important for those who customarily take their evening meal between nine and ten. Villagers usually have a light evening meal at around seven.

Regardless of the meal, in Malta men are served first, and they usually receive the largest and choicest portions. But Maltese meal service is generally pleasantly casual; enjoying food takes precedence over formal manners. Thus there are no frowns when succulent bones are eaten with the fingers.

SPECIAL OCCASIONS

Together with special family occasions such as weddings, christenings, birthdays, and funerals, the Maltese calendar includes Roman Catholic festivals, national holidays, and many local *festas*. It would be difficult to spot a time of year when nothing exciting is happening.

Special occasions are the time for sweet treats more than special main dishes. They are made extra-special because they are served or prepared only for specific festivals. Some of these include the following:

Christmas: Roast stuffed turkey and steamed plum puddings are the Christmas specialties. The Christmas pudding is usually made near the beginning of November then soaked with rum each following Sunday till the festive day. Hot chestnut soup (**mbuljuta**), flavored with cocoa and tangerine peel, and specially baked treacle rings (**qaghaq tal-ghasel**) are also made. The latter is a white pastry filled with a rich treacle and semolina filling and shaped to form a round "sausage." Small slits in the white pastry reveal the rich filling beneath.

Carnival: Loud bands, winding parades, and costumed figures mark the three-to-seven-day celebrations preceding Lent. **Prinjolata**, a rich pine nut cake, almond chunks, and **qubbajt** (nougat) are the special sweets.

Lent: Lenten restrictions have been considerably relaxed. Usually no meat is eaten, but dairy products and fats are now allowed. **Kwarezimal**, a Lenten cake containing no eggs or fat but made from minced almonds and flour, sugar and citrus zest, is still a tradition.

Easter: It wouldn't be Easter without **figolli**, which are human and animal shapes cut from sugar-cookie dough filled with almond paste and brightly decorated with colored icing. Too good to save only for Easter and often made at other times are the tiny **Rikotta**-filled tartlets called **qassatat**.

Birthdays, Christenings: Biskuttini tal-maghmudija or christening biscuits are rich cookies shaped into rounds or oblongs. **Biskuttini tal-lewz** are delicately crisp almond meringues. Both are specialties of all christenings and most family gatherings and festas. But no Maltese birthday would be complete without **xkunvat**, fried twisted strips of rich pastry scented with orange-flower water and served in a golden crispy pile drizzled with Maltese honey (thyme-flavored) and colored "shot" (tiny pinheads of colored candies used for cake decoration).

GLOSSARY OF FOODS AND FOOD TERMS

Aljotta: the least expensive and least appealing fish is poached in a court bouillon, reserved and kept warm to be served as a second course. This fish broth (court bouillon) is then enriched with well-fried chopped onion and garlic, and seasoned with tomato paste and fresh marjoram. A handful of raw rice is thrown in twenty minutes before serving. (There is no limit to how much garlic can be added.) This is a meatless Friday specialty. Bread, cheese, wine and it is a meal.

Bragoli: thin pounded slices of beef are stuffed with chopped hard eggs, crumbled bacon, and fresh bread crumbs all lightly seasoned. The beef is rolled over the filling, tied with string, and browned in fat. Wine, browned onions and garlic simmer with the beef rolls. The dish may be served with canned peas or freshly cooked shelled peas.

Brodu: designates a hearty soup with visible chunks of meats and vegetables.

Brodu Tat-Tigiega: a whole chicken is slowly simmered in water with vegetables then removed and browned separately. Rice is added to the rich stock and finally a few eggs are beaten and slowly added. The **Brodu** is served with rice and chopped vegetables while the chicken makes the second course. This is an efficient way to cook an entire meal when ovens are tiny or not available. A similar **Brodu** includes the simmering of a whole chicken which has first been stuffed.

Brungiel Mimli Fil-Forn: **Brungiel** is eggplant, *mimli* means stuffed, and *fil-forn* means baked in the oven. This then is a dish of baked, stuffed eggplant, a varied combination of grated cheese, bread crumbs, capers, olives, and ground meat.

Fenkata: literally, a "rabbit dinner," so popular that rabbits are specially bred for the purpose, although wild hares are traditional. Jointed and well cooked, the tangy rabbit stew is served over rice or pasta and eaten together with Malta bread and red wine.

Ftira: Maltese sourdough bread baked in a flat round disk. It is often eaten split and filled with sliced plum tomatoes, salt and pepper. Other additions might be sliced onions, anchovies, olives, etc.

Kusksu: not to be confused with the **Couscous** of North Africa. This one is a pasta similar in appearance, coarse and granular. Fresh broad beans and green peas are added to browned onion (garlic and tomato puree if desired) and simmered with water. The **Kusksu** is added to cook then the soup is set aside. To serve, a poached egg and some crumbled fresh cheese (**Gbejna** and **Rikotta**) are placed in the soup bowl then the thick pasta soup with peas and beans is ladled over. Again, just add bread and wine and it is a superb meal.

Laham Bil-Patata L-Forn: a lengthy name but instantly recognized by any Maltese as referring to almost any meat well seasoned with onions, garlic, and strips of lard (if needed), and baked in the oven over a bed of sliced potatoes. In Malta, this is a Sunday dinner specialty usually baked in the communal oven.

Minestra: similar in name to the well-known Italian minestrone soup but this one is usually made with a variety of vegetables and legumes but no meat. At least three types of pasta are added near the end of the cooking and the soup is served with big spoonfuls of grated Parmesan cheese. Marrow, pumpkin, **qara tork** (lighter but similar to pumpkin), kohlrabi, onions and potatoes are some of the usual vegetables included.

Pastizzi: classic Maltese cheesecake served with tea or coffee. Usually it is made with light puff pastry filled with a mild **Rikotta** cheese filling. Can also be filled with peas, onions or even anchovies.

Pastizzi Tas-Summien: a circle of puff pastry filled with a quail then folded over, sealed, and baked.

Pulpetti Tal-Laham: meatballs prepared from any minced meat, seasonings, and flour. But they are not ball-shaped, they are round, thick and patted flat, then fried in lard. Served with rice, potatoes or spaghetti with or without a sauce.

Ravjul: tiny pillows of noodle dough stuffed with chopped spinach and cheese, well seasoned and served with tomato sauce.

Ross Fil-Forn: the classic Maltese baked rice. A rich blend of onions, garlic, minced meat (or cut-up tidbits), tomato paste, seasonings, saffron, and grated cheese, plus water or stock with raw rice. The whole mixture is slowly oven-baked to a crusty golden goodness. A Sunday or company specialty.

Soppa: the Maltese term for a smooth creamy soup, not the most popular type by far unless it is **Soppa Tal-Qara Bali**, a variety of zucchini found in Malta cooked with potatoes and onions, soothed to a puree and served with butter and egg yolks whipped in.

Soppa Tal-Armla: a vegetable-stock soup made with only green and white vegetables. Commonly called "widow's soup." A poached egg and crumbled **Gbejna** and **Rikotta** are arranged in soup bowls and the hot vegetable soup poured over.

Souffle: not really a souffle, nor is it of French origin. This is actually a dessert that could be described as a trifle with a Maltese accent. Sponge-cake fingers are arranged in a crystal bowl, sprinkled with sherry and layered with candied peels, fruits, and chocolate pudding and finished with a custard or an uncooked soft meringue of whipped egg whites, sugar, and flavoring.

Stuffat Tal-Qarnit or **Qarnita**: fresh octopus, tenderized by beating well and hard till grayish. After cutting in chunks the octopus is stewed and served with spaghetti or cut-up potatoes. The surprise comes in the seasoning: curry powder or a mix of walnuts and currants.

Timpana: classically Maltese, this dish is made with a deep puff pastry pie shell, layered with minced seasoned meats, tomato paste and grated cheese, and lightly cooked macaroni. Sealed with a top crust of pastry, the pie is well baked then served in slices.

Toqlija: a thick sauce made from well-browned chopped onions and garlic blended with tomato paste. A little or a lot is used to season almost anything.

Torto Tal-Lampuka: a dolphinfish pie. Baked in a pastry shell are layers of boned, breaded, and fried **lampuka** with assorted well-seasoned vegetables.

CHAPTER 35

MEXICAN

To millions of Mexicans and tourists alike, Mexico usually means Mexico City. That thriving metropolis carries her more than 600 years with dignity, charm, and a great deal of sophistication as she cradles more than 8,300,000 people on her plateau situated about 7,300 feet above sea level.

Mexico had a highly intelligent and predominantly agricultural civilization thousands of years ago when the rest of the world was in its infancy. It is believed that the original Indian tribes – Olmecs, Toltecs, Mayans, and Aztecs – who made up her population originally came from Asia across the Bering Strait to settle in the land and develop the crops from which the world now derives almost half of its food supply. These include corn, beans, potatoes, tomatoes, chocolate, eggplants, avocados, many varieties of squash, vanilla, and chilies.

In 1523 Hernando Cortes came to Mexico from Spain; and, because Montezuma believed him to be a former god returned to life, Cortes was able to conquer the land with little resistance. In return for all the Mexican foods which the Spaniards subsequently introduced to Europe, they left behind in Mexico much of their influence. Spanish architecture, the Spanish language, the Roman Catholic religion as well as Spanish foods: rice and wheat, oil and wine, olives, cinnamon, cloves, peaches and apricots, and the breeding of cattle, which added beef, butter, and cheese to the Indian cuisine. All were widely accepted and embedded themselves deeply into Mexican culture.

The brief rule of the Viennese Maximilian, and his wife, Carlotta, spread a wave of European manners and customs as well as the influence of French, Austrian, and Italian cookery (**sopa seca**, which is similar to a southern Italian pasta dish, is an example). But with the reinstatement of the Indian, Benito Juarez, as leader in 1910, Spanish and other influences were somewhat mitigated and once again Indian culture came to the fore. To this day it is the ancient Indian culture that has predominant influence, although the language is still Spanish – the Mexican Spanish varying somewhat from the classic Castillian Spanish – and the predominant religion is still Roman Catholic.

Contrary to popular belief, all Mexican food is not spicy hot. This is not to say that Mexicans don't take good-natured delight in watching a *tourista* attempt to eat some of their fiery dishes. What could be funnier than the involuntary tears shed by a novice sampling a *piquante* dish?

While Mexicans pride themselves on their supposed immunity to the many varieties of fiery chilies, the range of their dishes and the subtle seasonings commonly used are very wide indeed and go back several thousand years. Specialties can be found in every province and region of Mexico, and the techniques are handed down from mother to daughter with pride and meticulous attention to detail. Here are a few:

Mole Poblano – from Puebla (a spicy sauce made with unsweetened chocolate);

Tamales – from Oaxaca (meat filling steamed in corn husks);

Bunuelos – from Oaxaca (crispy fritters soaked in syrup);

Banana Dishes and Stewed Turtle – from Tabasco;

Barbacoa – from Mexico province (meat packed in the fleshy maguey leaves and buried in a pit with hot coals);

Ceviche Acapulco – from Guerrero (raw fish marinated in lime juice, well seasoned and served cold);

Beef and Beef Dishes – from Sonora.

But time is the best cooking pot, and although Mexican cuisine and food habits are a blend of Indian, Spanish, and other European influences, it is the native Mexican ingredients adapted over thousands of years that have given Mexican food immense variety and a unique quality all its own.

DOMESTIC LIFE

Many old but very practical cooking utensils are still widely used in Mexico. These include:

Cazuela: earthenware casserole used both for cooking and serving;

Olla: earthenware jug;

Comal: round iron or earthenware baking sheet used to cook tortillas;

Metate: three-legged oblong stone base used with a cylindrical stone called a *metlapil* to grind corn or chocolate.

And while most women can pat a tortilla to paper-thinness – a considerable skill – with just their hands, the use of a tortilla press is common, and store-bought tortillas are inexpensive and increasingly popular. The tortilla is the staple pancake-like bread, used by every class and present at every meal. It is prepared from simple ingredients of **masa harina** (flour ground from corn), warm water, and salt. Skill is required to attain just the right consistency to press out the tortillas. It can be used in many ways in a great variety of dishes, and also as a plate or utensil to scoop up and eat other foods.

Most modern Mexican kitchens consider the electric blender a necessity to puree sauces and grind spice mixtures and pastes to the right consistency, for those techniques are the most exacting and time-consuming in the Mexican kitchen.

It should be pointed out that although there exists in Mexico today a poor lower class and a wealthy upper class, the white-collar middle class is expanding rapidly thanks to newer and better schooling and living conditions. Annually more and more of Mexico's citizens are enjoying the benefits of these good living and working conditions. And while the poorer and rural people make excellent use of the many old yet practical utensils, the kitchens of the middle and upper classes rival any in North America: yet it is rare that the lady of the house is also the cook.

Since many fine markets with fresh produce abound, food storage is really not a problem as most families prefer to buy their foods fresh each day. In some homes this may even include a fresh daily supply of **tortillas** and the freshly baked rolls called **bolillas**. Refrigerators are common in middle- and upper-class homes, as are various small electrical appliances, especially blenders. But freezers are not widely used. Lower-class homes rely on earthenware vessels to keep foods cool as needed.

DAIRY PRODUCTS

Fresh milk is available but is not widely used. Canned evaporated and sweetened condensed milks are popular, perhaps because they keep better. These are used in beverages and especially to make the dessert **flan**. Mild cheeses are usually used grated as a topping or garnish to other foods.

FRUITS AND VEGETABLES

Despite the powerful influence of Spanish cuisine, the Mexican kitchen is still filled with the aromas of foods and dishes based on the Indian staples of beans, tomatoes, many varieties of chilies, and most especially corn in all its many forms. Corn cultivation dates back more than 7,000 years in Mexico. Many types of squash and pumpkin are used most widely, but other vegetables used in Mexican cuisine include peas, onions, tomatoes (both red and green types), **jicama** (bland, with an apple-like crispness), cactus leaves, beets, potatoes, squash blossoms, lettuce, radishes, **nopales** (prickly pear leaves), garlic, and

FOODS COMMONLY USED

The staples of the Mexican diet are:

Chilies: as many as 92 varieties are available, each varying both in hotness and flavor;

Chorizo: a fresh sausage made from pork and seasonings;

Frijoles: beans of many varieties but most commonly the small black beans which are usually well cooked then mashed with lard and reheated before eating;

Tomatoes and Onions;

Tortillas: flat, pancake-like bread made from specially ground cornmeal called **masa harina**. High in calcium content since it is made with lime water.

These staples are popular with every class level and are present in every day's meals. In fact, there is seldom a meal that does not have **tortillas** and **frijoles** on the table. Canned milk is favored over fresh, and mild cheeses are used mostly as a grated garnish to other dishes. Fish and seafood are plentiful especially in coastal areas. Fresh fruits and many seeds and nuts are used for snacking. Dried or candied fruits (and sometimes candied vegetables such as pumpkin or squash) are enjoyed but many prefer the taste of salted foods or spicy ones rather than sweet. There is a knowing hand with many types of seasoning and these are usually according to local tastes. Soft drinks and local beers are popular as well as tea, coffee, and hot chocolate. Restaurants featuring foods of many lands, as well as local traditional specialties, can be found in cosmopolitan Mexico City.

peppers. Many vegetable dishes take much preparation time and involve the intricate assembly of stuffed vegetables with sauces also prepared from vegetables, often with a tomato base. Both red and green tomatoes are used frequently for dipping and garnishing sauces and many vegetables are used for soups. Fresh salads of either fruits or vegetables are used mostly by upper classes.

Fruits include a wide and colorful range of tropical and subtropical varieties such as pineapples, bananas, avocados, strawberries, pomegranates, oranges, mangoes, papayas, coconuts, quince, cherimoyas, and apples. Limes are almost everywhere and appear often as a plate garnish and to heighten the flavor of spice mixtures. Bananas are enjoyed baked for dessert, but most other fruits are eaten more often as a fresh snack purchased from vendors.

MEATS AND ALTERNATES
Meat is too expensive for many tables, but pork and pork products including sausages and offal head the list of favorites. Goat, beef, chicken, lamb, turkey, turtle, and veal are also used. Fish and seafood are plentiful in coastal regions, including the **huachinango** (red snapper) and **camarones** (shrimp).

Beans are used daily, mostly as **frijoles** or **frijoles refritos** (refried) and eaten as a side dish with **tortillas** or other foods, or combined as fillings to other dishes. Nuts are enjoyed as snacks or more often finely ground and used to thicken sauces. As a snack they are preferred well-salted, toasted, and often dusted with spicy hot chilies. **Cacahuates** (peanuts) are abundant, but walnuts, cashews, and pistachios are also used. The toasted and sometimes well-seasoned seeds from pumpkins and varieties of squash may be crushed and used in cooking or nibbled as a snack.

BREADS AND GRAINS
Tortillas made from **masa harina** (ground cornmeal) are the ubiquitous staple for every table at every meal, either made by hand or purchased fresh daily. **Bolillas** are also very popular, especially in the cities. These are oval-shaped white rolls with a chewy crust, said to be baked hourly around the clock and made from wheat flour. There is some limited use of dry breakfast cereals in middle- and upper-class homes.

FATS
Lard is the most widely used fat for cooking, baking, and deep-fat frying. There is a limited use of oils. Some margarine is used and some butter, mostly as a table spread (for **bolillas**) or in specialty baking.

SWEETS AND SNACKS
The favorite sweet of all ages is candied or dried fruits, especially candied squash, candied sweet potato, and pumpkin. Tamarind is another favorite. Chocolates and candies are expensive, and many prefer tangy, salty, or spicy snacks rather than sweet. The Mexican dessert of Spanish influence is the **flan**, a slow-baked custard of eggs and condensed or evaporated milk, glazed with caramelized sugar and often flavored with vanilla or coconut. Very young children also enjoy nibbling on sugarcane when it is available. Fresh sliced fruits such as pineapple or **jicama** are often eaten as a snack first by dipping into little dishes of spicy hot sauces or bowls of blended dry seasonings.

SEASONINGS
There is a wide and general use of many seasonings, especially in particular areas. These include skillful blends of varieties of chilies, as well as cinnamon, cloves, cumin, anise, allspice, coriander seeds, vanilla, chocolate, nuts, coconut, limes, oranges, garlic and onions, capers, and many fresh Mexican herbs such as **cilantro** (like Chinese parsley), **epazote**, mint, marjoram, and sage. The use of unsweetened chocolate or cocoa powder in sauces (**mole**) originated in Mexico. Red tomatoes and small green ones are used so frequently that they must be considered a seasoning as well. Limes are used freely everywhere as juice, seasoning, and garnish.

The importance of chilies in Mexican cookery deserves a closer look. Because chilies frequently self-fertilize, identifying varieties is often difficult. Generally, green chilies are used fresh and red ones are used dried, but both may be available canned or pickled. Some are available in powdered form similar to cayenne. Removing seeds, stem, and veins usually reduces the fire and yields a milder sweeter taste. Common red and green chilies are listed below.

Red Chilies:
Ancho: comparatively mild and flavorful, about 2 to 3 inches long.
Chipotle: smaller than the Ancho, more of a brick red and very hot.
Morita: similar in size, color, and taste to the Chipotle and commonly in pickled form.
Mulata: similar in size to the **Ancho** but a brownish color and stronger in flavor.

Green Chilies:
Guero: pale yellowish green and sweet milk taste.
Jalapeno: very hot when veins and seeds are used; flavorful, mild when not.

Largo: light yellowish green, usually canned, very fiery but retains a delicate taste.

Poblano: varied sizes from small to as large as a bell pepper and can be mild or hot.

Serrano: slender and less than 2 inches long and very hot whether canned or fresh.

Valenciano: the most commonly found sweet green pepper in supermarkets everywhere.

Two chili-based sauces are classic in Mexican cookery:

Mole means a sauce prepared with chilies, but only the **mole poblana** from Puebla has bitter chocolate as an ingredient. Moles are prepared like Indian **curry** or Hungarian **lesco**.

Tingas represent the Spanish influence on Mexican cookery and may even have similar ingredients to the **mole** (chilies, garlic, onions, tomatoes, seasonings) but these are chopped, never puréed.

In both **moles** and **tingas**, seasonings including chilies are cooked in hot oil or fat (Mexico uses lard). The pre-cooking of the sauce eliminates the raw taste. This sauce is then added to pre-cooked meat, vegetables, or fish, simmered to marry the flavors then served.

BEVERAGES
Soft drinks are popular and inexpensive. Tea, coffee, and hot chocolate are used according to taste. Excellent local beer, an increasingly high quality selection of wines and even brandy are made in different areas. **Pulque**, fermented cactus juice, is an old tradition. **Tequila**, the national potent drink made from cactus, is traditionally enjoyed straight, first with a lick of salt, followed with a squirt of fresh lime.

MEALS AND CUSTOMS
Desayuno is breakfast in Mexico and as in many other places, it is eaten early and is usually a light meal. For the countryside farmer or the worker in Mexico City, the first meal may be **tortillas** with **frijoles refritos** sprinkled with mild grated cheese and washed down with hot chocolate or **cafe con leche** (coffee with milk). For the city person, the **tortillas** may be replaced with fresh **bolillas** or other breads, the hot drink will be the same, but the morning paper may be the accompaniment. Where time and money are no problem, a more leisurely *desayuno* may include fresh fruits, eggs (**huevos rancheros**), **tortillas**, and **frijoles refritos** garnished with grated cheese and a few wedges of fresh avocado, together with **cafe con leche** or hot chocolate.

The main meal of the day is usually the *comida* lasting a leisurely two or three hours (which may include a rest time), from 2:00 to 5:00 p.m. Most people try to take this meal at home with their family.

Mexicans also have a name for a special lunch at about 11:00 a.m. which they call *almuerzo*. This meal usually consists of one filling dish such as **sopa seca** or something based on **tortillas** such as **tacos** or **enchiladas**. But if *almuerzo* is taken, then the *comida* would be correspondingly a lighter meal.

And if either the *almuerzo* or the *comida* left some hunger pangs, there is a type of "sweet break" in the late afternoon that usually consists of sweet rolls or small pastries with coffee or chocolate and this is called *merienda*.

In spite of the many "official" meals, snacking is a national pastime and many vendors on city streets and along the highways make their living by carefully preparing fresh sliced fruits, fruit drinks like **horchata** (prepared from melon seeds, sugar, and lime), candied fruits and vegetables, salted and spiced nuts and seeds.

On special occasions, many villages have their own local sweet bakeries and small confections that are prepared in the homes then offered for sale to passersby. Some of the oldest traditional sweets and baked goods were prepared by nuns in the convents for special holidays. Within minutes a small stand can be set up to make fresh **tortillas**, and varieties of fillings and bottles of hot spicy sauces to be used to taste. Other stands are specially constructed to bake bananas where they are served hot with a sprinkle of sugar and a dribble of canned milk. **Chicarrones** (pork cracklings), fried **taco** chips and crispy-fried cookies all beckon the appetite of anyone walking by.

The evening meal is called the *cena*. In the rural areas this would, like the other meals, be based on the staples of **tortillas** and **frijoles** and may include a **cazuela** of vegetables, seasoned with a **mole** of garlic, onions, tomatoes, and chilies. This evening meal is taken very late in the city, eight to ten o'clock being a usual time. But this meal would not be a heavy one unless the family is dining out or there is a special occasion. Much entertaining is done out of the home, especially in the city. Home parties are likely to be buffet style.

SPECIAL OCCASIONS
The predominant religion in Mexico is Roman Catholic. But together with Christmas and Easter, many other typical Mexican festivals are observed and many of these are peculiar only to a province or town. Festivals are generally characterized with local costumes, street dancing, and vendors busily selling sweet cakes and confections for the occasion. Among those occasions celebrated nationally are:

January 1: New Year's Eve and New Year's Day, celebrated with parties, restaurant dinners, festive meals.

January 6: Fiesta de los Santos Reyes (the Coming of the Kings). Costumed wisemen roam the streets and give candies and treats to the children; in homes there is gift giving. Traditional *rosca de reyes*, a ring-shaped bread decorated with candied fruits, is eaten. Somewhere in the bread is hidden a tiny figurine, and the finder is obliged to make a party for all on February 2.

Shrove Tuesday and Easter Week: Most businesses and schools take this week (and Christmas week) as annual holidays. This time is characterized by visits to relatives, church services, and pilgrimages to shrines. In each locale specialty cookies, cakes, and confections are sold by vendors.

March 21: festival celebrating the birth of Benito Juarez, Mexico's liberal president (1861-1872 and reinstated in 1910) and a Zapotec Indian. Despite the colonization attempt of Napoleon and the brief rule of Austria's Maximilian and his wife, Carlotta, Juarez's government returned Mexico to the Mexicans, reformed the education system, built a railway, and set the country towards prosperity.

November 1 and 2: All Saints' and All Souls' days. Families visit the graves and leave offerings of *zempazulchitl*, bright fragrant flowers similar to marigolds, as well as specially baked bread called **pan de muerto**. These round breads, decorated with crossbones and teardrops and sprinkled with pink sugar, are baked and eaten by all social classes days before the solemn occasion.

November 20: Anniversary of the 1910 Revolution, restoring Juarez to power.

December 16-25: The happy time of the *posadas*, colorful parties with candy-filled *pinatas*, games for all, and a table laden with buffet dishes – the best the family can offer. **Ensalada de noche buena** is the Christmas Eve specialty: a huge salad of chopped fruits, crunchy peanuts, and red beets all lightly sprinkled with sugar and vinegar

Every festival, small or large, brings out regional and local specialties, alcoholic and fruit beverages, bright costumes and communal dancing. Small rich sweets, some specially wrapped in papers, candied fruits and hot spiced snacks provide the refreshment and energy for the celebrants.

GLOSSARY OF FOODS AND FOOD TERMS

Almuerzo: name given to an early (11:00 a.m.) light lunch, often a dish based on **Tortillas**.

Annatto: the seeds of a tropical tree, delicate in flavor but colors foods a bold orange-red. Called *achiote* in Mexico.

Arroz: rice.

Bolillas: crusty, torpedo-shaped rolls of white bread (wheat flour) popular at all meals, especially breakfast, and particularly in Mexico City.

Bunuelos: simple deep-fried fritter served with cinnamon sugar and often a syrup or molasses sauce. A specialty of the fiestas, especially the *posadas* of Christmas.

Burritos: **Tortillas** that are made of wheat flour, larger than the **Masa Harina Tortillas**, often served filled with **Frijoles**, spicy meat sauce, lettuce and cheese and rolled up like an envelope.

Cafe: coffee.

Cafe con Leche: a blend of coffee and hot milk specially favored for breakfast.

Cafe Negra: black coffee.

Carne: meat, usually referring to beef.

Cena: the late evening meal, usually light. One course perhaps followed by fruit and a beverage.

Ceviche: strips of raw fish marinated in lime juice and lemon juice with chilies, onions, and garlic. The flesh of the fish loses its translucency and turns white as if cooked. Delicious as an appetizer. Of ancient Peruvian origin.

Chipotle: a red hot pepper, smoked, available pickled or fresh, and brick red in color. Like a brick, it delivers a potent punch!

Chorizo: popular fresh sausage made of fresh pork, pork fat, and seasonings.

Comida: literally, "a meal." The term is usually used to designate the leisurely heavy meal served from 2:00 to 5:00 p.m.

Desayuno: breakfast, usually early and light.

Empanadas: crescent-shaped pastries with sweet or savory fillings. Of Spanish origin.

Enchiladas: **Tortillas** that have been rolled over a filling, ends open, covered lightly with a sauce, and baked in the oven or served without being baked.

Ensalada: salad.

Epazote: herb indigenous to Mexico (also called pazote, peqweed, or goosefoot). Dried and crumbled, it is used in bean and tortilla dishes, adding a strong distinctive flavor.

Flan: the most popular Mexican dessert, a slow-baked custard of eggs, condensed milk with a caramel or coconut glaze.

Frijoles: beans, the dried type. Any one of many cooked varieties.

Frijoles Refritos: beans that have been cooked then reheated by mashing in lard till a smooth thick paste is formed. Eaten as a staple side dish, usually with mild grated cheese on top.

Guacamole: a smooth but piquant paste made by mashing ripe avocados with lime juice, onion, seasonings. Used as an appetizer, more frequently as a garnish to other foods.

Horchata: a cooling drink prepared from ground melon seeds with added water, sugar and grated lemon rind.

Huevos: eggs.

Huevos Rancheros: a popular egg dish suited for *almuerzo* or a North American brunch. Eggs are cooked in spicy tomato sauce seasoned with onions, peppers and served traditionally with **Tortillas** and **Frijoles Refritos**.

Jicama: looks like a large turnip, and served sliced in thin flat rounds. Tastes crisp and very juicy, somewhat like an apple. Mexicans buy it from street vendors and douse it with peppery hot sauce.

Leche: milk.

Masa Harina: a special corn flour made by soaking the corn in lime water and grinding it very finely. It is used for the making of **Tortillas** and often to thicken stews and sauces.

Merienda: late afternoon snack of coffee or chocolate and sweet rolls or pastries.

Mole: the name given to many different sauces, each similar only in that the combination of seasonings, tomatoes (red or green), nuts, etc., are first ground to a paste then cooked in hot lard before the other parts of the dish are added. The most famous mole, **Mole Poblano**, is made the same way but with the addition of bitter chocolate (*poblano* means in the style of Puebla).

Ollas: earthenware jugs, often attractively glazed and decorated, used to store liquids.

Salsa: sauce.

Sopa: soup.

Sopa Seca: literally, "dry soup." Refers to a rice or pasta-type dish similar to Italian pasta casseroles, baked with sauce.

Taco: a fried crisp **Tortilla**, either rolled or folded with a filling.

Tamales: when prepared as a simple bread dough from **Masa Harina** and steamed in corn husks, **Tamales** are eaten like bread. When the dough part is filled with spicy mixtures of meats, **Tamales** become a complete meal.

Tinga: a stew of meat and vegetables with seasonings prepared by sautéeing onions, garlic, then tomatoes and seasonings and finally adding meat and then the vegetables. With Mexican ingredients and European method, these dishes are a blend of old and new world cuisine.

Tortilla: a flat, pancake-like bread made from specially ground corn flour called **Masa Harina**. It can be used as a bread, spread or layered with filling, rolled, baked, fried, shredded into soups, or shredded and fried and enjoyed as snacks. The uses are almost endless. The tortilla even serves as an edible plate and a utensil for eating other foods.

Tostada: when **Tortillas** are crisp-fired, still flat, and stacked with a filling – cooked ground meats, **Frijoles**, shredded lettuce or cheese for example – they are called **Tostadas**.

CHAPTER 36

Montenegrin. See The Southern Slavs

MOROCCAN

Morocco nestles on the northwest coast of Africa bordering the shores of the Atlantic and the Mediterranean with a finger of land pointing north-

ward to Spain. This is also part of the region known as the Mahgrib, where great extremes of climate occur between the coastal regions, the tips of the Atlas Mountains where snow is not uncommon year-round, and on the parched expanses of the Sahara Desert.

Despite only 20 percent arable land and the historic concern of drought in Morocco, modern farming and irrigation produce prodigious crops of grains – wheat, barley, corn, and oats as well as fruit and vegetables for export and domestic use. Ancient orchards still burst forth with the rich scents of blossoming trees that ripen into almonds, figs, olives, and many varieties of dates. Gnarled grapevines yield fine grapes that are pressed into a distinguished variety of wines. Herds of goats, sheep and some cattle are watched over in pastures and carefully guided along roadsides. As in most of North Africa and the Middle East, meat is usually in short supply and fish is consumed mainly where it is caught because of limited storage facilities.

Long referred to as Moors, the people of Morocco are actually a mix of Berber, Arab, and Black peoples. The 800-year occupation of Spain by Arabs and Moors (from the seventh to the fifteenth centuries C.E.) probably established the term "Moors" because most Christians at that time referred to all Muslims as Moors.

The Berbers were the first known inhabitants of Morocco and even today make up more than 75 percent of its population. These non-Arabic tribes inhabiting many parts of North Africa are a lean, hardy people, white to dark brown in coloring. Belonging to more than 200 separate groups each with distinctive customs and dialects, they live by

herding sheep, goats, and cattle and increasingly work as crop-raising farmers.

Two facts illustrated their individualism and fierce independence: adoption of both Islam and Judaism did not replace but enhanced their former beliefs and traditions; and the continued agitation of the Berber tribes against the French occupation of Morocco actually led to the Moroccan independence of 1956.

The fact that almost 80 percent of the Moroccan population is illiterate can be misleading. For it must be understood that most of the Berber dialects do not have a written form, knowledge having been carefully transmitted verbally to succeeding generations. However, these peoples have a great appetite for education. French and at least one Arab or Berber dialect is spoken by educated Moroccans, but today Arabic and French are commonly taught in the increasing number of schools springing up even in rural and mountain areas.

Despite successive foreign conquest by Phoenicians, Carthaginians, Romans, and Byzantines, the Berbers stoutly maintained their own lifestyles. It was the sweeping Arab conquest in 682 C.E. that left the deepest mark. The entire population, with the exception of the few Christians (from Roman times) and the Jewish settlers in the larger cities, intermarried and adopted Islam but never really replaced their own ancient Berber traditions. Even now, of all the many sects of Islam, the Berber brand is one of the loosest and varies from tribe to tribe.

In fact, the Berbers had a profound effect on the Arabs. The rituals of serving and eating foods as well as many classic dishes are definitely of Berber origin. These include the eating of foods with only three fingers of the right hand. However, the ceremonial handwashing that precedes the meal seems to be of Jewish rather than Arabic or Berber origin.

The classic dish of **couscous** – national dish of the entire Maghreb which includes Morocco, Tunisia, Libya, and Algeria – is also enjoyed in Egypt and other Middle Eastern countries. **Mechoui** (succulent roast lamb), with its many variations, is found all around the Mediterranean. **Bisteeya** or **pastilla**, the whisper-thin pastry layers shaped in an 18 inch to 20 inch pie enclosing scrambled eggs and pigeon meat, closely resembles the spring roll pastries of China.

The **tagine**, prepared and served in an earthenware dome-shaped dish, is the classic of all stews.

Berber traditions are deeply steeped in the supernatural. Arabs, Berbers, and even many Jews profoundly believe in the power of the color of blue to ward off evil spirits; it would be impossible to count the doorways and even the windows that are painted blue in Morocco and in many other areas of North Africa and the Middle East. And it is attributed to a mysterious supernatural power called *kimia* that lowly but faithful peasants are able to survive despite only subsistent levels of food – often only scant quantities of bread dipped in oil. Satiety is said to be attained more by faith than by food.

"What isn't known can't be stolen...." Who can say whether this ancient saying was born out of folklore or the reality of prevalent thieves? Nonetheless, in Morocco perhaps more than any other area of North Africa, the cloak of secrecy and the characteristic of self-debasing modesty exist side by side with scenes of secluded walled courtyards, hidden doorways painted a luminous blue, women clad in *burkas* (head-to-toe enveloping cloth "veils"), and *djellaba*-clad men together with vendors of amulets, potions, and formulas all guaranteed to ward off the evil eye.

Great wealth and lovely women, like other treasured Moroccan possessions, are never displayed openly. Even the great cuisine of Morocco is seldom tasted in public places but is reserved for the hospitality of the home. Such is the Moroccan world: a curious blend of faith and superstition, lore and legend, Arab, Berber, Black, and Jew all touched by history and ancient customs, yet secretive.

DOMESTIC LIFE

Just as it is impossible to make sweeping generalizations about the 200 distinctive Berber groups, so is it impossible to speak of the average Moroccan home. The great gap between rich and poor defies comparisons. How can one even speak in the same breath of the lifestyle of a nomadic Berber tribe of goatherders and a palatial servant-filled home of a Moroccan family serving a thirty-plate *diffa* (banquet)? Yet both are valid examples of Moroccan life.

But some things are the same. Everywhere, it is the women who cook. Everywhere, classic Arabian hospitality climaxes in the philosophy of *shaban*: abundance of satisfaction characterized by heaping plates of the best the household can offer. For even the lowliest of peasants *shaban* can be achieved if one has sufficient *kimia*. The Moroccan legends of endless exotic dishes preceded by long flowery speeches may not seem so lavish if one remembers that the arts of speech and the arts of the Moroccan cuisine have been carefully cultivated for centuries and just as carefully handed down from mother to daughter.

It also helps to bear in mind that many of these culinary wonders are actually prepared from the simplest and least expensive ingredients. They require, however, the agility of many knowing hands of which there is no shortage in Morocco.

Food preparation begins with the daily shopping for the freshest available ingredients found in the *souks* (marketplaces) or sold by vendors, sometimes from house to house. Everyone has a favorite source of fine spices, fresh vegetables, and fruits.

Despite the incredible quantity and endless variety of Moroccan food, the utensils needed in the kitchen are few. They include the mortar and pestle for grinding and pounding seasonings, a **couscousiere** (a two-layered pot for cooking stew in the bottom and the couscous in the perforated top), several pots and pans of universal design, earthenware **tagine slaouis** (their conical tops may be heaped with charcoal embers to simulate baking or for long slow simmering), shiny copper **taouas** (casseroles), a range of knives, and a small charcoal stove. If large amounts of food are to be prepared, neighborhood ovens are used.

Not evident in Moroccan kitchens are measuring utensils and electrical appliances. Like loving

FOODS COMMONLY USED

A variety of cultures have reached into Moroccan kitchens. Spanish chickpeas, Arabian spices, Portuguese fish dishes (especially in the coastal city of Essaouira), and African and Senegalese spicy sauces all take their places with the ancient Berber dishes of **couscous**, **tagine**, **bisteeya**, and **mechoui** and make artful use of local barley and wheat flour for breads and pastries, dates, olives and almonds, and seasonal fruits and vegetables. Grains and vegetables form the dietary staples: the larger the household the smaller the meat consumption. The commonest beverage is hot sweetened green mint tea sipped from small glasses. From the British the Moroccans learned "tea-dunking," and the country was a French protectorate for so long (1912-1956) that Gallic touches abound, especially in upper-class homes. The ancient staple of **harira** (legume soup) served with **harisa** (peppery hot sauce), bread and dates remain the rural staples and the universal "simple meal."

dedicated cooks throughout the world (only maybe more so in Morocco) amounts of ingredients are measured by experience, tasted knowingly, and seasoned deftly with shakes of this and pinches of that. Small wonder that Moroccan girls begin their training in the culinary arts very early. Electrical power is being increasingly produced from the country's many rivers but is still considered a luxury and is not widely available. For this reason as well as the enjoyment of the freshest foods, perishables are bought daily rather than stored.

The accomplished Moroccan cook will also have the following utensils for specialty dishes:

Gdra Dil Trid: earthenware dome used to stretch the thin pastry for **Trid** (similar to **Bisteeya**);

Gsaa: large wooden or earthenware kneading trough for bread dough (easier than a board);

M'ghazel: silver or brass skewers for meat and vegetable tidbits or meatballs (**Kefta**);

Tobsil: similar to **Gdra Dil Trid**, except this utensil is placed over heat or over boiling water and is used to make the **Warka** (paper-thin pastry for **Bisteeya**).

Included also would be a variety of brass, copper or silver trays for serving, ornate teapot and sets of glasses for tea serving, and small decorated kettles and basins for pouring perfumed waters in the handwashing ritual.

For rural Berber women, the arts of cookery are somewhat simplified. Both breads and main dishes are cooked over open fires with few utensils. Yet the serving of foods, though not as elaborate as a *diffa*, may be nonetheless gracious. Low tables are placed before the diners and the customary heaped platters are eaten with three fingers of the right hand, while the frequent trays of sweet tea or spiced coffee are just as much enjoyed as in the palatial city homes.

DAIRY PRODUCTS

Fresh milk consumption is considered to be low, but for good reasons. As in other areas of North Africa and the Middle East, transportation and storage facilities make it difficult to distribute perishables such as fresh milk.

Whether out of taste or out of necessity, **leben** is a favored beverage. It is similar to buttermilk except that the natural milk from which the butter is churned is first allowed to ferment in an earthen jug. The low-fat **leben** is widely used especially by lower-income groups; cream and natural whole milk is used sparingly by upper classes. Served cool or slightly chilled, **raipe** is a type of thickened milk dish eaten as a refreshment. The milk is warmed then thickened with the addition of the pulverized powder from dried wild Moroccan artichoke hearts.

FRUITS AND VEGETABLES

It was the Moors who introduced the fragrant almond, peach, and apricot trees and the bittersweet "Seville" oranges to Spain. They merely introduced luscious fruits with which they were already familiar. In season, grapes, figs, dates, and many varieties of melon are readily available even to the poor. Many varieties of olives are used in cooked dishes and salads. Green cracked olives are usually brine-cured and may be flavored with lemon, spices or garlic, the seasonings depending on the bitterness. Ripe olives, which may be any color from green to tan or purple, are usually preserved in a mix of olive oil, a little salt and lemon juice. Shriveled ripe black olives are either salt-cured or packed with the hot sauce called **hrisa** or **harissa**.

Dates are a staple everywhere in North Africa, but in one Morocean oasis alone – Erfoud – more than 30 varieties are grown. Dates may be nibbled as a dried fruit but they are also used to stuff fish, in combination with lamb, and also in vegetable dishes as well as desserts and sweets.

Main meals are concluded with platters of fresh fruits and assorted nuts. When fresh fruits are out of season, dried fruits take their place. Dishes of assorted nuts and dried fruits are common snacks at any time.

There are times in Moroccan cuisine when the line between fruit and vegetable is not as clearly delineated as in the western world. For example, jams and sweet preserves are frequently prepared from vegetables such as types of squash or tomatoes. Fruits as well as vegetables lend their aroma and taste to many a **tagine**. The smooth texture and tangy pickled flavor of preserved lemons are indispensable to Moroccan cuisine. Most are preserved in salt and lemon juice; Moroccan Jews preserve their lemons with the addition of olive oil. It is not uncommon to present a whole fish stuffed with one or more dried fruits, for instance a shad stuffed with dates. Fruits and vegetables are happy mates in salads too.

Basic vegetables and staples in almost every household include onions, tomatoes, turnips (widely used in cooking, salads and also as a preserve), carrots and many varieties of squash and pumpkin. Quinces may also be used fresh or preserved. Other basics are okra, zucchini, artichokes, green peppers, eggplants, string beans, sweet potatoes, cabbage, cauliflower, and many other common vegetables. Wild white truffles, wild cardoons, and wild artichokes also add their special flavors when picked in season.

MEATS AND ALTERNATES

Even though the consumption of meat is low by western standards, small amounts of meats are used so artfully in cookery that their taste permeates many dishes. The **tagine**, the classic Moroccan stew, can be made from any combination of meat, legumes, fruits, vegetables, and even grains. In fact, it seems if a mixture is cooked in the **tagine** cone-shaped casserole it is therefore a **tagine**, ingredients notwithstanding.

Lamb and kid head the list of preferred meats and are the most plentiful. Mutton and beef are also used and it goes without saying that no part of the animal is ever wasted; heads and innards are regarded as special treats. For festive occasions, lamb is most sought after, kid second in favor, and the poor may have to be satisfied with chicken or pigeon meat.

Moroccans cook their meats as part of a **tagine** (with endless combinations of fruits, vegetables, and spices), grilled as **mechoui**, or sometimes made into sausages (usually from innards). Any odd bits and pieces are usually finely ground and richly spiced to form **kefta**, which refers to any ground meat mixture. **Kefta** may have many variations; it may be shaped like finger sausages and skewer-grilled, formed into meatballs as part of a **tagine**, or stuffed into vegetables or fruits.

In coastal areas where fish is more often used, imaginative cookery adds ginger, cinnamon, sugar, sweet butter as well as incredible combinations of fresh or dried fruits and nuts. There are **tagines** of fish and seafood, baked fish dishes, poached fish dishes, and a great variety of tiny fluffy fish balls served with many accompaniments of seasoned sauces, fruits, or vegetables. The only combination that is wrong is the one that doesn't taste good!

Special mention must be made of the preserved meat called **chele** or **khelea**. This sun-dried, salted and spice-preserved beef is similar to the Romanian **pastrama** (which is also smoked) and the Greek or Turkish **bastourma**. The sun-dried beef is cooked in boiling olive oil and water, then stored in the fat until used.

Eggs are widely used but often prepared differently than in the western world. Street vendors hawk hard-boiled eggs and serve them with cumin-flavored salt for dipping. The Tunisian **brik** – a triangle of crisp thin pastry enfolding a raw egg, which is quickly fried and eaten immediately, is also a favorite, whether as a street snack or part of a home meal. Saffron-tinted hard eggs may garnish **tagines** or other platters. Eggs beaten with lemon juice and cooked into soft curds are a part of the famed **bisteeya**. Eggs may be poached in a zesty tomato sauce with tiny **kefta** or set into a **sefirna**, a casserole of meat and legumes baked overnight.

The **sefirna** is related to the Spanish **olla podrida** or **adafina**, a dish based on long-cooked beef, vegetables, legumes, and whole eggs in the shell.

Adafina (Spanish), **sefirna** (Moroccan), and the central European **cholent** are all believed to be derived from ancient Jewish dishes. (See Israeli and Jewish.) This meal-in-a-dish set to bake in banked ovens before the Sabbath could be eaten as a hot meal on the Sabbath without violating the commandment against work. The long slow cooking of the eggs in the casserole leaves them with tanned whites and mellow creamy yolks (these eggs are called **huevos haminados**).

Nuts are so widely used in Moroccan cookery that they must be viewed as a source of valuable protein. Almonds are most frequently used in whole blanched form, chopped, and often as almond paste. Nuts are also used in desserts and pastries and not uncommonly in many meat and fish dishes.

BREADS AND GRAINS

Bread is the essential of every meal. For the very poor the whole meal may be only bread, sometimes dipped into olive oil. The classic Moroccan bread is shaped into absorbent, chewy oval discs, made from a mixture of wholewheat and unbleached white flour and gently fragrant with aniseed.

Bread is much more than a meal accompaniment. Bread is viewed respectfully in deep recognition of its ability to satisfy hunger and as a gift from God. A piece of bread inadvertently dropped may be kissed and blessed as it is carefully retrieved. Broken pieces of bread become eating utensils as they scoop up moist foods and soak up tasty juices and sauces. Community bakers pride themselves on recognizing each family's special symbol stamped on their breads, for breads are made with loving attention in private homes then toted on trays to be baked in the communal ovens.

Moroccan diets can be described as "classic antique Mediterranean" because grains and oil form the basis. Wheat and barley are the principal grains and are used to make a great variety of breads. European-type white bread is increasing in popularity.

After weaning, the child's principal food is sweet tea and grains in the form of rice, corn, semolina, breads, and pasta.

Despite the importance of bread, no other food can compare in variety of preparation and importance to the legendary **couscous**. Of undisputed Berber origin, this incomparable dish may be called by various names, contain infinite varieties of ingredients and seasonings, and may be made from wheat, corn, barley, millet, green wheat, green barley shoots, or sprouts and even rice, tapioca, or bread crumbs. Named **seksu** by Moroccans, it may also be called **sikuk**, **sksu**, **utsu**, **ta'am**, and even **kouski** as in Tunisia. The principle is the same. Dry floury grains are dribbled with water and rubbed to form tiny pellets. These are carefully steamed with no cover over a perforated pot set upon a bubbling stew. The small pellets swell with moisture and absorb some of the flavors of the broth. Often two steamings are required to get the proper consistency of separate fluffy and tender granules. Frequently a light sprinkling of oil or **smen** (like clarified butter) is added. Today pre-cooked couscous speeds up meal preparation.

Couscous may be served upon one large platter, with meat, fruits, vegetables, and well-seasoned sauce heaped over the grain base. Or, as in the French or Algerian version, each part of the couscous may be served on separate plates. Couscous may be savory or sweet, and is usually served as a luncheon meal or at the very end of a *diffa* (banquet) solely for the purpose of achieving *shaban*, total satisfaction.

FATS
Many Moroccans use large amounts of oil in cooking and often a swirl of oil is added as a garnish to complete a dish. Oily sauces are frequent. Because it does not cloud and retains a shiny appearance, olive oil is used in many salads and cold dishes while vegetable oils or peanut oil is saved for cooking. Oil extracted from the nuts of the argan tree is used in the southwest region. A mix of honey, crushed almonds, and oil is called **amalou** and is popularly used on breads. When **amalou** is mixed with more honey and wheat germ it makes a kind of breakfast gruel called **zematur**.

Smen is a type of clarified butter widely used in soups and couscous. Sometimes it is flavored with herbs and often it is fermented and stored. The strong smell and pungent taste of **smen** is not too widely appreciated except by Moroccans.

SWEETS AND SNACKS
Many sweet pastries, chewy nougat-type candies, sugared dried fruits, and spicy sweet couscous as well as sugared fried pastries are readily available. But probably more sugar is consumed in the endless cups of heavily sweetened green tea scented with mint than in any other form.

The traditional dessert to end a meal is inevitably an array of available fresh fruits and nuts. Dried fruits may replace the fresh. Moroccans will likely enjoy their sweetly rich pastries at the start of a special occasion meal such as at a wedding or circumcision and especially during the month of Ramadan where the meal after sundown is often begun with sweet cakes called **shebbakia** or **mahalkra** hungrily downed together with bowls of spicy **harira** soup.

SEASONINGS
Basically, Moroccan food has humble beginnings; it is the artistry of careful preparation and complex seasoning that set it apart. Spices are used not only in foods but also in perfumes, medicines, and even in magical potions with mysterious powers.

Spices are not used to mask flavors; they are used with discretion and knowledge to enhance, to tantalize, and to blend. Each cook measures with her nose, her fingers, and her eye but never by actual measurement. These are the skills that are passed from generation to generation. So is the knowledge of exactly which *souk* (marketplaces) and which merchant has the best seasonings.

Salt and pepper are basic, but to the Moroccan cook ten basic seasonings are always at hand: black pepper and cayenne, cumin (subtler than caraway) and saffron, ginger and turmeric, paprika and cinnamon as well as sesame seeds and aniseeds. This is by no means the end to the list, for allspice, cloves, and gum arabic (**mksa**) as well as cardamom, coriander seeds, and many others too exotic for most western tastes subtly season many foods.

Much like the many varied blends of curries (**kari**) in India, Morocco too has its prized blends of seasonings called **ras el hanout**. These blends may contain almost anything including alleged aphrodisiacs such as ash berries, Spanish fly, and monk's pepper; they are purchased in prepared amounts or created in special blends by individual experts.

Chermoula is one example of a highly seasoned sauce made with a blend of herbs and strongly flavored with crushed fresh garlic, cayenne, and lemon juice. It is used mainly as a marinade for fish but other blends of seasonings may be specially prepared for soups and sauces. Not surprisingly, these seasoning blends are cherished family secrets.

Fresh mint or spearmint is used with steeped green tea while other fresh or dried herbs take their place with spices to enliven foods: green parsley, green coriander leaves, oregano, basil, grey verbena, and **za'atar**, a much-used herb similar in aroma and flavor to thyme and oregano.

Rosewater and orange flower water are used often in sweets and pastries and sometimes in the water used for ceremonial handwashing. Many dried herbs and even dried flowers and buds are used in mixing special medicinal potions and herbal teas.

A truly hot spiced relish made from crushed fresh garlic, chili peppers, salt, and olive oil is similar to the Indonesian **sambal oelek** and is called **harissa**. This hot condiment may be used as a dip or added judiciously to soups and sauces. It always accompanies **harira**, the staple legume soup.

BEVERAGES

Tiny decorated glasses of green tea served hot, sweet, and scented with fresh spearmint are the classic Moroccan beverage. Countless glasses are enjoyed every day at any time. But coffee is enjoyed too and helps many a Moroccan to begin the day. Coffee may be served black and sweet – it may also carry the surprise of a blend of sweet and peppery spices. Carbonated beverages are gaining in popularity but sweetened fruit drinks made from local produce and sometimes from crushed nuts are enjoyed as refreshers; these are called **sharbat**. Cool **leben**, similar to buttermilk, is also a frequent thirst-quencher.

Street vendors sell plain water, fruit juices, and even **sharbat**. Water is also the usual mealtime beverage accompanied by the main dishes with green tea following the meal. In rich homes, it is not unusual for the mealtime beverage of water to be lightly perfumed with the subtle addition of orange flower water, rose petal syrup, or other aromatic concentrates.

The prohibitions against alcoholic beverages that stem from Islamic traditions are kept to varying degrees. No such prohibitions exist in Jewish homes and many Jewish kitchens are known for their homemade wines and fruit brandies prepared from ancient recipes and distilled from a great variety of fresh fruits. Wine is a part of Sabbath and festival tradition in Jewish homes.

MEALS AND CUSTOMS

Moroccans commonly awake to the nose-tickling aroma of freshly brewed coffee. Tiny cups of coffee may be served black, heavily sweetened, or delicately spiced depending on the home and the location. Breakfast is not an important meal; the important meal of the day is most often the midday meal. Usually more than one set of talented hands prepare the noon meal from the freshest ingredients available and everything from grinding spices in mortar and pestle (or, if fortunate, in an electric blender) to cutting meats, trimming and chopping vegetables, scaling fish and washing and preparing fruits – everything will be done in the four to five hours preceding that meal.

The main meal of the day may begin with three tiny glasses of sweet green tea; or, in the south, with a plate of fresh dates and a bowl of milk; or, in the countryside, with plain biscuits, honey, and **smen**. More cosmopolitan areas may begin a meal with rounds of drinks and platters of appetizers such as miniature meatballs or fish balls or tiny stuffed crisp pastries (**braiwats**). Moroccan salads, usually a mix of spiced and sometimes sweetened vegetables which have been cooked and served at room temperature, may be one of the many dishes or may introduce the meal much as Italian **antipasti**.

Dining is almost always communal, the meal arranged on platters in the center of the table with diners helping themselves. The food is always eaten with the first three fingers of the right hand. Only soups and sometimes **couscous** (traditionally served at the end of a banquet and as the main course only in family meals) may be eaten from spoons. Adept fingers form foods into small balls, dip them with a calculated swirl into the savory sauces, and pop them into waiting mouths. More often, bread is used to scoop up food and soak up fragrant juices and sauces.

Festive occasions are not the only time when hospitality and a great show of abundance is important. Heaped platters and full stomachs are always the goal. But even when the platters are whisked away, hungry mouths will take care of the leftovers: nothing is ever wasted. To a Moroccan the great show of abundance is a matter of deep pride and is essential for any feast and for any guests. It is not, however, the dictum of restaurants.

Meals are always preceded and ended with ceremonial handwashing. This may be done humbly and simply or with great elaborate gestures and appropriate gracious words accompanied by elegant towels and perfumed water. Just as commonly, the custom of tea drinking – a minimum of three tiny glasses – often also precedes and concludes important meals.

The importance of the one midday meal can be understood when one realizes the great prevalence of vendors, souks, tiny shops and restaurants offering drinks and snacks at any time of day. Seldom is any work done or business discussed without a customary drinking of tea and often the offering of snacks. Thus the Moroccan is not so concerned with food upon awakening, nor is the evening meal of great importance; there has been a hearty meal at noon and many tidbits and sips throughout the day.

SPECIAL OCCASIONS

The population of Morocco is 99 percent Arab-Berber, and therefore Muslim, with a tiny minority of Christians and Jews. Religious holidays, family occasions, and guests all call forth gracious hospitality and an abundance of the best of foods. To mark the sweetness of the occasion it is not unusual for the festive banquet to begin with rounds of sweet pastries accompanied with glasses of sweet green mint tea. Eventually, many courses and dishes later, the *diffa* will likely end in the way it began: with sweetness as the theme.

For those Moroccans of the Muslim faith, the month of *Ramadan*, which calls for complete abstinence from food and drink through the daylight hours, is ended each day at sundown with the serving of the soup called **harira**. This is a thick soup of meats and legumes flavored richly with vegetables, lemon, turmeric or saffron, cinnamon and ginger and thickened with a fermented, slightly musty flour-water mixture called **tedouira** or sometimes with a clean tangy mixture of beaten eggs and lemon juice. This hearty soup is accompanied with **mahalkra** or **shebbakia**, pastries cooked in boiling honey. Platters of fresh dates, fruits, and coffee or milk complete the ceremonial meal.

GLOSSARY OF FOODS AND FOOD TERMS

Amalou: a smooth thick blend of crushed almonds, honey and olive oil used as a spread on **Khboz** (regular bread) or fried breads, and as an ingredient in a breakfast gruel called **Zematur**.

Barbary Figs: name given to a succulent pear-shaped fruit of a type of cactus plant. Also called prickly pear.

Bisteeya, **Pastilla**, or **Bastilla**: one of the most important Moroccan dishes, of Berber origin and inevitably part of any *diffa* (banquet). A large circular pie, composed of many buttery, tissue-thin layers of pastry (**Warka**) enclosing lamb, eggs, vegetables and usually pigeon meat all salted and spiced, redolent with cinnamon and almonds.

Boukha: sweet brandy distilled from figs.

Braiwats: similar to the Greek **Tiropetes**. Tissue-thin **Warka** pastry oiled or generously buttered and filled with cheese or other savory mixtures then pinched or folded and finally baked or deep-fried and served crisp and hot.

Brik: deep-fried meat turnovers but made with **Warka** pastry and often filled with a whole raw egg that cooks during the deep-frying. While eating, some care is needed not to dribble the soft-cooked yolk. Tunisian classic, eaten also in Morocco.

Chele or **Khelea**: a preserved form of beef used as a snack, appetizer or as flavoring in other dishes. The selected pieces of beef are spice-rubbed, sun-dried, then oil-cooked, and finally preserved in oil until used.

Chermoula: Tunisian dish of sautéed fish served with a sweet and sour sauce of raisins and wine vinegar touched with sugar.

Chorba: name given to any thin soup.

Couscous: classic Moroccan dish of Berber origin. Basically this is a dish of specially prepared grains over or beside which is served a stew of vegetables and meats with a well-seasoned sauce. The classic Couscous is prepared from wheat flour rubbed with dribbles of water to form tiny grains. Often the Couscous may be purchased in this form. Cooking is done by steaming (no cover) over a bubbling stew or boiling water in a pan with a perforated base. The two-layer pot used to prepare both the stew and the Couscous grains is called a couscousière. Note that Couscous may be made with any grain and sometimes even with sprouted grains or even dried bread crumbs.

Djej: chicken.

Doqq: salt-preserved lemons. Moroccan Jews often prepare **Doqq** by preserving their lemons in oil as well as salt. Indispensable to Moroccan cuisine.

Harira: one of the most famous of Moroccan soups, a meal in itself. It is made with browned pieces of lamb, lentils and garbanzos, noodles and vegetables all pungent with ginger, coriander, and pepper. The final touch may be threads of lemony eggs or a thickening of slightly fermented flour and water stirred in just before serving. Large bowls of this, accompanied with sweet pastries, dates, and other fruits are the usual sundown meal of the month of Ramadan.

Harissa: a smooth peppery sauce added to the **Couscous** by the diner according to taste. If it is true that Moroccan sauces are "everything," then the **Harissa** is truly important for it always accompanies the **Couscous** (unless it is a dessert couscous) and usually enhances many other foods. The base of this sauce is usually the slow-simmered juices of the stew accompanying the **Couscous**, thus the blend while being peppery is also one of subtle seasonings.

Hummous: a name heard all over the Mahgrib and many other places as well. It is a general name referring either to whole chickpeas or garbanzos, or to a purée of these legumes. The latter is usually blended with both garlic and pepper.

Hut Makali: crispy fried fish. Popular street snack found almost everywhere but especially in coastal areas.

Kaaki: Tunisian breadsticks prepared in many shapes and sold by street vendors. These are nibbled anytime and especially enjoyed by children.

Kebab: small morsels threaded on skewers and broiled usually over charcoal. The French call them **Brochettes**, the Spanish **Pinchitos**, but all around the Mediterranean they are called **Kebab**.

Kefta: the Moroccan version of ground meat used in large or small meatballs with the mixture usually sweetened and spiced with cinnamon.

Khboz or **Kisra**: typical Moroccan bread made from wholewheat flour and unbleached white flour (all white flour for guests), yeast, milk, or water and seasoned with anise, sometimes sprinkled with sesame seeds. Baked fresh daily, usually in communal ovens.

Kousha: a Tunisian stew of potatoes, tomatoes, chickpeas, and any variety of fish. May be garnished with prawns or shrimp.

Leben or **Lobon**: similar to buttermilk, used as a cooling beverage or in cookery.

Mahalkra: like biting into crisp honey, these saffron-tinted yeast pretzels are shaped then browned in hot oil and plunged into boiling honey. They are served with a sprinkle of sesame seeds (cool), adding a mouthful of sweetness to the sundown meal of Ramadan.

Mechoui: Moroccan specialty of spit-roasted whole lamb or sheep generously rubbed with ground coriander seeds and garlic cloves. It is eaten with the fingers while piping hot. Tidbits are dipped into a salt and cumin mixture. Moroccan bread is the accompaniment.

Mechouiya: a thick purée of tomatoes and peppers garnished with chunks of hard eggs and tuna. It is not to be confused with the succulent lamb mentioned above (**Mechoui**); this is a Tunisian appetizer salad resembling a very thick Spanish **gazpacho**.

Meshmel or **Djej Emshmel**: classic *diffa* (banquet) specialty. A **Tagine** of chicken, green olives, and preserved Moroccan lemons (**Doqq**).

M'Hanncha: a pastry that uses the thin **Warka** pastry, stuffed with a rich sweet mixture of sugared chopped nuts and tingling spices, then rolled up, coiled like a snake and baked crisply. This pastry is served in slices with cups of traditional sweet green mint tea as a snack.

Mikla: when the Moroccan bread dough is patted into flat rounds and baked to a brown crustiness on both sides on an open-fire griddle, the resulting bread is called **Mikla**.

Pita: Mahgrib and Middle Eastern bread, sometimes called Arabic bread. Rounds of simple yeast dough are rolled thinly, allowed to rise, then baked quickly in a hot oven. The resulting breads puff up high then slowly deflate upon cooling. The result is a thin tasty bun that is hollow in the center. Makes a convenient pocket for fillings.

Qodban: Mahgrib tidbits of lamb entrails first marinated then skewered and charcoal-broiled.

Raipe: a bland sweetened dessert resembling yogurt or junket but the whole or skimmed milk is set with the addition of the pounded dried pulp of wild Moroccan artichokes.

Ras el Hanout: a varying blend of spices used in meat and game dishes, stuffings, and even candies. Sometimes mystical properties are attributed to **Ras el Hanout**, which may be a blend of a few or over a hundred ingredients said to contain legendary aphrodisiacs.

Rghaif: Moroccan version of thin dessert pancakes or crepes. Served in many variations: greased, stretched, folded and deep-fried or layered and served with melted butter and honey. Sometimes a special breakfast dish.

Sefirna: the classic Moroccan Jewish Sabbath dish of legumes and meats nestled with whole eggs in the shell. The whole casserole is placed in banked ovens late Friday afternoon, then eaten as the Sabbath noon meal without violating the prohibition of work. Versions of this dish abound. It is said to have been taken by the North African Jews to Spain during the Moorish conquest where the Spanish version came to be known as **Olla Podrida** (literally, "rotten pot") because ingredients were always added to the leftovers and reheated and eaten over and over. In central European countries this practical and satisfying dish came to be known as **Cholent** and often included potato chunks, and/or a large flour dumpling. (See Israeli and Jewish.)

Shebbakia: luscious honey pastry, the same as **Mahalkra** but shaped into stars.

Smen: clarified butter. But the Moroccan version is more than clarified: it is often salted, spiced, or herbed and frequently has been preserved in underground crocks until it has the appearance and odor of very old cheese. Small amounts may be added to soups or **Couscous**. Most appreciated by Moroccans.

Souk: outdoor markets.

Tagella: bread eaten by the Tuaregs (a Berber group), made from a simple dough and baked in open fires on hot stones.

Tagine: meal cooked in one pot, the bottom of the pot being a rimmed shallow circle fitted with a classic cone-shaped cover. If the ingredients require, the **Tagine** can be cooked over a heat source or banked with hot coals to give the food a baked-in-the-oven effect. The ingredients may vary but usually include a spiced mixture of vegetables, legumes, meats, with almost as many regional and personal variations as the **Couscous**.

Tedouira: a floury mixture used for thickening sauces and soups. In Marrakesh, the classic **Tedouira** is left overnight to ferment and develop a sour flavor.

Warka: thinner even that the Greek phyllo pastry, the **Warka** is made from flour and water and most closely resembles the technique for making Chinese spring roll skins. The dough mixture is dabbed or rubbed over a flat or domed heated utensil, forming a sheer "skin" of pastry that is gently lifted off as soon as it firms. To keep it workable, it may be gently washed with oil or melted butter. Layered together, the final effect is similar to the French puff pastry.

Za'atar: a herb of sweet aromatic scent, similar to the thyme-oregano family.

Zebda: fresh butter.

Zematur: a thin breakfast porridge or gruel made from toasted wheat germ and the honey-almond butter called **Amalou**.

CHAPTER 37

NEW ZEALANDERS

It is almost as though it were the last place created. For carefully arranged on two main islands it seems that nature's awesome constructions display themselves solely for the delight of humans. Here is everything: snow-tipped mountains piercing the clouds, emerald green pastures dotted with sheep, glacial lakes spilling into waterfalls, and sunny beaches splashed with blue waters. Small scrubbed cities nestled into hillsides, a few bustling hustling cities where the main business gets done, and then miles and miles of peaceful but rugged natural beauty to calm the mind and quench the soul with serenity.

But most of the world thinks of New Zealand as a faraway place where people drink tea at four and spend the rest of their time tending sheep. No doubt this is the image deliberately perpetuated by the 3.5 million New Zealanders who are fully aware of their good life, beautiful land, and benevolent climate.

If New Zealanders have a reputation for pride, it is for good reason. Although they cannot take credit for the beautiful land or benevolent climate, they can take credit for creating a society where pollution, poverty, malnutrition, racism, and unemployment are almost non-existent. This is not to say that life for New Zealanders was always idyllic. There had to be friction between two peoples of such diverse philosophies: the Maoris and the English.

Well-preserved legends tell of the seven canoes in the Great Migration that brought the first Maoris in 1350 C.E. to the islands of New Zealand. They quickly disposed of a small population of simple people known today as the "moa-hunters"; those they favored they married, the others they ate. Surviving on the many indigenous birds and planting their own crops, the Maoris soon expanded into many powerful tribes.

Today most of the prominent Maori families trace their origin to these early adventurers who worked artistically with bone, stone, and wood, creating a highly developed culture that survived untouched for about 300 years. Then, in December 1642, the Dutch explorer Abel Janszoon Tasman arrived. His visit was brief. A skirmish resulting in the deaths of several of his men convinced him to return to sea. More than a hundred years later, in 1770, Captain James Cook carefully charted the coasts of both islands and the European influx began.

The first Europeans to create settlements were missionaries bent on saving souls and fishermen bent on hunting whales. The established Maori population did not take kindly to all of this and sporadic fighting ensued. The Treaty of Waitangi in 1840 gave Great Britain sovereignty over the islands but guaranteed the Maoris', right to their lands. English colonization was slow, and occasional uprisings and disagreements between the European and native populations did little to encourage peaceful growth of the new nation. But a gold rush in 1865 brought a swell of immigrants who later settled into farming pursuits when the gold fever exhausted itself. Production of mutton and lamb quickly exceeded local needs and the introduction in 1882 of refrigerated ships gave impetus to the production of fresh meat, stimulating both the intensity of farming and the flow of immigrants.

Light industries based on food and forest products, clothing and light machinery together with the small population probably account for New Zealand's lack of pollution problems. Although the sheep outnumber the people by twenty to one, farming only absorbs about 12 percent of the population. At its worst, the unemployment level is usually less than most countries. Likely it is a combination of climate and agricultural efficiency that accounts for the abundance of meats and dairy products and a year-round selection of fruits and vegetables that places nourishing foods on every table.

That the easygoing nature of the Polynesian Maoris can exist side by side with the work-oriented English (or *Pakehas* as they are called in New Zealand) is a tribute to both peoples. About 88 percent of the Kiwis (New Zealanders) are of European descent, with about 9 percent of Polynesian Maori origin and the rest small groups of mixed descent. "Kiwi," by the way, does not derive from the fruit by that name, but rather from the native kiwi bird which is flightless. Although some Maoris have adapted themselves into the mainstream of New Zealand society and can be found working in all types of industries and professions, great inequalities still exist.

A phenomenon called *musu* is often apparent among the Maoris, as it is among other South Pacific and even African groups. It is characterized by a deadpan expression and monosyllabic speech and is said to be caused by a combination of fear, shame, and perhaps a sense of unjust accusation. The intervention of a trusted person who speaks the language will usually calm the afflicted Maori. Regarding all property as communal and seeing no wrong in "borrowing" something he desires is another Maori cultural trait that has frequently caused misunderstandings.

But in the fabric that has built the New Zealand nation, the interweaving of the Maori spirit of nature and the *Pakehas'* ethic of work and order over more than 150 years have combined to produce a proud and pioneering people in a fresh clean land of boundless beauty, in a climate that is never too hot and never too cold and where no one needs to pray for rain. Maoris, Europeans, and others have retained their cultural identities, enriching each other and in the process creating an exemplary country.

DOMESTIC LIFE
The mutually appreciative and interdependent relationship shared by the peoples of New Zealand is depicted in the preparation, serving, and storing of homegrown foods. Certainly the Maoris' vast knowledge of and skill with local produce, fish and fowl added to the European larder.

Abundant water power produces hydroelectricity widely used in industries and homes. About 82 percent of New Zealanders cook by electricity while only 11 percent use gas. They enjoy the use of a wide range of electrical appliances including refrigerators, freezers, and small kitchen appliances.

The ability to bake has always been a criterion for the New Zealand homemaker, but today many other factors influence cookery skills. These include widespread travel and communications, increasing sophistication of restaurants, the burgeoning New Zealand wine industry, and the influence of other ethnic groups: Chinese, East Indian, Pacific Islanders, and the Dutch. Curiosity and pleasure in discovering new foods and food combinations have stimulated not only interest in cuisine other than British, but also interest in acquiring unusual cooking utensils, recipes, and menu patterns. Previously, a simple cook top and an oven produced the typical *Pakeha* dinner of roasted meat and roasted vegetables topped off with a creamy fruit dessert. But today, skewers for shish-kabob, woks for Chinese dishes and casseroles for moussakas, and electric blenders to create curry combinations are all a part of the New Zealand kitchen.

While eager to taste and adapt new food ideas, the Kiwis are also wise enough to retain at least one cooking tradition that has not only stood the test of time, but has proven to be a practical modern innovation as well. From earliest times, the Maoris cooked their main meal of the day in an earth oven which they called an **umu** or **hangi**. A pit would be dug and a wood fire kindled in the bottom. As the fire progressed, smooth stones would be placed on top. By scraping out the fire's ashes and retaining the red-hot stones in the pit, the Maoris created a well-insulated oven. Over the heated stones they placed joints of meat, leaf-wrapped fish and seafood and finally arranged **kumara** (sweet potatoes) or other vegetables on top. Liberally sprinkled water created steam, and woven mats set on top sealed in

FOODS COMMONLY USED

Because many of the plants brought by the first Polynesians who arrived in New Zealand more than a thousand years ago (such as coconut) would not grow, subtropical New Zealand differs from the rest of the South Pacific. It was the Maoris who, with diligence and patience, coaxed varieties of corn, kumara, taro, and species of weeds and bracken to become

part of their daily staples together with the plentiful fish, seafood, and varieties of birds and other flesh.

The basic food preferences and meal patterns of New Zealand are British. A great variety of home-baked scones, biscuits, quick breads, and cakes are visible at most meals and whenever tea is served – which means often.

Lamb is the favored meat and careful distinctions are made in regard to the age of the lamb, mutton being enjoyed only by the staunchest Brit. Abundance of local fish and seafood and a plentiful supply of a variety of fresh fruits and vegetables all make the New Zealand diet a good one.

the heat and moisture. After a period of undisturbed cooking time, a well-cooked tasty meal of meat, fish, and vegetables could be enjoyed by a large number of people. Today, many a large outdoor party, sports club, gathering or family picnic is highlighted with a feast made in a **hangi**.

Except for certain isolated areas, food storage has never been a problem in New Zealand. This is because of the combination of efficient agricultural methods and the variations from temperate to sub-tropical climates which allow for an almost continuous supply of fresh fruits, vegetables, and grains as well as meats and dairy products. Refrigerators and freezers are widely used and most Kiwis also enjoy convenience foods, delicatessen specialties, and a range of imported foods as well.

DAIRY PRODUCTS
Milk is taken by most children at most meals in the form of fresh whole milk. Where considered necessary, toddlers are provided with the New Zealand Whole Milk Biscuit, a cookie enriched with protein in the form of skim milk powder. Most adults take some milk in tea, soups, and creamy desserts. The use of skim milk, powdered skim milk, yogurt, and cottage cheese is still limited although increasing in popularity. Many varieties of cheeses are available but not widely used.

FRUITS AND VEGETABLES
Produce is mainly grown on the North Island where the climate varies from temperate to sub-tropical, allowing for an almost continuous growing period. Imported, frozen and canned fruits and vegetables are also used. Fruits include apples, pears, varieties of berries, plums, peaches, apricots, nectarine, and cherries. The more exotic fruits include **feijoas**, **tamarillo** (tree tomato), **kiwi** (Chinese gooseberry), passion fruit, and pineapple. Pumpkin and sweet potatoes (called **kumara**) are the staple vegetables but many other common vegetables and salad greens are also used.

MEATS AND ALTERNATES
Lamb is the number-one meat in New Zealand almost to the exclusion of beef, pork, and poultry. Distinction is made in the age of the lamb: the youngest and tenderest is called **spring lamb** and is aged from twelve to eighteen weeks; weaned lamb is aged from four and one-half to nine months old. **Hogget** is the deeper pink-fleshed lamb butchered from nine to twenty months. **Young mutton** is the next classification and includes lamb from twenty months to two years. **Mature mutton** is strong in taste, deep red in flesh color with brittle white fat, and for this the

sheep are butchered from two to five years old. The most common method of cooking is oven-roasting, with prepared vegetables added near the end of the cooking time. Currently lamb has been used more imaginatively in a variety of international dishes.

Popular fish include trout, cod, red snapper, groper, **terekihi**, **John Dory**, flounder and tuna, with whitebait considered a special delicacy. Oysters, mussels, and eels are widely used. **Toheroa** is a native bivalve considered a delicacy but not always available. Crayfish, similar to lobsters, are enjoyed and crayfish tails are exported. Fish is eaten in quantity, often as an ingredient in other dishes, sometimes as a garnish or side dish. Legumes are seldom used except for special dishes.

BREADS AND GRAINS
New Zealand is almost self-sufficient in wheat production. Few wholegrain breads or cereals are consumed; white wheat flour is favored. Oats as a baking ingredient and hot breakfast porridge are used occasionally. But there is increasing emphasis on "health foods" with the resulting interest in whole grains and varieties of different grains, including wheat germ. "Tea breads" or quick breads, biscuits, scones and cakes are served whenever tea is poured and often are a regular part of most meals as well.

FATS
New Zealand butter and cream are of fine quality and widely used. Butter, lard, cooking oil, and salt pork are all used in cooking.

SWEETS AND SNACKS
Much sugar is consumed in the form of sweetened tea, sweet pastries, and candies as well as preserves such as jams, jellies, and marmalades.

SEASONINGS
With traditional British restraint in seasoning, Kiwis have used little more than salt, pepper, and onions. However, more current interest and stimulation in imaginative cooking has brought an increase in both seasonings and condiments, although bland flavors still prevail.

BEVERAGES
Tea is the beverage for every meal and as a mid-morning snack usually with biscuits or breads. Tea is traditionally taken with milk and sugar. Local wines are appearing more frequently in homes and restaurants, and beer is enjoyed for quick lunches and outdoor parties.

MEALS AND CUSTOMS

The pattern of three meals a day is slowly making inroads into the long-cherished tradition of six meals: breakfast, morning tea, lunch, afternoon tea, dinner and supper (although often afternoon tea and dinner may be one and the same). The factors that are creating the changes in New Zealand are similar to those found almost worldwide: increased food costs, more married women joining the workforce, concern about obesity, and a distinct increase in nutrition awareness. Although morning and afternoon tea breaks are still widely observed both at home and at work, meals are becoming lighter and more varied. In spite of all these factors, British influence still predominates in most meals and the way in which they are served.

Substantial breakfasts, small lunches, and meat-and-vegetable dinners are punctuated by tea breaks. Ice and ice water are seldom seen although beer is usually served chilled. Most table service is on the formal side with a special knife always set for the sole purpose of buttering one's bread. And New Zealanders still frown on the habit of resting one's knife on the dinner plate; the main course is to be eaten throughout with knife and fork. Further, New Zealanders have no qualms about placing a spoonful of chilled salad on their main dinner plate right beside the roast and hot vegetables.

SPECIAL OCCASIONS

The New Zealand population is predominantly Christian with about 80 percent of the people being members of one of four denominations: Church of England, Roman Catholic, Methodist and Presbyterian. Ratana and Ringatu are the two main Maori sects, though many Maoris are Christian. Close to 4,500 New Zealanders are of the Jewish faith.

Although Christmas and Easter are celebrated with family gatherings, there is little question that the avidly sports-minded Kiwis generate more excitement over "rice dyes" (that's Race Days, of course) and the accompanying outdoor picnics or **hangis** (pit-cooked meals) than over any religious oriented occasions. Foods vary little from the daily fare except that Sunday dinner is almost invariably roast lamb and roasted vegetables with trifle or **pavlova** for dessert. Festive days may include meals that are more leisurely but differ little in content.

GLOSSARY OF FOODS AND FOOD TERMS
Note: See also Australian Glossary

Aruhe, **Parara**, or **Ruma**: a fern-like shrub, one of the first "greens" used by the Maoris. The steamed roots were pounded into cakes said to be both medicinal and nourishing.

Biscuits: cookies.

Chips: french-fried potatoes.

Colonial Goose: a stuffed, boned leg of lamb, roasted and served like goose. Probably originated as the pioneer's version of a holiday dinner, since they had no geese.

Corn Flour: cornstarch.

Essence: used to describe flavoring extracts, as in "vanilla essence."

Fell: the thin membrane covering cuts of lamb, usually cooked by roasting. Removing the fell helps to make carving easier as it is a thin but tough membrane; however, removing it before roasting may cause the roast to lose both shape and moisture.

Golden Syrup: light molasses, a frequent sweetener in cooking.

Hangi or **Haangi**: the Maori method of earth-pit cooking. A wood fire is kindled in the bottom of an earth pit then smooth stones are arranged over the embers and allowed to reach red-hot heat. Prepared joints of meat, fish, and seafood wrapped in leaves or placed in flax baskets and finally vegetables are set on the top. Water is sprinkled in to create steam then the whole thing is sealed over with straw mats. After a prescribed cooking time (usually about two hours) the food is removed and the feasting begins. This method of cooking is still enjoyed by Maoris and also by *Pakehas* (Europeans), especially for outdoor entertaining.

Hogget: lamb aged nine to twenty months, not as tender as younger lamb. Best used in ground meat dishes, casseroles, and stews.

Jam: jelly made from sweetened cooked fruits or berries.

Jelly: commercial or home-prepared gelatine desserts.

Kiwi: also called "Chinese gooseberry," this brownish-skinned fruit is about the size of a lemon with a vivid green soft pulp. Each kiwi contains only about 30 calories, and is rich in vitamin C. They are used in many fruit desserts, eaten from the skin as they are and are also considered as a steak tenderizer because of their acid juice.

Koura: a type of crayfish.

Kumara: Maori name for the yam or sweet potato, a favorite and staple crop in New Zealand, used as a vegetable and in making breads.

Lamb (**Weaned**): name used to refer to young lamb four and one half to nine months old.

Lollies or **Sweets**: candies.

Manuka: popularly called the "tea tree," a native shrub with fragrant leaves used by the early European pioneers as a substitute for tea. The Maoris use the fragrant **Manuka** twigs to make a fire for grilling fresh-caught fish.

Mutton: New Zealanders make a distinction between young mutton (twenty months to two years) with its pinky-red flesh and firm fat, and mature mutton which may be from two to five years, strong in flavor and with red flesh and brittle white fat.

Paraoa: Maori name for bread, baked in many varieties, both leavened and unleavened and made essentially from wheat flour.

Paraoa Takakau: probably the earliest form of Maori bread prepared simply with flour and water and shaped in large flat rounds.

Paua: a local type of abalone whose tough chewy flesh requires much pounding to tenderize before cooking.

Pavlova: favorite dessert in both Australia and New Zealand. It is made from a crisp baked meringue shell filled with fresh or cooked sweetened fruit and whipped cream. The dessert is said to be named after the Russian ballerina Anna Pavlova, who enjoyed a triumphant tour of New Zealand and Australia in 1926.

Pikelets: tiny flapjacks or pancakes served with preserves and whipped cream or lemon butter.

Pipis: tiny New Zealand shellfish similar to cockles.

Puha: a well-known New Zealand weed of many varieties, the coastal species being the best and used as both herb and vegetable. Can be lightly cooked and used much like spinach.

Savories: appetizers or dishes that are not sweet. Usually made with eggs, cheese or fish, and served for tea.

Spring Lamb: designates the youngest lamb. Most succulent and tender, aged from twelve to eighteen weeks, with very pale pink flesh and creamy fat.

Steak and Oyster Pie: cubed beef is browned and cooked in a thickened gravy then poured into a prepared piecrust. Fresh shelled oysters are arranged on top then covered with pastry and quickly oven-baked. A great favorite in a country where the more than three million population consume 100,000,000 oysters annually.

Tamarillo: also called tree tomato. May be eaten as a fruit or as a salad vegetable.

Toheroa: a bivalve native to areas of New Zealand's western shore. The flesh is very tough and is only edible when minced or finely chopped.

Toheroa Soup: famed New Zealand soup prepared from the finely minced flesh and green parts of the **Toheroa**. The smooth green soup is considered a special delicacy.

Tuatua: a smaller and more plentiful version of the larger **Toheroa**. Both are delicious fleshy bivalves enjoyed in season.

CHAPTER 38

NORWEGIAN

There is more to Norway and Norwegians than meets the eye. Outwardly the country is the most sparsely populated in all of Europe with less than 25 percent of the land inhabited and more than 75 percent of it a vast stillness of barren mountain ranges. Outwardly Norwegians appear to be a literate, calm and homogeneous people, with conformity appearing to be the key to their way of life.

Yet the Norwegians were the first in Europe to recognize the potential of water-powered electricity and in 1891 installed in northern Hammerfest the first hydroelectric plant in all of Europe – while the rest of Europe lit their candles and kerosene lamps. As early as the 700s, when the rest of civilization was still nascent, Norwegian Viking ships set out to far off coasts of the Arab world and even North America, to explore, to trade, and to plunder. Stone Age carvings visible throughout Norway on mountainsides and rocky strata are said to be more than 4,000 years old and depict a vivid way of life with images of the sea and the land and even well-drawn skiers.

Even today, with little more than 3 percent of the land arable, Norway has an efficient mechanized system of agriculture, a bustling industry in forestry and fishing products, and a merchant shipping fleet that is one of the largest in the world. And while much of the rest of the industrialized world concerns itself with problems of pollution, Norway exports an increasingly prized resource: pure springwater.

Norwegians freely admit to being hooked on sports and physical fitness and to being avid readers – there are said to be three times as many daily newspapers in Oslo as in New York. They also admit that alcoholism is one of their oldest problems. And while they enjoy parties after skiing, skating, sailing, or mountain climbing, there is sure to be at least one guest abstaining from alcoholic drinks in order to drive the others home. For in Norway impaired driving carries the stiff penalty of twenty-one days in jail and this is strictly enforced. Special government stores dispense alcohol at high prices and close for weekends. Perhaps it is a spark of the old Viking fire that accounts for the Norwegians openly adhering to the letter of the law, while many of them quietly make good use of a still hidden in the cellar!

And while 96 percent of the population profess to the Lutheran faith, complete with the celebration of Christmas, Easter, confirmation ceremonies and parties on the fifteenth birthday, examples of still older beliefs are much in evidence. Dotted throughout the rugged countryside are gnarled and grotesque rock formations which the Norwegians – only slightly hesitantly and more than half-jokingly – will tell you are fossilized trolls. Many inexplicable events are quietly attributed to the varying dispositions of the mischievous trolls inhabiting the rocks and trees throughout Norway and there are few who would dismiss their existence completely. There is scarcely a Norwegian family that would not set out a plate brimful of creamy **rommegrot** for *Julenisse*, the Christmas troll dressed in a red cap and sporting a white beard. With a full belly on Christmas Eve, he is not so likely to play tricks on the family the rest of the year.

The Norwegian's apparent contradiction between the inner and outer self is an ancient trait. Although daring and violence seemed to characterize the Viking abroad, at home he organized things – special meeting places where village grievances and disputes could be heard and settled. This surprisingly democratic system was in existence before the 600s. And while the Viking held the belief that to fall in battle meant a place in Valhalla with Odin in the afterlife, he also clung to a firm belief in *ragnarok*, "the final confrontation between Good and Evil," and the accounting of man's deeds.

But it is history as well as ancient cultures that have molded the Norwegian lifestyle. The flamboyant era of the Vikings ended in 1066 followed by almost 500 years of internal strife, domination by Sweden and Denmark in ill-fated unions and finally the Black Plague which reduced the population. Pressure from the German Hanseatic League controlled Norwegian trade for almost 200 years, while the Danes ruled and taxed the people and spread the Lutheran faith.

Finally, toward the end of the 1700s, with her population increased, her economy strengthened, and a resurgence in rich peasant art, Norway adopted English manners and culture and stepped towards independence.

The democratic constitution was signed on May 17, 1814, and is celebrated today with children's parades and a buoyant sense of freedom just as though "the ink were still wet on the paper."

Wherever Norwegians have emigrated, they have adapted themselves quietly into the community, retaining their Lutheran faith and their love of sports, everywhere their calm natures and gentle strength pervading their lifestyle. Unquestionably their long historic struggle with the elements of nature and their life in a vast quiet country have left them with a deep sensitivity to the concerns of others as well as a personal need for solitude.

DOMESTIC LIFE

Although Norwegians treasure their solitude and privacy, they do enjoy social occasions. In rural areas social occasions are often combined with cooperative efforts concerned with smoking, pickling, salting, and preserving meats and fish, preserving berries and other fruits and communal baking of huge batches of **flatbrod**, enough for a whole season. The dimpled crispy round bread keeps well and is the perfect accompaniment to the many cheeses made over the summer months when the sheep's and goat's milk is at its richest.

Refrigerators and freezers are used almost everywhere, but traditional foods and implements continue to play an important role in the Norwegian *kjokken*

(kitchen). Indeed, many large restaurants and modern homes proudly use the intricately carved wooden butter molds that were in use hundreds of years ago.

Although agriculture is fully mechanized, the Norwegian farmer still keeps a few cream-colored Westland "fjord ponies," more out of nostalgia than need. And dotted over the landscape are the *stabburs*, two-floor storehouses reminiscent of a time before electricity and freezers, yet still much in use. The main floor is used to store grains, apples and pears, home preserves, pickles and root vegetables. And the sweet and musty food smells mingle with the heady aromas of fermenting beer and wine and waft upward to the second story which is used as a guest house and where the Norwegian family proudly keep some of their best possessions. Travel throughout the more remote areas is often difficult, and guests are always welcomed and expected to stay at least overnight.

Also reminiscent of former times are *saeters*, the tiny cabins perched precariously on craggy ledges near the pastures. In summer months the women of the household would often spend weeks at a time at the *saeters* busily collecting, churning, and aging the creamy milk from sheep and goats into a variety of cheeses. Today most of the cheese making is carried out commercially in factories, and the picturesque *saeter* is treasured as a summer cottage by the solitude-hungry urban Norwegian.

DAIRY PRODUCTS

Glasses of cold milk, sour milk, and buttermilk are enjoyed by all ages at all meals and often as a refreshment. Many varieties of cheeses, mostly made from sheep's and goat's milk, range from creamy and sweet to the powerful **gammel ost**, a cheese so aged and

FOODS COMMONLY USED

Although ice cream vendors commonly hawk their wares at ski matches and shows throughout the winter, in other respects Norwegians are uncommonly conservative not only in foods but also in food preparation. This is not to say that Norwegian food is bland. It is not. Rather, care is taken to preserve the natural sea or earthy flavors inherent in all fresh foods. Freshly caught fish (often still alive), fresh meats, young vegetables and seasonal fruits are all enjoyed with a minimum of fripperies: simply boiled or gently stewed and served with their own freshness and taste intact.

Robust, pungent, and heartier flavors are evident in the many fermented, cured, pickled, and salted dishes that appear on the Norwegian table; fermented fish (especially trout, called *rakorret*) and smoked, cured meats, pickled herrings, pickled and salted vegetables and tangy salads all take their place with aged cheeses and sour, crisp, wholegrain breads. So much are natural flavors relished

that often soups, stews, and desserts are seasoned only with salt or sweetened with sugar. Dairy products are enjoyed daily and sour cream is as important an ingredient in many dishes as salt. Though fruits and vegetables have only a short growing season, they seem to make up in quality and taste what they lack in variety. Self-sufficient in meat (domestic and game), dairy products, and vegetables, Norway imports most of her grain needs, fruits, and some vegetables.

odiferous that it is always kept on its own covered plate.

Most commonly used is the caramel-colored sweetish goat cheese appearing at almost every meal and often blended with a roux, and smoothed with currant jelly to make a sauce for meats. A Norwegian kitchen is never without a supply of sour cream, for this is used in fruits, vegetables, stews, soups, and in pancakes, waffles, and baked goods. Even **rommegrot**, the traditional ending to a meal and an indispensable dish at country weddings, is made basically from flour-thickened sour cream and served with a dribble of clear melted butter and a drift of cinnamon and crunchy brown sugar.

FRUITS AND VEGETABLES
Apples, pears, and plums are the staple fruits, with some apricots and peaches being grown at Sjoholt. But when the wild berries ripen, almost half the population declares a holiday from work to attend to the urgent business of picking berries: **lingonberries**, **cloudberries**, blueberries, cranberries, and tiny wild strawberries. What cannot be eaten in short order is preserved in freezers or packed in jars as sweet preserves or sauces to be enjoyed all winter. Fruits, especially the variety of sweet and tart berries, are enjoyed sometimes slightly thickened and sweetened into puddings, enfolded into pancakes, layered in cakes, sprinkled into waffle batter, and frequently eaten as a side dish with roasted meats and game.

Norwegians enjoy all the commonly stored winter vegetables such as cabbages and potatoes, beets and carrots. But they especially savor young fresh vegetables in season, serving them simply boiled and lightly glazed with fresh butter, sour cream, and fresh dill sprigs. Freshly made **sauerkraut** still crisp and crunchy with caraway seeds, wilted cucumber salads, and bright tart pickled beets are year-round favorites.

MEATS AND ALTERNATES
Norwegians enjoy many meats, especially lamb and mutton either fresh or salted, dried, smoked, and eaten hot or cold. Pork (mainly in the form of ham, bacon, salt pork, and sausages), beef, veal, goose and duck appear less often on the menu.

Even more than lamb and mutton, Norwegians love fish. The almost endless varieties of fresh fish – salmon, trout, mackerel, flounder, herring, eel, turbot, halibut, and cod as well as shrimp and crayfish – are matched by the almost endless methods of preparation – salting, smoking, drying, marinating, poaching. The early dinner, simple but hot, is most likely to be poached fresh fish with a mustard or horse radish sauce accompanied by boiled vegetables, or a simple mutton and vegetable stew like **faar**

I kaal. There is surely no shortage of protein, for meats and fish may be consumed not only for dinner but often at lunch, as part of a sandwich, and frequently, together with cereals and eggs, as part of *frokost*, the ample Norwegian breakfast. Legumes are not widely used, except the dried peas so popular for soup. Almonds and almond paste are usual bakery ingredients.

BREADS AND GRAINS
A great variety of breads and rolls – crisp, dried, chewy, crusty, even soft and light – make their appearance at almost every meal. Most popular is the crisp dimpled circle of rye bread called **flatbrod** which is still made in huge quantities, often as a communal effort. Norwegian women take great pride in their baking and even though guests may drop in unexpectedly, there will always be crispy cookies and at least one cake to accompany the inevitable good strong coffee. Cooked and cold cereals are also very much a part of the popular *frokost* which also includes cheeses, meats, and fish. The Norwegians are firm believers in a hearty breakfast.

FATS
Butter is not only a cooking fat and a spread, it is also used as a flavoring and an ingredient in almost every dish. Cheeses, milks, cream, and sour cream are all rich in butterfat and skimmed milk is considered suitable for anything but humans. Smaller amounts of other fats such as rendered duck or goose fat, salt pork and lard are also used in cooking.

SWEETS AND SNACKS
The Norwegian preference is not for sweets, but an undeniable sweet tooth does exist. Although candies are eaten as well as cakes and pastries, they are seldom richly iced or syrupy. Most baked goods are only slightly sweet and coffee is usually preferred strong and black.

SEASONINGS
Natural tastes predominate in Norwegian cuisine, but there is a definite predilection for salted foods. Salty cheeses, salted and pickled vegetables, salt-cured meats and fish are a daily part of the diet. Only moderate amounts of other seasonings are used: bay leaves, peppercorns, caraway seeds, mustard, horse radish, dill, thyme, and of course, butter and sour cream are liberally used.

BEVERAGES
The general Scandinavian custom of *skaal* is as prevalent in Norway as it is in Sweden and Denmark: the raised glass of chilled **Aquavit**, the firm meeting of

eyes followed by a decisive gulp and then the triumphant raising of the emptied glass and the final meeting of the eyes. Frequently this is followed by chasers of beer and most often the whole ritual precedes a meal and is carried on throughout the dining. The final bottomless cups of coffee are perhaps a token attempt at sobriety. It is difficult to say for which of these beverages the Norwegian has the greatest capacity. Suffice it to say that all are consumed in Norway in quantities unrivaled in North America.

MEALS AND CUSTOMS

So keen on sports and the outdoor life are the Norwegians that it seems they rise deliberately early to have time to fortify themselves with a heroic breakfast selected at will from a **koltbord**. Typically, this consists of an assortment of cold roasted and cured meats and sausages, eggs, ham, bacon, hot and cold cereals, a selection of mild to strong cheeses, crisp and soft rye and wheat breads, fresh butter and several fruit preserves as well as fruit juices and fruits and coffee.

Then they are off to the day's activities. School and work begin very early but they also end early in the day, and most people are homeward bound to eat a simple early dinner at around 4:00 p.m. Throughout the day, small snacks of coffee, pastries or bread and butter and cheese may suffice to replenish and nourish; sometimes lunch is an abbreviated form of the breakfast **koltbord**: open-face sandwiches with coffee or beer.

Aside from breakfast, there is little doubt that food and its preparation are never really as important in the Norwegian mind as having time to ski or skate, sail or mountain-climb. The 4:00 p.m. dinner is always a hot though simple meal, sometimes a hearty soup and a filling dessert of waffles or pancakes with fruit, other times a fish soup and poached fish with boiled vegetables. At least once a week, **farikal**, a simple but substantial casserole of cabbage wedges and mutton, is served.

When the occasion demands a more leisurely and lengthy dinner, whether at home or in a restaurant, the three- or four-hour meal will be frequently punctuated with *skaal* as well as convivial conversation and laughter. Later in the evening, a small version of the **koltbord** will again make an appearance just as a "snack" to beckon sleep, or perhaps to signal the end of the evening.

Norwegians are fond of flowers. Even though they may be expensive, flowers always grace a special dinner table, and the best restaurants always have at least one fresh flower in a vase at each table.

Perhaps because of the isolation of many villages or perhaps just because of the Norwegian natural love for people, it is impossible to visit a Norwegian home and leave without at least having had coffee and cookies or cake. Usually a visitor will be expected to partake in the next meal with the family. Traditionally in Norway, wedding or confirmation guests are expected to stay for a few days: they may sleep over at a neighbor's but they will take all their meals with the host family, the food and drink mingling happily with songs, speeches, and dancing.

Blending with their love for natural flavors and their appreciation of life, Norwegians take more than ordinary delight in seasonal foods. Skipping school and work to pick the ripening berries is enjoyed just as much as gorging oneself on prawns. Spring and summer are so precious and so short that meals of berries or prawns are an unabashed national pastime. Even the fishermen must stagger their summer holidays so that no one will be denied the classic meals of prawns accompanied by crusty fresh bread with sweet butter and homemade mayonnaise with pauses only long enough for swallows of chilled white wine. In fact, bags of cooked prawns are bought from street vendors and munched like peanuts.

Firm about the food traditions of their own land, Norwegians are not much concerned about breaking so-called rules of eating and drinking. The order of courses in a meal is not of great urgency: if the main dish is ready first, it will be eaten first and the fish course may follow later. A fish soup may precede a main course of fish that may be garnished with a shrimp sauce: the duplication matters little. Frequently a robust red wine is served with a main course of poached cod and mustard sauce. Though unorthodox, the combination is delicious!

SPECIAL OCCASIONS

The Norwegians were the last of the Teutonic tribes to set aside their beliefs in Odin and Thor and the glorious afterlife in Valhalla, the warrior's final reward. This was followed by almost 500 years of Catholicism which in turn was suppressed in favor of Evangelical Lutheranism. Although the Norwegians are almost 96 percent Lutherans and devoutly celebrate Christmas, Easter, and confirmation at the age of fifteen, they are not avid churchgoers, nor have they completely relinquished their respect for the heavenly bodies (they celebrate Midsummer's Eve in honor of *solsnu*, the turn of the sun). The Christmas troll Julenisse has a definite place in Christmas celebrations, and Easter is as much celebrated for its religious connotation as for the fact that it marks the beginning of the annual mountain trekking.

There is a growing difference between urban and rural dwellers in the way everything from weddings to funerals is celebrated. Because most inhabited areas are generally isolated from each other in the countryside, lengthy and often difficult traveling conditions make it more practical for guests or visitors to stay at least overnight. This necessitates extensive cooking preparations and even the sharing of neighbors' accommodations. In contrast, urban dwellers are less gregarious, emotionally colder and tend to put forth less effort than the more traditionally minded country people.

This situation is probably most evident in funerals. In the country, the death of a villager will be mourned by the entire area with all flags at half mast and everyone coming out to attend the services, gathering afterwards to share sandwiches and coffee. In the city, cremation is popular and this together with the custom of hiring not only a preacher but also professional hymn singers and even mourners makes for a brief, rather dispassionate ceremony. After a city funeral only the immediate family gather quietly for **gravmat** (grave food) and **gravol** (grave beer).

Similarly, many villages are not only retaining, but in many cases reviving, age-old traditions for weddings. In the village of Voss, Saturday is the day for weddings with a traditional wedding cake made of towering layers of almond rings decorated with tiny Norwegian flags, sugary flowers, miniature crackers all topped with a tiny bride and groom. In Hardanger, a bridal outfit would be incomplete without an heirloom gold or silver crown (if necessary rented from the village goldsmith). Everywhere in rural areas, weddings are events of many days' duration, often going through the night, with courses of coffee and sandwiches or sometimes hearty soups and nibbles of cheeses and thinly sliced sausages to periodically revive the merrymakers. City weddings are briefer, increasingly becoming merely a one-day affair, but most still retaining the traditional wedding cake.

Birthdays are special in Norway, the most important being the fifteenth. This is Confirmation Day, and preparation is taken seriously with all the candidates preparing themselves both in knowledge of the Church as well as in new clothes. The confirmation service is announced with special invitations; the candidates appear at the service in long white gowns covering their new clothes as they nervously answer questions on their teaching before a hushed audience. The tenseness of the services is broken with lavish gifts, flower-decked tables, and hours of singing, eating (an enlarged *frokost*), and drinking.

While confirmation is an undeniable highlight on the birthday register, so is the fortieth, fiftieth, and sixtieth. In fact, these special birthdays are celebrated with beautiful gifts, flowers, and special cakes.

At the age of seventy the occasion is considered so important that photos of septuagenarians appear regularly in local papers, and women who reach a hundred are sent a special birthday cake by a Norwegian women's magazine.

From noon on Christmas Eve, Norwegian shops close, and exactly at 5:00 p.m. church bells throughout the country herald the holiday. But weeks before, the bustle of holiday baking, slaughtering of animals and curing of meats and the preparation of **lutefisk** as well as the sending of typical Norwegian Christmas cards – a jolly picture of Julenisse gobbling his plate of **rommegrot** – leave little doubt of the coming occasion. In western areas of Norway, the Viking tradition of serving dried salted lamb at this time is still enjoyed, while in most of the eastern areas traditional roast pork together with **lutefisk** and a delectable display of fruits, nuts, and bakery highlight the Christmas menu.

While there may be a difference in menu, other traditions are uniform throughout the country. Everywhere animals are given a special treat on Christmas eve in the belief that they shared in the holy event in the stable on the special eve; Norwegian cows get a special treat of salted herring. After the Christmas Eve dinner, carols are sung around the Christmas tree which is aglow with white candles or white lights. Then the exchanging of gifts ends the evening. Christmas Day is a quiet family day. The rounds of parties begin the following day.

Julebord is the special name given to the groaning table of Christmas delicacies whether at home or in a restaurant. Traditionally the display includes the finest specialties of the country: whole poached cod, whole smoked salmon, glazed roasted duck, and roasted pork stuffed with prunes and apples. By January, Oslo has only eight hours of daylight, but the Julebord and the white lights of Christmas as well as the parties and *skaal* make all oblivious to the outside gloom.

Lent and Easter are observed more casually. Easter Sunday services are followed by a hearty but brief dinner, for traditionally this is the day the mountain climbing begins.

Baptisms and birthdays, Christmas and Easter all compete on the festive calendar with ancient holidays closely related with the changing seasons, seasonal activities, and the enjoyment of fresh seasonal foods. The threads of paganism and even superstition that persist into the culture of the modern-day Norwegian, and indeed that of most Scandinavians, seem to be no more contradictory than their delight in parties and their craving for solitude.

GLOSSARY OF FOODS AND FOOD TERMS

Agurksalat: salad of salt-wilted cucumbers prepared by thinly slicing the fresh cucumbers and allowing them to stand after being liberally salted. The salting wilts the slices and helps to draw away any bitterness. Or the thin slices may be marinated in a sweet and sour mixture of vinegar, water, and sugar, and with onion slices and fresh dill.

Aquavit: colorless alcoholic drink distilled from grain or potatoes sometimes flavored with caraway seeds. Aquavit means "water of life" and is a great favorite in all Scandinavian countries.

Avkokt Torsk: poached cod steaks usually served with lemon and butter, hot or cold.

Blot Kaker: creamy dessert of alternate layers of sponge cake, fresh or preserved fruits or berries and whipped cream.

Faar I Kaal or **Faikal**: a stewed or oven-baked casserole of layered browned cubes of boneless lamb and wedges of cabbage cooked in stock or bouillon, and finished with peppercorns and flour-thickened sour cream. This dish is a weekly specialty.

Fattigman: crispy rich fried cookies prepared from a batter of egg yolks, butter and flour flavored with brandy. The rolled pastry is cut into squares, each square gashed and the point drawn through, then the shapes are deep-fried and served sugar-sprinkled.

Fenalar: thin strips of mutton that have been salted and wind-dried. Legs of lamb and lamb spareribs may be prepared in the same way.

Fiskepudding: a fish pudding – but what a fish pudding! On top of a baked mixture of chopped fish blended with cream and flour and touched with nutmeg are placed poached fish balls (of the sauce mixture). Before serving, a hot lobster or shrimp sauce is poured over all.

Flatbrod: thin and crisp, large round dimpled circles of whole rye bread which are often baked in huge quantities to last the winter. Villagers make it a social occasion to gather and bake the breads in hearth ovens then hang them through a hole in the center on long poles to dry.

Gammel Ost: a distinctive Norwegian cheese, brown in color and tangy sharp in taste. It is also distinctive in odor and for this reason is always served from its own covered dish.

Goro Wafers: a thin dough of eggs, flour, cream, and vanilla is cut to fit the patterned **Goro** iron pan. When the pan's two sides are pressed together, a pattern is baked on. Quickly rolled into crisp tubes while hot the wafers are a coffee treat.

Gravlaks: thick fillets of very fresh salmon from Norway's icy waters are pressed after being rubbed with salt, sandwiched with sprigs of fresh dill, and allowed to stand overnight. This is made in all Scandinavian countries and in Russia as well, but the special Norwegian touch is a splash of brandy. Washed and wiped after their "bath," the slabs of translucent salmon are sliced very thinly crosswise.

Gravmat: name given to the sandwiches and other foods eaten after the funeral service.

Gravol: name given to the ceremonial beer drunk after funerals.

Grott or **Grotte**: commonly called porridge but it is not a grain cereal. It is a thick pudding made from sour cream or sour milk and is the usual end to a Norwegian dinner.

Julebord: name given to the multi-dish buffet prepared for Christmas Day. Features all the Norwegian specialties including roast duck and roast pork stuffed with apples and prunes, many salads, cooked vegetables, fish dishes and **Gravlaks**.

Kirsebaersuppe: a cold cherry soup to warm the heart! Made with pitted fresh cherries simmered with lemon, sugar, and cinnamon then finished with more than a splash of sherry.

Kjott: the generic name for meat. For example, lamb is **Lammekjott**.

Kling-Korg: the special wooden basket used by brides to serve breads and cakes throughout the wedding festivities. A tradition of Hardanger, Norway.

Koltbord: the bountiful Norwegian buffet of many fish dishes, assorted cheese and cold sliced meats, fruits and jugs of fresh cold milk, breads and rolls and of course coffee. A **Koltbord** makes its appearance early for breakfast, but is on display at holidays, weddings, funerals, and birthdays.

Kransekake: a many-layered almond meringue cake decorated with icing and caramel-sealed with tiny flags, crackers, petit-fours, sugared flowers. A must for weddings and confirmations.

Lefser: tiny triangle-shaped cakes filled with butter and sour cream.

Lutefisk: a Scandinavian specialty for Christmas Eve dinner, made from dried salt cod which has been soaked in water and then a water-and-lye solution and finally gently poached. The resultant fish is bland with the jelly-like consistency and is served with sauce.

Middag: the name given to the early Norwegian dinner, usually served at about 4:00 p.m.

Multer: tart yellow cloudberries, sweetened then served as a Christmas dessert with whipped cream.

Oplagt Melk: freshly made clabbered cream, slightly tart, served with a sprinkle of sugar and cinnamon and eaten as a snack.

Pytt I Panne: meat and potato hash pancakes served with eggs cooked on top.

Rok Orret: strong (in smell and flavor) fermented trout.

Rommegrot: traditional Norwegian dessert and Christmas Eve meal for the mischievous troll Julenisse. Cooked sour cream thickened with flour and served in soup plates drizzled with melted butter and touched with cinnamon and brown sugar.

Ryper Med Tyttebaer: a special dish of butter-braised ptarmigan served with a sour cream and goat's milk cheese sauce and garnished with lingonberries.

Skarke: another name for thinly sliced meat that is salt-sprinkled and wind-dried.

Smalefotter: grilled, smoked and wind-dried lamb's legs.

Smorrebrod: sometimes used as a name for lunch, since the most usual Norwegian lunch is open-face sandwiches.

Stockfish: air-dried cod. Though an abundance of fresh fish is available, Norwegians enjoy smoked, pickled, dried, and fermented fish as well. It is said that five kilos of fresh cod is equal to one kilo dried.

Surkal: a dish of cooked shredded cabbage smoothed with a cream sauce sharpened with a splash of vinegar and sprinkled with black caraway seeds.

Syltete Rodbeter: a salad of pickled beets, frequently garnished with hard-cooked eggs.

Tyttebaer: sweet-tart lingonberries.

CHAPTER 39

PEOPLE OF THE FERTILE CRESCENT:

IRAQI, JORDANIAN, LEBANESE, AND SYRIAN

In the area of the Middle East known as the Fertile Crescent, where the summers are dusty and hot and the winters cool and rainy, lie the four Arabic nations of Iraq, Jordan, Lebanon, and Syria. They share a common heritage, many common problems, and a very similar cuisine.

It is difficult to believe that in the parched hills north of Iraq lies an area that is believed to be the home of modern agriculture. Here primitive peoples are said to have first tamed sheep, grown wild wheat, and even cultivated fruits. The sheep were used for wool, milk, meat, and as a source of fat. The wild wheat, carefully nurtured, formed the basis of early man's existence. It was used in the form of porridges, gruels, and assorted types of simple breads baked on stones from coarse flour and water mixtures.

Craggy olive trees were first cultivated for their oil but it was not long before the fruit was also appreciated as a food: green olives, ripe black olives, and olives that were cured in oil or vinegar or spiced. Even the pruned olive branches could be used as fuel or carved to form implements.

Grapes were enjoyed as a fresh fruit and fermented to form wines. The delicately luscious fresh figs were at first eaten only in local areas where they grew, but when sun-drying was used to preserve them, they became a favored fruit in many other areas.

The Fertile Crescent was so named not only because this was the area believed to be the start of agricultural and pastoral occupations, but also because in ancient history it was a "mentally fertile" area as well. About 1700 B.C.E. Syria itself was the home of an advanced culture, much affected by the complex systems of law and religion and even the art of writing is believed to have developed very early in the ancient Iraqi area of Mesopotamia.

It is this same area that attracted waves of conquerors throughout history, each bringing their own culture and each leaving behind some indelible mark on the peoples of those lands. Attacks by Assyrians and Chaldeans were soon forgotten when Syria, Jordan (then part of Palestine), Iraq and Lebanon (then part of Phoenicia) were melded as part of Alexander the Great's empire in 332 B.C.E. Hellenistic culture and customs touched everything from the architecture of the cities to the food on the tables:

meze, assorted small appetizers taken with **Arak** (anise-scented liquor similar to **Ouzo**); tart egg-lemon sauces and rice-stuffed vegetables; even the sweetly-rich phyllo pastries.

The Roman Empire and then the Byzantine Empire each held its place for a time in the affairs of the Fertile Crescent. But the greatest influence was to come in 636 C.E. when the Muhammedans conquered Syria from the Byzantine Empire and established Damascus as the center of the Muslim Caliphate. With the spread of Islam came the practice of the Laws of the Koran which included Friday as the day of rest, prescribed hours of daily prayer, a man's acquisition of as many as four wives and their carefully secluded position within the home, and the dietary laws proscribing wine and pork. Today, the entire area is still predominantly Muslim, but this has not brought the end of wars or hardship.

Yet another empire was rising, and it was to be so powerful that its grip over this coveted area would last for 400 years. In 1516 C.E., the Fertile Crescent fell to the Turkish Ottoman Empire.

IRAQI

Today in Iraq, the same ancient foods form the dietary staples. Every part of the sheep is enjoyed: meats are roasted, offal simmered in broths made from cracked bones; milk is used for cheeses and fat from the fat-tailed sheep is used in cookery. **Turshi**, a mix of pickled vegetables, accompanies a usual meal of broth, wheat bread, and select bits of sheep such as the tongue, sheep's head or stomach. Olives are a staple and frequent food; grapes and figs too. The Tigris and Euphrates Rivers yield fish that require only the simplest of broiling and seasoning to make a memorable meal.

JORDANIAN

The Hashemite Kingdom of Jordan is also part of the Fertile Crescent where, because of present arid conditions, the once-fertile area now only barely supports camels, sheep, goats, and cattle. Today, as in many other Arab countries, special cultivation of legumes such as beans and lentils, vegetables such as okra, eggplant, and varieties of pumpkins and squashes, and fruits such as citrus and bananas all add to the daily diet.

LEBANESE

Lebanon traces its ancestry to the ancient merchants and seafarers known as Phoenicians. It is an ancestry that still boldly characterizes the Lebanese penchant for travel and business. Although frequently listed as "Syrian" in foreign immigration files, a more careful study shows that 95 percent of the emigrants from the Near East to other parts of the world are in fact from Lebanon. Beirut, the capital of Lebanon, is also known as "the Paris of the Middle East." Beirut has earned this title not only as a cosmopolitan city of culture and entertainment, but also as a vital commercial and banking center and one of the most important seaports of the area.

Lebanese have emigrated from their homeland partly because of their adventurous spirit but also because of poverty and persecution. The largest flood of emigration occurred after 1860, a date marking one of the most vicious religious persecutions which sent Christian Lebanese to any part of the world where they could find religious freedom. The majority settled into business or professional activities, but most have retained their fluent Arabic, native celebrations and customs, deep devotion to the Church, and food specialties.

Because France had occupied both Lebanon and Syria during World War I, she was given a mandate over both countries by the League of Nations. In 1920, therefore, Lebanon became officially "detached" from Syria but actually did not attain independence until 1943. Both Lebanon and Syria simmered with hostility under French rule, which lasted twenty years and was disrupted by British intervention in 1943. By 1946, Syria, too, gained independence. To this day, not only Arabic but French and English are fluently spoken by the educated upper class of both countries.

Lebanon's population is almost equally divided between Druses and Christians. The Druses are a religious sect considered to be an outgrowth of Islam but with both Judaic and Christian ideals.

SYRIAN

Life moves more slowly in Syria than in Lebanon. Most of Syria's population is concentrated in the

FOODS COMMONLY USED

There is little difference in the basic cuisine of the Iraqi, Jordanian, Lebanese, or Syrian kitchen. The staple foods include wheat which is used for many types of breads, and the popular **burgul**, as well as rice, which is the basis of many dishes; **leban**, yogurt, and **madzoon** are all forms of cultured (soured) milk served at any meal and eaten with bread, pilafs, meats, or fruits. Olives and dates are the most useful and widely planted fruits; tropical and semi-tropical fruits are eaten seasonally as available and according to means. Eggplant, tomatoes, onions, and potatoes head the list of vegetables most widely available, but in many areas wild greens also supplement the diet. Aside from milk and local cheeses, legumes are the most widely used protein source in the form of many varieties of peas, beans, and lentils used as soups and stews and nibbled as spicy snacks. The favorite meat is lamb eaten several times a week by those who can afford it and only on special occasions by the poor. The use of many exotic herbs and spices, especially garlic and cinnamon, are common, while olive oil adds its richness to many dishes. But spices and herbs were not only used to enhance foods, they have always been considered to have distinct therapeutic, medicinal and, some say, aphrodisiac properties.

In considering the foods commonly used by these peoples, the climate, topography, and agricultural systems cannot be overlooked. The varied topography and climate of Lebanon as well as its advanced technology and the fact that it is the most westernized of all Arab countries contribute to the important fact that while the staples are the same, the Lebanese diet invariably includes more quantity, quality, and variety than others. Both the Syrian herdsmen and the agriculturalists tend to work on a subsistence basis; that is, they plant or herd only enough to supply their own needs and contribute little to local markets. Combine this subsistence philosophy with the limited rainfall, primitive farming, and pastoral techniques, and the limitations of the Syrian, Iraqi, and Jordanian diet can be readily seen.

coastal region and cities; few live in the vast Syrian desert.

Syria's population is overwhelmingly Muslim with the next largest group being Bedouins, then small groups of Druses and still fewer Jews.

Agriculture and animal husbandry provide the main occupations for 75 percent of Syria's population. Lebanon is one of the few countries in the Fertile Crescent whose gross national product (GNP) is not from agriculture but from commerce. This accounts for the different pace of life and lifestyle between Syria and Lebanon.

The nomadic Bedouin tribes are principally the inhabitants of the desert and there are approximately 300,000 tribes in this area. They profess the faith of Islam, but such is the power of the sheiks of various tribes that they grant themselves some latitude in interpretation of the faith. They can be divided into three broad groups: "Bedouins of the Camel," "Bedouins of the Sheep," and "Settled Tribes."

"Bedouins of the Camel" are truly nomadic and roam the driest desert areas. Their tents, clothing, even their food is derived almost entirely from camels. They use the camel hair for cloth and the milk and meat for food. Dates are also important in their diet; anything else they may require is bartered.

The "Bedouins of the Sheep" are less nomadic than the first group and tend to live nearer large cities. Wool from their sheep is used to make tents and clothing and the sheep also supply milk and meat. This diet may be supplemented with bartered rice and some local vegetables. Honey, locusts, and lizards also form a part of their diet.

The "Settled Tribes" follow general agricultural pursuits and in many cases have adapted themselves to the customs of the areas.

The many peoples who inhabit the Fertile Crescent share a common heritage of historic conquerors all of whom were intensely aware of the strategic value of this crossroads location. The people share, too, the common problems of poverty and illiteracy, as well as periodic political and religious upheavals. But hope for the future lies in the warm and unstinting sense of hospitality that is also common to all these peoples. The open door and the dual symbols of the olive branch and the fig tree bespeak the hope of peace and plenty for all.

DOMESTIC LIFE

Here there is no average lifestyle, only contrasting extremes. The wealthy lead an entirely different lifestyle from the poor; the nomads differ greatly from those who are settled in groups. All share the gracious and generous display of hospitality, the typical Mediterranean sense of time, and a pride in food traditions.

Even the humblest shopkeeper takes time to converse and offer tiny cups of sweetened tea or coffee before conducting business; Bedouins invite passing strangers to dine with them; and hospitality in private homes invariably offers a buffet of local delicacies. It is not unheard of that the poorest widow may slaughter her only goat to present a meal for a visitor. One can then only imagine the sumptuous repast presented by the wealthy.

The Mediterranean sense of time, although often suggested by the saying "If Allah wills it," really has little to do with the Muslim faith. Mealtimes, social and business engagements, and even international appointments may be delayed hours or even days much to the chagrin of punctual foreigners. Every minute seems to count to the bustling westerner, but people of the Middle East move about their daily affairs with a sense of eternal time. What is not done today will be surely be accomplished tomorrow, "if Allah wills it."

Perhaps as an extension of hospitality, larger cities – especially Beirut – offer foods for the homesick tourist; anything from English fish and chips to Japanese **sake** can be found in restaurants catering to these desires. But in every home it is likely that traditional dishes and local specialties hold the spotlight. Small appliances and kitchen gadgets can never gain great popularity where the hands of many servants are still readily available, but those who can afford them enjoy the use of small refrigerators. With only few exceptions, most women still make their homes the center of their interests, supervising children and cookery with the aid of as many servants as they can afford. But this too is changing. In rural areas, the women add many agricultural tasks and care of animals to their daily work routine.

DAIRY PRODUCTS

Necessity and availability dictate food customs. Thus it is not surprising that the combination of a dry hot climate and the lack of storage and transportation facilities combine to make the use of soured milk products most practical. Milk is used from whatever is locally available: sheep, goats, cows, or camels. Soured or fermented milk produces yogurt, **leban**, and **madzoon**. **Labneh** is a delicate fresh cheese prepared in most homes simply by allowing yogurt to drip overnight in a cloth bag. **Ushta** is thick clotted cream prepared from simmered buffalo's or cow's milk but in Iraq it is called **gaimer**. Some locally made cheeses are preserved in salt brine or olive oil.

Fresh fluid milk is not popular or practical. Pasteurization of milk is available in some of the larger cities only, otherwise fresh milk may be sold locally in small quantities. But unhygienic handling is common and often the milk may be skimmed or adulterated with the addition of water. Sometimes boiled milk with bread may form a breakfast dish.

FRUITS AND VEGETABLES

The fruit of the vine, grapes, and the versatile fruits of the olive tree and date palm are important additions to almost everyone's table. Wine is not used by observant Muslims but fresh grapes of every variety are eaten in season and dried as raisins or used to make a type of molasses. Olives are eaten green or ripe and in many forms including spiced, oiled, brined, and vinegared. Melons and citrus fruits, stone fruits such as peaches, cherries, and apricots as well as dates and figs, quinces, pomegranates, apples and plums are all enjoyed seasonally, locally, and as budget permits. **Aarak**, a national drink in Lebanon, is distilled from grape alcohol. Dried figs, dates, and raisins are also enjoyed, but **kamaradine**, a form of dried apricots pressed into sheets, is especially popular. A sweet syrup can be made from dates or raisins.

Middle East homemakers often have their own small vegetable gardens where they grow fresh beans, cabbage, scallions, cucumbers, tomatoes, squashes, okra, and even their own onions and garlic. The eggplant is a special favorite. Vegetables may be cooked, puréed, and blended with garlic and olive oil to be used as an appetizer dip with bread. Stuffed vegetables, well-spiced and vinegared pickled vegetables as well as salads of fresh vegetables dressed with lemon juice, olive oil, and fresh black pepper are enjoyed and used when available. A side plate of cucumbers, fresh onions, and olives is a common sight at most meals.

MEATS AND ALTERNATES

More than any other food, meat takes on class distinctions. The rural poor rarely if ever eat meat and then it is usually an old animal about to die anyway, or on a special occasion warranting an animal's slaughter for food. The preferred meat is lamb—and nothing is wasted. Offal and bones lend their meaty taste to many dishes while other parts of the lamb may be roasted whole or skewered for **kababs** and frequently used as ground lamb in the national dish of **kibbe** (ground lamb and **burgul**) or in the many **pilafs** (rice dishes) and stuffed vegetables. Chicken and beef are also used. Except for lamb (which is slaughtered very young and therefore tender), most other meats used by Syrians and Lebanese require either marinating or slow moist cooking for tenderness as cattle and poultry tend to be lean and tough.

All legumes have an important place in the diet. Soups made of orange, green, or brown lentils, chickpeas, and dried beans of many varieties, as well as vegetable and bean stews are all well liked and may form the main dish or at least an important part of the meal. Legume dishes may be enjoyed at any meal (even breakfast) and are served warm or cold.

Fish is usually prepared in a complex way: browned fish pieces heavily seasoned with cayenne and garlic then simmered in a broth and served chilled (**yakhnit samak el harrah**); sautéed onions and pine nuts tossed with cooked rice and saffron then served with olive-oil fried fish (**riz bi samak**); or the classic **samak tahini**, an elaborately baked fish served with a sauce of sesame seed oil and lemon juice. In Syria this dish is liberally touched with onion while in Lebanon the same dish is preferred liberally flavored with garlic.

Eggs are not plentiful but are enjoyed scrambled, sometimes with powdered cumin seed for breakfast. Omelets chunky with vegetables are enjoyed hot or cold with meals or as snacks.

Although minimum food preservation techniques are used, especially in rural areas, the fat-tailed sheep do provide important winter food for many. The mutton is heavily salted and rolled in its own fat for later use.

Almonds, walnuts, and pistachios are widely grown and used in desserts, pastries, rice dishes and eaten roasted and salted as nibbles.

BREADS AND GRAINS

Bread is unquestionably the "staff of life" and the basis of every meal. For the poor it may often be the only food augmented at times by olives and some form of soured milk. Wheat breads in many varieties are preferred but breads made from corn, barley, or millet – sometimes in varying quantities with wheat flour – are used by the rural poor. The exact type of bread depends on locality and income.

Wheat that has been boiled, sun-dried, and cracked into fine, medium, and coarse grains is called **burgul** in Arabic, while **bulgur** is the common western name. This versatile nourishing grain forms the basis for several classic dishes:

Kibbe: lean lamb meat is pounded to a smooth paste and combined with **burgul**, seasoned with garlic and cinnamon, layered in a pan and oven-baked. Served with melted butter poured over and cut in diamond shapes; this is called **Kibbe Bil Sineeyah**. Raw **Kibbe** mixture is called **Kibbe Neyee**. The same mixture shaped into ovals, hollowed out with one finger and stuffed with ground lamb and pine nuts then fried in hot butter is called **Kras Mihshee**. In whatever shape, cooked or raw, **burgul** and lamb make **Kibbe** the classic dish of Syria and Lebanon.

Tabouleh or **Tabooley**: soaked **bulgur** is drained and tossed with fresh minced parsley and other greens and flavored tartly with fresh lemon juice. A favorite salad and appetizer.

Rice is the next commonly used cereal. Many varieties are used: polished, unpolished, and brown. All find their way into aromatic mixtures for stuffed vegetables (often with ground lamb and pine nuts) or molded into **pilafs**. Iraqis have a distinct preference for the fragrant **basmati rice**.

FATS
The most widely used fats are olive oil and clarified butter. The latter is made from sheep or goat's milk and is commonly called either **ghee** or **samneh**. Clear golden olive oil is used both in cooking and frequently as a final shimmering touch to pureed vegetables, **pilafs**, cold cooked vegetables or bean dishes.

SWEETS AND SNACKS
Throughout most of the Middle East, sweets are very sweet. Confections of seeds and nuts, fruit drinks and even tea and coffee are heavily sugared, and pastries are layered and drenched in honey or sugar syrups. These treats are taken at the end of meals or as mid-afternoon or evening snacks, sometimes with seasonal fruits. The poor seldom taste such luxuries, their treat being the sweetened tea or coffee or the occasional use of dried fruits, most likely dates, when available. For many villagers, **dibs**, a type of molasses made from fruits, is an important sweetener.

SEASONINGS
Spices are the great deceivers; in places where foods are simple, the arts of seasoning reach great heights in order to deceive the body that a great meal has been eaten. The Fertile Crescent provides no exception. **Sfeeha**, those peppery little meat pies that are a specialty of Syrian homemakers, can be made of fine ground lamb and pastry or a highly spiced filling of legumes. **Kishik**, a fine powder made from **leban**, flour, and spices, is used for adding flavor to soups and even some egg dishes; sometimes it may form a soup simply by adding water. **Taratour** is a classic sauce made from sesame seed oil and lemon juice often zipped up with garlic and used for many dishes, especially fish, or simply as a dip for bread. **Zahter** is a blend of thyme and sumac and is used to season breads. Iraqis like a mix of allspice, pepper, and paprika or use **baharat** (a spice mix) when available.

Cinnamon, coriander and mint, olive oil, yogurt, and lemon juice — scarcely a dish can be prepared without at least one. But even more common is the pungency of onions and garlic and the peppery-hot of freshly ground black and white peppers and cayenne. Syrians tend to favor onions, while Lebanese show a preference for garlic. Iraqis use dried limes to heighten all flavors.

Toasted nuts and seeds spread their richness through many dishes, while crushed nuts and seeds, syrup and honey and the perfumes from rosewater and orange flower water as well as anise lend an exotic touch to desserts and pastries.

BEVERAGES
Nbeeth (wine) is enjoyed by the Christians. **Aarak**, an anise-flavored liquor, is enjoyed by many as an appetizer with the varied **mezes**, dozens of small morsels of pickled and spiced vegetables and olives, salted and roasted nuts, legumes and seeds, purees of spiced garlic-rich seeds and vegetables and many other tidbits. Many drinks made from mixtures of fruit juices or fruit syrups (such as rose petal syrup) blended with plain or sparkling bottled water as well as locally made beers are all popular refreshers. It should be kept in mind that beer was reputedly prepared as early as 3000 B.C.E. by the Sumerians of this region.

Sweetened tea spiced with cinnamon or flavored with mint is called **shai** (note similarity to Chinese name **ch'ai**) but the most honored beverage of all and the symbol of hospitality is **kahwah**, coffee.

Yet in countries where water is at such a premium, a humble drink of plain water is highly esteemed and often will be taken from a **breek**, a special water jug. The art of pouring water from the **breek's** spout into the mouth without either touching or spilling takes practice.

MEALS AND CUSTOMS
Arab peoples have a deep respect for elders and family. Early risers love to stroll through their walled gardens or go out at a very early hour to take coffee and fruit with friends or relatives, even before breakfast. Bread, cheese, and olives can make a meal anytime, and for the *fellaheen* (rural peasants) probably do. For others, freshly prepared coffee will be accompanied with wheat bread and fresh cheese, olives and perhaps eggs scrambled with **zahter**. A serving of fresh seasonal fruit such as melon or ripe figs may conclude the **futoor** (breakfast).

Gatha, the main noon meal, is often the largest of the day unless guests are expected for the evening meal, which is usually taken at sundown. **Gatha** may consist of one or two filling dishes, dessert, and coffee. In wealthier homes many courses are served, preceded by **aarak** and **mezes**. There is never any problem of leftovers as these become the food for servants. **Asha** is the name given to the customary light meal at sundown. It consists of salads, bread, cheese, vegetable stews or vegetable **pilafs**.

In traditional Muslim homes and in the Bedouin tent, an ordered ritual of hospitality is followed. It matters little whether the meal offered is only bread and cheese or a few dates or the Bedouin festive fare of **mansaf** (shredded cooked lamb heaped on a mound of cooked rice with soured milk poured over all) and **shrak**, the thin layers of wheat bread baked on a dome, or a many-course display of **kababs**, **kibbe**, **tabouleh**, stuffed grape leaves and cabbage leaves, rice-stuffed young zucchini and tomatoes. Whatever the main meal, it will be preceded with ceremonial handwashing and prayers of grace. Frequently the host will stand apart and enjoy watching his family and guests enjoy the meal, eating only with three fingers of the right hand; sometimes he will join the feast. Traditionally only men eat together and only manservants wait upon them. After they have completed their meal, with belt-loosening, lip-smacking, and even a few belches of satisfaction, the leftovers are removed and eaten in another area by the manservants. What they leave becomes the meal for women and children.

Traditional meals are served on carpeted floors bedecked with white cloths and surrounded with many plump pillows for the comfort of the diners. In most areas of the Fertile Crescent and Middle East, it is common to place all foods for the meal on the table, with diners selecting and eating as they wish. Modern homes provide tables and chairs but still enjoy settling into soft pillows after dinner for the *narghile* (water-pipe) and coffee and the inevitable platter of **baklava**.

Christian homes follow some of the above traditions, except that women are a part of the meal with the men. For both Christians and Muslims, many small dishes of assorted appetizers and many rounds of **Aarak**, usually diluted with water to a milky white, precede the main meal.

SPECIAL OCCASIONS

Syrians, Jordanians, and Iraqis are mostly of the Muslim faith, while the Lebanese are about 52 percent Christians (Maronites, Greek Orthodox, and Greek Catholic) and the remainder are predominantly Muhammedans, mostly Druses. The creed of the Druses is basically Muslim with some elements of Judaic-Christian principles.

Since legendary hospitality is an everyday matter among the Arab peoples, as is the elevation of simple ingredients to gastronomic creations, the gracious manners and display of special foods for special occasions know no limits — except perhaps the budget of the host. Days of preparation precede any feast or happy family occasion: lamb, kid, or camel are ritually slaughtered and knowing hands prepare the classic dishes, such as:

Baba Ghanouj: smooth smoke-flavored puree of cooked eggplant (charring of the skin gives smoky taste), minced garlic olive oil, and lemon juice. Eaten with pieces of bread.

Dolmahs: the wrapping may be any green leaves: chard, spinach, grape leaves, cabbage. The filling will likely be a blend of cooked rice, pine nuts, cinnamon and ground lamb.

Huumus bi Tahini: pureed chickpeas brightly seasoned and blended with sesame seed paste (**Tahini**), garlic, and lemon juice. This smooth mix is spread flat on platters and swirled with a decoration of olive oil and sprinkled pine nuts or parsley (coriander).

Kibbe bis Sineeyah or **Sayniyyi**: bulgur and finely minced lamb seasoned with spice (cinnamon, allspice, pepper) and layered in a pan, drizzled with olive oil and/or melted butter, marked into diamonds and baked.

Kibbe Nahyeh: same mixture as above but served raw in a mound on a platter to be eaten with broken pieces of bread.

Lubia Bishmi: a slow-simmered stew of lamb (kid or camel) with tomatoes and green beans. Served with a rice pilaf of saffron, pine nuts, melted butter and/or yogurt.

Syrian Sfeeha: peppery hot little meat pies made with thin yeast dough.

Tabouleh: a tangy fresh salad made of soaked, drained bulgur tossed with chopped vegetables such as parsley, onions, tomatoes, etc. All tartly flavored with lemon juice.

The above list represents only the classic festive dishes of the Syrian-Lebanese cuisine. There are many other lesser dishes. Besides the tidbits that have been previously mentioned and many that may come to mind, there are many exotic specialties such as miniature **sfeeha**, pickled grapes, pickled tomatoes, pickled walnuts, pickled eggplant, spicy vegetable or legume purées to be scooped up with broken bread, and many variations of the **bourek** or **borek** which are tiny rolls or triangles of butter-drenched **phyllo** pastry filled with cheese, meat, or vegetable mixtures.

That is still not the end. To complete the picture, the leisurely ending of the feast would be **kahwah**, tiny cups of Arabian coffee enjoyed with the passing around of the *narghile* and interrupted only by conversation and a few platters of **baklava** and/or many other varieties of syrup drenched pastries luscious with nuts and fruits and fragrant with rosewater or orange flower syrup.

The sweetness of weddings is emphasized by a series of festivities preceding the special day. Guests are served trays of sweet pastries, nuts, confections, and **kahwah**. Candy-coated almonds are a special symbol of a sweet and prosperous life. The wedding feast itself features all the traditional dishes with kid and lamb forming the main festive dishes.

For Christians, Lent marks the beginning of a pensive period of fasting and abstinence, but it is introduced with festivities featuring games, dancing, and costumes. *Marfeh* is the name given to the preceding two weeks: the first is a week of meat-fare dishes followed by a week of cheese-fare dishes. Meat and cheese, indeed all foods of animal origin, will not be eaten again by Orthodox Christians until Easter itself. The forty somber days of Lent as observed by pious Christians follow a dietary pattern of mostly cold foods made from olive oil, legumes, vegetables, grains and breads. These same fast-day foods are also served at other fast days during the year:

January 5: Eve of Epiphany

June 29: Fast of the Holy Apostles for one week from All Saints' Sunday to the Feast Day of the Holy Apostles (June 29)

August 1-15: Fast of Theotokas

August 29: Fast of the Beheading of St. John the Baptist

September 14: The Elevation of the Holy Cross

November 15-25: Fast before Christmas

It should be noted that many strictly observant Orthodox Christians also conduct fasts on Wednesdays and Fridays of each week throughout the year. The Wednesday fast is said to be in memory of the betrayal of Christ, while the traditional Friday fast is in memory of Christ's death on the cross. The very elderly, those who are sick, and young people under the age of twenty-one do not observe the fasts.

Easter is one of the most important occasions on the calendar of Christians and the colorful ceremonies are concluded with the eating of eggs to break the abstentions of the previous weeks. With joyous gatherings, the festival is ended with the classic dishes of feasting.

But not all Christian religious occasions are ones of penitence and fasting. There are also twelve special feast days, some with specific foods to mark them, and all with as many classic festive dishes as the family can afford. Some of these include:

March 25: Annunciation of the Virgin Mary, when seafoods are eaten.

August 6: Transfiguration of Christ, when a special fish (**Samak**) meal is served.

August 15: Assumption of Mary.

December 4: St. Barbera, when **Iyuok**, a traditional yellow barley pudding is served.

January 6: Feast of Epiphany, the oldest and one of the most important feast days. The day is spent in prayer and church services followed by the priests visiting homes to bless every corner of each room with prayers and holy water. **Awam** and **Zalabee** (ring-shaped fritters and doughnuts made from sweet yeast dough and sprinkled with sugar) are served to family and guests.

Christian funeral rites also follow traditional patterns. Before the burial of the deceased, family and friends gather together and each in turn says a few words about the departed. Forty days after the death and again on the first anniversary, an ancient tradition is followed in the preparation, blessing, and serving of a cooked wheat dish. A mound of cooked wheat, spices, raisins, and nuts is symbolically decorated to reaffirm faith and the "sweetness of everlasting life."

Similarly, Muslim feast days and family occasions display as many of the classic festive dishes as can be afforded by the household. As a part of their faith, Muslims are cautioned at all times to eat foods for health and survival and never to overindulge. The important annual fast takes place for the entire ninth lunar month: *Ramadan*. During the daylight hours of *Ramadan* a total abstinence of all food and drink is observed by the faithful; food and drink are only taken before sunrise or after sundown. The fasting ends with a great feast on the first day of the next month: *Bairam*. Those who are ill, or for some other reasons unable to fast during *Ramadan*, traditionally make up those fast days at some other time.

GLOSSARY OF FOODS AND FOOD TERMS

Aarak or **Arak**: clear potent liquor which may be distilled from grapes, rice, etc. It is flavored with anise and most often served slightly diluted with water, which causes it to turn a milky color.

Baba Ghanouj: classic appetizer made from eggplant. The skin of the eggplant is removed by scorching over a flame which lends a smoky taste. The cooked, puréed eggplant is highly peppered and seasoned with minced garlic and lemon juice. It is eaten by scooping it up with broken pieces of flat Arabic bread.

Batinjan Wia Joban: a baked casserole of egg-dipped eggplant slices browned in olive oil then layered with cheese and tomato slices. A custard of beaten eggs, chopped onions and tomatoes is poured over the top, then the whole mixture is oven-baked. Served as one of the many buffet dishes.

Bourek or **Borek**: rolls or triangles of thin **Phyllo** pastry stuffed with varying mixtures of spiced meat, cheese or vegetables, sometimes legumes. Usually served as appetizers. Of Greek origin, but brought to the Middle East during the time of the Ottoman Empire.

Breek: spouted water jug. Refreshment is taken from the jug by adjusting the water stream into the mouth without touching lips to it. Experts never spill a drop.

Burgul or **Bulgur**: wholegrain wheat that has been boiled, sun-dried then cracked into categories of fine, medium, or coarse. It may be soaked then drained and eaten in a salad with chopped vegetables (**Tabouleh**) or cooked as part of many dishes, most notably **Kibbe**.

Dolmahs: another Turkish introduction into the Syrian-Lebanese cuisine, but originally from Greece. Any fresh green leaves – cabbage, chard, spinach, grape leaves, etc. – wilted with hot water (to make handling easier) then stuffed with fragrant mixtures, most commonly rice, ground lamb, cinnamon, and pine nuts. After cooking, they may be served hot or cold with a dribbling of olive oil and lemon juice, sometimes yogurt. Served as appetizers or part of a dinner buffet.

Dugag Mahshi: chickens stuffed with **Hashwa**, a mixture of cooked rice, lamb, cinnamon, and pine nuts. Kid, lamb, game fowl, pigeons, rabbit, etc., may all be prepared in the same way. The stuffed, trussed meat is boiled in stock first, then browned in the oven or in oil in a pan.

Halawa: confection of ground nuts and seeds, sold by the piece.

Hashwa: a flavorful mix of cooked rice, finely ground lamb, pine nuts, and cinnamon. Sometimes the meat is omitted. Usually used to stuff meats, leaves, or other vegetables such as squash, peppers, eggplant, tomatoes. Very much a part of this cuisine.

Huumus bi Tahini: puréed, cooked chickpeas, usually well peppered, with lemon and garlic. **Tahini** refers to a milky thick paste of puréed sesame seeds, and sometimes to sesame seed oil. The mix of the two purées, flavored generously with pepper, lemon and garlic, constitutes one of the flavored appetizers. It is spread flat on a platter, a swirl made with a knife and olive oil poured into the indentations. The final touch is a sprinkle of parsley or fresh minced coriander. It is eaten by dipping into with broken pieces of bread.

Kahwah or **Qawah**: Syrian-Lebanese name for Turkish coffee.

Ka'ick: anise-flavored Syrian bread.

Karishee: cheese made from yogurt or other cultured milk products hung in a bag overnight. A fresh cottage-cheese type.

Kathamee: roasted chickpeas (**Garbanzos**).

Khobaz: a large thin circle of bread with a crisply blistered top. Usually made from wheat flour (whole wheat) but may also include varying proportions of maize flour, millet, or sorghum depending on the locality and income. Never sliced, the bread is eaten by breaking off pieces. Diameter of bread may be from 14 to 16 inches.

Khobaz Arabee: general term for Syrian bread.

Kibbe, **Kibbi**, or **Kibbeh**: classic dish made with pounded lamb blended with **Burgul**, pine nuts, cinnamon, and allspice. The mixture may be served raw in a heaped mound on a platter to be eaten with bread; it may be layered in a baking pan (layers of alternating **Burgul** and ground lamb), scored lightly into diamond-shaped servings and baked with olive oil and melted butter on top (**Kibbe Bil Sineeyah**). Or it may be formed into ovals, hollowed with a finger and stuffed with more ground lamb and pine nuts and then deep-fried (**Kibbe Mahshee**). Or the **Kibbe** mixture may be formed into tiny balls and dropped into hot broth (**Shurbat Al Kibbe**).

Kishik: similar to the Egyptian **Kishk**. A mix of flour and dried yogurt, seasoned with hot spices. Used to flavor dishes or can be mixed with hot water or stock to form a soup.

Kitchri: a deliciously satisfying and spicy Iraqi dish of rice and red lentils (which cook up to a golden color) heightened with tomato paste, turmeric, and a whiff of cloves and cumin.

Klitcha: Iraqi pastries simply prepared with a short pastry of butter and flour and a filling of dates.

Konafa or **Kadaif**: Lebanese and Syrian name for Middle Eastern crisp shredded pastry.

Kurban: Christian holy bread distributed by the priest every Sunday.

Mansaf: the main and festive dish of the Bedouins. Thin sheets of wholewheat bread (**Shrak**) are placed in layers on large platters, cooked rice is mounded on top and then shredded boiled lamb over that. As the dish is served, well-seasoned butter and sometimes cultured milk is poured over.

Maqaali: general term for cooked vegetables. Usual preparation of most vegetables involves frying either before or after boiling.

Maza or **Meze**: small name that covers the huge range of simple and exotic appetizers routinely served with a round of diluted **Aarak** preceding a special meal.

Nbeeth: wine.

Pilaf: originally a Turkish dish of cooked rice. At its very simplest, long grain rice is tossed in melted butter or oil till glazed, then water or broth is added to cook. **Pilafs** may contain any combination of seasonings, fruits, vegetables, meats, even fish or legumes. A popular **Pilaf** is one tossed with cooked lentils or browned rice pasta or vermicelli crisply browned in oil.

Qamardine or **Kamaradine**: a thick sheet of pressed dried apricots.

Qatayef: small pancakes filled with cheese then folded into half moons and deep-fried. They are served with honey or syrup.

Roz: actually just means rice, but most popular is the rice dish dotted with browned grains of rice pasta (pasta in the form of long grain rice).

Salata: a tossed salad of any combination of vegetables, meats, etc. Always dressed with lemon juice or vinegar, olive oil, fresh black pepper.

Samak: fish.

Sfeeha: tiny Syrian meat pies, made in quantity for nibbles or appetizers. Rounds of yeast dough are spread with meaty filling, then the sides brought up and pinched. Served hot.

Snoober: pine nuts.

Tabouleh: fresh tart "salad," the main ingredient being soaked drained bulgur (uncooked) tossed with chopped seasonal vegetables and liberally dressed with lemon juice.

Tahini: a thick creamy paste made from sesame seeds.

Taratour: a classic sauce made from the sesame seed paste (**Tahini**) with the addition of lemon juice, pepper, and garlic. **Taratour** may also refer to a thick paste made from beans, avocados, etc., all flavored with lemon juice and garlic.

Yukhnee: a stew with basic ingredients of tomato paste or tomatoes and other mixed vegetables in season, flavored with lemon, garlic, coriander seeds; sometimes containing cubed lamb. May be served hot or cold.

Zahter: a seasoning mixture of powdered sumac and thyme, used in egg dishes and some breads.

CHAPTER 40

POLISH

Her neighbors invaded her, fought with her, divided her into pieces, and for a time even erased her name from the map of Europe. Over a period of about  400 years, from the 1300s to the late 1700s, intermittent wars with Sweden, Russia, Turkey, and Germany continually changed the borders of Poland until she was swallowed up and divided into Russia, Prussia, and part of the Austro-Hungarian Empire and finally disappeared. At least her name disappeared, but the western Slavs known as "Polanians" or "dwellers of the plains'" clung tenaciously to their own traditions and held fast to their beloved church. And, despite the influence of three foreign masters at one time for a period of more than a hundred years, the Polish spirit proved indestructible.

Under the oppressions of the 1800s, the parts of Poland under Prussia and Austria did not fare as badly as those parts under Russia. These latter areas were subjected to forced Russification which included sharp restrictions in the use of the Polish language and even in the attendance of religious services. Feudal land systems prevailed widely and so did illiteracy. And while the princes and the aristocracy dined at sumptuous banquets, the laboring peasants survived on cabbage and potatoes and their deep religious faith.

These difficult times witnessed many Polish uprisings, and following each unsuccessful attempt, waves of soldiers, political refugees, and peasants made their way to North America. With the outbreak of World War I Poles conscripted into both the Russian and the German army resulted in Pole fighting against Pole.

But on November 3, 1918, Poland accomplished a miraculous resurrection and proclaimed the Republic of Poland. Establishment of the republic was only the beginning. Poland also hoped to regain her lost territories and these hopes led again to conflicts, mainly with Russia. In the ensuing years, problems with minority groups, financial crises, and government turmoil added to the difficulties and the weakening of Poland. These problems culminated in 1939 with the Third Reich's sweep of Poland and the beginning of World War II.

This history of repeated conquest and subjugation drained the spirit of the people, as well as taking a serious toll on the country's natural resources and arable lands. It also intensified family relationships and the enjoyment of special occasions. Today, many ancient pagan rituals blend with religious ceremonies and festive celebrations that demand a great flurry of fine cooking and baking, decorations and party clothes. Poles, in common with all Slavs, love having parties, enjoy wearing their best clothes, and sharing an abundance of good food and drink in celebrations that often last several days before finally coming to an end.

While it is inevitable that the turbulent history of conquerors and oppressions should have affected Polish life, traditions, and cuisine, it is also interesting that two royal romances, an influx of refugees, and a brief rule by a French dandy also affected the Polish culinary arts. In the early 1300s, the love Casimir III bore for Esterka, a Jewess, resulted in Poland's welcoming Jewish refugees from all the oppressed regions of Europe, particularly western Germany. The introduction into Polish cuisine of potato puddings (**kugelis**) from Lithuania, honeycakes (**piernik**), and sweet and sour dishes like the classic jellied carp with raisins and almonds from Germany are all attributed to Jewish influence.

Two hundred years later when the Polish King Sigismund I wed Italy's Queen Bona Sforza, Poland not only gained a queen but also a retinue of Italian chefs and gardeners. They introduced pastas, pastries, and ice cream desserts. Italian gardeners cultivated many vegetables new to the Poles, including tomatoes. And it was the son of Catherine de Medici and Henry II of France – Henry III – who briefly ruled Poland in the late 1500s and left as probably the only redeeming aspect of his rule, a Polish appreciation for sauces and mayonnaise.

Also entrenched in the Polish cuisine are evidences of Russian, German, and Austrian culinary arts. Sour cream and dill, baked grains (**kasza** in Poland, **kasha** in Russia), cabbage soups and beet soups, **zakaski** and **vodka** are all as familiar in Poland as they are in Russia. Sausage-making, a taste for sweet and sour foods, and specialty potato dishes can be traced as favorites in Germany as well. And the influence of the far-flung Austro-Hungarian Empire (before 1918) was no doubt responsible in large part for the Polish predilection for paprika from Hungary, dumplings and bread-crumb sauces from the Czechs, and strudels, tortes, and other delectable bakery from Austria.

The ingenuity of Polish peasant women combined the produce of their own land with the tastes that history meted out to them from other countries and developed the great classics of Polish cuisine. These include:

Babka: a rich delicate yeast cake of eggs and dried fruits, special for Easter.

Bigos: a hunter's stew of layered cabbage or sauerkraut, mixed meats, game, and sausage.

Cholodnik: a cold beet and sour-cream soup garnished with sliced fresh vegetables and shrimp.

Pierogi or **Pierozki**: boiled dumplings made of filled noodle dough.

Pieczony Schab: roast pork loin.

DOMESTIC LIFE

For the most part, in cities, only the most privileged can afford modern kitchen appliances. Country kitchens have changed little in hundreds of years: enamelware and cast-iron cooking pots, wooden implements for stirring and pounding, heavy rolling pins for doughs, mortar and pestle for crushing and blending, and sturdy, well-scrubbed wooden tables. All utensils and furnishings have been time-tested and in many cases used for many generations.

Food storage poses little problem for city dwellers: in good times and bad, preference is for foods freshly purchased. Age-old methods of food preservation prevail in rural areas: brining of vegetables, salting of fish, drying of wild mushrooms and garlic and large quantities of home-preserved fruits and jams all carefully stored in cellars or kitchen shelves are the pride of every peasant household. The tradition of a full pantry remains, and many Polish households take pride in this.

DAIRY PRODUCTS

Fresh whole milk is used mainly by children with the adults preferring soured milk or buttermilk. Sour cream is widely used as an ingredient, as a dressing or a sauce, blended into soups, gravies and as a side dish. Cheeses are available, but the bland smoothness of pot or cottage cheese is preferred both as a spread and in many cooked dishes.

FRUITS AND VEGETABLES

Some fresh fruits and vegetables are eaten in season, but Poles enjoy fruits in the form of compotes and stews and they like their vegetables either well cooked or pickled. Plums, apples, and pears are the most readily available fruits and these are used as compotes, thick richly sweet preserves, fillings for cakes and yeast bakeries and even as condiments with meats for a sweet-sour flavor (but mostly sweet). Vegetables widely used are potatoes, red and green and savoy cabbages, beets, kohlrabi, and smaller quantities of carrots, peas, and beans. Wild mushrooms, fresh or dried, are used in many dishes. Both mushrooms and sauerkraut are used not only alone, but in so many other dishes they can also be considered as flavorings.

MEATS AND ALTERNATES

Poles enjoy their meats well cooked, tender and juicy and with accompanying sauces or gravies. Broiling or dry roasting are not a part of their culinary practices.

FOODS COMMONLY USED

The food tastes of conquerors and the ingenuity of the Poles in hard times is evident in the general taste for hearty substantial dishes based on local produce. The staples of the Polish diet are the homegrown grains, basic vegetables (beets, potatoes, and cabbages) that store well, and the many smoked and cured meats and sausages prepared from pork.

Among dairy products a preference is shown for sour cream and soured milk. Simple pot cheese is prepared and served in many satisfying ways to make complete meals.

The rich flavor of abundant wild mushrooms appears in many thick soups and stews, and few homes are without their own barrels of sauerkraut which are used in many ways. The Polish taste for sweets is evident in their honeycakes and fine baked goods, and is characterized in a definite touch of sweetness in soups, fish dishes, and even salads made with vinegar and a generous taste of sugar. Dill, garlic, paprika, and sour cream are laced through many dishes, while baked goods are redolent with honey, raisins, and almonds. Beer and coffee are not as frequently taken as vodka and tea.

Pork and beef are the favorites but chicken, duck, turkey, game fowl and game animals are eaten when available.

Except for herring in many different forms and occasional baked or poached pike or carp, Poles seldom eat fish or seafood. Eggs are used generously in baking and cooking, occasionally as main dish omelets, more frequently as appetizers. Legumes are not widely used. Nuts, especially almonds, find a place in baking or as a garnish.

BREADS AND GRAINS
Rye, wheat, buckwheat, barley, and oats are grown in quantity. Wheat flour is used in all bakery but rye flour is preferred for breads. Barley and buckwheat groats are used almost daily as stuffings, fillings, in soups, or as side dishes to meat and vegetables. This type of side dish is called **kasza**. Rye bread is a staple at all meals especially in the country, but potatoes often supplant bread at a meal, especially at dinner.

No crumb of bread is ever wasted. **Polonaise sauce**, famed in many other lands besides Poland, is actually not a sauce in the usual sense, but a toasted mixture of crumbs browned in butter. Cooked vegetables, especially green beans and cauliflower, benefit from this "sauce." Bread crumbs also form the basic ingredient for poached dumplings served either with meats or with a fruit sauce or sour cream as a dessert. Many fine cakes are made from light mixtures of separated and beaten eggs folded together with fine bread crumbs and ground nuts.

FATS
Butter is preferred for cooking and baking and as a spread. Lard, salt pork and bacon fat, rendered chicken, goose or duck fat are also used. Vegetable oils and margarine are used only sparingly.

SWEETS AND SNACKS
Poles have an insatiable sweet tooth that encompasses a great array of fine baked goods and pastries, tortes, strudels, and **mazurkas** (rich, buttery cakes). They also enjoy munching raisins and almonds together as a treat. There is a general use of much sugar in beverages, and honey in cakes and drinks. Polish dishes that are purportedly "sweet and sour" are always very sweet with only a hint of the sour. An added sprinkle of sugar is felt to enhance everything from soups and meat dishes to pickles and fish specialties.

SEASONINGS
Polish seasonings include sour cream, dill, garlic, paprika, and dried or fresh wild mushrooms. Horse radish is used alone or in combination with finely grated beets as a sauce for fish. Lemons and the fermented juices from grains and pickled vegetables are used for tartness, always tempered with sugar or honey. As mentioned above, sugar is believed to enhance all flavors.

Without diminishing the importance of that little touch of sugar in so many Polish dishes, the Poles also retain a reverence for salt. Perhaps nowhere else in the world is this depicted as beautifully as in the salt mines of Wieliczka where workers have carved a small chapel graced with statues and candlesticks sculpted from salt.

BEVERAGES
Tea is the most common beverage, served clear or with lemon and sugar. Coffee is generally only served after a more formal meal and then it is served strong and black or with sugar. Beer served in small glasses may accompany meals; wine is used only by the more affluent or "more refined." Polish vodka is believed to be the finest available, even by Russian standards. It is made from grains or potatoes and is taken straight with appetizers (**zakaski**). In recent years it has been consumed by rich and poor alike in such quantity as to constitute somewhat of a problem. **Krupnik** is a fine liqueur prepared from honey, spices and vodka, served warm.

MEALS AND CUSTOMS
Polish women take great pride in their culinary abilities; even daily foods are prepared with loving care. Festive foods are often simply the daily fare in larger quantity, because (so-called) daily fare is of classic quality.

Polish meal patterns are similar to both Ukrainian and Russian in that soups, grains in the form of breads or **kasza**, and vegetables (mostly cabbage and potatoes) are really the mainstays of the diet. Before tea and coffee became popular beverages, it was customary to start the day with a hot filling bowl of soup accompanied by dark bread. More recently, tea or coffee plus breads and preserves start the day's meals.

The noon meal most often includes filling soups based on grains and vegetables, accompanied by bread and beer. The evening meal may be similar, but if guests are expected or the occasion is special, the dinner will be preceded by an array of pickled appetizers, stuffed cabbage rolls (**golabki**), and salted and pickled fish dishes all accompanied by vodka. Soup, braised or stewed meat with cooked vegetables, and stewed fruits or home-baked or purchased pastries will complete the meal. Also enjoyed are light suppers consisting of sweet fruit soups made from seasonal berries or fruits, or light vegetable soups. A filling dessert completes the meal. These desserts may be fruit dumplings with sour-cream rice dishes, pancakes (**nalesniki**), puddings, or most often, cooked noodles sprinkled with cottage or pot cheese, poppy seeds or chopped nuts and sugar.

Poles are hearty eaters, and foods are always enjoyed in large servings. Most meals are served family style with diners helping themselves.

SPECIAL OCCASIONS

The majority of Poles are members of the Roman Catholic Church. An estimated 3 million out of the total population of over 35 million were of the Jewish faith before 1931, but members of this group were almost all victims of Nazi annihilation before and during World War II. Very small groups of Poles are members of the Orthodox Church and of some Protestant denominations.

Since Poland is a Christian country, Christmas and Easter are occasions for lavish preparations of feasts, singing and dancing and family gatherings. A day of abstention from meat is culminated in a somber and ritualistic dinner (called the Vigilia) on Christmas Eve. The meal contains no meat dishes and opens with the ceremony of bread-breaking; the mother holds in her hand a white communion wafer – symbol of love, forgiveness and friendship – and all at the table share it. An old tradition of a sheaf of wheat or a bit of hay sprinkled under the white tablecloth is still carried on in many homes today as a remembrance both of the agricultural blessings and the holy manger.

Some still carry on the tradition of twelve meatless dishes served in remembrance of the twelve apostles: three types of soups, three different fish dishes (one of which is sure to be jellied sweet and sour carp slices), three side dishes of grains or vegetables or noodles, and finally three desserts. Diners helps themselves to at least one serving of each dish.

And out of Poland's pagan past, there will surely be at least one dish with poppy seeds to symbolize the peaceful sleep of the dead. Another dish will be sure to contain honey to provide a year of sweet content for all.

Christmas Day is one of quiet family togetherness. Even the mother of the house enjoys peace and rest, for all the cooking and baking has been done in the frenzied days before. On this special day the family enjoys a buffet of cold meats: sliced ham and chicken, salads made with potatoes, pickles or sauerkraut, delicious pastries and finally coffee. And what better way to combine all the leftovers than in a hunter's stew (**bigos**) to be served the next day.

To the Poles, a party is always a reason to dress up, and at no time is this more meaningful than on New Year's Eve. Candy, flowers, and wine are brought by the guests, and the evening's food will include an impressive diversity of **zakaski**, hot and cold meat dishes, pickled salads and vegetables, **bigos**, and finally dessert pastries, liqueurs, coffee, and of course vodka.

Members of the predominantly Catholic population celebrate Easter with deep devotion. The fast period of Lent is usually observed with two to three meatless days a week; meals on these days consist of pasta or noodle dishes or a main course of cold fish, poached, baked, or pickled.

The final week of Lent includes many special prayer services at church and a frenzy of cleaning and painting in the homes. Special baking and cooking for the Easter luncheon increase the anticipation of the Holy weekend. Good Friday is traditionally spent visiting the church displays of Christ in a tomb, surrounded by floral displays, bathed in colored lights, and guarded by groups of costumed children. A humble dinner of vegetable or barley soup followed by bread and herring or potatoes and the decorating of Easter eggs completes the day's activities.

The large traditional buffet table for the Easter Sunday luncheon is arrayed with the finest foods of the year: cold sliced Polish ham, roasted pig, beef or veal, pickled salads and relishes and **cwikla** (traditional Easter relish of grated beets and horse radish). Sliced **babka**, fingers of **mazurka**, tortes and cakes with nuts, fruits, and poppy seeds will be served for dessert with vodka or liqueurs. But before the Easter meal is enjoyed with family and guests, a special food basket containing hard-boiled eggs, salt, butter, sausages, and sliced **babka** will be taken to church for blessing. The Easter table itself will not be considered complete unless a display of painted eggs shares the center of the table with a molded lamb (a symbol of Christ) made of sugar and candies.

Easter Monday is a restful day, the quiet broken only by a meal of **bigos** and often a surprise dousing of cold water – a bit of traditional fun which is considered good luck and called *smigus* or *dyngus*.

GLOSSARY OF FOODS AND FOOD TERMS

Baba or **Babka**: literally, "grandmother," but in food terms refers lovingly to the light, rich Easter bread leavened with yeast and dotted with blanched almond slivers and golden raisins.

Barszcz: Polish soup similar to Russian or Ukrainian **Borsch**. Made from beets or cabbage plus other ingredients. Tartness often achieved by adding fermented beet juice, sauerkraut juice, lemon juice, or juice from fermented rye. A special meatless **Barszcz** is made for Christmas Eve, using mushroom stock and beets.

Bigos: the classic Polish "hunter's stew." A medley of sauerkraut, apples, and mushrooms with layered mixed meats including game and sausage all slowly simmered.

Chlodnik: a classic Polish soup of beets and sour cream, garnished with shrimp or crayfish and thin slivers of fresh radishes and scallions. Served chilled.

Dodatki Do Zup: soup accompaniments. Includes croutons, **Kasza**, noodles, dumplings, etc.

Golabki: cabbage rolls made by steaming cabbage leaves to soften, then filling with a mixture of mushrooms, barley or buckwheat with onions and mushrooms, ground meat, or seasoned sauerkraut. The filled, rolled cabbage leaves are then simmered and served with butter and sour cream.

Kapusniak: cabbage soup.

Kapusta: cabbage.

Karp po Zydowski: sliced, poached carp chilled in its juices to form an aspic. Served with raisins and almonds, this dish is a favorite Polish Christmas Eve dish. Of Jewish origin.

Kasza: common name given to all steamed or baked grains (i.e., wheat, buckwheat, barley) served frequently as side dishes.

Kielbasa: a Polish sausage made from ground pork and beef and well flavored with garlic. May be fresh or smoked; usually cooked before serving.

Kisiel: a thickened fresh fruit puree, served as a dessert; similar to Russian **Kissel**.

Klopsiki: meatballs.

Kluski: noodles.

Kompoty: stewed, sweetened fresh or dried fruits or a combination of both.

Konfitura: jam.

Krupnik: a hot mead. A mixture of honey, spices, and alcohol or vodka heated together. Known by the same name is a spiced honey liqueur, and a Polish barley soup usually prepared with a meat base and served with browned mushrooms.

Kwas: a tart liquid fermented from sour rye bread and water. Used for flavoring and as a beverage.

Makowiec: a special Christmas cake made with pastry or yeast dough thinly rolled, filled with poppy seeds, nuts and raisins, shaped like a jellyroll and baked. Served in slices.

Mazurka or **Mazurek**: rich, buttery cakes, often with nuts and fruits, baked in a thin sheet then cut in fingers. May be iced.

Nalesniki: thin pancakes or crepes which may be filled with sauces or fruits. With meat or vegetable filling, may be served as appetizers or main dishes.

Oplatek: the bread of love. The thin white wafer of unleavened bread blessed and eaten to open the Christmas Eve meal.

Paczki: filled jelly doughnuts enjoyed year-round but especially on New Year's Eve.

Pieczen Huzarska: boneless braised beef, stuffed and tied for cooking. Served with potatoes and gravy.

Pieczony Schab: roast pork loin. Served with stewed fruits or fruit sauce.

Piernik: honeycake aromatic with citrus rind and spices. Reputedly of Jewish origin.

Pierogi or **Pierozki**: dumplings or "dough pockets" made by preparing thinly rolled noodle dough, cutting into squares and filling then poaching the sealed triangles till cooked. Fillings may be of meat, mushrooms, cheese, cabbage, or potatoes — all seasoned. These are served with drawn butter, meat gravy, or sour cream.

Polonaise Sauce: not a sauce in the usual sense — a toasted mixture of crumbs browned in butter and poured over vegetables.

Powidla: a thick fruit butter. Most popular is plum butter lightly spiced with anise.

Salatki: salad. Most often made with cooked ingredients or pickled vegetables. Frequently sweetened with sugar.

Smietana: sour cream.

Wloszczyzna: literally, "things Italian," refers to vegetables. Dates from Italy's Queen Bona Sforza's marriage to Polish King Sigismund I, when she introduced to Poland the preparations and produce of her Italian chefs and gardeners.

Zakaski: savory, salted, tart "nibbles" or appetizers served with vodka to open the evening meal.

Zupa: soup, without which most Polish meals would be incomplete.

Zupa Grzybowa: favorite Polish mushroom soup with a chicken or vegetable base, served with sour cream and dill.

Zupa Nic: a "nothing" soup made by heating milk with sugar and vanilla and thickening slightly with beaten egg yolks. This is poured over a soup plate of cooked rice and garnished with poached meringue balls.

PORTUGUESE

Why are the Portuguese so similar to the Spanish and yet so distinctly different? Portugal and Spain share the Iberian Peninsula, and the Portuguese themselves are an ethnic mix of Iberian and Moorish (Moroccan) elements, as are the Spanish. Yet a range of jagged mountains isolates Portugal and causes her to turn inward on herself.

The Portuguese express their difference in many ways. There is the exuberant burst of song and dance that seems to be a part of any group of working Portuguese. Many writers describe the favorite foods and drinks of the Portuguese not merely as "favorites" but as "obsessions," "passions," or even "manias." This innate intensity of feeling is a part of every Portuguese. A cup of coffee or a glass of wine can become that obsession. Any one of the several hundred dishes made with salt cod (**bacalao**) may well be described as a passion. And the Portuguese delight in rich sweets does indeed border on a mania.

The same intensity of feelings appears again and again. The Portuguese ability to lose oneself temporarily in melancholia is called *saudade* and periodically surfaces, especially when in the atmosphere of a candlelit cafe and the soulful *fado* songs. The national love for artifice, ornament, and color satisfies itself in the Portuguese bullfight, religious parades, and festivities and even in architecture, especially that of the Manueline period.

On only two subjects does a Portuguese ever show the slightest signs of nonchalance or vagueness. These are the subjects of time and distance. After all, what does time matter, or even distance, so long as one is enjoying oneself?

Until the Middle Ages, Portugal and Spain did indeed share their destiny as part of the Iberian Peninsula. So it is not surprising that the Portuguese language bears many similarities to the Spanish and this is especially noted in the Spanish dialect in the provinces of Galicia and Asturias. Portuguese dishes bear a distinct resemblance to many Spanish ones but veer off in combinations that the Spaniards would never dare.

The Portuguese are still influenced daily by Spanish customs such as the formalities observed in addressing strangers, the tendency to flamboyancy in the use of adjectives, and the rigid codes involving the dating and chaperoning of daughters. In Portugal as in Spain the main festivities of the year center around family and church, with each locale devoting special festivities and rites to local legends and saints.

Probably the earliest traders to touch and influence Portugal were the Phoenicians who brought with them the roots and twigs that stand to this day as craggy olive trees and rows upon rows of sprawling vineyards over the entire Iberian Peninsula. In the eighth century C.E. the Moorish Muslims swept northward from Morocco introducing rice culture, sugar plantations, and groves of lemon, almond, and fig trees as well as the persistent "mania" for rich sweet desserts. For the next several hundred years the land of Portugal was so often a part of Spain in many seesaw battles, that Spanish tastes, traditions, and customs melted into Portuguese.

Portugal's Golden Age of the 1400s and 1500s was preceded by a period of calamities. In 1346 a massive earthquake occurred in Lisbon. Two years later plague ravaged the country and it was said that "six bodies were buried in every grave." A heatwave in 1354 scorched crops and killed cattle. About the same time, Spain was gripped with the evils of the Inquisition while tales of monsters in the seas and the flatness of the world were told and retold.

Yet from the calamities, evils, and superstitions of the times, one man dared to set a different pace and launched Portugal as one of the great world powers. With the intensity so typical of his people, Prince Henry, son of King Joao I, and later known simply as Henry the Navigator, set up a planned system of navigation, dispelled the fantasies of the times with scientific facts, and launched a sailing craft called the caravel.

The caravel won such a reputation for reliability that for several hundred years it was believed only a Portuguese-built ship could navigate African waters successfully. Inspired and encouraged by

Henry the Navigator, Portuguese adventurers and explorers relentlessly searched for new routes and discovered the Madeiras and the Azores, acquired parts of Morocco and Africa, and under Bartholomeu Dias opened a sea route to the Orient in 1487.

Portuguese daring and expertise of the seas shine in names that are legends today: Vasco da Gama, Pedro Alvarez Cabral, Ferdinand Magellan. The Portuguese were among the first to visit Labrador (which they mistook for a part of Greenland) and named it after a captain who was called "Lavrador," meaning "farmer." It was they who brought back tales of seas so laden with fish that the ships could scarcely move. To this day the "beef of the sea" are the great catches of fresh cod later to be salted and dried in Portugal and cooked in hundreds of dishes. The **bacalao**, one of Portugal's passions, is still found, but in diminishing quantities, in the North Atlantic seas.

Portuguese explorers revolutionized the taste buds and markets of Europe. They brought back gold and diamonds from Brazil as well as pineapples, corn, potatoes, squash, pumpkin, tomatoes, tiny fiery chilies, and beans of many types. From African ports they loaded their ships with yams, cocoa, and vanilla pods. Vasco da Gama's crews — at least those who survived the scourge of scurvy — became rich beyond dreams. The black pepper they brought back from India is said to have alone financed churches, monasteries, and street-widening, and made Manuel I one of Portugal's richest kings. With the pepper selling at more than sixty times its cost, Lisbon became a commercial center, one that could well afford the flamboyant ornate architecture that came to be called "Manueline."

The audacity of Portugal's seafaring adventurers and the merchandising skills of the Jews who had fled to Portugal to escape the Spanish Inquisition were factors that quickly led Lisbon to the title of the world's leading commercial capital. But the Inquisition spilled over Portugal's borders and Manuel was forced to threaten expulsion of the Jews unless they were willing to change their faith and become *conversos*.

Portugal lost much of its vital merchandising middle class when many Jews left Lisbon. Portugal was further weakened in the 1500s with the growth of French, Danish, Dutch, Swedish, and English fleets, who "cut their slices of East India cake and New World pie," effectively breaking the Portuguese monopoly of the seas.

Only the areas of Africa and Brazil were left open to Portuguese traders who once again revolutionized European tastes and social life with the gradual introduction of a new beverage called coffee and a new institution called the coffeehouse.

Despite Portugal's decline as a world power in the late 1500s, her successful diplomatic trade with China cannot be overlooked. Of all the world sea powers, the Portuguese were the first to reach China, to settle in Macao, and to set up a viable volume of trade that lasted unchallenged for more than 300 years. Elegant Chinese goods of porcelain, lacquer, and silks were traded for silver and furs from North America and sandalwood from the Hawaiian Islands. From China came oranges, limes, peaches, walnuts, and coriander. And, while the Portuguese passion for wine and coffee continues unabated to this day, there is still a place for tea on the Portuguese menu. Originating from her trade with China, the Portuguese call tea **cha**, a name hauntingly reminiscent of its origin, for the Chinese call their tea **ch'a**.

FOODS COMMONLY USED

Cooking in Portugal is hearty, simple, and distinctively regional. The penchant for fresh ingredients simply prepared is as important in Portugal as it is in Spain. But the Portuguese delight in unusual combinations such as seafood and pork in the same dish, and take pleasure in a stronger use of garlic and the frequent surprise of a stinging hot sauce made with the Brazilian fiery peppers called **piri-piri**.

Dishes of pork, seafoods of all kinds — especially the beloved dried salt cod called **bacalao** — form the main dishes together with any variety of available vegetables and greens. Every meal is accompanied with bread, whether it is the cornmeal bread called **broa** in northern Portugal, or the many types of wheat breads in the south. Rice, widely used as a base for other foods, appears well sugared in many dessert dishes. Rich sweets in the forms of puddings, baked custards, imaginative confections and pastries are the specialties of many monasteries and special pastry shops. Each region is proud of its own sweet delights.

Portuguese red wine is abundant and considered so superior to the white that it is consumed with every dish, even fish. In fact, drinking red wine with fish dishes is considered to be a tradition in the Algarve. But the drinking of red wine in no way diminishes the Portuguese love for good coffee which appears after meals and frequently accompanies the many tempting sweets.

Portugal may have declined as a world power in the annals of history but the products she brought back and the instigation of sea adventure that she nurtured still deeply affect the tables of the world and are still reflected in the agriculture and cuisine of her own land. Today Portugal is almost self-sufficient in grains, fruits, and vegetables.

But despite a rich harvest of fresh fish and seafood, the Portuguese still passionately manage to consume salted and dried cod at the rate of 100 pounds per person per year. Northern Portugal's language and cuisine still reflect the tastes and ties of Brazil, from crusty white bread and fine coffee, to **piri-piri**, that fiery little hot pepper that becomes a favored seasoning for fowl or seafood when ground and blended with oil. And southern Portugal's Algarve district still leans heavily on Moorish cuisine: almonds in so many dishes and as a sweetmeat, and crusty wholewheat bread to mop up sauces in the Moroccan style.

Said to be prepared in at least 365 different ways (one for each day of the year), **bacalao** was introduced into Portugal in the early 1400s as a result of barter with the English.

English fishermen gathered huge catches of cod off the Grand Banks of Newfoundland, salting and drying the fish for preservation. With little market for the cod in Great Britain, the English tried elsewhere and so began to barter with the Portuguese — a coarse red Portuguese wine for dried salted cod. The English called the wine "Red Portugal." This early trade formed the basis for strong English-Portuguese ties and is known to this day, some 500 years later, as the Port Wine trade.

There is a story of the sons of a Liverpool wine merchant who journeyed to Portugal to select wines firsthand and decided to add a "dollop of brandy" to the kegs to fortify the wine for its journey to England. The fortified wine is said to be the origin of port wine. There may be some debate about the story but there is no debating the English taste for port wine. The Methuen government in 1703 agreed to allow Portuguese wine to enter England at a lower tariff than French wines in exchange for Portuguese importation of English wools.

In 1756, Prime Minister Pombal laid down strict rules in regard to the growth and production policies of port wine. These policies form the basis of the rules today. During the next 200 years, Portugal was to suffer through the Napoleonic Wars, which left the Portuguese with a taste for French furniture and French silver; through Brazil's formation of an autonomous republic in 1889, but with no diminution of the Portuguese passion for coffee; and through the grim years between 1910 and 1926 when it is said that the Portuguese "averaged one revolution and three governments a year." The Portuguese port wine trade was still so important after 200 years that it was considered Portugal's sole stable institution when Dr. Antonio de Oliviera Salazar took the job of prime minister in 1932 and ruled for 36 years.

Beneath the rumblings and political upheavals, the Portuguese people have remained steadfastly absorbed in the intensity of life itself and with their passions, obsessions, and manias for food and drink, and for work and play.

DOMESTIC LIFE
Portuguese domestic life follows traditional patterns and in many rural areas regional costumes are much in evidence. Discipline of children and courtship follow strict patterns. These factors may result in adjustment problems when Portuguese emigrate to Canada and the United States. The father is the household head, but Portuguese women frequently work side by side with their husbands in agriculture, fishing, or factories. In fact, many work activities are considered family affairs. After the work of shucking corn, beating trees for olives, or picking grapes is completed, a family picnic ending with singing and dancing is more the rule than the exception.

It is typical of Portugal that modern methods are only implemented where traditional ones are no longer feasible. If the old method works, why toss it out? In the fields, ancient agricultural techniques are practiced alongside modern mechanization.

This is true too of the Portuguese kitchen. Since three-quarters of Portugal's people are engaged in agricultural pursuits, the country home and kitchens dominate the country's way of life. Self-sufficiency is a matter of great pride. Many types of homemade pork sausages, sausage-like strings of lard, barrels of salted bacon flavored with bay leaf and garlic, and of course a good supply of homemade wines, stores of fruits, vegetables and grains stock the pantries and cool storage areas of the Portuguese home. This is still a source of pride today.

Many communities share a huge cement and stone oven where breads and confections may be baked. Kitchens glow with tiled floors and walls and often tiled cooking areas. Few electrical appliances are used as traditional mortar and pestle, hand coffee-grinders and strong arms do the blending, crushing, chopping, mixing, and beating of kitchen chores.

Southern Portugal reflects many dishes of the Spanish cuisine such as **gaspacho**, the cold vegetable soup; **pudim flan**, the sweet caramel custard; and many dishes that are cooked all in one pot by steaming. The **cataplana** is used especially in the Algarve, the southernmost province of Portugal. Two rounded lids are clamped tightly together, cooking food on the stove top like a type of pressure cooker and giving any food combinations a moist freshness.

DAIRY PRODUCTS

Cows and ewes supply milk which is used more to produce the many varieties of local cheeses than to take as a beverage. Five- and six-course meals are not uncommon in Portugal, especially in the North where hearty eaters abound in the cooler, moister weather. Some form of white soft or mild local cheese appears either before or with the fruit course. **Queijo do Alentejo** and **Serra** are two popular soft cheeses made from ewe's milk. They are especially good with apples and walnuts and washed down with a velvety red wine like **Dao**. Other good cheeses include **Queijo da Serpa** and **Queijo da Azeitao**. **Flamengo** is a cheese often proffered to tourists; it is similar to a **Gouda** but considered not as good as other local cheeses.

FRUITS AND VEGETABLES

Most of the fruits of Portugal come from area orchards and vineyards and are enjoyed in season: oranges, apples, figs, melons, limes, peaches. Imported fruits such as pineapples and bananas also form an important part of the fruit intake. Monks in the 1300s are credited with teaching the peasants the arts of fruit growing. Fruits, enjoyed in their fresh ripe state, are often eaten with cheese as a meal course before the sweet desserts. The famed plums of Elvas are eaten liquored and iced or fresh.

Portuguese vegetables are enjoyed garden-fresh frequently as soup or casserole ingredients but seldom overcooked. Turnip greens are a great favorite as is the strongly flavored kale, the principal ingredient in the northern specialty **caldo verde**. This is a very popular soup, made from potatoes and finely shredded kale or other greens, well seasoned with pork sausages (**linguica** or **chourico**) and garlic. Fresh coriander with its clean lemon-like taste is used in so many dishes that it can almost be regarded more as a food than as a seasoning.

Potatoes belong at the top of the list of vegetables. They are used in soups and stew-type dishes with either meat, fish, or seafood and they are a part of almost every dinner or supper. So fond are the Portuguese of their potatoes that these vegetables often appear beside rice as the second starchy food of the meal.

The Portuguese enjoy a wide variety of vegetables but prefer them in cooked form rather than fresh in salads. Many soups are made predominantly with vegetables and highlighted with garlic browned in olive oil and the pungent garlic sausages of which there are so many types.

Garlic and onions, scallions and leeks are a large part of Portuguese cuisine. And the ancient olive trees deserve special mention. Olives are used in cooking, adding their color and taste to many dishes. They are enjoyed brined, pickled, black or green.

MEATS AND ALTERNATES

Porco (pork) is the staple meat of the Portuguese table. Nothing is wasted; trimmings and odd pieces as well as fat and offal are used in the many varieties of sausages, some spicy and some mild but almost all pungent with garlic. **Presunto** is the name given to smoked hams, while **paio** is salted, smoked, and spiced pork tenderloin. The spicy casserole called **porco con ameijoas** is only one of many combining stewed or braised pork with some form of seafood, in this case cockles.

Some beef is used but it is leaner and tougher than beef found in North America, for the most part requiring slow moist cooking or else held in marinades to tenderize before grilling. Chicken, duck, and game are also used when available. Meat of young animals is favored; veal, lamb, kid, suckling pig.

So important is fish in the Portuguese diet that at least one meal a day will be based on a fish dish, and even if meat happens to be the main dish of the meal, it will be preceded by both soup and a fish course. In June, the sardine season, almost everyone grills sardines outdoors on small charcoal-heated braziers. Lampreys have the height of their season in March and these are used mainly in stews. It should be noted that grilled fish is the one dish that is often accompanied with a salad of freshly sliced tomatoes and onion rings. Herring, cod, salmon, and trout are plentiful as are every variety of shellfish and seafood.

Beans are served frequently, especially in stews and casserole-type dishes. **Dobrada** is a hearty peasant dish of tripe and beans. Incidentally, the natives of Oporto are so noted for their love of tripe and the many ways of preparing it, they are often called *Tripeiros* or "tripe-eaters."

While chicken meat may not be so important, chicken eggs certainly are. Where would all the lusciously sweet yolk-rich desserts, the airy-light sponge cakes and delicate meringue confections with exotic names like "nun's nipples" and "nun's breasts" be without eggs? Hardly a sweet rice pudding or the ubiquitous **pudim flan** (caramel custard) could possibly exist without eggs. Aside from the multitude of sweetmeats and confections that are based on eggs, eggs are also served hard-cooked or poached as colorful garnishes to other dishes like fish casseroles or codfish cakes. **Tortilha** is the name for omelet, and the omelet, aside from eggs, may also contain a satisfying portion of onions, potatoes, other vegetables, and a garnish of spicy sausage.

The trees in Portugal offer many things: fruits for eating, pine boughs to add aroma to the bake ovens, cork for wine bottles, olives for eating and making oil, and, last but not least, almonds, walnuts, and chestnuts: nuts for roasting, munching, salting, sugaring, and making into cakes and pastries. Almonds are especially plentiful in the southern Algarve district.

BREADS AND GRAINS

The basket of fresh bread is probably the first thing that is put on any Portuguese table for any meal. If the meal is breakfast, then the local bread – whether made from cornmeal or corn flour, rye flour or coarse, nutty wholewheat flour – will be accompanied by fresh butter, sweet preserves and, depending on the area, either hot tea or coffee.

The slightly sweet heavy bread made from the flour of maize is the bread of northern Portugal and is called **broa**. Crusty and warm, it is particularly good served with **caldo verde**, the national soup of greens and potatoes.

Crusty breads of rye or wholewheat flour are more popular in the mid and southern regions where they are commonly used in the Moroccan way to mop up gravies, juices, and sauces from meat or seafood dishes. Breads are only taken from the table when the desserts are brought out.

The Moors brought rice cultivation to Portugal, and rice is much used in many savory and sweet dishes. It seems that the Portuguese cannot decide if they prefer rice or potatoes, so commonly are both served on the same plate.

FATS

Fats are consumed in many forms: fatty sausages made mainly from pork and lard; the fat contained in egg yolks and used so widely in desserts and confections; but most of all, olive oil. Portuguese olive oil, called **azeite**, is produced for domestic consumption and is rarely exported. **Azeite** is the principal cooking fat and is also used by the canners of anchovies and sardines. The characteristically strong color and flavor of the Portuguese olive oil is due to the processing. Olives are allowed to remain in the field from two to ten days before pressings and are deliberately run through hot water to bring out the strength of taste and depth of color. In other countries pains are taken to rush the fresh olives for pressing and to pass them through cold water to give a product light in both taste and color.

SWEETS AND SNACKS

Only the sweets of Iran, Turkey, Greece, and Morocco can vie with the confections, pastries, puddings, cakes, and other desserts of Portugal for honey-rich syrupy sweetness. It is not difficult to see that Portuguese sweets must have originated with the Moorish occupation, but the Portuguese have gone further with the addition of egg yolks and feathery-light meringues to create a confectioner's heaven of desserts. Each small village proudly displays at least one fancy pastry shop and most villages even have their own specialties for the sweet tooth.

From olden times, the nuns in monasteries were famed for their exquisitely wrought sweets rich in sugar, eggs, vanilla, chocolate, and almonds. Tinted sugar and almond paste molded sweets are called **macapao** or marzipan. Similar sweets may be shaped like tiny sausages, fish, shellfish, fruits or vegetables and some are more suggestive with shapes and names like "nun's kisses," "nun's nipples," and "nun's breasts." At least one place, Amarante, is famed for its phallic-shaped brioches, probably survivors of ancient fertility rites common in many European areas and now melded into religious festivals.

SEASONINGS

Staple seasonings include garlic, coarse sea salt, lemon juice and wedges, and the generous use of fresh or freshly dried herbs such as mint, coriander, and parsley. **Azeite**, the Portuguese olive oil, must also be considered a national seasoning for the special flavor it imparts to many dishes. Fresh eggs, fresh butter, and vanilla together with grated lemon or orange rinds scent bakery and desserts but almonds must take an important place too. Curry blends also find a place, hearkening to Portugal's ties with India.

BEVERAGES

With wine appearing at every meal except breakfast, there can be little doubt as to what constitutes Portugal's favorite beverage. Yet, many writers speak of Portugal's passion for coffee too. And some areas prefer tea over coffee as the beverage both for breakfast, after meals, and with the many sweets taken as snacks or between-meal treats.

More than 240,000 people in Portugal are permanently engaged in some aspect of wine-growing or processing, while more than 1.25 million depend directly on the wine trade for their income. These are startling figures considering Portugal's size. The variety of her wines usually startles outsiders as well. The world is familiar with port and Madeira but many should familiarize themselves with the varieties of port: vintage port, crusted port, wood port, vintage tawny and the lesser-known white port made from white grapes to produce a fine dry aperitif which is excellent when chilled.

Similarly, Madeira wine is infrequently known in all its varieties from the dry aperitif *sercial* Madeira to the light dry *verdelho*, good also as an aperitif or with a first course. The *bual* Madeira is considered to be in the middle range, rich but versatile, while the well-known richly full Malmsey Madeira is best served as a sipping wine or with dessert.

The **Vinho Verdes** of the northern Minho province (named from the grape) are zesty wines that come in either red or white. Aromatic whites are produced in Obidos while the whites of Alcobaca and Bucelas are richly golden, reminiscent of fine Rhine wines. The grapes of the Duoro are used mainly for the production of a popular red table wine called **consumo**. About one-quarter of the grape production is used for port wine. The muscatel grapes of Azeitao produce a sweet dessert wine whose flavor is heightened with the addition of fresh muscat skins giving it the perfume of fresh fruit.

Lisboans enjoy the many wines as well as tea and coffee. However in Lisbon, more than anywhere else in Portugal, foamy beer is also enjoyed, especially in the *cervejarias* (beer parlors) where the beer is accompanied by steaming plates of fresh fish or seafood specialties.

MEALS AND CUSTOMS
Few people feel more deeply about their native land, their childhood, or their food and drink than the Portuguese. They bring to their meals the same intensity as they bring to every other aspect of their lives. There is no philosophizing about food or drink as there is with the French, nor is there a plethora of cookbooks in Portugal. Portuguese prepare their food with simple dignity, making the most of nature's rich gifts and in the same humble way they eat quietly and appreciatively. Food is important and meals are generous but food is never glorified or categorized.

Dinners and suppers frequently run to five- or six-course menus and these include soup, fish, meat and vegetables with rice and potatoes, cheese, fruits, and a choice of sweet desserts of which at least two must be taken in order not to cause offense. Meals are usually leisurely with dinner from 1:00 to 3:00 p.m. and the evening supper sometime between 8:00 and 10:00 p.m. but not as late as the Spanish have theirs. The Portuguese enjoy eating meals with their children, who are not only included in the adult conversation, they also join their parents in drinking wine as freely as water.

Though dinner and supper are often filling meals, the typical Portuguese breakfast is simple and light, usually consisting of a hot beverage like tea or coffee and a variety of fresh breads and rolls to be eaten with honey, jams and butter.

SPECIAL OCCASIONS
The predominant religion of Portugal is Roman Catholic.

Every town has its special legends, saints, and festivities concerning every aspect of the seasons, the land, family occasions, and religion. In fine weather almost anything becomes excuse enough for a family outing that probably includes relatives, neighbors, and ample provisions of fresh breads, cheeses, cured hams, cold roasted chickens, boned and stuffed suckling pigs, salted herrings, and of course huge wicker-covered jugs of fine homemade or local wines.

Everything wild in Portugal is usually called "brave" or "royal" so a gathering that later turns into a party but is ostensibly for the purpose of branding young bulls may be called *festa brava*; while a dish of wild duck may be called **pato real**, recalling the days when all wild game was strictly for royalty to enjoy. It is well to remember that the Portuguese *brava* does not mean "brave" but "wild." Sometimes Portuguese may refer in faltering English to a young girl as being "brave" when they really mean that her dress and manner indicate her to be "wild" – at least by Portuguese standards, which tend to be conservative.

Any part of outdoor work that requires several hands is also turned into a special occasion. Gathering olives or grapes, shucking fresh corn, treading grapes for wine, in fact most rural jobs that others may consider simply as work, the Portuguese turn into a pleasure by working and singing, enjoying a meal of perhaps **broa** and **caldo verde**, then finishing with extra wine, sweets, and much music and dance.

An example of this is the *esfolhade*, the party for corn shucking. With everyone in best clothes, the work proceeds seriously enough until someone finds a cob of red corn and then the fun begins: the lucky holder of the red cob gets to kiss all the ladies present, or vice versa.

Incidentally, corn is an important crop in Portugal, but not just for reasons of fun or food. The thinnings are fed to the cattle; coarsest stalks are used to bed cattle while the emptied cobs are saved and dried to use as fuel.

In the summer months, especially in the North, there is an almost continuous round of fairs and special pilgrimages called *romarios*. Church services and processions are interspersed with feasting, singing and dancing, ornate decorations and often fireworks.

One of the more interesting festivals, the *Feast of Tabuleiros*, is held every three to five years in the town of Tomar. Girls march in processions with huge layered headdresses made of loaves of bread decorated with wheat sheaves, flowers, and ribbons. The clergy follow bearing richly decorated silver crowns on small black pillows and several young bullocks bring up the end. Later the cattle are slaughtered and portions of meat and breads from the headdresses are distributed to the poor of the area.

Country fairs sell everything from pottery and ribbons to boots and donkeys, but the most celebrated of all is the Feast of St. Martin held in mid-November in Golega. It is a horse fair and a national occasion, a spectacle of Lisbon *sociedade*, visiting dignitaries and royalty, army horsemen, *cavalheiros* who fight the bulls on horseback, and the great horse breeders of Ribatejo and Alentejo, dressed in their special attire of trim gray jacket and trousers and the wide gray flat-brimmed hats. Each group dresses in its finest, with the horses prancing in their best manner and everyone there to see everyone else. Nearby dining rooms are ready with fine foods and wine always on tap.

All Saints' Day, November 1, always brings with it memories of that same day in 1755 when almost three-quarters of Lisbon crumbled in a brief but violent earthquake. Then as now it is a solemn day set aside for quiet church services and memorials for all who died. After services, street vendors sell **broas dos santos**, saints' cakes and other sweets, a brief reminder of the sweeter side of life.

GLOSSARY OF FOODS AND FOOD TERMS

Acordas: similar to the **migas** of Spain, these are bread soups made with bread crumbs or a slice of day-old bread moistened with water or garlic-scented broth. Often served with a poached egg and a sprinkle of freshly chopped coriander.

Almondegas: seasoned meatballs rolled in flour and browned in oil then simmered in a sauce of browned onions, broth, and chopped parsley. Served with rice and potatoes.

Azeite: strongly flavored olive oil typical of the country.

Bacalhau or **Bacalao**: dried salt cod for which the Portuguese are said to have 365 different recipes, one for each day of the year, each one so enjoyed as to gain the title of a "national dish."

Batatas a Portuguesa: thinly sliced new potatoes browned in a skillet with butter and olive oil, salt and pepper.

Broa: the cornmeal bread of northern Portugal. Sweetish and heavy but crusty and satisfying – and wonderfully absorbent of tasty sauces.

Caldierada: a melange of freshly caught fish simmered in a soup-stew with whatever else is at hand, usually served with potatoes and fresh bread.

Formas con Laranja: tender waffles served with orange wedges.

Laranja: the sweet juicy oranges of Portugal. Those are enjoyed fresh in wedges or slices, scooped out and refilled with mixed fruits in the shells, or served in a sweet candy-syrup. Still another favorite is candied orange peel.

Medronho: a clear liqueur distilled from arbutus berries. Brandy mel is the same liquor with the addition of honey – easier to take. Neither is exported, but are the specialty of the Algarve region.

Migas: a dish of pork fillets or chops surrounded by lard-soaked bread.

Paio: pork tenderloin that has been salted, smoked, and spiced.

Pao de Trigo: a bread of southern Portugal made with wholewheat flour, coarse and crusty, and used to soak up sauces.

Papas de Frieiras: small sweet pastries with the earthy name of "nuns' nipples."

Percebos: local shellfish, similar to barnacles.

Porco con Ameijoas: one example of many types of casseroles combining pork and shellfish. Both these ingredients are prohibited by the dietary laws of both the Muslims and the Jews and are said to be typical of the dishes prepared and eaten during Inquisition days to prove "Christian zeal."

Presunto: smoked ham.

Queijadas da Sintra: small cream-cheese and almond-paste tarts.

Queijo: cheese.

Sardinha Asada: grilled sardines.

Tortilha: omelet.

Vaca Estufada: beef stew with vegetables.

CHAPTER 42

Quebecois. See Canadian

ROMANIAN

The Romanian is a study in contrasts. Like the Romanian climate which is icily cold in winter and fiercely hot in summer, the Romanian can be consumed with melancholy listening to the *doine* (poignant country songs of love and longing) or elevated to a passionate frenzy when dancing the *hora* or the *colusari*. Gypsy violins can make him cry, but the sound of flutes and *nai* (panpipes) or *cimpoi* (bagpipes) will evoke songs and laughter. He likes his tea very weak and his coffee very strong, his pickles very hot and his desserts very sweet. Like the powerful wind called the *crivetz*, which whips up the snow in the winter and drives the yellow dust in the summer, the Romanian soul is alternately gay and animated or sad and despairing – but seldom dull.

Aside from these extremes of temperament and taste, the two-thirds of the Romanian population engaged in agriculture do show a form of moderation when it comes to their work. The rich fertile lowlands and the Wallachian Plains yield bounteous crops with little effort, and for centuries the people contented themselves with their own needs and little more.

Probably it is those same fertile pastures, orchards, vineyards, and fields of grain that enticed the Roman conquerors about 100 C.E. In exchange for the grain and the gold that they took from the land, they built bridges and roads; but more important they built the beginnings of an identity and left a language and culture that is proudly preserved to this day. The strength of the Roman cultural identity can be better appreciated when one realizes that Romania was and still is almost surrounded by Slavic peoples and even counts within her own population more than a dozen ethnic groups. Despite this, more than 85 percent of the population speak Romanian, which is closely related to the other Romance languages of Latin, Spanish, French, and Italian. Further, their homogeneity is displayed not only in their almost universal temperament and tastes but also in their religion, for the vast majority of the population are members of the Romanian Orthodox Church.

Romania today is composed of the areas of Transylvania, Banat, Wallachia, and Moldavia, with the Transylvanian Alps and parts of the Carpathian Mountains forming her interior. In former times, Bucovina and Bessarabia were also a part of Romania

– but never all these areas at one time. Because of the tug-of-war for her lands, parts of Romania developed differently, strongly influenced by invaders. For example, Transylvania, originally a Romanian province, before 1000 C.E. became a Hungarian province, but in the 1200s was settled by German colonists, thus adding to the population of Romanians, Hungarians, and Szecklers (of non-Hungarian origin). At this time Hungarian domination spread to most of Romania, and the original Romanian population was kept in ignorance and subservience for almost 800 years.

In the 1400s, the Turks conquered Moldavia and Wallachia and placed Greeks on the thrones. In the late 1600s a contest of power between Austria and the Ottoman Empire further suppressed the Romanians and added Hungarian peasants to the oppression.

By the late 1700s, Russia joined the battle for Romania's lands and by 1812 Bessarabia became Russian. But a surge of Romanian nationalism resulted in the creation of Romania as an independent kingdom in 1881, and rather than wars, she made treaties with Russia and the Austro-Hungarian Empire and gained some internal stability.

In the powerful desire to throw off their subservient yokes and gain independence, the Moldavian peasants began a surge of anti-Semitism that later became government policy and led in the early 1900s to a mass exodus of Romania's Jews.

Towards the end of the First World War, Romania's siding with the Allies gained her more territory at one time than she had previously ever known. Back into her fold came Transylvania, Bucovina, most of Banat and Bessarabia. In the wake of this good fortune, Romania rescinded its anti-Semitic policies and attempted much-needed land reform policies. This too was short-lived and growing political pressures and Fascist sympathies led again to Jewish repression, censorship, and alignment with the Germans during the Second World War. By 1944, Russian armies swept into Bessarabia and Bucovina and deep into Romanian territory to secure her surrender. The gradual spread of communism began, as did the shift from a basically agricultural economy to a more industrialized one.

Because of the repressive history of Romania, it is all the more intriguing that the country has retained her ancient Roman cultural identity and language – even the Romanian Orthodox religion. With the many territorial exchanges and foreign rulers, and despite the sufferings of her people, Romania mirrors her history in her cuisine but not in her identity. From the Southern Slavs of the former Yugoslavia came the **sarmales** and **ghiveciu**, from Hungary the **tokany**, **gulyas**, and **paprikash**, from Austria the **strudels**, **tortes**, and **wiener schnitzel**, from Turkey the **pilafs**, **baklava**, **halva**, **dolmas**, and strong Turkish coffee, and finally from Russia the taste for soured soups, **blini**, and a variety of dark breads made from rye and coarse wheat flours. In some areas the German love of potatoes predominates over the inherent Romanian love of **mamaliga**, Romania's staple "bread of gold" made from cornmeal.

Aside from cuisine, one other Slavic tradition has become important in Romania. This is the reverence for wheat as the symbol of life. A part of the Romanian Orthodox funeral service is the blessing of a plate of mounded wheat sprinkled with sugar, raisins, and nuts. This is similar to the Ukrainian **kutya**, the Russian **kutija**, and the Serbian **koljivo** or **zito**.

Romanians are noted for extremes in temperament and taste, and diversity in history and cuisine, but some things have remained comparatively consistent. Although increasingly Romanian women are stepping into full-time jobs away from their homes, they still retain their age-old respect for their men; the Romanian man comes first. And although Romanians are devotedly religious, they have embraced Christianity in addition to, not instead of, paganistic rites and superstitions.

All share one other characteristic: they believe firmly that old age is simply a disease, not an inevitability. Health spas, mineral baths, drinking waters, the assiduous application of herbs and sometimes even a spell or two are believed to do the trick. From infancy to adulthood the taking of special waters, teas, and herbal brews are as much a staple as their beloved **mamaliga**. Hence too the serious devotion paid to the skills of the kitchen by all Romanian women: what can be more important than food and herbs?

DOMESTIC LIFE
Romanian homes are brightly decorated with wall hangings, curtains, coverlets and tablecloths of richly intricate embroideries. Displays of folk pottery and carved wooden objects attest to an artistic people who are seldom idle with their hands. Even much of the furniture is handmade and beautifully carved and finished.

The center of most homes, whether rural or urban, is the kitchen. This same room is not only the largest in the house, it is also the living room, the dining room, and the children's bedroom. One other small room will be the parents' bedroom and a still smaller one will be the food storage room or the pantry. A large wood-burning stove with ovens, cooktop, and open hearth will be centered against one wall of the kitchen's whitewashed interior. Not only do all the good foods come from here, but so does the heat.

Colorful earthenware dishes, mixing bowls, and casseroles for baking the many popular vegetable stews are basics of the kitchen as are the heavy cast-iron pots for soups and cooktop stews like **gulyas** and **tokany**. But most important are the utensils involved in the preparation of **mamaliga**. This thick cornmeal porridge that is almost all things to a Romanian is so special it is cooked in a special cast-iron pot called a **ceaun** and stirred with a carved wooden stick called a **facalet**. Finally, it is turned out on to its own wooden board to cool and is cut with a special string into hearty wedges; that is, if it is not prepared to be eaten in one of countless other ways.

FOODS COMMONLY USED

The single most important staple of the Romanian diet is **mamaliga** (the name is of Turkish origin from *mama*, and means food). Many peasants have survived almost solely on this cornmeal porridge while even the upper classes make it almost a daily part of the menu. Romanians are also fond of spicy and tangy appetizers, cheeses, sour soups, stews of vegetables and meat, grilled and roasted meats and fish as well as sweet desserts and pastries. All of this is enjoyed with good wine, potent plum brandy (**Tuica**), thick Turkish coffee and sometimes weak tea. Simple or complex, Romanian foods all have distinctive flavors, and as in everything else, contrasts are much enjoyed.

Romanians prefer fresh fruits and vegetables, each in its own season. But the pantry area does hold cabbages and root vegetables that can take storage: to preserve them for winter use, vegetables that are more perishable are sometimes wrapped in leaves and buried in an earthen pit. Mostly, however, seasonal fruits are preserved as jams, fruit butters to be used for pastry fillings, dried, or cooked in heavy syrup to produce **dulceata**, thick sweet preserves of whole or sliced fruits or berries eaten with a spoon between sips of icy cold water and finally washed down with strong Turkish coffee. Cabbage may also be stored as barrels of sauerkraut; other vegetables will be preserved for winter and year-round use as spicy hot, sweet, or sour pickles.

DAIRY PRODUCTS

Yogurt, soured milk, and cottage cheese head the list of dairy products in the Romanian diet for these are not only eaten by themselves but enjoyed as parts of many other dishes. Sweet cream is widely used as whipped cream in pastries, and sour cream finds a place in many Hungarian and Slavic-inspired dishes.

Even when other protein sources such as meat and fish are scarce or expensive, cheese is consumed at least once daily and often more often. Most cheeses are made from sheep's or goat's milk and include the **Kashkaval**, a firm yellow cheese, and **Brinza**, a soft creamy cheese. Together with the fresh cottage cheese, all cheeses are eaten as they are with breads, with **mamaliga**, atop casseroles, or enfolded in cakes and dumplings, yeast doughs and **clatite** (thin crepes). Some sharp and pungent cheeses are eaten as an appetizer with **Tuica** (clear plum brandy) and black olives.

FRUITS AND VEGETABLES

The climate and fertile lands produce an abundance of quality fruits: peaches, apricots, pears, apples, plums, cherries, grapes, and many varieties of melons and berries. In season these are eaten fresh or as a compote. Some fruits are dried, others made into fruit butters and jams and the famed **dulceata**.

Many varieties of vegetables are available and are eaten in quantity and variety commensurate with the budget. The staples are cabbage and potatoes as well as the usual root vegetables. In season, many vegetables such as tomatoes, cucumbers, radishes, and scallions are eaten raw as a side dish. Cabbage may be stored as sauerkraut, and peppers, cucumbers, etc., will be made into spicy pickles. Eggplant is one of the more popular vegetables because of its versatility as an appetizer. **Vinete tocate** is a vegetable stuffed with meat and rice or as the important part of **musaca**.

The uses and nutritional values of vegetables are well appreciated by Romanians. Infants are fed finely puréed vegetables as one of their first solid foods. The cultivation of herbs for flavoring and medicinal purposes is widely pursued. Vegetables in colorful profusion are munched raw, nibbled as appetizers, enjoyed raw, or cooked for salads, may be stuffed, pickled, wrapped, layered, stewed, or simmered in hearty soups.

At the very least, most vegetables will be accorded the "simple" Romanian treatment of being chopped, shredded, or diced then tossed with lard and browned onions with a little water. They are then cooked till tender, sloshed with sour cream or yogurt and blended with a little vinegar just before serving. Finally, most Romanian sauces are really only a puree of vegetables blended with oil. One way or another, everyone in Romania gets their vegetables.

MEATS AND ALTERNATES

Pork and veal are the favorite meats and there is no part of the animal that is not used. Meats are grilled or roasted but most often are a part of vegetable soups and stews. One of the favorite snacks is **mititei**, sausage-like fingers of highly seasoned ground meat grilled over an open fire and served with sour cabbage, hot pickles, and dark bread. Often tidbits of variety meats and offal – heart, liver, kidney, lungs, brain, or udder – are grilled too. Some chicken, duck, and game birds are occasionally used, but the birds are often scarce and expensive. Chicken and egg production is low and chickens are often tough.

From the Black Sea coast, the Danube River and countless smaller rivers and lakes comes quite a good supply of fish. Sturgeon, trout, carp, pike, perch, and bream are baked or grilled and often made into soups or stews. Sturgeon roe (caviar) is expensive, but carp roe is often prepared by mashing and blending into a thick sauce with olive oil. This appetizer is called **icre** and may be a part of the appetizer assortment together with salted olives and tangy cheese.

Beans are used quite often in soups, salads, or casseroles.

BREADS AND GRAINS

Corn, wheat, oats, buckwheat, rye, barley, and rice are all grown in Romania but nothing exceeds cornmeal in popularity. From this is made **mamaliga**. This food's versatility equals the pasta, rice or potato staples of other peoples, and even the most affluent Romanian succumbs at least occasionally to a meal based on **mamaliga**. This is not difficult to enjoy, for **mamaliga** in its bland sweetness seems the perfect foil for meats and gravies, cottage cheese, yogurt, butter or sour cream, various vegetable sauces or simply a mound of browned mushrooms or onions. Cold, it can be sliced into wedges and eaten as a bread or sliced thinly and dipped in egg and breaded and fried in squares, layered into vegetable and/or meat casseroles, or served in the bottom of a soup plate. Sometimes **mamaliga** is the companion to fried or scrambled eggs, or even just sauerkraut or pickles. With **mamaliga** who can be hungry?

Wheat flours are processed in various stages of refinement and used for the many pastries, cakes, tortes and desserts so beloved by the Romanians. If **mamaliga** is not on the table, it is certain there will be an assortment of dark and sour rye breads or crusty coarse wholewheat breads to accompany the meal. Rice and barley are used in soups and stews, in stuffed vegetables and as a base for meat and gravy dishes.

FATS
Lard, butter, olive oil, and sunflower seed oil are used in cooking and baking. The latter two also serve as salad dressings.

SWEETS AND SNACKS
Romanians are fond of sweets and they like their sweets very sweet, perhaps as an antidote to the hot peppers.

Dulceata (fruits preserved in heavy syrup) and sweet thick Turkish coffee plus the whole range of rich tortes, layer cakes, filled cakes, honey and syrup-drenched Turkish pastries, sticky-rich dried fruits, strudels filled with fruits, nuts, poppy seeds – the list is endless. Chocolates in every form, plain or filled, are a specially treasured treat. Failing chocolates, Romanians will munch happily on raisins.

SEASONINGS
As in other parts of the Romanian cuisine, the intertwining of Slavic and Oriental tastes is evident. Olive oil, sour cream, onions and leeks, garlic, black olives (**masline**), paprika, wine, and a wide range of herbs are used not just for flavor but for their other properties as well. Babies enjoy sucking sprigs of sassafras tied to their wrists. Parsley and garlic are believed to purify the blood, yogurt to aid digestion, and caraway to act as a mild laxative.

In order to prepare the many sour soups that are a frequent part of the menu, fermented grains, fruits, beer or vinegar or the juice from pickles or sauerkraut is used.

BEVERAGES
Romania's vineyards produce a variety of good local wines enjoyed with dinner and supper and often in between, especially when mixed with soda water as a **shpritz**. The most popular aperitif is the clear plum brandy called **Tuica** or **Tzuica** enjoyed straight but always with appetizers such as **icre**, **vinete tocate**, **masline**, **mititei**, tiny hot peppers, pickles, or sharp cheeses. **Must** is an autumnal beverage of lightly fermented grape juice.

On the sober side, clabbered milk called **lapte batut** is often a part of breakfast with breads or rolls (croissant or brioche) or even **mamaliga**. Sweetened soft drinks and cola are increasingly available, and fruit drinks called nectars are also enjoyed.

Turkish coffee, tea, and herbal teas are also taken.

MEALS AND CUSTOMS
Breakfast may of necessity have to be only **mamaliga** and yogurt or clabbered milk, but Romanians prefer a hearty breakfast including soft-boiled eggs or omelets, sliced ham and sausages, cheeses and dark bread. Lunch or dinner is considered the biggest meal of the day and may be anytime between 1:00 and 4:00 p.m. It usually begins with a **gustare** or "taste" of cheeses, olives, scallions, and **Tuica**, then on to soup, followed by a good stew of meat or fish with vegetables, a dessert of fruit or pastries or **clatite** (rolled thin pancakes). This is accompanied by wine and completed with Turkish coffee. The evening meal will be lighter and taken around 9:00 p.m. It is usually made up of leftovers from dinner, noodle or dumpling dishes, or something based on **mamaliga** (cottage cheese and butter atop a plate of **mamaliga** for instance). Large servings are the rule.

Casual visitors are always offered a tray with **dulceata**, cold water, and tiny cups of Turkish coffee. The procedure is to take small spoonfuls of **dulceata** followed by sips of water. Turkish coffee completes the ritual. In some areas the offering of the second cup of coffee means that the visit is over and it is time to leave.

Meals at home tend to be not only generous in portions, but simple and hearty. The many-course meal is a rarity except in affluent homes or restaurants. There is little home life in the cities, because of the congested and sparse living quarters, so people enjoy the evening stroll (like the *korzo* of the former Yugoslavia and the *paseo* of Spain) with a stop for drinks, snacks, and gossip. Meals in restaurants feature fine-quality beef and all of the complex dishes that require skilled preparations: **ciorbas**, **tocanas**, **ghivetcu**, **tortes**, **strudels**, and other specialties. Coffeehouses serve tea and coffee but mostly aperitifs with appetizer plates of olives, pickles, and cheese.

Street vendors sell fresh fruits in season, dried fruit snacks, and the Romanian specialty **mititei**.

SPECIAL OCCASIONS

Over 85 percent of the population is Romanian Orthodox. Very small minorities of Roman Catholics, Protestants, and Jews make up the remainder. The Romanian calendar burgeons with fast days and feast days, lucky days and unlucky days, rites for spring and rites for winter, sheep milking festivals, harvest and seeding festivals, wine festivals and festivals for the invocation of rain. All have traditional songs and dances and often costumes and much wine and good food.

Funeral customs exemplify many ancient pagan rites, beliefs, and symbols: dirges and funeral songs are played, special dawn ceremonies are held and many don special masks while keeping the vigil with the corpse. In the church service, the priest blesses a special plate of cooked grain, nuts and sugar in memory of the dead.

Weddings are gay, colorful, and bursting with exuberant song and dance. One of the oldest country wedding traditions is the fertility rite of "the song of the hen." Feasting and good times may continue more than one day.

In Wallachia, Gypsy children parade in green-leaved costumes, knocking at each house, singing, dancing and being splashed with water by the villagers. This *paparude* is intended to invoke rain and is usually performed in the spring or during a drought. More water-throwing accompanies June 24, St. John's Day, when little girls dress in costumes and hats decorated with ears of corn, singing, dancing, and uttering occasional shrieks destined to reach the ears of some unnamed corn god – another ancient tradition.

Christmas is celebrated more quietly with caroling and good food. But the stress on agricultural themes can be seen again in many villages. New Year's is celebrated by carrying a decorated plough from house to house accompanied with songs to ensure the next year's good crops.

GLOSSARY OF FOODS AND FOOD TERMS

Balmos: boiled cheese balls.

Bors or **Borsh de Miel**: sour soup (like Russian **Borsch**) with pieces of lamb.

Branza de Burduf: cheese flavored with pine.

Budinca: rich steamed puddings made with eggs, meat and/or vegetables, cut in squares to serve.

Cartofi: potatoes.

Cas: unsalted country cheese.

Ciorba: soups that may be made with meat and/or vegetables or even just grains. Characteristic is the sour taste created with the addition of vinegar or the fermented juices of fruits, grains, sauerkraut, pickles or beer.

Ciorba de Fasole: a soup of dried white beans thickened with an onion roux. Tartness comes from the addition of vinegar and sour cream.

Ciorba Pescareasca: sour fish soup.

Ciuperci: wild mushrooms.

Clatite: thin dessert pancakes served with nuts and sugar or fruit.

Coltzunash cu Smintina: cheese-filled, poached dumplings encased in noodle dough. They are served with sour cream and a sprinkle of sugar.

Dulceata: selected whole or sliced fruit preserved in a very heavy syrup. Eaten in small spoonfuls with sips of ice water, followed by Turkish coffee.

Ghiveciu: a mixture of vegetables and herbs browned first then slowly cooked or baked in one pot. Occasionally meat is a part of this dish. Top may be finished with grated cheese, or a custard of beaten eggs and yogurt. To the Romanians not only a culinary delight but a symbol of their own country: many diverse elements living in harmony and enhancing each other. The Romanian classic via the former Yugoslavia.

Gustare: just "a taste," the term used to refer to a small appetizer.

Icre: well-seasoned carp roe mashed and blended with oil and served as an appetizer, usually with black olives. From the Greek **Taramosalata**.

Lapte Batut: clabbered (fermented) milk served as a beverage.

Mamaliga or **Mamaliga de Aur**: Romania's "bread of gold," her staple in good times and bad, regarded almost as a symbol of reverence and security. **Mamaliga** is simply cornmeal cooked in boiling salted water to a porridge. It is eaten hot or cold and in countless forms with endless combinations often making the entire meal, whether breakfast with the addition of cream or milk, dinner with meat and gravy, or a light supper served with cottage cheese and sour cream.

Masline Frecate: an appetizer paste made of black olives, sweet butter and seasoned with chives, parsley, fennel, and pepper.

Meze or **Mezelicuri**: appetizers.

Mititei: ground, seasoned meat shaped into fingers and grilled.

Musaca: a casserole of potatoes layered with cubed pork or veal, topped with beaten eggs and cream and baked in the oven. Of Greek origin.

Pastrama: any smoked meat: pork, lamb, mutton, even goose.

Patricieni: similar to **Mititei** but even more spiced and covered with pork intestine.

Praz cu Masline: a chilled appetizer of leeks, onions, and olives cooked in garlic and olive oil.

Sarmales: ground meat and rice stuffed into cabbage sauerkraut, spinach, or grape leaves.

Supa: soup other than **Bors** or **Ciorba**.

Tocana: Hungarian stewed meat with onions and paprika.

Tzuica or **Tuica**: clear distillate of plums taken straight and called **Apa Chiora** (cross-eyed water) by country people. For those who can take it, it is considered the national drink of Romania.

Urda: cheese made from sheep's milk.

Varza: cabbage.

Varza ala Cluj: layers of sauerkraut, meats and rice topped with sour cream.

Vinete Tocate: an appetizer prepared from cooked mashed eggplant well seasoned with garlic and served with black bread.

CHAPTER 43

RUSSIAN

Note: Political events cannot be ignored. Borders and ideologies shift and transform, but the general ethos and cultural traditions of the peoples – with regional distinctions – are stubbornly retained because they represent stability and identity.

Nobody can find more excuses for eating than the Russian. The generous, gregarious Slav spirit can make a party with only one herring and a bottle of homemade vodka. Even the grayest, most depressing day will be greeted by the Russian with a gathering of chairs to the table and comments like, "It's a good day for eating." And the visitor who protests the endless flow of food and the pressing of drinks is reminded that "God created everything in pairs," a rough translation being, "How can you eat just one?"

Religious feast days and fast days, saint's days and name days are further excuses for the Russian creative ingenuity to produce a veritable flood of culinary delights for which it is said the Russian soul pines when away from home. So closely intertwined are food and happiness that it is even rumored that concert artists traveling abroad bring with them a special delegation whose sole task is to locate and provide black bread, **borsch**, vodka, and perhaps with luck even **kasha**.

In 1875, John Murray commented in *A Handbook from Travelers in Russia* that "hospitality is still ... one of the chief virtues of the Russian people." One hundred years later, hospitality – whether it be the traditional welcome of bread and salt, a sumptuous dinner beginning with **zakusky**, or even the offering of a glass of tea with lemon and sugar cubes – still characterizes the generous sharing spirit of the Russian. Whatever is offered will be accompanied by excited talk, which will sometimes lapse into soulful songs and the melodic strumming of the *balalaika*, and the guest will be left with an aura of hearty warmth and conviviality.

The passion with which Russians describe (often in beloved diminutives), cook, and serve food may have its roots in the many long periods of suffering endured over their almost 2,000-year history. The pleasures of guests were too infrequent pleasures for a people who were often isolated not only by miles and transportation difficulties but also by long, severe winters. And food itself could never be taken for granted by a people who still retain memories of the great famines of the 1100s and 1200s when straw and bark were soup ingredients and when more than one family survived only by resorting to cannibalism. Nor can the stinging memories of hundreds of years of oppressive rule by callous royalty (with few

exceptions) more concerned with territorial acquisition and sumptuous banquets and extravaganzas than with the tortured, starving, and illiterate serfs be quickly erased. To have food and drink and to share these with family and friends – these simple pleasures have been elevated to artistry unequaled elsewhere, perhaps because the Russian's passionate appreciation is not equaled elsewhere.

Spilling over two continents with its more than 240 million people spread over fifteen republics, the Soviet Union was formed after the Russian Revolution of 1917. It embraced more than 170 ethnic groups speaking predominantly Russian but also almost 200 other languages and dialects. The largest group of these are the Slavs making up Great Russia and Little Russia or Ukraine. Others include the Turko-Tatar, the Japhetic peoples of the Caucasus, the northern people mainly in the Baltic states of Finno-Ugric origin, as well as much smaller groups of Jews, Greeks, Bulgarians, Koreans, Chinese, and others.

Entering the twenty-first century, the former Russian Empire up to 1917, and the Russian Soviet Federated Socialist Republic from 1917 to 1991, is now Russia or the Russian Federation. As such it no longer encompasses the Baltic States, Ukraine, Belarus (or Belorussia or White Russia), Georgia, Azerbaijan, Kazakhstan, or Mongolia. Russia now embraces at least 60 ethnic groups, and over 80 percent of this population of more than 147 million, are Russians.

What is perhaps most interesting is that despite a history of migrations, wars, and fluctuating borders, not only each of the republics, but frequently each of the ethnic groups, clung to individual food customs. Further, much of what we consider today as Russian cuisine can be traced to influences of the early Slavic paganism. The reverence for bread and water is an example. The Russian Orthodox

Church's proclamation of Wednesdays and Fridays as meatless days leads to the inclusion of more fish and imaginative flour-based dishes. The adoption of tea and noodles and dumplings from the Chinese, wine from the Greeks, pastas from the Italians, and sauerkraut and sausages from the Germans has greatly enriched the Russian cuisine.

The basis of the Slav cuisine is grain. Rye bread and **Kvass**, a fermented slightly alcoholic beverage made from rye, are important in the north; wheat flour and wheat breads predominate in the south, while corn is the staple in the southwest. From the dawn of the Russian Empire under the rule of the Scandinavian chief Rurik, breads and meats were the staple foods. They were plainly cooked and plainly eaten with dried or fresh fruits such as apples and pears forming desserts, and salted or seasonal vegetables adding some variety.

From this period of Scandinavian influence comes the Russian **zakusky**, an array of assorted appetizer foods adapted from the Swedish **smorgasbord** (*see* Swedish) and now an integral part of the evening meal. The conversion of Vladimir the Great (980-1015) to Greek Orthodox Christianity and its subsequent acceptance by the people through the slightly differing Russian Orthodox Church led to taboos regarding the eating of wild animals and the consumption of meats with blood. Further, the meatless fast days as well as Lent led to the increased used of fish, dairy products, and vegetable oils.

But perhaps most influential of all was Peter the Great (1672-1725) who attempted to "Westernize" the semi-Oriental society of his country. He stimulated the organization of the military, increased industrialization, acquired territory and supremacy in the Baltic, and brought home from his travels chefs, artisans, officers, and boatbuilders. The latter introduced

French soups and sauces, Italian pastas, pastries and ice cream, German sausages and sauerkraut. But it was the Russians themselves who added their own touches of mushrooms and sour cream, dill and brined vegetables and butter.

With increased production, improved transportation, and exciting possible imports from neighboring republics, the Greater Russian diet could include exotic Caucasian and Central Asian fruits, Siberian canned gamed meats, a greater variety of vegetables from Ukraine, and cakes and sweets from the Baltics. Nonetheless, the "soul food" of Great Russia will always be cabbage, beets and **borsch**, black bread and **kasha**, and what is life without vodka to wash it down?

DOMESTIC LIFE

The center of the traditional Russian kitchen is a remarkable stove called the **pleeta**. Remarkable because it not only often provides the heat for most of the house, serves as a warm bed at night (with a mattress on top), but also cooks meals and bakes foods in either one of two ovens: a slow oven and a fast oven. Further, an area near the ovens is perfect for broiling **shashlyk** (skewered meats), while a covered hole in the chimney carries the charcoal fumes away from the heating **samovar**. This latter could be described as the second most important piece of equipment in the traditional Russian kitchen for the huge polished **samovar** is used to heat water for tea, and unquestionably tea has a special place in the Russian home.

Upon the heavy **pleeta** can be found an array of practical cooking utensils, almost all of cast iron. These include pots, skillets, and the special griddle, which is actually a series of round "nests" all in one piece, used for preparing **blini**. Of special importance

FOODS COMMONLY USED

The staples of Great Russia are few but are prepared in many classic variations that form a hearty and filling repertoire of cookery. Basic grains include dark wholegrain rye breads, coarse wheat breads, and the all-encompassing **kasha** which usually refers to whole fluffy grains of buckwheat but may also refer to barley, corn, or millet.

Basic year-round vegetables such as cabbage, potatoes, beets, and mushrooms appear in the guise of thick soups, tart and tangy pickles, well-cooked casseroles, or encased in satisfying envelopes of chewy noodle doughs, flaky buttery pastries, or airy yeast doughs. Liberally laced through the grains and vegetables are generous servings of soured milk, cream, sour cream, and especially butter. Russians are fond of butter and like to add some to almost every food. Beef, game and fish, like fresh salad vegetables, are enjoyed when available.

Fruits are relished but are most commonly used in some cooked form. To the Russian, such hearty natural foods require little seasoning except perhaps dill and garlic, sugar, sour (acid) crystals, and usually a little more butter. There are many fermented drinks, soured milk drinks, and fruit drinks, but tea and vodka are the most important. Tea is elevated to an important social ritual with the samovars while any gathering is an excuse for endless toasts with vodka.

is the earthenware pot used especially for baking **kasha**. Characteristically there are no individual-sized baking or cooking dishes, because limiting anyone's food is contrary to Russian thinking. A big wooden table for working, wooden mixing bowls, and a set of scales complete the important items for cooking and baking.

In the country areas of modern-day Russia, the traditional kitchen and utensils are still used. But many people living in urban apartments have little time to fuss over cooking. They prepare simpler meals in smaller kitchens.

Traditionally, home preserves of fruits and jams and barrels of pickled vegetables and cured meats all formed a part of the family's winter supply. More and more, foods are purchased on an almost day-to-day basis as city dwellings have little storage space and refrigerators are costly. In fact very few electrical appliances or gadgets are used, which means that water boiling, puréeing, etc., are all done by hand as needed rather than by electric kettles, juicers, and blenders.

DAIRY PRODUCTS

Smetana (sour cream) is an indispensable staple. Too many dishes would be unthinkable and uneatable without a topping of **smetana**. Whole cow's milk, mare's milk, and fresh cream are widely used in many dishes and as beverages but usually well cooked. Sour milk in many forms, pot cheese and cottage cheese, baked milk or **kaimek** and many varieties of excellent local cheeses are used abundantly.

FRUITS AND VEGETABLES

The most available fruits are those that can survive the generally extreme climate or are imported: apples, pears, cherries, plums, cranberries, and lingonberries. Other berries such as raspberries, strawberries, currants, gooseberries, blackberries, and huckleberries are savored when they can be obtained. Some fruits are enjoyed fresh, others are preserved or prepared as stews, compotes, or the puréed fruit dessert served everywhere called **kissel**. Fruits are also used well sweetened as fillings for dumplings, as fruit sauces or served as a "spoon sweet" to be taken with tea.

Most-used vegetables include cabbage, potatoes, beets, onions, black-skinned radish (**rediska**), carrots, turnips, and squash. Enjoyed but used less frequently are green beans, green peas, cauliflower, eggplant, spinach, sorrel, and pumpkin. The greens are used in soups and the less-used vegetables are considered a special garnish to other dishes. Cucumbers are avidly enjoyed fresh with salt to form a type of fresh salad-pickle, or brined to form pickles that will be used all winter. Homemade barrels of **sauerkraut**

(sometimes with fermented apples) are used year-round in many ways too. Mostly the vegetables are used well cooked in soups, used as fillings or served pickled. When served cold as salads, they have been cooked first then chilled and chopped or sliced and served with sour cream or mayonnaise. Russian salads are never green leafy mixtures and seldom include raw vegetables.

Citrus fruits are not in abundant supply, but very thin slices of lemon are a special treat in hot tea.

MEATS AND ALTERNATES

Beef, veal, pork, and mutton are first on the list of meats. Most chickens are tough unless they are capons; geese, ducks and turkeys as well as game birds, deer, and hare are used when possible.

Fish is eaten fresh, salted, or smoked. Salmon, herring, crayfish, and caviar from sturgeon are considered special delicacies.

Soft-cooked or scrambled eggs are beaten occasionally for breakfast, but most eggs are consumed as garnishes, appetizers (pickled, stuffed, chopped), in meat mixtures, and as fillings for **blini**, doughs, dumplings, and other baked goods. Legumes are not widely used except in some regions and occasionally in soups. Except in the republics, especially Georgia, nuts are only used in baking or as an occasional confection.

BREADS AND GRAINS

Dark and heavy wholegrain rye breads, coarse firm wheat breads, and the ubiquitous casserole of **kasha** (usually buckwheat) are the most firmly entrenched Russian staples. But there are countless shapes and types of breads and rolls – **kulitch**, **krendel**, and **bagel** – to make even a diet solely of breads an interesting one.

To this list of breads may be added the hearty list of large and small pancakes, kulebiaka, noodle dough and yeast dough dumplings that may be baked, boiled, or fried and filled with anything from chopped cabbage to meats, mushrooms, or fruits, and one can see the importance and variety of grains. Further, every kitchen and countless bakeries produce sweet cakes, tortes, rolls, pastries, and fruited yeast doughs (kulitch) that daily find a place on the Russian menu, if only as an accompaniment to tea.

Bread and salt are the traditional symbols of welcome.

FATS

To a Russian, no dish ever contains quite enough butter. Butter is used during cooking, after cooking and more is added during eating. Sunflower oil or peanut oil are used for some dishes.

SWEETS AND SNACKS

Ice cream, available from street vendors or in ice cream parlors, is a frequent snack. Snacks of toasted sunflower, pumpkin and squash seeds as well as many candied fruits are munched frequently. Chocolates or candies are special occasion treats and not used as often as sweets in other forms. Rich baked desserts are enjoyed whenever possible and for any excuse (one never drinks without eating). But it is more common to sip one's tea with a sugar cube held between the teeth for maximum sweetness or to enjoy a small saucer of sweet rich fruit preserves, a spoonful at a time, with hot tea.

SEASONINGS

The main seasonings include dill, onion, sour cream, sour crystals (citric or acetic acid crystals), the fermented juices from sauerkraut or pickles, sugar and salt, butter, parsley and many types of dried or fresh mushrooms. Foods are generally not highly seasoned; the predominant flavors are either buttery and creamy or a blend of sweet and sour. There is a frequent use of equal measures of both sugar and salt to heighten flavor.

BEVERAGES

Tea and vodka rank as the great Russian beverages. Tea is always served very weak. **Kvass**, a fermented drink made from black bread, sugar and yeast, is said to be the drink of the Russian peasants. **Kumiss** (or **Koumiss**) is an ancient Tatar drink said to have legendary nutritive and restorative powers. It is made from mare's milk that has been fermented in wooden tubs or horse skins. It is drunk mainly in the Central Asian Kirghiz region. Other fermented beverages include pear and raspberry liqueurs, cider, beer, and **Med** (similar to mead). Soured or clabbered milk and whole milk are also enjoyed as beverages.

REGIONAL SPECIALTIES

(See also Armenian; Belorussian; Baltic Peoples: Latvian, Lithuanian and Estonian; Czech and Slovak; Polish; Ukrainian)

AZERBAIJAN

Lamb, rice, and yogurt predominate the cuisine while soups and stews are the favored forms of cooking. A custard of eggs sprinkled liberally with fresh green herbs forms the final garnish to many dishes, and exotic seasonings include saffron, cinnamon, pomegranate seeds, and the dried powder of plums and barberry. Other Central Asian dishes include **pilafs** (a base of seasoned rice served with meat or fish together with vegetables or fruits) and **shashlyk** (skewered broiled meats). **Kyurdyuk**, the fat rendered from fat-tailed sheep, is used liberally both in cooking and as a final flavor fillip (like a dab of butter). The **keufta** or meatballs are astonishing in size, many weighing several pounds, sometimes cooked with a whole chicken inside. But it is **piti**, the Azerbaijan thick lamb soup served in earthenware bowls that is considered the outstanding specialty. Generally, a preference for tart and sour flavors predominates, an example being **dovga**, a thick soup of yogurt, rice, and greens served as dessert.

CAUCASUS

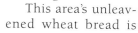

Eastern Mediterranean cuisine predominates in this region with rice as the staple, along with stuffed vegetables, yogurt both as beverage and ingredient, and

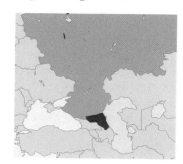

great variety in fruits and vegetables. Lamb is the favored meat, lamb fat is preferred for cooking, olive oil is used for salads and stuffed vegetables, while butter is used only occasionally in baking.

This area's unleavened wheat bread is made only with flour and water. Onions and garlic are much beloved; walnuts and pine nuts are pounded into sauces or used in dishes and fillings, while the exotic fragrance of rosewater, cumin, mint, and coriander enhance many other dishes.

CENTRAL ASIA

A huge area in large part consisting of a dried-up sea basin whose plateaus and deserts are visited with extremes of climate, the Soviet Central Asian republics include Turkmen and Uzbek, Tadzhik and Kirghiz and the Kazakh republic north of those.

Nomads still roam the lands with herds of horses and camels, goats and sheep, yaks and cattle and live primarily on cheeses, lamb, mutton, and horsemeat. Their beverages include green tea and the fermented mare's milk called **kumiss**. When meats and rice are available, they are cooked usually by steaming in a sheepskin pouch that is lowered into a pit of hot coals then banked with earth or sand. Open fires are used for broiling skewered meats and heating water for tea.

The rest of Central Asian cuisine is similar to Azerbaijan cookery with few exceptions. These include the use of sauces made of crushed garlic and broth, and crushed garlic and yogurt to be poured over meats, general use of carrots in most Uzbek dishes, and the popularity of stuffed steamed dumplings of which **manty** is the most famous. **Pilafs** are the most popular rice dishes while many types of flat almost unleavened breads accompany most meals.

Other than the nomads, the peoples of Central Asia live in permanent homes and consequently have a wider variety of cooking utensils and techniques which include chopping foods into small morsels and cooking by stir-frying; steaming foods in a type of double boiler; and cooking foods by dipping into a **Mongolian hot pot** where the food morsels are eaten first and the broth served later. Staple vegetables include pumpkin, onions, and turnips and more recently tomatoes and potatoes. Fresh green herbs, spicy hot peppers, onions and garlic all add zest to what is basically a well-balanced diet of meats, milk and cheeses, seasonal fruits (or preserved fruit syrups) and vegetables.

Some Central Asian specialties are:

Bozbash: a thick Azerbaidzh mutton and vegetable soup.

Chikhirtma: a chicken or lamb soup finished with beaten yolks and lemon juice.

Chup Oshi: an Uzbek dish of tossed cooked noodles, fried onions, and sour milk.

Dyushbara or **Byushpere**: the Caucasian form of dumplings.

Palov: the Uzbek name for pilaf.

GEORGIA

One cannot think of Georgian cuisine without thinking of walnuts. Pounded into a paste and combined with garlic and fiery-hot peppers, walnuts make a sauce that is used to flavor and garnish many dishes.

But that is not all. Walnut oil is used in cooking, walnuts are made into candied treats, and chopped walnuts are a nutritious ingredient in stews, soups, and appetizers. Corn and many varieties of beans as well as soured milks (sheep, buffalo) and curds form the staples, but in good

times there is also an abundance of stone fruits eaten fresh and dried and used as syrups, sauces, preserves, and even in soups.

Fresh green herbs are often eaten out of the hand as snacks or liberally used in the form of garnishes, salads, or seasonings. Eggplants, pumpkins, squash, cucumbers, radishes, onions and scallions precede most meals of which a plate of beans is usually a part, together with stewed or roasted lamb, kid, or fowl.

Georgians enjoy wines but are not big sweet-eaters. A great variety of bread from the thin crisp **lavashi** to the heavy corn bread called **tchadi** or **mchadi** as well as the elliptical **puri** baked from wholegrain wheat and leavened with sourdough starter is a part of all meals.

Some Georgian specialties are:

Chicken Tabaca: young chickens split, flattened, butter-browned, and served with pickled vegetables.

Khadja Puri: a dessert of hot bread filled with cheese.

Lobio: a cold appetizer dish of cooked beans dressed with **Satsivi**, one of the walnut sauces, or a sauce of pomegranate seeds and juice.

Tchadi or **Mchadi**: a coarse heavy bread of cornmeal often baked with a layer of cheese or onions in the middle.

MEALS AND CUSTOMS

The Russian day begins traditionally with a light breakfast of breads and tea and occasionally an egg or two fried or boiled. Lunch is most often a light meal, usually a hot meat or fish dish and often a **pirog** (type of pie). Even more frequently for a family lunch, the main attraction is a huge pot of **kasha** and a pitcher of milk with perhaps a fish or pot cheese dish for variety. A simple milk pudding or stewed fruit finishes the meal.

Since breakfast is small, snacks in the morning rare, and lunch generally a humble light meal, the true Slav spirit (obviously not in full bloom till later in the day) really appears with dinner. *Obed* or dinner begins anytime from 3:00 to 5:00 p.m. and though seldom punctual always begins with **zakusky** plus vodka. The **zakusky** appetizer may be as simple as a plate of salt herring or **ikra** (chopped eggplant) or as elaborate as an array of fish and pickled vegetable dishes as well as one or two hot dishes. Small or large, the **zakuskies** are all eased down with many toasts of vodka and then the meal begins with hearty soup and probably **piroshki** followed by meat, fish or game birds, a vegetable and whatever elaborate desserts the hostess can conjure.

For a typical dinner, family and guests will sit down to a table set with a centerpiece of crystal or cut glass filled with fruit, and at each setting will be a small top plate for the appetizers and a larger plate below for the main dish. Soup is always served from a tureen into ample soup plates, and all the dishes that follow will be arranged on platters or in serving bowls. There is no place in the Russian kitchen or on the Russian table for "individual servings," for in the Slav idiom a serving is not only what a person wishes to eat, but the hope is always engendered that he or she can be coaxed into "just a little more." It would therefore be an insult to provoke the suspicion that the food had been measured at all.

Meats are always discreetly carved in the kitchen or on a side table, and heaping dishes are the sign of generous hospitality. While the hostess always sits at the head of the table, the host sits wherever he pleases. Both share in the responsibility to urge their family and guests to enjoy, that is, eat.

The vodka that was downed from one-ounce glasses following appropriate toasts during the sampling of the **zakuskies** is continued in a steady flow throughout the meal. All drink when toasts are made, for to decline is considered unfriendly. Though wine sometimes accompanies meals among more cosmopolitan families, it is generally regarded with suspicion and gulped down like a soft drink.

Meals end with many thanks to the host and hostess whose warm reply of *"Yeshte na zdorovie"* – "Eat and have good health" – congenially sums up the entire meal. Another ritual of delightful warmth and courtesy is the traditional welcome to guests or newlyweds: *"chleb ee sol."* These words mean "bread and salt" and are presented with a freshly baked loaf of bread and a mound of salt as visitors enter the home. They must cut a slice and dip it in salt before eating. The beautiful symbolism indicates that the guests are welcome to share whatever the household can offer, and expresses the hope that there will always be at least bread and salt, the necessities of life.

Though life today in Russia is often more hectic and there is little opportunity to practice time-honored traditions, the customs associated with foods are still honored. Perhaps the most pleasurable tradition of all is the fourth meal of the day – *vechernyi t'chai* – that intimate get-together of friends and family around the samovar.

Over glasses and cups of tea – all scalding hot – and between hearty bites of breads, meats and cheeses and finally a torte or two, the talk is as continuous as the tea and sometimes as hot. There is a choice of thin lemon slices, sometimes apple slices, and always sweet preserves to enjoy with clear weak tea and cubes of sugar to suck. It is believed this practice of fruit or preserves added to tea was adopted from the ancient Chinese caravanserais. Glasses for tea drinking are favored by the men and usually the glasses are set into ornate straw or metal holders. But it is not unusual to see tea being sipped while the glass is held casually between thumb and third finger, the thumb resting on the upper rim and the third finger acting as the bottom stand. It would be a good bet that unaccustomed hands could scarcely touch the glass even after it was emptied. Women prefer to take their tea from cups and both men and women like to have a small cut-glass side dish from which to spoon up their preserves.

Even in the most modest of dwellings it is likely that a gleaming **samovar** will be one of the proudest possessions. Contrary to some notions, the **samovar** does not dispense tea from its spout. It is a large chamber heated by a central chimney containing charcoal embers and its sole purpose is to boil and dispense water. The embers are dropped in the chimney after the water is poured in the surrounding section. The top of the **samovar** is then connected to that special section of the **pleeta** (kitchen stove) in order to draw off the charcoal fumes. A strong essence of good tea is brewed in a small pot. When the water is boiling, the small pot of tea is placed on top of the samovar and the whole thing is transported from the kitchen to the dining room and placed at the right side of the hostess.

To serve tea, a small amount of the strong essence is poured into the bottom of the cup or glass which is then filled with boiling water from the tap of the samovar. A lemon slice is floated on top, sugar cubes or preserves are placed on the tiny side dishes. And though a tray of vodka and perhaps a few liqueurs may be visible during the evening tea, unquestionably it is the samovar and the good talk that highlight the *vechernyi t'chai.*

SPECIAL OCCASIONS

The predominant faith is represented by the Russian Orthodox Church founded by Vladimir the Great in 988 C.E. as an offshoot of the Greek (Byzantine) Orthodox Church. The main difference between the two is the translation of the service in the Russian Orthodox Church into what was known as Church Slavonic. Other Christian religious groups include Baptist, Lutheran, and Roman Catholic, the latter being found mainly in Lithuania and the extreme westerly regions of the former Soviet Union. Islam is the predominant religion in the Central Asian republics, while almost two million Jews live mostly in the larger cities.

In 1918, the Soviet government nationalized all properties of religious groups and disestablished the Russian Orthodox state church. In 1936, the constitution has stated that "Soviet citizens are granted freedom of religious worship and antireligious propaganda ..." though in practice the churches became more like museums, with seasonal and national holidays replacing those with religious connotation, and overt atheism seeming to be the rule.

Since the collapse of the former Soviet Union, churches and any remaining synagogues and mosques have begun to open their doors not only for prayer, but also to link people to their former heritage. For many, the Russian Orthodox Church is a revered symbol of Russian spirit and identity even as the Greek Orthodox Church was for the Greeks under Turkish rule. Those who professed overt atheism are now gradually returning with renewed piety to their religious and spiritual traditions.

The Slavic spirit has always been attuned to mysticism, spirituality, and cherished superstitions and rituals. (See Ukrainian; Polish). And these blend seamlessly with the symbols and rituals of each special occasion.

The highlight of the Russian calendar is Easter. It is a day observed by all with a Slavic heart whether out of nostalgia, faith, or simply because it is so good to have a celebration to welcome the long-awaited spring.

Traditionally the festival begins during still-wintry days with a week-long festival called *Maslyanitsa*, a gay time of carnivals, parties, and above all contests of **blini**-eating. Slathered with melted butter and dollops of sour cream, jam, sliced smoked fish or herring, **blini** are consumed in gargantuan quantities. Following this cheerful gorging of the "Butter Festival" are the forty days of Lent which the Orthodox Russian observes with a strict diet of vegetables, vegetable oils, and grains. This strict period is sometimes softened by a preceding week of the "Little Fast" in which dairy products and fish are permitted, but no meat. After the Little Fast and the Great Fast, Easter is traditionally celebrated with midnight mass, a service beginning with each worshiper carrying glowing tapers and ending with the victorious cries of "Christ is risen!"

With warm hearts the worshipers hurry home to festive tables laden with the preparations of previous days: ham baked in rye dough, pates, salads of beef herring and sour cream, **pirogi**, **mazurka**, and gaudy decorated eggs. The highlight of the rich meal is the towering rich fruited bread called **kulitch** served side by side on a special plate with the creamy smooth **pascha**, rich cream cheese molded with fruit and nuts.

In modern times the traditional Easter feasts and fasts and worship services are celebrated mostly by those Slavs living in other countries. In the Russian Federation, the Maslyanitsa is reduced to rounds of blini parties in villages or private homes. Few fast, and those who attend services probably do so more out of nostalgia than faith. Nonetheless the Easter buffet of good foods is still ruled by the **kulitch** and **pascha**.

Although Russians adore any excuse for a party such as birthdays, anniversaries, name days, weddings, picnics, seasons, national holidays, the beginning of Lent, Easter, and Christmas, very often the gathering of friends and family and the spirit of conviviality overrides the need for special foods. If it is a gathering then it is a party!

Russians claim that their own patron saint, St. Nicholas of Myra, was the origin of one of the world's most beloved Christmas traditions — the joyous gift-laden visit of St. Nicholas. It is said that when Prince Vladimir declared Christianity the official religion of Russia in the latter part of the eighth century C.E., he also named St. Nicholas as the protector of the poor and oppressed.

For as long as people can recall, some speak of "Old Russia," it was the beloved grandmother, called *Babushka* — after the kerchief worn over her hair and tied beneath her chin — who really brought small gifts to good children.

The traditional Christmas was always a quiet family festival and Orthodox Russians fasted (abstained from meats) for six weeks before. The traditional Christmas Eve dish was **kutija**, a blend of boiled grains mixed with sugar, honey, nuts and raisins. This dish has ancient symbolic meaning, is prepared with slight variations (wholewheat grains or rice), is always served at Christmas Eve and also from a larger platter to all mourners at an Orthodox funeral. Traditional Orthodox Christmas is called *Rozjedestvo*. The Christmas Day family dinner almost always includes a roast goose garnished with baked apples and preceded by **zakusky**.

For a time under the former Soviet Union, the religious and spiritual festivities of Christmas were downplayed and New Year's Day became the major winter festival. The celebration included Grandfather Frost, with his long white beard and red costume, arriving in a sleigh, accompanied by the Snow Maiden distributing small gifts for children. These festivities, with music, clowns, magicians, dancers, and festive foods would take place with throngs of people in the "Palace of Congress."

Other occasions on the Russian calendar also demand traditional foods, for example, the name day or *Iminine*. Orthodox Russians are named after saints and the name day is also the day of the patron saint. It is celebrated with **pirogi krendel** and steaming hot chocolate served somewhere between the vodka and the **zakusky**.

Weddings (*Svadisa*) are traditionally solemnized with a church service, the entire congregation standing for the service. Weddings often take place on Sundays since according to tradition fast days, Tuesdays, Thursdays, and Saturdays, are forbidden for weddings. The "Happiness Cake," a rich yeast dough baked in a large round pan and topped with a small container of salt, symbolizes the bread and salt ceremony of welcome. Bride and groom have some first, then it is shared with the guests. Banquet foods, champagne, and vodka follow.

Picnics are a favored pastime and any collection of **zakusky** foods together with vodka and meat for **shashlyk** are deemed suitable for enjoying in the outdoors.

GLOSSARY OF FOODS AND FOOD TERMS

Beef Stroganoff: thin slivers of beef in a rich sour cream sauce lightly seasoned with hot mustard. Addition of tomato purée and mushrooms are North American adaptations.

Bitky: toothpick appetizer of tiny seasoned meatballs.

Blinchiky: small, thin pancakes usually served with jam for dessert. Diminutive of **Blini**.

Blini: round pancakes traditionally made with yeast and buckwheat flour. These are an ancient Slav symbol for the sun and are served in great quantities during the springtime pre-Lenten festival called *Maslyanitsa*. They are eaten with a generous quantity of melted butter plus sour cream, preserves, fish, etc.

Borsch: a classic Slavic soup originating in Ukraine. Usually prepared with a meat broth, beets, and other vegetables and served with a spoonful of sour cream. It can also be a clear sweet and sour beet broth. Sugar adds sweetness and the brine from saurkraut or pickles provides the sour balance.

Chalop: an Uzbek hot-weather soup of diced fresh vegetables and sour milk topped with chopped fresh herbs. Often served chilled and with an ice cube.

Chicken Kiev: Ukrainian dish consisting of butter-filled breast of chicken, crumbed and crisply browned.

Ditch: name used for any game meat.

Forshmak: general name for warm appetizers but usually referring to a baked casserole of potatoes, onions, apples and herring or ham blended with sour cream.

Galubtzi or **Golubtsi**: cabbage rolls filled with meat (beef and pork) and baked with a thin sauce of sour cream. There are many variations.

Grusheviikvas: alcoholic beverage made from pears.

Hvorost: traditional cookies for Christmas. They are shaped like branches.

Ikra: caviar. This name is also used sometimes for chopped, seasoned, and cooked eggplant, "the poor man's caviar."

Kaimek: "baked" milk. Milk is heated slowly in a low oven for several hours until a thick skin forms.

Kapusta: cabbage.

Kasha: the name used to refer to cooked grain. It most often means cooked buckwheat groats. Others include: **Mannaia Kasha**, semolina; **Ovsjanaia Kasha**, oats; and **Risovaia Kasha**, rice. Although always referred to simply as **Kasha**, the full correct name for a buckwheat variety is **Grechnevaia Kasha**. The Russians have a saying: "One cannot spoil **Kasha** with too much butter."

Keshka: a winter dish of thick porridge puréed with meat and served in a soup plate with butter and cumin.

Keufta: meatballs.

Khazan Pirog: a thick Tatar chicken pie served by placing a wedge in a soup plate and pouring hot chicken stock over it.

Kisel or **Kissel**: puréed cooked fruit that is thickened slightly with cornstarch or potato starch and served chilled.

Kopchenaya Senga: smoked salmon.

Kotletki: Russian meatballs made of finely ground beef, seasonings, and shaped into rounded ovals, crumbed and butter-fried. Diminutive of **Kotleti**.

Krendel: the traditional pretzel-shaped sweet yeast bread for Christmas, dotted with fruits and lightly iced.

Krupenik: Russian barley and mushroom soup based on broth and served with sour cream.

Kulebiaka: rich flaky pastry filled with a mixture of salmon, cabbage, and crepes then rolled up and baked. It is served hot or cold in thick slices, with the addition of extra butter and the inevitable sour cream.

Kulitch: the towering delicate yeast-leavened fruit cake, blessed by the priest and served with **Pascha** for Easter.

Kumiss or **Koumiss**: considered the oldest of Russian beverages and one cloaked in legendary attributes. Still a favored drink in the Kirghiz region, **Kumiss** is made from fermented mare's milk prepared in wooden tubs or horse skins.

Kutija: ancient Slavic dish of cooked grain, sugar, honey, raisins, and nuts usually prepared especially for Christmas Eve and also served to mourners at a funeral. In the south, rice replaces the whole grains of wheat used in most other areas of the Russian Federation.

Kvaschenaya Kapusta: sauerkraut.

Kvass: the "great drink of the Russian peasants," a fermented but non-alcoholic drink made from water, black bread, sugar, and yeast; repeated soakings and pouring off of the liquid yield **Kvass**.

Kyurdyuk: the fat rendered from fat-tailed sheep; used in cooking and as a final hint of flavor.

Lapsha: noodles. May also refer to a soup of milk and noodles.

Lox: uncooked fresh salmon that is cured by salting and/or smoking. It is served in very thin cross-grain slices as part of the **zakusky**. Adapted from Scandinavian influence.

Malinovoi: alcoholic drink made from raspberries.

Mazurka: a rich cake of fruit and nuts baked especially for Christmas. Of Polish origin.

Med: a beverage of honey and diluted wine similar to mead.

Okroshka: A cold soup of chopped fresh vegetables laced with either sour milk, buttermilk, or sour cream. Similar to **Chalop** and the Spanish **Gazpacho**.

Oladky: fluffy pancakes made with separated eggs, sieved cottage cheese and flour and fried in butter. Served with sugar and sour cream.

Ouha, **Oukha**, or **Ooha**: the classic clear Russian fish broth served with minced chives and lemon. The poached fish is served separately.

Pascha: creamed fine cottage cheese, eggs, and minced fruits combined and pressed into a special cheesecloth-lined mold. Unmolded, this delicious cream is served for Easter accompanied with slices of **Kulitch**.

Pashtet or **Paschtet**: a rich paste (pâté) of chicken livers, browned onions, and butter smoothly ground or puréed together. Eaten as part of the **Zakusky**.

Paramach: Tatar-originated pastry of a five-inch dough circle spread with filling, pinched up, and deep-fried. Salad completes the meal.

Pelmeni: Siberian half-moon-shaped dumplings of noodle dough usually filled with meat. Customarily these are prepared in huge batches and frozen by hanging outdoors on strings. Dropped into a boiling soup or water, they are often taken by travelers as "instant food."

Pirog or **Pirogi**: a flaky envelope of dough that can be filled with almost anything. This turnover is usually made large enough to feed six. The largest version is called **Kulebiaka**, while the smallest is called by the diminutive **Piroshki**. **Pirojok** is the singular, but is never used because who eats just one? After baking in the oven they are served piping hot, and a Slav will betray his origins by lifting the crust and adding just a little more butter.

Piroznaya Plate: a special small plate that accompanies almost all soup plates — especially to place soup accompaniments on.

Pivo: beer.

Pleeta: the common name for the built-in all-purpose Russian kitchen stove. **Pleeta** is really the name for the hot cooking plate.

Riba: fish.

Russkaya Piechka: proper name for the Russian built-in kitchen stove, maid's bed, baking oven, **Shashlyk** broiler, and extension for samovar — all in one!

Salat: salad.

Schav: a spinach or sorrel soup, tart in taste, served with sour cream and **Vatrushky**.

Schi: a classic cabbage soup served with **Kasha** and traditionally accompanied by **Vatrushky** (cheese tarts). Variations include: sour **Schi**, made with sauerkraut; green **Schi**, also called **Schav**, made with spinach, sorrel or both; and spring **Schi**, prepared from the first spring cabbage sprouts. That this soup is a classic is evidenced by this old saying: "Cabbage soup and kasha is our daily food."

Selodka: herring, the most important and sometimes the only accompaniment to vodka during the **zakusky**.

Shashlyk: skewered broiled meats.

Smetana: sour cream.

Solianka: a sweet and sour soup made by poaching any white-fleshed fish in court bouillon. The vegetables are strained, puréed, then returned to the soup with the fish pieces.

Soupi: soup.

T'Chai or **Chai**: Russian name for tea, probably derived from the Chinese name for tea, **ch'a**.

Tvorog: dry white cottage cheese or pot cheese.

Vatrushky: small open-face pastry tarts filled with cottage cheese and sour cream, traditional accompaniments to all varieties of **Schi**. (**Vatrushka** refers to a large cheesecake.)

Vodka: clear potent alcoholic drink distilled from grains or potatoes. Varieties include basic vodka flavored with anise, caraway, buffalo grass (**zubrovka**), lemon peel, cherries (**vishniowka**) and cherry pits. All varieties are drunk icy cold from one-ounce glasses in one gulp after an appropriate toast. Not to join in when toasts are proposed is considered close to an insult.

Zakusky: the elastic aperitif hour preceding the Russian dinner. It can be as simple as herring and vodka, or it can be an array of sliced smoked and salted fish, pâtés and salads and one or two hot dishes in casserole form.

Zrazi: similar to **Kotleti**, only the "hamburgers" are filled with mushrooms and **Kasha** then crumbed and butter-browned.

CHAPTER 44

SCOTTISH

A small, rocky country of streams and lakes, with a moderately cool climate, and proud, vigorous inhabitants, Scotland is also known for short-bread, marmalade, and Scotch whisky. Though about 5 million folk make their homes in the Highlands, Lowlands, and Uplands, it could almost be said that one of Scotland's principal exports is people; an estimated 20 million Scots have emigrated to other countries.

They have carried with them their kilts and their pipes, their brogue and their oats to whatever wee corner of the world they decided to call home. And several times a year they gather for their Scottish Games – a day of Highland flings and sword dancing, tug-of-war and the flinging of the mighty caber all to the stirring wail of the kilted bands. Always, Scottish souls are stirred by the foot-tapping rhythms, and Scottish eyes mist as "Scotland the Brave" fills the air. And though they may be heard to call themselves "Scotch and proud of it," they'd rather you refer to them as Scots and their fine smoky whisky as Scotch.

Early accounts show a predominance of oats, barley, and dairy products as the mainstay of both urban and rural diets in Scotland. Although sheep and black Angus cattle were raised, they were mainly for export rather than local consumption. The general porridge and milk diet was supplemented with kale or cabbage. Small amounts of fish were used in coastal areas and occasionally some meats in the interior.

By the 1800s, the rapid growth of urban areas in Scotland became the impetus for agricultural improvement and diversification. There was a sharp increase in the use of wheat bread, meats in broths and stews, and wider acceptance and use of potatoes. This soon made barley and oats a minor part of the daily fare except in the more remote agricultural settlements where economic factors still limited the variety of the diet.

Although people generally ate what was available and what they could afford, good food simply prepared is still the keynote in Scotland. Scots have never been keen on seasonings, sauces, or exotic mixtures of foods.

The earliest influences on the Celtic and Gaelic traditions of Scotland were English. But English influence gradually threatened to become English control.

In 1295, John de Baliol, King of Scotland, formed an alliance with France, making England the common foe. This alliance lasted several hundred years and through many successions of kings. To this day many Gaelic food names can be traced from the original French name: **flam** from *flan*; **tartan purry** from *tarte-en-puree*; **kickshaw**, *quelque chose*; **stovies**, *a l'etuvee*; and **jigget**, *gigot*.

Scottish food retains the individuality of its people. To this day Scottish foods preserve their simplicity while retaining the most delightfully endearing names – even if some of the sources are long forgotten.

DOMESTIC LIFE

Simplicity and practicality, so much a part of the Scottish diet, are also a part of the Scottish kitchen. Utensils are sturdy and useful rather than ornamental, and many pieces of kitchenware (as well as recipes) have been handed down from mother to daughter. There are few gadgets, fewer luxury-type electrical appliances, and a more limited spice shelf than typically found in North American kitchens. Refrigerators generally are smaller because cold pantries are frequently found as an adjunct to the Scottish kitchen, pantries being practical for food storage in a moderately cool climate.

Greaseproof paper is still widely used for baking pans, iron griddles are still favored for scones and bannocks, and carved thistle presses are still used to shape the traditional Scottish shortbread. But other traditional utensils are declining in general usage. These include the *spurtle*, a stick with a thistle-shaped handle used for stirring porridge; and the *ashete*, the traditional oval or rectangular enameled baking dishes with high sides to support a pastry crust. Surprisingly, these age-old utensils are being snapped up by collectors and treasured by novice gourmet cooks in other lands.

DAIRY PRODUCTS
Milk, cream, and butter are widely and generously used. Cheeses in great variety are assuming increasing importance in the Scottish diet. Some types commonly used:

Caboc: a log-shaped, soft, buttery cheese rolled in fine oatmeal and traditionally served with **Baps**.

Caithness: a soft cheese aged sixty days.

Hattit Kit: the Scottish version of cream cheese, often molded and served with fresh fruits and cream (French-food buffs will note its similarity to **Coeur a la Creme**, a classic French dessert prepared from a blend of cream cheese and cottage cheese pressed into a heart-shaped basket to drain off the whey. Unmolded, it is served with sugared fresh berries.)

Raasey Cheese: a thick, cooked mixture of milk, eggs, and cheese served on toast.

Rarebit: a thick sauce of melted cheese with beer or ale, seasoned with mustard and served on toast.

FRUITS AND VEGETABLES
Fresh fruits and vegetables are usually served in season and are often prepared with milk, butter, or cream. Staples for winter use include kale, seaweed, cabbage, and potatoes. Canned peas are often used as a garnish. Fruits are consumed as preserves, sweetened desserts, or in baked goods. Scots by tradition are not large vegetable eaters nor do they usually consume any great quantity of fresh vegetables or green fresh salads. Typical fruits include apples, plums, and many types of berries. To the staple vegetables listed above may be added turnips (**neeps**), leeks, onions, tomatoes, and parsnips.

MEATS AND ALTERNATES
Fish and, more recently, beef are the favored protein foods. Extended practical use of offal (heart, liver, kidneys, tripe, etc.) and economical cuts of meat are prepared simply. Usual methods of cooking include meaty soups, stews, or meat pies and broths. When the budget permits, beef, veal, and mutton are used most, with chicken and pork products less. The exception is bacon which is used often, and frequently lends its smoky taste to many economical dishes or light suppers. In some areas wild fowl and game are used. Fish is preferred over other seafood. Favored fish include salmon, trout, cod, haddock, kippers, and herring. There is some consumption of mussels, oysters, crab, winkles, and shrimp.

Eggs are mostly used as an ingredient in other dishes or prepared as a light supper. Legumes are used only occasionally in some soups.

BREADS AND GRAINS
Oatmeal is no longer the leading item in the Scottish diet. Nonetheless it is still the most important grain cereal used. Some of its ingenious variations include its use as a thickening and coating agent; as a breakfast cereal; toasted, baked, griddled, boiled or fried; as part of soups, beverages, desserts, dumplings, cookies, and meat mixtures. Scottish oatmeal is used in the fine ground form rather than as rolled flakes.

Each Scottish cook takes pride in the authenticity of traditional family recipes for breads, cakes, biscuits, and shortbreads. Most are made from wheat flour, very few use yeast as a leavening agent, and all are characterized by the delicate natural taste and aroma of fresh eggs and butter.

FATS
Butter, margarine, lard, and suet prevail as the favored fats in cooking and baking. Oil is seldom used. Fats are also consumed in the form of buttery cheese and cream.

SWEETS AND SNACKS
Candies, especially butterscotch, taffy, and hard sugar candies are frequent treats, found in many pockets

FOODS COMMONLY USED
Hearty soups, fish dishes, and a great variety of quick breads and cakes (leavened with soda or baking powder rather than yeast) are the staples in a Scottish kitchen. Fish may be considered one of the most important staples, but dairy products are also used in abundance. Fruits are used mainly in season and in the form of jellies, preserves, and marmalades rather than fresh fruits to satisfy the Scottish sweet tooth. Garden vegetables are popular but kale and seaweed, cabbage and potatoes are the favorites. Thistle leaves may be used as a food but usually only in times of necessity.

North Americans tend to think of oatmeal as a breakfast cereal and perhaps occasionally as a component of breads and cookies. But the Scottish use of oatmeal has stimulated an astonishing array of recipes including beverages, soups, meat and fish dishes, puddings, dumplings, stuffings and many desserts and baked goods. There is even a popular cheese which is sold coated in oatmeal.

Though Scottish food may be prepared with a minimum of seasonings and a maximum of cooking, it is nonetheless substantial and filling.

and often used to reward children. Jellies, jams, marmalades, and preserves such as fruit butters are on the table daily. Quick tea breads, plain un-iced cakes and crisp plain cookies (**biscuits**) are consumed in large enough quantities to form a significant part of the diet. Scottish **shortbread** is enjoyed in many countries and not only by Scots.

SEASONINGS

The Scottish spice shelf is one of the smallest in the world. Salt and pepper are used but seldom are other spices or any herbs called for. Onions add zest to many dishes, and butter and oats are used with such frequency that they could also be considered to be typical flavors. Ginger is the spice most used in baking, if at all. The pure natural taste of fresh ingredients is preferred to the addition of any spices or herbs or anything that may mask them.

BEVERAGES

It has been said that Scotch whiskey is the staple beverage of Scotland, and there's scarcely an individual who won't stoutly defend the attributes of a favorite brand. But a fair amount of beer and some imported wines are also consumed.

Tea is the beverage for breakfast and for a refreshing break. This is usually accompanied by at least a few of the famed tea breads and cakes for it wouldn't do to have tea alone. At its simplest, tea will at least be accompanied by bread, butter, and preserves.

MEALS AND CUSTOMS

It has been said that the best Scottish meals are breakfast and tea. But those who have enjoyed fine black Angus beef or rich Scottish salmon may well have a quarrel. And though there has long been a Scottish superstition (especially in the north) against shellfish and seafood as "the lice of the sea," many Scots do enjoy locally caught shrimps, mussels, winkles, crab, and lobster. But those persisting in the old beliefs hold that salmon, cod, haddock, or herring can't be beat for a fine meal.

Generally Scots prefer a few simple good dishes for a meal rather than many courses and elaborate service. What they lose in variations they make up in hearty servings. Scottish hospitality is legendary: no one leaves a table hungry no matter how simple the fare.

A Scottish breakfast will likely include oatmeal porridge made from finely milled, unrolled oats and served with cool milk or cream. Traditionally each spoon of hot porridge is dipped in milk to cool it. Toast with butter, preserves, and a cup of tea complete the meal. More elaborate breakfasts may include a fish dish, bacon, assorted cheeses and tea breads.

The noon dinner often consists of a hearty meat and vegetable soup, a dessert of steamed pudding, custard or baked bread pudding and tea.

Often the highlight of the day will be the tea served in the late afternoon at about five-thirty. Here will be the display of breads and cakes, preserves and marmalades that Scotland is famed for: **baps**, **bannocks**, **scones**, **tarts**, and **buns** all served with strong tea, milk and sugar. Chops or sausages with eggs or a dish of sole, kippers, or salmon may accompany the tea.

Perhaps because the late afternoon tea is so special, the evening meal is usually light and includes only one course: either sausages, bacon, chops with eggs and a garnish of peas or a mashed vegetable combination dish served with a glass of buttermilk. In humbler homes, the evening supper may be just a bowl of hot porridge made of oats or barley and served with milk.

SPECIAL OCCASIONS

The Presbyterian Church of Scotland has more than a million followers. The Roman Catholic Church is second in importance with other denominations following in much lesser numbers.

Christmas in Scotland is a one-day holiday highlighted with a festive family dinner at noon featuring roast chicken, mashed potatoes and turnips and climaxed with a flaming steamed fruit pudding.

But the merriest days on the Scottish calendar are *Hogmanay* and *Robbie Burns' Night. Hogmanay* is the day before New Year's and probably the only day in the year when everyone takes a holiday. This is the time for gifts and merrymaking, for nibbling nuts and eating juicy imported oranges. It is also the time for the finest bakery from the kitchen – **black bun**, fragrant cherry and currant cakes, crispy delicate shortbreads – all to be accompanied with port wine, ginger wine or Scotch whiskey. Later in the evening after midnight, all present enjoy a buffet meal of cold ham, roasted fowl and other meats, **scones**, **bannocks** and sweet butter to be followed yet again by the array of cakes and buns till all are happily sated.

Robbie Burns' Night is the celebration marking the birth of the great Scottish poet. It is celebrated on January 25 and is only slightly less important than *Hogmanay.* For public banquets both occasions may be marked with the almost-mystical preparation of the **haggis**, served with great ceremony to the accompaniment of the pipes and many a nip of Scotch whiskey.

GLOSSARY OF FOODS AND FOOD TERMS

Arbroath Smokies: tiny haddocks smoked slowly to a dark color and strong flavor. A specialty from the east coast near Dundee.

Ashet: an oval or rectangular baking dish with high sides and spout, especially used for pies.

Atholl Brose: a dessert made of honey, cream, and oatmeal moistened with Scotch whiskey and served in glasses.

Bannock: an original Scottish bread made of flour, water, and fat, leavened with baking powder and traditionally baked on a griddle (or **girdle**) as a flat round cake. When cut into farls (wedges), and then baked, the result is called **scones**. Sometimes milk or buttermilk as well as soda is added to the basic ingredients. Other variations include the addition of spices, molasses, currants, raisins or even cooked, mashed potatoes.

Baps: small dimpled oval rolls of yeast dough. Traditionally a breakfast bread.

Biscuits: this term may refer to the baking powder biscuits known in North America, but the term is mainly used to refer to cookies.

Black Bun: the traditional cake for *Hogmanay*, a rich very dark fruitcake baked in a dough crust.

Black Pudding: a mixture of oats, suet, and onions plus fresh animal blood cooked by steaming in a cloth.

Blenshaw: a beverage made by blending hot milk or hot water with a small amount of oatmeal.

Brambles: blackberries.

Brose: a very thick porridge made with oatmeal, hot water or milk with added fat.

Cabbie-Claw: cod.

Caboc: a soft, buttery cheese formed into a log shape and crusted with toasted oats. Served with **Baps**.

Caithness: a soft aged cheese for spreading.

Cake: may be taken to mean cake or cookies.

Car Cakes: a batter of oatmeal, milk or buttermilk and leavening dropped onto a griddle and cooked as pancakes.

Carrageen: also called "Irish Moss," a purplish, edible seaweed, gathered and dried and used to thicken gelled desserts, puddings, and custards.

Chicken Stovies: a baked casserole made of layered, sliced chicken, potatoes and onions seasoned with salt and pepper.

Clapshot: a popular side dish or supper dish of equal amounts of cooked mashed potatoes and turnips seasoned with salt and pepper and served with butter.

Clootie Puddin': a steamed dessert pudding made mainly of bread.

Cock-A-Leekie: a rich chicken broth made with leeks. Sometimes rice or prunes are added.

Colcannon: a combination of shredded cabbage, potatoes, carrots, and turnips all cooked together in water then drained and mashed and served with salt, pepper, and butter.

Collops: thin slices of meat, generally referring to beef or veal.

Cranachan: a dessert of sweetened whipped cream and toasted oatmeal. The addition of fresh fruit is optional.

Cream Cruddie: a bland dessert similar to junket, served in a round mold accompanied by crisp oatcakes.

Crud: curds.

Cullen Skink: a cream soup made with mashed potatoes and flaked, cooked, smoked haddock (*See* **Finnan Haddie**)

Dundee Cake: a light fruit cake.

Dunlop: a type of Cheddar cheese long popular in Scotland.

Feather Fowlie: a rich, creamed chicken broth seasoned with herbs and garnished with slivers of ham.

Finkadella: likely a corruption of the Danish **frikadiller**. Small meatballs made with ground meat and seasoning.

Finnan Haddie: fillets of fresh haddock prepared according to the traditional style – said to have been first used in Findon, Kincardineshire – brined then smoked.

Forfar Bridies: small pastry turnovers filled with ground meat, oatmeal and onions, seasoned with salt and pepper. Often these are garnished with cooked peas.

Girdle: a griddle.

Grosset or **Crosert**: gooseberries.

Haggis: the traditional Scottish dish to be served at special banquets, especially for *Robbie Burns' Night* or *Hogmanay*. A carefully blended mixture of finely ground sheep's heart and liver, beef suet and toasted oatmeal, onions, salt and pepper is stuffed into a well-cleaned sheep's stomach and then well steamed. Traditionally served with **Neeps and Nips** and mashed potatoes.

Hattit Kit: a freshly made cream cheese made from scalded milk and buttermilk allowed to stand about 20 hours at a temperature between 80°-90°F. The mixture is placed into a cloth-lined colander and allowed to drip to separate the whey. The resulting cheese mold is chilled and served with fresh fruit and cream.

Hodgils: poached dumplings made of suet and oats.

Hotchpotch: a very thick soup usually made with a variety of the first garden fresh vegetables cooked in a lamb stock.

Hough: broth.

Howtowdie and Drappit Eggs: a stewed chicken dish finished by garnishing with poached (**drappit**) eggs.

Jittet: a leg or haunch of veal or lamb.

Kilkenny: a mixture of cooked shredded cabbage and cubed cooked potatoes seasoned with salt, pepper, and fresh cream.

Kippers: smoked herrings.

Lemon Butter or **Lemon Curd**: a type of custard made with fresh lemons, eggs and butter sweetened with sugar. It is eaten as a spread on breads or toast or used as a filling for tarts or pies.

Lights: lungs.

Mealie Pudding: a mixture of oatmeal, onions, and suet steamed in a cloth.

Mealy Candy: a taffy candy made from sugar, molasses, water, and oats flavored with ginger.

Mince: ground meat, usually beef.

Mungo Chocolate Tablet: an uncooked chocolate fudge cut in squares.

Musselburgh Pie: oysters wrapped in strips of beef, placed in a pan and covered with stock and pastry and oven-baked.

Neeps and Nips: the traditional accompaniment to **Haggis**. Mashed turnips and "nips" of Scotch whiskey.

Nettles: another name for thistles. The young shoots are plucked, well washed and cooked and served much like spinach.

Oatcakes: very thin crisp rounds or farls (wedges) of a mixture of fat, oats and water toasted in the oven or on a griddle (or **girdle**).

Partan Bree: a creamed soup of crab meat with rice. "**Partan**" is the Scottish name for crab.

Potted Hough: a jellied aspic mold of cubed beef and veal.

Raasey Cheese: a teatime dish made of a thick sauce of eggs, milk and cheese served on toast.

Rumbledthumps: similar to **Kilkenny**, a mixture of cooked cabbage and potatoes, but oven-baked and topped with grated cheese.

Scotch Barley Broth: a well-known soup of lamb or mutton broth simmered with vegetables and barley.

Scotch Crumpets: small dessert crepes served with cinnamon sugar.

Scotch Eggs: peeled hard-boiled eggs wrapped in sausage meat, then coated with crumbs or oatmeal and deep-fried.

Scotch or **Irish Oatmeal**: unlike the familiar rolled oats commonly used in North America this is more like a coarse mealy flour made from oats.

Seed Cake: a rich pound cake flavored with caraway seeds.

Shortbread: crisp melt-in-the-mouth cookie made from sugar, butter and flour, or sometimes corn-starch. Traditionally pressed into thistle-shaped molds, or shaped into rounds, cut into *farls* (wedges) and pricked with a fork.

Skirlie: a mixture of oatmeal, onions, and suet *skirled* (stirred) in a pan.

Smoored Pullets: cut up chickens dredged in sea-soned flour and pan-fried then served with cream gravy.

Spurtle: the traditional wooden stirring spoon for porridge.

Stoorum: a hot beverage. (*See* **Blenshaw**.)

Stoved: stewed or cooked on top of the stove.

Stovies: a dish of pared, sliced, raw potatoes cooked in a pan on top of the stove with just a little water, salt and pepper.

Syboes: scallions or green onions.

Tatties: potatoes.

Treacle: Scottish name for molasses. **Treacle**, how-ever, is slightly thicker and sweeter than the North American version.

Whim-Wham: a rich layered dessert of cake or ladyfingers, jam and whipped cream.

CHAPTER 45

Singaporean. See Indonesian, Malay, and Singaporean
South American. See Latin American

THE SOUTHERN SLAVS

FORMERLY YUGOSLAVIAN: BOSNIAN-HERZEGOVINIAN, CROATIAN, MACEDONIAN, MONTENEGRIN, SERBIAN, AND SLOVENIAN

"Yugoslavia has six republics, five peoples, four languages, three religions, two alphabets – and one great desire for peace."

There is scarcely a piece of writing on the former Yugoslavia that does not quote this country saying. For good reason. After more than 1,500 years of separate kingdoms, foreign domination and influences, wars and suffering, these Southern Slavs agreed – after the collapse of the Austro-Hungarian Empire in 1919 – to patch together a union of their peoples to form Yugoslavia. But their mutually hostile existence continued. World War II, communism under Marshal Tito, and a fierce civil war only served to exacerbate hostilities between the ethnic groups. However, 1996 saw the end of the civil wars and serious efforts to cement a peaceful co-existence within secured borders.

This picturesque, mostly mountainous land borders on seven European countries: Italy, Austria, Hungary, Romania, Albania, Greece, and Bulgaria. So it is not surprising that many customs and many foods and ways of cooking have crossed the border into the neighboring states of the Southern Slavs.

The Romans first ruled the earliest peoples in this region. They divided the Southern Slavs into eastern and western regions. The Slovenes and Croats in the west adopted Roman Catholicism and western ways, while the Serbs and Macedonians in the east adopted Eastern Orthodox and Muslim religions and traditions. In subsequent years, Turkish, Venetian, and Austro-Hungarian domination took their turn in attempting to rule and subjugate these multiethnic and multinational peoples. But they succeeded only in impressing a few customs and some delicious foods.

The individuality and proud heritages of the Southern Slavs are distinctively portrayed in their cultural ethos. Although all the Yugoslavian peoples are historically considered Southern Slavs, very early in their histories they separated to become Serbians, Croatians, Slovenians, Montenegrins, Bosnians, and Macedonians. Each group differs politically, religiously, culturally, and even temperamentally.

Historically, the borders of their lands have shifted and wavered, but our focus is the people, their culture and their food traditions rather than their politics. The six republics that made up the former Yugoslavia include (in order of size): Serbia, Croatia, Bosnia-Herzegovina, Macedonia, Slovenia, and Montenegro. The five nations or peoples included in these lands are the Serbs, Croats, Slovenes, Macedonians, and Montenegrins speaking the three languages of Serbo-Croatian, Slovenian, and Macedonian. Both the Latin and Cyrillic alphabets are used, and in some regions it is necessary to publish textbooks in three or four languages. In addition, many people also speak Italian, Hungarian, Bulgarian, and Greek, and currently English is increasingly popular and is taught in many schools.

A combination of favorable lands and climate aids in the production of grain, vineyards, orchards and pasturelands for cattle and sheep. Despite long periods of hard times, generally food has not been a problem. Perhaps this is at least one of the reasons for the Southern Slav's proclivity for the intense enjoyment of the moment, whether it is strolling, working, or talking with friends. Envious outsiders have called this the "shepherd's complex," but this laid-back approach to life may also be one of the reasons that in the former Yugoslavia, even the communist regime differed markedly from that in other countries. Changes were always gradual, seldom forced.

Yet strong regional differences persist and ethnic differences entrench them even more deeply. Although country festivals and religious holidays are celebrated with enthusiasm, religious influence is said to be diminishing. Western clothing is fast replacing ethnic costumes and regional dress. Western methods of business, western technology, skyscrapers, films, and cola drinks are encroaching on the old ways. Yet despite foreign domination, civil wars, and suffering, the gentle romantic soul of the Southern Slav predominates. This region remains a multinational and multiethnic land where "a poet can become a millionaire."

DOMESTIC LIFE

As in most other countries, urban and rural life differ. In most newly industrialized countries, the flow of people to the cities makes apartments scarce, and most often these living spaces are small. Kitchens are simply a designated area with appliances and cupboards added by the tenants according to their means. Refrigerators and stoves are small by North American standards, as well as expensive, and many households simply do without. Seldom can a family afford to devote one room to only one purpose, so it is not unusual for the kitchen to be set up with a cot for sleeping, while table and chairs may be a permanent part of the living room. Where space permits, some apartments may have the typical ceramic-tiled stove, called a *pec* (commonly found in country peasant homes), used for heating as well as cooking. The *pec* may use oil or coal for fuel.

Food storage is no problem in the rural areas where sheds, cold pantries, or even earthen pits may be used. In the urban areas there is no problem in winter: foods are simply kept in a cool place. In summer it is seldom a problem because the people prefer to purchase their foods fresh and marketing is generally done on a daily basis.

Samo posluga, literally, "self service," is the name given to the supermarkets. Foods are also purchased in outdoor markets. Some prepared and convenience foods as well as frozen foods are gaining in popularity because of the many working women who have little time for food preparation at home – and few facilities as well.

Country people moving to the cities often adjust well, but retain a yearning for their own beehives, fruit trees and fresh produce. It is not unusual to hear of a city family managing somehow to find a place for their own chickens to supply fresh eggs and their own goat for milk.

Country living is simple and casual, and the food is substantial. The ceramic-tiled *pec* is the center of country homes, a vegetable garden, beehive, fruit trees, and a few animals always nearby. There are few roadside cafes for tourists but all have one thing in common: a huge charcoal stove with a spit as the feature of the open-air kitchen. Grilled foods and hearty soup-stews are the usual fare.

DAIRY PRODUCTS

Dairy products find a frequent place on the menu and soured milk and curds often form the staple protein foods of people with lower incomes. Buttermilk and yogurt are eaten with meals and as snacks. Many types of local cheeses are used but most popular are fresh, salted or fermented curd cheese, made from cow's, goat's, or sheep's milk. Cheeses are used as appetizers, condiments, and often in bakery. Sweet, rich cream and sour cream are frequently a finishing touch to stews and oven-baked casseroles of vegetables and meat. In fact, it is difficult to think of a Slav day without some form of cheese: as appetizers, spreads for bread, in dumplings and fritters, or in cheese-filled vegetables and bakery.

FRUITS AND VEGETABLES

With the Slavs' great love and appreciation of nature, it is not unusual to see their cornfields interlaced

FOODS COMMONLY USED

Just as the people differ, so do their foods. Most Southern Slav specialties are either grilled or slowly cooked in big pots or casseroles. Italian, Hungarian, Romanian, Bulgarian, Greek, and Albanian dishes all find a place in Yugoslavian cuisine but the strongest overall influence is Turkish. Stuffed vegetable dishes, grilled meats, enjoyment of dairy foods especially soured milk and yogurt, and many forms of curd cheese (fresh, salted, fermented) and a taste for syrupy and honey-drenched sweets, served with strong Turkish coffee, prevails. So does a taste and capacity for wine and strong brandies, the latter often a morning eye-opener. Strong flavors predominate: garlic and onions and spicy hot pickles. Strong alcoholic drinks and seasonings notwithstanding, the Southern Slavs also have a keen sense of taste and appreciation for water. (Future chlorination and fluoridation of water supplies will likely meet with strong resistance.)

Country foods are usually simple and may be based mainly on curds, coarse breads made of corn or coarsely ground wheat, fresh fruits and raw vegetables, soups based on beans or potatoes, and homemade pastries and pastas. But always cheese, breads, and hot pickles will be on the table, and always there will be homemade wine to wash it all down.

with pumpkin vines, fruit orchards buzzing with beehives, and vineyards large or small almost everywhere.

Vineyards, fruit trees, and olive groves abound, but most of all, this region is famous for fine plums. These are dried, preserved as jams, fillings and **slatko** (cooked fruit in very heavy syrup) and fermented into plum brandy called **Slivovitz** and **Klekovaca**, a plum brandy flavored with juniper berries.

Apples, pears, peaches, apricots, sweet cherries and sour cherries, figs, melons, berries (cultivated and wild), and several varieties of nuts are all enjoyed fresh when possible. Mostly, fruits are stewed with sugar for dessert or made into preserves or brandies. Pumpkin is used as a fruit for stewing, filling for bakery, and cooked in a heavy syrup as a special treat. There are many uses also for quinces: preserves, jellies, compotes, liqueurs, and even a type of quince "cheese," prepared by drying a thick quince paste and topping it with nuts.

Fruit juices are very popular and form a large industry, these regions being one of the first European countries to produce on a large scale quality juices and concentrates from a great variety of crushed fruits and berries.

Vegetables are almost as varied and abundant as fruits. They are eaten raw (especially onions, scallions, cucumbers, and radishes) or in the form of spicy hot pickles as well-cooked ingredients of a stew or soup.

Favorite vegetables vary, from potatoes and cabbage (also **sauerkraut**) in the north, to eggplant, tomatoes and zucchini, red and yellow peppers, green beans in the south, and always onions and garlic. In many wooded areas, wild mushrooms are collected and form the basis of many special dishes, if not the whole meal.

MEATS AND ALTERNATES

Depending on the area, pork and lamb are the favored meats, but beef, veal, and occasionally poultry are also used. Legumes are used especially in the mountain areas for soups and slowly cooked casserole meals. Fish is used only when fresh, mostly in coastal areas. Stews and grilled meats are most popular and a restaurant specialty almost everywhere. Especially in sidewalk cafés and garden restaurants, grilled meats served with spicy hot peppers, chopped raw onions, and bread are popular.

From the Adriatic Sea fishermen bring swordfish, tunny, sardines, anchovies, langouste, scampi, crayfish, octopus, squid, and mussels. Salmon and trout, carp and pike, sturgeon and sterlet, beluga and perch are also to be found in rivers and lakes. **Brodet** and **alaska corba** are two types of classic fish soups that

may be made with several types of fish or seafood and vegetables. Fish roe may be soaked in milk and served with chopped onions and a sauce of lemon juice, paprika, and olive oil poured over. Caviar is enjoyed with chopped onions and a squeeze of fresh lemon juice. Fresh-caught fish may be baked in the oven over a bed of chopped fresh vegetables or grilled over charcoal and seasoned with olive oil and lemon juice.

Eggs are frequently combined with pot or cream cheese and used in bakery. They are also used as a topping with cream for the famed meat and vegetable stews, and sometimes eaten by themselves.

BREADS AND GRAINS

Bread is a staple food and is found on every table at every meal. Wheat, corn, rye, oats, and barley are grown in various areas and breads are made from all these grains. Corn and wheat are mostly used. Grains are not used as porridge but may be a part of soups and stews or fillings for vegetables or pastries, or enjoyed as side dishes.

FATS

Fats are consumed in the form of sweet cream and sour cream as well as many varieties of cheeses. Cooking fats include olive oil, seed and vegetable oils, butter, pork or sheep's fat.

SWEETS AND SNACKS

Sweets are always a special treat, but exactly which sweets depends on where one is indulging. Ice cream and sherbets, syrup- and honey-soaked crisp nut pastries, and thick, sweet fruit preserves are all enjoyed. In desserts, as in all other foods, the influence varies from Austro-Hungarian to Italian, Greek, and Turkish. Street vendors tempt passersby with trays of tiny sweet pastries, and a frequent urban afternoon snack is pastries and coffee.

SEASONINGS

Southern Slav foods are all richly flavored and seasoned without timidity. Onions and garlic are used in abundance: there is even a famous casserole dish, **lonac**, made with whole heads of garlic. Sweet and sour soups of Romanian influence, sour fermented juices like **rasol** made from **sauerkraut**, pickles made with brine or sugar-vinegar solutions and hot chilies and spices, and salads (often made from cold cooked vegetables) dressed with lemon juice and olive oil testify to Slavic tastes, though of varied origin. Paprika, caraway and poppy seeds are of Hungarian influence, and grace main dishes, while sugar and honey, fruits and cheeses, all with their own distinct flavors, form the basis for the many cakes and pastries.

BEVERAGES

Sweet, strong Turkish coffee served in tiny cups is taken at breakfast, afternoon snack times, and after dinner. Wine is plentiful and inexpensive and accompanies lunch (the main meal) and dinner. The locally made beer **Pivo** is quite popular but not considered as good as the wines, which are drunk in quantity. **Slivovitz** or **Slivovka**, the clear, potent brandy made from plums, is the national drink and not only begins and ends many meals, but also begins and ends many days. The luscious fruit syrups, rich in taste and color, may be diluted with water or soda for a refreshing drink.

REGIONAL SPECIALTIES

The regions of the former Yugoslavia share many commonalities of domestic life and food customs, but there are also distinct regional differences consciously preserved and deeply cherished. The regions that were separate kingdoms for so long have developed historical backgrounds, traditions, and distinctive characteristics.

BOSNIAN-HERZEGOVINIAN

This inland republic is bounded by other former Yugoslavian republics and maintains a slow pace of  living, the religion of Islam, and the serious outlook on life imprinted by the Turkish domination. The almost cloistered existence of the women, the haggling at the marketplace, and the narrow winding streets and walled courtyards exist today almost as they did several hundred years ago.

Some Balkan dishes find their way into the diet, but the overall influence in the cuisine, as in the general way of life, is Turkish. Because of the Muslim restriction against pork, it is not used in this area. But the Mediterranean climate helps produce a variety of crops: grains, fruits and vegetables, all generously used in a healthful cuisine rich in vegetables, soured milk, simple cheeses, fresh fruits and some meat and fish. Turkish coffee begins and ends the day, accompanied with **Rakija** (clear potent spirits) and/or sweet Turkish pastries.

Some Bosnian-Herzegovinian specialties include:

Baklava: a Turkish pastry made with butter-drenched layers of thin **phyllo pastry**. The center layers are sprinkled with chopped nuts, spices and sugar. After baking, a hot spiced syrup is poured over and absorbed. The dripping sweet diamond cuts are eaten usually accompanied with Turkish coffee.

Bosanke Cufte: (**Cufte** is an Arabic word which means minced or finely chopped.) Bosnian meatballs oven-baked and topped with an egg-yogurt custard.

Bosanski Lonac: a casserole of cubed mixed meats layered with cubed vegetables (root), potatoes, onions, and often whole heads of garlic all baked with wine or diluted vinegar.

Bosnian Cheeses: **Travnicki** is a soft cheese, both salty and sour. Others enjoyed in this region are **Sjenicki** and **Livanjski**.

Halva: popular Middle Eastern (Turkish) confection with semolina and/or ground sesame seeds.

Kadaif: Turkish sweet of honey-soaked thin shreds of wheat.

Musaka: layered casserole of eggplant and meat with tomatoes, onions, and seasonings. Sometimes topped with cheese or an egg-yogurt custard. Of both Greek and Turkish origin.

Pita: the general Southern Slav name for most confections made with phyllo pastry. The Bosnian (and Macedonian) version is usually made in a round baking dish and cut in wedges like a big round cake. Similar to **Baklava**.

Ratluk: also called **Lokum** or **Turkish Delight**. Blandly flavored (rosewater water or orange flower water) jelled confection cut in squares and dusted with icing sugar.

Sis-Cevap: *sis* (pronounced "shish") is the Turkish word for skewer. So this is a dish of skewered meat cubes, green peppers, and tomatoes.

Sogan Dolma: *dolma* means "stuffed" in Turkish. This dish is stuffed onions filled with ground mutton, rice, **Kajma**, and tomato paste.

Suva-Pita: just like **Baklava**. (Perhaps having many names for the same thing means you can order it more often without sounding greedy.)

Turkish Coffee: made the Bosnian way, uses two **Dzezvas** (lidless, long-handled coffeepots), one to boil fresh water and the other to hold the coffee. Pouring from one to the other after the initial boiling increases the frothiness. Sugar may be added to the pot or crunched in the mouth while sipping the coffee.

Urmasice: a rich pastry of egg yolks, butter, yogurt, blended with flour. Small pieces are pulled off and shaped like fat dates. After baking, the rich cookies are soaked in honey-spice syrup.

CROATIAN

Croatia is one of the most ancient states in all of Europe. King Tomaslav created it as an independent Catholic realm in the late tenth century. At one time

in Croatia's later history, Dalmatia and Istria along the Adriatic Sea as well as the central areas of Bosnia-Herzegovina, were all part of Croatian territory. After the Turkish victory in the 1500s, Croatia came under Austrian control, which ended only with the collapse of the Austro-Hungarian Empire after World War I. In 1946, after World War II, Croatia became one of the reconstituted Yugoslavian republics.

By 1991 Croatia seceded from Yugoslavia, but the Serbs, with Yugoslavian military backing, seized almost a third of Croatian land that Croatia managed to regain by vicious fighting in 1995. The formal end of the war resulted in the return of Croatian territory but with simmering Serbian resentment. Peace remains a hope.

As a people, the Croats are among the most artistic and literary members of the great family of Southern Slavs. Zagreb is the capital of Croatia, but the Dalmatian city of Dubrovnik, with its ancient walled area housing a mixture of Catholics, Muslims and Orthodox Christians, Croats, Dalmatians and Montenegrins, even a few Gypsies, speaks most eloquently of its historic past. In so many ways, Dubrovnik seems to be the city most representative of the Southern Slav ethos and a microcosm of their history.

The Golden Age of Dubrovnik lasted about 300 years, from the 1400s to the 1700s. Despite continual political problems, it was a time of economic and intellectual flowering. Religious pressures and dominance from the Turkish Empire, the Hungarian Empire and later the Austro-Hungarian Empire not withstanding, the Croats treasured their principles and traditions and avidly kept them alive. In smaller villages, even illiterate peasants could recite poetry. It was these same traditions that served and continue to serve as inspiration to the Croats to preserve their national identity. They always retained a reputation as militarists and brave fighters but this prowess was never used to conquer, only to defend what was theirs.

The majority of Croats are Roman Catholic, a few are Muslims. All are devoutly religious. Together with an innate love of the arts and literature, and with a devotion to family and religion, Croats are also known for two other traits that are often misunderstood. Family and home are so important and jealously guarded that Croats are sometimes accused of "Croatian envy," a trait that can lead to feuds and

vengeance. And their strong self-determination that has made them often successful in business also serves to prevent unity in Croatian organizations. It is an individualism that often prohibits submission. In 1945 Tito suppressed both religious zeal and political independence in the cause of Communism, creating the first semblance of unity for the various religious and ethnic groups that formed Yugoslavia. Today the religious zeal of former times is somewhat diminished, but the will for political independence remains.

Nonetheless, the cult of the family remains an integral part of Croatian life. There are currently ripples of change, but for the most part the families are patriarchal, and relatives, even godparents, retain the lifelong concern of all family members. "Brothers-by-friendship," called *pobratimi*, and "sisters-by-friendship," called *posestrime*, are unique relationships entered into by mutual agreement. The vow is taken seriously and the relationship is as equally important as any other interfamilial bond.

Croatian domestic life, regardless of location and income, compares favorably with average North American lifestyles. Amenities such as VCRs, radio and television, personal computers and video games and the usual kitchen and laundry appliances are commonly found. A variety of dwellings are available, including single-family homes, multi-family homes, and apartments. These have separate bedrooms, living and dining rooms as well as well-equipped kitchens. Most families own a car even though public transportation is widely used.

Since Croatians rush through a busy workweek, they especially enjoy the weekend. Sunday lunch after church is the special time for a leisurely and more elaborate meal. Families come together and share this special time with guests and close friends.

Although many areas of the former Yugoslavia retain Oriental (Turkish) cultural characteristics, the 25 percent of the population that are Croats are basically western in outlook and culture due to their early acceptance of Roman Catholicism and influence from the Romans and Germans. Earliest immigrants were sailors and fishermen, later ones were mainly laborers and peasants, but all took care to retain their language, their arts and even their *tamburitza* orchestra. (*Tamburitza* is a string instrument plucked with a pick.)

Croatian cookery is simple, rich with eggs and cream, and for the most part resembles that of the Austro-Hungarian Empire intertwined with Balkan favorites. This means, above all, that a meal is not a meal without soup. Soups that are satisfying, warming, or cooling – there are soups for every mood and taste and often soup and bread may be the entire meal. The stuffed vegetable dishes vie with the grilled meats and layered casseroles, dumpling dishes and noodle specialties. Noodles are such a favorite they are often eaten as a dessert sprinkled with walnuts and cinnamon sugar, or as a light main dish with pot cheese. It is also not uncommon to taste **gulyas** and **paprikas**, cherry, apple or poppy seed **strudla**, or the bread dumplings so typical of Czech and Austrian cookery.

The coastal area of Dalmatia differs. Although here too Balkan and Austro-Hungarian dishes are found, the emphasis is on fresh fish from the Adriatic Sea prepared simply, often only with the addition of olive oil, or as a fish stew called **brodet**. Recipes for the latter are local, and family specialties are as varied as the 365 fish said to live in the Adriatic Sea. Corn breads and **gnocchi**, made from cornmeal and served with cheese and butter, seem to be "imports" from northern Italy, while a local predilection for swiss chard and spinach seem to be more typically Dalmatian.

Favorite desserts in Dalmatia, as in Croatia, are usually fresh, stewed, or preserved fruits. Ice cream is one of the favorite Dalmatian desserts often served together with the abundance of fresh local fruits. Croatians have a more pronounced sweet tooth, which can only be satisfied by the famed Austro-Hungarian pastries and then only if they are accompanied with whipped cream.

Some food specialties of the area include:

Dalmatian Cheeses: as everywhere in the regions of the former Yugoslavia fine local cheeses abound: **Primorski, Granicki, Krcki, Paski**. They are sold as soft unripened cheeses or allowed to age and used mainly for grating.

Knedla od Zemicke: a soft mixture of eggs, milk-soaked bread, and flour is kneaded together then shaped into a log and wrapped in a napkin for steaming. When done, the dumpling is sliced and served with butter and sour cream.

Knedle od Povrca: cooked cubed vegetables and toasted croutons of bread are mixed with beaten eggs, milk, and flour then shaped into round dumplings and poached in water. Served with butter or butter-fried bread crumbs and sour cream they, like other dumpling dishes, may form a meal with only the addition of a hot soup.

Licki Kupus: from the Lika district of Croatia, a casserole of layered cabbage and smoked pork (ribs or chops), served with boiled potatoes.

Marascas: sour cherries.

Pasta I Fazol: the spelling may vary slightly, but this dish of cooked pasta and beans, pungent with garlic and onions, and sometimes a bit of smoked meat or cheese, is originally Italian.

Pohovan Pile: Croatian specialty of breaded fried chicken.

Slavonski Cevap: Croatian barbecue dish similar to others made with cubed meats, peppers, onions, and tomatoes skewered and grilled. But the Croatian touch appears when the entire skewer is first wrapped in caul fat before grilling.

Zdenka: a fine processed cheese served and sold everywhere in the country, but especially popular in Croatia where it is served as a dessert cheese just before the fruit.

MACEDONIAN

Muslim and Greek Orthodox are the main religions and both Turkey and Greece the main influences in this area where life is still for the most part poor and primitive. The Macedonians are a mixed group counting among their numbers Albanians, Greeks, Bulgarians, and Serbians.

The variety of spices, especially tiny hot chili peppers, fresh herbs, garlic, onions and leeks, so much a part of both Turkish and Greek cookery, are very evident in the Macedonian cuisine. In fact so spicy is their food that it is purported to be the reason they eat such large quantities of bread with their meals.

Many types of local fish and locally made cheeses, lamb dishes, stuffed vegetables, and a lush variety of fruits and vegetables add to their diet. Macedonia is considered to be the "Southern Slav California," with a moderate climate conducive to the production of a variety of produce. Okra, spinach, eggplant, zucchini, olives, tomatoes, and peppers all flourish in this region. Rice as well as a pasta resembling rice, called **Tarana** (note similarity to the Hungarian **Tarhonya**), is used in soups and layered meat and vegetable dishes.

The Macedonians enjoy Turkish coffee and the sweet rich pastries so much a part of the Turkish and Greek cuisine; only some of the names differ. **Pita** is considered the Macedonian specialty and can be made with sweet or savory fillings rolled or layered with **katmer**, the phyllo pastry that is stretched, buttered, and layered for all the **pita** dishes.

Yogurt is a snack food and an ingredient in many other dishes. **Feta, Mandur** (a whey cheese in pear shape), and **Kefalotir** are the most popular cheeses. The latter is smooth and strong and favored for *meze* (appetizers) with **Rakija**, olives, and salted nuts.

Olive oil is used instead of animal fats, and the

egg-lemon sauce so popular in Greece is used here in soups, and as a sauce or topping for fish or vegetables or casseroles.

MONTENEGRIN

A small republic on the Adriatic coast situated south of Dalmatia and north of Albania, Montenegro, as  the name suggests, is a rocky and mountainous country with little arable land. Sheep graze on sparse pastures and here and there vineyards, orchards, and cornfields manage to produce the main food of the region: mutton and lamb, cheeses and yogurt from the sheep's milk, fruits, wine and corn for breads and pudding dishes. Beehives yield a fine honey that forms one of the main sweeteners used as it is and in a variety of spiced honey cakes and cookies such as **medenjaci**. The **kajmak** so enjoyed throughout the regions of the former Yugoslavia is also a favorite here and is eaten on coarse cornbread, layered between cornmeal puddings and as a filling in baked dishes.

The Montenegrins are tall gentle people, preferring their simple uncomplicated mountain life to the hustle and bustle of the urban world. From Muslim influence, they prefer lamb and mutton and eat little or no pork. There are also Venetian-inspired fish soups added to the basic cuisine of corn dishes and mutton.

SERBIAN

The Republic of Serbia borders on Hungary, Romania, and Bulgaria and contains a sizable minority of 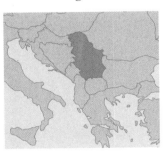 Hungarians in the north and Albanians in the southwest. Serbians form the largest racial group in the former Yugoslavia, almost 42 percent of the population. Most are members of the Serbian Orthodox (Greek) Church, although minorities of Muslims and Protestants do exist. Centuries of almost unceasing warfare and oppression by the Ottoman Empire finally ended in 1867 with the withdrawal of the last Turkish garrisons.

Serbians are especially sociable, talkative, and fun-loving. Warm-hearted hospitality is evidenced particularly in two traditions originated in Serbia and popular in nearly all of the former Yugoslavia. These are the customs of drinking plum brandy

(called variously: **Rakija, Slivovka, Slivovitz**, or **Klekovaca**) with Turkish coffee as the first "meal" of the day, and the special way of preparing the coffee – often called **Serbian coffee** – and the greeting of guests with **Slatko**.

The preparation of **Slatko** is the pride of every homemaker and a measure of her culinary prowess. The finest fruits are selected to be simmered in a thick, sweet syrup. These may include any whole perfect fruits (or attractive slices), for example, figs, green walnuts, cherries, and apricots. Many exotic preserves are made only from sugar and flower petals from violets, roses, and acacia – chosen for color and fragrance. The **Slatko** is served in tiny dishes arranged on a large tray with teaspoons and glasses of fresh cold water. Guests relish the perfection of the **Slatko** and enjoy its rich sweetness contrasted with sips of icy cold water. This tradition is usually followed by serving tiny cups of coffee, and is a ritual enjoyed throughout the former Yugoslavian republics, but may have its origin in Greece.

Serbian coffee is prepared in a lidless long-handled pot called a **dzezva**. Finely pulverized coffee, water, and sugar are measured into the **dzezva** and brought quickly to a boil. Some water is then poured off into a demitasse cup and the mixture is allowed to foam up again over high heat for only half a minute, then the amount previously poured off is added again and the coffee is ready to serve. (See also **Turkish coffee** as prepared in Bosnia.)

Serbian cookery is generally considered to be the richest in regional specialties: cheeses and cheese dishes, fine fish specialties and highly seasoned meats cooked in lard. Not only the **Slatko** and **Serbian coffee**, but also the custom of stirring a spoonful of rich preserves, especially plum jam, into a cold glass of water as a refreshment is widely copied in other regions. Similarly, the rich flavors of many Serbian dishes have also found wide popularity in Romania and Bulgaria.

Particular favorites are the **kisela corba**: a slow-simmering soup (said to be Serbia's national soup) of lamb, chicken, and chopped vegetables, thickened with rice and finished with a mixture of egg yolks, cream and vinegar added just before serving; and **gibanica**, a Serbian pastry made with butter-drenched layers of phyllo pastry sheets filled with a smooth mixture of cream cheese and eggs, baked till crispy golden and served in diamond cuts with fresh fruits or sweet fruit preserves.

Many Balkan and Hungarian dishes are a part of the Serbian cuisine, pork the favorite meat, lard the favored cooking fat, and a generous hand with paprika, garlic and onions, dill and caraway much in evidence.

Serbia is also fish and cheese country. The river fishermen are called *alasi*, and they bring in quantities of fresh sturgeon, carp, pike, sterlet, and sheatfish, all of which may be simply baked with lemon and butter or as **keciga u procepu**: the cleaned fish is wrapped in willow bark, packed with river mud, then cooked slowly over charcoal embers. When the mud and bark begin to crack, the fish is considered done. The **alaska corba** is a medley of simmered fish and vegetables with seasonings, strained then served with big pieces of cooked fish with the broth poured over. The broth itself is finished with the egg yolk-vinegar-cream mixture.

Soft white cheeses are served as **meze** (appetizers) with thin slices of smoked beef or pork called **prsuta**. Cream and cottage cheeses are used in bakery, in yeast buns, dumplings, fritters. In this area, the Turkish (filo or phyllo or strudel) pastry is called **pita** and is used in endless combinations just as it is used and enjoyed elsewhere. Most cheeses in Serbia are made from sheep's milk and are named for the area in which they are produced: **Javorski, Lipski, Zlatiborski**.

More recently, many successful imitations of other European cheeses have been made: **Liptaur**, a cream cheese flavored with onion, caraway, and paprika; **Imperial**, a soft cream cheese further enriched with added butter; and **Gervais**, a soft delicate cream cheese. A typical hard cheese with a pungent odor and taste made everywhere in the former Yugoslavia is **Kackavalj**. When this cheese is young it is eaten as *meze*; as it hardens with age it may be used grated or cut in pieces, batter-dipped and deep-fried.

A special Serbian dairy product, also much enjoyed in neighboring countries, is **kajmak**. Boiled milk is cooled in special shallow wooden bowls called **karlice**. The cooled cream is skimmed off and layered in wooden tubs called **cabrica**. The freshly made **kajmak** is eaten as a spread on breads, especially the heavy farmer's bread made with fat, flour and yeast, called **pogaca**, or the **srpska proja** (Serbian corn bread) made from cornmeal, fat, eggs, and milk. This latter bread may be made daily and split when half-baked, then returned to the oven to toast. Served warm with fresh **kajmak** and sauerkraut dishes or **sarma** (stuffed vine or cabbage leaves) it makes a memorable country meal. When the **kajmak** is allowed to ferment with the addition of salt, a stronger flavor develops. This aged **kajmak** is often used in combination with fresh curd and cream cheeses in many baked dishes and pastries, but most especially for the **gibanica**. Yogurts and soured cow's milk or sheep's milk are, together with the cheeses, a daily part of the diet in Serbia. These are prepared in every home and eaten not just as part of a meal but often as a snack.

Serbian food specialties are among the most widely copied elsewhere in the Southern Slav republics, and among the Serbs themselves their special dishes are so loved they are even considered "fit to cure the sick."

Some Serbian specialties are:

Cevapcici: grilled meatballs shaped like thick fingers, and well-spiced. Of Turkish influence.

Corba: a rich broth made with meat or fish plus vegetables. Just before serving, the soup is strained. The clear broth is blended with a mixture of egg yolks, cream, and vinegar and served with choice pieces of the meat or fish. Classic soup throughout the Balkans.

Djuvec: a layered casserole of a variety of meats and vegetables, sometimes with added rice cooked slowly with water and oil. The dish may have a topping of eggs and cream poured over and baked just before serving. Serbian version of the Romanian **Guivetch**.

Gurabije: rich honeycake cookies.

Musaka: a baked casserole of layered eggplant and meats richly flavored with garlic, onions, and tomatoes, sometimes cheese. Relic of the Turkish occupation.

Pihtije: a natural aspic prepared from simmered calves' feet. The meat and vegetables from the broth are chopped and jelled.

Pita: the thin, translucent sheets of pastry used to prepare many strudels, pies, and appetizer dishes. The **pita** is brushed with melted butter and filled with any mixture of flavored meats, fruits, pumpkin, nuts, then layered, rolled or folded, and baked.

Pljeskavice: grilled meat patties, often in oval or finger shapes.

Podvarak: cooked meats served with a specially prepared sauerkraut, made by simmering the kraut with onions then smothering the mixture with meat drippings and baking slowly in the oven till the mixture has caramelized throughout. Similar to the Hungarian **Czekely Gulyas**.

Raznjici: grilled cubes of meat on skewers. Like all grilled meat dishes, this is served with chopped raw onions and tiny hot chili peppers.

Sarma: meat-and-rice-stuffed grape (vine) or cabbage leaves. Many variations of this dish exist. For example, the leaves may be pickled as sauerkraut then wrapped around meat and rice and oven-baked with smoked spareribs with a roux (flour and fat) added near the end of cooking to thicken the juices. Tomato juice, cream, or broth may be used as the liquid to cook the **Sarma**.

Srpski Ajvar: "Serbian caviar," but actually a dish popular in so many countries it is difficult to name the origin. Grilled eggplant is cooled and mashed with pepper and garlic then served as a salad appetizer with pita.

Zito: ground cooked wheat is mixed with sugar and chopped walnuts and patted into a round mound on a platter, the top is dusted with fine sugar and more walnuts. This dish was prepared by the ancient Slav tribes as an offering to their gods and is a tradition still held in any Slav country or household. In Serbia, it is prepared for *Slava*, the special day of the patron saint of each family, and though this dish dates from pagan times, it is still very much a part of Orthodox Serbian custom.

SLOVENIAN

Located in a triangle area in the northernmost part of the former Yugoslavia, Slovenia is bordered by Italy,  Austria, and Hungary. The Southern Slav tribes, called Slovenes, settled in the area about 300 C.E., their strategically located land a veritable highway for the Germans and Huns. The Romans and finally Slovenia joined with the Hapsburgs in a struggle against the Ottoman Empire and ended up with a 1,000-year domination by the Austro-Hungarian Empire. It was a combination of their geographic location and their very early affiliation with the Holy Roman Empire and later the Austro-Hungarian Empire as well as its Roman Catholicism that gave the Slovenes a combination of western culture, folklore, education, and even a cuisine that is almost indistinguishable from that of its neighbors.

Slovenes retain the sociable easygoing characteristics of most Southern Slavs, but because of their early affiliations, they are probably the most intellectual and sophisticated of all. Slovenes are adept at languages, most being fluent in German and Italian, the intellectuals versed in French as well. Most Slovene children learn English in school. In spite of this inherent linguistic ability, many historians, and the Slovenes themselves, credit their very survival to the fact that above all, and indeed through all, they clung to their own ancient language, which is considered to be one of the oldest.

Slovenian *bifes* (snack bars) and *slascicarna* (tea shops) betray the national weakness for delectable cakes, tortes, strudels, and pastries in seemingly endless procession. Sweet bakery is not only a national snack, it is a national preoccupation. When one considers that the selection includes the finest of Italian, Austrian, Hungarian, and Turkish sweets, it is difficult to imagine a more delectable combination. With the frequent difficulty of deciding which pastry to select, it could indeed become a preoccupation.

Turkish coffee, pastries, grilled meats, Balkan sweets, hearty meat and vegetable casseroles, German varieties of excellent sausages, Italian sauces, pastas and risottos, the filling sweet dumplings and sweet noodle creations of the Austro-Hungarian Empire – with Slovenian cooks adept at all of these it needs little further explanation that a slim waistline must be one of the most pressing national problems. **Cvicek**, the omnipresent Slovenian rosé wine, is served everywhere with everything, although an excellent variety of red and white wines is also available, as is **Slivovitz**.

Close in importance to the sweets are Slovenian soups. Not only is a meal considered incomplete without soup, soup often comprises the entire meal, with only the minor accompaniment of bread and wine and perhaps a sweet noodle dish. This pattern is similar to Croatian tastes.

The heavily wooded areas of Slovenia yield game in abundance: quail, partridge, pheasants, hare, boar, venison. The Adriatic Sea supplies the ingredients for the numerous fish dishes, while the region's orchards produce not only peaches, apricots, and sweet and sour cherries, they are also famed for their apples. Almonds, walnuts and berries in generous amounts add their flavors to desserts. Mutton and pork are the favored meats (aside from game) and many excellent cheeses are locally produced.

Some Slovenian specialties include:

Cvicek: Slovenian rose wine used in such quantity and frequency that it is poured from casks rather than bottles.

Dunajski Zrezek: the pounded veal cutlet or scallop after it has been egg-dipped and crumbed then fried to a crisp perfection, otherwise known as **Wienerschnitzel**.

Idrijski Zlikrofi: small filled noodle pockets, poached and served with sauce. In Italy they would be called **Ravioli**.

Kranjske Klobase: German-style sausages in many varieties.

Mladic sa Pecurkama: whole baked river char stuffed with a bread and mushroom dressing. (Whether or not to use mushrooms in Slovenian cookery is not a problem. The problem is deciding which of the hundred varieties to use.)

Palacinke: those thin pancakes that the French call **Crepes**. Slovenians enjoy them mostly Hungarian style with apricot preserves and chopped walnuts, or with any other number of sweet combinations.

Pohana Piske: it doesn't matter what you call it, it is still breaded fried chicken. If the bird is not exactly tender, the dish may be finished by baking for a short time in the oven like the Austrian dish **Backhendl**.

Potica: from the Slovenian word *povitica*, which means "something rolled in." Usually it is taken to mean a many-layered coffee cake with generous nut filling.

Rezanci: freshly cooked noodles tossed with fresh curd cheese, poppy seeds, or chopped walnuts. Whatever proves to be the choice, melted butter and sugar will also be generously added. This dish may be a snack or, with soup, may make a light meal.

Ricet: stewed barley flavored with a small amount of smoked meat.

Struklji Od Sira: one of the infinite varieties of dumpling. Noodle dough is spread with a mixture of cottage cheese, egg yolks, sour cream, and whipped egg white. It is then rolled and placed in a crumb-sprinkled napkin and poached. The cooked dumpling is removed from the napkin then sliced and served with buttered crumbs.

Vipavska Corba: a thick soup of pork, potatoes, sauerkraut and beans, zesty with onion and garlic and served with sour cream.

MEALS AND CUSTOMS

Rakija, **Sljivovica**, **Slivovitz** or **Slivovka**, whatever it is called, is the national drink, a clear, potent plum brandy, its potency rendering the uninitiated literally breathless. Yet it is the morning drink accompanied by **Turska kafa**: a tiny strong sweet cup of Turkish coffee that sets most Southern Slavs on their daily routine. Some take a simple breakfast of coffee or weak tea and breads with jams or honey.

Almost everywhere in the regions of the former Yugoslavia the main meal of the day is at noon, followed by a rest period. The meal begins with soup, may include a fish dish or a meat and vegetable casserole, and probably ends with fresh or stewed fruits. Wine accompanies most meals. In some areas a course of cheese precedes the fruit dessert. The evening meal is usually a light one made up of dinner leftovers or soup and a sweet noodle dish or simply a vegetable casserole. Wine is a part of dinner and the evening meal and bread is indispensable. Further, the meal would likely be considered incomplete without a small salad of cooked dressed beans or vegetables or at the very least a dish of tiny hot peppers.

In the early evening, streets everywhere are congested with strollers and with people standing and talking. It is the time of the **korzo** (promenade). And no **korzo** is complete without a snack in a **kafana** (coffee shop) where always **Sljivovica**, **Turska kafa**, beer or a **Spricer** (wine and soda water) awaits. But who can drink without a little nibble? This is where

all the many tidbits grilled on skewers over charcoal fires are so enjoyed with tiny salads of spiced cooked vegetables, chopped raw onions and hot little peppers. Afternoon snacks may be the same, or they may lean to the sweet side. In the summer the popularity of sherbets and ice creams is evident. Always coffee and sweet pastries tempt the passerby.

The enjoyment of guests and generous hospitality is of utmost importance. Slovenians like to offer guests small dishes of sweetened cooked fruit: apple sauce, mixed fruit compotes. Montenegrins will be likely to offer a fresh, cool glass of milk, while the Bosnian-Herzegovinians will present a tray of Turkish coffee and **Ratluk** (a potent, clear plum brandy). In Serbia and Macedonia Turkish coffee will be accompanied by Rakija. Almost everywhere, the offering to welcome guests may well be the ornate tray with **Slatko**, with tiny spoons and glasses of fresh cold water. Eating and drinking together is the age-old symbol of friendship; to refuse would be a great insult.

SPECIAL OCCASIONS

Serbian Orthodox, Roman Catholic, and Muslim are the main religions amongst the Southern Slavs. Also there are minorities of Protestants and Jews.

Throughout the lands of the Southern Slavs, the year's calendar is dotted with special occasions. These include many local festivals, church festivities, regional fairs, and agricultural celebrations as well as saint's days and name days and more recently "The Day of the Republic."

During Marshal Tito's Communist regime throughout the former Yugoslavia, religious holidays were practiced quietly and sometimes furtively. In their place, the government promoted *Nova Godina*, a two-day New Year's celebration on January 1 and 2. This was widely celebrated with decorated trees, feasting, partying, and the exchanging of gifts with family and friends.

Croatia provides an example of the major religious groups and their festive celebrations. For the Catholic holy days and traditions these include Lent, Easter Monday, the Feast of Assumption of Mary on August 15, All Saint's Day on November 1, December 21 and 26 with Epiphany on January 6. For Muslims the holiest time is the month of *Ramadan*, the month of ritual fasting, ending with visiting family and friends and exchanging small gifts during the last three days. The days are called *Bajram* in Bosnia and *Ayd Al-Fitr* elsewhere. The Jewish minority celebrate Passover, *Rosh Hashana* and *Yom Kippur* as they do throughout the world.

Christmas, however, is still the most important festival on the calendar. Roman Catholics celebrate on

December 25 while the Serbian Orthodox members celebrate on January 7. But earlier, on the evening of December 6, Croatian children set out their shoes hoping St. Nicholas will remember them with small gifts.

For the Orthodox Christians the day before Christmas Eve is considered a fast day and no meat is eaten. But the atmosphere in the house is special: a yule log burns while a special 24-hour candle is lit and clean straw is scattered over well-scrubbed floors in memory of the manger scene. With the traditional Serbian Orthodox chant of "The Father, the Son, and the Holy Ghost, Amen," four whole walnuts are tossed, one into each corner of the room. The traditional evening meal will feature a soup, fish and vegetables with bread and cheese and fruit but no meat or meat fats. January 6, Epiphany Day, is considered to be the celebration of the visit of the three Wise Men and the baptism of Christ. This holy day, believed to be a holiday long before December 25 was celebrated as Christmas, is devoted to visiting with family and close friends. Especially important is the traditional Christmas cake cut in the shape of the Eastern Orthodox Cross with four "arms" and a center wedge removed and set with a cup of wine to be symbolically tasted by all adults.

When the Southern Slavs adopted Christianity in the 800s, each family took the name of a saint (on whose day the family was baptized) as their own patron saint. Coming soon after *Bozic* in January, the Family Saint's Day or *Krsna Slava* is celebrated. A platter of **Zito** or **Koljivo** is prepared. This is a mixture of boiled crushed wheat mixed with sugar and nuts and decorated with more nuts and often raisins as well as candles. This ancient dish was prepared by early Slavs as an offering to their gods; with the acceptance of Christianity the Slavs present this offering to their own saint after first being blessed in the church.

GLOSSARY OF FOODS AND FOOD TERMS

Note: Food terms and names of dishes are given under Regional Specialties. The following are the more general names and terms not described previously.

Boreks: Turkish appetizers made with phyllo pastry filled with savory meat or cheese mixtures, usually triangular in shape.

Bundeva: strips of pumpkin simmered in a flour-thickened dill sauce flavored with lemon and cream.

Corba od Pasulja: a thick bean soup with a mixture of chopped browned vegetables added just before serving. Paprika is the seasoning.

Dalmatinski Prsut: ham.

Djuvec: a baked mixture of meats and vegetables topped with grated cheese.

Flekice s Kupusom: a dish of shredded sautéed cabbage tossed with cooked tiny square noodles (the **Flekice**).

Jagnjeca Kapama s Jajima: an oven-baked stew of browned meat cubes, usually lamb and onions. Just before serving, a custard of eggs and yogurt is poured over the top and the dish is baked until set.

Kacamak or **Palenta** or **Mamajuga**: prepared in the former Yugoslavia as a thick, creamy corn soup, which is eaten with unleavened baked corn bread.

Kapama: a stew of cubed lamb, green onions, and spinach.

Lenja Pita: a cake made with a top and bottom of rich cookie crust; the in-between filling is made of sweetened spiced apples. When baked, the cake is served by cutting in squares.

Mastika: a spiced liqueur.

Pasulj: baked beans, sometimes flavored with a piece of smoked pork, always served with hot peppers.

Pekmez: a thick fruit butter, not as sweet as a jam.

Pelinkovak: a spiced liqueur.

Pilav: highly seasoned meat and rice dishes of infinite variety.

Pileca Corba: clear chicken broth.

Pita sa Medon: baked in a square pan, a ground lean pork filling is placed between a top and bottom crust of rich pastry. After baking, the top is spread with sour cream and sprinkled with grated cheese.

Pita sa Sljiva: a many-layered "pie" of rich pastry, sliced plums flavored with nuts, sugar, cinnamon and lemon zest, and well baked.

Plesk sa Kajmakom: small meatballs, cubed lamb, and green sweet pepper strips baked in **Kajmak**.

Pljeskavica: same as **Plesk sa Kajmakom** only grilled instead of baked in **Kajmak**.

Rasol: sauerkraut juice, taken as a beverage and used in cooking. If quinces are added, the juice is yellow; if beets are added, the juice is red.

Ratluk: a potent, clear plum brandy.

Ribasa Paprika: fish baked or cooked with paprika.

Sarma od Slatko Kupusa: a Macedonian dish of stuffed cabbage leaves (ground beef or pork and rice), flavored with dill and cooked on a bed of sauerkraut. An egg-lemon sauce (Greek **Avgolemono**) is served with the dish.

Slatka Pita sa Sirom: yeast dough pastry filled with cream cheese, raisins, and lemon zest, blended with beaten egg.

Spricer: a cooling drink of one-third white wine and two-thirds soda water.

Som u Mileramu: poached cod fillets baked with sour cream and garnished with anchovies.

Sovica Salata: lentil salad.

Struklji: a poached dumpling of cheese, plums, and nuts.

Sumadija Tea: plum brandy is poured over caramelized sugar with extra sugar or honey added as desired. Hot water is added to make a "warming" drink.

Tava: casserole for baking. **Tavce** is a smaller version.

Teleca Corba: a thick soup-stew with veal.

Usicka Prsuta: smoked beef.

Vinjak: brandy.

CHAPTER 46

SPANISH

It is common to refer to anything we don't understand as being "mystical." And more than any other country, Spain has long been tagged with this cloudy term. The contrasts of the country, the contradictory characteristics of the people, and the endless juxtaposition of the old and new jar the sensibilities and make slick summaries all but impossible.

Spain's 40 million people are spread over 9 regions, divided into 50 provinces and speak various dialects of 4 main languages. But one province overshadows them all. Since 1469, Castile has dominated Spain linguistically, geographically, and historically. For in that year, Isabella of Castile married Ferdinand of Aragon, launching not only Castile's influence over the rest of Spain, but also subtly but undeniably the dominance of women over men. It is interesting that Ferdinand and Isabella's rule is referred to by Spaniards as the rule of the "Catholic kings" in a phrase neatly depicting their strength and equality and the symbolism of "Spain's fervor for religious purity" that was to launch Christopher Columbus to the New World and herald Spain's global career, and at the same time catapult all of Spain into the degradation of the Inquisition.

The rule of the Catholic kings ended almost 800 years of Arab and Moorish occupation and united all the kingdoms of Spain. Probably because the Christians of that period identified all Moslems as Moors (inhabitants of what is today Morocco), the 800-year period is always called the Moorish period. Actually the first invasions were by Sunnites from Yemen and Shiites from Persia, and the combined Arab, Berber, and Moorish occupation was not all bad. The rule was seldom a unified one, and there was as much fighting among themselves as there was with the Spanish princes. There were also long periods of amiable coexistence. Christians practiced their religion and it was intellectual Arabs, Jews, and Spaniards together who perfected new ideas in medicine, mathematics, and astronomy and made Spain one of the most populous and wealthy countries in all of Europe at the time.

The 800 years left not only an intellectual and economic imprint but a gastronomic one as well. Much earlier in Spain's history (about 1100 C.E.) the Phoenicians had planted grape vines and olive trees. The olive oil supplanted the use of pork fat from Roman times, and the grapes added to the development of many wines. The Arabs, Berbers, and Moors did some planting too. They added gardens of fragrant peach, apricot, lemon and almond trees as well as the thick-skinned bitter orange for which Seville was to become famous. Exotic seasonings of cinnamon, nutmeg, cumin, and saffron found their way into Spanish dishes, and the planting of sugarcane and rice added new staples as well. Today Spanish **paella** seems so indigenous to Spain that its roots in many exotic **pilaus** of the Near East are all but forgotten.

Isabella and Ferdinand had launched Spain into an era of exploration, colonization, and conquest. Spain swelled to encompass a vast overseas empire that included Cuba, Puerto Rico, colonies in South America, Guam, and the Philippines. The world may remember that it was the Spanish *conquistadores* who brought corn, potatoes, beans, squashes and tomatoes as well as chocolate and vanilla from the New World. But the world also remembers that these were the results of plunder and destruction abroad, while a degradation of another sort was taking place in Spain itself. The Inquisition, also launched by Isabella and Ferdinand in 1481, began slowly with the tormenting of *Conversos* (Jews converted to Christianity) and *Moriscos* (Muslims converted to Catholicism) in Spain for the sake of "religious purity and unity." It ended with torture, death, and expulsion not only for Conversos and Moriscos, both of whom were thought to be secretly practicing their own religions, but finally for every person of a faith other than Catholicism.

To this day, Spaniards speak well of the great reign of the Catholic kings that brought unity and an overseas empire. They speak as if it happened but recently, and they dismiss critics of the conquests and the Inquisition as all part of a "Black Legend." But the results of that Black Legend still ominously haunt

Spain. For with the expulsion and deaths of the *Conversos* and *Moriscos* went some of the greatest minds of the country. There followed a gradual but undeniable slump in the country's intellectual, economical, cultural, and political affairs and achievements.

In later years Spain was left bereft by the declarations of independence by its colonies, the Treaty of Paris in 1898, which gave Puerto Rico, Guam, and the Philippines to the United States. Internal strife – the continuing and fundamental conflict of the Liberalists and the Absolutists – and bitter sporadic civil wars gradually led to Spain's isolation from the rest of the world.

Perhaps it is this isolation that furthers the image of the province of Castile as the symbol of Spain itself. Linguistically, Castilian Spanish is considered the purest. Geographically, Castile is located in the center of Spain, aloof and impenetrable. Historically and socially, the Castilians consider themselves descendants of royalty whose manners and sophistication are unexcelled. Yet to describe all Spaniards in the image of Castilians would be a mistake. For though the provinces have been unified for more than 500 years, the areas are fiercely individualistic and regard themselves as Basques, Aragonists, Catalonians, Andalusians, and so on. They treasure their linguistic differences as much as they savor their culinary specialties, and they cling to many old ways even as they enjoy materialistic changes.

Everywhere in Spain roads are shared by motorcycles, bicycles, Seats (the Spanish answer to the Italian Fiat), and mule-drawn Gypsy carts. Small scattered villages still store their daily water supply in earthenware jugs brought from the rivers while electricity lights their homes and television antennas bristle on their roofs. And in Madrid black-clad women jostle girls in miniskirts and blue jeans, outdoor cafes serve unhurried coffees, and snackers enjoy **tapas** (appetizers) in age-old bars with sawdust floors. But while relative prosperity seems to be merging the working class into the middle class, it is the Castilian legacy of rigid class structure that is making this inevitable movement a slow one.

The old is never quite removed from the new: the mule carts stubbornly demand their share of the road, and water is still the most important and unsolved problem in all of Spain. While television draws the men perhaps more than philosophical conversations, they traditionally prefer to talk and think rather than to do.

Other things have not changed. Did the vital force of women's influence begin with the Castilian Queen Isabella? Surely she must stand as the single most important figure of Spain, for it is not only her Castile that has dominated all of Spain, but for more than 500 years her impact has been felt, and is responsible for the quiet but driving force typical of Spanish women. Regardless of class or position, the Spanish male prides himself on his appearance, his authority, and his own great self-esteem. It is with a patience born of centuries of intuitive understanding that the Spanish woman has resigned herself to the combination of Don Juan and Don Quixote that is her husband. While he fantasizes and philosophizes, she quietly manages the finances and the household.

Time and influences from the outside world are making their influence felt all over Spain, from the fertile lush lands of the Basque country to the mountains and hard plains of the Castile and Estremadura and even to the lazy, sunny coastal areas of Costa del Sol and San Sebastian. Gently the old forces, customs, and patterns are making a place for the new as Spain herself emerges from the shackles of feudalism and the Black Legend, from fantasies and philosophies into realities and the pursuit of material pleasures. Likely the mysticism will always be there, but the clouds are parting.

FOODS COMMONLY USED

The most common misconception about Spanish food is that it is spicy hot. In fact, Spanish foods are noted for their fresh natural flavors and a minimum of seasonings, and many an authentic Spanish dish prepared elsewhere fails simply because of the lack of quality and freshness in the basic ingredients.

The staples of the Spanish kitchen include olive oil, tomatoes, garlic, and onions. Fresh bread is always on the table not only for each meal but also for each course except dessert. Partly because they are the freshest, and partly because of regional pride and preferences, the Spanish cook adds local specialties from land or sea to the staples to produce distinctive regional dishes. **Cocida** and **gazpacho** are national dishes of Spain, but there are as many variations as there are kitchens, and each variation is stoutly defended as being the best. Fruits and subtle light seasonings, combinations of fruits and nuts with meats and fish, and dishes based on rice are all influences from Muslim times. But the oldest additions to Spain's table — wine and olive oil — have never lost their importance.

DOMESTIC LIFE

The kitchens of Spain mirror old traditions side by side with the newest conveniences. The mortar and pestle is being replaced by the electric blender and a place is being found for imported electrical refrigerators even if that place is in the living room. Yet breads freshly baked in community hearth ovens and earthenware **ollas** (pots or casseroles) have not been cast aside. And as more and more women are entering the workforce, and as cooks and maids are becoming scarcer too, convenience foods and electrical appliances that make cooking easier and quicker are quickly finding a place.

DAIRY PRODUCTS

Milk as a beverage is almost non-existent in Spain except perhaps occasionally in some rural areas. Adults and children alike take coffee or chocolate (made with milk) for breakfast only. But milk is consumed in the form of cheeses and the favorite dessert, a caramel flan. Cheeses may be made from cow's, goat's, or sheep's milk or combinations thereof. Spain's cheeses are not of exceptional quality but they are often eaten as **tapas** (appetizers) and with fruits for dessert. Condensed and evaporated milk is used as well as fresh whole milk for the preparation of the baked custard called **flan** which is so popular it is often a part of the dessert course even with pastries or fruits.

FRUITS AND VEGETABLES

The Arabs, Berbers, and Moors brought with them not only a taste for fruits but the actual plants themselves. There is seldom a day in Spain when fruit has not been enjoyed either by itself as a snack, wine-soaked in **Sangria**, nestled in a casserole with meat or fish, or served as a refreshing dessert perhaps with cheese. Oranges, lemons, peaches, apricots, many types of berries, grapes, melons, dried fruits (dates, raisins, figs), candied fruits and even candied vegetables are all part of the daily fare.

Vegetables are seldom eaten raw; salads tend to be simple greens with tomatoes dressed with olive oil, salt and perhaps vinegar. Pickled or cooked vegetables dressed with oil and vinegar and served chilled are often a part of the **tapas** or **entremeses** (appetizers), but more usually vegetables are served as a separate course, simple but well cooked. A wide range of fresh vegetables are available almost year-round: potatoes, carrots, peas, fresh beans, cabbage, cauliflower, artichokes, zucchini, cucumbers, greens, eggplants, and of course tomatoes, peppers, onions, and garlic. Besides being served in salads and as appetizers, many vegetables are a part of soups and stews.

MEATS AND ALTERNATES

Still another reason for the difficulty in duplicating Spanish dishes is the wide variety of game used: rabbit, hare, partridge, boar, etc., as well as the use of suckling lamb and pig only little more than three weeks old. Domestically produced meats are tough and lack flavor, which is probably why the most popular method of cooking meat dishes is by stewing or braising. The national dish, **cocida**, whose ingredients vary from area to area, nonetheless makes practical use of meats and vegetables to produce three courses: a clear soup, a platter of mixed cooked vegetables, and finally a variety of boiled meats.

Fish and seafood abound in many varieties unknown in North America. Mussels, prawns, shrimps, clams, and oysters vie in popularity with lobsters and crayfish, crabs, barnacles, and sea spiders. Fish is a cornerstone of Spanish cuisine and is widely used because of its fresh availability and because it is inexpensive. Dried and salted cod (**bacalao**) is also used, but the fresh fish include bream, hake, mullet, flounder, tuna, fresh cod, sea bass, sole, and trout. Fish may be poached, fried or baked and is often prepared as a soup-stew. Common also in Spanish cookery is the combination of fish or seafood with meats or fowl in one dish, such as hake with ham and eggs, lobster with chicken, or the famed **paella valenciana** which, though made in many versions, classically combines chicken and seafood with rice.

Legumes, especially in the form of **garbanzos** (chickpeas) and lentils are widely used as an ingredient of the **cocida** and often as a simple but hearty soup. Eggs are consumed most frequently as ingredients in other dishes such as omelets, soufflés, and **flan**. Almonds are nibbled as a candied sweet, pounded and made into a beverage called **horchata**, used in sauces, pastries and in fish and meat dishes.

BREADS AND GRAINS

Except for the province of Galicia where a light bread is made from cornmeal, and the Canary Islands where corn is a staple, all of Spain enjoys fresh, crusty, white wheat bread. Bread is the staple that is always on the table. Hot or cold cereals are not eaten in Spain.

FATS

Olive oil is unquestionably the staple fat in all of Spain except in Basque country (Las Vascongadas) where pork fat is mostly used. Butter is used in some desserts and pastries, and with breads.

SWEETS AND SNACKS

Candied dried fruits, candied cooked fruits, and even candied vegetables such as pumpkin and squashes as well as candied nuts, especially almonds, are favorite nibbles. Taking late afternoon tea or coffee (*merienda*) with a variety of sweet pastries is customary in some areas. Almost everywhere, convents are famed for their sweet pastries and candies especially prepared for the frequent fiestas. The main meal of the day (*comida*) taken leisurely in the afternoon or the restaurant meal taken with friends is seldom complete without a sweet **flan** or pastries. Occasionally though, fresh fruit may complete the meal. Sweet flaky pastries and honey-drenched cakes reminiscent of the Muslim occupation are great favorites.

SEASONINGS

The lightest hand in seasonings is found in southern Spain; the garlic and onions become more pronounced as one moves northward. Saffron is almost indispensable in most rice dishes, cumin, nutmeg and cinnamon are found in desserts and sometimes meat and fish dishes. But the universal seasonings are garlic, onions, and tomatoes.

BEVERAGES

Coffee with hot milk, and hot chocolate made with milk are the usual breakfast beverages. Red wines and varieties of sherries from Jerez include *finos* and **olorosos**. The **finos** include **manzanilla** and **amontillado**: pale in color but with a rich dry taste. The **olorosos** include "brown" and "cream" sherries and their deep rich color matches their deep mellow taste. Local wines are made everywhere in Spain and wines commonly accompany the *comida* to the enjoyment of young and old alike. **Sangria** is the most known mixed wine drink consisting of sliced fruits marinated in brandy then combined with equal amounts of mineral or soda water and red wine. Another refreshing drink popular everywhere is **horchata**. It is milky in appearance, only slightly sweet and delicately almond. **Horchata** may be made from pounded melon seeds, chufa seeds (similar to almonds), or almonds.

A specialty served in Las Vascongadas (Basque country) is a mixture of equal amounts of red wine, white wine, and lemonade served chilled but without ice cubes and especially enjoyed with the Basque buffet called *merienda*.

REGIONAL SPECIALTIES

ANDALUSIA

Sometimes it is difficult to believe that the Strait of Gibraltar actually separates Andalusia from Morocco, so alike are these areas in lifestyle, climate, and appearance. Moorish architecture predominates, and the romantic Andalusians enjoy many originally Muslim dishes.

One of these is **gazpacho**, the quintessence of the Andalusian kitchen. At once light and refreshing yet satisfying, this now-classic soup of Spain actually has many variations. Occasionally grapes and even rabbit meat are added to the fresh vegetable base. Originally the name **gazpacho** referred to a cold soup based on water-soaked bread; today it commonly refers to a cold soup made with fresh tomatoes and cucumbers added to the water-soaked bread and usually flavored with at least a little garlic. Cold soups based on vegetables, garlic, or almonds are common in this area where the temperature may reach 130°F and life, of necessity, moves slowly.

Purists argue that although **gazpacho** is made throughout Spain, it cannot compare with the Andalusian version. Madrid **gazpacho** is said to be too thick, Estremadura's is said to be too thin.

A little farther inland, cool wintry weather makes cities like Granada appreciative of hot, thick soups. Although garlic, olive oil, and tomatoes are unquestionably the staples in this province, fish, seafood, and fresh fruits are much enjoyed. **Pote blanco** is a thick, satisfying soup of cod, cream, and potatoes. One of the most popular basic sauces is **salmorejo** made with garlic, eggs, bread crumbs, oil, and wine vinegar. In Granada, the term **escabeche** means anything that is pickled.

ARAGON

Bordering on France, Aragon shares France's love of sauces and dedication to fine foods and wines. **Chilindron** is a basic sauce similar to the **sofrito** used in many Spanish-speaking countries. It is a well-cooked blend of onions, garlic, tomatoes, and meat – in Aragon the meat is **serrano** ham. This sauce is used with meats, game, fish or seafood. One of the secrets of many dark, rich Aragonese sauces is the last-minute melting in of chocolate to blend all the other flavors, especially in a meat or game sauce.

But the great tradition of the area and popular in much of Spain is the **migas**, piping hot crisply fried croutons of stale bread. These are lightly salted and often fried and tossed with crispy bits of ham to make a light

delicious appetizer, but the **migas** also find their way into stews, soups, and sauces.

CATALONIA

Bordering the Mediterranean in the northeastern corner of Spain, the province of Catalonia is famed for its cosmopolitan and hardworking people who

are said to be more like Europeans than any of the other Spaniards except perhaps the Basques. Here, it is said, "everything edible is eaten." Perhaps it is the distinctive ruddy **romescu** sauce with its tangy sharp and sometimes hot taste together with the **ali-oli** (garlic and oil sauce) that helps to make any fish, sea-food, or game palatable.

In any case the sauces are almost as famous as the fine fruits grown in the area: peaches, apricots, cherries, pears, sweet berries, and especially the numerous melons. **Habas** (broad beans) are widely used in soups and stews, and, while a **zarzuela** in most of Spain means an operetta, in Catalonia it usually refers to a melodic blending of fish and seafood as a stew. The hearty Catalan appetites often consume brimming soup plates of **escudella**, a hearty thick soup made with a melange of pork products (**escudella cocida**) or a variety of meats (**escudella i carn d'olla**), then go on to finish a meal of several more courses. Another specialty is **potaje de garbanzos y espinacas**, a thick nourishing soup of spinach and chickpeas. The Catalan version of the **flan** dessert is called **crema catalana** and is served on a wide flat plate, a layer of creamy custard resting under a crispy topping of burnt sugar.

CENTRAL PLATEAU

Don Quixote's La Mancha is noted not only for windmills but also for wheat and olives. This southeasterly area of the Central Plateau can also boast some game: hare, rabbits and quail. **Manchego**, a cheese made from goat's milk, is produced in the area.

The rest of the Central Plateau includes New and Old Castile, and the general lack of game make very young lamb and piglets the specialties. Placed on an earthenware platter directly in an oven they are slowly roasted to an unbelievable tenderness. Together with ham, pork sausages, bacon and other pork products, veal is also commonly used. There are many versions of the Castilian **cocida** but most frequently it is made with varieties of sausages, cabbage, potatoes, and vermicelli.

Olla podrida (literally, "rotten pot") is a simple bean and pork stew, said to be the original **cocida**. But both the **cocida** and the **podrida** reputedly have their origins in an ancient Jewish dish called **adafina** which was a slow-cooked mixture of beef, vegetables, and hard eggs. Set in a slow oven late Friday afternoon, it provided a hot meal for the Sabbath without breaking the Sabbath commandment against work. During the times of the Inquisition, the Conversos and even the Moriscos demonstrated their pious Christianity by substituting pork for the eggs. (No Muslim or Jew would eat pork.) In time, the simple dish gained many variations and came to be the staple of Spain.

Other specialties of the area include **Sangria**, a light wine punch with sliced brandied fruit; **flan**, a baked milk and egg custard usually with a caramel sauce; and **sopa de ajo**, "garlic soup" made basically of oil-browned garlic and bread crumbs and served with a whole egg.

Like the rest of the area, Madrid itself prefers light simple food, but the city boasts restaurants that can serve any of the finest regional Spanish dishes. *Madrileños* themselves are famed for their endless eating and lack of sleep. They rise early, nibble frequently, and eat three or four meals a day, the last being anytime after 10:00 p.m.

ESTREMADURA

The area west of the Central Plateau is dry, moun-

tainous, and sparsely populated. Even the name means "extremely hard." Because it is one of the poorest regions in Spain, pork and potatoes form the staples and the **tortilla**, a potato and onion omelet, is a specialty.

GALICIA AND ASTURIAS

Located north of Por-tugal, in the northwest area of Spain, the province of Asturias is noted for its coal mining and the fine salmon that are caught from its rivers.

Galicia is the only place in Spain where the people play bagpipes and the provincial export is men. The area is so poor that the men leave their women to look after the few cornfields while they seek work

elsewhere. The staple foods are pork, potatoes, greens (especially **grelos**, turnip greens), and a moist bread made from cornmeal. Apple cider is used as a beverage and frequently in cooking.

Pote gallego, a specialty of Galicia, is a thick soup-stew made with any meat or vegetables available. **Caldereta asturiana**, a specialty of Asturias, is a type of bouillabaisse made from fish and seafood from the Bay of Biscay.

Most famous of all is the **fabada asturiana**, a stew of **chorizo**, ham and beef, cabbages, potatoes and white beans; and the **empanadas**, meat or seafood pies, usually served cold, and shaped in small triangles or cut in wedges from a large pie.

LAS VASCONGADAS (BASQUE COUNTRY)

Near France in the north-central part of Spain lie the Basque provinces where it is claimed that the simplest and finest cooking in all of Spain can be found. The Basques excel energetically in everything they

do. The greenest fertile lands, the highest per capita income, the most industry, the most banks, and the most beautiful women in all of Spain are said to be in Las Vascongadas. With all of that, it is difficult to believe that it is here too that gastronomy is a masculine art and that somehow the men find time to belong to the many serious societies dedicated solely to good food and drink.

While the midday meal may be taken at home and most weekends spent with the wife and family, the Basque male will be found most evenings dining with his gastronomic society – if not actually cooking.

Their many courses include egg dishes, fish, fowl, meat, cheese, **natillas** (soft custard tinged with cinnamon and lemon), fruits, pastries, coffee and brandy. Basque cooks are noted for the delicacy and unexcelled natural flavors of all of their dishes but especially cod. **Txakoli** is a dry white wine with a fresh apple-like taste, the specialty of Las Vascongadas. Unfortunately, it does not travel well so is enjoyed only there.

NAVARRE

Hemingway made famous Pamplona, the capital city of Navarre, and tourists as well as Spaniards flock there in July for the festival of San Fermin, the running of the bulls. The day of excitement is ended with a late special meal of rabbit pie and tangy cheese.

VALENCIA

The fertile and even swampy lands of Valencia make it Spain's principal rice-growing area. So it is not surprising that rice is the staple food, the base for

many meat and seafood dishes, is used in soups, and in flour form is used to prepare many cakes and pastries. Valencian women are renowned for their pastry-making skills.

Sweet Valencian oranges are enjoyed for their juice, which is a common refreshment, and oranges, like rice, appear in many dishes: salads, desserts, and in combinations with fish, seafood, and meats.

But the most famous dish of all is the classic **paella valenciana**, a succulent melange of chicken, seafood, and rice lightly flavored with saffron and a small garnish of red pimentos and green peas. But that is only one version. There are as many **paellas** in Spain as there are **cocidas**, and who can say which is the best? Here too, as in Catalonia, the garlic and oil sauce called **ali-oli** is used as a dip or sauce for meats, game, fish or seafood.

MEALS AND CUSTOMS

Spain's history has indelibly affected the life of her people. The Civil War of 1936-1939 was followed by a long period of isolation from the rest of the world. This was broken in 1951 by the signing of an aid and defense pact with the United States, the impact of which sent pulses of change throughout Spain and still affects the daily life of the people. The resulting trade and industrial explosion not only brought about the slow emergence of a middle class, but also the adoption of many western patterns in clothing, foods, sports, television, and the increasing emergence of women in the business and professional world. Increasingly young women went out unchaperoned. The availability of cars (the modest Seat) made travel easier with the result that Spaniards are getting to know each other as regional differences break down and communications increase.

No longer are regional food specialties available only in the respective provinces. No longer are Spaniards sipping only wine and sherry; now tourists sip the sherry while natives enjoy international cocktails. Domestic help is becoming scarcer but luckily a range of electrical appliances is helping to fill the gap.

Men and women are enjoying greater freedom, but some things have not changed. There is an overall general lack of domestic life: the center of the Spaniard's social life is not in the home. Guests or friends are invited to dine in restaurants, meet at a specific coffeehouse for *tertulia* (meeting and talking leisurely over coffee and pastries), or spend an evening *chateo* (a touring of bars and enjoying drinks and snacks called **tapas**). There is no end to superb restaurants, and many of the coffeehouses are regular hangouts for specific groups, for example, students, professors, doctors. But the age-old bars with their endless varieties of drinks and **tapas** are best for brief enjoyment. Usually the refreshment is taken standing up, debris is thrown on the sawdust floors and then the patrons move on.

While the Spaniard's hospitality is usually offered outside the home, an effusion of courtesy and compliments are offered everywhere, even without prompting. It is never enough to say thanks: in compliments, and courtesies superlatives are the rule. Prized even more than smiles, money, or the polite gesture, verbal compliments are a cultivated art. Perhaps the pinnacle of the fine art of compliments is to be found in the *piropos*, those delightfully risque remarks addressed by men to any passing female. Far from being insulted, a woman would be greatly upset if her walk elicited no *piropos*.

While the rural dweller's day and meal patterns are geared to his work and the seasons, the day of the *Madrileño* never ceases to astonish the tourist. The people of Madrid are early risers, beginning their day with a modest coffee or hot chocolate and a bread or pastry (commonly **churros**, cinnamon-dusted spiral doughnuts). Traditionally, an ample dinner followed by a siesta is taken in the early afternoon then work resumes at about four and concludes in the early evening. But with the increasing pressures and influences of the global economy and women in the workforce, old ways are slowly changing. The evening meal is, however, still usually taken no earlier than ten and often later. It is an incredible sight to see *Madrilenos*, men, women, and even small children,

thronging the streets close to midnight, simply out for a walk. No one seems to know when they sleep. But what they lack in sleep they make up in appetite: meals, snacks, and drinks are consumed in unbelievable quantities around the clock.

SPECIAL OCCASIONS

Roman Catholicism is the state religion of Spain. In 1967 Spain passed a decree guaranteeing religious freedom; this affected about 30,000 Protestants and 7,000 Jews. Previous to this, dating from 1481, laws still in effect forbade public worship or advertising of religious services by anyone other than Roman Catholics.

It is not enough to say that fiestas abound in Spain; they are in fact an almost daily occurrence. Perhaps in no other country of the world (with the possible exception of Italy) are there so many holidays and festivities to honor personal and local saints and special rituals relating to the seasons, work, weddings, and funerals. It has been said that there is scarcely a day on the Spanish calendar that is not marked by a fiesta for some region, village, or family.

These are a few of the main festivity days:

January 1: New Year's Day

January 6: Epiphany

March: *Fallas de San Jose*. Rice-planting festival in Valencia. Costumes, parades, every conceivable rice dish and varieties of fine pastries.

March 19: Feast of St. Joseph (*San Jose*) in rest of Spain

Holy Week Celebrations heralded with costumed processions and carnivals:

Good Friday

Holy Saturday

Easter Monday

Pentecost Monday

May 1

Ascension Day

Corpus Christi

June 24: Feast of St. John on the shortest night of the year, often celebrated with bonfires, especially in coastal beach areas

June 29: Feast of St. Peter and St. Paul

July 1: *San Fermin*. The running of the bulls in Pamplona, Navarre

July 18: National Feast Day

July 25: Feast of St. James, patron saint of Spain

August 15: Assumption Day

September 24: Feast of Our Lady of Mercy, patron saint of Barcelona

October 12: Feast of Hispanidad

November 1: All Saints' Day. Pumpkin is the symbolic All Saints' Day food in both French and Spanish Basque areas.

December 8: Immaculate Conception

December 19: *Pregon de Navidad*. The official opening of the Christmas festivities which last until January 6. Kings' Day or the Day of the Three Wise Men, the day of gift-giving to children.

December 25 or 26: St. Stephen's Day or Christmas. Celebrated as a family occasion. Christmas Eve is celebrated with decorations of the manger, Spanish carols, midnight church services, and a late family dinner with roasted pork, lamb or baked fish ending with special sweets prepared weeks ahead of time.

GLOSSARY OF FOODS AND FOOD TERMS

Albondigas: small fried meatballs, usually eaten as appetizers.

Ali-Oli: a basic sauce of pounded fresh garlic blended with olive oil and sometimes a dash of lemon juice. It is said this sauce was taken to France by Richelieu after he tasted it in Mahon in 1756. There, with the addition of eggs and the removal of the garlic, it was transformed into *mahon-aise*, presumably today's mayonnaise.

Angulas: tiny eels, lightly steamed and eaten whole.

Ardangozatza: a Basque wine punch made from equal portions of white and red wines and lemonade all well chilled. Probably the drink would be more popularly known if it was as easy to pronounce as **Sangria**.

Arroz: rice.

Ave: poultry and fowl.

Bacalao: dried salt cod. Spanish and Portuguese fishermen were among the first to sail to the Grand Banks of Newfoundland for great catches of cod which they cleaned and salted down in their holds. It is said the Basques excel in their recipes for **Bacalao**.

Bacalao al Pil Pil: a classic Basque specialty of dried salt cod pre-soaked and gently cooked in garlic and olive oil so that the natural juices form a delicate sauce. It is one of those "simple" dishes that could test the skills of the greatest chefs.

Basque Merienda: a large buffet of fish and meat dishes accompanied by **Ardangozatza**.

Bilboa: the ubiquitous Gallegan (from Galicia) bottle of olive oil always with fresh garlic cloves afloat.

Broa: a moist bread made from cornmeal. Popular in Portugal, Galicia, and Asturia.

Caldo: clear soup. Usually it is the skimmed broth from a **Cocida** where the broth, meat, and vegetables are then served as separate courses.

Carne: meat.

Chilindron: an all-purpose sauce made from simmered tomatoes, garlic, onions, peppers, and meat. In this case the meat is **Serrano** ham. The Basque version of the **Sofrito**.

Chorizo: a classic pork and garlic sausage found everywhere in Spain. The best is said to be made in Estremadura.

Cocida: also called **Pote**, **Olla**, **Podrida**, **Puchero**. It is a stew or thick soup made from beans, pork, and vegetables but there are countless variations depending on region, season, and simply "what is at hand." Sometimes it is served in small earthenware casseroles; sometimes the ingredients are served in separate courses as clear soup, meats then vegetables.

Crema: cream soup.

Crema Catalana: in this case, **Crema** means a soft custard served on a wide flat plate and topped with a crunchy burnt sugar crust. A favorite dessert and snack in Catalonia.

Ensaladas: salads. Usually served as a first or appetizer course. To the combination of dressed greens may be added fruits and vegetables (e.g., oranges and onions), seafood, fish or meat.

Entremeses (Variados): appetizers; almost unnecessary to add the *variados* as appetizers are almost always assorted.

Escabeche: in Granada, this term refers to anything pickled.

Estofada: though it may be often difficult to distinguish between a soup and a stew, the Spaniards do have a word for stew. This is it.

Fabada: Gallegan or Asturian "stew" of meats, beans, and vegetables.

Flan: a baked sweet custard of eggs, milk (whole fresh, evaporated, or condensed), and sugar. It is the classic dessert of all Spain and is almost always present in one form or another at the end of the meal.

Garbanzos: chickpeas. These, together with lentils and white beans, are Spain's favorite legumes.

Gazpacho: cold soup of Moorish origin. Literally, "soaked bread," the soup has many variations but most common is one of water, bread, tomatoes, and cucumber finely chopped or puréed and lightly flavored with garlic.

Habas: broad beans.

Horchata: a sweet milky chilled beverage. It can be made from seeds or nuts pounded to a paste, sweetened, and added to water. Chufa nuts, almonds, or melon seeds are used.

Legumbres: vegetables.

Mariscos: seafood.

Merienda: throughout Spain this is the name for the late afternoon refreshment of cakes and pastries served with tea or hot chocolate.

Merluza: hake. Next to cod, probably the most plentiful fish in Spain.

Natillas: soft custards made of eggs, milk, and sugar and delicately flavored with lemon and cinnamon. Served in individual molds.

Olla Podrida: another name for **Cocida**. Literally, "rotten pot." At the end of the meal a little water and a few more ingredients (beans, pork, vegetables) would be added to the leftovers to be simmered again and again. When the smell became unbearable, it would be thrown out and the pot started again.

Paella: you immediately think of **Paella Valenciana** because this dish originated in Valencia, the rice-growing area of Spain, but **Paella** simply means any dish based on rice, and the combinations are many.

Pao de Lo: a simple light sponge cake delicately touched with vanilla, lemon, or almond.

Pasteleria: pastry shop.

Pescados: fish.

CHAPTER 47

SWEDISH

Maintaining neutrality in two world wars, and historically the benevolent ruler of parts of the Baltic, Germany, and Finland, Sweden stands today as the wealthiest, most cosmopolitan country of Northern Europe. Sweden's population of approximately 8.5 million makes her the fourth-largest nation in Northern Europe. Despite the fact that only 9 percent of her land is arable, Sweden is almost self-sufficient in agricultural and dairy products, meats and fish due to the efficient application of the most modern techniques of fertilization, mechanization, animal and poultry production and fishing procedures. In the late 1800s, Sweden gradually emerged as one of the important industrial nations of the world, maintaining to this day a great respect in business circles and a high reputation for fine products from industrial steel to glassware and modern furniture.

The southern portions of Sweden enjoy moderate climate due to the prevailing westerly winds and the warming Gulf Stream. But the northern areas bordering on Finland and Norway and stretching into the Arctic Circle brave bitter temperatures and long dark winters, though they delight in two months of near continuous daylight. The many lakes and long rivers contribute to a great potential of hydroelectric energy of which only a portion is presently used.

Making the most of her natural resources and industrial potential is only a part of Sweden's success story. The other part must be the Swedish people themselves. Known for their lilting musical language, which has borrowed words both from French and German roots, the Swedes are also noted for their serene dispositions. Perhaps a part of their serenity stems from confidence and pride in their country; perhaps a part stems from their ordered, relaxed daily way of life. Swedes have the enviable ability to enjoy each day. And rituals are an important part of that enjoyment. Everything from coffee-drinking to **skoal**,

from table manners to holiday festivities, follow prescribed and predictable procedures. Most Swedes are Lutheran, and their relaxed attitudes also extend into their religious life.

DOMESTIC LIFE
Swedes enjoy most modern kitchen facilities and appliances, use electricity widely, and should they lack anything, it is sure to be imported. Beautiful tableware is prevalent in all homes and there is scarcely a meal where flowers do not grace the table.

Enjoying a variety of produce in season and imported fruits and vegetables in the winter months, Swedes are said to be second only to the United States in their consumption of frozen foods. Convenience products, delicatessens, canned and frozen foods all combine to make the Swedish kitchen as up-to-date as any in the world.

DAIRY PRODUCTS
Children may take milk with their meals; adults prefer beer or coffee. The main form of milk consumption is in a wide variety of mostly mild cheeses which are eaten for breakfast, as appetizers, as part of the **smorgasbord** (sliced cheeses and sliced meats), or for dessert with fruits.

FRUITS AND VEGETABLES
A wide variety of fruits and vegetables are used fresh in season, grown locally, or imported. Also used are canned, dried and frozen fruits and vegetables. The most popular of the fruits are apples and lingonberries, while the humble potato still outshines imported artichokes and white asparagus in most homes as the daily standby. Fruit preserves and pickled and brined vegetables are much enjoyed year-round.

MEATS AND ALTERNATES
Pork and pork products are most important, but other meats are used: veal, beef, lamb, offal products, chicken, and goose. Game fowl and wild animals are quite plentiful. The Laplander's domesticated reindeer meat is sold frozen, fresh, or smoked. Herring is the staple fish and is served fresh, salted, smoked, pickled, fried, or with a variety of sauces such as onion, mustard, cream, etc.

Other fish used include **rakor** (shrimp), **svardfisk**

(swordfish), smelts, perch, flounder, halibut, sole, haddock, and **lax** (salmon). Not only herring, but also these other fish are frequently served with sauces of which the most popular are white sauce, mustard sauce, and horse radish. Fish may be prepared by poaching, steaming, grinding, and forming into balls; fish may be pickled, smoked, or smoked then baked, or made into soufflés. Only occasionally is fish served breaded and fried.

Eggs are consumed in baked goods, as omelets or souffles, pickled or chopped into salads. The most-used legumes are the dried yellow peas made into the traditional Thursday soup: **arter med flask**. Small white dried beans are used for Swedish baked beans, a traditional dish which is part of almost any **smorgasbord**. Nuts, especially almonds, are used in desserts and in sweet bakery and pastries.

BREADS AND GRAINS
Rye breads and thin rye crispbreads are very popular. These may vary from very dark, heavy, and sour breads to light breads that are slightly sweet such as the Swedish **limpa** bread. Cooked cereals, gruels, and porridges are not used by the Swedes. The frequent serving of coffee is always accompanied with a selection of yeast coffee cakes, light plain sponge cakes, and crisp plain cookies – after meals, between meals, and as a form of hospitality.

FATS
Butter or pork fat (lard) is used in cooking and baking. Fats are also consumed in the many cheeses, in cream, which is used generously, and in whipped cream, which is enjoyed with desserts. Only occasionally is sour cream used.

SWEETS AND SNACKS
The Swedish sweet tooth is well satisfied by all the delicately sweet baked goods that accompany the many daily cups of coffee. A supply of these in any Swedish home is considered as much a staple as bread.

SEASONINGS
Brining, marinating, and smoking are ways of flavoring and preserving meats and fish, while dill and onions are the seasonings. Sometimes the addition of creamy sauces mellows the flavors of salt and smoke. Vegetables are cooked in soups or stews or otherwise well cooked then sauced with mustard and/or horse radish. Vegetables are also used in salads with a marinade of vinegar, onions, and spices. Fresh eggs, sweet butter, and cream lend their gentle rich taste to most bakery.

The centuries-old river trade with Kiev brought the first spices to Sweden: saffron, cardamom, cinnamon and cloves, cumin and coriander, anise and even pepper. There is variety on the Swedish spice shelf, but the hand that measures spices has a light touch: natural flavors from good ingredients is the overall preference.

BEVERAGES
Coffee is not only a staple in Sweden, it is a ritualized institution. No meal is complete without it, and it must be hot, strong, and black. Similarly, an evening appetizer or the famed **smorgasbord** is scarcely complete without the ritual of *skoal*: you hold an icy glass of **Akvavit** up high, eyeing your companion, say "Skoal!" and down the drink in one gulp with a final nod to your companion as you display the emptied glass. Some Swedes like to follow the **Akvavit** with beer, most others blithely continue with more **skoal** punctuated with salty morsels from the appetizer trays.

MEALS AND CUSTOMS
Once again, the predominant word for this discussion

FOODS COMMONLY USED

The Swedish cuisine, like its people, is a cosmopolitan one. Indigenous Scandinavian cooking makes the most of fine dairy products, rye, wheat and barley grains, domestic meats, game and herring. All are prepared with the combination of centuries-old skills, concern for appearance and natural flavors, and the gentle intermingling of French and German dishes that have filtered down into daily use from the royal courts of old.

Swedes prefer the robust natural flavors induced and preserved by salting and smoking, stewing and simmering. Seldom are any Swedish foods deep-fried. And the pride of the Swedish cuisine – baked delicacies – take their taste from fresh eggs, butter, and cream gently enhanced with cardamom, ginger, and freshly grated citrus peel.

Great eaters of meat, potatoes, and fish, the Swedes prefer to take their milk in the form of cheeses, and their grains in the form of pastries, light rye breads, and crackers.

on meal patterns is "ritual." Incredible as it may seem for such a sophisticated people, the Swedes delight not only in drinking according to prescribed ritual (as in the *skoal* tradition) but they eat certain foods in a specifically prescribed way, and they prepare festive foods exactly in the traditional way following centuries-old patterns.

The ritual of the **smorgasbord** is but one example. Accompanied by suitable **skoals**, salty herring dishes with tiny potatoes are always the first foods eaten from the huge array of selections. Each subsequent "course" follows a special order (never varied) and is eaten from a separate clean plate: other fish dishes and cold marinated salads, cold meats and varieties of pickles, a selection of hot dishes containing meats, eggs, fish, and, finally, on still another plate, a dessert of sliced cheeses and fruits.

It is even more interesting that this type of ordered procedure also applies to individual dishes. The familiar **smaland ostkaka** (previously made at home in a copper mold, but now available in stores everywhere in Sweden) is a rich but delicate molded cheesecake savored as a special dessert. Even at a party, the custom is for each person to taste a spoonful of the various **ostkakas** on display, but to take their taste from the center of the mold so that the cake may be fruit-filled the next day and served as a new dessert.

The potato dumplings of northern Sweden demand their own special ritual, too. A wedge is cut into the dumpling and the center filling of ground seasoned pork is removed to be immediately replaced with a golden lump of butter. As the butter melts in its warm potato cavern, the diner cuts off small pieces of filling and dumpling and after dunking each into the melted butter, pops them into the mouth.

Aside from carefully preserved traditions in drinking and eating, the Swedes also have a cherished way of thanking their hostess for a meal. The guest to the left of the hostess expresses thanks first, followed in order by every person around the table.

There are eating rituals for certain days of the week as well. Traditionally, on Thursday night, it is said that everyone in Sweden, from the king on down, enjoys a supper of yellow pea soup with pork, followed by tiny pancakes with lingonberry preserves. And on every Tuesday during Lent, the dessert can be counted on to be buns filled with almond cream (**semlor**) enjoyed with a glass of milk.

The Swedish day begins with coffee, which is essential for breakfast. One or two open-face sandwiches with coffee will likely take the hardworking Swedes happily off to their jobs, but those at home and children will often have yeast coffee cakes or bread and butter with their morning coffee. Children often take milk.

Lunch is most likely to be a small basic version of the **smorgasbord** called simply *sos*, meaning herring, cheese, and bread with butter. Or it may be the full splendor of the **smorgasbord** itself.

The evening meal, most often taken at home together with the family, is the hot meal of the day, often featuring a satisfying soup or a hearty meat or fish casserole always accompanied by potatoes. It finishes with a dessert and strong black coffee.

Throughout the day, coffee and pastry shops, sandwich shops, and fruit stands are all arrayed to tempt the unwary. It is certain that the Swede will have at least one coffee and pastry bread in the day. And at the close of a pleasant evening with guests, there is sure to be an offering once again of coffee and pastries or a savory hot casserole with beer as a **nattmatt** (nightcap) to assure that the guests will not suffer hunger pangs on the way home!

SPECIAL OCCASIONS

Although tolerant of all religious beliefs, most Swedes are Lutheran. Church affiliation is begun almost at birth, but holidays and festivities are celebrated more out of tradition and sheer enjoyment than out of any deep religious convictions.

Perhaps it is to allay the cold and the months of darkness, or perhaps it is an inextricable part of their penchant for ritual and order. Whatever the reason, the Swedish calendar is dotted with important reasons for special celebrations, each demanding special foods.

It is of particular interest that while Christmas and Easter are undoubtedly the most important festivals, the three most joyous festivals, are pagan in origin – May Day Eve (*Valborgsmassoafton*), Midsummer Even on June 24; and most beloved, St. Lucia Day, on December 13. For though Sweden can be classified as a modern sophisticated community, as recently as a hundred years ago almost 90 percent of her people were rural – deeply bound up in the land, the changing seasons, and the path of the sun in the sky. With traditions such a deeply ingrained part of Swedish life, it will likely be a very long time before any of these fade, if indeed their warmth and symbolism are discarded at all.

CHRISTMAS

The Swedes accepted Christianity in 1537 and joined the celebration of Christ's birthday with the ancient festival of "greeting the returning sun." Christmas actually begins on December 13 with the celebration of St. Lucia's Day. The early church assimilated the pagan tradition of Lussi Queen of Light with the Italian St. Lucia. In the home, the oldest daughter rises early in the morning and, dressed in a special white gown, a wreath of burning candles in her hair, she delivers to her parents a tray of fragrant saffron buns (**lussikator**) and fresh hot coffee. In the cities, a Lucia Queen is chosen and a huge party is given at which everyone enjoys the saffron buns and coffee.

The very next day, the hectic baking and preparations for Christmas begin in earnest. In the Swedish countryside it was always customary to slaughter a pig for Christmas with every portion being utilized: fresh meat cuts, hams and bacon, with the blood, feet, head, and offal all used in soups, sausages, puddings, and pates. In the past these dishes were served specifically in the Christmas season, but today they are readily available in specialty stores.

In pagan times, pigs, symbol of fertility, were sacrificed during the mid-winter bacchanal, and the Christmas ham of today is a symbol of that tradition. In fact the noon meal before Christmas Eve follows the ritual of **Doppa I Grytan**: dunking chunks of bread into the broth from the simmering ham and sausages. This too has its origins in the ancient belief that eating certain parts of the animal recaptured the animal's vigor for the diner. Modern-day Swedes may be unaware of the symbolism; they just happily enjoy the delicious feast.

The highlight of the Christmas Eve dinner is the **lutfisk**. There is a ritual to the preparation of this dish too. About three weeks before, the dried salted cod is set to soak in a daily change of fresh water; an immersion in lye and ashes for a period, then it is ready to be scrubbed and again immersed for at least seven days in a daily changing bath of fresh water. Finally it is considered ready for gentle poaching then a glaze of velvety white sauce completes the festive fish. Boiled potatoes accompany the **lutfisk** and then everyone is ready for the suspense of the dessert. Although it appears to be a simple creamy rice pudding, the dessert has one whole almond hidden in it. The lucky finder of the almond may win a special prize, and, if a girl finds it, she will be wed in the next year. In some homes, no one is allowed to sample their rice pudding until they have recited a poem.

To complete the cheerfulness of Christmas Eve, the tree is decorated, gifts distributed and everyone enjoys delicious samplings of the many Christmas cakes and cookies all washed down with **glogg** (hot spiced wine punch with almonds and raisins, made especially for Christmas).

At each place on the Christmas breakfast table a delectable **julhog** awaits demolishing: this is an edible stack consisting of rye bread, a sweet yeast ring, a currant saffron bun, a crisp flat cookie, and finally a red apple on top. Add hot coffee and that is a Swedish Christmas breakfast.

The Christmas ham becomes the center of what is really a magnificent feast: the Christmas **smorgasbord**. For even today, many Swedish women pride themselves in preparing all of the festive foods in traditional Christmas splendor. The centerpiece of fruits and nuts is a reminder of sacrifices made to the gods at this time to bless and provide plenty for the table.

Once again **Akvavit** is served with many **skoals**, although some prefer **Glogg** (hot spiced wine punch). Meanwhile the children eat, laugh, and play happily with their gifts, comparing those from *Jultomte*, the Swedish elf-like version of Santa Claus. And the woven straw *julbocken* (Christmas ram woven of straw) will swing from the chandelier as a reminder that long ago a Swedish Christmas was celebrated with straw strewn all over the floor.

ANNANDAGEN
This is the name given to the days between Christmas and New Year's, days of parties, drinking, eating and, above all, gatherings of family and friends.

EPIPHANY – JANUARY 6
This holiday is the solemn commemoration of the Three Wise Men, celebrated quietly in the home or in the church.

ST. CANUTE'S DAY
This falls on January 13 and is also called affectionately, if a little sadly, Knut's Day. This is the day when all the festive decorations of the holiday season are carefully put away. Even the Swedes know that there is a time to return to the realities of everyday living.

SHROVE TUESDAY
This is the day before Ash Wednesday, and throughout Sweden light yeast buns filled with almond paste and whipped cream or almond paste and hot milk are served for lunch. Each Tuesday through Lent the dessert will be these same buns, called **semlor**.

It has always been a Swedish rural custom to give gifts of sweets such as buns, cakes, and biscuits for special occasions or just out of appreciation or affection. This may be the origin of the Shrove Tuesday custom of giving sweet treats to children.

WAFFLE DAY
Waffle Day takes place towards the end of March, and was originally called *Var Fru*, meaning "Our Lady," to commemorate the Virgin Mary's Annunciation Day. Later the name became *Vaffer* and finally Vaffel. And for each of the three meals of that day waffles are served.

EASTER

Many old country superstitions have full sway at Easter time. After the house is cleaned, the broom is locked up so that the Easter Witch cannot spirit it away. During Lent birch twigs are picked and placed in the house; if they sprout green leaves by Easter it is said to symbolize growth in nature. There are many more such legends, and most are not taken seriously but followed out of fun or for tradition's sake.

Good Friday is a quiet, solemn day; simple humble foods are eaten such as herring and boiled potatoes and a sweet soup of cardamom-flavored ale is often the dessert. Easter Eve is celebrated with a **smorgasbord** but this time the highlight of the table is the mass of hard eggs which the children share in delightful competition, to see who can eat the most. For eggs with all their symbolism of life, growth, and vitality are an important Easter symbol.

VALBORGSMASSOAFTON

Also known as *Walpurgis Night*, the eve of May Day is celebrated with outdoor gatherings, singing, and the lighting of huge bonfires.

CHRIST'S ASCENSION DAY

Celebrated forty days after Easter, this occasion usually coincides with the fishermen's first good catch of the season, so the menu features fresh-caught fish with horse radish sauce.

PINGST OR WHITSUNTIDE

A happy flower-filled holiday, just ten days after Christ's Ascension Day. Most often celebrated with happy announcements of First Communion, engagements, etc. The menu invariably features fresh fish.

MIDSUMMER EVE

The festival to celebrate the longest day of the year, June 23, features dancing and the crowning of the Midsummer Queen in most North American Swedish communities. In Sweden, however, this is the special night when spells can be cast and dreams dreamed. With a mystical sun dazzling for almost twenty-four hours and resting for a brief two hours of dusk anything can happen. So this is the night that young Swedish girls gather nine different flowers to tuck under their pillows to conjure special dreams of their lovers.

AUGUST

The last of the bright soft summer nights coincides happily with the crayfish season, and outdoor parties abound. Lit by colored lanterns or flickering candles, the diners gather around a table set with a huge platter of crayfish, bibs for everyone, beer and **Akvavit**. For more reasons than one, it may be difficult to tell whether it is night or day by the time the party ends.

MARTINMAS OR ST. MARTIN'S DAY

Martin Luther's Name Day, November 11, also happens to coincide with traditions much older than Christianity in Sweden. The slaughtering of animals, with all the attendant rendering of fat, smoking, and sausage-making, began, in olden times, towards the end of October in order to prepare for the feast at the end of December. November 11 was the time for the geese slaughter, and to this day, *Martinmas* is celebrated with roast goose stuffed with apples and prunes, preceded by a rich soup made from the goose blood. The spectacular dessert specialty of the day – **spettkaka** – is a wondrously intricate cake baked by dribbling an egg and sugar batter on a rotating spit.

GLOSSARY OF FOODS AND FOOD TERMS

Akvavit: the clear, faintly caraway-flavored liquor without which there could be no *skoal*, that formidable Scandinavian ritual of the raised glass, the joint meeting of eyes (as if in agreement to the intent) followed by the downing of the potent brew, a nod, and the raising of the emptied glass. **Akvavit** may be distilled from potatoes or grains, and though the caraway flavor is available here, many other varieties of herb-, spice-, and even flower-flavored **Akvavit** are available in Sweden. Always served very cold, the bottle can also be placed in a container of water to be frozen and unmolded for serving, the liquor is then served by tipping the bottle, ice and all. (This is done in Russia using vodka.)

Appelkaka: apple cake.

Doppa I Grytan: the Christmas custom of dipping chunks of rye bread into the broth where the Christmas ham and sausages are simmering. This forms the lunch before Christmas Eve.

Fasan: cut up pheasant pieces placed in a casserole over fruits and oven-baked with white wine. Served with oven brown potatoes.

Fisk: fish.

Frukt Kram: a compote of fruit or berries, slightly thickened with potato flour and served with milk or cream.

Glogg: hot spiced wine punch that includes **Aquavit** and vermouth. A combination to make any occasion festive!

Gos: bass.

Grolangkaalsuppe: a thick hearty winter soup made with salt pork, kale, and potatoes.

Gronsaks: vegetables.

Inlagd Gurka: freshly pickled cucumbers.

Inlagd Sill: pickled herring.

Julglogg: a hot spiced wine punch with almonds and raisins, served especially on Christmas Day.

Julhog: an edible stack, consisting of rye bread, a sweet yeast ring, a currant saffron bun, a crisp flat cookie, and finally a red apple on top. Usually consumed at Christmas.

Julsinka: Christmas ham.

Kaldolmar: meat-stuffed cabbage rolls.

Knackebrod: the crisp dimpled Swedish flatbread, made mostly of rye flour.

Kottbullar: essential on the **smorgasbord** table. The famed tiny Swedish meatballs made with a blend of beef, potato and seasonings, browned in butter. Usually served dry for the buffet table, a sauce may be prepared to serve them for a meal.

Krans: turban-shaped yeast coffee cakes fragrant with spices and almonds.

Lax: salmon.

Leverpastej: liver pate, usually prepared in a mold and glazed with aspic.

Limpa: round Swedish rye bread flavored with molasses and finely grated orange peel.

Lussikator: the saffron and raisin yeast buns served warm with fresh coffee especially for the St. Lucia Day's breakfast.

Lutfisk: dried salt cod that undergoes a ritual of special soaking for several weeks before being presented as the main course for the Christmas Eve meal. Gently poached and served with a glaze of white sauce.

Nors: smelts.

Ost: cheeses.

Plattar: light crisp little pancakes made with a simple egg, flour and milk batter and cooked in butter. These are always served with lingonberries, fresh or preserved.

Rakor: shrimps.

Saffronsbrod: saffron yeast bread.

Sjomansbiff: sailor's beef. A hearty stew of layered, thinly sliced and pounded beef, sliced potatoes, stock and dark beer. Served with pickled beets.

Smavarmt: the warm dishes of the **smorgasbord**, eaten only in small sampling amounts. These include omelets, creamed dishes, custards, souffles of vegetables or fish, livers, mushrooms, sweetbreads, ground meat dishes, rolls, and vol-au-vent specialties.

Spettkaka: the most original and intriguing of all Swedish cakes. Baked on a rotating spit by dribbling the egg and sugar batter in trickles. The final result is a tall cone of intertwined delicate bakery that dissolves in the mouth with a soft powdery sweetness. Specialty of St. Martin's Day, November 11.

Spritsar: rich short butter cookies.

Stekt Kyckling: butter-roasted chicken served with creamy gravy and boiled or mashed potatoes.

Svardfisk: swordfish.

Vaffel: waffles. The specialty of the March waffle festival when they are eaten for the three meals of the day.

CHAPTER 48

SWISS

If the Swiss have a gentle but perceptible air of superiority, it is well deserved. For over 675 years, Switzerland has maintained her status as an independent nation – no small feat for a nation in the heart of Europe.

Switzerland is made up of 22 separate cantons, each almost a country in miniature, with its own history, food specialties, local government, and even a distinctly local dialect. The 6.7 million Swiss profess membership in 18 faiths (but predominantly Protestant), 3 main ethnic groups – Italian, German, and French – and speak 4 languages – German, French, Italian, and Romansh. Although German predominates, most Swiss can speak several languages, and the Latin-based Romansh is spoken mostly in the Grisons area.

This diversity in ethnic background and languages, as well as the number of distinct areas, is a unique situation, for no other country as small as Switzerland can claim such a patchwork, and a peaceful one at that. In fact, it is probably because each Swiss is a member of a minority group that they are so tolerant of other nationalities, languages, and lifestyles. However, their national tolerance stops short at any indication of autocracy or bureaucracy; it is believed that true Swiss will sell their souls to no one.

So loyal are the Swiss to their hometown that marriage outside of their canton is considered a "mixed marriage." Emotional and traditional ties are strong: the family comes first, then the hometown, the canton, and finally Switzerland itself. Swiss society, like Swiss loyalty, is traditional and well ordered, and perhaps this too is a factor in individual security and self-confidence.

The Swiss characteristically rise early and work hard and often late hours. Quality and value-for-money are basic concepts. They expect this same seriousness from everyone else and will not tolerate either shoddy work or inferior products. More than half the population is engaged in agriculture in small rural areas; the rest are involved in a diversity of specialized industries such as watchmaking and precision machines and tools. Yet Switzerland suffers from a chronic labor shortage and each year approximately half a million laborers are imported from other countries, even from as far away as Greece and Turkey.

It is also no accident that some of the finest chef and hotel administration schools are located in Switzerland. Not only do the Swiss have a penchant for education and culture, they are also famed for their hospitality and politeness. Customers are always considered as personal guests and their comfort and happiness are of prime importance. Guests enjoy warm, clean surroundings, bountiful food servings, and a surfeit of "good days" and "thank yous" as well as the idyllic scenery of picturesque towns, green valleys, and snow-tipped mountains. Yet although their chef schools teach "haute cuisine" and their hospitality is all-inclusive, the Swiss are quietly reserved in their friendships and domestic life and prefer the simplest of menus.

Swiss life, as Swiss food, is very much influenced by neighbors: France, Germany, Austria, and Italy. Specialty dishes from each of these countries have long been intertwined with local regional specialties to produce a simple but substantial cuisine centering on soups, breads and nourishing cheese, egg and vegetable dishes. Recent trends in foods have attempted more exotic fare adapted from Chinese and Malaysian cooking but retaining mildness in flavor.

One of the most successful "food movements" was started by Dr. Bircher-Benner in Zurich. He invented **muesli**, a combination of toasted oats, shredded dried apples and nuts. His movement stresses the inclusion of fresh salads and wholegrain cereals, but it is **muesli** that has attained almost a worldwide reputation as a "Swiss breakfast."

Switzerland is many things: mountains and lakes, specialized schools and industries, a peaceful mix of people and languages, a huge wheel of Swiss cheese or a chunk of smooth Swiss chocolate. But probably most of all, Switzerland is people – people who have learned more than any other nation in the world the consummate art of blending tolerance and politeness with innate simplicity, to end up with a subtle sophistication entirely Swiss. It is a phenomenon as incredible as their mix of foods adopted from other countries. Somehow, in Swiss hands, these foods become purely Swiss.

DOMESTIC LIFE
The Swiss reputation for hard work, orderliness, and simplicity is evidenced in the home. Swiss homemakers are "scrubbers": every corner is scrupulously clean and ordered. Swiss kitchens vie with any in the western world for efficiency, appliances and convenience, but gadgets are used only if they are truly timesaving. Shoddy materials and poor quality are as little tolerated in the kitchen as they are in industry.

Although the true origin of Swiss **fondues** is lost in antiquity, the fondue remains a favored meal and a form of entertainment. Most Swiss homes have the necessary accoutrements: the *caquelon*, a shallow but sturdy earthenware casserole for heating the cheese fondue, a supply of long-handled forks for dipping, and a practical stand and heat source usually for alcohol heating. For **fondue friture** (dunking foods in hot oil), the Swiss home will be equipped with a deep heavy metal pot, wider at the base than at the top to prevent tipping and possible spattering while frying. For the newly introduced chocolate fondue (introduced in New York by Beverley Allen for the Swiss Chalet Restaurants), a small candle-heated earthenware pot is used.

Finally, for the delightful Swiss supper of **raclette**, an efficient gadget that not only keeps plates warm but also holds a big wedge of cheese firmly in place for melting is also a part of the culinary equipment. Mountain cheeses such as **Gomser**, **Raclette**, **Belalp**, or **Bagnes** are best for melting.

The Swiss standard of living is very high and this is reflected in the many specialty shops for bakery and pastries, meats and fancy delicatessen. Preparation of foods, packaging and displays reach such a high standard that they can seldom be duplicated elsewhere. Huge varieties of imported goods of every type await the shopper and convenience foods abound. Even raw meats in butcher shops are displayed with artistry, garnished with sprigs of greens and trimmed and shaped so that the homemaker need only cook them. In addition, a growing variety of prepared foods awaits the harried homemaker. The long tradition of daily shopping to ensure the freshest produce and baked goods is slowly declining as more and more women join the workforce. Even the sale of deep freezers is increasing.

DAIRY PRODUCTS
There is no shortage of quality dairy products in the Swiss diet. Fresh milk is almost a staple food in the form of coffee and milk (**cafe au lait** or **milchkaffee**) which is served so frequently that it is considered more of a food than a mere beverage. Milk and cheese are almost daily a part of soups or quick dishes that make up light meals, while the **fondues** and **raclettes** of Switzerland are well known.

There is scarcely a canton in Switzerland without its own special version of a cheese soup: thick, thin or baked with bread as a pudding or casserole. Cheese is also an integral ingredient in soufflés, sauces, dumplings, fritters, croquettes, and garnishes as well as pies and tarts. One of the oldest traditional dishes is **fanz**, made like a thick white sauce with flour, milk, and butter and then eaten with bread and **cafe au lait**.

FRUITS AND VEGETABLES
Orchards abound in Switzerland, but when fresh fruits are scarce, much use is made of canned or dried fruits. Fruits are served fresh in season, stewed, or made into puddings or tarts. Apples and cherries are special favorites and these are made into fritters (**fnutli**, Basel apple fritters, or **chriesitutschli**, fresh cherry bunches dipped in batter and delicately fried), puddings or fruit soups. A bowl of stewed fruit accompanied with **cafe au lait** is a popular finish to a meal. More recently fruit and yogurt combinations have been gaining in popularity.

FOODS COMMONLY USED
Quality of ingredients and simplicity in preparation and serving of foods are typical of Swiss menus. There is stress on the importance of soups and many dishes made from cheese. Much bread is consumed and is a part of all meals. Meats and fish are often expensive so are purchased and cooked with care, often extended with vegetables or cereal foods.

The recent food reform movement stressing fresh vegetable salads and the use of wholegrain breads and cereals has made a definite impression; there is an increase not only in the fresh vegetables eaten and wholegrain bread preference, but also more concern for the cooking of vegetables.

Staple foods include bread, potatoes, and cereals with a good consumption of milk and cheese. Favorite methods of food preparation are soups, stews, and simple casserole dishes.

Green beans, spinach, Swiss chard, turnips, leeks, asparagus, cabbage, squash, and many other vegetables are available in profusion but none can reach the popularity or versatility of the potato. Potato soups, dumplings, baked puddings, pancakes, fritters, cheese and potato casseroles – the number and variety of potato dishes is staggering.

But one potato dish is supreme: **kartoffelrosti**. This dish is so popular it is known everywhere as simply **rosti**. Mealy parboiled potatoes are coarsely shredded, then are packed into a large hot skillet sputtering with butter. When the bottom is crisply browned the whole cake is inverted (easy if inverted on a platter held over the pan, then slid carefully back) to brown the second side. Served in wedges, the crisply browned **rosti** accompanies almost any meat, fish, or even cheese dish and often stands alone as a light supper.

MEATS AND ALTERNATES
Meat, fish, and game are expensive in Switzerland and are purchased, cooked, and eaten with care and respect. The amount consumed depends very much on the family income, but traditional frugality usually results in every part of the meat being carefully used. Fats will be rendered, bones and trimmings will make soups, and meat will be generously accompanied with vegetables or cereals such as rice, cornmeal, or pasta to extend the meaty flavor.

In many areas, meat is for Sundays only, while the poor may taste it only once in a year. Only recently have *rotisseurs* (restaurants specializing in expensive broiled or roasted meats) become popular. Part of the reason may be that Swiss cattle are raised mainly as milk cows and work animals with the result that their flesh is too often tough and stringy and best suited to soup-making and the long simmering of stews or the well-seasoned mixtures that make sausages. Swiss sausages are so varied and so popular that they probably represent the favored form of meat, and there is a type of sausage for every taste and use from mild to spicy, whether for snacking, picnicking, leisurely dining or light suppers. Meats used include veal and beef, pork, venison and kid. Chickens, affectionately called **guggeli** or **mistkratzerli** (manure-scratchers) in German-speaking Switzerland, form the base of many a soup or stew.

Fish is not a staple, but is considered a delicacy. It is cooked with simplicity: usually simply baked or poached and served with butter or lemon. Trout, salmon, perch, and pike as well as eels and scampi are available, but largely only in the cities.

Eggs and legumes are seldom eaten as individual dishes; mostly they are consumed as ingredients. Eggs are a part of most cheese and milk baked casseroles as well as souffles, omelets and pancakes. Dried peas and beans are used in lesser quantities in soups.

BREADS AND GRAINS
It is almost an impossibility to think of a Swiss table set for a meal without bread. Breads and rolls are often the main part of breakfast, they accompany soups, they crumble or cube into casseroles and puddings with cheese or fruits or even vegetables, they are squeezed with water or milk to form stuffings, dumplings, fritters, and chunks of bread are dunked into cheese fondues, and even mop up creamy sauces and gravies.

Cereals have been a Swiss food staple from earliest times. Gruels, porridges, and soups made from grains and flour are seldom used anymore except for the one traditional dish that has survived: **fanz**. Now popular mostly with shepherds, it is a thick white sauce made with milk, flour, and butter and served with bread and **milchkaffee** and is considered a satisfying meal.

Noodles and many pasta forms are served in the Italian way and also in typically Swiss style: cooked noodles tossed with butter-browned onions and sprinkled with cheese. Pasta is also a frequent ingredient in soups and a popular means of stretching meat dishes. In the area of Ticino (close to Italy), cooked cornmeal or polenta is frequently served as a bread, side dish, or as part of a baked dish with cheese. Rice is gaining in popularity and used as an emergency staple because of its versatility and excellent keeping qualities.

Not to be overlooked is the increasing use of whole grains in breads, rolls, and especially in the popular breakfast dish of toasted oats, shredded dried fruit, and nuts served with milk or yogurt called **muesli**.

FATS
Considerable fats are consumed in the form of cream and of course in the many varieties of cheese. Butter is favored for baking and cooking because of its flavor and abundant good quality, but the efficient homemaker makes good use of all fats whether beef drippings, chicken fat, lard or bacon fat. Oils are not widely used for cooking but are a salad dressing ingredient.

SWEETS AND SNACKS
Confiseries, those exquisite pastry shops, are located frequently enough in the cities to defy any resistance. A definite Swiss sweet tooth does exist, but it is more often assuaged by bread and butter with jam, or a "sweet supper" (pancakes or dumplings with sweet

sauce) than with ornate rich pastries. Chocolate, however, to the Swiss mind is more food than treat and will often be a part of a child's lunch or a hiker's pack for "quick energy."

SEASONINGS

Depending on the area and the predominating influence, the spice shelf in the Swiss kitchen may look more familiar to a German, French, or Italian cook. Dill, caraway, garlic, tarragon, white wine or tomatoes, garlic, basil, oregano or even a melange of all may be used in the Swiss kitchen.

Overall, Swiss foods are well cooked and not strongly flavored. Much use is made of **Maggi**, a seasoning sauce similar in taste and color to soy sauce, and **Aromat** or **Fondor** – popular trade names for monosodium glutamate, all of which are used frequently and sometimes overdone. But the array of bottles, jars, and tubes of condiments, spices, and herbs makes cooking in any language possible and probable in Switzerland.

BEVERAGES

The most popular beverage is strong coffee mixed with hot milk called **cafe au lait** or **milchkaffee**. It may be served at any meal, to all ages, and fresh **cafe au lait** will always be prepared for guests. Hot chocolate is also a popular drink, mostly for breakfast. Teas of all types including herbal brews are also popular, especially after the evening meal. Switzerland's famed **cheese fondue** may be accompanied with a single small glass of **kirsch** and followed by hot tea, never with cold drinks of any type as is so often the custom elsewhere. Areas influenced by the French or Italian drink wines, German-speaking areas favor beer. An overall sense of moderation in drinking alcoholic beverages predominates.

MEALS AND CUSTOMS

Hotel administration schools and internationally famous chefs' schools may teach sophisticated cuisine while Swiss restaurants may cater to every taste sensation, but in the Swiss home, light and simple meals are the rule.

Muesli and **milchkaffee** are a popular Swiss way to begin the day, but **cafe complet** or **chocolate complet** are still traditional. With either **cafe au lait** or hot chocolate as the mainstay, this simple breakfast revolves around an assortment of breads and rolls served with fresh butter and a variety of preserves.

The main meal of the day takes place at noon. Beginning with a hearty soup, dinner may go on to a main dish based on potatoes, cheese, fish or meat accompanied by a small salad and ending with fruit and cheese. The adults will usually have wine or water and the children will sip only water with the dinner.

A late afternoon snack at about four o'clock called *zvieri* will consist of sausages or ham with pickles and bread together with a quenching drink of hard cider or perhaps beer. Children will snack on bread and butter, women sometimes on **milchkaffee** or one of many teas with simple cakes or buns.

The evening meal may be one of the lightest and simplest of the day, consisting of bread, cheese, and **cafe au lait**, or a simple casserole of potatoes and a side salad and bread.

If these typical meal patterns sound too simplistic, then the reader is underestimating the quality of fresh foods and the consummate skill of preparation so typical of Swiss cuisine. Probably no meal can be simpler than the **raclette**. Here a wedge of fine mountain cheese is melted before a special heater or an open fire. Just at the right moment, the melted cheese is scraped onto a waiting hot platter and served at once accompanied with a crunchy sweet pickled gherkin and a few tartly sharp pickled onions. The final touch in both flavor and texture is a boiled mealy potato. Few dishes are simpler both in preparation and service and yet the contrasting tastes and textures are worthy of the most complex gastronomic masterpiece.

More widely known is the Swiss **cheese fondue**. There are many versions and variations but basically a shredded mixture of **Swiss Emmenthaler** and **Gruyere** cheeses are melted in simmering wine then lightly touched with a sniff of garlic (often just rubbed in the **caquelon**) and a splash of **kirsch**. Diners spear chunks of crusty bread and dip into the melted cheese mixture, giving a stir and a swirl at the same time. At the end of the meal, a tasty crust will have formed at the bottom of the pot and this should be lifted and served to all. A small glass of **kirsch** is served in the middle of the eating, while hot tea is usually served to complete the fondue dinner. Sometimes servings of sausages and pickles with bread may be added to the meal.

SPECIAL OCCASIONS

More than 18 religious groups claim members in the 6.7 million Swiss population. By a slight majority, Protestants predominate.

The many festivities that dot the Swiss calendar focus on the change of seasons, the movement of the cattle, planting and harvesting, and of course religious celebrations. All have in common an abundance of good food and a colorful flurry of regional costumes. Both Catholics and Protestants celebrate Christmas with a variety of special cakes and cookies but no special menu; the best that is available is served with pride. In the German-speaking areas, Christmas Eve is celebrated with gifts and a candlelit tree. Customs and ceremonies in each home may be traced to either French, German, or Italian influences, together with individual family preferences.

As in the Netherlands, the Swiss have no Santa Claus, but they do set aside December 6 as the special evening when St. Nicholas brings fruits and candies and small gifts to all deserving children, and for the naughty ones only a switch! This holiday has no religious connotation and is celebrated by almost everyone.

As in many other countries, Easter is celebrated with the fresh exuberance of approaching spring: chocolate bunnies, colored eggs, special cakes and cookies – as well as the sober rejoicing accompanying church services. The many popular meatless dishes make Lent less of a hardship, and one of the traditionally favorite dishes is **basler mehlsuppe**. This is a typical "brown roux soup" prepared by browning flour in butter then adding water to form a stock. Often little more than a bit of seasoning is added, and in the case of the **basler mehlsuppe** the flavor is of bay leaf and cloves.

Celebrating the coming and passing of the seasons is a Swiss excuse for more festivities. Effigies of "Winter" are joyously burned to hasten the departure of the cold and to welcome the gentle warmth of spring. The end of summer and the beginning of autumn is heralded with animals decorated with garlands of flowers and people dressed in local or national costumes. They gather in the towns to welcome the descent of shepherds and their flocks from the high mountain pastures of summertime, happy that they will be home for winter. Later in the fall season, the wearing of golden sun masks on St. Martin's Day (November 11) marks the beginning of wintry days.

GLOSSARY OF FOODS AND FOOD TERMS

Aromat: trade name for monosodium glutamate.

Berner Platte: a massive platter of green beans, boiled potatoes, and sauerkraut artfully topped with smoked and salted pork, boiled tongue, and several types of spicy sausages. Served with side dishes of mustard sauces.

Bindenfleisch: meat that is cured then dried in clear mountain air, retaining a fine flavor and bright color. Served very thinly sliced together with wholegrain bread and red wine. A specialty of the Grisons area.

Cholermus Pancakes: typical of a "sweet" country supper, huge pancakes reputedly first made by the herdsmen who then tore them with forks and browned them in butter. Served with fruits and sugar and steaming mugs of **Cafe au Lait**, this is considered a satisfying supper.

Chriesitotsch: Zurich's traditional baked cherry pudding.

Chriesitutschli: fresh bunches of cherries dipped in batter, deep-fried, and served with cinnamon sugar.

Fanz: a thick sauce of flour, butter, and milk eaten with bread and **Milchkaffee** to make a light supper. Typical of the many soup and gruel-like mixtures that were early staple foods for the Swiss. One of the oldest traditional herdsmen's dishes.

Fondor: trade name for monosodium glutamate.

Gonterser Bock: a light supper meal of hard-cooked eggs or cored apples that are batter-dipped and fried then sliced and eaten with fruit compote.

Kabisuppe: a soup made of shredded browned cabbage, beef broth, and rice all well cooked together.

Kartoffelkuchen: a baked potato pudding from Grisons made from boiled riced potatoes that are packed into a baking dish. A mixture of eggs, cream, and grated cheese is poured over and the whole casserole is baked in the oven.

Kartoffelplatzli: another Grisons dish made from a soft dough of potatoes, flour, cheese, and eggs. The dough is shaped into a long roll then sliced and browned in butter.

Kasuppe: cheese soup, a favorite in every area of Switzerland. Countless variations.

Lattich und Speck: minced onions and tomatoes sautéed with small heads of Romaine lettuce and crisply fried bacon. This dish makes a complete meal when served with **Rosti** and fresh fruit.

Maggi: a trade name representing many manufactured food products but especially noted for a liquid seasoning of flavor extracts made from blended grains. Looks and tastes like soy sauce.

Maluns: another famed potato dish from the Grisons area. Cold, finely grated potatoes are stirred in quantities of sizzling butter until they form tiny crisp balls. A dish of **Maluns**, a dried fruit compote, and endless cups of **Cafe au Lait** of fresh milk make a meal.

Metzgette: pig-slaughtering day in rural areas. Accompanied by much food and drink with only the pig's squeal being allowed to escape the endless smoking, curing, salting, sausage-making, and fresh meat-cutting.

Milchkaffee: a satisfying blend of hot milk and hot coffee.

Muesli or **Musli**: the Swiss breakfast cereal invented by Dr. Bircher-Benner, made of toasted uncooked oats, grated apples, and nuts. The mixture is usually refrigerated overnight with cold milk and eaten in the morning with a topping of fruit, wheat germ, brown sugar, or any desired combination.

Omeletten: pancakes of any type. German-speaking areas in Switzerland often make a supper of a fruit tart, a rice and milk pudding, or pancakes and fruit all served with the usual **Milchkaffee**. It is these light sweet suppers that often cause dissension between the Swiss homemakers and the workers from other countries; they are not satisfied with such a light evening meal!

Paiuolo: Ticino follows many of the food patterns of northern Italy, and the making of polenta (cornmeal) is one of them. The **Paiuolo** is the big tinned copper kettle used to cook the polenta over an open hearth. It is stirred with a special wood paddle.

Pfnutli or **Fnutli**: Basel apple fritters.

Potato Gnocchi: mashed cooked potatoes blended with flour to form a dough which is then shaped into little fingers. After drying for about thirty minutes, the little shapes are poached in salted water and served with a buttery tomato sauce. As popular in Ticino as they are in Italy.

Raclette: derived from the French verb *racler*, which means "to scrape off," refers to a supper plate of melted cheese (**Gomser**, **Belalp**, **Raclette**, or **Bagnes**) served with a boiled potato, pickled gherkins, and onions. As many plates are eaten as desired.

Rettich Salat: a salad of coarsely grated white radishes blended with a dressing of oil, vinegar, and mayonnaise and flavored with Dijon mustard, salt and pepper.

Rosti: the national potato pancake. This dish appears so frequently in homes and restaurants that it is unlikely that many days go by without the Swiss enjoying their **Rosti** together with **Lattich und Speck**, **Leberspiessli** (skewered liver and bacon) or any number of other dishes. **Rosti** is made from long shreds of boiled potatoes packed into a pan sizzling with butter. After browning one side, the huge pancake is flipped (a plate placed on top and then inverting the whole is the easiest method) to crisp the second side. Served whole to the table, wedges are cut to serve.

Saure Pflumli: traditional sweet and sour purple plum relish served with meats, game, and cold cuts.

Schwartztee: Indian tea.

Schweinspfeffer: jugged pork.

Stierenaugen: though eggs are seldom served alone, if they are then it is in the form of "bull's eyes" – the name of this dish is for simple fried eggs.

Wiworm: a New Year's drink of diluted spiced wine served hot.

Zuchertopf: a Zurich dish of meat and rice.

Zuger Kirschtorte: cherry tart, another Zurich specialty.

CHAPTER 49

Syrian. See People of the Fertile Crescent.

THAI

Images of Thailand, formerly known as Siam, undulate through the memory as gently as a Thai smile and as gracefully as a Thai dancer. In the capital of Bangkok there are still smiles and somewhere there are also dances. But the reality of city streets includes wafts of purple pollution, honking horns, and sticky heat. This contrasts with the calm of shimmering rice paddies in the countryside and the floating markets in the canals selling everything from flowers, vegetables, and fruits, to snacks, ice cream, and hot coffee.

Emanating from gilded temple halls and private funeral meetings, one can hear tinkling bells and thumping gongs in mystical rhythm with chanting monks. All of these images, sounds, and smells impress the senses as surely as the sharply etched flavors and exquisitely carved garnishes of a Thai meal. Ancient Siam has only cautiously given way to bustling modernity – ancient ways continually emerge and reveal themselves as Thailand's firm cultural foundation.

Thai gentleness seems to belie their reputed origins as feisty T'ai tribes escaping the Mongolian invasions of southwestern China in the early tenth century. It also seems to belie their ensuing history of ravaging wars with their neighbors, the Burmese, Cambodians, Laotians, and Vietnamese. But the wars were real and the memory of the sad destruction of their ancient capital of Ayuthaya by the Burmese in 1767 is still commemorated today. Perhaps their history is proof of the strength and love for independence that hovers under the gentle face and manners.

Another Thai characteristic is their genuine love and deeply felt respect for their royal family. Thais have never forgotten the wisdom and diplomatic finesse of Thai royalty who, over several hundred years, successfully fended off foreign traders, missionaries, and colonizers. For unlike most of Southeast Asia, foreigners never colonized Thailand, trade was strictly controlled, and more than 92 percent of the people remain Buddhists. A bloodless coup by the military in 1932 replaced the absolute monarchy with a constitutional one, but did not displace Thai respect for their royalty.

Thai confidence and tranquility is enhanced by unwavering religious devotion. Distinct from the more widespread Mahayana Buddhism (in China, Japan, Tibet, Korea, and Mongolia), Theravada Buddhism (confined to Sri Lanka (Ceylon), Burma (Myanmar), Cambodia (Khmer), and Thailand) centers on monks and monasteries and emphasizes individual responsibility and practice of correct behavior. This includes tolerance, avoidance of criticism, anger, and conflict. Merit is achieved through practicing meditation, feeding the monks, and making donations to the temple. Each Thai male will voluntarily spend a period of time as a monk in a monastery, engaged in work and study, practicing meditation and living a strict personal discipline that will be a part of his entire life. The presence of more than 32,000 *wats* or Buddhist monasteries throughout the land attests to the importance of Thai religious devotion.

Thai smiles may be interpreted as warm and welcoming, but a Thai smile may not always connote approval, enjoyment, or agreement. It may simply be a means of soothing anger, softening criticism, avoiding confrontation, or hiding embarrassment. Thais also smile or laugh in sad situations – their way of hiding their despair or sorrow. And sometimes Thai smiles radiate from a special attitude rooted in a favorite saying, "*Mai pen rai*," meaning "Never mind; it doesn't matter." "*Mai pen rai*" is the Thai way of getting out of a rut and moving on with daily life.

If a smile does not always mean pleasure and approval, there is no doubt that in Thailand fun always means fun. What matters very much in Thai culture is the notion of *sanuk*, meaning fun. This element of enjoyment pervades all activities, relationships, and communications whether business or social. Mealtimes especially are a time for fun and giggles, hearty laughter and enjoyment of food and people; business and serious matters are not part of meal conversations. Friends and guests who can spark humor and enjoyment will delight their Thai hosts.

Despite Thai pride in cultural traditions, many of these bear imprints of influence from others. The Thai language has been adapted from the Chinese, the Thai alphabet from the Cambodians, aspects of democracy and corporate management have been distilled from the west, and even important elements of cuisine have been adapted from China and India. Yet each aspect of Thai culture remains somehow distinctively and irrevocably Thai.

There are traceable influences from other cultures threading through Thai cuisine too. Chinese influence is strong. Thai dishes and meals are cooked on stovetops often in Chinese woks, and meals consistently balance flavors as in the Chinese Five Flavor Principles of sweet, sour, hot, salty, and bitter. And most of Thailand has adopted long grain rice for everyday meals while only the northern sections still use short grain sticky rice. The Thais have simplified sauces, use mainly two kinds of dips, and never thicken sauces with starch as Chinese cooks do.

Even the complex and diverse curries of India have been simplified to four formulaic curries: yellow, green, red, and **musaman** (from the Muslim style). Like the Chinese, Thais do not use dairy products

FOODS COMMONLY USED

Despite roots in China and the strong influence of neighboring cuisines, Thai food stands distinctively apart in simplicity and organization. Steaming hot white **khao** (rice) is the center of each meal accompanied by **kaeng chud** (soup), **kaeng** (dishes with sauce, like curries), **kreung kieng** (dishes that are dry like steamed, grilled foods or salads [**yum**]). Most **kaeng** soups are herb-fragrant broths sipped throughout the meal – a boon to chili-seared mouths. Before eating with a spoon and fork came into fashion, the **kaeng** dishes were always mixed deftly with rice then eaten from the fingers. Platters of intricately sculptured fresh fruits may sweetly finish the meal.

Chinese-style fried rice is considered a snack in Thailand and can comprise any mixture of meats, fish, seafood, and vegetables with leftover rice.

While rice is the staple of most meals, noodles (**phat**) made from wheat, rice flour, mung bean starch (cellophane noodles), or egg are widely enjoyed. If Thais are eating with chopsticks, they are either in a Chinese restaurant, or they are enjoying a bowl of garnished noodles for a quick lunch.

The key flavors are sweet, sour, hot, salty, and bitter. Sweetness is most often provided with the flavorful touch of palm sugar, actually made from the sap of the coconut palm, in taste similar to brown sugar.

What really separates Thai food from the cuisines of other Southeast Asian cultures is the deft combination of chilies, garlic, and **nam pla** (fermented fish sauce) or **kapi** (dried shrimp paste) with the refreshing tartness of tamarind, lemon grass, or **kaffir** lime leaves and rind. The warm fragrance and taste of freshly roasted peanuts can be detected from the peanut cooking oil, tasted in the fiery hot peanut dipping sauce or easily seen as ground or crushed peanut garnishes.

Other distinct flavors starring in Thai cuisine include fresh herbs – coriander, basil, and mint that are used generously not only in cooking but also as part of fresh vegetable plates served with dips. In addition, four distinct curry pastes – red, yellow, green, and **musamam** (from the Muslim style) embellish cubed poultry, meats, fish, seafood, and vegetables, transforming them into delectable, and usually fiery, Thai curries. At least one curry dish will be part of the main meal.

Fish and seafood are enjoyed especially in cities and coastal regions. Chicken and duck are eaten more often than beef or pork. All meats, fish, and seafood are prepared in classic ways that vary little from one table to another: in one of the four curries, fried, steamed, or grilled. Thai street vendors are famed for serving tasty skewers of **satay** of chicken, pork, or beef, with spicy hot peanut sauce for dipping.

A plethora of tropical fruits and vegetables vie for a place on the table – their bounty emerging from Thai fields, orchards, both from the fertile valleys and from the northern temperate regions. Fish, seafood, and poultry enjoy a place with vegetables and rice, and the luscious variety of tropical fruits sometimes served with sticky rice provides a sweet finish to a main meal.

Tiny side bowls used for dipping sauces and dry garnishes deserve a word. These dishes are used freely by diners so that each morsel may be seasoned to taste not only with sauces but also with crushed nuts, roasted ground rice, finely chopped chilies or vegetables or whatever is appropriate to the foods served.

Thai-produced beer and wine as well as whisky find their place at meals, but salted fruit drinks of many varieties are also very popular. Clear soups are often taken with meals in the same way as westerners may sip a fruit drink.

(used so generously in India) and use few soy products. Instead, Thai sauces, soups, and stews are smoothed and mellowed with coconut milk.

Thai cooking was already spicy with black and green peppercorns before the Portuguese traders introduced varieties of hot chilies. But ever since, Thais have used a variety of chilies with consummate skill, and black and green peppercorns have been relegated to a secondary level of importance.

A very important influence on Thai food over the centuries has been the royal palace cuisine inspired by the food expertise of some of Thailand's kings as well as visiting dignitaries and traders. Although northerners prefer simple basic dishes based on vegetables with little meat or fish, and serve these with sticky short grain rice, the southerners prefer hotter more elaborate dishes, sumptuously garnished. Palace foods provided inspirational combinations and artful decorations that are now classic Thai.

No other cuisine in the world takes decorative food sculpture and colorful arrangement to such heights. Humble onions and turnips become lilies and chrysanthemums, brilliantly colored chilies become feathery flowers, and many varieties of vegetables and fruits become butterflies, cameos, fishes, and birds. A simple plate of fresh vegetables and green herbs can delight the eye as surely as a delicate watercolor painting.

DOMESTIC LIFE

In almost constant sweltering heat and humidity, more than 80 percent of the Thai population of about 55 million live and work in rural and mountain regions. Here the simple practical homes are built upon stilts to avoid flooding during the monsoons and to provide cool shade for work and storage areas for cows and chickens. The upper levels are for the family, mainly for eating and sleeping. Everywhere cow dung and chicken droppings mingle their penetrating odors with drifts of spicy cooking and fragrant herbs. Most cooking is done outdoors near the house. The people walk, cycle, or pack into rickety buses to visit health centers, reading centers, and markets. Electricity and running water have been extended to most of the rural population. Small markets and roadside vendors are everywhere, providing fruits, flowers, vegetables, and other necessities as well as instant snacks and ready-cooked meals.

The two main cities are Bangkok, the capital and tourist destination, and Chiang Mai located in the northern mountain region. Both cities lack planning and efficient sewage, water, garbage and electrical systems. Construction and repairs clog the streets, making the slow-moving traffic of black-spewing exhaust fumes almost impenetrable to foot traffic. Yet somehow people maneuver their way through it all with grace and good humor.

In Bangkok, elaborate houses and tall apartments cluster along the same streets with ramshackle slum dwellings, elegant formal buildings, and traditional Buddhist temples called *wats*. Here and there, these high towers and curved rooflines of the glistening, dazzling gilded *wats* seem to guide the eye and mind to higher things, but sidewalks are clustered with vendors of snacks, meals, clothing, souvenirs, and flowers of indescribable variety and beauty.

The nearby *klongs* (canals) are dotted with *sampans* (boats) selling everything from clothing and housewares to ready-to-eat meals and snacks, fresh fruit, flowers, herbs and vegetables. The cacophony of city streets assaults the ears with the calls of hawkers, chatter of pedestrians and children, and the honking horns, belching buses, cars and trucks seem to form an impenetrable mass.

Somehow, bicycles with two or three passengers or bundles dangling over the wheels, as well as bicycle rickshaws, wobble between the vehicular traffic and find their way through the dense purple smog. Somehow, too, pedestrians manage to press their way, carrying briefcases and parcels, and clutching their children while balancing a parasol to shade from the unrelenting sun. And they do this with tolerance, purposefulness and a smile.

Perhaps the loveliest time in Bangkok is just after dawn, when, through the barely wakened misty streets, saffron-clad barefoot monks pad quietly along the streets as women step from doorways to silently and respectfully spoon food into their humble bowls.

Despite exotic appearance and skillfully blended tastes and textures, Thai food is simple to prepare – all foods are cut in bite-size pieces as in China – and quickly cooked by stir-frying, steaming, frying or grilling. Even curry pastes are widely available already mixed in powder or paste forms. Meals are composed from what is fresh and locally available, and rice is the center of each meal.

No matter how small or large – or even if the kitchen is a small outdoor space – Thai kitchens are models of efficiency. Cooking methods are based on Chinese ways of steaming, frying, boiling, and stir-frying and therefore make use of classic Chinese cooking implements, plus a few distinctively Thai ones.

Thai basic kitchen equipment includes a wok with ladles, paddles and skimmers for stirring and lifting, a rice steamer, and a three-tiered steamer for other foods, a large stockpot and a small saucepot. In addition to an assortment of sharp knives and cleavers, there will be an array of small sharp implements used for carving ornate garnishes from vegetables and fruits. A mortar and pestle for pounding and blending small quantities of seasonings and an electric blender for bigger jobs, as well as a coconut grater, are necessities.

All Thai kitchens will also have an assortment of baskets for serving long grain rice and sticky rice. Many serving plates and dishes are embellished with rich blue abstract designs on white china, making a pleasing background for vivid food colors. A variety of small bowls will be used to serve individual portions of accompanying sauces.

DAIRY PRODUCTS

Dairy products have limited use in most Asian countries but ice cream is a special treat as a snack, and canned sweetened condensed milk is used in desserts. Milk is not used as a beverage, cheese is not a part of the diet, and dairy products are not used in the preparation of meals. Where **ghee** (clarified butter) might be used to brown onions, garlic, and spices, the Thai use peanut oil – darkly rich in flavor. And where dairy products may be used in sauces and soups, the Thai use coconut milk or coconut cream.

FRUITS AND VEGETABLES

A luscious abundance of fresh tropical fruits dazzles the eye and tempts the taste buds even after a richly satisfying meal. And no wonder! Thai fruits are rarely served in simple slices; instead they greet the diner in intricately carved shapes of birds, flowers, fish and leaves, so beautiful it seems a shame to eat them.

Fruits are enjoyed as snacks and desserts. Mangosteen, pawpaw (papaya), mangoes, mandarins, pineapples, varieties of bananas, **rambutans**, as well as temperate fruits like melons, apples, and varieties of berries are widely available. **Durians** are large melon-like fruits with the unenviable reputation for being the only fruit in the world that is banned on airlines and in some hotels. It does have a horrendous smell like rotted cheese but the flesh is sweet and delicious, and those who can get past the odor are admittedly addicted to its taste.

Common vegetables like potatoes, cabbage, spinach, eggplant, zucchini, cucumbers, carrots, baby corn, and snow peas share the shopping list with vegetables such as **snake beans**, bitter melon, pumpkin, white radish, tiny purple and white eggplants the size of grapes and green ones the size of peas. Long slender Japanese eggplant, **Thai eggplant** that looks like tiny green grapes, **Thai papaya** that resembles a big green cucumber, countless varieties of mushrooms, delicate frilly greens – all of these astound the eye and delight the palate. Bundles of fresh green herbs such as **Thai basil**, mint and corian-der would delight any cook and are available fresh and fragrant throughout the year. Stems and roots of coriander are used as well as the leaves.

MEATS AND ALTERNATES

Thais freely mix meat, fish, and seafood not only in recognizable chunks in curries and mixed vegetable dishes, but also in sausages. Poultry is the most used meat, but pork and beef are also used. Meats, fish, and seafood usually comprise a small proportion of any meal, the rest being rice (or noodles) and many different vegetables.

Fresh legumes are used, but dried peas, beans, and lentils are seldom a part of Thai foods. However, soybean curd and **tempeh** (fermented soybean curd) are used as part of curries or stir-fried dishes or may be marinated in salads.

Peanuts find their way into many dishes. Deeply roasted peanut oil is darker and more flavorful than any processed peanut oil sold in the west. It is this oil that is used to brown spices, chilies, and garlic or to brown prepared curry pastes. Raw peanuts either whole or chopped may be toasted in a hot wok then set aside while the rest of the dish is prepared, the toasted peanuts added to the mixture just before serving. Or peanuts may be toasted then crushed, ground or finely chopped before adding to sauces or sprinkled as a light garnish on a finished dish. Other nuts such as cashews and sataw nuts may be used in the same way, but peanuts are most prevalent.

BREADS AND GRAINS

Rice is the staple grain in Thailand, with a preference for sticky white rice in the northern regions, and long grain white rice everywhere else. Rice is always served fluffy and hot with nothing added. It is served in a separate covered dish or covered basket. The preferred jasmine rice is bright white in color and lightly scented when cooked. Fried rice is a dish prepared from leftover cooked rice mixed with bits of meats, seafood and vegetables, very similar to the classic **Chinese fried rice**. Thais do not consider this dish as part of a meal, but enjoy it occasionally as a snack food.

But the use of rice does not begin and end with a mound of fragrant steaming white rice! As in China, there are many varieties of rice noodles, some as thick as pasta noodles, others as fine and thin as vermicelli. Round rice paper sheets are moistened in warm water and used to wrap prepared greens, seafood, etc., for appetizers ready for dipping in hot sauces. Bean starch noodles too can be thick or very thin as can egg noodles and wheat flour noodles. These various noodles, dressed with sauces and tossed food tidbits, can be a meal in a bowl or just a snack.

White glutinous rice and black glutinous rice are often used for desserts. In Thai cookery, they are often cooked with coconut milk and palm sugar resulting in a sweet stickiness, ideal for shaping into ovals, balls or cakes. Usually these are served with intricately sculptured fresh fruit. The addition of coconut milk or cream, sesame seeds, tapioca flour, rice flour, or mung bean flour added to the sticky rice produces delicious custards, cup-shaped pancakes, and other treats. As in the rest of Southeast Asia, Thais like to tint their desserts with vivid pastel food coloring, especially in shades of green, yellow, and pink.

FATS
Peanut oil is used most frequently in all cooking or frying.

SWEETS AND SNACKS
Thais like to eat small amounts of food at a time and enjoy nibbling various snacks and enjoying cool fruit drinks or beer during the day and into the evening between meals. Everywhere, vendors sell snack foods to be eaten out of hand, nibbled off bamboo skewers, or enjoyed more leisurely at roadside tables or open food stalls. Snack foods may include smaller versions of main dishes, **satays**, or a meal of noodles with garnishes all in one bowl and slurped up with chopsticks. Snacks may also be a cool drink and a sweet based on fruit and glutinous rice.

SEASONINGS
Thai foods lack complexity and classic dishes follow simple cooking rules. Although there are innovations, traditional dishes are seasoned in specific ways and even these seasonings follow traditional patterns. For example, spices, garlic, and onions as well as any of the curry pastes are always heated or lightly browned in peanut oil before other ingredients are added. Similarly, meats are always cut in bite-size pieces and boiled to tenderness before joining seasonings and vegetables in either a "dry" or "wet" dish.

Coconut milk and coconut cream find their way into almost every Thai dish from soup to dessert. While these can be prepared from scratch, they are also widely available in dry powder form or in cans. The range of dried, powdered, canned, frozen, and prepared ingredients is wide, and a busy city householder can prepare a meal, complete with steamed rice, from the electric rice cooker in a short time.

Freshly made coconut milk is prepared by finely grating the flesh of a fresh coconut then pressing it hard with added boiling water. The liquid from a first and second pressing with boiling water is called the "milk." When this is left to set, the thick top layer is called the "cream" and this can be skimmed off. The milky juice inside a freshly cracked coconut is just the sweet "water" and is not used in cooking.

It is said that the Thai consume garlic – fresh, fried, pickled – in quantities second only to the Koreans. Garlic adds its pungency, and chilies of many varieties add their mouth-searing fire, but many other seasonings round out Thai flavors. These include tiny red shallots, large sweet purple onions, black and green peppercorns, several varieties of ginger, galangal, and sweet green onions. Salty **nam pla** (fermented fish sauce) and **kapi** (dried shrimp paste) obviate the need for a saltshaker. Tangy citrus-like flavors come from kaffir lime rinds, juice and fresh leaves, also from tamarind dried or in paste form and from the roots of lemon grass. Finally, fresh green herbs are used generously, often together with leaves, stems, and roots: coriander, mint, pandanus leaves, garlic chives, chives, and many varieties of basil.

Contrary to popular tales, Thai food is not all blast furnace hot. Usually the dipping sauces, served separately, are added according to the diner's taste. Most of these have chilies and garlic, but are gentled with ingredients like palm sugar and coconut milk, **nam pla** or **kapi**. Dilution with vinegar or water helps too.

A variety of chilies from mildly hot to the pale orange, devilishly hot ones called **prik leung** (also known as "mouse droppings") find their way to most Thai dishes either as garnish or ingredient. If chilies are not minced into the sauces, they may be dried and sprinkled on top, deftly slit into flower-like petals as an edible garnish or sliced in tiny thin rounds to float atop sauces. If there is Thai food, there are probably chilies close by!

Four main types of curry pastes are used: red, green, yellow, and a milder one called **musamam** that is based on a traditional Muslim recipe. The ingredients for the paste are either prepared fresh or mixed from packaged dried powders. The term "paste" denotes a thick concentrated mixture of curry ingredients. Only a few teaspoons of any curry paste is heated in oil then blended with coconut milk to form the velvety curry sauce accompanying meat, or seafood sometimes with added vegetables.

BEVERAGES
Popular beverages are Thai beer – varieties from **Singha** (like lager) to a lighter sweet beer called **Kloster**. Rice whisky and a strong rice wine called **Anak** are widely enjoyed and often prepared privately. Coffee will likely be of the instant variety, although there is some locally grown, roasted, and ground coffees. Coffee bars are increasingly popular in Bangkok, with all the European types served, but

most popular is coffee with sugar and sweetened condensed milk. Tea is less commonly served in Thailand, except of course in Chinese restaurants. As with coffee, when tea is ordered, it may be served in a glass with sugar and sweetened condensed milk unless otherwise requested.

Fresh fruit juice drinks, sometimes made with blended fruits, sometimes with coconut milk added, are still pressed out by ancient machines and sold by hawkers everywhere. In fact, wherever people pass by, there will be juice stands. Juices include those made from green coconut, mango, pineapple, orange, sugarcane, and whatever fruits are readily available. All juices will be generously seasoned with salt – refreshing in Thailand's humid heat.

Commercial bottled mineral water and popular soft drinks are available everywhere.

MEALS AND CUSTOMS

From court and palace kitchens comes the tradition of eating small portions of food, always artistically presented. Appearance is considered as important as balance and taste. Dips and sauces as well as rice are always served in small individual bowls. Traditionally, all plates of foods, dipping sauces, and a large covered bowl or basket of steaming plain fragrant rice is the centerpiece. Diners take foods as they like, in any order and any combination. Clear soups or soups creamed with coconut milk may be served through the meal. Beverages may include cool fruit drinks or Thai beer; coffee may be served later.

Noodles are eaten from small deep bowls with chopsticks, and soup is eaten with Chinese-style porcelain spoons. Thai food is eaten from a plate with a fork and large spoon; the fork is used to push the food onto the spoon and the spoon is taken to the mouth. Although Thai food is always served in bite-size pieces, the tip of the spoon is sometimes used to cut food.

Dipping sauces are served in tiny side bowls for each diner or may be served in a small bowl surrounded with appetizers or vegetables for communal dipping. These provide added seasoning to be used for any food the diner wishes. Sauces are not thickened with any starchy mixture but instead take their creamy or chunky texture from the ingredients.

Thais begin their day with a small bowl of **congee** – a bland Chinese rice gruel that starts the stomach gently for the day. Sometimes eggs may be poached in the gruel. Tea or instant coffee will complete the quick meal.

Most commonly a brimming bowl of noodles with assorted garnishes and a choice of sauces to add will be the quick hot lunch taken from vendors and roadside stands and eaten with chopsticks. If time

permits, a meal of several dishes including steamed fish, curried chicken and/or stir-fried vegetables with rice and dipping sauces will be served, but in smaller portions than will be presented for the main meal in the evening.

The evening meal will be more leisurely, taken with friends and family and often in restaurants. Similar to the leisurely lunch, several dishes including rice, a curry, stir-fry, steamed dish, and a variety of dipping sauces will be presented on the table together. This will be preceded by a variety of delicate and beautifully presented appetizers with their own dipping sauces. The evening meal is often served with Thai beer. Desserts are rarely served except at special dinners or banquets and these are usually delicately carved fruits with sweet sticky rice or sweet cakes.

But with all the tempting vendors and hawkers and the Thai penchant for snacking, three meals a day hardly suffice. And who wouldn't be tempted with the aroma of sizzling **satay**, the cool freshness of tangy green mango lightly dusted with sugar, chili pepper flakes and salt, not to mention steaming noodles with delectable garnishes?

The graciousness of Thai manners is in evidence everywhere, but especially at the table. It is expected that a guest will be taken to a restaurant, that small portions of all the foods will at least be tasted and that the eating will be delicately done with spoon and fork unless noodles are served. If sticky rice is a part of the dessert, it is usually taken with the fingers. In the home, the hostess may not eat, but rather will hover over the table to be sure that all the guests are enjoying themselves.

An important Thai custom is the greeting of **wai**, a prayerful clasping of the hands and slow bowing. This is used for hello, goodbye, to say thank you and to say sorry.

SPECIAL OCCASIONS

Buddhist customs and traditions are very strong in Thailand, and permeate every aspect of daily life. The more than 32,000 *wats* (or monasteries) throughout the land and the fact that 92 percent of Thais are Theravada Buddhists provides a conformity in celebrations and special occasions not seen in countries where larger minority groups are represented. Nonetheless, like other Asian cultures, old ways, myths and superstitions are just below the surface, emerging throughout the year and throughout the life span.

At some time in his life, usually after school and before marriage, every Thai male is expected to spend a period of time as a monk. The traditional duration is three months. Women also can become nuns and spend periods of time in the *wats*. Monks wear the traditional saffron robes and shave their heads, and women wear white robes and also shave their heads. But a *wat* is much more than a place for meditation. It is a center for festivities, study, health services, a transient guesthouse, and even a sauna. It houses not only valued statuary and reliquaries but also an extensive library.

A very much smaller but equally important edifice in Thai life is the "spirit house," an active symbol of Thai belief in the spiritual world where particular spirits reign over certain realms. Every important Thai building and home has a spirit house usually located just outside. The **phra plum** will be decorated with flowers and filled with food offerings, incense, and candles to keep the vagrant spirits happy outside rather than inside the building or home where they may be troublesome.

Thais are also fervent believers in astrology and numerology and most astrologers and numerologists are Chinese, who determine auspicious dates and times for life's important events. Beyond religion or mysticism, a simple Thai proverb is worth remembering: Do good and receive good; do evil and receive evil.

Thai holidays are based on a lunar calendar, Thai special events center around the local *wat*, with music and meditations led by the monks, and with small refreshments provided to family and guests. Thai funerals can last as long as a week depending on the stature of the deceased. All women wear black – Thais only wear black for funerals – and a period of time is spent each evening listening to the monks chants and their music of horns, gongs, and bells. Funeral participants are seated in rows and talk softly but no one is weepy or overtly sad. After a time, small refreshments of juice and tiny sweets are passed around, then everyone files out. Thais are usually cremated.

The Thai annual calendar is dotted not only with national holidays, but also with countless regional festivals. The most known is *Songkran*, marking the Thai new year with a water festival occurring in April. Similar to the Indian *Holi*, it is a time for throwing water everywhere ostensibly to wash away evil spirits, but also to have fun. January 1 is also celebrated with as much festivity as the Thai New Year. The holiest of all Buddhist festivals occurs on the first full moon in May, *Wisaka Bucha*, to mark the birth of the Lord Buddha with parades, incense, food offerings, and candles.

In fact, each month of the year brings at least one special occasion to mark royal birthdays, Buddhist festivals, labor and plowing holidays as well as historical dates.

GLOSSARY OF FOODS AND FOOD TERMS

Coconut Milk: not the fluid inside a ripe coconut but the milky residue prepared from freshly shredded coconut soaked in boiling water then strained. If fresh coconuts are not available, most Asian food stores carry packets of dried coconut milk or tins of liquid coconut milk that make preparation easier and quicker.

Durian: probably the only fruit in the world that has been banned from hotels and airlines because of its unforgiving stench. Available all over Southeast Asia, sought after by those who love its soft and sticky golden pulp and enjoy its strong fermented cheese-like taste. Its outward appearance is large, round, greenish brown, and spiky. Could it be that those who are addicted to **Durian** really believe in its aphrodisiac properties?

Green Curry Paste: probably the hottest curry paste, takes its color and fire from the deceptively innocent small green chilies. Shallots, garlic, and shrimp paste add further pungency and lemon grass and kaffir lime add the tang while spices round out the taste.

Green Pawpaw (Papaya) and **Mango**: just a reminder that many tropical fruits are cooked and eaten like vegetables while they are still green.

Jackfruit: not an attractive fruit either when picked or when growing straight out of the tree trunk. It has a mild cheese-like taste and its soft juicy flesh is similar to that of melons.

Kapi: dried shrimp paste, pungent and salty and used as an ingredient.

Khao Chi: originally from the court of King Chulalongkorn, a presentation of cold iced rice enjoyed with side dishes of miniature crisply fried beef strips, stuffed banana peppers (capsicum) wrapped in egg lace, tiny fried shrimp balls, and thinly sliced fresh vegetables. Cold cooked rice is steeped in water and ice cubes and scented with jasmine then quickly served with the side dishes.

Khao Niew Ma Muang: probably the most popular dessert in Thailand, especially when mangoes are in season. Generous fresh slices of luscious ripe mango are lightly carved with a floral or leaf impression then served beside a patty of sticky sweet rice tinted pale green.

Lemon Grass: a delicately lemon-scented herb that can be grown almost anywhere. Only the firm white stem above the root is used, finely chopped in dishes, and left whole for soups or stocks then removed before serving.

Longans: a tenderly delicious fruit, white and smooth, with a slight crunchy texture similar to fresh lichees. These can be purchased canned when they are not available fresh.

Mangosteen: a dark reddish brown fruit. Sweet white lobes of juicy fruit emerge when the purple skin is peeled away. Even with purple stained fingers, the luscious taste is worth it.

Mee Krob: one of the most intricate and famed of Thai special dishes. It is presented on a platter as a peaked mountain of stir-fried pork, shrimp, and garlic, tossed with a syrupy sauce and crisply fried rice-stick noodles. This mound is topped with egg lace and red chilies shredded to look like flowers. Bean sprouts snuggle around the base. Of course, fluffy fragrant rice accompanies each mouthful.

Musaman (Muslim) **Curry Paste**: also called "regular curry paste" it is a blend of dried chile peppers with mixed spices, garlic, coriander seeds and roots, lemon grass and **galangal**.

Nam Pla: the fermented amber fish sauce, salty and pungent in taste used by Thais in cooking and as a condiment.

Nam Pla Prik: the dipping sauce created when chilies are added to **Nam Pla**.

Namtan Peep: usually called "palm sugar" because it is made from the boiled-down sweet sap of coconut palms. Available in solid chunks or packed in jars, but dark brown sugar or demerara sugar can be substituted.

Peanut Oil: in Southeast Asia darker and stronger in peanut flavor than the western colorless and tasteless version. When used for cooking, it adds a rich roasted peanut flavor to the food.

Red Curry Paste: dried or fresh red chilies are the basis of this curry paste with **Kha**, onions, garlic, spices, and coriander as essential ingredients.

Thai Ginger: comes in many varieties – common or green ginger, **Kha** or **Laos** or **Galangal** and **Kra Chai**. Each differs slightly in texture, flavor, and use. **Kha** has a hard texture and is used in salads in northern Thailand, while elsewhere it is sold dried as a powder and used as a seasoning. The sweet, peppery green ginger is commonly sliced, grated or chopped, may be pickled, used fresh or candied. **Kra Chai** is used as a raw vegetable or in fish curries.

Thai Sweet and Sour Sauce: one of the few Thai sauces that is thickened with cornstarch and thus has similar ingredients to Chinese sweet and sour sauce with, of course, chiles added.

Tom Yam Kung: Thailand's most famed hot sour soup prepared from a broth seasoned with lemon grass, shrimp paste, **Nam Pla**, ginger, lime juice, and chilies and garnished with floating fresh shrimp.

Yellow Curry Paste: considered a mild curry paste, prepared from yellow chilies and takes its color from turmeric and dry mustard. Flavor is enhanced with spices, garlic, and shallots.

Yum: represents the food category of salads. These salads include sliced, shredded, grated, cubed vegetables either raw or briefly steamed to heighten color then served, arranged like flowers in a garden or heaped into a delicate mountain, with appropriate dipping sauces.

CHAPTER 50

TIBETAN

Tibetans live in one of the highest altitudes and in one of the most isolated countries in the world. The lofty snow-dusted mountains, high-altitude  deserts, and barren wind-swirled plains are as much a part of the Tibetans' rugged daily life as the profound religious devotion and spirituality permeating each aspect. This long-isolated land is for only the hardiest and most persistent traveler, but the reward of sharing even a little of this indomitable land and her quietly persistent people is to return home with newfound serenity.

Religious beings and historic figures are everywhere evident in Tibetan art, sculpture, murals, and statuary. *Lamaism* is the Yellow Sect of Tibetan Buddhism that emerged from the interaction of the ancient Tibetan shaman religion of *Bon* and the *Mahayana* Buddhism from northern India. It was during the reign of the Tibetan king Songsten Gampa (600s C.E.) and through the practice and persistence of his Nepalese queen and especially his Chinese queen (both fervent Buddhists) that Buddhism and many Chinese customs were instilled into general Tibetan practice.

By the 900s, however, the Tibetan Dynasty was torn apart by regional strife, slave uprisings, and disparate military forays that weakened any existing Tibetan authority. The Chinese Song Dynasty (960-1279 C.E.) took advantage of the disarray and divided the isolated land into provinces more or less submitting to Chinese authority. This type of rule continued until 1949, when the People's Republic of China formally claimed the Tibetan Autonomous Region and declared it under China's control.

In the early Communist period, many teenage Tibetan Red Guards (like the Chinese Red Guards in China), swept with newfound allegiance, helped to destroy their own ancient monasteries, monuments, and priceless libraries in their revolt against the intel-

lectuals. These Tibetans today work hard to erase past deeds and gain merit with prayer and good works.

It is said that many factors intertwine to make the Tibet Autonomous Region one of the poorest of China. These factors include the continuing influx of ethnic Chinese, the failure of Communist development methods, and the severe and harsh repression of Tibetan monks and nuns. When these factors are added to the historical difficulties of the constantly forbidding land and often treacherous climate, it is not difficult to understand Tibet's isolation and poverty.

With patient steadfastness and a profound belief in their land and way of life, Tibetans still twirl their prayer wheels, thoughtfully fondle their prayer beads, and tie colorful prayer flags to bushes and trees. Tibetan children still listen avidly to the history, legends, and myths from the *Chochunj*, the ancient Tibetan scholarly books that guide their everyday actions. To both children and adults, the invisible *Mimayim*, those good or bad ghostly spirits with inhuman powers, seem nonetheless very real entities to be reckoned with. Religion suffuses every moment of Tibetan daily life, affording a serenity and pleasure not always evident in the harsh struggles of day-to-day life.

Symbols of Lamaism are everywhere. Women cherish necklaces with heavy carved reliquaries containing sacred prayers. Household and courtyard shrines, *stupas* (the cylinder and dome-like structure found in Buddhist lands) and monasteries, and *thankgas* (scroll-like painted or embroidered banners) are everywhere. *Mandalas* (geometric renditions of the cosmos), believed to exude the powers of the universe to those who meditate on them, decorate walls and buildings. Some monasteries display *Mandalas* skillfully created with colored sand. These are said to depict not only the enlightened mind, but also act as a reminder of the transitory nature of life itself.

And while China is rebuilding some roads and monasteries, Chinese authorities are limiting the number of monks and nuns; while more children are being educated at least to grade 3, they are learning Chinese language, foods, and customs as well as Tibetan. Despite this, Tibetan still remains the primary language and is enthusiastically supported by Tibetan television, radio stations, plays, operas, and publications.

Despite the Chinese presence and the exile of the Dalai Lama, Tibetan culture remains strong. Perhaps most important, religious practice retains its fervor in every aspect of Tibetan daily life, precipitating pleasure, peace, and enlightenment together with the hope for independence.

DOMESTIC LIFE

To describe the domestic life of the Tibetans, it is necessary to distinguish four ways of living: the nomad herders, the valley farmers, the city merchants, and the monks and nuns in monasteries.

THE NOMADS

Only nomads live in the high plateaus, traveling when necessary with their herds of yaks and flocks of sheep and their ever-present fierce mastiffs that guard and help to herd their livestock. Nomads erect four-sided tents with sloping roofs made from tightly woven yak hair. Groups of families set their tents within shouting distance, but remain far enough apart so there is ample grazing room for all. For each group of families, the tents are the center of camp life and daily living. This means that the tents are for cooking, eating and gathering to talk, although in the summer, talking and sleeping is enjoyed in the open air.

Cooking takes place near the entrance to the tent, in a fire pit over which a stove is built to hold a few large covered pots. Kitchen utensils are few, sturdy and practical and are stored with swords and saddles hung on the tent walls. Food stores are nearby in sacks and boxes. The family will take meals sitting on sheepskins at a low table. Members will have their own personal bowl and spoon for beverages, soups, and stews. Other foods are eaten simply with the fingers. This way of eating is common for most Tibetans, except those in the city. Chinese use bowls and chopsticks.

In one corner of the tent is the family shrine with its butter lamps and images of Buddha. The clarified yak butter is the commonest form of illumination. Near the shrine there is usually a handsome wood and silver chest for family valuables. In this, the women store precious belongings as well as the gold and silver jewelry that even the poorest own.

For both men and women, their belongings are few but sturdy and practical for ease in packing and moving. Year-round the men wear long trousers and well-worn sheep's fur but their hats, made of felt for summer and fur for winter, may take various shapes. Both men and women wear boots. Women's clothing includes a long sleeveless robe over a long-sleeved shirt with a brightly woven apron.

FOODS COMMONLY USED

In Lhasa, the capital city, markets and restaurants provide an increasing variety of foods and cuisine. But in the rural areas, **tsampa**, hot buttered Tibetan tea called **poja** or **cha suma, momos** (dumplings), and **thukpa** (noodle soup with meat and vegetables seasoned with yak butter) still form the daily fare.

Tibetan staple foods are **tsampa**, fermented yak butter, and black tea. **Tsampa** is a mixture of roasted, ground barley and fermented yak butter moistened with tea that is used as a bread or a snack as well as a seasoning for soups and stews.

Peas and beans as well as wheat, corn, and rice are used. Vegetables, wild herbs, and berries add variety to the diet, as do dairy foods such as yogurt, buttermilk, and dried cheese. Vegetables and legumes are used when available. Beverages include **poja** or **cha suma**, salty, hot buttered tea, and **cha ngamo**, the milky sweet black tea, and **chang** (beer).

Poja is the favorite but sometimes **cha ngama** is served. **Chang**, a beer brewed from roasted barley, is enjoyed by all ages, especially on festive and special occasions.

Nomads make many meals of beef or mutton and enjoy dairy products in addition to the staple **tsampa** and hot buttered tea. They drink little or no alcohol, often setting up their tents outside the towns to avoid the **chang**-drinking city dwellers on those occasions when they come to the towns.

Nomads do, however, enjoy smoking. The elders especially like to smoke their long pipes made from sheep's bone.

Monks eat sparsely and simply and often rely on what others place in their bowls or donate to their monasteries. In doing so, they permit others to gain merit by providing them with food. Their staple foods too are the **tsampa** and hot buttered tea.

Chinese influence is evident in the increasing use of Chinese cookery utensils, cooking methods like steaming and stir-frying and in an increased use of wheat, rice, and vegetables as well as Chinese seasonings and condiments.

THE VALLEY FARMERS

Tibetan farmers like to build their two-to-three-storey houses on high ground but near rivers and usually facing south. The walls of the houses, though built of layers of flat rocks or pounded earth, have many windows. Several houses are grouped together and built around a central courtyard. As with the nomads, fierce dogs guard the homes and families, yet these dogs are gentle and loyal to their own families. The lowest floor of each home is for storage and/or livestock while upper floors house the family living quarters. Cooking facilities are simple, sturdy, and practical but may be more elaborate than those of the nomads.

As with the nomads, each pastoral farmhouse has a family shrine or prayer room, which may just be an area set apart, decorated with blankets or rugs, images and butter lamps. In this designated space, members of the family express their devotion in prayers, chants, or in serene meditation.

THE CITY MERCHANTS

Sturdier dwellings built of stone, finely woven Tibetan carpets made of wool and colored with softly toned vegetable dyes, and carved furniture set apart city merchants' dwellings from those in rural areas. Their higher standard of living is also reflected in their clothing, jewelry, servants and varied diet. Each home has its family shrine or prayer room, with more elaborate setting and decorations.

MONASTERIES

The Dalai and the Panchen Lamas, together with their councils made up of abbots and noblemen, governed Tibet in isolation from the rest of the world for more than 1,000 years. These monasteries (*gampas*) formed independent landowning units and had local people working as serfs. Each monastery housed several thousand to several hundred monks all engaged in the study of art, Buddhist philosophy, literature, or medicine. Each Tibetan family is still expected to give one son, and sometimes a daughter, to the local monastery. To do so has always been considered an act of high merit, and for a long time this religious life was also the only means to education, status, and power.

Despite the treasures in statues, religious images and relics, priceless murals, and exquisitely carved architecture, life in the monastery has always been rigorous. Early rising and an intensive program of religious obligations, long hours of study, and chores occupy every waking moment for the monks. Their clothing includes the *kasaya*, a quilted outer vest in red and purple tones worn over a flowing long-sleeved shirt. The Lamas are renowned for their gracious saffron and scarlet robes and variously designed hats especially worn for occasions of religious importance.

DAIRY PRODUCTS

Milk is used from sheep and goats, but the most popular is milk from yaks. This is churned into butter then fermented to preserve it and used for all cooking. The pungent smell and slightly sour taste of yak butter is considered delicious, especially in the salted black tea. Buttermilk and yogurt are used by the nomads, and a dried cheese made from buttermilk is also a nomad favorite since it is portable and satisfying, especially when stirred into a bowl of buttery hot tea.

Fresh milk and a variety of fresh cheeses are also used.

FRUITS AND VEGETABLES

Arable rural land is at a premium in Tibet so cultivation of fruits and vegetables is minimal. Wild greens and herbs are eagerly gathered in season. Vegetables that can be stored such as carrots, cabbage, and potatoes are used in stews and for gruel. Varieties and use of vegetables are increasing with Chinese influence, but most of these are available only in the Lhasa markets.

Onions, garlic, potatoes, radishes, carrots, turnip, cabbage, cauliflower, bamboo shoots and bean sprouts, spinach and tomatoes are all enjoyed when available and affordable.

In season, wild berries are picked in the rural areas for eating fresh while some are dried to be eaten in winter and to be used for prayer offerings. Fruits such as grapes, oranges, mangoes, apples, pears, apricots, and bananas are not widely available but are relished.

MEATS AND ALTERNATES

Lamaism does not forbid the eating of meat or fish. Cattle, goats, pigs, and chickens are used, but yak meat is used most of all. Autumn and spring are considered the best times to slaughter animals, so meat is preserved in several ways to last the year and nothing is wasted. Nomads and pastoral people preserve meat by drying it in the sun and wind and by freezing it outdoors. Choice fat meat is wrapped in yak hide and stored in special boxes made from dried yak dung over which fresh yak dung is spread. The choice meat will be saved for special occasions.

For a long time Tibetans ignored the fish in their lakes and streams but in recent years they have been using fish more frequently. Chinese influence has increased the use of fish.

Dried meat and **tsampa** washed down with hot

buttered tea may be a meal especially for the nomads. Or the preserved or fresh meats may be cooked into a stew or gruel flavored and thickened with **tsampa**.

Varieties of peas and beans are used fresh and dried. Tofu or soy curd is being used in mixed dishes with vegetables.

BREADS AND GRAINS
Wheat, corn, buckwheat, and rice are used for food, but barley, roasted and crushed, is the staple for Tibetans. Wheat production and rice imports increased with the influx of ethnic Chinese and both rice and wheat are gaining popularity.

For the Tibetan, **tsampa** is bread, snack food, seasoning, and thickener for cooked foods. To prepare it, barley must be roasted and pounded to a flour – still done in many regions between two rocks – before being mixed with yak butter and moistened with black tea. Sometimes crushed roasted peas may be added. **Tsampa** is eaten for a snack or as bread with a meal. By rolling the mixture into a ball with the fingers, Tibetans form a moist ball that may be dipped into a stew or eaten as is. The dried barley flour keeps well and can be combined with yak butter and tea whenever required thus making **tsampa** an inexpensive, nourishing, and portable food.

So popular is **tsampa** that one can easily overlook the use of grains in other ways. Steamed breads and noodle dishes of Chinese origin and pancakes and flat breads similar to those in India are made from grain flours and add variety. Steamed or boiled meat dumplings, probably of Mongolian origin, add further variety and can be frozen and reheated. In their frozen form they can be carried while traveling.

FATS
The predominant fat used for eating, drinking, and cooking is fermented yak butter. Fat is also consumed in the form of fatty meats especially on special occasions. Chinese prefer to use oil and this is used in small quantities now by Tibetans, but does not add the flavor and aroma of the yak butter.

SWEETS AND SNACKS
Cha Ngamo, the sweet milky tea, dried fruits, and dried wild berries are the common sweets. A candy is made from browning sugar and some candies can be purchased. **Tsampa** is the most usual snack. Sometimes dried meat or dried cheese is also eaten with **tsampa** as a more filling snack.

Dried bread, dried cheese, cooked potatoes, or dried meat carried in string bags tied to the waist are snacks to take when traveling. These can be nibbled alone or if hot tea is served, these will be stirred into the tea for a substantial snack or small meal.

SEASONINGS
Salt and sugar are used but the distinctive yak butter permeates most Tibetan cooking and most foods. Chinese spices like five-spice powder and black pepper, seasonings like chili oil and vinegar, condiments like soy sauce, black bean sauce, and hot chilies are being imported and used increasingly. Cinnamon, caraway, and cardamom are used to spice cookies and cakes.

BEVERAGES
The ubiquitous hot buttered tea – **cha suma** or **poja** – is the Tibetan's favorite drink whether farmer, nomad, merchant, or monk. For more than 1,000 years Tibetans have imported blocks of fermented black tea from Yunnan province in China. A small piece of the block tea is broken off and boiled in water with soda made from wood ashes. The mixture is then poured into a specially made wood churn, and boiling hot water, salt, and yak butter are added and churned together forming a thick soup-like tea. This may be sipped immediately from their bowl, or may be poured into a thermos for later refreshment.

Cha ngamo, the heavily sweetened milky tea, is taken less regularly than **poja**, while coffee – **cha kbi** – is beginning to find favor.

Chang, the beer prepared commercially and privately from roasted barley, is flat and slightly sour in taste but every Tibetan enjoys it, and not just for special occasions. Imported beer is also available.

Fresh milk, Chinese-style tea, soda, vodka, and wine are used but not widely.

MEALS AND CUSTOMS
Barley is not only an ancient staple crop and the main part of the diet, for Tibetans it is as sacred as corn is for some North American aboriginal peoples.

Tibetans in rural areas begin their day by burning offerings of juniper branches, dried fruits, and **tsampa**. As the sweet-scented smoke drifts upward, all family members participate in the ritual with prayers and chants. Later the fire will be used to cook food or to boil water. Families then gather for the morning meal, each person filling their personal bowl with hot buttered tea and adding dried cheese, yogurt, or some meat.

In the evening, rural families gather to talk and enjoy the evening meal, usually a soup or stew with boiled meat, rice, or barley or perhaps dumplings and a few vegetables. Just past dusk everyone is ready for sleep but not until prayers are said before flickering butter lamps.

In the city, the morning ritual will be performed in the family prayer room or in front of the family shrine by lighting a butter lamp and igniting grain while prayers are said. **Thukpa**, the noodle soup, is still a Tibetan breakfast favorite, often to eat on the run. Eggs in many forms, together with bread or toast, fresh cheese and types of porridge are finding their way to the Tibetan breakfast table. City families may use more dishes and cutlery while eating but most still prefer to drink their beverage from a bowl, and eating with the fingers is quite usual.

Tibetan courtesy is as much a part of everyday life as prayers. Tibetans greet each other with open arms and palms raised upward. On more formal occasions, white or blue silk *hadas* (long narrow scarves) are proffered on outstretched palms as a sign of respect. This hospitable greeting is often followed with gifts of food such as yak butter, fine preserved meats or dried fruits.

SPECIAL OCCASIONS

The nomads and the pastoral people of the rural areas in Tibet hold fast to traditions and practice ceremonies and rituals with profound intensity and rapt pleasure rarely seen elsewhere. Each person is totally involved; their many prayers and quiet meditative periods are wholly voluntary. This is a devotion that is not just part of everyday life, it is life for them.

The deep devotion, values and rituals of Lamaism suffuse every aspect of Tibetan daily life from birth to death. The Tibetan calendar, a combination of solar and lunar calendars, reveals festivities and ceremonies mostly based on religious traditions.

Losar, the Tibetan New Year, is celebrated for three to five days in the first week of January. Wearing their best clothes and jewelry, Tibetans join together to pray for a good year, visit friends and relatives, and enjoy cultural events like plays and operas. Some wear masks, disguising themselves as gods while they sing and dance through the streets to drive away *mimayin* (ghosts).

January 15 brings the Lantern Festival when large intricate sculptures carved from hardened yak butter are paraded through the streets especially in the capital city of Lhasa. Streets are festooned with lanterns also carved from yak butter and people dance all night long under them.

Nyungne is a more solemn introspective time lasting four days. While participation is voluntary, those who do partake in the practice of *Nyungne* are believed to accrue merit for the next life. Accumulating deeds of merit through one's lifetime is believed to lead to a higher state of being at rebirth, and to offset the sins of daily life. *Nyungne* includes abstention from work, sex, conversation, as well as a period of fasting from food and drink. The first day begins with burnt offerings of juniper, dried fruits and **tsampa** to local gods, the second day with

prayers and recitations culminating in a noon meal. Chanting, prayers, and an evening feast of celebration on the fourth day follow the long fasting period. The feast is eagerly welcomed, for the fasting means no food or drink for more than twenty-four hours.

FUNERAL PRACTICES

Tibetan funeral practices vary according to the social status of the deceased. High-ranking Lamas may have a *Stupa Burial*. This may involve either cremation or the special preservation of the corpse with saltwater, drying and coating with spices. Whether cremated or dried, the remains are then sealed in a specially marked *stupa* so that others may visit and meditate on the person's life and teachings. Lamas of lower rank may be given a *Fire Burial*; widows and people of low social status are given a *Water Burial*.

The fourth funeral practice common in Lamaism is the *Sky Burial*. The accompanying rituals, though initially horrifying to western minds, actually underlie the cycle of life and death and the interdependence of all life. The *Sky Burial* also honors the vulture, a bird respected by Buddhists because it never kills for food but only eats dead flesh. For the *Sky Burial*, the corpse is carried to a high plateau where, accompanied by chants and prayers, and the solemn precision and steady rhythm of long experience, it is hacked to pieces by men garbed in white coats. Attending this ceremony are a small group of friends and some family members as well as a monk in saffron and red robes. The pieces of flesh and bones are pulverized in a stone pit then mixed with **tsampa** to make a paste. This sacred mixture is fed to the waiting vultures. Thus **tsampa**, the staple and consecrated food and drink of the Tibetan, is not only interwoven into daily life, it is also an essential aspect of the ceremony for the dead. Periodically, the men rest with cups of **cha suma** and talk quietly.

Throughout the funeral rituals, there are no signs of mourning, no tears, just rapt respectful silence. After it is over, tea is served again.

BIRTH RITUALS

Tibetan babies, especially in rural regions, are welcomed into the world a few days after birth with a little dab of **tsampa** placed on their foreheads. When the baby completes the first month of life, the parents touch the child's nose with soot to keep away evil ghosts and the family will go to the nearest monastery to pray for protection, and for the baby's well-being and wealth in adulthood.

WEDDING PRACTICES

Although in the past Tibetans accepted differing family structures, today monogamous family relations prevail although some marriages are still arranged but only with the agreement of the future partners.

As in many rural regions around the world, mischief and playfulness are a traditional part of the marriage rituals. When the families are unfamiliar with each other, they designate a friend to make the initial approach and inquiry for them. The friend will first present the *hada* (traditional silk scarf proffered on open palms) and bring generous gifts of meat, butter, and cheese. Such gifts are also generously exchanged between the parents if all is going well.

As well as Lamaism, Tibetans also believe in consulting an astrologer for all-important decisions, and marriage certainly is important. The astrologer pronounces on whether the couple is suited and ordains an auspicious wedding date.

Food gifts and horses figure largely especially in a nomad wedding. The bride will be hiding in her tent while representatives of the families jokingly complain about the food being served and mischievously hurl insults to each other. When this tradition is completed, the bride leaves her parents' tent on her brightly decorated new horse – or white yak – to go to the groom's family. The signal for the bride to start whining, crying, and complaining about leaving her parents' home is the appearance of her mother-in-law carrying a bucket of milk. Not until the scene ends with a relative of the bride flicking milk off her fingers to the sky does the whole group sit down to a wedding feast.

GLOSSARY OF FOODS AND FOOD TERMS

Ashom: corn.

Chadang: plain black tea.

Cha Kabi: coffee.

Chang: Tibetan barley beer, brewed almost everywhere.

Chura Soba: fresh cheese.

Churd Gambo: dried cheese prepared from buttermilk.

Dray: rice.

Gaw-Nga: fresh eggs.

Gwn-Dre: an omelet.

Hru Jaudza: meat dumplings served in soup.

Mentau: plain steamed buns or bread.

Moma or Momos: steamed meat-filled dumplings. If these are prepared Mongolian style, they will be frozen and stored before cooking by steaming or boiling. They may be filled with spinach or potatoes and cheese or meat.

Nay: barley.

Oma: milk.

Palay or **Ruti**: bread.

Poja or **Cha Suma**: salty Tibetan black tea with fermented yak butter.

Sha Paly: a fried pancake filled with chopped meat.

Sho: yogurt, usually prepared fresh daily.

Thien Momo: steamed plain bread shaped into a fan and usually served with the main meal of the day.

Thukpa: Tibetan noodle.

Tsampa: a mixture of roasted, ground barley and fermented yak butter moistened with tea, that is used as a bread or snack as well as a seasoning for soups and stews.

CHAPTER 51

TURKISH

The area of land occupied by present-day Turkey has an ancient history of conquerors and the conquered, extending from the early Hittite peoples, through the 600-year Ottoman Empire to today's nation. For hundreds of years the area of Asia Minor has geographically, culturally, and even linguistically bridged the gap between Asia and Europe.

As early as 1900 B.C.E. the Hittites inhabiting the plains of Anatolia raised cattle and sheep and cultivated crops of wheat and barley. They were also adept at making pottery and metal objects and it is believed that they were among the first people to work in iron. About 1000 B.C.E. the Hittites succumbed to Assyrians and later to groups of Arameans and Phoenicians (present-day Lebanese) and then to Thracian tribes from Greece. These peoples encouraged great prosperity and this drew the attention of the neighboring Persians who dominated the area for about 200 years, up to the early fourth century B.C.E.

Each of the early conquerors left some lasting influence, but none as much as the Greeks. Even the Persian conquest could not subdue the effects of Greek culture, the prosperity, or the vitality of Greek enclaves in the cities. To this day, ancient Greek ruins dot the landscape, Greek words for fish and vegetables exist in the Turkish language, and many daily foods can be easily traced to Greek origin. So entrenched was Hellenism, that even Roman rule in the first century C.E. – which brought Christianity, roads, buildings, and general unification – could not replace the general widespread acceptance of Greek culture. The Christianity brought by the Romans lasted in the area in calm coexistence with Hellenism, paganism, and the small Jewish communities for about 800 years.

It was the Romans who changed the name of Byzantium to Constantinople, made it the center of the Eastern Roman Empire, and introduced Latin. But the coexistence of religions, languages, and cultures was paralleled also by the interplay of Greek, Roman, and Oriental influences in arts and architecture. Asia Minor not only bridged the Asian-European land gap, it mirrored the cultural imprints of its conquerors.

Around the 900s C.E., there was a brief conquest in the area by the Armenians. But they in turn were quickly subdued by the powerful surge of Arab-Islamic conquests which reduced the Byzantine Empire to a small area around Constantinople. This remained mainly a market area for Oriental and Occidental trade of foods, cloths, pottery, and spices.

The next conquerors – the semi-nomadic Seljuk Turks – ousted the last influences of the Roman-Byzantium-Christian rule. These were the peoples from Persia, the chiefs of the Turk-omans, powerfully influenced by Islamic-Persian culture, who were to gain the longest and strongest hold on the coveted Asia Minor. Only the periodic raids of the Crusaders in the next 200 years delayed the firm establishment of Turk rule, but it was inevitable.

By the early 1200s C.E. the Seljuks were overpowered by the Turkomans whose leader, Osman, gave his name to the Ottoman Empire. During this period, there was some influence from the Genoese but more importantly from the Mongol raids. The Mongols, being mainly meat-eaters, left the field crops in ruin and encouraged only stockbreeding. Not only agriculture declined; the general prosperity of the area disintegrated as the Turkomans became attracted to conquests around the Mediterranean, leaving the Anatolian area exploited and neglected.

For the next 500 years, as the Ottoman Empire sprawled over the Balkans, Persia, parts of North Africa, Arabia, Yemen, Greece, Bulgaria, areas of southern Russia, and Italy, Asia Minor absorbed still other influences. Providing the subject peoples were "People of the Scriptures," the Muslims were tolerant rulers, yet wherever they lived they built their walled homes and walled cities often side by side or even surrounded by Christian or Jewish suburbs. While Greek words had long been used for foods, gradually Italian words entered the language for shipping, commerce, and banking and later French words were added to express ideas. The Ottoman Empire was ruled from its center in Istanbul (Constantinople) by an educated group of bureaucrats so loyal to the Sultan that they commonly referred to the rest of the populace as *raya* (the herd).

But Istanbul was not only the seat of Ottoman rule, it was also the stronghold of the Turkish culinary tradition. Historical documents dating as early as the 1400s C.E. record details of the special buildings constructed beside the Topkapi Palace by the Great Sultan Mehmet. These were specifically for food preparation and housing for the food artisans such as confectioners, tinsmiths (required to reline copper cooking vessels), vegetable chefs, and yogurt-makers.

Even the most cursory review of the dishes reflects clearly the cultural imprints of earlier times. Pilafs and yogurt from Persian sources; rich sweet pastries such as **baklava** of obvious Greek origin, as well as the widespread use of the egg-lemon sauce (**avgolemono**) so characteristic of Greek cooking; thick bean and lentil soups and flat Arabic breads from Egypt and areas of North Africa; layered vegetable casseroles and **corbasi** so reminiscent of the Romanian classic **guvech** and **corbas**; and an unquestionable echo of Maltese cookery in the Turkish version of meat **borek** served in a tray, so similar to the Maltese "cheese-cake" with its layers of flaky puff pastry and meat or cheese filling. Even the popular confection called **lokum** or **lukum** (Turkish delight) is well known and beloved in all Arabic countries.

The lengthy periods of Ottoman excursion around the Mediterranean and their subjugation of other lands gradually declined in the 1800s, coinciding with two other gradually emerging influences: the strengthening of the neighboring nations both nationalistically and militaristically and the internal struggles occurring within Asia Minor. The latter included deteriorating finances, political power struggles, and Muslim versus Christian domination.

At this crucial point in Turkey's history a new ferment had begun. A group of Turkish patriots, counterpart of similar nationalistic movements in other lands, used their European education to bring about needed reforms in the ancient land. With the final dismemberment of the Ottoman Empire at the end of World War I and the proclamation of the Turkish Republic in 1923 with its new capital at Ankara, the stage was set for the new Turkey. It was largely the efforts of Mustafa Kemal that gained the Turks world recognition of their right to their own country and the need for the sweeping reforms which he instigated. Primarily he sought modernization by disentangling Islam from government (which brought changes in daily lifestyles to everyone including women), and encouraged the return to Turkey of Muslim refugees from Greece, Bulgaria, and even Chinese Turkestan.

The modern republic of Turkey was founded in 1923 and presently has a population of about 51 million. More than 90 percent of the people speak Turkish and are Muslims, and about 80 percent are engaged in agriculture. The Ottoman Turks had a threefold origin: Turkish, Arabic, and Persian with a culture strongly influenced by the early Greeks. The origins and cultural influences remain, but a distinct Turkish society is emerging. The opposition to the newer ways comes mainly from the Kurds, a strong Muslim minority who retain their predominantly oral tradition in dialects of Kermanji, Zaza, and Gurani and have a reputation for extreme and sometimes unorthodox devoutness. Some of the Kurds are farmers, others are city dwellers, while a small group retain their ancient nomadic lifestyles,

FOODS COMMONLY USED

Asia Minor has an ancient history of fine agricultural produce including wheat, barley, fruits and vegetables. To this day, the basic diet includes unleavened breads made from wheat or rye flours, locally grown fruits and vegetables in season and a variety of cheeses and sour milk products. Barley is used mainly for brewing varieties of beer. Beef, mutton, and lamb are enjoyed but are often too expensive to constitute a regular part of the fare. Muslims do not eat pork and many eschew shellfish and

snails. Fish, fresh or dried, and served in many ways are an important protein source especially in the coastal regions where they are plentiful. Even in difficult times, most Turks eat well from their small household gardens and the sheep and goats that are typical of homes in rural areas. Diluted yogurt and buttermilk are widely consumed as beverages; beer is enjoyed, and **raki**, made from fermented raisins and flavored with anise, is considered to be the national beverage.

While the adult population enjoys a well-balanced diet, malnutrition is still widespread among infants and small children mainly as a result of feeding them starchy water and cereal gruels upon weaning with no other additional foods. More recently, increased availability of medical professionals provided by the government's Ministry of Health has improved health care, but still more so in urban rather than rural areas, where there is little change.

roaming with their herds for their winter migrations. Still smaller minority groups include some Christians and Jews.

DOMESTIC LIFE

Largely due to the influence of Islam, the "true Turk" is devoted to Sunni Islam, speaks Turkish, and makes family life the center of existence. But there is something more. An important value in Turkish life is *durustluk*, that sense of trust and reliability conveyed by personal contact. *Durust* can motivate business deals, and family relationships, and can prove more important than wealth, education or ability. Small rural communities are more influenced by these traditional values than are the Turkish communities in urban areas, yet changes are slowly occurring even in isolated regions. Urban Turks have modified their lifestyles because of European influence, and the migrating Turkish workers returning to their small villages from European centers have also carried with them the seeds of change.

Yet despite outside influence, Turks do retain a strong preference for home styles and home life that is distinctly and traditionally Turkish. Middle-class Turks still delight in decorating their homes with fine carpets, copperware, and ceramics and disdain the European penchant for paintings and sculpture; rural homes still devote the first floor of their homes to animals and remove their shoes when entering the second floor, which is designed for the family. Larger homes still have separate facilities for men and women; women are still rarely seen in public alone, and Turkish men still feel somewhat ill at ease with feminine company in public.

While many homes have adapted western cookstoves and even some kitchen gadgetry, the work of willing hands still dominates in meal preparation. Foods and water are still kept cool in earthenware jugs and jars called **testi**. Homes have collections of brightly decorated wooden spoons used for cooking and eating.

DAIRY PRODUCTS

Yought (yogurt), believed by some to be a Turkish invention, is widely used as a finishing touch to soups, vegetable dishes and as a sauce. It is also used as a dressing mixed with chopped fresh or cooked vegetables and provides a cooling refreshment when taken as is or diluted with ice water and lightly salted. Buttermilk may be used in the same way as **yought**.

Many varieties of local cheeses, both fresh and aged, are also widely used in many dishes. They are eaten in cubes as appetizers or may be a main part of a meal accompanied with bread and olives. Fresh milk is an important ingredient in the many types of sweetened desserts based on milk-cooked rice.

FRUITS AND VEGETABLES

Turkish peaches and figs, melons, oranges and lemons are outstanding for quality and flavor, but because of the climatic variations, fresh fruits are available in any season and these are enjoyed especially at the end of the meal.

Favorite Turkish vegetables are **aubergines** (eggplant) and okra. These are prepared in many ways and always served well cooked, as are tomatoes, onions, cucumbers, large-disc artichokes, zucchini, many varieties of squash, cabbage, cauliflower, beans of all kinds, and canned or fresh peas. **Aubergines** are such a favorite that household fires are common when the vegetable's season is at its height. The cooking oil used to fry the slices of **aubergine** readily catches fire and burns the wooden homes.

Leaves of many kinds, but especially vine leaves (from grapes), are used to prepare rolled **dolmas**, but any available vegetable may be served cooked and filled. Small squash, tomatoes, **courgettes**, **aubergines**, **asma kabagi** (marrow squash), and tomatoes and cucumbers may all be prepared as **dolmas**. At all times vegetables are plentiful and are used generously.

Thick conserves prepared from sweetened fruits and even flowers are often a part of meals. Purple and green, fresh or dried figs, many varieties of large grapes (**cavus**), tiny perfumed strawberries, and many colorful types of sweet melons grow throughout the area. Some regions are noted for their exceptional produce: peaches and apricots from Bursa; hard round pears from Ankara; Jaffa oranges from Fethiye and Hatay; sultana raisins and of course the dried figs exported all over the world from Izmir (Smyrna).

MEATS AND ALTERNATES

Meats do not form a large or important part of Turkish meals. Beef, mutton, and lamb are the favorites. Pork is not used as eating it is against Muslim dietary laws. Veal and poultry as well as occasional game are enjoyed when available. Most meats are prepared either by slow simmering in vegetable sauces, in soups, or marinated then cooked on skewers. A traditional Turkish specialty is the **doner kebab**: marinated serving pieces of lamb threaded on a tall vertical spit that rotates slowly in front of a specially constructed **doner** broiler; the huge oval of rotating broiled succulent lamb is sliced vertically to serve. When chickens or turkeys are used, they are well cooked and often stuffed with a **pilaf** of rice, pine nuts, and currants. Offal such as brains, kidneys, liver, lungs, and tripe are used to add meaty flavor to soups and vegetable dishes and stuffings.

Sea bass, mullet, swordfish, bluefish, dory, and plaice are the most widely used fish. Fish is often prepared with a base of vegetables called a **pilaki**, a well-chopped mixture of carrots, garlic, and onions cooked in olive oil and flavored with parsley, dill, and tomato sauce. Fish may also be baked in parchment; dipped in oil then flour then deep-fried in more oil; poached with vegetables to form both a broth and a main dish; or steamed by baking in a covered casserole in the oven. **Kilich sheesh** is a popular dish of cubed marinated swordfish broiled on skewers. Tuna, mullet, and swordfish may also be smoked and served in pieces or thinly sliced. Lobsters, prawns, sea scorpions (**iskorpit**), and mussels are also used by some who are not so strict about Muslim dietary rules. Red roe, the luxury **botargo** (gray mullet roe), as well as the very expensive sturgeon caviar are used as appetizers; red roe is used to prepare **tamara** (a salty-fish roe-appetizer paste of Greek origin).

Eggs are not plentiful but are enjoyed when available. A traditional preparation is to cook a pan of chopped vegetables lightly then make "holes" and drop the eggs in to cook together with the vegetables. Eggs are also blended with fresh lemon juice to form the tart egg-lemon sauce, of Greek origin, used in so many dishes and soups.

Peas, beans, and lentils are used to prepare thick and hearty soups and they are also served cooked and chilled then dressed lightly with seasonings, olive oil, and lemon juice and enjoyed as a salad dish. Lightly toasted salted nuts, especially Turkey's famed hazelnuts, are a special snack treat.

BREADS AND GRAINS
The importance of cereal grains in the Turkish diet can be readily seen by a glance at a typical full-course meal. Not only is the typical **pida** (Arabian flatbread) in evidence throughout the meal to serve as plate, cutlery, and food, there will likely be at least one course featuring a **bulgur** (cracked wheat) or rice **pilaf**, and yet another offering hot baked and filled pastries made from wheat flour.

Wheat and rye flours are widely used for breads and the finer flours to create the many pastries of stretched doughs, noodle pastries (**manti**), and delicate sweets made from **yufkas** (paper-thin dough brushed with butter). Rice is the main ingredient in daily **pilafs** of many varieties and may be cooked with consommés, vegetables, or the popular combination of nuts, currants, and spices. Many desserts are based on thick mixtures of rice that have been well cooked in milk then sweetened. **Bulgur** may replace rice in stuffings and **pilaf** dishes.

FATS
Olive oil is used not only as a cooking fat, but also drizzled over many cooked dishes to add a pleasing glossy finish. Olive oil is not only the basic fat, but it is used with a generous hand in almost every dish and bakery item. Second to olive oil is butter which is also used generously in the preparation of the many delicate layered pastries and sweets. Paprika-tinted butter melted to a glowing sauce is often used as a garnish. **Kaymak**, a rich thick clotted cream used as a topping for puddings and pastries is yet another source of fat in the Turkish diet. It should also be noted that even the milk and yogurt used is preferred with a high fat content. Skim milk products have no place here.

SWEETS AND SNACKS
While it is an easy matter to select random dishes and specialties in the Turkish cuisine and assign their likely origins, so popular are sweets that it is clear that the Turks have happily adopted the desserts and confections of almost every people with whom they have come in contact. The myriad varieties of shaped pastries either baked or fried then drenched in rich sweet syrup include **sekerpare**, **tatlisi** (of many types), **kadaifes**, and triangles of **baklava**. These would be as familiar to the Turk as to the Greek or Iranian. So would the meltingly tender cookies called **kurabiye** and the sweet cake squares called **helva**. A popular dessert made of stewed pumpkin in rich syrup then served cold with walnuts would delight Turks and most peoples of North Africa. A final course of ripe fresh fruits and small dishes of salted toasted nuts is a familiar meal ending to most peoples living near the Mediterranean.

But sometimes the pang of between-meal hunger cannot be satisfied by sweets no matter how tempting. **Muhallebici** (milk shops) stand ready to serve light meals of soups, boiled chicken dishes, many types of milk and **yought** refreshments or servings of milk-rice puddings. **Kebapci** are restaurants specializing in small meals or snacks of various types of **kebabs**. For those who have overindulged, **iskembeci** are the shops dedicated to serving a strong vinegar-garlic soup made from tripe and believed to soothe many ailments. Finally there are the Turkish coffee-houses, where everything from conversations to full-course meals are available – but mainly for males.

SEASONINGS
The delicacy of fine olive oil, fresh butter, sweet young vegetables and the tart overtones of **yought** and egg-lemon sauce predominate in the Turkish cuisine. Flavors are subtle and delicate with only the gentlest touches of mint, garlic and onions, dill and

in some dishes the aromatically sweet cinnamon, all-spice, and coriander.

BEVERAGES

Ayran, diluted **yought** lightly salted, the staple drink of the Anatolian peasants, is enjoyed by almost every-one. Local beer made from barley, wine made from grapes, and **raki** distilled from fermented raisins are used everywhere. Some of the more devout Muslims follow the prohibition against wine, but freely use beer and **raki**. Thrace province produces some pop-ular wines: **Buzbag** (red), **Kavilkedere** (red or white), and **Doluca** (dry white). Whiskey, gin, rum, and brandy are also taken by many Muslims with the conviction that these couldn't be prohibited as they were not known in the Prophet's time.

In many areas of the Middle East coffee is referred to as "Turkish coffee" even though it originated in Arab lands and was brought to Asia Minor by devout Muslims who made it their staple beverage. So impor-tant is coffee to the Turks that traditional marriage vows include a promise from the groom to provide his wife with coffee. Basically, the Turks prepare their coffee from pulverized beans boiled with varying amounts of sugar and sometimes spices in a funnel-shaped pot and serve it still foaming in tiny cups from which it is slowly sipped, leaving the grounds at the bottom. Any excuse is reason enough for serving coffee in one of many ways: **sade** is bitter; **az seker-li** is sweetish; **orta** is medium; while **cok sekerli** is very sweet.

Strong good coffee seems to be synonymous with Turkey, so it often comes as a surprise to learn that tea is of great importance throughout the Turkish day. Tea is everywhere: accompanying large and small business deals; trays bearing glasses of hot tea mirac-ulously balanced on shoulders are hustled along the streets; and hundreds of tea gardens (*cay bachesi*) tempt the weary to rest and sip. Teas prepared from fruits and fruit extracts like apple, kiwi, lemon, melon, and berries, and teas prepared from flower infusions like rose, hibiscus, and other exotica, as well as herbal teas, all put ordinary tea to shame. For the Turks, all teas are to be taken strong and hot without the "adul-teration" of sugar or milk.

REGIONAL SPECIALTIES

It is from the leisurely prepared meals in the Sultan's palaces in Istanbul that the cuisine of Turkey devel-oped. Yet over the countryside favorite dishes and traditions still prevail. The province of Bursa, noted for its fine orchards and some of the best butter and cheeses, also prides itself on a simple and classic meal style including a first course of fresh vegetables dressed with olive oil, then a meat stew accompanied with

some type of seasonal **dolma** (whatever greens are in season) and ending with **yought**, a bowl of fresh fruit, and a quiet session with the *narghile* water pipe). **Kavurma** or **haslama** are two typical types of coun-try stews containing some meat, mostly vegetables and varying amounts of fats.

Predominantly, meat is rare but vegetables and **yought** are in abundance. Olives are a daily famil-iar staple everywhere except near the Black Sea coast where walnuts are used. Circassian chicken is a dish prepared with a garnish of crushed, well-peppered walnuts. In the same area the **hamsi** (small anchovy) is also widely used. In the southeast, hot **kebabs** and spicy raw meatballs (**cig kofte**) are the favorites and pulses are used daily, especially mashed seasoned chickpeas.

European customs and manners prevail in Turkish cities, but traditional customs such as eating with bread, spoons and fingers from cloth-covered car-pets prevail, as does the custom (as in Greece) of entering restaurant kitchens to inspect and taste foods before eating one's meal.

MEALS AND CUSTOMS

Urban Turks may enjoy a simple European-type breakfast of breads, fruit, and coffee; rural Turks will wake up to clear tea, breads and goat's cheese, olives and jam; Anatolian peasants will start their day with hot satisfying soup. Typically throughout the day hunger will be sated with snacks from the many ven-dors and small shops and restaurants, which also provide small meals of **meze** (appetizers) and **raki** or simply hot soup.

Turks enjoy extending hospitality to respected guests, most especially those with education or *durust* education. The traditional six-course meal is not a daily occurrence but will be reserved for special guests or special occasions. One or more of the courses may comprise a usual evening meal. **Meze** and **raki** of themselves can be so elaborate and varied that they can constitute a meal known as **raki sofrasi**. But for the traditional meal, they comprise but the first course: tidbits of meats, fish of all types, vegetables hot and cold, stuffed and dressed with oil in endless varieties, cheeses, breads, olives and salted nuts. **Lekerda**, **balik yumurtasi**, **tarama**, **pastirma** (sun-dried beef spiced with paprika, cumin, and garlic), **midia dolmasi** (stuffed mussels), and many others add to the tasty varieties of appetizers.

The second course, **hamur isi**, consists of varieties of stuffed pastries all served hot, some with sauces. Fillings may be of cheeses, rice, meats, or vegetables. The meat course would be served next, usually a form of **kebab**, to be followed by a refreshing cold vegetable dish with olive oil.

The last two courses of a traditional dinner could be considered as the desserts, with a milky rice pudding or one or more forms of the rich syrup-soaked pastries coming first, to be followed by an array of fresh seasonal fruits and Turkish coffee.

While changes are occurring, traditionally, women are more in the background socially, and in some homes and areas they may even dine separately from the men. But overall, the innate sense of generous hospitality is prevalent and the respected guest (education, authority, and fine manners having priority over mere wealth) can be assured of the finest that the family may have to offer.

Traditionally food was eaten from trays called *tepsi* which were placed either on carpets or on small low tables for each diner or several diners. Luxurious cushions and exquisite carpeting made dining, either sitting or squatting, a comfortable matter. Foods would always be prepared and served in such a way that diners needed only to use wooden spoons for eating, but more recently the European forks and knives have been used more widely.

SPECIAL OCCASIONS

It has already been noted that the great majority of Turks profess the faith of Islam: "There is no God but God, and Muhammad is His Prophet." Yet while the call of the *muezzin* is heard throughout the land, few Turks observe the daily set of five prayers or adhere to the ban on alcohol. Most do retain the ambition of the pilgrimage to Mecca and many observe Friday prayers although Mustafa Kemal (or Kemal Ataturk, president of Turkey, 1923–1938) decreed Sunday the day of rest. Further, few Turks will eat pork, seafood or snails, and those Muslims who follow the precepts of the Prophet's son-in-law Ali and call themselves *Alevi* include the dietary prohibition against eating hare.

One of the most important religious festive occasions is the *Sunnet Dugunu* (circumcision) performed when a boy is about seven years of age (based on the Mosaic law of circumcision which is performed on the male infant at the age of eight days) to mark his initiation from infant to adolescent. But the occasion is not just one of joyous family celebration for very often it also contains a heartwarming deed: wealthy families traditionally sponsor the circumcision of a poor boy as well.

Popular at *Sunnet Dugunu* is not only food, music, and dancing but also the traditional *Karagoz*, a type of shadow-show featuring the adventures of witty characters and sometimes critical or even crude but humorous dialogues.

Turkish weddings or *dugun* are almost as festive as the circumcision but differ from the country to the city. City weddings are brief refined ceremonies followed by musical receptions where **meze** and sweetened soft drinks are served. Country weddings delight in ancient traditions which include the lively bargaining for the "bride-price," the *baslik*, and the inclusion of as many guests and musicians as can be afforded all happily participating in processions, dancing, eating and drinking often throughout the night while the marriage is consummated.

The peak of religious observance for the Turks is the holy month of *Ramazan* when all fast (totally refraining from food, drink, smoking) during the daylight hours. In many areas, drums waken the people one hour before sunrise so that a meal may be taken. And later at sundown, a cannon may sound to signify the end of the day's fast; traditionally this time is determined when the light is such that a black thread cannot be distinguished from a white. A two-day period called *Seker Bayram* marks the end of the holy month with floodlit monuments and mosques, festivities for children, parades and exhibitions and family gatherings featuring lengthy traditional dinners. Perhaps it is because of the sincere devotion to *Ramazan* that many consider the Turks to be "night people." Certainly every province and village has its favored coffeehouses (for men only) where men and boys commonly spend the entire night during *Ramazan*, eating, drinking, and being entertained by the great oral tradition of Turkey, the wandering folk poets, singers, and balladeers accompanied by the *saz*, a three-string, lute-like instrument.

Other special occasions include the Festival of *Mevlana Konya*, in memory of the founder of the whirling dervishes; *Kurban Bayrami*, especially celebrated in rural areas as the lamb sacrifice; and October 29, when the anniversary of the Turkish Republic is celebrated with parades and special events.

GLOSSARY OF FOODS AND FOOD TERMS

Aubergine: eggplant. This is the favorite Turkish vegetable and is prepared in imaginative ways such as **borek**, cooked strips of eggplant sandwiched with cheese then egg-dipped, crumbed, and deep-fried; or **kofte**, cooked pureed eggplant blended with grated cheese and bechamel sauce then chilled to thicken and finally shaped into walnut balls and deep-fried.

Bamya: okra.

Borek: small squares of phyllo pastry dabbed with cheese and rolled like cigarettes then butter-brushed and baked till golden.

Bulgur: specially prepared cracked wheat (sometimes the term is also used for buckwheat) prepared like rice. Common preparation: chopped onions are browned in butter then the **bulgur** is stirred in and cooked till tender with boiling stock poured over. Grains are always separate, never mushy. A Turkish country staple.

Doner Kebap or **Kebab**: classic favorite of selected strips of lamb wound on a vertical broiler and cooked by slow rotation then served by slicing vertically.

Dugun Corbasi: traditional "wedding soup." A rich vegetable and meat soup finished just before serving with egg-lemon sauce.

Ekmek: an imitation of the **Kadaifes** that may be prepared from leftover bread, crisply fried then served with syrup, nuts, and cream.

Gullac: soft noodle-like layers cooked in sweetened milk and scented with rosewater. Served with **Kaymac**.

Hamur Isi: general term for the third course of hot filled pastries in a traditional Turkish dinner.

Ic Pilaf: rice is soaked in hot water then drained. Pine nuts, chopped onions, chopped, browned lamb's liver, currants, spices (allspice, cinnamon, and pepper), and cubed tomatoes are added to the rice then hot consomme is poured over to cook. After resting twenty minutes, the dish is served.

Imam Biyaldi: the legendary Turkish dish of stuffed baked eggplants said to taste so exquisite that the priest fainted when he ate it.

Izgara: a grill of either meat or fish, usually served after **meze** (appetizers).

Kadaifes: crispy shreds of wheat fried in butter, drenched in hot syrup, cooled, garnished with chopped nuts, and served with cream or **Kaymak**. An imitation of this classic dish may be made from leftover bread, crisply fried then served with syrup, nuts and cream. This is called **Ekmek**.

Kilich Sheesh: cubes of swordfish marinated in olive oil, vinegar, salt, and pepper then threaded on skewers with onions, bay leaves, and tomatoes and grilled. Lemon wedges accompany the serving.

Kofte: balls of ground meat of any size.

Kokorec: a grilled type of sausage sold by street vendors.

Kurabiye: a tender buttery round cookie studded with clove and heavily dusted with icing sugar.

Lekerda or **Lakerda**: salt-cured fish steaks sliced very thinly and served with sliced onions. (Similar to smoked salmon or **Lax**.)

Manti: rich noodle pastry is prepared from flour, egg, and water then thinly rolled and cut into squares. These are filled with minced beef and onions then sealed tightly into triangles, placed on buttered sheets, and baked till crisply browned. Boiling hot consomme is poured over and baking continued until the **Manti** swell to cover the baking sheet. Finally a sauce of melted butter and **Yought** is poured over to serve. This dish likely has its origins in the steamed dumplings of China. A Turkish classic.

Maruli: a type of long, thin, delicately flavored Turkish lettuce served with tomatoes and onions as a first course.

Mastic: an aromatic resin from a Mediterranean tree of the cashew family. The resin is used as a flavoring.

Moussaka: this renowned eggplant casserole made Turkish style involves scooping out the vegetable and draping the purple skins over the baking pan then refilling it with the mashed eggplant, rice, and seasonings and baking. Serve unmolded from the pan to stand on a platter entirely encased in the shiny purple skin.

Mucver: grated onions and grated squash blended with fresh dill, salt and pepper, eggs and crumbled white cheese then formed into patties and fried.

Pastirma: appetizer of sun-dried beef spiced with paprika, garlic, and cumin.

Pastries: the list would be endlessly mouth-watering, but here are a few: **Sekerpare**, **Yought Tatlis**, **Tulumba Tatlisi**, **Hanim Gobeci** (lady's navel), **Samsa Tatlisi**. Each are variously shaped pastries then baked or fried before soaking in sweet syrup and serving with nuts and **Kaymak**.

Peynir: a cheese prepared from a blend of cow's and sheep's milk. Mild when fresh, becoming dry and salty as it is aged.

Pida or **Pides**: flat, round Arab bread.

Pilaki: sometimes used to refer to an entire dish but is actually the well-cooked vegetable base with which meat or fish may be cooked then finished by dribbling with olive oil.

Puddings: **Keskul** is a rice and milk pudding stuffed with almonds and garnished with ground almonds, pistachios, and coconut. Served cold. **Sutlac** is a plain sweetened milky-rice pudding; the top may be oven-browned. Sometimes served with ice cream. **Tavuk Gogsu** is a pudding in which a cooked chicken breast is pulled into threads then combined with a thick sauce of strained and sweetened rice and milk. This is poured into a flat pan to cool then sprinkled with cinnamon and served cold.

Puf Moreks: half-moon shapes of delicately thin pastry filled with a blend of milk cheeses and parsley then served hot after deep-frying.

Rahat Lukum or **Lokum**: the confection dusted with sugar and flour and called **Turkish Delight**. Prepared from cornstarch-thickened syrup and flavored with either rosewater or orange flower water or ground **Mastic**. Sometimes slivered almonds or pistachios are added.

Salma: a Persian pilaf of plain rice first cooked in water then drained and added to boiling consommé and recooked.

Sis Kebap: small pieces or cubes of meat skewered and grilled.

Tas Kebap: cubed stewed meat with various vegetables.

Tulum: sharp goat's cheese aged in goat skins.

Yalac Chorbasi: a soup broth of chicken, thickened with barley and seasoned with mint, butter, and browned onions. Just before serving, **Yought** is stirred in.

Yought: yogurt.

Yufkas: thin delicate sheets of phyllo pastry used by brushing with butter then shaping, filling, rolling, or layering to prepare desired foods.

UKRAINIAN

Famed both as the "Mother of Russia" and the "Breadbasket of Europe," Ukraine's reputation has been well earned. Her earliest history is in effect the early history of Russia itself. From the ninth to the thirteenth century C.E., under Prince Yaroslav, the Ukraine was the center of the first Russian state known as *Kievan Rus*. Kiev was the center of culture, education, and the institution of the first Russian law: *Russkaya Pravda*.

But Yaroslav's attempts to consolidate the Russian Empire disintegrated after his death not only because of feuding between the Rus principalities, but also because of intermittent invasions by neighboring Poles, Lithuanians, and Teutonic knights. Subsequent divisions of the Ukraine lands found them alternately under control of Russia, Poland, and later Austria. For example Galicia, once a state of the Ukraine, at first challenged the supremacy of Kiev and in later history ended up as a part of Poland, then Austria, and finally today finds itself divided between Poland, Russia, and Austria. Each conquest left the marks of suppression of Ukrainian nationalism as well as some cultural and gastronomic influences of the conquering nations.

Despite the suppressions and reversals caused by the relentless path of history, Ukrainian peoples have retained a distinct cultural, literary, and linguistic pattern that distinguishes them from other Slav nations (*see* the Southern Slavs) and one which they proudly maintain wherever they live.

Throughout history, Ukraine was always a tempting acquisition for any nation because of her vast fertile steppes that produced not only an abundant variety of grain crops but also fruit, and nut-laden orchards and fine pastures for beef and dairy cattle.

Her rivers – the Danube, Dnieper, Dniester, Donets, and the Southern Buh – once famed for varieties of fish, are now, unfortunately, like the estuaries of the Black Sea and the Sea of Azov, heavily polluted. During the Soviet period, collective and state farms were organized to increase crop and livestock and poultry production. Under restructuring processes, there has been a gradual return to small-scale vegetable, fruit, and livestock production by private farmers. More recently the large collectives provide research and technology while the smaller family-owned farms do the actual farming.

Today, Ukraine is still justly famed for her production of fine wheat and the world's largest production of sugar beets. Historically, as now, she is self-sufficient – generously so – in all aspects of food production.

It was the great natural gifts of fertile land interlaced with many river systems and combined with a mild and moist climate that made Ukraine, together with her population of sturdy, hardworking people, an asset to any conqueror.

Although Ukrainians are Eastern Slavs together with the Great Russians and Belorussians, their language as well as many aspects of their culture and cuisine differs. Russians may insist that Ukrainian is nothing but a Russian dialect, but Ukrainians feel that the historical events of 1918 have divided them from the Russians in outlook as well as language. Ukrainians point to the fact that their language differs in phonetics and alphabet. Further, Ukrainians feel that their appearance and personality sets them apart from other Europeans, profound individualism being their noted characteristic.

The influence of historical conquests means that the Ukrainian cuisine contains many elements of Russian and Polish cookery. The **borsch**, however, is claimed to be of Ukrainian origin and the myriad breads baked by Ukrainians are said to be unexcelled (though copied) elsewhere.

DOMESTIC LIFE

The rural areas of Ukraine have changed little from hundreds of years ago. Typically, families lived in small cottages surrounded by gardens and fences. Older cottages may have had only one or two rooms; more recently only an increase of rooms may be noted as a sign of modernization.

The center of the main room would be the stove built against one wall of clay or stone. The traditional stove would include ovens, cooking top, and an opening in the forepart called the *prychipok*, usually also made of clay or bricks. To one side of the stove would be a firebox, and to the other side a hanging cupboard with shelves for dishes and implements. Kerosene or oil lamps would be used for light; in north Ukraine, wood splinters placed in a holder would provide lighting. In wooded areas wood would be the fuel; straw and sweet rush were and are used as fuel in the southern parts; dried manure would provide fuel in Eastern Ukraine. More recently, the use of electricity is spreading through the countryside, but as in olden times, running water and proper sewage facilities remain problems in some rural areas.

Age-old methods of food preservation also prevail in country areas. Winter food storage is crucial and much care is taken to assure adequate winter provisions. Hollowed tree stumps, wooden chests, and large bins or granaries are used for grain storage. Vegetables such as beets and potatoes are commonly stored by burying them in the ground. In some areas funnel-shaped pits plastered with clay and straw are used to store grains and even sauerkraut. Fish and some vegetables could be preserved by drying in the wind and sun or over a fire; meats could be brined, smoked or dried. Food storage is not a problem in cities as frequent shopping is the rule.

DAIRY PRODUCTS

Dairy products form a daily part of Ukrainian diet. **Smetana** (sour cream) is used as a topping for fresh chopped vegetables, in soups, with noodle and dumpling dishes, and with cooked or fresh fruits. **Smetanka** is the fresh sweet cream used in bakery served with grains or fruit desserts. Fresh milk is used, but sour milk, buttermilk, and **huslyanka** (clabbered milk) are preferred as beverages and in cookery.

Pot cheese or dry curd cottage cheese is used widely as the base for many dishes and the filling in baked goods, noodle or dumpling dishes. Also available in Ukraine are a number of varieties of hard and soft, fresh and aged local cheeses made from sheep's or cow's milk.

FRUITS AND VEGETABLES

The vegetable staples are beets, cabbage, and potatoes. In western Ukraine corn is also an important staple where it may be classed both as a grain that is dried and ground and used as hominy or cornmeal and cooked into breads, gruels, and cereals; or it may be eaten off the cob as a vegetable. Other vegetables used in much lesser quantities include carrots, turnips, onions, tomatoes, cucumbers, greens (spinach, sorrel), pumpkin, eggplant, and many varieties of wild mushrooms. Garlic is important and used generously.

Vegetables are eaten coarsely chopped and raw in salads, and well cooked in soups. Many stuffed vegetable dishes utilize the leaves of cabbage, spinach, grape leaves, or beet greens. Pickled and brined vegetables such as dill pickles, beet relishes, fermented apples, sauerkraut, and dilled green tomatoes, are enjoyed.

A variety of cultivated fruits and wild berries are enjoyed in season or preserved as relishes or jams. Fruits may be eaten fresh in season but are more often preferred stewed with sugar in compotes; cooked and puréed then thickened with starch as in **kysil**; and cooked and sweetened to use as filling for **varenyky** (noodle dumplings). Fruits may also be simply stewed, sweetened and thickened, then served with **smetanka**. Others may be prepared as sharply tart or else in sweet and sour fruit soups.

MEATS AND ALTERNATES

Pork and pork products are most enjoyed. Very occasionally veal or lamb may be used. Mostly, meats are considered expensive and are eaten only on special occasions; all edible parts are well used. Salt pork is considered the staple of the peasant's diet. Also used when possible are chicken, turkey, wild duck, goose, rabbit, pigeon, and venison. Many types of sausages

FOODS COMMONLY USED

Ukrainian cooking is primarily Slavic; it resembles Russian cooking in eastern Ukraine and takes elements both from Polish and Czech cooking in western Ukraine. Tea drinking, emphasis on substantial soups and **kasha** as well as the **zakuska** preceding dinner are all threads of Russian influence; some flour mixtures such as noodles, honeycakes, and certain breads may all be of Polish origin, while the judicious use of bread crumbs as well as dumplings could be traced to Czech origin. But the hearty soup of beets and/or cabbage the Russians call **borsch** and the Poles called **barshch** is considered to have originated in Ukraine. Ukrainian baking of sweets and breads based on their fine quality of wheat and rye flours is unexcelled both in variety and quality. Ukrainians also use more garlic in their foods; pork is the favored meat when available; but the general basic diet depends upon grains and vegetables, dairy products and occasionally fish.

are widely used because they are economical and tasty. These include mildly flavored veal and pork sausages; **kyshka**, a homemade or commercially prepared sausage containing mostly fat and flour; **sardelky**, a spicy sausage; and hunter's sausage, thin, hard, well-cured, and durable.

There is a good supply of fresh water (hopefully the many rivers in Ukraine will be cleaned of pollution) and sea fish include herring, perch, pike, sturgeon, and carp. Fish is usually prepared by poaching, jellying, frying, pickling, or baking. Eggs are produced abundantly and used unstintingly in baking. Eggs are occasionally served boiled or fried for a breakfast. Legumes are not used extensively, except dried peas may be used in soup. Nuts are used in bakery for a garnish and as a filling.

BREADS AND GRAINS

The sheaf of wheat is a fitting symbol for the Ukraine Republic. Grain is not only the basic ingredient for the **kasha** and breads that are a part of almost every meal, it is an important and holy symbol on many sacred occasions, from the Christmas **kutya** (a mixture of cooked wheat grains, honey, poppy seeds, and nuts) to the grains of rye that are often strewn in the coffins of the deceased. Specially baked breads highlight each special occasion as well. In fact, there is no aspect of Ukrainian life or afterlife that is not celebrated with the holiness of grain. If a daily meal has neither breads nor **kasha** (which would be most unusual), it would certainly have noodles (**lokshyna**) in some form, or the many types of **pyrohy** or **varenyky**, little noodle pockets of fruit, meat, or vegetable filling served with cream, fruits, or **smetana**, or afloat in soups.

FATS

Lard, rendered salt pork and bacon ends add characteristic smoky taste to most Ukrainian cookery. Butter is used when available. There is a preference for whole milk rather than skim. Much fat is also consumed in the creams and cheeses. Vegetable oils, sunflower seed oil, and also oils from flax and hemp are used by the Orthodox on fast days and Lent when meat or meat products are not traditionally used.

SWEETS AND SNACKS

While rural Ukrainians serve desserts only on special occasions, urban Ukrainians consider a meal completed only when cakes or desserts have been served. Desserts with honey are a special favorite. Tea is often enjoyed Russian style, with a small accompanying saucer of sweet fruit jams to spoon up with each sip. Because of the frequent use of honey as a sweetener, bee-keeping is important in Ukraine. Toasted and salted sunflower and melon seeds are enjoyed as a snack.

SEASONINGS

Tart flavors, fermented sour flavors, and the combination of sweet and sour are prevalent. Juice from pickles and relishes, the juice squeezed from sauerkraut, and a specially made fermented liquid called **kvas** (from fermented rye bread or fermented beet juice) – any of these may be used to add that special touch to soups and other dishes. And tart or soured pickled vegetables are frequent meal additions. In general cookery, foods are rich with well-cooked natural tastes enhanced occasionally with dill seeds or caraway seeds, dill, butter, or **smetana**. Onions and mushrooms also add their touch to many dishes, but garlic is probably the most used of all. Honey is the favorite sweetener.

BEVERAGES

Tea is the most important beverage. Milk and sugar may be added according to taste. **Kvas**, as well as being used for its unique soured taste, is also a popular country beverage. Coffee is enjoyed but considered to be a luxury. Ukrainian wine or vodka may be a part of the evening meal. Tea, water, or bottled mineral waters are most usually taken with breakfast or lunch.

MEALS AND CUSTOMS

The Ukrainian emphasis on grains permeates each meal and most customs and special occasions. The traditional four meals of the day – breakfast, dinner (before noon), *pidvechirok* (the afternoon snack), and the evening supper – all feature bread. It is also said that in Ukraine a meal would be incomplete without a soup course. In fact, very often the nourishing thick soups together with **kasha** (buckwheat or barley groats oven-baked so each grain is fluffy and separate) and bread are satisfying enough to be the entire meal. Typical country meals include large helpings of soup, **kasha**, and bread together with noodle or dumpling dishes that may sometimes include meat, fish, or vegetables. Pickles and **smetana** complete the meal. Depending on the time and family budget, the evening meals in the cities may include more courses or more elaborate dishes: herrings, cheeses, **pashtet** (baked pate served hot or cold), sliced meats, sausages, varieties of breads, and dessert.

Meals are traditionally served family style with the foods placed on platters and diners helping themselves. Hearty eating is encouraged and taking more than one helping is considered to be flattering to the hostess. Tables are often set with hand-embroidered cloths traditional to the various regions of Ukraine.

SPECIAL OCCASIONS

The principal religions of Ukraine are represented by the Ukrainian (Greek) Catholic Church and the Ukrainian Greek Orthodox Church with others in various Christian denominations, as well as a small population of Jews. Most of the latter were listed variously as Poles, Ukrainians, Austrians, or Russians in the immigration waves following the turn of the century and both world wars.

Although Christianity predominates in the religious feelings of Ukrainians, many of the festivals are intertwined with agricultural celebrations and carry overtones of ancient Slavic festivals as well as local superstitions and mysticism.

The majority of Galician Ukrainians belong to the Ukrainian (Greek) Catholic Church, distinct from the Roman Catholic Church in many features but especially in allowing married men to be ordained as priests. The majority of Ukrainians from Bukovina (southwestern Ukraine, now a part of Romania) belong to the Ukrainian (Greek) Orthodox Church. Since most Ukrainians not only attempted to live near their own peoples and preserve their language and customs, as well as retain their religious affiliation, the community and the church became an integral part of social life.

Special occasions are described here as traditionally celebrated in Ukraine. For a time religious observances were not encouraged in the Communist Soviet Union; however, agricultural and seasonal festivities were celebrated by all. In North America, most Ukrainians celebrate two Christmases: one on December 25 with a Christmas tree (*yalynka*) and gift giving, and the other more solemn occasion of January 6 when the Ukrainian traditions of Christmas together with the symbols of family unity, respect for the dead, and the importance of agriculture intertwine in a memorable Christmas Eve celebration.

In Ukraine, traditional folk customs and rites are connected with the "Folk Calendar," with each season bringing its special days which are interlaced with family, agriculture, and religion, not excluding spells, sorcery, and protection against evil spirits or the "evil eye."

Winter festivals are mostly centered around Christmas and New Year's but begin with a special holiday for young men and unmarried girls on December 13. For this day special breads are baked, some concealing charms or coins which will tell the lucky finder that she or he will wed within the year. The breads are called **balabushky**. Games, the casting of spells, and telling of fortunes are commonplace on this day, one of the favorites being the pouring of hot wax on cold water to predict the future. This special day ends with a huge honeycake called **kaly-ta** which is tied and hung from the rafters and becomes the center of games and teasing until finally eaten.

December 19 is called St. Nicholas' Day, St. Nicholas being considered the guardian saint of orphans, animals, and the poor. His day is one of merrymaking and gifts for the children.

January 6 is the start of the Christmas season, which ends on January 19 with Epiphany. It is considered the most important family celebration and its preparations begin many weeks before. In the early morning of *Sviat Vechir*, the mother lights a new fire from twelve pieces of wood that have been carefully selected and dried for twelve days. The ritual evening meal will start with blessings and a speech from the father, and the entire family will be present around the table with a special place set to remember the dead. Symbols of the sacredness of agriculture in the life of the family will be found in the farm implements that are placed under the dinner table, the sheaf of wheat placed in the holy corner under the icons, garlic placed on four corners of the table, and hay or straw strewn over the entire floor and some under the tablecloth. In the middle of the table will be placed a special round loaf of bread (**knysh** or **kalach**) with a lighted candle in the center.

The ceremonial meal will begin with the **kutya**, a dish of cooked grain mixed with poppy seeds, honey, and nuts. A handful of this may be mixed with the food for the animals in the stable because it is believed that on this night even the animals have the power of speech. Another handful of **kutya** is thrown out of doors – "let the frost eat **kutya**" – and a last handful is flung up at the ceiling "so that the bees may swarm." Finally, all at the table take some to eat and this ritual food is followed by eleven meatless dishes to complete the meal. The total of twelve dishes is said to be symbolic of the twelve apostles. Vegetables, fishes, and grains are the basic ingredients of the twelve dishes which may include **kasha**; boiled dumplings filled with fruit, grains, or vegetables; cabbage, peas, beans, or potatoes dressed with oil and garlic; boiled corn (**kokot**); **pyrohy** with poppy seeds; and fruit dishes. Children play an important part in this ritual meal for it is they who eagerly watch the sky to sight the first star – a signal that the ritual meal may begin.

The day of Christmas is celebrated usually with caroling, dancing, and a roast suckling pig. The festivities continue till January 9.

New Year's Eve, January 13, is called *Malanka* or *Shchedryi-vechir* ("Generous Eve") and is celebrated with parties. Each area of Ukraine prepares its specialty dishes, which may include **pyrohy** filled with meat or cottage cheese, buckwheat pancakes and sausages, and bagels or **bublyky**. In addition, a plate of **kutya** completes the festive meal. The following day the festivities continue with costumes and entertainment, dancing and fortune-telling.

January 19 and 20 ends the Christmas season more solemnly with church services commemorating Christ's baptism by St. John the Baptist in the Jordan River. This is called Epiphany or Jordan's Day and the evening meal is similar to that of Christmas Eve, ending this time with the **kutya** being driven away.

The many spring festivals are centered around Easter and Whitsuntide or the "Green Festival." *Miasnytsi* is the carnival period that precedes Lent; the traditional food, **varenyky** (boiled dumplings made with fine noodle pastry and filled with fruits or cheese fillings), and **hrechanyky** (pancakes) are served.

This period is marked by intensive housecleaning, washing, repairing and painting. Refuse is collected and burned. And all of this work is accompanied by prescribed rituals and incantations ending with the carrying of a plow around the village and the sacrificial burning of a black rooster. Although the cleaning takes place about the home, there seems to be an accompanying cleansing of the soul said to culminate in the burning of the rooster – perhaps symbolic of the end of evil deeds and sins.

Since palm branches are not available, willow branches are substituted for blessing on Willow Sunday, the Sunday before Easter.

Maundy Thursday, the Thursday before Easter Sunday, is celebrated with a solemn *strasti* or "passion" service in the church with all the congregants hurrying home afterward, each carrying a specially lit candle. This candle is considered to have special significance the whole year through; it is relit and placed near the icons during a severe thunderstorm and is lit and placed in the hand of a dying person. In eastern Ukraine strong beliefs persist that the dead return on that night to hold a Divine Mass in the church.

Easter Sunday's joyous service is ended with the congregants singing "*Khrystos Voskres*" ("Christ Is Risen") and hurrying home with baskets of foods and decorated eggs (**pysanky** and **krashanky**) blessed by the priest. These are eaten as part of the festive meal: a fine array of sausages, smoked meats, roast suckling pig, cheeses, breads, relishes, and the specialty Easter cakes, **paska** or **babka**.

Summertime is similarly laced with festivities that intertwine the mystical and the religious and pay special homage to the good earth which produces the bounties of Ukraine. Young love, weddings and births, even funeral ceremonies are symbolic of the agricultural life of the people. Coffins may be strewn with rye so that the dead will not go hungry; poppy seeds may be sprinkled on the coffin so that the dead

may rest peacefully. Sometimes food is left at the graveside, usually a dish of **kolyvo**, a mixture of grains and honey. Traditionally upon returning from the funeral, no one must look back, and all must purify themselves by washing and touching the stove before eating the funeral meal which itself begins with the traditional **kolyvo**.

A freshly baked loaf of bread topped with a small mound of salt is traditionally called **khlib I sil** and is the age-old welcome for special guests and for newlyweds. Perhaps it comes as no surprise that a Ukrainian wedding cake is also replete with tradition. Seven bridesmaids grind flour taken from seven different sources and bake it into an ornamented loaf of bread called **korovai** which will be tasted by each wedding guest at the wedding feast. The **korovai** is considered to be the wedding cake.

Few Ukrainians in North America keep all the old world traditions, but certain customs and rituals are held dear by some families. Many celebrate two Christmases and most celebrate Easter with all its joyous symbols.

GLOSSARY OF FOODS AND FOOD TERMS

Babka: rich yeast cake with fruit. Baked especially for Easter.

Borsch or **Borshch**: pride of Ukraine, and adopted in other countries, a hearty soup based on cabbage and/or beets. Made in many variations from a soup full of meats and other vegetables to clear ruby red broth.

Borshchok: a soup specialty of western Ukraine, made mostly with beets.

Brazhka: beer. Traditionally, the Ukrainians seldom drink beer.

Breads: there are said to be more than 780 varieties of breads baked in Ukraine. Each festival has its specialty bread.

Balabushky: small sourdough rolls or breads sprinkled with poppy seeds. A few are baked with coins or charms, which will tell the lucky finder that he or she will wed within the year. These are baked for December 13.

Bublyky: bagels. Small doughnut-shaped rolls dipped in boiling water before baking to make a chewy crust. In some areas, a New Year's specialty.

Drahli: a **Zakuska** (appetizer) dish of molded aspic made from simmered pig's feet and vegetables, chopped, arranged and set in their own juices. Sliced and served cold.

Easter Syrnyk: a cheesecake made of pot cheese and eggs served with the main course. Can also be sweetened and served as a dessert.

Egg Barley: tiny dumplings made of firm dough (milk, eggs and flour) finely grated into boiling water, and poached. When served with browned onions and sour cream, the dish is called **Halushky**.

Holubtsi: cabbage leaves stuffed with a mixture of ground meat and buckwheat, well seasoned with garlic.

Horokhivka: thick soup made from dried green peas, often enriched with salt pork or ham bone.

Hrechanyky: buckwheat pancakes leavened with yeast and served with melted butter. A specialty, together with **Varenyky**, during the pre-Lenten carnival of *Miasnytsi*.

Huslyanka: a clabbered milk eaten with mashed potatoes or **Kasha**. Can be made by adding a few spoonfuls of buttermilk or sour cream into fresh milk and allowing the mixture to stand at room temperature overnight or until thickened. Chill before serving.

Kalyta: a large, round, sweet yeast dough cake coated with honey and hung from the ceiling as the highlight of special games on December 13.

Kapusnyak: **sauerkraut** soup.

Kartoplyanka: a creamy potato soup. Sometimes called "white borsch."

Kasha: refers to any cooked grains, but most often used to refer to cooked buckwheat groats. **Kasha** is cooked so that each grain is separate; it is not a mushy mixture. Sometimes browned chopped onions are added.

Khala: a slightly sweet twisted yeast bread golden with egg yolks and sprinkled with poppy seeds.

Kholodynk: chilled fresh vegetable soup served with buttermilk or sour milk.

Knysh or **Kalach**: may be a simple white yeast bread, or when shaped into a high round, with a candle in the middle and set upon the table, it becomes the special bread baked for Christmas Eve and other festivals.

Kokot: corn.

Kolach or **Kalach**: a white yeast bread.

Kolyvo: cooked grains mixed with honey. This dish is left at the graveside. Also eaten at the meal following the funeral.

Komora: storehouse for grains and vegetables.

Korovai: the special large bread baked for weddings. Seven bridesmaids traditionally grind flour from seven sources. The bread is shaped with flowers, doves, and other decoration all made from the dough. Everyone at the wedding tastes a piece.

Kotlety: any combination of meats that are pounded or ground, then shaped into patties, dipped in crumbs and browned in butter. (Ground beef, pork, veal, brains, etc.)

Kotlety Po-Kyivskomu: the renowned chicken Kiev: boned, flattened chicken breasts rolled up with a firm pat of butter inside then breaded and deep-fried.

Krupnyk: barley soup made with vegetable stock and flavored with fresh or dried mushrooms.

Kulesha: cornmeal.

Kutya: the ritual grain dish served at the beginning and end of the Christmas festival. It is a combination of cooked wheat grains, honey, nuts and poppy seeds.

Kvas: name used to refer loosely to any fermented liquid made from beets or rye dough. The rye **Kvas** is a common peasant beverage.

Kyshka: a frequently homemade sausage made by cleaning intestines and stuffing them with a flour, cereal or blood mixture. These are then cooked and served whole or in slices.

Kysil: sweetened, cooked and puréed fruit served as a dessert.

Lokshyna: noodles.

Mid: mead, a honey wine.

Mlynsi: plain griddle cakes.

Nalysnyky: small pancakes like crepes.

Pashtet: a finely ground seasoned mixture of meats and bread crumbs pressed into a mold and baked. After unmolding and chilling it is often served for a **Zakuska**.

Paska: another name for the special fruited Easter bread.

Pyrohy: western Ukraine name for **Varenyky**. Small envelopes of noodle dough filled with potatoes, cabbage, cheese, meat, grains, or fruits.

Pyrizhky: tiny dumplings filled with vegetables, cheese or meat, served as an accompaniment especially to clear soups.

Pysanky: colorful and intricately decorated Easter eggs.

Rosolnyk: a mildly tart soup made with diced kidney and sliced dill pickles.

Smetana: sour cream.

Smetanka: sweet cream.

Stebky: northern Ukraine vegetable storerooms.

Syrnychky: cottage cheese pancakes, flour dipped and butter browned. Served with sour cream.

Shashlyk: mixed meats broiled on skewers.

Vushka: another name for **Pyrizhky**.

Varenyky or **Vareniky**: see **Pyrohy**.

Zakuska: appetizers eaten before the meal, usually accompanied by vodka. Ukrainian **Zakuska** consists of usually one dish, with several dishes served on special occasions.

Zrazy: meatballs.

CHAPTER 53

Uruguayan. See Latin America
Venezuelan. See Latin America

VIETNAMESE

The name Vietnam has historically caused confusion, and for good reason. The mixed ethnic population has seldom known long periods of freedom, security, or peace.

There is South Vietnam and North Vietnam. Originally the area was known as French Indochina. In fact, just before 1800, the area known as South Vietnam was called Cochin China and South Annam while North Vietnam territory was known as Tonkin and North Annam.

The huge S-shape of North and South Vietnam, curving from the Gulf of Tonkin and bulging outward to the South China Sea, is the home of a population made up of 90 percent Annamite stock from the Hindu-Buddhist Kingdom of Annam. These peoples are believed to have migrated as a Paleomongoloid people from the area that likely was the flat wooded swamp of lower Tonkin, long ago called Yue state, in the Vietnamese language, Viet state; and so the people came to be called Vietnamese.

The first capital of the Vietnamese Kingdom of Nam Viet or South Yue was Hanoi. By 42 C.E. Nam Viet had become a Chinese province and in the almost thousand-year occupation by China both the people and the country reflected the powerful "elder brother" influence in every aspect of daily life.

Chinese influence in the countryside remains to this day. Chinese-style villages, autonomous leadership, ancestor worship, and the patrilineal kinship system, coupled with a high degree of nationalism and individual reserve, characterize most of the South Vietnam villages. Dikes and canals constructed against annual floods, layout of irrigation patterns for the fields, the introduction of fertilizing fields with human feces as well as the use of the iron plowshare and the bucket-wheel all greatly increased rice production. In fact, some areas were able to glean two annual crops with the use of these methods. The Chinese also introduced and helped to develop crafts and craft guilds, which promoted the rapid development and pride in creativity.

To the basic animism, the Chinese introduced Taoism, Mahayana Buddhism, and the morals and philosophy of Confucianism. As in China, government officials were a hierarchy of Confucian intellectuals. Temples, pagodas, and gracefully curved roof lines (warding away evil spirits) became a part of the skyline just as the Chinese vocabulary permeated the Austro-Asiatic language of the Vietnamese.

Even today Chinese influence is clearly distinguishable at the table as well. Most Vietnamese eat their foods with chopsticks. Only in scattered mountainous regions, where the Chinese influence did not penetrate, do people eat with their fingers as is customary in most of Southeast Asia. Chinese cooking 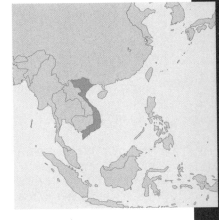 implements, which include charcoal braziers, ladles and stirring spoons, many bowls and woks, knives and choppers, are as familiar and lovingly used as in any Chinese kitchen. Vietnamese prefer their rice served plain and white. The northerners show a preference for long grain rice (**tamthom**); the southerners prefer short grain rice (**nanhchon**) served separately rather than mixed with other foods.

Yet while Vietnamese enjoy many fried foods and stir-fried dishes, they have a further distinct preference for lean meats (lean chicken and pork) and fatless soups, and a dislike for foods that taste greasy. Because of this, most dishes are steamed or boiled or very quickly stir-fried, and all foods that may have any suspicion of grease are skimmed, trimmed, or otherwise handled to remove grease.

By the late 900s C.E. Vietnamese drove out the Chinese and extended their sense of strength by pressuring their southern neighbors in the Kingdom of Cham (predominantly under Indian influence). The population of Malayo-Polynesian origin engaged in rice culture soon came under Vietnamese domination. By the 1600s Viets had annexed the entire "rice-bowl" of the Mekong Delta region. It is probable that Viets might have even gone further in their "annexing" had it not been for the incredible influence of both the Catholic French missionaries and the development of the French East India Company in the 1600s, which helped to engage France's interest in this area.

It was the French who moved into the Mekong Delta and established the colony of Cochin China and the protectorate of Cambodia in 1865. Gradual French influence was seen in the extension of industrialization and in the spread of Roman Catholicism. Gradually too, Vietnamese of means began sending their children to study in Europe. French culture, language, cuisine, and religion found a place in the Vietnamese lifestyle. The increase of these overseas-educated led to a small middle class and a gradually burgeoning intelligentsia soon joined by Chinese moving into the cities and towns as traders, craftspeople, clerks, and merchants. Saigon's twin city of Cholon was founded by the Chinese.

It was not long before the growing minority ethnic groups of approximately 6 million Khmers, 2.5 million Laotians, 3 million mountain tribesmen, and 1 million Chinese all came to view the 33 million Vietnamese with the same attitudes of hostility and fear as the Vietnamese traditionally had towards the Chinese.

Although the French united much of the area for administrative purposes, a slow-simmering nationalism brewed. Ignoring the French extension of ports, canals, highways and railroads, the Annamese pressed for independence of their Vietnam or "Indochinese Union," as it was called by 1900.

France's collapse to Germany in 1940 gave further impetus to the nationalistic tide but was quelled when the Allies divided Indochina arbitrarily into a northern zone to be held by the Chinese and a southern zone to be held by the British-Indian troops pending the arrival once again of the French.

The embattled Vietnamese, torn by strife, starvation, and corruption from within, and tugged by opposing outside forces, became the pawn in a chess game called the Cold War. In the belief that it could contain the Communists (under Ho Chi Minh in North Vietnam), the Americans poured men and arms into South Vietnam.

From the earliest Hindu-Buddhist to Chinese to French, the Communists and most recently the Americans — these historic influences and upheavals have left their imprint on the land, and almost every aspect of the people's culture. Ethnic antagonisms and deep contrast between the rich and the poor, the various religions and between the lowlanders and the mountain people will take kinder turns of history to heal.

DOMESTIC LIFE

The domestic life of the Vietnamese closely resembles that of traditional China even with the distinguishing characteristics of the village, town, and city. Close family life, respect for elders, and the dignified politeness of children are all apparent. Some elements of

FOODS COMMONLY USED

The tropical-monsoon climate of most of Vietnam, the land and the freshwater and inshore fishing contribute to bring the Vietnamese staples to the table: rice, **nuoc mam**, fish, fruits and vegetables, pork and poultry. Rice is the most important food, present at all main meals but close in use and importance is the condiment added to most dishes at all times: **nuoc mam**. This is made from salt and fish well fermented. The first liquid produced is the best quality **nuoc mam**; the result of pressing the remaining fish and salt (stronger flavor and more pungent smell) is of lower quality. Inland fishing is less costly than deep-sea, but every type of fish and seafood is enjoyed in the Vietnamese diet. Both wild and cultivated fruits are abundant, and consumption of vegetables has increased since North Vietnam refugees brought market garden culture to the southern "rice bowl." Both meat and fats come from hogs, although some chicken, beef, small animals, and reptiles are also eaten. Almost as widely used as **nuoc mam** is the spicy hot condiment **nuoc cham**, each cook preparing it in her own special way with chili peppers, garlic and onions, vinegar and a sprinkle of citrus juice to heighten the tang.

The northerners prefer long grain rice, the southerners round grain rice. Both areas also enjoy "hot-pot cookery" where a bubbling pot of broth centered on the table receives tidbits of foods held by chopsticks for quick-cooking. At meals, diners assemble their own tidbits of meats, fish, fruits and vegetables and then wrap them in packets of edible rice paper, various green leaves, noodle dough, all to be sauce-dipped before devouring. Although many similarities have been noted between the two groups, northerners and southerners insist not only upon their rice preferences, but that southerners enjoy more spiciness, the use of more fresh fruits and raw vegetables, simpler dishes and a lot of coconut. They will tell you this is because of their more tropical climate. However, while northerners consider the southern food something less than subtle, the southerners may counter that they think the northerners' food flat!

traditional animism, Taoism, and Buddhism show in family celebrations and festivities and even in everyday affairs. Few Vietnamese homes fail to give at least cursory homage to several personal gods.

Despite the modernization of the cities, the presence of French and later the Americans, despite even education abroad, old traditions hold dear. A child is considered one year old at birth and counts birthdays not on the day of birth but on each New Year's; scholars still lead in the traditional hierarchy of society followed by agriculturalists, salaried workers, and finally merchants; belief in herbal teas and the medicinal qualities of certain foods persist and remain important.

Similarly, Vietnamese kitchens and tables reflect much of China's influence. Facilities and utensils vary according to means: many small electrical appliances find a useful place in city kitchens while the age-old methods of food storage and meal preparation hold sway in traditional village kitchens. Women enjoy preparing their foods for meals in a separate kitchen that is often also a separate building from the main living quarters. This is not only practical from the standpoint of fire hazards, but also provides the women a special place to talk together. Three-stoned stands set in clay or stone hearths hold charcoal embers and efficiently heat steamers, iron kettles, or woks. Sharp knives and cleavers make quick work of slicing, slivering, chopping, mincing, while quick and artful fingers carefully arrange platters of foods to be placed attractively on the meal table. Among the wealthy, the cuisine of the household may be very continental and varied, with dishes from local and western cultures. For all Vietnamese, the dishes of Chinese origin (but given a special Vietnamese fillip) appear for all special occasions.

Tradition persists not only in the home and kitchen, but even in the diets of expectant mothers. Vietnamese women are fearful of eating too much food lest their babies become too heavy, and many fear that certain foods may be harmful to the fetus. Rice, soy sauce, some vegetables, and **nuoc mam** (the fish-sauce condiment) are taken as required, but many believe that fish and meats may generate poisons in the child and refuse to eat them as part of the daily diet during pregnancy. These are typical of food beliefs in the countryside and are not commonly found among women in Saigon.

DAIRY PRODUCTS
Vietnamese share the general Oriental distaste of milk and cheese. Some canned evaporated milk is used, but the quantity is small. Soybean curd in the form of creamy-white sponge-like squares is used in many dishes and is sometimes called "Oriental Cheese." There is a growing tendency for milk and cream to appear at the tables of the well-to-do (milk for children and cream in coffee for adults) but not among the poorer country dwellers.

FRUITS AND VEGETABLES
Consumption of fruits and vegetables varies according to location and income. Wild fruits are abundant and used green or ripened. These include mangoes and bananas as well as coconuts and a range of common tropical fruits. Pineapples are enjoyed in season and by those who can afford this cultivated fruit. Both fruits and vegetables may be mixed in different dishes containing meats or fish. Often fruits may be used and seasoned in the same way as vegetables: for example, green slices of papaya are eaten with a mixture of salt and chili peppers and a sprinkle of vinegar.

All leafy green vegetables, onions, scallions, garlic, as well as many varieties of mushrooms, radishes, and cabbages are enjoyed. Perhaps the only category of vegetables not a part of the Vietnamese diet are the roots and tubers such as yams and cassava.

Together with the general Vietnamese disdain of fatty or greasy foods goes the predilection for quantities of fragrant fresh herbs such as mint, dill, coriander, various sprouts, basil, and green onions. These are taken as generous garnishes to many dishes including **pho**, the Vietnamese noodle dish that is really a meal. Popular too are little bundles of mixed fresh herbs wrapped in rice paper or lettuce and dipped in **nuoc mam** or **nuoc cham** then into a small dish of crushed roasted peanuts before nibbling. Fresh dill and green spring onions are a special accompaniment to fish dishes.

Fruits may be used in their green state in cooked dishes to impart a sour tang and enliven other flavors, or enjoyed for their own taste. Other fruits may be served fresh as dessert. Most vegetables are served raw, steamed, boiled, or stir-fried.

MEATS AND ALTERNATES
In Vietnam cattle and buffalo are considered animals of burden rather than food sources. Hogs are the principal source of meat and fat for cooking. Chickens and ducks are seen everywhere but their meat is generally lean and tough, and the production of eggs is not high. Some beef is used in various dishes, especially in the larger towns and cities where tastes are more cosmopolitan and income higher; again the beef is lean and requires moist cooking or marinating to tenderize before grilling.

Fish is the most important protein in the Vietnamese diet. Since inland fishing is less costly, the majority of fish eaten is taken from inland water sources. Deep-sea fisheries are increasing. Fish may be steamed with vegetables and seasoning, poached, made into minced fish cakes, or barbecued over coals.

Both meats and fish are used in small quantities, cooked with great care to gain maximum flavor from minimal amounts, and served attractively. Many soups are prepared by the basic Chinese method of browning a few meat strips in a small amount of fat with some seasoning, then adding water to form the basic soup broth. Both meat- and fish-based soups may be prepared in the same way. The practice of thinly slicing or shredding meats or fish or seafood, or cooking them together with quantities of minced, sliced, or slivered vegetables also extends their flavor.

Oriental medicine ascribes great value to eggs, especially incubated eggs, and the Vietnamese are very fond of these although the high price and scarcity makes them only a small portion of the diet. Eggs may also be pickled, boiled in tea (to color), and served in slices or wedges as a garnish to other dishes or appetizers. Tiny pancakes, made basically with eggs, and the shredded egg pancake used as a soup garnish, are used according to income.

Soybeans are used in the Chinese way and in as many forms (see Chinese or Korean). Sprouted greens of many types of beans, as well as seasoned mashed beans, used in condiments and for fillings, and the popular soybean curd, served in many ways in soups and with vegetables (usually stir-fried), add to the protein consumption.

BREADS AND GRAINS
Rice is the principal staple Vietnamese food and one of the most important crops. For the poor, rice with only a sprinkling of low grade **nuoc mam** is considered a meal and an occasional addition of fish and few vegetables may constitute the whole diet. For other Vietnamese, rice still comes first but the addition of fish, meats and poultry, as well as a variety of vegetables and fruits round out the diet more completely. Without rice – simply boiled white and fluffy – it is scarcely a meal.

Rice flour is used in the making of many dumplings and pastry dishes that are cooked usually by steaming. One such soft dumpling dish is called **banh cuon**, made by rubbing a ball of soft dough over cheesecloth stretched tightly over a pot of boiling water. The steam cooks the circle of dough which is then lifted off, filled with a minced mixture of meat, fish or vegetables, then rolled and dipped in **nuoc cham** before popping in the mouth. "Papers" of almost cellophane consistency are made usually commercially out of rice flour and are called "rice papers." Cut into small squares these are used at the table to wrap variously prepared tidbits, then a preliminary sauce-dunking makes them the special dish called **cha gio**.

Some western-type breads and rolls are available in Saigon in restaurants catering to European or western tastes but these are not a regular part of the Vietnamese diet.

Noodle dishes, as in other East Asian countries, often form the basis of a quick lunch. Noodles may be prepared from rice, wheat, or buckwheat flours. As with almost every other type of dish, what makes it distinctly Vietnamese is the addition of **nuoc mam**.

FATS
The only animal fat used is pork fat. All foods are served well skimmed of any fats as Vietnamese do not like greasy foods. Coconut oil and groundnut (peanut) oil are also used.

SWEETS AND SNACKS
Sweet chunks of juicy fruits in season and specially prepared sweet small cakes and steamed dumplings for festivities are the main sources of sweet foods for the Vietnamese. More recently, consumption of sweetened bottled beverages and imported candies has increased. Sugar is used in cookery much like any other seasoning to heighten and distinguish flavors.

SEASONINGS
The Chinese seasonings of garlic, scallions and onions, fresh ginger root and soy sauce are all part of Vietnamese cookery. But what makes the cuisine most distinctive is the addition of two special condiment sauces used both in cookery and at the table: **nuoc mam** and **nuoc cham**. These two sauces represent the essence of what separates Vietnamese cookery from most other eastern cookery. **Nuoc mam** is the liquid that is produced from layered salted fish which has been allowed to ferment in barrels. Almost equally important is **nuoc cham**. Every cook has a special recipe for the addition of fiery spices and pungent flavors to the basic **nuoc mam**. Garlic and onions, chili peppers, black pepper, cayenne, sugar, citrus juices, coconut juice, and vinegar may all be a part of the final fiery hot combination. Both of these sauces are used as ingredients in many other dishes – almost the way westerners use salt and pepper – or as added sauces or condiments for dipping savory mouthfuls.

The delicate flavors of coconut and lemon grass also permeate many Vietnamese dishes. Roasted peanuts, crushed or chopped, add a special flavor to many sauces.

For the Vietnamese, fragrant fresh herbs are eaten in such quantities as to be considered part of the daily vegetable intake as well as seasoning prepared foods in typically Vietnamese ways: for example, mint leaves and fresh coriander accompanying grilled beef; fresh dill and green onions used in fish cookery; bean sprouts, fresh coriander, slivered hot chilies and lime added to **pho bo** (beef noodle soup); fresh ginger, lemon grass, garlic and green onions with a sprinkle of brown sugar added to a boned chicken dish.

BEVERAGES
Some upper-class city children drink milk as a beverage but this is not common. Flavored and sweetened bottled beverages, sweetened or natural fruit juices, tea, coffee, and beer all take their place as mealtime accompaniments or as refreshments. Where French influence is evident, wines may be used. Vietnamese-grown tea is exported as is the high quality Vietnamese beer.

MEALS AND CUSTOMS
Vietnamese are the only peoples in the Pacific and Southeastern Asia region whose eating customs are dominated by Chinese influence. This is most evident in the use of chopsticks both for eating and as an aid in lifting, beating, and stirring while cooking. Table service also borrows heavily from traditional Chinese customs: white tablecloth, individual rice bowls and beverage glasses or tea bowls with most foods being served buffet style for the diners to help themselves.

The reverence for rice is shown on the Vietnamese table by serving rice in a separate bowl, never mixed with other foods. Diners take rice into their own small rice bowl then nibble other foods with their rice.

The Vietnamese recognize three types of meals. Whenever rice is served with or without anything else it is considered to be a "filling meal"; a meal of refreshing beverages or sometimes only soup is considered to be a "cooling meal"; a meal consisting of sweetmeats and locally prepared delicacies is called a "greed meal." People in most other lands frequently enjoy the same types of meals but seldom label them. These three types of meals represent nutrition, refreshment, and pleasure. Festive meals, or large meals in well-to-do homes, may well contain the elements of all three types, but for most Vietnamese one type at a time suffices.

Street vendors are seen everywhere in stalls and along roadsides or carrying their wares upon their heads. Snacks and nibbles and drinks and even soups are always available to satisfy the faintest hunger pang. These may vary from slices of fresh fruit with dipping sauces, to bowls of hot soups, steamed dumplings, or local fish or specialties.

There is a difference not only in the foods eaten but also in the meal patterns among the well-to-do, the middle class, and the poor. Well-to-do families enjoy a wide variety of local dishes, western dishes as well as Chinese delicacies, the latter usually served daily on all festive occasions. Breakfast may feature eggs, breads, preserves, and coffee with cream and sugar. Lunch and dinner will likely be similar, with rice at both meals, and a variety of meat or fish, eggs, vegetables and fruits or fruit preserves or compotes for dessert. **Thit-kho** (pork) is the favored meat and may be served as sausages, minced raw or cooked, diced and fried and served with vegetables, noodles, or in steamed doughs. **Nuoc mam** and coconut juice will add flavor to almost all dishes, while soy sauce will flavor Chinese-type foods. Sugar and vinegar are also widely used. Tea, wine, or beer may appear at meals, and often the choice of all three is given. Some well-to-do homes may also include butter and quality oils at the table and in their cooking. Fruits in season may be offered as a refreshment to guests or for dessert.

Middle-class homes prepare a varied menu combining local foods, Chinese and even western-type foods. A typical breakfast may include a minced pork broth with **hu-tien** (rice noodles) – a Chinese soup that becomes definitively Vietnamese with the addition of **nuoc mam**. Dinner and supper are usually similar, featuring rice and several dishes of vegetables plus meat, fish, poultry or eggs. Vegetables are used more frequently and in more variety than fruits.

The poorer class consumes mostly rice, but varies this by preparing both steamed rice or **nep**, sticky rice. Some vegetables or fish may be steamed on top of the rice or the fish may be sliced and eaten raw.

More **nuoc mam** is consumed by the poorer classes than the middle or upper classes, but it is of the lowest quality and pungently strong in flavor and fishy odor. Cooking is done mostly with lard, occasionally with vegetable oils.

SPECIAL OCCASIONS
Animism, Taoism, Buddhism, Confucianism, and more recently Christianity, have each in turn influenced Vietnamese daily life. Even those professing Christianity may still cherish personal deities and specific household idols and shrines and often on special occasions there will be a symbolic return to ancient traditions.

As in China, Korea, and Japan, Vietnamese special occasions may be separated into family, seasonal, as well as religious. Throughout, despite religious preferences, Chinese festivals, traditions, and foods predominate.

Tet is the lunar New Year celebrated for seven days. Great importance is attached to family togetherness, to serious reflection on the past year, and to pleasure in the present while thoughtfully contemplating the future. But all of this is accompanied with parades and fireworks and musical and sporting events. Even the presence or absence of sun on the seventh day is taken as a portent of the coming year. A particularly Vietnamese tradition is the creation of a paper bird covered with a detailed report of the family's year-long activities. Beside the bird is an array of rich and sticky sweets. It is hoped that while the fire is set to this special offering, the god will dine as he reads the report, then be forced to keep his mouth shut (at least in regard to any bad deeds) by the sticky candy.

The fifth day of the third lunar month is *Thanh Minh*, a special time to visit the departed souls, leaving offerings of flowers, joss sticks and food on their graves. Autumn and the school opening are heralded in the eighth lunar month with the eating of sticky rice **moon cookies** and colorful lanterns hung everywhere. The festival is call *Trung Thu*.

Some special occasions are celebrated with dates in the Gregorian calendar. In North Vietnam, Ho Chi Minh's birthday is celebrated on May 19. The celebration of the Declaration of Independence of the Democratic Republic of Vietnam is held on September 2. Christians celebrate Christmas in the larger cities with church services.

GLOSSARY OF FOODS AND FOOD TERMS

Banh Cuon: a variation on the Chinese **Dim Sum** (steamed filled dumplings), where only the dough is steamed then filled. The dough is made into a ball from rice flour and water then rubbed over a cheesecloth tautly stretched over a pot of boiling water. As the steam cooks the "wrapper," it is pulled off, rolled up with a minced filling of pork, shrimp, mushrooms and onions then dipped in hot sauce before being eaten. Commonly made and served by street vendors or at market stalls.

Banh Hoi Nem Chua: cooked rice noodles served with raw pork.

Banh Hoi Tom: cooked rice noodles served with lobster.

Banh Trang: rice-paper wrappers made from rice flour, water, and salt. These are moistened in warm water then quickly filled to be fried, or used uncooked as wrappers for slivers of meat or fish and fresh herbs. Usually dipping sauces are provided for the diners.

Ca-Kho: raw fish.

Ca Ran Chua Ngot: a special main dish of quickly fried whole fish served with a delicate sweet and sour sauce touched lightly with chilies and onions, **nuoc mam**, vinegar, and sugar. The stir-fried slivered tiger lily buds, mushrooms and scallions form the garnish.

Cha Gio: the general name for wrapped tidbits of fish, seafood, vegetables, which are eaten as is after being dipped in various sauces or which may be deep-fried in their wrappers (as when using ricepaper wrappers). The finger-sized rolls may be served as appetizers or as part of a meal.

Hoisin Sauce: a thick, sweet and spicy sauce used especially to glaze **Peking Duck;** also to enhance many meat, fish or poultry dishes. May be used also as a dipping sauce. It is prepared from a base of wheat or soybeans with sugar, garlic, and chilies.

Hu-Tien: a broth with noodles often served as a hot satisfying breakfast dish.

Mang Tay Nau Cua: soup based on chicken stock with crab meat and asparagus and mushroom pieces. The soup is thickened with cornstarch and served garnished with slivers of scallions and crumbled hard egg yolk.

Micha Trong Kroeuny: strips of plaice fillets dusted with rice flour and briefly browned in fat then lightly cooked in a spicy sauce of garlic, scallions, chilies, and **Nuoc Mam**.

Mien Ga: light, flavorful chicken broth (fat-free), served with cellophane noodles and thinly slivered scallions to garnish.

Mut: a sticky sweet candy that can be prepared from fruits, vegetables, or seeds cooked in syrup until translucent.

Nanhchon: the short grain rice preferred by the South Vietnamese.

Nems: deep-fried pastry-wrapped delicacies very similar to Chinese egg rolls and eaten after being dipped into **Nuoc Mam** or **Nuoc Cham**.

Nuoc Cham: to the basic **Nuoc Mam** the cook adds chilies, black pepper, cayenne, scallions, onions, garlic to taste in order to produce a fiery hot sauce, **Nuoc Cham**, to the diner's liking.

Nuoc Leo: a peanut dipping sauce made by mixing **Nuoc Mam** with chicken broth and **Hoisin Sauce** then garnishing with slivers of chilies, garlic, and crushed roasted peanuts.

Nuoc Mam: the single most important sauce of Vietnamese cuisine. It is prepared (mostly commercially) by layering fish and salt in barrels and allowing them to ferment. The first liquid that oozes off naturally is considered to be of high quality. The liquid that results after pressing the fermented mixture is stronger in color, flavor, and odor and is considered to be of lower quality. This sauce is as common as salt and pepper is to the western table. No dish is complete without at least a little **Nuoc Mam**, but each diner adds more, according to taste.

Pho: the only Vietnamese dish that is served in individual portions. All other dishes are served in dishes to be shared at the table. Lengthy cooking and careful seasoning produces the beef or chicken broth that is poured over cooked noodles. The shredded meat of your choice is arranged on top. Each diner adds fresh green herbs, garlic, and chilies. Sauces are served in tiny side dishes for dipping meat slivers with chopsticks. A porcelain soup spoon may be used to aid the delivery of slippery noodles to the mouth.

Tamthom: the long grain white rice preferred by the North Vietnamese.

Thit-Kho: pork. The preferred meat, eaten frequently by the upper class, often by the middle class, and almost never by the poorer class.

CHAPTER 54

WELSH

The Welsh name for Wales is *Cymru*, "land of comradeship," and a place where traditions are deep-rooted and well preserved, not only in the

castles, customs, and philosophy of the people, but also in their love of music and poetry. The "musical" Welsh language seems natural for a people who love to sing and who are world famous for their voices. In fact, of all people in the British Isles, it is the Welsh who are considered to be the "most truly British of all."

They proudly trace their ancestry to the original Celts who fled foreign invaders by hiding in the mountains and valleys of what is today called Wales. Here they carefully preserved their love of community and their kinship ties – to this day families proudly trace relationships "even to the 9th degree" – and the early principles of Welsh society which always stressed unity rather than class distinction.

The earliest Welsh poetry is thought to date from the 500s C.E., and has served as a model of inspiration not only for other literary forms but also for language and even "masculine heroic ideals." Queen Elizabeth, in 1563 C.E., insisted upon having the Bible and Common Book of Prayer translated into Welsh (in the hope of gaining Welsh sympathies), which had the effect of preserving not only the Welsh language but Welsh nationalism as well. The early Calvinist churches deeply affected Welsh life by fostering a strong individualistic sense, which much later resulted in the development of radical and even socialist thought.

Further effects of religious influence on Welsh life were to come later with the Methodist Movement, its exaggerated emphasis on "saving souls," its consideration of music and dance as "sinful occupations," even insisting that the Sabbath (Sunday) be a day of sanctity with no sound of music.

The good effect of these conflicting religious

movements, the Calvinist and the Methodist, was twofold: it promoted a literate nation and made the people strongly concerned with theology, politics, and literature. To this day, the stimulation of religious thinking and the proud preservation of language, especially in the Sunday schools, has continued to unify the people and make *Cymru* much more than just a name.

Despite the sweep of industrialization in the 1800s, despite repeated attempts by the English to integrate them, and despite many periods of dismal poverty, the Welsh have retained their solidarity and think of the whole of Wales as "home." Their intense love of language, music and poetry is reflected in their annual *Eisteddfod* festival in August, the Welsh national holiday honoring music and poetry.

Although they are known in England as "Welshmen," the people distinguish themselves as North Walian and South Walian. Black is the prevailing color of South Wales, for more than 50 percent of the population is concentrated in the Glamorgan county famed for coal mining. As if to remove the blackness from their lives, every collier wears a bright white scarf when off work and every housewife has a fetish about whitewashed doorsteps! Intertwined with their religious feelings is more than a thread of respect for the supernatural, and with great wit, the South Walians love to tell jokes, and hair-raising ghost stories as well. North Wales is more industrialized than South Wales and some claim that the greatest social reformers, statesmen, and orators were all born in the hills of North Wales. But that is a matter for Walians to debate.

However, there is no debate about the need to strengthen Welsh culture. Sustaining the Welsh language is high priority evidenced by the formation in 1966 of the Welsh Language Society and in the 1980s with the establishment of a Welsh language television channel. In addition, radio, the arts, opera, and literature have gained increasing support and recognition. And youngsters can learn Welsh in their schools.

While the Welsh are making every effort to retain and enhance Welsh culture, they are almost always concerned about unemployment and the resulting emigration of the young. Declining heavy industries and increasingly capital-intensive agriculture exacerbated this situation. However, more recently foreign investment has spurred new industrial growth.

It is from their ancient Celtic inheritance that a linguistic link connects the Welsh with the Irish, Scots, Cornish, and even the Bretons of Brittany, France. In fact, there are many interesting culinary links between Wales and Brittany based on their mutual love of onions and leeks, pork, seafood, spices, and the presence of cheese, red wine, ale and cider in so many of their traditional dishes.

Many different forms of pancakes are common to all Celtic countries, differing only in the names: Scotland has thick **drop scones**, Brittany enjoys delicate lacy cakes called **crepes dentelles**, while the Welsh call them **crempog**. Similarly, a raisin- or fruit-flecked cake served well buttered is called **barmbrack** in Ireland, **selkirk bannock** in Scotland, and **morlaix brioche** in Brittany, while the Welsh call the same beloved cake **bara brith**. Here are some other similar dishes:

Brittany	Wales
Flan de Poireaux	**Tarten Gennin**: leek tart
Pomme de Terre a la Boulangere	**Teisen Nionod**: onion cake
Sauce Vinaigrette	**Suryn Cyffaith Poeth**: a potent and spicy garlic sauce served with veal.
Crepine or Crepinettes	**Faggots**: called **Mock Duck** or **Savoury Ducks** in English; meatballs of pig liver, seasoned and wrapped in lacy pig's flead or caul fat and baked.

DOMESTIC LIFE

Against a backdrop of snow-tipped mountains and nestled into rolling green countrysides are the traditional stone and slate houses. Inside each house the most important room has always been, and still is, the kitchen. Here the family gathers for meals around a table; a *deal-top* (similar to pine wood) table scrubbed to a glowing white and covered with a cloth for dinner and on Sundays. If there were more children than could be seated at once, they quietly took their turns. Guests, whether relatives or strangers, were always seated on the hearth bench called *mainc y simnai*, where it would be warm, and bowls of soup were traditionally offered together with entertaining songs and stories. Family and visitor alike were warmed inside and out in the hospitality of the kitchen.

Traditional Welsh kitchens boast utensils of earthenware and wood. Earthenware mixing bowls and pudding bowls and many sizes of wooden spoons for beating, measuring, and mixing are a part of every kitchen. As in most Celtic countries, the griddle or bakestone is the utensil most used for preparing the popular quick breads and pancakes. Some bakestones have a removable handle, others are set on legs ready to be placed over an open hearth fire. Many homes still take pride in their home-baked breads and ancient stone ovens that result in crispy-crusted bread.

The area of the kitchen called the scullery includes the sink for washing and the shelves where dishes, pots and pans are stored. Storage shelves may be openly displayed or covered with curtains. Perishable foods are stored in stone crocks or in earthen cellars under the house. The week's bread may be suspended in a cage called a bread crate, hung from the ceiling and worked on pulleys. The bread is thus kept safe from animals or vermin. Sides of bacon and pieces of ham, carefully meted out for the week's meals, may also be kept in suspended cages hung

FOODS COMMONLY USED

The staples of the Welsh table reflect the products of the land: pork and succulent lamb and mutton, oats and wheat for breads and cakes, local cheeses and buttermilk, homemade cider, ale and wine, locally caught fish and seafoods, and onions, leeks, and potatoes as well as seasonal vegetables, fruits, and herbs. In poorest times, bread forms the staple food accompanied by milk or soups based on "drippings" (leftover rendered fats). Meats, except on special occasions, are used thriftily, their flavor spread as far as possible in soups and stews and quick supper dishes based on breads, pancakes, or potatoes. Large cuts of meat are a Sunday dinner tradition, together with two or three cooked vegetables and a slow-baked rice pudding to complete the meal. The Welsh enjoy sprightly seasoned cakes fragrant with lemon, caraway, cinnamon, and nutmeg. Wild mountain herbs such as mint, marjoram, thyme, rosemary, and wild garlic are used liberally in roasted meats, fish dishes, and casseroles as well as soups and stews.

from the ceiling.

Modern homes, especially those in the cities, boast electrical refrigerators and gas-heated ovens and cooktops. However, coal is still widely used in rural areas, both for heating and cooking. The thrifty no-nonsense approach that the Welsh use in every aspect of their lives applies also to the kitchen: there is little use for frivolous gadgets or for unnecessary electrical conveniences.

DAIRY PRODUCTS

Milk is considered by most Welsh to be a food not a beverage. Therefore, water is commonly served with meals for children while milk is an ingredient in custards and puddings, and usually served with tea. Breakfast coffee or cocoa is usually prepared liberally with milk, but the consumption of milk in the many daily cups of tea should not be underestimated. Soured milk and buttermilk are enjoyed, especially accompanied by pancakes of many kinds, potato dishes, or one of the many light supper dishes.

Wales produces and enjoys many fine local cheeses, fresh as well as aged. The most famous is **Caerphilly** originating from Caerphilly in Glamorgan County. It is a moist mild cheese good both for eating and cooking.

Chunks of local cheese, fresh bread, and a few pickles together with a mug of ale constitute the famed **ploughman's lunch**, a popular meal in any pub. The well-known **Welsh rarebit** consists of cheese melted and poured over toast points then browned in a grill. Grated cheese often garnishes homemade soups and tops baked casseroles. But the most creative cheese dish of all is **Glamorgan sausages** or **selsig Morgannwg**: a mixture of lightly seasoned soft bread crumbs and grated cheddar cheese bound with egg yolk, shaped like sausages, then dipped into beaten egg white and dried bread crumbs and fried to a golden crispiness. Served with creamed potatoes and peas, it is a hearty meal.

FRUITS AND VEGETABLES

Fruits and vegetables are enjoyed fresh only in season. Salads of fresh vegetables are not a common part of the Welsh menu, nor are fresh fruit desserts, with the possible exception of berries. Pears, apples, and plums, as well as many types of berries – blackberries, elderberries, gooseberries, strawberries, and **blaeberries** (similar to blueberries) – are available in season. Berries are served fresh, but are enjoyed still more in preserves, pastries, and desserts, where they are well cooked and sugared.

Onions and leeks head the list of Welsh vegetables, followed very closely by potatoes – used in everything from soups and stews and the Sunday roast (**tatws rhost**) to many light supper dishes of layered potatoes, onions and bacon, even a moist potato pastry from which **teisen datwys** is made (thick potato cakes cooked on the bakestone and served with butter and glasses of buttermilk). Pumpkin is a traditional Welsh favorite, pre-cooked then crumbed and fried, and is also popularly cooked with mutton or spiced and baked in a pie. Could it have been the early Welsh settlers who introduced pumpkin pie for Thanksgiving? Swedes (turnips), carrots, peas, and the vegetables in the cabbage family (cabbages, cauliflower, brussels sprouts) are all served well cooked, mostly as a part of soups or stews.

Special mention should be made of **chips**. There is scarcely a Welsh kitchen without a sturdy pot and a wire basket used especially for deep-frying potato strips called **chips**. There is scarcely a meal served in a pub that is not accompanied by **chips**: steak and chips, fish and chips, prawns and chips. Almost as ubiquitous are peas: considered as a garnish, canned peas or well-cooked fresh peas nestle on plates of meat pies, casserole dishes, and quick supper dishes.

A Welsh favorite is **laverbread** or **bar lawr**. Called **sloke** in Scotland and Ireland, this is the fine silken seaweed, washed and cured (dried) and served boiled. It can be eaten as is or mixed with fine oatmeal and fried into cakes for breakfast, used as an appetizer, or made into a soup. It is said to be an acquired taste that can become "a passion."

MEATS AND ALTERNATES

Pork, lamb, mutton, beef, and chicken, as well as the occasional rabbit or **rook** (a type of crow) supply meat for the Welsh table. Great use is made of every part of the animal or bird for soups, sausages, stews and ground meat mixtures, and probably most popular of all is the sweet smoky flavor of ham and bacon. In fact, bacon is a staple of the Welsh kitchen and it not only forms the base of many quick supper dishes, it is often used as a garnish for dishes such as **cardiganshire savouries** or **tocyn y cardi** (flour and oat cakes fried in bacon fat and served with sliced tomatoes and rashers of bacon); as a flavoring for soups such as **leek and potato soup** or **swp cennin a thatws** and the delicious **brithyll a chig moch** or trout laid and topped with bacon then oven-baked (known as **truites au lard** in Brittany).

Large roasts of meat are saved for Sunday dinner, when the roasted meat is accompanied by two or three well-cooked or roasted vegetables and the Sunday special rice pudding **pwdin reis dyddsul** for dessert.

Pig's liver is used in many ways. The most well known is probably in baked **faggots** or **mock duck**, called **ffagod sir benfro**. Usually made around pig-killing time, balls are shaped from a mixture of pig's liver, bread crumbs and oatmeal, minced onions, and liberally seasoned with mace, sage, thyme, and salt and pepper. The minced balls are covered with the lacy fat-veined membrane called **pig's head** or **caul fat** then baked in a pan until well done. They are good eaten hot or cold and are a popular dish for those carrying their lunch to work as well as those eating at home.

Although special occasions may warrant a boiled ham served with parsley sauce (**cig moch wedi ei ferwi a saws persli**), or Welsh salt duck with onion sauce (**hwyaden hallt cymreig**) or even a sage-stuffed roasted goose, most Welsh meals contain small quantities of meats and these are carefully used to provide the most flavorful and satisfying meals.

Not to be overlooked are the fine salmon and trout in many varieties caught in local waters. Coastal areas, such as Swansea, are especially noted for their fresh seafood and Welsh enjoy a variety of clams, cockles, prawns, shrimp, mussels, and scallops. Herrings are used for sousing (pickling) and served in casseroles with potatoes for supper. Oyster soup, **cockle cakes** and **cockle pie**, potted herrings, baked with seasonings then pounded to a paste and served cold with oatcakes or toast, and trout baked with bacon are popular dishes.

Beans are not a frequent part of the Welsh menu, but dried peas are. These are cooked in a cloth bag so that they swell and form a firm mold which is then served as a side dish with dinner (similar to the English **pease porridge**).

Eggs may form part of a hearty breakfast menu, but more frequently are served as part of light supper of fried eggs, omelets, or pancakes.

BREADS AND GRAINS

Bread is an important part of every meal: homemade bread with homemade soup is considered a hearty meal. Bread forms the staple of the diet for rich or poor. Fine breads are made from white wheat flour or whole meal (wholewheat or wholegrain), while many types of flat thin "cakes" are made from oats. The Welsh prefer the fine oatmeal rather than the rolled or flaked oatmeal popular in Canada and the United States. Fine oatmeal is also used to thicken soups, sauces, and stews and to coat foods for frying. Cornstarch, called corn flour, is used to thicken puddings and desserts and sometimes in baked goods.

Every Welsh cookbook has a large section devoted to breads, mostly quick breads, biscuits, scones and cakes of many kinds. Few, however, are rich or very sweet: the simple natural flavors are most enjoyed and spices such as cinnamon, nutmeg, and ginger are widely used, while raisins, currants, and caraway seeds dot and flavor many breads and cakes. Fancy baking is traditionally done on Saturdays so that there will always be something especially nice to serve at tea on Sunday afternoons. Pancakes, crumpets, and pikelets (variations of thin and quick breads) all prepared on the iron bakestone are a teatime specialty and are served with generous quantities of butter and sometimes preserves.

Pasties are savory or fruit-filled pies and tarts that are not only snacks but may also form the main part of a meal. Large pastie rounds may be oven-baked or browned on a bakestone and carefully turned to brown the other side. A traditional Welsh **pastie** is called **teisen blat** or **harvest cake**. This is a fruit-filled pastry but is unusual in that it is baked on a thick plate, then cut and served warm with buttermilk to drink.

FATS

Lard and drippings as well as bacon fat are used to brown meats and vegetables before stewing or preparing as a soup and in baking as well. Butter is used generously as a spread and for flavoring other foods from oatmeal porridge to vegetables and fish. Oil is used very little.

SWEETS AND SNACKS

The Welsh sweet tooth is satisfied daily in the sugar taken in frequent cups of tea and in the sweet cakes and sweet breads that accompany most cups of tea. **Cyflaith** or **treacle toffee** is a special New Year's treat, but candies are not consumed in great amounts.

SEASONINGS

Welsh prefer to begin their cookery with fresh seasonal foods, adding spices and herbs in judicious but never in overpowering quantity. Ginger, nutmeg, mace, cinnamon, and cloves are the common spices, while sage, thyme, marjoram, parsley, mint, and wild garlic are the most used herbs. The smokiness of bacon and ham cannot be ignored as a taste that delights the Welsh, nor can the special touch of ale, cider, and red wine be ignored for they add much to treasured traditional Welsh dishes. Vinegar is used to sharpen flavors; in other countries lemons or limes would be used. Currants, raisins, caraway seeds and lemon add delicious taste and aromas to many cakes and special bread.

Eog rhost (roast salmon) is a fine example of the Welsh sense of seasoning: nutmeg, cloves, and bay leaves spread with butter are rubbed and placed in the salmon cavity and the fish is roasted covered in paper or foil then served with the pan juices blended with more butter, thin orange and lemon slices, and a splash of vinegar.

Another example of the Welsh touch with herbs and spices is to be seen in **granville sauce**: the frequent accompaniment with fish made with sherry, pounded anchovies, pepper, nutmeg, and mace all smoothed into a creamy base of cream, flour, and butter.

BEVERAGES

Tea with milk and sugar is a mealtime and snack beverage, afternoon tea being a popular ritual in many Welsh homes. Coffee is taken rarely, mostly at breakfast, if at all. Soured milk and buttermilk are preferred over plain milk as a beverage. At meals water is served and men usually drink ale. Local ales, ciders, and wines are often prepared in homes. In fact, many unusual wine recipes are treasured traditions: wines prepared from elderberries, potatoes, rhubarb, oak leaves, pumpkin, beetroot, daisies, parsley, parsnip – the list seems endless. Also a favorite – **Ginger Beer (Diod Sinsir)**.

MEALS AND CUSTOMS

The simplest and oldest traditional Welsh breakfast is a basin of **flummery**: prepared from flour and milk like a soft porridge or the more widely favored bacon and eggs served with bread fried in the bacon fat till crisp. Plentiful cups of tea with milk and sugar complete the classic breakfast. Sometimes a porridge of fine oatmeal is prepared in winter and served with hot cocoa, or with coffee with milk. Whatever the breakfast choice, the Welsh are seldom off to work without at least tea and bread and butter.

In some areas, businesses close between 1:00 and 2:00 p.m., when everyone goes home for the main hot meal of the day, consisting usually of fish or meat with two vegetables and a dessert of steamed or suet pudding, canned fruit with cream, trifle or a custard. Tea with milk and sugar is taken by children and women, while most men prefer beer or ale with their meals.

In the late afternoon a light quick meal, again with tea, is taken. This may consist of a plate of cold meats and pickles served with buttered bread, or anything cooked quickly: sausages and beans, fish and chips, warmed leftovers or sandwiches. So inconsequential is the evening meal that many restaurants serve only the main hot meal at noon and close in the evening.

Mid-morning snacks of tea with breads, **pikelets** (pancakes), or little cakes are taken by almost everyone. This is similar to a snack time in the evening at about 9:00 p.m., when tea and "something small" is eaten again. To the Welsh, tea is so satisfying that the kettle is always on; there is always a comforting cup of tea with milk and sugar available.

The Welsh prefer their foods served on individual plates. Food service is similar to the English style, with dessert eaten with a spoon and fork.

SPECIAL OCCASIONS

The great traditional Welsh family pride and communal interest makes almost any occasion a special one. Helping hands are always available, whether it is for the hard work of harvesting, sadness of funerals, or the joy of weddings. **Teisen blat**, fruit-filled **pasties** baked on old heavy China plates and traditionally served up in large quantities together with fresh cool buttermilk, make all work seem lighter. When a neighborhood wedding is in the offing, neighbors and relatives help with the preparations – pig-killing, fowl-plucking – and delicious smells from the many spiced breads and cakes fill the air. Light fingers of sponge cake, often tied in bundles with black ribbons, would be baked for funerals together with several caraway seed cakes, **bara carawe**, all to be eaten with sips of wine or sherry for the mourners.

The national holiday of Wales, held during the summer, the *Eisteddfod*, is a merry week-long celebration of what the Welsh hold dearest – music and poetry. To sustain the singers and orators, ale, cider, and wine accompany the many savory **pasties**, especially **katt pie**, made from ground spiced mutton and currants, and the **treacle toffee**. Katt pie is a favorite snack that also appears at fairs, markets, and festivals.

Many other special foods help to mark special days on the Welsh calendar. When everyone gathers together to help shear the sheep, **cacen gneifo** (also called **shearing cake**) is made in quantity. This dark cake is made with brown sugar, nutmeg and caraway seeds. On All Hallow's Eve, October 31, it is traditional for costumed young men to go house to house collecting small gifts, and children chant old rhymes and are given fresh fruits. Eating oatcakes (**bara ceirch**) near a blazing bonfire is the traditional way to celebrate May Day Eve, St. John's Eve, and All Hallow's Eve. The purpose of the bonfire is to drive away all evil spirits. Various area specialties are prepared to help celebrate these occasions. Sometimes a meat and vegetable stew is shared after the huge bonfire, or a special sweet dish called **whipod**, made of dried fruits, rice and white bread, is enjoyed by all. Whatever the specialty, it is followed by beer and dancing.

The Feast of Epiphany or Twelfth Night is a more festive occasion than Christmas, which is usually observed quietly as a religious day. The Twelfth Night festivities are highlighted by the serving of a roast dinner, such as stuffed goose, two or three vegetables, and steamed pudding for dessert. The special **Twelfth Night cake** is a rich mellow fruitcake topped with almond paste and thick white frosting – and hidden somewhere in its fruity sweetness is a bean or pea, which is supposed to bring good luck to the finder. An ancient Christmas tradition still followed in some homes is *Plygain*, a Christmas morning service held between 3:00 and 6:00 a.m., usually preceded by decorating the house, making **treacle toffee**, or playing card games in between refreshments of various buttered cakes, **pikelets** and tea. The *Plygain* ends about 8:00 a.m. with carol singing and feasting. The special foods enjoyed at this time include **Welsh rarebit** and ale, assorted cold meats and breads, **brewis**, and other local specialties or family favorites.

New Year's is celebrated in some areas by young boys calling on houses carrying skewered apples or oranges brightly decorated with mistletoe and holly, said to be symbolic of fruitfulness in the coming year. Coins and gifts of little cookies called **calennig** are presented to the boys after they offer verses. **Treacle toffee (cyflaith)** is the traditional New Year's sweet and everyone is greeted with: *"Blwyddyn Newydd Dda!"* (Happy New Year!).

Heralding spring, the fifth Sunday of Lent is called Pea Sunday (*Sul-y-pys*) and roasted peas or a soup made of dried peas form the traditional fare. Roasted lamb, chicken, and colored eggs help celebrate Easter.

Courtship is another time in Welsh life that carries special traditions and superstitions. Most famous of all are the Welsh love spoons. It is customary for a young man to carve a wooden spoon with suitable symbols and designs to be presented to the girl he wishes to court. Some girls collected more than one, keeping them as treasured heirlooms, while others were lucky to have just one. Today these spoons are considered museum pieces for there are few carvers left. Pricking a clean-picked blade bone of mutton nine times (a magical Welsh number) was used by girls to divine their future husbands, especially on the night of All Hallow's Eve. Similarly, stored onions would be named after suitable bachelors: the first one to sprout would become the loved one, while those that refused to sprout were designated as future bachelors! Various love potions presumed to increase the ardor of a loved one were also used. One of these was a mysterious mixture of herbs and wines placed into a drinking horn together with small crumbs of dough preserved from nine bakings. It was believed that this drink offered to a loved one would ignite the fires of passion.

GLOSSARY OF FOODS AND FOOD TERMS

Aberffraw Cakes: thin-rolled cookies served with whipped cream and raspberry jam. (Cookies are frequently called biscuits or cakes.)

Bakestone: a heavy flat iron piece used for cooking. It can have a handle for hanging or it can be set on three legs to stand over a fire. Depending on the area in Wales, it can also be called **Llechfaen, Gradell, Maen**, or most commonly **Planc**. Modern Welsh kitchens may replace it with an electric fry-pan.

Bara Brith: the speckled (spiced and fruit-dotted) bread common to all Celtic countries can be made with yeast or baking powder leavening – many in Wales favor the use of self-raising flour – and is finished with a brushing of warm honey to glaze it. Served in buttered slices.

Bara Carawe: there are many versions of this caraway seed cake, but most often it is a light pound cake flecked with caraway seeds.

Bara Ceirch: traditional thin oatcakes (thinner than the Scottish version), eaten especially on May Day around the bonfires, but enjoyed any time with spreads such as butter, preserves, or lemon curd, and may be eaten with any dish as a bread. Usually buttermilk is the accompanying drink.

Bara Lawr: **bara** means bread, though often it refers to cakes, and in this case refers to a food that is neither cake nor bread. Also called **Laverbread**, this is a well-washed seaweed that is boiled for hours then served in many ways: eaten as is with a squeeze of lemon juice served on toast; as an hors d'oeuvre when mixed with olive oil, salt and pepper, and lemon juice; as a sauce for mutton when mixed with Seville orange juice and heated; mixed with fine oatmeal and formed into small cakes to be fried in bacon fat (a breakfast treat); or eaten with a splash of vinegar as they do in Cornwall. Traditionally, **Bara Lawr** is never touched with a metal spoon or iron pan, but used only with wooden or silver cutlery and an aluminum saucepan.

Bara Sinsir: Welsh gingerbread darkened with black molasses and brown sugar and perfumed with chopped peel of a citrus fruit. The taste is reminiscent of ginger, although none is added, except perhaps candied ginger on top to decorate. A traditional country fair treat.

Basin: Welsh name for the traditional wide-lipped soup plate.

Brawn: a spicy, peppery, jelled dish prepared from well-boiled pig's head and trotters (feet). The carefully picked-off bits of meat are set in small bowls to gel with the seasoned cooking broth.

Brewis: the "great filler-up in hunger years." A type of milk-toast called **Sowans** in both Ireland and Scotland, **Brewis** was originally made from oat bread or oat husks over which was poured boiling water to soften, then cooked and served with milk, butter, seasonings, or a lump of bacon.

Brithyll a Chig Moch: widely used Welsh (and Breton) method of cooking fresh-caught trout by wrapping the fish in rashers of bacon and baking quickly in a hot oven.

Cawl or Swp: soup or broth.

Cawl Ail-Dwyn: leftover and reheated broth drunk for breakfast.

Cawl Cennin: soup prepared with leeks, potatoes, and chicken broth finished with a splash of cream, and freshly chopped mint.

Caws Pobi: the famed **Welsh Rarebit.** The dish uses a strong cheese, such as Cheddar or Cheshire, blended with seasonings and heated with milk or beer then spread over toast and broiled under a flame.

Cig Moch Wedi ei Ferwi a Saws Persli: traditional dish of boiled ham, served with creamy parsley sauce and dumplings made of fine oatmeal and studded with currants.

Crempog: general name given to many types of pancakes made from eggs, milk (fresh or soured) and sometimes fine oatmeal. May also be called **Pikelets, Scones, Pancakes, Crumpets**. All are served while hot with generous spreadings of butter.

Cyflaith: treacle toffee. Made from sugar, butter, and corn syrup boiled to the "hard ball" stage. A favorite Welsh sweet.

Faggots: similar to Breton **Crepine** or the English **Savoury Ducks** or **Mock Ducks**. Rounded balls made from a mixture of pork liver, seasonings, bread crumbs, and oatmeal. Each large ball is wrapped in a thin membrane veined with fat called pig's flead or caul fat. Baked in the oven, they may be served hot or cold and are often taken for lunches.

Gammon: ham.

Hwyaden Hallt Cymreig: a traditional Welsh dish of duck that has been salt-rubbed for two to three days then rinsed and slowly cooked or baked, and finally served with a creamy onion sauce.

Katt Pie: a traditional dish from Pembrokeshire prepared especially for Fair Day (November 12). It is a deep-dish pie lined and topped with lard pastry enclosing layers of minced lamb, currants, and brown sugar. Can be served in slices or made into small pies.

Leeks: not only the symbol of Wales, but a great tradition in custard tarts, stews, and soups and even served as a vegetable dish; it is a vegetable related to the onion but milder in taste, having a white root end and flowing long green leaves.

Mead: wine made with honey.

Pwdin Caws Pobi Cymreig: a Welsh cheese pudding that is more like a soufflé. Layers of stale or toasted bread and grated cheese are soaked with an egg-milk mixture then oven baked till puffed and golden. (Called **Cheese Strata** in North America). Eaten as a light meal or a "savory" with tea.

Pwdin Reis: rice pudding. Baked slowly in the oven with the roast and vegetables and served as the Sunday special dessert. Creamy with eggs and milk, the pudding is spiced with nutmeg and served with honey or preserves and sometimes fruit compote.

Spiced Beef: a favorite in Ireland too, this can be an economical dish as the inexpensive, tougher cuts of beef are suited to this preparation. Boned beef is rubbed with salt, sugar, spices, and saltpeter, and turned daily for ten days to two weeks. It is then covered, boiled or roasted slowly, drained and pressed, then served hot or cold.

Stwns Rwdan a Iau: a **stwns** is a mashed cooked mixture usually of vegetables or vegetables and meat, in this case liver, onions, potatoes, and **swedes** (turnips).

Swp Cennin: leek or leek and potato soup. The vegetables are cooked in milk, puréed or strained then the mixture is thickened with a butter-flour roux and garnished with grated cheese and crisp-fried bacon.

Swper Scadan: a herring supper dish of layered sliced apples and potatoes, fillets of fresh herring rolled up with mustard, moistened with water, salt and pepper, and seasoned with onion and sage.

Tatws Rhost: a "hot-pot" of layered sliced potatoes and onions and rashers of bacon covered and slowly baked. A supper dish good with ale or beer.

Teisen Blat: also called **Plate Cake** or **Harvest Cake**. A layer of pastry is pressed on a large round china plate, then fruit filling is placed over that and finally another layer of pastry pressed over. After baking, it is served warm in wedges with glasses of buttermilk. Considered a meal for the workers at harvest and sowing time.

Teisen Datwys: a dough made from cooked mashed potatoes, flour, and eggs, seasoned with cinnamon and shaped into one-inch-thick flat patties to be browned on a bakestone and served hot with lots of butter. The dough may also be used as a pastry, rolled and filled then baked in large crescents. If filled with grated cheese it is called a **Cheese Cake** and served with buttermilk to drink.

Teisen Gocos: pre-cooked cockles dipped in batter and deep-fried. Served with lemon wedges and wholemeal bread and butter.

Trollies: dumplings, usually made with fine oatmeal.

Welsh Stew: a stew of cubed beef, simmered in water with cubed potatoes, **swedes** (turnips) and carrots added as it cooks. Eaten very hot with pieces of bread and butter.

W E S T   I N D I A N

"All mixed up and born in the islands…" This phrase refers to one definition of the term "Creole." But it could so easily refer to the complex diversity that is the West Indies of today.

The West Indies are also known by two other names: the Greater and Lesser Antilles and the Caribbean Islands. Historically they have shared periods of conquest, piracy, oppression, slavery, and revolution. They also share incredibly beautiful landscapes of mountains, plains, and beaches and a remarkably stable climate warmed by the tropical sun and tempered by the easterly trade winds. It is these trade winds that are believed to have brought the many seeds, spores, and coconuts to the islands' fertile soils. And it is these same trade winds that brought the European explorers.

Christopher Columbus landed on these islands in 1492. The 2,600-mile arc of islands enclosing the Caribbean Sea and arching outward to the Atlantic Ocean must have seemed like paradise to the European explorers. The beauty of the landscape and the pleasantness of the climate were marred only by the group of warring native peoples whom the Spanish called the *Caribs*, from the Spanish word meaning "cannibal." However the other native peoples, the Arawaks and the Ciboney, were peaceful and hospitable. They introduced the Europeans to their fruits: avocado, papaya, guava, pineapple, as well as to their staple food crops of corn and cassava root. They taught the Europeans how to smoke tobacco and how to sleep in a hammock. They even taught them a delicious way of cooking fish and fowl by coating the foods with wet mud and burying them in hot embers (later to be known as clay-baking) and a method of cooking meat with a smoky flavor by laying thin strips of meat over green boughs placed atop burning embers. The early settlers called this latter method of cookery **boucan**, while the

Arawaks themselves called it **barbacoa**, from which we derived the "barbecue." And from this, much later, came the term "buccaneer," identifying the men who sustained themselves by preparing their meats in this way.

In spite of the sad fact that strains of the original inhabitants of the West Indies today are almost extinct, their important culinary contribution to the culture of the islands cannot be forgotten because it is ever-present. Aside from the fruits and vegetables – and the distinctions between those that are edible and those that are poisonous – the smoking of tobacco and the use of hammocks as well as clay-baking and barbecuing, the Indians (as the Europeans called them) left two other important contributions: they taught the settlers how to make **cassava bread** and **pepper-pot**. Presently, the few Aboriginal peoples remaining in the West Indies rely on these as their staples.

Because the raw juice of the bitter cassava root is poisonous (containing prussic acid), the root is prepared for use by first grating then squeezing to extract the juice. The last moisture is removed by spreading the grated mixture to dry in the sun. From this, a coarse meal is prepared which, when mixed with water and "baked" on a metal griddle, produces a satisfying crusty bread enjoyed to this day. **Pepper-pot** is also a sustaining food, especially important to the poorer people. A huge pot is kept simmering over coals, perhaps the simplest method of food preservation long before the development of refrigeration and easier than salting, drying, or smoking. Any available foods including meats, fish, or fowl and a variety of vegetables plus water could be added to the constantly simmering **pepper-pot**. But most important was the seasoning of chili peppers and **cassareep**, the boiled juice from the **cassava** root that lends a peculiar bittersweet flavor. Always the contents of the pot would be eaten in little amounts so as to leave a continuing source of food. In fact "a good pepper-pot is so highly valued that it may be willed from one generation to another."

The Spanish were the first explorers and settlers in the area of the West Indies and they took over the islands of the Arawaks – Cuba, Hispaniola, Puerto Rico, and Jamaica – ostensibly looking for gold. The Papal Donation of 1493 allocated to Spain all territories (land and sea) west of a boundary set in the mid-Atlantic Ocean.

This did not last long. By the 1500s piracy was common, and France and England disputed the papal rights coinciding with the decline in Spain's marine powers. The Netherlands allied itself with the French and English naval powers against the Spanish, and even set up the Dutch West India Company in 1621. The Dutch were seeking not gold but salt. Portugal's union with Spain in 1580 had deprived the Dutch of the use of Portuguese sources of the salt vital for their fisheries and so an alternative source had to be found: the Dutch discovered the Araya saltpans of Venezuela and later those in Curacao.

In the 1600s, the French settled in Martinique, Guadeloupe, and Grenada. The British acquired Jamaica around 1658 by defeating the bucanneers who had made it their headquarters, living on wild pigs and selling hides and smoked meats (**boucan**) to passing ships and adding piracy for greater profits.

Another group of people came to the West Indies in the 1600s. These were Sephardi Jews seeking to escape the Inquisitions of both Spain and Portugal and bringing with them some of the techniques of sugar processing and the capital necessary to establish the industry. Many came from Brazil in the early 1600s; they had used their expertise and wealth to increase sugar production in Brazil (then under Dutch control), but when the Jews were pressed to become "new Christians" they moved northward to Barbados, Jamaica, and Nevis. Ancient tombstones and old synagogues found on the islands, now being restored, testify to the presence of early Jewish settlers.

Those who had settled on the lands — British, Spanish, Dutch, and French — all sought profitable crops that could be exported and so began the trade of cacao, cotton, coffee, tobacco, and sugar.

It did not take long for the settlers to realize that their most profitable crop was sugar. It could be easily shipped (requiring no special care to prevent spoilage), it was a great luxury to the European market accustomed mainly to honey as a sweetener, and, most important, several crops a year could be harvested from the same piece of land.

The first sugar plantation workers were Europeans hired as indentured laborers. This meant that they agreed to work for a given period of time and then were given small areas of land of their own. But when sugar replaced tobacco as the important crop, the small landholders were wiped out. As using indentured workers became unfeasible, the growing shortage of labor and the huge sugar profits started a new trade — slavery.

It is important to note that the slaves were brought to the trading companies from many different areas of Africa. From 1698 onwards, more than 40 English slave-trading companies were established on the west coast of Africa. Some masters favored Africans from certain areas because of their purported characteristics; for example, the Mandingoes were said to be the most gentle. Other Africans included the Yorubas from West Nigeria, the Ashanti and Fanti from the Gold Coast, and the Ibos and Dahomians. Although they shared the fact that they were Africans, they were forced to subdue their individual native cultures and, bonded by their common plight of slavery,

FOODS COMMONLY USED

Again, there may be different names used in different areas, but the staple foods of the West Indies bear a striking similarity from island to island. The naturally grown fruits and vegetables, together with those brought and introduced by the waves of immigrants, blend together to form the culinary pattern. **Cassava bread** and **pepper-pot**, introduced by the earliest inhabitants, continue to form the staples of the poorer classes especially in the south and southeastern areas of the West Indies. **Salt beef**, **salt pork**, and **salt fish** keep well in the tropical climate and are widely used to add needed protein to a diet that largely depends on root and starchy vegetables such as **cassava**, **tarp plantains**, many varieties of squashes, yams, sweet potatoes, corn, and okra and a variety of greens. Meats are added to the diet by those who can afford them: fish and seafood increasingly plays an important part in the cuisine. Another important staple combination is beans and rice: the Jamaicans may call beans "peas" and cook a dish with coconut milk and red beans; to the Cubans black beans and rice are a specialty; and the Haitians cook a combination of local black mushrooms, rice and lima beans; while the Puerto Ricans sauté their rice in hot fat and serve it with beans or peas such as cowpeas, chickpeas, or pigeon peas. However, for the Puerto Ricans, red or kidney beans are the favorites. Most popular beverages include cold fruit drinks of many types; while coffee with hot milk or hot chocolate are enjoyed for breakfasts. Tea is popular in the areas of English influence. Rum is the alcoholic beverage of the islands. Desserts based on fruits, but especially coconut and bananas in many different forms, are popular everywhere.

developed their own customs and language under the West Indian conditions.

The slaves learned foreign languages rapidly and made their own adaptations of mixtures of languages. Many, forbidden to converse while working, learned to gossip while singing and thus was born the enchanting words and rhythms of calypso.

They built their own homes from mud-plastered timber or woven leaves and grass. On tiny plots of land near their homes they carefully cultivated yams, sweet potatoes, and other vegetables and prepared dishes based on these and flavored with bits of salt meat or salt fish supplied to them by their masters. Often they were fed foods that were rejected by their masters, but a taste from "home" could be evoked by preparing dishes from the plants of okra, **callaloo**, **taro** and **akee**, which they had brought with them from Africa. To make these simple foods more palatable, they made clever use of natural herbs and pungent spices, much as they had done in their homeland.

The slave and sugar trade was also called "the triangular trade." The West Indies shipped mostly sugar but also cotton and tobacco to the British Isles. From the British Isles went ships carrying iron tools, kitchen utensils and cutlery as well as wool and cotton cloths to be used for barter in return for the human cargo of slaves at the ports in West Africa. Ships laden with their unhappy cargo made for their markets both in the West Indies and also South America (particularly in Brazil where the Africans were to play a key role in the developing Brazilian cuisine). The completion of the triangular voyage for one ship from the West Indies to the British Isles and then to Africa and finally back to the West Indies took twelve months.

Wars and disputes continued among the marine powers, all vying for territories and hoped-for riches. Blockades often prevented the shipment of salt cod from the New England states in exchange for rum and molasses from the West Indies, so other foods had to be found to feed the slaves. Young **akee** trees were brought from West Africa, **breadfruit** trees from Tahiti (it was breadfruit trees that the much-maligned Captain Bligh on the *Bounty* was attempting to save with rations of the crew's water) and mangoes from Asia. For almost 200 years, despite the human suffering involved, the slave and sugar trade was ruthlessly pursued so that the words "West Indies," "sugar," and "slaves" became synonymous.

However, changes came. Two seemingly unrelated occurrences were destined to change both "sugar" and "slavery" and thus, inevitably, the West Indies. In 1756, the arrival of the first missionaries from Germany (Moravian Protestants) was met by strong opposition from the plantation owners. With good reason: they feared the education of their slaves might lead to intermarriage and the consequences of being taught the precept that "all men are equal."

At about the same time a German scientist, Marggraf, discovered sugar in beet juice and by the end of the 1700s many European countries unable to grow sugarcane were busily producing their own sugar from beets which could be easily grown.

The combination of competition in sugar manufacturing and revolution among the slaves led, in 1772 in England, to the pronouncement that "a slave becomes free the moment he sets foot on English soil." Other nations followed suit, with the Portuguese, repeatedly the first in the slave trade, being the last in 1836 to put a legal end to it. But the end of slavery was not an end to misery. Both the English and Dutch seemed unprepared for the handling of the freed slaves and viewed the black people's slavery as synonymous with inferiority. Spanish slaves, upon being freed, were treated generally as people who had suffered; while the French treated the freed slaves slightly less well than the Spanish but better than either the English or the Dutch.

Although the general economy of the West Indies had slowed, the huge plantations still had to be worked and labor had to be found. Many freed slaves became small independent farmers with fruits and vegetables as their produce.

The answer to the labor shortage was found in bringing in Chinese and Indians as indentured servants, and they in turn brought with them their culture, customs, and food preferences. The Chinese planted vegetables and the Indians planted rice crops. Both groups came to be respected members of the community, many ending up as merchants and businesspeople.

Many Indians settled in Trinidad and Tobago, introducing their flat breads called **roti**, and a taste for blended spices called curry. As the foods and tastes spread, the Dutch called it **kerry**, while the French gave it the name **colombo**, all agreeing that the perspiration caused by eating the spicy hot curries, caused them to feel cooler.

The 1800s and early 1900s in the West Indies saw the development of racial stereotypes that persist in many areas to the present time: Africans showing disdain for the Indians and Chinese arriving to undertake what they still consider to be slave labor. The close family life of these groups and their distinctive customs helped to intensify their separateness. But more and more, children went to schools, women minded their homes, and the men went to work. Neither the African nor the European pattern of society was distinct. Instead, a loose family structure developed, often not even bound by formal marriage contracts.

The 1930s witnessed a sudden blossoming in West Indian identity. Increase in population led to expansion of social services, growth of cultural groups, trade unions and political parties, and the surge for self-government. Overpopulation in some islands led to emigration, causing, unfortunately, a loss of the most skilled. And during World War II when the United States used the West Indies as military bases, the inhabitants opened their eyes to higher living standards and labor-saving devices, all of which reinforced the need for development and change.

In the last years of the twentieth century, many countries of the West Indies have independent status. These include Cuba, Haiti, Dominican Republic, Jamaica, Trinidad and Tobago, St. Vincent and the Grenadines, St. Lucia, Grenada, Bahamas, Barbados, St. Kitts and Nevis, Antigua, and Barbuda.

Several other West Indies countries remain dependent: the British West Indies includes Anguilla, Cayman Islands and the British Virgin Islands; the Netherlands Antilles encompass Aruba, Curacao, Bonaire, Saba, St. Eustatius, and part of St. Martin; both the Virgin Islands and Puerto Rico remain dependent on the United States, while Guadeloupe, Marie Galante, and Martinique remain dependent on France.

Although other islands can be clearly seen on the horizon from almost any one of the West Indian islands, it is a curious phenomenon that the ties have in the past always been closer to the European country of influence rather than to a nearby island. A peculiar state of insularism and self-imposed isolationism that has persisted for so long is more recently showing signs of abating. Colonialism at least seems to have given way to dependence. Both colonialism – though for the most part fading now – and dependency, leave deep cultural imprints in the daily life of the islanders. A hopeful portent is the development of economic unions including the Central American Common Market to establish a regional free trade zone, the Caribbean Community and Common Market promoting cooperation among English-speaking countries and the African, Caribbean and Pacific Group of States receiving preferential tariffs with the European Economic Community.

Thus the culture, political ties, and even the food preferences and the language can be readily predicted by understanding the past ties of the island. The religious diversity of the islands includes those of the Muslim faith, Christians, Sephardi Jews, and many varieties of primitive cults. Some adapted form and rituals from Christianity to their own African-born religions and customs and so found solace for their woes.

The population is diverse with black Africans dominating, followed by Afro-Europeans who are called "brown" or "colored," while both these groups together may be called "creole." The smaller minorities of Amerinds, Asians, and Europeans are "white." Only in Puerto Rico is the majority of the population white (80 percent) and the minority "non-white" (20 percent). Status is determined by material possessions and by color and language. The closer the language is to "white" the higher the status.

Four hundred years of human influx, blending a diversity of colors, languages, customs, religions, and cultures and suffering a common history of oppression, slavery, and revolution has created a unique and interesting region.

Diversified though their people and their pasts may be, there is a new pride in local culture and a movement towards unifying the complex elements of the West Indies. This is reflected in the establishment in 1957 of the West Indian Federation. This federation suggests that all peoples are capable of assuming all positions and class levels in human society regardless of color, race, or religion, and gives the sense that while a nation may be small, nonetheless its independence is important to its image and future.

It is further an example of how people add their foods and food customs to those already established. Together with the influences of the early Amerinds, then the Europeans and the Africans, Chinese and Indians, still another group is adding its influence: the tourists. And it is the combination of the desire of tourists to taste "the real Caribbean flavors" and the pride of the West Indians themselves, regardless of traditional imperial ties, that causes the flowering and promotion of the greatest appreciation of the West Indian cuisine.

DOMESTIC LIFE

Although there is a rapidly growing movement in all the islands to improve living conditions, "most West Indians can afford only the meanest accommodations" and status is undeniably linked to color, with black being synonymous with poverty. Lower classes tend to be matriarchal, middle classes (mostly the "colored") tend to be patriarchal, and the upper classes "agnostic and scientific." Poverty, poor health, lack of medical services, and lack of sanitation are almost constant neighbors to examples of luxuriant living. But the fertile soil and the benevolent climate help to alleviate some hardships.

Most homes are wooden structures with galvanized metal roofs. Cooking and toilet facilities are usually separate from the main dwelling. Small coal pots and boards nailed between trees may serve as cooking and working areas. Most kitchens have the necessary tools for making cassava bread: a grater, sifter, and metal griddle for cooking. And most homes, too, depending on the area and the circumstances, will have a large heavy pot for the **pepper-pot**. A treasured implement is the **baton lele**: an African swizzle stick used deftly as a whisk for beating and whipping. The growing middle class is enjoying increasingly better accommodations and facilities, and in most areas modern supermarkets stock an array of convenience foods as well as quality local produce.

In Puerto Rico, the traditional kitchen stove will be shaped like a built-in box, made of cement, tiles or brick with grates on top for cooking and using charcoal as the fuel. This is called the **fogon**. Upper-class homes will have a **fogon** with a decorated ceramic tile and a hood above to collect smoke and odors and direct them through a chimney to the outdoors. Traditional kitchen utensils include a **rallo** (a grater used especially for coconut); **pilon y maceta** (mortar and pestle to grind spices); **caldero** (a large heavy pot to cook rice); and **habichuelas guisadas** (an aluminum covered kettle used to cook legumes). The latter two implements are indispensable for Puerto Rico's staples: rice and beans. Although the implements may be similar from island to island, each area in the West Indies has its own name for each.

DAIRY PRODUCTS
Milk as a beverage is not widely used in the West Indies, but canned evaporated milk or canned condensed milk is used in cooking and mostly for desserts, confections, and as hot milk in coffee or hot chocolate. Imported Dutch cheeses are used in the islands of Dutch influence, French cheeses are preferred in the islands of French influence, but there is little dairy product produced locally.

FRUITS AND VEGETABLES
All West Indians enjoy an abundant variety of native fruits, many unknown in other areas because of their short season, perishability, and difficulty in transporting and storing. The more familiar fruits include pineapples, coconut, guavas, bananas, mangoes, papayas, oranges, grapefruit, and limes. Others include tamarind, **soursop**, **otaheite**, gooseberry, pomegranates, **tangelo**, **ugli**, star apple, passion fruit, **cherimoya**, **hog plum**, **cocoplum**, **granadilla**, sugar apple, and **genip**.

Unusual as many of these are, they are catalogued as to nutrient composition by the Caribbean Food and Nutrition Institute in their pamphlet. It should be noted that many of these fruits are not only used ripe but are also prepared while in their green state

and often cooked as a vegetable. Papaya and mango are both used in their green state, cherished for their tartness, and also for the enzymes they contain that are known to tenderize meats. Many fruits are eaten fresh while others may be used as preserves, made into many types of refreshing drinks, or prepared as fruit sherbets or ice creams. Starchy fruits, roots and tubers commonly form the main part of many meals and these include breadfruit, plantains, **taro** (also called **coco** or **dasheen**), yams, sweet potatoes, Irish potatoes, cassava (also called **malanga**, **yautia** or **yucca root**) yambean. Squashes include those commonly known in temperate climates, such as pumpkin, but also others such as **calabaza**, **christophene** or **chayote**. Greens are also used: **taro** leaves, turnip and beet tops, mustard greens, endive, radish leaves. **Akee** is another vegetable-fruit that frequently forms part of a main dish, while okra, an African favorite, is also used widely.

Most of the starchy roots, tubers and green fruits can be used in a variety of ways: boiling, mashing, frying, or made into specialty dishes. Corn is frequently prepared into a thick pudding similar to the Romanian **mamaliga** or the Italian **polenta**, only here it is called **funchi** or **fungee**. Curacao is famed for its **funchi** served with **fish chowder**. Other areas commonly serve okra plus **funchi** and it is called **coo-coo**. Okra cooked with mashed plantains is called **foo-foo**. **Funchi**, **coo-coo**, and **foo-foo** are West Indian dishes originating in Africa.

Plantains too enjoy great popularity as thinly fried crisp plantain chips, and as **mofongo**, the Puerto Rican appetizer made by mixing ripe fried plantains with garlic and pork cracklings and spreading the mixture on bread.

Garlic, onions, scallions, leeks, avocados, **leren** (a root vegetable with a corn flavor), red peppers and green peppers, eggplant, tomatoes and cucumbers round out the list of widely used vegetables. Vegetables are seldom served raw or as salads (except for tourists); they are cooked as vegetable main dishes with highly seasoned sauces often with chilies or have their flavor enhanced by the use of small amounts of salt meat or salt fish. Soups and stews also make use of well-cooked vegetables.

MEATS AND ALTERNATES
Although vegetables are cooked and eaten in common ways (though sometimes with different names throughout the West Indies), the preparation and eating of meats differs by technique, climate, and influence of the European powers. It was the Spanish-speaking islands that early in history imported cattle, horses, pigs, and sheep from Spain, and to this day these same islands use more beef dishes than the

others. **Picadillo**, **ropa vieja**, and **sancocho** are the classic dishes of the Spanish-speaking islands, but so too are **lechon asada** (spit-roasted young pigs); **chicharrones** (pork cracklings served as snacks); and **pasteles** (meat mixtures wrapped in plantain leaves then steamed).

Guadeloupe and Martinique favor sheep and lamb, probably a preference inherited from Algeria via France. Surely their **mechoui** (spit-roasted sheep) points to indisputable Algerian influence. Another French-influenced specialty is **pate en pot**: finely chopped sheep and lamb parts cooked to form a thick, rich soup generously seasoned with garlic and hot peppers and a whiff of cloves, thyme, bay leaf, and celery. Rich as this dish may be, it is usually served as the first course of a dinner, probably preceding a main course of roast mutton or lamb.

Barbados is often called "little England" and many English customs persist unchanged from the mother country. However, some acknowledgment to West Indian food culture may be noted in the use of rum as a meat marinade, and the festive **conkies**, similar to **pasteles**, a banana-leaf-wrapped meat mixture steamed before eating. Roast pork, roast lamb, and roast fowl are sure to grace the Sunday or festive dinner table.

The Dutch-owned islands enjoy two specialties: **stoba** (a stew made from goat or lamb, well seasoned with garlic, chilies, and spices); and the showy **keshy yena** (a scooped-out whole Edam cheese refilled with a mixture of chopped cheese, mixed beef, olives, onions and tomatoes, all oven-baked).

The **pepper-pot** of the more southern islands may be a blend of any available meats, with additions of what is available.

Although meats may be scarce on the menu of the poorer people, they are prepared as regional specialties and the favorite meats used include beef, pork, chicken, duck, goat or kid, and rabbit. The offal and variety meats of all types are carefully used in minced dishes, sausages and in soups and stews. Many areas consider kid and rabbit as special delicacies, while **curried goat** and meat, chilies and vegetable-filled **roti** are particular favorites in Jamaica.

While a glance at the map would indicate that fish and seafood must have an important place on the West Indian menu, the facts are otherwise. Lacking a history or tradition of seafaring or fishing, most West Indians are better suited to farming. Thus it is not surprising that the fishing industry is only carried out on a small and local scale. The lack of proper transportation, storage and packing facilities aggravates the situation. Probably more fish and seafood is consumed by tourists than by the local populace.

Dating back to sugar and slave trade days, **salt cod** or **baccalao** is widely used and very popular. Mixtures of flour batter or batters made with any of the starchy vegetables plus flaked salt cod are prepared by frying in small patties. These are called **stamp and go** in Jamaica; **marinades** in Haiti; **codfish cakes** in Barbados; **acrats de morue** in Guadeloupe and Martinique; **bacalaitos** in Puerto Rico and **accra** in Trinidad. Another favorite is conch (pronounced conk) and called by the *Carib* name **lambs** or **lambie**; by the Spanish name **concha**; or by the French name **conque**. By whatever name, the large white fleshy mollusc is first pounded then marinated to tenderize before cooking in soups or stews or serving cooked but chilled in salads.

The third most popular fish dish could be **escabeche** prepared by pouring a tangy dressing of oil, vinegar or lime juice and spices over pieces of grilled or fried fish. Note that **escabeche** is made with cooked fish, while the Mexican and South American **ceviche** is made with raw fish "cooked" with lime juice and spices. **Escabeche** may be eaten hot or cold and keeps well. Fish chowders are often prepared with coconut milk.

Other available fish and seafood include snapper, grouper, kingfish, Caribbean dolphin (not related to the mammal type), Spanish mackerel, sea eggs, green turtles, Caribbean lobster and shrimp. Also popular are sea crabs and land crabs. These are usually prepared by steaming or boiling then removing the flesh and preparing it as a stuffing with crumbs and seasonings, served in the crab backs.

Probably the most important protein source, and the most widely used, is legumes: lima beans, black beans, green beans, cowpeas, chickpeas, pigeon peas, all usually prepared from the dried legumes, and most frequently served together with rice – in many homes more of a staple than bread. Many soups are also based on legumes.

Eggs are not abundant because of low local production, but are used when available, baked or scrambled, or most frequently as omelets or **tortillas** mixed with vegetables.

BREADS AND GRAINS
Rice as served with beans, breads made from cassava and wheat flours, cornmeal served as **funchi** or **fungee**, provide the main sources of cereal staples. Many varieties of other breads such as banana bread, corn bread and coconut bread are used. White, brown, and rye breads are also prepared but not as widely used by the indigenous population as by the tourists. **Cassava bread**, rice with beans and peas and cornmeal pudding (**funchi**) – related to the African staple **fufu** – remain the West Indian bread and cereal staples.

FATS

Fried foods of all kinds are very popular, particularly those made from starchy vegetables into patties, fritters, and cakes. Lard is used most frequently for deep-frying but many seed and vegetable oils as well as margarine are also available. Butter is used at the table and for special baked goods, while **ghee** (clarified butter) is favored by the Muslims (East Indians). Jamaicans use coconut oil for sauteeing; French-speaking islands (e.g., Haiti) prefer butter and olive oil.

SWEETS AND SNACKS

Sweetened fruit drinks, icy fruit desserts, such as sherbets and ice creams, and many mousses, souffles, custards and flans use sugar and fruit as their base. Sweet confections made from sugar and coconut are traditional. Fresh fruits in combination are served frequently. Citron, **cocoplum**, **guava**, bitter orange, and other fruits are especially used in sweet preserves and jams. Pound cakes, simple light sponge cakes, and caramel baked custards called **flans**, are especially popular in the Spanish-speaking islands. Puddings and desserts are also made from pumpkin, sweet potatoes, and rice. Brown sugar is commonly used.

Snack foods are most likely to be nibbles in a great variety of crisply fried savory treats: plantain chips, fried corn sticks (**surullitos**), and the variety of East Indian fried vegetable specialties often sold by street vendors, especially in Trinidad: **palouri**, **baras**, **kachouri**, and **baigani** (all vegetable fritters dipped in batter and fried crisply).

SEASONINGS

Although the Africans brought with them a taste preference for spicy hot sauces to add to their mild **coo-coo** and **foo-foo** and **funchi**, the Amerinds also enjoy the use of spices and chilies. The East Indians added the taste for blended seasonings called curries, and while these became a favorite, most West Indians prefer to buy blended curry powder rather than crush and grind their own blends as those from India do so skillfully. In the Spanish-speaking islands the basic sauce that finds its way to many dishes and adds its own distinct taste and aroma is the **sofrito**, a highly seasoned thick sauce based on tomatoes, garlic, onions, and chili peppers.

Two other important ingredients in the **sofrito**, which add to its distinctiveness, are cilantro (also called Chinese parsley) and **annatto seeds**. In fact, cooking of the annatto seeds in lard to make a reddish-orange paste serves as a base for many dishes. Annatto seeds are called **achiote** on the Spanish Islands. Annatto seeds or **achiote** were used by the Amerinds, the Caribs, the Ciboney and the Arawaks to anoint and color their naked bodies as a protection against insects and the sun. Puerto Ricans also consider these seeds useful as a flavoring ingredient. **Aceite de achiote** is a preparation of **annatto seeds** cooked with olive oil until the color is deep orange, then strained, cooled and bottled.

The French-influenced islands of Martinique and Guadeloupe use seasonings of wines, herbs, and especially **onion pays**, also called **cive**, a herb combining an onion and garlic flavor.

The southern islands, especially Trinidad, are strongly influenced by their large East Indian population. Thus, as in the East Indian cuisine, many fried vegetables served in appetizer form (**pakoras**), many Indian breads under the general name **roti**, and **curries** are all popular. The distinction between dry and wet **masalahs** is also observed. (**Masalah** is the correct East Indian term for any mixture of seasonings. See Indian.) **Ghee** (clarified butter) is frequently used and adds flavor as well.

While there are definite seasoning preferences in the different areas, many seasonings are common to all. A **pepper-pot** without **cassareep** could hardly be considered authentic. And a bottle of **coui sauce** is as common on a West Indian table as salt and pepper is on the North American table. **Coui sauce** is as often used in place of salt and pepper for it is a potent mixture of hot peppers and cassava juice. **Cassareep** and **coui** are two more traditions from the Amerinds. Everywhere too, tomatoes and hot peppers are a traditional combination for many dishes. There is little doubt that the rich color and taste of these pungent seasonings help to make the simplest foods tasty: even meats and fish are commonly marinated with herb seasonings before cooking.

Ginger, cloves, allspice, and nutmeg are often included in soups, stews, meats, and fish preparations. A most interesting custom is the common use of cinnamon. In fact, in many areas, cinnamon is synonymous with "spice." Grenada is famed for its use of nutmeg and mace.

BEVERAGES

While milk is not a popular or widely used beverage, the abundance of fresh and unusual fruits of the West Indies is made into a great variety of cooling fresh drinks and punches. Those that are alcoholic usually contain the local varieties (many types) of rum. Puerto Rican drinks are familiar in all Spanish countries: **horchata**, a cooling drink of milky appearance made from pressed almonds, melon seeds, or sesame seeds then sweetened and diluted to taste; **cafe con leche**, equal parts of hot milk and hot coffee, sweetened to taste, is a popular breakfast beverage, while hot chocolate is also an old favorite.

In Puerto Rico, hot chocolate enriched with butter and egg yolks was a traditional hot beverage for weddings. Two drinks that may be familiar only to the Spanish-speaking islands are **mabi**, a fermented beverage prepared from a water extract of mabi bark, sweetened with brown sugar, and **garapina**, a heady drink made from the peelings of pineapple allowed to ferment with water then strained, sweetened, and served well chilled.

The most famous beverage of all the islands is rum, prepared from sugarcane. What is not so well known is that rum comes in many varieties and each locality takes pride in its specialty. Rum may be light, medium, or heavy. The light or clear rum is delicate in taste and often used in cocktails; the heavy rum in strong punches, or by the experienced rum-toter. In the middle range are rums of every hue and flavor from deepest mahogany to a gentle yellowish tone. Rum is the only spirit distilled from sugarcane; most other spirits are made from grains and a few from grapes.

MEALS AND CUSTOMS

Caribbean history produced a profound sense of isolationism in the islands that has only recently begun to withdraw its hold on the people. So it is not surprising to find that the sense of allegiance and influence of the European "owners" was felt at every level of culture and in the people's daily life, including at the table. If you imagine that a Sunday Jamaican planter's table would bear some resemblance to an Englishman's Sunday table, you would be right. On both would appear an abundance of cooked vegetables together with a large roast ready for carving. But to the French mind, carving a huge roast at the table is not a part of the etiquette, and so the custom of presenting platters of sliced, ready-to-eat meats at the table will be seen in Martinique and Guadeloupe.

By simply adding the local produce, seasonings, the fresh fruit beverages, many concocted from rum, it is not difficult to conjure up West Indian tables or eating customs. Add the color of the tropics: clear, bright colors for tablecloths and flowers for centerpieces, the steel drums of Trinidad or the gentle calypsos of Jamaica, and you have a typical West Indian picture.

SPECIAL OCCASIONS

People in the West Indies, like those the world over, enjoy a festive occasion. Arts and music festivals and local Independence Day festivities as well as special days to mark family and religious festivities are all characterized with feasting, drinking, and merry-making, with everyone decked out in their best clothes.

Religious tolerance is characteristic of the West Indies. Many primitive cults, animism, and others coexist with those professing the Muslim faith, Sephardi Judaism, and various forms of Christianity. Roman Catholic festive days predominate in the Spanish-speaking islands, while the celebration of many Muslim festivities prevails in Trinidad and Tobago where approximately 40 percent of the population are of Indian-Pakistani descent.

Trinidad and Tobago mark Christmas with a fury of house cleaning and decorating with balloons, tinsel, flowers and colored electric lights -- as well as by the sending of greeting cards and singing of carols. Children bursting bamboo and carbide-in-tins with loud noises and much laughter starts before Christmas and is punctuated by the friendly house-to-house visiting. While adults drink rum, beer, and whiskey, children enjoy sorrel, ginger beer, and sweet fruit drinks and great amounts of nuts, cakes, and fruits. The Christmas dinner is a buffet featuring chicken and turkey, ham and goat meat.

New Year's in Trinidad and Tobago is a quieter festival celebrated especially the night before, which is called "Old Year's Night." An interesting tradition is to stay awake for midnight "to feel the New Year's breeze blowing in...." Many also attend midnight church services. During New Year's Day beach picnics are common and so are spectator sports.

The most famous festival of Trinidad and Tobago is the Carnival. Here, the cultural elements of French, African, and Indian are evident. Held on the Monday and Tuesday preceding Ash Wednesday, Carnival is a raucous and colorful blend of brilliant costumes, steel bands, calypso singers, kalinda stickfighting, and competitions for the best of each. To feed the masses of paraders, dancers, musicians and onlookers, Indians set up stands and booths and sell coconut confections and fruit beverages, but most of all a tempting array of crisply fried batter-dipped vegetable snacks (**pakoras**). Other stands scoop steaming ladles of spicy stews and vegetable curries into **roti** to be gobbled up by the hungry revelers to fortify them for more singing and dancing.

Easter weekend in Trinidad and Tobago also involves ancient pagan rituals and modern rites: on Good Friday it is traditional to pour the white of an egg into a glass of lukewarm water and analyze the shape formed to foretell a fortune; children make a Judas by stuffing old clothes with grass or dry leaves then beat it up. The stuffed image may also be called "Bobolee." Easter Sunday may be spent as a beach day, or a time to attend a goat race or a boat race.

The Indian-Pakistanis of Trinidad and Tobago celebrate their own festivities with great color and festivity. These include *Dewali*, or the Feast of Lights, when hundreds of small *deeyahs* – candles fueled by wicks floating on **ghee** – are prepared and lit during prayer sessions. Special baths are taken before the ceremonies, singing and dancing are interspersed with eating. *Kartik Nahan* is the ceremonial river-bathing for the devout, followed by eating of special foods and sweetmeats. *Phhagwah* or *Holi Festival* is characterized by the splashing of red paint (actually just a red liquid) on anyone that can be "caught." Food and drink are taken at various homes, while rhythmic pelvic dances and suggestive songs fill the merry time. The whole month of *Ramazan* for Muslims is spent with fasting from dawn to dusk prayers, alms for the poor, and visits to friends and relatives. The special foods of *Ramazan* are: **sawine**, a special mix of noodles, milk, sugar, raisins, and spices; curried chicken and goat meat eaten with **parathas** (like pancakes).

Many of the people of African descent in Haiti believe in ritual dancing, animal sacrifices, possession by *loas* (spirits), magical potions and charms, and Zombies or Jumbies who are characterized by their dazed expressions and servile mien. Many of the rituals are accompanied by specially prepared offerings of food or drink. Because of these traditional beliefs, a proper funeral may be of more importance to a Haitian than any material goal. Believing that a soul incorrectly mourned (and thus not freed) may remain in the area and turn evil, great care is taken to provide a good "wake." This means much loud weeping and wailing followed by the best foods and drinks available as well as songs and games so that the spirit may enjoy its last hours on earth. Traditional burials are held just before dawn with a devious route to the cemetery "to confuse the spirit about the way back to its house."

Puerto Ricans celebrate their festive occasions with a Spanish touch. **Cena de Nochebuena** is the Christmas Eve supper served at midnight or after the family returns from mass services. It is an occasion for family gatherings and a special menu: eggnog or rich fruit punch followed by **crullers**, **hayacas**, and **yostones**. Then the family and relatives sit down to a festive dinner of chicken with rice or a whole ham baked in wine or stewed rice (with **sofrito**) and pigeon peas. **Ponque**, nuts and raisins, coffee and more drinks will finish the great meal. Christmas Day and New Year's Day are spent quietly and are usually highlighted with a family meal of a stuffed roast turkey, a large chicken pie, or a roast suckling pig. Side dishes of eggplant, plantain, or stewed beans give the meal the Puerto Rican touch for the tradition of the turkey is taken from the United States. Cakes, nuts, puddings, and flans end the meal on a sweet note and coffee marks the finish. A special dish for most holidays and "essential" for feeding Christmas carolers, who go from house to house, are **pasteles**:

a mixture of chopped meats, raisins, almonds, and spices steamed in plantain leaves with a filling of mashed plantain or cornmeal. Fragrantly sweet and filling, **pasteles** fortify the singers and traditionally must be kept hot for any hour of the evening that the singers may appear. Perhaps most popular of all is the **lechon asado**, or roast pig, special for Christmas but popular also for picnics or any outdoor family gathering; the blood is saved for sausage (**morcilla**) and variety meats used for a special stew, **gandinga**. The pig is roasted on a pole and turned and basted with **achiote**, while charcoal burning over a stone bed keeps a constant heat.

Puerto Ricans also enjoy *Trulla*, or Three Kings' Day, noted for singing groups that go from house to house and are greeted with the serving of **Sangria** and appetizers, such as **tostones**, **chicharrones**, **morcella**, sweets and coffee. Fish and egg dishes are frequently eaten by Puerto Ricans during Lent, when the most devout do not eat meat. **Cocas**, sardine pies, fish stews, and omelets, as well as more familiar vegetable dishes and rice and beans are served.

GLOSSARY OF FOODS AND FOOD TERMS

Achiote Oil: annatto seeds cooked in oil until deep orange in color; used as a coloring and flavoring in many dishes and as a basting for roast suckling pig.

Ajilimojili: a spicy sauce made with ground sweet and hot peppers, peppercorns, garlic and salt blended with oil and lemon juice. Served especially with pork and other meats. (Puerto Rican)

Akee: Caribbean fruit with yellow flesh and black seeds used in Jamaica as a vegetable especially in **Akee and Rice**. Salt cod, bacon and spices are mixed with shredded **Akee** and after cooking, served with rice.

Allspice: also called **Jamaican Pepper**, discovered in the West Indies, has a flavor and aroma resembling a blend of cinnamon and cloves.

Apem: baby plantains – like bananas but used as a vegetable and cooked before eating.

Ariles: the edible part of the peach-like **Akee** with a flavor similar to that of scrambled eggs and added to casseroles of salt fish and rice. Especially enjoyed in Jamaica.

Arroz con Dulce: sweet rice pudding, cooked, then chilled and cut in squares. Flavored with cinnamon, ginger, cloves, coconut, milk, and brown sugar. (Puerto Rican)

Arroz con Gandules: sofrito, rice and pigeon peas, all cooked together. (Puerto Rican)

Asopao: a soupy version of **Paella**, richly flavored chicken pieces and seafood with rice. (Puerto Rican)

Bajans: what people in Barbados call themselves.

Callaloo: a thick, spicy soup made with the large green leaves of the taro plant (similar to spinach). Also called **malanga** or **elephant ears**.

Cassareep: juice from the **cassava** root giving a distinctive bittersweet flavor to the classic **Pepper-Pot**, the continually simmering pot based on whatever is available and flavored by everything that was in the pot before ... sometimes willed from one generation to another.

Cassava Chips: crispy snacks of thinly fried slices of **cassava**. (Jamaican)

Chicharrones: crispy snacks of pork crackling. **Chicharrones Pollo** refers to tiny crisp snacks of pieces of chicken chopped with bone and skin into little morsels then marinated with lime juice and soy sauce and fried crisp after a dusting with flour.

Citron: looks like a big lemon with warts but its pulpy bitterness makes a great marmalade and the skin is widely used as candied peel.

Cocido: a thick stew of beef, ham, **Sofrito**, Spanish sausages and hearty chunks of cabbage, carrots, potatoes, and green beans. (Puerto Rican)

Conkies: patties made from a mixture of cornmeal, coconut, yam, pumpkin, and spices then stewed in plantain leaves, said to be introduced by the Arawaks. More recently prepared and served in Barbados like mashed potatoes.

Coo-Coo: okra cut in pieces and cooked with cornmeal pudding (**Funche**).

Coui Sauce: used in place of salt and pepper, made of hot peppers and cassava juice.

Duckanoo: one of a large range of delicious "packets" of food mixtures placed in banana or plantain leaves, folded and tied then steamed. Originated in Africa,

can be made sweet or spicy and savory, and the filling is any mixed vegetables grated then steamed. **Alcapurrias** is the Spanish name for the same thing. **Pasteles**, **Conkies**, and **Hayacas** all have meat fillings and the addition of raisins, nuts, spices, and some mashed plantain.

Daiquiri: a cocktail of chilled lime juice, sugar and rum, invented by an American mining engineer working near the town of Daiquiri in Cuba.

Dulce de Leche: creamy caramel sauce for desserts or eaten as is, prepared (usually commercially) by slow-simmering of milk and sugar to a thick rich brown sauce.

Escabeche: fish dish enjoyed all over the West Indies, called **Escovitch** in Jamaica. Prepared by grilling or frying fish then marinating in a mixture of oil and lime juice plus spices. Eaten hot or cold.

Foo-Foo: a staple dish of okra plus cooked mashed plantains. Of African origin.

Funchi or **Funche** or **Fungee**: plain-cooked cornmeal, served hot or cold as a firm "bread" or a base for other foods. Of African origin.

Funche con Coco: a sweet made by cooking cornmeal with coconut milk and serving cinnamon and brown sugar. (Puerto Rican)

Gazpacho: Spanish dish with a West Indian accent, a hearty "salad" of salt cod, cooked plantains, yautias, potatoes, all tossed with bananas and avocados. In Spain it is a soup; not here.

Gumbo: begun with a roux and a court bouillon plus a variety of vegetables, always including okra, plus seasonings of cumin, thyme, and chilies. In the last few minutes of cooking, cut up seafood is added. The whole dish is served with fluffy white rice.

Habicueles Guidadas: Puerto Rican-style "bean pot" made with small pink beans hotly seasoned with chili peppers, and often with ham and calabaza. Served over rice.

Jerk: a spicy hot blend of seasonings – allspice, cinnamon, garlic, black pepper, Worcestershire sauce, scallions and hot pepper sauce – rubbed into chicken or other meat or fish a few hours before cooking. (Jamaican.)

Jug Jug: a kind of pudding made with salted ground meats, pigeon peas, and corn flour steamed together. Some say it was first prepared by Scottish settlers as a substitute for their **Haggis**. A dish from Barbados especially for Christmastime.

Mofongo: a dish based on mashed cooked plantain, garlic and pork cracklings but served in many ways: as a spread for bread, rolled in tiny balls and deep-fried, or baked like a large pancake, crisply brown, to be served in wedges as a side dish for meat or fish or for breakfast with eggs. (Puerto Rican)

Ortaniques: a hybrid of sweet oranges and tangerines. They have a loose skin and somewhat flattened appearance belying the sweet juicy fruit within.

Pan de Agua: crusty, chewy white bread. (Puerto Rican)

Papas a la Hunacaina: a tart yellow dressing made from fresh cheese and lime juice and seasoned with cayenne and turmeric cooked in oil. Served over hard eggs, potatoes or green salad.

Pawpaw: also called **Papaya** – familiar as a golden pear-shaped fruit with pleasant peach-colored flesh and shiny round black seeds.

Peanut-Rice Salad: a salad of seasoned cooked rice dressed with lime juice and peanut oil, garnished with fresh orange and pineapple slices and topped with chopped roasted peanuts.

Petit Punch or "**Tee Paunsh**": traditionally served on a tray with each ingredient separate for the drinker to mix to taste: rum, lime wedges, ice, and a small bottle of thick sugar syrup.

Picklises: relish made in Haiti by placing cleaned, cut up vegetables in a crock and topping with vinegar. After one week in a cool place they are considered ready to eat.

Piononos: long strips of fried plantain wrapped and secured around a well-seasoned meat filling. The whole is then egg-dipped and quickly fried. Served with rice and beans.

Pomelo: the largest of all the citrus fruits and not as juicy. Also called **Shaddock**.

Ponque: simple light Puerto Rican sponge cake, or pound cake.

Rice and **Peas**: really a dish of rice and red beans. Jamaican and well spiced.

Ropa Vieja: cooked sliced flank steak strips cooked in a casserole with a sauce made from **achiote**, garlic, pepper, chilies, tomatoes, cinnamon, and cloves. Served with rice and peas or fried plantains. Literally, "old clothes," the dish could actually be made with any leftover cooked meats cut into thin strips.

Roti: an East Indian generic name for breads, but used in Jamaica to mean a flat Indian bread filled with a spicy hot meat mixture or a similarly hot vegetable curry.

Run Down: a mixture of lime-marinated fish, coconut milk, tomatoes, and seasoning, like Mexico's **Ceviche**. Eaten with boiled bananas as a main dish or as an appetizer, or the mixture may be used as a stuffing, e.g., in breadfruit. (Jamaican)

Sancocho: vegetable stew flavored with bits of pork, beef flank, and ham, often including **yautias**, onions, yams, peppers, and sometimes small "dumplings" of mashed plantain. (Puerto Rican.)

Sapodillo or **Naseberry:** It looks like a small brown potato but is a fruit with sweet juicy orange flesh eaten (like a kiwi) by scooping out from the inedible skin.

Sazon Preparado: a blend of peppers and tomatoes, garlic, onions and seasonings all well simmered then cooled and bottled, ready to be used as a base for cooking or a seasoning to be added; a type of **Sofrito**. (Dominican Republic)

Sopa Borracha: literally, "drunken soup," a light cake, poured over with a hot wine syrup then covered with meringue.

Sopon de Garbanzos: a hearty vegetable soup made with pig's feet, chickpeas, tripe, and mixed available vegetables.

SOURCES

Chapter One: African

Badenhorst, Judy, Glenda Moddy, and Sarah Seymour. *The Old Cape Farmstall Cookbook*. Cape Town: Citadel Press, 1983.

Barbour, Andrew. *Fodor's South Africa*. New York: Fodor Travel Publications, 1996.

Berry, LaVerle, ed. *Ghana: A Country Study*. Area Handbook Series. Washington, DC: US Government Printing Office, 1995.

Canada. Department of Manpower and Immigration, 1974. *Immigration '73: Quarterly Statistics*.

Chapin-Metz, Henen, ed. *Somalia: A Country Study*. Area Handbook Series. Washington, DC: US Government Printing Office, 1993.

Cheifitz, Phillippa, and Shirley Friedman. *Meals for a Month*. Cape Town: David Philip, 1977.

Collelo, Thomas, ed. *Chad: A Country Study*. Washington, DC: US Government Printing Office, 1990.

Copage, Eric V. *Kwanzaa: An African-American Celebration of Culture and Cooking*. New York: William Morrow & Co., 1991.

De Andrade, Margarette. *Brazilian Cookery: Traditional and Modern*. Rutland, Vermont: Charles E. Tuttle Co., 1965.

De Villiers, Marq, and Sheila Hirtle. *Into Africa*. Toronto: Key Porter Books, n.d.

Der Haroutunian, Artero. *North African Cookery*. London: Century Publishing, 1985.

Funk and Wagnalls Standard Reference Encyclopedia. New York: Standard Reference Works Publishing Co., 1967.

Gelfand, Michael. *Diet and Tradition in an African Culture*. Edinburgh: E. & S. Livingstone, 1971.

Gibril, Martin. *African Food and Drink*. UK: Wayland Publishers, 1989.

Hafner, Dorinda. *Taste of Africa*. Berkeley, CA: Ten Speed Press, 1993.

Handloff, Robert E., ed. *Côte d'Ivoire*. Area Handbook Series. Washington, DC: US Government Printing Office, 1991.

Harris, Jessica B. *Africa's Gifts to New World Cooking: Iron Pots & Wooden Spoons*. New York: Macmillan, 1989.

The Johannesburg Women's Zionist League. *International Goodwill Recipe Book*. Johannesburg, South Africa, 1969.

Karle, Marina. *Fodor's Touring Guides: Kenya*. New York: Prentice Hall, 1991.

King, Maurice. *Nutrition for Developing Countries*. Nairobi: Oxford University Press, 1972.

Knight, C. Gregory, and James L. Newman. *Contemporary Africa: Geography and Change*. Englewood Cliffs, NJ: Prentice Hall, 1976.

Lewis, I. M. *A Modern History of Somalia: Nation and State in the Horn of Africa*. London: Westview Press, 1988.

———— *Understanding Somalia: Guide to Culture, History & Social Institiutions*. London: Haan Associates, 1993.

May, Jacques. *Ecology of Malnutrition in Middle Africa*. New York: Hafner Publishing Co., 1965.

————. *The Ecology of Malnutrition in the French-speaking Countries of West Africa and Madagascar*. New York: Hafner Publishing Co., 1968.

————. *The Ecology of Malnutrition in Eastern and Western Africa*. New York: Hafner Publishing Co., 1970.

Meditz, Sandra W., and Tina Merrill, eds. *Zaire: A Country Study*. Maryland: Bernau Lanham, 1994.

Mendes, Helen. *The African Heritage Cookbook*. New York: The Macmillan Co., 1971.

Nelson, Howard D., ed. *South Africa: A Country Study*. Area Handbook Series. Washington, DC: US Government Printing, 1991.

Newton, Alex. *Central Africa: A Survival Kit*. Berkeley CA: Lonely Planet Publications, 1989.

Oka, Odinchezo. *Black Academy Cookbook*. Buffalo, NY: Black Academy Press Inc., 1972.

Osman, Anab Mohamed. *Notes on the presentation of Somalis in Canada*. The Somali Canadian Association of Etobicoke, 1992.

Reader's Digest South African Cookbook. Cape Town: The Reader's Digest Association, 1988.

Rosen, Myrna. *Cooking with Myrna Rosen*. UK: Howard Timmins Publishers, 1980.

————. *The New Myrna Rosen Cookbook*. Cape Town: Don Nelsom, 1986.

Ross, Sue. *The Defy Cookbook for South Africa: Countrywide Cooking*. Cape Town: David Philip, 1981.

Sandler, Bea. *The African Cookbook*. New York: World Publishing, 1972.

Trillo, Richard. *The Real Guide: Kenya*. New York: Prentice Hall, 1989.

Ullendorff, Edward. *The Ethiopian: An Introduction to Country & People*. 3rd ed. Oxford: Oxford University Press, 1973.

Van der Post, Laurens, et al. *African Cooking*. New York: Time-Life Books, 1970.

Wasserman, Ursula. "Afrique Gastronomique." *Gourmet*, November, 1962.

Webster's New World Dictionary. New York: The World Publishing Co., 1966.

Chapter Two: Albanian

Gottman, J. *A Geography of Europe*, Vol. I, 3rd ed. New York: Holt, Rinehart and Winston, 1960.

May, Jacques. *The Ecology of Malnutrition in East-Central Europe*. New York: Hafner Publishing Co., 1963.

Nelson, Kay Shaw. *The Eastern European Cookbook*. Chicago: Henry Regnery, 1973.

Rowland, Jean. *Good Food from the Near East*. New York: M. Barrows and Co., 1957.

Seranne, Anne, and Eileen Gaden. *The Best of Near East Cookery*. Garden City, NY: Doubleday & Co., 1964.

Wright, John, ed. *The New York Times 1998 Almanac*. New York: Penguin Group, 1998.

Chapter Three: American

Castle, Coralie, et al. *Peasant Cooking of Many Lands*. San Francisco: 101 Productions, 1972.

Harris, Jessica B. *Africa's Gifts to New World Cooking: Iron Pots and Wooden Spoons*. New York: Macmillan, 1989.

Hewitt, Jean. *New York Times Heritage Cookbook*. New York: G. P. Putnam's Sons, 1972.

Krause, Marie V., and Martha A. Hunscher. *Food, Nutrition and Diet Therapy*. Philadelphia: W. B. Saunders Co., 1972.

Seranne, Anne, ed. *General Federation of Women's Clubs Cookbook: America Cooks*. New York: G. P. Putnam's Sons, 1967.

Shenton, James P. *American Cooking: The Melting Pot*. New York: Time-Life Books, 1971.

Tannahill, Reay. *Food in History*. New York: Stein and Day, 1973.

Thomas, Gertrude I. *Foods of Our Forefathers*. Philadelphia: F. A. Davis Co., 1941.

Walter, Eugene, et al. *American Cooking: Southern Style*. New York: Time-Life Books, 1971.

Chapter Four: Armenian

Encyclopedia Canadiana. Toronto: Grolier of Canada, 1970.

Leaf, Alexander. "Observations of a Peripatetic Gerontologist." *Nutrition Today*, Sept./Oct. 1973.

Norman, Barbara. *The Russian Cookbook*. Toronto: Bantam Books, 1970.

Papashvily, Helen, and George Papashvily. *Russian Cooking*. New York: Time-Life Books, 1969.

Polvay, Marina. "Cuisines of Russia." *Gourmet*, February 1974.

Rowland, Joan. *Good Food from the Near East.* New York: M. Barrows and Co., 1957.

Uvezian, Sonia. *The Cuisine of Armenia.* New York: Harper and Row, 1974.

Wright, John, ed. *The New York Times 1998 Almanac.* New York: Penguin Group, 1998.

Chapter Five: Australian

"Australians Told to Eat Less Steak, More Curries." *London Free Press,* August 24, 1974.

CD-ROM. *Brittanica CD.* Encylopedia Brittanica Inc. 1995.

Chambers, Elaine. *Australian Dried Fruit Cookbook.* Rigby Ltd., 1972.

Commonwealth Bureau of Census and Statistics. *Australia at a Glance.* 1973.

Hembrow, Sally. *Outdoor Cookbook.* Rigby Ltd., 1972.

Howat, Val, and Gwen Mierisch. *Presbyterian Women's Missionary Union Cookery Book.* Melbourne: Lothian Publishing Co., 1973.

Marshall, Anne. *Australian and New Zealand Complete Book of Cookery.* Sydney: Paul Hamlyn, 1971.

Nation, Rhoda. *Mary Bought a Little Lamb and This Is How She Cooked It.* Wellington: A. H. and A. W. Reed, 1973.

Osborne, Charles, ed. *Australia, New Zealand and the South Pacific: A Handbook.* New York: Praeger Publishers, 1970.

Rabling, Harold, and Patrick Hamilton. *Under the Southern Cross: The Story of Australia.* London: Macmillan and Co., 1961.

Skimer, Gwen. *The Cuisine of the South Pacific.* Auckland: Hodder & Stoughton, 1983.

Steinberg, Raphael, et al. *Pacific and Southeast Asian Cooking.* New York: Time-Life Books, 1970.

Wright, John, ed. *The New York Times 1998 Almanac.* New York: Penguin Group, 1998.

Chapter Six: Austrian

Encyclopedia Canadiana. Toronto: Grolier of Canada, 1970.

Langseth-Christensen, Lillian. *Gourmet's Old Vienna Cookbook: A Viennese Memoir.* New York: Gourmet Distributing Corp., 1959.

May, Jacques. *The Ecology of Malnutrition in Central and South-Eastern Europe.* New York: Hafner Publishing Co., 1966.

Morton, Marcia Coleman. *The Art of Viennese Cooking.* Garden City, NY: Doubleday & Co., 1963.

Rhode, Irma. *The Viennese Cookbook.* New York: Grosset & Dunlap, 1951.

Waldo, Myra. *Myra Waldo's Travel and Motoring Guide to Europe, 1974.* London: Collier Macmillan, 1974.

Wechsberg, Joseph, et al. *The Cooking of Vienna's Empire.* New York: Time-Life Books, 1968.

Chapter Seven: Baltic Peoples

Aavik, Johannes, et al. *Aspects of Estonian Culture.* London: Boreas Publishing Co., 1961.

Bilmanis, Alfred. "Latvia as an Independent State." Washington, DC: Latvian Legation, 1947.

Blodnieks, Adolfs. *The Undefeated Nation.* New York: Robert Speller and Sons, 1960.

Encyclopedia Canadiana. Toronto: Grolier of Canada, 1970.

Estonia, A Story of a Nation. New York: Estonian House, 1974.

Florinsky, M. T., ed. *McGraw-Hill Encyclopedia of Russia and the Soviet Union.* New York: McGraw-Hill Books, 1961.

Gerutis, Albertis, ed. *Lithuania 700 Years.* New York: Manyland Books, 1969.

Gibbon, John Murray. *Canadian Mosaic: The Making of a Nation*. Toronto: McClelland and Stewart Ltd., 1938.

Norman, Barbara. *The Russian Cookbook*. Toronto: Bantam Books, 1970.

Orav, Liia. *Eesta Rahva Vanu Kombeid*. 1965.

Papashvily, Helen, and George Papashvily. *Russian Cooking*. New York: Time-Life Books, 1969.

Ratsep, A. *Matkates Mooda Kodumaad*. Tallin, 1964.

Saviauk, V. *Tuhandeist Sudameist*. Tallin, 1956.

Sild, E. *Keedu-ja Majapidamis Raamat*. I Osa, Iosa.

Suziedelis, Simas, ed. *Encyclopedia Lituanica*. Boston: J. Kapocius, 1972.

Note: Thanks and sincere appreciation to Kaljo and Asta Loone and their daughter Hilja, of London, Ontario, for translating the above Estonian sources and providing much background material.

The World Book Encyclopedia. Chicago: Field Enterprises, Educational Corp., 1970.

Wright, John, ed. *New York Times 1998 Almanac*. New York: Penguin Group, 1998.

Chapter Eight: Belgian

Beal, Doone. "The Appeal of Antwerp." *Gourmet*, February 1973.

Donovan, Maria Kozslik. "Gourmet Holidays: The Belgium Coast." *Gourmet*, April 1971.

Encyclopedia Canadiana. Toronto: Grolier of Canada, 1970.

Hazelton, Nika. *The Belgian Cookbook*. New York: Atheneum, 1970.

Langer, William. *An Encyclopedia of World History*. Boston: Houghton Mifflin Co., 1952.

Chapter Nine: Belorussian

Encyclopedia Canadiana. Toronto: Grolier of Canada, 1970.

Funk and Wagnalls Standard Reference Encyclopedia. New York: Standard Reference Works Publishing Co., 1967.

Norman, Barbara. *The Russian Cookbook*. Toronto: Bantam Books, 1970.

Stankevich, M. *Greatlitvanian (Byelorussian sic)Cookbook*. Ottawa: National Museums of Canada, 1972.

The Globe and Mail, Toronto, Canada. June 24, 1994.

Chapter Ten: Bulgarian

Castle, Coralie, et al. *Peasant Cooking of Many Lands*. San Francisco: 101 Productions, 1972.

Encyclopedia Canadiana. Toronto: Grolier of Canada, 1970.

Field, Michael, and Frances Field. *A Quintet of Cuisines*. New York: Time-Life Books, 1970.

Focus on Bulgaria. *Globe & Mail*, April 29, 1995. Toronto.

Funk and Wagnalls Standard Reference Encyclopedia. New York: Standard Reference Works Publishing Co., 1967.

May, Jacques. *Ecology of Malnutrition in Central and South Eastern Europe*. New York: Hafner Publishing Co., 1966.

Nelson, Kay Shaw. *The Eastern European Cookbook*. Chicago: Henry Regnery Co., 1973.

Perl, Lila. *Yugoslavia, Romania, Bulgaria: New Era in the Balkans*. Toronto: Thomas Nelson and Sons, 1970.

Rowland, Jean. *Good Food from the Near East*. New York: M. Barrows and Co., 1957.

Seranne, Anne, and Eileen Gaden. *The Best of Near East Cookery*. Garden City, NY: Doubleday & Co., 1964.

Chapter Eleven: Canadian

Abrahamson, Una. *God Bless Our Home*. Toronto: Burns & McEachern Ltd., 1966.

Anderson, Olga H. "Boiled Dinner Still Preferred." *Canadian Hospital*, February 1962.

———. "Posies and Doughboys." *Newfoundland Home Economics Association Newsletter*, May 1969.

Assiniwi, Bernard. *Indian Recipes*. Toronto: Copp Clark Publishing, 1972.

L'Association Canadienne des Educateurs de Langue Française. *Facets of French Canada*. Montreal: Editions Fide, 1967.

Barbeau, Marius. *Indian Days on the Western Prairies*. Ottawa: National Museum of Canada, 1968.

———. *Quebec: Where Ancient France Lingers*. Toronto: Macmillan Company of Canada, 1936.

Beaulieu, Mirelle. *The Cooking of Provincial Quebec*. Toronto: Gage Publishing Co., 1975.

Benoit, Mme. Jehane. *The Canadian Cookbook*. Toronto: Pagurian Press, 1970.

Benson, George. *Historical Record of the Edwardsburg and Canada Starch Companies*. 1958.

Canada. Department of Agriculture. *Canada's Agriculture, The First 100 Years*. Ottawa: Queen's Printer, 1967.

Canada. Department of Secretary of State, Citizenship Branch. *The Canadian Family Tree*. Ottawa: Queen's Printer, 1967.

Careless, J. M. S. *Canada: A Story of Challenge*. Toronto: Macmillan Company of Canada, 1972.

CD-ROM. *The 1998 Canadian & World Encyclopedia*. Toronto: McClelland & Stewart, 1997.

Clark, S. D. *The Developing Canadian Community*. Toronto: University of Toronto Press, 1962.

Deering, Rosemary. *Life of the Loyalists*. Toronto: Fitzhenry & Whiteside, 1975.

Doiron, Nancy. "Fish and Seafood in PEI. Foodways." Student paper. Charlottetown: University of Prince Edward Island, 1975.

Doyle, Leona. "Festive Foods on PEI." Student paper. Charlottetown: University of Prince Edward Island, 1975.

Drucker, Philip. *Cultures of the North Pacific Coast*. New York: Chandler Publishing Co., 1965.

Eccles, W. J. *The Canadian Frontier 1534-1760*. New York: Holt, Rinehart and Winston, 1969.

Ellis, Eleanor. *Northern Cookbook*. Ottawa: The Queen's Printer, 1967.

Encyclopedia Canadiana. Toronto: Grolier of Canada, 1970.

Finnegan, Joan. *Canadian Colonial Cooking*. Toronto: NC Press Limited, 1976.

Flowers, A. D. *Loyalists of Bay Chaleur*. Saint John, New Brunswick.

Fort George, Quebec. Traditional Indian Recipes. Cobalt, ON.: Highway Book Shop, 1971.

Gagne, Mme. Charles. *Quand les bateaux reviennent. Recettes typiques de la Gaspésie et des Iles-de-la Madeleine*. Ottawa: Leméac Inc., 1973.

Gesner, Abraham. *New Brunswick with Notes for Emigrants*. London: Simmonds & Ward, 1849.

Guillet, Edwin C. *Pioneer Days in Upper Canada*. Toronto: University of Toronto Press, 1964.

———. *The Great Migration: The Atlantic Crossing by Sailing Ship Since 1770*. Toronto: University of Toronto Press, 1963.

Halpert, Herbert, and G.M. Story. *Christmas Mumming in Newfoundland*. Toronto: University of Toronto Press, 1969.

Hatheway, C. L. *The History of New Brunswick from Its First Settlement*. Fredericton: James P. A. Philips, 1846.

Heidenreich, Conrad. *Huronia*. Toronto: McClelland & Stewart Ltd., 1971.

Henrikson, Georg. *Hunters in the Barrens*. St. John's, Newfoundland: Institute of Social and Economic Research, Memorial University of Newfoundland, 1973.

Houston, James. *The White Dawn*. New York: Harcourt Brace Jovanovich, 1971.

Johnston, Charles M., ed. *The Valley of the Six Nations*. Toronto: University of Toronto Press, 1964.

Ladies Auxiliary of the Lunenberg Hospital Society. *The Dutch Oven*. Lunenberg Nova Scotia: Progress Enterprise Printers, 1953.

Lawson, Jessie I, and Jean Maccallum Sweet. *This is New Brunswick*. Toronto: The Ryerson Press, 1951.

Leechman, Douglas. *Native Tribes of Canada*. Toronto: Gage Publishing, n.d.

Lindal, Valdimar Jacobson. *The Saskatchewan Icelanders: A Strand of the Canadian Fabric*. Winnipeg: Columbia Press, 1955.

Lowenberg, Miriam, et al. *Food and Man*. New York: John Wiley and Sons, 1968.

MacGibbon, Duncan. *The Canadian Grain Trade*. Toronto: Macmillan Company of Canada, 1932.

Macklem, Michael, trans. *Champlain: Voyages to New France (1615-1618)*. Ottawa: Oberon Press, 1970.

Magrath, C. A. *Canada's Growth and Some Problems Facing It*. Ottawa: The Mortimer Press, 1910.

McAlduff, Angela. "Small Fruits and PEI Foodways." Student paper. Charlottetown: University of Prince Edward Island, 1975.

McFeat, Tom, ed. *Indians of the North Pacific Coast*. Toronto: McClelland and Stewart Carleton Library, 1966.

Mowat, Farley, and John de Visser. *This Rock Within the Sea: A Heritage Lost*. Boston/Toronto: Atlantic Little, Brown Books, 1968.

Moyles, R. G. *Complaints is Many and Various But the Odd Divil Likes It: 19th Century Views of Newfoundland*. Toronto: Peter Martin Associates, 1975.

Murray, Jean, ed. *The Newfoundland Journal of Aaron Thomas 1794*. Toronto: Longman Canada, 1968.

Nightingale, Marie. *Out of Old Nova Scotia Kitchens*. New York: Charles Scribner's Sons, 1971.

Norris, John. *Strangers Entertained*. Vancouver: Evergreen Press, 1971.

Olsen's Loyalist Day Scrapbook. In Saint John Regional Library Scrapbook Collection, Saint John, New Brunswick.

Paget, Amelia M. *The People of the Plains*. Toronto: William Briggs, 1909.

Parkham, Francis. *The Jesuits in North America in the Seventeenth Century*. Toronto: George N. Morang and Co. Ltd., 1900.

Peterson, Martin S, and Donald K. Tressler. *Food Technology the World Over*. Westport, CT.: Avi Publishing Co., 1963.

Powers, William K. *Indians of the Northern Plains*. New York: G. P. Putnam & Sons, 1969.

Pyke, Magnus. *Synthetic Food*. London: John Murray Ltd., 1970.

Quimby, George Irving. *Indian Culture and European Trade Goods*. Madison: University of Wisconsin Press, 1966.

————. *Indian Life in Upper Great Lakes*. Chicago: University of Chicago Press, 1960.

Reaman, George Elmore. *The Trail of the Black Walnut*. Toronto: McClelland & Stewart, 1957.

————. *The Trail of the Iroquois Indians*. Toronto: Peter Martin Associates, 1967.

Ritzenthaler, Robert, and Pat Ritzenthaler. *The Woodland Indians of the Eastern Great Lakes*. Garden City, NY: Natural History Press, 1970.

Robotti, Frances D., and Peter J. Robotti. *French Cooking in the New World*. Garden City, N.Y.: Doubleday and Co., 1967.

Rush, Gary B. *The Supermarket Storybook*. Vancouver, 1972.

Schaeffer, Otto. "When the Eskimo Comes to Town." *Nutrition Today*, Nov./Dec. 1971.

Smallwood, J. R. "Life Today in Newfoundland." *The Book of Newfoundland*. St. John's: Newfoundland Book Publishers Ltd., 1967.

Societe St. Thomas d'Aquin. *La Cuisine Acadienne/Acadian Cuisine*. Charlottetown, PEI, 1976.

Stephanson, Vilhjalmer. "Food and Food Habits in Alaska and Northern Canada." *Human Nutrition Historic and Scientific*, edited by Iago Galston. New York: International Universities Press, 1960.

Surtees, Ursula. "LAK-LA HAI-EE." *Interior Salish Food Preparation*. Lamont, Surtees, Canada, 1974.

Szezawinski, Adam F., and Nancy J. Turner. *Wild Green Vegetables of Canada*. National Museums of Canada. 1980.

Tannahill, Reay. *Food in History*. New York: Stein and Day, 1973.

Thompson, Charles Thomas. *Patterns of Housekeeping in Two Eskimo Settlements*. Ottawa: The Queen's Printer, 1969.

Traill, Catharine Parr. *The Canadian Settler's Guide*. Toronto: McClelland & Stewart Ltd., 1969.

Vanstone, James. *Athapaskan Adaptations: Hunters and Fishermen of the Subarctic Forests*. Chicago: Aldine Pub. Co., 1974.

Walworth, Arthur. *Cape Breton, Isle of Romance*. Toronto: Longmans Green and Co., 1948.

Waterston, Elizabeth. *Canadian Portraits, Pioneers in Agriculture*. Toronto: Clarke, Irwin and Co., 1957.

Wherry, Joseph H. *The Totem Pole Indians*. New York: Wilfred Funk, 1964.

Wright, E. C. *The Loyalists of New Brunswick*. Available from the author, P. O. Box 7110, Wolfville, Nova Scotia.

Chapter Twelve: Chinese

Bodde, Dirk. *Annual Customs and Festivals in Peking*. Hong Kong: Hong Kong University Press, 1965.

Burkhardt, V. R. *Chinese Creeds & Customs*. Hong Kong: South China Morning Post Ltd., 1982.

CD-ROM. *The 1998 Canadian & World Encyclopedia*. Toronto: McClelland & Stewart, 1997.

Castle, Coralie, et al. *Peasant Cooking of Many Lands*. San Francisco: 101 Productions, 1972.

Chang, K. C. *Food in Chinese Culture*. New Haven & London: Yale University Press, 1977.

Dore, Henry. *Researches into Chinese Superstitions*. Taipei: Ch'eng-Wen Publishing Co., 1966.

Froud, Nina. *Far Eastern Cooking for Pleasure*. London: Hamlyn, 1971.

Gall, Timothy L., ed. *World Encyclopedia of Cultures and Daily Life*. Vol. 3. Detroit: Gale Publishers, 1998.

Hahn, Emily, et al. *The Cooking of China*. New York: Time-Life Books, 1968.

Hsu-Balzer, Eileen. *China Day by Day*. New Haven: University Press, 1974.

Hu, Chang-Tu, et al. *China: Its People, Its Society, Its Culture*. New Haven: Hraf Press, 1960.

Kaplan, Frederic M., Julian M. Sobin, and Arne de Keijzer. *The China Guidebook*. Boston: Houghton Mifflin, 1993-94.

Kolb, Albert. *East Asia: China, Japan, Korea, Vietnam: A Geography of a Cultural Region*. London: Methuen and Co., 1971.

Lo, Keweth. *The Encyclopedia of Chinese Regional Cooking*. London: Octopus Books, 1984.

Ma, Nancy Chi. *Mrs. Ma's Chinese Cookbook*. Rutland, Vermont, and Tokyo: Charles E. Tuttle Publishers, 1970.

May, Jacques. *The Ecology of Malnutrition in the Far and Near East*. New York: Hafner Publishing Co., 1961.

Miller, Gloria Bley. *The Thousand Recipe Chinese Cookbook*. New York: Grosset & Dunlap, 1970.

Munro, Ross H. "China Molds Minds of Minorities." *Globe & Mail*, June 2, 1976, Toronto.

Ramondt, Joanne. "1,000 Londoners Celebrate Advent of Chinese 'Year of the Tiger.'" *London Free Press*, January 24, 1974.

Rosenberg, Monda. "Chinese Feasts Will Launch Year of Dragon." *Toronto Star*, January 28, 1976.

Spunt, Georges. *The Step-by-Step Chinese Cookbook*. Toronto: Fitzhenry and Whiteside, 1973.

Stokes, J., and G. Stokes. *The People's Republic of China*. London: Ernest Benn Ltd., 1975.

The Globe and Mail, "International news," Toronto, Canada. May 23, 1997.

Waley, Arthur. *Translations from the Chinese*. New York: Alfred A. Knopf & Co., 1941.

Wang, Lydia. *Chinese Cookbook*. Tokyo: Kamakura-Shobo Publishing Co., 1971.

Winfield, G. F. *China: The Land and the People*. New York: Wm. Sloane Assoc., 1948.

Wittfogel, Karl A. *Food and Society in China and India: Human Nutrition, Historic and Scientific*. New York: International Universities Press, 1960.

Witzel, Anne. "Chinese Immigrants and China: An Introduction to the Multi-Medium Package on China." Research Department, Toronto Board of Education, 1969.

Wright, John W., ed. *The New York Times 1998 Almanac*. New York: Penguin Group, 1998.

Yeung, David L., Lillian W.Y. Cheung, and Jean H. Sabry. "The Hot-Cold Food Concept in Chinese Culture and its Application in a Canadian-Chinese Community." *Journal of the Canadian Dietetic Association*. Vol. 34, no. 4, winter 1973.

Chapter Thirteen: Czechs & Slovaks

Brizova, Joza, et al. *The Czechoslovak Cookbook*. New York: Crown Publishers, 1965.

Canada. Department of the Secretary of State, Citizenship Branch. *The Canadian Family Tree*. Ottawa: Queen's Printer, 1967.

Castle, Coralie, et al. *Peasant Cooking of Many Lands*. San Francisco: 101 Productions, 1972.

Funk and Wagnalls Standard Reference Encyclopedia. New York: Standard Reference Works Publishing Co., 1967.

Kane, Robert S. *Eastern Europe A to Z*. Garden City, N.Y.: Doubleday & Co., 1968.

May, Jacques. *The Ecology of Malnutrition in Central and South-Eastern Europe*. New York: Hafner Publishing Co., 1966.

Nelson, Kay Shaw. *The Eastern European Cookbook*. Chicago: Henry Regnery Co., 1973.

The Globe & Mail. "International News", Toronto, Canada. May 23, 1997.

Wechsberg, Joseph. *The Cooking of Vienna's Empire*. New York: Time-Life Books, 1968

Wechsberg, Joseph. "Traditional Czech Cookery." *Gourmet*, April 1973.

Chapter Fourteen: Danish

Barry, Naomi. "Gourmet Holidays: Copenhagen." *Gourmet*, May 1970.

Brown, Dale. *The Cooking of Scandinavia*. New York: Time-Life Books, 1968.

Castle, Coralie, et al. *Peasant Cooking of Many Lands*. San Francisco: 101 Productions, 1972.

Encyclopedia Canadiana. Toronto: Grolier of Canada, 1970.

Fielding, Temple. *Fielding's Travel Guide to Europe*. 1973 ed. New York: Fielding Publications Inc., 1972.

Funk and Wagnalls Standard Reference Encyclopedia. New York: Standard Reference Works Publishing Co., 1967.

Hardisty, Jytte. *Scandinavian Cooking for Pleasure*. London: Paul Hamlyn, 1970.

Hazelton, Nika. *The Art of Danish Cooking*. New York: Doubleday & Co., 1964.

Waldo, Myra. *Myra Waldo's Travel and Motoring Guide to Europe, 1974*. London: Collier Macmillan Publishers, 1974.

Chapter Fifteen: Dutch

Bates, Johanna (van der Zeijst), and Jan Walrabenstein. *Let's go Dutch Again*. Regina, SK.: Centax Books, 1994.

Bennett, Margaret. "Tiptoe through the Spargel." *Gourmet*, June 1972.

Brown, Dale. "A Dutch Celebration." *Gourmet*, December 1971.

Encyclopedia Canadiana. Toronto: Grolier of Canada, 1970.

Field, Michael, and Frances Field. *A Quintet of Cuisines*. New York: Time-Life Books, 1970.

Funk and Wagnalls Standard Reference Encyclopedia. New York: Standard Reference Works Publishing Co., 1967.

Halverhout, Helen A. M. *The Netherlands Cookbook*. Amsterdam: De Driehoek, 1957.

Mario, Thomas. "Hot Dutch Treat." *Playboy, n.d.*

Stirum, Countess Van Limburg. *The Art of Dutch Cooking or How the Dutch Treat*. New York: Doubleday & Co., 1961.

The Globe and Mail, "St. Nicholas Under Attack as Christmas Symbol," Toronto, Canada. December 14, 1996.

Thomas, Gertrude I. *Foods of Our Forefathers*. Philadelphia: F. A. Davis & Co., 1941.

Waldo, Myra. *Myra Waldo's Travel and Motoring Guide to Europe, 1974*. London: Collier Macmillan, 1974.

Chapter Sixteen: Egyptian

Baldachin, Yolande. "Savoury Secrets from the Middle East." *Globe & Mail*, April 25, 1974.

Funk and Wagnalls Standard Reference Encyclopedia. New York: Standard Reference Works Publishing Co., 1967.

Jacob, Heinrich Eduard. *Coffee: The Epic of a Commodity*. New York: Viking Press, 1955.

May, Jacques. *The Ecology of Malnutrition in the Far and Near East*. New York: Hafner Publishing Co., 1961.

Nickles, Harry G., et al. *Middle Eastern Cookery*. New York: Time-Life Books, 1969.

Rowland, Jean. *Good Food from the Near East*. New York: M. Barrows and Co., 1957.

Seranne, Anne, and Eileen Gaden. *The Best of Near East Cookery*. Garden City, N.Y.: Doubleday & Co., 1964.

Zane, Eva. *Middle Eastern Cookery*. San Francisco: 101 Productions, 1974.

Chapter Seventeen: English

Bailey, Adrian, et al. *The Cooking of the British Isles*. New York: Time-Life Books, 1969.

"Cumbria." *Lakeland Cookery*. Clapham, England: Dalesman Publishing Co., Ltd., 1973.

Dunan, Marcel, et al. *Larousse Encyclopedia of Modern History: From 1500 to the Present Day*. New York: Paul Hamlyn, 1975.

English Tourist Board Information. *Traditional English and Regional Food*. London: British Government Office.

Evans, Hilary, and Mary Evans. The Victorians: *At Home and at Work*. New York: Arco Publishing Co., 1973.

Hart, Roger. *English Life in Chaucer's Day*. London: Wayland Publishers, 1973.

Hutchins, Sheila. *English Recipes and Others*. London: Methuen and Co., 1967.

Know Your Foreigner: The British. Toronto: Southam Business Publications.

Lands and Peoples: Europe. Vol. 1. New York: Grolier Inc., 1972.

Langer, William, ed. *An Encyclopedia of World History*. Boston: Houghton Mifflin Co., 1962.

Morris, Jan. "Rolls-Royceness." *The New York Times Magazine*, February 2, 1975.

Ogrizek, Dore, ed. *Great Britain: England, Scotland and Wales*. New York: McGraw-Hill Book Co., 1949.

Priestley, J. B. *The English*. New York: Viking Press, 1973.

Pullar, Philippa. *Consuming Passions*. London: Hamish Hamilton, 1970.

Spicer, Dorothy. *From an English Oven*. New York: Women's Press, 1948.

The Globe & Mail, "Tea Council Wants Britons to Fill Their Cups," Toronto, Canada. March 4, 1995.

Trager, James. *The Foodbook*. New York: Avon, 1972.

Chapter Eighteen: Filipino

Alejandro, Reynaldo. *The Philippine Cookbook*. New York: Coward-McCann Inc., 1982.

Brennan, Jennifer. *The Cuisines of Asia*. New York: St. Martin's Press, 1984.

Castle, Coralie, et al. *Peasant Cooking of Many Lands*. San Francisco: 101 Productions, 1972.

Day, Beth. "Philippine Fare." *Gourmet*, June 1974.

De Roos, Robert. "The Philippines: Freedom's Pacific Frontier." *National Geographic*, September 1966.

Froud, Nina. *Far Eastern Cooking for Pleasure*. London: Paul Hamlyn, 1971.

Funk and Wagnalls Standard Reference Encyclopedia. New York: Standard Reference Works Publishing Co., 1967.

London Free Press, "Filipino Family Sometimes Has to Live with No Income." November 13, 1974.

Nelson, Raymond. *The Philippines*. New York: Walker and Co., 1968.

Steinberg, Raphael, et al. *Pacific and South-East Asian Cooking*. New York: Time-Life Books, 1970.

Wernstedt, Frederick L. *The Philippine Island World: A Physical, Cultural and Regional Geography*. Berkeley: University of California Press, 1967.

Chapter Nineteen: Finnish

Brown, Dale. *The Cooking of Scandinavia*. New York: Time-Life Books, 1968.

Castle, Coralie, et al. *Peasant Cooking of Many Lands*. San Francisco: 101 Productions, 1972.

Encyclopedia Canadiana. Toronto: Grolier of Canada, 1970.

Fielding, Temple. *Fielding's Travel Guide to Europe*. New York: Fielding Publications, 1972.

Funk and Wagnalls Standard Reference Encyclopedia. New York: Standard Reference Works Publishing Co., 1967.

Graves, William. "Finland, Plucky Neighbour of Soviet Russia." *National Geographic*, May 1968.

Heinonen, Rev. Arvi I. *Finnish Friends in Canada*. United Church of Canada, 1950.

Ojakangas, Beatrice. *The Finnish Cookbook*. New York: Crown Publishers, 1974.

Simpson, Colin. *The Viking Circle*. London: Hodder & Stoughton, 1967.

Waldo, Myra. *Myra Waldo's Travel and Motoring Guide to Europe, 1974*. London: Collier Macmillan, 1974.

Chapter Twenty: French

Barry, Naomi. "The Basque Country." *Gourmet*, July 1970.

Child, Julia, Louisette Bertholle, and Simone Beck. *Mastering the Art of French Cooking*. New York: Alfred A. Knopf, 1968.

Claiborne, Craig, and Pierre Franey. *Classic French Cooking*. New York: Time-Life Books, 1970.

Curnonsky, Prince Elu des Gastronomes. *Cuisine et Vins du France*. Paris: Larousse, 1953.

De Gramont, Sanche. *The French: Portrait of a People*. New York: G. P. Putnam's Sons, 1969.

Escudier, Jean-Noel, and Peta J. Fuller. *The Wonderful Food of Provence*. New York: Harper and Row, Publishers, 1988.

Feibleman, Peter S., et al. *American Cooking: Creole and Acadian*. New York: Time-Life Books, 1971.

Fisher, M. K. F., et al. *The Cooking of Provincial France*. New York: Time-Life Books, 1968.

Funk and Wagnalls Standard Reference Encyclopedia. New York: Standard Reference Works Publishing Co., 1967.

Hughes-Gilbey, Ann. *French Country Kitchen*. New Jersey: Chartwell Books Inc.,1983.

La Cuisine Francaise. New York: The Cultural Services of the French Embassy, 1964.

McCall's Introduction to French Cooking. New York: McCall Publishing Co., 1971.

Montagne, Prosper, and Gottschalk, Dr. *Larousse Gastronomique: The Encyclopedia of Food, Wine and Cooking*. London: Paul Hamlyn, 1961.

Root, Waverley, et al. *The Cooking of Italy*. New York: Time-Life Books, 1968.

Sangster, Dorothy. "In Search of France's Nouvelle Cuisine." *Globe & Mail*, January 31, 1976.

Waldo, Myra. *Myra Waldo's Travel and Motoring Guide to Europe, 1974*. London: Collier Macmillan Publishers, 1974.

Waugh, Alec, et al. *Wines and Spirits*. New York: Time-Life Books, 1968.

Wolfert, Paula. *The Cooking of South-West France*. New York: Doubleday & Company, 1983.

Chapter Twenty-One: German

Adam, Karl Hans. *The Wine and Food Society's Guide to German Cookery*. Cleveland: World Publishing Co., 1967.

Bielefeld, Dr. August Oetker. *Dr. Oetker German Home Baking*. Hannover, Germany: Ceres-Verlag Rudolf-August Oetker KG, Bielefeld, 1970.

Castle, Coralie, et al. *Peasant Cooking of Many Lands*. San Francisco: 101 Productions, 1972.

Fodor, Eugene, ed. *Fodor's Germany West and East, 1976*. New York: David McKay Co., 1976.

Hazelton, Nika Standen, et al. *The Cooking of Germany*. New York: Time-Life Books, 1969.

Jacob, Heinrich Eduard. *Coffee: The Epic of a Commodity*. New York: Viking Press, 1935.

Kahler, Eric. *The Germans*. Princeton, NJ: Princeton University Press, 1974.

Langseth-Christensen, Lillian. "Christmastime in Germany." *Gourmet*, December 1972.

————. "The Cuisines of Germany." *Gourmet*, June 1973.

May, Jacques. *The Ecology of Malnutriton in East-Central Europe*. New York: Hafner Publishing Co., 1963.

Morey, George. *West Germany*. London: Macdonald Educational, 1974.

Morgan, Dr. Roger. *Germany 1870-1970*. London: BPC Publications, 1970.

Nelson, Kay Shaw. *The Eastern European Cookbook*. Chicago: Henry Regnery Co., 1973.

Reaman, George Elmore. *The Trail of the Black Walnut*. Toronto: McClelland & Stewart, 1957.

Schuler, Elizabeth. *German Cookery: Mein Kochbuch*. New York: Crown Publishers, 1968.

Sheraton, Mimi. *The German Cookbook: A Complete Guide to Mastering Authentic German Cooking*. New York: Random House, 1965.

Wright, John W., ed. *The New York Times 1998 Almanac*. New York: Penguin Group, 1998.

Chapter Twenty-Two: Greek

Antoniou, C. *Greek Family Life*. Address presented at Greek Intercultural Seminar, Toronto, 1974. Courtesy of Estelle Read, Ministry of Culture and Recreation, Citizenship Bureau, Toronto, Ontario.

Encyclopedia Canadiana. Toronto: Grolier of Canada, 1970.

Gage, Nicholas. *Portrait of Greece*. New York: American Heritage Press (McGraw-Hill), 1971.

Lands and Peoples: *Europe*. New York: Grolier Inc., 1972.

Lianides, Leon. "Easter in Greece." *Gourmet*, April 1974.

Mahaffy, J. P. *What Have the Greeks Done for Modern Civilization?* New York: The Knickerbocker Press, 1909.

May, Jacques. *The Ecology of Malnutrition in East-Central Europe*. New York: Hafner Publishing Co., 1963.

Nickles, Harry G., et al. *Middle Eastern Cooking*. New York: Time-Life Books, 1969.

Paradissus, Chrissa. *The Best Book of Greek Cookery*. Athens-Thessalonika: Estathiadis Bros., 1972.

Report on the Greek Intercultural Seminar Held at St. Barnabas Anglican Church, Toronto, 1974. Courtesy of Estelle Read, Ministry of Culture and Recreation, Citizenship Bureau, Toronto, Ontario.

Rowland, Jean. *Good Food from the Near East*. New York: M. Barrows and Co., 1957.

Selected Recipes of Creek Cooking. Ottawa: Royal Greek Embassy, Press and Information Office, 1972.

Seranne, Anne, and Eileen Gaden. *The Best of Near East Cookery*. Garden City, N.Y.: Doubleday & Co., 1964.

Stubbs, Joyce. *The Home Book of Greek Cookery*. London: Faber & Faber, 1970.

Vickery, Kenton Frank. *Food in Early Greece*. Chicago: University of Illinois, 1936.

Vlassis, George. *The Greeks in Canada*. Ottawa: 1942.

Zane, Eva. *Greek Cooking for the Gods*. San Francisco: 101 Productions, 1970.

Zotos, Stephanos. *The Greeks: Dilemma between Past and Present*. New York: Funk & Wagnalls, 1969.

Chapter Twenty-Three: Hungarian

Ausubel, Nathan. *Pictorial History of the Jewish People*. New York: Crown Publishers, 1962.

Bennett, Pogany, and Clark Bennett. *The Art of Hungarian Cookery*. Garden City, N.Y.: Doubleday & Co., 1954.

CD-ROM. Britannica CD. *The 1998 Canadian & World Encyclopedia*. Toronto: McClelland & Stewart, 1997.

Donovan, Maria Kozslik. "A Hungarian Rhapsody." *Gourmet*, August 1971.

Encyclopedia Canadiana. Toronto: Grolier of Canada, 1970.

Fallon, Steve. *Hungary: A Survival Kit*. Australia: Lonely Planet Publications. 1994.

Funk and Wagnalls Standard Reference Encyclopedia. New York: Standard Reference Works Publishing Co., 1967.

Gall, Timothy L. *Worldmark Encyclopedia of Cultures & Daily Life*. Detroit: Gale, 1997.

Gundel, Karoly. *Hungarian Cookery Book*. Budapest: Athenaeum Printing House, 1956.

Hungarian Review. Budapest, No. 10, 1974.

Isaacson, Rabbi Ben, and Deborah Wigoder. *The International Jewish Encyclopedia*. Prentice-Hall, 1973.

Kosa, John. *Land of Choice: The Hungarians in Canada*. Toronto: University of Toronto Press, 1957.

Lang, George. *The Cuisine of Hungary*. New York: Atheneum, 1971.

———. "The Pastries of Budapest." *Gourmet*, August 1971.

May, Jacques. *The Ecology of Malnutrition in Central and South-Eastern Europe*. New York: Hafner Publishing Co., 1966.

Tannahill, Reay. *Food in History*. New York: Stein and Day, 1974.

Timar, L. J. *A Short History of the Hungarian People in Canada*. Toronto: Across Canada Press, 1957.

Wechsberg, Joseph, et al. *The Cooking of Vienna's Empire*. New York: Time-Life Books, 1968.

Chapter Twenty-Four: Icelandic

Gjerset, Knut. *History of Iceland*. New York: The Macmillan Co., 1924.

Icelandic Food Specialities. New York: Icelandic National Tourist Office.

Leaf, Horace. *Iceland, Yesterday and Today*. London: George Allen and Unwin Ltd., 1949.

Lindal, Amalia. *Ripples from Iceland*. New York: W. W. Norton and Co., 1962.

Lindal, Valdimar Jacobson. *The Saskatchewan Icelanders: A Strand of the Canadian Fabric*. Winnipeg: Columbia Press, 1955.

Simpson, Colin. *The Viking Circle*. London: Hodder and Stoughton Ltd., 1967.

Swaney, Deanna. *Iceland, Greenland & the Faroe Islands*. Australia: Lonely Planet Publications, 1994.

Wright, John W., ed. *The New York Times 1998 Almanac*. New York: Penguin Group, 1998.

Wylie, Betty Jane. "Paradise Revisited." *Gourmet*, March 1961.

Chapter Twenty-Five: Indian

Ballentine, Martha. *Himalayan Mountain Cookery: A Vegetarian Cookbook*. Pennsylvannia: Himalyan International Institute of Yoga Science and Philosophy, 1978.

Beyersbergen, Joanna. "Indian Nutritionist Claims Poverty Not 'Taboos' Cause of Poor Diet." *London Free Press*, June 15, 1974.

Chaudhuri, Amiya. *Traditional Indian Cookery*. New Delhi: Orient, 1990.

Collins, Ruth Philpott. *A World of Curries*. New York: Funk and Wagnalls, 1967.

Fernandez, Jennifer. *100 Easy to Make Goan Dishes*. India: Tarang Paperbacks, 1982.

Funk and Wagnalls Standard Reference Encyclopedia. New York: Standard Reference Works Publishing Co., 1967.

Grosvenor, Donna K., and Gilbert H. Grosvenor. "Ceylon." *National Geographic*, April 1966.

Hare, Rap. *Tasty Dishes of India*. India: D. B. Taraporevala, n.d.

Harris, Marvin. *Cows, Pigs, Wars and Witches*. New York: Random House, 1989.

Jaffrey, Madhur. *An Invitation to Indian Cooking*. New York: Alfred A. Knopf Inc., 1973.

Kaufman and Lakshmanan. *The Art of India's Cookery*. New York: Doubleday & Co., 1964.

Lahnoy, Richard. *The Speaking Tree: A Study of Indian Culture and Society*. London: Oxford University Press, 1971.

Lowenberg, Miriam, et al. *Food and Man*. New York: John Wiley and Sons, 1968.

Marks, Copeland. *The Varied Kitchens of India*. New York: M. Evans & Co. Inc., 1991.

May, Jacques. *The Ecology of Malnutrition in the Far and Near East*. New York: Hafner Publishing Co., 1961.

Mehta, Jeroo. *101 Parsi Recipes*. Bombay: Vakils, Feffer and Simons Private Ltd.,1973.

Norris, John. *Strangers Entertained: A History of the Ethnic Groups of British Columbia.* Vancouver: Evergreen Press, 1971.

Pandya, Michael. *Complete Indian Cookbook.* London: Paul Hamlyn, 1980.

Rau, Santha Rama, et al. *The Cooking of India.* New York: Time-Life Books, 1969.

Reejhsinghani, Aroona. *Delicious Begali Dishes.* Bombay: Jaico Publishing House, 1991.

Rogers, Alisdair, ed. *Peoples & Cultures.* New York: Oxford University Press, 1992.

Sacharoff, Shanta Nimbark. *Flavors of India: Recipes from the Vegetarian Hindu Cuisine.* San Francisco: 101 Productions, 1972.

Sakr, Amid. "Dietary Regulations and Food Habits of Muslims." *Journal of the American Dietetic Association*, February 1971.

Sekiguchi, Shindai. "Zen Diets Condemned." *Journal of the American Dietetic Association*, January 1972.

————. *Zen: A Manual for Westerners.* Japan Publications Inc., 1968.

Singh, Dharam Jit. "Saffron, Sandalwood and Spice." *Gourmet*, September 1958.

Singh, Manju Shivraj. *A Taste of Palace Life: Royal Indian Cookery.* New York: Marshall Cavendish Limited, 1987.

Stroup, Herbert. *Four Religions of Asia.* New York: Harper and Row, 1968.

Taneja, Meera. *The Indian Epicure.* London: Mills & Boon Limited, n.d.

Tarrant, John, ed. *Farming and Food.* New York: Oxford University Press, 1991.

The Roastrian Stree Mandal. *ZSM Cook Book.* Hyderabad. 1986.

Thomas, P. *Festivals and Holidays of India.* Bombay: Taraporevala Sons & Co. Private Ltd., 1971.

Trotta, Geri. "Intriguing India." *Gourmet*, May 1974.

World Graphical Encyclopedia. New York: McGraw-Hill Inc., 1995.

Wright, John W., ed. *The New York Times 1998 Almanac.* New York: Penguin, 1998.

Zaener, R. C., ed. *The Concise Encyclopedia of Living Faiths.* New York: Hawthorn Books, 1959.

Chapter Twenty-Six: Indonesian, Malay, and Singaporean

Brennan, Jennifer. *The Cuisines of Asia.* New York: St. Martin's Press, 1984.

Brooks, Guy, and Victoria Brooks. *Malaysia: A Kick Start for Business Travelers.* Vancouver: Self-Council Press, 1996.

Business Travel Guide: Asia and Pacific. Toronto: SP Travel Books, 1989.

Devine and Bragmati, eds. *Asian Customs and Manners.* New York: St. Martin's Press, 1986.

Finlay, Hugh, and Peter Turner. *Malaysia, Singapore and Bunei.* Australia: Lonely Planet Publications, 1994.

Fuller, Barbara. *Berlitz: Discover Singapore.* UK: Berlitz Publishing, 1993.

Jaffrey, Madhur. *Far Eastern Cookery.* London: BBC Books, 1989.

Jarolim, Edie, ed. *The Wall Street Journal Guides to Business Travel: Pacific Rim.* UK: Fodor, 1991.

Kon, P. C. *The Malaysian Cookbook Two.* Vista Productions Ltd., 1986.

Law, Ruth. *Southeast Asia Cookbook.* New York: Donald I. Fine Inc., 1990.

Malik, Michael, ed. *All-Asia Guide.* Hong Kong: Review Publishing Co., 1991.

Passmore, Jack. *The Encyclopedia of Asian Food and Cooking.* New York: Hearst Books, 1991.

Solomon, Charmaine. *Encyclopedia of Asian Food.* Vancouver: Raincoast Books, 1996.

Turner, Peter, and Tony Wheeler. *Singapore: A Lonely Planet Guide*. Australia: Lonely Planet Publications, 1994.

Wright, John W., ed. *The New York Times 1998 Almanac*. New York: Penguin Group, 1998.

Chapter Twenty-Seven: Iranian

Batmanglij, Najmiah. *Food of Life: Ancient Persian & Modern Iranian Cooking and Ceremonies*. Washington, DC: Mage Publishers Inc., 1986.

Funk and Wagnalls Standard Reference Encyclopedia. New York: Standard Reference Works Publishing Co., 1967.

Iny, Daisy. *The Best of Baghdad Cooking*. Toronto: Clarke, Irwin and Co., 1976.

Langseth-Christensen, Lillian. "Gourmet Holidays: Isfahan." *Gourmet*, March 1971.

London Free Press. "Iran Nation that Cannot Feed Itself: Government Has Program to Eliminate Poverty." London, Ontario 1974.

May, Jacques. *The Ecology of Malnutrition in the Far and Near East*. New York: Hafner Publishing Co., 1961.

Mazda, Maideh. *In a Persian Kitchen*. Rutland, Vermont: Charles E. Tuttle, 1968.

Nickles, Harry G. et al. Middle Eastern Cookery. New York: Time Life Books. 1969.

Rowland, Jean. *Good Food from the Near East*. New York: M. Barrows and Co., 1957.

Seranne, Anne, and Eileen Gaden. *The Best of Near East Cooking*. Garden City, N.Y.: Doubleday & Co., 1964.

Wright, John W., ed. *The New York Times 1998 Almanac*. New York: Penguin Group, 1998.

Zane, Eva. *Middle East Cookery*. San Francisco: 101 Productions, 1974.

Chapter Twenty-Eight: Irish

Bates, Margaret. *The Belfast Cookery Book*. Oxford: Pergamon Press, 1967.

Craig, Elizabeth. *The Art of Irish Cooking*. London: Ward Lock and Co., 1969.

Encyclopedia Canadiana. Toronto: Grolier of Canada, 1970.

Facts about Ireland. Dublin: Department of Foreign Affairs, 1972.

Ferguson, Jeremy. "Northern Ireland." *Globe & Mail*. Feb. 2, 1995.

Fitzgibbon, Theodora. *A Taste of Ireland*. Boston: Houghton Mifflin Co., 1969.

Guillet, Edwin C. *The Great Migration: The Atlantic Crossing by Sailing Ship since 1770*. Toronto: University of Toronto Press, 1963.

Laverty, Maura. *Feasting Galore: Recipes and Food Lore from Ireland*. New York: Holt, Rinehart and Winston, 1961.

O'Hanlon, Thomas J. *The Irish*. Don Mills, ON: Fitzhenry and Whiteside, 1975.

Robinson, Walter V. . "A Rented House." *Globe & Mail*, March 9, 1996.

Tucker, Gilbert. "The Famine Immigration to Canada." *American Historical Review*, April 1931.

Waldo, Myra. *Myra Waldo's Travel and Motoring Guide to Europe, 1974*. London: Collier Macmillan Publishers, 1974.

Chapter Twenty-Nine: Israeli and Jewish

Ausubel, Nathan. *Pictorial History of the Jewish People: From Bible Times to Our Own Day throughout the World*. New York: Crown Publishers, 1962.

Bar-David, Molly Lyons. *The Israeli Cookbook: What's Cooking In Israel's Melting Pot*. New York: Crown Publishers, 1973.

Barer-Stein, Thelma, Esther Schwartz, and Risa Vandersluis. *To Life! Setting a New Standard for Delectable Healthy Eating within Cherished Kosher Traditions.* Toronto: Culture Concepts Inc., 1996.

Baron, W. Salo, et al. *Great Ages and Ideas of the Jewish People.* New York: The Modern Library (Random House), 1956.

Cornfeld, Lillian. *Israeli Cookery.* Westport, CT: The Avi Publishing Co., 1962.

David, Suzy. *The Separdic Kitchen.* New York: Jonathan David Publishers Inc., 1984.

Eban, Abba. *My People: The Story of the Jews.* New York: Behrman House (Random House), 1968.

Epstein, Morris. *All about Jewish Holidays and Customs.* New York: Ktav Publishing House, 1959.

Funk and Wagnalls Standard Reference Encyclopedia. New York: Standard Reference Works Publishing Co., 1967.

Gaster, Theodor. *Festivals of the Jewish Year: A Modern Interpretation and Guide.* New York: Wm. Sloane Assoc., 1953.

Haase, Richard. *Jewish Regional Cooking.* London: Quarto Publishing Ltd., 1985.

Hertz, Dr. J. H. *The Pentateuch and Haftorahs.* London: Soncino Press, 1972.

Isaacson, Rabbi Ben, and Deborah Wigoder. *The International Jewish Encyclopedia.* Jerusalem: Masada Press, 1973.

Levi, Zion, and Hannah Aqabria. *The Yemenite Cookbook.* New York: Seaver Books, 1988.

Machlin, Edda Servi. *The Classic Cuisine of the Italian Jews.* New York: Giro Press, 1981.

Marks, Copeland. *Sephardic Cooking.* New York: Donald L. Fine Inc., 1992.

May, Jacques. *The Ecology of Malnutrition in the Far and Near East.* New York: Hafner Publishing Co., 1961.

Nahoum, Chef Aldo. *The Art of Israeli Cooking.* New York: Holt, Rinehart & Winston, 1960.

Nickles, Harry G., et al. *Middle Eastern Cooking.* New York: Time-Life Books, 1969.

Perry, Ruth. "Cooking the Sephardic Way." *Women's League Outlook.* Spring 1974.

Raddock, Charles. *Portrait of a People: The Story of the Jews from Ancient to Modern Times.* New York: The Judaica Press, 1965.

Rowland, Jean. *Good Food from the Near East.* New York: M. Barrows and Co., 1967.

Seranne, Anne, and Eileen Gaden. *The Best of Near East Cookery.* New York: Doubleday & Co., 1964.

Stavroulakis, Nicholas. *Cookbook of the Jews of Greece.* New York: Cadmua Press, 1986.

Waugh, Alec, et al. *Wines and Spirits.* New York: Time-Life Books, 1968.

Chapter Thirty: Italian

Andrieux, Maurice. *Daily Life in Venice in the Time of Casanova.* London: George Allen and Unwin Ltd., 1972.

Barzini Luigi. *From Caesar to the Mafia: Sketches of Italian Life.* New York: The Library Press, 1971.

Bodd, Dirke. *Annual Customs and Festivals in Peking.* Hong Kong University Press, 1965.

Boni, Ada. *Italian Regional Cooking.* New York: E. P. Dutton and Co., 1969.

Candler, Teresa Gilardi. *The Northern Italian Cookbook.* New York: McGraw-Hill Book Co., 1977.

Castle, Coralie, et al. *Peasant Cooking of Many Lands.* San Francisco: 101 Productions, 1972.

Cowell, F. R. *Everyday Life in Ancient Rome.* New York: G. P. Putnam's Sons, 1966.

De'Medici, Lorenza. *The Renaissance of Italian Cooking.* New York: Fawcett Columbine, 1989.

Dilke, O. A. W. *The Ancient Romans: How They Lived and Worked.* Chester Springs, PA: Du Four, 1975.

Donovan, Maria Kozslik. "Epiphany in Italy." *Gourmet,* January 1973.

Encyclopedia Canadiana. Toronto: Grolier of Canada, 1970.

Field, Carol. *Italy in Small Bites.* New York: William Morrow & Co. 1993.

————. *The Italian Baker.* New York: Harper & Row, 1985.

Fitzgibbon, Theodora. *A Taste of Rome: Traditional Food.* Boston: Houghton Mifflin Co., 1975.

Fodor, Eugene, ed. *Fodors Italy*, *1976*. New York: David McKay Co., 1976.

Harris, Valentine. *Recipes from an Italian Farmhouse.* London: Conran Octopus Limited, 1989.

Jones, Evan. "Tastes of Tuscany" *Gourmet*, March 1971.

Langseth-Christensen, Lillian. "To Genoa by Sea." *Gourmet,* June 1970.

Levine, Irving. *Main Street Italy*. Garden City, N.Y.: Doubleday and Co., 1963.

Lucas-Dubreton, Jean. *Daily Life in Florence: In the Time of the Medici.* London: George Allen & Unwin Ltd., 1960.

Mondadori, Arnoldo, ed. *Feast of Italy*. New York: Thomas Y. Crowell & Co., 1973.

Muffoletto, Anna. *The Art of Sicilian Cooking.* Garden City, N.Y.: Doubleday & Co., 1971.

Root, Waverley, et al. *The Cooking of Italy*. New York: Time-Life Books, 1968.

Tucker, Ninetta. *Italy*. London: Thames and Hudson, 1970.

Whelpton, Eric. *A Concise History of Italy*. New York: Roy Publishers Inc., 1964.

Chapter Thirty-One: Japanese

Brennan, Jennifer. *The Cuisines of Asia*. New York: St. Martin's Press, 1984.

"Briefly About Japanese Cooking." *Practical Japanese Cooking* (sent from Japanese Trade Offices).

Castle, Coralie, et al. *Peasant Cooking of Many Lands.* San Francisco: 101 Productions, 1972.

Chie, Nakane. *Human Relations in Japan.* Ministry of Foreign Affairs, Japan, 1972.

Facts about Japan. Public Information Bureau, Ministry of Foreign Affairs, Japan, Code no. 05103, April 1972 (Geography of Japan).

Facts about Japan. Public Information Bureau, Ministry of Foreign Affairs, Japan, Code no. 05104, April 1974 (Chronological Outline of Japanese History).

Facts about Japan. Public Information Bureau, Ministry of Foreign Affairs, Japan, Code no. 05502, March 1973 (Religion).

Facts about Japan. Public Information Bureau, Ministry of Foreign Affairs, Japan, Code no. 05507, March 1973 (Chanoyu).

Funk and Wagnalls Standard Reference Encyclopedia. New York: Standard Reference Works Publishing Co., 1967.

Griffin, Stuart. *Japanese Food and Cooking.* Tokyo: Charles E. Tuttle and Co., 1968.

Jaffrey, Madhur. *Far Eastern Coookery.* London: BBC Books, 1989.

Japanese and their Food. Radio Japan News, June 1973.

Kohno, Sadako. *Homestyle Japanese Cooking in Pictures.* Tokyo: Sufunotomo Co. Ltd, 1977.

Kokku, Ryoichi (Russ Rodzinski). *Japanese Country Cookbook.* San Francisco: Nitty Gritty Productions, 1969.

Oto, Tokihiko. *Folklore in Japanese Life and Customs.* Tokyo: Kokusai Bunka Shinkokai, 1963.

Pfeiff, Margo. "Sake: Japanese Culture by the Sip." *Globe & Mail.* February 26, 1994.

Shinojima, Tadashi. *Japanese Cookery.* Shufunotomo Cooking Text, Japan, 1968.

Skurka, Norma. "The Way of Tsutsumu: Design: An Art in Packaging." *The New York Times Magazine*, February 9, 1975.

Steinberg, Raphael, et al. *The Cooking of Japan*. New York: Time-Life Books, 1969.

Tanaka, Heichachi. "The Pleasures of Japanese Cooking." *Gourmet*, August 1963.

The Japan of Today. Ministry of Foreign Affairs, Japan, 1972.

Trager, James. *The Foodbook*. New York: Avon Books, 1972.

Wenkam, Nao S., and Robert J. Wolff. "A Half Century of Changing Food Habits among Japanese in Hawaii." *Journal of the American Dietetic Association*, July 1970.

Wright, John W. *The New York Times 1998 Almanac*. New York: Penguin Group, 1998.

Chapter Thirty-Two: Korean

Castle, Coralie, et al. *Peasant Cooking of Many Lands*. San Francisco: 101 Productions, 1972.

Choong-Ok, Cho. *The Art of Korean Cookery*. Tokyo: Shibata Publishing Co., 1963.

Facts about Korea 1974. Seoul: Korean Overseas Information Service, 1974.

Froud, Nina. *Far Eastern Cooking for Pleasure*. London: Paul Hamlyn, 1971.

Kolb, Albert. *East Asia: China, Japan, Korea, Vietnam: Geography of a Cultural Region*. London: Methuen & Co., 1971.

Korea. Seoul: International Publicity Corp., 1974.

Osgood, Cornelius. *The Koreans and Their Culture*. New York: The Ronald Press Co., 1951.

Wright, John W., ed. *The New York Times 1998 Almanac*. New York: Penguin Group, 1998.

Chapter Thirty-Three: Latin American

Adams, R. N. "Food Habits in Latin America: A Preliminary Historical Survey." *Human Nutrition, Historic and Scientific*. New York: International Universities Press, 1967.

Autumn, Violetta. *A Russian Jew Cooks in Peru*. San Francisco: 101 Productions, 1973.

Carpenter, Allan, and Jean C. Lyon. *Enchantment of South America: Uruguay*. Chicago: Regensteiner Publishing Enterprises Inc., 1969.

Castle, Coralie, et al. *Peasant Cooking of Many Lands*. San Francisco: 101 Productions, 1972.

Chile. Courtesy of the Embassy of Chile, Ottawa, Canada.

De Andrade, Margarette. "Brazilian Cookery." *Gourmet*, June 1963.

————. *Brazilian Cookery: Traditional and Modern*. Rutland, VT: Charles E. Tuttle Co., 1965.

Direccione National De Tourismo, Grafica, Ham, S.A. *Argentina*.

Dobler, Lavinia. *The Land and People of Uruguay*. Philadelphia: J. B. Lipppincott Co., 1965.

Funk and Wagnalls Standard Reference Encyclopedia. New York: Standard Reference Works Publishing Co., 1967.

Guevara, Susan. "Memories of a Chilean Kitchen." *Gourmet*, September and October 1960.

Hafner, Dorinda. *A Taste of Africa*. Berkeley, CA:10 Speed Press, 1993.

Jacob, Heinrich Eduard. *Coffee: The Epic of a Commodity*. New York: Viking Press, 1935.

Leonard, Jonathan N., et al. *Latin American Cooking*. New York: Time-Life Books, 1968.

Montagne, Prosper, and Gottschalk, Dr. *Larousse Gastronomique*. London: Paul Hamlyn, 1961.

Ortiz, Elisabeth Lambert. "Brazil." *Gourmet*, December 1973.

Republica Argentina. Courtesy of the Embassy of Argentina, Ottawa, Canada.

Rozin, Elizabeth. *Blue Corn and Chocolate*. New York: Alfred A. Knopf, 1992.

"Tasty Colombian Dishes." Reprinted from *Gourmet*, n.d. Consulate of Colombia. Colombian Information Service.

Wright, John W., ed. *The New York Times 1998 Almanac*. New York: Penguin Group, 1998.

Chapter Thirty-Four: Maltese

Bradford, Ernle. "Democracy's Fortress: Unsinkable Malta." *National Geographic*, June 1969.

Carbonaro, Carmen. (Translated and explained by Melrose Micallef Paquet). *Maltese Dishes*. Hamrun, Malta: Luxprinting Press, 1967.

Galizia Caruana, Anne, and Helen Galizia Caruana. *Recipes from Malta*. Valetta, Malta: Progress Press Co., n.d.

Malta Handbook, 1974. Issued by the Office of the Prime Minister, Kastija, Valletta, Malta.

Trotta, Geri. "Malta: A Journey through Time." *Gourmet*, December 1975.

Chapter Thirty-Five: Mexican

Aaron, Jan, and Georgina Sachs Salom. *The Art of Mexican Cooking*. New York: Doubleday & Co., 1967.

Booth, George C. *The Food and Drink of Mexico*. Toronto: Ward Ritchie Press, General Publishing Co., 1964.

DeLeon, Josefina Velasquez. *Mexican Cookbook*. Mexico City: Culinary Arts Institute, 1971.

Funk and Wagnalls Standard Reference Encyclopedia. New York: Standard Reference Works Publishing Co., 1967.

Leonard Jonathan N. *Latin American Cooking*. New York: Time-Life Books, 1968.

Ortiz, Elisabeth Lambert. *The Complete Book of Mexican Cooking*. New York: Evans and Co., 1967.

Rojas, Pedro. *The Art and Architecture of Mexico*. New York: Paul Hamlyn, 1968.

Rozin, Elizabeth. *Ethnic Cuisine: The Flavor Principle Cookbook*. Vermont: The Stephen Green Press, 1983.

Wason, Betty. *Cooks, Gluttons and Gourmets*. New York: Doubleday & Co., 1962.

Chapter Thirty-Six: Moroccan

Ausubel, Nathan. *Pictorial History of the Jewish People*. New York: Crown Publishing Inc., 1962.

Carrier, Robert. *A Taste of Morocco*. New York: Clarkson Potter, 1987.

Castle, Coralie, et al. *Peasant Cooking of Many Lands*. San Francisco: 101 Productions, 1972.

Croft-Cooke, Rupert. "Tunisian Cookery." *Gourmet*, November 1970.

Eban, Abba. *My People: The Story of the Jews*. New York: Behrman House (Random House), 1968.

Ellingham, Mark, and Shaun McVeigh. *The Real Guide: Morocco*. New York: Prentice Hall, 1989.

Englebert, Victor. "Trek by Mule among Morocco's Berbers." *National Geographic*, June 1968.

Feibleman, Peter. *The Cooking of Spain and Portugal*. New York: Time-Life Books, 1969.

Field, Michael, and Frances Field. *A Quintet of Cuisines*. New York: Time-Life Books, 1970.

Funk and Wagnalls Standard Reference Encyclopedia. New York: Standard Reference Works Publishing Co., 1967.

Hafner, Dorinda. *A Taste of Africa*. Berkley, CA: Ten Speed Press, 1993.

May, Jacques. *The Ecology of Malnutrition in Northern Africa*. New York: Hafner Publishing Co., 1967.

Szulc, Tad. *Portrait of Spain.* New York: American Heritage Press, Div. of McGraw-Hill Book Co., 1972.

Trotta, Geri. "Morrocco's Imperial Cities." *Gourmet*, February 1974.

Wolfert, Paula. *Couscous and Other Good Food from Morocco.* New York: Harper and Row, 1973.

Zane, Eva. *Middle Eastern Cookery.* San Francisco: 101 Productions, 1974.

Chapter Thirty-Seven: New Zealanders

About New Zealand. Washington, DC: New Zealand Embassy.

Benchley, Peter. "New Zealand's Bountiful South Island." *National Geographic*, January 1972.

Facts about New Zealand. Wellington: New Zealand Information Service, Tourist and Publicity Dept., 1974.

Flower, Tui. *New Zealand Recipes.* Wellington: New Zealand Information Service, Tourist and Publicity Dept., 1973.

Funk and Wagnalls Standard Reference Encyclopedia. New York: Standard Reference Works Publishing Co., 1967.

Gall, Timothy L., ed. *Worldmark Encyclopedia of Cultures & Daily Life.* Detroit: Gale Publishers, 1998.

Hooper, Keith. "Booklet on Understanding Polynesians Prepared for White New Zealanders." *London Free Press*, December 10, 1974.

McCarry, Charles. "New Zealand's North Island: The Contented Land." *National Geographic*, August 1974.

Nation, Rhoda. *Mary Bought a Little Lamb and This Is How She Cooked It.* Wellington: A. H. and A. W. Reed, 1973.

New Zealand Background: Fish Recipes from New Zealand. Wellington: No. 27, Government Publicity Division, 1965.

Rome, James, and Margaret Rome. *New Zealand.* London: Ernest Benn Ltd., 1967.

Skinner, Gwen. *The Cuisine of the South Pacific.* Auckland: Hodder & Stoughton, 1983.

Special New Zealand Recipes. New Zealand Tourist Office, March 1956.

Wright, John W., ed. *The New York Times 1998 Almanac.* New York: Penguin Group, 1998.

Chapter Thirty-Eight: Norwegian

Barry, Naomi. "Norwegian Journey." *Gourmet*, June 1959.

Caraman, Philip. *Norway.* London: Longman's Green & Co., 1969.

Encyclopedia Canadiana. Toronto: Grolier of Canada, 1970.

Funk and Wagnalls Standard Reference Encyclopedia. New York: Standard Reference Works Publishing Co., 1967.

Langseth-Christensen, Lillian. "Bergen." *Gourmet*, July 1971.

Ovstedal, Barbara. *Norway.* London: B. T. Batsford Ltd., 1974.

Chapter Thirty-Nine: People of the Fertile Crescent: Iraqi, Jordanian, Lebanese, and Syrian

Allan, Donald Aspinwall. "Flavors of Lebanon." *Gourmet*, August 1974.

Casella, Dolores. "The Welcoming." *Gourmet*, March 1960.

Corey, Helen. *The Art of Syrian Cookery.* Garden City, N.Y.: Doubleday & Co., 1962.

Encyclopedia Canadiana. Toronto: Grolier of Canada, 1970.

Funk and Wagnalls Standard Reference Encyclopedia. New York: Standard Reference Works Publishing Co., 1967.

Mallos, Tess. *The Middle East Cookbook.* New York: McGraw-Hill, 1979.

May, Jacques. *The Ecology of Malnutrition in the Far and Near East*. New York: Hafner Publishing Co., 1961.

Nickles, Harry, et al. *Middle Eastern Cooking*. New York: Time-Life Books, 1969.

Rodin, Claudia. *Mediterranean Cookery*. New York: Afred A. Knopf, 1987.

Rowland, Jean. *Good Food from the Near East*. New York: M. Barrows and Co., 1964.

Sakr, Ahmad H. "Dietary Regulations and Food Habits of Muslims." *Journal of the American Dietetic Association*, February 1971.

Seranne, Anne, and Eileen Gaden. *The Best of Near East Cookery*. Garden City, N.Y.: Doubleday & Co., 1964.

Tannahill, Reay. *Food in History*. New York: Stein and Day, 1974.

Zaehner, R. C., ed. *The Concise Encyclopedia of Living Faiths*. New York: Hawthorn Books, 1959.

Zane, Eva. *Middle Eastern Cookery*. San Francisco: 101 Productions, 1974.

Chapter Forty: Polish

Castle, Coralie, et al. *Peasant Cooking of Many Lands*. San Francisco: 101 Productions, 1972.

Encyclopedia Canadiana. Toronto: Grolier of Canada. 1970.

Field, Michael, and Frances Field. *A Quintet of Cuisines*. New York: Time-Life Books, 1970.

Funk and Wagnalls Standard Reference Encyclopedia. New York: Standard Reference Works Publishing Co., 1967.

May, Jacques. *The Ecology of Malnutrition in East-Central Europe*. New York: Hafner Publishing Co., 1963.

Ochorowicz-Monatowa, Marja. *Polish Cookery: The Universal Cookbook*. New York: Crown Publishers, 1973.

Zeranska, Alina. *The Art of Polish Cooking*. New York: Doubleday & Co., 1968.

Chapter Forty-One: Portuguese

Bridge, Ann, and Susan Lowndes. *The Selective Traveller* in Portugal. London: Chatto & Windus, 1967.

Feibleman, Peter, et al. *The Cooking of Spain and Portugal*. New York: Time-Life Books, 1969.

Funk and Wagnalls Standard Reference Encyclopedia. New York: Standard Reference Works Publishing Co., 1967.

Kelly, Marie Noelle. *This Delicious Land Portugal*. London: Hutchinson & Co., 1956.

Kempner, Mary Jean. *Invitation to Portugal*. New York: Atheneum, 1969.

Kolb, Albert. *East Asia: China, Japan, Korea, Vietnam: Geography of a Cultural Region*. London: Methuen and Co., 1971.

Maas, Carl. "Beyond the Tagus." *Gourmet*, April 1974.

———. "The Cookery of Northern Portugal." *Gourmet*, August 1973.

"Report on the Portuguese Seminar Held at St. Helen's Portuguese Community Centre, November 21, 1973," and "Adjustment Problems of the Portuguese Mother," Fatima Pires.

Thomas, Veronica. "The Allure of the Algarve." *Gourmet*, May 1973.

Waldo, Myra. *Myra Waldo's Travel and Motoring Guide to Europe, 1974*. London: Collier Macmillan, 1974.

Waugh, Alec. *Wines and Spirits*. New York: Time-Life Books, 1968.

Chapter Forty-Two: Romanian

CD-ROM. Brittanica CD. *Encyclopedia Brittanica* 1995.

Funk and Wagnalls Standard Reference Encyclopedia. New York: Standard Reference Works Publishing Co., 1967.

Levi, Avraham. *Bazak Guide to Romania.* Tel Aviv: Bazak Israel Guidebook Publishers, 1970.

Mackintosh, May. *Rumania.* London: Robert Hale Ltd., 1963.

Matley, Ian M. *Romania: A Profile.* New York: Praeger Publishers, 1970.

May, Jacques. *The Ecology of Malnutrition in Central and South-Eastern Europe.* New York: Hafner Publishing Co., 1966.

Nelson, Kay Shaw. *The Eastern European Cookbook.* Chicago: Henry Regnery Co., 1973.

Perl, Lila. *Yugoslavia, Romania, Bulgaria: New Era in the Balkans.* Toronto: Thomas Nelson and Sons, 1970.

Seranne, Anne, and Eileen Gaden. *The Best of Near East Cookery.* Garden City, N.Y.: Doubleday & Co., 1964.

Stan, Anisoara. *The Romanian Cookbook.* New York: The Citadel Press, 1969.

Chapter Forty-Three: Russian

Castle, Coralie, et al. *Peasant Cooking of Many Lands.* San Francisco: 101 Productions, 1972.

Funk and Wagnalls Standard Reference Encyclopedia. New York: Standard Reference Works Publishing Co., 1967.

Funk and Wagnalls Standard Reference Encyclopedia Yearbook: Events of 1973. New York: Funk and Wagnalls Inc., 1974.

Gall, Timothy L. *Worldmark Encyclopedia of Cultures & Daily Life.* Detroit: Gale Publishers, 1997.

Kropotkin, Alexandra. *The Best of Russian Cooking.* New York: Charles Scribner's Sons, 1964.

Nelson, Kay Shaw. *The Eastern European Cookbook.* Chicago: Henry Regnery Co., 1973.

Nicolaieff, Nina, and Nancy Phelan. *The Art of Russian Cooking.* New York: Doubleday & Co., 1969.

Norman, Barbara. *The Russian Cookbook.* Toronto: Bantam Books, 1970.

Papashvily, Helen, and George Papashvily. *Russian Cooking.* New York: Time-Life Books, 1969.

Petrova, Nina. *Russian Cookery.* Harmondsworth, England: Penguin Books, 1968.

Polvay, Marina. "Cuisines of Russia." *Gourmet,* February 1974.

Rand McNally Premier World Atlas: New Census Edition. Chicago: Rand McNally & Co., 1972.

Stearns, Anna. *New Canadians of Slavic Origin: A Problem in Creative Orientation.* Winnipeg: Trident Press, 1960.

Thompson, Sue Ellen, and Barbara Carlson. *Holidays, Festivals & Celebrations of the World Dictionary.* Detroit: Omnigraphics Inc., 1993.

Wren, Christopher, "Ho Ho Ho, Soviet Style." *New York Times,* n.d.

Wright, John W., ed. *The New York Times 1998 Almanac.* New York: Penguin Group, 1998.

Chapter Forty-Four: Scottish

Bailey, Adrian, et al. *The Cooking of the British Isles.* New York: Time-Life Books, 1969.

Barker, T. C., J.C. McKenzie, and J. Yudkin. *Our Changing Fare: 200 Years of British Food Habits.* London: Macgibbon and Kee, 1966.

Cameron, Sheila MacNiven. *The Highlander's Cookbook: Recipes from Scotland.* New York: Ward Ritchie Press, 1966.

Costa, Margaret. "The Highlands of Scotland." *Gourmet,* August 1972.

Encyclopedia Canadiana. Toronto: Grolier of Canada, 1970.

Funk and Wagnalls Standard Reference Encyclopedia. New York: Standard Reference Works Publishing Co., 1967.

Howells, J. Harvey. "Home to Arran: Scotland's Magic Isle." *National Geographic.* Vol. 128, no. 1. July 1965.

Lindsay, Ann McColl. Proprietor of Ann McColl's Kitchen Shop, London, Ontario. Interview with author, 1976.

Walker, Sara Macleod. *The Highland Fling Cookbook.* New York: Atheneum, 1971.

Chapter Forty-Five: The Southern Slavs (formerly Yugoslavian)

Donovan, Maria Koszlik. "Yugoslavia I." *Gourmet,* January 1972.

———. "Yugoslavia II." *Gourmet,* June 1972.

Encyclopedia Canadiana. Toronto: Grolier of Canada, 1970.

Esterovich and Spalatin. *Croatia: Land, People, Culture.* Vol. I and Vol. II. Toronto: University of Toronto Press, 1964.

Fodor, Eugene, ed. *Fodor's Yugoslavia 1970.* New York: David McKay Co., 1970.

Gall, Timothy L., ed. *Worldmark Encyclopedia of Cultures & Daily Life.* Detroit: Gale Publishers, 1998.

Goldring, Patrick. *Yugoslavia.* Chicago: Rand McNally, 1973.

May, Jacques. *The Ecology of Malnutrition in East-Central Europe.* New York: Hafner Publishing Co., 1963.

Markovic, Spasenija-Pata. *Yugoslav Cookbook.* New York: Lyle Stuart Inc., 1966.

Nelson, Kay Shaw. *The Eastern European Cookbook.* Chicago: Henry Regnery Co., 1973.

Perl, Lila. *Yugoslavia, Romania, Bulgaria: New Era in the Balkans.* Toronto: Thomas Nelson and Sons, 1970.

Seranne, Anne, and Eileen Gaden. *The Best of Near East Cookery.* Garden City, NY: Doubleday & Co., 1964.

Wechsberg, Joseph. "Dubrovnik." *Gourmet,* June 1972.

Wright, John W., ed. *The New York Times 1998 Almanac.* New York: Penguin Group, 1998.

Chapter Forty-Six: Spanish

Aguilar, Jeanette. *The Classic Cooking of Spain.* New York: Holt, Rinehart & Winston, 1966.

Castle, Coralie, et al. *Peasant Cooking of Many Lands.* San Francisco: 101 Productions, 1972.

Feibleman, Peter, et al. *The Cooking of Spain and Portugal.* New York: Time-Life Books, 1969.

Fodor, Eugene, and William Curtis, eds. *Fodor's Spain, 1969.* New York: David McKay Co., 1969.

Funk and Wagnalls Standard Reference Encyclopedia. New York: Standard Reference Works Publishing Co., 1967.

Hatheway, Maruja. *Authentic Spanish Cooking.* New York: Paperback Library, 1970.

McDonough, Jean. "All Ranks of Basques Work Gourmet Wonders." *London Free Press,* March 21, 1974.

Mitchell, Fanny Todd. "Buena Sopa." *Gourmet,* February 1973.

———. "The Riches of Granada." *Gourmet,* February 1971.

Passmore, Jacki. *The Complete Spanish Cookbook.* Vancouver: Raincoast Books, 1992.

Szulc, Tad. *Portrait of Spain.* New York: American Heritage Press, Division of McGraw-Hill Book Co., 1972.

Waldo, Myra. *Myra Waldo's Travel and Motoring Guide to Europe, 1974.* London: Collier Macmillan, 1974.

Wason, Betty. *Thirty-eight Delectable Dishes from Spain.*

Chapter Forty-Seven: Swedish

Adlerbert, Elna. *Cooking the Scandinavian Way*. London: Paul Hamlyn, 1969.

Brown, Dale. *The Cooking of Scandinavia*. New York: Time-Life Books, 1968.

Castle, Coralie, et al. *Peasant Cooking of Many Lands*. San Francisco: 101 Productions, 1972.

Coombs, Anna Olsson. *The New Smorgasbord Cookbook*. New York: Hill & Wang, 1958.

Encyclopedia Canadiana. Toronto: Grolier of Canada, 1970.

Funk and Wagnalls Standard Reference Encyclopedia. New York: Standard Reference Works Publishing Co., 1967.

Howard, Irene. *Vancouver's Svenskar: A History of the Swedish Community in Vancouver*. Vancouver Historical Society, 1970.

Langseth-Christensen, Lillian. "Swedish Yuletide Baking." *Gourmet*, December 1973.

Lindahl, Mac. "'God Jul': A Swedish Christmas." *Gourmet*, December 1959.

Chapter Forty-Eight: Swiss

Castle, Coralie, et al. *Peasant Cooking of Many Lands*. San Francisco: 101 Productions, 1972.

Cowie, Donald. *Switzerland: The Land and the People*. Cranbury, NJ: A. S. Barnes and Co., 1971.

Field, Michael, and Frances Field. *A Quintet of Cuisines*. New York: Time-Life Books, 1970.

Hazelton, Nika Standen. *The Swiss Cookbook*. New York: Atheneum, 1967.

Hofer, Heinz P. *La Fondue: A Collection of Authentic Fondue Recipes from Switzerland*. Switzerland Cheese Association, 1970.

Hofer, Heinz P. *Recipes from Switzerland*. Zurich: Swiss National Tourist Office, 1970.

Kampfen, Werner. *Switzerland*. Zurich: Swiss National Tourist Office.

Chapter Forty-Nine: Thai

Asia and Pacific Business Travel Guide. Toronto: SP Travel Books, 1989.

Brennan, Jennifer. *The Cuisines of Asia*. New York: St. Martin's Press, 1984.

Cummings, Joe. *Thailand: A Lonely Planet Survival Kit*. Australia: Lonely Planet Publication, 1995.

Devine, Elisabeth, and Nancy L. Braganti. *The Traveler's Guide to Asian Customs and Manners*. New York: St. Martin's Press, 1986.

Ferguson, Jeremy. "Thai Foods Can be Hot-and-Spicy Adventures." *Globe & Mail*. March 1995.

Gall, Timothy L., ed. *Worldmark Encyclopedia of Cultures & Daily Life*. Detroit: Gale Publishers, 1998.

International Life Sciences Institute (ILSI) and ILSI "Southeast Asia Conference, Singapore 1995." *Nutrition Today* 31, no. 2 (March/April 1996).

Jaffrey, Madhur. *Far Eastern Cookery*. London: BBC Books. 1989.

Kanchananaga, Suraphong, ed. *All About Thailand: Thai Religion, Festivals & Ceremonies*. Bangkok: Suraphong Kanchananaga, Publishers, 1978.

Langseth-Christensen, Lillian. "Gourmet Holidays: Bangkok." *Gourmet*, August 1970.

Law, Ruth. *Southeast Asian Cookbook*. New York: Donald I. Fine. 1990.

Ortiz, Elisabeth Lambert. "A Thai Christmas." *Gourmet*. December 1971.

Osbourne, Christine. *Essential Thailand*. U.K: Automobile Association, Publications Division, 1990.

Pinsuvana, Malulee. *Cooking Thai Foods in American Kitchens*, Book II with ASEAN Recipes. Bangkok: Thai Watana Panich Press. 1987. (ASEAN is Association of South East Asian Nations.)

Pinsuvana, Malulee. *Cooking Thai Foods in American Kitchens*. Bangkok: Thai Watana Panich Press, 1981.

Royal Thai Embassy. *Thai Food*. Ottawa, n.d.

Sananikone, Keo. *Keo's Thai Cuisine*. Berkeley, CA: Ten Speed Press, 1986.

Segaller, Denis. *Thai Ways*. Bangkok: Thai Watana Panich Press, 1980.

Smith, Huston. *The Religions of Man*. NY: Mentor Books, 1959.

Solomon, Charmaine. *Asian Collection: More Than 700 of Her Best Recipes*. Vancouver: Raincoast Books, n.d.

———. *Charmaine Solomon's Thai Cuisine*. Vancouver: Raincoast Books, 1989.

———. *Encyclopedia of Asian Food*. Vancouver: Raincoast Books, 1996.

Spitzer, Dan. *Fielding's Budget Asia: Southeast Asia and the Far East*. NY: Fielding Travel Kits, 1990.

Wall Street Journal Guide to Business Travel: Pacific Rim. UK: Fodor, 1991.

Western, Tasnee Sarikananda. "From Thai Kitchens." *Gourmet*, March 1963.

Chapter Fifty: Tibetan

Ash, Niema. *Flight of the Windhorse: A Journey into Tibet*. (With a foreword by the Dalai Llama) UK: Rider, 1990.

Booz, Elisabeth. *Tibet*. Licolnwood: Passport Books, 1986.

Gall, Timothy L., ed. *Worldmark Encyclopedia of Cultures & Daily Life*. Detroit: Gale Publishers, 1998.

Goldstein, Melvyn C. *Tibet Phrasebook*. Berkeley, CA: Lonely Planet Publications, 1987.

Gyatso, Palden. *Fire Under the Snow: Testimony of a Tibetan Prisoner*. UK: Harvill Press, 1997.

Jung, Betty. *The Kopan Cookbook: Recipes from a Tibetan Monastery*. San Francisco: Chronicle Books, 1992.

Norbu, Thubten Jigme (elder brother of the Dalai Llama), and Colin M. Turnbull. *Tibet: An Account of the History, Religions and the People of Tibet*. New York: Simon & Shuster, n.d.

Richardson, Hugh E. *Tibet and Its History*, 2nd ed. Boston: Shambhala, 1962.

Snelgrove, David, and Hugh Richardson. *A Cultural History of Tibet*. UK: George Weidenfield & Nicholson Ltd., 1968.

Taylor, Chris. *Tibet: A Lonely Planet Travel Survivor Guide*, 3rd ed. Oakland, CA: Lonely Planet Publications, 1995.

Wong, Jan. "Tibet: Life at the Top of the World." *Globe & Mail*. December 10, 1994.

Chapter Fifty-One: Turkish

Barish, Mort, et al. *Mort's Guide to Festivals, Feasts, Fairs and Fiestas*. International Edition. Princeton, NJ: CMG Publishing Co., 1974.

Erturk, Ilyas. *Turkish Kitchen Today*. Istanbul: Istanbul Matbasi, 1967.

Funk and Wagnalls Standard Reference Encyclopedia. New York: Standard Reference Works Publishing Co., 1967.

Gall, Timothy L., *Worldmark Encyclopedia of Cultures & Daily Life*. Detroit: Gale Publishers, 1998.

Iny, Daisy. *The Best of Baghdad Cooking*. Toronto: Clarkes Irwin and Co., 1976.

Jacob, Heinrich. *Coffee: The Epic of a Commodity*. New York: Viking Press, 1955.

Mango, Andrew. *Discovering Turkey*. New York: Hastings House Publishers, 1971.

Newman, Bernard. *Turkey and the Turks*. London: Herbert Jenkins, 1968.

Nickles, Harry G., et al. *Middle Eastern Cooking*. New York: Time-Life Books, 1969.

Nyrop, Richard, et al. *Area Handbook of Turkey*. Washington, DC: U.S. Government Printing Office, 1973.

Salter, Cedric. *Introducing Turkey*. London: Methuen and Co., 1961.

Seranne, Anne, and Eileen Gaden. *The Best of Near East Cookery*. Garden City, N.Y.: Doubleday & Co., 1964.

Walker, Warren, and Ahmet Uysal. *Tales Alive in Turkey*. Cambridge, MA: Harvard University Press, 1966.

Chapter Fifty-Two: Ukrainian

Canada. Department of the Secretary of State, Citizenship Branch. *Canadian Family Tree*. Ottawa: Queen's Printer, 1967.

Encyclopedia Canadiana. Toronto: Grolier of Canada, 1970.

Funk and Wagnalls Standard Reference Encyclopedia. New York: Standard Reference Works Publishing Co., 1967.

Gall, Timothy L. *Worldmark Encyclopedia of Cultures & Daily Life*. Detroit: Gale Publishers, 1998.

Hawrish, Mary-Beth. "Age-Old Customs: Ukrainian Families Enjoy Christmas Twice." *London Free Press*, January 7, 1974.

Kubijovyc, Volodymyr, ed. *Ukraine: A Concise Encyclopedia*. Vol. I. Toronto: University of Toronto Press, 1963.

Norman, Barbara. *The Russian Cookbook*. Toronto: Bantam Books of Canada, 1970.

Papashvily, Helen, and George Papashvily. *Russian Cooking*. New York: Time-Life Books, 1969.

Schopflin, George, ed. *The Soviet Union and Eastern Europe: A Handbook*. London: Anthony Blond, 1970.

Statistics Canada. *1970 Immigration*. Ottawa: Department of Manpower and Immigration, Canada Immigration Division, Information Canada, 1971.

Stechishin, Savella. *Traditional Ukrainian Cookery*. Winnipeg: Trident Press, 1967.

Webster's New World English Dictionary. Toronto: Nelson, Foster and Scott, 1966.

Young, Charles H. *The Ukrainian Canadians: A Study in Assimilation*. Toronto: Thomas Nelson and Sons Ltd., 1931.

Chapter Fifty-Three: Vietnamese

Brennan, Jennifer. *Cuisines of Asia*. New York: St. Martin's Press, 1984.

Foley, Dylan. "Some Snake wine with my snake." *Globe & Mail*. Oct. 11, 1997.

Froud, Nina. *Far Eastern Cooking for Pleasure*. London: Paul Hamlyn, 1971.

Funk and Wagnalls Standard Reference Encyclopedia, New York: Standard Reference Works Publishing Co., 1967.

Jaffrey, Madhur. *Far Eastern Cookery*. London: BBC Books, 1989.

Kolb, Albert. *East Asia: China, Japan, Korea, Vietnam: Geography of a Cultural Region*. London: Methuen and Co., 1971.

Law, Ruth. *South East Asia Cookbook*. New York: Donald Fine Inc., 1990.

May, Jacques. *The Ecology of Malnutrition in the Far and Near East*. New York: Hafner Publishing Co., 1961.

Rutledge, Len. *Maverick Guide to Vietnam, Laos & Cambodia*. Gretna, LA: Pelican Publishing, 1993.

Steinberg, Raphael, et al. *Pacific and South-East Asian Cooking*. New York: Time-Life Books, 1970.

Tao-Kim-Hai, Andre M. "Disciple of Ong Tao." *Gourmet*, June 1958.

Chapter Fifty-Four: Welsh

Fitzgibbon, Theodora. *A Taste of Wales*. London: Pan Books, 1973.

Gall, Timothy L. *Worldmark Encyclopedia & Cultures in Daily Life*. Detroit: Gale Publishers, 1998.

Haldane, Rhian. President, London Welsh Society. Interview with the author. London, Ontario, 1975.

Jones, R. Brimley. *Anatomy of Wales*. Glamorgan, Wales: Gwerin Publications, Peterston-super-Ely, 1972.

Lands and Peoples: Europe. Vol. 4. New York: Grolier Inc., 1972.

Llewellyn, Sian. *The Welsh Kitchen: Recipes from Wales*. Swansea, Wales: Celtic Educational Services Ltd., 1972.

Lloyd, D. M., and E.M. Lloyd. *A Book of Wales*. London: Collins, 1954.

Ogizorek, Dore, ed. *Great Britain: England, Scotland and Wales*. New York: Whittlesey House, McGraw-Hill, 1949.

Price Jones, Iris. *Celtic Cookery*. Swansea, Wales: Christopher Davies, 1979.

Smith-Twiddy, Helen. *Celtic Cookbook*. Y. Lofa: Wales 1989.

Wales. London: Alabaster, Passmore and Sons, n.d.

Welsh Gas Board. *Croeso Cymrig: A Welsh Welcome*. Cardiff: Tudor Graphic Ltd., 1963.

Chapter Fifty-Five: West Indian

Cabanillas, Berta, and Carmen Ginorio. *Puerto-Rican Dishes*. Puerto Rico: 1966.

The Caribbean Food and Nutrition Institute. *Food Composition Tables for Use in the English-speaking Caribbean*. Kingston 7, Jamaica, 1974.

Castle, Coralie, et al. *Peasant Cooking of Many Lands*. San Francisco: 101 Productions, 1972.

Clark, E. Phyllis. *West Indian Cookery*. Hong Kong: Thomas Nelson & Sons, 1986.

Eneruwa, Linda. *The West Indies*. London: Longman's, 1962.

Gall, Timothy L., ed. *Worldmark Encyclopedia of Cultures & Daily Life*. Detroit: Gale Publishers, 1998.

Hamilton, Jill. *The Taste of Barbados*. Barbados W.I.: Letchworth Press Ltd., n.d.

Harman, Carter, et al. *Life World Library: The West Indies*. New York: Time-Life Books, 1966.

Harris, Jessica B. *Iron Pots & Wooden Spoons*. New York: MacMillan Publishers, 1989.

Horowitz, Michael M., ed. *Peoples and Cultures of the Caribbean: An Anthropological Reader*. Garden City, NY: Natural History Press, 1971.

Lowenthal, David, ed. *The West Indies Federation*. New York: Columbia University Press, 1961.

Ortiz, Elisabeth Lambert. "De Leyritz of Martinique." *Gourmet*, October 1972.

———. "Puerto Rico." *Gourmet*, January 1973.

———. *The Complete Book of Caribbean Cooking*. New York: Evans and Co., 1973.

Pearcy, G. Etzel. *The West Indian Scene*. Princeton, NJ: Van Nostrand Co., 1965.

The Trinidad and Tobago Government Office. Toronto: Series of pamphlets, recipes, printed sheets, etc., prepared and presented courtesy of this office. (Particularly useful was M. P. Alladin's *Festivals of Trinidad and Tobago*, published by the Director of Culture, Ministry of Education and Culture, National Museum and Art Gallery, Trinidad and Tobago).

Waddell, D. A. G. *The West Indies and the Guianas*. Englewood Cliffs, NJ: Prentice Hall Inc., 1967.

Wolfe, Linda, et al. *The Cooking of the Caribbean Islands*. New York: Time-Life Books, 1960.

Wright, John W., ed. *The New York Times 1998 Almanac*, New York: Penguin Group, 1998.

nimono, Japanese, 276, 280
nips, Scottish, 379
nockerl, Austrian, 54
nohond basti, Armenian, 44
nomads, Tibetan, 423-24
Nonya cookery, Chinese, 224
noodle dumplings, Ukrainian, 437
noodle pastry, Turkish, 431
noodles:
    Chinese, 95, 100, 102; Croatian, 386; Hungarian, 190, 194; Italian,
    264; Japanese, 274, 276, 280; Korean, 285-86, 290; Polish, 350;
    Russian, 373; Slovenian, 390; Southern Slavs, 391; Swiss, 410;
    Thai, 415, 417; Tibetan, 427; Ukrainian, 438, 441, 442; Uzbek,
    369; Vietnamese, 446
noodle soup, Tibetan, 423, 426
nopales, Mexican, 311
nori, Japanese, 277
norimaki-zushi, Japanese, 274
Norouz, Iranian, 230
nors, Swedish, 407
Northern Italy, 260-61
Northumberland aniseed cake, English, 129
Northumberland pie, English, 129
Northumbrian sweet pie, English, 129
Northwest Territories Tribes, 81
Norwegian, 330-36
    domestic life, 331; history, 330-31; meals and customs, 333; special
    occasions, 333
nougat, Maltese, 308
Nova Scotia, 76-77
nsiko, African, 30
nuoc cham, Vietnamese, 444, 445, 446, 449
nuoc leo, Vietnamese, 449
nuoc mam, Vietnamese, 445, 446, 447, 448, 449
nutmeg, Belgian, 62
nuts:
    Albanian, 31; Armenian, 43; Bulgarian, 68; Chinese, 95, 98; Danish,
    109; Eastern Woodlands Nations, 81; Egyptian, 120; Fertile
    Crescent, 340, 341; Filipino, 138; French, 158; Greek, 176;
    Hungarian, 190; Indian, 204; Iranian, 228, 230; Japanese, 279;
    Moroccan, 319; Portuguese, 356; Southeast Asian, 220; Turkish, 431
nyama ne nyemba, Zimbabwean, 23

O
oatcakes:
    English, 130; Scottish, 379; Welsh, 452, 454, 455
oaten biscuits, Irish, 238
oatmeal:
    Belgian, 62; Czech, 106; Dutch, 114; English, 128; Icelandic, 198;
    Irish, 234, 236, 238; Israeli, 245; Nova Scotia, 77; Scottish,
    376, 379; Welsh, 453
oats:
    Russian, 372; Welsh, 451
oca, Latin American, 291
octapothi, Greek, 185
octopus:
    Greek, 185; Maltese, 309
odamaki-mushi, Japanese, 276
oeufs a l'Auvergnate, French, 159
ofe nsala, African, 30
offal:
    African, 20; Australian, 48; Czech, 104; Danish, 109; Finnish, 144;
    Scottish, 376
ogede, African, 30
ogilie, African paste, 21

oilcakes, Dutch, 117
oils:
    American, 35; Austrian, 52; Bulgarian, 68; Chinese, 95-96; Iroquois,
    83; Valencia, 398. See also specific oils
oi-sobaki, Korean, 289
oka cheese, Quebec, 86
oka esiri esi, African, 30
okazu, Japanese, 280
okopa arequipena, Peruvian, 303
okra:
    African, 28, 30; American, 38; Armenian, 44; Egyptian Jews, 247;
    Israeli, 243, 255; Turkish, 430, 433; West Indian, 460, 462, 467
okro:
    Brazilian, 295; soup, Nigerian, 27; West African, 26
okroshka, Russian, 373
Oktoberfest, German, 171
oladky, Russian, 373
olele, Nigerian, 30
oliebollen, Dutch, 115, 117
olilie, African seasoning paste, 30
olive oil:
    Albanian, 32; American, 35; Armenian, 42; Bulgarian, 68; Fertile
    Crescent, 341; Filipino, 138; French, 155; Greek, 176, 179;
    Iranian, 228; Israeli, 245; Macedonian, 386; Portuguese, 356, 358;
    Romanian, 362; Spanish, 394, 395; Turkish, 431; West Indian, 464
olives:
    Chinese, 94; Egyptian, 121; Fertile Crescent, 338, 340; Greek, 176,
    178; Israeli, 243; Moroccan, 318; Portuguese, 355
olla:
    Mexican, 311, 315; Spanish, 395, 400
olla podrida:
    Spanish, 319, 323, 401; Spanish Central Plateau, 397
ollebrod, Danish, 111
olorosos, Spanish, 396
olykoeks, Dutch, 117
oma, Tibetan, 427
omelets:
    Bordeaux, 157, 162; Chinese, 101; Danish, 111; Iranian, 230, 231;
    Israeli, 245; Portuguese, 355, 358; Southeast Asian, 224; Tibetan,
    427
omeltten, Swiss, 413
omija-wha-chai, Korean, 287
o-mochi, Japanese, 276
onde, African, 20
onesooe, Prince Edward Island, 77
onion cake, Welsh, 451
onion pays, West Indian, 464
onions:
    Armenian, 42, 43; Chinese, 96; Czech, 105; Egyptian, 119, 121;
    Filipino, 137; French, 155, 163; Indian, 202, 203; Mexican, 311;
    Russian, 367; Spanish, 394, 396; Sri Lankan, 208; Syrians, 341;
    Vietnamese, 446; Welsh, 451, 452
ontbijtkoek, Dutch, 117
oogiot sumsum, Sephardi Jews, 249
ooha, Russian, 373
oolichan, British Columbia First Nations, 79
oolong, Chinese tea, 96
oplagt melk, Norwegian, 336
oplatek, Polish, 350
oporo ukwu, African, 30
orange flower water, Greek, 180
orange julep, American, 39
oranges:
    Egyptian, 119; kafir, 20; Portuguese, 358; Valencia, 398
oregano, Greek, 180